W9-BYF-165

FIFTEENTH EDITION

Sports and Recreational Activities

Dale P. Mood
Professor
Department of Integrative Physiology
University of Colorado, Boulder

Frank F. Musker
Formerly Professor of Physical Education,
Boston University; Supervisor of Physical Education,
Peabody Public Schools, Peabody, Massachusetts

Judith E. Rink
Professor
Department of Physical Education
University of South Carolina
Columbia, South Carolina

McGraw Hill

Connect
Learn
Succeed™

SPORTS AND RECREATIONAL ACTIVITIES, FIFTEENTH EDITION

Published by McGraw-Hill, an imprint of The McGraw-Hill Companies, Inc., 1221 Avenue of the Americas, New York, NY 10020. Copyright © 2012 by The McGraw-Hill Companies, Inc. All rights reserved. Previous editions © 2007, 2003, and 1999. No part of this publication may be reproduced or distributed in any form or by any means, or stored in a database or retrieval system, without the prior written consent of The McGraw-Hill Companies, Inc., including, but not limited to, in any network or other electronic storage or transmission, or broadcast for distance learning.

Some ancillaries, including electronic and print components, may not be available to customers outside the United States.

✪ This book is printed on recycled, acid-free paper containing 10% postconsumer waste.

1 2 3 4 5 6 7 8 9 0 QDB/QDB 1 0 9 8 7 6 5 4 3 2 1

ISBN 978-0-07-802248-7
MHID 0-07-802248-7

Vice President & Editor-in-Chief: *Michael Ryan*
Vice President EDP/Central Publishing Services: *Kimberly Meriwether David*
Publisher: *Beth Mejia*
Executive Editor: *Christopher Johnson*
Managing Editor: *Marley Magaziner*
Executive Marketing Manager: *Pamela S. Cooper*
Project Manager: *Erin Melloy*
Design Coordinator: *Brenda A. Rolwes*
Cover Designer: *Studio Montage, St. Louis, Missouri*
Photo Research Coordinator: *Sonia Brown*
Cover Image: Front Cover Images: *Woman Sitting on a Weight Lifting Bench:* © Corbis RF; *Woman Doing the Butterfly:* © PhotoLink/Getty Images RF; *Man's Hand Lifting a Dumbbell:* © Thinkstock/PunchStock RF; *Male Archer:* © Comstock/Jupiter Images RF; *Soccer Player:* © Brand X Pictures/PunchStock RF; *Dancer:* © Stockbyte RF; *Man About to Throw Flying Disc:* © Getty Images RF; *Woman Performing Forearm Stand:* © Ingram Publishing/ SuperStock RF. Back Cover Images: *Track Meet:* © Getty images RF; *Woman Lifting Weights:* © Jupiter Images RF; *Lacrosse Player:* © Corbis RF; *Side Profile of a Woman Performing Bow Pose:* © Ingram Publishing/SuperStock RF
Buyer: *Laura Fuller*
Media Project Manager: *Sridevi Palani*
Compositor: *Laserwords Private Limited*
Typeface: *10/12 Minion*
Printer: *Quad/Graphics Dubuque*

All credits appearing on page or at the end of the book are considered to be an extension of the copyright page.

Library of Congress Cataloging-in-Publication Data

Mood, Dale.
    Sports and recreational activities / Dale P. Mood, Frank F. Musker, Judith E. Rink.—15th ed.
       p.   cm.
    ISBN 978-0-07-802248-7 (alk. paper)
    1. Sports. 2. Group games. 3. Physical education and training—Study and teaching. I. Musker, Frank F.
II. Rink, Judith. III. Title.
    GV704.M66 2011
    796—dc22

                                                                                      2006046643

Consultants

HEALTH-RELATED PHYSICAL FITNESS
James Morrow
Department of Kinesiology, Health Promotion, and Recreation
University of North Texas

AEROBIC DANCE (GROUP EXERCISE)
Rochelle Slayback
Rancho Pico Junior High Santa Clarita, CA

ARCHERY
Frank Thomas
Department of Health and Kinesiology
Texas A&M University

BACKPACKING
Jeff Steffen
Department of Physical Education
University of Wisconsin—La Crosse

and

Jeff McNamee
Health, Human Performance and Athletics
Linfield College

BADMINTON
Donald Paup
Department of Exercise Science
George Washington University

BASKETBALL
James LaPoint
Department of Health, Sport, and Exercise Science
University of Kansas

and

March Krotee
Department of Physical Education
North Carolina State University

and

Paul Blair
Academy of Sport and Leisure Studies
University of Trinidad and Tobago

BICYCLING
Chris Harnish
Exercise Physiologist and Coach
East Falmouth, MA

BOWLING
Curt Fowler
Department of Kinesiology, Health Promotion and Recreation
University of North Texas

DANCE: CONCERT AND RECREATIONAL FORMS
Toby Hankin
Theater and Dance Department
University of Colorado at Boulder

DISC SPORTS: ULTIMATE AND DISC GOLF
Mike Whitaker
University of Colorado

FIELD HOCKEY
Karen Collins
USA Field Hockey

GOLF
Kimber Westbrook
St. Louis, MO

GYMNASTICS AND TUMBLING
William Cornelius
Department of Kinesiology, Health Promotion, and Recreation
University of North Texas

IN-LINE SKATING
Liz Miller
Danville, CA

JOGGING AND WALKING
Don Torok
Department of Exercise Science and Health Promotion
Florida Atlantic University

and

Jim Hesson
Exercise Science Department
Black Hills State University

KARATE
Rick Schmidt
Nutrition and Health Sciences
University of Nebraska

KAYAKING AND CANOEING
Dan Henderson
Seattle, WA

LACROSSE
Dan Finck
Lone Tree, CO

and

Keith Bugbee
Physical Education Department
Springfield College

MOUNTAINEERING
John Bicknell
Colorado Mountain School
Boulder, CO

ORIENTEERING
Miki Snell
Dallas, TX

PICKLE-BALL
Janet Valentine
Seattle, WA

RACQUETBALL, PADDLEBALL, AND HANDBALL
Robert Maughan
Department of Kinesiology, Health Promotion and Recreation
University of North Texas

RUGBY
Kevin McAllister
Department of Sport Management and Recreation
Springfield College

SELF-DEFENSE
Aaron Banks
Department of Health and Exercise Science
Gustavus Adolphus College

SOCCER
March Krotee
Department of Physical Education
North Carolina State University

and

Paul Blair
Academy of Sports and Leisure Studies
University of Trinidad and Tobago

and

James LaPoint
Department of Health, Sport, and Exercise Science
University of Kansas

SOFTBALL (SLOW PITCH)
Jimmy Disch
Kinesiology Department
Rice University

SPEEDBALL
Aaron Banks
Department of Health and Exercise Science
Gustavus Adolphus College

SWIMMING
Ian Ratz
U.S.A. Swimming
Colorado Springs, CO

TABLE TENNIS
Steve Hopkins
Warwick, RI

TEAM HANDBALL
Paul Blair
Academy of Sport and Leisure Studies
University of Trinidad and Tobago

and

March Krotee
Department of Physical Education
North Carolina State University

and

James LaPoint
Department of Health, Sport, and Exercise Science
University of Kansas

TENNIS
Randy Hyllegard
Department of Kinesiology
Western Illinois University

TOUCH FOOTBALL AND FLAG FOOTBALL
Jack Holik
Athletic Department
Springfield College

TRACK AND FIELD
Mark Wetmore
Department of Athletics
University of Colorado

VOLLEYBALL
Lyndsay Benson
Athletics Department
University of Northern Colorado

WATER POLO
Rich Corso
Athletic Department
University of California, Berkeley

WEIGHT TRAINING
Jay Dawes
National Strength and Conditioning Association
Colorado Springs, CO

WRESTLING
Gerald Landwer
Department of Kinesiology
University of Nevada

YOGA
Aaron Banks
Department of Health and Exercise Science
Gustavus Adolphus College

Contents

Preface

PURPOSE OF THE BOOK

The purpose of the fifteenth edition of *Sports and Recreational Activities* is to provide current fundamental knowledge about a broad spectrum of physical activities. The physiological, psychological, and social benefits of participation in physical activities have long been proclaimed by physicians, physical educators, and recreation directors, and it appears that their advice is receiving the public's attention. Most evidence suggests that the number of people engaging in regular physical activity is higher than in the past, although it is still considerably lower than the goals set by national health agencies. There is some evidence that the number of people, especially young people, participating in regular physical activity in the United States might actually be declining after several years of increase. For reasons of safety, enjoyment, and motivation, it is important that participants start out correctly and that they are exposed to a variety of possibilities. We believe that participation in physical activities can enrich the quality of life and that use of the basic concepts provided in this book will promote this enrichment.

Sports and Recreational Activities is written for two groups of readers—participants and instructors (or instructors-to-be). People who decide to embark on a personal program of sports and recreation can benefit from this book's excellent overview of 46 popular physical activities in its 39 chapters. Physical educators, recreation leaders, playground directors, and camp counselors, no matter how well trained, seldom have the time to learn the fundamentals of all the activities covered in this book. For these instructors or students who will become instructors, the book should serve as a valuable resource when they are called upon to teach an unfamiliar activity.

In most cases, each chapter includes a brief historical perspective of the activity, including Olympic history where applicable; information about the selection and care of required equipment; a digest of the basic rules; a discussion of the fundamental skills and techniques required; ideas about strategies; safety concerns; a list of teaching considerations, terminology, and selected references, including written materials, visual aids, and Web sites. Armed with this knowledge, both the participant and the instructor should find increased enjoyment in physical activities.

CHANGES IN THE FIFTEENTH EDITION

The revision process for this edition was extensive. Although much about sports and recreational activities remains constant over the years, there also is much that changes. For example, we have updated the text to reflect the invention of new equipment, changes in the rules, the discovery of new techniques, and the increase in available references, including Web resources. Occasionally, significant rule changes occur between editions (an example this time is that badminton has begun to adopt rally scoring), and these are detailed in this edition. The focus of the health-related physical fitness chapter now stresses the research-confirmed importance of physical activity. The increasing participation of women in sports and recreational activities has brought about many rule changes during recent years (consider basketball, for example). The conversion of various dimensions to metric units and the simple need to update photographs as new apparel and techniques become available are other reasons revision is necessary. Along with these updating needs, many other changes have been made in this fifteenth edition to make it a more useful book.

CHAPTER CONSISTENCY

Particular attention has been given to present this wealth of diverse material as consistently as possible from chapter to chapter. In general and where appropriate, each chapter proceeds from behavioral objectives, to history, to equipment and facilities, to rules and etiquette, to fundamental skills and techniques, to strategies, to teaching considerations, and finally to ancillary information such as a glossary, suggested readings, audiovisual materials, and Web sites.

NEW ILLUSTRATIONS

Many new photographs and drawings have been added and others replaced or modified to illustrate the latest developments in technique and instruction. If a picture is worth a thousand words, then the hundreds of illustrations in the book provide an efficient method for communicating a great deal of information. However, it is not always a simple task to obtain just the right photograph or drawing to capture the intent. A great deal of effort was spent on improving the illustrations for this edition so that the reader can truly "see" the nuances of each activity.

NEW TO THIS EDITION

Each chapter has been revised to include only the latest rules and regulations. Photos and illustrations have also been updated to include current and easy-to-follow pictures and drawings. Additionally, you will find:

- References to the most recent Olympic achievements throughout
- A new chapter on yoga
- A totally rewritten chapter on self-defense
- Major additions or revisions to the chapters covering health-related physical fitness, bicycling, bowling, in-line skating, kayaking and canoeing, speedball, team handball, weight training, and wrestling
- Significant modifications to the chapters covering backpacking, jogging and walking, women's lacrosse, rugby, tennis, and touch football and flag football

ANNOTATED REFERENCES

Recognizing that a book such as this cannot present every facet of every activity, we present a list of suggested readings or resources for each chapter. Beginning in the ninth edition and continuing through this edition, we have provided a short annotation for many of these references. This will allow readers who wish further details about an activity to select readings that are germane to their particular interests.

VIDEOS

Appendix C lists pertinent video resources that specify where relevant videotapes may be found. Videotapes and DVDs of talented performers and of classic events are being used for instructional purposes at an increasing rate. We hope this additional resource will continue to prove helpful.

APPENDIX MATERIAL

Appendix A contains some playing field and court dimensions, for activities not presented as individual chapters. New to this list for the fifteenth edition is bocce ball. Appendix B provides a guide for converting metric and English units, and as mentioned, Appendix C contains sources for relevant videos.

ONLINE RESOURCES

Book Web Site

www.mhhe.com/mood15e

An online instructor's manual and test book has been prepared for use with the fifteenth edition. It includes chapter outlines, test questions, and suggestions for discussion. The chapter outlines can be used to obtain a quick synopsis of the chapter contents. They are useful for organizing class lectures and could be reproduced for students as study guides. Objective test questions (true-false, matching, and multiple choice) are provided *only* as a source of ideas from which an instructor may build a valid examination over the factual materials presented in each chapter. It is much better, from a validity viewpoint, for each instructor to build his or her own examination than to rely only on the suggested questions in the instructor's manual. The suggestions for discussion include questions that can be used either as essay questions on examinations or as stimuli for discussions. They generally require the student to demonstrate comprehension of the chapter information by applying learned material and summarizing important concepts contained in the chapter.

McGraw-Hill Create Custom Publishing

Craft your teaching resources to match the way you teach! With McGraw-Hill Create, www.mcgrawhillcreate.com, you can choose to build your own custom sports and activities book using only the chapters that you use in your physical education or recreation program. Add your own materials on local or state standards to customize the book for your students.

Create allows you to easily rearrange chapters, combine material from other content sources, and quickly upload content you have written such as your course syllabus or teaching notes. Find the content you need in Create by searching through thousands of leading McGraw-Hill textbooks. Arrange your book to fit your teaching style. Create even allows you to personalize your book's appearance by selecting the cover and adding your name, school, and course information. Order a Create book and you'll receive a complimentary print review copy in 3–5 business days or a complimentary electronic review copy (eComp) via email in about one hour. Go to www.mcgrawhillcreate.com today and register. Experience how McGraw-Hill Create empowers you to teach your students your way.

ACKNOWLEDGMENTS

A book with as diverse and broad a scope as this is obviously the result of the work and ideas of many people. We wish to express a very large thank you to all the consultants and contributors for their valuable insights and helpful suggestions for this revision.

Special thanks go to the officials of the various sporting goods companies and publishers for giving us permission to reproduce many drawings and photographs.

We also want to thank the survey respondents for their valuable contributions in developing the fifteenth edition of the text.

Reviewers

Robert S. Christenson
Oklahoma State University

LaTonya Conner
Albany State University

Patty Hacker
South Dakota State University

Robert M. Isosaari
University of West Florida

Mark Kutame
Chicago State University

James LaPoint
University of Kansas

Dawn Lewis
CSU Fresno

William McCullough
University of Southern Maine

Deborah Myers
University of Texas–Pan American

David Oatman
Missouri State University

Steve Phillips
Faulkner University

Bennie Prince
University of Arkansas at Little Rock

Celia Regimbal
University of Toledo

Elaine Rydze
Coe College

Dave Thorn
East Central University

Callie Traub
Southern Illinois University–Edwardsville

Henry E. White
North Carolina Central University

Jeff Word
East Central University

We wish to express our gratitude to Marilyn Rothenberger, Marley Magaziner, Christopher Johnson, Erin Melloy, and all the other folks at McGraw-Hill for providing feedback and guidance and for keeping us to our deadlines. Their suggestions and gentle reminders are much appreciated.

Dale P. Mood
Frank F. Musker
Judith E. Rink

Introduction

*T*here is almost unanimous agreement that optimum health is our most prized possession. Schopenhauer, the German philosopher, expressed this idea when he remarked, "The greatest of follies is to neglect one's health for any other advantage of life."

A tremendous amount of research has verified that there is a direct causal link connecting optimum health and participation in physical activity. However, there is wide variation in the types of activities recommended for different age groups.

The latest information on guidelines for the amounts, durations, and intensities of physical activity that should be done by children and adolescents (ages 6–17), adults (ages 18–64), and older adults (ages 65 and older) are presented in Chapter 2 of this text. The most recent large-scale endorsement for physical activity is its inclusion as an important component of *Healthy People 2010,* a concerted effort of the Office of Disease Prevention and Health Promotion and the U.S. Department of Health and Human Services. Healthy People 2020 is now in the developmental stage.

In addition to the value of physical activity in maintaining optimum health, there are often social and recreational benefits as well. These benefits are becoming even more important than in the past.

Although in some high schools, colleges, and universities students are required to participate in physical activity classes, several institutions have eliminated this requirement. Some have replaced the requirement with an elective program, while others have simply eliminated the requirement altogether. At the high school level, this has generally resulted in a decrease in students participating in structured physical activity classes, while at the college level, the number of students taking physical activity classes has remained constant or decreased.

There is little doubt that the number of adults participating in sports and recreational activities in the United States has increased somewhat in recent years. However, this number is still far short of goals set by national health agencies.

Recent increases in the proportion of the population that falls into the obese category demonstrate the high level of inactivity in the United States. Ironically, the number of children being exposed to high-quality, daily physical activity in physical education programs in the public schools continues to decrease. Local economic shortfalls are the primary cause for this phenomenon, and the trend has public health officials concerned. Obesity among children as well as adults is a growing concern. A large amount of scientific evidence is now available to demonstrate that early and continued participation in physical activity can significantly improve the overall health of this country. The mechanism to provide this exposure (physical education in the public schools) is available but is currently being curtailed. This may prove to be very shortsighted in the long run.

The slight increase in activity participation noted among adults can be attributed to increased awareness of the health benefits of physical activity and to an increase in the amount of leisure time available to most Americans. We have shorter work weeks and more and longer vacations than in the past. In addition, sports and recreational facilities have become

increasingly abundant and accessible to larger and more diverse segments of the population.

The increased leisure time, however, does not explain why Americans choose to use this time engaged in sports and recreational activities; it merely provides the opportunity to do so. Likewise, increased facilities reflect only that larger segments of the population choose to participate, but they do not supply a reason for this choice.

A number of theories have been proposed by educators, sociologists, medical personnel, and others to explain why we engage in physical activity. These theories are diverse, yet contain many overlapping concepts. The satisfaction of creative desires, expression of inherent basic instincts, use of excess energy, preparation for other types of life situations, and exposure to risk to provide excitement are a few of the concepts that have been proposed.

People have become increasingly aware of several benefits of physical activity, particularly in the physiological and health areas. Some of these benefits and relevant considerations are presented in Chapter 2, "Health-Related Physical Fitness." In addition to the physiological benefits, the following are other areas believed to be affected positively by participation in sports and recreational activities.

PSYCHOLOGICAL FACTORS

Many life situations are conducive to producing tension and emotional stress, resulting in worry, anxiety, fear, frustration, and depression. Although the evidence is not as definite because the factors involved are more difficult to measure, there is some indication that physical activity under the proper conditions can be helpful in improving emotional stability and mental fitness, just as it aids in developing physical fitness. Participation in an interesting sport takes the mind off other things and prevents it from dwelling on problems. Exercise also helps release emotions through socially approved channels. It is a means of satisfying certain universal primitive urges, and it provides for self-expression.

Experiencing success in developing skills and participating in a physical activity are excellent means of developing confidence and reaping satisfaction that comes from successful accomplishment. Through individual activities such as archery, bowling, running, swimming, gymnastics, and golf, it is possible to compete against oneself as well as against others. The personal gains and achievements possible through participation in physical activities have been shown to be related positively to motivation and self-confidence.

Although participation in almost any sport or any physical activity involves a degree of risk, an interesting phenomenon, sometimes called "extreme sports," has emerged in the recent past. In about the mid-1980s, in-line skates (see Chapter 15) began to replace standard roller skates, and now over 26 million people in the United States in-line-skate at least once a year. In 2008 nearly 18.5 million mountain bikes were sold. Indoor climbing walls are now found in gyms, private athletic facilities, and even some department stores. Large increases in the number of people who snowboard, skydive, hang glide, bungee jump, and mountain climb have been recorded in the early 2000s. Some TV sports networks have broadcast extreme sports competitions, and mountain biking and half-pipe snowboarding appeared in the 1998 Winter Olympics.

Whether this increase in risky sports is a passing fancy or a historical trend is difficult to determine at this time. Certainly for now there is an undisputed increase in the participation and interest in the psychological trait of risk-taking through involvement in dangerous physical activities. See the Web sites listed at the end of this chapter for additional information about extreme sports.

KNOWLEDGE

A dominant factor in the American way of life is the ability of the average citizen to know about and understand sports, if not as a participant, then as a spectator. Therefore, it is beneficial to learn the rules and strategies of various sports and physical activities. In addition, knowledge of etiquette, safety, equipment, history, values, techniques, and other factors can enhance the enjoyment of watching or participating in team, dual, or individual activities.

SOCIAL VALUES

An important aspect of physical activity is to help in the socialization of the individual. Because we are living in an age of social conflict, it is highly important that positive social habits are instilled in the members of our society. A program of physical activities offers unlimited opportunities for developing broad social understandings. In fact, initial contacts between previously distant cultures or societies are sometimes made through a common interest in sports.

One facet of common social interests of Americans is shown by the wide publicity given to sports through radio and television, sports pages of newspapers and magazines, and discussions between individuals of all ages. There is possibly no better way to learn how to get along with and to live with others than through participation in sports and physical activities. In these settings the individual must show the same qualities that are necessary for successful and happy living in a democratic society. To be most successful, courtesy, self-control, initiative, cooperation, and loyalty must be acquired. The experience of being both a follower and a leader can be gained. Successful participation in sports implies that the participant must learn to be a good sport and to give credit where it is due, regardless of who wins or loses. Participation in team games, particularly, can teach the individual to work with others to the best advantage of the team and to control emotions.

People are often motivated by the social instinct of belonging. One way the desire to associate with others can be satisfied is through participation in physical activities. The congenial atmosphere of sports presents the opportunity to develop friendships that may have lasting value.

RECREATION

Technology has liberated us from much physical work, and recreation has assumed an important place in modern life as a result of the increasing amount of leisure time available.

It is evident that people can use leisure time constructively or destructively. One of the aims of a physical activity program is to teach the wise use of leisure time. People should be made aware of the vital place that wholesome recreation, and especially sports, can play in the full enjoyment of life.

Recreation, to be helpful, need not be elaborate or expensive. Many of the simple forms of recreation available to all are the most satisfying and of the greatest help in maintaining

physical, mental, and emotional health. (See the section on walking in Chapter 16.)

FACTORS ASSOCIATED WITH A PHYSICAL ACTIVITY PROGRAM

To profit most from participation in sports and physical activities, a number of things should be considered.

Training and Conditioning

Some physical educators and sports directors make a distinction between "conditioning" and "training." Conditioning is usually considered to be related to such notions as proper nutrition, resting, relaxing, sleeping, and exercising regularly, as well as working toward the improvement of skills in a particular activity. Training, on the other hand, is considered by some to be the practice of certain movements by constant repetition until a skill is established or mastered. An example of this would be attempting to improve—and master to the greatest possible extent—skills required in such sports as swimming, golf, tennis, or track. The meanings of the words *training* and *conditioning* overlap, for gains in one generally lead to increases in the other.

To improve and maintain a reasonably modest level of *physical fitness,* it is necessary to participate in vigorous physical activities at regular intervals. It is generally recommended by the U.S. Department of Health and Human Services that, at a **minimum,** a healthy adult under the age of 65 should participate in at least 2½ hours of moderate-intensity or 1¼ hours of vigorous-intensity, or an equivalent combination of moderate and vigorous physical activity per week. In addition, they should do muscle strengthening activities involving all major muscle groups at least 2 or more days per week. It is best to begin with mild exercise and to increase the intensity gradually during subsequent periods. This is recommended to prevent undue stress and strain on muscles. The duration of physical activity periods should be governed by the response of the individual to activity and past training periods. Other factors, such as age and initial physical condition, will dictate the starting intensity and duration of activity periods. To develop the greatest overall muscular efficiency, one should participate in activities that require some use of all the major muscles of the body. Many sports require repeated use of only a limited set of muscles; thus, it is best to take part in a wide variety of sports.

Recently, however, epidemiologists examining the *health* benefits of physical activity (defined mainly as living longer and with a higher quality of life) have determined that even modest participation is valuable. Indications are that 30 minutes per day of rather modest energy expenditure (even if it takes the form of three bouts of 10 minutes each) produce health benefits such as reduced risk of heart disease and increases in longevity. The value of an activity as simple as taking a brisk walk periodically has been determined to be an important predictor of improved health. It is unwise to engage in any strenuous activity before the body is in condition for it. To *improve* the physical condition of the body requires application of a stress or overload. However, to *maintain* a particular state of physical condition requires less intense activity than is required to get to that level. It is also

generally accepted that if participation is discontinued, the degree of physical condition will decline at about the same rate required to build it.

Good physical condition is sufficient for participation in most sports. However, it must be kept in mind that certain sports require special training. Age makes a difference in conditioning and training; younger people can train and condition more rapidly than older people.

Physical Examination

No one should participate in prolonged and strenuous physical activity without first having a complete medical examination by a physician. A medical examination including an exercise stress test is so important that it cannot be overemphasized, especially after the age of 40, and regular examinations should be repeated periodically throughout life. The results of medical examinations show that most people do not need to restrict physical activity; however, if certain conditions are present, such as a defective heart, participation in unrestricted strenuous exercise can be very damaging.

Precautions

It should be apparent that an exercise program needs to be structured to fit each individual. Beginning level of fitness, medical condition, interests, age, and availability of facilities are examples of factors that need to be considered.

Before one engages in strenuous physical activity, common sense dictates that there should be a period of gradual *warming up* and stretching of the muscles to eliminate some of the danger of muscle injury. Large-muscle groups, including the arms, legs, and trunk, should be warmed up first. In fact, they should receive major attention throughout the warming-up and limbering-up period.

It is usually recommended that vigorous and strenuous physical activity be tapered off. Sudden and complete relaxation after vigorous exertion without tapering off can cause

dizziness, nausea, and even fainting if the exercise has been particularly strenuous. Giving the body processes a chance to slow down gradually is a precautionary measure observed by practically all champion athletes.

There are good reasons for *tapering off* following vigorous or strenuous activity. During activity, the heart rate speeds up to keep the muscles supplied with sufficient oxygen and nutrients. The increased heart rate sends the arterial blood to the muscles and eventually to the veins. Because the venous system has no forceful mechanism like the heart to help move blood back to the heart, the action of muscles must be depended on to help the return flow of blood. When the veins fill with blood, the pressure of contracting muscles produces a pumping action on the thin-walled veins to propel the blood back toward the center of the body. If vigorous activity ends abruptly, the heart continues for a time to send extra amounts of arterial blood to the muscles. Because the muscles are suddenly inactive, there is not sufficient force for returning the extra blood to the heart. Consequently, the extra blood tends to pool in the muscles, and the imbalance may leave some organs, such as the brain, with an inadequate supply of blood. During the tapering-off process following strenuous activity, the muscles continue to squeeze blood from the extremities of the body back into the main circulation.

Regardless of the care taken in beginning training and conditioning for sports, muscles may become sore and stiff. Mild activity, in cases of this sort, helps the pumping action of the heart that is necessary to bring blood to the sore muscle and thereby speeds up the carrying away of waste products.

Another precaution is *avoidance of overexertion*. Excess emotional stress can greatly add to the seriousness of overexertion. The ability to recuperate after strenuous activity is a good guide at any age to the amount and extent of activity to participate in at one time. The recovery should be reasonably prompt. However, if the breathing and heart rate are still greatly accelerated 10 minutes after activity, and if there is marked fatigue or weakness after a few hours of rest or a sense of definite fatigue the day following, the activity likely has been too severe or prolonged.

As a last precaution following strenuous activity, an adequate *cool-down period* should follow the tapering-off process. From three to six minutes should elapse between tapering off and entering the shower. Otherwise, the warm water will prevent loss of heat from the body, and it will continue to perspire. Heavy perspiration following a shower and dressing may cause chilling, with the same results as chilling after being drenched by a cold rain.

Of course, local and environmental conditions may require other precautions. For example, physical activity in very warm temperatures requires extra attention to fluid replacement and core body temperature. Acclimation to unusually high altitudes may be required before engaging in strenuous physical activity. In most cases, common sense should be used to prevent discomfort or injury.

Rest and Sleep

Sufficient rest and sleep are necessary for maintenance of good physical, mental, and emotional health. Although it is thought that the average person needs eight to nine hours of sleep each night, the amount varies with the individual and with age. Growing children require more sleep than adults. Some people require more sleep than others who have similar activity levels. Regularity in rest and sleep is very important. If one is not getting sufficient rest and sleep, participation in strenuous and vigorous physical activities can be more harmful than helpful. It is recommended that each individual learn to judge the amount of sleep and rest necessary to maintain physical and mental alertness and a feeling of well-being.

Diet and Nutrition

A balanced diet is necessary for maintenance of good nutrition. Nutrition is basic to physical, mental, and emotional health. Those who participate in physical activity usually require more food than those who lead sedentary lives. Participation in physical activities requires energy, and food is the main source of energy for the body. Replacement of fluid and electrolytes lost through physical activity is also important.

It is usually best not to eat heavy meals before strenuous physical activity, especially if emotional stress is present, as in a competitive activity. It is difficult for the body to digest and assimilate food under such circumstances.

Finally, together with activity, diet is a controlling factor in body weight. Although physical activity is helpful in weight reduction, the number of calories eliminated through exercise is minimal when compared with the number of calories that can be eliminated through a sensible diet. If the overweight person uses activity to reduce weight and then refrains from overeating, the activity can be helpful.

Clothing and Cleanliness

Proper clothing is important when participating in sports. It is essential to change from street clothes to sports clothing when participating in vigorous activities that will cause perspiration and body odor. Even sports clothing can become so soiled by dirt and perspiration that it becomes objectionable to others. Therefore, it is important to have sufficient sports clothing and to keep it as clean as possible. It is particularly important that shoes and socks be selected properly. Gymnasium or other sports shoes should fit properly to safeguard the feet. Blisters form easily if shoes or socks do not fit properly. Clothing that fits too tightly or that may hinder performance should be avoided.

A shower should be taken after participation in vigorous physical activity for both hygienic and social reasons. Showers not only cleanse the skin, but also reduce chances of infection. Some people like a warm shower followed by a short, cold shower; others prefer that water temperature be tapered from warm to comfortably cool. Prolonged hot showers are not recommended because they interfere with the body's ability to recover from the changes in blood flow brought on by the exercise.

Injuries and Illness

A considerable amount of recent research supports the hypothesis that increases in the efficiency of the immune system are associated with improvements in physical condition. Just as muscles adapt to the stress of overload by becoming stronger, it is postulated that the immune system adapts by becoming increasingly resistant to infection. However, due to the significant increase in energy required to fight off a cold or the flu, once contracted, it is best to refrain from participation in physical activities during any illness caused by infection.

Care should be given to even slight injuries received while participating in physical activities. Small scratches and cuts should be treated as soon as possible. Any cut or scratch that seems to have become infected should have the attention of a physician immediately. Various infections can be contracted in gymnasiums and shower rooms. Participants should be careful with taking showers and drying in the dressing rooms to avoid "athlete's foot." Serious sprains and bruises should be treated with immediate first aid and then examined by a physician.

Safety

Sports and physical activities should be as safe as possible. Participants should take every precaution to prevent injury to themselves and to others. Equipment and rules and regulations of games and sports generally are designed to protect players as much as possible. Some sports (e.g., football) and activities require special protective equipment, and playing them without such equipment risks serious injury.

The beginner in certain sports should recognize that some advanced activities may be dangerous to attempt. For example, a beginner attempting advanced tumbling stunts would be in danger of injury because of a lack of skill. Everyone should give attention to safety, because a high percentage of the injuries and deaths from accidents can be prevented.

REFERENCE

Healthy people 2010: The cornerstone for prevention. 2005. ODPHP Communications Support Center (Stock No. H0020). Rockville, MD: U.S. Department of Health and Human Services.

WEB SITES

Information about the American College of Sports Medicine: www.acsm.org
Information about extreme sports: www.allextremesports.com www.extremesportsblog.org
Information about *Healthy People 2010*, and *Healthy People 2020*: www.healthypeople.gov
Information about the National Guidelines for Physical Activity: www.physicalactivityplan.org

Health-Related Physical Fitness

After completing this chapter, the reader should be able to:

- Understand the importance of physical activity and how it relates to health, quality of life, and total well-being
- Define and identify the components of health-related physical fitness
- Develop an activity or training program that will increase aerobic endurance, positively influence body composition, and increase muscular strength and endurance and flexibility
- Assess one's health-related physical fitness

The term *physical fitness* means many things to people. For some, it conjures up visions of a large muscular "Adonis" weight lifter whose rippling muscles testify to the great shape he or she is in. Others envision a marathon runner, a lean individual who has trained to run great distances and has a physique quite different from that of the weight lifter. Actually, neither of these individuals is the best illustration of physical fitness. Rather, a physically fit individual is one who can conduct the functions of daily life without undue stress on the body and, perhaps more importantly, has a healthy body and is not at risk for disease as a result of his or her fitness level or physical inactivity. Thus, the term often used today for physical fitness is *health-related physical fitness* (HRPF). This chapter focuses on HRPF: how it differs from the historical definition of physical fitness, the components of HRPF, how to achieve HRPF, the scientific literature defining how one can develop HRPF and maintain it throughout life, and how to assess your own level of HRPF.

The science of epidemiology—the study of diseases, their causes, and their impact on society—has been widely used in the past 60 years to illustrate the relationship between a physically inactive lifestyle and increased morbidity and mortality. Many diseases can be said to be hypokinetic in origin because they result from physically inactive lifestyles. The scientific literature was so supportive of the relationship between physical inactivity and disease that the U.S. Department of Health and Human Services, the U.S. Centers for Disease Control and Prevention, and the U.S. Surgeon General released a document entitled *Physical Activity and Health: A Report of the Surgeon General* (1996) summarizing this influence and calling for national dedication to increasing the physical activity levels of all Americans.

The American College of Sports Medicine and the American Heart Association created guidelines for physical activity for adults (see Haskell et al., 2007; Nelson et al., 2007; and Williams et al., 2007). Importantly, in 2008 the U.S. Department of Health and Human Services developed Physical Activity Guidelines for Americans (http://www.health.gov/PAGuidelines/). These were the first physical activity guidelines developed at the national level in the United States. The guidelines provided further documentation of the relationship between physically active lifestyles and a wide number of morbidities and mortality. A complete scientific report is also available (http://www.health.gov/PAGuidelines/). Physical activity guidelines are provided for active children and adolescents, active adults, and active older adults. Subsequent to the guidelines' development, processes are underway for creation of a National Physical Activity Plan (see Table 2.1) (http://www.physicalactivityplan.org/).

Looking to the future, the U.S. Department of Health and Human Services developed *Healthy People 2010,* a set of objectives to be achieved by the year 2010. The objectives were developed based on input from states, communities, professional organizations, and individuals to help improve the health of U.S. citizens. *Healthy People 2010* was built on the initiatives set forth in the 1979 Surgeon General's Report, *Healthy People* (Healthy People, 1979) and *Healthy People 2000: National Health Promotion and Disease Prevention Objectives* (Healthy People, 1990). The two goals of *Healthy People 2010* are (1) to increase quality and years of healthy life and (2) eliminate health disparities among segments of the population. *Healthy People 2010* identifies 10 leading health indictors: (1) physical activity, (2) overweight and obesity, (3) tobacco use, (4) substance abuse, (5) responsible sexual behavior, (6) mental health, (7) injury and violence, (8) environmental quality, (9) immunization, and (10) access to health care. It is interesting that the first five leading health indicators are lifestyle characteristics. Health-related physical fitness is directly related to the first two leading health indicators.

Our understanding of the importance of exercise or physical activity and its impact on quality of life can be traced back at least as far as Hippocrates (460–370 BCE), who stated that "eating alone will not keep a man well; he must also exercise." Over the years, attention to fitness components and the reported lack of fitness has often been associated with times

Table 2.1. NATIONAL GUIDELINES FOR PHYSICAL ACTIVITY (http://www.physicalactivityplan.org/)

Children and Adolescents (aged 6–17)

- Children and adolescents should do 1 hour (60 minutes) or more of physical activity every day.
- Most of the 1 hour or more a day should be either moderate- or vigorous-intensity aerobic physical activity.
- As part of their daily physical activity, children and adolescents should do vigorous-intensity activity on at least 3 days per week. They also should do muscle-strengthening and bone-strengthening activity on at least 3 days per week.

Adults (aged 18–64)

- Adults should do 2 hours and 30 minutes (150 minutes) a week of moderate-intensity or 1 hour and 15 minutes (75 minutes) a week of vigorous-intensity aerobic physical activity or an equivalent combination of moderate- and vigorous-intensity aerobic physical activity. Aerobic activity should be performed in episodes of at least 10 minutes, preferably spread throughout the week.
- Additional health benefits are provided by increasing to 5 hours (300 minutes) a week of moderate-intensity aerobic physical activity, or 2 hours and 30 minutes (150 minutes) a week of vigorous-intensity physical activity, or an equivalent combination of both.
- Adults should also do muscle-strengthening activities that involve all major muscle groups on 2 or more days per week.

Older Adults (aged 65 and older)

- Older adults should follow the adult guidelines. If this is not possible due to limiting chronic conditions, older adults should be as physically active as their abilities allow. They should avoid inactivity. Older adults should do exercises that maintain or improve balance if they are at risk of falling.

Table 2.2. RESEARCH HAS ILLUSTRATED THE RELATIONSHIP BETWEEN PHYSICAL ACTIVITY, PHYSICAL FITNESS, AND ENERGY EXPENDITURE AND VARIOUS HEALTH OUTCOMES IN A WIDE NUMBER OF POPULATIONS.

Health outcomes

Bone health
Coronary artery disease
Cancer
Cardiovascular disease
Death
Functional limitations
Hypertension
Mental health
Metabolic syndrome
Stroke
Type 2 diabetes

Populations

Men
Women
Children
Elderly
Europeans
North Americans
Chinese
Danes
Japanese
Native Americans
Scandinavians

of war, when individuals were found to be unfit for military service. However, those individuals' "unfitness" really had little to do with fitness as it is perceived today. For example, many were declared unfit for military service because of poor eyesight, flat feet, or syphilis. The *Army Times* reported in 2009 that the Pentagon estimates that 35 percent of Americans aged 17 to 24 are unqualified for military service because of physical and medical conditions,

Also, historically, "physical fitness" tests measured a number of characteristics that were greatly influenced by genetics (e.g., speed, agility, quickness) and thus were not easily modifiable. Fitness tests from 60 years ago measured speed, agility, and power through the use of dashes, shuttle runs, softball throws, and long jumps. Many of these items are not significantly affected by training and have not been shown to be related to health. Conversely, HRPF components are trainable and modifiable and, most importantly, are related to health, disease, and quality of life.

EXERCISE OR PHYSICAL ACTIVITY?

For years the focus about physical fitness was on "exercise." The phrases "No pain, no gain" and "maximum performance" expressed common expectations about what was necessary for becoming fit. However, evidence from exercise physiologists, physicians, epidemiologists, and other researchers has given us more accurate knowledge of how to develop physical fitness in healthy adults.

This chapter illustrates activities that result in improved quality of life and protection against disease. Certainly, people who are physically fit (i.e., have achieved higher levels of fitness as a result of greater-intensity exercise) are generally healthy. However, we will provide evidence to support this claim and steps that you can take that will improve your HRPF, your health status, and your quality of life without turning you into a muscle-rippling weight lifter or a marathoner.

A list of diseases known to be related to levels of physical activity, energy expenditure, and/or physical fitness is presented in Table 2.2. The generalizability of the relationship between physical activity and disease is illustrated in this table. Its impact is seen in many different diseases and many different populations. Many professional organizations have developed position statements on the important role that physical activity plays in health (Table 2.3). Evidence by Morrow et al. (1999) suggests that people are aware of the cardiovascular benefits of physical activity but less aware of the metabolic benefits derived from a physically active lifestyle.

COMPONENTS OF HEALTH-RELATED PHYSICAL FITNESS

The three major components of HRPF are aerobic capacity, body composition, and musculoskeletal development (muscular strength and endurance, and flexibility). We will consider each of these components and why they are important to HRPF.

Aerobic Fitness

The term *aerobic fitness* is often used synonymously with the term *physical fitness*. Aerobic (or cardiorespiratory) fitness is probably the aspect most commonly agreed to be a part of physical fitness. Essentially, aerobic capacity is the maximum amount of oxygen your body can extract from inspired air and utilize at maximal exercise. Many studies have shown a relationship between aerobic capacity and a number of health factors. For example, persons who are aerobically fit are less likely to prematurely die due to heart disease, and they are less likely to have a stroke, develop diabetes, be overweight,

Table 2.3. ORGANIZATIONS WITH STATEMENTS OR POSITION PAPERS ON THE POSITIVE EFFECTS OF PHYSICAL ACTIVITY ON HEALTH AND/OR QUALITY OF LIFE

American Academy of Pediatrics
American Cancer Society
American College of Sports Medicine
American Diabetes Association
American Heart Association
International Federation of Sports Medicine
International Society and Federation of Cardiology
Royal College of Physicians
Surgeon General of the United States
U.S. Centers for Disease Control and Prevention
World Health Organization

have high blood pressure, or develop certain cancers. Your aerobic capacity is related to the frequency, intensity, duration, and type of exercise or physical activity in which you engage (the ACSM [1998] and Kesaniemi et al. [2001] report). A "dose response" to the level of physical activity has been demonstrated. The term *dose response* refers to the fact that as you increase your "dose" (amount) of aerobic exercise, you can expect better health outcomes and quality of life.

Figure 2.1 illustrates the findings from six studies on the dose response resulting from increased physical activity. You can increase the "dose" in a number of ways. You can increase the frequency, intensity, and/or duration of the aerobic exercise that you do. However, this does not mean that you must do a great deal of exercise to have a health benefit. Various national studies have reported wide ranges of physical activity behaviors in adults. Figures 2.2 and 2.3 illustrate this variation. Figure 2.2 suggests that most adults are NOT regularly physically active. Yet, Figure 2.3 suggests that most people meet guidelines for physical activity sufficient for health benefits. These discrepancies illustrate the difficulty in assessing physical activity behaviors with self-reported data. Objectively measured physical activity behaviors through electronic tracking suggest that less than 5 percent of American adults actually engage in sufficient physical activity for a health benefit. Clearly, additional research on physical activity behaviors is necessary. The greatest benefit in risk reduction is often seen as people move from the lowest level of fitness to the next level of fitness. Figure 2.4 shows that, for males and females, the relative risk of mortality from all causes of death declines as one moves to a higher level of fitness. Figure 2.5 presents similar information for prevention of stroke in persons who are physically active.

Body Composition

The body composition aspect of HRPF refers to the amount and relative distribution of fat in your body. Americans of all

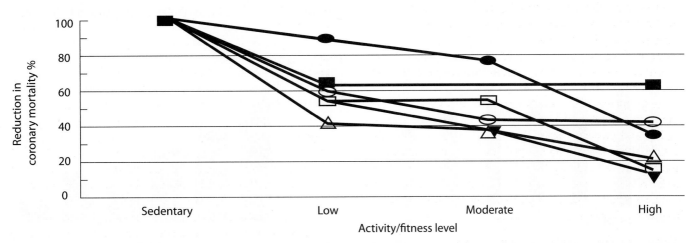

Figure 2.1. Results from six studies illustrating the dose-response effect on reduction in coronary mortality associated with increased physical activity/fitness level. (Source: Blair and Connelly 1996. Reprinted with permission from *Research Quarterly for Exercise and Sport*, Vol 67, No. 2, 193–205, copyright 1996 by the American Alliance for Health, Physical Education and Dance, 1900 Association Drive, Reston, VA 20191.)

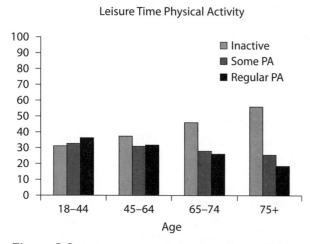

Figure 2.2. Leisure time physical activity. (Source: Blair et al. 1989)

ages are now carrying more fat than their ancestors of just a few decades ago. The U.S. Centers for Disease Control and Prevention reported that about two-thirds of U.S. adults and one-fifth if U.S. children are obese or overweight. Excessive body fatness is related to a variety of negative health consequences, including heart disease, hypertension, and diabetes. Figure 2.6 illustrates the risk associated with increased body fatness. Figure 2.6 essentially indicates that as one's fatness increases, the risk of developing coronary heart disease (CHD), type 2 diabetes (adult onset), and hypertension also increases. There are conflicting research results about the relationship between body size and various diseases. Suffice it to say that increased weight is associated with some notable diseases (e.g., high blood pressure, diabetes, heart disease, stroke, gallbladder disease, osteoarthritis, sleep apnea, and a number of other concerns). Evidence indicates that even those who are overweight are at reduced risk if they are physically fit (Blair and Brodney 1999; Blair and Church 2004). This suggests that physical fitness plays a more impor-

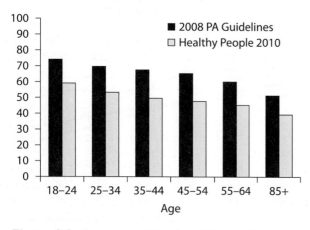

Figure 2.3. Prevalence of Americans Meeting Physical Activity Guidelines. (Source: Blair 1993)

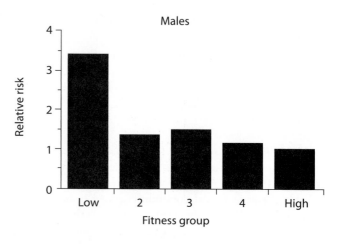

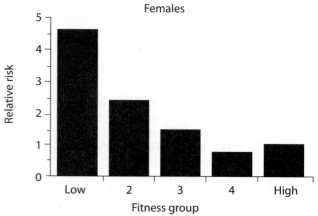

Figure 2.4. Age-adjusted all-cause death rates per 10,000 person-years of follow-up. (Source: Blair et al. 1989.)

tant role than body weight alone in some disease development (see Barlow et al. 1995, and Brodney et al. 2000).

It is important to realize that it is not weight alone that is the risk factor. One's body can be "compartmentalized" into several different components. One model suggests three body compartments: fat, lean (muscle and bones), and

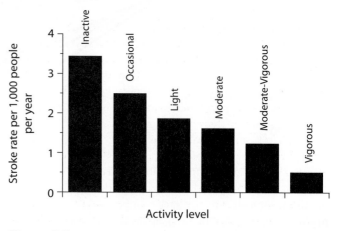

Figure 2.5. Age-adjusted reductions in stroke rate per 1,000 persons per year. (Source: Blair 1993.)

	BMI (kg/m²)	Obesity Class	Disease Risk* Relative to Normal Weight and Waist Circumference†	
			Men 102 cm (40 in) or less Women 88 cm (35in) or less	Men > 102 cm (40 in) Women > 88 cm (35 in)
Underweight	<18.5		–	–
Normal	18.5–24.9		–	–
Overweight	25.0–29.9		Increased	High
Obesity	30.0–34.9	I	High	Very High
	35.0–39.9	II	Very High	Very High
Extreme Obesity	40.0+	III	Extremely High	Extremely High

* Disease risk for type 2 diabetes, hypertension, and CVD.
† Increased waist circumference can also be a marker for increased risk even in persons of normal weight.

Figure 2.6. Relationship between body composition/fatness measures and disease risks. (From National Heart, Lung, and Blood Institute, 2010 [http://www.nhlbi.nih.gov/health/public/heart/obesity/lose_wt/bmi_dis.htm].)

other tissues (e.g., organs). If a person has a high weight but the weight is largely lean tissue, the health risks associated with the high weight might not be as great as if the weight were made up of a higher percentage of fat. An additional consideration is how the weight is distributed on the body. Individuals whose weight is stored at the waist have a greater risk of disease than those whose body fat is stored throughout their body or in the hips. The American Heart Association suggests that both men and women should strive to have a normal BMI (less than 25 kg/m²) and men should have a waist circumference less than 40 inches (102 cm) and women a waist circumference less than 35 inches (88 cm). Waist circumference is measured at the natural waist, just above the navel. You will learn more about the measurement of body composition in the pages to come.

Musculoskeletal Fitness

The arguments and support for health-risk reduction are not as great for the musculoskeletal component. There is increasing evidence that musculoskeletal fitness is related to a variety of diseases and mortality (FitzGerald et al. 2004, Ruiz et al. 2008 and 2009, and Jackson et al. in press). The primary reason musculoskeletal fitness is included in HRPF is because one needs sufficient muscular strength to conduct daily activities. Certainly muscles that are trained increase in size (hypertrophy) and strength. That is, the musculoskeletal aspect of HRPF is largely "functional" in nature because sufficient musculoskeletal strength permits one to conduct daily activities requiring some degree of strength and endurance. There are, however, two important health-related aspects to sufficient strength and endurance. Many fitness tests contain items of abdominal strength and endurance because of the theoretical relationship between abdominal strength and reduced risk of low back pain. This relationship has not been well supported in the scientific literature, but from theoretical and physical therapeutic perspectives, abdominal strength and endurance are important in holding the spine in correct alignment. Another area where strength is important is the development of strong bones. Much attention has been directed at the development of osteoporosis in women. Osteoporosis is becoming more important as a health consequence because people are living longer, and thus the disease has a longer time to have an effect on people. Both males and females suffer from osteoporosis, but it is found much more frequently in females. A good protection against the development of osteoporosis as you age is to have strong, solid bone tissue when you are young. Everyone's bones become less dense as they age. It is important to develop as much bone tissue as possible so that when the deterioration begins, it will take longer for the bone to "demineralize" and reach the "fracture threshold" where it is more easily broken. Although dietary supplements and pharmaceuticals have been suggested for increasing bone density, another good way to help develop bone density is to stress the muscles connecting the bones. As these muscles are stressed, the bones connected to them are also stressed and become more fully developed. For example, a tennis player's dominant arm is more dense than the nondominant arm, because the dominant arm is used much more during practice and play. Thus, stressing bones through physical exertion is a means of creating bone density. Marcus (2001) presents evidence of the relationship between exercise and osteoporosis. In addition, a report by the U.S. Surgeon General, *Bone Health and Osteoporosis* (2004), illustrates the important role that physical activity plays in bone health.

TRAINING FOR HEALTH-RELATED PHYSICAL FITNESS

A few overall guidelines must be considered when training for health-related fitness. These are presented in Table 2.4. Additionally, there are guidelines that are specific to each component of health-related fitness. Recall that the focus here is on improving one's health and decreasing risk of disease, not on making you an Olympic athlete. Thus, the guidelines provided herein can result in improved health status. Increased levels of physical activity will improve your health and quality of life.

Aerobic Fitness

Becoming aerobically fit does not require spending money to join a club or buying expensive workout clothes. Many simple lifestyle changes can help you improve your aerobic fitness level. The key point (as previously presented in Table 2.1) is to accumulate 150 minutes of moderate to vigorous physical activity each week. It is also important to incorporate resistance exercises a minimum of two days per week. Lifestyle changes such as walking during lunch, parking farther from the entrance at work or the store, or taking the stairs can help improve your health. Household tasks (gardening and raking leaves, moving furniture, caring for children, etc.) that cause an increase in your metabolic rate will have a positive effect on your aerobic fitness. A suggested aerobic training program is presented in Table 2.5.

Table 2.4. GENERAL PRINCIPLES FOR HEALTH-RELATED PHYSICAL FITNESS TRAINING

Specificity principle

Training must be specific to the type of effect desired. Aerobic training will improve aerobic capacity. Strength training will improve strength. Flexibility training will improve flexibility. Additionally, strength and flexibility training must be specific to the muscle group or joint that you wish to train.

Overload principle

An improvement in fitness level is achieved when the system (aerobic, musculoskeletal, or flexibility) is required to go beyond its current capacity. That is, the fitness level is increased as one progressively increases the "load" placed on the body as training occurs. If you are happy with your current level of fitness, keep doing what you are doing. If you would like to increase your level of fitness, you will have to progressively overload your system to improve your fitness level.

Progressive resistance principle

Improvements in fitness levels are best achieved through progressive increases in the amount of work conducted. The work may be aerobic or muscular in nature. One should begin at a comfortable level and then gradually increase the amount of energy expended in the activity.

Reversibility principle

Unfortunately, this principle simply means that if you stop training or being physically active, your body will revert back to a deconditioned state.

Table 2.5. AEROBIC TRAINING PROGRAMS

Warm-up portion	10 to 15 minutes of flexibility and general calisthenics
Activity portion	
For health benefit	20 to 30 minutes of moderate to vigorous physical activity
For fitness benefit	15 to 20 minutes of vigorous activity according to the U.S. Department of Health and Human Services presented in Table 2.1
Cool-down portion	10 to 15 minutes of flexibility activities

Body Composition

You don't just "train" to maintain your body composition characteristics within a healthy range. Changes in your body weight and composition are a function of "caloric balance." You are in caloric balance if the number of calories you ingest from food is equal to the number of calories that you expend through simply being alive plus the number of calories you expend in physical activity. If you take in more calories than you expend, you are in a "positive caloric balance," and you will gain weight (and fat). If you expend more calories than you take in, you are in a "negative caloric balance," and you will lose weight. It is as simple as that. Assuming that your current caloric balance is neither positive nor negative, if nothing else changed in your life for the next year except that you expended an extra 50 calories per day through physical activity (walking for about 7 to 8 minutes) and you decreased your caloric intake by 50 calories per day (the approximate number of calories in one cookie), you would lose 10 pounds of fat in one year. Your negative caloric balance would be approximately 100 calories per day for 365 days (or 36,500 calories for the year), and it takes about 3,500 calories to gain a pound of fat (positive caloric balance) or to lose a pound of fat (negative caloric balance). Unfortunately, most people don't pay sufficient attention to their caloric balance; as a result, most people gain about 45 pounds of fat from age 20 to age 45! However, their total weight might not change that much. As they decrease their physical activity, their lean tissue is replaced by fat tissue. As the fat level increases, the risk of developing disease increases. A good goal is to attempt to lose one pound of weight every year after you reach age 25. You don't really plan to lose a pound each year (ultimately, you might disappear!)—the point is to make lifestyle changes and decisions that result in your being aware of your caloric balance so that you can maintain your weight throughout adulthood and not reach a state where your weight causes you to be at an increased risk for degenerative diseases.

An important point to note regarding weight loss is that "spot reduction" does not work. Often you will hear of people who attempt to lose inches around the abdomen or inches off the hips by purchasing special equipment or engaging in special "fad" diets. Unfortunately, most of these devices and diets do not work. The key is to develop and maintain lifestyle changes that you can live with. Working specific muscle groups to lose fat in a particular body area

Table 2.6. ESTIMATED CALORIES EXPENDED FROM VARIOUS PHYSICAL ACTIVITIES

Moderate Physical Activity	Calories Burned per Hour[a]
Hiking	370
Light gardening/yard work	330
Dancing	330
Golf (walking and carrying clubs)	330
Bicycling (less than 10 mph)	290
Walking (3.5 mph)	280
Weight lifting (light workout)	220
Stretching	180

Vigorous Physical Activity	Calories Burned per Hour[a]
Running/jogging	590
Bicycling (more than 10 mph)	590
Swimming (slow freestyle laps)	510
Aerobics	480
Walking (4.5 mph)	460
Heavy yard work (e.g., chopping wood)	440
Weight lifting (vigorous workout)	440
Basketball (vigorous)	440

[a]These values are average for a 154-pound person. Lighter people burn fewer calories and heavier people burn more. From *Your Guide to Physical Activity and Your Heart*, NHLBI, U.S. Department of Health and Human Services, NIH Publication No. 06-5714, June, 2006.

will simply not work. It certainly will increase the muscular strength in that body part, but the best way to lose body fat is through general aerobic conditioning that results in a negative caloric balance. This will result in fat being removed from wherever it is stored in the body.

Since maintaining body weight is a function of caloric balance, it is interesting to determine how many calories you expend in physical activity (and in simply being alive) and how many calories you consume through food intake. You can estimate the number of calories that you take in by recording calories from food labels. You can also estimate the number of calories that you expend from vari-

ous tables listing caloric expenditure for different physical activities. The caloric expenditure values presented in Table 2.6 for selected activities are estimates based on a 154-pound person. If you weigh less, you would burn fewer calories. If you weigh more, you would expend more calories. You can use Table 2.6 to estimate how many calories you might expend when engaging in these physical activities.

Musculoskeletal Fitness

The principles of specificity, overload, and progression are also important in the development of musculoskeletal strength, endurance, and flexibility. Exercises must be completed with specific body segments to effect changes in musculoskeletal fitness in these body segments. A few definitions are necessary for you to understand a strength-training program:

repetition maximum (RM) The maximum weight that can be lifted a specific number of times. For example, 1–RM is the maximum amount of weight that can be lifted one time, while 10–RM is the maximum amount of weight that can be lifted 10 times.

repetitions (reps) You might conduct 10 repetitions of a specific exercise.

set The number of times you complete the repetitions. You might conduct 3 sets of 10–RM.

A key concept is to begin the activity with weights that you can lift and slowly increase the number of sets and repetitions until you reach the level of strength and endurance you desire. Generally, the use of higher weights lifted with fewer repetitions results in greater strength development, and the use of lower weights lifted with a higher number of repetitions results in increased muscular endurance. There are many types of weights to choose from (e.g., free weights, machines, constant resistance), and each type of weight equipment can be used to increase muscular strength and endurance. Table 2.7 provides an example of a training

Table 2.7. MUSCULOSKELETAL STRENGTH AND ENDURANCE TRAINING PROGRAM

Training for muscular strength				
Weeks	**Frequency**	**Sets**	**Repetitions**	**Resistance**
1–3	2 days/week	2/session	6–10 set	12–RM
4–20	3 days/week	3/session	6–10 set	6–RM
21+ (maintenance)	3 days/week	3/session	6–10 set	6–RM

Training for muscular endurance				
Weeks	**Frequency**	**Sets**	**Repetitions**	**Resistance**
1–3	2 days/week	2/session	15/set	40% 1–RM
4–20	3 days/week	3/session	15+/set	60% 1–RM
21+ (maintenance)	1–2 days/week	3/session	15+/set	60% 1–RM

Source: From Howley and Franks 2003. Adapted by permission from E. T. Howley and B. D. Franks, 2003, *Health Fitness Instructor's Handbook*, 4th ed. (Champaign, IL: Human Kinetics), 308.

program for improving musculoskeletal fitness. Also see Chapter 37 on weight training.

Similar training concepts can be used for flexibility training. Start slowly by moving the joint of interest through its unrestricted range of motion. Gradually add to the amount of movement that you do and attempt to increase the range of motion over a period of weeks. For example, a common flexibility movement is to touch one's toes. You can attempt this exercise in either a standing or a sitting position—but a seated position may be safer to begin training. However, your first attempts might result in your being able to reach only somewhere near your ankles. Flex and hold this position for 5 to 10 seconds and then relax. Repeat this for 8 to 10 repetitions. Over a period of a few weeks, you will see increased flexibility, resulting in your ability to reach farther toward your toes. Flexibility is an area particularly vulnerable to the reversibility principle. It is easy to lose flexibility if you don't continue to practice the movements.

GETTING STARTED WITH AND MAINTAINING HEALTHY LIFESTYLE HABITS

Deciding to change one's behavior and adopting healthy lifestyle behaviors are not easy. See Table 2.8 for data illustrating the prevalence of healthy lifestyle behaviors. As you can see, less than 5 percent of men and women engage in all of these four healthy lifestyle characteristics. Starting a physical activity, diet, or exercise program is not easy. Sticking with a program is not easy. The dropout rates for such programs are significant. A key factor in continuing your exercise program is to determine what you can currently do and then choose activities that you know you can and will continue. Starting too quickly can result in increased fatigue and/or injury, and this results in lack of motivation. The program you start must match your needs, if you are to begin, continue,

and then maintain healthy lifestyle behaviors. This is true no matter what the behavior change, whether it is physical activity, diet, smoking, seatbelt wearing, or flossing your teeth. Intervention strategies for motivating individuals to engage in physically active lifestyles must be consistent with the individual's desires and current levels of interest. Much research has been conducted on "stages of change" in order to create intervention strategies consistent with individual goals and objectives. Table 2.9 illustrates stages of readiness to change related to physical activity. Note that individuals at each of these stages will need to be motivated differently, and the intervention strategy that might work for one group of people could well be ineffective for another group. Additionally, Martin et al. (2000) report that individuals who believe physical activity to be important to health are more likely to engage in sufficient physical activity to achieve a health benefit.

ASSESSMENT OF HEALTH-RELATED PHYSICAL FITNESS COMPONENTS

Aerobic Fitness

Aerobic fitness is best assessed through a treadmill test where you are taken to maximum performance, and the maximum amount of oxygen that you can extract and utilize is measured. Unfortunately, because of the equipment and expertise needed, such a test is generally unavailable to most individuals. Thus, field tests of aerobic fitness have been developed. The most popular of these tests involves

Table 2.8. HEALTHY LIFESTYLE CHARACTERISTICS AMONG ADULTS IN THE UNITED STATES, 2000

Percentage Meeting Healthy Lifestyle Definition

Gender	Non-smoking	Healthy Weight	Fruits and Vegetables	Regular Physical Activity	Healthy Lifestyle (does all 4)
Males	75	32	19	23	2
Females	77	48	28	22	4

Healthy Weight: BMI = 18.5 to 25.0
Fruits and Vegetables: 5 or more per day
Regular Physical Activity: moderate intensity for 30 minutes or more per day for 5 or more days per week
Healthy Lifestyle: Met all four individual lifestyle indicators.

Source: Reeves, M. J. & Rafferty, A. P. (2005). Archives of Internal Medicine, 165, 854–857. Data from Behavioral Risk Factor Surveillance System. Centers for Disease Control and Prevention

Table 2.9. STAGES OF READINESS TO CHANGE

Precontemplation
I do not exercise/walk regularly, and I do not intend to start in the near future.
Contemplation
I do not exercise or walk regularly, but I have been thinking of starting.
Preparation
I am trying to start to exercise or walk regularly, or I exercise/walk infrequently.
Subaction
I am doing vigorous exercise less than 3 times per week or moderate exercise less than 5 times per week.
Action for moderate physical activity
I have been doing moderate exercise more than 5 times per week (or more than 2.5 hours per week) for the last 1 to 6 months.
Maintenance for moderate physical activity
I have been doing moderate exercise more than 5 times per week (or 2.5 hours per week) for more than 7 months.
Action for vigorous physical activity
I have been doing vigorous exercise 3 to 5 times per week for 1 to 6 months.
Maintenance for vigorous physical activity
I have been doing vigorous exercise 3 to 5 times per week for 7 or more months.

measuring the time it takes you to complete a specific distance (e.g., 1 mile) or the amount of distance you can cover in a specific time (e.g., 12 minutes). Table 2.10 provides results of a 1-mile walk/run test and evaluative categories for performance on the test.

Body Composition

There are a number of ways to determine your level of body fatness and the risk associated with your level of fatness. Three ways are described in this chapter.

The first is assessment of your body mass index (BMI). BMI is a measure of weight relative to height. If two people are the same height, the person who weighs more generally is at greater risk for developing disease, if the extra weight consists of body fat and not lean tissue. BMI is calculated by dividing your weight in kilograms by your height in meters squared (wt in kg/ht in m^2). Alternatively, you can calculate BMI as (703 × weight in lb)/(height in in)^2. Use Table 2.11 to determine your BMI and Table 2.12 to determine the category into which your BMI places you. You can also compare this to the values presented in Figure 2.6.

A second simple test is to determine your waist circumference. A greater waist girth correlates with greater risk for cardiovascular disease. Males are at increased risk if the waist girth is greater than 40 inches (102 cm), and females

are at greater risk when the girth is greater than 35 inches (88 cm).

The third method of determining your body composition is the estimation of body fatness from measures of the fat levels that underlie the skin. Skinfold measures of subcutaneous fat obtained by using skinfold calipers (see Figure 2.7) are used to estimate total percent body fat. Because males and females generally store their fat in different places, different sites are used in males and females to assess skinfold fat. Measurements are taken for males at the chest, abdomen, and thigh, while measures for females are taken at the triceps, suprailium, and thigh. Figure 2.8 illustrates how these measures are obtained. Table 2.13 can then be used to estimate your total body fatness. You can then use Table 2.14 to evaluate your body fatness. Percent fat greater than 25 percent for men and 33 percent for women puts you at increased risk for disease.

Musculoskeletal Fitness

It is difficult to measure strength and flexibility because of the specificity of the associated movements. See the weight-lifting guidelines in Chapter 37 for more information. However, Tables 2.15 and 2.16 provide normative data that are expressed relative to one's body weight and for upper-body endurance.

A variety of tests can measure abdominal strength and endurance. One widely used test is to determine the number of sit-ups one can perform in 1 minute. To start the test, lie supine on the floor with the knees flexed so that the angle between the thighs and the calves is about 90 degrees. Cross your arms in front of your chest and place your hands on the opposite shoulders. A partner should hold your feet to keep them in contact with the floor (see Figure 2.9). When timing starts, do as many sit-ups as you can in 1 minute. The sit-up is performed by touching the elbows to the thighs, with the arms maintaining contact with the chest, and returning to the starting position with the middle of the back touching the floor. Use Table 2.17 to interpret your results.

Likewise, flexibility can be measured in many different ways because of its specificity to body part and joint. A commonly used test is the sit-and-reach test. A special piece of equipment is needed for this test (see Figure 2.10). To perform the test, remove your shoes and sit down with your feet against the board and your legs fully extended. Extend your arms forward with one hand on top of the other with the palms facing downward and fingertips even. Reach as far forward as possible while keeping your knees straight. Repeat four times and hold the maximum reach on the fourth trial for 1 second. The score is the farthest reach achieved, to the nearest centimeter. When performing this test, do not use a forceful bobbing motion; use a smooth forward slide. Compare your results with the norms presented in Table 2.18.

Table 2.10. NORMATIVE DATA FOR 1-MILE WALK TEST

Subjects aged 30–69 years		
Rating	Males	Females
Excellent	<10:13	<11:41
Good	10:13–11:42	11:41–13:08
High average	11:43–13:13	13:09–14:36
Low average	13:14–14:44	14:37–16:04
Fair	14:45–16:23	16:05–17:31
Poor	>16:23	>17:31

Subjects aged 18–30 years		
Percentile[a]	Males	Females
90	11:08	11:45
75	11:42	12:49
50	12:38	13:15
25	13:38	14:12
10	14:37	15:03
Poor	>16:24	>17:32

Source: Jackson, Solomon, and Stusek 1992. Reprinted with permission from *Research Quarterly for Exercise and Sport,* Vol 63, No. 1, A52, copyright (1992) by the American Alliance for Health, Physical Education, Recreation and Dance, 1900 Association Drive, Reston, VA 20191.

[a]A percentile represents the percentage of people who score at this value or poorer. For example, if you are a 20-year-old male who completes the 1-mile walk test in 11:08, you scored better than 90 percent of the males who completed the test.

Table 2.11. CALCULATING BODY MASS INDEX (BMI)

Weight (lb)	Height (in)																Weight (kg)
	48	49	50	51	52	53	54	55	56	57	58	59	60	61	62	63	
100	30.6	29.3	28.2	27.1	26.1	25.1	24.2	23.3	22.5	21.7	20.9	20.2	19.6	18.9	18.3	17.8	45.5
105	32.1	30.8	29.6	28.4	27.4	26.3	25.4	24.5	23.6	22.8	22.0	21.3	20.5	19.9	19.2	18.6	47.7
110	33.6	32.3	31.0	29.8	28.7	27.6	26.6	25.6	24.7	23.9	23.0	22.3	21.5	20.8	20.2	19.5	50.0
115	35.2	33.7	32.4	31.2	30.0	28.8	27.8	26.8	25.8	24.9	24.1	23.3	22.5	21.8	21.1	20.4	52.3
120	36.7	35.2	33.8	32.5	31.3	30.1	29.0	27.9	27.0	26.0	25.1	24.3	23.5	22.7	22.0	21.3	54.5
125	38.2	36.7	35.2	33.9	32.6	31.4	30.2	29.1	28.1	27.1	26.2	25.3	24.5	23.7	22.9	22.2	56.8
130	39.8	38.1	36.6	35.2	33.9	32.6	31.4	30.3	29.2	28.2	27.2	26.3	25.4	24.6	23.8	23.1	59.1
135	41.3	39.6	38.0	36.6	35.2	33.9	32.6	31.4	30.3	29.3	28.3	27.3	26.4	25.6	24.7	24.0	61.4
140	42.8	41.1	39.5	37.9	36.5	35.1	33.8	32.6	31.5	30.4	29.3	28.3	27.4	26.5	25.7	24.9	63.6
145	44.3	42.5	40.9	39.3	37.8	36.4	35.0	33.8	32.6	31.4	30.4	29.3	28.4	27.5	26.6	25.7	65.9
150	45.9	44.0	42.3	40.6	39.1	37.6	36.2	34.9	33.7	32.5	31.4	30.4	29.4	28.4	27.5	26.6	68.2
155	47.4	45.5	43.7	42.0	40.4	38.9	37.5	36.1	34.8	33.6	32.5	31.4	30.3	29.3	28.4	27.5	70.5
160	48.9	47.0	45.1	43.3	41.7	40.1	38.7	37.3	35.9	34.7	33.5	32.4	31.3	30.3	29.3	28.4	72.7
165	50.5	48.4	46.5	44.7	43.0	41.4	39.9	38.4	37.1	35.8	34.6	33.4	32.3	31.2	30.2	29.3	75.0
170	52.0	49.9	47.9	46.6	44.3	42.6	41.1	39.6	38.2	36.9	35.6	34.4	33.3	32.2	31.2	30.2	77.3
175	53.5	51.4	49.3	47.4	45.6	43.9	42.3	40.8	39.3	37.9	36.7	35.4	34.2	33.1	32.1	31.1	79.5
180	55.0	52.8	50.7	48.8	46.9	45.1	43.5	41.9	40.4	39.0	37.7	36.4	35.2	34.1	33.0	32.0	81.8
185	56.6	54.3	52.1	50.1	48.2	46.4	44.7	43.1	41.6	40.1	38.7	37.4	36.2	35.0	33.9	32.8	84.1
190	58.1	55.8	53.5	51.5	49.5	47.7	45.9	44.3	42.7	41.2	39.8	38.5	37.2	36.0	34.8	33.7	86.4
195	59.6	57.2	55.0	52.8	50.8	48.9	47.1	45.4	43.8	42.3	40.8	39.5	38.2	36.9	35.7	34.6	88.6
200	61.2	58.7	56.4	54.2	52.1	50.2	48.3	46.6	44.9	43.4	41.9	40.5	39.1	37.9	36.7	35.5	90.9
205	62.7	60.2	57.8	55.5	53.4	51.4	49.5	47.7	46.1	44.5	42.9	41.5	40.1	38.8	37.6	36.4	93.2
210	64.2	61.6	59.2	56.9	54.7	52.7	50.7	48.9	47.2	45.5	44.0	42.5	41.1	39.8	38.5	37.3	95.5
215	65.7	63.1	60.6	58.2	56.0	53.9	51.9	50.1	48.3	46.6	45.0	43.5	42.1	40.7	39.4	38.2	97.7
220	67.3	64.6	62.0	59.6	57.3	55.2	53.2	51.2	49.4	47.7	46.1	44.5	43.1	41.7	40.3	39.1	100.0
225	68.8	66.0	63.4	60.9	58.6	56.4	54.4	52.4	50.5	48.8	47.1	45.5	44.0	42.6	41.2	39.9	102.3
230	70.3	67.5	64.8	62.3	59.9	57.7	55.6	53.6	51.7	49.9	48.2	46.6	45.0	43.5	42.2	40.8	104.5
235	71.9	69.0	66.2	63.7	61.2	58.9	56.8	54.7	52.8	51.0	49.2	47.6	46.0	44.5	43.1	41.7	106.8
240	73.4	70.4	67.6	65.0	62.5	60.2	58.0	55.9	53.9	52.0	50.3	48.6	47.0	45.4	44.0	42.6	109.1
245	74.9	71.9	69.0	66.4	63.8	61.5	59.2	57.1	55.0	53.1	51.3	49.6	47.9	46.4	44.9	43.5	111.4
250	76.4	73.4	70.5	67.7	65.1	62.7	60.4	58.2	56.2	54.2	52.4	50.6	48.9	47.3	45.8	44.4	113.6
	1.22	1.24	1.27	1.30	1.32	1.35	1.37	1.40	1.42	1.45	1.47	1.50	1.52	1.55	1.57	1.60	

Height (m)

(continued)

IT'S NEVER TOO EARLY OR TOO LATE TO START

Some might believe that they have been deconditioned, overweight, or inflexible for so long that it is useless to begin a physical activity program. Quite the contrary; it is never too early or too late to start. Evidence indicates that elementary-school-age children can be trained to increase their aerobic fitness, body composition, and muscular strength. Table 2.19 has guidelines for physical activity in children and adolescents that were developed as a result of a national consensus conference. Note the similarity those guidelines have with those suggested for adults in terms of daily physical activity levels. Similarly, research conducted on octogenarians indicates that they, too, can show increases in functional capacity with training.

Figure 2.11 shows results from a study on patients at the Cooper Clinic in Dallas, Texas, indicating the changes in disease risk from one physical examination to another. At the first examination, these adults had a specific risk factor (e.g., were physically inactive, smoked, had high cholesterol, had high blood pressure or high fat level). Upon returning for their second examination, they were no longer at risk, because they had changed the risk behavior (i.e., were physically active, no longer smoked, had normal cholesterol, had normal blood pressure or no longer had excessive body fatness). Note that the individuals who were physically inactive at the first visit but were then physically active at the second visit significantly reduced their risk. Physically active at the second visit did not mean that they were marathoners or highly trained runners. They had simply increased their fitness as a result of increased physical activity. This suggests that increasing your physical activity to increase your aerobic fitness level has a significant health benefit.

Table 2.11. CALCULATING BODY MASS INDEX (BMI) (Continued)

Weight (lb)	Height (in)															Weight (kg)
	64	65	66	67	68	69	70	71	72	73	74	75	76	77	78	
100	17.2	16.7	16.2	15.7	15.2	14.8	14.4	14.0	13.6	13.2	12.9	12.5	12.2	11.9	11.6	45.5
105	18.1	17.5	17.0	16.5	16.0	15.5	15.1	14.7	14.3	13.9	13.5	13.2	12.8	12.5	12.2	47.7
110	18.9	18.3	17.8	17.3	16.8	16.3	15.8	15.4	14.9	14.5	14.2	13.8	13.4	13.1	12.7	50.0
115	19.8	19.2	18.6	18.0	17.5	17.0	16.5	16.1	15.6	15.2	14.8	14.4	14.0	13.7	13.3	52.3
120	20.6	20.0	19.4	18.8	18.3	17.8	17.3	16.8	16.3	15.9	15.4	15.0	14.6	14.3	13.9	54.5
125	21.5	20.8	20.2	19.6	19.0	18.5	18.0	17.5	17.0	16.5	16.1	15.7	15.2	14.9	14.5	56.8
130	22.4	21.7	21.0	20.4	19.8	19.2	18.7	18.2	17.7	17.2	16.7	16.3	15.9	15.4	15.1	59.1
135	23.2	22.5	21.8	21.2	20.6	20.0	19.4	18.9	18.3	17.8	17.4	16.9	16.5	16.0	15.6	61.4
140	24.1	23.3	22.6	22.0	21.3	20.7	20.1	19.6	19.0	18.5	18.0	17.5	17.1	16.6	16.2	63.6
145	24.9	24.2	23.5	22.8	22.1	21.5	20.8	20.3	19.7	19.2	18.7	18.2	17.7	17.2	16.8	65.9
150	25.8	25.0	24.3	23.5	22.9	22.2	21.6	21.0	20.4	19.8	19.3	18.8	18.3	17.8	17.4	68.2
155	26.7	25.8	25.1	24.3	23.6	22.9	22.3	21.7	21.1	20.5	19.9	19.4	18.9	18.4	17.9	70.5
160	27.5	26.7	25.9	25.1	24.4	23.7	23.0	22.4	21.7	21.2	20.6	20.0	19.5	19.0	18.5	72.7
165	28.4	27.5	26.7	25.9	25.1	24.4	23.7	23.1	22.4	21.8	21.2	20.7	20.1	19.6	19.1	75.0
170	29.2	28.3	27.5	26.7	25.9	25.2	24.4	23.8	23.1	22.5	21.9	21.3	20.7	20.2	19.7	77.3
175	30.1	29.2	28.3	27.5	26.7	25.9	25.2	24.5	23.8	23.1	22.5	21.9	21.3	20.8	20.3	79.5
180	31.0	30.0	29.1	28.3	27.4	26.6	25.9	25.2	24.5	23.8	23.2	22.5	22.0	21.4	20.8	81.8
185	31.8	30.8	29.9	29.0	28.2	27.4	26.6	25.9	25.1	24.5	23.8	23.2	22.6	22.0	21.4	84.1
190	32.7	31.7	30.7	29.8	28.9	28.1	27.3	26.6	25.8	25.1	24.4	23.8	23.2	22.6	22.0	86.4
195	33.5	32.5	31.5	30.6	29.7	28.9	28.0	27.3	26.5	25.8	25.1	24.4	23.8	23.2	22.6	88.6
200	34.4	33.4	32.3	31.4	30.5	29.6	28.8	28.0	27.2	26.4	25.7	25.1	24.4	23.8	23.2	90.9
205	35.3	34.2	33.2	32.2	31.2	30.3	29.5	28.7	27.9	27.1	26.4	25.7	25.0	24.4	23.7	93.2
210	36.1	35.0	34.0	33.0	32.0	31.1	30.2	29.4	28.5	27.8	27.0	26.3	25.6	25.0	24.3	95.5
215	37.0	35.9	34.8	33.7	32.8	31.8	30.9	30.0	29.2	28.4	27.7	26.9	26.2	25.5	24.9	97.7
220	37.8	36.7	35.6	34.5	33.5	32.6	31.6	30.7	29.9	29.1	28.3	27.6	26.8	26.1	25.5	100.0
225	38.7	37.5	36.4	35.3	34.3	33.3	32.4	31.4	30.6	29.7	28.9	28.2	27.4	26.7	26.1	102.3
230	39.6	38.4	37.2	36.1	35.0	34.0	33.1	32.1	31.3	30.4	29.6	28.8	28.1	27.3	26.6	104.5
235	40.4	39.2	38.0	36.9	35.8	34.8	33.8	32.8	31.9	31.1	30.2	29.4	28.7	27.9	27.2	106.8
240	41.3	40.0	38.8	37.7	36.6	35.5	34.5	33.5	32.6	31.7	30.9	30.1	29.3	28.5	27.8	109.1
245	42.1	40.9	39.6	38.5	37.3	36.3	35.2	34.2	33.3	32.4	31.5	30.7	29.9	29.1	28.4	111.4
250	43.0	41.7	40.4	39.2	38.1	37.0	35.9	34.9	34.0	33.1	32.2	31.3	30.5	29.7	29.0	113.6
	1.63	1.65	1.68	1.70	1.73	1.75	1.78	1.80	1.83	1.85	1.88	1.91	1.93	1.96	1.98	

Height (m)

Source: Morrow et al. 2005.

Table 2.12. INTERPRETING BODY MASS INDEX

Underweight	<18.5
Healthy	18.5–24.9
Overweight	25.0–29.9
Obesity	>29.9

Based on U.S. Centers for Disease Control and Prevention and American Heart Association guidelines.

Many of the other chapters in this text can help you develop skills for remaining active throughout your life. Not everyone likes to swim, or run, or jog. Choose an activity that you like and that will help you remain physically active throughout your life. It will improve your health, quality of life, and general well-being.

PHYSICAL ACTIVITY

Historically, interest has focused on "exercise" or "physical fitness" for a health benefit. More recent attention has been directed at "lifestyle physical activities." The intent is to encourage people to adopt and maintain lifestyle behaviors that result in choosing alternatives to sedentary behaviors. In fact, there is increased interest in sedentary behaviors because many people spend much of their waking hours in sedentary behaviors. Pate et al. (2008) present the importance of measuring sedentary behaviors. Matthews et al. (2008) report that the majority of adults' waking hours are spent in sedentary behaviors. Katzmarzyk et al. (2009) report that time spent in sedentary behaviors is related to cardiovascular disease. Lifestyle behaviors include parking farther from the building at work or school, walking rather than taking the bus, taking the stairs instead of the elevator, using fewer labor-saving

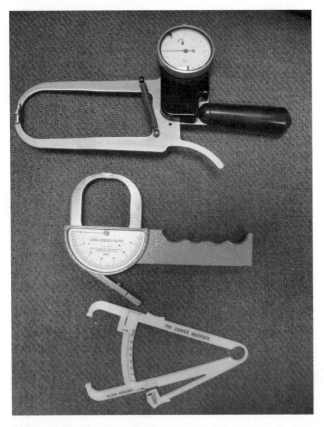

Figure 2.7. Skinfold calipers.

Figure 2.9. Sit-up test.

Male sites

Chest
A measure taken diagonally, halfway between the front of the armpit and the nipple

Abdominal
A vertical measure taken 2 cm lateral to the umbilicus

Thigh
A vertical measure taken at the midpoint of the right thigh, with the leg relaxed and knee slightly bent

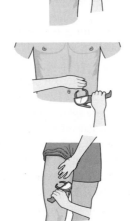

Female sites

Triceps
A vertical measure taken on the back of the upper arm halfway between the elbow and "point" of the shoulder, with the arm extended and the elbow relaxed

Suprailium
A diagonal measure taken above the hip at an imaginary vertical line extending down from the front of the armpit

Thigh
A vertical measure taken at the midpoint of the right thigh, with the leg relaxed and the knee slightly bent

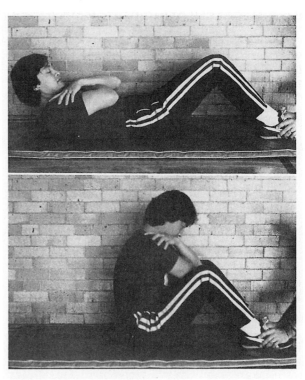

Figure 2.8. Descriptions of skinfold measurements.

Table 2.13. CONVERTING SKINFOLDS TO PERCENT FAT—MALES—SUM OF CHEST, ABDOMINAL, AND THIGH SKINFOLDS

Sum of skinfolds (mm)	Age to the last year								
	Under 22	23 to 27	28 to 32	33 to 37	38 to 42	43 to 47	48 to 52	53 to 57	Over 58
8–10	1.3	1.8	2.3	2.9	3.4	3.9	4.5	5.0	5.5
11–13	2.2	2.8	3.3	3.9	4.4	4.9	5.5	6.0	6.5
14–16	3.2	3.8	4.3	4.8	5.4	5.9	6.4	7.0	7.5
17–19	4.2	4.7	5.3	5.8	6.3	6.9	7.4	8.0	8.5
20–22	5.1	5.7	6.2	6.8	7.3	7.9	8.4	8.9	9.5
23–25	6.1	6.6	7.2	7.7	8.3	8.8	9.4	9.9	10.5
26–28	7.0	7.6	8.1	8.7	9.2	9.8	10.3	10.9	11.4
29–31	8.0	8.5	9.1	9.6	10.2	10.7	11.3	11.8	12.4
32–34	8.9	9.4	10.0	10.5	11.1	11.6	12.2	12.8	13.3
35–37	9.8	10.4	10.9	11.5	12.0	12.6	13.1	13.7	14.3
38–40	10.7	11.3	11.8	12.4	12.9	13.5	14.1	14.6	15.2
41–43	11.6	12.2	12.7	13.3	13.8	14.4	15.0	15.5	16.1
44–46	12.5	13.1	13.6	14.2	14.7	15.3	15.9	16.4	17.0
47–49	13.4	13.9	14.5	15.1	15.6	16.2	16.8	17.3	17.9
50–52	14.3	14.8	15.4	15.9	16.5	17.1	17.6	18.2	18.8
53–55	15.1	15.7	16.2	16.8	17.4	17.9	18.5	19.1	19.7
56–58	16.0	16.5	17.1	17.7	18.2	18.8	19.4	20.0	20.5
59–61	16.9	17.4	17.9	18.5	19.1	19.7	20.2	20.8	21.4
62–64	17.6	18.2	18.8	19.4	19.9	20.5	21.1	21.7	22.2
65–67	18.5	19.0	19.6	20.2	20.8	21.3	21.9	22.5	23.1
68–70	19.3	19.9	20.4	21.0	21.6	22.2	22.7	23.3	23.9
71–73	20.1	20.7	21.2	21.8	22.4	23.0	23.6	24.1	24.7
74–76	20.9	21.5	22.0	22.6	23.2	23.8	24.4	25.0	25.5
77–79	21.7	22.2	22.8	23.4	24.0	24.6	25.2	25.8	26.3
80–82	22.4	23.0	23.6	24.2	24.8	25.4	25.9	26.5	27.1
83–85	23.2	23.8	24.4	25.0	25.5	26.1	26.7	27.3	27.9
86–88	24.0	24.5	25.1	25.7	26.3	26.9	27.5	28.1	28.7
89–91	24.7	25.3	25.9	26.5	27.1	27.6	28.2	28.8	29.4
92–94	25.4	26.0	26.6	27.2	27.8	28.4	29.0	29.6	30.2
95–97	26.1	26.7	27.3	27.9	28.5	29.1	29.7	30.3	30.9
98–100	26.9	27.4	28.0	28.6	29.2	29.8	30.4	31.0	31.6
101–103	27.5	28.1	28.7	29.3	29.9	30.5	31.1	31.7	32.3
104–106	28.2	28.8	29.4	30.0	30.6	31.2	31.8	32.4	33.0
107–109	28.9	29.5	30.1	30.7	31.3	31.9	32.5	33.1	33.7
110–112	29.6	30.2	30.8	31.4	32.0	32.6	33.2	33.8	34.4
113–115	30.2	30.8	31.4	32.0	32.6	33.2	33.8	34.5	35.1
116–118	30.9	31.5	32.1	32.7	33.3	33.9	34.5	35.1	35.7
119–121	31.5	32.1	32.7	33.3	33.9	34.5	35.1	35.7	36.4
122–124	32.1	32.7	33.3	33.9	34.5	35.1	35.8	36.4	37.0
125–127	32.7	33.3	33.9	34.5	35.1	35.8	36.4	37.0	37.6

(continued)

devices, and doing things "the old-fashioned way." In other words, expend more energy in each of the activities you conduct throughout the day, and the number of calories burned and the potential health benefit from being physically active increases. Morrow et al. (2004) report that adults are generally more knowledgeable about traditional fitness activities than they are about the potential health benefits of lifestyle physical activities.

As a result of the focus on physical activity, pedometers have become increasingly popular. Pedometers come in a variety of makes and models (read that, expensive to inexpensive). Some pedometers measure activity minutes only; others measure distance, time, and estimated caloric expenditure. The simplest pedometers measure steps only. Others measure distance, steps, and time and estimate calories. Some newer pedometers use steps-per-minute to estimate slow, moderate, and vigorous activity. It is difficult to determine the number of steps one should take for "health benefits." While a variety of goals have been presented for achieving a health benefit, the most often reported goal is 10,000 steps per day. However, this goal has not been well validated. One method is to determine the number of steps

Table 2.13. CONVERTING SKINFOLDS TO PERCENT FAT—FEMALES—SUM OF TRICEPS, SUPRAILIUM, AND THIGH SKINFOLDS (Continued)

Sum of skinfolds (mm)	Age to the last year								
	Under 22	23 to 27	28 to 32	33 to 37	38 to 42	43 to 47	48 to 52	53 to 57	Over 58
23–25	9.7	9.9	10.2	10.4	10.7	10.9	11.2	11.4	11.7
26–28	11.0	11.2	11.5	11.7	12.0	12.3	12.5	12.7	13.0
29–31	12.3	12.5	12.8	13.0	13.3	13.5	13.8	14.0	14.3
32–34	13.6	13.8	14.0	14.3	14.5	14.8	15.0	15.3	15.5
35–37	14.8	15.0	15.3	15.5	15.8	16.0	16.3	16.5	16.8
38–40	16.0	16.3	16.5	16.7	17.0	17.2	17.5	17.7	18.0
41–43	17.2	17.4	17.7	17.9	18.2	18.4	18.7	18.9	19.2
44–46	18.3	18.6	18.8	19.1	19.3	19.6	19.8	20.1	20.3
47–49	19.5	19.7	20.0	20.2	20.5	20.7	21.0	21.2	21.5
50–52	20.6	20.8	21.1	21.3	21.6	21.8	22.1	22.3	22.6
53–55	21.7	21.9	22.1	22.4	22.6	22.9	23.1	23.4	23.6
56–58	22.7	23.0	23.2	23.4	23.7	23.9	24.2	24.4	24.7
59–61	23.7	24.0	24.2	24.5	24.7	25.0	25.2	25.5	25.7
62–64	24.7	25.0	25.2	25.5	25.7	26.0	26.7	26.4	26.7
65–67	25.7	25.9	26.2	26.4	26.7	26.9	27.2	27.4	27.7
68–70	26.6	26.9	27.1	27.4	27.6	27.9	28.1	28.4	28.6
71–73	27.5	27.8	28.0	28.3	28.5	28.8	29.0	29.3	29.5
74–76	28.4	28.7	28.9	29.2	29.4	29.7	29.9	30.2	30.4
77–79	29.3	29.5	29.8	30.0	30.3	30.5	30.8	31.0	31.3
80–82	30.1	30.4	30.6	30.9	31.1	31.4	31.6	31.9	32.1
83–85	30.9	31.2	31.4	31.7	31.9	32.2	32.4	32.7	32.9
86–88	31.7	32.0	32.2	32.5	32.7	32.9	33.2	33.4	33.7
89–91	32.5	32.7	33.0	33.2	33.5	33.7	33.9	34.2	34.4
92–94	33.2	33.4	33.7	33.9	34.2	34.4	34.7	34.9	35.2
95–97	33.9	34.1	34.4	34.6	34.9	35.1	35.4	35.6	35.9
98–100	34.6	34.8	35.1	35.3	35.5	35.8	36.0	36.3	36.5
101–103	35.3	35.4	35.7	35.9	36.2	36.4	36.7	36.9	37.2
104–106	35.8	36.1	36.3	36.6	36.8	37.1	37.3	37.5	37.8
107–109	36.4	36.7	36.9	37.1	37.4	37.6	37.9	38.1	38.4
110–112	37.0	37.2	37.5	37.7	38.0	38.2	38.5	38.7	38.9
113–115	37.5	37.8	38.0	38.2	38.5	38.7	39.0	39.2	39.5
116–118	38.0	38.3	38.5	38.8	39.0	39.3	39.5	39.7	40.0
119–121	38.5	38.7	39.0	39.2	39.5	39.7	40.0	40.2	40.5
122–124	39.0	39.2	39.4	39.7	39.9	40.2	40.4	40.7	40.9
125–127	39.4	39.6	39.9	40.1	40.4	40.6	40.9	41.1	41.4
128–130	39.8	40.0	40.3	40.5	40.8	41.0	41.3	41.5	41.8

Source: Pollack, Schmidt, and Jackson 1980. Reprinted with permission. © American Society of Contemporary Medicine & Surgery. (Michael L. Pollack, PhD; Donald H. Schmidt, MD; and Andrew S. Jackson, PED. Measurement of Cardio-Respiratory Fitness and Body Composition in the Clinical Setting. *Comp Ther.* 1980; 6[9]: 12–27.)

that you typically take during your daily activities and then add approximately 3,500 steps to this amount. If your typical daily steps are 5,000, your goal would be 8,500 steps per day. Note that the additional 3,500 steps should come in three bouts of at least 10 minutes and be truly purposeful in nature. Alternatively, it could be one 30-minute bout. The steps also should be moderate or vigorous in nature. Another strategy is to determine the number of steps you take in a day and then gradually increase the number until you have increased the number of steps to 3,500–5,000 above baseline. Here again, these should not be just "walking around" the office or workplace but should be in bouts of 10 minutes or more that accumulate to 30 minutes most days of the week.

Tudor-Locke and Bassett (2004) suggest the steps-per-day guidelines presented in Table 2.20. The use of a pedometer serves as a great self-monitoring device to let you know when you have had a sedentary day.

DIETARY GUIDELINES

Dietary Guidelines for Americans were revised in 2005. Specific comment is made to energy balance as it relates to loss and maintenance of weight. The Guidelines "provide science-based advice to promote health and to reduce risk for major chronic diseases through diet and physical activity." The Guidelines provide insight into selecting foods and nutrients, weight-management activities, and physical

Table 2.14. INTERPRETING PERCENT BODY FAT

Males

Rating	Age (years)					
	18–25	**26–35**	**36–45**	**46–55**	**56–65**	**66+**
Very lean	4–7	8–12	10–14	12–16	15–18	15–18
Lean	8–10	13–15	16–18	18–20	19–21	19–21
Leaner than average	11–13	16–18	19–21	21–23	22–24	22–23
Average	14–16	19–21	22–24	24–25	24–26	24–25
Fatter than average	18–20	22–24	25–26	26–28	26–28	25–27
Fat	22–26	25–28	27–29	29–31	29–31	28–30
Overfat	28–37	30–37	30–38	32–38	32–38	31–38

Females

Rating	Age (years)					
	18–25	**26–35**	**36–45**	**46–55**	**56–65**	**66+**
Very lean	13–17	13–18	15–19	18–22	18–23	16–18
Lean	18–20	19–21	20–23	23–25	24–26	22–25
Leaner than average	21–23	22–23	24–26	26–28	28–30	27–29
Average	24–25	24–26	27–29	29–31	31–33	30–32
Fatter than average	26–28	27–30	30–32	32–34	34–36	33–35
Fat	29–31	31–35	33–36	36–38	36–38	36–38
Overfat	33–43	36–48	39–48	40–49	39–46	39–40

Source: Reprinted from *Y's Way to Physical Fitness,* 3rd ed., with permission of the YMCA of the USA, 101 N. Wacker Drive, Chicago, IL 60606.

Table 2.15. NORMATIVE DATA ON STRENGTH TESTS (1–RM LB/LB BODY WEIGHT)

Males

Rating	Age (years)				
	20–29	**30–39**	**40–49**	**50–59**	**60+**
Excellent	>1.26	>1.08	>0.97	>0.86	>0.78
Good	1.17–1.25	1.01–1.07	0.91–0.96	0.81–0.85	0.74–0.77
Average	0.97–1.16	0.86–1.00	0.78–0.90	0.70–0.80	0.64–0.73
Fair	0.88–0.96	0.79–0.85	0.71–0.77	0.65–0.69	0.60–0.63
Poor	<0.87	<0.78	<0.71	<0.64	<0.59

Females

Rating	Age (years)				
	20–29	**30–39**	**40–49**	**50–59**	**60+**
Excellent	>0.78	>0.66	>0.61	>0.54	>0.55
Good	0.72–0.77	0.62–0.65	0.57–0.60	0.51–0.53	0.51–0.54
Average	0.59–0.71	0.53–0.61	0.48–0.56	0.43–0.50	0.41–0.50
Fair	0.53–0.58	0.49–0.52	0.44–0.47	0.40–0.42	0.37–0.40
Poor	<0.52	<0.48	<0.43	<0.39	<0.36

Based on norms from *The Physical Fitness Specialist Manual,* The Cooper Institute for Aerobics Research, Dallas, Texas, revised 1988; used with permission.

Table 2.16. NORMATIVE DATA FOR BENCH PRESS ENDURANCE TEST

Males (80 pounds with 30 repetitions per minute)

	Age (years)					
Rating	**18–25**	**26–35**	**36–45**	**46–55**	**56–65**	**66+**
Excellent	45–38	43–34	40–30	35–24	32–22	30–18
Good	34–30	30–26	28–24	22–20	20–14	14–10
Above average	28–25	25–22	22–20	17–14	14–10	10–8
Average	22–21	21–18	18–16	13–10	10–8	8–6
Below average	20–16	17–13	14–12	10–8	6–4	<5
Poor	13–9	12–9	10–8	6–4	4–2	<3
Very poor	<9	<6	<6	<3	0	0

Females (35 pounds with 30 repetitions per minute)

	Age (years)					
Rating	**18–25**	**26–35**	**36–45**	**46–55**	**56–65**	**66+**
Excellent	50–36	48–33	46–28	42–26	34–22	26–18
Good	32–28	29–25	25–21	22–20	20–16	14–12
Above average	25–22	22–20	20–17	17–13	15–12	11–9
Average	21–18	18–16	14–12	12–10	10–8	8–5
Below average	16–13	14–12	11–9	9–6	7–4	4–2
Poor	12–8	9–5	8–4	5–2	3–1	<3
Very poor	5–1	<3	<3	<2	0	0

Source: Reprinted from *Y's Way to Physical Fitness,* 3rd ed., with permission of the YMCA of the USA, 101 N. Wacker Drive, Chicago, IL 60606.

Table 2.17. ONE-MINUTE SIT-UP NORMS

Males

	Age			
Fitness level	**29 or under**	**30–39**	**40–49**	**50+**
Excellent	>60	>45	>42	>38
Good	48	37	32	26
Fair	40	23	20	15
Poor	25	18	15	10
Very poor	<18	<12	<10	<6

Females

	Age			
Fitness level	**29 or under**	**30–39**	**40–49**	**50+**
Excellent	>50	>40	>35	>25
Good	40	34	26	20
Fair	32	15	10	7
Poor	20	12	6	3
Very poor	<12	<8	<2	<1

Table 2.18. SIT-AND-REACH NORMS (IN CENTIMETERS)

Males

	Age			
Fitness level	**29 or under**	**30–39**	**40–49**	**50+**
Excellent	>42	>48	>48	>43
Good	36	43	41	38
Fair	30	23	25	20
Poor	16	18	13	13
Very poor	<10	<12	<8	<5

Females

	Age			
Fitness level	**29 or under**	**30–39**	**40–49**	**50+**
Excellent	>42	>53	>53	>48
Good	38	50	48	46
Fair	32	36	30	30
Poor	22	30	25	23
Very poor	<18	<20	<15	<15

activity. The Guidelines for physical activity are presented in Table 2.21. The Guidelines suggest the amount of physical activity necessary to achieve a health benefit and/or weight management. Working to maintain healthy dietary and physically active lifestyles is important to garnering lifelong health benefits.

INTERNET RESOURCES

Table 2.22 provides a list of Web sites related to health and physical fitness. Visit these sites regularly; many of them are updated as new evidence is obtained about the relationship between physical activity and health, quality of life, and total well-being.

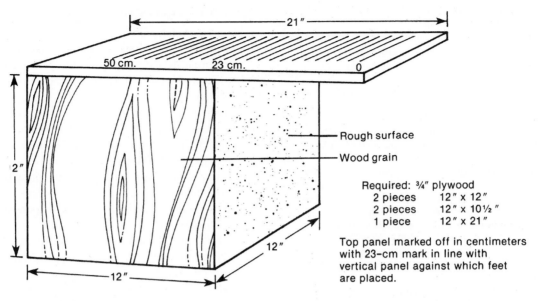

Figure 2.10. Apparatus necessary for sit-and-reach test.

Table 2.19. A CONSENSUS ON PHYSICAL ACTIVITY GUIDELINES FOR ADOLESCENTS

Physical Activity Guidelines for Adolescents. The health-related rationale for optimizing physical activity during adolescence is twofold: first, to promote physical and psychological health and well-being during adolescence; second, to enhance future health by increasing the probability of remaining active as an adult.

Guideline 1: All adolescents should be physically active daily or nearly every day, as part of play, games, sports, work, transportation, recreation, physical education, or planned exercise, in the context of family, school, and community affairs.

Adolescents should do a variety of physical activities as part of their daily lifestyles. These activities should be enjoyable, involve a variety of muscle groups, and include some type of weight-bearing activities. The intensity or duration of the activity is probably less important than the fact that energy is expended and a habit of daily activity is established. Adolescents are encouraged to incorporate physical activity into their lifestyles by doing such things as walking up stairs, walking or riding a bicycle for errands, having conversations while walking with friends, parking at the far end of parking lots, or doing household chores.

Guideline 2: In addition to daily lifestyle activities, three or more sessions per week of activities lasting 20 minutes or more at a time, that require moderate to vigorous levels of exertion, are recommended.

Moderate to vigorous activities are those that require at least as much effort as brisk or fast walking. A diversity of activities that use large muscle groups are recommended as part of sports, recreation, chores, transportation, work, school physical education, or planned exercise. Examples include brisk walking, jogging, stair-climbing, basketball, racquet sports, soccer, dance, swimming laps, skating, strength (resistance) training, lawn mowing, strenuous housework, cross-country skiing, and cycling.

Source: Sallis and Patrick 1994. Reprinted by permission from J. F. Sallis and K. Patrick, 1994, "Physical Activity Guidelines for Adolescents: Consensus Statements," *Pediatric Exercise Science,* 6(4):306–308.

Figure 2.11. Reduction in relative risk for all-cause mortality with change in risk behavior. (Source: Blair 1993.)

Table 2.20. PEDOMETER STEPS PER DAY GUIDELINES[a]

Steps per day	Index
<5,000	Sedentary lifestyle
5,000–7,499	Low active
7,500–9,999	Somewhat active
≥10,000	Active
>12,500	Highly active

[a]Based on Tudor-Locke and Bassett (2004)

Table 2.21. DIETARY GUIDELINES FOR AMERICANS 2005

- Engage in regular physical activity and reduce sedentary activities to promote health, psychological well-being, and a healthy body weight.
  - To reduce the risk of chronic disease in adulthood: Engage in at least 30 minutes of moderate-intensity physical activity, above usual activity, at work or home on most days of the week.
  - For most people, greater health benefits can be obtained by engaging in physical activity of more vigorous intensity or longer duration.
  - To help manage body weight and prevent gradual, unhealthy body weight gain in adulthood: Engage in approximately 60 minutes of moderate- to vigorous-intensity activity on most days of the week while not exceeding caloric intake requirements.
  - To sustain weight loss in adulthood: Participate in at least 60 to 90 minutes of daily moderate-intensity physical activity while not exceeding caloric intake requirements. Some people may need to consult with a health-care provider before participating in this level of activity.
- Achieve physical fitness by including cardiovascular conditioning, stretching exercises for flexibility, and resistance exercises or calisthenics for muscle strength and endurance.

TEACHING CONSIDERATIONS

1. Health-related physical fitness can be taught as a separate unit or integrated into other units of a school or broad-based program. Long-lasting effects, in terms of attitudes and habits, are probably best achieved when a concern for fitness is imparted in programs with enough activity to both develop and maintain fitness. Fitness is part of healthy lifestyle behaviors.
2. Teach the "why" as well as the "how-to" of fitness components. Make instruction activity-based as well as information-based. Talk about adopting behaviors.
3. The most effective programs for older students teach how to assess, design, and conduct personal programs of fitness.
4. Use preassessment and postassessment to gear the program to individuals and to assess both their and the program's effectiveness. Share information with the student about personal progress and where the student is relative to program and individual goals.
5. Plan lessons to include work in more than one aspect of fitness. Emphasize all fitness components.

Table 2.22. WEB SITES

American Cancer Society
  http://www.nci.nih.gov/
American College of Sports Medicine
  http://www.acsm.org/
American Diabetes Association
  http://diabetes.org
American Heart Association
  http://www.americanheart.org/
Arthritis Foundation
  http://www.arthritis.org/
Body Mass Index Calculator
  http://www.nhlbisupport.com/bmi/bmicalc.htm
Bone Health and Osteoporosis: A Report of the Surgeon General
  http://www.hhs.gov/surgeongeneral/library/bonehealth/
CDC Division of Nutrition, Physical Activity and Obesity
  http://www.cdc.gov/nccdphp/dapao
Center for Nutrition Policy and Promotion
  http://www.usda.gov/cnpp/
Centers for Disease Control and Prevention
  http://www.cdc.gov/
Dietary Guidelines for Americans 2005
  http://www.healthierus.gov/dietaryguidelines/
Duke University Diet and Fitness Center
  http://www.dukehealth.org/services/diet and fitness/
Food Pyramid Guide
  http://www.nal.usda.gov/fnic/Fpyr/pyramid.gif/
Global Health Network
  http://www.pitt.edu/HOME/GHNet/GHNet.html
Healthier US
  http://www.healthierus.gov/
Healthy People 2010
  http://www.healthypeople.gov/
National Cancer Institute
  http://www.nci.nih.gov/

National Coalition for Promoting Physical Activity
  http://www.ncppa.org/
National Heart, Lung, and Blood Institute
  http://www.nhlbi.nih.gov/
National Institute of Arthritis and Musculoskeletal and Skin Diseases
  http://www.niams.nih.gov/
National Institute of Diabetes and Digestive and Kidney Diseases
  http://www.niddk.nih.gov/
National Institute of Mental Health
  http://www.nimh.nih.gov/
National Institute on Aging
  http://www.nia.nih.gov/
National Institute on Alcohol Abuse and Alcoholism
  http://www.niaaa.nih.gov/
National Institute on Drug Abuse
  http://www.nida.nih.gov/
National Osteoporosis Foundation
  http://www.nof.org/
Physical Activity and Health: A Report of the Surgeon General
  http://www.cdc.gov/nccdphp/sgr/sgr.htm
Physical Activity Guidelines for Americans
  http://www.health.gov/PAGuidelines/
Shape Up America
  http://www.shapeup.org/
The President's Council on Physical Fitness and Sports
  www.fitness.gov
U.S. Department of Agriculture: Food and Nutrition Information Center
  http://www.nal.usda.gov/fnic/
U.S. Physical Activity Plan
  http://www.physicalactivityplan.org/
United States Government Consumer Information
  http://www.consumer.gov/
Weight Control Information Network
  http://www.niddk.nih.gov/index.htm

6. Use recovery time from exercise to teach physical fitness concepts.
7. Promote responsibility. Encourage work on fitness outside of class and give students the ability to design fitness programs using a variety of exercise types. Stress lifestyle behaviors related to increasing physical activity.
8. Testing should be only a small part of the program. Reduce testing time by assigning partners or station work where possible.
9. Choose ways to conduct activities that promote maximum participation. Use space, equipment, and time maximally.
10. Be sure that activities are being done correctly.
11. Be familiar with information on exercises that can be harmful.
12. Use the "stages of readiness to change" model to help individuals determine the amount of physical activity they currently do and then intervene in their physical activity behaviors at the point where they are.
13. Evidence suggests that the most commonly reported reason for not engaging in physical activity is "lack of time." However, with proper time management and attention to the "accumulation" of physical activity over time, everyone can find enough time in the typical day to engage in sufficient physical activity for a health benefit.
14. Self-motivation has been shown to be an important determinant of who adopts and maintains a physically active lifestyle. Discuss self-motivation and ways to get individuals motivated to be physically active (e.g., the health benefits, the social aspects, feeling better about themselves, increased energy, and better psychological outlook).

GLOSSARY

aerobic exercise Activity that uses the oxygen system. Typically the aerobic system is used when continuous physical activity lasts longer than approximately 4 or 5 minutes.

aerobic fitness Fitness that positively influences the cardiorespiratory system so that one's endurance level is increased.

anaerobic Without oxygen. Anaerobic activities are conducted over short periods of time and do not require a great deal of oxygen consumption. Weight lifting and brief sprints are anaerobic activities.

body composition The analysis of the body into fat, lean, and tissue components.

body mass index (BMI) The ratio of weight in kilograms to height in meters squared.

chronic diseases Diseases that develop over time.

duration The length of an exercise or physical activity session.

epidemiology The study of diseases, their causes, and their impact on society.

exercise frequency The number of times per week that an individual exercises.

exercise intensity The vigor or energy level of physical activity. Often measured in terms of heart rate during the activity. One's perception of the exertion can also be used.

health-related physical fitness Physical fitness based on components that have been shown to be related to health, quality of life, and reduced disease.

hypertension High blood pressure.

hypertrophy Enlargement of muscle cells.

hypokinetic diseases Diseases that result from physical inactivity.

lean body mass Muscle, bone, and other nonfat tissues of the body.

maximum heart rate The maximum heart rate that one can achieve at maximum exercise. Usually estimated as 220 minus one's age.

maximum heart rate reserve The difference between maximum heart rate and resting heart rate.

musculoskeletal fitness Fitness that positively influences the muscular system to increase muscular strength and endurance and joint flexibility.

obesity Excessive amount of body fat. Often defined as BMI ≥ 30.

osteoporosis Demineralization of bone, resulting in bones that are less dense and, as a result, more easily broken.

overload principle Imposing a greater than normal stress on one or more body systems.

reversibility The fact that increases in fitness level are not fixed and will reverse if the person does not continue to train to maintain or further increase fitness level.

RM Repetition maximum. 1–RM is the maximum amount of weight that can be lifted 1 time. 10–RM is the maximum amount of weight that can be lifted 10 times.

skinfold measurements Assessment of subcutaneous fat by measuring a fold of skin as an indicator of underlying fat.

specificity The concept of distinctiveness as it relates to a particular influence of physical activity or exercise.

REFERENCES

Blair, S. N. 1993. C. H. McCloy research lecture: Physical activity, physical fitness, and health. *Research Quarterly for Exercise and Sport, 64:* 365–76.

Blair, S. N., and Brodney, S. 1999. Effects of physical inactivity and obesity on morbidity and mortality: Current evidence and research issues. *Medicine and Science in Sports & Exercise, 31*(Suppl):S646–62.

Blair, S. N., and Church, T. S. 2004. The fitness, obesity, and health equation: Is physical activity the common denominator? *Journal of the American Medical Association, 292*(10):1232–34.

Blair, S. N., LaMonte, M. J., and Nichaman M. Z. 2004. The evolution of physical activity recommendations: How much is enough? *American Journal of Clinical Nutrition, 79:* S913–20.

Bone health and osteoporosis: A report of the surgeon general. 2004. Rockville, MD: U.S. Department of Health and Human Services, Office of the Surgeon General.

Brodney, S., Blair, S., and Lee, C. 2000. Is it possible to be overweight or obese and fit and healthy? In C. Bouchard (Ed.), *Physical activity and obesity* (pp. 355–71). Champaign, IL: Human Kinetics.

Dietary guidelines for Americans. 2005. Washington, DC: Department of Health and Human Services.

FitzGerald, S. J., Barlow, C. E., Kampert, J. B., Morrow, J. R., Jr., Jackson, A. W., and Blair, S. N. 2004. Muscular fitness and all-cause mortality: Prospective observations. *Journal of Physical Activity & Health, 1:* 7–18.

Golding, L., Myers, C., and Sinning, W. 1989. *Y's way to physical fitness*. Champaign, IL: Human Kinetics.

Haskell, W. L., Lee, I. M., Pate, R. R., Powell, K. E., Blair, S. N., Franklin, B. A. et al. 2007. Physical activity and public health: Updated recommendations for adults from the American College of Sports Medicine and the American Heart Association. *Circulation, 116,* 1081–1093.

Health, United States, 2005. 2005. Hyattsville, MD: National Center for Health Statistics.

Howley, E. T., and Franks, B. D. 2009. *Fitness professionals handbook*. 5th ed. Champaign, IL: Human Kinetics.

Jackson, A. W., Lee, D-C., Sui, X, Morrow, J. R., Jr., Church, T. S., Maslow, A. L., & Blair, S. N. (in press). Muscular strength is inversely related to prevalence and incidence of obesity in adult men. *Obesity.*

Jackson, A., Solomon, J., and Stusek, M. 1992. One-mile walk test: Reliability, validity, and norms for young adults [Abstract]. *Research Quarterly for Exercise and Sport, 63:* A52.

Katzmarzyk, P. T., Church, T. S., Craig, C. L., & Bouchard, C. 2009. Sitting time and mortality from all causes, cardiovascular disease, and cancer. *Medicine and Science in Sports & Exercise, 41,* 998–1005.

Kesaniemi, Y., Danforth, E., Jr., Jensen, M., Kopelman, P., Lefebvre, P., and Reeder, B. 2001. Consensus statement: Dose-response issues concerning physical activity and health: An evidence-based symposium. *Medicine and Science in Sports & Exercise, 33* (Suppl): S351–58.

Kohrt, W. M., Bloomfield, S. A., Little, K. D., Nelson, M. E., Yingling, V. R. 2004. Physical activity and bone health. *Medicine and Science in Sports & Exercise, 36:* 1985–96.

Marcus, R. 2001. Role of exercise in preventing and treating osteoporosis. *Rheumatic Diseases Clinics of North America, 27*(1): 131–41.

Martin, S., Morrow, J., Jr., Jackson, A., and Dunn, A. 2000. Variables related to meeting the CDC/ACSM physical activity guidelines. *Medicine and Science in Sports and Exercise, 32:* 2087–92.

Matthews, C. E., Chen, K. Y., Freedson, P. S., Buchowski, M. S., Beech, B. M., Pate, R. R. et al. 2008. Amount of time spent in sedentary behaviors in the United States, 2003–2004. *American Journal of Epidemiology, 167,* 875–881.

Morrow, J. Jr., Jackson, A., Bazzarre, T., Milne, D., and Blair, S. 1999. A one-year follow-up to *Physical Activity and Health: A Report of the Surgeon General:* What Americans know about physical activity and disease. *American Journal of Preventive Medicine, 17*(1):24–31.

MMWR. 2008. Prevalence of self-reported physically active adults—United States, 2007. *Morbidity and Mortality Weekly Report, 57,* 1297–1300.

Morrow, J. R., Jr., Jackson, A. W., Disch, J. G., and Mood, D. P. 2005. *Measurement and evaluation in human performance* 3rd ed. Champaign, IL: Human Kinetics.

Morrow, J. R., Jr., Krzewinski-Malone, J. A., Jackson, A. W., Bungum, T. J., and FitzGerald, S. J. 2004. American adults' knowledge of exercise recommendations. *Research Quarterly for Exercise and Sport, 75:* 231–37.

Nelson, M. E., Rejeski, J., Blair, S. N., Duncan, P. W., Judge, J. O., King, A. C. et al. 2007. Physical activity and public health in older adults. Recommenation from the American College of Sports Medicine and the American Heart Association. *Circulation, 116,* 1094–1105.

Pate, R. R., O'Neill, J. R., & Lobelo, F. 2008. The evolving definition of "sedentary." *Exercise and Sport Science Review, 36,* 173–178.

Physical activity and cardiovascular health: NIH consensus development panel on physical activity and cardiovascular health. 1996. *Journal of the American Medical Association, 276:* 241–46.

Physical activity and health: A report of the surgeon general. 1996. Atlanta: U.S. Department of Health and Human Services, Centers for Disease Control and Prevention. National Center for Chronic Disease Prevention and Health Promotion.

Pollack, M. L., Schmidt, D. H., and Jackson, A. S. 1980. Measurement of cardiorespiratory fitness and body composition in the clinical setting. *Comprehensive Therapy, 6*(9):12–27.

Reeves, M. J., & Rafferty, A. P. 2005. Healthy lifestyle characteristics among adults in the United States, 2000. *Archives of Internal Medicine, 165,* 854–857.

Ruiz, J. R., Sui, X., Lobelo, F., Lee, D. C., Morrow, J. R., Jr., Jackson, A. W., Hébert, J. R., Matthews, C. E., Sjöström, M., & Blair, S. N. 2009. Muscular strength and adiposity as predictors of adulthood cancer mortality in men. *Cancer Epidemiology Biomarkers & Prevention, 185*:1468–1476.

Ruiz, J. R., Sui, X., Lobelo, F., Morrow, J. R., Jr., Jackson, A. W., Sjostrom, M., & Blair, S. N. 2008. Association between muscular strength and mortality in men: Prospective cohort study. *British Medicine Journal, 337,* a439doi:10.1136/bmj.a439.

Sallis, J. F., and Patrick, K. 1994. Physical activity guidelines for adolescents: Consensus statement. *Pediatric Exercise Science, 6:* 302–14.

Troiano, R. P., Berrigan, D., Dodd, K. W., Masse, L. C., Tilert, T., & McDowell, M. 2008. Physical activity in the United States measured by accelerometer. *Medicine and Science in Sports & Exercise, 40,* 181–188.

Tudor-Locke, C., & Bassett, D. R., Jr. 2004. How many steps/day are enough? Preliminary pedometer indices for public health. *American Journal of Sports Medicine, 34,* 1–8.

U.S. Department of Health and Human Services. 2008. *2008 Physical activity guidelines for Americans* Washington DC: U.S. Department of Health and Human Services.

U.S. Department of Health and Human Services. 2000. *Healthy people 2010: Understanding and improving health.* 2nd. Washington, DC: Government Printing Office.

U.S. Department of Health and Human Services. 2008. *Physical activity guidelines advisory committee report, 2008.* Washington, DC: U.S. Department of Health and Human Services.

Williams, M. A., Haskell, W. L., Ades, P. A., Amsterdam, E. A., Bittner, V., Franklin, B. A. et al. 2007. Resistance exercise in individuals with and without cardiovascular disease: 2007 update: a scientific statement from the American Heart Association Council on Clinical Cardiology and Council on Nutrition, Physical Activity, and Metabolism. *Circulation, 116,* 572–584.

Your Guide to Physical Activity and Your Heart, NHLBI, U.S. Department of Health and Human Services, NIH Publication, No. 06-5714, June, 2006.

SUGGESTED READINGS

ACSM. 1998. Position stand: The recommended quantity and quality of exercise for developing and maintaining cardiorespiratory and muscular fitness, and flexibility in healthy adults. *Medicine and Science in Sports & Exercise, 30:* 975–91.

American College of Sports Medicine. 1993. Physical activity, physical fitness, and hypertension. *Medicine and Science in Sports and Exercise, 25*:i–x.

American College of Sports Medicine. 1995. ACSM position stand on osteoporosis and exercise. *Medicine and Science in Sports and Exercise, 27*:i–vii.

Barlow, C., Kohl, W., Gibbons, L., and Blair, S. 1995. Physical fitness, mortality and obesity. *International Journal of Obesity, 19*: S41–S44.

Blair, S. N. Cheng, Y., and Holder, J. S. 2001. Is physical activity or physical fitness more important in defining health benefits? *Medicine and Science in Sports & Exercise, 33*(Suppl): S379–99.

Blair, S. N., and Connelly, J. C. 1996. How much physical activity should we do? The case for moderate amounts and intensities of physical activity. *Research Quarterly for Exercise and Sport, 67*: 193–205.

Blair, S. N., Dunn, A. L., Marcus, B. H., Carpenter, R. A., and Jaret, P. 2001. *Active living every day: 20 weeks to lifelong vitality.* Champaign, IL: Human Kinetics. A behaviorally based program to encourage people to become and maintain an active lifestyle.

Blair, S. N., Kampert, J. B., Kohl, W. H., III, Barlow, C. E., Macera, C. A., Paffenbarger, R. S., Jr., and Gibbons, L. W. 1996. Influences of cardiorespiratory fitness and article precursors on cardiovascular disease and all-cause mortality in men and women. *Journal of the American Medical Association, 276*: 205–10.

Blair, S. N., Kohl, H. W., III, Barlow, C. E., Paffenbarger, R. S., Jr., Gibbons, L. W., and Macera, C. A. 1995. Changes in physical fitness and all-cause mortality: A prospective study of healthy men and women. *Journal of the American Medical Association, 273*: 1093–98.

Blair, S. N., Kohl, H. W., III, Paffenbarger, R. S., Jr., Clark, D. G., Cooper, K. H., and Gibbons, L. W. 1989. Physical fitness and all-cause mortality: A prospective study of healthy men and women. *Journal of the American Medical Association, 262*: 2395–2401.

Calle, E. E., Thun, M. J., Petrelli, J. M., Rodriguez, C., and Heath C. W., Jr. 1999. BMI and mortality in a prospective cohort of U.S. adults. *New England Journal of Medicine, 341*: 1097–1105.

Carlson, S. A., Densmore, D., Fulton, J. E., Yore, M. M., & Kohl, H. W., III. 2009. Differences in physical activity prevalence and trends from 3 U.S. surveillance systems: NHIS, NHANES, and BRFSS. *Journal of Physical Activity and Health, 6 Suppl 1,* S18–S27.

Corbin, C. B., Welk, G. J., Corbin, W. R., and Welk, K. A. 2008. *Concepts of physical fitness: Active lifestyles for wellness* (15th ed.). New York: McGraw-Hill.

DiPietro, L. 1995. Physical activity, body weight, and adiposity: An epidemiologic perspective. *Exercise and Sport Science Reviews, 23*: 275–303.

Fahey, T. D., Insel, P. M., and Roth, W. T. 2004. *Fit & well: Core concepts and labs in physical fitness and wellness.* 6th ed. New York: McGraw-Hill.

Fuemmeler, B. F., Pendzich, M. K., & Tercyak, K. P. 2009. Weight, dietary behavior, and physical activity in childhood and adolescence: Implications for adult cancer risk. *Obesity Facts 2,* 179–186.

Ford, E. S., Ford, M. A., Will, J. C., Galuska, D. A., and Ballew, C. 2001. Achieving a healthy lifestyle among United States adults: A long way to go. *Ethnicity & Disease, 11*: 224–31.

Franklin, B. A., Fagard, R., Farquhar, W. B., Kelley, G. A., and Ray, C. A. 2004. Exercise and hypertension. *Medicine and Science in Sports & Exercise, 36*: 533–53.

Glassberg, H., and Balady, G. J. 1999. Exercise and heart disease in women: Why, how, and how much? *Cardiology in Review, 7*: 301–08.

Gordon, P. M., Newcomer, R., and Krummel, D. A. 2001. Physical activity and osteoporosis: Disparities between knowledge and practice. *West Virginia Medical Journal, 97*(3): 153–56.

Haapanen, N., Miilunpalo, S., Pasanen, M., Oja, P., and Vuori, I. 1997. Association between leisure time, physical activity, and 10-year body mass change among working-aged men and women. *International Journal of Obesity Related Metabolic Disorders, 21*: 288–96.

Haapanen, N., Miilunpalo, S., Vuori, I., Oja, P., and Pasanen, M. 1996. Characteristics of leisure time physical activity associated with decreased risk of premature all-cause and cardiovascular disease mortality in middle-aged men. *American Journal of Epidemiology, 143*: 870–80.

Haapanen, N., Miilunpalo, S., Vuori, I., Oja, P., and Pasanen, M. 1997. Association of leisure time physical activity with the risk of coronary heart disease, hypertension and diabetes in middle-aged men and women. *International Journal of Epidemiology, 26*: 739–47.

Healthy people 1979: The Surgeon General's report on health promotion and disease prevention. Washington, DC: Government Printing Office (Stock Number 017–001–00146-2).

Healthy people 2000: Midcourse review and 1995 revisions. 1995. Washington, DC: U.S. Department of Health and Human Services, Public Health Service.

Healthy people 2000: National health promotion and disease prevention objectives, full report, with commentary. 1990. DHHS Publication Number (PHS)91–50212. Washington, DC: U.S. Department of Health and Human Services, Public Health Service.

Hockey, R. V. 1996. *Physical fitness: The pathway to healthful living* (8th ed.). Dubuque, IA: W. C. Brown/McGraw-Hill.

Hoeger, W. W. K., and Hoeger, S. A. 2006. *Lifetime physical fitness and wellness: A personalized program.* 9th ed. Stamford, CT: Wadsworth/Thomson Learning.

Jackson, A. W., Morrow, J. R., Jr., Hill, D. W., and Dishman, R. K. 2004. *Physical activity for health and fitness: An individualized lifetime approach.* Champaign, IL: Human Kinetics.

Kavanagh, T. 2001. Exercise in the primary prevention of coronary artery disease. *Canadian Journal of Cardiology, 17*: 155–61.

Kodama, S., Saito, K., Tanaka, S., Maki, M., Yachi, Y., Asumi, M. et al. 2009. Cardiorespiratory fitness as a quantitative predictor of all-cause mortality and cardiovascular events in healthy men and women: A meta-analysis. *Journal of the American Medical Association, 301,* 2024–2035.

Kohl, H. W., III. 2001. Physical activity and cardiovascular disease: Evidence for a dose response. *Medicine and Science in Sports & Exercise, 33*(Suppl): S472–83.

Kravitz, L. 2009. *Anybody's guide to total fitness.* 9th ed. Dubuque, IA: Kendall/Hunt.

Lee, I. M., Manson, J. E., Hennekens, C. H., and Paffenbarger, R. S., Jr. 1993. Body weight and mortality: A 27-year follow-up of middle-aged men. *Journal of the American Medical Association, 270*: 2823–28.

Lee, I. M., Sesso, H. D., and Paffenbarger, R. S., Jr. 2000. Physical activity and coronary heart disease risk in men: Does the duration of exercise episodes predict risk? *Circulation, 102*(9):981–86.

Lee, I., and Skerrett, P. J. 2001. Physical activity and all-cause mortality: What is the dose-response relation? *Medicine and Science in Sports & Exercise 33*(Suppl): S459–71.

Loustalot, F., Carlson, S. A., Fulton, J. E., Kruger, J., Galuska, D. A., & Lobelo, F. 2009. Prevalence of self-reported aerobic physical activity among U.S. States and territories—Behavioral Risk Factor Surveillance System, 2007. *Journal of Physical Activity and Health, 6 Suppl 1,* S9–S17.

Lowry, R., Lee, S. M., Fulton, J. E., & Kann, L. 2009. Healthy people 2010 objectives for physical activity, physical education, and television viewing among adolescents: national trends from the Youth Risk Behavior Surveillance System, 1999–2007. *Journal of Physical Activity and Health, 6 Suppl 1,* S36–S45.

Marcus, B. H., and Forsyth, L. H. 1999. How are we doing with physical activity? *American Journal of Health Promotion, 14:* 118–24.

McCauley, E., and Randolph, D. 1995. Physical activity, aging, and psychological well-being. *Journal of Aging and Physical Activity, 3:* 67–96.

Morbidity and Mortality Weekly Report. March 9, 2001. Physical activity trends—United States 1990–1998, 166–69.

Nutrition and your health: Dietary guidelines for Americans. 5th ed. 2000. Washington, DC: U.S. Department of Agriculture, U.S. Department of Health and Human Services.

Oguma, Y., Sesso, H. D., Paffenbarger, R. S., Jr., and Lee, I. M. 2002. Physical activity and all cause mortality in women: A review of the evidence. *British Journal of Sports Medicine, 36*(3):162–72.

Paffenbarger, R. S., Jr., Hyde, R. T., Wing, A. L., Lee, I-M., and Kampert, J. B. 1993. The association of changes in physical activity level and article lifestyle changes with mortality among men. *New England Journal of Medicine, 328:* 538–45.

Pate, R. R., Pratt, M., Blair, S. N., Haskell, W. L., Macera, C. A., Bouchard, C., Buchner, D., Ettinger, W., Heath, G. W., King, A. C., Kriska, A., Leon, A. S., Marcus, B. H., Morris, J., Paffenbarger, R. S., Jr., Patrick, K., Pollock, M. L., Rippe, J. M., Sallis, J. F., and Wilmore, J. H. 1995. Physical activity and public health: A recommendation from the Centers for Disease Control and Prevention and the American College of Sports Medicine. *Journal of the American Medical Association, 273:* 402–07.

Powell, K. E., and Blair, S. N. 1994. The public health burdens of sedentary living habits: Theoretical but realistic estimates. *Journal of the American Medical Association, 248:* 1073–76.

Pratt, M., Macera, C. A., and Wang, G. 2000. Higher direct medical costs associated with physical inactivity. *Physician and Sportsmedicine, 28*(10): 63–70.

Promoting physical activity: A guide for community action. 1999. Champaign, IL: Human Kinetics for the U.S. Department of Health and Human Services.

Rejeski, W. J., Brawley, L. R., and Schumaker, S. A. 1996. Physical activity and health-related quality of life. *Exercise and Sport Sciences Reviews, 24:* 71–108.

Rockhill, B., Willett, W. C., Manson, J. A. E., Leitzmann, M. F., Stampfer, M. J., Hunter, D. J., and Colditz, G. A. 2001. Physical activity and mortality: A prospective study among women. *American Journal of Public Health, 91:* 578–83.

Sacco, R. L. 2001. Newer risk factors for stroke. *Neurology 57*(Suppl): S31–34.

Sattelmair, J. R., Pertman, J. H., & Forman, D. E. 2009. Effects of physical activity on cardiovascular and noncardiovascular outcomes in older adults. *Clinics in Geriatric Medicine, 25,* 677–702.

Scarmeas, N., Luchsinger, J. A., Schupf, N., Brickman, A. M., Cosentino, S., Tang, M. X. et al. 2009. Physical activity, diet, and risk of Alzheimer disease. *JAMA, 302,* 627–637.

Seidell, J. C., Verschuren, W. M. M., van Leer, E. M., and Kromhout, D. 1996. Overweight, underweight, and mortality: A prospective study of 48,287 men and women. *Archives of Internal Medicine, 156:* 958–63.

Seiger, L., Kanipe, D., Vanderpool, K, and Barnes, D. 1998. *Fitness and wellness stragies,* 2nd ed.. Boston: McGraw-Hill.

Sesso, H. D., Paffenbarger, R. S., Jr., and Lee, I. M. 2000. Physical activity and coronary heart disease in men: The Harvard Alumini Health Study. *Circulation, 102*(9):975–80.

Shephard, R. J., and Shek, P. N. 1995. Cancer, immune function, and physical activity. *Canadian Journal of Applied Physiology, 20:* 1–25.

Sui, X., Laditka, J. N., Hardin, J. W., & Blair, S. N. 2007. Estimated functional capacity predicts mortality in older adults.*Journal of the American Geriatric Society, 55,* 1940–1947.

Sui, X., LaMonte, M. J., Laditka, J. N., Hardin, J. W., Chase, N., Hooker, S. P. et al. 2007. Cardiorespiratory fitness and adiposity as mortality predictors in older adults. *JAMA, 298,* 2507–2516.

Troiano, R. P., Macera, C. A., and Ballard-Barbash, R. 2001. Be physically active each day. How can we know? *Journal of Nutrition, 131*(Suppl): S451–60.

Vuori, I. M. 2001. Dose-response of physical activity and low back pain, osteoarthritis, and osteoporosis. *Medicine and Science in Sports & Exercise, 33*(Suppl): S551–96.

Wannamethee, S. G., and Shaper, A. G. 2001. Physical activity in the prevention of cardiovascular disease: An epidemiological perspective. *Sports Medicine, 31*(20):101–14.

Williamson, J., and Pahor, M. 2910. Evidence regarding the benefits of physical exercise. *Arch Intern Med., 1702,* January 25, 124–125.

3 | Aerobic Dance (Group Exercise)

After completing this chapter, the reader should be able to:

- Recognize the benefits associated with regular participation in aerobic dance
- Organize and design a safe and effective aerobic dance class, including the sequencing of activities
- Select appropriate music, movement patterns, and exercises for an aerobic dance program

HISTORY

The activity referred to as "aerobic dance" is undergoing a change, mostly a broadening of the definition. The focus is less on the spandex, thong leotard, dance imagery and more on inclusion of the general population, including men, seniors, and overweight individuals.

Group exercise may be defined as exercise in a class-type setting where participants are all following a format predetermined by a group exercise instructor. Group exercise is usually, but not always, performed to music. Group exercise may include a wide variety of class formats as well as varying modes of exercise such as aerobic dance, step aerobics, slide aerobics, stationary indoor cycling, water exercise, muscle conditioning, and flexibility work.

Aerobic dance, defined as continuous and rhythmic movement to music, was introduced by Jacki Sorenson in 1969. The combination of vigorous dance steps and exercises performed to popular music in a group setting soon became one of the fastest-growing leisure activities in the United States. According to the American Academy of Podiatric Sports Medicine (AAPSM), "More than 24 million people participate in aerobics" (www.aapsm.org/aerobics.html). Virtually every community offers some form of aerobic dance class. Even home exercisers can participate in this physically demanding activity by following popular group exercise leaders on television programs and DVDs.

Aerobic dance has evolved from rigidly choreographed dance routines intended for female participants to freestyle routines that incorporate random combinations of dance, sport, and exercise movements designed to attract men and women. In 1990, step aerobics was introduced, and by 1996, participation in step aerobics exceeded participation in either low- or high-impact aerobic dance (American Sports Data Inc. and Fitness Products Council). In addition, participation continues to grow in other group exercise modalities such as slide, water fitness, and indoor cycling.

Professional fitness associations are helping meet the demand for qualified instructors. Organizations such as the International Association of Fitness Professionals and the Aerobic and Fitness Association of America (AFAA) provide their members with services that include subscriptions to exercise journals, access to fitness conventions and workshops, and opportunities to become certified as a group exercise instructor. Since 1983, the AFAA has issued over 180,000 certificates to fitness professionals from 73 countries.

BENEFITS OF AEROBIC DANCE

Aerobic dance is an excellent activity for developing overall physical fitness. Balancing the health-related components of fitness, aerobic dance can improve a participant's flexibility, strength, cardiovascular fitness, and body composition. The rhythmic movements performed to music also help develop coordination and balance. In addition, exercising in a group setting provides opportunities for social interactions not afforded by many other aerobic activities (Figure 3.1).

FACILITY

The ideal setting for conventional aerobic dance includes:
1. Good ventilation with a room temperature of 60° to 70° F.
2. A floor that will absorb shock while controlling lateral motions of the foot and providing adequate traction. A hardwood sprung floor is an ideal aerobic dance surface.
3. Space for each participant to move comfortably. A good guide is enough space for each participant, with arms outspread, to take two large steps in any direction without touching anyone.
4. Acoustics that allow the instructor's voice to be heard over the music.
5. For large groups, a raised platform for the instructor.
6. Mirrors to help participants observe and correct their posture and exercise positions.

Figure 3.1. Aerobic dance class.

Other settings include shallow or deep-water pools and outdoor courses for walking and in-line skating.

EQUIPMENT

Equipment needs vary according to the type of facility and the size of the class. Most programs require a sound system and a collection of audiotapes or CDs. A wireless microphone for the instructor may be necessary if the class is in a large space (Figure 3.2). Many other possibilities for equipment and/or props are available, such as steps (benches), slides, rubber tubes or bands, hand weights (1- to 10-pound dumbbells are commonly used), ankle weights, stability balls, mats, stretch straps, jump ropes, boxing gloves and/or tape, spinning cycles, water mitts, noodles, wings, and water steps.

APPAREL AND SHOES

Participants should wear lightweight, well-ventilated clothing. Cotton fabrics are recommended because they absorb moisture while allowing air to circulate through the material. Many of the fabrics used for exercise apparel are made of cotton blends. Knee-length tights or fitness shorts worn with a leotard or T-shirt provide the greatest comfort and mobility. Cotton socks will help absorb perspiration and reduce the likelihood of blisters. Participants should be encouraged to layer their clothing in cool facilities and remove outer garments (such as a warm-up suit) as the body temperature rises with increased levels of activity.

Shoes are the most important item worn by the participants in aerobic dance and step classes. Because certain high-impact aerobic dance and step moves can generate vertical

forces on the feet of up to four times one's body weight, participants need to select a shoe designed to help absorb these impacts. Cushioned athletic socks can provide additional protection for the feet. A well-constructed aerobic shoe has a sole adequately cushioned, especially under the ball of the foot, to help absorb the shock of forefoot movements characteristic of most aerobic steps. Proper support and stability are particularly important for lateral movements. The traction provided by the shoe should match the surface on which activities are being performed. For example, less traction is needed on a carpeted surface while greater traction is necessary on a hardwood floor. Shoes should be selected for their durability, flexibility, and lightweight characteristics. Finally, regular checking of the shoes is important to insure they continue to provide support. Although expensive, shoes do not last forever.

FUNDAMENTAL SKILLS AND TECHNIQUES
Components of a Typical Aerobic Dance Class

A well-designed format for group exercise consists of:
1. Warm-up and prestretch (10 minutes)
2. Aerobic activity (20 to 30 minutes)
3. Cool down (2 to 5 minutes)
4. Strength work (5 to 10 minutes)
5. Final stretch (5 to 10 minutes)

Warm-up and prestretch

The purpose of the warm-up is to increase blood flow to the muscles, increase the rate of oxygen exchange between blood and muscles, increase the speed and force of muscle

Figure 3.2. Using a wireless microphone.

contraction, increase muscle elasticity as well as the flexibility of tendons and ligaments, and reduce the risk of cardiac abnormalities. Movements during the warm-up should include rhythmic, full-range-of-motion exercises designed to prepare the body for movements used during the aerobic segment. The initial warm-up should concentrate on large movements for the shoulders, arms, and legs. A warm-up routine might consist of shoulder rolls, arm circles, marches, step touches, and toe and heel raises. After the muscles have been warmed, static stretching exercises should be performed to increase joint range of motion. Stretching positions should be held for at least 10 to 30 seconds, paying special attention to muscles of the shoulders, chest, hips, low back, thighs, calves, and feet.

Aerobic activity

The purpose of the aerobic segment is to improve cardiovascular endurance. The physiological benefits of aerobic activity include increased heart and lung efficiency, improvement of the respiratory system, and decreased body fat. Aerobic benefits are achieved by using prolonged and continuous movement of the large muscles. Ideally, the aerobic segment of class will last 20 to 30 minutes, performed at an intensity of 60 to 80 percent of the heart rate reserve.

To determine appropriate exercise intensity, participants need to monitor their exertion using heart rate monitoring, a perceived exertion chart, or both throughout the class. This serves two purposes. First, it is a gauge by which participants can assess the intensity of their workout at any point. Second, it is a motivational tool allowing participants to measure, objectively, their progress over a 3-month program. Verifying improvement in their fitness level will encourage participants to make aerobic activity part of their lifestyle.

Heart rate monitoring. There are three heart rates about which each participant should be knowledgeable, and each of them indicates something about his or her level of physical fitness. They are the resting heart rate, the working heart rate, and the recovery heart rate. The **Resting Heart Rate (RHR)** is the rate at which a heart beats after sitting quietly for a while. It is usually 15–20 beats per minute (bpm) lower than a participant's usual heart rate and is a good indicator of physical fitness. A person in good aerobic condition ordinarily has an RHR lower than someone who is in poor aerobic condition. To determine the RHR, lightly place the middle and index finger on either the carotid artery (at the neck) or the radial artery (on the thumb side of the wrist) and count

Figure 3.3. Taking the heart rate.

the number of beats occurring in 60 seconds (Figure 3.3). The participant then uses that number to calculate his or her personal heart rate zone using Table 3.1. The target heart rate zone lies between the two values from the table that appear at the intersection of the resting heart rate and age. The **Working Heart Rate (WHR)** is the rate measured during the aerobic activity. It is an excellent indicator of the intensity of the aerobic activity. As exercise becomes more vigorous and more oxygen is required, the heart increases its rate to supply oxygen to the muscles, thus developing aerobic fitness. Use the same carotid or radial spot to count a heart rate for 6 seconds immediately after aerobic activity. Adding a zero to this number gives the bpm (beats per minute). The WHR drops off quickly, so it is imperative to measure it quickly. A 10-second count does not increase the accuracy significantly, and the mental math is a bit more challenging. A 15-second count is not accurate because the exercise has been stopped for too long. The **Recovery Heart Rate (RecHR)** is measured 5 minutes after aerobic activity has stopped. It is measured for 15 seconds and multiplied by four. It should be 120 bpm or lower. If not, additional cooling down is called for until it does measure at this level. Participants should be cautioned to refrain from moves that place the head below the heart until this heart rate level or lower is reached.

Table 3.1. WORKING HEART RATE RANGES

	Beats per Minute (BPM)							
				AGE				
Resting Heart Rate*	30 and under	31–40	41–45	46–50	51–55	56–60	61–65	65+
50–51	137–195	131–185	128–180	122–170	119–165	116–160	110–150	107–145
52–53	138–195	132–185	129–180	123–170	120–165	117–160	111–150	108–145
54–56	139–195	133–185	130–180	124–170	121–165	118–160	112–150	109–145
57–58	140–195	134–185	131–180	125–170	122–165	119–160	113–150	110–145
59–61	141–195	135–185	132–180	126–170	123–165	120–160	114–150	111–145
62–63	142–195	136–185	133–180	127–170	124–165	121–160	115–150	112–145
64–66	143–195	137–185	134–180	128–170	125–165	122–160	116–150	113–145
67–68	144–195	138–185	135–180	129–170	126–165	123–160	117–150	114–145
69–71	145–195	139–185	136–180	130–170	127–165	124–160	118–150	115–145
72–73	146–195	140–185	137–180	131–170	128–165	125–160	119–150	116–145
74–76	147–195	141–185	138–180	132–170	129–165	126–160	120–150	117–145
77–78	148–195	142–185	139–180	133–170	130–165	127–160	121–150	118–145
79–81	149–195	143–185	140–180	134–170	131–165	128–160	122–150	119–145
82–83	150–195	144–185	141–180	135–170	132–165	129–160	123–150	120–145
84–86	151–195	145–185	142–180	136–170	133–165	130–160	124–150	121–145
87–88	152–195	146–185	143–180	137–170	134–165	131–160	125–150	122–145
89–91	153–195	147–185	144–180	138–170	135–165	132–160	126–150	123–145

*The ideal time to take your resting heart rate (RHR) is before you get out of bed in the morning. Otherwise, make sure you sit quietly for at least 15 minutes.

This chart is based on the medically-proven Karvonen Formula, which uses your age and resting heart rate as a basis, then indicates what your working heart rate range should be in order for you to actually be receiving aerobic benefit. The lower number of each range is the minimum WHR that you should maintain for an aerobic workout. The higher number is the maximum WHR and is used to caution you against overexertion. However, for safety, we strongly advise you not to exceed 140 BPM during the first two weeks of your first-ever aerobic program.

Source: Sorensen, J. and Bruns, B. 1983. *Jacki Sorensen's Aerobic Lifestyle Book.* NY: Poseidon Press. pp 20–23.

Perceived exertion. During exercise it is important for the participant to monitor his or her intensity to make sure the exercise is at a pace that is challenging enough so that fitness is improved, yet not so high as to be detrimental to physical or emotional well-being. The standard perceived exertion scale is the Borg Rating of Perceived Exertion (RPE), which ranges from 0–20. Most gym and physical fitness centers post an adapted scale with a 10-point range (Table 3.2) to help make personal measurement easier. For most participants, a level of 5–6 during aerobic activity is desirable. If interval training is the goal, strive to work in a range from 4–9. Working at a level of 10 is not recommended for most participants. By self-monitoring and checking the chart, participants can adjust the intensity of the activity, increasing it by speeding up and lifting knees and arms higher, or slowing down by doing the steps at a more moderate level and minimizing arm movements to pace. Participants need to consider the total feeling of exertion and not just breath, physical stress, effort, or muscle fatigue.

To help gauge the pace of the class, the instructors should always monitor their heart rates with their students. Each participant's rate is individual and instructors should tell participants that regardless of rate, the aerobic activity should feel comfortable without unnecessary strain or fatigue. A good rule of thumb is that the participants should be able to have a conversation with others around them if they want.

The aerobic segment of an aerobic or step class consists of movement patterns choreographed to music. Movement patterns can be extremely varied, ranging from calisthenic exercises such as jumping jacks to dance movements such as leaps and lunges. Instructors can enhance their movement repertoire by using steps common to other dance forms,

Figure 3.4. Leg kick.

including jazz, modern, folk, and ballet, or by borrowing movement patterns used in sports and games, such as basketball dribbling.

Common basic steps used in aerobic dance include jogs, marches, hops, jumps, knee lifts, kicks, twists, step touches, jumping jacks, and lunges. These steps can be varied by changing the rhythm (half time, double time) or the direction of movement (forward, backward, sideways, diagonally, or in circles) or by adding arm positions to accompany the leg movements (Figures 3.4 and 3.5). Common moves used in step aerobics include the basic step (up, up, down, down), V step, travel step with alternating lead, over the top, lift step, lunge, L step, repeater, and turn step. There are several possible approaches to the step: front, side, end, corner, top, and astride.

Steps can be combined into movement patterns in several ways. Routines can be rigidly choreographed, repeating the same movements each time the routine is performed. Choreographed routines help participants become secure with a movement sequence, allowing them to concentrate

Table 3.2.

Perceived Exertion Chart	
10	**Very Very Hard Activity** Completely out of breath, unable to talk
9	**Very Hard Activity** Can speak only one word at a time
7–8	**Hard Activity** Out of breath, can speak a sentence or two
4–6	**Moderate Activity** Can still carry a conversation
2–3	**Light Activity** Breathing is easy
1	**No Activity**

Waehner, P. Perceived Exertion Scale. http://exercise.about.com.

Figure 3.5. Knee lift.

is an example of a linear progression in traditional aerobic dance:

> **Base movement:** 4 knee lifts in place (8 counts)
> **Add arms:** Overhead presses (8 counts)
> **Add direction:** Travel forward with 4 knee lifts and overhead presses (8 counts)
> **Change direction:** Travel backward with 4 knee lifts and overhead presses (8 counts)
> **Change arms:** Arm curls while traveling forward and backward with knee lifts (16 counts)
> **Change legs:** 4 step kicks with arm curls traveling forward and backward (16 counts)
> **Change arms:** Chest presses with step kick traveling forward and backward (16 counts)

Notice that only one variable was added or changed whenever a new movement was introduced.

Freestyle movements can also be sequenced into combinations. A combination is defined as two or more movement patterns that are sequenced together and repeated in a cycle. The following is an example of two simple combinations:

Combination 1
- 4 knee lifts traveling forward while pressing the arms overhead (8 counts)
- 4 step kicks traveling backward while curling the arms down and up (8 counts)

Combination 2
- 8 jogs forward with alternating arm curls (8 counts)
- 4 jumping jacks backward with hand claps (8 counts)

Combination 1 can be taught and repeated several times before combination 2 is introduced. Combination 2 can then be added to combination 1, producing a more interesting and challenging sequence of movements.

The first aerobic routine following the warm-up should be performed at a moderate pace to give the cardiovascular system ample time to adjust to the increasing demands of exercise. As the class progresses through the aerobic segment, the intensity and music tempo should be increased. Participants should be instructed to adjust the intensity of their movements to correspond with their level of cardiovascular fitness.

Cool down

The purpose of the cool down is to gradually lower the heart rate toward normal, prevent excessive pooling of blood in the lower extremities, and promote removal of metabolic waste products from the muscles. Slow but continued rhythmic contraction of the leg muscles is important to help return the blood from the lower extremities to the heart. A cool down of 2 to 5 minutes can consist of walking around the room while gently swinging the arms or doing a slow aerobic routine.

on the intensity of exercise and correct exercise positions. However, choreographed routines require a great deal of preparation by the instructor and can take extra class time to teach. Many instructors prefer to use a freestyle approach to combine movement patterns with music. Rather than using routines, instructors using the freestyle technique select movements in a random fashion, building combinations of step patterns as the music progresses. When skillfully led, participants enjoy the movement variety associated with the freestyle method. If, however, the step patterns are too complex for the group, participants may be unable to maintain appropriate exercise intensity as they struggle with unexpected and unfamiliar movements.

Freestyle choreography can be taught using a linear progression or by sequencing movement patterns into combinations. A *linear progression* is defined as a movement that advances into another, changing only one variable at a time, such as the leg or arm movement, the direction of movement, or the rhythm. This type of freestyle choreography is easy to follow, especially for beginners. The following

It is wise to take a recovery heart rate at the end of the cool down. A decrease in recovery heart rate over time is a measure of improved cardiovascular fitness. For comparative purposes, the recovery heart rate must be taken the same number of minutes following the end of the aerobic segment. A record sheet for recording exercise and recovery heart rates is useful for observing the progress of participants.

Strength exercises

Muscular strength is important for preventing injuries by helping the participant maintain proper alignment and body mechanics. It is therefore important to strengthen the muscles that help maintain good posture and aid in the proper execution of aerobic dance routines and floor exercises. Weak upper back muscles (upper trapezius and rhomboids) contribute to rounded shoulders, while weak abdominals can lead to a swayback posture. Aggravated by vigorous movements on the feet, these anatomical deviations can result in neck, shoulder, and low back pain. Therefore, it is prudent to strengthen the upper back muscles and abdominals in each class session. Rowing exercises and prone shoulder raises can be used to strengthen the upper back while curl-ups, diagonal curls, reverse curls, and pelvic tilts will help strengthen the abdominals.

It is also important to strengthen muscles of the shins (tibialis anterior). One of the most common injuries reported in aerobics is shinsplints. Although there are many causes for shin pain, a typical problem results from a muscle imbalance between the strong calf muscles (gastrocnemius), which contract vigorously for a prolonged period of time during the aerobic dance segment, and the weak shin muscles, which are used less frequently during class. Various forms of toe tapping, walking on the heels, and ankle flexion with light weights or rubber bands can help to strengthen tibialis anterior muscles.

If time allows, instructors can include strength exercises for other parts of the body. These include side leg lifts for the hip abductors and adductors, leg curls and lifts for the hamstrings and gluteals, knee extensions for the quadriceps, arm curls for the biceps, elbow extensions for the triceps, one-arm bent-over rows for latissimus dorsi, and lateral raises for the deltoids. Muscular strength is achieved by overloading the muscle with adequate resistance so that the student can complete 8 to 12 repetitions of an exercise. Surgical tubing, elastic bands, or weights can provide appropriate resistance. In addition, holding a contraction for 5 seconds at different points in the movement pattern can provide added resistance to the muscles. To continue strength gains, the resistance for each exercise should be increased when participants can comfortably complete three sets of 8 to 12 repetitions.

To encourage controlled movements during the strength exercises, music tempos should be moderately paced, and participants should be instructed to adjust the tempo (half time or double time) and the number of repetitions required to meet their personal levels of strength. To encourage proper exercise technique, the instructor should move around the room and provide appropriate exercise cues while observing and critiquing performance.

Final stretch

The purpose of the final stretch is to improve overall flexibility, which helps maintain good posture and proper body mechanics throughout the day. Stretching after a vigorous exercise session is often easier than stretching before because the joints are well lubricated, and the temperature of the muscles is increased following the aerobic workout. It is best to perform these stretches on the floor, allowing participants an opportunity to relax and concentrate on each stretch. The final stretch is most effective when performed to slow background music that does not have a strong beat. Flexibility exercises, held for 10 to 30 seconds, should include stretches for muscles of the low back, hip flexors, calves (Achilles tendinitis is a common injury in step aerobics), hamstrings, chest, shoulders, and neck (Figures 3.6 and 3.7).

Low, moderate, and high impacts

In the past, most aerobic dance routines consisted of high-impact movements, including variations of jogs, hops, and jumps. High-impact aerobics (HIA), characterized by movements that require both feet to leave the floor frequently, can produce vertical forces of up to four times the weight of the body. Researchers reporting on injuries suffered by aerobic dancers found a fairly high incidence of injury to the shins, feet, knees, and lower back. Although the injuries were seldom serious enough to require medical attention, concern that high-impact movements were in part responsible for these aches and pains led to the development of a new form of aerobic dance called low-impact aerobics (LIA). LIA, characterized by movements that use a wide base of support while keeping one foot on the floor at all times, has not been without its share of unique problems and injuries.

In an attempt to stay close to the floor during LIA, the use of a wide base of support and the extreme lowering and raising of the center of gravity produces a great deal of prolonged and often extreme knee flexion. This can result in a number of knee injuries for individuals already suffering from structural knee problems. In addition, the larger arm movements used to maintain exercise intensity during LIA have resulted in shoulder injuries among participants using uncontrolled arm-flinging motions.

Generally, LIA is not recommended for anyone who complains of knee discomfort during prolonged knee flexion or for well-conditioned individuals who are unable to achieve appropriate intensity levels using low-impact movements. On the other hand, HIA is generally not recommended for individuals who are deconditioned, especially if they are obese; for women in the latter stages of pregnancy; for anyone who is susceptible to injuries related to impact shock,

Figure 3.6. Quadriceps stretch.

Figure 3.7. Hamstrings stretch.

such as shinsplints; or for individuals who are uncomfortable with high-impact steps, such as people suffering from incontinence. To accommodate individual differences in each class, many programs use a combination of high- and low-impact steps throughout the aerobic routines. This results in a decrease in the number of high-impact steps being performed.

A compromise that combines the best elements of HIA and LIA is called moderate-impact aerobics (MIA). MIA movements require that one foot remain on the floor most of the time, as in LIA, although the base of support is narrower and the center of gravity is lifted up and down as in HIA. MIA steps are therefore characterized by a springlike motion. All MIA movements should begin by lifting the body upward, rising onto the balls of the feet. Each step should be completed by gently pressing the heels against the floor. The advantages of MIA include less-prolonged and -extreme knee flexion than often associated with LIA, and smaller vertical impacts than found in many HIA movements.

Other aerobic training modes

Traditionally the aerobic segment of an aerobic dance class consisted of continuous exercise. Today interval and circuit training have become common in both aerobics and step.

Aerobic interval training involves high-intensity work bouts (near maximal heart rate) followed by active rest or recovery periods of an equal length of time. Exercise and rest intervals vary from 1 to 3 minutes in length and are repeated 5 to 12 times during the aerobic segment of class. Because interval training requires high-intensity exercise during the work bouts, high-impact or propulsive movements such as jumps are commonly choreographed to fast-paced music. During the active rest, moderately paced movements such as walks and step touches are performed. Due to the fast-paced, high-intensity nature of interval training, this activity is recommended only for the more advanced participant. Interval training is associated with more physical pain than is experienced in continuous forms of training, because more metabolic waste products are produced and accumulated in the muscles during the near-maximal efforts of the activity.

Circuit training is another popular technique used in aerobic dance programs. A circuit consists of a specified number of exercise stations used to promote all-around physical fitness. The emphasis is on development of muscular strength and endurance, cardiovascular endurance, flexibility, and sometimes coordination and balance. Most circuits have 10 to 20 stations. Each area is posted with a sign indicating the task to be completed. Participants are instructed to remain at a station for a set amount of time (30 to 60 seconds) and move to the next station on command. The circuit moves in a clockwise or counterclockwise direction and can be repeated two to three times. Many other creative formats are possible. For example, cardio/strength intervals are popular. This type of class might alternate a 4-minute cardio segment (either step or aerobic dance) with a 4-minute muscle-conditioning segment. The muscle-conditioning segments might include squats and standing side leg lifts, unilateral bent-over rows and triceps extensions, overhead presses, biceps curls, and abdominal work. An advantage of this type of format is the increased amount of total work accomplished.

TEACHING CONSIDERATIONS

Patterns of Class Organization

Group exercise class should be arranged so that everyone can hear the instructor's verbal cues and see the demonstrations. Above all, it is important that the instructor be able to observe all class participants. In a typical class, the instructor stands at the front of the room with the participants facing forward. The disadvantage of this system is that the advanced participants usually stand at the front of the room while the less skilled stay at the back. The instructor cannot clearly observe those who are in greatest need of feedback. To resolve this problem, the instructor can periodically move from the front of the room to the back or the sides, asking participants to turn and face the instructor. A system of rotation is another effective way of observing class participants. At the end of each song, the teacher instructs the participants to rotate. The front line moves to the back of the room while every other line moves forward one row. Other patterns of class organization include circle formations (where the instructor stands at the center) and movement patterns that travel from one end of the floor to the other.

Cuing

Cuing is a very important part of teaching group exercise, particularly when the moves must be performed to music. Participants depend on the instructor's verbal and nonverbal cues for every step they take. Each anticipatory verbal cue should be brief and called on the preceding measure, giving ample time to move smoothly from one step to the next. Instructors can use a combination of types of anticipatory cuing, including footwork cuing (indicates whether to move the right or left foot), directional cuing (refers to the direction of movement: forward, backward, left, or right), rhythmic cuing (indicates the correct rhythm of the routine, such as slow or quick), numerical cuing (refers to counting the rhythm, such as "one, two, three, and four"), and step cuing (indicates the name of the step, such as "step touch"). Initially participants will be most dependent on footwork, directional, and numerical cuing. Once they become somewhat skilled and learn the names of each step or movement pattern, the participants will rely more on step cues and pay most attention to nonverbal cues, such as hand signals indicating direction. In addition to anticipatory cues, skilled instructors provide educational cues (or information), safety and alignment cues, and motivational cues. An example of an educational cue would be "This exercise is for your lats, which are *here*" (instructor points to her own lats). "Be sure to control the movement on the way down to minimize stress to the joints" is an example of a safety cue. "Terrific!" and "I like the way you're all concentrating on good form!" are motivational cues.

When leading most aerobic routines, the instructor should face the class and use mirroring techniques (the instructor moves to the left when the class moves to the right). To avoid potential collisions between students, instructors should begin lateral movements to the same side each time. Most instructors prefer moving first to the right and then to the left.

Music

Music provides the timing and style for exercise movements. In addition, it adds fun, variety, and excitement to class. The tempo, or rate of speed, at which music is played determines the progression and intensity of exercise. Instructors can determine the tempo of the music by counting the beats per minute (bpm). Over the years, the following guidelines have been adopted by instructors for selecting appropriate music tempo for land-based aerobic classes:

Warm-up, prestretch, and cool-down: 120 to 140 bpm
Floor exercise: 110 to 130 bpm
Aerobic activity: 130 to 160 bpm (LIA); 144 to 160 bpm (HIA)
Step aerobics: 120 to 128 bpm
Final stretch: under 100 bpm

Instructors must be cautious when using fast music tempos (more than 150 bpm). To avoid uncontrolled movements, participants should be encouraged to use the arms through a small range of motion and to take short steps. Because beginners are not proficient enough to perform fast movements under control, they should not be expected to exercise to fast-paced music. When using music with fast tempos, instructors should be aware that participants with long arms and legs need more time than participants with short limbs to cover the same spatial area. For example, people with short arms can raise them above their heads more quickly than people with long arms. Tall participants should therefore be encouraged to bend their arms in order to keep in time with fast music. The most efficient way to use music in class is to record a 40- to 60-minute audiotape that includes music for the warm-up, prestretch, aerobic segment, cool down, floor exercises, and final stretch. However, instructors reproducing and playing music in an aerobic dance class should be familiar with the copyright laws. The Copyright Act of 1976 states that a person wishing to play copyrighted music for a "public performance" must obtain permission from the copyright owner. Using music during a group exercise class constitutes a public performance. Because it would be time-consuming to obtain permission from the copyright owner of each piece of music used in a class, instructors can save valuable time by joining performing rights societies (ASCAP and BMI). These societies have been assigned the nondramatic rights of copyright owners and grant their members permission to play the music of numerous artists. Under the "fair use" doctrine, instructors teaching in the public schools or at institutions of higher education may be exempt from having to obtain copyright permission. It is wise, however, for instructors to consult with an attorney to determine if their use of music qualifies as "fair use."

Developing music tapes can be one of the most time-consuming tasks for the instructor. To save valuable time and to stay current with popular music selections, instructors can subscribe to a number of music services that provide complete audiotapes for all segments of many different types of classes (see the Resources section at the end of this chapter).

SAFETY CONCERNS

To ensure the safety of class participants, instructors should comply with the following guidelines:

1. Screen participants for common anatomical problems, such as kyphosis, lordosis, and excess pronation of the feet. Also evaluate them for tight or weak muscles. Early detection and correction of such problems can reduce the risk of injuries.
2. Encourage appropriate body alignment throughout the class period. Proper posture includes head up, shoulders back, chest up, buttocks tucked under the hips, and knees relaxed.
3. Avoid or minimize the use of the following potentially harmful exercise positions: (a) sustained and unsupported forward flexion in a standing position, (b) unsupported forward flexion in a standing position with rotation, (c) trunk rotation against a fixed axis, (d) neck hyperextension, (e) fast head circles, (f) the yoga plough, (g) deep knee bends, (h) hurdler stretch, (i) hyperextension of the elbows and knees, (j) straight-leg sit-up, (k) double leg raises, and (l) side leg lifts supported on the knees and hands or elbows.
4. Avoid ballistic stretching. Static stretching is effective and tends to be safer than bobbing or bouncing techniques.
5. Insist that participants wear shoes during the aerobic segment of class.
6. Be aware of the placement of class members to avoid collisions during rapid movements across the floor.
7. Encourage participants to control the placement of their arms, avoiding any flinging motions. Shoulder injuries are becoming increasingly common in aerobic dance and step.
8. Avoid having the participants keep their arms at or above shoulder level for a prolonged period of time. This increases blood pressure, places stress on the tendons and muscles of the shoulder, and increases heart rate in a manner not beneficial to increased cardiovascular conditioning.
9. Avoid prolonged and excessive deep knee flexion. Make sure the knees of participants remain over the first and second toes.
10. Be cautious of lateral movements on carpeted surfaces. The added friction associated with carpet can result in ankle inversion sprains.
11. Avoid impact on concrete surfaces.
12. Reduce the risk of common musculoskeletal injuries during aerobic activity by progressing slowly and by not exceeding intensity levels of 85 percent of heart rate reserve, exercise durations of 30 minutes, and exercise frequencies of 4 days per week on alternate days.
13. Avoid too many consecutive movements on one foot, such as dozens of hops.

14. Avoid rapid changes of direction.
15. Participants should avoid staying on the balls of their feet for extended periods of time. The lowering of the heels to the floor provides additional shock absorption for the feet.
16. Face the class as often as possible to effectively observe everyone's performance.
17. Do not allow the participants to hold their breath while performing strength exercises. Encourage them to exhale on exertion.
18. Control the movement of hand and ankle weights at all times.
19. Be aware of exercise restrictions and modifications for special populations. For example, people with high blood pressure should not perform isometric contractions and should avoid keeping the arms above shoulder level for extended periods of time.
20. Platform height: deconditioned participants should begin on 4 inches; highly skilled and experienced steppers can use up to 10 inches. The knee joint should not flex deeper than 90 degrees when the knee is fully loaded.
21. When stepping up, lean from the ankles and not the waist to avoid excessive stress on the lumbar spine.
22. Contact the platform with the entire sole of the foot. To avoid Achilles tendon injury, do not allow the heel to land over the edge of the platform.
23. Step close to the platform (no more than one shoe length away) and allow the heels to contact the floor to help absorb shock. On lunges and repeaters, do not push the heel into the floor.
24. Change the leading foot after no more than 1 minute.
25. Do not perform propulsion steps (both feet off the floor or platform at the same time) for more than 1 minute at a time. Propulsion steps result in higher vertical impact forces and are considered an advanced technique.
26. Do not perform more than five consecutive repeaters on the same leg.
27. It is recommended that weights be reserved for the strength segment of a step training class, due to the increased potential for shoulder joint injury when weights are rapidly moved through a large range of motion (Reebok International 1993).

GLOSSARY

aerobic dance Continuous and rhythmic movement to music intended to improve cardiovascular fitness.

choreographed routine Formally arranged step patterns taught in the same sequence each time the routine is performed to the same music.

circuit training A form of exercise that promotes all-around physical fitness by incorporating various stations involving strength, aerobic, and agility activities.

combination Two or more movement patterns that are sequenced together and repeated in a cycle.

continuous training A form of aerobic training that requires the continuous performance of moderate to vigorous movement over a specified period of time.

cuing Verbal and nonverbal techniques that inform participants of upcoming movements, safety, and alignment and that increase motivation.

duration of exercise The total time of each exercise session.

flexibility The range of motion possible at a joint.

freestyle routine Aerobic movements performed in a random fashion, building combinations of step patterns as the music progresses.

frequency of exercise The total number of exercise sessions per week.

HIA (high-impact aerobics) An aerobic dance style characterized by movement that frequently requires both feet to leave the floor simultaneously.

intensity of exercise the amount of exertion required by exercise, measured by the percent of the heart rate reserve used.

interval training A form of aerobic and anaerobic training that involves performing a series of high-intensity work bouts alternating with active rest periods.

LIA (low-impact aerobics) An aerobic dance style that minimizes the amount of vertical impacts by keeping one foot on the floor at all times while covering a larger spatial area with the feet and arms.

linear progression A movement that advances into another, changing only one variable at a time, such as the leg or arm movement, the direction of movement, or the rhythm.

MIA (moderate-impact aerobics) An aerobic dance style requiring that one foot remain on the floor most of the time while lifting the body high onto the balls of the feet and then gently pressing the heels to the floor.

muscular strength Maximum force exerted by a muscle or muscle group against resistance.

step aerobics An aerobic mode performed to music utilizing a 4- to 10-inch step bench.

target heart rate zone The number of heartbeats per specified period of time necessary to achieve aerobic benefits while minimizing possible musculoskeletal injury.

tempo Rate of speed music is played, determined by counting the number of beats per minute (bpm).

REFERENCES

Centers for Disease Control and Prevention (CDC.gov), 1600 Clifton Rd, Atlanta, GA 30333.

IHRSA/American Sports Data Health Club Trend Report, 1996. American Sports Data Inc, Hartsdale, NY.

Sorensen, Jacki. 1989. *Jacki's instructor textbook*. Northridge, CA: Jacki's Inc. Publishing.

Sorensen, Jacki with Bruns, Bill. 1983. *Jacki sorensen's aerobic lifestyle book*. New York: Poseidon Press.

Sorensen, Jacki with Bruns, Bill. 1979. *Aerobic dancing*. New York: Rawson, Wade Publishers, Inc.

Step Manual, 1993. Reebok International, Reebok University Press Publisher, Boston, MA.

INTERNET REFERENCES

Centers for Disease Control and Prevention. "Perceived Exertion (Borg Rating of Perceived Exertion Scale)." 29 March 2010 http://sportsmedicine.about.com

Quinn, Elizabeth. "Rating of Perceived Exertion Scale," 09 March 2004 http://sportsmedicine.about.com

Waehner, Paige. "Perceived Exertion Scale." 19 December 2008 http://exercise.about.com

SUGGESTED READINGS

Aerobic and Fitness Association of America; Jordan, P. 2002. *Fitness theory and practice.* 4th ed. Sherman Oaks, CA: HDL Publishing.

Mangili, L., and Mazzeo, K. 1999. *Step training plus.* 2nd ed. Stamford, CT: Wadsworth /Thomson Learning. Explains how to structure a complete physical and mental training workout.

Mazzeo, K. S. 2007. *Fitness through aerobics and step training.* 4th ed. Stamford, CT: Wadsworth/Thomson Learning.

Spitzer, T., and Hoeger, W. 2003. *Water aerobics for fitness and wellness.* 3rd ed. Stamford, CT: Wadsworth/Thomson Learning. Contains information on shallow and deep water exercises, nutrition, weight management, and behavior modification.

Stanforth, D. 1997. *Movement that matters.* Dubuque, IA: McGraw-Hill.

Stokes, R., and Trapp, D. 2004. *Aerobic fitness everyone.* 3rd ed. Winston-Salem, NC: Hunter Textbooks, Inc. Tips on flexibility, nutrition, stress reduction, and exercises for older adults are included.

Yarbrough, M. 2001. *Aerobic exercise.* Boston, MA: American Press.

RESOURCES

Aerobic dance associations

Aerobic and Fitness Association of America (AFAA), 15250 Ventura Blvd., Suite 310, Sherman Oaks, CA 91403.

American Council on Exercise, 5820 Oberlin Dr., Suite 102, San Diego, CA 92121.

International Dance Exercise Association (IDEA), 6190 Cornerstone E, Suite 204, San Diego, CA 92121.

Reebok Professional Instructor Alliance (a free service to aerobic dance instructors), 100 Technology Center Dr., Stoughton, MA 02072.

Videos/DVDs

Beachbody Aerobics, www.beachbody.com/aerobics

Twombly, G. *Creative Instructors Aerobics, Inc.* Telenium Center, 525 Mildred Ave, Primos, PA 19018 www.ciavideo.com

Music performing rights societies

ASCAP, 2675 Paces Ferry Rd SE, Suite 350, Atlanta, GA 30339.

BMI, 10 Music Square East, Nashville, TN 37203-4399.

Music services

Dynamix Music Service, 9411 Philadelphia Rd, Rosedale, MD 21237-4168.

Muscle Mixes Music, Inc., 1617 Hillcrest St., Orlando, FL 32803-4809.

Music Flex Aerobic Tapes, 15934 90th St., Howard Beach, NY 11414-3114.

Power Plus Productions, 3155 W. 5400s, Kearns, UT 84118-2271.

WEB SITES

Aerobics and Fitness Association
www.afaa.com

American Academy of Podiatric Sports Medicine (AAPSM)
www.aapsm.org

American College of Sports Medicine
www.acsm.org

American Council on Exercise
www.acefitness.org

IDEA
www.ideafit.com

Jacki's Aerobic Programs
www.jacki's.com

Archery

After completing this chapter, the reader should be able to:

- Recognize and select appropriate archery equipment
- Understand rules and scoring procedures
- Describe the best technique for stringing the bow
- Describe the steps involved in shooting
- Identify and use proper safety procedures
- Instruct a group of students in the fundamentals of archery
- Recognize and use archery terms correctly

HISTORY

The bow and arrow is one of the oldest mechanical weapons and remains the weapon of many aboriginal peoples in certain parts of the world. The bow and arrow was first used by primitive peoples for hunting. It was the chief weapon of the American Indians, both for hunting and for war. It was used as a weapon by the Egyptians in overthrowing Persia and in many other wars.

With the development of gunpowder and firearms in comparatively recent times, the bow and arrow has been retired to the realm of sport. In this capacity, it has sporadically interested groups in various parts of the world, particularly in England and the United States, but archery has not flourished to the same extent as many other sports.

The earliest archery contest, the Ancient Scorton Arrow, was created by the Ancient Scorton Arrow Society in England in 1673. This tournament is still in existence.

In the United States, the first archery club, the United Bowmen of Philadelphia, was organized in 1828. The first tournament was held in Chicago in 1879, and tournaments sponsored by this club are still being held.

The formation of the Federation Internationale de Tir l'Arc (FITA) in 1931 gave a great boost to target archery. A demonstration sport in the 1900 and 1904 Olympics, archery was given full status in 1908, and then was dropped after the 1920 Games. Through the efforts of FITA, archery was reinstated as a gold medal sport in the 1972 Olympic Games. The United States dominated the early years after archery's return to the Olympics. However, the Koreans have recently started to win the majority of Olympic medals. Beginning the winning tradition for the U.S. men was John Williams, 1972 gold medalist. Darrell Pace won in 1976 and 1984, and Jay Barrs placed first in 1988. The 1996 Olympic Games held in Atlanta, Georgia, were a huge success for U.S. archery. Justin Huish won the individual gold medal and was joined by Richard "Butch" Johnson and Rod White to win the team gold. The United States continued its strong showing in the 2000 Olympics, claiming the individual silver medal (Vic Wunderle). Wunderle joined with Butch Johnson and Rod White to capture the bronze team medal in Sydney. The U.S. women archers dominated the 1972 Olympic Games (Doreen Wilbur, gold medalist) and the 1976 Olympic Games (Luann Ryon, gold medalist); but since the boycott of the 1980 Moscow Olympics (won by Keto Losaberidze, USSR), dominance has shifted to the South Korean women. The South Korean women continued this dominance in 2000 by taking both the individual and team gold medals. In 2004 the Korean men and women won the team gold. In the individual competition, Park Sung Hyung of Korea won the women's gold medal while Italy's Marco Galiazzo took the men's gold.

A new shooting format was used at the 1996 Olympic Games in order to increase public awareness and gain television viewer support for archery. The format includes an elimination round, which was first introduced by FITA in 1986. The current Olympic system includes a 72-arrow ranking score shot at 70 meters. Because the new Olympic format allows for only 64 men and 64 women to attend the Games, each archer is ranked according to the 72-arrow score and placed in a bracket, then shoots the first round of the eliminations (two ends of six arrows for a possible score of 120). The elimination bracket continues to work in the same way (two ends of six arrows) until the semifinals, where the format changes to matches of four ends of three arrows with an alternating shot format.

At the 2004 Olympic Games in Athens, archery was one of only two sports (marathon) to hold its competition in Panatinaiko Stadium. This was the stadium in Athens that hosted the introduction of the modern Olympic Games in 1896.

In the 2008 Beijing Olympic Games, South Korea was once again a powerhouse in the sport of archery. In the team competitions they captured the gold medal for both the men and women. However, in the individual competition there was a surprising turn of events. South Korea was not as dominant as in years past. In fact, the Korean women's reign of winning the individual gold since 1984 came to an end. China's Zhang Juan Juan ousted Park Sung-Hyun of Korea to capture the gold for the host country. A similar scenario happened in the men's competition, where Ukrainian Viktor Ruban beat South Korea's Park Kyung-Mo to win the gold.

In 1971, the College Division of the National Archery Association (NAA) was founded in order to coordinate and promote collegiate archery throughout the United States. A national tournament is hosted and rotated each year throughout the United States. For more information on the College Division of the NAA, contact the NAA (One Olympic Plaza, Colorado Springs, CO 80909).

Today archery continues to hold interest for several reasons: (1) the introduction of the elimination round and head-to-head competition, (2) development of more efficient bows, arrows, and other archery equipment, and (3) the fascination many people find in the activities possible for the archer, ranging from target shooting, clout, field shooting, and novelty shoots to the hunting of small and large game.

EQUIPMENT

The Bow

The two types of bows most commonly used are the recurve bow (Figure 4.1) and the compound bow (Figure 4.2). The compound bow's pulley system and its sophisticated weighting, balancing, and sighting devices have completely revolutionized the sport of archery. Of course, these advances have increased the cost of the sport substantially, so the recurve bow is still popular, especially among beginners and Olympic hopefuls.

One should select a bow that one can pull back to full draw and hold steady while aiming. This is determined by the weight of the bow—that is, the number of pounds of pull it takes to pull the arrow to its full length. Proper bow weight varies with the age, sex, and strength of the archer. These are general recommendations for bow weights: teenage girls, 20 to 25 pounds (9 to 11.25 kg); teenage boys, 20 to 30 pounds (9 to 13.5 kg); women, 20 to 30 pounds (9 to 13.5 kg); and men, 25 to 40 pounds (11.25 to 15 kg).

The proper length of the bow is related to the length of the draw.

Draw length (inches)	Recommended bow length (inches)
24 or less (61 cm or less)	60 to 64 (152 to 163 cm)
25 to 26 (63.5 to 66 cm)	65 to 66 (165 to 168 cm)
27 to 28 (68.6 to 71.1 cm)	67 to 68 (170 to 173 cm)
29 or more (73.7 cm or more)	69 to 70 (175 to 178 cm)

Today's bows are made of fiberglass, wood, fiberglass-laminated wood, carbon, synthetic foam, ceramic, and aluminum alloy. Bow prices run from around $20 for a child's bow to $2,000 for a top-of-the-line target bow. Several

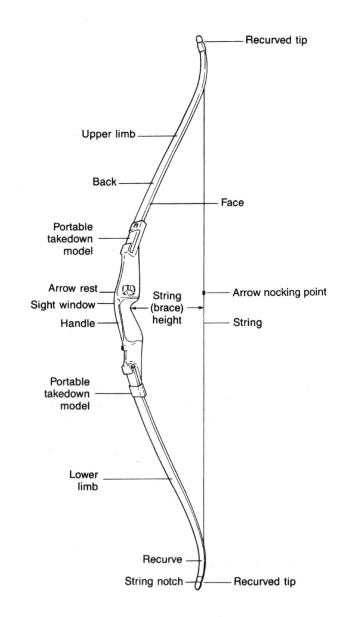

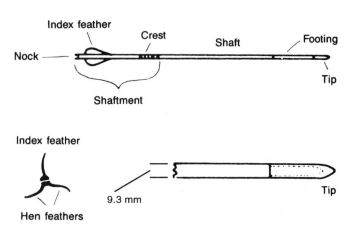

Figure 4.1. Parts of the bow and arrow.

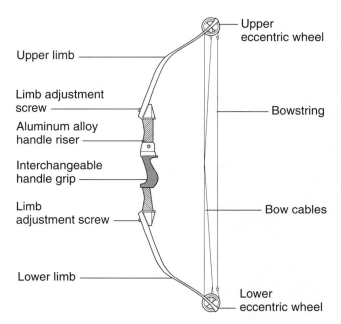

Figure 4.2. Compound bow.

Figure 4.3. Eye dominance.

bowmakers supply both recurve and compound bows costing around $200 that make respectable beginner bows.

Strings are usually made of Dacron or Fast Flight. Dacron strings are still used in most school and camp programs and in some compound bows. Most serious archers use Fast Flight, which gives a more consistent brace height and is as durable as Dacron.

Points to consider when selecting a bow
1. Purpose: Will the bow be used for target shooting, hunting, or both?
2. Shooting right- or left-handed: See the following section on eye dominance.
3. Bow weight: Select a bow that can be held without straining.
4. Limbs: Make sure they are straight, not twisted.

Eye dominance

Most coaches believe that an archer's potential is increased if he or she shoots with the hand on the same side as the dominant eye. Eye dominance must be determined if the archer chooses to shoot with both eyes open. If the archer chooses to shoot with one eye closed, eye dominance is not a determining factor in shooting right- or left-handed and the archer should shoot on the side he or she is accustomed to using. If the archer is unable to keep an eye closed, a patch can be used to cover the eye.

To determine eye dominance, stretch your arms out to their full length. Put your hands together to form a hole between the thumb and fingers (Figure 4.3). Aim at a spot while keeping both eyes open. Bring your hands toward your face, continuing to aim at the same spot. When your hands reach your face, the opening will be in front of your dominant eye.

The Arrow

Arrows are made of four types of material: wood, fiberglass, aluminum, or carbon graphite. Arrows made of wood are the most inexpensive, but they are rarely straight and they warp easily. Fiberglass arrows are much straighter and more durable than wood. They can take quite a bit of abuse and still be in good shape, which makes them a good choice for beginners.

For serious archers, aluminum and carbon graphite arrows are the most logical choices. These arrows are straighter and lighter and can be matched to suit each archer's individual needs. These characteristics increase the flight speed of the arrows and allow for better flight out of the bow. Aluminum and carbon graphite arrows are more expensive and possibly less durable than wood and fiberglass, but for the experienced archer, the benefits of shooting this type of arrow outweigh the consequences.

The arrow is one of the most important pieces of equipment in archery, so be sure to select the type of arrow that works best for you. If you need help, ask a staff person at an archery pro shop to advise you on arrow selection or use an arrow chart to determine what size arrow will best meet your needs.

When selecting arrows, there are three factors to consider: arrow length, arrow shaft, and the type of vane or fletching. To determine arrow length, draw an oversized arrow to full draw. The arrow should be marked in 1-inch increments. Select the arrow length that is closest to 1 inch past the back of the bow.

"Arrow spine" refers to the stiffness of the arrow shaft. The arrow shaft should have a maximum diameter of 9.3 mm. Arrows with different spines will fly differently when shot from the same bow. When you have a choice of spines, consult an arrow spine chart to determine the best selection. Experimentation will allow you to find the arrow length, spine, and point size that work best for you.

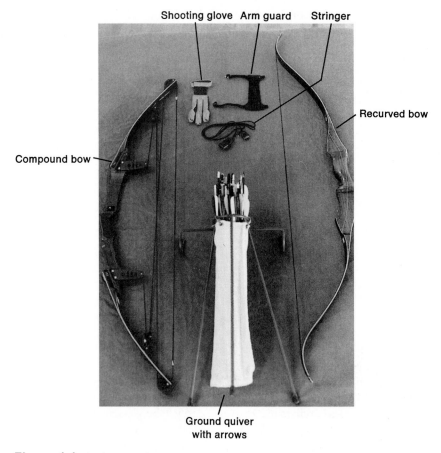

Shooting glove   Arm guard   Stringer

Recurved bow

Compound bow

Ground quiver
with arrows

Figure 4.4. Archery equipment.

Once you have selected the arrow size, you must determine whether to use vanes or feathers and what size is best. Feathers are most suited to indoor archery because they stabilize the arrow's flight more quickly than vanes and reduce the arrow's speed, which causes them to drift in the wind when used outdoors. Vanes are made of several types of plastic and are best suited for outdoor shooting. Vanes do not stabilize arrows as well as feathers, but they help arrows fly much faster. Both feathers and vanes come in a variety of sizes, so experimentation will be necessary to find what works best for you.

Protective Devices

Finger protection (see Figure 4.4) is necessary for all archers. Without it, the archer's shots will be inaccurate and painfully executed. There are two types of finger protection: (1) the finger tab, a leather tab patterned to fit the index, middle, and ring fingers; and (2) the shooting glove, similar to an ordinary glove without the thumb and little finger. A compound bow may be shot with a mechanical release aid. The arm guard protects the forearm of the bow arm from string contact.

The Target

Homemade targets and stands are usually considered the least expensive and best option for beginning archers.

The tripod stand should consist of three pine boards, 3 inches × 1 inch × 6 feet (7.5 cm × 2.5 cm × 1.8 m) long. It should incline backward about 10 to 15 degrees from the vertical (Figure 4.5).

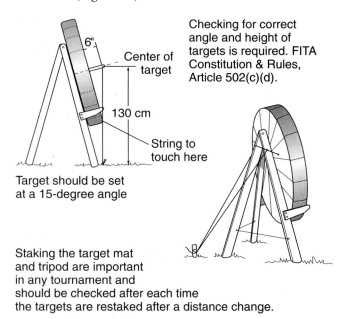

6"

Center of
target

130 cm

Checking for correct
angle and height of
targets is required. FITA
Constitution & Rules,
Article 502(c)(d).

String to
touch here

Target should be set
at a 15-degree angle

Staking the target mat
and tripod are important
in any tournament and
should be checked after each time
the targets are restaked after a distance change.

Figure 4.5. Target height and angle.

The target butt is approximately 4 feet (1.2 m) in diameter and 4 or 5 inches (10–12.5 cm) thick. It is constructed from rye straw or marsh hay wound tightly in a coil and held firmly together with tarred cord. Ethafoam targets have recently been used in target shooting due to their light weight, durability, and easy maneuverability.

The target face is made with heavy reinforced paper. Five colored circles are painted on the face with two scoring rings being represented by each color. The center is painted gold, followed by red, blue, black, and white circles. The target should be hung so that the exact center of the gold circle is 4 feet from the ground. Different sizes of target faces are used for different distances (Figure 4.6).

RULES (USA)

The three major organizations governing the sport of archery are the National Archery Association (NAA), the National Field Archery Association (NFAA), and the International Bowhunters Organization (IBO).

NAA tournaments are conducted under FITA international rules, which place limitations on the equipment used. See Table 4.1 for various types of tournaments. For example, a release aid and sight magnification may be used by compound shooters but not by recurve shooters. Compound shooters are also limited to a 60-pound maximum draw weight.

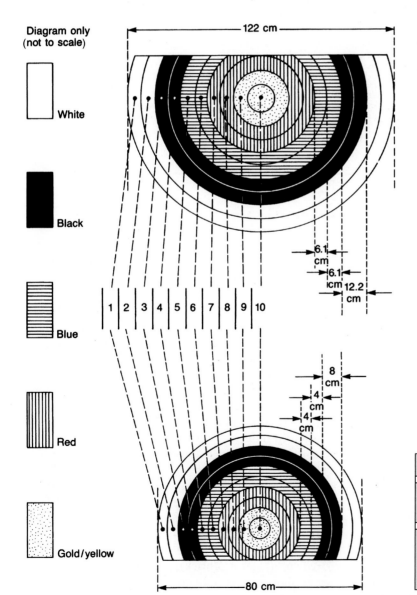

d	x	y	z
Diameter of face	Scoring zone	Color zone	Diameter of inner 10 ring
122 cm	12.2 cm	6.1 cm	6.1 cm
80 cm	8 cm	4 cm	4 cm
60 cm	6 cm	3 cm	3 cm
40 cm	4 cm	3 cm	3 cm

Figure 4.6. Ten-ring target. (To convert centimeters to inches, multiply centimeters by 0.4.)

Table 4.1. TARGET ROUNDS

FITA round	Number of arrows	Distance (m)	Face (cm)
Men and junior boys	36	90	122
	36	70	122
	36	50	80
	36	30	80
Women, junior girls, and cadet boys	36	70	122
	36	60	122
	36	50	80
	36	30	80
Cadet girls	36	60	122
	36	50	122
	36	40	80
	36	30	80
900 m round: men, women, intermediate boys and girls	30	60	122
	30	50	122
	30	40	122
Junior 900 m round	30	50	122
	30	40	122
	30	30	122
Cadet 900 m round	30	40	122
	30	30	122
	30	20	122
Easton 600 m round*	20	60	122
	20	50	122
	20	40	122
Collegiate 600 m round*	20	50	122
	20	40	122
	20	30	122

FITA round	Number of arrows	Distance (m)	Face (cm)
New Olympic round (64 individuals seeded 1 to 64) Round of			
64	12†	70	122
32	12	70	122
16	12	70	122
8	12†	70	122
4	12	70	122
2	12	70	122
Indoor FITA round I§	30	18	40
Indoor FITA round II§	30	25	60
Miniature round (indoor)‖	60	15	2 ft.
Range round (indoor)‖	60	#	2 ft.
Junior scholastic round‖	24	30††	122
	24	20††	122
Columbia round‖	24	50††	122
	24	40††	122
	24	30††	122
Junior Columbia round‖	24	40††	122
	24	30††	122
	24	20††	122
Clout round**			
Men and intermediate boys	36	165††	—
Women and intermediate girls	36	125††	—
Junior and Cadet boys and girls	36	110††	—

*Four ends of five arrows per end at each distance.

†Two ends of six arrows.

§Arrows are shot in ends of three arrows, and scoring is tallied after each end. A 2½-minute limit is allowed for each end.

‖Not an official NAA round, but may be used in school or camp tournaments.

#Sixty arrows from a single distance of 50, 40, 30, or 20 m (55, 44, 33, or 22 yards).

**The clout target is circular, 14.5 m (48 feet) in diameter, divided into five concentric scoring zones each 1.22 m (4 feet) in width. The target may be marked on the ground, or the scoring lines may be determined by steel tape or nonstretch cord marked off at the dividing lines. The center is marked with a white marker, not more than 36 inches (90 cm) nor less than 30 inches (75 cm) square, standing perpendicular to the ground. Scoring values of each scoring zone from the center outward are 9, 7, 5, 3, 1.

††Yards

The NFAA tournament structure also includes many classifications and categories (such as limited and unlimited) that govern the equipment each archer may add to the bow.

Tournaments conducted by the IBO involve competitions that simulate hunting. Various categories, including types of bows and age separation, are used.

Crossbow archers shoot in competitions organized by the National Crossbow Association; they do not compete officially against recurve or field shooters.

SCORING

According to FITA, in an outdoor tournament, six arrows are shot before scoring. The number of arrows shot before each scoring period is referred to as an "end." An end in an indoor tournament consists of three arrows. An arrow hitting the wrong target counts as a shot, but its score is forfeited. A line located 3 meters in front of the shooting line will serve to indicate the maximum distance that a missed shot or dropped arrow may travel before being considered "shot." The arrow must lie completely beyond the line to be considered shot.

An arrow that cuts two colors is always given the higher value of the two, even if the greater part of the arrow is in the ring of lower value. In tournament shooting, all arrow holes are marked when arrows are pulled from the target. If an arrow rebounds or passes through the target mat, the score is recorded as that of the unmarked hole. Scores are always listed with the highest score first, awarding 10, 9(gold), 8, 7(red), 6, 5(blue), 4, 3(black), and 2, 1(white) points for each arrow shot. Arrows must remain in the target until all are scored.

SAFETY PRECAUTION WHILE SHOOTING IN GROUPS

Each archer may approach the shooting line following two blasts of a whistle. The arrows are shot after one blast of a whistle. Each archer backs away from the shooting line, and all arrows may be retrieved when the whistle is blown three times. The cycle begins again when all archers are behind the shooting line and the whistle is blown two times. More than three blasts of the whistle means that a dangerous situation exists, and the archers should stop shooting immediately and remove all arrows from their bows.

NAA TOURNAMENT SHOOTING

In NAA outdoor tournaments, arrows are shot and scored at four distances (six ends of six arrows at each distance). Men shoot at 90 m, 70 m, 50 m, and 30 m. Women shoot at 70 m, 60 m, 50 m, and 30 m. A perfect score for 144 arrows is 1,440.

In an NAA indoor tournament, arrows are shot and scored at 18 m. Ten ends of three arrows are shot for a possible score of 300. A tournament consists of four rounds being shot for a possible total score of 1,200.

Both male and female archers are classified as follows:

Adult/Senior	**20 years old and older**
Junior	**through the 20th birthday**
Cadet	**through the 17th birthday**
Cub	**through the 14th birthday**
Bowman	**through the 12th birthday**

The distances shot in a tournament vary according to the division in which you shoot.

Field Shooting

Because of the vast increase in bow hunting in this country, the National Field Archers' Association of Redlands, California, sponsors a type of tournament and practice range called "field shooting." Fourteen or 28 targets of different sizes are placed at random over a course with both hills and valleys.

Groups of four archers shoot a "field round" and advance from target to target. Targets are black and white and have a bull's-eye that counts 5 points and an outer ring that counts 3 points. Four arrows are shot at each target. The archer with the highest score is the winner.

FUNDAMENTAL SKILLS AND TECHNIQUES

Stringing the Bow

The safest way to string a bow is to use a bow bracer, often called a "bow stringer" (Figure 4.7). A bow bracer is a length of braided cord with leather cups that fit over the tips of the bow limbs. To string the bow, place the top loop of the string over the top limb and slide it down until the bottom loop can be placed in the grooves of the lower limb. Then place the leather caps of the bow bracer over the tips of the limbs. Hold the bow parallel to the ground with the back of the bow

Figure 4.7. Stringing the recurved bow.

facing up. The bow bracer cord should be on the ground. Step on the cord and pull the bow up. Guide the upper loop along the limb and slip it into the grooves at the end of the limb. Let the bow down slowly, and check to see if the loops are securely in the grooves.

Checking the Bow after Stringing

Make sure that the loop is slipped completely into the notch and that the bowstring is centered. The distance from the string to the deepest part of the handle should measure about 8½ to 9½ inches (21.6 to 24.1 cm), which may be measured roughly by making a fist and letting the thumb extend perpendicularly from it. This is called the "fistmele" or "brace height."

Unstringing (Unbracing) the Bow

The process is exactly the same as stringing, except that the string is pulled out of the notch, and the loop is slid down over the upper limb.

PREPARATION FOR THE DRAW

Stance

The archer stands astride the shooting line in such a way that the body is perpendicular to the line. The bow arm is held at a 90-degree angle to the body and pointed directly toward the target. The archer's feet should be spread about shoulder-width apart, and the body and head should be held in a normally erect, comfortable position. This posture should allow for a complete absence of tension. Three types of stances are shown in Figure 4.8. Choose the stance that feels most comfortable to you. Beginners usually start with the open or square stance.

Possible errors in stance

1. Both feet on the same side of the line
2. Feet too close or too far apart
3. Too much weight on one foot

Position of the Bow Hand

As you raise the bow to shooting position, allow the hand to bend at the wrist so that the pressure of the bow is against the part of the palm just inside the base of the thumb. Allow the thumb and fingers to encircle the bow very lightly—just enough to keep it from falling. Never tightly grip or squeeze the bow (Figure 4.9).

Position of the String Hand

For best release of the arrow, begin by hooking the first, second, and third fingers of the drawing hand onto the string. The index finger should be above the arrow and the other two fingers below it with the first joint of each finger wrapped around the string.

NOCKING

For best clearance, make sure that the index feather (odd colored) is perpendicular to the string, pointing away from the bow on a recurve bow. On a compound bow, the index feather position varies according to what type of arrow rest is being used. A nock locator used as a reference point is placed on the string at a position such that the arrow will make a 90-degree angle when placed on the string. The nock locator

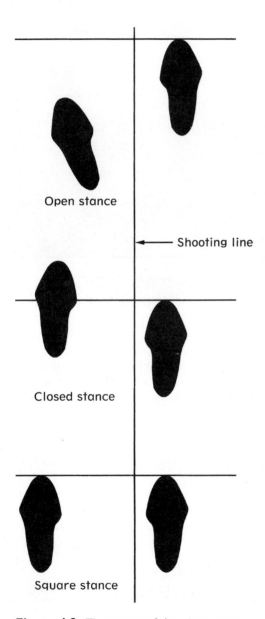

Open stance

Shooting line

Closed stance

Square stance

Figure 4.8. Three types of shooting stances.

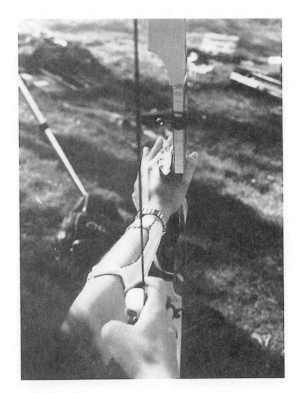

Figure 4.9. Bow-hand position.

should be tight against the string, and the arrow should be nocked below the nock locator (see Figure 4.10).

THE DRAW AND TRANSITION PERIOD

To begin the draw, the bow arm should be lifted to the desired shooting position, followed by a simultaneous pushing of the bow arm and pulling with the string arm. As the draw is made, equal pressure should be placed on the bow arm and string arm.

At full draw, the bow arm should be raised to shoulder height, and the elbow should have as little bend as possible. In sight shooting, the string hand is brought back to the face with the index finger placed under the chin in constant motion along the jawbone. The string bisects both the chin and the nose for additional reference points. Either a side anchor position (Figures 4.11 and 4.12) or a front anchor position (Figures 4.13 and 4.14) may be used. A consistent transition period is one of the most important phases in becoming a good archer. At full draw, the elbow of the string arm should be in line with the arrow.

Possible errors in the draw

Bow arm:

1. Elbow straight or hyperextended
2. Elbow bent too much
3. Left shoulder hunched

String arm:

1. Anchor point too far forward, too high, or below the chin
2. Some part of the hand other than the end segment of the forefinger or the string touches the anchor point
3. Elbow too high or too low

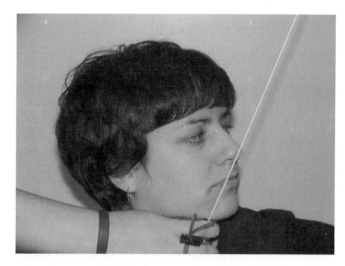

Figure 4.11. Close-up view of side anchor.

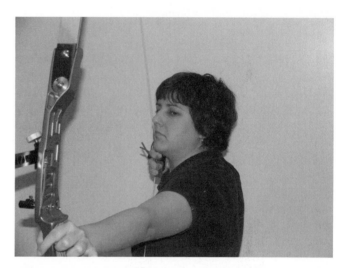

Figure 4.12. Distant view of side anchor.

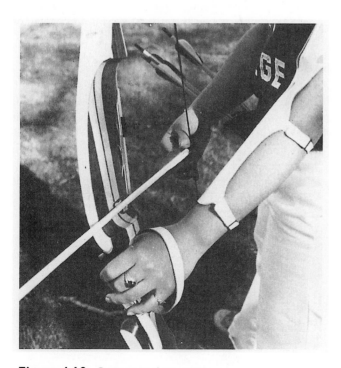

Figure 4.10. Correct nocking position.

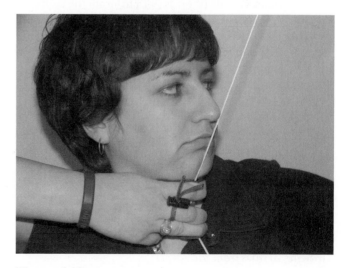

Figure 4.13. Close-up view of front anchor.

Figure 4.14. Distant view of front anchor.

Aim, Release, and Follow-through

Bow sight (freestyle)

A device that is used for sighting and is attached to the back of the bow is termed a *bow sight*. It has vertical and horizontal adjustments and is good for all ranges. In use, the line of vision is through the sight to the center of the target. For a right-handed archer (one who draws the string back with the right hand), the left eye should be closed and the sight should be placed by the target's center. For a left-handed archer, the right eye is closed.

Pin sight

One of the most economical types of bow sights today is the pin sight, in which the shooter uses masking tape or weather stripping with one or two large pins for sighting. Other shooters may use a tongue depressor held to the bow by adhesive tape and a pin or matchstick for sighting.

When adjusting the sight:

1. Always start about 10 yards (9.14 m) from the target.
2. Set the pin about 4 inches (10 cm) above the arrow rest. Sight through the pin to the yellow of the target.
3. Shoot a group of three arrows. If the arrows land high on the target, set the pin higher; if they are low, set the pin lower. Always move the pin in the direction the arrows are missing.
4. After resetting the pin, try again. Aim at the gold (yellow) and shoot.
5. When changing distances, adjust the pin sight. As the archer moves away from the target, the pin sight should be lowered to compensate for the longer distance. If the arrows are missing to the left or right, you push the pin in or pull it out. Remember to move the head of the pin in the direction you are missing.

Drawing Arrows from the Target

The back of one hand is placed against the target in such a way that the arrow is between the first and second fingers

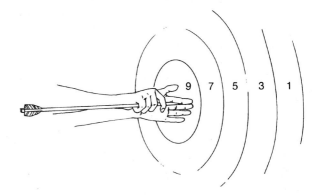

Figure 4.15. Drawing the arrow from the target.

(Figure 4.15). Grasp the arrow close to the target with the other hand and pull the arrow from the target. Care must be taken to draw the arrow straight out so that it will not be bent or kinked. After it is drawn out, drop the arrow on the ground, leaving the hand free for removing the remaining arrows. If an arrow penetrates to where the feathers have entered the target, it must be drawn on through the back of the target to prevent roughing or stripping off the feathers. If the arrow has penetrated one of the wooden legs or the wooden support of the target, it should be loosened with a pair of pliers before removal. At times, arrows that miss the target slither along the ground and into the grass. These must be pulled from the point end, much in the same manner as removing an arrow that has penetrated the target past the feathers. When looking for arrows that have missed the target, keep your eyes on the ground so you do not step on an arrow and break it.

SAFETY PRECAUTIONS

Archery contains certain elements of danger if participants become careless. Proper conduct while shooting or taking care of equipment off the range is exceedingly important. Safety rules are as follows:

1. Do not go to the target while others are shooting. All participants should retrieve arrows at the same time.
2. When finished shooting, step back three paces and wait.
3. Draw an arrow only when directed at the target.
4. Shoot at targets only from the shooting line.
5. Remember that bows and arrows are not toys.
6. Faithfully obey the starting and stopping signals.
7. While shooting, be certain that there is an adequate backstop behind the target or, if there is no backstop, that the area is clear behind the target.
8. Never leave bows and arrows unguarded where children or careless persons might handle them.
9. Never shoot straight up into the air under any circumstance.
10. Never shoot with a faulty bow or arrow or permit others to do so.

11. Never take chances or be careless.

12. Do not pinch the arrow between the thumb and finger to shoot. Always use three fingers for drawing the arrow so you cannot accidentally release the arrow.

TEACHING CONSIDERATIONS

1. Teach safety procedures with no flexibility and with strong consequences for any rule infractions. Establish and use consistent signals.

2. When teaching students, have the bows strung before the first class so that time is not wasted on this procedure and students get an opportunity to shoot during the first class period.

3. Assign bows and arrows to students the first day that they will use throughout the entire unit unless adjustments need to be made.

4. Teach stringing and unstringing of bows on the second day.

5. Give students the whole idea of the skill before breaking it down into parts. This can be done through demonstration or the use of audiovisual aids with a description of cues during the demonstration.

6. Practice stance, draw, and aim without an arrow, establishing clearly that the string is not to be released. Practice until each of these aspects is done correctly and with proper form. Do not continue on to the next step until students have mastered the basics of each of these principles. Walk through each step, if need be, one step at a time, until mastered. In large classes, use partners for feedback on:
   a. Straddling the line.
   b. Raising the bow with the bow weight on the palm of the hand.
   c. String-hand position using the first three fingers and whole first joint.
   d. Level, straight pathway of the elbow as it draws the string back (9 o'clock position).
   e. Slightly flexed elbow on bow arm.
   f. Correct transition period.

7. When students have mastered these steps, add nocking arrow, draw, anchor, aim, and release. Walk students through each step using cues before going to self-paced practice. Reemphasize rules for stepping in front of the shooting line before students release any arrows.

8. Teach students how to retrieve arrows and how to score arrows at one target before directing them to retrieve and score their own arrows.

9. Reemphasize point of aim and form after students have had an opportunity to shoot an end.

10. Help students analyze their errors in form based on clustering of arrows after enough practice results in consistent errors.

11. In longer units, develop skills for shooting rounds and add novelty shooting (balloons, golf archery, etc.).

GLOSSARY

addressing the target Assuming the proper stance; ready to shoot. Feet should straddle the shooting line.

archer's golf An archery game simulating golf; sometimes played on a golf course.

arm guard A protective cover for the lower part of the bow arm.

back The side of the bow away from the body and facing the target.

belly The inside of the bow; the side facing the string.

bow arm The arm that is extended in preparation for release.

bow sight A device attached to the bow used to assist in aiming.

brace To loop the string in the nock when stringing the bow.

broadhead An arrow point used for shooting live game.

butt Any object against which the face is placed.

cast The distance an arrow may be shot.

clout shooting Usually 36 arrows shot at a 48-foot (14.5 m) target placed or marked on the ground, from a distance of 120 or 140 yards (108 m or 126 m) for women and 180 yards (162 m) for men.

Columbia round A women's round consisting of 24 arrows shot at 55, 44, and 33 yards (50, 40, and 30 m).

crest The marks identifying the arrow.

double round A round shot twice in succession.

drift The motion of the arrow caused by wind or weather.

end Usually the shooting of six arrows, either in succession or in two groups of three.

eye The string loop.

face The front of the target.

field captain Usually the tournament director.

fistmele The height of the fist with the thumb raised (brace height).

fletch To place feathers on an arrow.

flight shooting The contest of distance shooting.

grouping Shooting a group of arrows close together on the target.

head The pile tip of the arrow.

hen feathers The two similar-colored feathers.

hit To strike the target anywhere.

in Second unit to be shot in a round.

index feather That feather of an arrow set at a right angle to the nock; the odd-colored feather.

instinctive shooting Shooting without the aid of any sighting device.

jerking Jolting caused by too much recoil of the shooting hand on release.

Junior Columbia round For boys and girls; 24 arrows shot at each of 33 and 22 yards (30 and 20 m).

Junior Scholastic round For boys and girls; 24 arrows shot at each of 33 and 22 yards (30 and 20 m).

keeper A piece of binding used to keep the loose end of the string fastened to the unstrung bow.

lady paramount Woman directing a tournament.

let fly To release an arrow.

limbs Upper and lower parts of the bow.

loose The release of the bowstring after the draw.

low strung Less than a fistmele between the string and bow.

miniature round Indoor shooting; 60 arrows shot from 16.7 yards (15 m) on a 2-foot (60 cm) target.

nock The groove at the end of the arrow.

nocking point The point on the string at which the arrow is placed.

out First unit to be shot in a round.

overbowed Using a bow too heavy in draw weight.

perfect end To put six shots in the gold.

petticoat On the target face but outside the rings; beyond the white ring. If hit, no score is given.

pin sight A device on the bow to help in aiming.

point The metal tip of the arrow.

point of aim The auxiliary object used in hitting the center of the target when the archer is not at point-blank range.

point-blank range The single distance where the true aim is on the bull's-eye.

quiver A device to hold arrows.

range Shooting distance.

range finder A device used to determine various distances.

range round Indoor shooting; 60 arrows shot from a single distance—55, 44, 33, or 22 yards (50, 40, 30, or 20 m).

reflexed bow A bow with limbs that curve out.

release To shoot an arrow.

round To shoot a definite number of arrows at specific distances.

roving Shooting a given number of arrows at targets placed at varied distances over an outside course.

Scholastic round Twenty-four arrows shot at each of 44 and 33 yards (40 and 30 m).

self arrow An arrow made from one piece of wood.

self bow A bow made from one piece of wood, as opposed to a composite bow.

serving The thread wrapped around the bowstring.

shaft The long center part of the arrow.

shaftment The part of the arrow holding the crest and feathers.

shooting line The line where one stands to shoot; the archer straddles this line.

shooting tab A protective device for fingers.

sight An aiming device that enables the archer to aim directly at the gold.

snake An arrow lost in deep grass.

spine A characteristic of the arrow's strength and flexibility.

spot Aiming center.

stringing To place the string on the bow and make it ready to shoot.

stroke Shooting position.

tackle Archery equipment.

tassel A bunch of fabric or a piece of cloth to wipe off wet arrows.

timber "Heads up"; a call of warning that an arrow is to be released. Used in field archery.

toxophilite One who has studied and mastered the art of shooting.

trajectory The flight of the arrow; the path that the arrow takes.

underbowed Using a bow that is too light in draw weight.

unit A 14-target course, including all official shots.

vane A plastic feather on an arrow.

wand shoot Shooting at an upright stick.

weight The number of pounds it takes to fully draw a bow.

windage The adjustment on the sight for right and left errors.

wobble Erratic motion of an arrow as it travels in flight.

SUGGESTED READINGS

Boga, S. 1997. *Archery.* Mechanicsburg, PA: Stackpole Books. Contains an introduction to the history, equipment, and techniques of archery.

Chase, C. 1997. *Archery: Guidelines to excellence.* Dubuque, IA: Eddie Bowers. Focuses on the archer on the shooting line. Written from the perspective of an experienced field archer.

Engh, D. 2005. *Archery fundamentals.* Champaign, IL: Human Kinetics.

Fadala, S. 1999. *Traditional archery.* Mechanicsburg, PA: Stackpole Books. Explains how to select the classic longbow and recurve bow, arrow selection, equipment tuning and maintenance, shooting technique, accessories, safety, history, and resources.

Haywood, K. M., and Lewis, C. F. 2006. *Archery: Steps to success.* 3rd ed. Champaign, IL: Human Kinetics.

Ruis, S. and Stevenson, C. 2004. Precision archery. Champaign, IL: Human Kinetics. Covers advanced technique and form of recurve, compound, and barebow archery.

Titlow, S., and Johnson. 1997. *Archery.* 3rd ed Boston, MA: American Press.

RESOURCES

Videos

Archery right on, 16 mm film, sound, color. Archery from caveman to the Olympics. A complete overview. Fred Bear Sports Club Film Library, 25921 W Eight Mile Rd., Detroit, MI 48235.

Several hunting films are available from Fred Bear Sports Club Film Library, 25921 W Eight Mile Rd., Detroit, MI 48235.

See Appendix C for other video sources.

WEB SITES

Dedicated to tournament archery and bowhunting traditions
www.archerynetwork.com

Home page for the national governing body for U.S. Olympic archery
www.usarchery.org

Home page of FITA—the International Archery Federation
www.archery.org

Home page for the National Field Archery Association
www.nfaa-archery.org

Home page for Junior Archery
www.aasinfo.demon.co.uk

Backpacking

5

After completing this chapter, the reader should be able to:

- Select and care for proper backpacking equipment
- Plan a safe backpacking trip
- Recognize the importance of conditioning and safety in backpacking
- Understand trail etiquette
- Teach a group of beginners the fundamentals of backpacking

HISTORY

Throughout history, people have carried loads on their backs as a basic means of transporting the necessities of life. With the introduction of horses, wagons, railroads, motor vehicles, airplanes, and other more efficient forms of transportation, the need to carry loads over long distances has disappeared. The backpacker of today transports basic necessities in primitive fashion as a means of independence, recreation, and fun. With minimum equipment and little knowledge, the hiker can reach places that are inaccessible by any other form of transportation. The rewards to the backpacker are magnificent scenery, solitude, and a sense of awe inspired by the magnitude of natural surroundings. There is a great thrill and feeling of accomplishment in being completely self-reliant and "doing it the hard way." There is challenge in the unknown and adventure on the trail. With a reasonable amount of preparation, any person in relatively good health and who is willing to exert the effort can enjoy the vigorous life of the backpacker. To move about freely in the wilderness is to experience the adventures of our heritage and to learn of some of the most important lessons Earth has to offer.

EQUIPMENT

Modern backpacking equipment is highly efficient and well-designed to minimize the weight and maximize comfort. It is also rather expensive, and a full outfit may call for an investment of a thousand dollars or so. Such an investment calls for judicious scrutiny of all items before purchase, and it may be found that alternatives to large cash outlays can be achieved. If at all possible, equipment should be borrowed, or rented, to find out whether it lives up to expectations. Only the necessary pieces of equipment should be bought at first, and additions can be made as experience and resources allow.

Hiking Boots, Socks, and Gaiters

Good-quality heavy-duty hiking boots are essential for the serious backpacker. All sorts of footgear may be seen on the trail, even sandals; but good boots offer protection and comfort (Figure 5.1). The boot selected should be sufficiently durable to last over many miles and should have a sole that will withstand wear from rocks and gravel and provide traction for walking on a variety of surfaces. Boots for backpacking should be made of a durable material such as leather or nylon. Many boots include waterproof and breathable material such as Gore-Tex. Most boots manufactured today have soles made of a synthetic rubber product known as Vibram, which is very durable. Lightweight hiking shoes also offer protection at a reasonable cost and decreased break-in time.

Beginners tend to buy boots that are heavier and more expensive than necessary; a reputable outfitter selling quality merchandise can be of great help. It is extremely important that boots fit properly and that they be long enough

Figure 5.1. Backpacking foot gear.

so that the toes do not contact the front of the boot while walking downhill. Proper fitting procedure should include standing on a slant board to check toe position. A good indication of a proper fit is when the toes do not contact the end of the boot after kicking a solid object several times. In all instances, boots must be well broken in before attempting to hike on the trail. They should be worn at every opportunity before making a long hike, to make sure that they will not cause blisters. Opinions vary regarding the best way to break in boots, but wearing them frequently is recommended. To increase wear and comfort of boots, a protective waterproofing should be applied to the exterior surface. This will prolong the life of the boot and keep feet dry.

Socks are important companion pieces to boots, and most hikers use two pairs. The inner pair is usually lightweight wool, polypropylene, or a similar material to wick moisture away from the feet. The outer pair is usually a heavyweight wool to provide cushioning of the feet within the boots. Dry and relatively clean socks should be worn to start each day. For shorter trips (2–3 days) it is advisable to bring enough socks for a clean pair each day. On longer trips, bring at least two pairs of liners and four to five pairs of wool socks. They can usually be laundered and dried at night, or pinned to the outside of the pack if they are not dry when it is time to start hiking.

Nylon or Gore-Tex gaiters will assist in keeping debris such as dirt and snow from entering into the top of the boots. Gaiters usually have side or rear zippers to allow the wearer to put them on or take them off without having to remove the boot.

Camp shoes can be a foot saver for many backpacking enthusiasts. Camp shoes should be fairly light, durable, and preferably have a covering over the toes. An old pair of lightweight running shoes or a pair of sandals suitable for wading across rivers are good choices for camp shoes.

Packs

The pack (Figure 5.2) is a major investment and should meet the needs of the person using it. The frame size should be matched to the individual. The pack size, or volume capacity, should be determined by the length and type of the anticipated trips. The volume may vary from 3,500 to 7,000 cubic inches (57.4 to 114.7 cu/dm). Pack prices will vary with size and quality. A quality pack of 5,400 cubic inches (88.6 cu/dm) will cost between $300 and $500.

Traditional packs are mounted on external frames (Figure 5.3A). It should be possible to remove the pack from the frame in case one wants to use the frame for carrying loads other than the pack. Frames are made of lightweight metal, usually tubular aluminum alloy.

Internal frame packs (Figure 5.3B) are currently the more popular choice for backpackers. Internal stays are inserted into the material of the pack to provide strength and shape. Often the stays can be removed and shaped to conform to the contours of the back. Internal frame packs should be equipped with compression straps to allow the user to adjust the size of the pack.

Both internal and external frame packs should come equipped with well-padded shoulder, waist, and sternum straps. Shoulder straps should be fully adjustable, include load-lifter straps, and allow the wearer to secure a heavy load to the shoulders without it slipping. A sternum strap allows the wearer to connect the shoulder straps in the front to prevent the pack from slipping from side to side. A padded, adjustable waist belt will allow the wearer to bear much of the weight of the pack on his or her hips. The amount of weight distributed between the hips and shoulders is a matter of personal preference and can be adjusted while hiking.

The packsack is often made of nylon or a tough Cordura fabric. Inspection of the stitching and seams is an important consideration. The number of stitches per inch reflects

Figure 5.2. Internal and external frame packs. A, Back view; B, Front view.

A
B

Figure 5.3. A, Backpackers carrying external frame packs. B, Backpackers carrying internal frame packs.

the strength of the seams; generally, the more stitches, the greater the strength. Weak seams can pull apart under the stress of heavy loads. The seams should also be taped or waterproofed, from the inside, with a seamsealer.

Packs are usually loaded from the top, but access from the side or bottom is an option some manufacturers incorporate. Additional accessories, such as detachable side packs and storm flaps, will allow the wearer easier access to commonly used items and will increase the pack's waterproofness.

The choice between an internal or external frame should be based on comfort and purpose. External frame packs are preferred for durability. Some backpackers believe that external frames provide more comfort because they are positioned farther from the wearer's back. Internal frame packs are preferred for extended expeditions involving climbing and skiing. These packs provide for better balance due to location on the body and the many straps that can be used to secure the load.

Rucksacks or daypacks, which allow the hiker to carry basic essentials on short excursions from camp, are helpful. Some packs have detachable tops that convert to fannypacks for this purpose. This saves space and weight.

Clothing

The major requirements for clothing used for backpacking are that it be comfortable and adequate for temperatures likely to be encountered on the trail. Much backpacking is done in fairly cool climates, and wool or pile clothing is usually welcome at night and in the early morning. In some instances, a set of polypropylene long underwear can provide extra warmth during the day and be a sleeping garment at night. Wool has an advantage over most other materials in that it will maintain some of its insulating qualities when wet. Pile or fleece will wick away moisture faster than wool, is substantially lighter, and will also insulate when wet. Clothes made of cotton or a cotton blend are the least desirable. There is a saying among backpacking enthusiasts, "cotton kills," because cotton is a poor insulator when it is wet and it dries

slowly. It is usually best to "layer" clothing and adjust the number of layers to suit the temperature and degree of physical activity. When layering, start with a wicking base layer, (synthetic, polypropelene, wool, or silk T-shirt and underwear) followed by an insulating layer and cover with a weatherproof layer. Weatherproof layers should protect from both wind and rain and ideally be breathable. Some examples of waterproof material include Gore-Tex and the less expensive but not as breathable option, nylon. Down jackets and vests are lightweight and highly efficient in retaining body heat, but they lose their insulating qualities when wet.

Some type of adequate rainwear is necessary if rain is likely to be encountered, and it should be compatible with other clothing worn. Lightweight rain suits that protect the wearer from the elements are available. Some types of rain suits are made of materials that permit body moisture to accumulate inside; "breathable" fabrics eliminate this problem. Rain chaps—sleeves that cover the legs and tie to the belt—are often used with a rain parka or poncho. The poncho is a large waterproof sheet of fabric or plastic with a hole in the middle through which the head is thrust to form a cloak-type garment. The poncho may also double as a ground cloth to prevent absorption of ground moisture by the sleeping bag or tent. Lightweight plastic raincoats or jackets likely to tear easily should be avoided, as they may fail at the time they are most needed.

For cooler weather, a wool watch cap or fleece ski hat is advisable. Approximately 50 percent of the body heat can be lost through the head, neck, and ears if uncovered. Also, such a hat can be worn while sleeping if the sleeping bag does not cover the head. In extremely cold weather, a glove or mitten system that includes a synthetic fleece lining separate from a nylon or Gore-Tex shell allows for increased warmth and protection.

Clothing for warmer hiking conditions should be made of lightweight synthetic material, such as polypropylene. This will allow perspiration to wick away from the hiker's body during exercise. Care should be taken to protect the skin from the sun with sunscreen or maximum coverage with clothes. Hats with broad bills and bandanas to protect the hiker's neck from the sun are advisable. Long-sleeve T-shirts and underwear will protect the skin from the sun, as well as from insects. Additional mosquito netting may be necessary for the head and neck in some environments.

It is wise to include in the clothing some reflective material that can be seen in the dark when a light shines on it. This could be very important if a member of the party becomes lost.

Sleeping Bags

The memories of minor discomforts of a hard day's hiking can be quickly erased by a good night's sleep. A sleeping bag adequate for low temperatures encountered will contribute to such a night. Sleeping bags come in all sizes and shapes and with several types of insulation. Remember that no sleeping bag generates heat; it only serves to stop heat loss. The mummy-style bag is probably most popular with backpackers. Down is often selected for its insulating value. However, down loses its efficiency when wet, and it is then of little value to stop heat loss. The synthetic fibers used for insulating sleeping bags, such as Dacron, Hollofil II, Polarguard, Fiberfil II, and Hollowbound II, are almost as efficient as down and have the advantage of being less influenced by moisture. However, synthetic-insulation-filled bags are approximately 30 percent heavier than down bags of equivalent warmth. Regardless of whether the sleeping bag is filled with down or synthetic fibers, it should never be stored tightly stuffed or rolled. Such storage will compress and break the insulating fibers. Sleeping bags should be stored in a dry place and in a hanging position. Most sleeping bag covers are made of ripstop nylon and are available in numerous colors. Although color is of little importance for other than aesthetic purposes, a light, tough cover that will permit body moisture to escape is essential. Sleeping bag covers should never be made of waterproof material, as large amounts of body moisture will collect in the bag and cause rapid heat loss. Often a bivouac sack (or bivy sack) is used to provide warmth and protection to a sleeping bag.

In the campsite, sleeping bags should be allowed to breathe. Rolling your bag out early in the evening allows the bag to regain its original insulating qualities. Likewise, hanging your bag in a tree in the morning allows the moisture that has accumulated from your body to evaporate.

Sleeping Pads

In addition to a ground cloth to prevent ground moisture from being absorbed by the sleeping bag or tent floor, some means of blocking heat loss through the ground is desirable. This can be accomplished through the use of a foam or inflatable sleeping pad. Specialized inflatable sleeping pads such as Thermarest™ are lightweight, small (when deflated), and provide some insulation combined with comfort. Foam pads provide much more insulation than inflatable pads. The two basic types of foam pad are of closed-cell and open-cell construction. Closed-cell pads need no additional cover and can serve as ground cloths, but open-cell pads will absorb moisture and a ground cloth is needed. Foam pads enclosed in waterproof material offer added protection from wetness. Winter backpackers often carry both types in their packs.

Tents and Shelters

One of the heavier items frequently carried in a backpack is a small tent, usually made of ripstop nylon or similar lightweight material, with aluminum poles and stakes. In some situations, no shelter at all may be needed, but it is highly advisable to have some sort of covering to remain dry during rain or snow. A lightweight tarp (or tube tent) is the choice of some hikers, while others prefer a tent. The tarp works well in light rain, but it is not nearly as effective as a tent in avoiding mosquitoes or other insects.

It is advantageous if the tent has a waterproof floor to serve as a moisture barrier and to eliminate the need for carrying a special ground cloth. The walls and roof of some tents are also made of waterproof material, which causes moisture to condense inside the tent, usually near the top. A more desirable arrangement is a tent with waterproof floor and walls and a roof of material porous enough for moisture to escape (Figure 5.4). This makes an additional covering necessary, that is, a tent rain fly stretched over the entire top of the tent (Figure 5.5).

Tents are often described as "two-person," "three-person," and so on. The prospective buyer should always see the tent set up before buying, to make sure that space in the tent is as extensive as described. Most two-person tents provide barely enough space for two average-sized people and little or no room for packs or other gear. Tents traditionally have an A-frame shape, but there are many options to choose from. Geodesic-shaped tents are popular for backpacking in extreme weather. I-pole-shaped tents with no floor are a popular choice when weight is a critical factor. Most back-

Figure 5.4. Hoop or tunnel backpacking tent with porous roof.

Figure 5.5. Dome backpacking tent with tent fly.

Figure 5.6. Cooking and eating utensils.

packers choose aluminum poles over composite fiber due to cost. Vestibules will provide additional room for storage. Mountaineers are sometimes forced to cook inside a vestibule. It is extremely dangerous to use a stove or other open flame inside a tent. Cooking in the vestibule is generally not recommended.

Tent seams should be well stitched, with reinforcement at points of strain. The typical tent designed for backpacking weighs 3 to 8 pounds (1.4 to 3.6 kg), depending on size, type of material, and weight of poles and stakes. Tent closures should fit tightly and are usually of the zipper type. It is important that zippers are of high quality. Mosquito netting that closes tightly is a must if the tent flaps are to be left open in warm weather. Regardless of the weather, the tent should be secured to the ground with stakes to prevent it from blowing away if a high wind develops.

Cooking and Eating Equipment

Many types of cooking and eating utensils are available at most outfitters. Cooking kits are designed for light weight and compactness (Figure 5.6). Pots and pans should fit into one another to decrease volume required. The pots and pans should be of thick enough aluminum to resist collapsing. Fry pans coated or treated with Teflon will increase menu choices and ease of cleanup. Pots require sturdy handles and lids that also can be used with the fry pan. Commercial pot holders are available; however, a pair of rubber-coated channel locks make a great universal pot holder.

Stainless steel or plastic tableware is adequate. Plastic is lighter than steel and will not stick to your lips in extremely cold weather. Plastic plates or bowls are preferred over metal for serving. Food cools quickly when served on metal. Connecting the spoon and bowl with a utility cord will keep your personal serving set together. A bowl with a tight-sealing lid (such as Tupperwear™) allows for carrying leftovers to be eaten for lunch the next day. The lid can double as a cutting board. Insulated plastic cups with lids will keep drinks warm, will not burn your lips, and will reduce camp spills.

Additional cookware—such as a large spoon, spatula, funnel, and heavy aluminum foil—may be desirable. Experience will assist the hiker in deciding what type of equipment to take. After a few trips, such selection will pose no problem.

Trail Stoves

However desirable open-fire cooking may be, most wilderness areas do not allow it. In an attempt to minimize the impact on the wilderness, many backpackers carry small trail stoves (Figure 5.7). As the number of campers increases, the restrictions on open fires will also increase. The use of stoves will thus increase in popularity as our concern for the environment increases. Most backpacking stoves are lightweight and very efficient at all altitudes. Trail stoves burn several types of fuel, including white gasoline, kerosene, compressed propane gas, or butane gas. White gasoline is the most popular. Other fuels such as Sterno or hexamine may be used, but these usually deliver considerably less heat. In the case of butane fuel, the fuel tank must be kept above freezing for effective use. This may make it necessary for the hiker to sleep with the fuel tank to have usable fuel to cook breakfast! Transporting stoves and fuels can be dangerous, and they should always be stored in the pack properly. Liquid fuel, such as white gasoline, should be transported only in metal bottles designed for that purpose. Fuel bottles should be carried in an outside pocket of the pack, at the bottom, so that leaks can be observed in time to prevent the pack from becoming a torch through accidental ignition. Be sure to carry a stove repair kit and to try out the stove before an overnight trip. In extreme climates, an aluminum wind shield will increase the efficiency of the camp stove.

It is the mark of the conscientious backpacker to "camp without a trace" and to protect the surroundings for the future enjoyment of others. Be sure to choose a durable surface, such as a rock outcropping, for your kitchen. Prepare all meals in such a way as to minimize the number of trips

Figure 5.8. Using a lightweight backpacking stove on a durable surface.

Figure 5.7. Two types of trail stoves.

necessary to the kitchen area (Figure 5.8). Minimize garbage and waste by planning ahead.

Pocket Equipment

Several items should be carried in the hiker's pants pockets or at the top of the backpack. A reserve supply of wooden matches, enclosed in a waterproof container, should be carried in the pocket, in addition to a supply in the pack. A folding pocketknife, or multi-tool, should also be carried, and special effort must be made to know the whereabouts of the knife at all times. Knives are probably the most "losable" items carried, and they are also one of the most important.

A small whistle should also be carried in the pants pocket, to use as an emergency signal if needed. The whistle can be heard over greater distances than the voice, and the whistle will still make noise long after the sound production of the vocal cords has been diminished to a whisper. In areas unfamiliar to the hiker, a map and compass should also be carried in an accessible pocket.

These items must be carried on the person in the event that the pack is lost. They are of prime importance to survival in an emergency and must be kept readily available in a location separate from the pack.

Equipment Selection

The prospective backpacker with limited funds will be forced to make many careful choices when buying equipment. It is better to buy fewer items of high quality than to buy a larger number of items and compromise on quality. Again, it is advisable to borrow or rent equipment and actually use it before investing in an item intended for long-term service. Gaps in noncritical equipment can be filled in with simple makeshift gear until further knowledge is gained and the right equipment is bought.

The following list is offered to aid the novice in planning equipment purchases. The list is intended to present equipment needed in most areas of the United States, but additions or deletions may be appropriate depending on local conditions. Always consider quality of construction, weight, bulk, and durability. Remember, there are no equipment stores in the wilderness!

Backpacking Checklist

Backpack with rain cover

Personal equipment
synthetic underwear
synthetic shirts
synthetic pants
synthetic socks liner
wool socks
boots
synthetic jacket
synthetic or wool insulating layer
parka
windpants (may double as
    rain gear)
rain gear
hat
gloves/mittens
camp shoes

Sleeping
sleeping bag
sleeping pad
tent with fly
ground cloth
stakes

Cooking
stove
fuel bottles/fuel
cooking pot/frying pan
plastic bowl/spoon
mug
water filter
water bottles
dish scrubber

Food
breakfast
lunch
supper
trail food
drinks
emergency foods

Miscellaneous items
first aid kit
flashlight with extra bulb and
    batteries
matches/lighter
map/compass
repair kit
camera and batteries
nylon cord
notebook/pencil
trash bags
whistle/mirror
sunglasses
insect repellent
lip balm
sunscreen
personal toilet articles
pocket knife
watch
prescription medicine
contacts
towel
camp sandals/shoes

Always check with land managers or experienced backpackers from the area where you plan to backpack to determine special equipment needs.

PLANNING THE TRIP

Where to Go

A major decision confronting the hiker planning a trip is the selection of a suitable area. One of the great features of backpacking is the freedom it offers, within limits of particular areas. Many people enjoy the "bushwhack," that is, cross-country travel in any direction desired without confinement to established trails. In areas where this is permitted, it can offer solitude that may not be attainable otherwise. The beginning packer will quickly find that characteristics of the landscape may make the bushwhack difficult and that established trails offer better routes. Generally it is considered best to stick to existing trails until experience has been gained that would benefit the hiker in the cross-country venture. Some areas of the country have become well

known for excellent trails and beautiful scenery, so much so that agencies in charge of many areas have been forced to establish a quota system that permits a limited number of people on a trail at a given time. Otherwise, the trails literally become worn out from excessive use and the abuse of overcrowding in campsite areas. Persons wishing to hike in such areas should determine whether permits are required. Most areas open for backpacking are public-use areas and include land controlled by state parks, the U.S. Forest Service, the National Park Service, conservation departments, or similar agencies. Many of the controlling agencies publish information about their respective areas and will furnish it on request. When selecting an area, you should consider the nature of the terrain, existing trails, area rules, and the availability of such things as water and places to camp. Established trails originate at a trailhead, and parking facilities are usually provided for a limited number of vehicles. If plans call for the trip to end at the same place it begins (called an out and back), it may be desirable to leave vehicles at that point. Should it end at some other access to the trail, it will be necessary to arrange a car shuttle or to enlist the aid of someone to deliver hikers to the start of the hike and pick them up at its end.

For first-timers, a good approach is to camp out in the backyard, using the equipment to be taken on the trail. Thus, if something goes badly, experience can be gained without the discomfort or danger of being miles from home. Another good idea is to make a short overnight hike near home to "shake down" equipment and determine its adequacy. The things that the hiker can carry will be limited; needed things not carried will be unavailable, and things carried and not needed only add useless weight to the pack. There is no substitute for an actual trial to determine those things that must be taken and those that are better left at home.

Leave No Trace

Although the Leave No Trace (LNT) program was developed in the early seventies by the U.S. Forest Service, it has only recently been adopted by public and private agencies as the standard for minimum-impact camping in the United States. Four federal agencies, the Bureau of Land Management, the U.S. Forest Service, the National Park Service, and the U.S. Fish and Wildlife Service, along with private agencies like the National Outdoor Leadership School (NOLS), have continued to refine the LNT program. The program's goal is simple: reduce the damage caused by outdoor activities, particularly nonmotorized recreation (Pokorny, 2001). The following seven principles were developed to ensure that damage resulting from the presence of humans in nature is minimal.

- Plan ahead and prepare
- Travel and camp on durable surfaces
- Dispose of waste properly
- Leave what you find

- Minimize campfire impacts
- Respect wildlife
- Be considerate of other visitors

For a more detailed description of the LNT principles and how to effectively implement them, review the Leave No Trace Skills and Ethics handbook published by LNT and NOLS.

Checklists

One of the most valuable things that the beginner can do is make a list of things that are to be taken on the trip and check them off as the pack is loaded. This helps avoid leaving a critical item of equipment at home and brings organization to the process of preparation.

Food

An adequate supply of food is essential. The planner must realize that energy expenditure in hiking is much greater than in normal daily activities, and thus appetites are often much greater than normal on the trail. Certainly a good practice for the novice is to take what seems to be an adequate amount of food and then add a little more. A matter for prime consideration is the weight of the food. Much of the weight of most food is water, and any process to reduce water contained in food will aid in reducing the total load to be carried.

The major area where weight can be reduced is food, and dehydrated foods of some sort are essential if the trip is to be of more than a few days' duration. Well-prepared foods are available that have been freeze-dried or have had the major portion of water removed by some other process. Wide choices are available from the typical outfitter. The major hindrance to such foods is their high cost. Freeze-dried foods may be the only resource for long trips, but many equally nutritious foods that weigh only slightly more can be purchased at a supermarket. Pretrip activities should include a visit to a supermarket to find dry foods that suit the palates of the persons involved. When such foods are selected, they should be removed from their bulky commercial wrappings and repackaged into smaller, space-saving units. Preparation instructions should be retained for each item.

Drying your own food before a trip is a good and economical alternative to purchasing prepackaged foods. There are commercially available food dehydrators that are relatively inexpensive. Dehydrating your own food provides a limitless number of possibilities for fun, unique, and healthy meals while on the trail. Some foods that are excellent for drying include fruits of any kind, vegetables, some meats, and sauces.

One means of food acquisition often espoused by backpackers is "living off the land." Not only is this uncertain, but it may be impossible because of low availability of natural food or local regulations that prohibit it. It is true that in some areas the diet may be supplemented by fish, berries, and sometimes fruit, but the wise packer will take an adequate supply of food along until sufficient experience is gained to be able to forage effectively.

The amount of food necessary will be dictated by the climate and the length and strenuousness of the trip. Cold weather and difficult terrain add to caloric needs. An "average" woman on an "average" hike might require 2,500 to 3,000 calories per day. An "average" man might require about 3,500 to 4,000 calories per day. Teenagers are likely to require twice as much.

Menus

Although some hikers detest any sort of formal organization, it will aid the beginner to take a written plan for each meal to be eaten on the trip. Changes can always be made, but it may be difficult to determine the amount of food needed without such a specific plan. When food is purchased, a good procedure is to group the items to be eaten at each specific meal. Then each of these groups should be placed in a plastic bag and labeled according to its intended time of consumption, such as "breakfast Saturday" or "supper Sunday." Such organization may not appeal to everyone, but it will ensure an orderly approach to the problem of providing adequate meals. Although unusual diets will probably not cause significant problems over a few days, the general procedure should be to follow the same guidelines in meal planning as one would at home; that is, plan a balanced diet that contains a variety of foods. Because energy expenditure will be high, a diet containing large portions of carbohydrates is desirable, but other food elements should not be neglected.

Trail food

It is usually desirable to plan lunches that require little or no cooking. In addition, most hikers find it advantageous to eat small amounts of high-energy foods during the course of the day's hike. A favorite is a mixture called "gorp." The origin of this word is obscure; it is sometimes said to mean "good old raisins and peanuts." Whatever the origin of the term, the mixture is often a creation of art. Depending on the taste of the preparer, it may include such items as dried fruit, chocolate, nuts of various kinds, cereals, and any other food that is high in energy but that will not become sticky when warm.

Water

Water is essential for the hiker, and it should be consumed frequently. There is a tendency for the inexperienced hiker to drink less water than is desirable, and effort may be necessary to ensure adequate consumption. It is better to drink more than is needed than to chance becoming dehydrated. This is particularly true in hot weather, and regular water stops should be planned.

A powdered sports drink can be added to some of the water to help replace electrolytes lost during hiking.

Lakes, rivers, and streams are all adequate sources of water, but none should be considered safe for drinking without treatment or filtering. Making water safe for drinking (potable) is imperative in most of the wilderness areas of the world. There are very few places where the water is safe to drink untreated from the source. There are a number of microorganisms, invisible to the human eye, that inhabit water sources. Of specific concern is a parasite called *Giardia lamblia,* which causes diarrhea, cramping, and intestinal discomfort that can last for months.

The type of water treatment is a personal preference as there are several methods available. Water filters are often the preferred choice as they do not alter the taste of the water. When choosing a water filter, be sure that it's suitable for eliminating *Giardia.* Chemical additives are another method of treating water that will protect against *Giardia* and other microorganisms. Iodine and chlorine are the most commonly used chemical methods. The advantages are that they are lightweight and easy to use. The disadvantages are that they may change the taste of the water and require suitable contact time to be effective. Adding flavorings to water, such as Gatorade powder or Kool-Aid, can hide the chemical additive taste. The final method of treating water is by boiling it for at least one minute at low altitudes, increasing to five minutes of boiling when at a higher elevation.

Maps and Guidebooks

Local guidebooks are of great help in assessing terrain and general physical characteristics of the area selected for hiking. They give many features of the land areas represented, including elevations, contours, water sources, campsites, area histories, and much more. Maps can be purchased from many outfitters, and if not available locally, they may be obtained from the Geological Survey and Water Resources Agency in each state (Figure 5.9). For information on maps of areas east of the Mississippi River, contact the Geological Survey Office in Washington, D.C.; for areas west of the Mississippi, contact the Geological Survey Office in Denver. Index maps of each state are available; maps for specific areas may be ordered after consulting the index map. The use of maps and a compass is discussed in detail in Chapter 21 of this book.

Loading the Pack

Once all of the items to be taken are assembled, they should be placed in the pack in some sort of order related to their function. Generally, lighter and noncrushable items are loaded near the bottom of the pack, and heavier items should be loaded near the top and close to the front. It is important to keep the greater portion of weight high on the back near the shoulders. Items that are likely to be used

Figure 5.9. Backpackers taking a break and reviewing their maps.

frequently or those that might be needed quickly should be placed in the side pockets on the pack to avoid the process of unpacking when the item is needed. Certainly rainwear should be readily accessible, and many packs provide special pockets for rainwear and maps. The most effective organization of the pack involves the use of multiple stuff sacks—for example, extra clothes in a blue stuff sack, food in a red stuff sack, etc.

Try to keep the basic pack unit to a weight of 35 to 60 pounds (15.9–27.3 kg) or less. This weight includes all necessities—such as pack, tent, sleeping bag, and the like—and excludes expendable items, primarily food. The total maximum weight carried may vary considerably from one person to another, but a general rule of thumb is for the total weight to be carried not to exceed one third the body weight of the person carrying it. This is a *heavy* load, and the beginner will do well to limit the load to a considerably lower weight.

First-Aid Kit

A first-aid kit should be a basic part of the backpacker's equipment. Commercially prepared kits are available, but a satisfactory one can be put together from items readily available from a local drugstore. The following is a suggested list of items for such a kit:

antibiotic ointment
gloves
Band-Aids (several sizes, including extra-large)
sterile gauze pads
moleskin
adhesive tape (cloth or athletic)
lip balm
tweezers
needle
safety pins
triangular bandages (3)
prescription medications
other items as anticipated needs may indicate (such as personal
    medications, extra contact lenses, etc.)

The Essentials

The essentials is a group of items that are suggested as necessary for survival in the back country. Essential lists differ among backpacking experts and should be specific for the trip and person. A typical essential list may include:

- Map and compass (may be supplemented with a GPS)
- Extra food
- Water
- Extra clothes
- Headlamp or flashlight (batteries)
- First aid kit
- Fire starter and matches
- Knife
- Prescription medications
- Sunglasses, sunscreen, and lip balm
- Signaling device (whistle, mirror, etc)
- Tarp for shelter
- Water treatment

ON THE TRAIL

Conditioning and Safety

It is important that the hiker be in good physical condition and able to walk for extended periods while carrying a pack. See Chapter 2 of this book for a discussion of physical fitness issues. Conditioning before the hike will improve stamina and make the trip more enjoyable. Conditioning should be accomplished over a reasonable period of time and may include walking, jogging, and similar activities that promote overall conditioning. In any event, the hiker should build up to the activity and not attempt greater distances than can be covered in the time allotted. Enjoyment, not exhaustion, is the objective. During the first few miles of a hike, it is wise to start slowly and "warm up" to the task. This is especially advisable if there is considerable increase in altitude in the first portion of the trail.

Particular care must be given to the feet, and at the first sign of irritation, action must be taken. The first warning is a burning sensation or a hot spot, often on the heel or toes. When this warning signal occurs, *stop!* Continued walking will quickly result in a blister, and the hiker may be "crippled" with the hike hardly started. Boot and socks should be removed and the area of irritation inspected. A moleskin cover may be applied over the area affected. This material, available at drugstores, has a smooth surface to reduce friction and an adhesive backing that causes it to stick to skin. After applying moleskin, the hiker can apply foot powder and replace socks and boot, paying close attention to the way the foot feels after walking is resumed. It is much better to avoid blisters than to treat them, but if one occurs, it should be taken care of at once. A Band-Aid and powder can be applied if the blister is small. Opening the blister should be avoided if possible. If the blister must be opened, this should be done with a needle that has been heated until the point is red hot and sterilized. The skin should be disturbed as little

as possible, antibiotic ointment applied, and the spot covered with a Band-Aid or similar dressing. It may be necessary to delay hiking a day or so if blisters become severe, and care must be taken to avoid infection and otherwise making them worse. Applications of a commercial preparation of benzoin (Tuf-Skin) several days in advance of the trip will help to toughen the skin on the feet and reduce the likelihood of blisters.

When hiking in groups, there are usually some individuals who wish to walk faster than others. It is irritating to walk behind a person who walks slower than you do, and it is good to let the sprinters pass—but keep the party together! One rule is to keep the person behind you in sight by looking back frequently and stopping to rest when the group gets spread farther than is desirable. Although it may cause some irritation on the part of those who wish to walk faster, a sure way to keep the group together is to put the slowest hiker in front and allow no one to pass. It is advisable to hike with at least one partner and to know the whereabouts of each other at all times. The "buddy system" allows one person to go for help in case of serious emergency.

Falls are a primary source of injury to backpackers, and precautions should be taken to avoid unnecessary risks. A broken leg or sprained ankle is no fun at any time, and on the trail deep in a wilderness area, it becomes a serious problem. Travel over ice, wet rocks, and loose rocks poses special problems and should not be attempted without special knowledge and training. Hiking poles can be a valuable aid in avoiding falls on difficult terrains. Some models of hiking poles are collapsible and thus easily carried in a pack when not being used. Each hiker must be responsible for her or his own safety and be ready to assist others.

A trip control plan (TCP) should be left with someone before starting to locate a hiker in an emergency and to enable emergency aid to be directed to the proper place if it should become necessary. TCPs should be as specific as possible, including information on mileage, elevation gain or loss, anticipated travel time, and identification of landmarks and probable campsites. Most established trails have some sort of registration procedure, either at a ranger station or a drop box a short distance up the trail from the trailhead. A good plan is to have someone start looking for you if you are not in contact with them at a specified time. In the event of a delay that is not an emergency, the party with whom you have the arrangement should be notified of your safety as soon as possible.

Extra precaution should be observed when descending trails, especially near the end of a trip, when fatigue is most evident and accidents are most likely to occur. During downhill travel, hazards may be more likely to be hidden by vegetation, and loose rocks, rotten logs, and other dangers may appear without warning. Lightning in the mountains poses an extremely dangerous threat, and in the event of an electrical storm, hikers should retreat to the lowest available area, avoiding high ridges and lone trees.

Trail Pests

The degree of irritation caused by trail pests is usually inversely proportional to the size of the pest. The uninitiated hiker may fear mountain lions, grizzly bears, and other wild creatures, but mosquitoes, black flies, "no-see-ums," and similar insects can cause far more discomfort than larger animals. Generally, it must be understood that it is the hiker who is the interloper in any confrontation with an animal. Most animals wish only to be left alone. Snakes are often feared, but most are harmless. Small garter snakes frequent springs in some mountain ranges, but they are there for the same purpose as the packer: to get a cool drink. Rattlesnakes are dangerous, and most can be avoided by careful observation during walking and especially when sitting down beside the trail or reaching along a rocky ledge. A good insect repellent will help considerably in dealing with insects, and common sense should prevail in dealing with other animals. No animal should be teased or antagonized. Remember, you are the intruder in the animal's home!

Personal Hygiene

Habits of personal hygiene should not vary markedly from those practiced at home. It is important to maintain personal cleanliness, and although baths may not be taken as regularly as at home, they may be even more necessary. Small mountain streams should **not** be used as bathtubs or as a place to wash dishes or clothes. The water is usually cold, and the aquatic balances that influence fish and other life can be easily affected. Water can be heated in the cooking pot and used for washing clothes or for bathing. Use biodegradable soap, because the soil can break it down much more rapidly than ordinary soaps. Soapy water should not be discarded where it can run into a stream. The idea of washing socks and cooking in the same pot may not be attractive to some, but the matter of weight makes it essential to leave the wash basin at home. A thorough rinsing and boiling of water in the pot after use for washing will make it safe and ready for the next meal. Thorough rinsing of the pot is essential, because soap acts as a strong laxative if ingested.

Good toilet habits should be practiced, including depositing fecal material in a small hole at least 200 feet (60 m) from the trail and any surface water. A "cat hole" should be at least 6 inches (15.2 cm) deep and covered with soil near other organic material.

Trail Etiquette

All travelers on the trail have the same rights and privileges, and all should respect other travelers. On a narrow trail, let faster hikers pass by simply stepping off the trail and greeting them cordially. In Western areas, horse pack trains use the same trails as backpackers, and often the packers do not rate very highly with the horse wrangler. Even though the packhorses see hikers frequently, they are sometimes "spooked" by them. If you see a pack train approaching or one overtakes you, move off the trail at least 20 feet (6 m) on the downhill side and stand quietly as the animals pass. Sudden movement or loud noise may cause horses to bolt and may result in runaways or horses falling down the side of the mountain. On Eastern, as well as some Western, trails, backpackers encounter snowmobiles, cross-country skiers, and mountain bikers. It is best to just move off the trail and allow these individuals to pass.

Campsites

On some trails, camping may be permitted in designated areas only. It is important to adhere to such regulations to prevent damage to the surroundings and to keep the area in a near natural state for others who will follow. When camping is unrestricted, it is convenient if the campsite can be located near water. Level ground is also desirable, but it may be difficult to find in some areas. Fires must be used with great discretion, and the campsite must be made as natural as possible before leaving. Fires must be completely extinguished and the fire scar covered. Many wilderness areas have fire restrictions. Contact the local ranger station before your trip to determine if an open fire is allowed. All garbage that will not burn completely must be packed out. Backpackers are the self-appointed guardians of the wilderness, and they must use it with the least possible damage and leave no evidence of their presence in the area. Popular phrases such as "low impact camping," "carry in, carry out," and "take pictures and leave only footsteps," should guide hikers in campsite management.

Hypothermia

A real threat in the outdoors is hypothermia. This condition occurs when the body core temperature falls below normal. Unless the condition is reversed, death results. Hypothermia is not freezing to death! Most often hypothermia occurs when the outdoor temperature is between 30 and 50°F. Hypothermia may be a problem at lower temperatures, but usually a person prepares more effectively for such situations. Sudden changes in weather may occur, and hikers caught unprepared in cold rainstorms are prime candidates for hypothermia. The combination of wet clothing and exposure to wind most frequently causes the problem. Such conditions remove heat from the body surface faster than it can be generated by normal body functions, and the decrease in temperature results. The hiker should be familiar with wind-chill factors.

It is extremely important that early symptoms of hypothermia—continued shivering, loss of alertness, and loss of control of the hands—be recognized and treated immediately. All of these things occur without the victim being aware of what is happening. The four basic defenses against hypothermia are these:

1. Stay dry and out of the wind.
2. If chilling has already started, get out of the wind and rain, give up objectives for the day, if necessary, and

"hole up" in a sheltered spot. Erect a tent and take advantage of such natural shelter as may be available.

3. Detect hypothermia by checking party members for uncontrolled shivering, slurred speech, memory lapses, stumbling, drowsiness, and apparent exhaustion.

4. Treat hypothermia as follows: Get the victim to shelter, strip off his or her wet clothes and put on dry ones, get the victim into a warm sleeping bag, give warm drinks, and, if at all possible, build a fire. Keep the victim awake. Remember, *think* hypothermia and be prepared to deal with it at the first sign of difficulty. Don't wait!

Heat Stress

Another problem that can confront the hiker is heat stress. Precautions should be taken to avoid heat exhaustion and heat stroke, but it is equally important to recognize their symptoms and to treat them if they occur.

Heat is eliminated from the body by conduction, convection, radiation, and evaporation. The most important process for regulation of body temperature is sweating, which promotes cooling through evaporation. While hiking, some heat is lost through perspiration, but it is minimal. Evaporation of sweat is influenced by the relative humidity, wind velocity, and outside temperature. High humidity is especially troublesome, because it reduces the rate of evaporation that can take place.

The steps of prevention, recognition, and treatment of heat stress are as follows:

1. Carry and ingest adequate amounts of liquid and salt to prevent depletion of these basic body requirements.

2. Ensure adequate rest and opportunity for cooling. Take frequent rest stops in shady areas.

3. Detect heat exhaustion from such symptoms as fatigue, muscle cramps, abdominal pain, and nausea. The pulse will be normal, the skin will be moist and pale, and there might not be an increase in temperature, although more commonly there will be. The tongue and mouth may be dry, and the hiker will feel weak and uncoordinated and may appear mentally dull.

4. Treat heat exhaustion by moving the hiker to a cool area and replenishing the liquid content of the body. Electrolytes or sport drinks will replace fluids and minerals simultaneously.

5. Detect heat stroke from such symptoms as fever; a rapid pulse rate; hot, dry, flushed skin; involuntary limb movements; and possible unconsciousness.

6. Treat heat stroke immediately by lowering body temperature through use of cold water, fanning, and massaging the limbs. Heat stroke is a medical emergency that requires advanced medical care. If heat stroke is suspected, seek medical help immediately.

TEACHING CONSIDERATIONS

Only instructors with a great deal of experience in backpacking and wilderness first aid should guide others on a trip.

Training is advisable through an organization such as the National Outdoor Leadership School in Lander, Wyoming. Having adequate training is particularly important when backpacking in wilderness areas where help in emergency situations is not likely to be available. All instructors should consider the conditioning and experience of their group in planning a trip and should not consider more than casual day trips with unconditioned, unprepared, or ill-equipped backpackers.

GLOSSARY

A-frame A triangle-shaped tent.

benzoin A commercial preparation used in advance to toughen the skin of the feet.

biodegradable soap A type of soap that should be used when backpacking because the soil can break it down very quickly.

bivouac A temporary camp.

bivouac sack An external covering for the sleeping bag.

campsite An area for sleeping and/or fire building. On some trails, camping may only be permitted in designated areas.

checklist A list of things that are to be taken. This is critical so that nothing is left behind.

dead out The condition every fire must be in before leaving the campsite.

external frame pack A pack with a frame on the outside of the pack sack.

first-aid kit A kit that contains all the immediate remedies for the hazards encountered along the trail.

fleece Synthetic fabric that adds insulation and dries fast.

foam sleeping pad A pad used for blocking heat loss through the ground.

gaiters Nylon or cloth anklets used to keep snow and dirt from falling into boots.

geodesic dome A dome-shaped tent.

giardiasis/giardia A waterborne disease.

gorp A high-energy food eaten during the course of the day's hike; "good old raisins and peanuts."

heat stress A common problem that confronts the hiker. High humidity is especially troublesome.

hip belt A padded waist belt.

hypothermia A condition that occurs when the body core temperature falls below normal. It is the greatest killer of people in the outdoors.

internal frame pack A pack with the frame enclosed in the pack sack.

I-pole tent A lightweight tent with one pole in the middle.

leave no trace (LNT) Use of skills and ethics to support the sustainable use of wildlands and natural areas.

liquid fuel One source of fuel for camping; should be kept in a metal container and carried in a pocket on the outside of the pack.

loft The thickness of a sleeping bag.

maps Guides for assessing the terrain and general physical characteristics of the area selected for hiking.

menus Written plans for food consumption for each meal.

moleskin Bandaging material to prevent blisters.

mummy-style bag A sleeping bag adequate for temperatures encountered and most popular with hikers.

pack A compartmentalized bag mounted on a metal frame.

pile A soft fabric made from polyester.

potable water Water that is safe for human consumption.

rain chaps Sleeves that cover the legs and may be tied to the belt.

seam sealer A special glue used to waterproof material where seams come together.

sternum strap Nylon straps that connect shoulder straps of the pack.

storm flap Panel of material on a garment or tent that prevents moisture and wind from getting in.

stuff sack A nylon bag with drawstring closure.

trail etiquette Observance of respect for other travelers.

trailhead A place where established trails originate.

trail pests Animals that may cause discomfort or danger; remember that the hiker is the interloper in any confrontation with an animal and that a good insect repellent will help deal with insects.

trip control plan (TCP) A detailed description of the trip, including departure and return times, and route description.

vestibule An extension of the tent that secures to the front or back.

REFERENCES

Pokorny, T. 2001. *Leave no trace skills and ethics.* North America, Boulder, CO: LNTINOLS.

SUGGESTED READINGS

Curtis, R. 2005. *The backpacker's field manual.* 2nd ed. New York NY: Three Rivers Press.

Fletcher, C., and Rawlins, C. 2002. *The Complete Walker IV.* New York, NY: Random House.

Harvey, M. 1999. *The national outdoor leadership school's wilderness guide.* New York, NY: Simon and Schuster.

Kemsley, W. *Backpacker and hiker's handbook.* Mechanicsburg, PA: Stackpole Books.

Kestenbaum, R. 2001. *The ultra light backpacker: The complete guide to simplicity and comfort on the trail.* New York, NY: McGraw-Hill.

Tilburg, C. 2005. *Introducing your kids to the outdoors.* Mechanicsburg, PA: Stackpole Books. How to plan, pack, and organize trips with children.

Wilderness Education Association, 2008. *Hiking and backpacking,* Champaign, IL: Human Kinetics.

Yaffe, L. 2003. *Backpack gourmet.* Mechanicsburg, PA: Stackpole Books. Explains how to prepare food at home and how to dehydrate and package it for eating on the trail.

RESOURCES

Dupont Fibrefill Marketing Division, Centre Road Bldg., Wilmington, DE 19898. For information on Hollowfil II, Quallowfil, and Thermolite.

Mountain Equipment Co-op, 1655 W Third Ave, Vancouver, BC Canada V6J 1K1. For a general catalog of outdoor clothing and gear.

Patagonia, 1609 Babcock St., P.O. Box 8900, Bozeman, MT 59715. For information on Patagonia products.

WL Gore, Rte 213, P.O. Box 1220, North Elkton, MD 21921. For information on Gore-Tex.

Videos, films, and filmstrips

See Appendix C for sources of videos

WEB SITES

Schools

National Outdoor Leadership School
www.nols.edu

Outward Bound
www.outwardboundwilderness.org

Trails Wilderness School
www.trailsws.com

Maps

National Geographic
http://maps_nationalgeographic.com/trails

Trails
www.trails.com

U.S. Geologic Survey
http://topomaps.usgs.gov

Environmental

Leave No Trace
www.lnt.org

National Park Service
www.nps.gov

Badminton

After completing this chapter, the reader should be able to:

- Appreciate the versatility of the game of badminton
- Know the important considerations for selecting and caring for badminton equipment
- Understand the rules and scoring procedures of the game
- Describe the correct grip, wrist action, ready position, footwork, strokes, and shots
- Understand badminton strategy and etiquette
- Instruct a group of students in the fundamentals of badminton
- Emphasize skill, stamina, and athletic ability necessary for badminton competition
- Recognize and use badminton terms correctly

HISTORY

A game with some sort of racquet and a feathered object goes far back into history. A game similar to badminton (shuttlecock kicking) was played in China as early as the fifth century CE, and there is mention of the game as long ago as the twelfth century in the Royal Court records of England.

Battledore shuttlecock was popular in the era of King James I, so it is not surprising that the game was played by early English settlers in the United States.

The portrait *Young Prince Sulkonsik,* by Adam Mangoki, who lived during the 1700s, shows young members of the Royal Family of Poland holding a shuttlecock and racquet with a stance similar to that used by a modern player preparing to serve. A portrait by Jean Simeon Chardin (1699–1779) hanging in the Uffizi Gallery in Florence depicts a girl with a racquet and shuttle.

Portrait of Master Stephen Crossfield hangs in the Metropolitan Museum of Art, New York. Painted by American William Williams (1727–1791). It depicts a young man holding a battledore (racquet) and shuttlecock.

It is generally accepted that the modern game of badminton, involving court boundaries and a winning objective, was named when a group of British army officers home on leave from India around 1873 played the game at Badminton, the country estate of the Duke of Beaufort in Gloucestershire, England. Since then there have been several important dates in the history of badminton. See Table 6.1. In 1878, the Badminton Club of New York City was founded. Records in the New York City Museum of History substantiate that this is the oldest organized badminton club in the world. The club was a leading social rendezvous in New York for 25 years. Such names as Astor, Roosevelt, Rockefeller, and Vanderbilt appeared on the membership list. Badminton had its heyday in the United States in the 1930s, when thousands of players, including famous athletes and Hollywood stars, enjoyed the game.

The American Badminton Association was founded in 1936, and in 1977 changed its name to the United States Badminton Association.

The second organized badminton club was founded in Ireland in 1899. This organization was a founding member of

Table 6.1. IMPORTANT DATES IN HISTORY OF BADMINTON

Year	Event
1873	The sport of badminton established in England and India
1879	New York Badminton Club, first in the world, founded
1893	English Badminton Association, first association in the world, founded
1899	First All England Badminton Championship held, with winner traditionally considered world champion
1903	First International competition, contested between England and Ireland in Dublin
1907	*Badminton Gazette,* first badminton journal, published
1934	IBF, governing body of international badminton, founded
1936	ABA, governing body of badminton in the U.S., founded
1937	First U.S. National Championships held, Chicago
1947	First U.S. National Junior Championships held
1948	Thomas Cup, international team competition for men, started
1956	Uber Cup, international team competition for women, started
1969	First Intercollegiate badminton championship for women held, New Orleans, LA
1975	First Intercollegiate badminton championship for men held, Toledo, OH
1977	WBF founded; governs world badminton championships, on alternate years to Thomas Cup
1977	ABA changed name to USBA; offered individual memberships
1981	First World Games held, included first participation by People's Republic of China in open international competition, San Jose, CA
1989	Sudirman Cup, world mixed team championship, established
1992	Badminton full medal sport in Olympic Games, Barcelona, Spain
1996	Mixed doubles a medal event in Olympic Games, Atlanta, GA

the International Badminton Federation (IBF) in 1934. The first badminton played internationally was a match between England and Ireland in Dublin in 1903. The original IBF included 9 national badminton organizations. By 1939, the tally had risen to 15; today there are more than 130 member organizations worldwide. The Thomas Cup competition for men's teams was started in 1948; the Uber Cup competition for women's teams was started in 1956. Strangely, no European country has yet won either trophy. Malaysia, Indonesia, and China have split the 18 competitions for the men's trophy. The Uber Cup was won three times by the United States between 1956 and 1964. The other 12 cups have been held by China, Japan, and Indonesia. The Thomas and Uber Cups are now staged every even year. The Sudirman Cup, world mixed-team championship, initially held in 1989, is staged every odd year and has been won by Indonesia, Korea, and China. Additional international competition is provided by the Asian games, the British Commonwealth games, the South East Asian games, and the Pan American games. In 1977, the first official world championship was held in Malmo, Sweden; tournaments are now scheduled every odd year.

Badminton was a demonstration sport in the 1972 Olympics and an exhibition sport at the 1988 Olympics. In 1992, it was a full medal sport for the first time at Barcelona, Spain. Table 6.2 depicts the number of the 57 Olympic medals that have been won by various countries since 1992. China has dominated the games by winning 35 percent of the medals, followed by Korea (26 percent) and Indonesia (23 percent). The chart reveals that China dominates the ladies' singles and ladies' doubles events, Indonesia dominates the men's singles, and Indonesia and Korea have split 10 of the 12 men's doubles medals. Of the 19 gold medals awarded since 1992, 8 have gone to China, 5 each to Indonesia and Korea, and 1 to Denmark.

CARRYOVER VALUES

Badminton offers fun and fitness for everyone. It is a sport that is easy to learn but difficult to master. A beginning player receives pleasure and exercise immediately, and an advanced player can get an extremely vigorous workout by playing just one game with an equally skilled opponent. Research studies of movement show that a badminton player uses more arm action in one match than the average baseball pitcher does in a nine-inning baseball game. Also, a top-flight badminton player runs more in one match than a running back or end does in a 60-minute football game.

Badminton is a family sport, played by women, men, and children. Adaptability to small areas, indoors and outdoors, at a minimal cost provides an opportunity for everyone to participate. For advanced players who wish to compete, indoor tournament play is available almost anywhere in the United States. Tournaments sponsored by local badminton clubs and sanctioned by USA Badminton provide local, regional, and national singles, doubles, and mixed doubles competition for both sexes for the following: Junior, Open, and Senior levels: Junior, under 21, 18, 16, 14, and 12; Open, any age; and Senior, 35 years up to 80+ years, at 5-year intervals.

SELECTION AND CARE OF EQUIPMENT

In all sports, good equipment is a prerequisite to good play. Badminton is no exception.

The Racquet

1. Most racquets are constructed of aluminum, steel, or various blends of carbon, graphite, ceramic, or boron. The carbon graphite racquets are popular among advanced players because they are very light and powerful.
2. Racquet weight depends on the strength of the individual and the feeling of comfort with the racquet. Most school and tournament racquets weigh 3 to 4 ounces (86 to 114 g).
3. Racquets should be evenly balanced or slightly lighter in the head.
   a. Doubles players usually prefer lighter racquets because quicker shots are possible.
   b. Point of balance is normally 11 to 13½ inches (27.5 to 33.8 cm) from the bottom of the handle.

Table 6.2. DISTRIBUTION OF OLYMPIC MEDALS WON IN BADMINTON BETWEEN 1992 AND 2008

	Men's Singles	Men's Doubles	Ladies' Singles	Ladies' Doubles	Mixed Doubles	Total
China	3	1	5	8	3	20
Denmark	2	0	1	0	1	4
Great Britain	0	0	0	0	2	2
Indonesia	5	5	2	0	1	13
Korea	1	5	3	4	2	15
Malaysia	1	1	0	0	0	2
Netherlands	0	0	1	0	0	1

4. Handle (grip):
   a. Size depends on size of hand.
   b. Normal racquet grips vary between 3¼ and 3⅜ inches (8.3 to 9.1 cm) in circumference.
   c. The player should try several sizes and pick the one that feels best.
5. Strings:
   a. Nylon is relatively immune to moisture, inexpensive, longer lasting than gut, and preferred for class use and beginners because of its serviceability and cost.
   b. Gut is expensive, less durable than nylon, not moisture proof, and requires special care. Synthetic gut is preferred by advanced and tournament players because of its resiliency and playability.
   c. Gut and nylon are normally strung at tensions from 14 to 20 pounds (6.4 to 9 kg).
6. Care of the racquet:
   a. Frayed strings should be replaced before they break to prevent loosening of string tension.
   b. Racquets should be kept away from extreme heat or extreme cold. (i.e., < 32°F or > 100°F)

Shuttlecocks (Shuttles)

Shuttles are made either of goose feathers or nylon. There are several kinds of feather shuttles, and the price varies depending on the quality of the feathers and construction of the shuttle. Feather shuttles are usually used for tournaments, but because of feather breakage, these shuttles usually last only one or two games. Feathers can be pointed or rounded on the tip. The feather shuttle should be kept in a moist environment to prevent the feathers from drying out. This can be done by wrapping a moist towel around the tube 24 hours before use or by placing a damp paper towel in the end of the tube. Nylon shuttles are best for class use because they last several weeks and require no special environment; however, they also last longer if humidified.

The International Badminton Federation has defined the correct speed of a shuttlecock. Law 4 indicates a shuttlecock has correct speed if a player of average strength strikes it with a full underhand stroke from a spot immediately above one back boundary line, in a line parallel to the sidelines, at an upward angle, and it falls within 9 inches (22.9 cm) on either side of the opposite long doubles service line (Figure 6.1).

Students and teachers of badminton should know how to test a shuttle and should test those in use. It is recommended that shuttles, whether feathered or nylon, test properly for speed as shown in Figure 6.1. Climatic conditions (temperature and humidity) and altitude have significant effects on shuttle speed. If the shuttle tests correctly, the game becomes one of matching speed, finesse, deception, control, and power rather than one of just brute strength, as can happen if the shuttle is too fast or too slow.

The Net and Standards

The net is 5 feet 1 inch (1.53 m) in height from the surface of the court at the post. The posts are placed on the side boundary lines of the court and should be sufficiently firm to keep the net stretched. Where this is not practicable, some method must be used for indicating the position of the side boundary line where it passes under the net, such as by the use of a thin post or strip of material, not less than 1.5 inches (3.75 cm) in width, fixed to the side boundary line and rising vertically to the net cord. On a court marked for doubles, it should be placed on the side boundary line of the doubles court, regardless of whether singles or doubles are being played.

The net is made of fine natural cord or artificial fiber of a dark color and an even thickness not exceeding ⅝- to ¾-inch (1.6- to 1.9-cm) mesh. It should be firmly stretched from

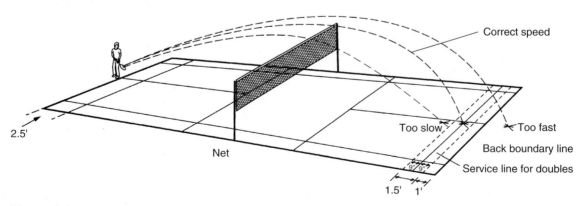

Figure 6.1. Testing the speed of shuttlecocks. They should land within 9 inches (22.9 cm) of either side of the service line for doubles.

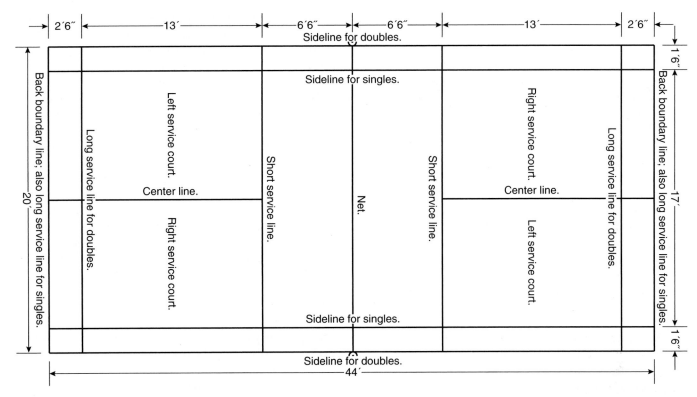

Figure 6.2. Double and single badminton court dimensions.

post to post and is 2 feet 6 inches (75 cm) in depth. The top of the net is 5 feet (1.5 m) from the floor at the center and 5 feet 1 inch (1.53 m) at the posts, and it is edged with 3-inch (7.5 cm) white tape doubled and supported by a cord or cable run through the tape and strained over and flush with the top of the posts.

HOW TO LAY OUT A COURT

If two or more courts are laid out side by side, a minimum of 4 feet (1.3 m) should be allowed between them. In laying out a home court in the backyard, either tape or dry lime can be used for the boundary lines. For the gymnasium, the boundary lines are defined by white or yellow lines 1.5 inches (3.8 cm) wide. In laying out a badminton court at home, the singles and doubles courts can be combined. The doubles playing court is the same length 44 feet (13.4 m) as the singles playing court, but is 3 feet (0.92 m) wider (Figure 6.2).

The ceiling height of a court used for international competitive play is a minimum of 30 feet (9 m) from the floor over the full court.

RULES

The object of the game is to hit the shuttlecock back and forth across the net with the racquet without permitting the shuttlecock to touch the ground, attempting to hit the shuttlecock into the opposing court so that it cannot be returned.

Scoring (Traditional System)

The doubles and men's singles games consist of 15 points. When the score is 14 all, the side that first reaches 14 has the option of "setting" the game to 3. After a game has been set, the side that first scores 3 points wins the game. The option to set the game must be made before the next service is delivered, after the score has reached 14 all.

The women's singles games consist of 11 points. When the score is 10 all, the player who first reaches 10 has the option of setting the game to 3.

The opposing sides contest the best of three games. The players change ends at the start of the second game and also at the start of the third game (if any). In the third game, the players change ends when the leading score reaches 8 in a game of 15 points or 6 in a game of 11 points. School tournaments and some consolation tournament matches play one game to 21 points. Under this format, players change sides when one player has 11 points and there is no setting at a score of 20–20. If players forget to change ends, the ends are changed as soon as the mistake is discovered, and the existing score stands.

Faults

A fault made by a player of the side that is in (has the serve) puts the serve out; if made by a player whose side is out, it counts a point to the in side.

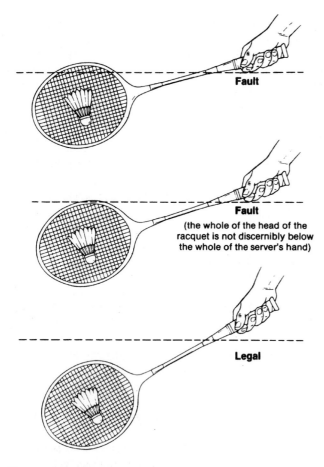

Figure 6.3. Delivery of service.

It is a fault:

1. If, in serving, the shuttle at the instant of being struck is higher than the server's waist, or if at the instant of the shuttle being struck, the shaft of the racquet is not pointing sufficiently downward that the whole head of the racquet is discernibly below the whole of the server's hand holding the racquet (Figure 6.3).

2. If, in serving, the shuttle falls into the wrong service court (into the one not diagonally opposite the server) or falls short of the short service line, beyond the long service line, or outside the side boundary lines of the service court into which service is in order.

3. If the server's feet are not in the service court from which service is at the time being in order, or if the feet of the player receiving the service are not in the service court diagonally opposite until the service is delivered.

4. If, before or during the delivery of the service, any player makes preliminary feints or otherwise intentionally balks (tries to deceive) the opponent, or if any player deliberately delays serving the shuttle or getting ready to receive it, so as to obtain an unfair advantage.

5. If, either in service or play, the shuttle falls outside the boundaries of the court, or passes through or under the net, or fails to pass the net, or touches the roof or side walls, or touches the person or dress of a player. A shuttle falling on a line is deemed to have fallen in the court or service court of which such line is a boundary.

6. If the shuttle in play is struck before it crosses to the striker's side of the net. The striker may, however, follow the shuttle over the net with the racquet in the course of the stroke.

7. If, when the shuttle is in play, a player touches the net or its supports with racquet, person, or dress.

8. If the shuttle is held on the racquet (that is, caught or slung) during the execution of a stroke, or if the shuttle is hit twice in succession by the same player with two strokes, or if the shuttle is hit by a player and partner successively.

9. If a player obstructs an opponent.

General

The server may not serve until the opponent is ready, but the opponent is deemed to be ready if a return of the service is attempted.

The server and the player served to must stand within the limits of their respective service courts (as bounded by the short and long service lines and the center and sidelines), and some part of both feet of these players must remain in contact with the surface of the court in a stationary position until the service is delivered. A foot on or touching a line in the case of either the server or the receiver is held to be outside the service court. The respective partners may take up any position, provided they do not obscure the view or otherwise obstruct an opponent.

If, in the course of service or rally, the shuttle touches and passes over the net, the stroke is valid and play continues. It is a good return if the shuttle, having passed outside either post, drops on or within the boundary lines of the opposite court.

If, in service or during a rally, a shuttle, after passing over the net, is caught in or on the net, it is a let.

If the receiver is faulted for moving before the service is delivered or for not being within the correct service court, and at the same time the server is also faulted for service infringement, it is considered a let.

A "let" may be given by the umpire for any unforeseen or accidental hindrance. When a let occurs, the play since the last service does not count and the player who last served serves again.

If the server in serving misses the shuttle completely, it is a fault.

If a player has the chance of striking the shuttle when quite near the net, an opponent must not extend the racquet near the net. A player may, however, hold up the racquet for protection to avoid being hit in the face if this action does not result in obstructing the opponent's stroke.

It is the duty of the umpire to call "fault" or "let" should either occur, without appeal being made by the players, and to give a decision on any appeal regarding a point in dispute, if made before the net service, and also to appoint line judges and service judges at the umpire's discretion. The umpire's decision is final, but the decision of a line judge or service judge should be upheld. This does not preclude the umpire also from faulting the server or receiver.

Singles Play

The players serve from and receive service in their respective right-hand service courts only when the server's score is 0 or is an even number of points, with the service being delivered from and received in their left-hand service courts when the server's score is an odd number of points. Setting the game does not affect this sequence.

Both players change service courts after each point has been scored.

Doubles Play

After it has been decided which side is to have the first service, the player in the right-hand service court of that side commences the game by serving to the player in the service court diagonally opposite. If the latter player returns the shuttle before it touches the ground, it is to be returned by one of the in (serving) side and then returned by one of the out (receiving) side, and so on, until a fault is made or the shuttle ceases to be in play. If a fault is made by the in side, its right to continue serving is lost, as only one player of the side beginning a game is entitled to serve, and the opponent in the right-hand service court then becomes the server; but if the service is not returned or the fault is made by the out side, the in side scores a point. The in-side players then change from one service court to the other, the service now being from the left-hand service court to the player in the service court diagonally opposite. So long as a side remains in, service is delivered alternately from each service court into the one diagonally opposite, the change being made by the in side when, and only when, a point is added to its score.

The first service of a side in each inning is made from the right-hand service court. A service is delivered as soon as the shuttle is struck by the server's racquet. The shuttle is thereafter in play until it touches the floor or playing surface or until a fault or let occurs. After the service is delivered, the server and the player served to may take up any position they choose on their side of the net, regardless of boundary lines.

Only the player served to may receive the service; however, should the shuttle touch or be struck by his or her partner, the in side scores a point. No player may receive two consecutive services in the same game.

Only one player of the side beginning a game is entitled to serve in its first innings. In all subsequent innings, each partner has the right, and they serve consecutively. The side winning a game always serves first in the next game, but either

of the winners may serve and either of the losers may receive the service.

If a player serves out of turn or from the wrong service court and the serving side wins the rally, it is a let, provided that such let is claimed and allowed or ordered by the umpire before the next service is delivered.

If a player of the out side standing in the wrong service court is prepared to receive the service when it is delivered and the receiving side wins the rally, it is a let, provided that such let is claimed and allowed or ordered by the umpire before the next service is delivered.

If, in either of the previous cases, the side at fault loses the rally, the mistake stands and the player's position is not corrected.

Should a player inadvertently change sides incorrectly and the mistake is not discovered until after the next service has been delivered, the mistake stands, a let cannot be claimed or allowed, and the player's position is not corrected.

Play shall be continuous from the first serve until the match is concluded, except for an interval of 90 seconds between the first and second games and an interval not exceeding 5 minutes between games two and three. Coaching is allowed during both of these time intervals.

Rally Point Scoring System

Simplified Scoring System—adopted by the IBF and USBA in 2006

1. A match consists of the best of 3 games of 21 points.
2. The side winning a rally adds a point to its score.
3. At 20 all, the side that gains a 2-point lead first wins that game.
4. At 29 all, the side scoring the 30th point wins that game.
5. The side winning a game serves first in the next game.

Intervals and Change of Ends

1. When the leading score reaches 11 points, players have a 60-second interval.
2. A 2-minute interval between each game is allowed.
3. In the third game, players change ends when a side scores 11 points.

Points—Singles

1. At the beginning of the game and when the score is even, the server serves from the right service court. When it is odd, the server serves from the left service court.
2. If the server wins a rally, the server scores a point and then serves again from the alternate service court.
3. If the receiver wins a rally, the receiver scores a point and becomes the new server.

Points—Doubles

1. At the beginning of the game and when the score is even, the server serves from the right service court. When it is odd, the server serves from the left court.

2. If the serving side wins a rally, the serving side scores a point and the same server serves again from the alternate service court.
3. If the receiving side wins a rally, the receiving side scores a point. The receiving side becomes the new serving side.

FUNDAMENTAL SKILLS AND TECHNIQUES

Gripping the Racquet

1. Standard forehand grip: The handle of the racquet is held as if the player were shaking hands with the racquet. Lay the handle across the hand parallel with the distal lifeline (Figure 6.4A). Grip the handle with the middle, ring, and small fingers (Figure 6.4B). The index finger and the thumb are used for control (Figure 6.4C).
2. Backhand grip: Similar to the forehand grip except that the hand is rotated slightly to the left and the thumb is placed flat against the side bevel for additional power (Figure 6.4D). The changing of grips during play becomes somewhat automatic.
3. The standard grip can be used for both forehand and backhand strokes.
4. The hand, wrist, and arm should be relaxed, but the fingers should tighten on the handle just before the racquet contacts the shuttle.
5. Compared to other racquet sports, the badminton racquet is gripped by the fingers and not held in the palm of the hand.

Wrist Action

1. Wrist action is used to disguise intentions. A simple flick of the wrist aids not only in directing the shuttle, but also in sending the opponent in the wrong direction, since the flight is concealed until the last fraction of a second.

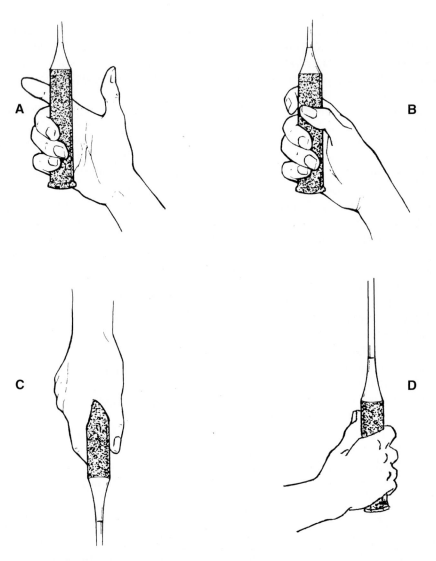

Figure 6.4. Gripping the racquet (right-handed player).

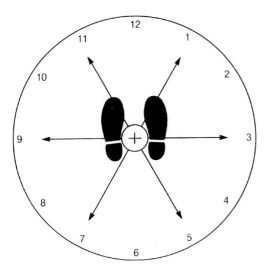

Figure 6.5. Footwork.

2. In starting all shots, the player should keep the racquet well back by hyperextending the wrist. The racquet's forward swing should not be checked; follow-through is very important.

Ready Position and Footwork

To move properly on a badminton court, the player must start from a constantly maintained "ready position." The ideal starting position on the court is approximately midway between the doubles long and the short service lines and straddling the center line. The player who does not reach this ideal position on the court before the opponent hits the shuttle should stop and react to where the shuttle is hit. A player should never be moving as the opponent is hitting the shuttle.

The correct stance is similar to that of a baseball infielder expecting a grounder. Weight should be on the balls of the feet, with the feet far enough apart to ensure stable balance, approximately 2½ feet apart. The body should be ready to spring in any direction. The knees should be slightly bent.

The racquet head should be held at about shoulder height, comfortably away from the body.

In the ready position, the feet are in the 12 o'clock position (Figure 6.5). To cover the court properly, the player should be ready to move quickly to the 1 o'clock, 3 o'clock, and 5 o'clock positions for a forehand stroke. Movement to the right, for a forehand stroke, at these positions on the court involves moving the body's center of gravity in the direction of the shuttle. For the backhand stroke, the player should be ready to move to the 7 o'clock, 9 o'clock, and 11 o'clock positions.

STROKES

The badminton strokes consist of overhead, sidearm, and underhand swinging patterns from both the forehand and backhand sides of the body. The in-front-of-the-body stroke is hit with the backhand swinging pattern. The serves and all other shots are executed with these stroking patterns and are identified by height and location of shuttle trajectory (Figure 6.6).

Service

High, deep serve

The high, deep serve is an underhand forehand serve hit high so that the shuttle will land in deep court, near the back boundary line (Figure 6.7).

1. Starting position: Feet in stride position with left foot in front for right-handed players. Shift weight to the rear on backswing, then forward as racquet comes forward. Both feet must remain in contact with the court; "stepping" is a fault (Figure 6.7A).
2. A full backswing is made with the wrist cocked (Figure 6.7B).
3. The wrist is uncocked just before contact (Figure 6.7B, C).
4. Follow-through: Shuttle contact is made well in front of the body, not at the side. On the follow-through of the underhand stroke, the racquet carries over the left shoulder (Figure 6.7D).

Low, short serve

The low, short serve should be made in such a manner that the shuttle barely clears the net, is on a downward trajectory

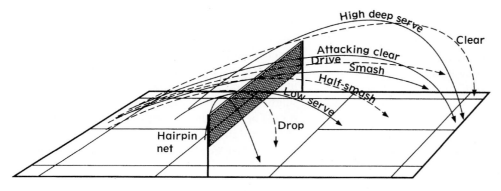

Figure 6.6. Badminton strokes.

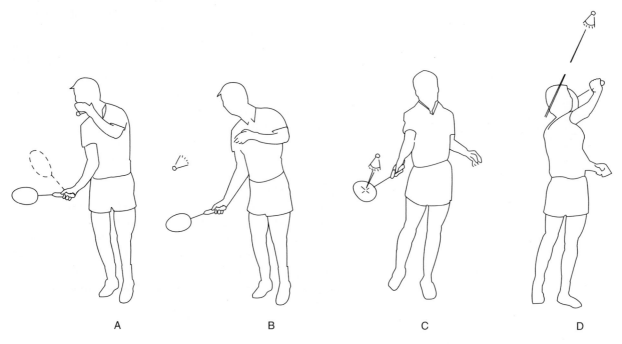

Figure 6.7. Forehand service mechanics.

the moment it passes over the net, and lands close to the short line in the opponent's court.

All basic techniques for the low, short serve—starting position, body rotation, shift in weight, and so on—are the same as for the deep, high serve except:

1. This is a "push" type of serve, accomplished with the wrist remaining almost fully cocked throughout the serve, with little rotation of the forearm (Figure 6.7B).
2. The server should attempt to contact the shuttle as close to the waist height as possible to achieve the desired flat trajectory.

Drive serve

The drive serve is comparable to hitting a line drive in baseball. This serve can be driven at the opponent preferably to hit just below shoulder level.

Basic techniques for the drive serve—starting position, body rotation, and so on—are the same as for the deep, high serve except:

1. The wrist is partially uncocked at contact with the shuttle, and the upper arm extends toward the net.
2. Inasmuch as the racquet does not go beyond half cock, there is not a complete follow-through in a full arc, as in the high, deep serve (Figure 6.7C).

Flick serve

This serve is designed to force players who are getting tired or are relatively slow on their feet to move to the baseline to retrieve the shuttle. It is hit with the power of a drive but with

a trajectory to just clear the opponent's extended racquet. Its effect and trajectory are similar to those of the attacking clear shot, described later. See Figure 6.8 for the trajectories of the various types of serves.

Forehand Overhead Strokes

The forehand overhead stroke begins with the player's weight on the back foot, followed by shifting of weight from the right to the left foot. Body rotation occurs here. During the shots, the forearm is rotated inward to produce power at the instant of contact (Figure 6.9).

1. Ready position with both arms up for balance and shuttle coming down over the right shoulder (Figure 6.9A).
2. Backswing phase with player pushing up and forward with the right leg, wrist cocked (hyperextended) and racquet taken back well behind the body. It is important to notice that the racquet head can be seen as perpendicular to the net from the side view (Figure 6.9B).
3. Racquet-shuttle contact occurs with forearm pronation, upper arm inward rotation, and uncocking the wrist to full extension. Figure 6.10 shows the angle of racquet-shuttle contact to hit the various overhead shots. It should be noted that the body is driving upward as weight is shifting from the racquet to nonracquet leg, and both feet are airborne at racquet-shuttle contact (Figure 6.9C).

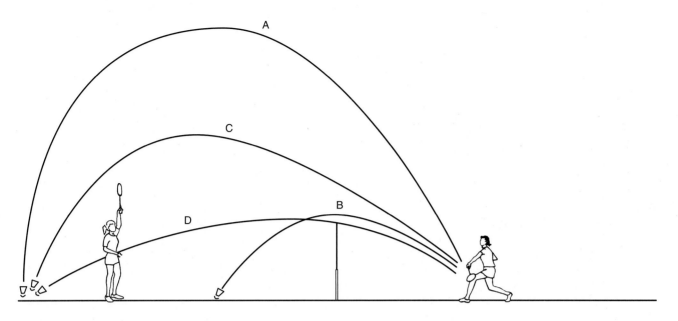

Figure 6.8. Trajectories for various serves. A, High, deep serve. B, Low, short serve. C, Flick serve. D, Drive serve.

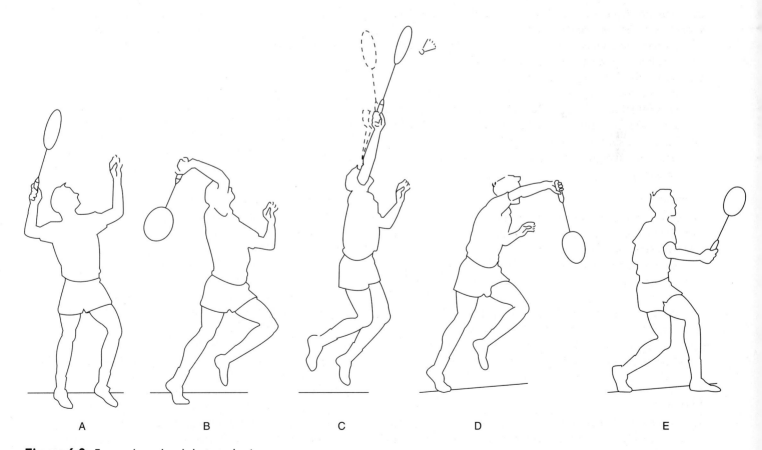

Figure 6.9. Forward overhead shot mechanics.

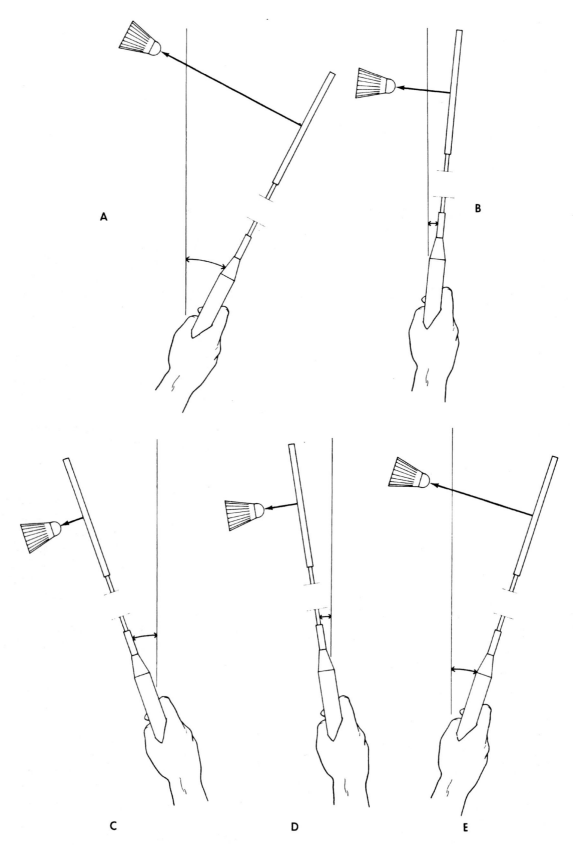

Figure 6.10. Racquet contact points for various shots. A, Contact point for defensive clear. B, Contact point for attacking clear. C, Contact point for smash. D, Contact point for fast attacking drop. E, Contact point for loop drop.

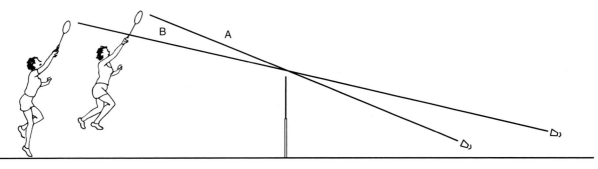

Figure 6.11. Trajectories for smash shots. A, Steep smash. B, Flat smash.

4. Follow-through occurs with completion of forearm rotation (pronation) and upper arm inward rotation (note racquet head down and perpendicular to the net). The elbow and hand are still elevated at head height, and the player has just landed on the left foot (Figure 6.9D).
5. Player steps toward base position to be ready for the next shot (Figure 6.9E).

Defensive clear shot

1. The racquet is angled slightly back from the perpendicular to attain a high trajectory (Figure 6.10A).
2. Contact with the shuttle is high and over the player's right shoulder (or head).
3. The player should hit the shuttle high and deep and assume proper court position as a receiver.

Attacking clear shot

1. This is the same shot as the defensive clear, except the head of the racquet is almost perpendicular to the floor on contact with the shuttle, giving it a flattened trajectory (Figure 6.10B).
2. This is a quick, hard hit used primarily to place the shuttle deep and out of reach of the opponent.
3. The object of this shot is to get the shuttle past an out-of-position opponent.

Smash

1. This shot is an extension of the overhead clear, except contact is made with the shuttle farther in front of the body, and the angle of the racquet is slightly forward (Figure 6.10C).
2. The body should be facing the net on completion of the shot.
3. One should lead with the elbow as the body rotates. The arm should be almost fully extended on contact with the shuttle.
4. Deception on this put-away, or kill, shot is accomplished by making it appear that the return will be a clear or drop.

5. Vigorous forearm rotation and wrist flexion just before contact provides the velocity for the smash.
6. A steep smash is more difficult to return than a hard flat smash. See Figure 6.11.

Drop

1. For a fast attacking drop, the racquet is held at approximately the same angle as for the smash at contact. It should be hit like a smash, except with a softer touch (Figure 6.10D).
2. For a loop drop, the racquet angle is similar to that of a defensive clear (Figure 6.10E).

Backhand Overhead Stroke

1. When taking the last step to hit a backhand shot, the player's back should be facing the net (Figure 6.13A). See Figure 6.12 for trajectories of overhead shots.
2. Backswing with player elevating the right elbow and rotating forearm inward (pronating) as player steps toward shuttle with right leg. The wrist should not be in a flexed position in hitting backhand shots (Figure 6.13B).
3. Acceleration toward racquet-shuttle contact. Elbow has extended fully, and racquet face is perpendicular to the net (Figure 6.13C).
4. Racquet-shuttle contact with outward rotation (supination) of the forearm and hyperextension of the wrist. Immediately after racquet-shuttle contact, the elbow remains stable and the racquet head is directed toward the net as there will be a great loss in power. See Figure 6.10 for the angle of the racquet at shuttle contact for hitting the various overhead shots. Racquet-shuttle contact should occur at or just before the racquet foot lands on the floor. Most shuttles are hit with both feet being airborne. Racquet-shuttle contact occurs at the side of the body in about the 1 or 2 o'clock position rather than directly over the right shoulder (Figure 6.13D).

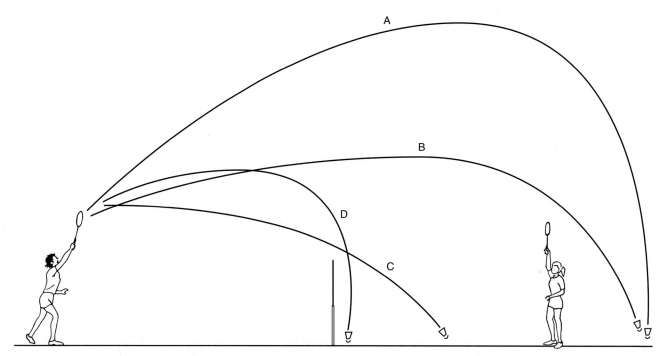

Figure 6.12. Trajectories for overhead shots. A, Defensive clear. B, Attacking clear. C, Attacking drop. D, Loop drop.

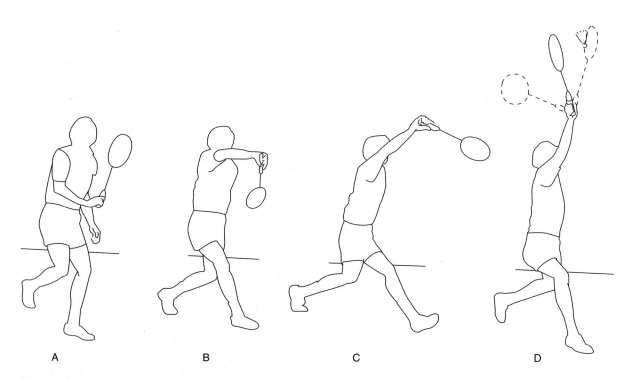

A   B   C   D

Figure 6.13. Backhand overhead stroke mechanics.

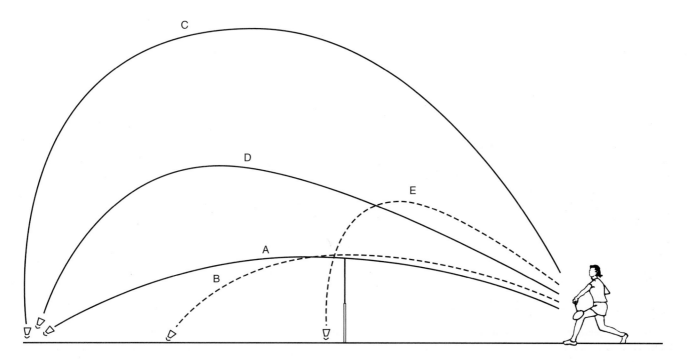

Figure 6.14. Trajectories for various sidearm shots. A, Hard drive. B, Half-court drive. C, Defensive clear. D, Attacking clear. E, Loop drop.

Sidearm Strokes

Drive

The shuttle is hit quickly, forehand or backhand, with a variety of trajectories to produce hard drives, half-court drives, defensive and attacking clears, and loop drop shots (Figure 6.14). The forearm drive action is similar to that of throwing a baseball sidearm.

1. In both forehand and backhand, one should lead with the elbow and hit from a cocked to uncocked position.
2. The arm should be straight on contact with the shuttle.
3. Drive shots are generally hit to defend against the smash.

Underhand Stroke

The player swings up and through with the wrist moving from a cocked to an uncocked position, using the same mechanics as in the serve. Underhand stroke shots include defensive and attacking clears, loop drops, and half-court drives (Figure 6.15).

Net Strokes

Net shots require a delicate stroke. The racquet, therefore, does not need to be held as firmly as it is in other shots.

1. Contact the shuttle as near the top of the net as possible.
2. Use arm movement with wrist remaining cocked instead of forearm rotation. This applies to both forehand and backhand net shots.

3. Stretch and reach for the shuttle.
4. Most players choke up on the racquet handle when hitting drop shots and in net play.

Around-the-Head Strokes

Such shots are within an arc around the head, above the shoulder, and on the left side of the body.

1. Body faces net, with weight shifting from the right to the left foot at contact.
2. Right leg swings forward at completion of stroke.
3. The angle of the racquet at the time the shuttle is hit determines whether a clear, smash, or drop shot can be executed.
4. A cross-court smash is particularly effective with this stroke.

STRATEGY

Singles

1. Serve long unless opponent is playing back for just such a serve; in that case, serve short to take advantage of opponent's poor position.
2. Base use of long or short serve on opponent's strengths and weaknesses.
3. Return a high serve with a drop or clear shot.
4. Use an attacking clear or drive shot for a low serve; or if it can be reached before falling too far below the net, use a net shot.
5. Use down-the-line smashes or smash at opponent's right hip or shoulder.

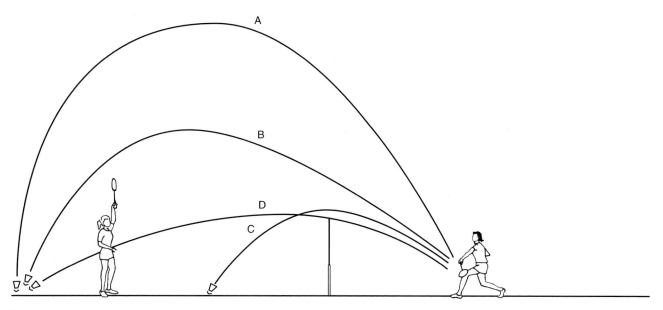

Figure 6.15. Trajectories for various underhand shots. A, Defensive clear. B, Attacking clear. C, Loop drop. D, Half-court drive.

6. Return a smash with a drop to the point on the court farthest from the point at which the smash was made.
7. Drive down the sidelines.
8. Play your position; do not try to outguess your opponent.
9. Take advantage of your opponent's weaknesses, but not to the extent that such repeated effort rectifies the weakness.
10. Alternate shots deep in court with drop shots to make the opponent run farther to return the shuttle. Once your opponent is out of position, hit a smash to win the point.
11. Most cross-court shots should be returned with a straight-ahead shot. This is a safe shot that forces your opponent to run cross-court to retrieve the return.
12. Hit risky shots when you are serving so you don't lose a point if it doesn't work. Play your most consistent shots when your opponent serves so you don't give any free points away.

Doubles
1. Play formations:
   a Side by side: Each person is responsible for half the court, from front to back. Disadvantages are that it is hard to run from the net to the back court and make a good smash or a good attacking shot, and returns to the center cause confusion as to who will hit them. This is the best defensive position.
   b. Front and back: One person plays the front court and one the back, with the front player taking all net shots and any other shot that can be returned with a better shot than the partner can deliver. Although this is a popular formation for doubles, a disadvantage is the resulting poor defense against smashes and drives down the sidelines. This is the best attacking formation.
   c. Combination: This formation combines the best features of the other two. The partners rotate in a counterclockwise circle, so that the backcourt player need never return for a backhand shot in the near court. When the team using this formation is on the attack, the players should be playing front and back; when on defense, they should be playing side by side.
2. Play shots that will give an opening for your partner on his or her return. Do not hit short clears, which may leave your partner open to an attack from the opponents.
3. Serve low and short, preferably to the corner formed by the center line and short service line.
4. Smash long serves, but occasionally use a drop shot.
5. Rush forward to attack short serves.
6. Do not play too close to the net. A position just behind the short service line is best for playing the net.
7. If servers are playing in front-and-back formation, the best return of a low serve is a shot down the sidelines to about half court.
8. Almost all high, deep shots should be returned with smash shots directed between the center line and the opponent playing straight ahead in a side-by-side defense. When in the front and back attacking formation, this smashing strategy generally forces a return directed to the forecourt player, who can hit a winning shot.

CONDITIONING FOR BADMINTON

When badminton players are of equal skill, whether novice or advanced, fitness becomes an important factor in deciding the winner. To increase stamina, strength, and speed, the fitness training program for badminton players must consist of drills and play patterns that simulate actual play patterns used in competition.

Three general categories of fitness training programs based upon the demands of the sport should be followed:

1. *Traditional fitness training.* This involves wind sprints, running, rope skipping, circuit weight training, and calisthenics—some examples are listed below:
   a. Wind sprints: six sets of very high-intensity exercise; 10 seconds of exercise with 30-second recovery periods.
   b. Running: six to eight sets of relatively high-intensity exercise; 30 seconds of exercise with 60-second recovery.
   c. One set of continuous aerobic exercise (run/cycle/jump rope); 10 to 60 minutes at 120 skips/minute.
   d. Weight training or circuit weight training: These are exercises using various machines (e.g., Universal Gym, Nautilus) or free weights to work trunk, lower-body, and upper-body major muscle groups. Badminton players should emphasize toe raises, leg flexion and extension, trunk flexion and extension, triceps extension, forearm, wrist, and shoulder exercises.
2. *Shadow drills.* Shadow drills are running and jumping exercises designed to simulate play patterns and improve balance, footwork, and court speed as well as fitness. For maximum benefit, the player should carry a badminton racket and simulate the execution of a badminton shot at each court position. Shadow drills can be set patterns or can be directed by the instructor and use the same time periods as wind sprints (10-second drill/30-second rest; 30-second drill/60-second rest; 1- to 3-minute drill/2- to 3-minute rest). The instructor uses hand signals to direct the player about the court at the fastest rate at which the player can maintain good balance.
3. *Pressure training.* These are continuous high-intensity badminton playing drills that require the player to move to all areas of the court, either in set patterns or in variation, to return a shuttle hit by the instructor or other players. Pressure training fitness programs become more effective as the player's skill increases to a level where long rallies can be played without making an error.

WARMING UP AND COOLING DOWN FOR BADMINTON

Warm-up for badminton consists of low-intensity exercise with gradually increasing activity over a period of 3 to 5 minutes until the player begins to sweat. Stretching exercises can be introduced at this time to increase or maintain player flexibility. The player can then do calisthenics, lunges, jumps, and racquet swinging exercises. These activities can be done off the court. Once the player moves onto the court, the warm-up consists of skill activities in which the player hits a variety of clears, drops, and smashes with power and accuracy.

Stretching exercises are recommended following a hard workout or competition to maintain or improve flexibility and/or prevent muscle soreness. Stretching exercises can *also* be done as the last portion of the warm-up if the player has low flexibility or is recovering from an injury. One to three sets of static stretching (no bobbing) of 20- to 30-seconds' duration are recommended.

BADMINTON ETIQUETTE

When playing badminton it is important that the players know and behave in accordance with certain rules and behaviors. This is especially important in badminton because few matches are overseen by linesmen and umpires. Below is a list of expected rules of etiquette:

1. "Calling the lines": Most of the time players call their own lines to determine whether a shuttle lands "in" or "out" of court on their side of the net. If a player is uncertain a "let" could be called and the point played over. Generally, if you are uncertain the player should award the point "in." If the shuttle lands on a line it is "in." Lines should be called honestly, quickly, and accurately.
2. When you are serving, call out the score and make sure your opponent is ready to receive serve.
3. Make sure your serve is legal.
4. If your opponent is serving and the shuttle is on your side of the net at the end of a rally, return the shuttle directly to your opponent.
5. Players should not cause any undue delays in continuous play.
6. During warm-up, hit the shuttle to your opponent so you both get warmed up.
7. Do not use abusive language or throw your racket.
8. Avoid interrupting or distracting other matches in progress.
9. Learn the rules well and follow them on and off the court.
10. Shake hands with the opponent(s) before and after each match.

TEACHING CONSIDERATIONS

1. For school-age populations, establish the grip and ready position as well as a basic underhand and overhead shot. It is not necessary to teach specialized shots until students can keep the shuttlecock going continuously across the net cooperatively with these basic shots.
2. Design warm-up activities that include combinations of skills using both forehand and backhand strokes.

3. Begin with singles, even if it means using half a court for practice.
4. Design experiences to have students change the placement, force levels, and trajectory of the shuttlecock from these basic shots. For example:
   a. Move your opponent from the net to the back line (up-and-back strategy using drop shots and clears).
   b. Tape four 3-foot by 3-foot squares in each of the back corners of the court. Have students practice getting the shuttlecock inside the squares or give each student an extra point if the shuttlecock lands inside the square during game play.
5. Teach the low, short and high, deep serves.
6. After minimal amounts of practice of a skill in basic conditions, put that skill back in the context of game play. Students can perform many badminton shots efficiently and effectively without having to execute the shot using correct form. Correct form allows the shot to be disguised in a game (for example, drop shot and smash).
7. Introduce competitive play and stress placement of shuttlecock away from opponent. Introduce the clear and drop shots as students attempt to place the shuttlecock in front of the service line and near the back boundary. Practice the specialized skills and put them back into the game. Modify the games, if need be, by giving extra points for points won using one of these shots.
8. Begin doubles play with side-by-side strategies. Introduce combination up-and-back and side-by-side as soon as students are consistently returning to their home base position after being pulled out of position defensively.

ROAD TO THE OLYMPIC TEAM

The WBF (Badminton World Federation) sets all guidelines [National Ranking, World Ranking (about top 45 in ranking), player development program, etc.] that have to be met to be considered for the Olympic team.

Requirements:

U.S. Citizen
World Ranking—in top 45 in world singles, doubles, and/or mixed doubles
Financial—can raise travel expenses
World Grand Prix playing record: The year before the Olympics the player must play in 8 of 10 Grand Prix tournaments, which are evaluated by player record on the following basis:

Class	Pay-off
1 Star	$ 15,000
2 Star	35,000
3 Star	60,000
4 Star	90,000
5 Star	125,000
6 Star	165,000+

Players who wish to try out for the Thomas, Uber, or Sudirman Cups or for any sanctioned event must be sanctioned by the USBA, IBF or WBF.

GLOSSARY

alley The 1.5-foot wide area on the sides of the court between the singles and doubles sidelines.

around-the-head A stroke hit from the backhand side of the body with a forehand stroking pattern.

backhand Strokes hit on the side of the body opposite to the racquet hand (left side of the body for right-handed players).

base Ready position to which players try to return after each shot.

bird Slang term for a shuttlecock or shuttle. The object hit back and forth over the net.

carry (sling, throw) A shot in which the shuttle slides across the face of the racquet and is misdirected from the intended shot. Since 1981, this shot is legal if hit unintentionally.

clear (lob) A shot hit high and deep to the opponent's backcourt.

combination doubles formation Partners play side-by-side on defense and up-and-back on offense.

cross-court A shot hit diagonally from one side of the court to the other.

defense A situation in which your opponent has the opportunity to hit a smash at you.

doubles A game played with two players on each side.

drive A sidearm stroke hit so as to land between the opponent's short service line and the back boundary line.

drop shot A shot hit from any position that passes close to the net and lands in the opponent's front court (in front of the short service line).

even court The side of the court corresponding to the right service court.

fault A violation of the rules.

forehand Strokes hit on the racquet side of the body.

game A badminton game is played to 15 points in all events except women's singles, which is played to 11 points, unless the game has been set.

grip (a) The covering of the racquet handle, usually leather. (b) The positioning of the hand in holding the racquet handle.

half-court shot A shot hit down the sideline that lands in the opponent's court midway between net and back baseline.

IBF (International Badminton Federation) Governing body for international competition.

kill (put-away, winner) A smash hit to win the rally.

let An incident that requires the replay of a rally.

long serve A high serve directed toward the receiver's back baseline.

match The best two out of three games.

mixed doubles A game contested with a male and female on each team.

net shot A shot played to the opponent's forecourt, dropping close to the net.

odd court The side of the court corresponding with the left service court.

offense A player or team on the attack or with the opportunity to smash.

overhead Strokes hit above head height.

power shots Shots that are hit very hard; clears, drives, and smashes.

racquet The implement used to strike the shuttle.

rally The exchange of shots during play or during warm-up.

receiver The player who receives the service.

server The player who hits the serve.

service The act of putting the shuttle in play to begin a rally.

service court The singles or doubles court boundary into which the service must be delivered.

setting A method of extending the game when tied near the end of the game.

short serve A serve hit just over the net to land near the short service line. The primary serve in doubles.

shot A clear, drive, drop, or smash that has been hit from one of the stroking positions.

shuttlecock (shuttle, bird) The object hit back and forth over the net.

side-by-side formation A doubles defensive formation in which the players play side-by-side in the midcourt.

smash A hard overhand shot hit with a downward angle.

strokes The basic hitting patterns from which all shots are executed.

T Court Area near the intersection of the short service line and the center line.

Thomas Cup An international men's team competition held every 2 years.

toss Before a match begins, players "toss" a coin, spin a racquet, or hit a shuttle to determine who will serve and defend court end.

Uber Cup An international women's team competition held every 2 years.

underhand A stroke in which the shuttle is contacted below the waist and in front of the body.

up-and-back formation A doubles formation providing the best attack positioning. Classic mixed-doubles positioning with the women in the forecourt and the men in the backcourt.

USA badminton The national governing body for badminton in the United States (formerly Badminton USA).

winner (see *kill, put-away***)**

SUGGESTED READINGS

Grice, T. 2008. *Badminton: Steps to success.* 2nd ed. Champaign, IL: Human Kinetics.

Grice, T. 2009. *Badminton.* 6th ed. Boston, MA: American Press.

Johnson, D., Rong Rong, L., and Johnson, M. 2000. *Badminton.* Boston, MA: American Press.

Kim, S., and Walker, M. 2002. *Badminton today.* 2nd ed. Stamford, CT: Wadsworth/Thomson Learning.

Paup, D., and Fernhall, B. 2000. *Badminton.* Scottsdale, AZ: Holcomb Hathaway Publishers. Comprehensive sequential illustrations of most important shots, stroking error analysis, solutions and drills, sport psychology, and advanced strategy and drills.

Schoppe, D. 2003. *Badminton for physical education and beyond.* Winston-Salem, NC: Hunter Textbooks. Cues, teaching progressions, and skills for the player, coach, or teacher in an easy-to-read format.

Song, C., and Li, M. 1999. *Badminton everyone.* Winston-Salem, NC: Hunter Textbooks.

U.S. Badminton Association. *Official rules of play (USBA handbook).* Current edition. USBA, One Olympic Plaza, Colorado Springs, CO 80909.

RESOURCES

Videos

Badminton Instructional Videotapes. 817 23rd St., NW, Washington, D.C. 20052. Offers guidance on (1) grip, footwork, serves; (2) basic strokes; (3) basic strategy.

Badminton Movies. Louisville Badminton Supply, 9411 Westport Road, Louisville, KY 40222.

Badminton: Winning Fundamentals. HL Corporation, P.O. Box 3327, Manhattan Beach, CA 90266.

Breen, J., and Paup, D. *Winning Badminton,* West Palm Beach, FL. The Athletic Institute.

USBA Video Library (rental of videocassettes of national and international events, weight training, International Badminton Federation instructional videos). USA Badminton, One Olympic Plaza, Colorado Springs, CO 80909. (719) 578-4808, Fax. (719) 578-4507. E-mail: usab2004@rmi.net. USBA home page: http://mid1.external.hp.comm/stanb/usba/usba.html.

See Appendix C for other video sources.

Magazines

Badminton USA. USA Badminton, One Olympic Plaza, Colorado Springs, CO 80909.

World Badminton. The International Badminton Federation, 4 Manor Park, Mackenzie Way, Cheltenham, Gloucestershire, England GL51 9TX.

Basketball

After completing this chapter, the reader should be able to:

- Tell the history of the game of basketball
- Explain the basic rules of the game and the slight differences that exist between the men's and women's game
- Demonstrate the fundamental skills of passing, dribbling, and shooting
- Explain the general principles of offensive and defensive strategy
- Instruct a group of students in the basic skills of basketball

HISTORY

Basketball was introduced in 1891 by Dr. James A. Naismith, then physical education director at the YMCA College in Springfield, Massachusetts. The first official game was not played until 1892. Basketball was principally designed as a game to create interest in the gymnasium during the winter months.

A peach basket was first used as the hoop. After each score, the ball had to be taken out of the basket before play could be resumed. After a basket was scored, play was restarted with a jump ball at center court. It was not until many years later that the team scored against got the ball out of bounds under its own basket.

The game spread rapidly to the nation's playgrounds, community centers, gymnasiums, schools, and colleges. Today nearly every boy and girl learns to play basketball.

In 1899 women formulated their own rules, and in 1901 the first women's *Basketball Guide* was published.

Men's Olympic Basketball History

Although basketball was included as a demonstration sport in the 1904 St. Louis Olympic Games, it was not finally adopted until 1936. The United States defeated Canada (19 to 8) for the gold medal in the 1936 Berlin Games, but the game was played outdoors on a clay court in the rain. The United States dominated Olympic basketball by winning the gold medal in 1948 (65 to 21 over France), 1952 (36 to 25 over U.S.S.R.), 1956 (85 to 55 over U.S.S.R.), 1960 (81 to 57 over U.S.S.R.), 1964 (73 to 59 over U.S.S.R.), and 1968 (65 to 50 over Yugoslavia). The United States lost for the first time in Olympic history in the famous final game of the 1972 Munich Olympics when the Soviet team, after protesting, was awarded the chance to replay the final 3 seconds of the game and won 50 to 49. In 1976 the United States regained the gold medal by defeating Yugoslavia 95 to 72. Yugoslavia defeated Italy 86 to 77 in 1980, the year the United States boycotted the Moscow Olympics. In Los Angeles (1984) the

U.S. team once again claimed the gold medal by defeating Spain 96 to 65. In the 1988 Seoul Olympics the U.S. men's team had its worst finish ever by claiming the bronze medal.

To compensate for their third-place finish in 1988, the U.S. men's team elected to allow professional players from the National Basketball Association to try out for the Olympic team. This team, known as the "Dream Team," was composed of 11 professional players and 1 collegiate player. The American team defeated Croatia 117 to 85 to win the gold medal in the Barcelona Olympics in 1992. In the 1996 Summer Olympics, held in Atlanta, Georgia, the U.S. men's team, known as "Dream Team 2," composed of NBA players, easily won the gold medal by defeating Yugoslavia, 95 to 69. Yugoslavia and Lithuania won the silver and bronze, respectively. At the 2000 Summer Olympics in Sydney, Australia, the United States defeated France for the gold medal and Lithuania won the bronze. In the 2004 Olympic Games, held in Athens, Greece, Argentina defeated Italy for the gold medal. The United States won the bronze medal. The American team of all professional players failed to claim the gold medal for the first time since professional players had been permitted to compete in the Olympics. At the 2008 Beijing Olympics, the United States captured the gold medal by defeating Spain. Argentina won the bronze medal.

Women's Olympic Basketball History

Women's basketball was added to the Olympics in 1976, and the gold medal was claimed by the Soviets, with the U.S. team picking up the silver medal. In 1980 the Soviet women defeated Bulgaria 104 to 73. The U.S. women's team won its first gold medal by defeating South Korea 85 to 55 in 1984 and its second straight gold medal with a victory over Yugoslavia in 1988. Following the 1988 Olympics, USA Basketball voted to allow women professional players to play in international competition, including the World Games and the Olympics. In the 1992 Olympics in Barcelona, Spain, the U.S. women's team defeated Cuba 88 to 74 for the bronze medal.

In the Atlanta Olympic Games, the U.S. women's team captured the gold medal by defeating Brazil, 111 to 87. Brazil won the silver and Australia the bronze. In Sydney, Australia, at the 2000 Summer Olympics, the U.S. women won the gold medal by defeating Australia, 76 to 54. Australia took the silver and Brazil the bronze medal, respectively. The United States team in 2004 defeated Australia for the gold medal, and Russia claimed the bronze medal. History repeated itself at the 2008 Beijing Olympics with the United States defeating Australia for the gold medal and Russia winning the bronze medal.

The game of basketball has flourished at all levels of competition, including youth, high school, college, and professional. The number of girls and young women participating in these leagues has increased dramatically. In the summer and fall of 1997, two new professional leagues for women emerged, the Women's National Basketball Association (WNBA) and the American Basketball League (ABL). After one season, the ABL folded, leaving the WNBA as the primary professional league for women. The number of spectators attending these games indicates that women's professional basketball in the United States may have been finally accepted on a permanent basis.

COURT AND EQUIPMENT

The playing court is a rectangular surface free from obstructions, having maximum dimensions for college of 94 × 50 feet (28.65 × 15.24 m) and for high school of 84 × 50 feet (25.60 × 15.24 m) (Figure 7.1). However, many courts are smaller. The court dimensions are the same for men's and women's basketball.

The backboard, 6 feet (1.83 m) wide and 4 feet (1.22 m) high (smaller for high school), is located at the center of each end of the court, 4 feet (1.22 m) in from the end line and 9 feet (2.74 m) above the floor. It can be made of hardwood, metal, or glass (Figure 7.2).

The basket is an open hammock net, suspended from the backboard on a metal ring 18 inches (45.7 cm) in diameter, which must be 6 inches (15.2 cm) from the rigid surface to which it is fastened and 10 feet (3.05 m) above the floor.

The ball is spherical, and the one used by men measures 30 inches (76.2 cm) in circumference. The ball used by women is 28.5 to 29.0 inches (72.4 to 73.7 cm) in circumference.

Foot comfort and protection should be a primary concern of both coach and player. Shoes and socks that fit well and that are designed for use by basketball players help avoid unnecessary injuries and discomfort, including blisters, sprained ankles, and bruised heels.

GENERAL RULES

Rules governing the game are revised each year by the joint Basketball Rules Committee, representing the Amateur Athletic Union (AAU), National Association for Girls and Women in Sport (NAGWS), National Collegiate Athletic Association (NCAA), Young Men's Christian Association (YMCA), National Federation of State High School Associations (NFSHSA), Canadian Amateur Basketball Association, USA Basketball, and chartered boards of officials.

The Game

The home team provides the game ball, and traditionally the visiting team is given the choice of end of court for the first half. If a neutral court is used, a coin toss determines home team and choice of ends. The teams change sides of the court at halftime. Half of the court is the frontcourt of one team and the backcourt of the other team.

The ball is passed, thrown, bounced, handed, or otherwise moved among players of one team, with the intent of scoring a basket and preventing the other team from scoring.

Teams consist of five players: two forwards, two guards, and one center. Generally the forwards play closest to the basket, the guards play farthest from their team's basket, and the center plays between the forwards and the guards. In basketball played at all levels, new terminology is replacing the traditional names of the positions played by the players. The players are now recognized by their position numbers. The number one position is typically the point guard. This player is responsible for bringing the ball down the court and setting up the offensive pattern. The number two position is referred to as the shooting guard. This player is an excellent ball handler and is expected to be more of a scorer than the point guard. If a team is utilizing a three guard offense, then the player in the number three position is the big guard. This player is capable of slashing to the basket and drawing fouls from the defense. If a team is utilizing a two guard, two forward system, then the number three player in this system is called the small forward. This player's job is to get rebounds, and to be a really good scorer. The number four position is the power forward. This player is usually taller and stronger than the number three player. The major responsibility of the number four player is to get rebounds and score easy buckets around the basket. This player is sometimes referred to as the high-post player. Player position number five is the center. This is usually the tallest player on the team and is also referred to as the low-post player. The center is needed to get rebounds, score inside, and cause the opposing team to foul. All players should be good free-throw shooters.

The game is started with a jump ball between any two opponents (usually the centers) at center court. After each field goal, the ball is put into play by the team not scoring, from the out-of-bounds area behind the basket at which the score was made.

After a free throw awarded because of a personal foul, the ball is put into play by the opponent from behind the opponent's basket. If the free throw is the result of a technical foul, the ball is put into play from out of bounds at midcourt by the free thrower's team.

A player is out-of-bounds if he or she touches the floor on or outside the boundary line. If a player causes the ball

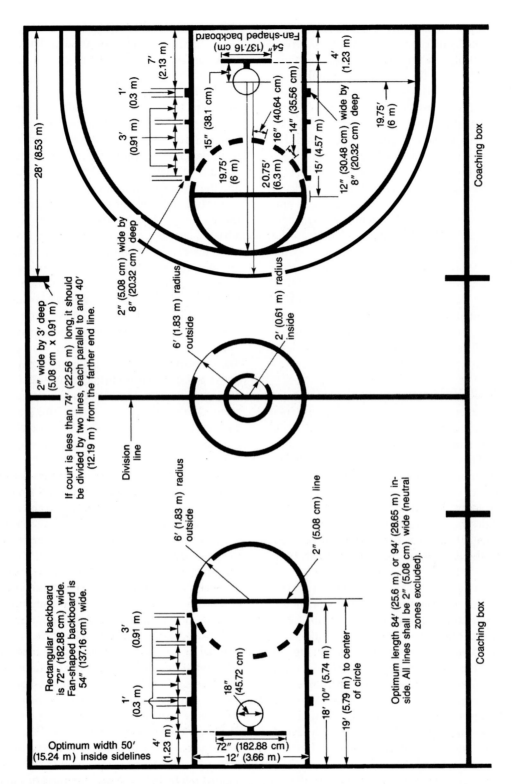

Figure 7.1. Basketball court for men and women. Left end shows large backboard for college games; right end shows small backboard for high school games. For the broken semicircle in the free throw lane, it is recommended that there be eight marks 16 inches (40.64 cm) long and seven spaces 14 inches (35.56 cm) long. There should be a minimum of 3 feet (0.91 m) and preferably 10 feet (3.05 m) of unobstructed space outside the court. If this is impossible, a narrow broken 1-inch (2.54 cm) line should be marked inside the court parallel with and 3 feet (0.91 m) inside the boundary. The three-point line is 19.75 feet (6 m) from the basket for high school courts. For the start of the 2008–2009 basketball season, the three-point shot line for college men was moved from 19 feet 9 inches (6.0 m) to 20 feet 9 inches (6.3 m). The three-point line for college women remained at 19 feet 9 inches (6.0 m). Most college basketball courts now have two, three-point lines of contrasting colors. The three-point line is an arc drawn from the center of the rim.

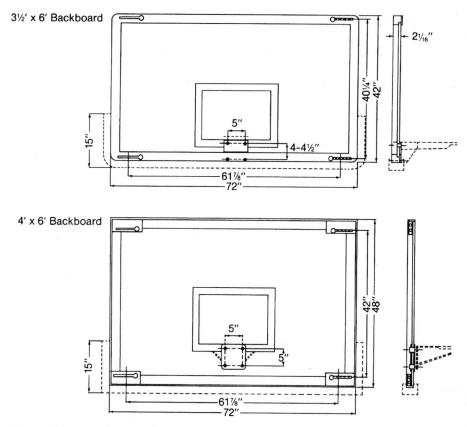

Figure 7.2. Basketball goals.

to pass over the boundary line, the ball is put into play by an opposing player from that spot. Any player can make the throw-in. The player throwing the ball in must stand out-of-bounds where the referee designates, may take one lateral step to the left or right, jump up or take two or more steps backward, and may use either one or two hands to make the throw-in, which must be completed within 5 seconds.

Rules Common to Men's and Women's Basketball

1. Numbers must be worn by players on front and back.
2. A jump ball is taken following a double foul.
3. The hand is considered to be a part of the ball on tie balls, shots, dribbles, interceptions, and the like.
4. The penalty for a violation is loss of possession of the ball.
5. The following are not considered dribbles:
   a. Successive tries for goals
   b. Fumbles
   c. Attempts to gain control of the ball by:
      (1) Tapping it from the control of another player
      (2) Tapping it from the reach of another player
      (3) Blocking a pass and recovering the ball
      (4) Blocking a shot and recovering the ball
6. The number of players permitted on the free throw lane is six. The opponents of the free thrower shall occupy the inside lane spaces; teammates of the free thrower may occupy the second spaces.

7. On jump balls, opponents are entitled to alternate positions around the restraining circle if they so indicate before the official is ready to toss the ball.
8. On jump balls, the players must hold their established positions around the restraining circle until the ball has been tossed.
9. After the opening jump ball to start the game, any jump ball situation results in the teams' alternating possession of the ball. The team losing the opening jump ball is awarded the first possession, with teams alternating possessions for the rest of the game.
10. The game clock is stopped after successful field goals in the last minute of the game and the last minute of any overtime period, with no substitutions allowed during this stoppage.

Rule Differences

It must be pointed out that there are basic differences between high school and college rules and regulations. At the high school level, for example, there is no shot clock used.

Two important differences in the rules for college men's and women's basketball are:

1. Use of a 30-second shot clock in women's basketball and a 35-second clock in men's basketball. After securing possession of the ball, the offensive team must attempt a shot at the basket that hits the rim before the time clock goes to zero or give up possession of the ball.

2. In men's basketball, the ball must be advanced into the frontcourt within 10 seconds, but in women's basketball (with the shorter, 30-second clock) there is no such rule.

Violations Common to Men's and Women's Basketball

1. Taking more than one step with the ball without passing, shooting, or dribbling
2. Kicking the ball with the foot or lower leg
3. Stepping out of bounds with the ball
4. The center's leaving the circle before the ball is tipped in beginning play
5. Staying in one's own free-throw lane for more than 3 seconds
6. Failure to observe free-throw regulations
7. Failure to inbound the ball within 5 seconds
8. Double dribbling
9. Moving the ball into the backcourt once it has been advanced to the frontcourt (over-and-back)
10. Technical fouls include:
    a. Taking time out too often
    b. Failure of substitutes to report to proper officials
    c. Unsportsmanlike conduct
    d. Use of illegal numbers or uniforms
    e. Touching the backboard or rim illegally
11. Personal fouls include:
    a. Charging
    b. Blocking
    c. Pushing
    d. Holding
    e. Tripping
    f. Hacking or kneeing

When a violation is committed, the ball is given to the opponents out-of-bounds. When a foul is committed, the opponents may be given a free throw, an opportunity to make two free throws if the first one is made, or the ball out-of-bounds. The decision as to which of these options is awarded depends on the particular foul committed, the level of play (high school or college), and the number of fouls that the offending team has previously committed. At the collegiate level, the opportunity to shoot the one-and-one (bonus) goes into effect following the sixth team foul on the opposing team. Following the tenth team foul on the opposing team, players shoot two free throws. A player fouled in the act of shooting gets two free throws. If the basket is made, one free throw is awarded and the basket is counted. Only personal fouls disqualify a player. A player is allowed only four personal fouls; a fifth sidelines the player for the remainder of the game.

Officials

At lower levels of play (sub-varsity), the officials include a referee and an umpire. At the college level, there are three timekeepers and two scorers (one timekeeper and one scorer are assistants). The third timekeeper runs the 30- or 35-second shot clock. At the men's college division 1A level, there are three officials utilized to referee the game. There is a referee and two umpires. At the collegiate level, the three referees wear a miniature microphone attached to their whistle, which sends a signal to the timing system to automatically turn off the game clock when their whistle sounds. This was implemented to prevent loud crowd noises from interfering with the timers' hearing the whistle and then stopping the clock manually. The game officials now start the clock with their precision timing devices as well. Because of the speed of the players and the complexity of the offenses and defenses, many high school state associations have adopted the three-officials system.

Scoring

Two points are awarded for each basket from the floor, and one point is awarded for each free throw. Three points are awarded for field goals made from outside the three-point line.

Coaching Box

A coaching box is outlined outside the side of the court on which the officials' table and players' benches are located. The area is bounded by the endline extended, the sideline, the midcourt marker extended, and the players' bench. The endline and midcourt mark lines are 3 feet (0.9 m) long and 2 inches (5 cm) wide, and their color contrasts with that of the midcourt mark line and endline.

DURATION OF GAME

College men and women play for two halves of 20 minutes each, with a 15-minute rest at halftime. If the score is tied at the end of the game, as many 5-minute periods as needed to break the tie are played.

High school teams play four quarters of 8 minutes each, with a 10-minute halftime rest and 1 minute between quarters. If the score is tied at the end of the fourth quarter, as many 3-minute periods as needed to break the tie are played.

FUNDAMENTAL SKILLS AND TECHNIQUES

Passing

Passing is the key to successful basketball. A team must be able to handle, control, and move the ball downcourt quickly and accurately to create scoring opportunities.

First, learn to catch as well as pass. When the ball is thrown to you, spread your fingers but keep them relaxed. When the ball hits your fingers, let your arms give slightly toward the body. When the ball is under control, finger it into passing position by placing your hands on each side of the ball so that you can get it away quickly or get set for a shot.

Some practical hints

1. Remember that the cause of most fumbling is holding the arms too stiffly while catching.
2. Watch the ball all the way into your hands.
3. Do not fight the ball; that is, do not pass until you have full control of the ball.

4. Stay relaxed, and try not to rush passes.
5. Keep your head up, and use peripheral vision to spot any free teammate.
6. When a teammate calls for the ball, check the position of the defender before making a pass, and make the pass to the side farthest from the defender.
7. Move toward a pass rather than away from it.
8. Passes to moving teammates should lead them so they do not have to slow down or reverse direction.
9. When some mastery in controlling the ball has been gained, learn to pass with deception—for example, looking one way and passing another or faking high and passing low.
10. Rely on "split vision," actually looking straight ahead but seeing the receiver out of the corner of your eye.
11. Do not pass blindly.

Chest or push pass

Hold the ball with both hands, elbows close to the body, fingers spread with thumbs pointed inward. Step toward the receiver and whip the ball with a strong wrist snap and push of thumbs and fingers, making the arms follow through in the direction of the pass (Figure 7.3).

Flip pass

A pass that can be used when there is to be a close exchange of the ball is a flip pass. This pass is executed by flipping or almost handing the ball to a teammate when the defense is applying heavy pressure. The person making the pass should try to position the body between the defensive player and the teammate to whom the pass is being made. To allow the other player the best chance to catch the ball, it should be flipped up softly. This passing technique is very effective in getting the ball to a teammate who is driving to the basket off a screen set by another player.

Bounce pass

A bounce pass can be executed with either one or two hands and is often used to get the ball past a defensive player between the passer and the teammate who is to receive the pass. For the two-handed bounce pass, hold the ball in much the same manner as for the chest pass except somewhat lower, about waist high. Then push the ball out and down with enough force and at such an angle that the ball bounces to the teammate. The one-hand bounce pass is often executed directly from the dribble. The bounce pass should only be used for short passes, and it should travel between one half and three quarters of the distance in the air.

Two-hand overhead pass

Hold and throw the ball with both hands. Bring the ball well above and slightly behind the head with both hands and release it with a strong wrist snap and extension of the arms. Arms and hands follow through in the direction of the pass (Figure 7.4).

Off-the-dribble pass

This pass can be used by players who have mastered the dribble. In this pass, the player will see the open teammate and, without stopping to pick the ball up, make a pass with the dribbling hand. This pass gets the ball to the open player before the defense can react, and it is very effective in fast-break situations.

Baseball pass

Shift the ball in front of the waist to the throwing hand, turn the opposite side of the body in the direction of the pass, and then whip the ball back, as in an infield throw. Step toward the receiver and throw the ball with a full arm motion and wrist snap. Permit the fingers to follow through without a twist so that the movement does not cause the ball to curve (Figure 7.5).

Figure 7.3. Chest pass.

Figure 7.4. Two-hand overhead pass. A, Midway; B, End.

Figure 7.5. Baseball pass.

One-hand hook pass

With the opposite side turned in the direction of the receiver, bring the ball from the hips, up and back. Cradle the ball on the wrist with the fingers well spread behind it for control, and throw it with a hook motion of the arm and strong wrist action over the head, following through with the hand (Figure 7.6).

Pivoting

Pivoting is a skill used to elude an opponent when a player has the ball. A forward pivot is executed by keeping one foot in place on the floor and moving the other forward and across the foot in place (Figure 7.7). A reverse pivot is executed by keeping one foot in place and moving the other backward in a semicircle.

Figure 7.6. One-hand hook pass.

Figure 7.7. Pivot and pass.

Dribbling

Learn to dribble with the body low for protection and the head up. Dribble with the hand farthest from the defender, and use the body to protect the ball. Spread the fingers and relax the wrist and fingers. Control the ball with the fingers, pushing it down and forward; do not bat it.

Keep the ball low, below the waist. Avoid a high-bounce dribble. The ball can be moved downcourt faster by passing than by dribbling, so never dribble when you can pass.

Up-and-under fake pass and dribble

Stand for the shot in front of the opponent and go through the motion of bringing the ball up for a jump shot. As the guard closes in or leaps to block the shot, duck low and drive past to one side, dribbling with the hand farthest from the opponent.

Fake pass and dribble

Hold the ball waist high on receiving it; then fake to the right with the ball and head. As the guard goes in that direction, turn quickly to the left and cross-step with the right foot and dribble the ball on the left side with the left hand, which is farthest from the guard (Figure 7.8).

Shooting

Basic mechanics of shooting

Shooting is a fundamental, learned skill. To become a good shooter, a player should know the basic mechanics of the shot and become aware of the common shooting faults. The following shooting methods can be practiced by looking into a mirror. Do not be afraid to look at the wrist action and follow through until a natural release can be attained. This is the reason it is wise to shoot off a wall or backboard; striving for accuracy should not be the primary objective until the smooth release has been learned.

Before becoming involved in the mechanics of shooting, the player should have a fundamental knowledge of the basket and the point at which to aim. Good shooters do not follow the flight of the ball with their eyes; they concentrate on the basket during the entire shooting process. Coaches and teachers vary in their opinions on what part of the basket the shooter should look at. Some believe the front of the rim should be the focal point, while others suggest focusing on the back of the rim. In selecting either method, it might be wise to analyze the ball-basket relationship.

Although it often doesn't seem to be the case, a basketball has a considerable clearance through a basket (see Figure 7.9). This suggests that looking at the approximate center of the basket would be the best because you can compensate for your margin of error in the following manner: If the shot is short, the ball can still be put in by aiming for the center. If the shot is slightly long, the ball can be put in by glancing off the back lip of the rim. If long by a large margin, the player can put the ball in off the backboard (Figure 7.10).

Figure 7.8. Fake right.

Front view of shooting positions (Figure 7.11). *A,* The ball should be rolled off the fingertips with a backspin effect. The backspin will cause the ball to become dead upon impact with the rim. *B,* The wrist should be cocked with the ball resting on the fingers and not touching the inside palm of the hand. *C,* The elbow should be on line to the target area. A slight lateral shift of the elbow, if comfortable, should be permitted for some shooters. *D,* The opposite hand should be

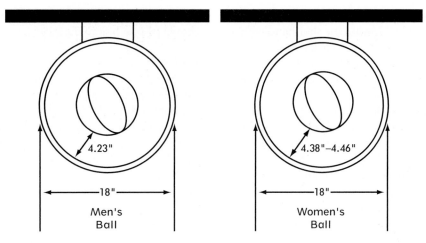

Figure 7.9. Basket size.

Figure 7.10. Aiming the shot.

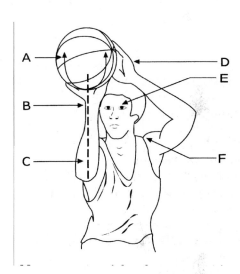

Figure 7.11 Front view of the shooting positions. See text for details.

placed on the ball in a position that is comfortable. However, this hand should not interfere with the shooting motion. *E,* The eyes should be focused on the basket. Watch for the common fault of following the ball. *F,* The shoulders should be squared off to the basket.

Shot from the side (Figure 7.12). *A,* The edge of the ball should be approximately in line with the shooting elbow. *B,* The off-hand should be placed on the ball in a position that is comfortable to the shooter, but it should not interfere with the shot motion. *C,* The ball should rest on the fingertips. *D,* The eyes should be focused on the basket during all phases of the shot, especially the release. *E,* The shoulders should be squared away with the basket.

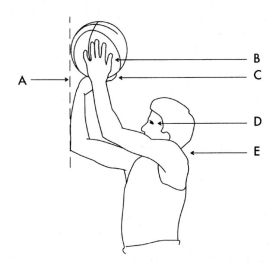

Figure 7.12. Shot from the side. See text for details.

View of shot from behind shooter (Figure 7.13). *A,* The fingers should be spread, with the ball leaving the shot hand with a reverse spin. The ball should leave the area between the first and second fingers last to ensure the proper backspin. *B,* The spread of the thumb and first finger should be in the form of a V. *C,* The wrist should be cocked. *D,* The shooter's forearm should be in line with the basket. *E,* The ball should be released in a position over the shooting eye and on line with the target. The shot should be a natural motion without actually aiming the ball.

Release action (Figure 7.14). *A,* The ball should be rolled off the finger. *B,* The wrist should be coiled. *C,* The eyes should remain focused on the rim. *D,* The release should preferably be over the shooting eye so that concentration will not be broken, with the ball passing through the sight of the shooter. *E,* After the release, the follow-through should be emphasized. The shooter should think of reaching inside the rim with the shot hand on the follow-through. *F,* The elbow should be pointing to the basket.

Jump shot

The jump shot is the most common one in basketball. It is often executed from a dribble, but players should be able to accomplish it in almost any situation. Come to a stop from the dribble and execute a controlled jump. At the same time, bring the ball overhead, with the shooting hand behind and the elbow of the shooting arm under the ball and the other hand in front. At the peak of the leap, remove the balance hand and release the ball with extension of the shooting forearm and good wrist extension (Figure 7.15).

One-hand set shot

Hold the ball chin high with both hands, the fingers spread along the sides and slightly behind the ball, the thumbs directed inward behind the ball, and the feet close together with one slightly ahead of the other. Turn the ball so that the shooting hand is behind and under the ball. Bend the knees, bring the ball up, removing the left hand if shooting with the right, and shoot with a strong wrist action and extension of the arm, letting the feet come off the floor, and follow through. At the high school level, many players employ this shooting technique when attempting the longer three-point shot (Figure 7.16).

Layup shot

Stop dribbling when the right foot is on the floor, step with the left foot, bring up the right knee and jump off the left foot, leap high into the air, shifting the ball to the shooting hand, and raise the shooting hand as high as possible above and in front of the head. Release the ball off the fingertips, laying it softly against the backboard (Figure 7.17). *Note:* Use both hands to bring the ball up for the shot, and do not remove the balancing hand too soon.

Hook shot

Hold the ball high with both hands, bring the ball to the hand on the side away from the basket, and remove the other hand (left). Shoot with a full sweep of the right arm, keeping the arm perfectly straight. In starting the shot, take a short step with the foot away from the basket and take off on it. The ball is released farthest from the guard, making the shot difficult to block (Figure 7.18).

Defense

There are two principal types of defense: one-on-one and zone. In one-on-one defense, each player is responsible for one opponent. In zone defense, each player is responsible for a certain area, or zone.

One of the main reasons for using a zone defense is to tightly guard the opponent's free-throw-line area to prevent drives for easy layup shots. All players shift on defense as the

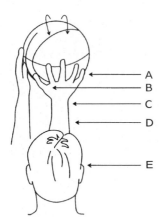

Figure 7.13. View of shot from behind the shooter. See text for details.

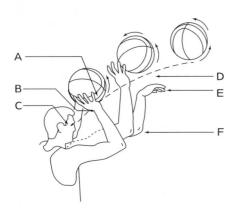

Figure 7.14. The release action. See text for details.

Figure 7.15. Jump shot.

Figure 7.16. One-hand set shot.

Figure 7.17. Layup shot.

Figure 7.18. Hook shot.

ball moves, to cut off passing lanes to the basket. It is considered strategically sound to use a zone defense when:

1. You are playing on a small floor.
2. Your team is in foul trouble.
3. You have an exceptional rebounder you want to keep near the opponent's basket.
4. The opponents have a height advantage.
5. The opponents have weak outside shooting.
6. The opponents have an exceptional player or two that your best defenders cannot handle one-on-one.

Stance

The feet should be in a forward stride position, knees and hips slightly bent, and the back straight. If the left arm is raised and the right arm extended to the side, the left foot should be forward. If the right arm is up, the right foot should be forward. From this position, one should be able to quickly move in any direction.

Role of defensive player

A defensive player should attempt to position the body between the opposing player and the player's own basket. If a pressing defense is being used, the defensive player should get into position so that one arm and hand are in the passing lane, between the ball and the player being guarded.

Objectives of defensive players

1. To harass the opponent by playing in close and moving arms in a distracting manner
2. To block the shot by staying with the ball as the opponent attempts to throw it (do not jump too soon)
3. If the opponent holds the ball unprotected, to tie up the ball by grabbing it

4. To knock an unprotected ball out of the opponent's hands
5. To steal a ball that is being dribbled
6. To deflect a ball that is being passed by an opponent to a teammate
7. To intercept a passed ball

Player-to-player and zone defenses

For students just learning the game of basketball, it is important to understand the differences between a player-to-player defense and a zone defense. In a player-to-player defense, each player is responsible for guarding an opposing player wherever he or she goes on the court. This is a very effective type of defense if the players are in excellent physical condition. Another advantage is that players can be matched up to guard an opposing player of the same approximate height, as well as the same position. For example, a guard versus guard, forward versus forward, and center versus center. When a team does not have a good matchup against the other team in terms of speed, height, rebounding skill, and shooting skills, it might be best to use a zone defense.

In a zone defense, each player is responsible for guarding a certain area of the court, rather than an opposing team player. The primary emphasis in a zone is on the ball, not the player. It does not matter where the opposing players move to; each defensive player covers a prescribed area of the court. Four popular zone defenses are the 2-1-2, 2-3, 1-3-1, and the 1-2-2. The defensive zone assignments for each of these configurations are shown in Figure 7.19.

A. *2-1-2 zone defense.* This is a zone defense that applies most of the defensive pressure in and around the free-throw line. It forces the offensive team to move the ball to the side positions for open shots at the basket.

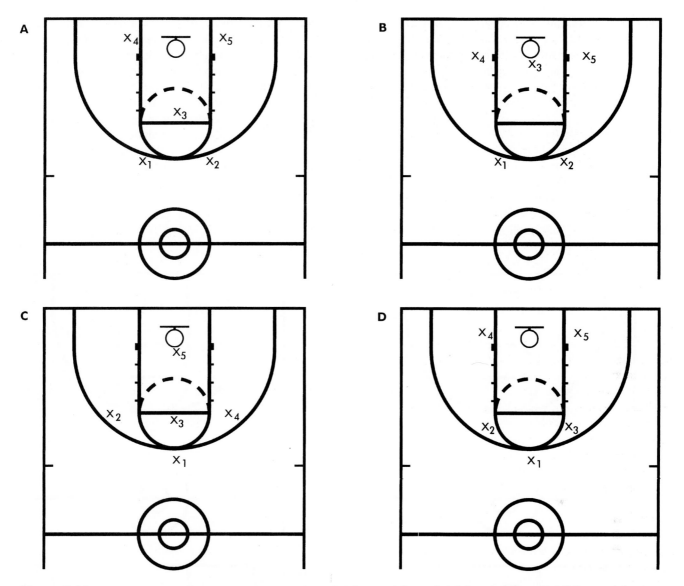

Figure 7.19. Basic defensive positions. A, 2-1-2 zone defense. B, 2-3 zone defense. C, 1-3-1 zone defense. D, 1-2-2 zone defense.

B. *2-3 zone defense.* This is a defense that puts three tall players around the basket, forcing the offense to take shots from farther out. If you do not have three tall players, select players who are above-average jumpers and rebounders.

C. *1-3-1 zone defense.* In this defensive setup, you are forcing the offensive team to play the ball over the top of the defense, hoping to force a bad pass, resulting in a turnover.

D. *1-2-2 zone defense.* A pressure-type defense that forces the opposing team to set up their offense farther out from the basket. You might need to utilize shorter, more active players to make this zone work.

Offense

Offensive tactics will vary with the defensive play patterns employed by an opposing team throughout a single game of basketball. One type of offensive tactic must be employed to meet a 2-1-2, 2-3, 1-3-1, or a 3-2 zone defense and another type to meet a player-to-player defense.

The most common method of offense against the zone defense is to use quick, sharp passing with the intent of penetrating the zone and forcing an opposing player out of an assigned position. Other tactics commonly used are mismatching (1-3-1 offense against a 2-1-2 defense) and overloading (putting an extra offensive player in a weakly defended area of the zone).

Basic maneuvers against the player-to-player defense are the give-and-go and the pick-and-roll. The intent is to screen a defensive player and then get the ball to the open offensive player. Spontaneous player-to-player offense, called *freelancing,* is quite common, but it is more common to use sets of plays.

Basic offensive formations

When determining the best offensive patterns to use, it is important to be aware of the abilities of the personnel on the team. Extensive details about complex offensive formations are beyond the scope of this text, but the top college teams in the United States use what is called a *motion offense.* This is an advanced and complicated system wherein players have the opportunity to freelance in the offensive area. However, there are some basic concepts that are important. As the players move about, they are constantly looking to screen for one of their teammates to allow an open shot or a drive to the basket. They always look for the easy pass and try to get the ball to a teammate who has a closer shot at the basket. This offensive system is built on a very strong team concept: All players contribute to the offensive attack. The scoring and the assists in this system will be distributed more evenly among the players than in the single- or double-post offenses, where one or two players are called on to do a majority of the scoring.

The alignments for four basic offensive formations are shown in Figure 7.20.

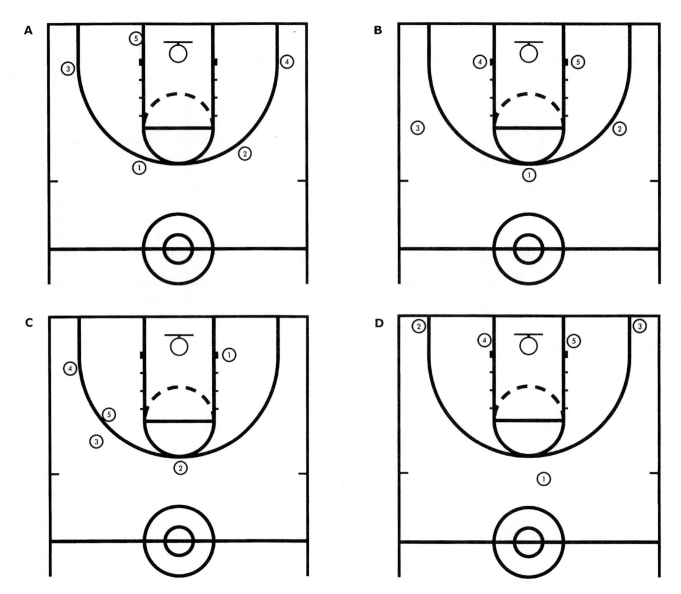

Figure 7.20. Basic offensive positions. A, Single-post offense. B, Double-post. C, Shuffle offense. D, Flex offense.

A. *Single-post offense.* This offense is designed for a team that has one tall center who can work around the basket area. This player should be a reasonably good shooter close to the basket.
B. *Double-post offense.* This setup is similar to the single post, except that you have two tall players to operate around the basket.
C. *Shuffle offense.* This offense relies on quick, accurate passes, with players passing in one direction, then moving in the opposite direction to set a screen for a teammate.
D. *Flex offense.* This type of offense spreads the defensive players out much more, allowing for many screens to create open shots.

TIPS TO REMEMBER

1. Dribble only when necessary to set up a shot or pass.
2. Move the ball by passing rather than dribbling. It is faster.
3. Practice being able to pass and catch the ball with no wasted motion. This is essential to an effective offense.
4. Improve your shooting percentage by developing a consistent shooting form and concentration.
5. Become proficient at layups and other short-range, high-percentage shots before working on more difficult shots.
6. Practice most often those shots you expect to get in games as a result of your team's offensive patterns.
7. Be aware of floor balance. Your team should always have one or more rebounders when a shot is taken and one player back on defense to prevent an easy fast-break basket by the opponents.
8. Make an extra effort to get the inside position on opponents at both ends of the court to improve your rebounding.
9. Learn to position yourself on defense so as not to lose sight of either the ball or the person being guarded.
10. Work on proper physical conditioning. It is as important to be able to get from one end of the court to the other and back again as it is to play good offense and defense.
11. Stay in condition year-round. Injuries result from inactivity followed by hard workouts with little or no adjustment period.
12. Remember that basketball is a team sport. The best individual players do not always make the best team players. Good team players develop an ability to help others play at their peak performance.

TEACHING CONSIDERATIONS

1. For younger learners, use smaller and lighter balls to develop basic skills.

2. Develop individual skills of dribbling for control of the object in simple conditions first (in one spot; moving forward, to the left, to the right, and backward; changing speed and level of dribble; stopping and starting; and dribbling to avoid others or objects).
3. Develop passing skills in a stationary position first, varying the level of pass. As soon as some degree of proficiency has been established, practice passing to a moving receiver, varying the distance and adding the pass on the move. Emphasize quick passes and the idea of the lead pass (passing the ball ahead of the moving receiver).
4. Combine dribbling and passing skills with an emphasis on a smooth transition from one skill to another (pass to a dribble and dribble to a pass). Add several players and emphasize cutting into a space to receive a pass in cooperative group work.
5. Teach basics of the foul shot, set shot, and layup. Combine the set shots and layup with combinations of dribble and pass as soon as basic proficiency in simple conditions has been established.
6. Begin offensive and defensive play with one-on-one situations. Teach students defensive positions to get the ball from a dribbler and offensive strategies to maintain possession.
7. Beginners should spend adequate time in two-on-two and three-on-three situations to learn about basketball as a "space" game. Offense must be able to create space and opportunities for passes, and defense must be able to close up space and passing opportunities. Teaching focus on offense should be on the person with the ball, the receiver, as well as the person without the ball. On defense the focus should be on cutting off angles of opportunity for the offense.
8. With large groups of learners, decrease the amount of space for game play, particularly when less than five-on-five work is being developed.
9. Manipulate the rules to bring out better play (e.g., no dribbling, three passes) and to encourage continuous play (e.g., be flexible when calling traveling, eliminate foul shots and jump balls).
10. Consider introducing zone defense as a concept of defending space. Three defensive players can constitute a zone defense. Add different patterns of zone defense as the number of defensive players increases.
11. Mix some game play with skill work in each lesson once a unit gets started. Progress with skills over the unit. Do not establish units that do all the basic skill development in the first few lessons and all the play in the last few lessons.
12. See Figure 7.21 for official signals.

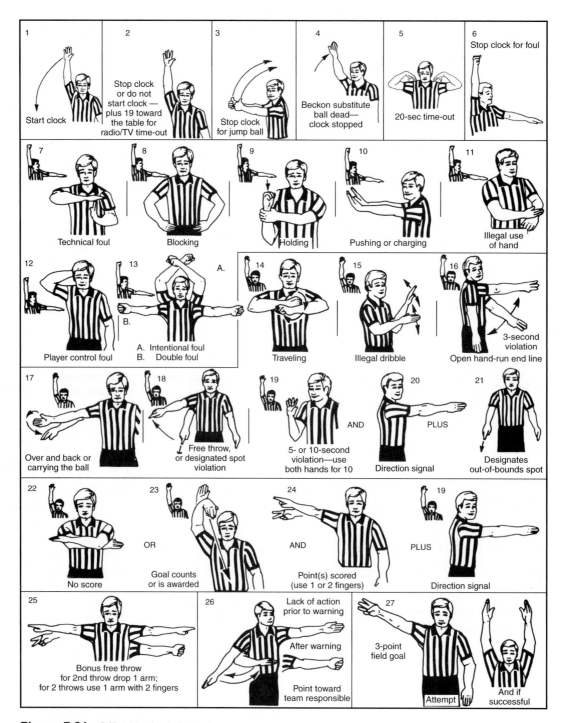

Figure 7.21. Official basketball signals.

GLOSSARY

alternate-possession rule The rule where any jump ball situations after the opening jump ball result in each team gaining possession of the ball. The team losing the opening jump ball will be awarded the first possession, with teams alternating possession for the rest of the game.

assist A pass or handoff resulting in a basket by a teammate.

backboard The surface of wood, metal, or glass to which the basket is affixed, used to carom shots into the basket.

backcourt The half of the court away from the basket under attack; the guards are often called "backcourt players."

basket (*a*) The iron hoop through which goals are scored; (*b*) a field goal.

bench The reserve strength of a team, apart from the starting five players.

blocking A foul by a defensive player who blocks the legal path of an offensive player.

center jump The method of putting the ball into play at the beginning of a game by having the referee toss up the ball between the rival centers.

charging A foul by an offensive player who runs into a defensive player who has established court position.

double dribble Dribbling again after the first dribble has ended.

dribble To bounce and control the ball continuously with one hand while walking or running. To double dribble is to stop and then resume dribbling, which is a violation.

dunk To leap to or above the basket and stuff the ball through the hoop. Such a movement with great vigor is called a "slam dunk."

fast break A style of offense in which a team attempts to race to the offensive basket before the defense can get set.

field goal A basket scored from the floor.

free throw An unobstructed shot from the foul line, worth one point, awarded as a penalty for a foul by the opposing team.

free-throw lane The area on the floor bounded by the free-throw line, the end line under the basket, and two connecting lines forming a 12-foot (3.6 m) (collegiate) or 18-foot (5.4 m) (professional) lane; also called "foul lane."

free-throw line A line, 15 feet (4.5 m) from the basket, behind which the shooter must stand in attempting a free throw; also called "foul line."

frontcourt The half of the court in which a basket is under attack.

give and go A play in which one player passes to a teammate and drives toward the basket to receive a pass for a layup.

handoff Handing the ball to a teammate (instead of passing it).

held ball Simultaneous possession of ball by opposing players, leading to use of the alternate-possession rule.

hook shot A sweeping, one-handed field goal attempt, with the shooter's back at least partially to the basket.

hoop (*a*) The rim of the basket; (*b*) a basket or score.

jump ball A means of putting the ball into play by having an official toss it upward between two players. This only occurs at the start of the game.

jump shot A field goal attempt in which the ball is released at the top of a vertical jump; also called a "jumper."

layup A shot from alongside the basket, using the backboard as a guide.

offensive foul A personal foul committed by a member of the offensive team, usually not involving a free throw as part of the penalty.

over and back Moving the ball into the backcourt once it has been advanced to the frontcourt.

palming An illegal means of carrying the ball along while dribbling.

personal foul Any of a variety of body-contact fouls; five, or in professional ball, six personals disqualify the player who commits them.

pick A legal method of providing shooting room for a teammate by taking a position that "picks off," or blocks, a defensive player.

pick-and-roll A maneuver in which a player moves suddenly (rolls) toward the basket for a pass from the teammate for whom a pick has been set.

pivot A position taken by a player with his/her back to the basket, at the head or alongside the free-throw lane, from which he/ she can spin and shoot or hand off to teammates moving past him/her toward the basket; also the floor area where pivot play is feasible.

player-to-player defense A style of team defense in which each player is assigned to a specific opponent to guard anywhere on the court.

post A position on the offensive end of the court where the player places himself or herself just outside of the free throw lane. Low post means the player is closer to the basket, while high post means the player is closer to the free-throw line.

press A style of defense in which offensive players are closely guarded and harried. A "full-court press" is applied all over the floor; a "half-court press" only after the ball is brought across the midcourt line.

rebound A shot that caroms off the basket or backboard and remains in play, to be recovered by either team.

set shot A field goal attempted from a stationary position with both feet on the floor when the player releases the ball. This shot is usually taken relatively far from the basket.

steal Capture of the ball from the hands of a player by the defender; an intercepted pass.

switch A defensive technique in which players who have player-to-player assignments switch responsibilities with each other as their offensive players cross paths.

technical foul A foul imposed for misbehavior or some technical rule infraction. The penalty is a free throw plus possession of the ball for the offended team.

ten-second rule The requirement that a team bring the ball across the midcourt line within 10 seconds after gaining possession.

three-pointer A field goal made by a player who is fouled in the act of shooting, plus the free throw that is made; also a basket scored from outside the three-point line on the court.

three-second rule The restriction against offensive players taking up set positions within the free-throw lane for more than 3 seconds.

tip-in A field goal made by tipping the ball into the basket while airborne for a rebound.

trailer A player who follows behind his/her teammates on a fast break as a passing option if they are unable to get off a shot.

trap Convergence of two or more defenders on a ball handler to force a turnover or steal.

traveling Illegally moving the ball by violating the dribbling rules.

turnover Loss of possession of the ball without attempting a field goal.

twenty-four-second rule In the National Basketball Association (NBA), the requirement that a team make a field goal attempt within 24 seconds after gaining possession of the ball; in international amateur competition, the limit is 30 seconds; in college basketball, the limit is 35 seconds for men and 30 seconds for women.

violation Any infraction not classified as a foul. The penalty is loss of possession of the ball.

zone A style of team defense in which each player is assigned to guard a designated floor area rather than a specific opponent.

SUGGESTED READINGS

The following represent only a very small subset of books available on basketball.

American Sport Education Program. 2007. *Coaching youth basketball.* 4th ed. Champaign, IL: Human Kinetics.

Atkins, K. 2004. *Basketball offenses and plays.* Champaign, IL: Human Kinetics.

Giannini, J. 2009. *Court sense: Winning basketball's mental game.* Champaign, IL: Human Kinetics.

Krause, J. 2002. *Coaching basketball.* 3rd ed. Dubuque, IA: McGraw-Hill.

Krause, J., Meyer, D. and Meyer, J. 2008. *Basketball skills and drills.* 3rd ed. Champaign, IL: Human Kinetics.

Minisalco, K. and Kot, G. 2009. *Survival guide for coaching youth basketball.* Champaign. IL: Human Kinetics.

NCAA official basketball rules. Current edition. College Athletics Publishing Service, Shawnee Mission, Kansas.

Newell, P. and Nater, S. 2008. *Pete Newell's playing big.* Champaign, IL: Human Kinetics.

Nix, C. 2000. *Skills, drills and strategies for basketball.* Scottsdale, AZ: Holcomb Hathaway Publishers.

Oliver, J. 2004. *Basketball fundamentals.* Champaign, IL: Human Kinetics.

Prudden, J. 2006. *Coaching girls' basketball successfully.* Champaign, IL: Human Kinetics.

Prusak, K. 2005. *Basketball fun and games: 50 skill-building activities for children.* Champaign, IL: Human Kinetics.

Paye, B., and Paye, P. 2001. *Youth basketball drills.* Champaign, IL: Human Kinetics.

Rose, L. 2004. *The basketball handbook.* Champaign, IL: Human Kinetics.

Wilkes, G. 1998. *Basketball.* 7th ed. Dubuque, IA: McGraw-Hill. Discusses essential basketball skills, information on offensive and defensive patterns of play, strategy, rules of the game, and sportsmanship.

Wissel, H. 2004. *Basketball—steps to success.* 2nd ed. Champaign, IL: Human Kinetics.

Women's Basketball Coaches Association. 2007. *The women's basketball drill book.* Champaign, IL: Human Kinetics.

Wootten, M. 2003. *Coaching basketball successfully.* 2nd ed. Champaign, IL: Human Kinetics.

RESOURCES

Web-based search engines identified nearly 38 million basketball instructional videos.

Videos

Coach to coach: The ultimate clinic on the art of coaching. The top coaches of the NBA lead in-depth clinics on their areas of expertise. West One Video, 1935 Bailey Hill Rd., Eugene, OR 97405.

See Appendix C for other video sources.

WEB SITES

American Youth Basketball Tour
www.aybtour.com

Basketball Congress International
www.bcibasketball.org

National Association of Basketball Coaches
http://nabc.fansonly.com

National Wheelchair Basketball Association
www.nwba.org

Women's Basketball Coaching Association
www.wbca.org

Youth Basketball of America
www.yboa.org

8 Bicycling

After completing this chapter, the reader should be able to:

- Explain how to select the proper size bicycle and how to adjust it correctly
- Describe which kind of cycling equipment is required to ride safely and comfortably
- Demonstrate how to start, steer, shift, and stop a bicycle
- State the rules of the road and execute them for maximum safety when road riding
- State the rules of the trail and execute them for maximum safety when mountain biking
- List basic training skills that enhance bicycling enjoyment

HISTORY

In stark contrast to the sleek modern racing machine, the first bicycles were crude, cumber-some contraptions that were inefficient and impossible to steer, making them less than desirable for everyday transportation. Yet they did have a simple advantage over walking: they used muscle power to move horizontally rather than vertically. When we stand up, muscles must be tensed and bones compressed to support body weight. This muscle tension expends energy even though no motion takes place, and walking triples the load on the legs. By sitting on a seat or board with two wheels attached to it, we save much of the expended vertical energy lost through standing muscle tension. Thus, the first bicyclists could sit on a seat and pedal the bike with their feet and glide along to their destination, using less energy than walking requires.

One of the first changes made to the bicycle was to increase the size (circumference) of the front wheel, increasing the distance the bike traveled with each pedal stroke. High wheelers, also known as *ordinaries* or *penny-farthings,* were in use from 1870 to 1885.

The development of the chain-driven-rear-wheel "safety bicycle," which first appeared in 1885, is considered one of the most important innovations in bicycle development. As the name implies, this type of bike is inherently safer because it does not have a huge front wheel. This design, still in use today, also removed the restriction of direct drive from pedals to wheels. Perhaps the most significant change to the bicycle since the introduction of the safety design was the addition of the derailleur in the 1930s. A derailleur enables one to select an appropriate gear, making possible the proper matching of pedal rate with changes in the terrain. For example, if the pitch of the road suddenly increases, one can shift the bike to a lower, easier gear. Before the development of the derailleur, most bikes had only one gear; today,

high-performance road bikes have 18 to 20 gears and mountain bikes (MTB) have up to 30 gears.

As the primary mode of transportation in many countries, the modern bicycle (Figure 8.1) is a marvel of complex simplicity: light, agile, versatile, and efficient.

The sport of bicycle racing has undergone immense change over the past century, driven in large part by technology and sponsorship. Cycling's inclusion in the first modern Olympic Games in 1896 highlights its early importance, but, like many sports, the results are skewed by the exclusion of black athletes, for example, the first black world champion (in any sport), Marshall "Major" Taylor. Despite his absence from the Olympics, Taylor was widely regarded as the world's finest living cyclist in the late 1800s and early 1900s. And while his story is largely unknown, Taylor should be recognized not just for his achievements as a black man in segregated America, but as an athlete of all races, with a story of triumph to rival any athlete in U.S. history. The sport itself has extended well beyond the simple time trial and track events of its origins to encompass more than 30 disciplines on road, track, or trails, lasting as little as several seconds to days. Cycling, like running, is egalitarian, offering nearly anyone an opportunity to achieve success.

Until recently, cycling's place in American culture has largely taken a backseat to its heyday prior to World War II; most would be surprised to learn that Madison Square Garden was originally used for track racing before the 1940s. This all changed in the early 1980s. First, in 1983 Greg LeMond won the World Road Race Championship, and this was followed in 1984 when U.S. cyclists took home gold in the men's and women's road race, as well as a number of track events. Until then, no U.S. cyclist had won an Olympic medal since 1908. However much the Soviet absence contributed to the success of the U.S. cycling team is open to debate, but the outcome still came as somewhat of a surprise and provided

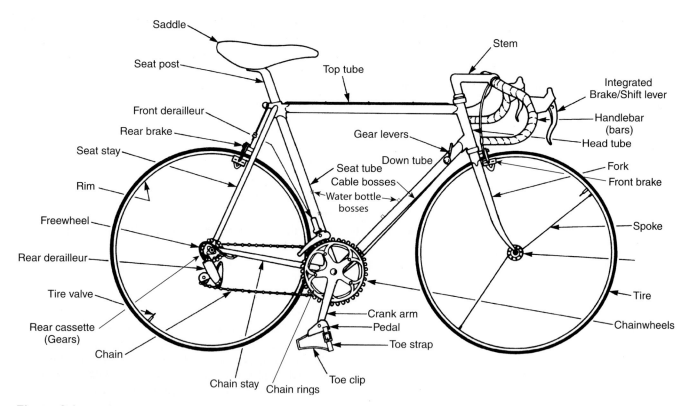

Figure 8.1. Modern road bicycle.

a much needed boost to U.S. cycling, propelling a number of Americans to stardom. Although the list of successful U.S. riders has grown too large to cover here, a handful have earned a defining place in both American and international cycling history. In 1986, Greg LeMond marked the United States' return to the pinnacle of cycling by becoming the first American to win the Tour de France. LeMond, already a World Champion in 1983, overcame immense pressure and internal team strife to accomplish his first victory, but this would prove nothing compared to his victory in 1989. Heralded as the next super champion, LeMond's career and life were nearly cut short by a gun-shot wound the following year. LeMond, however, would not be deterred from recapturing some of his potential by taking victory in the 1989 Tour de France by what remains to be the narrowest margin in history, a scant 8 seconds. LeMond would go on to claim another world title that year and a third Tour de France victory the following year. Meanwhile, American cyclists would show continued success in other major events, but it would be nearly a decade before another U.S. comeback would begin the longest Tour de France reign in history.

Before LeMond's retirement in 1994, several up and coming riders began making waves in Europe, each with their own promise, but none more than a young Texan named Lance Armstrong. However, Armstrong proved to have the wrong body type and skill set to succeed at the Tour. Further, Armstrong's career and life, like LeMond's, were nearly

ended prematurely, with a diagnosis of advanced testicular cancer. Again, like LeMond, Lance Armstrong defied the predictions, including those of his doctors, by recovering from cancer then returning to world-class cycling 20 pounds lighter and with a new objective, the Tour de France. After his recovery, Armstrong returned to professional racing in 1998, achieving several impressive results. However, his finest hour came on July 25, 1999, when he became only the second American to win the Tour de France. Overnight he became the "poster-child" of cancer survival and an inspiration to people around the world. Doubters to his win were silenced after Armstrong defended his title not just once, but went on to become the winningest rider in Tour de France history after capturing his seventh consecutive title in 2005. Armstrong's retirement that same year left many wondering if American cycling would be devoid of a new group of champions. However, the boon would continue with some new faces and eventually a very familiar one.

As the first decade of the 21st century winds down, both U.S. and Canadian pro cycling appear to be on the upswing. In the last few years the Colorado-based Garmin-Slipstream pro cycling team has moved from a small, novel racing team with good ideas to a topflight team built around a core group of world-class North American, like David Zabriskie and Christian Vande Velde. And, after nearly four years of retirement, Lance Armstrong marked his return to professional cycling in 2009 with a third-place finish in the Tour de France, the highest American finish since his 2004 victory. With Armstrong's return and record growth of the sport in the U.S., cycling should remain healthy for years to come.

Of all the changes within professional and Olympic cycling over the last decade, perhaps the greatest has been the development of a professional mountain bike racing circuit and the inclusion of road and mountain biking in the Olympics. These changes to the Games first occurred in the 1996 Atlanta Olympics. As with other Olympic sports that have allowed professionals to compete, the cycling professionals have won the majority of the Olympic cycling events since 1996, including the men's and women's road and mountain bike race, road time trials, and nearly all the track races, which consisted of more than 10 events for both genders combined, making track cycling one of the most gender balanced sports in the Olympics.

THE BICYCLE AND THE CYCLIST

Types of Bicycles

There are many different types of bicycles, each designed for a different purpose. *Road racing bikes* feature drop handlebars and short wheelbases and are lightweight (Figure 8.2). *Touring bikes* are equipped for carrying loads: they have heavy-duty wheels, luggage rack attachments, and "granny gears" for climbing steep hills. Designed for rugged trails and steep hills, modern mountain bikes (Figure 8.3) have wide, knobby tires, "granny" gears, and, very often, some type of suspension system that enhances handling on rough terrain. The upright position of the mountain bike and its ease of use spurred many manufacturers to develop a crossover or hybrid bike that blends the agile efficiency of a road bike with the upright flat bar and position of a mountain bike. The *cycle-cross* bike is essentially a road racing bike fitted with knobby tires and ridden with mountain biking cleats and pedals over off-road courses that force the rider to dismount and run frequently. This fall-winter sport, a long-time favorite in Europe, has seen tremendous growth in the U.S.

over the last decade. *Track bikes,* using the same frame design as road bikes, do not have brakes and use a single fixed gear that is set up so that the rider cannot stop pedaling unless the bike is brought to a complete standstill. Track bikes are raced only on specialized banked tracks. *BMX (Bicycle Motor Cross)* bikes, which are smaller than other bikes, are ridden in a sprint-like fashion around 1/4 mile (400m) dirt tracks that contain many small hills. Popular among children and young adults BMX has produced a number of great riders, including John Tomac, a premier U.S. off-road racer in the 1990s, and Belgian Sven Nys, who remains one of the world's dominant cyclocross riders. *Commuter bikes* are average "around town" vehicles that come in all shapes and sizes. Often equipped with fenders and reflectors, they provide reliable transportation and recreation.

Posture

One of the most important considerations in choosing a bicycle is its fit. A bicycle that does not fit will be uncomfortable and will not handle correctly. Most people believe that the bicyclist sits on the seat, pushes with the legs, bends the back, and steers with the hands. In reality, the cyclist straddles the seat, spins the pedals, leans forward from the hips, and steers by leaning. The basic components of a correct cycling posture include bike size and saddle height, tilt, and fore-aft positioning, along with proper handlebar height and stem length.

Frame Size and Saddle Positioning

A high-quality bicycle frame's geometry is specific to its use and is made of several measurements (Figure 8.4). A bicycle's geometry can have a profound effect on its comfort, ride quality, and agility. A simple and fast way to assess frame size is to straddle it. If the bicycle is the proper size, there should be 1 to 2 inches (2.5 to 5.1 cm) of clearance between the tires and the ground. In contrast, when sizing a mountain bike, there should be about 7.5 to 12 inches (20 to 30 cm) between the tires and the ground when the top tube is lifted against the

Figure 8.2. Road racing bike.

Figure 8.3. Fully suspended mountain bike.

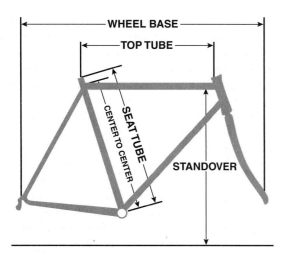

Figure 8.4. Common frame geometry measurements

Figure 8.6. Positioning of the cleat. Notice the ball of the foot is directly over the pedal spindle when the pedal is in the 3 o'clock position and is pointed nearly straight ahead.

crotch. The saddle should be positioned so that it is just possible to place the heels on the pedals at the bottom position and pedal backward without rocking the hips. A final check for saddle height is the angle between the upper and lower leg. When the leg is fully extended and fixed to the pedal, there should be a slight (5–10 degrees) bend in the knee.

After adjusting the saddle height, one needs to adjust saddle tilt and fore-aft positioning, because they are important factors for attaining a proper bike posture. Saddle tilt is an easy adjustment; all you have to do is make sure the saddle is level from the tip to the back. To check the tilt, place a level across the top of the saddle and adjust accordingly by loosening the nut that affixes the saddle to the seat post (Figure 8.5). If the saddle is tilted backward (with the tip higher than the back of the saddle), you may experience discomfort and numbness in the crotch while riding. If the saddle is tilted forward (with the tip lower than the back), you will slide off the front of the saddle while pedaling, which greatly increases neck, shoulder, and upper-arm fatigue.

Unlike the saddle tilt adjustment, fore-aft positioning is a bit tricky. First you have to adjust your cycling shoes precisely, a procedure that is extremely personalized, although there are two rules of thumb that serve as a good starting point: Position the cleat so that the ball of your foot lies directly over the pedal axle, and make sure your foot is pointing straight ahead, in the so-called neutral position (Figure 8.6). Most people do not need to have their shoes pointed inward (pigeon-toed) or outward (duck-foot), positions that often increase the risk of knee injury.

After setting up your cleats, you can then adjust the fore-aft position of your saddle. The first part of this adjustment is to find the area on the inside or outside of your knee where the thigh bone and lower leg meet. You should be able to feel a small indentation in this area—the joint line of the knee—when your leg is fully extended (Figure 8.7). Mark

Figure 8.5. Proper saddle tilt.

Figure 8.7. A plumb line dropped from the joint line of the knee past the crank arm when the pedals are at 3 and 9 o'clock bisects the pedal spindle.

this indentation with a big X. Next, sit on your saddle and place your feet on the pedals, rotating them at the 9 and 3 o'clock positions; the foot of the marked leg should be at 9 o'clock. (It helps to lean against a wall, doorjamb, or friend for this procedure.) Once accomplished, drop a plumb line from the mark on your leg to the pedal. The line will bisect the pedal axle if your fore-aft positioning is correct. If not, move your saddle forward or backward by loosening the nut that affixes the saddle to the seat post.

The final aspects of attaining proper bike posture are setting handlebar height and choosing stem length. A good rule of thumb for handlebar height is that the bars should be about 1 inch (2.5 cm) lower than the tip of your saddle. To check stem length, sit on the saddle, reach forward, and place your hands on the hooks or drops of a road handlebar or the handlebar grips of a mountain bike. (Again, it helps to lean on a wall, doorjamb, or friend.) If the handlebars obscure your view of the front hub while you are so positioned, the stem length is correct. If not, you will need a longer or shorter stem. It is a good idea to check stem length when you purchase a bike; most shops will replace the stem for free at this time.

Choosing a Saddle

A properly fit rider should enjoy hours of pain-free riding, and no other piece of cycling equipment can impact comfort more and be more tedious to choose than the saddle (seat). Moreover, once many riders find a saddle they like, they rarely change. Case in point, Lance Armstrong has raced on the same saddle for nearly 20 years, even after it was discontinued; the saddle was later returned to the market because Armstrong created a high demand for it. When selecting a saddle (seat), it is important to understand its function and that the rider does not sit on the saddle, but straddles it, using the seat as a prop for the pelvic, or "sit bones." The best saddle is smooth, flexible, and just wide enough to support your weight—a wider saddle will cause chafing on the inner thighs. Most saddles today are flexible plastic covered with foam and leather, and are quite comfortable once you become conditioned to riding. Numerous models exist, with some designed specifically for a woman's wider pelvis. If long distance (e.g., 1 hour or more) is your objective, then avoid cheap vinyl saddles, which are too hard, or large mattress saddles, which are simply too wide for comfortable riding.

Tires

There are three kinds of bicycle tires. The most common type—"wired-on" or clinchers—are so named because of the wire bead that seals the tires to the rim. In contrast to clinchers, tubular tires, used almost exclusively by racers, are glued on to the wheel rim. Finally, the tubeless tire is like car and motorcycle tires. Here, a special rim and valve are used in combination with a liquid tire sealant and what is essentially a clincher tire. The end product is a lighter, highly flat-resistant tire, more common on high-end mountain bikes. Tubeless tire development remains a high priority of many manufacturers. Tubes within the tires also come in two types (actually, it is the valves that are different), so it is important that the tire pump carried fits the type of valve on the bike. Schrader valves are large and sturdy, like automobile valves. Presta valves are narrow and require the little button on the valve tip to be unscrewed to use them. Each takes a different hand pump to fill with air. Because tires fail more frequently than any other part of a bicycle, it is worth the investment to purchase quality, medium- to high-priced tires. Morever, knowing how to change tires and fix flats will save a lot more time and money than buying "bargain basement" tires.

Changing clincher tires is not difficult, and with a little practice you can fix a flat in about 5 minutes. All you need is a spare tube, some tire irons, and a pump. Begin by removing the wheel from the bike and insert a tire lever near the valve stem scoop side out, until you catch the edge of the tire bead. Pry down until the bead pops over the rim. Note: Some levers have a hook on the opposite end to allow you to hook it around the nearest spoke (Figure 8.8A). While holding the first lever down, place the second lever a few inches away and repeat the above steps. Continue sliding the second lever around the tire until the bead is off on one side (Figure 8.8B). Once off, pull the tube out. Before replacing the tube, run your fingers SLOWLY, to avoid cutting your fingers, around the inside of the tire to be certain the cause of the flat is not embedded in the tire. If it is, remove it. Prior to installation, fill the tube with a little air to give it some "shape"; doing so helps prevent the tire from getting caught between the rim and bead (Figure 8.8C). Insert the valve stem first, then the remaining tube. Once it is installed, be certain the valve stem is straight, and, by hand, begin pushing the bead back onto the rim starting opposite the valve. Work the bead on around BOTH directions, deflating the tube when it gets too difficult to push the bead on (Figure 8.8D). Adept cyclists can "seat" the tire bead without tools. However, difficult tires may require using a tire lever to pry the last part onto the rim. If this is the case, be careful not to pinch the tube with the lever. Once it is seated, pump up the tire, replace the wheel, and ride on.

Clothing

Like the other components, cycling clothing has undergone substantial improvements (Figure 8.9). Forget buying generic, low-quality clothing. Numerous manufacturers are in business to make your riding experience pleasant and also to make sure you look cool. Moreover, many companies now offer custom clothing designs for cycling clubs and teams, and use that same technology to bring individuals pro-level clothing.

Today's best clothing is designed and manufactured with cycling comfort in mind. Cycling shorts are made from stretchable Lycra and a high-quality chamois lining to

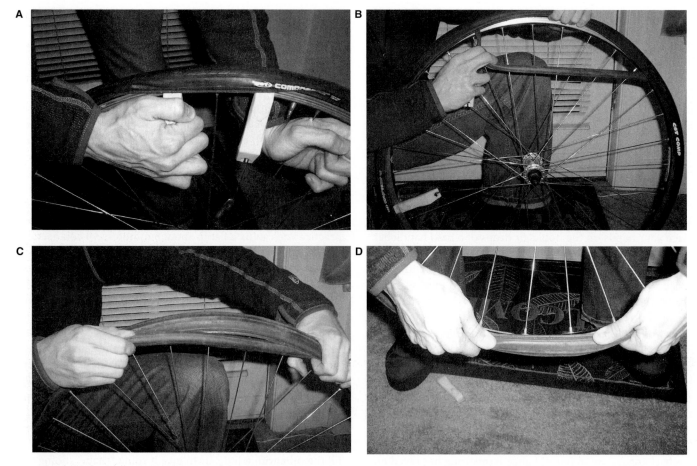

Figure 8.8. Major sequences of changing a tube: A, remove one side of the tire with levers. B, remove the old tube. C, inflate the new tube enough to give it "shape" before inserting it into the tire, and. D, install or seat the clincher, working your way around the tire starting at the valve and ending opposite to the valve. With practice, most tires can be completed by hand.

prevent saddle chafe and sores, while jerseys are made with special fabrics that wick moisture from the skin. This keeps a bicyclist cooler in the summer and warmer in the winter. In addition, many have long zippers in the front for added ventilation and pockets in the back for carrying identification, spare tire tubes (flats are common), and energy snacks. All quality clothing is also anatomically designed — i.e., cut to fit the cyclist in the seated position, and some clothing is designed specifically for women. Fingerless gloves, worn by many bicyclists, can be used to rub bits of glass off tires and protect the palms of the hands should a fall occur.

Shoes and Pedals

Cycling shoes are specifically designed for riding as well, with stiff soles that distribute the forces generated from pedaling over a larger area of the foot, a characteristic that reduces foot discomfort and fatigue. While many high-end shoes have universally moved to carbon fiber soles, care should be taken when buying very stiff-soled shoes, as many experienced riders report foot numbness and pain, proving that stiffness is not the most important factor.

Most modern road and mountain bikes utilize some type of "clipless" pedal system (Figure 8.10). One of the greatest bike innovations in the last 25 years, clipless pedals allow cyclists to clip into a pedal using a cleat mounted to the sole much like a ski binding. Not surprisingly, the first clipless pedal was developed by Look, a ski binding company. These pedals allow for a better foot–pedal connection, increasing peddling efficiency for all types of riding. Mountain bike pedal systems differ from road systems in a few small ways. Shoe soles are more flexible, with an aggressive tread and recessed cleat to allow for running, and the pedal is designed for easier release and greater reliability in muddy conditions.

Eyewear

Eyewear has become as much a part of cycling over the past 15 years as any other piece of equipment, and thus deserves a few words. The fact that most cycling-specific sunglasses are on the cutting edge of technology and style means you cannot go wrong here; Rudy Project, Oakley, Smith, and others offer a wide selection. While these glasses can be pricey, they will last many years and protect the eyes from the elements

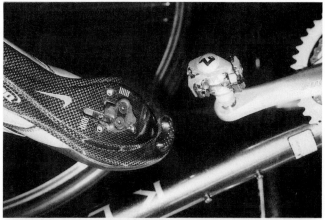

Figure 8.9. Cycling gear. Note the difference between the "aggressive" mountain bike shoes on the left and the streamlined shoes on the right. Also note the modern eyewear and interchangeable lenses.

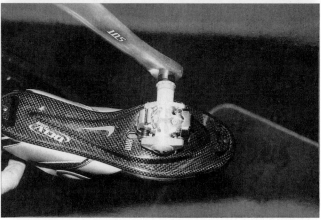

Figure 8.10. While numerous clipless pedal variations exist, the basic premise remains unchanged since the mid-1980s: a special cleat attached to the shoe "locks" the foot onto the pedal. Contrary to its appearance, the shoe will disengage in the event of a crash.

and reduce eye fatigue without obscuring vision (like low-priced generic eyewear sometimes does). Moreover, companies like Rudy Project and Oakley provide different color lenses for variable light conditions and even models that allow for use of your prescription lenses. Shop around and find the pair that looks and feels best to you.

Helmets: The Final Piece of the Puzzle

Whereas cycling shorts and jerseys are relatively unimportant to the short-distance rider, all cyclists should wear a helmet. Almost all deaths and most serious injuries incurred in cycling accidents are caused by head injuries. Where there is the chance of the head striking an immovable object—as in football, hockey, auto racing, and other contact sports—protective headgear can save a life (Figure 8.11).

Forget the leather strapped helmets of the 70s and the bucket helmets of the 80s; today's bicycling helmets are made of Styrofoam injected into a thin plastic shell. Helmets, like the Rudy Project helmet pictured here, are well-ventilated and very light, weighing only about 6 ounces, and look great. Moreover, the newest helmets are easy to adjust and stay in place to properly protect your head; Figure 8.11 shows how your helmet should look when properly adjusted. Any good

bike shop will carry a wide range of helmets and can help you adjust yours properly before you leave. As with many aspects of cycling equipment, you should expect to pay more for a quality helmet. While low-cost department store helmets appear comparable, they are often difficult to adjust and poorly ventilated.

Basic Maintenance

Before starting a ride of any distance, be sure to give the bicycle a quick safety check. Grip the brake levers and make sure that the brakes work. Look for worn brake blocks and loose cables. Make sure the handlebars, seat, and wheels are not loose and see that the wheels are true—that is, they do not wobble from side to side when you spin them (they do not rub on the brake pads). Check the tires for the proper pressure and for worn or cut places. Underinflated tires greatly increase rolling resistance and increase the chance of damaging the rims. Lubricate the chain if necessary. Make sure to have a spare tube, tire irons, and a pump. Taking a

Figure 8.11. The modern cycling helmet. Avoid allowing the helmet to slide back on the head, exposing the front of the head to injury.

few moments before a ride could save a long walk home, but more importantly, it could prevent an accident. Take your bike in for a good tune-up each year as well.

Tips for Purchasing a Bike

Shopping for a new bike can be a daunting task, particularly if you are new to the sport. However, with a little research and patience, you can find a satisfactory bike at a reasonable price. The following is a list of things to remember when looking for a new bike:

- **Know what you want**—If commuting to work is your goal, then a high-tech racing bike is of no use to you. Know the bike fit basics and stick to them; don't be pushed into buying something that doesn't fit your riding style or your body.
- **Avoid large chain stores**—It cannot be overstated: bikes are not toys. The best place to buy a bike is a reputable bike shop. Not only are the bikes higher in quality, the employees are more knowledgeable and more responsible about providing a quality machine; remember, if it doesn't work, they not only can fit it, they will fix it. Moreover, most bike shops have good shop warranties for their bikes.
- **Ride before you buy**—Any good bike shop will let you take a bike for a test ride to find the bike that is best for you. Avoid buying a bike that's uncomfortable for you.

- **Be prepared to pay**—While you do not need to spend thousands of dollars for a bike, you should expect to pay five or six hundred dollars for a quality, long-lasting bike. If you can, go shopping in the spring or fall/winter, as most shops are interested in reducing their stock of bike models. Avoid bikes with lots of plastic parts, particularly if you're expecting to do some trail riding, as they tend to break easily.
- **Stick to the basics**—Don't be pressured into buying fancy equipment. Special lightweight, aerodynamic wheels may look nice, but they are often difficult to repair and costly to replace. Your number one concern should be reliability/durability, then price, and finally the "bells and whistles"!

BIKE RIDING BASICS

Starting

Grasp the top of the handlebars and swing a leg over the seat to straddle the bicycle. Backpedal until one pedal is forward and high. Place the ball of the foot on the high pedal and kick off with the other foot. This will start the bicycle moving. Place the other foot on its pedal and ease the crotch backward up onto the saddle.

Braking

Use both brakes to stop safely by applying pressure first to the rear brake and then to the front brake. Gradually brake harder until coming to a stop or until the rear wheel starts to skid. If this happens, let up on both brake levers until the wheels start to turn again.

Never use only the rear brake in traffic. It cannot provide enough deceleration to stop in the event of trouble. Also, never brake hard with only the front brake, as you may be thrown forward over the handlebars. Use extra caution when riding in rain, as the brakes do not work as well; it is not uncommon to feel a sensation of increasing speed until the brake blocks wipe the rims dry. Riding on steel rims in wet weather is more dangerous than riding on alloy rims, as it takes longer to slow down. Remember to leave extra stopping distance. To prevent the rear wheel from locking up on steep descents or wet roads, continue to pedal lightly when braking.

Stopping

Apply the brakes to slow down. Put the pedals in the high and low positions, transfer your weight to the low pedal, and slide forward and off the seat. Remove the foot from the high pedal and reach for the ground while slowing to a stop. Just before the stop, turn the front wheel away from the free foot to tip the bicycle. If timed correctly, the bicyclist will stop and lean onto the free foot just as it touches the ground. Backpedal to the starting position.

Steering

Steering is accomplished more by leaning than by turning the handlebars. This effect can best be tested by walking along, pushing the bike forward, and holding on to only the saddle. A slight tip to the left or right will naturally turn the front wheel in the same direction. This action occurs when the bicyclist is in the saddle. The hands and arms on the handlebars primarily support the body's upper torso.

Shifting Gears

The premise of variable bicycle gear ratios on multispeed bikes is that the bicyclist is most efficient when pedaling at a constant rate in revolutions per minute. (One revolution is two complementary strokes, one from the left leg and one from the right.) Due to the variable terrain a bicyclist encounters while riding, it is impossible to keep a constant pace with only one gear. For example, the average bicyclist would be unable to keep the same pace going uphill as on the flat. Other variable conditions include wind and weight carried. Shifting gears allows the optimum in mechanical efficiency.

Shifting gears on a bicycle has become very easy—almost foolproof—since the advent of index, or "click," shifting in the mid-1980s. To shift, you simply move the gear lever—be it integrated in the brake lever, on the down tube, or on the handlebars (integrated shifters) (Figure 8.12)—until a click is heard. In general, shifting the right down tube shifter up will move your chain to a smaller cog (i.e., harder gear), while shifting the left lever up will move your chain to a smaller chain ring (i.e., easier gear). If the derailleur cables are properly tensioned and the frame is aligned, the bike will now be in a new gear. It is as easy as that. Sometimes it helps to reduce pedaling force so as to facilitate the shift, but this is usually unnecessary except in extreme situations, such as shifting while riding at a low pedal frequency on a steep incline. In general, it is best to anticipate the shift; that is, shift before the pedal cadence drops dramatically. It is wise to practice shifting on a flat, lightly traveled road so you can shift smoothly and safely in all situations.

Pedaling Technique

The mark of a good bicyclist is the smooth, steady way in which she or he pedals the bike. The foot must be placed on the pedal so it can push the pedal as far around the circle as possible. To do this, you use the foot as a lever with the ankle as fulcrum while pedaling on the ball of the foot. At the bottom of the circle, the heel is up and the toe is down. At the top of the circle, the heel is down and the toe is up, thus pulling the pedal back. This is called "ankling." Smooth ankling is achieved only by using cycling shoes equipped for clipped or clipless pedals, but this technique should be practiced even if tennis shoes or rubber pedals are used.

The feet should rotate the pedals at a rhythmic, constant pace (cadence), twice as fast as walking, A slow cadence is 60 revolutions per minute; 80 is normal; and 90 to 100 is racing pace. An easy way to determine cadence is to count the number of times one leg pedals down in 10 seconds (e.g., 15 down strokes with one leg in 10 seconds equals 90 RPM).

Figure 8.12. Close-up of modern dual brake/shift lever integration, which allows a rider to shift gears using the brake levers.

RIDING ON THE ROAD
Rules of the Road

The rules of the road for bicyclists are the same as for automobile drivers. Automobile drivers cooperate with each other within the rules of the road, and motorists usually cooperate with bicyclists who obey these rules. Conflict arises when bicyclists or motorists, through ignorance or design, act unreasonably on the roadway.

Where to Ride on the Road

Bicycles are vehicles and have a right to a safe corridor along the road. Unfortunately, some people do not recognize bicycles as legitimate vehicles. This often results in actions inconsistent with standard traffic engineering practice and common sense rules of behavior in traffic situations. Nevertheless, courtesy toward others will pay in increased respect and safety. Bicycles are vehicles, and the following are recommended rules governing the place of bicycles on the roadway.

As the rider of a vehicle, always ride with the flow of traffic. The greatest number of car-bicycle collisions are caused by riding against traffic. Moreover, riding on the wrong side of the road also increases the risk of bicycle-bicycle collisions with other cyclists riding correctly. When riding on a road of standard width, the bicyclist should ride inside the traffic lane at the right-hand side of the road. Cars will usually have ample room to pass within or nearly within this lane. On roads that are too narrow to permit safe passing either within the lane or over the centerline, the bicyclist should ride in the center of the right lane. If riding as fast as or faster than the other traffic, use the lane as if operating a car. Do not weave in and around parked cars.

It is important not to ride in the motorist's blind spot, especially when approaching intersections or driveways, where a motorist might make a right turn. Overtake on the right only when the cars are stopped or are barely moving. Never overtake on the right where it is possible for the motorist to make a right turn, and never overtake on the right when the road is too narrow to do so safely.

Right Turns

Make a right turn in the same manner as a car does: from the farthest right of the roadway. Some roads have right-turn-only lanes. When riding in the right-hand portion of a right-turn-only lane, the bicyclist must turn right (Figure 8.13B). If the bicyclist attempts to go straight through, he or she could be hit by a motorist legally turning right. When a bicyclist encounters a right-turn-only lane but does not wish to follow it, the alternative is to merge to the left and ride on the right-hand edge of the next straight-through lane (Figure 8.13A). Merge left by looking over your left

shoulder before changing the path of travel. Change lanes only when overtaking traffic has cleared or slowed to allow you to move over.

Left Turns

Never attempt a left turn from the right side of the street. The bicyclist stands a good chance of being hit by an overtaking car by making a left turn in front of it. To make a safe left turn, the bicyclist must follow the same procedure as an automobile driver. The first step is to merge left. Look back over your shoulder for overtaking cars. It may help to signal, but never signal without looking. A signal is a matter of courtesy; the look is a matter of life and death. After looking over the left shoulder for overtaking cars, move into the left lane if the way is clear. When occupying a left-turn-only lane, ride at the *right* edge of the lane (Figure 8.14A). This will allow motorists to also occupy the lane and turn simultaneously when the way ahead is clear. If the lane is not a left-turn-only lane, stay as close to the centerline of the road as possible (Figure 8.14B). This will allow motorists who wish to go straight through to pass on the right while the bicyclist is waiting for the oncoming traffic to clear.

After completing a left turn, you should turn into the right lane of the new street. But before doing this, check for traffic in that lane. Remember to check for oncoming traffic that may make a right turn on red and enter the inside lane as you approach.

When riding on multilane streets where the traffic is so heavy that it is not possible to make a left-hand turn as described, it may be best to use pedestrian rules, ride to the

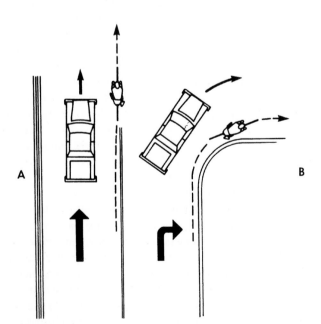

Figure 8.13. Right turns. See text for details.

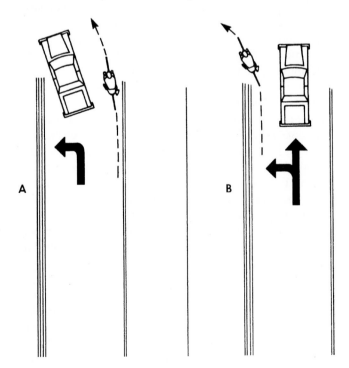

Figure 8.14. Left turns. See text for details.

far corner of the intersection, and turn the bicycle in the proper direction and wait for the light to change. At an intersection without a signal, wait for the traffic to clear in all directions.

RIDING ON THE TRAIL

Rules of the Trail

With the increasing popularity of the mountain bike and off-road riding, it is imperative that you follow a few simple rules when trail riding. In so doing, you will insure the safety of all trail users, while also helping to preserve the trail. To start, only ride where it is legal to ride. Some trails are closed and to ride on these may mobilize public sentiment against any trails being open to off-road riding. Once on the trail, be aware of your speed, particularly on sharp bends, remembering that other trail goers may be present. It is best to yield to hikers and horses, the latter of which are easily startled, Remember, the example you set affects all riders. While on the trail, do not leave it to take a shortcut, as this cuts new trails and increases erosion, which could lead to trail closures. Finally, volunteer to maintain the trails that you use. Responsible trail use and frequent trail maintenance means that you will always have trails to ride on.

Mountain Biking Skills

In general, mountain biking is similar to road riding with regard to starting, stopping, and shifting. However, trail riding can require different techniques for climbing steep hills, descending steep or bumpy hills, and traversing "loose" turns. When climbing a steep hill, the main concern is usually traction, so avoid standing, which will cause your rear wheel to slip, forcing you to dismount. A good approach is to shift to your granny gear and maintain a fairly high cadence, while spreading your weight over the bike by keeping your forearms parallel to the ground. This allows you to maintain traction in the rear and steering control in the front. Also, pick a clean line; that is to say, find the smoothest route up the hill and pedal smoothly. With any luck, you'll make it; otherwise hop off and either carry or push the bike.

Descending and steering on the trail can be trickier than on the road, so remember to use caution, and, if necessary, dismount. When descending, avoid "locking-up" your rear wheel, as it can make controlling the bike more difficult. On bumpy descents, maintain a controlled speed, pick a clean line, keep your upper body loose to help absorb bumps, and maintain control by keeping the wheels in contact with the ground. When making a tight turn, brake before the turn to reduce speed, then release while turning to avoid having the rear wheel slide out. You may want to put your inside foot out as you lean into the turn. To better maintain rear wheel ground contact and control, it is best to lean, or hang back off the saddle and maintain constant, but not heavy brake pressure as your descend. The bottom line is to stay calm and in control, otherwise you risk crashing.

Two important notes on equipment: First, many mountain bikes are now equipped with disc brakes, which provide superior braking performance, but require more finesse when applying them to avoid loss of control. If you are unfamiliar with disc brakes, use extra caution on descents until you become familiar with their use. Second, tire pressure can have a dramatic impact on traction and control of both mountain and cyclocross bikes. While too broad a topic to cover here, it is generally recommended that riders use a pressure lower than the maximum PSI for the tire—one that leaves the tire soft and pliable (e.g., 30–40 psi).

SAFETY

Statistics show that in the majority of bicycle accidents, the rider simply falls off the bicycle for some reason. The most frequent serious injury resulting from a fall is a cranial contusion. For this reason it is imperative that you always wear a helmet when road or off-road riding. The remainder of accidents are collisions with automobiles, fixed objects, and other bicyclists. Studies also show that experienced cyclists, like those who belong to organized clubs, have one-sixth to one-seventh the accident rate of other cyclists. This implies that the greatest cause of accidental injury is inept bicyclists.

First, it is important to know how to ride a bicycle. The bicyclist should adopt riding procedures that are reasonable and proper, always be observant, recognize potential problems, and be able to cope in emergency situations. Second, it is important to operate a bicycle as a vehicle. This provides operating procedures that are predictable and expected by drivers of automobiles and by other bicyclists. Because of unexpected turning and crossing maneuvers into streets from bike paths and sidewalks, it is much safer to ride a bicycle in the street than in these off-street facilities.

All cyclists should be self-sufficient on every ride. The road cyclists should carry a working pump, spare inner tube, patch kit with fresh glue, a piece of tire casing to fix a torn sidewall, money for food, a cell phone, and identification, all of which will easily fit in the rear pockets of a jersey, or in an under-the-saddle seat pack. The off-road cyclists should carry the same things as a road cyclist, plus a few tools, as mechanical failure is more common off-road. Tools should include a chain breaker, a few extra chain links, and a multi-tool with a variety of tools suitable for emergency repairs.

BICYCLING ACTIVITIES

Safe and proper bicycling offers a lifetime of enjoyment and fitness. Social and other benefits are also possible by joining a local bicycle club. Bicycle club members can supply a wealth of knowledge and are happy to help newcomers become more knowledgeable and more skillful bicyclists. Usually club members are aware of the latest equipment. On club rides, the novice can rapidly learn what others spent years finding out: where the best rides are, bicycling techniques that make riding easier, and favorite lunch stops.

There are many types of cycling clubs for a range of interests, including touring and all manner of racing endeavors (Figures 8.15, 8.16 and 8.17). Check with a local bicycle shop to find out about club activities. The novice is wise to investigate joining a touring club. Touring clubs usually have three levels of rides: short, medium, and long, or easy, moderate, and strenuous. Initially pick an easy ride and go with the club.

Figure 8.15. Bicycle road racing.

Figure 8.16. Mountain biking.

BASIC TRAINING TIPS AND RIDING SKILLS

Cycling is an activity that can be enjoyed throughout your life, either with a group or by yourself. Getting started is easy, but many cyclists ultimately seek to enhance their riding ability, usually in anticipation of a "big" ride. Therefore, a progressive riding program is needed to continually tax the rider to improve. Your cycling regimen may, however, be part of an overall fitness program, which involves flexibility work (Chapter 3 outlines some basic stretching techniques) and strength training exercises (as outlined in Chapter 37). Regardless of your goals, moderation is the key to long-term improvement, and always be cautious when beginning a new exercise program.

Every ride should begin with an initial warm-up period of about 10–20 minutes of easy riding. Once warmed up, you can begin your ride in earnest. Whether you're an aspiring racer or a bike tour rider, it is important to vary your riding from day to day to avoid boredom and improve all facets of your cycling fitness. For example, on some days you can ride longer at an easy to moderate pace, while on others you can perform a shorter, faster ride. These "fast" rides can be broken into intervals: for example, you could do two or three 5-minute "fast" stretches interspersed with 5 minutes of easy riding, or a series of 15- to 30-second sprints interspersed with long, easy stretches. Such varied training helps improve all facets of your riding, thereby improving your overall enjoyment by making it easier when you need to ride into a headwind or climb a hill.

The above is just a simple training outline to get new riders started. If serious long-distance riding, or even racing, is your aim, obtain one of the books on training listed in the

Figure 8.17. Cyclocross racers prepare to dismount from their bikes and run over barriers. Held in the fall and winter, "cross" has seen immense U.S. growth in the past decade.

Suggested Reading section at the end of this chapter. The books contain a wealth of training and tactical knowledge on road and MTB training and racing. Some books even help you outline entire yearly plans. Another approach is to hire an experienced cycling coach. A good coach can help you avoid many pitfalls and overcome training hurdles a book cannot. Many qualified coaches have their own Web sites and are only an e-mail away.

Tips for Your Ride

When heading out on a ride, it is a good idea to be prepared for the road or trail ahead. Bring along a tool pack for roadside repairs, and some money (just in case), and dress appropriately. In cool weather, always wear more clothing than you think you need; you can always take something off if too warm, but if you're cold, you can't add what you don't have. Carry sufficient food and drink for your ride. Experienced riders have a saying: "Eat before you're hungry and drink before you're thirsty." By the time you are thirsty, you are already dehydrated, and hunger likely means you have waited too long before eating. Fortunately any quality bike will allow you to install a water bottle cage (or two) to be fitted to the frame. One large water bottle (20 oz) for each hour is sufficient under most conditions. If you're riding more than 1 hour, a sports drink like Gatorade may be useful because the sugar helps to maintain energy levels; the best energy drink is the one that tastes the best to you. Alternately, you can make your own drink by using Kool-Aid and a pinch of salt. As for food, companies like Powerbar offer a range of options, or you can just bring a sandwich.

Now that you're heading out on the road, take a few skills to heart. Whether riding up long, gradual hills or into a headwind, you should maintain a good cadence, even if you must shift to an easier gear. The primary consideration with riding uphill or into the wind is effort, not speed. Speed will drop, so do not attempt to maintain your speed, as riding into a hard wind or up a hill with a high gear wears you out quickly, sapping valuable energy reserves that you might need later. A big energy saver when riding into the wind, or anywhere for that matter, is drafting. When drafting, ride about 6 to 12 inches (15 to 30 cm) behind the rider in front of you. By doing this, you reduce your effort at the lead rider's expense by about 30 percent; that is, it is easier to go faster or farther. When drafting, pay close attention to the task; keep hands on the brake hoods or levers and eyes focused on the road in front of the lead rider, not on his or her rear wheel. In so doing, you can anticipate when the lead rider will have to alter course or speed, which permits proactive rather than reactive riding. Drafting takes practice but it is an essential skill, one that allows experienced riders and beginners to ride together enjoyably.

These are the most basic riding skills. Any aspiring rider, and most certainly racers, should pick up a recent cycling text (see suggested readings). Many offer a wealth of information on riding skills. Another great resource is your local club, where experienced riders/racers can help you develop your bike handling skills.

TEACHING CONSIDERATIONS

1. Define the purpose of the instruction in terms of road or off-road riding.
2. Check equipment for safety and fit.
3. Teach bicycle safety and etiquette. For cyclists who do not have a license to drive a car, spend some time practicing the rules of the road. Use videotapes of different driving conditions, if necessary. Take students out on the road with no traffic to practice until hand signals and understanding of the rules of the road become automatic.
4. Combine more lecture-type material with opportunities for activity.
5. Provide opportunities to cycle. Where possible, conduct these activities in the environment to be used by the student. Choose less heavily traveled areas or less technical trails to begin practice and then move to more demanding areas.
6. Design an obstacle course in a parking lot for improving bike handling skills. The course can contain cones for steering or logs for jumping depending on class emphasis.
7. Hold a 5-mile time trial, starting individual cyclists at 30-second intervals.
8. When planning initial trips, organize a buddy system.
9. Do not take large groups of cyclists into heavy traffic.
10. Have students play "bumper-bike" on a grassy field. The students ride *slowly* and bump into each other on a grassy field, which teaches them how to handle bikes in tight situations.

GLOSSARY

bicycle clothing Special clothing, such as chamois-lined shorts, that prevent saddle chafe and sores.

brake hoods Rubber portion of the brake lever/shift lever mechanism. A good place to rest your hands while cycling.

braking Bringing the bicycle to a stop by using both brakes properly.

clincher tires Tires that have either a wire or kevlar bead, which holds the tire to the rim. Kevlar is more expensive, but much lighter. The lighter weight aids acceleration, which makes for a livelier ride.

double crank A crank assembly that has two chain rings up front. Found on road racing and recreational bikes.

drafting Following closely behind the lead rider to reduce energy expenditure.

frame geometry Used to describe the general structure of the bicycle frame and is typically categorized as traditional or compact for road bikes. Traditional frames have a horizontal top tube, while compact frames have a sloping top tube similar to a mountain bike. Frame geometry is made up of a series of measurements and can have a large impact on a bike's maneuverability.

gear shifting (derailleur) Varying the gear ratios on multispeed bikes; the bicyclist is most efficient when pedaling at a constant rate of revolutions per minute.

granny gear The universal (smallest) chain ring on a triple chain ring crankset—allows climbing up steep hills with less effort.

helmet Lightweight headgear designed for bicycle riding.

presta valve European bike tire valve that has a small knob at the end of the valve stem. The knob must be screwed out to inflate the tire.

rear sprocket The cogs on the rear wheel. The big cogs are the low gears and the little cogs are the high gears. Part of the freewheel on older bikes and the freehub on newer bikes.

RPM The number of revolutions per minute the crank-arms turn. A higher cadence or RPM is generally better than a low one.

rules of the road Rules that apply to both cyclists and automobile drivers.

rules of the trail Always yield to hikers and horses, stay on the trail, stay in control, and ride where it is legal. Do not rim puddles and skid around bends in the trail on downhills. Maintain trails: be a builder as well as a user.

saddle A smooth leather seat just wide enough for good support and not so wide as to chafe.

safety check Checking that the parts of the bicycle are in good working order before a ride.

Schrader valve Bike tire valve that is similar to one found on automobile tires in the United States.

steering Guiding the bicycle more by leaning than by turning the handlebars.

tools for the road Pump; spare tire, patch kit, and piece of tire casing to repair tire sidewall; a few dollars for food and either a cell phone or some change for a phone call.

tools for the trail Chain breaker, chain links, and chain lube; allen and box-end wrenches suitable to your bike's needs; pump; spare tire, patch kit, and a piece of tire casing to repair tire sidewall; screwdriver.

triple crank A crank assembly that has three chain rings up front. Found on touring and mountain bikes.

true A bike wheel that is perfectly straight.

tubeless tire A special clincher tire that relies on a special rim-tire seal to negate the need for an inner tube to hold air. Used with a tire sealant, tubeless tires are highly flat resistant.

SUGGESTED READINGS

Armstrong, L., and Jenkins, S. 2000. *It's not about the bike: My journey back to life.* New York, NY: Putnam Publishing Group.

Baker, A. 1998. *Bicycling medicine: Cycling nutrition, physiology, injury prevention and treatment for riders of all levels.* New York, NY: Fireside.

Borysewicz, E. 1985. *Bicycle road racing: Complete program for training and competition.* Boulder, CO: Velo Press. While outdated in a number of areas, this book can provide new cyclists and racers with a good starting point for a program, and provides some very good information on technical skills that benefit all cyclists.

Brunel, P. 1996. *An intimate portrait of the Tour de France.* France: Bounpame Publishing.

Burney, D. S. 2007. *Cyclocross: Training and technique.* 3rd ed. Boulder, CO: Velo Press. This book provides a complete guide to cycle-cross racing.

Clark, J. 1995. *Mountain biking the national parks.* San Francisco: Bicycle Books. This guide shows where mountain biking in the U.S. national parks is permitted. It covers the parks most suitable for sustainable trail riding.

Edwards, S., and Reed, S. 2000. *The heart rate monitor book for outdoor and indoor cyclists: A heart zone training program.* Boulder, CO: Velo Press. Describes training rides to (1) improve fitness, (2) train for fitness, and (3) enhance performance.

Friel, J. 2009. *The cyclists training bible.* 4th ed. Boulder, CO: Velo Press. An excellent resource for beginning and experienced cyclists. Contains information about constructing a yearly training plan, goal setting, and weight training. Friel has also published similar books for mountain bikers and triathletes.

Lopes, B., & McCormack L. 2010. *Mastering mountain bike skills.* 2nd ed. Champaign, IL: Human Kinetics. Lopes, a former pro mountain biker, provides a thorough written account of how to conquer the trails. This book provides some of the best material on the hows of mountain biking, as well as some of the whys. If serious trail riding is your goal, this is worth the read.

Mills, S., and Mills, H. 2001. *Mountain biking.* Mechanicsburg, PA: Stackpole Books.

Mountain Bike Magazine's complete guide to mountain bike skills. 1996. Emmaus, PA: Rodale Press. This book is designed to help all riders perform better on the trail, from beginners to experts.

Older, J. 2001. *Back-road to off-road biking.* Mechanicsburg, PA: Stackpole Books. Contains information on how to choose a bike and accessories, riding techniques, training, safety, and touring destinations.

Ollivier, J. 2001. *The Maillot Jaune.* Boulder, CO: Velo Press. A history of the most famous cyclists from 1919 to the present.

Parkin, J. 2008. *A dog in a hat: An American bike racer's story of mud, drugs, blood, betrayal, and beauty in Belgium.* Boulder, CO. Velo Press. Former pro cyclist Parkin delivers an engaging tale of his years as a blue-collar cyclist in Europe. An excellent read for those who want a glimpse of cycling behind the cameras.

Pevelar, W. 2009. *The complete book of road cycling and racing.* Camden, ME: McGraw-Hill.

Prehn, T., and Pelkey, C. 2004. *Racing tactics for cyclists.* Boulder, CO: Velo Press. Written for the experienced road cyclist, this illustrated book shows team riders how to ride in a race, explains the importance of position, and discusses individual and team racing tactics. A great resource for the aspiring racer.

Richards, B. 1997. *Mountain biking.* Mechanicsburg, PA: Stackpole Books.

Ritchie, A. 2009. *Major Taylor: The fastest bicycle rider in the world.* San Francisco, CA: Van der Plas Publications

Stevens, T. 2001. *Around the world on a bicycle.* 2nd ed. MechanicsMburg, PA: Stackpole Books.

Zinn, L. 2001. *Zinn and the art of mountain bike maintenance.* 3rd ed. Boulder, CO: Velo Press.

Zinn, L. 2001. *Zinn and the art of road bike maintenance.* 3rd ed. Boulder, CO: Velo Press.

Periodicals

Bicycling, published 11 times per year by Rodale Press, Box 7308, Red Oak, IA 51591-0308.

Cycle Sport, published monthly by Cycle Sport USA, 704 Hennepin Ave., Minneapolis, MN 55403. European publication, which provides good racing stories and behind-the-scenes information.

Mountain Bike Magazine, published 11 times a year by Rodale Press, Box 7308, Red Oak, IA 51591-0308.

Procycling, published monthly by Highbury-Lifestyle of Europe. European publication, which provides the best English language coverage of professional road racing.

Velo News, published 20 times a year by Inside Communications, Box 21450, Boulder, CO 80308-4450. Large newspaper format. Provides coverage of professional mountain and road bike racing, covers amateur racing, training tips, and lists U.S. race events by region.

RESOURCES

Videos & DVDs

Blood, Sweat + Gears. 2009. First Run Features, New York City, NY, Documentary filmmaker Nick Davis chronicles the dramatic story of "the clean team" throughout 2008, a year in which the team leader was superstar David Millar—making a comeback after a doping scandal sidelined his career—and sees Slipstream, now Garmin-Transitions, win their first invitation to the Tour de France.

Only one road. AAA Foundation for Traffic, Falls Church, VA.

Performance mountain biking, 1996. This video from Velo covers all aspects of mountain bike racing. *www.velocatalogue.com.* Velo, 1830 N. 55th Street, Boulder, CO 80301-2700.

Surviving the trail, 1993. This video from Velo covers all aspects of mountain bike maintenance on the trail. *www.velocatalogue. com.* Velo, 1830 N. 55th Street, Boulder, CO 80301-2700.

World Cycling Productions, 704 Hennepin Ave., Minneapolis, MN 55403. They sell videos that cover all the major European pro races.

WEB SITES

The definitive source for professional bike racing news from around the world.
www.cyclingnews.com

Free podcasts delivering the latest training, nutrition and athlete features to your computer or MP3 player.
www.esppodcast.libsyn.com

Probably the best-known online bike store. Performance provides everything except complete bikes at reasonable prices. Numerous other good online stores exist, so don't be afraid to shop around.
www.performancebike.com

For those interested in racing, USA Cycling is the place to start. This site provides a full list of contact information on how to become a licensed bike racer, on or off the road.
www.usacycling.org

Companion site to *Velo News* cycling magazine.
www.velonews.com

Bowling

After completing this chapter, the reader should be able to:

- Display a knowledge of the rules of bowling
- Demonstrate the correct grip, stance, approach, and delivery in bowling
- Identify three styles of delivery
- Instruct a group of students in the fundamentals of bowling
- Recognize and use bowling terminology correctly

HISTORY

Bowling is one of the most popular sports on our planet. It has been enjoyed for many years. In fact, bowling can be traced as for back as about 5,200 B.C.E., since evidence of crude bowling objects were found in an ancient child's grave in Egypt.

The game of modern tenpins had its inception in northern Italy, being derived from variations of games played by the ancients. The Italians called their game "bowls." Rounded stones without finger holes were used as balls and held in the open hand.

In the thirteenth century the game spread to Germany, The Netherlands, and England, where it was known as "ninepins." The playing area was known as the bowling green because the game was usually played on grass. In 1623, Dutch settlers introduced the game to America. It was first played on grass or clay and later on a single wide board. The game attracted considerable interest, and people began to bet extensively on it. In response, laws banning ninepins were passed in several states in the 1840s. Later, to circumvent the law, a Dutchman added one more pin and called it *tenpins.*

In 1895, the American Bowling Congress (ABC) was organized, and, to help standardize the game, it formulated rules governing alleys, balls, and pins. Over the following years, several other organizations were created. In 2005, however, the United States Bowling Congress (USBC) was formed through a merger of the ABC, the Women's International Bowling Congress (WIBC), the Youth American Bowling Alliance (YABA), and USA Bowling (USAB).

Colleges and universities often include lanes in their student recreation centers. In many colleges bowling is a popular course in the physical education curriculum, and some colleges have competitive bowling teams.

Contests on television have done much to increase the popularity of bowling. It was a demonstration sport in the 1988 Olympics, and efforts are underway to make it a permanent part of the Olympics.

SOCIAL VALUES

Bowling is a sport that appeals to everyone: weak or strong, young or old, men or women. It requires the learning of comparatively few skills. It requires only a change of shoes and no special uniform. One can bowl during lunchtime, after work, or in the evening, which is appealing to the average American. It requires no great strength. One can bowl alone or with others for enjoyment, or join a local team either for fun or the opportunity to improve. rhythm, relaxation, and coordination. Once mastered, it is an art. Around the bowling alley, social interaction is pleasurable and tensions seem to disappear. There is always the challenge, as in golf, to turn in a better score. Bowling, because it uses many muscles, is one of the best recreational sports skills, and it is relatively inexpensive.

EQUIPMENT AND FACILITIES

In bowling, 10 wooden or plastic pins are set in a triangular position at the far end of a wooden runway called a "lane" (Figure 9.1). The lane is 60 feet (18.3 m) long from the No. 1 pin to the foul line. It is about 42 inches (1.1 m) wide. On each side of the lane, a channel (also called a gutter) approximately 9 inches (22.5 cm) wide runs from the foul line to the pit, behind the pins. Behind the foul line is the approach, which must not be less than 15 feet (4.6 m) long. The pit, which is behind the pins, must have a drop of at least 9½ inches (23.8 cm) from the lane floor.

Pins are set 12 inches (30 cm) apart from center to center (Figure 9.2). A pin is 15 inches (37.5 cm) in height, with a base diameter of 2¼ inches (5.6 cm). It is typically constructed of clear, hard maple covered with a plastic coating.

Balls are constructed of synthetic plastic, hardened rubber, urethane, or reactive resin. The circumference is not more than 27 inches (67.5 cm), the diameter is about 8½ inches (21.3 cm), and the official ball weighs from 10 to 16 pounds (4.54 to 7.26 kg). Balls usually have three bored holes, two for the bowler's fingers and one for the thumb. These holes

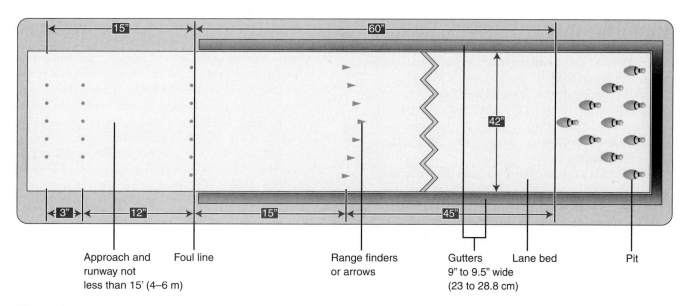

Figure 9.1. The lane.

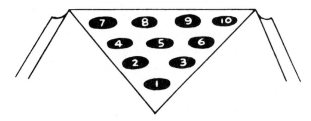

Figure 9.2. Positions of pins and their numbers.

aid in holding and accurately delivering the ball. Special balls with four or five finger holes are now available.

RULES

1. There are 10 frames, and 2 balls are rolled per frame.
   a. Exception #1: If a strike is bowled in frames 1-9, then only one ball is rolled in that frame.
   b. Exception #2: If a strike or spare is bowled in the 10th frame, then 3 balls are rolled in that frame.
2. A ball is legally delivered when it leaves the bowler's hand and crosses the foul line.
3. A strike occurs when all of the pins are knocked down with the first ball.
4. A spare occurs when all pins are knocked down, but it takes two rolls to accomplish this.
5. All pins knocked down by the ball or other pins are counted.
   a. Exception: If the ball bounces out of the gutter or from the rear cushions at the back of the pit and knocks down a pin(s), it does not count. If this happens on the first ball, the pins should be reset and then the second ball rolled. If it happens on the second ball, no pins illegally knocked down should be counted.

6. Any pin moved but still standing is still considered standing. If it is knocked down by the pinsetter, it should be reset.
7. No pins are counted when a foul occurs. A foul occurs when any part of the body touches the lane, gutter, division board, wall, upright, or similar items, beyond the foul line.
   a. If a foul occurs on the first ball, the pins should be reset if necessary and the second ball bowled.
   b. If a foul occurs on the second ball, any pins knocked down should not be counted.
   c. A foul is designated by an "F" on the score sheet.
8. No pins are counted when a dead ball occurs. The pins are reset and the ball rolled again. A dead ball occurs when:
   a. There is interference with the ball when it is on the alley.
   b. Pins are missing in the set-up.
   c. Someone bowls on the wrong lane or out of turn.
   d. Someone is interfered with during the approach.
   e. A pin is bothered before the ball reaches it.

League Bowling

The rules for league bowling are the same as for individual bowling, with these exceptions:

1. The two teams bowl on adjoining lanes. Each team starts on its own lane, then switches lanes on each frame thereafter.
2. Every ball delivered is counted, unless it is a dead ball.
3. If a player bowls on the wrong lane or out of turn, is interfered with by someone else, or comes in contact with an obstacle on the lane, the ball is called dead and is bowled again.

Scoring (See Figure 9.3)

Although many alleys have automatic scoring these days, it is beneficial to be able to determine your own score and the possible scores for others. To do this, use the following:

1. A strike (signified by an X mark) = 10 plus the number of pins knocked down by the next 2 balls. (A strike followed by a spare = 10 + 10 or a 20-pin addition. A strike followed by 2 more strikes = 10 + 10 + 10 or a 30-pin addition.)
   a. Exception #1: If a strike is made on the second ball of the 10th frame, add only 10 plus the number of pins knocked down by the one remaining ball.
   b. Exception #2: If a strike is made on the third ball of the 10th frame, only 10 is added since it is the final ball.
2. A spare (signified by a / mark) = 10 plus the number of pins knocked down by the next ball. (A spare followed by a strike = 10 + 10 or a 20-pin addition.)
   a. Exception: If a spare is made on the third ball of the 10th frame, only 10 is added to the first ball since the spare made was the final ball of the game.
3. A dash signifies when all pins are missed.
4. An open frame occurs when a strike or spare is not made.
5. When the first ball of a frame is circled, this indicates a split remains.

FUNDAMENTAL SKILLS AND TECHNIQUES

Ball Selection

Select a ball by tossing it up and catching it. It should not feel too heavy or too light. The fingers should fit comfortably in the holes. A comfortable fit is essential to good delivery. Select a ball with finger holes that are neither too close nor too far apart from thumb to fingers (i.e., finger span). A good method to determine finger span is to insert the thumb into the thumb hole up to the second joint, or about four-fifths of its length, then lay the hand flat on the surface of the ball with the fingers spread over the holes. The knuckle joints of the fingers should extend about ¼ inch beyond the nearest edge of the finger hole. This allows for proper looseness or slack, which is essential for a comfortable grip. When you grip the ball, this slack, or play, between the palm and the ball should be about ¼ inch (about the width of a pen or pencil). This method of fitting does not apply to fingertip or semifingertip balls.

Grip

The three-finger, or conventional, grip is the most commonly used and is recommended for beginners and young bowlers. It causes less strain on the wrist and arms, and the popular hook ball can be delivered better with this grip than with others. If a person has an excessively weak grip, a four- or five-hole ball is recommended. Bowling balls supplied by bowling establishments are nearly always three-hole balls (Figure 9.4).

In the beginning stance of the approach, the ball should be held in the shake hands position—thumb at 10 o'clock and fingers at 4 (lefties at 2 and 8 o'clock respectively). This position is held throughout the approach to achieve a hook on the ball, which increases the probability of bowling a strike. It is also best to start with the elbow and ball in line with the shoulder. This makes it easier to keep everything in line during the swing and delivery. At the end of the approach, when the ball is released, the thumb should come out first, then the fingers.

Scoring Example

1	2	3	4	5	6	7	8	9	10
8 −	7 /	X	− /	F 9	X	X	7 /	⑧ −	9 / X
8	28	48	58	67	94	114	132	140	160

Frame	Score
1	8 only (an open frame)
2	8 + 10 (a spare) + the next ball (a strike or 10) = 28
3	28 + 10 (a strike) + the next 2 balls (a spare or 10) = 48
4	48 + 10 (a spare) + the next ball (a foul or 0) = 58
5	58 + 9 (an open frame) = 67
6	67 + 10 (a strike) + the next 2 balls (a strike and 7, or 17) = 94
7	94 + 10 (a strike) + the next 2 balls (a spare or 10) = 114
8	114 + 10 (a spare) + the next ball (8) = 132
9	132 + 8 (a split and open frame) = 140
10	140 + 10 (a spare) + the next ball (a strike or 10) = 160

Figure 9.3. Sample method of scoring.

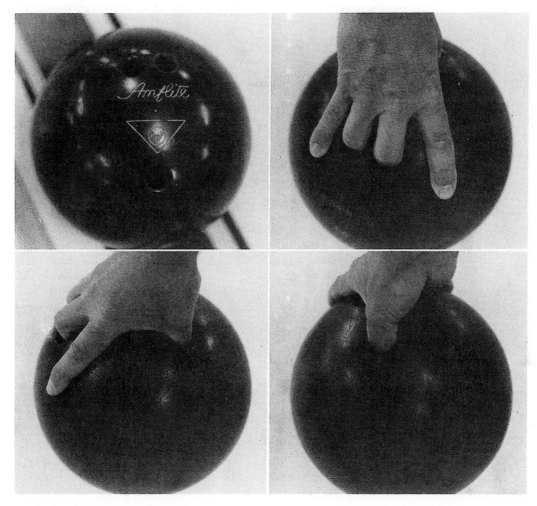

Figure 9.4. Conventional grip.

Stance

The bowler assumes a stance with the body facing the pins, erect or slightly crouched. The left foot is slightly in front of the right (Figure 9.5A) or the feet are even (Figure 9.5B). The ball is held with the right hand on the side of the ball and the left hand supports the ball from underneath. Normally the ball is held about waist high, although some bowlers hold it a bit higher and some lower.

Footwork

The most essential and fundamental skills confronting the beginning bowler are footwork, balance, and rhythm. Bowlers take three, four, or five steps before delivering the ball. There are many good bowlers using each style. The least acceptable style is the three-step approach due to the difficulty in timing with the arm movements. Probably the most popular among bowlers, because timing with the arms is more natural, is the four-step approach. However, each bowler should experiment until he or she finds the number of steps that work.

After this is accomplished, the bowler is ready to synchronize the footstep pattern with the arm movements while delivering the ball. The result of this practice is rhythm and timing. While doing this, you should also practice footwork so that the feet move parallel to each other, remaining on the same board on which they start.

Delivery and Approach to Foul Line

There are many styles of delivery. Usually the ball starts anywhere from waist high to chest high. It may be carried in the center of the body, but as mentioned earlier, to keep your swing straight, it is best to start with the ball in line with the shoulder. In general, the approach has four phases: the push-away, the back swing, the forward swing, and the release of the ball. The approach starts slowly and accelerates toward the end. The last step must stop short of the foul line (see rules), and the ball should contact the lane about 12 to 16 inches (30 to 40 cm) beyond the foul line.

The bowler starts the four-step approach by pushing the ball slightly down and away from the body so that it is extended

Figure 9.5. The stance.

outward between chest and waist height (Figure 9.6). At the same time, a step forward with the right foot is taken. If a five-step delivery is used, the left foot starts first.

The push-away places the ball forward about waist high, and the weight of the ball and gravity give the impetus in making the backward swing arc that is the next phase in the series of movements (Figure 9.7).

In executing this arc, the bowler should not try to shorten or lengthen it; i.e., it should be a natural swing. When the ball reaches the apex of the back swing, it is then ready to gain momentum from this pendulum swing downward and forward smoothly for the release and follow-through (Figure 9.8).

Release

If the bowler has achieved perfect timing, the ball should be coming forward in its well-executed arc just as the last step (left foot) is being taken. The body weight should be perfectly balanced over this last step with the left foot (Figure 9.9).

With continued practice, the series of arm and feet movements blend into a graceful, coordinated, rhythmic pattern.

Follow-through

At the finish of the arm movement, the bowler's left foot will be in front, the right foot balanced on the floor like a rudder behind, and the bowling arm extended forward and upward in the follow-through with the hand still in the shake-hands position. The follow-through should be emphasized since it is as essential in bowling

as in any other throwing motion. The final movement of the approach is an easy sliding glide that is controlled to stop about 2 to 4 inches (5 to 10 cm) short of the foul line (Figure 9.10).

The bowler's posture at the finish should be smooth, easy, and relaxed, with a bend at the knees and very little at the hips. The opposite arm is used as an aid to balance. A straight ball should be rolled smoothly onto the alley beyond the foul line and about 6 to 8 inches (15 to 20 cm) from the right channel. For a hook or curve ball, this distance will vary depending on the amount of curve.

Delivery

The skill techniques just described are common to all delivery styles. The bowler is now confronted with the choice of three styles of delivery: straight ball, hook, and curve (Figure 9.11). The young beginner might first try the straight ball. It is the easiest delivery to accomplish, and positive results are seen in a short amount of time. But older bowlers should experiment with the hook from the start because it is the most efficient way to bowl and is used by almost all professional bowlers.

Straight ball

To throw a straight ball, the thumb is placed on top of the ball in a 12 o'clock position (Figure 9.12A). When bowling for a strike, the bowler directs the ball at the headpin so that the ball will roll in a straight line. The most universal approach is from the right corner of the lane, so that the aim is directed

Figure 9.6. The push-away.

Figure 9.7. The backswing.

Figure 9.8. The forward swing.

Figure 9.9. The release.

Figure 9.10. The follow-through.

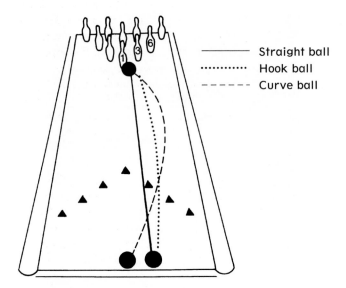

Straight ball
Hook ball
Curve ball

Figure 9.11. Types of deliveries.

in a diagonal crosslane path between the No. 1 and No. 3 pins. Some bowlers use the straight ball when attempting to pick up a spare to take away the effects of the lane conditions on their hook. This might be especially good, for example, for picking up the 7 or the 10 pin.

Hook ball

The hook ball is the most effective of all bowling styles for producing strikes. This style is universal with high-scoring teams. The technique recommended for the beginner's hook ball is as follows: The thumb is placed at the 10 o'clock position and the fingers at the 4 o'clock position, so that the V formed by the thumb and forefinger points down the lane (Figure 9.12B). In a natural hook, the wrist and/or fingers do not turn or rotate. The thumb's coming out first allows the fingers to lift their side of the ball, and a hook results. The ball is released near the right channel. The aim is at the 3-6 pocket. The ball then rolls with a forward motion and breaks sharply toward the left at the 1-3 pocket (see Figure 9.11). With the ball coming in at such a sideward angle, the pins are effectively swept off the lane. Unlike other styles, the hook ball, even thinly hitting the headpin, leaves few single pins remaining and few splits.

Curve ball

The curve ball is not recommended for beginners because of its inconsistency and the difficulty in controlling it. Much practice is required for its mastery (see Figure 9.11).

The technique is as follows: On the backswing, the wrist is rotated to the right, and on the forward swing to the left, which gives the ball a wide, sweeping curve (Figure 9.12C and D). The release is the same as for the hook ball. The ball

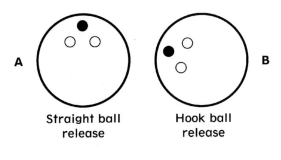

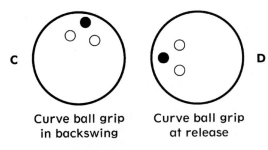

Figure 9.12. Grips for various types of delivery. See text for details.

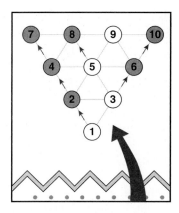

Figure 9.13. The 1-3 pocket.

is laid down near the center of the lane. The follow-through is forward.

Methods

Determining the approach starting position

When learning how to bowl there are two basic methods that can be used, either individually or in combination. But no matter which is used, there is a need to first find the strike position.

To find the strike position, first the approach length needs to be determined. To do this, start near the foul line facing away from the pins. With heels on the dots near the foul line, walk four and a half steps toward the back of the alley and turn around. After locating this distance, the next step is to find where to start from side to side. This is done by starting from a position where the right arm is in line with the second arrow from the gutter on the right side. The arrows on the alley, the dots at the foul line, and the two sets of dots at the back of the approach all line up. To line the arm up with the second arrow, the bowler should line the arm up with the second dot from the outside of the alley. Once the ball goes over the second arrow, the bowler can adjust properly. If the ball is left of the pocket, the bowler moves left, and if it is right of the pocket, he or she should move right. The amount of the move should be based on the 3-1-2 strike adjustment system.

The 3-1-2 strike adjustment system uses the boards on the floor of the alley to help adjust properly when off target.

Using the arrows as targets, for every three boards the ball is off at the pins the bowler needs to move two boards one way or the other from the previous starting point. For example, if on the strike attempt the ball goes over the second arrow but contacts the 3 pin solidly, adjustment would need to be made. Since the bowler is trying to hit the 1-3 pocket (Figure 9.13), and there are six boards from center of pin to center of pin, the bowler should move the ball impact position left three boards by moving the starting position right two boards. After this adjustment, the ball should hit the middle of the 1-3 pocket if bowled over the second arrow. The inside edge of the left foot should be used to make these board adjustments. Of course the bowler would use any ratio of 3 to 2 to determine how much to move. For example, if off one and a half boards at the pins, move one board on the approach, or if off six boards at the pins, move four on the approach. Remember to make adjustments only when the ball goes directly over the proper arrow; otherwise the adjustment will be wrong. On finding the strike position, to be successful, there is a need to decide on a method of bowling.

Bowling systems

Two basic ways of bowling are presented. They are the 3-6-9 system and the 4-8-12/3-6-9 system. If using the 3-6-9 system, once the strike position is known, the 10 pin starting position must also be found before adjustments for spare situations can be made. To do this, the bowler starts at the outside dot on the left side, walks at an angle toward the 10 pin, and delivers the ball over the third arrow on the right side. If the ball is left of the pin, the bowler moves left, or if it is right (i.e., in the gutter), the bowler moves right. Although this seems incorrect, thinking of the arrow as a fulcrum may help. Remember the 3 to 2 board ratio as any adjustments are made.

Once the strike and 10 pin positions are set, spare adjustments can easily be made. The bowler will always move three, six, or nine boards to the right side. Starting from the strike position, move three boards to the right for the

2 pin, six boards right for the 4 pin, and nine boards right for the 7 pin. All balls are bowled over the second arrow, and the approach is angled toward the pin. However, with spare pins on the right side, the ball is bowled over the third arrow and adjustments are three and six boards from the 10 pin starting position. This means moving right from the 10 pin position three boards for the 6 pin and six boards for the 3 pin. Again, the approach should be angled toward the target pin.

On the other hand, with the 4-8-12/3-6-9 system, once the strike position is found, the bowler is set. The starting adjustments for the left side pins are made to the right—three boards right for the 2 pin, six boards right for the 4 pin, and nine boards right for the 7 pin. For the pins on the right side, the adjustments are made to the left side, four boards for each pin (four left for the 3 pin, eight left for the 6, and twelve left for the 10). The important thing to know when using this system is that for the final two outside pins on the right side (the 6 and 10), one should bowl over the third arrow instead of the second arrow.

One of the distinct differences between the two systems is the approach. With the 4-8-12/3-6-9 system the approach is straight, not angular as in the 3-6-9 system. The bowler should check to see where the left foot is at the end of the approach by using the dots near the foul line. Since all the approach dots are coordinated, the bowler can look down after the release and easily tell if he or she is within one to two boards of the starting board. If off more than this, there is a need to correct the approach by straightening it out. The adjustment for angular shots is made by twisting the upper body slightly and being sure to bowl over the proper arrow rather than walking at an angle and bowling over the proper arrow. This should make bowling very consistent, since the approach would not vary from shot to shot.

No matter which system is used (these or others), they all deal with having targets. In spare situations especially, this is true. When there are pins remaining, they are often in a cluster or group. The best way to knock them down is to aim at the target or key pin. The target pin is the one the bowler needs to focus on, and any stance adjustments should be made based on it alone. For example, when two pins are together, the closest pin is key, but for groups of three pins, the middle pin is the target. On the other hand, if the head pin (the #1 pin) is left in a group of four or more, then the head pin is the key pin.

While grouped pins are fairly easy to pick up, when splits occur things are different. In the case of a baby split, where the ball can knock down both pins by going between them, the key pin is the one that is missing between the remaining pins. An example of this would be the 3-10 baby split. With this split the missing 6 pin would be the target, and the stance, approach, and target arrow would be adjusted for the 6 pin. In the case of the 2-7, the 4 pin would be the target. These are just two of the baby split illustrations.

The main thing to remember is to aim for the missing middle pin.

When there is a split greater than a baby split, however, it should be looked at in another way. If the pins left are on different rows, such as in the case of the 4-10 or 6-7 split, the bowler should first look at the closest pin. The adjacent pin behind it on the side away from the split should be the target whether it is present or not. Two examples of this would be that the bowler would aim for the 7 pin on the 4-10 split or the 10 pin on the 6-7 split. In the same manner, when there is a 4-6 split, the procedure is identical, with the bowler aiming for either the 7 or 10 pin to make the pickup.

COMMON ERRORS AND CORRECTIONS

Errors	Corrections
Ball travels directly to right or left gutter when released.	Keep the ball close to your body on backswing and forward swing.
Ball does not have adequate speed.	Increase the speed of your approach or push the ball higher as you complete the push-away.
Bowler releases ball too late or too soon.	Release the ball past the foul line as the hand starts going up.
Path of the ball is inconsistent.	Keep shoulders square to the pins and the sliding or forward foot pointed toward the target. Follow-through should be toward target.
Bowler fails to start approach with the correct foot.	For the four-step approach, right-handers should start with the right foot. Left-handers should start with the left foot.
Bowler frequently fouls.	Make the first step in your approach very short or move your starting position back.
Bowler lofts the ball.	Bend more at the knees than at the waist at point of release and/or release the ball earlier.
Ball falls from bowler's hand during swing.	Check size of finger holes and length of span.

TIPS TO REMEMBER

1. Develop an even speed in rolling all shots, and use whichever speed develops the most accuracy and consistency.
2. Concentrate on the spot to be hit.
3. Relax.
4. Be sure that the approach is not too fast or too slow.
5. Do not force a delivery; let the weight of the ball do the work. The arm merely serves as a pendulum.
6. In rolling the straight ball, be sure that the fingers are behind the ball when it is released, to prevent the ball from curving.

7. Learn to let the thumb come out of the hole first.

8. Hold the wrist firm when releasing the ball.

9. Lay the ball on the lane smoothly.

10. In follow-through, let the arm continue in the direction of the pins.

TEACHING CONSIDERATIONS

1. Basics of bowling can be taught in a gymnasium without real balls by using softballs and a target area. Stance, footwork, approach, and delivery can be effectively practiced before going to the lanes.

2. If needed, lanes can be set up inside the gymnasium using hard rubber bowling balls, 2 × 4s, and plastic pins.

3. If lanes are available for instruction, begin with selection of the ball. Teach stance, delivery, and approach with proper footwork without using the ball. Then add the ball. Concentrate on the push-away action.

4. Teach a four-step approach. For young bowlers it is best to teach the straight ball first. This can be modified later as needed.

5. Begin practice without the pins set up, and initially disregard foul-line infractions. Add rule infractions as learners develop consistency in the coordination and rhythm of their delivery and are placing, rather than dropping, the ball onto the alley.

6. Once pins are set up, the instructor may vary the approach to strike and spare bowling. Some instructors effectively teach strike bowling by setting up only the 1-3 pins to encourage bowling at the 1-3 pocket. Students will not be successful unless they hit the pocket most desirable for strike bowling. Eventually all pins should be set up, and both strike and spare bowling strategies need to be communicated and practiced.

7. Several students can be involved on one lane by charting the path of the *first ball* rolled in each frame for each other. This is a good exercise for evaluating consistency. Students would have to be given pencils and diagrams of the lanes. Evaluating the diagrams would help the instructor correct problems.

8. All aspects of scoring do not have to be introduced until learners are using two balls to get down all the pins. All students should be expected to learn how to score.

9. Bowling systems can be introduced once some consistency has been achieved.

10. Introduce spare bowling by setting up different spare combinations with pins in front of the learner and having the learner make decisions about which pin to hit and where to hit it. Another way to do this is to roll the first ball without strike intent and then try to pick up the remaining pins with the second ball.

11. Based on the students' previous bowling scores, compute their handicaps and put them into teams for a tournament. All groups will be equal, regardless of skill level, with the use of handicaps. If time permits, alternate instruction with actual games so students are bowling games early in the unit and are still receiving instruction throughout the unit.

GLOSSARY

ABC American Bowling Congress.

anchor The last bowler on a team.

approach That part of the lane, or runway, on which the bowler takes steps to proceed to the delivery point, the foul line.

arrows The arrows (called *range finders* in Figure 9.1) start at 15 feet (4.57 m) out from the foul line and are numbered 1-3 from each gutter; the center arrow is numbered 4.

average Total number of pins credited to a bowler divided by the number of games bowled in one season in a sanctioned league.

baby split The 3-10 split for right-handed bowlers and the 2-7 split for left-handed bowlers.

backup ball A ball delivered in such a manner as to curve toward the arm that delivered the ball. For a right-handed bowler, the ball curves to the right.

bedposts The 7-10 split.

big four The 4-6-7-10 split.

blind score Score for an absent bowler. This is usually the average minus 10 pins.

blow Same as error or miss.

boards The strips of wood on the lane.

box Same as frame.

Brooklyn or crossing over Hitting the headpin and adjacent pin on the opposite side of the lane from which the bowler released the ball on the delivery.

channel Another name for "gutter."

cherry Knocking down one or more of the front pins in a spare and leaving others standing.

cluster Pins next to one another.

convert To make a spare.

dots or spots The dots on the approach are use to standardize the approach starting and ending positions.

double Two consecutive strikes.

error A complete failure to knock down any remaining pins after the first ball is rolled.

foul The act of touching the foul line with the foot or hand. If a foul is made on the first throw, all 10 pins are respotted; if it occurs on the second throw, only the pins knocked down with the first ball count.

foul line The line at the end of the approach at the beginning of the alley (Figure 9.1). If this line is crossed, the ball does not count.

frame The box on the score sheet in which the scores are recorded. Ten frames constitute a game.

gutter Trough, or channel, on each side of a lane.

gutterball A ball that falls off the lane into the gutter.

handicap System used to equalize competition.

headpin The No. 1 pin.

hook A ball that is caused to curve from outside in on its way to the pins.

kingpin The No 5 pin.

lane The alley bed.

lane conditions The amount of oil on the lane. It is inversely related to the amount of curve on the ball.

leave Pins left standing after the first ball has been rolled.

lift An upward motion given to the ball by the fingers during the release.

line A complete game recorded in the 10 frames across the score sheet.

loft Throwing the ball onto the lane rather than placing it down near the foul line.

mark A strike or spare.

open frame Failure to achieve a strike or spare in a frame.

perfect game A score of 300.

pitch Angle at which holes are drilled into the bowling ball.

pocket The gap between the No. 1 and No. 3 pins for right-handed bowlers and between the No. 1 and No. 2 pins for left-handed bowlers.

rack The trough holding the balls beside the runway.

return The ball returned from the pit to the bowler by way of a trough alongside or under the alley.

setup The arranging of 10 pins in regular formation.

sleeper A pin that is hidden behind another pin.

spare Bowling down all pins with two balls in any one frame.

strike Bowling down all pins with the first ball rolled.

striking out Rolling strikes for any part of a remainder of a game.

tandem Any two pins in a spare formation arranged one behind the other.

triple or turkey Three consecutive strikes at any time in a game.

WIBC Women's International Bowling Congress.

YABA Young American Bowling Alliance.

SUGGESTED READINGS

Ange-Traub, C. 1998. *Bowling.* 8th ed. Dubuque, IA: McGraw-Hill. Provides readers with all the basics, including up-to-date information on equipment and advanced techniques.

Edginton, C. 1993. *Bowling.* Dubuque, IA: Eddie Bowers. Features a step-by-step approach to the game of bowling, and discusses techniques, strategies, lane markers, pin placements, and scoring.

Grinfelds, V., and Hultstrand, B. 2007. *Right down your alley.* 6th ed. Stamford, CT: Wadsworth/Thomson Learning. Contains advice on how to improve bowling efficiency, accuracy, and consistency, and how to correct common errors.

Hinitz, D. 2003. *Focused for bowling.* Champaign, IL: Human Kinetics.

Jowdy, J. 2009. *Bowling execution.* 2nd ed. Champaign, IL: Human Kinetics.

Martin, J. 2000. *Skills, drills and strategies for bowling.* Scottsdale, AZ: Holcomb Hathaway Publishers.

Mullen, M. 2004. *Bowling fundamentals.* Champaign, IL: Human Kinetics.

Wiedman, D. 2006. *Bowling: Steps to success.* 3rd ed. Champaign, IL: Human Kinetics.

RESOURCES

Video

Bordon, F., and Yakobosky, R. 2004. *Essential keys to better bowling.* DVD. www.sportsvideos.com.

See Appendix C for other video sources.

WEB SITES

Bowling equipment
  www.bowling.com

College bowling
  www.collegebowling.com

Complete bowling index
  http://www.bowlingindex.com/

International Bowling Museum and Hall of Fame
  www.bowlingmuseum.com

pin bowling
  www.10pinbowling.com

United States Bowling Congress
  www.bowl.com

Dance: Concert and Recreational Forms

After completing this chapter, the reader should be able to:

- Distinguish among various forms of dance and appreciate their development
- Demonstrate the fundamentals of movement
- Understand how elements of movement (space, time, and effort) and creativity apply to modern dance
- Organize and teach square dancing
- Organize and teach folk dancing
- Recognize forms of social dancing

Dance offerings today at all academic levels are increasingly broad in scope and rich in content. On the national level, the diversity of dance programming makes generalization difficult. Curriculum frameworks for dance exist in both physical education and the arts, and are mandated at the state level. They have changed substantially over the past few decades. One significant shift has been toward framing dance as a cultural activity, relating it to social studies and humanities curricula. Another has been to teach dance at the elementary level using Rudolf Laban's movement concepts and developmental theory.

School programs often include two broadly defined types of dance: recreational forms and concert (performance) forms. The first category might include international folk dance (world dance), social (ballroom), square dance, hip-hop (club dance), and country line dance. These types of dance are done largely for health benefits, socialization, and the enjoyment of participants. They are primarily leisure activities having some aspects of cultural appreciation.

By contrast, concert dance forms use the body and movement as a means of communication, usually with an audience. In concert dance, with its emphasis on performance outcomes, the process of making and performing dances is central. Students can be taught the basic skills for creating and performing their own dances. The goals of dance performance are varied: they may be to entertain, inform, educate, enlighten, or provoke an audience. In most cases, however, the primary goals are aesthetic rather than recreational. Although modern dance and creative dance (movement education) are the forms often taught in schools, there is increasing recognition of ballet, jazz, and non-western dance forms in dance curricula and a desire to embrace dance as a global art form.

The growth of participation in recreational dance forms is indicated by the proliferation of clubs, classes, performances, festivals, conferences, publications, and videos. Recreational forms of dance undergo regular changes in popularity from time to time. Over the past decade, there have been many changes in vogue, from break dance to country line dance, to tango and lambada, to Irish step dancing. Many dances experience a resurgence of popularity after a period of decline—for instance, disco, tap, and swing dance have all had renewed interest in the past decade.

As a nonverbal means of communication, dance can quickly transcend barriers of language and promote cultural understanding. In fact, international folk dance has been used in American education since the beginning of the century to enhance cross-cultural understanding. At the community level, dance often plays an important part in the affirmation of cultural identity, shared history, and values. Ethnic communities throughout the United States regularly host festivals, parades, and special events designed to celebrate and strengthen culture, share it with others, educate children, and enhance political presence. In many of these cultural events, dance plays a key role.

Experts in dance education, supported by Howard Gardner's theory of multiple intelligences, which identified and validated the bodily kinesthetic intelligence, tend to recommend creative dance as an important component of general education in the early years. Creative dance emphasizes body awareness, knowledge of the fundamental elements of movement, problem solving, creativity, and self-expression. This is the best time to involve boys (who are often not encouraged to dance in American culture), as they quickly find it exciting, challenging, and gratifying to participate in dance. When it is developmentally appropriate, there may be a shift in emphasis to technical skills and the mastery of more complex choreography, without sacrificing the creative component of dance making. In this schema, both creative exploration and technical training have a contribution to make to dance education.

It is quite possible to develop a wide and deep appreciation of dance through reading and watching dance in performance or on film and video. However, only through active participation in dance does one develop the bodily kinesthetic knowledge needed for teaching or fully understanding any kind of dance. Specialized training is needed for any teacher who wishes to integrate dance activities into the curriculum. College courses in dance are offered for those majoring in dance, physical education, and elementary education. Professional development workshops in dance are useful for educators who wish to expand their teaching competencies.

As a subject area, dance is malleable and can be successfully introduced or adapted within almost any context. Dance programming is most effective when determined by assessing the needs of a particular population. However, it often happens that a dance program, once established, shifts its focus as it grows. One common sequence is that dance is first introduced perhaps for recreational purposes, but as participants increase their dance knowledge, ability, and self-confidence, performance opportunities are sought out as a natural and satisfying culmination.

HISTORY OF DANCE

People have always danced. They have used some form of rhythmic movement as a part of their life experience from the beginning of time. Scholars argue that dance is one of the first forms of human communication. History indicates that dance has been used in worship, as part of ritualistic ceremonies connected to important rites of passage, for entertainment, for socialization, for education, for healing, in preparation for war, and as means of expressing ideas and emotions. Recent research, conducted worldwide, defines dance as cultural activity and reveals the rich and varied forms of dance in different cultures.

FUNDAMENTALS OF MOVEMENT

An understanding of the fundamentals of movement is an important element in the education of a dancer. The fundamentals may be thought of as the basic ingredients of movement—the ABCs of a complex and varied language—which combine and interact in innumerable ways to give movement its richness as an expressive art form.

Theorists through the years have attempted to articulate the basis of movement for purposes of studying, analyzing, and teaching dance. Rudolf Laban spent his entire career developing a conceptual and practical framework for penetrating the complexities of movement. His ideas have been widely incorporated in dance and physical education programs throughout the United States, Canada, and Europe.

Laban observed that every movement may be described in terms of three interconnected aspects: body, space, and effort.

Body

Laban suggested that there are at least six basic body actions: weight shift, gesture, traveling (locomotion), jumping, turning, and balancing. Weight shift is any movement that causes the body to transfer weight from one part to another. The most obvious example is stepping. Another example might be shifting weight from one hip to another in a seated position.

Gesture is defined as any non-weight-bearing movement, such as flexion, extension, rotation, bending, stretching, reaching, collapsing, or spiraling. See Figures 10.1 and 10.2.

Traveling causes the body to move from one location in general space to another. There are many ways to travel, and they might include some of the other body actions. Examples of ways of locomoting include walking (with different body parts), running, rolling, crawling, creeping, and sliding.

When considering just foot patterns in traveling, there are only five possible ways to transfer the weight of the body using the feet:

walk, run, or leap (Figure 10.3) Transfer of weight from one foot to the other foot.
hop (Figure 10.4) Transfer of weight from one foot to the same foot.
jump (Figure 10.5). Transfer of weight from two feet to two feet.
assemble Transfer of weight from one foot to two feet.
sissonne Transfer of weight from two feet to one foot.

With the exception of walk and run, the rest of these patterns are aerial. They can only be performed with a push-off and landing component.

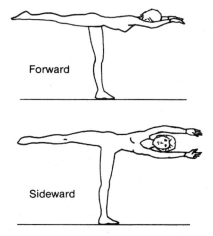

Figure 10.1. Flexion.

Forward

Sideward

Figure 10.2. Extension.

Figure 10.3. Leap.

Figure 10.4. Hop.

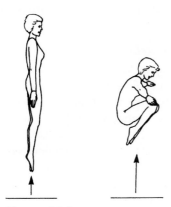

Figure 10.5. Jump.

Once the five basic weight transfers are mastered, it is easy to see how all other dance steps are simply combinations or variations of them. The following dance steps are commonly found in many dance forms:

gallop Combination of a leap and a walk. The leap, the first part of the movement, is rhythmically long, and the walk onto the other foot is rhythmically short.

skip Combination of a walk and a hop. The movement is performed on the same foot. The step, which is the first part of the movement, is rhythmically long, and the hop, the second part of the movement, is short.

slide Combination of two walking steps. The forward step, or the first part of the movement, is rhythmically long, and the second step, in which the other foot is brought up to the forward foot and the weight placed on it, is rhythmically short.

two-step Combination of two quick steps followed by one slow step.

schottische Combination of three walks and a hop. Each movement is rhythmically the same length as the others. The hop creates a fun variation on weight transfer.

step-hop Combination of a walk followed by a hop on the same leg. The first and second parts of the movement are rhythmically equal.

In particular, the skip, slide, and gallop have an identical rhythmic pattern and can easily be linked together in dance combinations. Adding changes of direction or floor pattern (see the section on space) can make for interesting and delightful challenges.

Turning is defined as a change of body facing. Turns can be performed to varying degrees ranging from one-eighth of a turn to multiple turns.

Balancing is momentary stillness in movement, where the body finds dynamic equilibrium and the shape of the body takes on heightened importance.

The basic body actions can be used quite effectively as a starting point for making dance combinations. For example, a teacher might easily create an interesting dance combination using the following sequence: perform a gesture while also shifting weight, followed by some type of traveling pattern, climaxing in a turning jump, and resolving with a balancing shape. This phrase would be both challenging and fun for students to perform.

Space

Dancers inhabit space and also shape it with their bodies. Therefore, a knowledge of the basic space elements is a necessary part of dance education. The basic elements of space include personal space, general space, directions, levels, floor patterns, and shape.

Personal space is defined as the area directly around the body that can be reached without stepping or traveling. (Laban termed it "kinesphere." Educators who teach young children sometimes refer to it as a "space bubble.") Individuals can never leave their personal space; it travels with them when they move through general space. Teaching students to have an awareness of personal space has many advantages, not the least of which is empowering students to create a large enough personal space away from others for their bodies to move freely and safely.

Dance, like all movement, must take direction in space. It is possible for the dancer to move forward, backward, up, down, side right, side left, and diagonally. Exploring directions in space can easily lead to creating interesting patterns of movement, particularly if other ideas are included, such as levels (up and down), facing changes (turns), rhythm (fast and slow), and floor patterns (pathways).

Floor patterns are spatial pathways taken by a dancer while traveling. Some common floor patterns are linear, curved, zigzag, and spiral.

Dancers may also create "writing" in the air with the movement of their bodies through space. For example, one might poke a hand directly above the head in a one-dimensional pathway, toss an arm in an undercurve creating a two-dimensional pathway, or swing an arm in a spiraling figure eight creating a three-dimensional pathway.

Dancers, teachers, and choreographers would be wise to consider how the use of space may contribute to the expressive impact of a dance. A dance that is restricted to a small square of light in one corner of the stage, for example, will communicate very differently than one in which the dancers travel energetically throughout the performing space.

Effort: Movement Qualities

Movement qualities are related to the dynamics and expressive aspects of movement. A dancer can intentionally use energy in different ways to color or shade movement, deeply altering the effect it has upon the viewer.

Laban and F. C. Lawrence observed that human movement reveals the inner attitude of the mover through the presence of four motion factors: time, space, weight, and flow. The mover's approach to each of these factors is manifested in various dynamic/effort qualities, which combine to give movement its expressive impact.

Time relates to the mover's attitude toward time—is it rushed or languid? Movement that slows down or is prolonged reveals an indulgent attitude toward time and is described as sustained (as in a leisurely yawn). Movement that accelerates, that is abrupt or urgent, is described as sudden (as in a surprised jump of fright).

Space relates to the focus of the dancer. It can be indirect and flexible, attending to a wide span of overlapping foci. Or it can be direct and pinpointed to a very specific focus.

Weight pertains to an active use of body weight. Light is experienced as resisting gravity, decreasing pressure, and moving delicately. Strong is increasing pressure, power, and forcefulness. A passive use of body weight leads to collapse and heaviness.

Flow is experienced as greater or lesser amounts of bodily tension. A free-flow movement is one that is uncontrolled, abandoned, and difficult to restrict or stop. A bound movement is one that is controlled or restricted. It has a sense of holding back.

By exploring all the efforts singly and in combinations, dance students learn a wide range of expressive possibilities.

Aileene Lockhart categorized movement qualities in a different way, using the mechanical properties and release of energy into the various parts of the body as criteria. She classifies movement qualities into swinging, sustaining, percussing, suspending, vibrating, and collapsing.

Swinging is the most frequently used and naturally occurring of the body's movements. Swings are characterized by a slight impulse, a pause, a giving away to gravity, and then a rebounding into another suspension. These movements convey feelings of freedom, openness, and ease.

Sustained movement is even, smooth, and free of sudden and sharp actions. This requires maximum muscular control. Sustained movement elicits feelings of calmness, self-control, restraint, and sometimes mystery.

Sharp, aggressive movements in which energy appears and disappears quickly symbolize percussive movement quality. Emotions of vigor, explosiveness, directness, and aggressiveness are evoked through percussive movement.

Movement is described as suspended when two opposing forces are equated. The instant at the peak of a leap when the upward force and the force of gravity are equal is an example of this movement quality. It is used to express anticipation, ecstasy, and breathlessness.

Vibrating movement results from quickly recurring, small percussive movements. It is characterized by intermittent spurts of energy within a limited range. Most commonly this quality of movement is used to denote fear or rage.

Collapsing movements occur when muscular tension in the body is released and gravity is permitted to take over. This can be accomplished in a gradual and controlled manner or suddenly. Emotions such as acquiescence, resignation, and helplessness are elicited through this movement quality.

Rhythm and Its Relationship to Dance

Rhythm is what makes the world go around; it is the pulsation of the universe, the foundation of the world. We would not and could not be alive today if rhythm was not a part of us. The beating of our hearts and exhalation of air from our lungs are excellent examples of rhythm. Changing of seasons, patterns in rock formations on the coast, stars in the heavens, tides, and patterns of trees and flowers are all rhythmic examples given to us by nature. We also find rhythm in the pattern of our lives. These rhythmic patterns may be seen in changes in the fashion world, politics, economics, and in the many social changes that come upon us during a lifetime.

Rhythm, by definition, is a series of pulsations that can be even or uneven, weak or strong. These are grouped in small groups of time. Some rhythmic elements a dancer is concerned with are:

accent   Stress or force of movement that can vary from very strong and hard to light and weak.
phrase   A group of several meters giving a feeling of unity and completion to the rhythmic sentence and movement pattern.

underlying beat Constant pulsation that takes place throughout the dance. This beat is divided into units, thus designating the meter or time in which the dance is performed.

Concert Forms

MODERN DANCE

At the turn of this century in the United States, a new form of dance was created. Five pioneers rebelled against the styles of dance imported from Europe (ballet, social dance, and musical revues) and set out to forge a new form of dance befitting American culture and spirit. The results were the beginning of modern dance.

Isadora Duncan, considered by many to be the matriarch of what is now known as modern dance, retreated from the artificial movements, rigid style, and royal court settings of ballet. She explored free and natural movements generated from the center of the body (solar plexus). She also shed the restrictive clothing and many corsets of Victorian-era women. She danced barefoot, in loose and flowing Greek-inspired tunics.

An American contemporary of Duncan was Loie Fuller, who experimented with lighting, props, and fabric to create illusions on stage. Both artists struggled to find success in the United States, but were immediately embraced by European audiences that better understood their artistic contributions.

Following closely upon Duncan and Fuller came Ruth St. Denis and Ted Shawn, who reintroduced theatricality and technique into dance and founded the first school for modern dance in Los Angeles in 1915, the Denishawn school. A major contribution of Ted Shawn's was bringing men into American modern dance, and founding Jacob's Pillow, a modern dance retreat in the Berkshires of Massachusetts that is an international showcase for dance.

The Denishawn company helped to promote the young art form by making 13 cross-country performance tours in the 1920s while the school provided training for future teachers and performers. These included three pioneers of the second generation of modern dancers: Martha Graham, Charles Weidman, and Doris Humphrey. All three of these artists established themselves in New York City in the late 1920s, where they taught, performed, created new choreographies, and eventually opened schools.

The fifth pioneer to contribute to the development of modern dance in this country and to musical theater was a German dancer, teacher, and choreographer, Hanya Holm. Holm represented the best of the German tradition in modern dance, which began with Rudolf von Laban in the early 1900s and was furthered by the great German expressionist dancer Mary Wigman. The German and American modern dance forms originated at almost the same time, but Germany's was disrupted by World War II when many German dancers emigrated to the United States or England.

During the 1930s, New York City became the hub for modern dance and modern art. During this period at Bennington College in Vermont, many college teachers of physical education participated in dance classes taught by these outstanding artists and in turn taught dance to the students in their classes, in effect spreading modern dance ideas and technique throughout the nation. As a result, today many universities house a dance department either within physical education or the arts. University dance programs offer comprehensive study in a variety of areas, including pedagogy, history and philosophy of dance, music, production, choreography, movement analysis, and injury prevention, as well as training in a variety of movement styles. Dance has become a professional orientation for many students who eventually become teachers, performers (in television, film, or on stage), choreographers, dance therapists, and scholars.

Historically, modern dance has been characterized by innovation, individual expression, and continuous evolution. The face of what is commonly called "modern dance" is in constant flux. Whereas in decades past modern dance classes were likely to be influenced by the techniques developed by the "pioneers," today it is common to see contemporary modern styles that reflect a broad range of stylistic and semantic influences. Although there is a broad range in modern dance vocabulary; its ongoing emphasis on individual voice and creativity make modern dance a valuable study for students of any age (Figure 10.6).

Technique

Modern dance technique develops control of the body, and kinesthetic awareness and increases the range of movement. Warm-up exercises prepare the body for the more demanding work to follow. Subsequent patterns develop strength and flexibility, alignment, and balance and expand the movement vocabulary. Combinations using the length of the studio develop the ability to travel through space and to move in and out of the floor with ease. Classes often culminate in a dynamic dance phrase that gives participants the opportunity to practice the skills they have been learning in previous activities. Each section of the lesson is designed to prepare for the next.

To teach dance rather than a series of exercises to music, the leader must be technically skilled to the level of competent demonstration. Phrasing must be clear, with interesting rhythmic variations. Many kinds and variations of movement must be presented to increase the beginner's vocabulary of movement. While dance classes vary in content and style, students at any level should be helped to experience dance as an expressive art form. Students should dance in class as if they were on stage, with total concentration and intensity.

All individuals can be creative in movement to some degree, if only because we are creative in movement in the way we go about our daily tasks. Modern dance develops

Figure 10.6. A modern dance student performs. (Source: Ashley Hartka)

further the individual's creativity in movement (Figure 10.6). In a modern dance class, the student has the opportunity to explore movement and then to solve movement problems. The student learns to improvise, or move on the spur of the moment without any previous plan, and then to plan a dance pattern or dance study. Beginning dance studies ask students to explore elements of movement in a personal way. For example, a study might be about changing meter and rhythm, contrasts in dynamics, or elements of space. As dancers gain choreographic experience, they may be given the opportunity to create longer, more developed compositions. This composition has a theme or idea and has a beginning, a development, a climax, and an ending.

Sources of inspiration come from the world around us and the world within us. A dance study may be based on an idea or emotion, an interesting movement phrase, or art forms such as music, poetry, literature, painting, or sculpture. There are as many approaches to making dances as there are individuals who make them. Some choreographers begin before knowing what the dance will be about. Others come in to the dance studio, driven by a specific image or a need to communicate a specific idea. Sometimes the choreographer's intention shifts while rehearsing with the dancers. Choreography is a process of trial and error, and, just like writing an essay or a poem, many rough drafts generally precede the polished final product.

In evaluating the composition, it is useful to ask the following questions: Are my choreographic intentions clear to the viewer? Have I made a unified statement in which all parts contribute to the whole? Have I fully investigated the movement material (the language of the choreographer) to find a vocabulary that is fresh, personal, and well suited to the choreographic goals?

The following are ideas that may help the beginning dancer get started in creating a movement study:

1. Create your own phrase that includes locomotion, a balance, a jump, a turn, a swing, a collapse, a leg gesture, and a head gesture, in any order. This is your theme. Try varying it by doing it twice as fast, twice as slow, making it smaller or larger, doing it all on a low level, changing its direction, finding a way to make the whole thing jump. Try your phrase to two contrasting selections of music and see how it changes in response. How else can you vary your phrase? You might create a brief dance that uses the new material you've discovered.

2. Explore opposites in movement—forceful and delicate, for example. Try each of these qualities in isolated body parts and then in the whole body. Try them traveling and in one place, near the floor and in the air. Try them fast and slow, large and small. Notice the different feelings created by the contrasting qualities. Do you have a preference for one of them? Create a study (a brief dance composition) that demonstrates the contrast between these two qualities. Other pairs that might be explored include rigid and floppy, percussive and smooth, near and far. Find your own!

3. With a partner, play with interesting body shapes and relationships. How can you fill the negative space created by your partner's shape? Find a relationship in which your own weight is counterbalanced by your partner's. Check out contrasts in level. How about shapes that are intertwined or others that are more spacious? Find four duet shapes that you really like and figure out how to move interestingly from one to the other. Transitions may be longer or shorter in duration.

4. Examine autumn leaves, pine needles, seashells, coral, or other natural objects. Notice shapes, textures, weight, and density. How might these characteristics be expressed in movement? You are not being asked to look like the object in question, only to express its essence through movement.

Choreography is a form of creative research. It takes time, perseverance, and imagination. The dancer spends many hours experimenting in the studio, testing movement ideas. The completed work is the culmination of an in-depth investigation process. This is a mental, physical, and emotional challenge, but the final outcome is well worth the effort, because that is when the complete expression and discovery of the individual are realized.

BALLET

History

Ballet technique emerged from court dances of the sixteenth century. The basic steps were codified by Beauchamps at the Royal Academy of Dance in Paris in the seventeenth century. In the early nineteenth century, Carlo Blasis published two books that described the theories and procedures of that day. His descriptions are the basis of ballet training of the intervening years and of today. Ballet moved through a period of acclaim in the eighteenth and early nineteenth centuries, but public interest declined in the latter part of the nineteenth century. When Serge Diaghilev's Ballet Russe, a group of émigrés from Russia, went to Paris in 1909, western Europe was astonished by the artistic daring and innovation of Russian ballet. This created renewed interest throughout the Western world. Although Diaghilev's Ballet Russe only functioned for 20 years, in that time it transformed ballet into a vital art form.

By the 1940s, the United States could claim two major companies, Ballet Theatre (later changed to American Ballet Theatre) and the New York City Ballet. Since that time, ballet has flourished throughout the United States, with many ballet companies active today, including a large number of civic and regional groups.

Ballet in Education

Ballet is considered the backbone of training in dance programs in higher education and is more frequently a part of the secondary school dance program today than in the past. The highly disciplined training builds a strong technique (Figures 10.7 and 10.8). Youngsters are most responsive to ballet, much to the surprise of some teachers who have been hesitant to include it in the school dance offerings. As in all other aspects of dance, the caliber of the teaching will determine the eagerness and enthusiasm of the students, the amount of progress made, and the suitability of the form in the total dance offerings.

JAZZ

History

Jazz dance grew out of the African heritage, the Irish clog dance, minstrel shows, vaudeville, social dances, and other sources. It is truly American in origin. Syncopation makes jazz rhythmically stimulating.

Figure 10.7. A modern dance student experimenting with gravity. (Source: Alina Prax)

Figure 10.8. A ballet student performs an arabesque. (Source: David Andrews)

Jazz Dance in Education

Jazz in the educational setting ranges from popular movements or steps taken from disco dancing to work that is original and varied, exciting for the movement style as well as the rhythm. It is changing continually because of its strong relationship to contemporary popular culture.

When jazz dance is taught with an awareness of its rich history, students begin to appreciate the significance of this art form as an exuberant expression of contemporary American life.

TAP DANCING

History

Tap dancing is an American dance form that originated from the merging of African, Irish, and English cultures. It began in the southern United States when blacks and whites copied each other's dance styles, and developed further in the mid-1800s in northern urban settings. Tap dance was made popular through touring minstrel shows and later during the vaudeville tours; however, blacks and whites were segregated as performers, which led to the peculiar use of blackface characterization (white performers blackening their faces to imitate African American performers.)

A combination of Irish jig, English clog dancing, and African-based dance steps mixed with complex African rhythms distinguish tap dancing from all other forms of dance. The earliest forms were flat-footed and used the edges of the foot in a style called "buck and wing." The 1900s brought about a new and complex set of steps that were more rhythmic, smooth, and steady. Tap dancing became extremely popular during these times through vaudeville shows, on showboats, and especially on Broadway stages in Ziegfeld Follies and other shows. In the 1920s and 1930s, Bill "Bojangles" Robinson invented and popularized a new style of tap dancing that was up on the toes, elegant, and rhythmically very precise.

Tap dancing reached a zenith during the 1930s on Broadway and in Hollywood musical films, when enormous productions were mounted, sometimes employing hundreds of tap dancers. Many of these shows and films are now considered "classics" in the history of American entertainment. Some examples are the opulent art deco films of Busby Berkeley, the romantic films of Fred Astaire and Ginger Rogers, and the films of Gene Kelly, which blend athleticism with tap dancing. During the 1960s and 1970s, tap dance experienced a period of decline in popularity, with the exception of a few masters like Honi Coles who kept performing and teaching throughout the United States and Europe.

In the 1980s, a revival of interest in tap dancing as a form of recreation and entertainment led to reconstruction of many Broadway classics such as *Singin' in the Rain, On Your Toes, Showboat,* and *42nd Street,* and the making of new films such as *White Nights* and *Tap.* Other new shows such as *Sophisticated Ladies, A Chorus Line, The Tap Dance Kid,* and

Jelly's Last Jam featured new talented artists like Gregory and Maurice Hines and Savion Glover.

In the 1990s, enormous, sustained public interest in shows like the traditional Irish step-dancing production *Riverdance,* percussion-filled *Stomp,* and Broadway's *Bring in Da Noise, Bring in Da Funk* have fueled the success of many similar shows such as Australian *Tap Dogs* and the spin-off of *Riverdance, Lord of the Dance.*

Tap Dance in Education

Tap dancing instruction began in public schools around the early 1900s. Today there are hundreds of teachers, primarily in private dance studios and recreation centers, who continue to teach this art form. Since the late 1970s there has been a sustained public interest in tap-dance instruction, which has recently been boosted by the growing interest in its parent form of traditional Irish step dancing.

Tap dance has a standardized vocabulary, as do ballet and certain jazz and modern styles. The marked difference between these forms is that tap dancing might be considered drumming with the feet. Mastering precise rhythmic patterns and a sense of musicality are an important part of the art form. It is recommended that children begin creative forms of dance before moving on to tap dancing, which requires sophisticated control of the feet and balance.

Recreational Forms

All recreational dance involves people moving together and enjoying the group or partner as well as the rhythmic movement. These forms are an ideal coeducational activity, as they provide an easy, casual basis for mixing and working together. There are dances suitable for every age level.

A major stimulus to the growth of recreational dance has been the development of good recordings. Having appropriate, inexpensive music readily available eliminates the cost and trouble of an accompanist. Moreover, authentic music is motivating to beginning dancers. They can tape music for home practice and small parties. Where once only large groups could afford dance music, now the individual can bring an "orchestra" home for a family swing lesson.

If teachers, recordings, and dances are up-to-date, students can move readily from the classroom to local clubs and recreational classes for leisure enjoyment. Some teachers take their classes to community dances or require attendance once during the semester to increase the likelihood of participation after graduation.

Fun is part of any recreational dance class from the first day. There is no long period of learning before the student can enjoy the satisfaction of accomplishment. At the same time, challenging new figures, steps, or dances should constantly be presented, as should more complicated combinations or more intricate rhythms. The range of skill possible in recreational dance forms is extremely wide.

Limitations of space preclude discussion of all the types of recreational dance, and new variations are constantly becoming popular. For example, country-western round dance, country-western swing, and round dancing are currently very popular. Thus, only square dancing is presented in detail; folk and social dances are introduced briefly.

AMERICAN SQUARE DANCE
History
The American square dance (Figure 10.9) had its beginning in England with the English country dance, a dance form that developed among the people in rural districts. In the early 1600s, the dance did not enjoy tremendous popularity, especially in larger cities. The impetus that propelled it into prominence came in 1651 when John Playford published the first English country dance book. Most of the dances compiled for this publication were known as "longways," or what the French later called *contre* dances. In the contre, participants arranged themselves in two lines facing each other. Through various sequences of movements, dancers moved from one position in the line to the next or from one line to the other.

Before the introduction of Playford's book, the dances of the royal court had been in vogue. These dances sometimes contained intricate dance steps and suggested a romantic or

Figure 10.9. Square dancers doing a left-hand square.

flirtatious attitude on the part of participants. To understand the significance of Playford's publication in regard to the people's choice of dances, it is necessary to investigate the conditions that prevailed in England during the early part of the seventeenth century.

Segments of England's population had been agitating for change in government. This led to civil war and the eventual beheading of the king. Before this event, a group of Puritans, who had been urging separation of church and state, managed to sail to America in an attempt to set up its own government. As evidence of the desire for a government of their own and as a sign of their rebellion, the Puritans and other sympathetic groups refused to participate in the dances of the court, preferring the more simple English country dances. Playford, a Puritan, attempted to meet this need with his publication. Not only was his book accepted with great acclaim among England's discontented, but it also met with favor in America.

From this beginning, the American square dance evolved. Instead of the pomp and circumstance attending the dances of the court and the social etiquette marked by favors given to the most prestigious persons at a dance, participants took their places in lines according to their order of arrival. Gone was the intricate, delicate footwork, and in its place was a steady, even movement of the feet to each beat of the music. The flirtatious attitude among participants of the court dances was replaced by emphasis on movement patterns and the coordination of all dancers in an attempt to work together to effect these patterns of movement. The dance emphasized the cohesiveness of the people and stressed democracy in action. Today the American square dance is still based on these principles.

From its beginning, the American square dance has exemplified the ideals on which the country was founded and that its citizens have attempted to realize in the intervening years. It is the folk dance of North America, not only because it has been a part of the culture since its colonial beginnings, but also because the essence of the dance reflects the philosophy and values of its people.

In the early 1700s, the French, who had also found enjoyment in the longways, introduced the square formation. It was believed that the contre did not allow for sufficient activity or excitement. The French realized that they could effect figures similar to those used in the contre in the square formation, thereby assuring more activity for all participants. The new style of dance that emerged as a result of this innovation was called the *cotillion*.

The advent of the French Revolution added further innovations to the cotillion. A faster tempo and more intricate dance steps grew out of the cultural changes taking place in France. People were demanding change and excitement, and they found an outlet in their dance.

By the mid-1800s, the cotillion no longer satisfied the people. Its rather short, simple movement patterns were not enough to sustain interest. All facets of the culture were becoming more complicated, and it was inevitable that the dance should also articulate this growing complexity. The French combined five to six cotillions into one dance for greater intricacy in dancing. The French *quadrille* became popular in England and the United States soon after its inception.

The first American innovation to the dance came with the introduction of the "caller." It is the caller who sets the American square dance apart from all other dances and that provides the major justification for labeling it the American folk dance. Before the advent of the caller in the early 1800s (during or soon after the War of 1812), participants memorized each dance. However, with a caller presiding over the dance program, it was possible to perform a new, unfamiliar dance as long as one knew its "basics" or dance patterns (circle, do-si-dos, promenade, and such). This change heralded a new method of learning how to dance. Sequences of basics no longer needed to be committed to memory. The patter call evolved as an adjunct to this concept. The caller would make up dances as he or she went along. This introduced the element of anticipation—not knowing what will be called next—that has drawn many people to the square dance over the years. Participants rely on their knowledge of basics, listening ability, coordination, timing, and rhythm to complete a dance successfully.

In the mid to late 1800s, the singing call emerged. Currently popular music was used (the practice when choreographing new dances), and a figure was developed by the choreographer in which there was an exchange of partners. This figure was constructed in such a way that if repeated three more times, dancers would be back with their original partners in their home positions.

In the late 1800s, the waltz, polka, and other couple dances became overwhelmingly popular in Europe and in the eastern United States. Consequently, ballroom dancing took over as the favorite form of social dancing in the cities, and the contre and square dances were eliminated from the dance program. In the eastern United States, the American square dance receded into small towns.

Meanwhile, it was enjoying tremendous popularity in the West. The visiting-couple figure predominated, as did rhyming patter depicting life on the plains. However, by the early 1900s, ballroom dancing became popular in the newly formed cities of the West, and here, too, square dancing became associated with the small town, the roundups, and the granges.

Little change occurred in the American square dance from the early 1900s until after World War II. For the most part, those who participated in dancing were content to perform the dances of yesteryear. A study of the evolution of the American square dance shows that change in the dance has occurred during times of social unrest and political upheaval. Thus, it was inevitable that World War II would precipitate a new style of American square dance.

During the war, United Service Organizations, church groups, and other organizations presented social activities for service personnel. The square dance seemed a logical activity to inspire congenial social cohesiveness among strangers. After the war, many of the young men who had enjoyed this experience turned to calling to provide hometown neighbors with a similar experience. Overnight, it seemed, the American square dance gained tremendous popularity, and with this popularity came many changes in the dance.

The wave of popularity grew in the West and quickly spread eastward. In southern California in 1941, there were approximately 10 clubs and 5 callers. By November 1948, there were some 30 callers and 75 square-dance clubs. Six months later, in May 1949, the number had risen to some 400 active groups in the same area. By the end of 1950, there were an estimated 50,000 square dancers in Los Angeles alone and 5 million in the nation.

By the time the wave of popularity hit the East Coast in the late 1940s and the early 1950s, a new dance style—the modern American square dance—had developed. There were few differences in dancing from one section of the country to the other. For this reason, dance historians believe it was at this point that the square dance finally emerged as the national dance—the American folk dance.

The square dance as it developed from the 1940s to the 1970s is vastly different from the square dance of the early twentieth century. From some 10 or 12 basic movements prior to 1940, there are now over 800. Twenty or more new singing calls are released each month from the 15 or so commercial square-dance record companies now in existence. One to two years' instruction is required to prepare participants for community dancing. The simple visiting-couple figure of the Western square dance is no longer performed. Instead, the line, posting, and star-thru figures are used, along with the traditional circle formation. Participants learn to perform basics, not dances. They rely on their ability to listen to the calls; to coordinate their movements with each other; to time each basic correctly while dancing; to move to the beat, tempo, and phrasing of the music; and to space their steps appropriately for the various formations and basics used in the dancing.

It is estimated that some 6 to 10 million people belong to square-dance clubs in the United States. For many, square dancing takes up at least two evenings a month, while for others, dancing two or three evenings a week is not unusual. The American folk dance knows more participants than any other national folk dance. It continually changes as the culture changes. It is a vibrant, living folk dance articulating the values of its people.

Objectives of Square Dancing

1. To provide satisfaction and pride by giving the participant a new ability

2. To promote gracefulness
3. To develop coordination
4. To help develop self-discipline
5. To help develop good timing and rhythm
6. To provide an opportunity to learn to relax with the opposite sex
7. To provide an opportunity to develop emotional and social values
8. To provide an activity that will promote togetherness and fun for everyone

Square-Dance Formation

The square dance is performed by sets of four couples. The woman is always situated to the right of the man. The couple in front of the caller is couple 1. Couple 3 faces couple 1. These two couples are the *head* couples unless otherwise designated. Couple 2 is to the right of 1. Couple 4 is opposite 2. Couples 2 and 4 are the *side* couples. Home position is the starting position. If a mistake is made by a couple while performing a figure, "Square the set" is called, and all couples return to their starting positions.

Relative Position of Partners

The woman on the man's right is always his *partner;* the one to his left is his *corner.* The man to the woman's left is her *partner;* the man to her right is her *corner.* During the dance, the man may be separated from his starting partner. If he is separated and the word *partner* is called, he must take the woman who at that time is to his right. Partners hold hands whenever possible.

Shuffle Step

The dance should be performed in a light-footed, lively shuffle step, with the dancers changing from one basic to another. One step is taken on each beat, or count. The feet slide forward on the floor. When moving to the right, as in "Circle right," dancers step right foot to the side, then left foot in front of the right. They continue this sequence with toes pointed toward the center of the circle.

Square-Dance Composition

basics Individual movements—for example, "Go forward and back."

dance Enough figures to take a couple through a song.

figure A group of phrases, usually 64 counts, in which the couples start at and return to home position.

name of square dance Usually the main figure—for example, "Ducking for the Oyster" or "Taking a Peek." The dance can be identified by the name of the music to which it is danced.

phrase A number of basics making 8 or 16 counts.

Starting the Dance

The call "Honor your partner" starts the dance. Participants bow first to their corners and then to their partners.

Fundamental Skills of the Square Dance

allemande left Eight counts. The man joins left hand or arm with whomever allemande is to be made. Both then shuffle counterclockwise around each other, back to starting position.

around that couple, take a peek Sixteen counts forward and back. Couple 1 faces Couple 2. Couple 1 goes forward, splits, goes past Couple 2, peeking at each other, and then backs up to starting position. The call may be for heads or for sides to take a peek.

balance Dancers take two steps back from partner and curtsy.

balance and swing Couples balance, then take two steps forward, joining hands or arms, and rotate twice around each other.

circle Eight beats halfway; 16 beats all the way. Designated dancers join hands, turn slightly in the direction designated, and shuffle-step around. This may be to the left or to the right. The call may be for women, for men, or for everybody.

dive for the oyster Sixteen counts. First and second couples face by shuffling together. All hold hands and circle halfway to the left. Second couple joins hands and raises arms while the first couple goes four steps under and four steps back. Again all join hands and circle halfway around and back to starting position.

do-si-dos (pronounced doe-see-doe) Eight counts. Partners, corners, or opposites shuffle forward, go back to right of each other past each other's right arm, go back-to-back, and then back out to starting position.

forward and back Eight beats, or counts. Designated couples take four steps toward the center of the circle and then four steps back out.

grand right and left Eight counts halfway; 16 counts all the way. Partners face each other and hold right hands. They walk by each other and take the opposite hand of the dancer they are facing. They advance around the circle, alternating from side to side until they meet. Men go counterclockwise; women advance clockwise.

grand square Thirty-two counts. Simultaneously all dancers walk a small square in their corner of the full square (Figure 10.10A). Couples 1 and 3 walk forward four steps, meeting in the center of the set, while partners in Couples 2 and 4 face each other and walk four steps backward to the outside corners of the set (Figure 10.10B). Partners in Couples 1 and 3 face each other with backs to side walls, join inside hands, and walk back four steps (they will now be in home position of Couples 2 and 4); at the same time, man 4 and woman 2 and man 2 and woman 4 face each other and walk four steps forward to arrive at original home position of Couples 1 and 3 (Figure 10.10C). They continue this sequence as shown in Figure 10.10D and 10.10E, at which point all couples should be back in their home positions. The entire sequence is then reversed (first four counts shown in Figure 10.10F) by beginning with Couples 2 and 4 walking to the center while Couples 1 and 3 move backward to the outside corners of the set.

ladies' chain Eight counts. Women, heads or sides, shuffle across the set, touching right hands as they pass each other in the center of the circle. They then extend their left hands to the men. The men take the women's left hands with their left hands, place their right hands on the women's waists, and all turn counterclockwise to home and starting position.

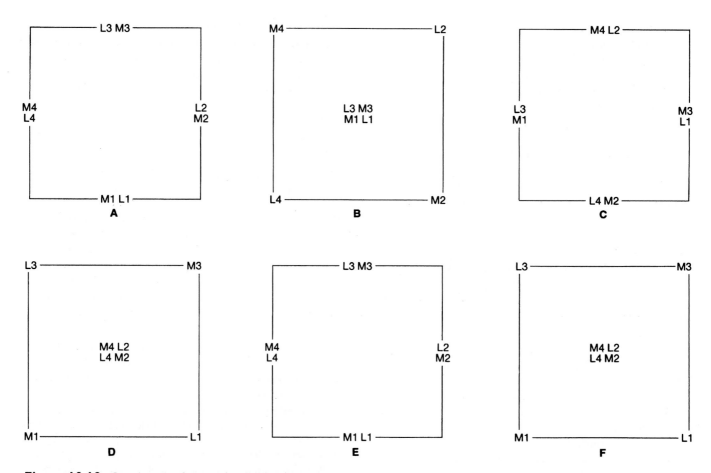

Figure 10.10. Grand square. See text for details.

promenade Eight counts halfway; 16 counts all the way. Pairs take right hands as though shaking hands and position themselves side by side, facing counterclockwise with the man on the inside of the circle and the woman on the outside. The man reaches under his right arm with his left hand and grasps the woman's left hand. They then shuffle-step together around the circle.

right and left thru Eight counts halfway; 16 counts all the way. Two couples face each other. Couples extend their right hands to the persons opposite them and pass them on the right, then immediately give their left hands to each other, and men put their right arm around their ladies to courtesy-turn them around to face each other (couples have exchanged places).

right hand round the partner Eight counts. Partners face each other holding right hands and go around each other moving in a clockwise direction, then return to starting position. This basic is opposite to allemande left (and is sometimes called "allemande right").

sashay round your corner Eight counts. Using sideward sliding steps and always facing the center, the man goes to the left, outside and around his corner, and returns to his original position.

seesaw round your own Eight counts. The man uses sideward sliding steps to the right, outside and around his corner, returning to his original position.

star Eight counts. Designated partners extend designated hands into the center of the circle and shuffle around in an inner circle one full circle, returning to starting position. Dancers may be called to do a right or left star.

weave the ring Eight counts halfway; 16 counts all the way. Same movement as the grand right and left except hands do not touch.

Construction of the Figure

"Bow to your corner, bow to your partner, and all join hands"

Circle to the left halfway	8 counts
All go forward and back	8 counts
Circle right halfway	8 counts
Circle to the left all the way	16 counts
Circle to the right all the way	16 counts
All go forward and back	8 counts
	64 counts

"Bow to your corner, bow to your partner"

Do-si-dos your corner	8 counts
Do-si-dos	8 counts
All join hands and circle left	16 counts
Heads go forward and back	8 counts
Sides go forward and back	8 counts
All join hands and circle right	16 counts
	64 counts

"Take a peek"

Circle left all the way	16 counts
Heads "take a peek" round the couple on the right	16 counts
Sides "take a peek" round the couple on the right	16 counts
Circle right all the way	<u>16</u> counts
	64 counts

Music for Square Dancing
Patter, or hoedown, music
Patter music is used for timing and rhythm. It usually does not have a familiar melody, and as a rule, it is used to teach the basic skills.

Singing call
Singing call music has a definite melody, and there is a specific set of figures written for it. Examples of singing calls are: *Oh Johnny!, Hot Time in the Old Town Tonight, Hello, Dolly!, Cabaret, Buffalo Girls,* and *Pop Goes the Weasel.*

FOLK DANCE
Folk dances (Figure 10.11) are traditional dances, part of the cultural heritage of a group, nation, or religion. They developed as ethnic dances in which ordinary folk participated. In contrast, some ethnic dances evolved as art forms danced by highly skilled performers.

Sources
Folk dances are international. Some had their start as a means of celebrating some special occasion, such as the harvest, a wedding, or a feast day. Others grew out of work practices, religious ceremonies, or military customs. But most evolved as recreational pastimes, a means of having fun.

Because folk dances are "of the people," they often are changed "by the people." Someone may add a clap here or a turn there to make a dance more enjoyable. Others follow along, and the change thus spreads. This continues today. There may be a local variation on almost any dance, but basic styles, steps, and formations tend to endure and give each dance its special flavor.

Forms
Folk dances take many forms. In some, individuals dance alone without touching anyone else. In others, the individual is in a line or circle or broken circle (with a leader at one end) in contact with those on either side. Neighbors may join hands, hook arms, put hands to shoulders or about the waist, or just interlace little fingers. Sometimes they wear loose belts that are grasped by dancers on either side, especially in line dances for men where the action is very vigorous.

Dances for two, three, six, or eight are more structured. Group formations vary from short lines to single circles, double circles, parallel lines, squares, stars, and even triangles. In dances for partners, there is a definite dance position or way they relate to each other—for example, closed (facing and close as for ballroom dance), open (side by side), shoulder-waist (man's hands at the woman's waist and her hands on his shoulders), and butterfly (partners facing, hands joined, and arms outstretched at shoulder height).

Currently, nonpartner dances for any number seem to be most popular. They are quickly organized and make it easy for anyone to join the group. They suit the casual atmosphere of many folk gatherings. Couple and group dances take more organization to get started, and some persons may be left out.

Basic Dance Steps
Basic movements used in folk dances are walking (or stepping), running, leaping, jumping, hopping, skipping, sliding, and galloping. Traditional folk dance steps are composed of combinations of these basic movements put to various rhythms. Following are brief descriptions of some common folk dance steps. ("Close" means to bring the feet together and step, and *L* is left, *R* is right.)

two-step (2/4 or 4/4 meter) The rhythm is quick, quick, slow as the last count is held.

step	close	step	hold
L	**R**	**L**	

polka (2/4 meter) The hop is quick, coming on the pick-up beat just before count 1. The rhythm changes from the two-step to ah quick, quick slow.

hop	step	close	step
L	**R**	**L**	**R**

schottische (4/4 meter) Four movements on four counts with a steady rhythm. Sometimes the action is step, close, step, hop; sometimes runs are used in place of steps.

step	step	step	hop
L	**R**	**L**	**L**

Figure 10.11. Folk dance students practice a line dance.

waltz box (3/4 meter) Six steps on six counts (two measures of music) with an even rhythm. The rhythm is slow, slow, slow.

step forward	side	close
L	**R**	**L**

step backward	side	close
R	**L**	**R**

mazurka (3/4 meter) Three actions on three counts in even time. Styling includes sweeping the left foot backward across the right shinbone on the hop.

step	close	hop
L	**R**	**R**

Combinations of the basic movements changing direction, rhythm, and style appear in amazing variety in the hundreds of folk dances recorded and performed. The steps described here are a small sampling that have become set through frequent use.

Regional Dance Characteristics

The following brief highlights point up some regional differences in dance styling. There is much fascinating material available (see sources listed at end of chapter) in this area for the student dancer.

England. Country dances for couples moving with light, springy, running steps have a smooth, gliding effect. With arms hanging freely and bodies erect, the dancers interweave in interesting patterns.

Germany. Couple dances with regular patterns, such as waltzes, polkas, and schottisches, are typical. Also there are dances featuring intricate clapping sequences and much slapping of the body with rhythmic precision.

Greece. Common are broken-circle dances led by a man waving his handkerchief to signal step changes. He improvises with much flamboyance as the line keeps the basic step. Often the women are in separate lines and are much more restrained in their movements.

Hungary. Sudden changes in tempo, clicking of the heels, stamping of feet, and individual improvisation are part of such dances as the csárdás.

Ireland. Intricate, exact footwork characterizes Irish solo dances, such as jigs and hornpipes. Reels call for simpler, more gliding steps.

Israel. Religious dances express hope, joy, and courage. National dances serve to unify the many ethnic groups in Israel, blending movements from Europe, Asia, and the Mideast. The use of circle formations in Israeli dances reflects the strength of their ties. Accomplished choreographers create new dances based on traditional steps and forms. The hora is Israel's national dance.

Mexico. Fast footwork with crisp stamping and heel-toe tapping gives excitement to flirtatious couple dances. Action centers in the legs and feet as the man clasps his hands behind his back and the woman holds her full skirt.

Scandinavia. Smoothly turning couple dances are typical. Best known is the Swedish hambo. There are also vigorous dances for men and some clowning, light-hearted dances.

Scotland. To traditional bagpipe music, precise Scottish dancers perform with toes pointed, bodies erect, and hands carefully placed. Flings, reels, schottisches, and sword dances are familiar.

Yugoslavia. Most typical is the kolo, with a leader waving his handkerchief to signal step changes. The many kolos are as varied as the diverse Slavic peoples of this country. Some are quiet, some are bouncy, and some are lively and noisy as the dancers punctuate their steps with exuberant shouts.

SOCIAL DANCE

Popular couple dances without set patterns are classified as social or ballroom dances (Figure 10.12). They have a casual, relaxed quality not possible in patterned dances. Each couple moves independently of others, and in some dances, partners are quite independent of each other, improvising at will. But most social dances are characterized by the man leading and the woman partner following whatever steps, styling, and rhythmic variations he chooses and indicates.

Sources

Formal social dancing began with the European court dances of the Renaissance. Dance masters were employed to develop and teach proper steps to the aristocracy. Today dancers and dance teachers continually invent new steps and styles. Popular music, films, television, and stage shows have all inspired new dances that have swept the United States.

The social dances of one era tend to become the folk dances of later eras. Whenever pleasing combinations begin to be repeated and take set forms, the dance can be recorded and copied by others. The waltz, polka, schottische, and mazurka were all early social dances. Only the waltz continues as a modern ballroom dance, although the polka appears occasionally in the ballroom. The Charleston of the Roaring Twenties already is appearing in folk dance books. Some of the current fad dances may well have the same fate in time. Continual change seems to be the only certainty in popular social dancing. However, set standards and required steps are spelled out for establishing dance forms, especially those used in dance competitions.

Basic Steps

"Anyone who can walk to music can dance!" This common introduction to a social dance class points up the fact that every form of social dance is based on walking steps. Differences of style and rhythm and patterns set to distinctive music distinguish the different forms. A few variations on the basic steps that are common to all forms include:

balancing Taking a long step followed by two closes. Often the shift of weight is minimal on the closes.

closing Stepping one foot next to the other and transferring the weight. Steps may be forward, backward, or sideways.

hesitating Pausing by touching the free foot to the floor without transferring weight.

pivoting Rotating in either direction. Dancers may stay in place or travel on a pivot.

rocking Staying in place stepping forward and back or from side to side.

SOCIAL DANCE FORMS

To indicate the rhythmic patterns of the common social dances listed below, the symbol *S* indicates slow and the symbol *Q* indicates a quick step.

Fox-trot. The fox-trot is an American dance evolving from a trotting dance performed by Harry Fox in a Ziegfeld show in 1913. Present forms tend to be smooth, with dancers gliding around the dance floor with little up-and-down motion. Fox-trots may be dreamy and slow or quick and light. They can be adapted to in-place dancing in a small space or be expansive where space permits (one step *QQQQ*, two step *QQS*, magic step *SSQQ*).

Swing. From the lindy of the 1920s and the jitterbug of the 1930s comes our modern swing. The basic step is still the six-count lindy with variations. Though the music may be bouncy, good swing dancers smoothly execute the individual turns, exchanges, and position variations typical of Eastern swing. On the West Coast, a slower, more complicated swing form has developed.

Figure 10.12. A social dance: the fox-trot.

Waltz. The oldest ballroom dance form and the first to be danced in closed (or waltz) position, the waltz was considered shocking when first introduced to Americans in the early nineteenth century. Previously it was the rage in Vienna, with Strauss waltzes filling the air. It probably originated in seventeenth-century Germany. The name comes from a German word meaning "to revolve," and turning with smooth, gliding steps continues to be characteristic of waltzing (*SSS*).

Cha-cha. A Cuban dance growing out of the earlier mambo in the mid-1950s, this dance is characterized by three quick steps. The dancers often are apart, allowing much freedom of movement around the basic "step, step, cha, cha, cha" of the dance. The Latin rhythm is catchy and distinctive (*SSQQQ*).

Rumba. The rumba was introduced to the United States from Cuba in 1930. Like the cha-cha, action is from the waist down, with a subtle swaying of the hips resulting from careful knee and foot action. The dancers weave interesting patterns as they change positions in this relatively restrained Latin dance (*SQQ*).

Tango. From Argentina this "dance with a stop," as it was called, came by way of Europe to the United States in 1913. Characterized by sudden changes of direction interrupting the catlike slow steps, the tango is a distinctive form with its many fan (flaring) and corté (dipping) steps (*SSQQS*).

Samba. From Brazil comes this bouncy, vibrant dance. It involves much knee action, with the dancers' bodies resembling a swinging pendulum as they sway and turn. It was introduced to the United States at the New York World's Fair in 1939 (*QQS*).

Contemporary dances. Always of interest to students are the currently popular dances. Now and then, one endures to find its way into dance literature. For some years, through the 1960s and 1970s, discotheque, no-contact, partner dances were the fad. Then the line hustle came along, and there was no partner at all, just individuals doing essentially the same steps at the same time. At present there is a resurgence in the popularity of ballroom and couple dancing. New steps come out regularly, with studios competing to create interesting combinations. These are enjoyable, stimulating dances that add a contemporary spice to the classroom scene.

TEACHING CONSIDERATIONS

Square Dance

1. Explain the activity and let participants hear a recording of the fundamentals.
2. Use a chalkboard, draw a "set," explain positions: home, head, sides, partner, corner.
3. Explain what is meant by "Honor your partner," and have students practice: bow to the corner, bow to your partner.
4. Teach the class the shuffle step. Have them perform and repeat it until all students do this well. Have them hold hands, go forward and backward, and circle right and left.

5. Explain and demonstrate the beat, or count, of the square dance, and explain how square dances are phrased. Play a recording and let the class hear the beats and phrases as you count.

6. Teach each basic until all participants are familiar with the mechanics and the call and until they react quickly.

Folk and Social Dances

1. If possible, provide students with the opportunity to see the dance performed with the music.

2. With complex step patterns, teach the basic step directly (not necessarily in the appropriate group formation). Slow down the speed, if needed, using word cues (e.g., step, close, step, hold). Increase speed of practice until it approaches correct speed. Add the music to practice. Allow sufficient individual practice to have the step be automatic before using the group formation of the dance.

3. With complex group formations (folk dance), teach the chorus first and then other patterns. Walk through parts of the dance with the students—first slowly, then more quickly, and then with the music—before adding parts to the whole.

4. Repeat parts as new ones are added.

5. Keep the atmosphere and learning climate informal, but stress good technique. The dances are more enjoyable that way.

6. As the number of dances students learn increases, provide opportunities for review. Try not to have whole lessons of just new dances.

7. Intersperse giving regional information with learning dances (folk dance).

8. Use the names for the steps to provide later transfer to other dances that use the same steps.

9. Use mixers to provide opportunities for students to dance with different partners.

SUGGESTED READINGS

General

Laban, R. 1963. *Modern educational dance*. London: MacDonald & Evans.

Laban, R. 1966. *The mastery of movement*. London: MacDonald & Evans.

McGreevy-Nichols, S., Scheff, H., and Sprague, M. 2005. *Building dances*. 2nd ed. Champaign, IL: Human Kinetics.

Scheff, H., Sprague, M., and McGreevy-Nichols, S. 2005. *Experiencing dance—from student to dance artist*. Champaign IL: Human Kinetics.

Concert forms

Hammond, S. 2004. *Ballet basics*. 5th ed. New York, NY: McGraw-Hill.

Kassing, G. 2000. *Beginning ballet*. Champaign, IL: Human Kinetics.

Laban, R., and Lawrence, F. C. 1947. *Effort*. London: MacDonald & Evans.

Penrod, J., and Plastino, J. 2005. *The dancer prepares: Modern dance for beginners*. 5th ed. New York, NY: McGraw-Hill. Introduces students to the techniques, combinations, and vocabulary of modern dance.

Recreational forms

General

Bennet, J., and Riemer, P. 2006. *Rhythmic activities and dance*. 2nd ed. Champaign, IL. Human Kinetics.

Lane, C. 2000. *Christy Lane's complete book of line dancing*. 2nd ed. Champaign, IL: Human Kinetics.

Laufman, D., and Laufman, J. 2009. *Traditional barn dances with calls and fiddling*. Champaign, IL.: Human Kinetics.

Social dance

Wright, J. 2003. *Social dance*. 2nd ed. Champaign, IL: Human Kinetics.

Tap and jazz dance

Hatchett, F. 2000. *Frank Hatchett's jazz dance*. Champaign, IL: Human Kinetics.

Kraines, M., and Pryor, E. 2005. *Jump into jazz: The basics and beyond for jazz dance students*. 5th ed. New York, NY: McGraw-Hill.

Lihs, H. 1993. *Jazz dance*. 2nd ed. Boston, MA: American Press.

Periodicals

Dance Teacher Now, SMW Communications, 3020 Beacon Blvd., West Sacramento, CA 95691.

Dancemagazine, 33 W. 60th St., New York, NY 10023.

Journal of Physical Education, Recreation and Dance, American Alliance for Health, Physical Education, Recreation and Dance, 1900 Association Dr., Reston, VA 22091.

Sets in Order, National Square Dance Magazine, 462 N. Robertson Blvd., Los Angeles, CA 90048.

RESOURCES

Dance instructions and recordings

American Alliance for Health, Physical Education, Recreation and Dance, 1900 Association Dr., Reston, VA 22091. Provides books, tapes, films, lesson plans, and resource guides for all types of dance.

World of Fun, 819 NW 92nd St., Oklahoma City, OK 73114. Offers a complete collection of beginner folk dance instructions and records for children and adults.

World Tone Music, 230 Seventh Ave., New York, NY 10011. Offers extensive collections of audiotapes and records, some with instructions, for teaching folk and square dances.

Videos

Many videotapes are available for preview, rental, or sale from the following organizations or libraries:

Home Vision, P.O. Box 800, Concord, MA 01742.

Kimbo Educational, P.O. Box 477K, Long Beach, NJ 07740. Distributes many records, audiocassettes, filmstrips, and videotapes.

Media for the Arts, 360 Thames St., Newport, RI 02840.

Princeton Book Company/Dance Book Club, P.O. Box 57, Pennington, NJ 08534.

University of California, Extension Media Center, 2176 Shattuck Ave., Berkeley, CA 94704. Provides titles for preview, rental, or purchase.

See Appendix C for sources of other videos.

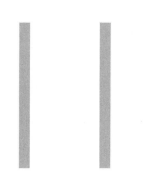

Disc Sports: Ultimate and Disc Golf

After completing this chapter, the reader should be able to:

- Appreciate the versatility of the games of ultimate and disc golf
- Demonstrate the correct grip, stance, approach, and delivery of three throwing styles
- Display a knowledge of the rules and strategy for ultimate and disc golf
- Display a knowledge of the variety of skills, sports, and games associated with throwing and catching discs
- Instruct a group of students in the fundamentals of ultimate and disc golf

Ultimate and disc golf are two extraordinary examples of modern-day sport evolving from the use and popularity of a commercial toy product. The invention of the flying disc, which only after many years came to be called Frisbee, is credited for the development of these two sports.* Ultimate and disc golf are the most popular of flying disc sports, others being Guts, Discathon, and Freestyle. Both sports require players to throw a Frisbee or disc toward targets—moving players in ultimate, and pole-mounted baskets in disc golf. The discs come in a variety of sizes, shapes, and weights. Each sport involves players moving and changing positions to prepare themselves and execute throws. Both ultimate and disc golf invite players to compete in various versions of games and activities where the skills needed to be successful are easily acquired. Rules are simple and easy to follow and may be easily modified to extend or reduce the complexity of the skill or the physical challenge of the sport. Few popular sports today appeal to such a diversity of players regardless of age, size, or physical or intellectual ability.

HISTORY

The games of ultimate and disc golf are modern examples of hybrid sports that appeal to players because the play in each game requires a combination of physical and mental skills. Ultimate combines the playing skills of soccer and football; disc golf resembles the play of traditional golf. Learning to throw the disc for distance and accuracy is the main skill component needed to be successful in both sports.

The histories of both ultimate and disc golf began with the invention of the plastic flying disc, originally called the *Pluto Platter*, by Fred Morrison in 1949. This prototype was derived from earlier handcrafted models by Morrison and Warren Fancioni in 1948. Morrison sold the rights to this flying disc to a leading toy manufacturer, Wham-O, Inc., in 1955,

which in turn developed and marketed its own model by 1957. In 1959, Wham-O instituted the trademark label and the ever-popular name Frisbee for all such flying discs, then began selling them in stores across the country. Wham-O is reported to have renamed its flying disc Frisbee after observing Yale University students playing catch with metal pie pans from the Frisbie Pie Company. When a thrown pie pan veered too close to people passing by, the players would yell "Frisbie!" The evolution of the sports of ultimate and disc golf developed along similar paths in that the flying disc was the instrument of play and each player was the prime mover and individual performer of each disc throw. However, the inception of each sport is unique, with its own history, rules, styles of play, equipment, players, and separate sport associations that exist today.

Disc Golf

Wham-O continued to market versions of the Frisbee, experimenting for a number of years with sizes, shapes, and aerodynamic designs. Ed Headrick became CEO of Wham-O Toys in 1964 and is credited with finding, in the years to follow, new applications and formalizing the game of disc golf from an unorganized activity. The original version of the game of disc golf developed during these years. In 1975, Headrick designed and invented the Disc Pole Hole to serve as the fixed target for aiming disc golf shots. The first Disc Pole Hole and, subsequently, first disc golf course were in Oak Grove Park in La Canada, California. Ed Headrick is known as the "father of disc golf" and has personally designed over 200 disc golf courses around the world. His visions and ambitions for disc golf were to improve a park's environment by designing an activity that might deter vandalism and loitering and provide a fun sport in pleasant surroundings that would appeal to all people, including people with mental and physical impairments.

In 1976, only three disc golf courses existed in the United States. Since that time, over 2,000 courses have been installed

---

*Frisbee is a term often associated with flying discs and is a registered trademark of Wham-O, Inc.

and there are courses now in all 50 states. Disc golf courses are most prevalent in California, Michigan, Wisconsin, and Texas, with the DeLaveaga Disc Golf Course in Santa Cruz, California, on the West Coast, and the Winthrop Lakefront Disc Golf Course in Rock Hill, South Carolina, on the East Coast, considered by some players to be among the best in the world. Disc golf courses can be designed to conform to a variety of geographical locations and land forms, including forests, deserts, and mountains, making them challenging and appealing to all players. The widespread popularity of disc golf has expanded internationally. There are more than a hundred disc golf courses in Canada, Europe, and Japan.

Many local parks and recreation departments have capitalized on this recreational trend and installed disc golf courses for less than it might cost to install one lighted tennis court. A typical 18-hole disc golf course might cost less than $10,000, where one lighted tennis court could cost twice that amount. The revenue generated in disc golf could come from sales of golfing discs, user fees to play the course, and entry fees from sponsored tournaments. The phase-in installation process for disc golf holes and minimal maintenance costs for grounds and target baskets are attractive to community parks and recreation departments with budget constraints. The cost for players is remarkably inexpensive, with virtually indestructible golfing discs costing less than $10 each. Experienced players will carry with them during play a disc golf bag that might hold a dozen or more discs designed differently for different types of throws. For example, a "driving" disc is aerodynamically designed to throw farther than a "putting" disc for short accurate tosses.

The typical disc golf hole has a tee area, similar to traditional golf, a fairway and rough, hazards, out-of-bounds, and a "hole" consisting of a 5-foot-tall durable galvanized steel basket. The basket is mounted on a metal pole and consists of a circular top plate or rim with hanging chains arranged above a circular metal basin. The chains act to catch the disc and then drop it down in the basin.

Playing disc golf is much like playing traditional golf. The objective is to take as few attempts (throws) as possible to land your disc in the basket. A disc golf course may be laid out with different-length holes sporting various trees, bushes, and other hazards along the fairway to call for strategy and variation in the type of throws taken by the player approaching the hole. Novice players will attempt their most basic shots with a standard delivery style that they feel confident will keep the disc straight and go far. However, more experienced players will select a disc of particular size or weight and, using their own particular delivery style, make a throw toward the target with a particular design to maximize air flight and roll distance on the ground.

The game of disc golf appeals to many players because it is both fun and challenging. It can be learned and played by individuals from any economic or cultural background. Equally inviting to the young and old, male and female,

physically talented and physically limited, and novice and expert players, it is recognized as a lifelong sport where one can enjoy the outdoors, walk for exercise, throw for accuracy, and find a challenge in every toss. Disc golf is fast becoming a popular sport that brings people together for fun and recreation.

Paralleling the popularity of disc golf has been the growth of its official organizing association, the Professional Disc Golf Association (PDGA) founded in 1984 and now numbering over 10,000 members. PDGA annually sponsors over 175 tournaments worldwide with over $300,000 in prize money.

Ultimate

In 1968, the first version of the game of ultimate, at that time called Ultimate Frisbee, was played at Columbia High School in Maplewood, New Jersey. Students arranged in teams passed the disc from one end of the field to the other to score a goal. Much like football and soccer, the team in possession of the disc was on offense. The team trying to intercept passes or throws was on defense. In 1998, in tribute to the inception of Ultimate Frisbee at this school, the Thirtieth Anniversary Maplewood Ultimate Frisbee Tournament was held. The first reported collegiate game of ultimate was held in 1972, with Rutgers University playing Princeton University. The first collegiate championship was held in 1974 with eight colleges participating. Since 1979, when Tom Kennedy founded the Ultimate Players Association (UPA), ultimate has become an international sport. The UPA has more than 30,000 members and acts as the official governing body for the sport of ultimate in the United States.

Ultimate is a very active team sport that requires a great deal of running in addition to throwing and catching skills. It can be enjoyed by players of almost any skill level and physical ability. The action of the game involves players for the team with possession of the disc running to an open space and catching a disc thrown to them. It is a noncontact sport involving a team on offense advancing the disc down the field, much like football, toward its opponent's end zone. The disc can be passed forward and backward between teammates, much like soccer, as long as each pass is caught in the air by a teammate. A dropped pass or missed catch reverses possession of the disc to the other team, and the team that previously held possession now becomes defenders. The action of the defensive team is to cover offensive players and knock down or intercept throws made by the offense. An incomplete pass, whether knocked down by the defense or simply not caught by an offensive teammate, results in a turnover, with the defensive team now on offense. Throughout a game, turnovers have teams changing from offense to defense very quickly.

The defensive player marking the thrower also initiates a stall count. If the defender reaches 10 seconds before the disc is released, the result is a turnover. The defender is responsible for counting to 10 at an appropriate speed.

Players agree that an appeal of the sports is in generating speed and force in the act of throwing and releasing a disc using smooth and graceful form, with the result being a uniquely flying disc. Selecting different types of shots and using various strategies gives players a feeling of artistic control and thrill of athletic accomplishment. The added elements of throwing to specific targets to score, inviting cooperation from teammates, and competition with other players define both ultimate and disc golf as sport.

SOCIAL VALUES

Ultimate and disc golf have been tremendously popular with youth in recreational programs and school settings, and more recently with coed students in collegiate recreational and intramural sports. Public park directors frequently report that disc golf courses are popular in their communities and deter vandalism and unwelcome individuals. They also report that players are environmentally conscientious, careful to respect the trees, bushes, flowers, and grounds, and are often seen picking up their trash and the trash of other park users.

Both ultimate and disc golf invite the use of basic and elementary motor skills, making either sport a proper choice as a developmental activity. With only minor modifications to the rules, procedures, and facilities of either sport, individuals with particular mental and physical conditions and limitations can have fun and be successful. Both sports have social value, combining cooperation and competition in proper balance to be considered fun, physically challenging, and socially rewarding for all players. Camaraderie would

seem essential for playing and practicing disc sports, yet many of the skills for both games can be rehearsed individually or with partners and teams. In both sports, the "spirit of the game" involves players acting as their own referees to enforce the rules of play and etiquette, and displaying sportsmanship and respect for other players in the true spirit of competition.

FUNDAMENTAL SKILLS AND TECHNIQUES REQUIRED

Many people associate "playing Frisbee" with unstructured fun and imagine people at beaches, parks, and picnics engaged in a loosely organized activity. For this reason, many beginners may be challenged to remain focused and attentive to the detail required to be capable of competent play in these sports. Once provided with the proper instruction and direction on the fundamental skills and techniques for throwing and catching the disc, it is important that players experiment with their own personal technique and perfect their own unique style.

The situations and circumstances that arise during play in ultimate and disc golf often require a little inventiveness and imagination from a player who is called upon to execute a throw around or over other players and obstacles (Figure 11.1). The development of the ability to execute these throws is dependent upon body coordination and consistent mental concentration. The key to successful throws in either sport is the total development and use of the body's lever systems to project the disc by generating force and imparting spin onto the disc. Before describing the three major styles of

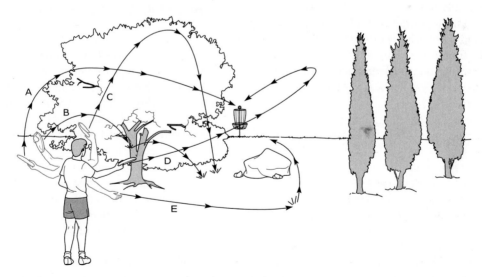

Figure 11.1. Selecting the right approach requires keen evaluation. A, A backhand roll curve or a sidearm skip curve: the backhand might roll down the incline after landing—choose the sidearm depending on the wind. B, A backhand curve roller: might carry too far and head down the incline. C, Sidearm lob: probably won't carry far enough because of the height of the tree. D, Sidearm roll curve or backhand skip curve: again, choose the skip curve in this case. E, A backhand veer roller: with a ground obstacle, might not be able to cut it back sharply enough to reach the pole hole.

throws, we will introduce some basic terminology. This terminology is accompanied by a discussion of hand positions and grips, body positioning and stance, typical disc flight patterns, and catching skills.

Hand Positions and Grips

Hand positioning for the three most basic grips on a disc is simple yet critical. To identify the disc, remember to think of the top as the part having the label or logo inscribed; the bottom, then, is underneath and does not have a logo. The circular span of the disc is referred to as the flight plate with a center and rim, the top part of the rim called the lip, and the bottom part of the rim called the edge.

To learn the first basic grip (Figure 11.2), grab the disc with your thumb on the topside, your index finger stretched out along the lip, and your remaining fingers fanned out underneath (as if to fan yourself). In this manner you have positioned your hand for the most elementary of throwing styles, referred to as the cross-body backhand or simply backhand. The degree to which one fans out the underside fingers is individual; however, a power grip is attained by closing the fingers down toward the edge and cupping the rim, which enables the thrower to generate greater force. A minor modification of dropping your index finger off the rim and curling it partially below the edge produces the Berkeley grip, now preferred by most players. Many players experiment with this grip and throwing style first because it is recognized easily in other players and is chosen by most players as the most forceful and accurate of all throwing styles.

A second basic grip used for the sidearm or forehand style is called the two-finger grip (Figure 11.3). Grasp the disc with your middle finger positioned underneath and along the inside edge of the disc, with your thumb on the topside. Your index finger should lie neatly on top of your middle finger for support while your ring finger and small finger are cupped into the palm of your hand. A variation of this grip

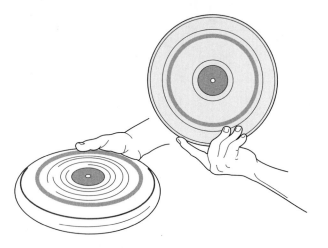

Figure 11.2. Basic grip for cross-body backhand throw.

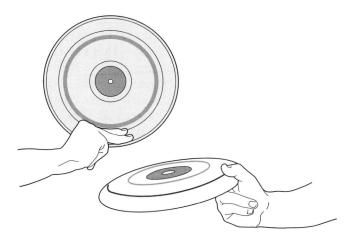

Figure 11.3. Grip for sidearm or forehand throw.

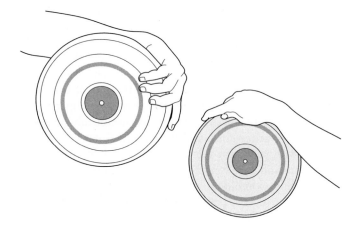

Figure 11.4. Grip for overhand throw.

is to cup your middle finger into your palm as well and place only the index finger along the inside edge of the disc.

The third basic grip to be introduced is used for the overhand style throw (Figure 11.4). Grasp the disc with your thumb on the underside edge of the disc and your index finger extended along the outer rim. The rest of your fingers are fanned out across the top of the disc. If you are able to follow these descriptions and practice them on a disc, you will notice that the first two grips are underhanded with your thumb on the topside of the disc positioned skyward, while the last grip, the overhand, has your thumb on the underside of the disc facing the ground.

Body Positioning and Stance

To simplify discussions of left side and right side for right- or left-handed throwers, the terms on-side and off-side are introduced. On-side always refers to the side of the body that is handling the disc. The other side, then, is the off-side. When the on-side arm initiates a throw or makes a catch on the off-side, it is said to be cross-body. This may help you understand why the most easily recognized and most popular throwing style is called the cross-body backhand. The disc is positioned on the off-side of the body, and the action of throwing brings the arm across the body. Both sidearm (also called forehand) and overhand styles are on-side. It might be argued that the arm will cross the body during the action of throwing sidearm or overhand styles, but one must note that the disc is positioned on-side to initiate the throw.

Stance is important to generate force and angle of delivery. A throw facing square to a target is in a facing stance, and if facing away from a target, is in a blind stance. The blind stance is used in ultimate or for trick throws and stunts. The terms open and closed stance are useful for understanding throwing style. An open stance, as is used for sidearm throws, has the arm and hand positioned away from the body in the cocked position as the throw is initiated. The closed stance, used for backhand style throws, has the arm and hand tucked inside and close to the body as the throw is initiated.

Disc Flight Patterns

Think of the disc in flight as divided into four quarters. Regardless of how much spinning the disc does, the front or forward quarter is referred to as the "nose." The back quarter is the "tail," and the lateral or side quarters are the "shoulders." During the flight, the angle of the nose to the tail is called the attack angle. A nose-up position, with the nose above the tail, is considered a negative attack angle, and the disc will tend to stall before dropping. Conversely, a positive attack angle, with the nose down or below the tail, will cause the disc to dive forcefully without slowing or losing speed.

In each flight there is a skip shoulder and a roll shoulder, which are directly related to the direction of spin on the disc. The side or shoulder of the disc that is spinning forward during flight (imagine that being the left side for a right-handed backhand thrower) is the skip shoulder. Upon striking the ground surface, given enough force and speed, the disc may bounce or skip (Figure 11.5). The side or shoulder of a disc that is spinning backward during flight is the roll shoulder. Upon striking the ground surface, it will likely roll with enough force and speed. These terms remain constant for every flight except a boomerang flight. At the apex of its outward motion, as the disc stalls and begins retreating toward the thrower, the nose becomes the tail, the tail becomes the nose, and the skip and roll shoulders switch sides as well.

Once in flight, the disc tends to display a definite tendency in flight pattern. Basically straight and level flights (Figure 11.6) remain that way, while curving flights continue curving in the same direction, in a more or less dramatic fashion. While it is convenient to refer to curving throws as curving either "right" or "left," in each case the curve should be properly designated as skip curve or roll curve, depending on which shoulder of the disc the curving motion is headed toward. For example, a right-handed thrower who uses a cross-body backhand style will observe a throw curving to the right in its downward flight as a roll curve (Figure 11.7). This curve is also referred to as an outside-in curve. This

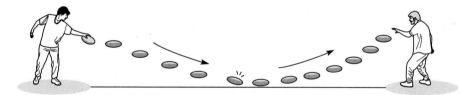

Figure 11.5. The skip shoulder.

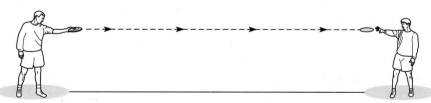

Figure 11.6. Straight and level flight.

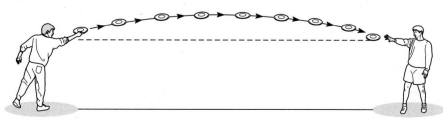

Figure 11.7. Roll curve flight.

makes sense because upon striking the ground, the tendency of the disc is to roll. If that same thrower with the same throwing style observes a throw curving or bending left, it is a skip curve, also called an inside-out curve (Figure 11.8).

One other flight worth mentioning is called the hover (or floater) flight (Figure 11.9). As one might imagine, at some point, usually toward the end of its flight, a disc will slow down and stall before descending. At that point before it begins to drop, it is said to be hovering or floating. Even with a hover flight, the descending action may curve in one direction or the other. For the sake of simplicity, it is still considered a hover flight because of its predominant attitude.

Beginners often throw discs where the flight curves in an extreme fashion and "turns over" the disc. In most cases where this occurs, the skip shoulder is lifting toward a vertical position caused by the combination of excessive arm action and minimal wrist action. Some degree of skip shoulder lifting is part of almost every flight, but practice is required to minimize excessive lifting action. This correction feature, used to compensate for excessive skip shoulder lifting and the tendency of the disc to turn over, is called hyzer. By determining the exact angle of flight and angling the skip shoulder slightly away from the direction it will lift, the delivery should compensate for the lifting action. In one sense, the term hyzer refers to the correction or adjustment for lifting; in another sense, it is used simply to mean the angle of delivery.

Adjustments for lifting are critical, because prior to and at the moment of release, the positions of both the wrist and the disc, combined with the amount of pressure used to grasp the disc, determine the characteristics of the flight. The pressure on the disc produced by one's grasp at the moment of release may be called the pinch point. To minimize excessive lift and reduce the likelihood of wobble or unstable flight, both wrist and disc must pivot around the pinch point on the same level plane as the disc snaps out of one's grasp. In addition, the wrist and disc must be in the same alignment with the angle of flight. The thrower must first visualize the angle of flight and attempt to keep the wrist and disc on the same plane at the moment of delivery. Achieving this co-planar alignment can be visualized with a basically flat throwing motion using a backhand or sidearm delivery. If the desired flight path is a flat level throw, and the arm motion, as well as the wrist and disc, are basically flat and level, the likelihood of wobble or flutter is minimized.

Catching Skills

There is an art to catching as there is an art to throwing. In fact, there are almost as many styles for catching a disc as there are for throwing one. Intuitively, most players understand that a successful catch entails reading the flight of the disc and tracking it to position oneself within reach of it during descent. Once within reach, the skill of eye-hand coordination is combined with cupping the hand and grasping the disc with a "giving" or retreating action of the arm. This action means simply bringing the catching motion in line with the motion of the disc and avoiding a tense and rigid posture of the arm and body as the catch is made. It is important as well to position oneself to catch the disc between the farthest reach of the outstretched hand and one's body. This sets up the receiving motion of the arm and hand to be moving toward the body as opposed to away from the body. The

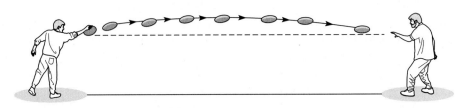

Figure 11.8. Skip curve flight.

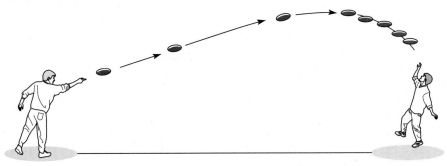

Figure 11.9. Hover (or floater) flight.

following pointers will be helpful in developing better catching skills.

A catch, by definition, is any time the flight of the disc is arrested by a player. Essentially, the cupping action of the hand to form a "C" between the thumb and the fingers is how a true catch is made. Determining whether to catch the disc with the thumb in a down position where the thumb will grasp the underside of the disc, or in the up position with the thumb on the topside, is a matter of adjusting to the height at which the disc is received. Generally, one should be able to visualize catching low throws with a thumb-up position and high throws with a thumb-down position. Develop this skill using both hands together, then the dominant hand alone, and lastly, the nondominant hand alone. A catch made between both hands held flat with fingers extended, as if to clamp down from the top and up from the bottom, is a trap or a pancake catch. A trap can also occur between a hand and another part of the body. Additionally, one can develop skills, referred to as discwork, where manipulating the flight of the disc during flight will set up a catch. Examples of this are tipping, brushing, or slapping the disc to slow down its action, or fingertipping the disc with the tip of one's finger to control its spinning action and make a catch.

Regardless of catching method, the first challenge is to move to be in position to make a catch. The secret to success in this skill is in the ability to read the flight of the incoming disc and react quickly with footwork, balance, and body positioning. There is much visual information to be used even prior to the disc's flight, beginning with the body position and throwing action of the thrower. The direction of spin on the disc is determined by the releasing action of the thrower's wrist and hand, so it is important to immediately recognize the thrower's style of delivery and associate it with direction of spin and the typical flight pattern.

The spin direction of the incoming disc is important as you decide which hand and what method you will use to catch the disc. It is helpful to know whether the disc will spin into or out of the palm of your hand. A disc spinning out of your hand or away from you will require you to close your grasp more quickly and firmly. Though developing an eye for reading the spin direction quickly is beneficial, the exact amount of pressure applied by the hand and fingers during a catch must be experimented with and practiced in order to improve on this skill.

The height, angle of attack, angle of delivery, and speed of the incoming disc must also register immediately with the receiver as positioning action is taken. Adjustments for height can be made by advancing toward or retreating away from the disc. The angle of attack (nose to tail) helps you determine if and how much a disc will rise, hover, fall, and drop. The hyzer (shoulder-to-shoulder) angle controls the lateral curve of the flight. In each flight, the disc has the tendency to continue this flight pattern, often with more or less emphasis, depending on wind variation. Experienced players

will include reading the wind conditions as a determining feature for both throwing and catching. As one might imagine, the speed of the incoming disc is greatly affected by wind direction. Disc speed at the moment of catch is also determined by the distance between the catcher and the thrower and the amount of force generated by the throw. The beginner should be experimenting with applying various amounts of force in throwing as well as learning to catch discs thrown at various speeds.

Being knowledgeable about the basic principles of grip, stance, and flights of throws, and having added to that an appreciation for some catching skills, we can move on toward developing an understanding of throwing and delivery styles. Familiarity with the terminology introduced above will aid in the understanding and appreciation of the following three major styles of throws: the cross-body backhand, the sidearm or forehand, and the overhand.

The Cross-Body Backhand

To throw a disc using the cross-body backhand style, grip the disc with your thumb on the topside and your fingers fanned out on the underside (see Figure 11.2). As introduced earlier, the index finger may run along the rim or slightly bend and partially curl beneath the edge. Novice throwers may spread the underneath fingers apart for stability, but then curl them up to the rim as their proficiency develops. The degree of firmness with which to grasp the disc must be experimented with individually; usually a firm but relaxed grip is required.

The stance and approach used for a step throw is the basic delivery skill that the novice must practice, after which the full walk-up or run-up delivery can be developed. To execute the step throw, position your throwing shoulder toward the target and place your feet along the line of the intended flight; this is basically a closed position (Figure 11.10). With most of your weight on your rear foot from the target, curl your throwing arm, shoulders, and hips behind you. As you step forward down the target line and your weight transfers to the lead foot,

Figure 11.10. Cross-body backhand throw.

release your hips, then shoulders, then arms, wrist, and disc. The transfer of weight to the lead foot is timed to immediately precede the beginning action of releasing your hips. With practice, a smooth, graceful, and powerful delivery can be developed. To generate maximum throwing force and use full-body action, a walk-up or run-up approach initiates the throw. The forward momentum of the walk or run approach must be controlled and applied to the torque action of the legs and hips. Immediately prior to the weight transfer step, the trailing leg should be planted behind the throwing-side leg. With the weight on this backside leg, the hips, shoulders, and throwing arm should be rotated back. As the lead foot steps forward and the weight transfer begins, the hips, shoulders, and arm should release and rotate forward toward a natural follow-through. Foot placement must be practiced and perfected to achieve complete balance and full momentum (Figure 11.11).

To achieve success in throwing discs with different flights using this throwing style, it is important to recognize that body motion and arm action constitute only part of the

Figure 11.11. Cross-body backhand delivery motion.

throw. Indeed, every throw is critically dependent on the angle of the forearm and wrist at the release point, and the amount of additional force imparted on the disc using wrist flexion and extension.

Setting up for the cross-body backhand throw involves cocking the wrist in an accented flexed position and timing the release from that position with the pressure and release of the fingers on the disc. One should attempt to release the disc flatly, at first, with an easy and smooth motion. Note the way the arm, wrist, and fingers feel during each attempt and make subtle corrections in a trial-and-error fashion. Experiment with finger placement and pressure, wrist action, and arm motion between each throw.

A skip curve thrown by a right-hander will curve left from the intended target line, whereas a roll curve will curve right. Remember, the direction of the curve, either right or left of the target, is related to which shoulder the disc is curving toward. In most throws, it is well to intend to have some degree of curve during flight. The amount of curve is determined by a sensitive adjustment, either lowering or raising, of the angle of the skip or roll shoulder. Again, this adjustment is the hyzer. To correct for excessive roll curve, where the skip shoulder is lifting toward vertical, you must experiment with hyzer, or the degree of angle of the skip shoulder during delivery. An excessive roll curve taken to its extreme results in a turnover, which can be corrected for in the delivery by angling the skip shoulder slightly away from the direction of lift.

The hover throw can be practiced by attempting to throw a basically straight shot with the nose of the disc elevated. This shot is intended to slow down and stall out at some point during flight, then drop down over the target. This feature is useful in both ultimate and disc golf.

Skip shots and roll shots that strike and move along the ground are not applicable for ultimate but are extremely useful for disc golf, and they must be practiced by the disc golfer. With the right purpose and intention, skipping a shot toward a target or rolling a shot down a fairway makes perfect sense. In the right situation, using a throw that exaggerates the angle of the skip or roll shoulder during delivery will produce the skip or roll shot. Although the angle of the shoulder appears to be the critical element of the shot, the player must be able to recognize and predict the effect of the ground or surface on the action of the disc.

The Sidearm or Forehand

The sidearm and forehand throws are one and the same, keeping in mind that the natural forward throwing motion of the arm can be delivered from the various arm angles used for throwing in other sports. Similar to a pitcher's delivery in baseball, the arm can come forward and through in a flat or sidearm position, directly over the top of the shoulder as in a tomahawk motion, or somewhere in between, often referred to as a three-quarter delivery. In all cases, the forward throwing motion of the arm is initiated by the shoulder muscles of that arm, while the delivery and release is led by the elbow, then followed by the wrist and hand.

The sidearm grip uses the middle finger and index finger on the underside of the disc with the thumb on top (see Figure 11.3). The thrower may position the middle finger against the rim together with the index finger, or spread the index finger toward the middle of the disc. An index finger only (underneath) is another grip variation. The amount of pressure applied by the fingers must conform to the extent that the disc can be held level at release while the wrist is allowed to snap freely and forcefully. The hand and wrist are cocked backward as the arm retreats behind the body. Forward arm motion and arm speed, along with wrist flexion, are primarily responsible for the force exerted in this throw.

Again, a step throw for the sidearm or forehand relies upon the weight transfer from the back foot to the front foot during delivery. Both feet should be positioned along the line of the intended flight, with the front foot stepping forward and slightly open to the target during delivery (Figure 11.12). This footwork is accompanied by leg, hip, trunk, and shoulder rotations that open up to the target as the arm comes forward toward release. To set up for this throw, the thrower must be able to turn the shoulders and hips away from the target, and coil the upper body to generate rotational force and momentum. The stepping motion and weight transfer must be practiced and timed to coincide with the releasing action of the hips, shoulder, and arm. Easy and rhythmic throwing action should be practiced at varying distances to establish comfort and control. Added force and additional arm speed should be practiced after a natural motion is established (Figure 11.13).

To generate optimum force and speed for this delivery style, as well as for others, a walk-up or run-up approach during delivery can be added. Again, it is important to main-

Figure 11.13. Sidearm delivery motion.

tain balance and rhythm and stay relaxed through acceleration to generate as much force as possible into the last moment of release. All energy generated by added footwork must be timed and directed into the last act of releasing the throw. Toward the final step in this approach, many players will use a short hop to plant the weight onto the back foot to begin uncoiling the body. They quickly follow by stepping and shifting the weight forward to the front foot, releasing the hips and shoulders and accelerating the arm forward.

For the disc to adopt the best angle of delivery upon release from the hand, it is critical to have the wrist and disc maintain a level posture. To enable this positioning to take place, the forearm should also approximate a level posture. For the forearm to be in a level posture, the arm must approach the release point from a sideways position versus a three-quarter or over-the-top position. Hence, most forehand throws are of the sidearm delivery. The action of positioning the arm toward vertical during delivery increases the likelihood of a rolling curve to the point where the disc will turn over. A forehand throw where the arm and disc are released in nearly vertical position, a tomahawk position, is observed to produce a turnover where the disc flies most of its flight

Figure 11.12. Sidearm stance and delivery.

upside down. This throwing style is effective for both distance and accuracy and should be experimented with and practiced. It is commonly called the hammer.

For the most part, however, a sidearm throw, keeping the forearm, wrist, and disc level during delivery, will achieve great distances and can be thrown with accuracy. It is critical to snap the wrist quickly and forcefully at the release point, otherwise the throw suffers from an excessive roll curve, where the skip shoulder lifts toward vertical and the flight of the disc descends rapidly.

The thrower must experiment with pressure applied and location (pinch point) of the thumb and fingers to hold the disc level. Practicing the snapping action of the wrist while holding the disc in place will afford additional control and sense of adjustment. At the release point, where in fact the wrist does snap, the arm should temporarily freeze or stop moving forward as the wrist, hand, and fingers release the disc. This freezing action, while brief and momentary, will inhibit any form of a long or extended follow-through. Developing throwers must practice throwing level flights by controlling the lifting action of either shoulder of the disc. Correcting for excessive lifting action was discussed under Disc Flight Patterns.

The release point will determine the direction the disc flies out of the hand. Minor adjustments produce major changes in direction. The amount of spin imparted on the disc can act to stabilize the disc during flight. Generally, a wobbly disc is the result of insufficient force applied by the snap of the wrist. The sidearm delivery can generate skip curves, roll curves, skip shots, and roll shots.

For skip curves and skip shots, maintaining an open stance improves the chance to angle the skip shoulder down and produce the desired results. An observant thrower will notice that successfully throwing skip curves and skip shots requires the arm motion to be more inside or closer to the body during delivery than with a straight shot or roll curve. The roll curve, then, will likely position the arm outside and away from the body to allow the roll shoulder to maintain a down position. The roll shot takes the disc to near vertical position with the roll shoulder very much in the down position. The flight paths of the roll curve can be varied from sharp and steep to soft and wide, with both paths exaggerated or compromised by wind conditions. The action from the roll shot (roller) obviously depends on ground surface conditions as well as the force, angle, and impact with which the disc strikes the ground.

The Overhand

The overhand delivery style might appear unorthodox at first and feel quite different from the first two styles of delivery mentioned. As noted earlier, the grip for this throw is different from the other three by placing the thumb on the underneath side of the disc with the fingers spanned out over the top of the disc (see Figure 11.4). Most throwers prefer

Figure 11.14. Overhand stance and delivery.

to place their index finger along the outside of the rim of the disc for better feel and control. With the disc held in this grip, as the arm retreats during the backswing, the wrist is fully cocked.

The position of the body has the feet aligned with the intended flight of the disc and the opposite shoulder pointed toward the target. As the backswing is started, the shoulders and hips rotate into a closed position. With the weight back on the rear foot, the body is coiled, cocked, and ready. The release begins with a step and transfer of weight on to the lead foot, followed by the immediate release of the hips and shoulders. As the arm comes around to make the throw, arm speed is generated toward the release point. It is important to maintain the forearm in a level position as wrist snap and release occur. It is helpful to learn this throw by practicing a delivery with the motion of the arm and wrist occurring at shoulder height. This enables the thrower to prematurely set the forearm in a level position (Figure 11.14).

Much force can be generated from a properly timed and coordinated release of the body and arm, but, as in other throws, a walk-up or run-up approach can greatly increase the amount of force. Much like the forehand throw from over the top, a short hop to set the weight on to the rear foot will start the momentum forward, and precede the release of the rotational action from the hips and shoulders. At the release point, with the forearm fairly level, the wrist will extend forcefully from the cocked position. From start to finish, a full-body motion delivery is the most effective and least stressful. A disc diving downward sharply, as in an extreme roll curve, is evidence that the wrist and forearm were not held in a level position during release.

Straight shots and hover flights are fairly easily performed if position of the forearm, wrist, and disc are virtually preset, level, and co-planar with the angle of flight the thrower is attempting to achieve. A roll curve can easily be thrown with the overhand delivery by simply modifying the arc of the throwing arm. Skip curves and skip shots are executed by simply dropping the angle of the arm from shoulder level to waist level as the arm proceeds through delivery and into release position.

ULTIMATE

General Description

Ultimate combines throwing and catching skills with simple strategies and a great deal of running. Generally, almost any number of individuals can play in a game, given teams of equal numbers and ability and a playing area large enough to accommodate them. Typically, ultimate is played by two seven-person teams. The rectangular playing field has an end zone at each end. Teams are posed against each other, with the offensive team in possession of the disc, attempting to advance the disc toward its opponent's end zone to score.

The object of the game is to score goals by passing the disc among teammates. A goal is scored if a pass from a teammate is caught in the end zone. One point is awarded for each goal. A player may not run with the disc. Upon catching a throw, a player must come to a stop and establish a pivot foot immediately. The disc may be thrown in any direction to players positioned anywhere in the field of play. A careful and controlled offensive team will throw the disc among its players, much like soccer and lacrosse, as it advances downfield toward the opponent's end zone. Because running with possession of the disc is not permitted, unlike in soccer and lacrosse, the ability to throw accurately and to catch successfully while moving and avoiding defenders is most important. Intentional physical contact, including pushing, shoving, tripping, and blocking, is not permitted. Shielding a teammate from a defender by positioning oneself between the players, and setting picks, are also illegal.

The defensive team attempts to prevent the opponents from reaching their end zone by guarding and covering the opponent's players and trying to knock down or intercept throws, or by causing an errant throw to be made. Two basic defensive strategies are zone or one-on-one coverage. Ultimately, possession of the disc when it is in the air is up for grabs. Once a disc thrown by the offense is intercepted, missed, knocked down, or lands on the ground, the defense immediately takes possession at that spot and goes on offense. They now proceed in the other direction to advance the disc toward their opponent's end zone. Once the game has started and a disc is "in play," it remains in play until a goal is scored and a restart ensues. The first team to score 15 points is declared the winner.

Play is continuous even as offense and defense exchange possession. There is no offsides, so any player positioned within the field of play by either team at any given moment is legal. Possession is reversed whenever a throw lands out of bounds, is intercepted, or hits the ground. In a friendly game of ultimate, players call their own fouls and referees are not used. When a foul is called on a player, that player has the option to contest or not to contest the call. In a game without observers, a contested foul essentially results in a do-over. However, for UPA-sanctioned competition, official observers are used to act as mediators for contested calls. What is unique to the sport of ultimate is the "spirit of the game." Players observe elements of etiquette, sportsmanship, and camaraderie not always found in other competitive team sports.

Field/Equipment

1. The field of play is a rectangular area measuring 70 yards (64 m) in length and 40 yards (36.6 m) in width, with end zones 25 yards (22.9 m) deep.
2. The perimeter lines are not considered part of the playing field and are out-of-bounds.
3. Any flying disc acceptable to both teams may be used. The standard disc for UPA events is the 175-gram Discraft Ultra-Star.
4. Players for opposing teams are identified by any method agreeable by both teams.

Abridged Rules

Starting and restarting play

1. Initial possession: A disc flip (where two discs are flipped and the caller calls whether they will land on the same or opposite sides), coin toss, or any other method acceptable to both teams decides which team receives the initial throw-off and/or which end of the field to defend initially. To begin the second half of the game, the throw-off will be made by the team that received the initial throw-off to start the game. This throw-off will occur at the same end of the field as the original throw-off.
2. The throw-off: A throw-off (also called the pull) is used to begin play in each half, and to restart play after a goal is scored. Each team must line up on its respective goal line. The receiving team must indicate its readiness to receive a throw before the disc is thrown by the opposing team. Any player for the offensive team may elect to make the throw-off, and any player on the receiving team may elect to catch the throw-off. The throw-off must land and remain in the field of play. At this point, whether the disc is caught in the air or not by a member of the receiving team, possession will begin with the receiving team at that spot. If it lands out-of-bounds, play is started in the center of the field at that point or at the brick mark (20 yards [18 m] out from the receiver's end zone). No member of the throwing team may touch the disc before the receiving team has had a chance to put the disc in play. After a goal is scored, the teams switch end zones; the team that was scored upon walks to the other goal line, and the scoring team lines up for the throw-off.
3. The check: When play is interrupted, the player who was in possession of the disc retains possession at the spot where he or she was located when play was

halted. All other players remain at their respective locations. The defender covering that thrower will hand the disc back to the thrower to resume play, or the disc will be tapped or checked back into play by the defender.

Offense

1. Thrower: The disc is advanced toward the end zone by passing. Passes may be made in any direction. The thrower must establish a pivot foot, as in basketball, in attempting to pass in any direction and in any fashion. If the thrower takes steps, or the pivot foot is "lifted," traveling may be called by the defender and play is immediately halted. This violation results in play being restarted with a check. The defender restarts play at the same stall count by tapping the disc. A throw-off that goes out-of-bounds is put in play at either a spot at the sideline where the disc crossed out-of-bounds or at a spot in the middle of the field, perpendicular to the point where the throw-off crossed out-of-bounds. The thrower establishes a pivot foot at either point to begin play.
2. Receiver: After catching a pass, a receiver is allowed the fewest number of steps, usually three, to come to a complete stop and establish a pivot foot. In situations where a pass is caught near the sideline or the end zone line, the receiver's first point of contact with the ground determines where the pass was caught and whether it is ruled in or out-of-bounds or a goal or not. If the catch is good and the player's momentum takes him or her out-of-bounds or over the goal line, the player must return to the point of contact with the ground, and play resumes without a check.

Defense

1. Marker: A marker is the defender, who may guard the thrower but must allow the thrower to pivot and must maintain a distance equal to the diameter of a disc away from the thrower at all times. Therefore, hitting or slapping a disc out of the hands of the thrower or receiver is illegal. The thrower cannot maintain possession of the disc indefinitely, and the marker, at any time, can initiate a 10-second stall count by counting 10 seconds aloud. If the thrower has not released the disc within the 10-second count, a turnover is called by the defender and a check ensues.
2. General: Double-teaming is not permitted in guarding the thrower. However, defenders against receivers may position themselves in any manner they feel is best suited to defend against the pass.
3. Basic strategies are zone defenses and one-on-one coverage.

Fouls and violations

Fouls are the result of physical contact between opposing players. A foul can be called only by the player who has been fouled and must be announced by calling out "Foul!" loudly and immediately after the infraction. A foul may be called by either an offensive or a defensive player. Once a foul is called, play is immediately halted. If the foul is called by a defensive player, the disc goes back to the thrower in possession before the foul occurred and a check is called before play resumes, unless a turnover occurs, in which case possession reverts to the defensive team. If the foul is called by an offensive player, play resumes at the point of infraction with a new stall count unless the pass is completed. In both cases, a check is called before play ensues.

Miscellaneous

1. Substitutions: Unlimited substitution is allowed but only after a goal is scored or for an injured player.
2. Dispute/confusion: If there is a dispute or confusion on the field, play is halted and the issue is resolved before a check is called to restart the game.
3. Length of game: The length of game can be adjusted according to constraints. An official game is to 15, although teams may agree to any number of goals necessary to win, preferably before the game begins.

Teaching Considerations

1. Before providing lengthy instruction on learning the fundamental skills and techniques used in playing ultimate, it may be helpful to have the rules of the game and basic procedures of play discussed and demonstrated. Players might associate greater relevance to variations in throwing styles and deliveries by experiencing or visualizing the variety of game situations and circumstances.
2. Throwing and catching skills improve with guided instruction and feedback. Initially, helping students find success with one basic style of throwing and catching might be the primary objective. With confidence in one skill, a student might be less apprehensive about trying other skills. Conversely, students might rely too much on one successful style and need to be encouraged and challenged to develop versatility.
3. Throwing and catching drill must accompany playing time. Correct and repeated practice is necessary for continued improvement of basic skills. Several drills are described in the next section, but instructors are encouraged to invent drills to challenge their particular learners as well as accommodate students with physical and mental limitations.
4. Drill work for throwing off a pivot foot under various conditions must be practiced. Faking, pivoting, and

throwing with low and high release points goes beyond the basic skills of throwing and catching.

5. Beginners might initially prefer games where the thrower is a greater distance from the defender than in regular play.

DRILLS

1. Rapid thrower drill: Space one player as thrower about 5 yards from the remaining players, who form a line of receivers. Receivers have the discs to begin the drill. The first player in line tells the thrower the intended pass route, gives a short, accurate toss to the thrower, and runs the pass route. The thrower throws to the player in motion, and the next receiver steps up to line and does the same. After catching or retrieving the throw from the thrower, the receiver returns to the line. After several times through the line, a new thrower is installed.

2. Throw-spin-throw drill: Identify one player as thrower in the middle of two groups of receivers lined up and facing a different direction from each other. The thrower has two discs on the ground next to him or her. On the command "Go!" the first receiver in each line takes off running as the thrower grasps one disc, sets up and throws, then spins and grabs the other disc, sets up, and makes a throw to the second receiver.

3. Guard drill: A modified version of drill number 1. The receiver who runs a pass route becomes a defender and shadows the next receiver before returning to the line.

4. Triangle and circle throwing: Players are arranged in either formation. Each player uses alternate throwing styles to a player positioned to the left or right in the group. Modifications: catch only in dominant hand or nondominant hand; sidearm and cross-body backhand delivery styles must follow catches made in the thumb-up position. Overhand deliveries follow catches made in the thumb-down position.

DISC GOLF

General Description

Disc golf is played like traditional golf. However, instead of hitting a ball with a club into a hole, you throw a flying disc and hit a target. The layout for a disc golf course is very similar to a regular golf course. There is a tee area or designated starting point for every hole from which your first throw to the target is made. The target, in disc golf, is a 5-foot-high metal pole supporting a circular metal basket consisting of hanging chains and a catch basin. To land "in the hole," the disc must be thrown into, and remain within, the basket. The object of the game is to take as few throws as possible to get from the tee area to the hole. Generally, a course is laid out with nine or eighteen holes. Each hole presents a challenge to avoid trees, bushes, and other obstacles as the disc golfer proceeds down the fairway from the tee to the hole.

Disc golf presents an interesting challenge for disc throwers. The course layout, and wind and ground surface conditions, make it nearly impossible to simply throw straight shots down the fairway. The disc golfer must often elect to throw discs that fly both long and straight or short and curve or roll and skip along the ground. As the distance from the tee to the target is covered, accuracy takes on greater importance, until the final shot, which must fall in the basket, is taken.

Practice for disc golf can take the form of throwing at any target (e.g., fence post, telephone pole) without having to have an actual course on which to play. Players can "make up holes as they go" and find it equally challenging and fun. Beginners must learn to develop consistency and control in disc throwing as well as power for long-distance throws.

Field/Equipment

Disc golf courses are laid out like traditional golf courses with nine or eighteen holes, each of which is composed of a tee-off area, a fairway, out-of-bounds areas, a hole or target, and obstacles and hazards. Holes are of varying distances with a predetermined average number of strokes to hit the target (par). Typically, most holes on a disc golf course are par 3, with few labeled par 4 or 5. Without an official course, players can invent their own course using a park or field for fairways and boundaries, and trees, bushes, fence posts, and telephone poles for targets. The cost to play is minimal; many courses are free to the public, and flying discs retail for under $10. There are no other requirements of a player except a throwing arm with which to propel the disc toward the target and the means to get from one throw to the next.

Play

Disc golf has adopted common courtesy rules of play that are similar to those for regular golf. With more than one player playing, players throw one at a time. It is inappropriate to distract or interfere with another player's throw by any means. Players are not permitted to handle other players' discs. Each player should make her or his throw, then wait in turn for the remaining players to throw. After all players have thrown, all proceed to their discs and prepare for the next throw.

Typically, the player whose throw has landed farthest away from the hole will be the first to throw again. Therefore, other players must remain behind and out of the way of the throw as they take their turns. To begin a new hole, the player who has scored the fewest number of throws on the last hole will throw first, and so on. Players record their own scores for each hole on a scorecard.

From one throw to the next, each player must mark the spot where the disc has landed and make the next throw from behind that mark. Many disc golfers use a marker disc to place on the ground immediately in front of and touching the disc where it landed. With the location marked, the disc is picked up and the thrower prepares for the next throw, which must be taken with one foot planted behind and within close proximity to the marker disc. If a walk-up or run-up approach is used from the tee or in the fairway, the planted foot must be as close to touching the marker disc as possible. The follow-through action can carry the throw past the marker disc, without penalty, except for throws of less than 10 meters (11 feet).

For any throw to the target from within 10 meters, the planted foot must be positioned behind the marker and the other foot must remain behind a line perpendicular to the intended line of flight. Any follow-through motion that causes a player to touch the ground in front of this perpendicular line is a violation and results in a one-stroke penalty and rethrow. A player may be warned one time concerning a putting infraction without penalty, although a rethrow must be taken if the illegal putt was successful.

Accurate foot placement on lies and tees is required and is self-policing. However, other players may inform a player of the violation and the ruling of a one-stroke penalty and rethrow after the first warning.

Abridged Rules and Procedures

Practice throws are not permitted. Each player is allowed a maximum of 30 seconds to prepare and make a throw to the target once the playing area is cleared and the previous player has thrown. This rule is self-policing, but other players may inform a player of the violation and the ruling of a one-stroke penalty and rethrow after the first warning.

If a throw comes to rest aboveground in a tree or bush or some other permanent feature of the course, the subsequent throw must be made from a marker directly below the elevated spot but no closer to the hole.

If a throw lands out-of-bounds, where boundaries are clearly determined and enforced, the disc is brought in-bounds at the point where it left the in-bounds area, and a one-throw penalty is assessed. Other hazards, including ponds, lakes, and other fenced-off or restricted areas, are played similarly to out-of-bounds areas.

If a disc lands within bounds in an unplayable area due to standing water, muddy grounds, or manmade objects, the subsequent throw must be made from a marker positioned directly next to the area but no closer to the hole.

TEACHING CONSIDERATIONS

1. The fundamental skills and techniques used in playing disc golf include the introduction and practice of various throwing styles and deliveries. It can be helpful for students to have the rules of the game and basic procedures of play discussed and demonstrated as many of these skills are practiced. Players might associate increased relevance to variations in throwing styles and deliveries by experiencing or visualizing the variety of game situations and circumstances.

2. Throwing skills improve with experimentation, guided instruction, and feedback. Helping students develop proficiency with one basic style of throwing is the first objective. A student who has developed confidence in one type of delivery might be encouraged to experiment with other styles. On the other hand, students might rely too much on one successful style and need to be encouraged and challenged to develop versatility.

3. Throwing drill work must accompany playing time. Correct and repeated practice conducted on and off a playing course is necessary for continued improvements of basic skills. Instructors are encouraged to invent challenging tasks and play scenarios for students as well as to accommodate students with physical and mental disabilities.

GLOSSARY

approach shot Any shot in disc golf thrown with the purpose of gaining putting position.

attitude The angle of the disc with reference to the shoulder axis. Nose up is called positive attitude. Nose down is called negative attitude.

backhand A cross-body throw with the thumb on top of the disc and the fingers on the underside.

barrel roll Exaggerated turnover in flight.

basket The target in disc golf.

bend A curve steep enough to have a pronounced peak.

Berkeley grip A backhand grip with the forefinger hooked around the rim and the other fingers curled back and beneath the edge.

birdie Hitting a target in disc golf in one throw under par.

bogey Hitting a target in disc golf in one throw over par.

bomb A long downfield pass in ultimate, also called a huck.

brush A glancing slap on a disc in flight, also called a mack.

check A momentary delay in game during ultimate where the defender holds the disc as players get settled before handing the disc over to the offense. Often the offensive player holds the disc and the defensive player taps it.

closed stance The throwing position for a backhand.

cross-body Any catch or throw made with the arm reaching across the chest.

deflection Any change in the course of the disc's flight caused by contact with the disc's lip.

delivery The entire throwing motion.

dip Any sudden drop during a disc's flight, particularly when the disc rises afterward.

disc golf hole A standardized golf hole and target.

discwork Any move or action of the body or hand to control a disc.

drop A missed catch in ultimate that falls to the ground.

eagle Hitting a target in disc golf in two throws under par.

edge The bottommost portion of the rim of the disc.

facing stance A throwing position in which the thrower faces directly toward the target.

fairway The playing area considered in-bounds on each hole in disc golf.

fan grip A backhand grip with the forefinger along the rim and the other fingers spread out on the flight plate.

flight axis An imaginary line through the center of a flying disc from nose to tail.

flight plate The surface of a disc from rim to rim.

floater A hovering disc.

give and go A passing technique used in ultimate in which one player, after completing a short pass, sprints to catch a return pass.

glide phase The most nearly level portion of flight in the descent of a throw.

hover A type of flight in which the disc has little or no forward momentum and descends slowly.

hyzer (1) The tendency of a disc to rotate around its flight axis (most discs lift slightly at the roll shoulder). (2) The degree to which this tendency must be compensated for in the angle of release to produce the desired flight.

lie The spot where a disc comes to rest after being thrown in disc golf.

lip The outside rim of a disc.

marker A defensive player in ultimate who is guarding an offensive player in possession of the disc.

marker disc A mini-disc used in disc golf to mark the spot where a throw landed.

move Any act of throwing, controlling, or catching a disc, often used to refer to a series of discwork tricks as well.

multiple skips A steep skip flight that results in two or more skips.

normal curve A term sometimes used for a skip curve.

nose The leading edge of a disc in flight.

open stance The throwing position for forehand and overhand throws.

out-of-bounds The area beyond the field of play in both disc golf and ultimate, marked with boundary lines or otherwise, where a disc or player is considered out of play.

pancake (1) Trapping the disc between both hands. Also called a sandwich trap or clap catch. (2) The flattening-out motion of an upside-down lob throw.

par The predetermined average number of throws the tournament players in disc golf take to hit the target on each hole.

pick-up Any technique used to retrieve a disc from the ground.

propulsion Any technique used to impart spin to a disc.

rim The outer portion of a disc—the lip, rim, and edge.

roll curve A curved flight in which the roll shoulder is lower so that the disc tends to roll when it lands.

roll shoulder The shoulder of the disc that spins back toward the thrower.

setup (1) Any method to impart spin on a disc without propulsion. (2) To get in position for a particular move.

shadow To guard or defend a receiver in ultimate.

shoulder axis An imaginary line through the center of a flying disc from roll shoulder to skip shoulder.

shoulders The sides of a disc in flight, 90 degrees from the nose or tail.

sidearm A forehand throw usually made with the middle finger underneath and against the inside edge of a disc with the thumb on top of the disc.

skip curve A curved flight in which the skip shoulder is lower so that the disc tends to skip when it lands.

spin axis An imaginary line through the center of the disc perpendicular to the flight plate.

stability The property of a disc to maintain flight at the angle of release—the ability to resist turnover.

stall A portion of some flights during which the disc loses forward momentum.

stall count The marker counts loudly to 10 seconds at an appropriate speed. Reaching 10 before the disc is released results in a turnover.

stalling A defensive call in ultimate when the passer is taking too much time; followed by a countdown.

stroke (1) Any throw in disc golf. (2) The forward-moving portion of the delivery.

tacking A disc's holding its course across a wind.

tail The rear end of a disc in flight.

tee-box The designated area in disc golf for taking the first throw for each hole.

throw-off The arrangement of teams in ultimate on their respective end zone lines and subsequent first throw by one team to the other. Also called a pull.

tipping Control of a disc by finger contact with the flight plate.

touch Appropriate speed and spin in the act of putting in disc golf.

trap A type of catch in which the disc is stopped between any two parts of the body or even a part of the body and another surface.

turnover (1) Rotation of a flying disc about the flight axis. (2) A discwork technique in which the disc is turned from upside down to right side up or vice versa. (3) A change of possession in ultimate.

wrist flip An overhand throw made with the thumb on the belly and the fingers fanned out on top.

ACKNOWLEDGMENT

The contents of this chapter contain information that has been copied and reproduced from earlier writings. Permission has been obtained to use all such material. The assistance provided by Dan "Stork" Roddick has been instrumental in the assembly of this information.

SUGGESTED READINGS

Baccarini, M. and Booth, T. 2008. *Essential ultimate: Teaching, coaching, playing.* Champaign, IL.: Human Kinetics

Gregory, M. 2003. *Disc golf: All you need to know about the game you want to play.* Chicago, IL: Trellis Publishing.

Parinella, J., and Zazlow, E. 2004. *Ultimate techniques and tactics.* Champaign IL: Human Kinetics.

UPA rules of ultimate. Current edition. Colorado Springs, CO: Ultimate Players Association.

World Flying Disc Federation. Current edition. *WFDF official rules of flying disc sports.* World Flying Disc Federation, 655 Rim Road, Pasadena, CA 91107. Copies of this publication can also be purchased through mail-order supply houses of disc sporting goods.

RESOURCES

Freestyle Players Association, P.O. Box 2612, Del Mar, CA 92014.

Professional Disc Golf Association (PDGA), 65 Front St. West, Suite 0116-24, Toronto, Ontario, Canada M5J 1E6.

Ultimate Players Association (UPA), 3595 E. Fountain Blvd., Suite J2, Colorado Springs, CO 80910.

United States Disc Sports, c/o Bob Verish, 8550 Tujunga Valley Street, Sunland, CA 91040.

World Flying Disc Federation (WFDF), c/o Dan Roddick, 655 Rim Rd., Pasadena, CA 91107.

Books, Films, and Videotapes

Distributors

Circular Productions, P.O. Box 793, Austin, TX 78767-0792.

Disc Golf World, P.O. Box 4474, Overland Park, KS 66204.

Discovering the World, Box 911, La Mirada, CA 90637.

Professional Disc Golf Association, 65 Front St. West, Suite 0116-24, Toronto, Ontario, Canada M5J 1E6.

The Wright Life, 200 Linden, Fort Collins, CO 80524.

Ultimate Stuff, C Associates, P.O. Box 14520, Washington, DC 20003.

Wham-O Sports Promotion, 3830 Del Amo Blvd., Suite 101, Torrance, CA 90501.

WEB SITES

Beach Ultimate Lovers Association
http://beachultimate.org/home.html

WFDF
www.wfdf.org/

PDGA
http://www.pdga.com

PDGA course directory
http://www.pdga.com/course_directory

The Huddle: An Online Ultimate Magazine
http://www.the-huddle.org

Ultimate in 10 Simple Rules
http://upa.org/resources/officiating/rules/

Ultimate Players Association (UPA)
www.upa.org

Field Hockey

12

After completing this chapter, the reader should be able to:

- Describe the history and development of field hockey
- Be aware of important equipment selection and care considerations
- Understand the rules of field hockey and related games
- Execute the correct grip, dribble, ball control, and passing skills
- Understand basic defensive and offensive strategies and formations
- Demonstrate fundamentals to a group of students
- Recognize and use field hockey terms correctly

HISTORY

About 2,500 years ago, the early Greeks and other ancient nations played a game very similar to our present-day hockey. Centuries later the game was being played in France and was called *hoquet*. Then the English began to play it under the name *hokay*. The game became generally known as hockey with its English spelling and pronunciation. However, later—when ice hockey, a similar game played on ice, became popular—the game of hockey was called *field hockey*, and so it remains today in North America.

Between 1880 and 1890, field hockey was played exclusively by men in England, France, and other European countries and is still popular with them. In the United States, men tried the game, but it met with little favor.

A group of women who formerly lived in England formed the Livingston Association—a field hockey club—on Staten Island, New York, about this time, but it was short-lived. Then in 1901, Constance M. K. Applebee, of the British College of Physical Education, demonstrated the game of field hockey during a visit to Radcliffe College. She recommended it as a health-building form of combative recreation for college women. Miss Applebee was then invited to several Eastern women's colleges (Smith, Vassar, Wellesley, Bryn Mawr, and Mount Holyoke), and on each campus field hockey was accepted with great favor. Women's teams were formed, and the first interclass contest was held in 1902.

The women enjoyed the game so much that they adopted it and revised the rules to make them uniform and suitable for women's play. In 1920 an American women's team traveled to England, and later an English team visited the United States to play games in Philadelphia, New York, Boston, and Baltimore, thereby establishing field hockey as an international game.

In 1922 the United States Field Hockey Association (USFHA) was formed in Philadelphia to govern the sport for women, its purpose being to advance the interests of hockey for women and girls. The game's popularity spread rapidly among schools, colleges, and clubs.

In 1927 the worldwide interest in field hockey brought about the International Federation of Women's Hockey Associations (IFWHA), and tournaments were held in Philadelphia and Denmark.

In 1963 the USFHA hosted 18 of the 25 IFWHA member nations. Plans were made for this federation to meet every four years for conference games and discussion of international rules and hockey problems.

The next conference was held in Cologne, Germany, in 1967, with the format unchanged. The first unofficial IFWHA World Championship was held in 1971 in Auckland, New Zealand. The Netherlands won the tournament, and the United States finished eighth. The first official World Championship was held in Edinburgh, Scotland, in 1975. England won the title, and the United States finished eleventh.

The second World Championship was held in Vancouver, Canada, in 1979. The United States improved to an amazing third in world standings. The Netherlands finished first and West Germany second.

The Fédération Internationale de Hockey (FIH)—until 1930 a men's group—controls Olympic hockey and has well over 50 members. Members conduct world championships between Olympics for both men and women. The IFWHA and the FIH united in 1981 to form a single international governing body.

With women's hockey introduced into the Olympics for the first time in 1980, a combined committee from both world organizations was formed to organize the methods, standards, and procedures for qualifying. The team from Zimbabwe won the round-robin tournament (six teams) to capture the first women's field hockey Olympic gold medal. The decision of the United States to boycott the Moscow Olympics cost the U.S. team the chance to compete, which they had earned in the 1979 World Championship. The appearance of both the men's and women's U.S. field hockey teams in the 1984 Olympics marked the first time in 28 years that they were in this competition together. Although they had been ranked among the top six teams in the world in the early 1980s, it nevertheless came as a mild surprise when the women's field hockey team took the bronze medal in the 1984 Olympics by winning a stroke-off against Australia to break the tie for third place.

In 1988 the men's team from Great Britain won the Olympic gold medal, as did the women's team from Australia. The U.S. women's team finished eighth. In 1992 the men's team from Germany and the women's team from Spain won gold medals at the Barcelona Olympic Games. The U.S. teams did not qualify. At the Centennial Olympic Games in Atlanta, the United States was guaranteed a spot in the 1996 Games by virtue of being the host country. The women secured their highest Olympic finish since 1984, finishing fifth out of eight, but disappointment was evident as the team had hoped to win a medal in front of the large home crowds. The men's team was more competitive than in previous Olympic experiences, but was unable to win a game and finished twelfth out of twelve teams. The men's Olympic champion was the Netherlands, and the women's Olympic champion was Australia. In the 2000 Olympic Games in Sydney, Australia, the men's gold medal was won by the Netherlands and the women's gold was won by the host country, Australia. The U.S. teams did not qualify. In the 2004 Olympics, the gold medal for men was won by the Australian team and the team from Germany took home the women's gold medal. Once again, the U.S. teams did not qualify.

The mean's 2008 Olympic champion was Germany, and the women's gold medal was won by the Netherlands. The United States women's field hockey team qualified for the 2008 Olympics by winning a qualifying tournament. They finished eighth in the Olympics.

Men's field hockey is popular around the world and has been in the Olympics since 1908. India and Pakistan dominated for years, but Germany, the Netherlands, and Australia have emerged as consistent world-class teams. The U.S. men's team has never been an influence in world competition. While most of the world focuses on producing a strong men's and women's team, the United States has struggled with the lack of a true player development system for male field hockey players. There are no college programs, and there are only limited club team opportunities for men to play their sport on a year-round basis. The U.S. team has made strides with additional Olympic funding and access to facilities, but it has a smaller development pool of young athletes than other nations one-tenth their size.

In 1974, the USFHA sponsored a national collegiate championship for the very first time. Powerhouses such as West Chester State College, Ursinus College, and Lock Haven University were perennially the best collegiate teams. With the advent of athletic scholarships in 1975, slowly the composition of the tournament field changed. Larger schools, such as Penn State University, the University of Maryland, and the University of Massachusetts, began to dominate the championship scene. Field hockey championships were held from 1975 to 1981 under the direction of the AIAW (Association of Intercollegiate Athletics for Women). In 1982, the NCAA (National Collegiate Athletic Association) integrated women's sports into its traditional all-male championship structure. Women's field hockey national champions are now named in NCAA Divisions I, II, and III. In the 1990s, collegiate dynasties have been established by Old Dominion University and the University of North Carolina at the Division I level, Lock Haven and Bloomsburg University at the Division II level, and the College of New Jersey and William Smith College at the Division III level.

The NCAA now sponsors championships for women in Divisions I, II, and III. Over 225 colleges play around the country, with the highest concentration being east of the Mississippi River.

Indoor hockey is now quite popular in the winter months. Played by six players (five plus a goalkeeper), the game produces high scoring and lots of end-to-end action. The USFHA now sponsors national tournaments for adult men, women, colleges, and high school girls. While still not up to the level of European competition, the United States has seen a growth in this particular version of the sport.

GENERAL DESCRIPTION

The official game is played by two teams of 11 players on a grass field or artificial surface. Each player has a stick with which to propel and receive the ball. Each team attempts to put the ball into the opponent's goal, which is defended by a goalkeeper, the only player with special privileges and equipment.

The game should be modified in a variety of ways for youngsters, physical education classes, and intramural sports for maximum participation and fun. Games having two, three, or four players on each team in limited space, using cones as goals, are appropriate in these situations.

EQUIPMENT

Sticks

The implement for propelling and receiving the ball in field hockey is a stick (Figure 12.1), which is commonly divided into two parts—the handle and the head—for discussion and selection purposes. The head, which is the playing part of the stick, is curved and must be flat on the left side and rounded on the right. Only the flat side may be used to play the ball. It is referred to as the "face" of the stick. The handle is thin and round for a comfortable grip. The handle is generally covered with toweling, rubber, or leather; the head of the stick is uncovered and is usually made of a composite material. All sticks are "right-handed," but it is possible to play left-handed (although rare).

The length of the stick can vary from 30 to 38 inches (0.77 to 0.97 m). Most high school and adult players should usually use 36- to 37.5-inch (0.93- to 0.96-m) sticks. Youngsters

Figure 12.1. Composite hockey sticks.

and junior high players use 30- to 34-inch (0.77- to 0.87-m) sticks. If the stick is slightly too long, the player can choke down a little or the stick can be shortened.

Ball

The official ball used in the United States is made of a hard polyurethane composition. The circumference is not more than 9¼ inches (23.1 cm) or less than 8¼ inches (22 cm), and the weight is between 5½ and 5¾ ounces (157 to 164 g). In international competition, the official ball is dimpled, like a golf ball.

Shin Guards

Many types of leg protectors are available. Most are plastic with light padding inside. Like soccer guards, they fit comfortably into knee socks, and some have elastic straps that fit around the calf of the leg. Players should wear shin guards to prevent injury.

Shoes

Cleated shoes are best for play on grass. The cleats may be rubber, plastic, or metal. On hard surfaces, basketball shoes are recommended. Turf shoes are now available for play on artificial turf.

Clothing

The traditional uniform for males is shorts, shirt, and socks. For females it is a kilt, shirt, and socks. The goalkeeper plays in ice-hockey-style shorts and/or Lycra pants with a long-sleeve goalkeeping jersey of a contrasting color.

Goalkeeper's Equipment

Pads. The goalkeeper needs to protect the legs up to midthigh. High-density foam pads have recently been introduced, and they provide great protection while enhancing mobility (Figure 12.2).

Kickers. These are pads that fit over and around the shoe. High-density foam is also being used for kickers, which dramatically increases the protection of the foot from a hard shot. They are strapped behind and around the foot.

Gloves. Gauntlet-style gloves or ice hockey gloves are commonly used. The left palm is heavily padded, while the right palm is thinner to allow a comfortable grip on the stick. Recently, high-density foam "blockers" have been designed to allow for even more hand protection. Now goalkeepers can redirect the ball away from the goal cage rather than actually catching the ball.

Upper-body protectors. Shoulders, arms, chest, and stomach are all areas that should be protected. Lycra padded "pullover" protection, as well as fitted padding, are a necessary extension of harder shots and a more active goalkeeper. This equipment should always be used.

Throat protectors. They are made of foam that wraps around the neck like a collar. They are recommended for advanced players.

Mouthguards. All players should wear mouthguards.

Helmets. Helmets are now required at every level of play. They are similar to ice hockey helmets and have a full faceguard. Some keepers wear custom-fitted face masks, but these are usually way beyond the typical budget.

Figure 12.2. Goalkeeper's equipment.

DIMENSIONS OF FIELD

The hockey field (Figure 12.3) is a little wider than a football field (100 × 60 yards) (91.4 × 54.9 m), with a goal at each end. Goalposts are 4 yards (3.7 m) apart and 7 feet (2.13 m) high, joined by a crossbar. The goal is enclosed by a net or wire screen supported by two additional posts 4 to 6 feet (1.2 to 1.8 m) behind the goal. The sideboards and backboard in the goal are 18 inches (45.7 cm) in height. A half-circle having a 16-yard (14.6 m) radius is drawn in front of each goal cage to designate the scoring area. A smaller field can be used for junior play.

RULES

Basic Rules

The game is played by two teams of no more than 11 players each. One player is designated goalkeeper.

Time of play varies according to the level of competition, but no more than two halves of 35 minutes each (30 minutes in high school), with a 5- to 10-minute halftime, are played. To play off a tie, up to two 15-minute overtimes

are played and the number of players per side is reduced to seven. If after the first 15 minutes the score is still tied, a second sudden-death period is played. If no goals are scored in the sudden-death period, the game can go into a stroke-off to determine a winner. In international rules, a tie play-off involves two 7½-minute periods with the number of players remaining at 11 per side. If the score is still tied, a "golden goal" (first goal wins) is played.

Center-pass

To start the game or to resume play after halftime and after each goal is scored, a center-pass is played at the center of the field. The center-pass for the start of the game is made by a player of the team who did not make the choice of ends, after halftime by a player of the opposing team, and after a goal has been scored by a player of the team that the goal was scored against. Teams may cross the centerline at first touch. The center-pass may be played in any direction.

Players other than the player making the pass-back must be in their own half of the field. Players on the opposing team must be at least 5 yards (4.6 m) from the ball. The clock

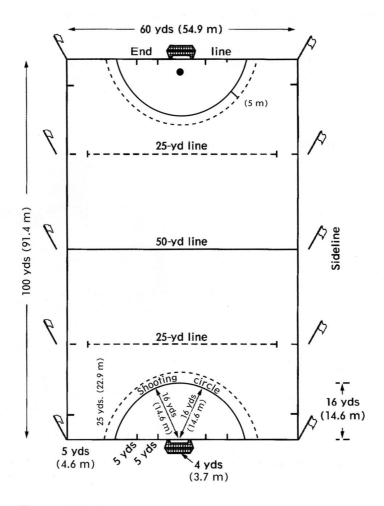

Figure 12.3. Plan of field of play.

is stopped on the official's signal for a goal and restarted on the official's whistle for a pass-back (in international rules, the clock never stops).

Coin toss

The captains toss a coin for choice of start or ends. The winner of the toss has the choice either of possession of the ball at the start of the game or of which end of the field to attack in the first half. The loser of the toss has the option not selected by the winner of the toss.

Scoring

Putting the whole ball over the goal line into the opponent's goal is a score. The ball must be touched by a member of the attacking team in the circle to count. Each goal counts 1 point.

Fouls

A player may not:

1. Play the ball with the round side of the stick.
2. Raise the stick in a dangerous way.
3. Propel the ball with any part of the body.
4. Play dangerously—that is, wildly or deliberately hit into an opponent or uncontrollably raise the ball.
5. Interfere in any way with an opponent's stick.
6. Trip, charge, shove, or interfere with any opponent's person or clothing.
7. Use the hand to stop or catch the ball.

Goalkeepers play by the same rules except that they may play the ball with their feet and may give an aerial ball slight impetus forward. Goalkeepers lose these privileges if they leave the circle.

No foul should be called when the fouled team is able to maintain an advantage and has the same or better opportunities than it had prior to the foul.

Penalties

1. When the foul occurs *outside the circle,* the opponents get a free hit from the spot where the foul occurred. An intentional, flagrant foul inside the 25-yard line results in a penalty corner.
2. When the foul occurs *inside the circle by an attacker,* the defenders have a free (16-yard) hit.
3. When the foul occurs *inside the circle by a defender,* the attackers have a penalty corner.
4. When a foul is committed *inside the circle by a defender and a certain goal was prevented,* a penalty stroke is awarded to the attackers.

Offside

In 1996, the offside rule was eliminated in field hockey, dramatically changing the defensive styles and scoring opportunities for the attack and expanding the role of the goalkeeper.

Free hit

The free hit is taken on the spot by any member of the fouled team. An exception is when the offense fouls in the circle. In this case, the defense may take the free hit anywhere in the circle. Usually it is taken 16 yards out in line with the foul.

The ball should be motionless, and the striker may use any legal stoke. The ball may not be raised dangerously. At the moment the free hit is taken, no player of the opposing team may be within 5 yards (4.6 m) of the ball. However, should the umpire consider that a player is standing within 5 yards in order to gain time, the free hit is not delayed.

For a free hit awarded to the attacking team for a breach of rules within 5 yards of the circle, at the moment when the free hit is taken, both teams must be 5 yards off of the ball. Hash marks have been added to the field markings to clearly depict this area. After a free hit is taken, the striker may not touch the ball again until it is touched by someone else.

Penalty corner

1. The corner injector (Player X$_A$ in Figure 12.4) hits or pushes the ball along the ground from a spot no closer than 10 yards (9.1 m) from the near goalpost on the side of the team's choosing. The hitter must straddle the endline. The player may not touch the ball again until it is touched by someone else.
2. Any of X$_A$'s teammates may be receivers. No member of the team may have any part of the body or stick in

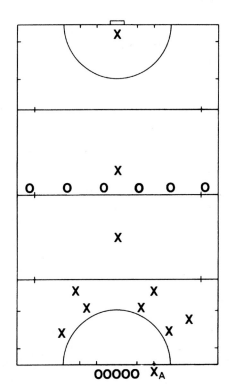

Figure 12.4. Field hockey penalty corner.

the circle until the ball is hit. No member may be closer than 5 yards (4.6 m) to the corner hitter. The receiver must control the ball outside the circle before shooting.

3. The defending team may have no more than five players on the endline. The remaining six must go to the 50-yard (45.5-m) line. Their bodies and sticks must be behind the line until the ball is hit; then they may move to defend. No defender may be closer than 5 yards to the corner injector at the point of injection.

Penalty stroke

The penalty stroke is between the goalkeeper and any member of the fouled team:

1. The goalkeeper is not permitted any change in dress or equipment. The keeper must have part of the feet on the goal line and may not move them until the ball is stroked. At the moment the ball is stroked, the goalkeeper may use all legal means to prevent the ball from going into the goal. The goalkeeper need not clear the ball.
2. The stroker is 7 yards (6.4 m) from the center of the goal line. The stroker may push, flick, or scoop but may not hit. The stroker lines up within reach of the ball. The ball may be touched only once, and the attacker must execute smoothly and continuously with no faking or deception.
3. All other players of both teams shall be beyond the nearer 25-yard (22.9-m) line and not in the goalkeeper's line of sight.
4. A successful goal is followed by a pass-back. An unsuccessful shot gives the defending team a 16-yard (14.6-m) hit opposite the center of the goal line.

Out-of-bounds

1. When the ball goes out-of-bounds *over the sideline,* the opponents receive a side-in.
2. When the defending team unintentionally sends the ball over the endline from within its 25-yard (22.9 m) area, a long hit shall be taken by the attacking team. A player from the attacking team shall hit the ball from a spot on the end line 5 yards (4.6 m) from the corner flag nearest to the side where the ball crossed the goal line.
3. When the ball is hit *over the endline by the attack,* a 16-yard (14.6 m) hit is awarded to the defense.

Side-in

Any member of the team may push or hit the ball into play from the spot where it went out-of-bounds. The player's feet may straddle the sideline. At the moment the side-in is taken, players on the opposing team must be 5.4 yards (5 m) away. After taking a hit-in, the player may not touch the ball again until it is touched or has been played by another player of either team. The side-in must be kept on the ground.

16-yard hit

The ball is hit from any spot not more than 16 yards (14.6 m) from the endline opposite the point where the ball went out-of-bounds. All rules of the free hit apply here.

Fouls on push-in or free hits

1. When the foul is by the hitter, the opponents are awarded a hit-in or free hit on the same spot. The exception is a foul by a player taking a free hit in the circle, in which case the opponents are awarded a penalty corner.
2. When the foul is by the opposition, the play is repeated only if the foul gives the opposition an advantage.

Fouls on penalty corners

1. When the foul is on the attacking team on a penalty corner, the defense has a free hit anywhere in the circle or 1 yard (0.91 m) outside the circle in line with where the foul occurred.
2. When the foul is by the defense, the play is repeated only if the violation gives the opposition an advantage.

Rules for Indoor Hockey

The rules are generally the same as for field hockey unless noted otherwise. Two exceptions are that no lifted balls (except on a goal) and no backswing strokes are allowed. The game is played by two teams of six players. Each half lasts a maximum of 20 minutes.

Starting and restarting the game

At the start of the game, a center-pass is made by the player of the team winning the toss, and after a goal it is made by a member of the team scored against. The pass may be played in any direction. All players must be in their half of the court, and no one except the passer may be closer than 3.3 yards (3 m) from the ball. No player shall cross the centerline until the ball is pushed.

Playing area

The court is rectangular, 43.8 × 21.9 yards (40 × 20 m). When possible, sideboards 4 inches wide and inclined slightly inward will surround the area.

Circle

The circle measures 10 yards (9.4 m) instead of 15 yards (14.1 m). On narrower-than-regulation playing areas, the circles will meet the sideline. Penalty corner marks will be 6.6 yards (6 m) from the goalposts, and the penalty stroke will be 6.6 yards (6 m) from the center of the goal mouth.

Fouls

A player may not:

1. Hit or play the ball in the air.
2. Take part in the play while lying on the ground unless the player is the goalkeeper.

3. Hit the ball.
4. Lift the ball outside the circle.

Free pushes

Free hits are referred to as "free pushes." All players must be at least 3.3 yards (3 m) from the pusher.

Penalty corners

Offense

1. The pusher is 6.6 yards (6 m) from the near goalpost.
2. No one may be within 3.3 yards (3 m) of the pusher.
3. The half or game shall be prolonged to complete a penalty corner. The corner is over when the ball leaves the circle or a goal is scored.

Defense All players may defend, but they are on the end-line opposite the side of the pusher. No player other than the goalkeeper is allowed in the goal at the start of the corner (Figure 12.5).

Out-of-bounds over the sideboards

Any ball that goes over the sideboards is put in play by a member of the opposite team 1.1 yards (1 m) from the sideboards but not in the circle. No one may be within 3.3 yards (3 m) of the pusher.

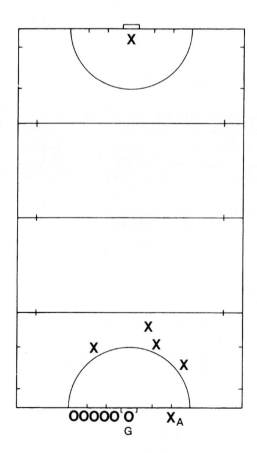

Figure 12.5. Indoor hockey penalty corner.

Out-of-bounds over the endlines

No matter who sends the ball over, the defending team gets a free push inside the circle. The exception is when a defender deliberately sends the ball over the endboard or makes no effort to keep it in play; then a penalty corner is awarded.

FUNDAMENTAL SKILLS AND TECHNIQUES

Stickwork

Key focal points

1. Grip: left hand at top; V of thumb and forefinger down the side of the stick; right hand comfortably wrapped around the stick midway down (Figure 12.6).
2. Eyes should be focused on a point about 2 yards (1.8 m) in front of the ball, but *scanning* is essential—you need to be able to see 180 degrees around you. Looking up is also very important!
3. Forehand dribbling: The ball should be positioned off the right (front) foot, slightly out to the side so that you can see the maximum amount of the field. There are two types of forehand side dribbles: close and loose.
   a. Close: The ball rests against the stick at all times—no tapping! This is to be done in traffic, and you *always* need to be ready for a sudden change of direction.
   b. Loose: The ball stays within 3 feet (0.9 m) of the stick; stick angle goes backward to a 45-degree angle underneath the ball; hands slide up the stick. The ball is pushed more in front of the right foot.
4. Backhand dribbling: The left hand controls the ball: the right hand may be off the stick. Be sure to make the grip change by rotating your top hand one quarter turn to the left. The ball is in front of the left shoulder, outside of the left foot. Be careful not to let the ball drop behind your left shoulder—unless you keep moving it's obstruction!

Spin Move

1. Your plan should be to end up with possession in a space with time to make a good pass or execute an elimination skill. Don't roll into traffic!
2. Begin your move by taking the ball on a slight angle toward one foot of your defender. You need to initiate your spin well *ahead* of the defender because you cannot make contact (no bump and run!), and you need to create the space for your body to move into.
3. Finish by going on a 45-degree angle to space—and look up!

Dribble

The ultimate objective is for each player to develop a rhythm and harmony between self and the ball, at speed, over varying distances, and against all kinds of opposition. The dribble (Figure 12.7) is needed to gain ground, to set up a pass by drawing an opponent, and to beat or eliminate an opponent. In open field the straight dribble (the ball moves in a

Figure 12.6. Grip.

Figure 12.7. Dribble.

straight line) is best. Before passing or beating an opponent, the Indian, or zigzag, dribble (the ball moves ahead but, in doing so, it alternately moves diagonally in any direction) is best because it is quicker and can be more deceptive.

Grip

Straight dribble. The back of the left hand now faces obliquely up and over the right shoulder. The back of the right hand faces backward. An instructional cue is to "read your wrist watch." In general, the stick is gripped firmly with the left hand and it glides through the right-hand grip.

Indian dribble. When the ball is moved left, the back of the left hand faces the same as in the straight dribble. When the ball is moved right, the back of the left hand faces the ground. The back of the right hand faces right or left throughout the dribble.

Wrists and arms

Straight dribble. The left wrist and forearm are a straight extension of the stick. The arm is at 90 degrees at the elbow, which is 10 to 12 inches (25 to 30 cm) from the body. The right wrist is hyperextended, and the right arm is straight.

Indian dribble. This is the same as the straight dribble except the left arm is almost straight out in front of the body and the right wrist is straight.

Body and head

Straight dribble. The body is slightly left of and behind the ball, and the center of gravity is slightly lower than when running without the ball. The head is up as often as possible for increased vision.

Indian dribble. The procedure is the same as in the straight dribble except the body is directly behind the ball. In a one-on-one play, the player swerves downfield rather than run in a straight line. Lifting the head frequently is essential.

Feet and legs

Straight dribble. Both feet are slightly left of and behind the ball. With balance, one can run quite fast without losing the ball.

Indian dribble. Both feet are behind the ball; the player runs fast, with sudden changes of pace and direction to get around opponents quickly.

Stick

Straight dribble. The stick is angled across the body at 45 degrees. The top of the handle is opposite the left thigh. The face of the stick faces the direction in which the player is moving and is ahead of and slightly to the right of the right foot.

Indian dribble. The stick is angled straight out in front of the body. The left-hand grip rotates one-quarter turn counterclockwise to accommodate the reverse stick. When moving the ball left, the face of the stick faces diagonally left.

When moving the ball right, the stick is turned over and the toe is down, moving the ball diagonally right. Playing the ball with the toe down is referred to as "reverse stick." The stick is turned by the left hand through a relaxed right hand.

Ball

Straight dribble. The ball is 14 to 18 inches (35 to 45 cm) in front of and slightly to the right of the right foot. It is propelled forward in a series of short taps.

Indian dribble. The ball moves alternately left and right diagonally out in front of and wide of the body. The ball should be allowed to get outside either foot.

Common faults

1. The player fails to keep the stick at 45 degrees away from the feet.
2. The ball is too close to the feet.
3. The eyes become riveted to the ball. The player no longer scans the field for options.

Push

The push (Figure 12.8) is used for passing over short distances. It is characterized by the absence of a backswing, which allows for quickness in execution and disguising the direction of the pass until the last instant.

Grip

Use the same grip as when dribbling. Rotate the stick as required for comfort and efficiency.

Wrists and arms

The hands work together in a common motion. Beginners tend to use a shovel motion rather than a dragging motion.

Body and head

The body is inclined forward with the head over the ball. The left shoulder faces the intended direction of the pass. The body weight is back on the right foot before the push. The weight shifts to the left foot as the right hand and wrist push the ball. The body on the follow-through is low and at full stretch. The follow-through provides power and direction.

Feet and legs

The left foot is forward a little more than shoulder's width from the right foot. The feet are parallel and slightly angled. The legs are bent, and the right leg extends on the follow-through. Ideally, the ball starts slightly behind the midline of the body.

Stick

The stick is angled about 45 degrees across the body, with the handle slightly ahead of the head of the stick. The face of the stick is directly behind and on the ball.

Figure 12.8. The push. A, Start point. B, Midpoint. C, Follow-through.

Common faults

1. The player is unable to coordinate weight transfer.
2. The left shoulder is not brought around.
3. The stick is held vertically instead of angled.
4. The player is too upright and does not bend from the knee.
5. The hands do not work together, moving across the body.
6. The player fails to follow through.

Receiving Skills

Ball control is the ability to bring any ball coming at you from any direction under control—to "catch" it. The ball's speed is deadened on the face of the stick. Ultimately, players should be able to play the ball immediately upon receiving it. Ideally the ball should never be tapped still, so that the defense cannot easily close you down.

Grip

Ball coming toward the player. Both hands are relaxed enough to absorb the ball and place it in the most advantageous attacking position. A 45-degree angle is sometimes used to "trap" the ball.

Ball coming from left. Allow the ball to come across your body and receive it off your right foot. The stick moves with the flow of the ball (Figure 12.9).

Ball coming from right. Allow the ball to come across your body and receive it off your left foot. The stick moves with the flow of the ball (Figure 12.10).

In receiving any ball, the right hand, which is comfortably down the stick, is very relaxed so that it can move the face of the stick behind the ball and then act as the major factor in cushioning the ball and preventing deflections.

Wrists and arms

Ball coming toward the player. The left wrist and forearm are straight extensions of the stick, with the left elbow bent at 90 degrees. The right wrist is hyperextended, and the right arm is comfortably positioned to cushion the ball.

Figure 12.9. A, Initial contact outside left foot. B, Receiving across the body. C, End point—ball outside right foot.

Figure 12.10. Ball control. Ball coming from the right. Receive outside right foot and play to left.

Ball coming from left. The left wrist and arm are straight extensions of the stick. The right wrist and arm are comfortably positioned to cushion the ball.

Ball coming from right. Taking the ball midstride, both arms and wrists are the same as when the ball is coming toward the players. Taking the ball reverse stick, both arms and wrists are the same as when the ball is coming from the left.

Body and head

When receiving any ball, the player must concentrate enough to see the ball make contact on the face of the stick.

Ball coming toward the player. The body is behind and slightly left of the ball.

Ball coming from left. The body is inclined forward.

Ball coming from the right. Taking the ball midstride, the body twists 90 degrees right from the waist to face the oncoming ball. Taking the ball reverse stick is the same as when the ball is coming from the left.

Feet and legs

Except when taking a ball from the right in midstride, the feet must be sufficiently behind the ball to prevent overrunning it. Ideally the ball should be received facing the attacking goal.

As in other sports, players must be prepared to go to meet the ball or the pass will be intercepted.

Stick

When fielding any ball and at the moment of contact, the face of the stick must squarely meet the ball. The face of the stick must be inclined slightly toward the ball to trap it and keep it on the ground.

Ball coming toward the player. The stick is angled 45 degrees across the front of the body. The handle is opposite the left thigh, and the head is on the ground forward of and slightly right of the right foot.

Ball coming from left. The stick is angled forward in front of the right foot. The toe is up.

Ball coming from the right. Taking the ball midstride, the stick is angled across the body with the handle slightly higher than and left of the left knee, and the head of the stick is on the ground out from but between the feet. In reverse stick, the stick is angled forward opposite the left foot with the toe down.

Ball

The ball, after contact with the stick, is in position to be dribbled, pushed, hit, or shot. Deflections and rebounds are acceptable as long as they are not dangerous.

Common faults

1. The face of the stick is not square to the oncoming ball.
2. The left wrist is bent.

3. The right hand is too tight, so the player does not feel the ball on the stick.
4. The player moves the stick into the ball rather than absorbing its speed.
5. The top of the stick is not angled forward, creating upward deflections.

Hit

The hit moves the ball far, hard, and decisively to any part of the field. It is a necessary complement to the push because it allows for the big game by opening up and spreading the play. A "good ball" is a hard, accurate pass that hugs the ground and can be handled by the receiver. Although the following are components of the hit, successful execution is one action; that is, the backswing, downswing, hit, and follow-through combine in one continuous motion (Figure 12.11).

Grip

Preliminary. The traditional grip is used with the back of the left hand facing the intended direction of the pass. The right hand is directly under and touching the left, with the back facing right. The V formed by the thumb and index fingers on both hands are in line with the toe of the stick. In most cases the right hand slides up to the left, but some prefer to slide the left hand down. Quickness, not power, is gained with this "choked down" grip.

Backswing. The same grip is used.

Hit and follow-through. The hands grip tighter at contact.

Wrists and arms

Preliminary. Wrists and arms are slightly bent and out from the body.

Backswing. The stick is brought back with the arms and wrists, which do not touch any part of the body. The wrists are about waist height, firmly cocked, so that the head of the stick is higher than the wrists. The arms move together on the backswing with the right arm rotated and slightly bent. The right elbow points back, about 6 inches (15 cm) away from the body. Hands are 5 to 7 inches (12.5 to 17.5 cm) off the hip. The toe of the stick should point up at the end of the backswing.

Hit and follow-through. Transfer the weight from the right foot to the left on the downswing with the left foot (even with the ball at contact). The arms, wrists, hip rotation, and weight transfer provide a strong hit. The muscles of the arms and wrists, like all muscles, must be tensed on impact but relaxed on the backswing and follow-through. Follow through in the same natural arc as the backswing.

Body and head

The head is over the ball throughout.

Preliminary. The body is turned so that the left shoulder faces the intended direction of the pass.

Backswing. The weight is shifted to the rear foot.

Hit and follow-through. The weight is shifted to the front foot just before the stick makes contact with the ball. The force of the swing should naturally bring the body through in the direction of the hit.

Feet and legs

Preliminary. The feet are about shoulder-width apart and pointed at right angles to the direction of the hit. The left foot is ahead of the right. The legs need to be firm, strong, and slightly flexed.

Backswing. Same feet and leg positions are used. A slight hip rotation is important.

Hit and follow-through. At impact, the leg muscles must be tense but not rigid. The left leg should be bent close to 90 degrees with the weight over the left leg. The right leg is used for balance only after contact.

Stick

Preliminary. The flat side of the stick is placed directly behind the ball, facing the intended direction of the pass.

Backswing. The stick goes straight back, not behind the right shoulder. The toe is above the wrists and pointing slightly upward.

Hit and follow-through. The stick is vertical at impact at or around the height of the left knee, and it clearly continues in the direction of the hit until the head reaches waist height and there is no more upward movement. The hit is a rotational skill. It is more like hitting a baseball than striking a golf ball.

Ball

Preliminary. The ball is a comfortable distance from the body and is in line with the left foot at the moment of impact to hit the ball straight (perpendicular to the body position).

Hit. After being struck by the middle of the face of the stick, the ball should travel smoothly along the ground.

Common faults

1. Choppy, lofted, or sliced hits because of poor arm and hip synchronization.
2. Topping the ball because of not keeping the eyes on the ball throughout the hit.
3. The left shoulder is not around far enough, causing misdirection.
4. The arms are too tight in on the body, restricting their movement.
5. Body weight is not transferred fully onto the left foot.
6. Only the wrists or only the arms are used. Power comes from the legs through weight transfer.
7. Failure to follow through.
8. Carrying the stick in a backswing position for several yards, thus telegraphing intentions.
9. Trying to "overhit" the ball. Timing is more important than force for control and accuracy.

Figure 12.11. Hit. A, Backswing. B, Contact. C, Follow-through.

Flick

The flick is a lofted stroke that is used to score goals and to clear over the opponents. The basics are the same as the push, with the following differences:

1. The stick must not only be behind the ball but also slightly under it.

2. The ball is positioned slightly more forward just prior to the flick.

3. The right shoulder and elbow drop behind the ball on a 45-degree angle to enhance the height of the flick.

4. Weight should be transferred through the ball in the direction of the flick, not falling away.

Tackle

The tackler wants to dispossess the opponent of the ball. If that is not possible, the player can, by the pressure exerted, force passes that can be intercepted by teammates.

Jab

The stick is held with a "frying pan" grip. The tackler attempts to jab underneath the ball and pop it over the dribbler's stick. The tackler needs to pull the stick back immediately and protect the feet. Body position for this tackle is in accordance with the attacker's movement.

Block

The player is square with and in front of the dribbler. The defender uses the length of the stick on the forehand or backhand side to "block" space and take the ball away. Both hands should be used to tackle, and the weight should be balanced evenly on both feet or forward to aggressively win the ball.

Common faults

1. Having center of gravity too high.
2. Hitting opponent's stick or leg.
3. Not being forceful enough on the ball.
4. Overcommitting or overstriking.

Passing

Passing is the heart of the game. It is the intentional movement of the ball by two teammates. Passes eliminate defenders.

Techniques

1. Pushing and hitting for delivering the ball.
2. Controlling or fielding skills to receive the ball.

Players without the ball

To receive a pass, teammates without the ball must take the initiative and get free of their opponents so they can receive a pass. Making short, hard cuts at speed is one way to lose an opponent.

Player with the ball

The passer makes the pass when he or she is sure there is no opponent in or close to the line of the intended pass. If the path of the pass is clear, then the passer must send the ball *accurately and properly paced* to a teammate. A ball hit too hard will go by the teammate, and too soft a hit gives the opponent time to move in and intercept. To make an accurate pass, the passer must assess the teammate's speed and direction so that the receiver does not break stride. The passer must time the pass. Players who get free without the ball do not have much time before the defender recovers. If the passer is slow to recognize the moment the teammate is free, the pass will be late and likely intercepted. Conversely,

the passer must recognize when to hold the ball momentarily because the teammate is getting free and will be available in a few steps. If the passer passes too soon, the teammate will not be there. Good vision, timing, and accuracy are important for successful passing.

Passing strategies

Upfield pass (Figure 12.12A).
When possible, passes should always go to an open teammate who is closer to the goal than the player with the ball is. Upfield passes will be at a variety of angles.

Through pass (Figure 12.12B).
This is the ultimate upfield pass. It runs parallel to the sideline and is very penetrating because it eliminates two defenders.

Square pass (Figure 12.12C).
This pass gains no field position because it runs parallel to the endline. It should not be used if there is any chance of an interception. The square pass is best used in a "give and go" (Figure 12.12D). This passing combination is most often associated with basketball, but it is equally useful and effective in field hockey. The player with the ball takes it close to an opponent. The player "gives" a square pass to a teammate and "goes" quickly to the open space behind the opponent for a return pass.

Back pass. Passing backward will often open up the field of play and allow the team to change the point of attack.

Shooting. Scoring a goal should be viewed as the final pass. It is a ball that goes by the goalkeeper into the goal.

BASIC DEFENSE

Simply stated, defense is the team not in possession of the ball. When the opponents have possession, the players on the defending team in the vicinity of the ball actively attempt to get it while their teammates not immediately involved move back into the best defensive position in case the ball suddenly shifts. Pressure, marking, and covering are the basic principles in defense (Figure 12.13).

Pressure. Pressure must be exerted against the opponent with the ball in such a way that a tackle is possible if ball control is lost. If a tackle is not possible, pressure reduces the passing angles.

Marking. Defense must be such that opposing attack players without the ball cannot receive the ball or are under instant pressure if they do. To mark effectively, the defender must be goalside and ballside of the opponent and the defender must be able to see both the opponent and the ball, unless front marking. The farther the opponent is from the ball, the less tightly the defender has to mark.

Covering. At the point of attack where the opponent with the ball is pressured and nearby teammates are marked, there is space behind the defenders. A player must be assigned to cover this space should a pass suddenly come through or an opponent get by.

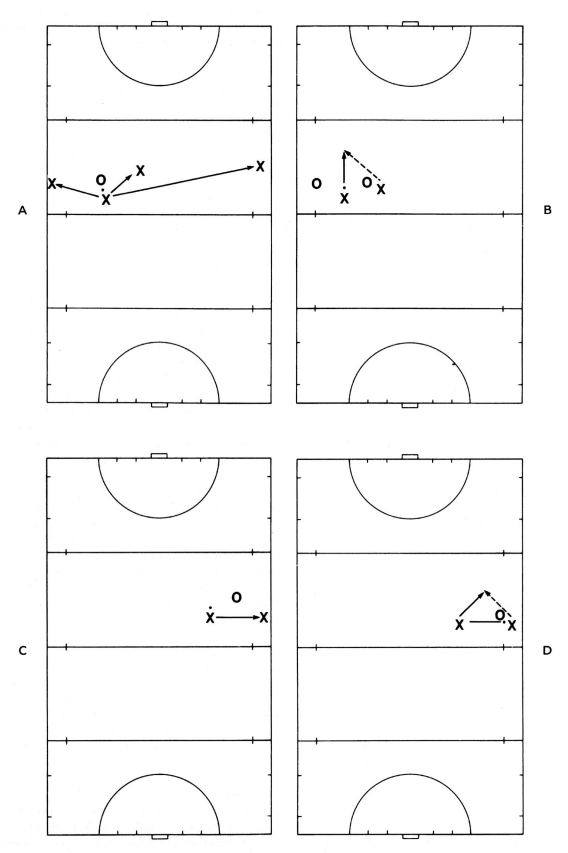

Figure 12.12. Passing strategies. A, Upfield pass. B, Through pass. C, Square pass. D, Give and go.

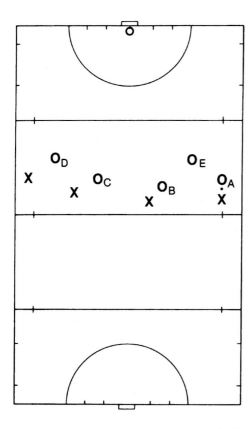

Figure 12.13. Defense. O_A is pressuring; O_B, O_C, and O_D are marking. O_E is covering.

BASIC OFFENSE

The offense is the team with the ball. At the moment a player gets the ball, every teammate thinks offense and the players in the vicinity of the ball become active participants in the attack.

Principles of Offense

Movement off the ball. The key to successful attacks is players without the ball seeking open space. The player with the ball should have a minimum of two open teammates to whom to pass.

Width. Crowding is one of the biggest problems in all team sports. The first move a player should make is wide—to the sidelines. This forces the defender into a decision. Does the defender go with the ball carrier or stay in position? By spreading out and stretching the defense, the ball carrier will be able to receive the ball and have some space to work with.

Depth. This principle encourages an uneven distribution of attack players rather than a straight line. This provides more passing opportunities for the player with the ball.

STATIC SITUATIONS

Free Hit

Offensively, the first priority is to take a free hit quickly, before the other team sets up. If this is not possible, the

player can delay slightly to give teammates a chance to organize. Movement by the receivers and deception by the passer are essential. Usually a short pass is most effective, and a long pass should only be used if a player is wide open.

Defensively, against the free hit, the team must recover quickly and set themselves up so there is no outlet for the free hit.

Side-in

Essentially, tactics of the side-in are the same as in the free hit. Offensively, it is important to keep possession of the ball, and the pusher should not make a back or square pass if there is any chance of interception, or if an attacking pass is available.

Penalty Corner

Offense. The player who hits-in must be able to accurately and smoothly hit the ball to the trapper, who then smoothly and with precision places the ball in position for the shooter to shoot. The shooter should be the player with the greatest ability to hit hard, accurately, and quickly. On the college and international levels, a "stick stopper" is employed to provide a controlled stop for the shooter. This is very common on artificial surfaces. The other forwards are in a position to get a goal from a deflection or a goalkeeper's rebound. Usually three defenders should be in a backup position should the ball come out of the circle. Tactically, it is best to take the penalty corner on the left because it is easier to inject and stick stop from this position.

Defense. There are numerous penalty corner defense strategies. In the most common strategy, the fastest player should go to the shooter, hoping to get the ball or at least disrupting the shooter's rhythm and concentration. Two players, one on each side, trail to get any deflections or dodges. One defender covers and one comes out on the opposite side from the corner in case the ball suddenly shifts. No one should block the goalkeeper, who comes out to reduce the angle of the shot. There is usually a player designated to protect the post and clear rebounds off the goalkeeper.

GOALKEEPING

The goalkeeper is the last line of defense. The goalkeeper needs the qualities of continual concentration, agility, quickness, strength, and power and the ability to anticipate and communicate effectively. If all these qualities are evident but there are signs, no matter how small, of lack of courage, aggression, or confidence, the player is not meant to be a goalkeeper.

Skills

Stopping and clearing. With the advent of high-density foam pads, goalkeepers will redirect 90 percent of all shots coming at them. The old days of "controlling" a ball and then clearing it (i.e., stop and clear) are gone, as keepers try to stay balanced and clear the ball at the same time (one-time clearing).

Aerial balls. Goalkeepers are forced to use their hands standing up as well as lying down. Most balls are immediately redirected away from the play. The keeper may not cover the ball at any time (as goalies are permitted to do in ice hockey).

Tactics

The basic tactic for goalkeepers is to take the shooting angles away from the forward. By coming off the goal line and being directly between the ball and goal, the goalkeeper reduces the shooter's opportunity for scoring, and the goalkeeper's chance for success is greater.

FORMATIONS

Other than the goalkeeper, whose position remains stable, the players can be arranged in any manner. It is now more common to employ a system where two or three defenders or attackers are made midfielders or links who play both offense and defense (Figure 12.14, top high school system, and Figure 12.15, top college or international system). It is thought that the defense is tighter and more secure and that the offense is more varied and unpredictable. Generally speaking, the team needs a sweeper, whose job it is to cover and to chase down through balls and take on breakaway forwards. In modern hockey the sweeper generally plays in front of the defense rather than behind it as in the past. The team needs three backs, whose job is primarily defense; two or three midfielders, who play about 60 percent

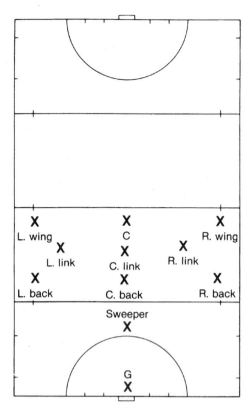

Figure 12.15. The 3-3-3-1 system.

defense and 40 percent offense; and three or four forwards, who are primarily responsible for scoring. However, all players need the ability to play attack and defense within a balanced structure. Most advanced teams have one system of attack and another system for defense.

PROGRAM

General

All players must have equipment they can handle. A stick that is too long or heavy forces the player to compensate, producing bad technique. In the early stages it is not important for beginners to know all parts of every technique. The techniques can be learned and improved by making minor adjustments to many children's games. All kinds of tag, relays, obstacle courses, "keep away," and "steal the bacon" types of games are useful and fun.

Small Games and Competitions

In the beginning, the game can be played one versus one and then gradually moved up to two versus two, three versus three, and so on. Interspersed with even sides should be uneven sides, such as two versus one, three versus two, and the like, to work on specific group play and to give one team a good chance of succeeding. These types of games contain all the skills and tactics of 11 versus 11, but they permit the players many more opportunities with the ball (Figure 12.16). Young players and

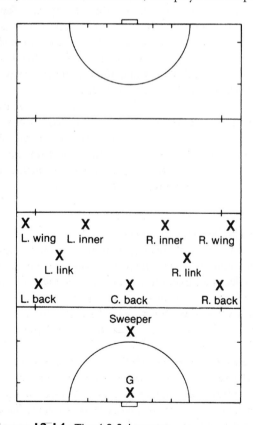

Figure 12.14. The 4-2-3-1 system.

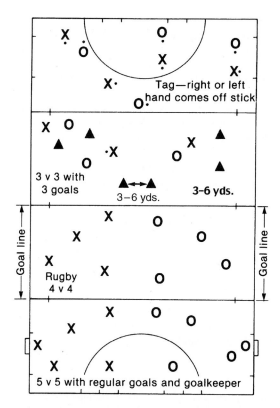

Figure 12.16. Small games and competition.

beginners should concentrate on skills and techniques through technical games and skill training. A basic technical level should be achieved before any tactics are introduced.

Scoring

The scoring objectives in these small games and competitions are many and varied.

1. No goals—"keep away"—object is to see which team can achieve the highest number of consecutive passes.
2. One, two, or multiple goals (cones) placed on the lines or indiscriminately in the playing area where scoring can come from either side, with or without goalkeepers.
3. Regulation goals, with or without goalkeepers, in limited space, depending on number of players.
4. Rugby—successfully having possession of the ball over any part of a line up to 25 yards (22.9 m) long. This game is excellent for spreading play. Players should think of that line as if it were the edge of the circle. If they control the ball over the line, then they can be certain they would have had a shot on goal.
5. Be creative.

FLOOR HOCKEY

Floor hockey is a popular game and is an excellent lead-in to field hockey. It is a combination of ice hockey and basketball, is strenuous, is ideal for boys and girls, and can be taught in a short time. However, the stick usage is very different in floor hockey, as a player can use both sides of the stick as opposed to only using one side in field hockey. Players need to be shown the differences in stick length and curve as well.

For safety, participants should play the puck, not the opponents. The stick must be carried below the waist at all times, and body checking is not allowed.

A basketball court can be used as the playing area, and either a puck or a floor hockey ball can be used. The mid-court line of the basketball court is the centerline. The basketball midcourt jump circle is the center circle, in which play always begins (after a goal or penalty). The goal area should not exceed 58×46 inches (1.45×1.15 m); hockey nets are recommended. A restraining line 5 feet (1.52 m) from the front of the goal and 4 feet (1.22 m) on each side of the goal defines the goal box.

Each team consists of six players. One is the goalkeeper, who can stop shots with the stick, feet, or hands. One is the center, who is the only player allowed to move full court and is the offensive leader. The stick of the center must be striped with black tape. Two players are defensive and cannot go past the centerline, and their main task is to keep the puck out of their half of the floor. Two players are forwards, who work with the center player on offense. These two players cannot go into their defensive half of the court.

The game consists of three periods, each 8 minutes in length, with 5-minute rest periods between them. A flip of a coin determines which team gets the puck to begin the game. Whichever team is behind gets the puck to start the second and third periods. Play begins with the referee's whistle. The center of the team in possession of the puck begins play with a pass. The center must have at least one foot inside the center circle during this pass, and all other players must be outside the 10-foot (3.05 m) restraining circle.

The clock begins when the puck is touched by any player following the center pass and runs continuously, except for a roughing foul, a misconduct call, or the scoring of a goal. Any player who accumulates a total of five fouls or a combination of three roughing fouls and a misconduct must be substituted for immediately. Free substitution is allowed at any time.

TEACHING CONSIDERATIONS

1. Passing, receiving, and dribbling work should dominate practice sessions for beginners working alone and with partners for maximum practice opportunities. Combine dribbling and passing as soon as possible. Be firm about safety rules regarding use of the stick. Do not forget to help fielders receiving a pass from the right to adjust to using only one side of the stick.
2. As soon as some degree of ball control has been achieved, work with two-on-one situations to emphasize opening up space, quickpasses, dodging, tackling, and defensive and offensive strategy. Two-on-one experiences can be designed as a "keep-away"

situation or as two offensive players shooting against a goalie.

3. All essential skills and strategies can be taught in five-on-five games or practice situations of four-on-three or five-on-three. It is critical that hockey be learned as a "space" game, and reduced numbers make basic strategies easier for the beginner to utilize. Games with fewer numbers also give more practice opportunities. Teach how to avoid defense and how to defend with few players.

4. Save specialty situations (e.g., penalty corner) for more advanced players. These tend to slow the game down.

5. Be strict in calling safety violations, but be more flexible for beginners on fouls such as offsides and obstruction.

GLOSSARY

ball control Maneuvering or maintaining possession of the ball.

clear Removing the ball from the scoring area.

cover Defender stationed behind a teammate challenging for ball so that the defender will be in a position should the teammate be beaten.

defender A player whose major contribution is to get the ball from the opponents; prevents opponents from scoring.

dribble Individual technique of moving and maintaining control of the ball with short taps off the end of the stick.

flick Push that is lofted; primarily a shot for getting the ball out of danger or used as a shooting technique.

forwards/strikers Primarily offense; the first line of the attack.

goal (1) The unit of scoring; (2) the cage on the endline into which a team tries to put the ball.

hit Stroke used for moving the ball over great distances and for shooting.

Indian dribble Controlling ball in front of body and propelling it forward in a zigzag pattern; ball is moved alternately with a regular dribble and reverse stick.

links/inside forwards Midfielders; play both offense and defense.

marking (1) Defender playing close enough to an opponent to prevent opponent from receiving a pass; (2) defender close enough to tackle or pressure an opponent immediately upon receiving the ball; (3) one-on-one defense.

pass Intentional moving of the ball from one teammate to another.

pressure Decreasing the time and space that an attacking player has in which to pass or dribble.

push The stroke used for short passes; there is no preliminary action before release, making it the quickest pass.

receiving Absorbing the ball's speed on the end of the stick so that it is immediately under control.

reverse (backhand) stick Playing the ball with the toe of the stick down.

reverse side (1) The left side of the player; (2) the side of the field away from the ball.

score Goal; the final pass.

square Pass that goes parallel to endline to a teammate moving forward and taking it on the run.

sweeper Free defender who covers and roams either in front of or behind defense, picking up all through passes and taking on a forward with ball who gets free.

system Arrangement of players on the field.

tactics Thinking level of play; the outwitting of opponents.

through pass Pass that goes parallel to sideline between opponents.

timing Releasing a pass at the right moment; involves good judgment of the positions of teammates and opponents.

SUGGESTED READINGS

Anders, E., and Myers, S. 2008. *Field hockey: Steps to success.* 2nd ed. Champaign, IL: Human Kinetics.

Davidson, J. and Stein breder, J. 2000. *Hockey for dummies.* 2nd ed. New York, NY: Hungry Minds, Inc.

Mitchell-Taverner, C. 2005. *Field hockey techniques and tactics.* Champaign, IL: *Human Kinetics.*

Rulebook for outdoor and indoor hockey. Current edition. Colorado Springs: United States Field Hockey Association.

RESOURCES

Longstreth Sporting Goods. Major U.S. supplier of current books, videos, and magazines from around the world. Contact: Longstreth Sporting Goods, P.O. Box 475, Parkerford, PA 18457; 800-322-7022.

United States Field Hockey Association. Various coaching publications and up-to-date rule books. Contact: USFHA, One Olympic Plaza, Colorado Springs, CO 80909; 719-866-4567.

Videos

Field hockey: The basic skills. Available from Longstreth Sporting Goods, P.O. Box 475, Old Schnylkill Rd., Parkerford, PA 18457.

Hockey for coaches, 5 videotapes. Available through Reedswain, Inc., 62 Byers Rd., Chester Springs, PA 19425.

See Appendix C for other video sources.

WEB SITES

FIH (Fédération Internationale de Hockey)
www.fihockey.org

IOC (International Olympic Committee)
www.olympic.org

USFHA (United States Field Hockey Association)
www.usfieldhockey.com

www.fieldhockey.com (resources and news) Field hockey information changes on a regular basis, and the reader is encouraged to contact the above suppliers for the latest resource materials.

www.fieldhockey.tv Twenty-four-hour free world-class hockey games available.

13 | Golf

After completing this chapter, the reader should be able to:

- Recognize the values and benefits of participation in golf
- Select proper golf equipment and explain the use for each club
- Practice proper technique in executing the basic golf swing and the several specialized shots
- State the rules of golf and be familiar with the etiquette of the game
- Teach a group of beginning students the fundamentals of golf
- Use properly the many colorful terms associated with golf

Golf is one of the most challenging and fascinating of modern sports. The thrill of striking a ball well over 200 yards (183 m) and the satisfaction of successfully executing the soft touch needed for a 4-foot (1.2-m) putt are of lasting pleasure. Whether one learns to play golf for relaxation and fun or aspires to achieve a high competitive level is the privilege of the individual. Few sports offer playing fields with such great variety and beauty as golf courses.

HISTORY

The game of golf is one of the most ancient of the modern sports. Historians do not agree on its origin, but it appears certain that golf was played in Scotland more than 500 years ago. As early as 1457, the Scottish Parliament ordained that golf should not be played because it was detracting from the practice of archery, which was deemed necessary for defensive purposes. Old paintings and drawings show that similar games were also played about that time in the Netherlands, Belgium, and France. The Dutch term *kolf*, meaning a "club," is considered by some to have given rise to the name of the present-day game. Regardless of how much Scotland invented on its own and how much it borrowed from others, it appears certain that Scotland was the source from which the game as it is known today spread to all parts of the world. St. Andrews in Fife, Scotland, is believed to be the oldest existing golf course.

Courses, or links, of the early days differed greatly from those of today. Golf was then distinctly a seaside game, played over stretches of land that linked the seashore with tillable lands farther inland. It was this condition that led to calling the scene of play "links," which in fact means a seaside golf course.

The location of holes followed no definite plan. The landscape was partially covered by bushes, trees, and the like. Open areas were chosen as finishing points or putting greens. No official number of holes was adopted as standard for a round of play until 1858, when 18 holes were designated as a round.

Golf clubs were organized in the United States in the closing years of the eighteenth century, but the game as we know it today had its start in the United States a little over 95 years ago. A few clubs were started in the eastern United States, and the rapid increase in popularity since then has greatly increased the number of private and municipal courses. Today class instruction in golf is found in most high schools and colleges. Colleges and universities often own and operate golf courses; high schools use private and municipal courses. In recent years, television coverage of major golf events has done much to stimulate interest in the game. In fact, in many urban areas of the country, the number of golf courses is insufficient to accommodate the demand. In 1980, the National Golf Foundation estimated that nearly 29 million Americans participate in golf, playing nearly 500 million rounds per year.

There are nearly 16,000 golf courses and over 17,000 golf driving ranges in the United States. Many people become enthusiasts and start playing golf as a result of experience on a driving range.

Golf today is no longer a game only for those with a high income. It is played by individuals from a variety of economic and ethnic backgrounds and includes the young and the old, duffers as well as masters, men and women.

Truly, golf is a sport that offers a life-long source of pleasure. One or two well-timed and well-directed shots often serve as the catalyst that causes the player to return for another round.

The social aspects of golf include the following: it encourages excellent compatibility of mixed groups; it clears and freshens the mind by diversion of interest; it brings urban dwellers into sunshine and nature; it provides restful activity for the working individual; the golfer is pitted against self as well as against opponents; each hole is a separate contest and challenge; and the game is played by people of all ages, sizes, and builds. As recreation, golf is one of the most desirable of all sports.

GENERAL DESCRIPTION

Eighteen holes make up the typical golf course. The first, ninth, tenth, and eighteenth holes are generally near the clubhouse. Any multiple of nine holes can be played, and each hole varies in length and general layout. Hazards are generally placed to penalize a poor shot. The object is to score as few strokes as possible for each hole. Play starts at the tee between two markers, continues along the fairway, which is generally bounded by rough, and finishes at the green, which is often surrounded by bunkers. The ball is rolled into the hole marked by the pin, or flagstick.

EQUIPMENT

The United States has contributed in large share to improvements in golf equipment—for example, the type of ball in use today; the steel-, graphite-, and titanium-shafted clubs; the peg tee; and utility clubs such as the sand wedge.

Clothing

Dress should be comfortable and in accord with local custom on the course played. Many courses have clothing restrictions (e.g., no T-shirts or jeans allowed).

Spiked golf shoes are an important part of a player's golfing equipment. However, if they are not available, a pair of tennis shoes will suffice. Recently, soft spikes have become mandatory at many courses because they cause less damage to the greens than metal spikes.

Clubs

It is not necessary to have the most expensive set of golf clubs on the market to enjoy playing golf and to play it satisfactorily. On the other hand, one should not handicap one's game by playing with inferior equipment. Purchasing clubs that are suitable to your characteristics and that are made by a dependable manufacturer is a sound policy for assurance of satisfaction and long wear.

Golf clubs come in a variety of lengths, weights, shaft flexibility, and other features (Figure 13.1). Club length is usually determined by a person's height, and club weight is often selected on personal preference in relation to feel. Usually, the faster the swing, the less whip you should have in your club shafts. Ask your golf teacher or club professional for advice on the type of clubs to purchase.

Starter set

The beginning golfer need not invest in an expensive, complete set of clubs. Options include purchasing a set of used clubs or a starter set. The advantages of purchasing a set of used clubs rather than a starter set are usually in the quality and number of clubs obtained for a comparable cost. In either case, the minimum clubs to start with include a 3 wood; a putter; and the 3, 5, 7, and 9 irons.

Woods

The three common woods are the driver, or No. 1 wood; the No. 3 wood; and the No. 5 wood (Figure 13.2). More recently, however, it is not unusual to see 7 and 9 woods in golfers' bags. They have longer shafts and weigh more than the iron clubs and, consequently, can give more distance than an iron club having a similar loft, or tilt, to the club face. Seldom are woods constructed of wood now; metal heads are the norm today. However, these clubs are still referred to as "woods."

It is difficult to state precisely the distance any individual can hit the golf ball, because there are so many variables (e.g., experience, gender, age). However, below are estimates of the distances one might expect.

Driver. This club is usually used to hit off the tee when long distances are required. Males typically drive the ball 180 to 260 yards (165 to 238 m); females typically drive the ball 150 to 220 yards (137 to 201 m).

No. 3 wood. This club is usually used off the fairway or when accuracy off the tee is more important than distance. Males typically hit the ball 165 to 240 yards (151 to 219 m); females typically hit the ball 140 to 210 yards (128 to 192 m).

No. 5 wood. This club is usually used off the fairway or on some par-3 holes. Males typically hit the ball 150 to 215 yards (137 to 197 m). Females typically hit the ball 130 to 190 yards (119 to 174 m).

Nos. 7 and 9 woods. These are utility woods used to get the ball out of the rough or bad lies. Many golfers have replaced their long irons (i.e., 2-3-4) with these more lofted woods.

Irons

Irons are used from the fairway or from the tee on short holes. Cast iron or perimeter weighted irons are more forgiving and better for beginning golfers. Forged irons or blades are recommended for experienced golfers who want improved control of ball flight. The player selects the proper iron according to the distance required (Figure 13.3). For various irons and distances achieved with each, see Figures 13.3 and 13.4.

Putter. This club is used for putting on the green or from just off the green. Putters are manufactured in a great variety of styles and are chosen on the basis of individual preference.

Pitching, sand, gap, or lob wedge. These clubs are used for short approaches from the rough and fairways, less than 125 yards (114 m), and as a trouble club from tall rough or sand traps. They are very versatile when properly used.

Golf Balls

Golf balls are made by many manufacturers. Their construction varies from a solid, one- or multipiece ball to a ball developed from a small, hard core wound with rubber bands and sealed with a durable cover.

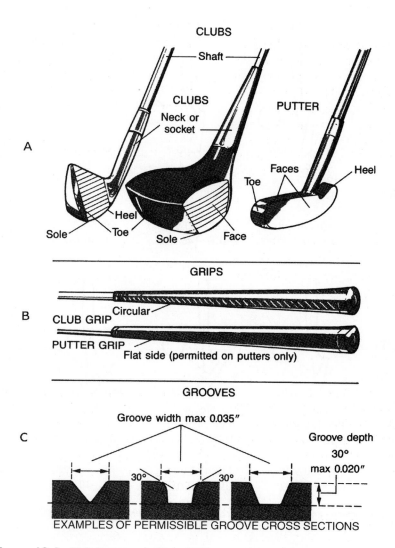

Figure 13.1. Club features. A, Clubs. B, Grips. C, Grooves.

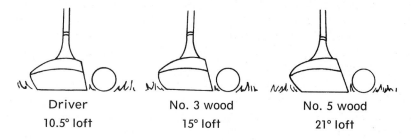

Driver
10.5° loft

No. 3 wood
15° loft

No. 5 wood
21° loft

Figure 13.2. The woods.

Ball preference is left up to individual feel and style of play. One should have several balls in the golf bag when going out to play.

Plastic balls may be used for the gymnasium, small field, or backyard practice.

THE COURSE

A golf course is actually built and constructed to best conform to the contours of the land. A complete golf course consists of 18 holes, which requires not less than 100 acres. In many communities, 9-hole or 18-hole courses are constructed on less acreage with shorter holes that require less time to play. Par-3 courses, on which 18 holes can be played in 3 hours or less, are becoming increasingly popular.

A well-constructed golf course is architecturally planned so that each hole differs from the rest, yet certain elements are common to all.

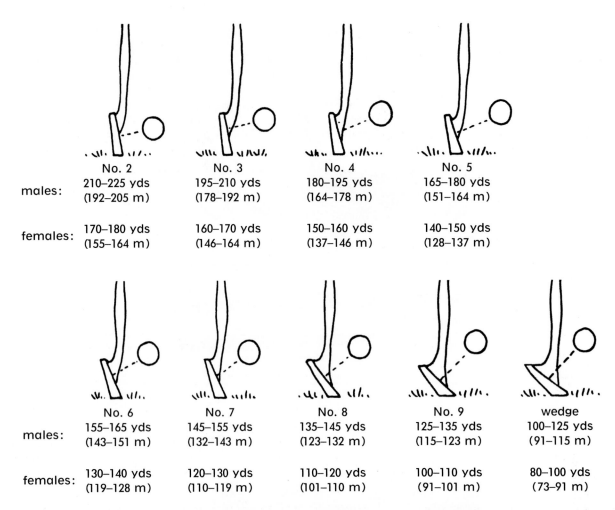

Figure 13.3. Various irons showing angle of pitch of each club and approximate distance obtained by experienced golfers.

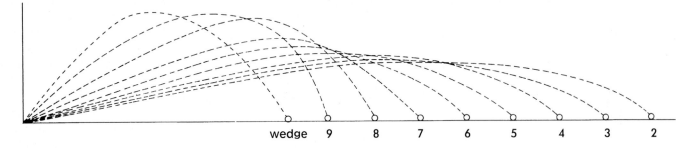

Figure 13.4. Trajectory or flight of ball using the same swing with each iron (male golfer).

Each hole is composed of a tee and tee markers, fairway, rough, trees, boundary, sand bunkers and sometimes water hazards, and a green, cup, and flag. The shape and size of the greens, as well as the placing of bunkers and water hazards, are left to the creativity of the golf course architect (Figure 13.5).

Par is determined by the distance of the hole from the middle of the tee down the middle of the fairway to the middle of the green. Holes up to 250 yards (229 m) are usually designated as par 3, holes from 251 to 470 yards (230 to 430 m) as par 4, and holes from 471 to 600 yards (431 to 549 m) as par 5. Par 3 is a score usually obtained by reaching the green in one shot and rolling the ball into the cup with two putts. On a par 4, the golfer should reach the green in two; and on a par 5, reach it in three. A championship course usually has a par of 72, or an average of four strokes per hole.

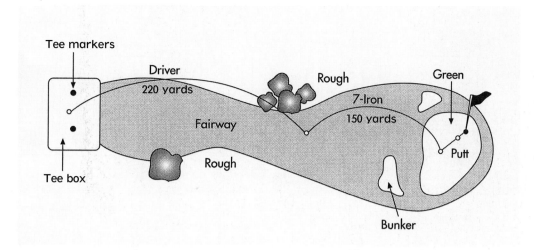

Figure 13.5. Example of 375-yard, par-4 hole.

A typical course has four par-3 holes, 10 par-4 holes, and four par-5 holes.

Par for women differs somewhat from that for men, depending on the difficulty of each hole as to distance, hazards, and the like.

Refer to the sample scorecard (Figure 13.6) with regard to par with men and women, distances of each hole, and hole handicap (a ranking of the holes by difficulty).

FACILITIES FOR PRACTICE

1. Outdoor driving range and putting green.
2. Any large room, preferably a gymnasium.
3. Two or three large pieces of canvas hung in front of a wall with fish netting along the sides to form a cage-type setup.
4. Mats from which to hit.
5. Clubs and balls (plastic balls may be used if nets are not available).
6. A large rug with short nap for putting.
7. Putting cups for individual putting (water glasses can be used).

FUNDAMENTAL SKILLS AND TECHNIQUES

Because certain clubs and types of shots fall into natural groupings, the following material has been arranged to take advantage of these categories. For the left-handed player, it will be necessary to reverse the techniques presented here because consideration has been given only to the right-handed player.

The Golf Grip

1. Ten-finger grip; sometimes used by players with small, weak hands or extremely short fingers (Figure 13.7).
2. Interlocking grip; preferred by some players who like a solid feel (Figure 13.8).
3. Overlapping, or Vardon, grip (Figure 13.9); the most popular grip, used by most players (described next).

To form the overlapping grip, the player first opens the left hand, and with the thumb and fingers together, places the club diagonally across the hand from the middle joint of the index finger across the heel of the hand. The hand closes over the club so that it is held by the fingers. The V formed by the thumb and index finger should point approximately to the right shoulder. When the club is held in the position of address, the player should see the first three knuckles of the fingers. Also, the thumb should be on top of the club, one quarter turn over the club with the pad of the thumb on the grip of the club. The correct rotation of the left hand allows cocking of the wrist at the peak of the backswing. It also allows the left arm to deal a backhand blow to the ball. At this point, the player should try swinging the club head with only the left arm, watching that the arm remains comfortably straight and that the wrist cocks at the top of the backswing.

To place the right hand in position, the player first places the right hand below the left hand and contacts the grip with the middle joint of the right index finger and then slides the joint up and down the club grip so that the left thumb will fit snugly into the palm of the right hand when it is closed. Next, the player closes the left hand, placing the right thumb to the left of the club and diagonally across the shaft. This will help the index finger securely grip the club, which is important because the feel of the club head is controlled mainly by the fingers to ensure optimal power and control. When the right hand is closed, the middle joint of the right index finger (the first part of the right hand placed on the club) must be on the right side of the grip, never directly under it. Finally, the little finger of the right hand should be wrapped around the crevice formed by the first two fingers of the left hand to form the overlapping grip.

It should be emphasized that, regardless of the grip used, the back of the left hand and the palm of the right should face squarely toward the target. Also, maintaining light grip

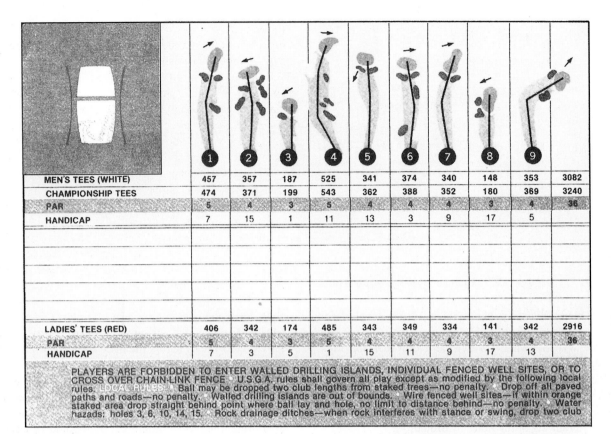

	1	2	3	4	5	6	7	8	9	
MEN'S TEES (WHITE)	457	357	187	525	341	374	340	148	353	3082
CHAMPIONSHIP TEES	474	371	199	543	362	388	352	180	369	3240
PAR	5	4	3	5	4	4	4	3	4	36
HANDICAP	7	15	1	11	13	3	9	17	5	
LADIES' TEES (RED)	406	342	174	485	343	349	334	141	342	2916
PAR	5	4	3	5	4	4	4	3	4	36
HANDICAP	7	3	5	1	15	11	9	17	13	

PLAYERS ARE FORBIDDEN TO ENTER WALLED DRILLING ISLANDS, INDIVIDUAL FENCED WELL SITES, OR TO CROSS OVER CHAIN-LINK FENCE   U.S.G.A. rules shall govern all play except as modified by the following local rules. LOCAL RULES   Ball may be dropped two club lengths from staked trees—no penalty.   Drop off all paved paths and roads—no penalty.   Walled drilling islands are out of bounds.   Wire fenced well sites—if within orange staked area drop straight behind point where ball lay and hole, no limit to distance behind—no penalty.   Water hazards: holes 3, 6, 10, 14, 15.   Rock drainage ditches—when rock interferes with stance or swing, drop two club

	10	11	12	13	14	15	16	17	18	IN	TOTAL	HDCP	NET
	404	348	487	166	366	363	375	178	439	3116	6198		
	411	369	506	184	380	381	394	203	466	3294	6534		
	4	4	5	3	4	4	4	3	5	36	72		
	2	10	14	16	6	8	4	12	18				
	383	340	418	149	351	347	358	155	441	2942	5858		
	4	4	5	3	4	4	4	3	5	36	72		
	4	14	2	18	10	12	8	16	6				

COURSE RATING
CHAMPIONSHIP TEES   70.1
MENS TEES   63.0

DATE _____

PLAYER _____

ATTEST _____

LADIES COURSE RATING 72.4

lengths—no penalty.   Out of bounds defined by white stakes or green stakes—white tops: No. 4 only—out of bounds right side as staked.   Driving range Out of Bounds as staked. COURSE RULES   Players will at all times observe the rules of Golf etiquette.   Practicing prohibited anywhere on course.   Replace turf and fix ball marks on greens.   Keep electric carts off tees and 30 ft. from greens.   Keep electric carts on paths and designated areas. Keep pull carts off tees, areas between traps and greens, and 10 ft. from greens. Lateral water hazard: Hole No. 4.

Figure 13.6. Typical scorecard.

pressure is important to enhance power and clubface rotation needed in the golf swing.

Stance

For various foot positions, see Figure 13.10.

Square stance. The feet, knees, hips, and shoulders are parallel to the line of flight. This stance is used for almost all long shots of both woods and irons because it allows free movement of either side of the body. The knees are slightly bent, the toes turned slightly outward, and the weight evenly distributed. The arms hang downward from the shoulders and away from the body but not forward. The body curves naturally, but not sharply, forward. The eyes are on the ball.

Open stance. The left foot is withdrawn slightly from the line of flight, but the knees, hips, and shoulders remain square. This stance is used rarely for wood shots but more often for the shorter iron shots. It tends to restrict the turning and pivoting of the left side, but allows a better follow-through. This stance encourages the fade, or slice, but can result in increased distance.

Closed stance. The right foot is withdrawn slightly from the line of flight, but the knees, hips, and shoulders remain square. This stance is often used for wood shots and encourages a draw, or hook.

Swing

For progressive steps in the golf swing see Figure 13.11.

Tempo

Maintaining an even tempo is one of the most important aspects of developing a proper golf swing. A player who is able to maintain good rhythm and smoothness throughout the swing will be able to develop an efficient and consistent golf swing. Most beginners attempt to hit the ball too hard, which results in an improper tempo or an uneven rhythm and causes many faults. In fact, as a variable, strength is much less important than proper tempo and clubhead speed in the successful

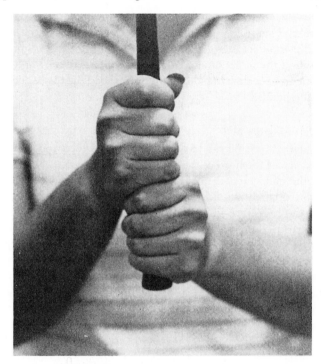

Figure 13.7. Ten-finger grip.

A

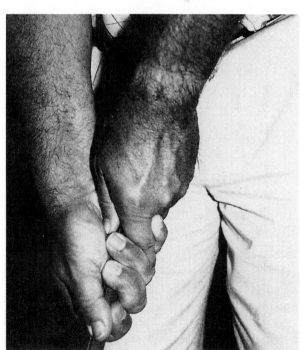

B

Figure 13.8. A, Interlocking grip (back view). B, Interlocking grip (front view).

general, the golf swing is developed by gradually increasing the speed. The golfer should begin slowly, then accelerate on the downswing, keeping a continuous rhythm throughout. It takes approximately the same time to take the club from the address to the top of the backswing as it does to complete the down-swing and the follow-through.

Selecting the target

The first step the golfer should take in preparing to hit the ball is to select a target. Often the ball will not end up pre-cisely at the target or along the intended target line, but it is difficult to realize the ideal shot unless the target is selected beforehand.

Addressing the ball

When addressing the ball, the player takes the proper grip and places the head of the club on the ground, with the sole of the club parallel to the turf. The feet should be placed approximately shoulder width apart or in a relative position for the club used—for example, wider for the longer clubs. The arms should fall naturally from the shoulders and not so far away from the body that the individual is stretching. For the woods, the ball is generally placed in line with the inside portion of the left heel. As the length of the club and the required distance decrease, the ball is addressed farther to the right of the left foot but seldom farther back than in the center of the stance.

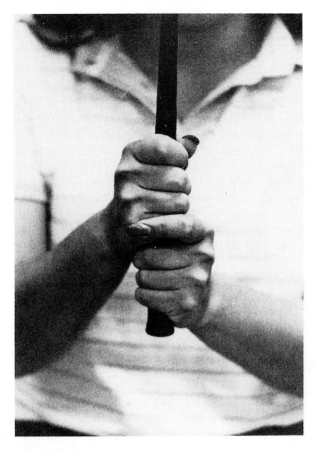

Figure 13.9. Overlapping grip.

Waggle

The waggle is a preliminary movement that takes a variety of forms, depending on individual preference. It is designed to help the golfer relax, adjust the grip, check alignment, and get ready to begin the swing. Usually, it involves slight body movement and the lifting of the club head several inches to check balance and position. When the golfer feels ready, there is a slight hesitation before the beginning of the full swing. This preliminary move tends to ease tension in prepa-ration for the shot.

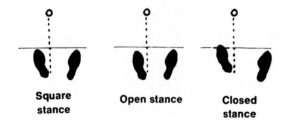

Square stance   Open stance   Closed stance

Figure 13.10. Various foot positions.

Backswing

Before beginning the swing, the golfer must fix his or her eye on the ball. The swing is started with a rotation of the shoulder and hips, which starts the club head moving to the back. The left arm should be relatively straight and the club head low to the ground. The wrists begin to cock approxi-mately halfway back on the swing. The right elbow points down toward the ground, and the weight is shifted from a balanced position to the right foot. The left knee is turned inward, and the left foot rolls to the right, keeping the left heel low to the ground. At the top of the backswing, the left shoulder is pointing at the ball and the club is approaching being parallel to the ground depending on the flexibility of the player.

golf swing. Beginning golfers should strive to achieve a con-sistent tempo or rhythm in all shots attempted. Often a simple key such as saying "Back," "Wait," and "Through" or "one, two, three" on the backswing and "One, two, three" on the down-swing and follow-through will help to develop the rhythm nec-essary for success. Once the idea of tempo is understood and accomplished, the beginner will have the necessary basis for the development of a sound golf swing. Without proper rhythm, it is difficult to hit the ball correctly and much power is wasted. In

Figure 13.11. Progressive steps of swing.

E

F

G

H

Figure 13.11. (continued)

Figure 13.11. (continued)

Downswing

To make a smooth change of direction, the downswing is started with the left leg. The left foot comes down flat to the ground, and the knees and hips turn toward the target. The knees are bent slightly to allow freedom of movement as the weight is shifted from the right side to the left. There should be a feeling of turning from the left side. The wrists should remain cocked until the arms are parallel with the ground. The weight is shifted to the left side, and the left side provides a strong hitting position by supporting the majority of the weight. At impact, there should be a straight line from the ball or club head through the hands to the left shoulder. The head must remain steady and the eyes remain focused on the ball after contact is made.

Follow-through

After impact, the right arm becomes just as straight as the left arm was on the backswing. The head rises naturally, but does not move forward as the right shoulder comes under. Both arms should be stretched out as far as possible toward the target. The wrists will begin to turn over after the arms have reached their limit, finishing with the hands high above the head.

Swing plane

When the golfer takes the club back from the ball, the club should come slightly inside the line of flight, maintaining a plane that will run back approximately between the shoulders and neck. One of the keys to a successful golf swing is to maintain this same plane on the downswing. To accomplish this, the golfer must maintain the proper sequence of body movements. The swing is started with the shoulders and arms, then the hips and legs turning about 45 degrees to the right. The wrists will naturally cock. The downswing starts with turning the hips and legs, then the shoulders and arms back to the left. The wrists will naturally uncock so that they are straight at the point of contact. This sequence will enable the golfer to swing from slightly inside the line of flight out through the ball, maintaining proper control of the shot. Any deviations from this sequence will allow the club head to break the plane and will cause inconsistency or initiate numerous faults or problems with the flight of the ball. This sequence and having the clubhead square to the intended line of flight at impact are the two most important factors in a successful golf swing.

Common errors

The following are errors often made by beginners when learning the golf swing:

1. Swaying or moving the head to the right instead of turning so that weight is on the right leg during the backswing
2. Backswing that is too fast, eliminating good tempo and throwing the golfer off balance
3. Not extending the left arm during the backswing
4. Raising the right shoulder during the backswing
5. Backswing too flat, too horizontal, or too inside the swing plane
6. Raising the head from its original position
7. Pausing too long or not long enough at the top of the swing
8. Not initiating the downswing with the lower body first
9. Uncocking the wrists too soon, which throws off the proper sequence and usually casts the club outside the correct plane
10. Hitting too hard with the right hand, which drops the right shoulder, causing contact behind the ball
11. Failing to complete the follow-through with the hands held high and weight turned onto the left leg
12. Hitting at the ball rather than swinging the club at the target.
13. Making an arms-only swing rather than coordinating arms, shoulders, torso, and legs

Short Swing

One of the consistent factors in golf is that it is not necessary to learn a different swing for each club. The plane varies slightly with the length of the club; however, there is no difference in what has to be learned to attempt the swing. When a shot requires less distance than produced by the shortest club in the bag, a shorter swing must be executed. The short swing is a breakdown of the full swing, and the distance of the shot is commensurate with the length of the backswing. If a half swing is required for a particular shot, then the golfer uses less body turn and less wrist action than in the full swing, where the wrist break is not completed until the club is brought to the top of the swing. The shorter the swing, the less wrist action and body movement occur. The follow-through is the same as in the backswing. A one-quarter backswing requires a one-quarter follow-through, a one-half backswing requires a one-half follow-through, and so on. The rest of the fundamentals are exactly the same as described for the full swing. The golfer should practice short swings of various lengths to determine how far the ball will travel and to obtain the correct feel for the distance required. Regardless of the distance of the shot, the club head must be accelerated through the ball.

Pitch Shot

The pitch shot (Figure 13.12) is usually executed with a pitching wedge, sand wedge, or lob wedge. This shot will fly high and is used to hit the ball over a bunker or hazard of some type and will stop on the green with very little roll. The stance should be square or slightly open, with the length of the backswing determined by the distance needed as described for the short swing. Some golfers prefer to choke down on the club for greater control, particularly for shorter shots. Inasmuch as the swing is shorter, body movement is kept to a minimum; there is little wrist cock, and the left arm is straight, but relaxed, throughout the swing. It is important that the follow-through be carried the same distance as the backswing, with care taken not to make any special effort to meet or hit the ball hard.

Tempo is just as important in the short swing or pitch shot as it is in the full swing. Regardless of the distance of the shot, it is important that one hit down through the ball and not try to scoop the ball into the air. The club is designed to give the proper lift to the ball.

The Chip Shot

The chip shot (Figure 13.13) is usually executed with a 7, 8, or 9 iron and is effective when the golfer has an open shot to the pin and does not have to hit over any type of hazard.

The stance is similar to that for the pitch shot, with slightly more weight forward at the address. The less-lofted clubface will allow the ball to travel low and run much farther than the pitch shot. Again, the distance of the shot is determined by the length of the backswing, and the follow-through should be commensurate with the backswing. One should practice taking the club back various distances to determine the proper length of the backswing for the distance required. Club selection for this shot is usually determined by selecting the club that will allow the ball to hit as close to the edge of the green as possible and roll the remainder of the way to the cup. A short chip can be executed in a manner similar to a putting stroke. Again, the key to the chip shot is proper tempo and rhythm, with care not to chop at the ball with an uneven tempo. A general rule for chipping is to carry the ball about one-third the distance to the pin and roll it the remaining two-thirds of the distance to the pin.

Figure 13.12. Pitch shot.

Figure 13.13. Chip shot.

Putting

Putting is individual in nature, although there are certain aspects of the stroke that must be maintained, regardless of the golfer's style or the type of putter used. For examples of the many styles and designs in which putters are manu-

factured, see Figure 13.14. The stance may be wide, narrow, open, or closed, depending on individual preference. However, there must be no body or head movement, and the putter blade should be taken straight back in line with the direction required for a straight-through motion toward the

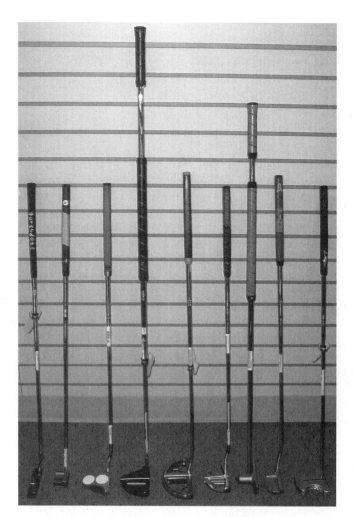

Figure 13.14. Putters.

hole. Better putters usually have their heads and eyes directly above the ball, neither behind nor ahead of the intended putting line. Figures 13.15 and 13.16 display two types of putting stances that can be used. The following description of putting can be used as a guide; however, technique can be varied according to personal preference. The distance of the putt is determined by the length of the backswing. A shorter putt requires a shorter backswing and a longer putt a longer backswing, but the tempo must be consistent throughout.

Stance

1. The stance is fairly upright, with the neck and shoulders bent slightly.
2. The feet are 8 to 12 inches (20 to 30 cm) apart.
3. The stance is square.
4. The weight is balanced.
5. The left arm is kept close to the torso.
6. The right forearm is close to the right thigh.
7. The ball is at the left instep.
8. The head and eyes are directly over the ball.

Figure 13.15. Neutral putting stance.

Figure 13.16. Crouched putting stance.

9. The ball is positioned in the middle of the face of the putter.

Grip
1. The back of the left hand and the palm of the right hand are square to the line.
2. Both thumbs are directly on top of the grip.

Swing
See "Checkpoints for the Golf Swing" box.
1. The swing is short and low to the ground.
2. It is in line with the intended roll of the ball.
3. It is completely relaxed, slow, and steady.
4. There are no body or head movements.
5. The club head follows through.
6. The ball should be struck firmly enough to reach the hole.

Reading the green
1. The player sights the hole from behind the ball to determine the angle of roll, more commonly called the break.
2. The player checks the grass to determine whether the putt will be with or against the grain. A lighter color indicates the intended path is with the grain, which allows the ball to roll faster.

Sand Bunkers
Properly executing the bunker shot can save the golfer many strokes. To control this shot, the player must hit the sand about 2 inches behind the ball and let the sand throw the ball out of the trap. The distance the ball travels is relative to the distance hit behind the ball. The object is not to bury the club but to continue to swing smoothly through the sand under the ball, with a strong follow-through and finish.

General principles
1. Because sand traps vary from deep, soft sand to shallow, hard clay and sand, each shot is different.
2. The trap is entered from the lowest point so as not to destroy the bank or unduly disturb the surface.
3. The player positions his or her feet and then moves them back and forth in order to sink into the sand and have a firm stance.
4. In addressing the ball, a penalty is incurred if the club head touches the sand before the ball is hit.
5. On leaving the trap, all irregularities made in the sand should be covered by smoothing them out with the club head or rake.

CHECKPOINTS FOR THE GOLF SWING

1. The overlapping grip
   a. Left hand is gripped with fingers to form V over right shoulder
   b. Right hand is not too far under shaft; the V formed should point over right shoulder
   c. The thumbs are placed on the side of the shaft
   d. The little finger of the right hand overlaps the first finger of the left hand
2. The stance
   a. Square: Both feet are equidistant from the line of flight
   b. Open: The left foot is a little farther from the line of flight than the right foot
   c. Closed: The right foot is farther away from the line of flight than the left foot
3. The swing
   a. Pick target
   b. Backswing
      i. Fix the eye on the ball; determine the proper position of the head
      ii. Start back with rotation of shoulder and hips
      iii. Keep the left arm straight, but relaxed
      iv. Keep the club head low to the ground
      v. Begin to cock the wrists approximately halfway back on the swing
      vi. Keep the right elbow pointed toward the ground
      vii. Turn and shift weight from left foot to right foot
      viii. At top of backswing, the left shoulder will be pointing at the ball and the club will be parallel to the ground, pointing toward the target

   c. Downswing
      i. Start with the left leg
      ii. Left foot comes down flat to the ground
      iii. Turn and shift weight from right foot to left foot
      iv. Bend the knees to allow freedom of movement
      v. There is a feeling of pulling from the left side
      vi. Uncock the wrists when the hands are parallel with the ground
      vii. At the moment of impact, the ball, the hands, and the left shoulder are almost in a straight line
      viii. The left leg straightens and becomes firm
   d. Follow-through
      i. The right arm is just as straight as the left was on the backswing
      ii. The head rises naturally with the pulling of the right shoulder
      iii. The grip must be firm but not tight throughout the swing
      iv. Arms are stretched out as far as possible
      v. The wrists will begin to turn over after the arms have reached the limit
      vi. Finish with the hands high
4. Suggestions for putting
   a. Keep the putter blade flat on the ground
   b. Keep toes parallel with the line of flight
   c. Putt the ball off the left foot
   d. Keep the blade low to the ground
   e. Use no body or head action at any time
   f. Place head and eyes directly over the ball

The explosion shot

See Figure 13.17.

1. The grip, stance, and swing are about the same as for the short, high approach.
2. The stance is open, with the feet fairly close together and well-set in the sand.
3. The grip must be firm but not tense.
4. The swing must be fairly long, upright, and U-shaped.
5. The club head must not stop in the sand because sand pushed ahead of the club will cause the ball to rise. The follow-through should be definite and powerful.
6. The amount of sand taken, or the distance back of the ball that the club head enters the sand, determines the distance the ball will travel. Thus the closer one is to the green, the more sand one must take.

Sidehill Lies

When playing from sidehill lies, the golfer must adjust the stance and ball replacement to conform to the contour of the ground. The golfer should avoid trying to overswing and should first take one or two practice swings to become familiar with the changes in swing feel.

General principles

1. Do not overswing.
2. Play for accuracy.
3. Allow the club head to follow the contour of the ground.

Uphill

1. There is a tendency to pull or hook, so aim to the right.
2. Stand close to the ball with the feet almost together.
3. Put more weight on the right foot.
4. Play the ball forward of the normal position in stance.

Downhill

1. There is a tendency to slice, so aim to the left.
2. On a steep slope, avoid wood clubs, because it is difficult to achieve a rise.
3. Play the ball back of the normal position in stance.
4. Level the shoulders parallel with the downslope to prevent hitting behind the ball.

Ball below feet

1. There is a strong tendency to slice, so play to the left.
2. The weight is on the toes, so open the stance somewhat.
3. Avoid topping by moving the grip closer to the top end of the club and concentrating on staying down until after the ball is contacted.
4. Do not pivot as much as on level ground; more of a U-shaped swing is natural.

Ball above feet

1. The tendency is to pull or hook, so play to the right.
2. Hold the club short.
3. Swing slowly; a fast swing will throw you back, causing you to top the ball.

Figure 13.17. The explosion shot.

4. There is a tendency to toe the ball with the club, so play it close.

Playing from the Rough

When playing from the rough, set yourself firmly with a slightly open stance. The club should be brought back in a more upright motion. Hit down through the ball and finish the swing strongly. Be sure to select the club with enough loft to get the ball out of the rough. This is the primary objective.

General principles

1. Do not press in trying for too much distance.
2. Use the U-shaped swing.
3. Play the shot safely rather than gamble on a "lucky one."

4. Open the face of the club slightly to cut the grass better and to give a quicker rise in long grass.

5. Each rough position will differ from the last, so judge each one individually.

RULES

The United States Golf Association (USGA), in association with the R&A in St. Andrews, Scotland, writes and interprets the rules of golf. The complete list of rules and decisions can be found at www.usga.org with the next revision occurring January 1, 2012. Following are some of the most referenced rules of golf:

1. The ball must be played as it lies except as outlined by the rules. Local rules may permit preferred lies, or "winter rules," in which case the ball may be placed within the distance defined by the local rule and not moved nearer the hole.

2. The ball must be fairly struck with the head of the club.

3. The player whose ball is farthest from the hole plays first.

4. If a ball goes out-of-bounds, the player must play the next stroke at the spot from which the ball was last struck. If the stroke was played from the tee, the ball may be teed; in all other cases it must be dropped. The penalty is loss of stroke and distance. (Add 2 strokes to score for the hole.) If any part of the ball lies in-bounds, the ball remains in play.

   Note: If a ball is believed to be out-of-bounds, a provisional ball may be played before the golfer leaves the point from which the first ball was played.

5. In match play, if a player's ball knocks the opponent's ball into the hole, the opponent shall be considered to have holed out on the last shot. A ball that has been moved by an opponent's ball may be left at that point or replaced in its original spot. In stroke play, the ball moved must be replaced as near as possible to its original spot. The golfer playing the putt has the right to ask the opponent to mark the ball.

6. The player has the option of having the flagstick attended or removed. If the putted ball strikes an attended flagstick or a person attending the flagstick in stroke play, there is a 2-stroke penalty. In match play, if the flagstick is held by an opponent or an opponent's caddie, the opponent loses the hole. If it is held by the player's caddie, the player loses the hole.

7. Irregularities of surface that might in any way affect the player's stroke may not be removed or pressed down by the player, any partner, or caddies, except when putting. Loose impediments may be removed from the line of a putt, and ball marks on a green may be repaired before putting.

8. A player may not move, bend, or break anything fixed or growing before striking at a ball in play. This applies to holding branches out of the way and to trampling weeds to improve the lie of the ball.

9. A ball lying on or touching an obstruction, such as clothing, lumber, vehicles, ground under repair, and the like, may be lifted and dropped away from such an object without penalty but may not be moved closer to the hole. The ball is dropped by holding it in front of the body and with the arm parallel to the ground, and must land within one club length, no nearer to the hole.

10. If a player's stroke is interfered with by any object such as just mentioned, relief is taken. The player finds the nearest point where a clear swing can be taken. Then the player drops the ball within one club length of this point, no closer to the hole, without penalty.

11. When a ball lies in a hazard, nothing shall be done that can in any way improve its lie; the club may not touch the ground in addressing the ball or during the backswing; nor may anything be touched or moved by the player before the ball is struck, or there is a 1-stroke penalty.

12. If a ball lies or is lost in a recognized water hazard (whether the ball lies in water or not, or in casual water in a hazard), the player may drop a ball, under penalty of 1 stroke, either behind the hazard, keeping the spot at which the ball crossed the margin of the hazard between himself or herself and the hole, or in the hazard, keeping the spot at which the ball entered the water between himself or herself and the hole. If the ball was played from the teeing ground, a ball may be teed under the penalty of 1 stroke, as near as possible to the spot from which the original ball was played. If a ball lies or is lost in casual water (unintentional hazard), the player may drop a ball without penalty on dry ground as near as possible to the spot where the ball lies but not nearer to the hole.

13. A golfer may have no more than 14 clubs when playing and must adhere to club shaft length and club head size limits.

14. A ball is considered lost if not found within 5 minutes.

ETIQUETTE

Students should study golf etiquette carefully and govern their conduct accordingly. Golf developed as a mannerly game, and it still remains so. One should play the game by the rules without exception.

1. There may be no more than four persons in one party, and each person must have a set of clubs.

2. No one should move or talk or stand close to or directly behind the ball or the hole when a player is making a stroke. This includes ensuring that electronic devices are turned off.

3. On the putting green, the player whose ball lies nearest the hole should hold the pin while other players putt.

4. Extreme care must be taken not to step on another golfer's intended putting line and not to step too close to the hole (to avoid damaging it).

5. No player should play until golfers playing ahead are out of range.
6. Players looking for a lost ball should allow other players coming up to pass them. They should signal to the players following them to pass, and having given such a signal, should not continue their play until these players have passed ahead and are out of range.
7. A player should see that any turf cut or displaced (a divot) by him or her is at once replaced and *pressed down.*
8. No practice shots should be attempted on any part of the course when other golfers are following.
9. A good pace should be kept and players should stay within one-half of a hole of the group in front of them.
10. Slow players should allow a faster group to play through.
11. Local course rules should be observed.
12. All shots should be played according to the rules of the game.
13. The player farthest away from the hole plays or putts first.
14. On the putting green, players should repair damage to the green made by the impact of the ball with any player's approach shot.
15. A player should avoid walking ahead of partners or opponents.
16. The tee shot must be played from between or slightly behind the markers.
17. If any person on the course is in danger of being hit by your shot, "Fore" should be called as a warning.
18. Carts and golf bags should always be kept off the green and placed between the green and the next hole.
19. Footprints in a sand trap should be smoothed out after a shot.
20. When holding the flag on the green, a player should stand so that a shadow does not fall across the cup.
21. When all players have holed out, the party should properly replace the flagstick and leave the putting green immediately for oncoming players.
22. When one member of a twosome, threesome, or foursome has lost a ball, all members of the group should help look for it.
23. Above all, players should be courteous.

Golf teaches the highest principles of etiquette and consideration for others. The game is no longer enjoyable when rules are broken at random. Golf etiquette is easily understood and, when correctly observed, affords pleasure and enjoyment of the game.

TEACHING CONSIDERATIONS

1. The basic swing is usually introduced with a No. 7, 8, or 9 iron as a full swing. It is advisable to practice without the ball until basic form is established. Golf whiffle balls are useful once the ball is introduced. This enables students to get a great deal of practice with limited equipment. Repetition is critical. Nets to hit into prevent time being wasted chasing balls.
2. As soon as possible, give students a target and distance goal to swing toward so that maximum force can be attained and the importance of form can be established.
3. Introduce woods and other irons as only slight variations of the basic swing. Emphasize the basic elements as well as critical differences between use of the woods and other irons. One wood and a No. 9 or wedge are all that are necessary for basic instruction before learners are introduced to playing a hole (or toward a distance target area).
4. Teach principles of putting, but permit variations in style.
5. After learners have had experience with a wood, several irons, and putting, introduce concepts regarding the short swing, pitch and chip shots, and strategies for different lies. Each of these situations should be practiced separately, not just alluded to in instruction.
6. If possible, have learners go to a golf course before the end of the unit and not just as a culminating event. Prepare them for a particular course and review golf etiquette and rules. Learners will return to instruction highly motivated and willing to share their experiences and problems when they have had an opportunity to actually play golf.
7. Emphasize safety considerations at the beginning of the golf unit. Be strict about the movement patterns allowed on the field or in the gymnasium. For example, some golfers will finish hitting their allotment of balls before others, and the tendency for those already finished is to collect their balls. This places these golfers in the line of fire from those still hitting. Also, be strict about maintaining an appropriate distance from other golfers, on all sides.

GLOSSARY

ace Making the hole in one stroke.
addressing the ball Placing the body and club in position to stroke the ball, and grounding the club.
approach shot A shot played to the green.
apron The area immediately surrounding the green.
away Ball farthest from the hole, to be played first.
banana ball Slang term for "slice."
birdie Making a hole in 1 stroke less than par.
bogey A score of 1 over par on any hole.
bunker Hazard, usually artificial, of exposed ground or sand.
caddie Assistant to the player, who watches the ball, carries the clubs, and the like.
carry The distance the ball travels through the air.
casual water Not a permanent water hazard. A ball lying in casual water may be lifted without penalty.
clubs Implements used to propel the ball.
course rating Comparative course difficulty.

cup Hole into which the ball is played.

dead Ball does not roll after flight.

divot Slice of turf cut out with club.

dogleg A hole that is bent in one direction.

driver No. 1 wood.

eagle Two under par for any hole.

face Contact surface of the club head.

fairway The mowed or well-kept part of the area between the tee and the green.

fat Term for a shot where the golfer hits the ground before contacting the ball, resulting in a large divot and a shorter distance.

flagstick Indicates the position and sometimes the number of hole. The flagstick is in the hole.

fore Warning signal that a ball is approaching another player.

foursome Four people playing as a group.

fringe See **apron.**

green Short-cropped grass around a hole.

grip Handle of the club or method of grasping.

gross score Actual score shot by a player in stroke play.

halved Tied score on a hole or in a complete game.

handicap Strokes given to a player to enable him or her to shoot a score of par, computed on the basis of the difference between the player's average score and par.

hazard Natural or unnatural obstacle on a course.

head Part of club used for hitting.

heel Inside part of the club head at base of shaft.

hole The cup into which the ball is rolled.

holed A ball is "holed" when it is in the cup.

hole high A shot hit the correct distance to the green but not on target.

hole out Final stroke for a hole.

honor Right to play first from a tee by low score on the previous hole.

hook A shot that curves to the left if hit by a right-handed golfer.

iron A club with an iron head. Most common club used on the fairway.

lie Position of the ball on the course.

links The entire course.

loft The elevation of a shot or angle of the clubface.

match A game.

match play Competition played on a hole-by-hole basis.

medal play Competition based on total strokes per round (also called "stroke play").

ninety-degree rule A rule to minimize the impact of golf carts on the golf course. Keep carts on path until even with the golf ball. Then drive straight across to the ball, play it, and return to the path.

par Expected score for a hole; a set number of strokes.

penalty stroke A stroke added to the score of a player or team for a rules violation.

pin The flagstick in the hole marking it.

play through When faster players are allowed to advance through slower players.

press Too much tensing of muscles or swinging too hard. Also, slight forward movement of the hands before putting or swinging the club.

pull-shot A shot hit diagonally to the left (right-handed golfer).

push-shot A shot hit diagonally to the right (right-handed golfer).

rim the cup A ball that rolls around the edge of the cup without falling in rims the cup.

rough Rough ground and long grass off the fairway.

round Any series of holes, generally 18.

sandy Successful one-putt following a bunker shot.

shaft The stick that holds the club head.

shank A severe mishit, where the ball is contacted by a part of the club other than the clubface, often the nose.

slice The ball curves to the right (right-handed golfer).

stance Position of the feet.

stroke Act of swinging at the ball even though it may be missed.

swing through A focus point a golfer uses prior to hitting the ball.

tee An elevation, generally a wooden peg, on which the ball is placed and from which it is to be driven.

teeing ground Starting point for each hole; a designated area between markers.

thin A term for a shot where the club head strikes the ball too high, resulting in low ball flight and often a slice.

toe Front portion of the club head away from the shaft.

topped A ball hit above the center that rolls on the ground.

trap Usually a sand pit in the fairway and around the green.

up The number of holes or strokes by which one leads an opponent.

up and down Successful one-putt following a pitch or chip shot.

waggle Preliminary movements with the club as the ball is addressed.

whiff A swing that misses the ball.

wood A club with a wooden head.

SUGGESTED READINGS

Burr, B. 1997. *Golf for lefties.* Indianapolis, IN: Masters Press. A book written with the left-handed golfer in mind. Covers the entire game from driving to putting.

Chmiel, D., and Morris, K. 2001. *Golf past 50.* Champaign, IL: Human Kinetics.

Craig, E. 2005. *Learn to play golf in a weekend.* New York, NY: Sterling Publishing.

Drane, D., and Block, M. 2006. *Accessible golf.* Champaign, IL: Human Kinetics.

Fuller, G. 2009. *I golf, therefore I am . . . nuts!* Champaign, IL: Human Kinetics.

Gilchrist, G., Hill, S., and Troesch, J. 2009. *Going for the green.* New York, NY: Sterling Publishing.

Jackowski, E. 2007. *Fit to a tee.* New York, NY: Sterling Publishing.

Johnson, J., and Armstong, B. 2000. *Golf: The game for everyone.* Boston, MA: American Press.

Madonna, B. 2001. *Coaching golf successfully.* Champaign, IL: Human Kinetics.

McCord, G. 2006. *Golf for dummies.* 3rd ed. New York: IDG Books Worldwide. Professional golfer/commentator takes a humorous approach to golf instruction with content for all playing levels.

Novosel, J., and Garrity, J. 2004. *Tour tempo.* New York, NY: Doubleday.

Schempp, P., and Mattsson, P. 2005. *Golf; Steps to success.* Champaign IL: Human Kinetics.

Snead, J., Johnson, J., and O'Connor, R. 2000. *Golf today.* 2nd ed. Stamford, CT: Wadsworth/Thomson Learning.

Stokes, R., Perkins, K., and Garriga, I, 1999. *Golf everyone.* Winston-Salem, NC: Hunter Textbooks.

St. Pierre, D. 2004. *Golf fundamentals.* Champaign, IL: Human Kinetics.

Suttie, J. 2006. *Your perfect swing.* Champaign, IL: Human Kinetics.

United States Golf Association. Current edition. *Rules of golf.* Far Hills, NJ: United States Golf Association. Official rules of the game.

Valiante, G. 2005. *Fearless golf.* New York, NY: Doubleday.

Williams, J. 2000. *Playing from the rough: The women of the LPGA hall of fame.* Reston, VA: American Alliance for Health, Physical Education, Recreation and Dance.

Golf Magazines

Golf Digest, 800-PAR-GOLF.

Golf for Women, 800-374-7941.

Golf Illustrated, www.golfillustrated.com.

Golf Magazine, 800-876-7726.

Golf Tips Magazine 800-283-4604.

Golf Week 800-996-4653

Golf World, 800-627-4438.

All are available on the newsstand or by subscription. Articles cover all facets of the game, from fundamentals, competition results, and travel.

RESOURCES

Videos

Golfworks, 4820 Jackson Rd., Newark, OH 43055.

Professional Golf Association, 100 Ave. of the Champions, P.O. Box 12458, Palm Beach Gardens, FL 33410.

See Appendix C for other video sources.

CD-ROMs

Fundamentals of a model swing, deluxe edition (Windows). Offers step-by-step instructions on how to master the perfect swing with over 8½ hours of drills and instruction.

Golf tips: Breaking 100 (DOS). Basic fundamentals for beginning and intermediate golfers.

WEB SITES

Provides information to help young men and women who aspire to earn college golf scholarships through competitive junior golf.
www.ajga.org

Interactive calculator provides personalized advice to help you improve your golf game.
www.golfonline.com/instruction

Provides links to help golfers, specifically women, improve their game.
www.lpga.com

Provides instruction on how to teach golf with course outlines.
www.pgtaa.com

Starts with basic fundamentals and offers advice for all aspects of the golf swing.
www.pga.com/instruction/guide

Free instructional videos from the U.S. Golf Teachers Federation.
www.usgtf.com

Provides information on rules, handicaps, clubs, balls, etiquette, and amateur status.
www.usga.org

Gymnastics and Tumbling

After completing this chapter, the reader should be able to:

- Appreciate the historical development of gymnastics and tumbling
- Understand the importance of safety and spotting techniques
- State the basic rules for dual-meet competitions in gymnastics
- Explain fundamental skills in vaulting, pommel horse, parallel bars, horizontal bar, rings, floor exercise, uneven bars, and balance beam
- Demonstrate fundamental skills and techniques in tumbling and apparatus activities
- Teach basic gymnastics and tumbling skills safely

Gymnastic

HISTORY

The word *gymnastics* means "naked art" and comes from the early Greeks. It is believed that the Chinese were the first to develop activities that resembled gymnastics. The Greeks worked *with* an apparatus rather than on it, whereas the Romans used an apparatus in the form of a wooden horse on which to practice in preparation for combat. The word *gymnasium* is also a Greek word and means the ground or place for gymnastic performances.

Johann Basedow (1723–1790) was the first European to teach organized gymnastic exercises. Johann Guts Muths (1759–1839), the "great-grandfather of gymnastics," published the first book on gymnastics.

After the Napoleonic victories over the Germans, a plan for building up the national strength of Germany was formulated by Frederick Jahn during the period from 1810 to 1852. Jahn is credited with introducing the parallel bars, the horizontal bar, the side horse with pommels, and the vaulting buck. He wanted the Germans to be united to protect themselves, so he took the boys of Berlin to nearby woods on hikes, and there they invented these different types of apparatus. In 1842, 10 years before Jahn's death, formally structured gymnastics was introduced into the German public school.

Mats were first used in Copenhagen, Denmark, when the Military Gymnastic Institute was opened to train teachers in gymnastics.

Around 1850, a wave of German immigration brought gymnastics clubs to the United States, where they were called Turner Societies.

In 1865, the American Turners established a Normal College of the American Gymnastic Union for training gymnastics teachers.

Gymnastics, through these Turner Clubs, YMCAs, schools, and colleges, became well established in the United States. Heavy apparatus, such as parallel bars, uneven parallel bars, vaulting horse, horizontal bar, side horse, rings, and balance beams, are the equipment used in most schools, colleges, clubs, and YMCA gymnasiums; the more elementary jungle gyms, teeter-totters, slides, rings, and swings are used in parks and community centers.

"Gymnastics" in modern usage and competition generally refers to body movements on apparatus and tumbling on mats.

The use of apparatus in American public schools and colleges was impeded by three factors:

1. Around 1800, Dio Lewis introduced exercises that did not require apparatus, and the schools accepted them enthusiastically.
2. The Swedish influence around 1900 emphasized calisthenics.
3. Between World War I and World War II, gymnastics did not occupy its rightful place in the total program of high schools and colleges in the United States. The trend was toward mild recreational activities for the majority, and strenuous competition was encouraged only for a few.

Following World War II, the pendulum swung back to resistive forms of exercise, including gymnastics. Today there is considerable emphasis on competitive gymnastics in the secondary schools, YMCAs, private gymnastics clubs, and colleges throughout the United States.

Noteworthy developments were the organization of the National Association of American Gymnastic Coaches in 1946 and the National Gymnastic Clinic in 1951. The current ruling body for gymnastics is USA Gymnastics (USAG).

Participation in gymnastics has increased dramatically in recent years, particularly in the private sector. This increase is probably in part due to the impact of the televised Olympic Games, during which names such as Olga Korbut, Nadia Comaneci, Kurt Thomas, and Mary Lou Retton became familiar. The tremendous success of the 1984 U.S. Olympic gymnastics team undoubtedly contributed to this trend. Because the strong Soviet team was not present at the 1984

Los Angeles Olympics, the first American gold medal in gymnastics since 1932 was won by the men's team. Mary Lou Retton's gold medal in the all-around event was the first individual Olympic gymnastics medal of any kind to be won by an American woman. By winning the team gold, all-around silver (Peter Vidmar); pommel horse gold (Vidmar); parallel bars gold (Bart Connors), silver (Mitch Gaylord), and bronze (Tim Dagget); and rings bronze (Mitch Gaylord), the 1984 U.S. men's team by far surpassed any previous U.S. gymnastics success. But perhaps the most dramatic moment of the 1984 summer Olympics came when Mary Lou Retton "stuck" her vault for a rare perfect score of 10 to win the all-around event. This highlight capped the best U.S. women's gymnastics performance ever with a team silver medal, vault silver (Mary Lou Retton), uneven bars silver (Julianne McNamara) and bronze (Mary Lou Retton), balance beam bronze (Kathy Johnson), and floor exercise silver (Julianne McNamara) and bronze (Mary Lou Retton).

The Soviet men and women returned to the 1988 Olympic Games with outstanding teams. Both won the team gold medal and most of the individual medals. The U.S. men's team finished a disappointing eleventh, and the women's team finished fourth, with Phoebe Mills capturing the only individual medal (a bronze on the beam).

The women's bid for the team bronze was crushed by a controversial 0.5-point penalty assessed by the head of the technical committee. In fact, many tremendous gymnastic performances were overshadowed by such controversies and questions about judging. Forty perfect scores of 10 were awarded to 14 gymnasts, and in the men's pommel horse, a three-way tie for the gold was awarded.

In the 1992 Olympics the former USSR team, then called the Unified team, won the men's and women's team gold. The U.S. men's team finished sixth; the women's team finished third. The highlight for the U.S. men's team was a first-place finish on the horizontal bar by Trent Dimas. Shannon Miller was the best performer of the women's team, earning second in the all-around and a silver and two bronze medals for individual events.

Although the 1996 Olympic Games in Atlanta were somewhat disappointing for the U.S. men's team (the only medal they won was a silver in the parallel bars by Jair Lynch), it was spectacular for the U.S. women's team. Dominique Dawes won the bronze medal in floor exercise, Amy Chow tied for the silver in the uneven bars, and Shannon Miller captured the gold on the balance beam—and the team gold was won by the U.S. women, just edging out the Russian team.

The U.S. men's and women's teams did not do as well as they had hoped in the 2000 Olympic Games in Sydney. The men's team did not win any medals, and the highest finish in an individual event was Blaine Wilson's sixth place in both the vault and the all-around competition. The men finished fifth in the team competition. The women's team also failed to win any individual medals, and Elise Ray's eighth place on the balance beam was the highest finish in an individual event.

It was apparent that in the Athens 2004 Olympic Gymnastic competition the U.S. had made significant improvement in its world standing. The U.S. won the silver in both men's and women's team competition. Furthermore, Carly Patterson and Paul Hamm, both of the U.S., won the women's and men's Individual All-around titles, respectively.

The Beijing 2008 Olympic Gymnastic finals again demonstrated U.S. presence among the top teams. U.S. women won silver and the U.S. men captured bronze in the team final, with China on top in both men's and women's team competition. The U.S. women excelled in the all-around competition with Nastia Liukin winning the gold and Shawn Johnson the silver.

SAFETY RULES

1. Apparatus should be inspected regularly to detect faults, make proper adjustments, and remove hazards.
2. Accidents on apparatus rarely "just happen." They are usually caused by carelessness.
3. An adequate number of clean mats should be placed around the apparatus. To extend their wear, mats should be carried, not dragged. To prevent landing injuries, especially to ankles, mats should not be overlapped when placed around the apparatus. They should be folded and put away when not in use.
4. Strength and skill are built progressively; the need for progression from the simple to the more complex must be recognized.
5. Instructors should master the art of spotting.
6. Magnesium chalk on the hands will help prevent slipping. To prevent hand tearing, wearing leather grips should be encouraged.
7. Horseplay should be absolutely forbidden in the gymnastics area.
8. Warm-up and stretching exercises are essential before and after practicing stunts. Stretching is also helpful as a warm-down at the completion of this activity. Strength development is also an important feature of any gymnastics program.

SPOTTING

Spotting is such an important safety and teaching skill that it deserves special attention. It involves the supporting, catching, or adjusting of the performer to aid in the completion of a stunt and to prevent possible injury from landing incorrectly. Spotting can aid the performer in "getting the feel" of a stunt or sequence of stunts. It is accomplished by hand spotting or with specialized equipment such as spotting belts. The most important purpose of spotting is for safety and to prevent injury, especially of the head, neck, and spine. Whether for teaching or for safety, the spotter should (1) know what the gymnast is about to perform, (2) know what and when possible mishaps might occur, (3) know what must be done to execute the spot and when the spot must occur, and (4) have sufficient muscular strength to optimize assisting the performer in facilitating learning and to reduce injuries to the spotter. Directions for spotting are given with many of the stunts described. Where required, the spot (•) shown on the figures illustrating most of the skills indicates the point(s) at which the instructor should offer assistance.

DUAL-MEET COMPETITION

Competition rules for high schools are written by the National Federation of State High School Associations. The USAG writes rules for competitions in colleges and clubs.

Order of Competition

Men

The events, in order of competition, for a dual meet are floor exercise, pommel horse, rings, long-horse vaulting, parallel bars, and horizontal bar. Usually a 2-minute warm-up period is allowed after the start in championship meets; however, none is permitted in dual meets.

Number of entries. Each team shall be limited to a maximum of six entries per event. Four of the men must be designated as all-around contestants. A gymnastics team shall be limited to 12 men.

Women

For women the order of events in competition is vaulting, uneven bars, balance beam, and floor exercise.

Number of entries. The number of gymnasts from each team to compete in each event should exceed the number of scores that will count for the final team totals (for example, five entries using three scores per team or four entries using three scores per team).

Score

The best three scores for each team in each gymnastics event are totaled to determine the team's score for that event. This includes the all-around score. The event scores are totaled to determine the final team score.

Judges

Four judges plus one superior judge conduct the competition. Each of the four judges flashes a score based on 10 points, 4 points for composition and 6 points for execution. Then the low and high scores are dropped and the other two averaged. If the middle two scores are too far apart, the superior judge's score is added to the average of these two scores and this sum is then divided by two to get the final score.

EQUIPMENT

1. Pommel horse
2. Long horse
3. Parallel bars
4. Uneven bars
5. Horizontal bar
6. Rings
7. Balance beam
8. Mats
9. Carbonate of magnesium
10. Emery paper to clean bars
11. Springboard
12. Floor exercise area: 40 × 40 feet (12 × 12 m)

FUNDAMENTAL SKILLS AND TECHNIQUES

The gymnastic exercises presented here are basic movements primarily for developmental purposes. Advanced stunts and routines may be found in other sources.

Vaulting

In all gymnastics events except vaulting, several stunts and movements are linked to produce a routine. In vaulting, a single stunt is performed and judged.

The vaulting event is slightly different for men and women. For men, the long horse over which the vaults are made is approximately 53 inches (1.35 m) in height, and the vaults are made over the length of the horse. In women's competition, the vaults are made across the width of the horse, which is approximately 43 inches (1.09 m) in height. There are preflight and postflight phases to all vaults. The preflight is designed to create opportunity for repulsion in a blocking technique. The shoulders elevate forcefully, as contact is made with the body of the horse in order to create maximum vertical and horizontal displacement in postflight.

The vaults described and illustrated in this chapter are fundamental and seldom used in anything but the most elementary gymnastics competition. On the other hand, they are fun to learn and in some cases require courage to try the first time. The use of a springboard is optional with the vaults presented here.

Squat vault

Use a two-foot takeoff, and as the hands contact the horse, push downward; as the body begins to lift, pull the knees to the chest. When the body clears the horse, extend the body. At the landing, flex at the knees, bring the arms forward for balance, and finish by standing as if at attention (Figure 14.1). The spotter should stand in front of the horse (to the left or the right).

Figure 14.1. Squat vault.

Flank vault

This is also called the "side vault." Use a two-foot takeoff and vault so that the side of the body passes over the horse. Keep the legs extended and the toes pointed. Land in a partial knee bend with the arms extended to the side (Figure 14.2).

Face vault

Use a two-foot takeoff and pass the body over the horse by doing a quarter turn so that the body faces the horse as it passes over it. Land with the side to the horse, with one hand on the horse and the other extended to the side (Figure 14.3).

Rear vault

In this vault, the rear (back) of the body passes over the end of the horse. If the vault is a rear vault to the left, the body makes a quarter turn to the left and passes over the horse in this position. After the body passes over the horse, place the left hand on the horse and extend the right to the side (Figure 14.4).

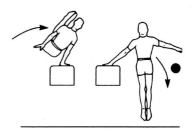

Figure 14.4. Rear vault.

Figure 14.5. Straddle vault.

Straddle vault

Do not stop on top of the horse, but pass the body completely over it. Keep the head up (Figure 14.5). (Stopping in a straddle position on top of the horse with an immediate push off into postflight might be used as a lead-up activity in learning this vault.)

This vault should be spotted closely. The spotter stands in front of the horse and grabs both upper arms of the vaulter. As the vaulter comes forward over the horse, the spotter moves backward.

Stoop vault

The stoop vault is the same as the squat vault except that the legs are kept straight rather than tucked as the body passes over the horse. This requires more height, and a vaulting board should be used. A spotter should stand in front of the horse and to one side of the performer. The spotter should grasp and lift the near shoulder and use the other arm to help lift the performer's hips as they pass over the horse (Figure 14.6).

Figure 14.2. Flank vault.

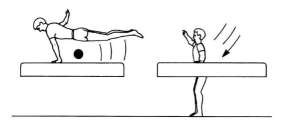

Figure 14.3. Face vault.

Figure 14.6. Stoop vault.

Pommel Horse

As with vaulting, the stunts described here are not normally seen in gymnastics competition, but are rather fundamental to this apparatus and are lead-up activities to more advanced stunts.

Squat to rear support

Use a two-foot takeoff and pass over the horse by lifting the hips high, keeping the head up, and bringing the knees between the arms. After the feet pass over the horse, the legs point straight down and the rear of the vaulter is supported by the horse (Figure 14.7).

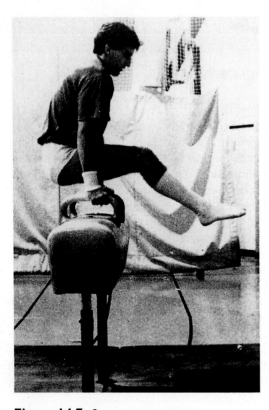

Figure 14.7. Squat to rear support.

Feint left or right

Do this from the front support. Swing the leg up and over the end of the horse, either the right side (the croup) or the left side (the neck). If the right leg passes over the horse, turn the face to the left; if the left leg passes over the horse, turn to the right. Keep the arms fully extended, legs stiff, and toes pointed. Pass the leg over the horse and then bring it back (Figure 14.8).

Cut left or right

From the front leaning support, pass the leg over the end of the horse and under one hand. To accomplish this, the weight of the body must be transferred to the opposite hand. Attempt to keep both arms and legs extended (Figure 14.9).

Right flank to rear support, reverse flank left to front support

If the weight is kept over the horse as the flank is performed, the catch to the rear support is not difficult. To perform the reverse flank, put all the weight on the right arm. The secret of the vaults and catch is proper weight distribution (Figure 14.10).

One-half alternating single-leg circles and return

Jump to a support, lean to the left, and lift the right leg and arm. Bring the right leg forward, and replace the right hand on the right pommel. Lean on the right hand, lift the left leg and arm, swing the left leg forward, and replace the left hand on the left pommel. The performer should now be in a rear support position. Shift both legs to the right, separate them as the right arm is lifted, and return the right leg to its original position. Finally, lean on the right hand as the left leg is returned to its original position (Figure 14.11).

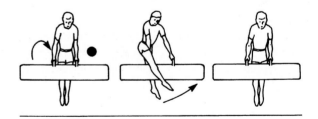

Figure 14.8. Feint left or right.

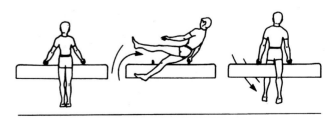

Figure 14.9. Cut left or right.

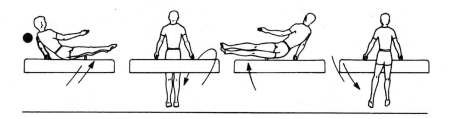

Figure 14.10. Rear flank to rear support, reverse flank left to front support.

Figure 14.11. One-half alternating single-leg circles and return.

Parallel Bars

Run and jump to cross support

Jump to a straight-arm support. Land in the forward-leaning position and then swing forward. *Spot for a collapse on the backswing.* Spot under the bar on the chest if a collapse takes place (Figure 14.12).

Hand traveling

1. Hand over hand, walk forward the length of the bars. Keep the chest hollow, head neutral, no arch in the back, and toes pointed (Figure 14.13).

Figure 14.12. Run and jump to cross support.

Figure 14.13. Hand traveling.

2. Hop the length of the bars in a straight-arm support position. In this hop forward, the hands are moved simultaneously.
3. Riding a bicycle with the legs increases the difficulty (Figure 14.14).

Figure 14.14. Bicycle riding.

Figure 14.15. Intermediate swing with hop.

Intermediate swing

From a cross-support position in the center of the bars, start to swing the body from the shoulders forward and backward. Learn to balance the center of body weight over the hand supports by leaning forward when the legs are moving back.

Intermediate swing with hop

In doing the intermediate swing, keep the arms extended, flex the body minimally on the front swing, and extend it to the back swing. The hop is executed on the front swing by using the uncoiling effect from the bars as the external force assisting in the upward swing and hop. *Spot this for a possible collapse right after the catch* (Figure 14.15).

Forward swinging dips

1. Swing from the shoulders.
2. At the end of the rear swing, flex the arms, keeping the back arched and head up (Figure 14.16).
3. Swing forward in a bent-arm position so that the chin is even with the bars in the middle of the swing.
4. At the front end of the swing, straighten the arms and shoot the feet forward.
5. Use the upward movement (uncoiling) of the bars to supply an upward force. This requires proper timing.

Hip rise

Swing forward vigorously in the upper-arm hang. Approaching the front end of the swing, pull backward and downward with the arms to receive a forward reaction force to a cross support (Figure 14.17).

Shoulder balance

Be in the center of the bar and extend elbows to be level with the shoulders. The forearms should be flexed at the elbow, with the hands on the bar. Flex the knees and place the feet on the bars for support. Roll the hips up first, then the legs, and arch the back to maintain balance. If you start to fall backward, keep the elbows well spread and swing downward, using the upper arms as rockers. *Always have a spotter on each side when practicing this* (Figure 14.18).

Dismounts

When trying dismounts for the first time, safety and success will be enhanced by using lower than normal bars (chest height or lower).

Figure 14.16. Forward swinging dips.

Figure 14.17. Hip rise.

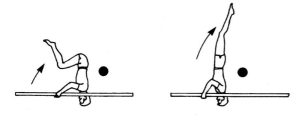

Figure 14.18. Shoulder balance.

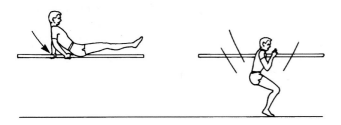

Figure 14.19. Rear vault dismount.

Figure 14.20. Single-leg cutoff.

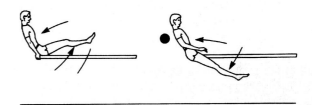

Figure 14.21. Double-leg cutoff.

From a cross support swing at the center of the bars, execute one of the following dismounts over either bar:
1. Rear vault dismount, in front of hands (Figure 14.19)
2. Front vault dismount behind hands
3. Side vault dismount facing outward, in front of the hands

Single- and double-leg cutoff
For safety, lower bars during initial learning phase.

Single-leg cutoff. At the end of the forward swing, push back and cutoff. *Keep the head back so that the face does not hit the bar. Spot this on both shoulders from the back.* The backward lean before the cutoff is very important (Figure 14.20).

Double-leg cutoff. Apply the same principle as in the single-leg cutoff. Cutoff with both legs. Use the same spotting technique as for the single-leg cutoff. Lean back just before the cutoff (Figure 14.21).

Another way to spot these two dismounts is to grasp the performer's wrist.

Split-off
This is nothing but a straddle vault. Be sure to keep the head up. Do not raise the hips too high. *Spot this forward on the chest and shoulders* (Figure 14.22).

Horizontal Bar
Swing
From a hanging position, execute a short underswing and dismount at the peak of the backswing.

Chins
1. Use the ordinary grasp and pull up to the chest six times.
2. Use the wide grasp and pull up to the back of the neck four times.
3. One hand grasps the bar and the other hand grasps the wrist of the chinning arm. Chin two times.
4. One hand grasps the bar and the other hand grasps the bicep of the chinning arm. Chin two times.

Skin the cat over the bar (front pullover)
From a hang position, pull the legs over the bar to a front-support position; do not allow the body to swing.

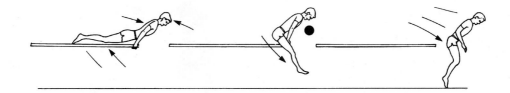

Figure 14.22. Split-off.

Skin the cat

From a hang position, bring the legs up through the arms and over the head until the feet point toward the floor. Return to original position.

Monkey hang

From a hang position, bring the legs up through the arms and over the head until the feet point toward the floor. Release one arm, swing a complete turn on one arm, and then regrasp the bar.

Seat swing-up from swing

Pull the legs up through the hands and then over the bar. Arch the back and quickly pull the body up over the bar into a sitting position on top of the bar. Keep the head back (Figure 14.23). Spot by placing one hand on the performer's upper back at the beginning of the swing and moving the other hand onto the thigh near the completion of the skill. This will prevent the performer from hitting the lower back on the bar when the leg direction is too high.

Kip, or upstart

Stress arching the back at the front of the swing. As the extended body approaches the height of the swing, bring the ankles to the bar. As the hips start to drop in the backswing, shoot the legs up, out, and down. Press down and in with the shoulder muscles. Get a little wrist flexion motion when going above the bar. Keep legs close to the bar. Do not push away from the bar. Force the shoulders well forward (Figure 14.24).

Single-knee mount

From a hang position with an ordinary grasp, swing one knee over and hook it on the bar, inside the arms, using either leg. Swing the free leg downward and backward and pull in with the arms, mounting to a cross seat on the top of the bar.

Hand and knee circles

From a cross-riding seat on the bar (one leg on each side of the bar) and with a forward grip (thumbs in direction circle is made), reach back with the rear leg and swing it downward hard and forward. The other leg is hooked at the knee over the bar, and a complete circle backward around the bar is made. The spotter assists at the upper arm.

Cast

From a hang position with a regular grasp, pull up to a half chin, lean the shoulders and head back, and at the same time raise the legs, holding the knees and ankles stretched and together. Shoot the legs forward and upward, at the same time extending the elbows. As the legs swing upward and shoot outward, also shoot the body forward by extending the arms at the elbows for a big swing (Figure 14.25). Practice this swing several times. Spot in case the hands slip off, particularly on the backswing.

Heel circle forward with reverse grip

Sit on top of and grasp the bar with a reverse or undergrip. Keep the legs extended, extend the arms, and raise the hips backward until the heels rest on the bar. Keep this position and let the body drop. Slightly alter the hand and leg relationship. Start the hip extension. Drive the legs over the bar. Return to a sitting position (Figure 14.26). Spot by reaching under the bar, grasping the wrist from the beginning of the skill and the back with the other hand returning to the sitting position.

Uprise

A requisite for this skill is a good cast. After the cast, swing down and back in an extended posture. At the end of the backswing, pike, raise the back and shoulders, and lift the

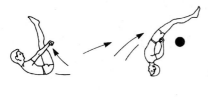

Figure 14.23. Seat swing-up from swing.

Figure 14.24. Kip, or upstart.

Figure 14.25. Cast.

Figure 14.26. Heel circle forward with reverse grip.

body above the bar by pushing down with the hands. Place the body weight over the bar by leaning over the bar and arching. Come to the front-leaning support (Figure 14.27). As the performer gets comfortable with this skill, reduce the amount of body bend and rely on an explosive swing at the beginning of the skill.

Hip circle forward

Pull over to a front-leaning support. Push down with the arms and raise the body so that the thighs rest on the bar. With the head held up, fall forward, keeping the thighs in contact with the bar. Hold this position. Shorten the radius after passing the horizontal, on the downswing, by forcing the head forward and bending the hips and arms. Come to a rest over the bar.

Cast to handstand

Practice this first on the low bar with both grips. Assume a front-leaning support position. Slightly flex the arms so that the bar contacts the lower abdomen, and swing the legs under the bar as the body leans forward. Forcefully hollow the chest while driving the heels backward and push with the arms as the body weight remains over the bar (Figure 14.28).

Half giant swing

Use the overgrip (palms down). Start cast as for a handstand, but push back. Swing down fully extended. At the 5 o'clock position, break at the shoulder joints and come to a rest on the bar (Figure 14.29). The spotter can assist by pushing on the back during the forward swing and catching the thighs near the completion of the skill. To gain confidence and

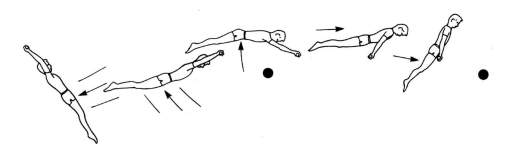

Figure 14.27. Uprise.

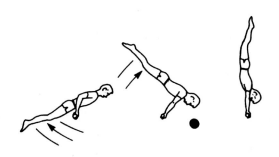

Figure 14.28. Cast to handstand.

Figure 14.29. Half giant swing (overgrip).

timing, begin by swinging repetitiously under the bar with spotter assistance. After developing confidence and the hollow chest position through the bottom of the swing, execute the last part of the half giant after passing through the bottom of the swing with spotter assistance.

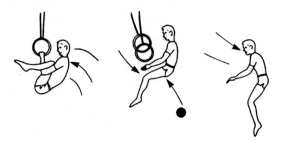

Figure 14.30. Double front cutoff.

Rings

Double front cutoff

From a pike hang position, rotate the body forward vigorously, bending the elbows, and at the same time bring the separated legs, with the knees bent, down across the elbows. Immediately afterward, while still rotating forward, release the rings and land standing on the mat (Figure 14.30). The spotter can assist in the upward and forward rotation. Rotation can be reinforced by elbow flexion and eye contact with the landing surface (chin on chest).

Straddled fly-away

From a bent-arm hang, swing the legs and hips upward vigorously, spreading the legs held straight until the crotch is astride the wrists. While the body still has momentum, release the rings and land in a standing position (Figure 14.31). Spot the lift of the hips and the front of the shoulder through the landing.

Front roll with arms flexed

This is a good stunt for the weight lifter, the bodybuilder, or the student who has been working apparatus for quite a while. It takes strength. Use a low ring to spot. Jump to the cross-support position. Lower the shoulders and raise the hips. Do not turn the hands as you perform this first move. As the body falls over, supinate the hands (palms upward). Do not let the shoulders drop. As the body turns forward, pull up as high as possible and pronate the hands. This move should bring the weight above the rings and on the arms. Now perform a push-up. Spot by lifting the performer above the rings (Figure 14.32).

Shoulder stand

Lower the rings to about 3 feet (0.91 m) from the floor. Now stand up on a chair or stool. Grasp the rings from the inside. Raise the hips slowly as the shoulders are lowered. On the first couple of tries, steady the body by locking the legs around the ropes (straddle legs). Keep the eyes at all times

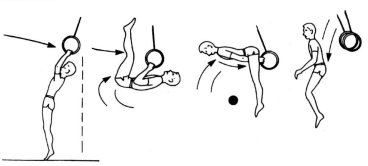

Figure 14.31. Straddled fly-away.

on the mats: If the head is flexed, the body will somersault. Eventually arch the back and bring the feet together. Keep the rings close to the shoulders at all times. Spot this by keeping the performer from turning over too quickly (Figure 14.33).

Muscle-up

Grasp the rings with the false, or high, grip. The body should be suspended on the wrists. Execute a pull-up as high as the chest. As the height of the pull-up is completed, the feet should be raised to about a 30-degree angle. Now drop the legs down and pronate the hands as the arms are inwardly rotated. This action should place you above the rings. Now push up, arch the back, and hold the head up. Spot this by helping to lift the performer above the difficult level (Figure 14.34).

Kip

Put the rings down to chest height. Grasp them from the outside. Now take a half step backward. Lift one leg and then the other into the pike position. Swing forward, and on the backward swing extend rapidly at the waist as you push

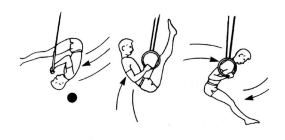

Figure 14.32. Front roll with arms flexed.

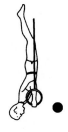

Figure 14.33. Shoulder stand.

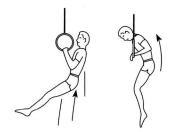

Figure 14.34. Muscle-up, or pull- and push-up.

down with the hands. Force the head and shoulders forward and up. This action should place the body in a straight-arm support position. Spot this in the middle of the back through the waist extension (Figure 14.35).

Standing back, or reverse, cutoff

This is not a difficult stunt to master. The important thing is the timing. The level of the rings should be just above the head. Grasp the rings from the outside. While holding the rings, fall off balance, pull up to a half bend, throw the shoulders back, and flex rapidly at the waist. Hold on as the body rotates until you can see the mat, and then release the hands. Spot with the spotter's right hand over the performer's left arm and on the chest, the left hand in the small of the back to turn the performer (Figure 14.36).

Reverse uprise, or back kip

Study the figures closely. On the forward swing, go into the pike. Immediately, without a swing in the pike position, lift the hips above the rings by quickly pulling up. Now, without losing momentum, extend the back at the hip joints to promote rotation of the body. Push down forcefully with the hands. End in a cross-support position. This is accomplished most easily with the false grip. Spot this under the shoulders on the up-swing and at the thighs near completion (Figure 14.37).

Uprise

The important move in this stunt is from the pike to hyperextension. The hips should drop out of the pike first. After the hips drop, whip the legs back and then up. Push down and outward hard with the hands, and bring the body to rest in the cross-support position (Figure 14.38). Spot a possible overthrow.

Floor Exercise

High-level competition in floor exercise is performed on "spring floors" made of certain types of wood, special springs, ethafoam, and covered by carpet. Those floors cover an area of 40 × 40 feet (12.2 × 12.2 m). This event in high schools and recreation facilities is often performed on wrestling mats.

Floor exercise contains dance movements, including leaps and poses, elements of dance combinations, acrobatics,

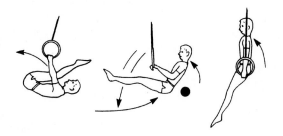

Figure 14.35. Kip.

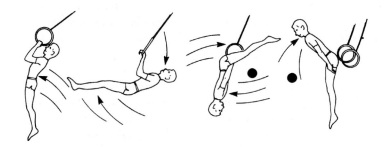

Figure 14.36. Standing back, or reverse, cutoff.

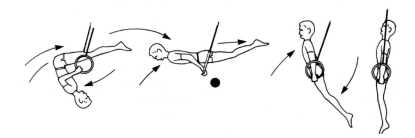

Figure 14.37. Reverse uprise, or back kip.

Figure 14.38. Uprise.

and tumbling grouped in rhythmic and harmonious patterns. Through these and other movements, the gymnast explores tempo, height, distance, mood, direction, and precision of form. The basic elements of form are balance, good body alignment, and full body extension (including pointed toes).

The routines, which are performed to music for women and without music for men, generally begin and end with a sequence of tumbling. The main part, or body, of the routine consists of dance movements, balances, flexibility stunts, and one or two additional tumbling passes.

The gymnast tries to create an artistic image. The composition is developed into a coherent pattern showing a change of pace, vitality, expression, individuality, and originality.

A great part of an individual's success involves adhering to an established and well-defined routine that includes elements that are not too difficult for the performer. Once the routine is composed, it must be practiced consistently.

Learning methods

The elementary movements and combinations must be adapted not only to the age and sex of the students but also to their mental and physical abilities.

1. Learn skills first—simple, fundamental, elementary movements. A spotter should be nearby to assist.
2. Combine various skills into series; combine dance steps and tumbling and make them into a simple routine.
3. Set routines to music for women gymnasts.
4. Warm up properly with stretching and flexibility exercises before trying the routine.

A few movements that may be used in a floor exercise routine are described in the following sections.

Toe rise, or stand

Take a standing position. Rise up on your toes and extend your arms sideward and back with the palms of your hands facing down and out, chest up, shoulders down. Lower your heels to the floor as you drop your arms at your sides to return to a full stand (Figure 14.39). This activity is often practiced as an ankle strengthener.

Body wave

Start with the body partially flexed—knees, hips, back, and head. Balance on the toes, with arms reaching forward but relaxed; then hyperextend the body and drop the arms down and back and the head forward. Last, extend the head, raise the body tall, and elevate the arms (Figure 14.40).

Split

Stand with one leg ahead of the other, and slowly lower the body downward into a split with the front knee on top and the rear knee under (Figure 14.41).

One-leg balance

Take a standing position. Raise one leg to the side as high as possible. Grasp the instep of your raised leg with one hand and extend the other arm to a horizontal or upward position (Figure 14.42).

Front scale

Take a standing position. Raise one leg backward and upward as the chest moves forward. As you balance on one foot, extend your arms in alignment with the upper torso and in front of you. Keep your head up and arch your back (Figure 14.43).

Arabesque

Take a standing position. Raise one leg backward. Balance on one foot and hold your arms out to the side and slightly back for balance. (One arm may be raised, the other one out to the side.) Allow your body to lean slightly forward and at the same time keep your head and chest almost vertical (Figure 14.44).

Handstand

Place your hands on the mat, shoulder width apart, with your fingers pointing forward. Keep your arms straight, head up slightly, and eyes focused between the hands. Kick upward. Extend the shoulders and hold stomach and buttocks tight. Do not arch the back (Figure 14.45). The spotter should catch the calf of the leg on the kick-up and place the beginner in a good handstand position.

Figure 14.39. Toe rise, or stand.

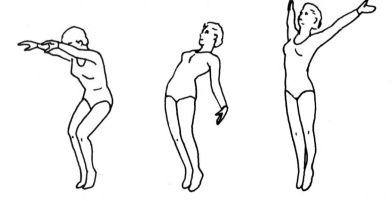

Figure 14.40. Body wave.

Figure 14.41. Split.

Figure 14.42. One-leg balance.

Figure 14.43. Front scale.

Figure 14.44. Arabesque.

Back walkover

From a standing position with the arms raised over the head, bring one leg (extended) up parallel with the floor. As the hips shift forward, reach back, arch the back, and place the hands with the fingers pointing forward on the mat. As the hands contact the mat, kick the leg that was originally raised and push with the other leg to complete the walkover. Spot by kneeling on the side of the raised leg, support the performer's back with an extended right arm, and use the left hand to assist the movement of the raised leg during the kicking portion of the stunt (Figure 14.46).

Front walkover

Take a standing position. Go into a handstand with the legs split (Figure 14.47). Shift the shoulders back as the lead foot continues over to the floor. Land on one foot. As the hips shift forward, lift your hands off the floor, bring your body to an upright position, and then bring your other foot to the floor.

Figure 14.45. Handstand.

Figure 14.47. Front walkover.

Figure 14.46. Back walkover.

Figure 14.48. Valdez to handstand.

Valdez to handstand

Sit on the floor. Place one hand on the floor in back of your hip. Raise your other arm shoulder high. Bend one leg so that the sole of your foot is on the floor near your seat and your knee is near your chest. Extend the other leg. (A Valdez can be done on the same arm with either leg bent. For some it is easier to have the bent leg on the same side as the supporting arm.) From this position, push with the support bent leg to lift the hips upward, raise your arm overhead and directly to the rear with the head following the arc of the arm thrown upward. (The hand is twisted, but the throw is directly back.) Lift the extended leg upward. (The move will be on one plane—a straight line back like a flip-flop.) Speed is picked up with a vigorous leg push and a strong head and arm throw. Keep the head between the arms for straight, clean lines and correct body position. A handstand is assured with an extended head throw (Figure 14.48).

A spotter should squat on the straight-leg side and assist with the right-leg throw.

Uneven Bars

One of the last pieces of apparatus to be added to the sport of gymnastics was the uneven bars. The routines performed on this apparatus are a cross between those performed on the horizontal bar and those on the parallel bars. Originally the routines included predominately pretty, graceful positions, but over the years the event has become one of fast, powerful swinging movements. The following stunts and their explanations are basic to more complex stunts but still require much time and practice to master.

Jump to front-leaning support

Stand facing the low bar. With the hands on the bar in an overgrip, jump so that the body comes to rest on a straight-arm support (Figure 14.49).

Figure 14.49. Jump to front-leaning support.

Back pullover

Grasp the low bar with an overhand grip. Kick one leg (extended) forward while pulling the hips toward the bar with the hands. Bring the legs together and rotate around the bar to a front support position (Figure 14.50). A spotter should help by pushing the hips and upper legs over the bar as well as supporting the back.

Cast to dismount

Start in a front support position on the low bar (facing the high bar), with an overhand grip. Pike at the waist around the low bar. Push back with the heels and against the bar with the thighs while pushing down on the bar with the arms. Continue to grip the bar until the body is parallel with the floor. As the descent from this position begins, push away from the bar, moving the arms upward into flexion at the shoulder joint, release the grip, and land on the feet facing the bar (Figure 14.51).

Back hip circle

Start from a front support position. Push away (cast) and then return to the bar. As the hips touch the bar, they allow the body to pike slightly at the waist and lean back with the

shoulders as the legs come forward around the bar. Rotate around the bar and extend from the pike as the rotation is completed. Learn this stunt on the low bar before trying it on the high bar, and use a spotter during the learning phase (Figure 14.52). The spotter should help keep the hips to the bar.

Forward mill circle

Start with one leg on either side of the bar (stride support) and an underhand grip (palms forward). Lift the body as high and as far forward as possible. As the rotation begins, extend the upper body out from the bar as far as possible. At the bottom of the downswing, curve the body slightly forward to shorten the radius and continue the rotation until the starting position is reached (Figure 14.53).

Front hip circle

Use an overhand grip and start in the front support position. Lean forward while pushing against the bar to extend the upper body. As the bottom of the downswing is reached, begin to pike slightly at the waist and pull against the bar to shorten the radius for the upswing. Continue the rotation until the original starting position is attained (Figure 14.54). The spotter should assist with upswing.

Figure 14.52. Back hip circle.

Figure 14.53. Forward mill circle.

Figure 14.50. Back pullover.

Figure 14.51. Cast to dismount.

Figure 14.54. Front hip circle.

Single-leg stem rise

Start by sitting on the low bar and grasping the high bar with an overhand grip. Flex one leg and place that foot on the low bar while raising the other leg (extended) to the high bar. Pull with the arms, push against the low bar with the support foot, and extend the straightened leg up against the high bar. Finish in a support position on the high bar (Figure 14.55).

Glide kip

Facing the low bar and about 3 feet (0.9 m) away from it, jump upward with the hips as the upper body reaches for the bar. Grasp the bar with straight arms and begin the downswing with a pike at the hips. As the rotation continues, straighten at the hips so that an extended position is attained. As the height of the forward swing is reached, immediately pike at the hips and bring the legs to the bar, creating a pike position. Immediately "shoot the legs up the bar" as the body extends and the arms push down on the bar. Finish with a front support position on the bar (Figure 14.56).

Balance Beam

Routines on the balance beam involve many of the stunts that are performed in floor exercise except that they must be accomplished on a beam only 4 inches (10.2 cm) wide and approximately 16 feet (4.88 m) long. The routine on the beam must be continuous and smooth and include tumbling, dance-type movements, and not more than three static, or balance, positions.

After mounting the beam (sometimes with the use of a spring board), various tumbling stunts (described later in this chapter) are interspersed with locomotor combinations. The routine is completed with some form of dismount. The routine performed in competition has a minimum and a maximum time limit.

Any number of sequences can be developed from the positions illustrated in Figure 14.57.

Tumbling

Tumbling is the art of manipulating the body in feats of skill without the use of apparatus. Tumbling maneuvers include rolls, somersaults, twists, springs, balances on hands, and manipulation of the body in unusual positions.

From primitive times and through all stages of development, people have nurtured the desire to learn new ways to move the body. Tumbling offers such an outlet.

HISTORY

The earliest historical records—in the form of painting, sculpture, and literature—indicate that tumbling was connected with the dance, a most fundamental activity. Tumblers of early times had an important influence on entertainment and the theater, and in Greece and Rome, tumblers entertained at private dinner parties and social occasions. Tumbling was also popular during the Middle Ages.

The word *tumble* is Teutonic in origin and means to dance violently or to dance with posturing, balancing, and contortions. The terms used by other nationalities have similar spelling, and embody the same activities of somersaulting, rolling, and contorting the body.

There is no question that springboard diving in swimming pools and rebound tumbling on the trampoline have been influenced by the tumbling art.

EQUIPMENT

A firm, padded, nonslippery mat is all that is necessary. Gymnastics slippers and a proper gymnasium uniform are adequate.

FUNDAMENTAL SKILLS AND TECHNIQUES

Tumbling provides an excellent means for developing agility, poise, balance, and coordination as well as being helpful in developing physical fitness. Success in learning new

Figure 14.55. Single-leg stem rise.

Figure 14.56. Glide kip.

Figure 14.57. Balance beam; pass-through positions.

skills gives the individual self-confidence, courage, and determination.

A great number of stunts and tumbling skills can be learned. Those presented are individual, elementary, and fundamental and form a basis to advance to the more difficult skills. A vast number of companion (or pairs) exercises can be introduced into a program. Pyramid building can also be used. Also, a routine in which several of the single stunts presented can be done in progression is an enjoyable and rewarding exercise.

Lead-Up Developmental Exercises

Animal walks (Figures 14.58 to 14.65) should be used as part of the conditioning program. The snail drag is especially good for developing the upper body.

First-Level Stunts

Beginning tumblers should never work without a spotter. Use safety belts when necessary. See that mats are always in place.

Figure 14.58. Galloping dog. Run on all fours.

Figure 14.59. Frog hop. Dive to hands and land in squat.

Figure 14.60. Crab walk. Belly up.

Figure 14.61. Elephant walk. Keep knees stiff and spread feet.

Figure 14.62. Wet-cat footwalk. Walk on three limbs and shake one.

Figure 14.63. Bear walk. Same as elephant walk but with feet together.

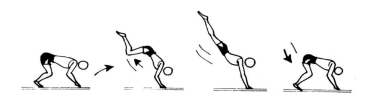

Figure 14.64. Kangaroo hop, or donkey kick. Place hands on mat, kick feet in air, and land in squat position with hands still on mat. Reach forward and repeat.

Figure 14.65. Snail drag. Keep legs inactive and drag body with arms.

Figure 14.66. Spinal rock.

Figure 14.67. Forward roll.

Figure 14.68. Forward roll to back.

Figure 14.69. Backward roll over shoulder.

The following are considered progressive-ability stunts of the first level of proficiency.

Spinal rock. Keep the head up, grasp the shins, pull tight, and rock (Figure 14.66).

Forward roll. Reach forward, take the weight on the hands, duck the head well under, round the back, roll, and tuck (Figure 14.67).

Forward roll to back. Place the hands on the mat, complete the forward roll, but do not lift the head after passing over it (Figure 14.68).

Backward roll over shoulder. Lie supine on the mat, place the right hand down by the side and the left arm out to the side, turn the head to the right, and bring the knees up and over the left shoulder. Land on the knees (Figure 14.69).

Backward roll. Begin in a squat position with the hands next to the ears. Make the back round and roll to the rear. Keep the chin tucked to the chest and the knees together throughout the movement.

Backward roll, pike. Bend forward with the knees stiff, place the hands behind the thighs, drop back to the seat, raise the

Figure 14.70. Backward roll, pike.

Figure 14.71. Backward extension roll.

Figure 14.72. Football roll.

Figure 14.73. Tripod.

Figure 14.74. Headstand.

Figure 14.75. Flying angel.

legs, relocate the hands beside the ears, and roll straight over the head (Figure 14.70).

Backward extension roll. Start as for the backward roll pike, but when the weight is on the shoulders, shoot the legs to the ceiling, maintain a neutral head position, and push hard with the hands (Figure 14.71). The spotter may grab the pelvis and thigh and lift.

Football roll. Spread the feet apart, bend over, and place the left hand on the mat. Reach under the left arm with the right. Drop to the right shoulder, roll over, and roll across the back from the right shoulder to the left hip. Get up on the left knee, and then step up on the right foot (Figure 14.72).

Tripod. Make a triangle with the head and hands. Slowly place the knees on the elbows (Figure 14.73).

Headstand. Be sure that the head and hands form a good triangle. Place the forehead on the mat at the hairline, not the top of the head. Raise the hips by straightening the back. Now raise the legs slowly (Figure 14.74).

Flying angel. Bottom performer lifts the top performer over the body slowly. The bottom performer turns feet slightly outward and along the top performer's hip joints to the pelvis. Top performer then arches the back and raises the head (Figure 14.75).

Cartwheel. Begin in a standing position with the side of the body facing down the length of the mat and the arms

extended overhead. Rock back on the back leg and then the forward leg. Place the front hand down on the mat. As the other hand comes over, place it on the mat in line with the first hand. At the same time, push with the front leg and swing the back leg up and over the body. Keep the head up and watch the hands as they are placed on the mat. The legs should be outward near a side-splits position when passing through the handstand. When the stunt is completed, the performer should be facing the same way as at the start (Figure 14.76).

Cheststand on partner. Place the chest on the back of the partner, grasp the upper arm and thigh, kick slowly into position, hold tight, and arch the back slightly (Figure 14.77).

Two high. The important move here is the hand position. The top performer stands in back of the bottom performer. The bottom performer reaches over the shoulders with the

Figure 14.76. Cartwheel.

Figure 14.77. Cheststand on partner.

palms up. The top performer places the palms in the bottom performer's hands. Holding this hand position, the two face each other. The position now should be like shaking hands with the left hands, right hands over the head. The top performer places the left foot on the bottom performer's left thigh. This is done from the side with the toe of the top performer pointing outward. As the bottom performer pulls with the right hand, the top performer steps up on the shoulder (Figure 14.78). The spotter should stand in front.

Headstand in hands. Place the forehead in the hands with the palms up and forearms on the mat (thumbs and forefingers form a triangle around the head). Kick up slowly (Figure 14.79).

Handstand support. Keep the head down, looking at the floor as you kick up. The catcher should stand to the side to prevent being kicked in the face (Figure 14.80).

Figure 14.80. Handstand support.

Second-Level Stunts

The following are exercises for those who have advanced to a more progressive level of tumbling skill. They represent the second level of proficiency.

Rolling. Begin in an all-fours position, jump sideward, landing on all fours, then immediately assume a stretched position during the roll (log roll). Bring arms and legs under the body to the all-fours position to complete the roll. Repeat in the other direction.

Triple roll. From the three-performer lying position, the middle performer rolls to the left, and the performer on the left springs from the hands and knees over the middle performer, landing in the middle. The middle performer always rolls under and executes a log roll with only one full turn and comes to rest on hands and knees. This is repeated from left to right (Figure 14.81).

Headspring over mat. The best way to learn this is to do a flexed handstand. Let the body fall off balance. Just as the balance is lost, kick hard and push with the hands (Figure 14.82). The spotter kneels in front (to the side) and places a hand on the performer's back.

Double roll with partner. Hold on to each other's ankles. Flex the knees and place the feet on the floor close to the thighs. Spread the knees apart so that the performer on top can duck the head and roll. This is important. Each person should work hard to help the other performer (Figure 14.83). A spotter should assist the top individual in the rolling action to prevent head or neck injuries. The spotter

Figure 14.78. Two high.

Figure 14.79. Headstand in hands.

assists in maintaining control by assuring that the head of the top individual gets safely under. The bottom performer applies some resistance as the knees bend and heels move to the buttocks. The resistance applied by the bottom performer assures that the top individual rolls under control.

Fish dive. Take a standing position. Kick either foot backward and upward and jump off the other foot. Land on the hands, with the feet over the head (handstand position). Now bend the arms and let the body down, rolling from the chest to the knees. Flex at the waist and push hard with the hands until the weight is back over the feet. Lift the body to the squat stand (Figure 14.84).

Dive cartwheel. To do this stunt properly, start with a run of a few steps, finish with a short hop, dive about 5 feet (1.5 m), and do a cartwheel (Figure 14.85).

Tiger stand. Try to keep the upper arm perpendicular to the floor and kick up slowly (Figure 14.86).

Mule kick. The best way to start this is from the handstand. Slightly bend the knees and bend the arms. Snap the legs downward and push hard with the arms. This is the true landing position: body bent forward and arms reaching backward and upward. Immediately use the lift of the arms, and jump back up into the handstand position. As the jump is made, keep the head down (Figure 14.87).

Round-off. Facing the far end of the mat, take several running steps and do a skip step. Throw the arms forward and downward and place the front hand on the mat. The second hand is then placed in front and slightly forward (not on the same line) of the first hand. Both hands are turned slightly in the direction of the turn. At the same

Figure 14.81. Triple roll.

Figure 14.82. Headspring over mat.

Figure 14.83. Double roll with partner.

Figure 14.84. Fish dive.

Figure 14.85. Dive cartwheel.

time, push with the front leg and drive the other leg upward. As the legs come overhead, bring them together, turn the body, and finish with a mule kick. At the finish, the performer should be facing the opposite direction from the start (Figure 14.88).

Fifteen-second handstand. Kick into a good balance and lock. Keep the head in line and use the fingers. Point the toes and tighten the muscles through the hips with the body in a straight alignment (pencil shape).

Pitch-back flip. The top performer stands in the palms of the bottom performer. On the count of three, the top performer throws the arms straight for the ceiling and jumps with all his or her strength. The top performer then moves the upper body back slightly and forcibly brings the knees up to give rotation. As the top performer jumps, the bottom performer lifts straight up and sits back to prevent being kicked in the face. The thing to watch for in this stunt is the overthrow. Be sure to have an experienced spotter or a safety belt. This is very important. Never attempt this skill without spotting (Figure 14.89).

Pitch from belly. This is a handspring with the assistance of the bottom performer. The top performer places the stomach and upper pelvis on the bottom performer's feet. The feet are placed in a V—heels together, toes apart. The bottom performer pulls the top performer forward, and as all the top performer's weight is felt, the bottom performer pulls the top performer's upper body forward and pushes hard with the feet. As the top performer's weight passes over, the bottom performer pushes with the hands. It is important to have at least one spotter assisting so that the top performer does not overthrow (Figure 14.90). The spotter should end with a hand on the chest of the performer to prevent overrotation.

Kip from mat. While in the lying position, place the hands over the shoulders on the floor and roll back until the weight is on the back of the head and shoulders. As the body is rolled forward slightly, shoot the legs up in the air and push hard with the hands. The legs should go up and forward (Figure 14.91). The spotter should kneel, help in facilitating the leg extension by throwing the thighs, and put a hand on the back in case an assist is needed.

Figure 14.86. Tiger stand.   **Figure 14.87.** Mule kick.

Figure 14.88. Round-off.

Figure 14.89. Pitch-back flip.

Figure 14.90. Pitch from belly.

Figure 14.91. Kip from mat.

Rollover kip from mat. Start this as a forward roll. Immediately on contact of the shoulders with the floor or mat, kip as in the preceding exercise (Figure 14.92). The spotter may have to lift.

Headspring. This is executed from the top of the head. Place the head on the mat with the hands slightly forward. Keep the hips flexed as the body falls off balance. As the body rolls past center, kick hard as in the kip and push hard with the hands (Figure 14.93). The spotter may have to provide support and assist in facilitating the leg extension.

Front handspring. Take about a 5-yard (4.6-m) run, hop, and whip the hands to the mat. Kick one foot hard backward and upward and push hard with the other. Keep the head up and the arms extended. As the legs pass over the head, push with the arms and shoulders and land on the feet. Emphasize explosively passing through a handstand position with all the body parts aligned (Figure 14.94).

Back flip. Stand with the arms outstretched. Drop the arms downward in a small circular action, and flex the knees to about a quarter knee bend. Throw the arms up just short of vertical as hard and fast as possible so that the body is lifted off the floor. Jump with the arms lifted as high as possible. Keep the head in a neutral position and bring the knees up to the chest. Tuck and let out. This should never be done without a spotter. The overhead mechanic should be used (Figure 14.95).

Front flip. There are many different ways to throw this stunt, but the best is the two-arm backward-upward lift. Take two or three running steps. Use a two-foot takeoff. From the takeoff, which is executed in a one-quarter forward bend, jump hard and throw the arms with much force backward and upward. Roll over in the air into a tight tuck, and let out. Beginners can learn this by landing on two or three loosely rolled mats (Figure 14.96). Spotting can be done with a hand belt. Spotters should watch for both over- and under-rotation.

Back handspring. This is performed as though sitting on a chair. Sit with the back straight, and swing the arms down and back. Keep the feet flat on the floor. Just as the body falls off balance, whip the arms over the head; emphasize throwing the head and arms backward as a unit. As the arms are thrown back, reach for the floor and throw the belly to the ceiling. Snap to the feet (Figure 14.97). Two spotters should use a hand belt or teach using an overhead belt.

Figure 14.92. Rollover kip from mat.

Figure 14.93. Headspring.

Figure 14.94. Front handspring.

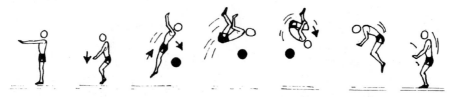

Figure 14.95. Back flip.

Figure 14.96. Front flip.

Figure 14.97. Back handspring.

TEACHING CONSIDERATIONS

1. Although the apparatus activities described in this chapter are basic to more-advanced skills, they require physical abilities not developed in many students. Particular amounts of arm strength, abdominal strength, and flexibility are necessary in many cases for students to be able to learn these skills successfully. Teachers must choose either to develop these prerequisites or to modify downward the expectations for learning. Students who attempt skills for which they do not have the prerequisite abilities create safety problems.

2. Many tumbling skills are basic to apparatus work. Because of this, many teachers choose to teach tumbling skills at first or build in tumbling skills with apparatus work. Tumbling skills permit more activity practice for larger numbers of students.

3. Checklists of skills on apparatus that go from simple to complex are often helpful for students to know what to work on and also for teachers to evaluate student progress. The emphasis must be on good form and not merely getting through an action.

4. It is often helpful to introduce a piece of apparatus to the whole group, but then use stations of different apparatus to practice. Teachers can make the decision to be at one or two stations for a period or to rotate as needed. Stations can be organized so that groups rotate at a signal from the teacher, or individuals can move freely from one station to another. Situations without teacher supervision can be assigned to a "group captain" who is a competent spotter.

5. Some students can perform some skills without spotters. Aerial skills in particular should be performed with trained spotters or should not be performed without the teacher. Instruction should continuously emphasize control of movement. Crashes and abandonment of control should never be permitted.

6. It is often desirable to have a culminating experience involving performance in gymnastics units toward which students can work. Students can choose one or two events and work to put sequences together. They can practice even the simplest moves until they perform them with smooth transitions and good form.

SUGGESTED READINGS

Ferralli, M. 2003. *A guide to beginner tumbling.* Baltimore, MD: American Literary Press.

Gruber, B. 2004. *Gymnastics for fun.* Mankato, MN: Capstone Press.

Jones, J. 2007. *Gymnastic skills: Beginning tumbling.* Mankato, MN: Snap Books.

Malmberg, E. 2003. *Kidnastics—a child-centered approach to teaching gymnastics.* Champaign, IL: Human Kinetics.

Mitchell, D., Davis, B., and Lopez, R. 2002. *Teaching FUNdamental gymnastics skills.* Champaign, IL: Human Kinetics.

National Collegiate Athletic Association. Current edition. *Official gymnastics rules.* Phoenix: College Athletics Publishing Service.

Ward, P. 1997. *Teaching tumbling.* Champaign, IL: Human Kinetics.

Werner, P. 2004. *Teaching children gymnastics.* 2nd ed. Champaign, IL: Human Kinetics. Shows how to use an innovative and individualized approach to teach gymnastics skills.

RESOURCES

Journal

International Gymnast Magazine, P.O. Box 721020, Norman, OK 73070.

Videos

United States Gymnastic Federation, P.O. Box 7686, Fort Worth, TX 76111.

See Appendix C for video sources.

WEB SITES

USA Gymnastics http://www.usa-gymnastics.org/
National Gymnastics Judge's Association, Inc.
www.ngja.org

In-line Skating

After completing this chapter, the reader should be able to:

- Appreciate the history, disciplines, and values of in-line skating
- Appreciate the significance and teach all aspects of in-line safety
- Select and maintain in-line skates and protective gear
- Introduce beginning skaters to a positive first-time experience
- Properly teach beginning and intermediate striding, turning, and stopping skills
- Demonstrate and teach agility improvement drills

HISTORY

Because in-line skating is such a convenient form of exercise and recreation and is so easy to learn, the number of nonathletes attracted to the sport exploded in the mid-1990s. Today, people of all ages are eager to gain its many recreational, social, and health benefits. Though others tinkered with placing wheels in a single row in the 1800s, modern-day in-lines were born in the early 1980s in the garage of an inventive athlete. An ice hockey enthusiast in Minnesota named Scott Olson designed the prototypes for today's in-line skates so he could use them for dry-land cross-training. He and his friends enjoyed those early models so much, they started skating for fun as well as hockey practice, and soon the recreation began to spread. With the infusion of cash from some forward-thinking investors, Rollerblade, Inc., was launched and so were the first mass-produced in-line skates.

Before long, skiers, bicyclists, speed skaters, rowers, and many other athletes began to cross-train on in-lines. In the 1990s this recreational boom generated several new competitive sports: extreme downhill trials, endurance and short-track speed events, street and ramp ("vert") competitions, and, of course, roller hockey, to name the most popular.

The International Inline Skating Association (IISA) standardized teaching techniques worldwide through its Instructor Certification Program, launched in the early 1990s. In 2006, the United Skate Schools Group (USSG) took ownership and management of the instructor certification programs in the United States, while the IISA continues as an international certifying body. Anybody planning to teach in-line skating to beginners or on a continuing basis should maintain certification through regularly scheduled programs offered by the USSG or the IISA.

The Fédération Internationale de Roller Sports (FIRS)—recognized by the IOC—lobbied hard for inclusion in the 2008 and 2016 Summer Olympics, but lost its bid in October 2009 after presenting its case along with six others to the International Olympic Committee. Despite this setback, the years of media attention resulting from the FIRS efforts yielded a greater global awareness of the athletic opportunities in roller sports. For now, competitive athletes are switching to ice skating for their chance at Olympic gold.

DISCIPLINES

Recreational/Fitness

Approximately 90 percent of the world's in-line skaters participate primarily for pleasure and fitness. Because the fluid in-line stride delivers nonimpact cardiovascular, body composition, and muscular benefits, in-line workouts are ideal for those who are interested in building and maintaining healthy bodies through sustained physical effort. Striding upright along a bike path at 8 to 12 mph, a skater can easily benefit from a workout that is comparable to biking. With practice, better balance makes it possible to assume a more aerodynamic stance and achieve a longer range of motion in the stroke; this style of skating increases the exertion to a level that compares to running.

Aggressive

Young skaters, especially boys, are often drawn to the thrills of launching off a ramp, doing aerial stunts on a quarter- or half-pipe, and curb grinding. Besides specialized equipment (or free access to public structures), aggressive skating demands precise footwork, excellent balance, and more than a little endurance, in every sense of the word (Figure 15.1).

Freestyle and Artistic

Freestyle in-line skating includes everything from line dancing to speed slalom to skate high jump. Both quad and in-line skates are used. However, with the 1997 model year, the first skates specifically designed for off-ice figure skating appeared on the market, complete with leather boots and a rolling toe stop that emulates the pick used for launching

Figure 15.1. Aggressive in-line skating.

into jumps or spins. Artistic skating competitions at the international level demonstrate an ongoing interest in this discipline.

Roller Hockey

Girls as well as boys are attracted to the fast action and excitement of roller hockey. Novices who give it a try report that the excitement generated by team dynamics, stick handling, and competitive play add up to a shorter learning curve for all striding and maneuvering skills. Players begin to think on their feet instead of about their feet. As for gear, each non-goalie player needs a hockey stick, protective gloves, helmet, a face shield and mouthpiece, hockey pants, shin guards, shoulder pads, and, for males, a jock strap and cup. Goalies need even more protective gear.

Marathons and Fitness Skating

For runners and joggers devoted to maintaining a fitness lifestyle, the thought of gliding over pavement rather than pounding it becomes increasingly appealing with each newly aching joint. Also, as experienced skaters begin upgrading to better, faster skates, they often seek instruction for achieving long, enjoyable, low-impact workouts. The growing interest in longer and harder skate workouts prompted a worldwide surge in the popularity of in-line skate marathons, with participation in the thousands at some of the most popular events.

Skate to Ski

The U.S. Ski Team and the Professional Ski Instructors Association (PSIA) discovered in-lines as a dry-land performance training program that improved the team's slalom skiing technique. Skaters who cross-train with ski poles not only become better, more centered snow skiers, they also learn how to manage both climbing and descending steeper asphalt hills.

Speedskating

In-line racing entered this decade on the urethane wheels of both ice and quad speedskating converts. It tends to cater to the elite athlete, due in part to the expense of lightweight custom boots, precision bearings, specialized wheel frames, and new or like-new wheels in sizes from 100 mm and up. Some race promoters add nonpro events such as fun rolls to their venues, which gives interested amateurs a taste of the race.

Non-Mainstream Activities

Just as the first modern-day in-line skates were invented by avid hockey players, other innovative skaters have created in-line versions of their favorite sports, including tennis, soccer, and basketball. Skating equipment has been adapted for use on unpaved terrain and for dry-land alpine and cross-country skiing, wind sailing, and downhill speed competitions.

VALUES

- Because pavement is easy to find in any town and equipment is compact, in-line skating is one of the most portable and versatile forms of fitness and recreation.
- In-line skating improves balance, strengthens every muscle from the lower back to the knees, and stimulates the upper body.
- The in-line learning curve is relatively short compared to other balance sports.
- Used for aerobic workouts, a fast pace with long strides produces a training heart rate similar to running without the high-impact penalty of joint stress.
- Used for cross-training, in-line skating can be used to complement specific and repetitive workouts geared toward improved sport-related performance.
- In-line skating is sociable, drawing participants together where the pavement quality is best. Combine fresh air, time to play, and healthy bodies, and friendships blossom naturally.
- Skating is just plain fun.

EQUIPMENT AND FACILITIES
Skates

In large cities, students may be able to find rental skates by contacting local retailers. Where rentals are not available, the best approach is to shop for new, good-quality skates that have been discounted by 30 to 40 percent. Stores do this to make space for manufacturers' annual release of newer models. Avoid shopping at a toy or discount department store because the quality of mass-market gear is horrendous. Cheap gear invariably leads to a disappointing introduction to the sport.

Shopping tips

- For children, purchase a model with features allowing it to accommodate four full sizes. These are made by the top manufacturers and retail for about $75.
- Adults should spend no less than $175 (list price) to get a decent skate. At the other end of the spectrum, beginning skaters should avoid high-end hockey or speedskates. These are too expensive and require better skills than a beginner will have for months. Usually a heel brake is not an option (Figure 15.2).
- Novices should purchase a skate with a high, molded-plastic cuff and at least one buckle at the top for good ankle stabilization.
- When trying on skates, wear a pair of thin socks manufactured specifically for athletic activity. Wear the same socks for skating to "wick" moisture away from the foot.
- Ladies' skate models are available from the better manufacturers. They usually compensate for the lower position of a woman's calf muscle and her narrower Achilles tendon. If the tag doesn't differentiate genders, the skate is probably made to fit men but sold as unisex.

Skate features

Fit. For the best performance, in-lines should fit snugly but without discomfort. With straight knees, the toes should lightly touch the end of the boot. Conversely, in the bent knee skating stance, the toes should pull away from the end of the boot as the shins press forward against the tongue.

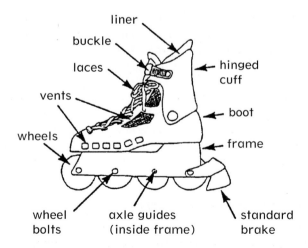

Figure 15.2. In-line skate components. (Source: From Liz Miller, 1998. *Get Rolling*. Ragged Mountain Press. Reproduced with permission of the McGraw-Hill Companies.)

When striding, the heel should be cupped by the boot so it doesn't slide up and away from the sole.

Boot materials. Molded plastic ski-style boots gave way to suede and mesh boots with plastic cuffs supporting the ankles in the late 1990s. Soft boot skates remain comfortable for a long day of skating and offer increased breathability.

Buckles or laces. Laces allow the close custom fit required by speed skating or a game of fast-action in-line hockey. Velcro "power straps" add ankle support and keep the laces tight. Buckles are convenient but often tricky.

Footbed. All good-quality skates feature preformed insoles, which are easily replaced with custom insoles or orthotics.

Wheel frames. Shorter frames are best for recreational, hockey, and artistic skating, and extended frames are built for stability at high speeds and to maximize the benefits of longer, more powerful strides. Frames can be equipped with "grind plates" to facilitate rail and curb grinding, or manufactured using the strong, lightweight composites used by speedskaters. Four-wheel frames are the most popular, although five-wheel frames were preferred for speed until 100 mm wheels came on the market in 2005.

Bearings. ABEC3 or ABEC5 precision-rated bearings are the standard on most entry-level skates. High-performance bearings (ABEC7 and above) might also feature removable shields to allow access to the inner balls and race, so that soaking in a solvent removes the grit that causes friction and loss of performance.

Wheels. A new skate's wheels feature the core type, hardness, profile, and diameter deemed to be best suited to the features of the skate on which they are mounted. When shopping for replacement wheels, you must know the maximum wheel size the skate's frame can accommodate (found in the owner's manual or printed on the wheel frame).

- Standard wheel **diameters** are: 70-72 mm for children's skates, 80 mm for hockey, 90 mm for fitness, and 100-plus mm for racing. The size is usually printed on the side of the wheel. Wheels in the low 50s and below are used on aggressive skates.
- The **profile** is the wheel's shape where it meets the road. Race wheels have the narrowest profile to reduce road drag. Fitness wheels are slightly wider to deliver a good grip on a variety of pavement surfaces. Hockey wheels are wider still to ensure stability and quick-turning maneuverability.
- Hardness, measured by **durometer** rating, dictates a wheel's shock absorption and grip qualities and is designated by a number ranging from 75 to 103 followed by the letter "A." Although softer wheels grip better and reduce vibrations on rough surfaces, they also wear out faster than harder ones.
- The **core** (also known as the hub) is a hard substance that the wheel's urethane bonds to, providing torsional stability and a solid seat for the bearings. Vented cores keep

bearings cooler at high speeds. Smaller aggressive-style wheels have no core at all, or the core might be hidden inside to provide better impact handling.

Brakes. Most standard brakes can be swapped from the right to the left skate as needed. Cuff-activated braking technology is for timid or wobbly beginners because they aren't required to balance on one foot in order to stop: all eight wheels remain on the ground. Typically, cuff-activated brakes cannot be swapped to the other foot.

Skate maintenance

Preventive maintenance is as simple as proper skate storage. The boot liners become warm and moist after half an hour of skating. To preserve boot fit, carefully arrange the tongue in its proper position, then buckle or strap the cuff closed to keep it there. This is even more important for long-term (winter) storage. Store skates in a well-ventilated area so they can dry out after each use.

Replace the brake pad once it is worn down to one-third inch or less. On most models, this is a simple matter of unscrewing the brake from the frame and inserting a new one. Usually the brake cannot be removed without also removing the rear wheel.

With time, wheels eventually begin to wear flat under the arch side of the foot. When rotating skate wheels, swap those with the most wear (usually the front and rear) with wheels showing the least wear. A scheme that works for most wear patterns is to trade wheel number 1 with wheel number 3, and wheel number 4 with wheel number 2 (Figure 15.3). At the same time, flip the wheels so that the worn-off side is mounted facing the outside ankle. During the process, wipe mud and dust from the boot and the inside of the wheel frame. Use an old toothbrush to remove grit from the outsides of the bearings.

Eventually, bearings may start making noise or become noticeably slower due to rust or extended use. This is when they are ready to be replaced. (However, for a low-end skate model, upgrading with new bearings is one way to

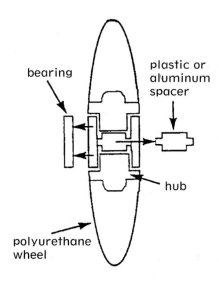

Figure 15.4. The in-line skate wheel.

improve performance.) Meanwhile, unless speedskating is the primary activity, it is not necessary to be concerned with regular bearing maintenance, although some skaters find the mechanics of the process just too fascinating to resist (Figure 15.4).

Helmet

Skate-specific helmets are offered by several manufacturers, usually providing extra coverage for the back of the head. A bicycle helmet works fine, however. No matter what the sport, the helmet should carry the ANSI or SNELL impact rating sticker. The N-94 standard was introduced in the mid-1990s to add an additional rating that withstands a series of impacts. This has been adopted by aggressive skating helmet makers.

Wrist Guards

Wrist guards offer abrasion protection for the palms, and plastic splints on the front and back prevent the wrist from hyperextending during crash landings.

Knee and Elbow Pads

A thick knee pad offers the best protection for a forward fall where the skater's body weight strikes the ground at the knees first. Elbow pads should be thick enough to take the full body weight in a sideways fall. Sleeved, slip-on pads stay in place better than those that strap on with hook and loop fasteners alone.

SAFETY CONSIDERATIONS

Basivc Skills

To ensure safety, the new skater absolutely must learn how to turn to avoid danger, how to fall properly, and how to slow down and stop. First-day skaters can learn to stride and turn on their own, but rarely learn how to use the heel brake without

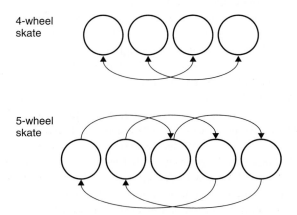

Figure 15.3. Rotation patterns to reduce wheel wear.

qualified instruction. Until they do, they remain either anxious and uncomfortable or ignorantly confident.

Protective Gear

The vast majority of in-line injuries can be prevented by wearing protective gear. The Consumer Product Safety Commission recommends that, at minimum, everyone should wear a helmet and wrist guards on every skate outing. Those items, plus knee and elbow pads, are a must for emergency stopping maneuvers, hills, and such aggressive moves as ramp skating and riding stairs. Street hockey should be played with all available safety gear; it doesn't take long to find out why.

Attitude

Unfortunately, the skaters least likely to wear protective gear have the greatest tendency to engage in high-risk behavior. According to a year-long study by the Centers for Disease Control and Prevention (CDC) using the National Electronic Injury Surveillance System, male skaters were treated for injury 30 percent more than females during the study period; for teens, the injury ratio leaped to 90 percent more for males.

The rules of the road should be prepared as class materials to educate every student about essential trail etiquette and safety habits. The following version is similar to the one originally distributed by the International In-line Skating Association and taught by certified instructors.

RULES OF THE ROAD
(SLAP: SMART, LEGAL, ALERT, POLITE)

Skate Smart

- Always wear your helmet, wrist guards, knee and elbow pads.
- Learn the basics: speed control, turning, and stopping.
- Keep all of your equipment in safe condition.

Skate Legal

- Observe all traffic regulations; on skates, you must obey the laws for wheeled vehicles.
- Skate with, not against, the flow of traffic.
- Don't "skitch." Never allow yourself to be towed by a motorized vehicle or bicycle.

Skate Alert

- Always skate in control.
- Stay away from water, oil, debris, sand, and uneven or broken pavement.
- Avoid areas with heavy traffic.
- Avoid wearing headphones or anything that makes it hard to hear.

Skate Polite

- Skate on the right side of the path and call out a warning before you pass on the left.
- Yield to pedestrians.

- Quit stroking to make room for passing cyclists (and to avoid catching a skate in their spokes).
- Be a goodwill ambassador for in-line skating.

FUNDAMENTAL SKILLS AND TECHNIQUES

Every in-line skating move involves one or more of the fundamental in-line skills: balance, pressure, upper body rotation, and edging. **Balance** starts from what is known as the ready position—a centered, bent-knee stance with weight evenly distributed over the feet. **Pressure** applied to alternate or both skates causes strides, turns, and all other skating dynamics. Varying degrees of upper-body **rotation** aid in turning when combined with **edging** or tipping the skates onto the outside, inside, or corresponding (both left or both right) wheel edges.

For the purpose of instruction without reference to right and left, the **support leg** (typically the left) is the one that is used for balance, while the **action leg** (typically the right) is stroking or performing other maneuvers. Identify nontypical students at the start of each teaching session for extra coaching if needed.

Skating Stances

Standing on dry lawn or another nonrolling surface, introduce the following in-line body positions.

Ready position. The in-line ready position is the same centered semicrouch that is used for tennis and skiing, among many other sports (Figure 15.5). Well-bent knees are the most important component of a balanced ready position, resulting in a platform of stability from which the skater can respond by moving in any direction, depending on the situation. With knees already straight, the usual upward response of a startled beginner often leads to a backward fall. Bent knees are also necessary to achieve stroke effectiveness. With straight knees, stroke power and efficiency are limited to the few inches the skate can remain in contact with the pavement.

1. Place feet shoulder-width apart.
2. Raise both hands to hip level and within peripheral vision.
3. Flex the ankles, knees, and hips to sink a few inches, keeping shoulders over hips and hips over heels. When looking downward (discouraged except for this test), the knee pads should block sight of the toes.
4. Practice the following in-line stances standing still, preferably on lawn or carpet.

A-frame. Ready position with feet wider than shoulder width, skates tipped onto inside edges (Figure 15.6).

V-stance. Ready position with heels nearly touching and toes pointed out at a 45-degree angle, with weight over heels.

A-stance. Ready position with toes nearly touching and heels pointed out at a 45-degree angle, with weight over toes.

Scissors stance. Ready position with knees together, skates parallel, with weight 75 percent over supporting leg; advance the action skate 6 to 12 inches, all wheels touching the pavement (Figure 15.7). Practice this on lawn or carpet to aid balance.

Figure 15.5. The ready position.

Figure 15.6. A-frame stance.

Balance and edging. Starting from the ready position, march in place, tip both skates onto corresponding (both left or both right) edges, and touch the toes. Make a small hop or two (if on lawn).

The Safe T

This skill allows the skater to stand stationary without rolling. Teach it before anything else to help students relax.

Figure 15.7. Scissors stance.

1. Starting from the ready position, place the skate without a brake (usually the left) so that its heel is tucked into the arch of the other skate. This places the feet in a T position. A slight angle is ok.
2. With weight evenly distributed and knees bent, roll skates backward if necessary until they feel locked together.

Falling and Getting Up

A controlled fall early in the lesson builds confidence in the protective gear and reduces the trepidation that can restrict some students' ability to progress. Encourage practice falls throughout the lesson.

1. In the ready position, move hands low and ahead of knees.
2. Fingers raised, reach forward toward the pavement until both knee pads come in contact, then finish by landing on both hands.
3. Tap both knee and elbow pads on the pavement hard enough to test the cushion. In a real skating situation, when you feel a fall coming, do your best to twist around and get your hands near your knees so you will land where the most padding is.

There are two ways to get up from the pavement. Weaker, inflexible, or obese students will require the second method.

Method 1

1. Start from "all fours," on hands and knees.
2. Lift one knee and place the skate of that foot on the pavement, close to your other knee.
3. Roll the upright skate back toward the skate still on the ground, to improve stability as you rise.
4. Leading with the head, rise straight up in one fluid motion. For added stability, place both hands on the raised knee and push down.

Method 2

1. Start from "all fours."
2. Lift one knee and place the skate of that foot on the pavement, with the thighs open at a wide angle.
3. Place both palms on the pavement between the knees, not in front of them.
4. Using the hands for support, pull the second knee forward and place that skate flat on the pavement, close to the first, wheels in a V-stance.
5. Push the hips up first, and then follow with the head and upper body.

Beginner Stride, Turn, and Stop

For the remaining skill instruction, it is assumed the skater will initiate the move from a stationary or rolling ready position, which should be reinforced throughout each lesson.

The V Walk

The purpose of this drill is to start the skater moving forward, transferring the weight from one skate to the other. Practice it on a nonrolling surface first.

1. Starting from the V-stance with toes pointing outward, take tiny steps forward.
2. Shift the weight from right to left between each short step, keeping the toes pointed out and heels as close together as possible.

Stride 1 (the beginning stride)

Stride 1 is used by all certified instructors to introduce stroking fundamentals that apply at every level of skating: weight on the heels, a lateral push, and full skate recovery before set down. But it is important to tell students that short strides are also the safest and most effective way to deal with slippery surfaces or rough uphills such as arching wood-slat bridges.

1. Building on the V walk, start pressuring the inside wheel edges at each step. That pressure results in a short glide on the support leg. The combination of pressure and glide becomes a stride.
2. Keep strides short at first to maintain balance and a slow speed. Relax into a coasting ready position if the speed picks up too much for comfort. Resist the temptation to bend forward at the waist, a common beginner's reaction that diminishes with practice and confidence.
3. Practice Stride 1 until you can build enough speed to coast 10 to 15 feet in the ready position. This qualifies you to learn proper heel-braking technique.

A-frame turn

Turning is a result of pressure along the sides of one skate's wheels, known as edging, coupled with upper body rotation.

1. Stride to gain a moderate speed.
2. Starting from a coasting ready position, push your skates into a wide A-frame stance with equal weight on both feet.
3. Rotate head, shoulders, hands, and hips toward the left, and press against the inside edge of the right skate's wheels at the same time, keeping the body centered evenly over both skates, without leaning. A turn to the left results. A typical mistake is to lean or tip the shoulders to the left, which prevents pressure on the turning (outside) skate.
4. To make a right turn, rotate the upper body to the right and pressure the left skate.

A fun drill to improve balance and coordination at this point is to have students skate in a large circle and respond to called-out instructions (e.g., play "Simon Says"). Direct them to coast in the ready position, touch their knees, toes, and then the pavement one hand at a time, if possible (getting upright in between calls). Allow them to rebuild speed as needed and use A-frame turns to turn the corners if skating in an oval pattern. Finally, from a coast, have them lift one skate and coast as far as possible on the other, an excellent balance drill and preparation for heel brake expertise. Success comes from shifting the weight fully to the support leg before lifting the action leg. Cue by calling out "shift, lift!"

Heel brake stop

Competent heel-brake technique is essential to safely deal with hills, intersections, traffic, and unpredictable crowds.

Unfortunately, the heel brake is not as easy to use as it looks. Simply raising the toe of the braking skate is not effective because the upper body tends to keep moving when the feet stop. For best results, the skater must learn how to push the brake ahead instead of down, which is not exactly intuitive.

Determine which skaters are left-handed. Most likely, they are also left-footed. It is important to get the brake swapped to the left skate early in the learning process. To help students learn how cuff-activated brakes work, have them kneel with the braking skate upright. Check to make sure the brake touches the pavement when the skater pushes the toe forward ahead of the knee. If not, lower it to ensure early success. Raise the brake later if it gets in the way of other skills.

The heel brake stop is a four-phased movement: from coasting ready position to scissors stance glide to light brake drag to a complete stop. For best results, the stance is low (bent knees), long (brake is well ahead), and narrow (skates no wider than hip width). Stress to the student "low, long, and narrow."

Note 1 for cuff-activated brake users: Stopping is accomplished in just three phases, from coast to scissors position to hip drop. The brake engages as soon as the skater achieves an effective scissors stance.

Scissors stance. Besides serving as an approach for heel brake stops, this is the best position to glide safely and easily over nasty patches of pavement, because the wheels form a longer platform that provides better front-to-back stability. (Figure 15.7).

Practice the scissors stance standing still before progressing to the rolling version.

1. Assume the ready position, with knees well bent, feet shoulder-width apart.
2. Shift weight to the support leg, keeping the braking skate in place.
3. Moving *only* your brake leg from the knee down, straighten the knee to push that skate forward. It won't go very far if your supporting knee is straight. From the side view, your lower legs should form a triangle over the pavement surface.
4. Make sure your skates are no wider than 4 inches apart and your toes are both pointing forward.

Note 2 for cuff-activated brake users: There are two versions of the scissors stance to learn. For stopping, keep the knees together but push the toe forward and down to engage the brake. This stance causes the calf muscle to move the cuff of the skate backward, which moves the brake arm down, automatically engaging the brake with all four wheels on the ground. To allow scissors coasting, separate the knees so that the lower leg remains perpendicular to the pavement, thus preventing the cuff from activating the brake.

Braking sequence. Teach and repeat each phase, advancing only after students master each turn.

1. Stride to gain a moderate speed (fast enough to stay in balance, slow enough to prevent fear).
2. **Phase 1:** Relax into a coasting ready position with hands hips high and in view. Repeat laps as needed.

Students need to be able to coast for at least 10 feet in order to learn how to stop with the heel brake. Later, this phase lasts just long enough to assume a good preparatory ready position.

3. **Phase 2:** Assume the scissors stance, shifting 75 percent of the body weight to the support leg (the one without the brake). Hold steady and continue to roll. Stride to regain speed and practice the scissors stance roll until it feels balanced, making sure to keep feet close together and both toes pointing in the same direction ("low, long, and narrow").

4. **Phase 3:** Coasting in the scissors stance, engage the brake and lightly drag it on the pavement. Repeat several times. Try to hear and prolong the light contact, but don't bother trying to stop yet. This is a balance-building drill.

   - **Standard brake:** Lift the toe of the brake skate until the rubber touches the pavement. Let it drag audibly but only very lightly on the pavement. If necessary, drop your toe to regain balance, then lift and drag again. Touch and then raise the brake several times over a long coast. Repeat until you can roll several feet while dragging the brake lightly.
   - **Cuff-activated brakes:** Press the big toe in the braking skate downward onto the pavement as you scissor that boot ahead, making sure to sink over the opposite heel rather than leaning forward over the brake. Feel the drag, and then retract the skate back under you. If the brake doesn't touch the ground when you scissor, lower the brake pad and/or shift more of your body weight to the support leg and bend that knee deeper.

5. Once you are able to brake lightly in a straight line, gradually increase the brake pressure by pushing the pad farther ahead. The only way to do this is to bend the support leg's knee.

6. **Phase 4:** To assertively finish the stop, drop your hips as though sitting down. This shoves the brake forward at the same time. Start with an upright torso, and resist bending forward by tightening up the abdominal muscles.

7. Quickly straighten up to avoid loss of balance.

To gain the most effective and instinctive heel-brake skill, make many practice stops on a line. Practice the light drag as a speed-control mechanism on gentle hills, making occasional full stops, keeping a long, low, and narrow stance.

Advanced Beginner Stride, Turn, and Stop
Stride 2 (the basic stride)

The difference between Stride 1 and Stride 2 is added pressure at pushoff and a longer glide.

1. Begin skating in Stride 1, focusing on pushing with heel pressure.
2. With torso upright, lower your hips closer to your heels by bending your knees. The stiff, lurching stride commonly seen in beginners results from throwing the arms to compensate for straight legs.
3. Try to prolong the duration of each glide by counting "one-two-three" before starting a new stroke. Think of waltz music here.
4. Attempt to recover the stroking leg fully beneath the hips before returning it to the pavement to begin a new stroke. This may prove difficult for first-time skaters who are nervous or lacking in balance.

Swizzle

The swizzle improves balance because it requires the skater to stay properly centered over both skates; it is a building block for learning how to make slalom turns and also introduces the concept of pushing to the side with the heel wheels to improve stroke efficiency for Stride 3 (Figure 15.8).

1. Standing in a V-stance, put both knee pads close together and push them 2 or 3 inches forward, letting the skates tilt onto the inside edges. The knees are bent into a "coiled" position.
2. With the torso upright, push outward against both heels; as the legs uncoil and heels separate, forward propulsion results in an A-frame stance. The more abrupt the push, the faster and farther the roll.
3. Keeping most of your weight over the heels, steer the knees and toes into a pigeon-toed position. Use momentum or inner thigh muscles to pull the skates close together again.
4. Once both skates are back under the hips, tip onto inside edges and sink to re-coil.
5. Push against both heels to start a new swizzle, which causes the body to rise as the legs straighten. Find the rhythm: kick, re-coil, kick, re-coil. Strive for a stronger push that resembles a swimmer's frog kick.

Figure 15.8. The swizzle.

Spin stop

The spin stop evolves out of the basic A-frame turn.

1. Stride to gain a moderate speed.
2. Begin a left A-frame turn by pressuring the right skate and rotating the upper body left without leaning left.
3. As the turn weights the right skate, raise the left heel (only) and balance on the left toe wheel as you pivot the heel inward. Keep the knees wide and the weight of the upper body centered between them.
4. Once you are heel-to-heel (both knees are pointed outward), return the left heel quickly to the pavement and balance your weight evenly between both thighs. A counterclockwise spin results, effectively terminating forward momentum (not recommended for stopping at high speeds).

Intermediate Stride, Turn, and Stops

Prerequisite: 20 hours skating beginning basics.

Parallel turn

The graceful parallel turn is made on one outside and one inside skate edge (corresponding edges). It is a core hockey skill and valuable for maneuvering in tight situations. This banked turn does not come easily to most first-day skaters because it requires the confidence and balance that typically only come with several hours on in-lines.

A good preparatory drill is to have students get used to coasting in a reversed scissors stance, left skate leading instead of right. The right-handed majority learns parallel turns to the left (counterclockwise) more easily.

The parallel turn is easier to learn on a slight slope—such as the drainage gutter in a parking lot—with a marker or object to swerve around.

1. Stride to gain a moderate speed, approaching the marker with arms open to the sides, airplane style.
2. Scissor the left skate forward and tuck your right knee behind the left.
3. In one assertive motion, shift your weight back onto the right tucked-under skate, while twisting head, shoulders, hands, and hips 180 degrees toward the left. This starts a turn because the twisting action forces the upper body across the left skate so that pressure is applied to the outside of the left skate's back wheel and the inside of the right skate's wheels.
4. Weight is now distributed 75 percent on the right supporting skate and 25 percent on the back wheel of the inside action skate. The upper body is tilted toward the center of the turn. Trust centrifugal force and seek its swinging pull.
5. Both skates will curve to the left, tilted onto their left edges. Straighten out once you have made a turn of at least 90 degrees.
6. Practice tightening up the turn until you can swerve close to the mark but still clear it; see if you can make a 180-degree parallel turn.

Forward crossover

Crossovers (Figure 15.9) are used to maintain or even gain speed through a corner. This skill presents a significant balance challenge because it requires the skater to lean the upper body and center of gravity momentarily outside the stable space between both feet. Crossover turns are easier to learn on a marked circle about 15 to 20 feet in diameter, such as those found on school playgrounds. Alternatively, place an object on the pavement that can serve as the center marker.

1. Begin skating in a circle at a moderate speed, traveling in a clockwise direction.
2. Outstretch both arms and rotate the upper body toward the center of the circle as though you are hugging the circle, right hand over the line ahead of you and left hand behind. The left skate's stride shortens.
3. Begin a glide on the left skate. Relax the left ankle so the left skate tips onto its outside edge. Combined with the upper-body rotation, this forces the upper body to tilt into the circle slightly.
4. Return the right skate to the pavement directly in front of the left, on the perimeter of the circle. Lift and advance the left skate, and return it to the pavement farther up the perimeter of the circle.

Figure 15.9. Forward crossover.

5. As you continue skating in a circle, gradually try to cross the right skate farther over the left skate. Beware: the more successfully you cross the right skate over the left, the faster you'll go. Stop stroking and coast if you find yourself moving too fast for comfort or begin to feel dizzy.

Backward swizzle

This easiest version of backward skating is nothing more than linked backward swizzles. Before starting any backward skating session, be sure the pavement is entirely clean of debris. Remind students to glance over their shoulders frequently during practice.

1. Standing still on the pavement, assume the A-stance with toes touching and heels angled out. The knees are bent. Skates are tipped onto inside edges.
2. Without leaning forward, push both skates' toe wheels out to the sides in one quick swipe. As the legs uncoil and the toes separate, rearward propulsion results. The more abrupt the push, the faster and farther the roll. Press your toe wheels straight out to the sides, not behind you; otherwise, you'll topple forward when you push!
3. Before your skates reach a full A-frame width, steer your heels together.
4. Once the skates are back under your hips, steer both heels outward again to achieve a new A-stance.
5. Lower your hips over both skates to begin another quick outward push against the toes.

Backward movement

1. Begin a series of rhythmic backward swizzles.
2. At the moment of the narrowest A-stance, shift most of your weight to the left skate. At the same time, begin a half-swizzle by pressuring only the right skate's toe wheel. The right skate begins its arc to the side.
3. Before the right skate passes behind your right hip, shift your weight onto it and begin to press the left skate into a half swizzle in a quick swiping motion. Make sure you keep both skates in constant contact with the ground, but apply the pressure with the toe wheels.
4. Continue alternating feet until you can get a short glide from each half swizzle.

Slalom turn

Slaloms are made on corresponding edges. Besides a thrilling way to embrace the pull of gravity once fully mastered, slaloms deliver speed control on wide downhill terrain as well as a near-perfect cross-training exercise for avid alpine-style skiers.

Slalom turns are best learned on a very gentle grade, with a long, flat run-out. Lacking a slope, stroke hard to build up speed before performing drills, or, if available, skate with a strong tailwind.

1. At slalom speed, begin coasting in the ready position.
2. Looking toward the left side of the "run," scissor the left skate forward to initiate a parallel turn to the left, with weight one-third distributed over the left skate's outside edge and two-thirds over the right skate's inside edge.
3. Midturn (when both skates are 45 degrees across the direction of travel), rotate head, hands, and shoulders to the right . . .
4. . . . scissor the right skate forward, tip onto both right corresponding edges, and swap the weight distribution so the most pressure is on the left (outside, downhill) skate.
5. Continue linking turns until the momentum or gravitational pull dies.

Once you are able to rhythmically link consecutive turns in both directions:

1. Sink into each turn by bending the knees as the skates tip onto the new corresponding edges. The resulting increased pressure on both uphill edges is what aids in speed control.
2. To initiate the next turn, rise and "uncoil" at the moment of weight shift.
3. Begin to phase out the parallel turn's upper-body rotation as much as possible, and instead, allow the edging, tipped skates to generate slalom turns as you rhythmically swap the scissors stance.
4. Practice making both big and small turns to feel the difference this makes in speed reduction. Tighter arcs deliver better speed control.

Lunge turn

Lunge turns are used in a fast-moving game of hockey or to make a wide turn at the bottom of a hill. Lunge turns are similar to parallel turns except that the skater's weight is more over the advanced skate than the behind skate (Figure 15.10).

Place an object down or mark the pavement for an imaginary corner.

1. Starting from at least 20 feet away, approach the mark at high speed.
2. About 3 feet ahead of the mark, assertively scissor the left skate forward and turn your head and upper body toward the direction of the turn.
3. Sink into a wide, low lunge as you enter the turn, making sure to center your chest over the left knee as you transfer most of your weight to that skate, tipping it onto its outside edge. The trailing leg carries enough weight to maintain pressure, with the knee slightly bent.
4. Allow centrifugal force to provide balance while both skates tip onto their left edges and press into the arc of the turn.
5. Close the gap between your skates and straighten up to resume forward momentum in the new direction.

Stride 3 (the power stride)

The skater who has achieved a competent basic stride is ready to learn a stronger, more efficient stroke. Stride 3

Figure 15.10. Lunge turn.

combines aerodynamics, proper use of the arms, stride angle and duration, and stroke initiation from the action skate's outside edge. Prepare the students with a lap of swizzles.

- **Aerodynamics:** Standing still with feet shoulder-width apart, fold both hands together, position knuckles under the chin, and touch elbows to knees. This resembles the most aerodynamic tuck used by serious speedskaters. Besides reduced wind resistance, the tuck's deep knee bend results in powerful, long strokes. Recreational skaters don't need to get quite this low. It takes most people months of practice to work up to maintaining a tuck position without back pain.
- **Arms:** The arm swing is front-to-back, not side-to-side, except for short sprints. The arm swing starts with the thumb close to the nose (bent elbow) and ends with the little finger pointing skyward (straight arm). For maximum energy conservation, the arms aren't swung, but are held close to the body with hands in the small of the back. To achieve this level of balance, start out with just one arm out of play at first.

- **Stride angle and duration:** When the support knee is bent into the tuck's deeper angle, the duration of each stroke can be longer and stronger because the stroking wheels maintain pressure on the pavement until the leg is fully extended. The stroke is pushed straight out to the side with all wheels in contact with the pavement, focusing pressure on the heel wheel. Stroking this way requires excellent one-footed balance and may not be possible in the first year of skating.
- **Outside edge:** To further maximize each stroke, the recovered skate is placed back on the pavement beyond the centerline of the direction of travel, touching down on its outside edge. The stroke, now lengthened by 1 to 3 inches, also gains power as it is pulled across the midline and rolled onto its inside edge to finish with a standard pushing stroke.

Find a teaching location that allows unhindered and fast skating for long distances. It's easier to learn Stride 3 by focusing on just one leg at first. Once a student can consistently perform it on one side, switch the focus to the opposite leg, then try it on both.

1. Begin skating at a fast pace, making long strokes with the heel wheel pressing to the side, not back. Swing the arms from front to back.
2. Begin landing just one skate across the centerline; this is Stride 3. Set down normally with the other leg (Stride 2).
3. Seek a feeling of pressure along the outside edge of the foot each time that skate hits the pavement; feel the short pull as it rolls from its outside to its inside wheel edges before the push.

180-Degree Transitions
Forward-to-backward

1. From a forward rolling coast at a moderate pace, begin a counterclockwise spin stop, riding the right skate while pivoting on the left toe wheel.
2. The moment the left heel wheel returns to the pavement (heel-to-heel with the right skate), shift your weight to the left.
3. Make the right skate parallel with the left by means of a quick pivot on the right toe wheel, finishing with the weight equally balanced on both skates.
4. Complete the transition by pushing off into backward skating.

Backward-to-forward

1. From a backward rolling coast, look over the right shoulder and, at the same time, push the right skate outward into a backward half swizzle. Transfer weight to the left skate.
2. While the hips are still sideways to the direction of travel, lift and rotate the right skate until the toe is pointing toward the direction of travel, then step forward onto it.

3. Utilize the pressure still on the left skate's inside edge to push smoothly off into a forward glide on the right skate.

Learn the following two versions of the 180-degree transition using raised arms as rotation and spotting guides; relax the arms when spotting is no longer needed. Try both movements standing still first.

Forward-to-backward pivot

1. From a forward rolling coast at a moderate pace, raise both outstretched hands to shoulder height—right hand straight ahead, left hand behind—lined up with the direction of travel. Advance the right skate slightly.
2. Eyes on your right hand, pivot lightly on both skates' *toe* wheels to rotate your hips, toes, and knees counterclockwise 180 degrees.
3. Return the heels to the pavement. Eyes and hands do not move during the entire movement. For best results, keep your knees bent and your upper-body movements smooth as you rotate the lower body.

Backward-to-forward pivot

1. From a backward rolling coast at a moderate pace, raise both outstretched hands to shoulder height—right hand straight ahead, left hand behind—lined up with the direction of travel. Without moving the positions of your arms, look over your shoulder at your left hand. Advance the right skate slightly.
2. Eyes on your left hand, pivot on both skates' *heel* wheels to rotate your hips, toes, and knees counterclockwise 180 degrees.
3. Return the toes to the pavement. Eyes and hands do not move during the entire movement. For best results, keep your knees bent and your upper-body movements smooth as you rotate the lower body.

Advanced Stops
T-stop

Skaters who have good one-footed balance are ready to try the T-stop. Be aware that this method can use up perfectly good wheels in a hurry. A heel brake is cheaper to replace and is a more effective tool when stopping really counts.

In the following T-stop drills, the support leg is the one bearing most of the weight, and the action leg is the one handling the braking activity.

1. Begin coasting in a ready position at a moderate speed.
2. Transfer all of your weight to your support leg as you . . .
3. . . . quickly lift and rotate the action skate and return all wheels to the pavement a few inches behind and perpendicular to the support skate's heel wheel.
4. Curve your tail bone forward over your supporting skate to better leverage the back skate's pressure and reduce knee stress.

5. Gradually increase the pressure on the dragging wheels by pulling the action skate closer to the balance skate.

6. Repeat the T-stop at progressively faster approaches while attempting to shorten the distance it takes your body to stop. For best results, practice stopping on a line.

Lunge stop

The lunge stop is used extensively in roller hockey. Prepare the students with lunge turning practice.

1. Skating forward at a moderate speed, fix your eyes on an object or mark on the pavement 15 feet ahead.

2. Begin a lunge turn toward the left, keeping your eyes fixed on the mark ahead of you.

3. Leaning over the left knee, begin to arc the right skate into the turn. As it swings around, begin transferring pressure from the lunging left leg onto the sharply angled wheels of the right skate.

4. Just before the right skate crosses between you and the mark on the pavement, begin to rise slightly from the lunge. This adds more pressure and friction to the extended braking leg.

Backward power slide

The power slide is used for stopping when skating backward. When accomplished correctly, this move ends in a lunge with the braking skate extended in the direction of travel, low on its inside wheel edges. Do not attempt to use the power slide to stop yourself in a high-speed emergency.

This drill uses the left leg as the support leg and the right leg as the action (braking) leg. Hips and shoulders begin facing away from the direction of travel, and finish rotated sideways 90 degrees.

1. Using your favorite backward skating method, relax into a moderately paced coast. Look over your right shoulder and spot an object or mark on the pavement 15 feet behind, in the direction of travel.

2. Drop your chest over the left knee and begin to arc the right skate out to the side and back, at the same time transferring pressure to its inside wheel edges.

3. Begin to rise from over the left leg so that you can increase the pressure on the braking leg's inside edge. Reach maximum pressure just before the right skate crosses between you and the mark on the pavement. This friction is what causes the stop.

TEACHING STRATEGIES, CONSIDERATIONS

Teaching Locations

A safe location for teaching first-time skaters is crucial. Beginners need a level, traffic-free environment for practicing their first strokes. Ideally, the first few moments on skates should be spent on carpeting or dry grass. The best outdoor site is a smooth concrete game court (basketball or tennis without the net) with a dry lawn nearby. Fine-grade asphalt parking lots are good, as long as auto traffic is blocked off with cones or other boundary markers.

Hills are the bane of the new in-line skater, and beginners must avoid them entirely until they learn how to use the heel brake or some other stopping method effectively. Even parking lots offer more than enough thrill, because, visible to the eye or not, there is always a drainage slope.

That said, a slight slope a short distance from the beginner area is a wonderful way to empower skaters near the end of a stopping lesson by having them first drag the brake lightly for speed control and, on the next pass, stop completely at a designated spot midslope.

Student Age and Previous History

As a rule, the most successful beginners have had several hours experience in ice or quad-style roller skating. Alpine or cross-country skiing is the next best previous experience because the student is already used to the gliding/sliding feeling. Lacking these, any sport that requires centered balance will help the beginner, whether it is cycling, gymnastics, snowboarding, or riding a horse. Even if it's been years since the last participation, the balance learned in the past can still be reactivated for skating. Thanks to better balance, which leads to better confidence, these students progress swiftly on the first day of instruction.

Young children and adults without a solid balance background require extra attention and tips on improving balance. For the average beginning skater, the initial awkwardness gives way to improved balance and coordination after about 20 hours on skates, as long as the time span is no greater than 6 months. Some of the intermediate skills may require a year or more to master. On the other hand, some beginners may never progress outside the learning environment or even off the non-rolling surface after hours of instruction.

Enhancing the Beginner Experience

For many beginning skaters, especially those over 30 years old, the fear of falling is the biggest hurdle. Add self-doubt, self-consciousness in front of others, lapses in concentration, or negative thoughts, and anxious novices tend to become even more awkward and prone to injury. Here are some ways to give the beginner a better sense of control:

- **Focus on safety.** Stress the benefits of wearing *all* protective gear and learning how to stop with the heel brake. Make sure the student takes a controlled practice fall early in the lesson. Bring a well-stocked first aid kit, injury report forms, and the local emergency numbers. Know the quickest route to the nearest emergency room. Maintain up-to-date CPR certification.

- **Reduce variables.** Stick with one teaching location for every skating session. Suggest that skaters practice on their own at one location until skills and confidence grow.

- **Encourage repetition.** Repeated drills build a foundation for more advanced skills later on, and this is one sport where repetition is rarely boring. To keep the learning curve in a strong upward arc, novices should practice no less than twice a week for several weeks. In many cases, they can progress beyond the basics without further instruction just by getting out on the pavement for hours of play.

- **Teaching strategies and considerations.** Skating agility and balance can always be improved. During lessons, instructors should review skills already taught through games that combine various forms of stopping, turning, or striding. Have students practice making turns around cones or chalk marks; use a broom to play limbo; call out yellow-light, red-light, and green-light, or have them stop on or near a marked location for braking practice. Drill on one-footed glides, stepping over a line or up and down a curb to reinforce one-footed balance. Have them pluck objects from the pavement while rolling by. Suggest yoga classes, balancing on one foot at all opportunities, or purchasing a wobble or rocker board.

GLOSSARY

ABEC A bearing precision rating system developed by the Annular Bearing Engineering Council: an ABEC5 bearing spins faster than an ABEC1.

action leg The leg that performs the work for a given movement, as opposed to the support leg.

A-frame stance An upright stance with skates positioned parallel and wider than shoulder width.

A-stance A version of the ready position where the toes are nearly touching and the heels are angled out.

axle guide The wheel frame inserts that can be rotated in some skate models to allow rockering the wheels or lengthening the wheelbase.

balance One of the four fundamentals of skating, balance on in-lines is achieved through life experience and proper stance using the ready position. The result is better equilibrium and confidence for learning new skills.

bearings The hardware behind a smooth-spinning wheel (two per wheel), using small balls that roll in a track called the race.

carving The act of riding one or both sets of wheel edges around the arc of a turn, commonly used in describing slalom turns.

center edge The place on the wheel that is in contact with the pavement when the skate is perpendicular to the surface.

centerline The imaginary line that bisects the direction of travel.

coasting ready position The rolling stance that results after the skater strides to attain a moderate speed (enough momentum to ensure good balance) and then rolls without striding in a balanced ready position.

coned The shaved-off state of a wheel that is worn on one side, indicating the wheel needs to be flipped over and rotated or replaced.

core See hub.

corresponding edges The outside edge of the right skate's wheels corresponds to the inside wheel edges of the left skate, and vice versa. When both skates are tipped in the same direction, they are said to be on corresponding edges.

cross-training Using in-line skating workouts to enhance performance for another sport, and vice versa.

cuff The portion of the in-line skate that encases the ankle.

cuff-activated brake A braking system utilizing a mechanism connected to the boot's hinged cuff, with a brake attached at the bottom. The brake automatically engages when the skate is pushed forward and the cuff angles back, allowing the skater to keep all four wheels in contact with the pavement.

diameter The measurement that determines wheel sizes, usually marked on the side of the wheel in millimeters.

durometer A rating system used to classify in-line wheel hardness, usually printed on the side of the wheel with a two-digit number followed by the letter A. The higher the number, the harder the wheel.

edges The portion of the wheel that contacts the pavement. There are three edges on a skate's wheels: the inside edge, the outside edge, and the center edge.

edging The act of tipping the skate onto the outside or inside edge to perform skating movements. Edging is one of the four fundamental elements of skating.

fall line On a hill, the direction with the most gravitational pull.

footbed The replaceable insole of the skate boot liner.

gliding The period of time when the skate rolls on the pavement after a stroke.

grinding Landing on the skate's wheel frame between the wheels to perform tricks like sliding across the edge of a tree planter or down a stairway banister; also performed on special apparatus during aggressive skating competitions.

half-swizzle A forward or backward swizzle performed with one action leg only; the other leg remains the support leg. Also known as sculling.

hub A hard substance that the wheel's urethane bonds to, providing torsional stability and a solid seat for the bearings.

inside edges The sides of the wheels below the foot's arch.

outside edges The sides of the wheels below the outside of the foot.

polyurethane The plastic material used to manufacture in-line wheels.

pressure The application of pressure is one of the four fundamentals of skating. Pressure application results in a wide range of skating skills when it is combined with rotation, weight transfer, and edging.

profile The wheel's shape when viewed from the edge. A wide profile results in quick-turning, slower skates; the narrowest-profile wheels are used for speed.

race The track inside a bearing around which the balls roll.

ready position The balanced alignment of the body that results in equilibrium and confidence. Feet are shoulder-width apart. Shoulders, hip joints, and arches are balanced along an invisible line that runs from head to foot through these joints. Knees and hips are flexed, hands and arms are at hip height within sight.

recovery The act of returning the skate that has just finished a stride to the proper position to push off into a new stride.

rockered A wheel configuration where the center wheels are mounted slightly lower than the end wheels, giving the skater more turning maneuverability (used in hockey and figure skating).

rotation Upper-body rotation is used for most turning skills. Rotary motion is one of the four fundamentals of skating.

safe-T The locked stance, standing still, where the brakeless heel is rolled up against the other skate's arch.

shield The exterior cover on the side of a bearing; can be permanent or removable for maintenance.

skitching Hitching a ride by grabbing onto a moving vehicle. Don't do it!

spacer The metal or plastic tube that sits within a wheel between the bearings.

Stride 1 The beginning stride, a variation that consists of short strokes with toes pointed out, used to introduce beginners to the glide and stride and to safely skate on slippery surfaces.

Stride 2 The basic in-line stride used for forward propulsion.

Stride 3 The power stride, a variation that combines an aerodynamic body position with an enhanced stroke and arm swing to maximize power and efficiency (used by fitness skaters and speedskaters).

striding The result of combining stroking and gliding.

stroking The leg action that propels the skater in forward or backward movement.

support leg The leg that bears the most weight during movements that require independent legwork. Sometimes referred to as the balance leg.

T-stop A stopping method accomplished by dragging the rear skate's wheels across the pavement perpendicular to the direction of travel.

V-stance A version of the ready position where the heels are nearly touching and the toes are pointed out.

wheelbase The length of a skate's wheel contact with the pavement.

wheel frame The chassis attached to the sole of the in-line boot into which the wheels are bolted (custom frames can be purchased for some skate models).

RESOURCES

Inline Information

Training and Travel

Camp Rollerblade, instructional camps and weekend clinics operated by Zephyr Adventures in conjunction with Rollerblade. P.O. Box 16, Red Lodge, MT 59068, 888-758-8687 toll free; http://www.CampRollerblade.com; info@CampRollerblade.com

Instructor certification programs offered in North America by the USSG and elsewhere by the International ICP.

Zephyr's MarathonSkating.com, training programs for all levels, P.O. Box 16, Red Lodge, MT 59068, 888-758-8687, http://www.marathonskating.com; info@marathonskating.com

Zephyr Skating Adventures operated by Zephyr Adventures, P.O. Box 16, Red Lodge, MT 59068; 888-758-8687 (toll free), http://www.zephyradventures.com/types-skating.htm; info@zephyradventures.com

News and Lists

About.com: Inline Skating with Carlesa Williams, Inline Skating Guide, http://inlineskating.about.com/; inlineskating.guide@about.com; newsletter, blog and forum available.

AskAboutSkating.com, Skating Forum and Chat Room Hosted by Kathie Fry, http://www.askaboutskating.com; skatelog@gmail.com

Inline Planet Skating Resources and News, editor Robert Brunson, http://www.inlineplanet.com/, info@inlineplanet.com; newsletter, forum and social network community available.

Kathy Fry's SkateLog.com, Articles and News about Inline and Quad Skating, http://www.skatelog.com/

Yahoo! Inline Instruction e-mail groups: http://groups.yahoo.com/group/inlineindustry

Organizations

General

Fédération Internationale de Roller Sports (FIRS), the international governing body of roller skating worldwide, recognized by the International Olympic Committee (IOC) since 1975. http://www.rollersports.org; info@rollersports.org

Inline Skating Resource Center (ISRC), http://www.iisa.org; info@iisa.org

National Sporting Goods Association (NSGA), 1601 Freehanville Dr. #300, Mt. Prospect, IL 60056, 800-815-5422 fax 847-391-9827, www.nsga.org, info@nsga.org; nsga1699@aol.com

Sporting Goods Manufacturers Association (SGMA), 8505 Fenton St., # 211, Silver Springs, MD 20910, 301-495-6321, fax 301-495-6322, www.sgma.com; info@sgma.com

USA Roller Sports, 4730 South St. (P.O. Box 6579), Lincoln, NE 68506-0578, Richard Hawkins, Executive Director, 402-483-7551, Fax: 402-483-1465, www.usarollersports.org, rhawkins@usarollersports.org

Aggressive

Amateur Inline League (AIL) 28621 Augusta Way, Tehachapi, CA 93561 www.inlineleague.com; office@inlineleague.com

World Rolling Series (WRS) www.worldrollingseries.com

Camps

Barry Publow Speedskating Workshops, 263 Front, Gatineau, Quebec, Canada J9H 6Z9 819-684-1528; http://www.breakawayskate.com/speedcamp/; barryp@breakawayskate.com

Camp Rollerblade, operated by Zephyr Adventures in conjunction with Rollerblade, P.O. Box 16, Red Lodge, MT 59068, 888-758-8687 (toll free) http://www.camprollerblade.com; info@camprollerblade.com

Eddy Matzger Skate Farm Camps for advanced fitness and speedskating techniques; 727-458-4420, www.skatecentral.com/page29.html;skatefarm@skatefarm.com

Woodward Camps, in California, Colorado, Pennsylvania, Beijing, China; and Wisconsin, www.woodwardcamp.com/inline

Freestyle

USA Roller Sports, 4730 South St. (P.O. Box 6579), Lincoln, NE 68506-0578, Richard Hawkins, Executive Director, 402-483-7551, Fax: 402-483-1465, www.usarollersports.org/; rhawkins@usarollersports.org

International Freestyle Slalom Association founded to promote the sport of freestyle slalom, speed slalom, and skate high jump. http://www.ifsasports.org/

Hockey

North American Roller Hockey Championships (NARCh), 521 Hidden Ridge Court #B Encinitas, CA 92024, 760-943-0049; darym@narch.com; www.narch.com

USA Hockey Inline, 1775 Bob Johnson Dr., Colorado Springs, CO 80906-4090, info@usahockeyinline.org, 800-888-4656, Fax: 719-538-1189, www.usahockey.com.

Hybrid sports

Roller Soccer International Federation, P.O. Box 423318, San Francisco, CA 94142-3318, Zack Phillips, 415-864-6879, www.rollersoccer.com; RSIF2@rollersoccer.com

WindSkate, P.O. Box 3081, Santa Monica, CA 90404, Jamie Budge, 310-829-9511, www.windskate.com, info@windskate.com

Speedskating

Amateur Speedskating Union (ASU), National Office: P.O. Box 450639, Westlake, OH 44145, Carol Bongers, ebongers@usspeedskating.org, 440-899-0128; www.speedskating.org

National In-line Racing Association (NIRA), 3234 So. Meridian, Wichita, KS 67217, Joe Cotter, Executive Director, www.sk8nira.com; nira@aol.com

USA Roller Sports, 4730 South St. (P.O. Box 6579), Lincoln, NE 68506-0578, Richard Hawkins, Executive Director, 402-483-7551, Fax: 402-483-1465, www.usarollersports.org; rhawkins@usarollersports.org

Trail Advocates

Rails-to-Trails Conservancy, HQ, 2121 Ward Ct. NW 5th Floor, Washington, DC 20037, 202-331-9696 www.railtrails.org

The Transportation Policy Project (TEA-21), 2121 Ward Ct. NW 5th Floor, Washington DC 20037; 888-388NTEC.

Printed Publications

Aggressive

BE-MAG print and PDF magazine, blog, online community; subscribe at http://www.be-mag.com/

One Magazine, San Diego / Los Angeles; subscribe at http://www.believeinone.com/; 800-284-3563.

McKenna, A. T. 1999. *Aggressive in-line skating.* Capstone Press, www.amazon.com (book, youth).

Roberts, Ben, Rainger, Tim, and Powell, Ben. 1999. *In line skating.* Barron's Educational Series, www.amazon.com (book, youth).

Kaminker, Laura 1999. *In-line skating! Get aggressive.* Rosen Publishing Group, www.amazon.com (book, youth).

Artistic

How to jump and spin on in-line skates by Jo Ann Schneider Farris, 1999. 1st Books Library, www.amazon.com. (book)

Fitness

Bradley, C. 1994. *Skate fit: The complete in-line skating workout.* New York: ABA, Inc. (video)

Humphrey, R. *Rollerdancing:* San Francisco: Movement in Motion Productions (606 Head St., San Francisco, CA 94132) Lessons 1-11 (Separate DVDs)

Nottingham, S., and Fedel, F. 1997. *Fitness in-line skating.* Champaign, IL: Human Kinetics. (book)

Hockey

USA Roller Sports-The Magazine, P.O. Box 6579, Lincoln, NE 68506-0579; 402-483-7551, ext 33.

Recreational

Miller, L. 2003. *Get Rolling: the beginner's guide to inline skating.* 3rd ed. Get Rolling Books, www.getrolling.com or www.amazon.com. (book)

Powell, M., and Svensson, J. 1998. *In-line skating.* 2nd ed. Champaign, IL: Human Kinetics. (book)

USA Roller Sports-The Magazine, P.O. Box 6579, Lincoln, NE 68506-0579; 402-483-7551, ext. 33.

Speedskating

Speed on skates: A complete technique, training and racing guide for in-line and ice skaters by Barry Publow, 1999. Champaign, IL: Human Kinetics (book).

USA Roller Sports-The Magazine, P.O. Box 6579, Lincoln, NE 68506-0579; 402-483-7551, ext. 33.

16 Jogging and Walking

After completing this chapter, the reader should be able to:

- State the guidelines for starting a jogging and walking program
- Select and care for proper jogging and walking equipment, particularly shoes and clothing
- Demonstrate correct running and walking form
- Construct a proper training schedule according to one's goals
- Prevent and treat jogging injuries
- Teach fundamental jogging and walking principles and skills
- Explain the difference between fitness walking and racewalking
- Explain the two basic rules of walking as a competitive sport

JOGGING

The popularity of jogging as a fitness activity has steadily progressed over the last 40 to 50 years. During the early 1960s, most organized jogging activities were directed by the YMCA, boys clubs, or college physical education programs. The physiological benefits of jogging were not widely known until a scientific study by Dr. Kenneth H. Cooper (Major, USAF Medical Corps) demonstrated a positive correlation between heart rate and oxygen consumption. He suggested a variety of types of exercise and explained how each helped build one's cardiorespiratory fitness. Cooper differentiated activities based upon the primary energy source required during their performance and substantiated the major role that aerobic activities, such as jogging, play in increasing cardiorespiratory fitness.

As the American public became increasingly fitness conscious, the high visibility of successful U.S. athletes such as Frank Shorter, Bill Rogers, Alberto Salazar, Mary Decker, and Joan Benoit Samuelson helped stimulate interest in jogging and running. The emergence of a number of running magazines and the writings of such authors as Jim Fixx, David Costill, Bill Bowerman, Fred Wilt, and George Sheehan helped to present the benefits of jogging to the ever increasingly fitness-conscious American public during the '70s and '80s. With this push, jogging moved into the mainstream of American pastime activities. The last 10 years have brought a number of new faces into the spotlight as a new set of American distance runners have emerged. This new, up-and-coming group has set a number of new American records and has won major medals in international races. This new group is comprised of the likes of Galen Rupp, Ryan Hall, Dathan Ritzenhein, Bernard Lagat, and Meb Keflezighi on the men's side and Deena Kastor, Shalane Flanagan, and Kara Goucher on the women's side. Media coverage has helped to increase the visibility and popularity of running events. Race Director Fred Lebrow, of the New York City Marathon, helped bring distance running into the public eye and led the way by bringing this event to television. The advent of this national attention and thousands of participants helped to bring other running events to live national television and Internet coverage.

Many national health organizations have started to use the popularity of running to help sponsor training programs and fund-raising in conjunction with popular road racing events. These programs enable individuals to train with others of similar ability and receive some running tips. The Internet has also created a new avenue for individuals in the running community. One is now able to find a complete array of running-related sites that provide free or paid running information (e.g., coaching tips, training programs, eating and drinking guides, injury treatment, stretching and strength training). Be sure to check the references at the end of this chapter.

Jogging may attract some individuals as a means of improving health and reducing the risk of heart disease. Others may be looking for a means of losing weight or reducing stress in their daily lives. And yet others find that jogging builds self-esteem and makes them feel good. Some are attracted to the social atmosphere often associated with many running events and participating in a type of activity where there is the potential to challenge oneself and others. Whatever the reason, jogging facilitates the improvement of one's quality of life.

GETTING STARTED

Jogging is usually defined as running slowly at a comfortable pace of about 9 to 12 minutes per mile. Running is an individual activity, so some will be able to run farther and faster than others with about the same effort. A good guideline for the beginning runner is to utilize the talk test: run just fast enough so that you are still able to carry on a conversation.

Running need not be a form of self-torture. To have a successful running experience, a sensible program should be initiated. The following guidelines are applicable to almost everyone:

1. Consult your physician before initiating any type of exercise program. This guideline increases in importance with an increase in age. You should answer the questions found in a general preparticipation health screening form, such as the Physical Activity Readiness Questionnaire (PAR-Q), before beginning a moderately intensive exercise program such as jogging. A diagnostic exercise test is generally not essential for apparently healthy men under 45 years of age and women under 55 if the exercise program is going to begin at the moderate-intensity level. This means exercising at 60 to 74 percent of one's maximal heart rate (see the General Suggestions section), an RPE (rating of perceived exertion) of 11 to 13 (very light to somewhat hard), or 40 to 60 percent of VO_2max (maximum oxygen capacity). Exercising at this level should be well within the individual's cardiorespiratory capacity and sustainable for about 60 minutes.

2. Start slowly. If you overdo it, your first day will probably be your last.

3. Be consistent. Set up a practical routine, and stick with it for at least 6 to 8 weeks. Jogging every other day gives the body time to recover from the previous workout.

4. Listen to your body. It will reveal your limits. Try not to become overly competitive and exceed those limits. If you become sore, back off for a day or two.

5. Take walking breaks frequently during the first few runs. Warm up and cool down by walking.

6. Get a pair of comfortable, properly fitting shoes (see next section). Clothing will be dictated by common sense and experience.

7. Do not always gear your schedule to how far you can run. Try using time as a guideline and increase your total time by no more than 10 percent per week. Start with as little as 5 minutes of walking and 5 minutes of easy running. Increase the time slowly, trying not to strain. By gearing your program to time, you allow the body to work to its own limits. Disappointment will not be part of your program when you fail to cover a set number of miles or kilometers.

Running can be enjoyable if it is done with a positive frame of mind.

SHOE SELECTION

Individual needs and requirements vary greatly from individual to individual, so one type of shoe cannot be recommended for everyone. Some things to be considered in your shoe selection are: comfort and shock absorption, body size and running-style mechanics, and skill and competitive level.

The running shoe (Figures 16.1 and 16.2) is designed to provide protection while leaving running motion unencumbered, so keep in mind that proper selection of a training shoe is essential for avoiding injuries while ensuring maximum performance and comfort.

As you begin the selection of a pair of running shoes, there are a number of factors that will assist in this process. You should identify your anatomical features, such as your arch structure and your gait. To determine your arch structure, you could perform the "wet test." Take a shallow pan or

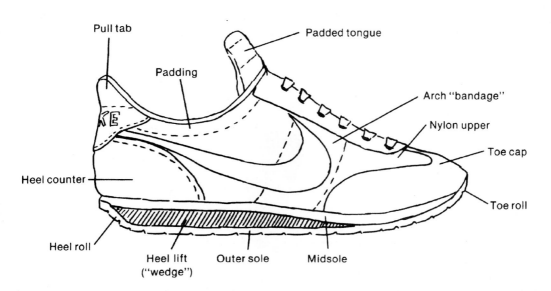

Figure 16.1. Anatomy of a running shoe.

Figure 16.2. Running shoes.

cookie sheet, which you can fit your foot into, and fill it with water. Then step into the pan to get the bottom of your foot wet, and then step on a bag or a surface where you can see your foot imprint. Look to see if you have a high, normal, or flat arch (Figure 16-3).

Checking the wear on the soles of your shoes will usually give you some good information about your normal gait. The soles will provide you with information about whether you are an overpronator or underpronator (supinator). If you are an overpronator (flat arches), then your feet roll excessively inward and your shoes will wear on the inside of your forefoot and heels. Look for a stability or motion-control shoe. If you are an underpronator (high arches), you don't roll inward or you land and run on the balls of your feet and the wear will be on the outside of the shoes. Look for a shoe that has a neural control or extra cushioning. If you have normal pronation (normal arch), you would see normal wear on the middle of the ball of the foot and the heel. You can select a shoe with normal cushioning.

Seek the assistance of a running shoe specialist, one who offers a wide variety of brands and models, during your selection of your first pair of running shoes. Try on several varieties and lace them up for a run. Check the shoes for minor defects (which are common in this age of mass production), and then take them out for a short run. Take your time in making a selection. Remember that major shoe manufacturers have a shoe selection guide on their website that will help guide you to the best shoe for you. They will utilize a number of specific characteristics of your running to help select the shoe best for you. Check this out before your visit to the store and it will help to narrow your shoe selection.

If you have orthotics, be sure that they fit in the shoes. You may have to pull out the sock liner to make room for them. You should also be sure to wear the same type of socks that you normally run in when selecting your shoes. You should have about a thumb's width between the toe of the shoe and your longest toe for a proper fit. Shoes that are too tight or too large will lead to blisters and will be uncomfortable.

Set your own requirements, keeping these questions in mind: Are you heavy on your feet, or do you run lightly with good form? What type of terrain will you run on (trails, roads, or grass)? Are you strictly a fun runner, or are you training for a specific distance or time? Find the shoes that fit your needs and buy the pair that fits your feet best.

Width sizing has become popular with the expansion of the running-shoe market in the past few years. Price is also a factor, but one should remember that high cost does not ensure a good fit or quality.

A good pair of shoes are a runner's most critical investment (outside of time), yet they are not a cure-all. The anatomy of your foot may call for something not offered by today's mass-produced shoes. If you cannot find shoes that fit comfortably, you may need to seek professional help from a qualified podiatrist or orthopedist.

Reserve your running shoes for running. Using them for casual wear causes different wear patterns, which will affect the life of the shoe.

normal
arch

flat
arch

high
arch

Figure 16.3. Various arch types.

Beginners should purchase a pair of training shoes. They offer more cushioning than a racing shoe. Always remember that it is important to wear high-quality socks when jogging. Socks capable of wicking moisture away from the feet are a must.

RUNNING FORM

Many people believe long-distance running requires little or no skill. Simple observation of different runners shows that some seem to float along almost effortlessly, whereas others pound along, struggling with each step and exhibiting contorted expressions. The obvious difference is cardiovascular conditioning, but technique and efficiency of movement are also involved to a great extent and require skill and practice.

Distance running is a natural activity, so a runner should do what comes naturally, as long as it is mechanically sound. The slower a runner travels, the easier it is to get away with poor form. Problems arise when the tempo is increased and mechanical inefficiencies become compounded by the increase in speed.

Foot Placement

The slower you go, the flatter the landing. Try to land lightly and gently; do not pound. As you run faster, you move higher on the foot, toward the toes. All runners land first on the outside edge of the foot, then roll inward. This absorbs shock. The precise point of contact varies with speed.

Stride

Stride is a function of speed. The short stride is more economical and also slower. As the pace increases, so does the length of stride. Keep in mind that you should lead with the knee first. The foot should follow and extend to meet the ground. Do not overstride; keep your feet under you. The point of foot contact should be directly under the knee, with the knee slightly flexed.

Body Carriage

Run tall and with a straight back (Figure 16.4). The head should remain level. Do not look at the sky or at your feet, but instead out in front of you about 10 to 15 feet (3 to 4.5 m). This approach ensures an erect, balanced running stance. The head should be in line with the trunk and the trunk in line with the legs.

The hips should be directly over the legs. Try not to "sit" or lean forward. A runner tends to "sit" when fatigue sets in, and this leads to a shorter, mechanically inefficient stride (Figure 16.5).

The arms should play an active role in running. They are there for balance and driving and should not be ignored. Arms help the legs go faster as long as they remain rhythmic. Hold the hands loosely cupped and relaxed, palms turned inward. Bend the elbow 90 degrees and bring the arms parallel to each other, slightly inward but not across the midline

Figure 16.4. Good running form.

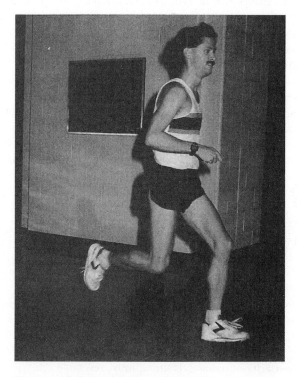

Figure 16.5. Runner who is "sitting."

of the chest. The hands should swing back, but not past the midline of the trunk. When a runner starts to fatigue, the hands and arms are no longer relaxed and they are much closer to the body. This is the time to drop the arms to your side and shake them out.

The best time to practice technique is during a short afternoon run. Stride six times over 50 to 60 yards (45 to 55 m) on a smooth, grassy surface, concentrating on any problem. Have someone watch you run several times and then make suggestions. All runners have innocent quirks in running styles that are their trademarks. If these quirks do not affect mechanical efficiency, they should be left alone.

TRAINING

Along with the increase in the number of joggers in the country, there has been a large increase in the availability of races in which to participate. Almost every weekend, a run is sponsored by some organization. Some are for serious runners, some for fun, some for raising money for charitable causes, and some for recognizing local traditions. Although it is possible to be a jogger and never enter a race, these events are motivational, much like the recital that piano teachers use to motivate students to continue practicing. These races also can be enjoyable social events. If you desire to enter a race, it shouldn't be done without advance preparation and training for the event's demands.

The word *training*, like the word *jogging*, can be ambiguous. The difference is sometimes artificial. Training indicates effort toward completing a specific distance or race; jogging is usually done on a more casual basis for fitness or health reasons.

There are several methods of starting training. Most are fairly simple. There are guiding principles, terminology, and systems of training for the beginning racer or jogger.

Fundamental Principles of Training

Four major components are necessary for the development of cardiorespiratory fitness: *mode of the exercise* (e.g., jogging or running); *frequency* (how often you do the activity; generally three times per week is the minimum); *intensity* (how hard you are working, or percentage maximum heart rate; generally 50 to 90 percent of maximum heart rate); and *duration* (length of time of workout; generally more than 20 minutes).

Stress. The body must adapt to stress if it is to improve its general condition. Training stimulates the type of stress the body will encounter during a race. A fine line separates training from stress and strain during the run.

Overload. Overload means taking on a little more work than is comfortable. It should be done for brief periods at first, perhaps every other day. Stretch your limits gradually. If done too quickly, it can result in injury or at least soreness.

Specificity of training. Training must resemble the type of race you are preparing for in both speed and distance.

Consistency. Body systems get into shape by regular training. Do not do a super workout one day and then be unable to walk the next. Be consistent.

Recovery. The body must be given adequate time to rejuvenate itself. Continuous hard training will bring you down eventually. Rest is just as important as exercise.

Pacing. Establish a long-view approach toward running. Both in races and training, focus on gradual improvement. At first, improvement comes quickly as mileage piles up. *Remember:* More does not always mean better.

Running surfaces. The surface that you run on will influence the amount of force that your body must absorb. Running on cement provides the greatest amount of stress. Cement has very little give and is very hard on the legs. Running on paved roads is a little less stressful than cement. Most modern running tracks are a little softer than running on the roads. A dirt or cinder track, grass, or a wood-chipped trail would provide the least amount of stress on the legs. Stay away from running in the sand along a beach, if you are just beginning. This type of surface is generally very uneven and requires a great deal of extra energy. The same would be true of trying to run in the snow. This surface can be very dangerous even with shoes that have excellent tread. Changing the type of surface that you run on can provide your legs with some needed stress relief. Selecting the proper surface can make your training program more enjoyable and reduce the possibility of injuries. Remember that as you increase your total time running, you are also increasing the amount of stress on your body.

Training Schedules

Individualize your training schedule. Find a system that fits your lifestyle and makes your running a part of you for the rest of your life. Keep yourself happy and eager. It is important to keep in mind that every workout should begin with an easy warm-up, followed by 10 to 15 minutes of static stretching, jogging, a cooldown, and some additional stretching. Do not increase your weekly mileage by more than 5 to 10 percent at one time. You will find that small increases are much easier for the body to handle than large increases. Undertrain rather than overtrain. Your daily workouts should alternate between hard/easy days to provide some recovery for the body. Too much hard training leads to injury and setbacks.

Another point that may help lessen the potential for injury in your training program is to reduce your training volume every fourth week. This will give your body a little better chance to recover and adapt to the training.

The warm-up and cooldown are very important parts of your workout. Before the muscles of the body are ready to begin an increased level of use, there must be sufficient time for the muscles to warm up and to increase the blood flow to these muscles. After 5 to 10 minutes of easy moving, you should spend an equal period of time in static stretching to increase or help maintain flexibility. A static stretch should be taken to the point where you can feel the stretch, but not to the point of pain. After holding the stretch for 10 to 20 seconds, relax and repeat the stretch two to four times. One generally starts with the larger muscle groups and works toward the smaller muscles (see the section "Beneficial Stretches and Resistance Training" for examples). A short period of time stretching should help reduce the potential for muscle strains and soreness. By the same token, the cooldown after a workout, where there is a gradual decrease in the level of activity, allows the body a period of recovery. The cooldown allows the muscle pump to keep the blood circulating and helps disperse a large portion of the built-up metabolites. Culminating the workout with a short stretching period will again help to increase one's flexibility.

Three different programs (beginner, intermediate, and advanced) are provided here as guides for developing your own jogging program. Each program will have a different focus and level of fitness required for successful completion. Remember to keep the goals for your jogging program realistic and practical. It should be fun and something that you look forward to.

Beginner program

The beginner program assumes that you have not had any prior training or have not trained for the last 6 months. Keep in mind that you want to find a level area to begin your jogging program. Running up and down hills in the beginning of a program may place too much stress on your joints and ligaments. If you are very overweight or your cardiovascular fitness is extremely low, you may want to begin with a 4- to 6-week walking program before starting to jog. See the section on walking later in this chapter.

The beginner program starts with a combination of walking and easy jogging done every other day. You can use a number of different methods (time, distance, steps) to monitor your training program. Select the one that is easiest for you and use it to guide your program.

Counting steps. When counting steps, it is easier to count only the number of times that one foot strikes the ground. Start with 5 to 10 jogging steps, followed by 5 to 10 walking steps. Repeat this cycle for 20 to 30 minutes. Be sure to monitor your heart rate and keep it at the lower end of your target heart rate (the method for determining your target heart rate is presented later in this chapter) or keep in mind the "talk test." This activity should not be labored activity. In the second week, increase the jogging to 15 to 20 steps, followed by 5 to 10 walking steps, for a total of 20 to 30 minutes. By week three, you should be able to jog for 25 to 40 steps, followed by 5 to 10 walking steps, for the full 20 to 30 minutes. In each succeeding week, try to increase the time that you jog before having to add the short walking segment. In a few months, you should be able to go a full 20 to 30 minutes without any walking and start working to increase the intensity of the runs.

Time. Start with 10 to 15 seconds of jogging, followed by 10 to 15 seconds of walking. Repeat this cycle for 20 to 30 minutes. Follow the same guidelines as previously mentioned. In the second week, increase the jogging to 20 to 30 seconds, followed by 10 to 15 seconds of walking, for a total of 20 to 30 minutes. By week three, you should be able to jog for 30 to 40 seconds, followed by 10 to 15 seconds of walking, for the full 20 to 30 minutes. In each succeeding week, try to increase the time that you jog before having to add the short walking segment.

Distance. This method requires that you have an area that is marked off for distances. This could be a running track, or a street with driveways, or telephone poles along the road. Start with jogging a specific distance, followed by walking for the same distance. You could start by jogging from one driveway to the next and then walking until you reach the next. Repeat this cycle for 20 to 30 minutes. Again, follow the same guidelines as given previously. In the second week, increase the distance that you jog, followed by the same walking distance as used in week 1, for a total of 20 to 30 minutes. By week three, you should be able to jog for three driveways, followed by walking for one driveway, for the full 20 to 30 minutes. In each succeeding week, try to increase the distance that you jog before having to add the short walking segment. In a few months, you should be able to go a full 20 to 30 minutes without any walking and start working to increase the intensity of the runs.

Intermediate program

The program for an intermediate jogger incorporates different training methods (Table 16.1). Training is carried out 4 days a week for 30 to 60 minutes per workout. This type of program is for someone who is interested in participating in an occasional road race in the 5K to 10K (3.1 miles to 6.2 miles) range. The program is based upon a 12-week preparation period for a road race, but the basic pattern can be used for longer or shorter preparation periods. The program for each week starts with a workout day, followed by a day off, followed by two consecutive days of training, followed by another day off, followed by a day of training, and finally a day off. The first 3 weeks are directed toward building a running base. The runs should not be hard, but work at a level where you can carry on a conversation throughout the run (the "talk test"). Use the fourth week as a recovery week.

The next 4-week cycle adds to the base that has already been created and adds some faster-paced runs into the workout schedule (Table 16.2). Now is a good time to introduce some "fartlek" training (see "Types of Training Systems") and some faster-paced repeats into your workout schedule. Alternating between a fast and a slow pace is repeated throughout the workout. The 400 m (366 yds) repeats (6 to 10) are done at a faster pace than you are normally accustomed to running. Each repeat is followed by an easy jog for the same distance.

Table 16.1. INTERMEDIATE TRAINING PROGRAM: FIRST 4-WEEK CYCLE

Training day	Week 1 time	Week 2 time	Week 3 time	Week 4 time
Day 1	20 minutes	22 minutes	25 minutes	20 minutes
Day 2	20 minutes	25 minutes	30 minutes	25 minutes
Day 3	20 minutes	20 minutes	25 minutes	20 minutes
Day 4	30 minutes	35 minutes	40 minutes	35 minutes

Table 16.2. INTERMEDIATE TRAINING PROGRAM: SECOND 4-WEEK CYCLE

Training day	Week 5 time	Week 6 time	Week 7 time	Week 8 time
Day 1 fartlek workout	25 minutes	27 minutes	30 minutes	25 minutes
Day 2	20 minutes	25 minutes	30 minutes	20 minutes
Day 3 400 m repeats	25 minutes (6 × 400)	30 minutes (8 × 400)	35 minutes (10 × 400)	20 minutes (6 × 400)
Day 4	40 minutes	45 minutes	50 minutes	35 minutes

Table 16.3. INTERMEDIATE TRAINING PROGRAM: THIRD 4-WEEK CYCLE

Training day	Week 9 time	Week 10 time	Week 11 time	Week 12 time
Day 1 Intervals	25 minutes (5 × 800)	27 minutes (6 × 1000)	30 minutes (6 × 800)	25 minutes (5 × 1000)
Day 2	20 minutes	25 minutes	30 minutes	20 minutes
Day 3 High-intensity runs	25 minutes (6 × 1000)	30 minutes (5 × 1200)	35 minutes (4 × 1600)	20 minutes (Easy)
Day 4	40 minutes	45 minutes	50 minutes	Race

The last 4 weeks of the 12-week program introduce some intervals and longer, faster-paced running (Table 16.3). The duration of the runs will not increase, but the intensity will be at a slightly higher level. The intervals should be 800 to 1200 m (732 yds to 1097 yds) at a 5K-race pace, with a 4- to 5-minute recovery between each interval. The high-intensity runs should vary in length, but be over 800 m (732 yds), and a little slower than your 5K-race pace. The recovery time between high-intensity runs should be rather short (1 to 1½ minutes).

By the time you finish this 12-week program, you should be able to finish a 5K or 10K road race.

Advanced program

A program for the advanced jogger—one who has been training for months and who is now interested in preparing for a 10- to 26.2-mile (marathon) run (16.1 to 42.3 km)—will now increase the number of days of training and the total time and mileage. The overall program can be based upon time or a combination of time and mileage, with more than one workout per day.

A time-and-mileage program might look like this:

Sunday. Long, easy run of 15 miles (24 km) or 1½ hours on a relatively flat terrain.

Monday. *Morning:* Easy 40-minute run. *Evening:* Brisk 45-minute run, followed by 8 to 10 strides on grass. Stretch and cool down. Do abdominal exercises.

Tuesday. *Evening:* Medium to hard 1-hour run on fairly hilly terrain. Start easy, finishing with a long, hard, sustained pace. Be sure to cool down.

Wednesday. *Morning:* Easy run of 3 to 5 miles (5 to 8 km). *Evening:* 40-minute run, according to the way you feel.

Thursday. *Morning:* 40-minute run. *Evening:* Fartlek workout over hills, changing the pace often; 1 hour total time.

Friday. *Evening:* Brisk 45-minute run.

Saturday. Try to find a race over 3 miles (4.8 km). Set a predetermined goal. Experiment with pace. *Afternoon:* Easy run of 4 to 5 miles (6.5 to 8 km).

This sample workout is equal to about 70 miles (113 km) a week, adequate even for a marathon of less than 3 hours.

In a time-based program, each week has one long run, a day of rest, and the other 5 days done at a comfortable pace. For the 14 weeks leading up to a long run or marathon, you should alternate the length of the long run to allow you to increase your mileage slowly and give you time to recover during the following week. The typical training program is illustrated in Table 16.4

Table 16.4. ADVANCED TRAINING PROGRAM: TIME-BASED

Week number	Time		
	Days 1 to 5	Day 6	Day 7
1	25–35 minutes	60 minutes	Rest
2	25–35 minutes	90 minutes	Rest
3	25–35 minutes	60 minutes	Rest
4	25–35 minutes	110 minutes	Rest
5	25–35 minutes	60 minutes	Rest
6	25–35 minutes	130 minutes	Rest
7	25–35 minutes	60 minutes	Rest
8	25–35 minutes	150 minutes	Rest
9	25–35 minutes	60 minutes	Rest
10	25–35 minutes	170 minutes	Rest
11	25–35 minutes	60 minutes	Rest
12	25–35 minutes	180 minutes	Rest
13	25–35 minutes	60 minutes	Rest
14	25–35 minutes	75 minutes	Rest

Table 16.5. RACE PACE PROJECTIONS

Min/mile	5000 m	10,000 m	Half-marathon	Marathon
6:00	18:36	37:12	1:18:36	2:37:12
6:30	20:09	40:18	1:25:09	2:50:18
7:00	21:42	43:24	1:31:42	3:03:24
7:30	23:15	46:30	1:38:15	3:16:30
8:00	24:48	49:36	1:44:48	3:29:36
8:30	26:21	52:42	1:51:21	3:42:42
9:00	27:54	55:48	1:57:54	3:55:48
9:30	29:27	58:54	2:04:27	4:08:54
10:00	31:00	1:02:00	2:11:00	4:22:00
10:30	32:33	1:05:06	2:17:33	4:35:06
11:00	34:06	1:08:12	2:24:06	4:48:12
11:30	35:39	1:11:18	2:30:39	5:01:18
12:00	37:12	1:14:24	2:37:12	5:14:24

You are now ready for a marathon or other long run during the next week. You should make sure to run easily during the first 3 days of the week and possibly take 2 days off before the race or, instead, run very easily. Some extra carbohydrates in your diet before a race of this length would also be beneficial. Using time as the basis for your program will allow you to individualize your training and respond to the way your body feels. If you feel good, cover more miles. If you need more time to recuperate, run fewer total miles. Get to know your fatigue symptoms because continual overstress will result in a reverse training effect. Table 16.5 provides an approximate race pace projection guide for different race distances if one were to maintain the same race pace throughout the entire race.

Beneficial Stretches and Resistance Training

There are a number of good stretches and some basic resistance training exercises that can easily be added to your program. These exercises can help you develop a little additional flexibility and strength to aid you in this new endeavor. It is a good idea to do your stretching after you have warmed your muscles up and after your cooldown. Each stretch should be held for 10 to 30 seconds and repeated a second time. Hold the stretch to the point where you can feel the stretch, but not to the point of pain. Try to stretch the larger muscles first and then move to the smaller muscle groups. It is a good idea to stretch every day. Here are some stretches that should help with your running program:

1. Lower back
2. Upper back
3. Groin
4. Hamstring
5. Hurdlers
6. Quads
7. Lower leg
8. Calf
9. Shoulders
10. Triceps
11. Ankle
12. Neck

Your resistance exercises should be done after your workout is completed. Some of these exercises require only the use of one's own body, or some homemade implements. You don't have to purchase any expensive equipment to get results. These resistance exercises will add a little strength without muscle bulk. If you need some weights, you can fill plastic milk containers with water or sand. Start with a small amount and gradually add more as your strength increases. Strive to do one to two sets of 10 to 15 repetitions of each exercise unless otherwise advised. These exercises are generally done only 2 to 3 times per week, with a day of rest between each workout. Try these out.

1. Sit-ups: Work up to 35. These can be done every day or every other day.
2. Push-ups: Work up to 25. These can be done every day or every other day.
3. Lunges: Forward. Step forward and extend so that your front knee is at a 90-degree angle. Don't extend so far forward that your knee extends beyond 90 degrees.
4. Lunges: Backward. Step backward and extend so that your front knee is at a 90-degree angle. Don't extend so far backward that your knee extends beyond 90 degrees.
5. Squats: Do not go beyond a 90-degree bend in your knees.
6. Overhead presses.
7. Upright rows.
8. Arm curls.
9. Tricep extensions with bike tube or towel.
10. Leg curls with bike tube.
11. Leg extensions with bike tube.

Most runners now include some core training as part of the normal training program. The goal is to strengthen the abdominals and lower back muscles to provide stability to the pelvis. Include two sets of 10 to 12 reps of the following exercises on three alternate days:

1. Crunches
2. Bicycle Crunches
3. Captains Chair or Hanging Knee Raises
4. Plank-Work to hold position for 30 seconds or more
5. Side Hover
6. High Bridge

There are other basic running drills that can be incorporated into ones training program to teach proper technique and improve efficiency. A number of the web links provided (see Resources) have good video clips of a variety of these specific exercises.

Types of Training Systems

Long, slow distance (LSD). In this method of training, a runner concentrates on running longer and farther, with little attention to speed. At least 95 percent of the time you should be able to converse and feel comfortable while on a training run. Keep pulse rate and respiration well within your limits. Do all things in moderation.

Fartlek. *Fartlek* is a Swedish word meaning "speed play." The basic principle is to change the pace endlessly by charging hills, stretching out going downhill, accelerating to a sprint, striding, jogging, and walking. Try to let changes in pace occur naturally, such as when forced to stop at an intersection or pausing to admire the mountain scenery. Do it off the track on uneven and changing terrain. Fartlek is not a long, easy distance run in the country with a 50-yard burst thrown in every mile!

Interval training. This method of training has five basic components: (1) distance of each fast run, (2) interval or recovery between the fast runs, (3) number of repetitions to be run, (4) duration of each run, and (5) activity done between runs (walking, jogging, or complete rest). *Cruise intervals* is another term that has been associated with this training technique. When trying to build endurance, run longer training runs with shorter rest periods or jog for recovery. To sharpen and become faster, run as fast as or faster than race pace, with almost complete rest for recovery. Interval training can bring quick results, but unless it is used in conjunction with a good endurance base, the results can be quickly wiped out by illness or injury. Intervals should not be added to your program until after you have put in at least 6 to 8 weeks of training.

Hard-easy-hard. This is more a philosophy toward running and training. The body must be given the opportunity to recuperate after being placed under stress. There should be days when the activity is varied or when little or no training is done. Supplemental activities such as swimming, cycling, or weight training may be incorporated.

Hill running. Most runners believe that hills should be an integral part of the training routine. Hill work is actually speed work in disguise, in that the heart rate is elevated and resistance work is done. Few runners enjoy hills, and many fear them when they are part of a race. However, by placing them on your training schedule, you may gain not only strength but confidence. Hill running does require that you adjust your normal stride length. During uphill running, you want to shorten your stride and lean forward slightly. During downhill running, you need to lengthen your stride and run "tall." Because of the force producing braking action of the striking leg, pain in the lower back, hip, or knee can result from downhill running. Downhill running should be done like sprinting or fast striding. Keep yourself balanced with the hips into the running action. Do not "sit." Land on the ball of the foot. Keep the arms in rhythm.

Tempo runs. This is a term that is used to describe a run where you try to maintain a set pace for a prolonged period of time. This time is usually around 20 minutes at around 90 percent of your max heart rate. You should try to keep the same pace throughout the run and not turn this workout into a race. As you progress, the pace that you can maintain for the complete run will decrease, as you are running faster.

SAFETY MEASURES AND CONSIDERATIONS

There are a number of different factors to be aware of when participating in any type of exercise program. First you must know how to recognize and prepare for different environmental factors during exercise. You need to recognize the potential dangers of both heat and cold. The cold can usually be dealt with by wearing several layers of clothing to wick the water away from the body's surface and protect you from the wind. One must also keep in mind that windy conditions will cool the body even in normal temperatures. The rate of heat loss is increased when the skin and clothing get wet. Heat is not always as easy to deal with because of the relative humidity. You must be prepared to take in fluids (generally water) at the rate of 150 to 250 ml every 15 minutes during high temperatures and high humidity. This will help reduce the possibility of dehydration during the workout. You should consider drinking another 500 ml of fluids for every pound lost during a run. Older adults and children need to be especially concerned with fluid replacement because they are less tolerant of the heat. By the time you become thirsty, the body has already lost about 1 percent of its weight. In addition to drinking fluids, you should wear light-colored clothing when exercising in the heat because dark-colored clothing retains more heat and increases the heat load on the body.

Other safety precautions to keep in mind include:

1. Always run facing traffic if you are running alongside a road, and wear some type of reflective apparel.
2. Always carry some form of identification in case an accident happens.

3. Never run alone at night or in areas that are not well lighted. Change your running routes and times; do not become too predictable.
4. Be aware of your general environment and other individuals around you. Listening to music while you run may be a great motivator, but music that is so loud that you can't hear what is going on around you can be dangerous.
5. Watch for animals, especially dogs. It is usually best to slow down and keep any dog in sight. If necessary, let a dog know that you want no part of it by yelling "No!" or "Get back!" If that fails, you may have to use some type of weapon (stick, stone, or spray).
6. Be considerate of others: Move out of the inside lanes of a track so that faster runners will not run you over; move to the side of a sidewalk when other runners are approaching from the opposite direction; and let others in front of you know beforehand that you are going to pass them from behind.
7. Stay away from secluded areas and try to find a training partner. This will be good motivation for both of you.

INJURIES

Most running experts suggest that a stretching routine before and, perhaps more importantly, after jogging can reduce injuries. If you start your jog easily, the initial stretching may not be as important, but a warm-down routine is important. This is true not only for limbering up but also to keep muscles constricting and pumping blood back to the heart. Even with adequate stretching, warming up, and cooling down, injuries will occur to most runners. Most runners try to ease through their injuries by taking time off or running easier for a while.

Minor irritations are a way of life for most runners. As one disappears, another arises; but they are usually not serious enough to make the runner give up the sport.

There are those who, through their own ignorance, are unwilling to heed the signs of trouble indicated by those minor irritations. Their excuse for avoiding medical attention is that the physician usually tells them to stop running for a while. However, the number of injuries to the lower limbs is on the rise and cannot be dismissed. Injuries present real problems, and the runner should seek a sensible solution based on fact rather than on hit-or-miss guesswork.

Problems with muscles or tendons are usually associated with fatigue or an aching pain. Burning or shooting pain may indicate nerve irritation. A consistent burning pain is probably caused by inflammation. Other injuries include blisters, bone spurs, Morton's toe, muscle strain and tears, plantar fascia inflammation, and sciatic nerve problems.

It is necessary to isolate the location of an injury and determine the type of pain and its depth and point of maximum tenderness. Also important to note are: How did the pain start? Was it from new shoes or running a long way on roads or sharp downhills? Did you have a proper warm-up? Did you make unusual demands on your body?

Most injuries can be attributed to simple overuse or overstress. During training, the foot can strike the ground 5,000 times in 1 hour—a tremendous amount of stress for the leg to sustain. This stress is magnified by the fact that each step is responsible for generating about three to four times your body weight. Unless you take a sensible approach to training, your legs will be unable to withstand this stress.

Biomechanical deformities, structural susceptibilities, and postural malformations that may not be evident in everyday walking can show themselves as injury when the runner has been overstressed. Add to this poor running shoes, improper training methods, and poor running surfaces, and the runner is at risk for injuries.

The overuse syndrome usually is evidenced by shin splints, Achilles tendinitis, chondromalacia of the knee, stress fractures, or bursitis. This syndrome can be treated by proper training, which includes a well-organized stretching program with a hard-easy approach to training. A well-planned conditioning period, proper shoes, and varied running surfaces all contribute to lessening the problems of overuse.

The knee is a common area of injury because it is a vulnerable hinge joint that takes most of the punishment inflicted by hard surfaces. The bottom edge of the kneecap is often irritated, a condition medically termed *chondromalacia*. This condition indicates joint instability and usually affects the hyaline cartilage on the joint side of the kneecap. It can be a result of excessive rotation of the knee at foot strike. The best way to prevent this injury is by stabilizing the foot with heel or arch supports and by strengthening the quadriceps, or thigh muscles, through weight training.

The Achilles tendon connects the heel bone and the calf muscles. It is synonymous with vulnerability. Running tends to shorten this tendon and cause inflexibility and tightness. The best way known to prevent this is to stretch before and after a run. The inclined wall push-up is a good exercise to specifically work on the Achilles tendon (Figure 16.6). One method of reducing the stress placed on the affected tendon is to place a ¼-inch lift in the running shoes.

The term *shinsplints* is a catchall for lower-leg problems. Shinsplints is a symptom, not a condition. It is primarily a swelling along the lower front of the legs and is usually a muscular problem. It results from (1) improper shoes; (2) insufficient shock absorption; (3) excessive training on hard surfaces, concrete, or all-weather tracks; (4) lack of flexibility; or (5) poor running form. Runners who suffer the least from shinsplints are those who keep their feet and knees in line with their hips. Other potential causes include an imbalance between an overly strong calf muscle and weak anterior, or front, muscles. Soreness in the shins can be a common complaint of the beginning runner. The legs are not used to this type of muscular activity and should be given time to adjust.

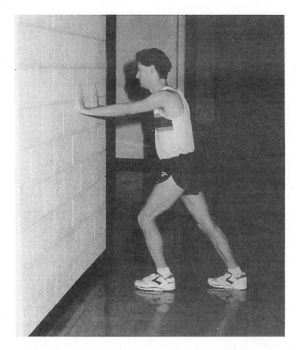

Figure 16.6. Inclined wall push-up (Achilles tendon stretch).

Cryotherapy, or ice treatment, has been used for all of these problems with excellent results for many years. The primary effect of cold—vasoconstriction (decrease in size of blood vessels)—takes place in the first few minutes of application. This is strictly a reflex action, with an accompanying decrease in the capillary blood pressure and an increase in the arterial blood pressure. Ice is used for the first 24 to 48 hours in acute muscular-skeletal injuries. The secondary effect is vasodilation, an increase in the rate of blood flow to the injured area. Massive hyperemia (blood congestion) is produced because of the increase in blood flow, with the peripheral blood vessels being constricted and the deeper blood vessels being dilated. (In contrast, with heat application there is dilation, with stagnation of blood in the area.) Cold also produces an anesthetic effect: a decrease in the spasticity of the muscles and an increase in the blood flow rate, rather than a gross increase in the circulation.

There are several methods of cold application. Crushed or shaved ice works best and produces a colder solution. A slush solution with a cold towel also works well. A massage with a frozen cup of ice is best for the knee and similar joint areas. The surface temperature when using ice treatments should be no higher than 55°F (31°C).

Remember: When ice therapy is first induced, the shock of the cold will cause an aching sensation. The skin will become numb in about 3 minutes and then redden. Therapy should be terminated at this point and repeated later.

One other method that can be used to either prevent or rehabilitate injuries is *cross-training:* use of multifaceted modes of training, either as an addition to or a temporary replacement for the activity. For the jogger, there are many modes of training that can be added to a program to add variety and to offset some of the stress of jogging. Cycling, swimming, cross-country skiing, rollerblading, stepping machines, and pool running all offer a change of pace for the jogger. Some will find that the use of these non-weight-bearing activities allows them the opportunity to maintain their aerobic activities during times of recovery from overuse or injury.

These are some of the most common types of injuries, preventive measures, and simple methods of treatment. If a problem persists, seek advice of a qualified podiatrist or orthopedic surgeon.

GENERAL SUGGESTIONS

1. Do everything in moderation.
2. Start out by improving your cardiovascular efficiency. Work up gradually to at least a 30-minute jog three times per week.
3. Use the hard-easy-hard approach, allowing your body time to recuperate. Understrain rather than overstrain.
4. Learn to calculate and measure your target heart rate (THR) and train at a pace to elicit this heart rate. THR is really a range, and the object is to keep your heart rate in this range while jogging. THR can be calculated by subtracting your age from the value of 220. The resulting value is an estimate of your maximum heart rate. Multiply this value by 0.70 and by 0.85 to obtain the two end points of the THR range, which is appropriate for young adults in good health. These percentages would be lower for older adults. For example, the estimated maximum heart rate for a 20-year-old is 200 (220 − 20). Multiplying this value by 0.70 and 0.85 results in a THR range of 140 to 170 beats per minute. (For a slightly more precise method of calculating THR, see Chapter 3.) Jogging at a pace to elicit a heart rate between these two values will produce a training effect over time. The use of a heart rate monitor makes it easy to keep your intensity level within your desired target range. Most of these monitors will make a sound when your heart rate exceeds or falls below the training limits that you set.
5. Keep an accurate record of your mileage or time. Find out how much stress your body can handle comfortably. Take your pulse before getting out of bed and about 1 or 2 hours after your evening workout. Place the numbers on a graph. This will allow you to see the progress being made toward cardiovascular efficiency.
6. The recovery phase is also important to the jogger. It will take between 3 and 5 hours for the heart rate to return to its preexercise level. By taking your pulse 1 to 2 hours after evening workouts, you will begin to see what type of adaptation your body is making to running stress.

7. Eat sensibly. With an increase in calorie expenditure, expect an increase in appetite. Eat a well-balanced diet. Be wary of fad diets.

8. Take fluids early if you are planning to run more than 1 hour, especially in warm weather. Water seems to work best for everyone. Be prepared and do not overextend yourself—whatever your goal!

9. Vary the training program.

10. Run with someone. Making your jogging sessions enjoyable through social interaction will help ensure that you stick with them.

TEACHING CONSIDERATIONS

1. Instructional programs for groups must deal with two major factors:
   a. For clear training effects to be achieved, students must exercise at least 3 days a week, a minimum of 30 minutes, for at least 5 to 6 weeks.
   b. Individuals will start at different levels of ability and will have different target goals.

2. If programs do not meet for the length of time required, additional work outside of the instructional period should be included.

3. Some type of preassessment should be used to determine beginning levels of students. Several tests using time (a 12-minute run-walk) or heart rate for a given work load are available. Programs should then be designed on this basis.

4. Heart rate is the best simple indicator of workload. Teach students how to calculate their target heart rates. Before set training programs are established, teach pacing for this rate. Begin increasing students' distance according to heart rate on a weekly basis. Have them keep records of progress. Give each student a target distance and time for the end of the program if possible.

5. Use the jogging experience to teach about the effects of exercise on the body and lifestyle of the student. Students are interested in this information. Jogging units can be combined with physical fitness experiences.

6. Provide a lot of encouragement, slow down overeager beginners, and be alert to adverse physical reactions. Become part of the class if possible.

7. Encourage students to be sensitive to their body to determine limits.

8. Begin your class instruction in an area that is easy to monitor—such as on a running track or large grassy field. When selecting this area, consider the potential problems and safety concerns that might arise. Do not select areas where students must cross roadways or encounter automobile traffic. You might want to consider a short loop for the beginners and a longer loop for the more advanced students, but keep in mind that you want to be able to visually monitor the whole class. Stay away from areas where your students must run along bushes or behind buildings.

Walking
HISTORY

Human walking on two legs has a long history, about 4 million years. There are references throughout the written history of the human race regarding the benefits of walking. Walking has long been recognized as a healthy activity, around the world, across cultures, and throughout history. During the last 40 years, we have learned a great deal about the human physiological response to an exercise stimulus. This new knowledge has increased our understanding as to why walking has always been beneficial. It has also allowed us to plan improved walking programs. All of the new research that has been published since the previous edition of this book continues to confirm the positive benefits of walking as a healthy life-long fitness activity.

Walking is the number one fitness activity of adults in the United States in terms of participation. More adults claim they walk for fitness than any other single fitness activity. With obesity, diabetes, and cardiovascular disease increasing, the importance of walking as a valuable fitness activity is also increasing. A sedentary lifestyle is one of the biggest contributing factors to health problems in the United States. A regular moderate walking program is part of the solution.

As a sport, racewalking has been officially included in the Olympic Games since 1908 for men and 1992 for women. The number of racewalking events in the Olympics and the official distances of the events have changed over the years. Since the 2004 Olympic Games in Athens, there have been three racewalking events: 20 km for women, 20 km for men, and 50 km for men.

EQUIPMENT
Shoes

As with jogging, the most important piece of equipment for walking as a sport, or as a recreational activity, is a good pair of shoes. Take your time when shopping for walking shoes to get good quality and a good fit. Try on both shoes and walk on a hard surface. Select your walking shoes based on comfort. Comfort is more important than appearance or price. A minor discomfort at this stage can become a major discomfort miles down the road. Don't look for the cheapest pair of shoes; look for the best pair of shoes for your feet. Ask around and find a knowledgeable athletic shoe professional who can help you pick out the best shoes for your feet.

The outer sole, or the bottom of the shoe, should be made from a durable material that will hold up for many, many miles. A good walking shoe should have a rocker-shaped sole to help your feet roll from heel to toe as you walk. The midsole provides a cushioning layer between the outer sole and the inner sole to absorb shock. The inner sole should have an arch support and a heel cup. The upper part of the shoe should be made from a durable, yet flexible, material. The upper is often made from leather, mesh, or some combination of the two. The toe box of the shoe needs to be wide enough so the front part of your foot can spread out but not too wide so that the toe box is loose on your foot. The toe box should bend at the ball of your foot. You may need to try on many different brands, models, and sizes before you find the most comfortable fit for your feet. Do not sacrifice comfort for brand, style, or price. This is an important investment in your health.

Clothing

Clothing for fitness walking should be comfortable, allow freedom of movement, and allow you to feel good about your appearance. Your socks should wick perspiration away from your skin and be comfortable. As with shoes, an investment in a couple of pairs of good-quality athletic socks that are comfortable with your walking shoes will prove to be a good investment in the long run.

Your walking clothing should keep you at a comfortable body temperature while walking. On hot days, light-colored and loose-fitting clothing should help keep you from overheating. On sunny days, a hat with a brim and sunglasses are recommended for protection from the sun. For a long walk on hot, sunny days, sunscreen would also be a good idea.

If you are walking in cool to cold weather, dress in layers. The first layer next to your skin should be a material that will keep you warm and dry. It should draw moisture away from your skin. The second layer should be a loose-weave fabric with air spaces that can hold a layer of warm air. Your outer layer should be waterproof and windproof but still allow you to vent excess body heat and perspiration. The advantage of dressing in layers is being able to adjust the layers as needed to maintain a comfortable body temperature. When you walk, your muscle contractions produce body heat. You need to plan your clothing to retain as much heat as you want and release excess heat to keep you at a comfortable temperature.

Because much body heat can be lost from your head, it is recommended that in cold weather you wear a hat or hood. In cold weather, you should also wear gloves or mittens to protect your hands and fingers.

Other Equipment

Other equipment, while not necessary, might make your walking experience more interesting, fun, and comfortable. Sunglasses can add to your comfort and protect your eyes on bright, sunny days. Reflective material may add to your safety if you need to walk when it is dark. A heart rate monitor might add to your interest if you want to be more precise about your exercise intensity. A pedometer can give you information about the distance you walk. Backpacks or fanny packs allow you to bring extra clothing layers, food, drinks, and other items while keeping your hands free.

Some like to carry hand weights when they walk. After you have been walking for some time, if you would like to try hand weights, start with a very light weight and progress to heavier weights very gradually. Generally, hand weights are not necessary and may result in unnecessary injury. If you wish to increase your upper-body strength, progressive resistance exercises for your upper-body muscles would be a better choice than carrying weights while walking. You might like to use walking poles or sticks to help you maintain your balance or for protection.

WALKING AREA

If you are walking as a recreational fitness activity, you can walk almost anywhere and almost any time. This is one of the great advantages of walking as a healthy, lifelong fitness activity.

If you are racewalking as a sport in a competition, it will be on a planned and measured course with trained officials as observers to make certain everyone in the competition is walking and not running.

RULES AND FITNESS WALKING GUIDELINES

Walking as a Sport

Walking as a competitive sport has two basic rules.

1. *The Straight-Leg Rule:* The knee must not be bent from the time the leading foot hits the ground until it passes under the center of the body.
2. *The Contact Rule:* During each step, the advancing foot of the walker must make contact with the ground before the rear foot leaves the ground.

Walking as a Recreational Fitness Activity

If you are walking as a recreational fitness activity, the guidelines concern adequate intensity, duration, and frequency to obtain the optimal health benefit from the activity.

Intensity

For adequate intensity, you should be between 55 and 90 percent of your maximum heart rate. You can estimate your maximum heart rate by subtracting your age from 220. As an example, if you are 40 years old, 220 minus 40 equals 180 beats per minute as your estimated maximum heart rate. The standard deviation for this estimate is 10 to 12 beats per minute; thus this is only an estimate and may not be your exact maximum heart rate, but it is safer than exercising until your heart can't go any faster. If you are 40 years old and have an estimated maximum heart rate (EMHR) of 180 beats per minute, multiplying 180 bpm by 55 percent results in an estimated threshold heart rate of 99 beats per minute. Multiplying 180 times 90 percent determines an estimated upper aerobic limit of 162 beats per minute. Therefore, if you are 40 years old, your heart rate should be between 99 and 162 beats per minute during your walk.

If you are a beginner, stay between 55 percent and 70 percent of your estimated maximum heart rate as long as you are comfortable and do not experience distress. If this is too fast, slow down. Use the talk test. You should be able to walk and talk at the same time.

After you have been walking for several months, gradually increase your intensity to 70 to 80 percent of your estimated maximum heart rate. This is a healthy intensity level to maintain if you are exercising for health benefits, including cardiovascular fitness and weight loss or weight control.

After you have been walking for a year or two, and if you feel like you would like to go even faster, move up to 80 to 90 percent of your maximum heart rate. However, keep in mind, most humans seek pleasure and avoid pain. If fitness walking is a pleasure, you are more likely to continue than if every walk is a painful experience.

Listen to your body. How you feel is more important than any number that represents exercise intensity. If you are walking uncomfortably fast and you are in pain, then you are walking too fast. If you are walking uncomfortably slowly and don't feel you are exercising at all, than you are walking too slowly. Moderation is the key to healthy exercise. A healthy level of exercise should feel good.

Duration

Appropriate duration for aerobic activities such as walking is 20 to 60 minutes. However, if you are just beginning a walking program, you may benefit from 10 minutes of walking at a low intensity. As your fitness level improves, you should gradually work up to 20 to 30 minutes of walking. Then increase your intensity to 70 to 80 percent of your estimated maximum heart rate. Twenty to 30 minutes at 70 to 80 percent of maximum heart rate is a healthy level of exercise for most adults. Increase your duration first, then your intensity.

Frequency

Appropriate frequency for aerobic activities is 3 to 5 days per week. You should walk at least 3 days per week with a rest day in between. This is a good idea for beginners whose muscles, bones, and joints need to adapt to this new demand. After a few weeks, progress to 5 days per week, starting with a low intensity (55 to 70 percent of EMHR) and a short duration (10 minutes). Once you get to 5 days per week and you are comfortable with the increase in frequency, then increase your duration to 15 minutes, then 20 minutes, then 25 minutes, and finally 30 minutes. When you are walking briskly for 30 minutes, 5 days per week, you have an excellent lifetime fitness activity.

Warm up, cool down, and flexibility

Begin each walk with approximately 5 minutes of walking at a slow pace. Walking is the best warm-up activity for walking. After about 5 minutes, or when you feel warmed up, gradually increase to your brisk cardiovascular exercise pace for the length of time you have decided on, then gradually slow down to cool down for approximately 5 minutes. When you stop walking, and while your muscles are still warm, perform stretching exercises to improve your flexibility. The following four exercises are recommended for walkers.

Standing lunge and shoulder stretch
- Stand up straight
- One leg back, one leg forward, front knee bent
- Back leg straight, back foot pointing straight ahead, heel on the ground
- Top of hips tilted back, lower back flat
- Both hands behind back, fingers interlaced, elbows straight
- Hold this position and stretch for 10 to 30 seconds
- Change legs and hold stretch for 10 to 30 seconds
- You should feel this stretch in the ankle of your back foot, the back of your lower leg, the front of your hip joint, the front of your shoulder joints, and across your chest.

Standing hip joint adductor, trunk, shoulder, and neck stretch
- Feet wide apart (two to three times your shoulder width)
- Hands overhead, grasp your left wrist with your right hand
- Bend your left knee and lean toward your straight right leg
- Feel the stretch along the inside of the right thigh (hip joint adductor muscles), the left side of your trunk, your left shoulder, and the left side of your neck
- Hold this stretch for 10 to 30 seconds
- Change sides, grasp your right wrist with your left hand, bend your right knee, and lean toward your straight left leg. Hold this stretch for 10 to 30 seconds

Standing quadriceps and shin stretch
- Start in a standing position on your left foot
- Bend your right knee, bringing your right foot up behind you
- Hold the toes of your right foot with your left hand
- Feel the stretch along the front of your thigh, the front of your hip joint, and along the front of your lower leg (shin)
- Hold this stretch for 10 to 30 seconds
- Change legs, hold the toes of your left foot with your right hand, and hold this stretch for 10 to 30 seconds

Standing hamstring and lower back stretch
- Place the heel of your right foot on a step, chair, bench, or some other solid object at a height that is appropriate for your flexibility
- Place both hands on your right leg
- Gently bend forward at your hip and waist
- Feel the stretch along the back of your thigh (hamstrings) and along your lower back muscles
- Hold this stretch position for 10 to 30 seconds
- Change legs and hold for 10 to 30 seconds

FUNDAMENTAL SKILLS AND TECHNIQUES

To receive the health and fitness benefits of walking as a recreational activity, you need to learn to walk at a brisk pace.

To be competitive in racewalking as a sport, you need to learn to walk very fast. The techniques for increasing walking speed are the same.

For a smooth fast walking motion, posture and body alignment are important. Your head should be level and directly above your body with your eyes looking straight ahead. Avoid tension in your neck and jaw. Your chest should be up, your back straight, your shoulders back, and your abdomen pulled in. Your elbows should be bent at a 90-degree angle with your palms facing inward and your hands in a relaxed fist position.

Your heel should contact the ground first; then you should roll forward across your foot from heel to toe and push off from your toes. Your arms should swing naturally and comfortably forward and backward to counterbalance your leg swing. Each arm should swing in a natural path and remain fairly close to your body. On the forward swing, your hand should rise to the level of the bottom of your rib cage and should not cross the midline of your body. On the backward swing, your hand should stop at the waist/hip area.

Your hip movement does not need to be exaggerated, but as you become stronger and more flexible, allow your hips to rotate more to lengthen your stride. As your stride length increases and your hip rotation increases, your chest and shoulder rotation will naturally increase to counterbalance your leg movements. Fitness walking gradually becomes quite an effective abdominal muscle exercise. However, don't force or exaggerate this twist because it can result in lower back pain. Let it happen naturally as you walk faster.

As you become stronger and more flexible your stride length will naturally increase. Don't force it. Both overstriding and understriding are undesirable. Your stride length should be comfortable and efficient for you.

TEACHING CONSIDERATIONS

When teaching walking to anyone, consider age, health, previous experience, and fitness level. Safety and enjoyment should be key considerations. The amount of instruction and supervision necessary will depend on the factors previously mentioned.

If you are teaching walking as a recreational fitness activity, start with low intensity (55 to 70 percent of estimated maximum heart rate), short duration (10 to 15 minutes), and low frequency (3 days per week). If there are individuals who are starting the class with a high level of cardiovascular and muscular fitness, you may want to work with them individually to develop a program more suited to their fitness level.

While there are general guidelines for fitness walking programs, it is important to adapt and individualize walking programs so participants are not being held back or pushed too hard. Exercise is like medicine: you need the right kind and the right amount for it to be beneficial. Each person needs an individualized program to find his or her personal training zone for intensity, duration, and frequency.

GLOSSARY

aerobic Running or walking that allows a near-normal breathing pattern; literally, "with oxygen."

anaerobic Running or walking involving labored breathing; literally, "without oxygen."

cardiovascular fitness The ability of the heart, blood vessels, blood and lungs to deliver oxygen to the cells, especially muscle cells, during long-term physical activity.

carotid artery A blood vessel in your neck often used to count heart rate.

cool-down Exercise movements designed to gradually reduce the intensity of activity.

cruise interval A type of interval training with short recovery times of 30 seconds to 1 minute.

duration Length of a single exercise session.

endurance Ability to run or walk for a long time.

estimated maximum heart rate 220 minus your age.

exercise heart rate Heart rate during exercise.

fartlek A style of training employing frequent changes of pace; from the Swedish word meaning "speed play."

fast distance Steady training running at slightly less than maximum speed.

fitness walking The type of walking that produces measurable health benefits.

flexibility The range of motion at each joint.

frequency The number of times one exercises, usually per week.

inner sole The bottom portion of a shoe that makes direct contact with the foot.

intensity How hard one exercises, usually determined by heart rate or perceived exertion.

interval training A formalized training program alternating fast running with rest periods.

lactic acid Chemical by-product of anaerobic, or oxygen-debt, running that produces fatigue.

long distance More than 6 miles (10 km).

marathon 26 miles, 385 yards (42.25 km); Olympic distance.

middle distance 880 yards to 6 miles (800 to 10,000 m).

midsole The cushioning layer between the outer and inner soles of a shoe.

outer sole The material on the bottom of a shoe.

overdistance Longer than one's racing distance.

oxygen debt Running or walking faster than one's normal breathing pattern can sustain body needs; shortness of breath.

pace Average rate at which a distance is run or walked.

radial artery A blood vessel near the wrist that is often used to count heart rate.

recovery Rebuilding energy after a hard effort.

repetitions Series of runs with recovery breaks between, as in interval training.

resistance Body's ability to withstand stress.

rocker-shaped shoe A shoe that is rounded from front to back.

specificity The principle that physiologic preparation for an activity must include training very similar to that activity.

static stretch A type of stretching in which the stretched position is held.

steady state The rate at which the body can operate aerobically.

tempo runs A sustained pace for about 20 minutes at about 90 percent of maximum heart rate.

training Running or walking program designed to increase the level of fitness and improve a runner's performance in racing.

upper shoe The top part of a shoe above the sole.

SUGGESTED READINGS

Benyo, R. 1998. *Running past 50.* Champaign, IL: Human Kinetics.

Benyo, R., and Henderson, J. 2002. *Running encyclopedia.* Champaign IL: Human Kinetics.

Beck, K. 2005. *Run strong.* Champaign IL: Human Kinetics.

Bowerman, W. J., and Freeman, W. H. 2009. *High performance training for track and field.* 3rd ed. Monterey CA: Coaches Choice.

Brown, R. L., and Henderson, J. 2003. *Fitness running.* 2nd ed. Champaign, IL: Human Kinetics.

Burfoot, A. 2009. *Runner's World complete book of running.* Emmaus, PA: Rodale Press.

Campbell, D. 2008. *Jogging.* 3rd ed. Boston, MA: American Press.

Clarke, B. 2006. *5K and 10K training.* Champaign, IL: Human Kinetics.

Cooper, C. 2010. *Long may you run.* New York, NY: Simon and Schuster.

Daniels, J. 2005. *Daniels' running formula.* 2nd ed. Champaign, IL: Human Kinetics.

Davis, K. 2005. *Fitness walking for everyone.* 2nd ed. Winston-Salem, NC: Hunter Textbooks.

Denison, J. 2004. *The greatest: The Haile Gebrselassie story.* Halcottsville, NY: Breakaway Books.

Dreyer, D., and Dreyer, K. 2009. *ChiRunning.* 2nd ed. New York, NY: Simon and Schuster.

Favor-Hamilton, S., and Antonio, J. 2004. *Fast track: Training and nutrition secrets from America's top female runner.* Emmaus, PA: Rodale Press.

Fenton, M. 2008. *The complete guide to walking.* Guilford, CT: Globe Pequot Press.

Fitzgerald, M., and Noakes, T. 2007. *Brain training for runners: A revolutionary new training system to improve endurance, speed, health, and results.* New York, NY: Penguin Books.

Floyd, P., and Parke, J. 2006. *Walk, jog, run for wellness everyone.* 5th ed. Winston-Salem, NC: Hunter Textbooks.

Galloway, J. 2002. *Galloway's book of running.* Bolinas, CA: Shelter Publications.

Gifford, C. 2008. *Running.* New York, NY: Evans and Co.

Glover, B., and Glover, S., 2007. *The competitive runner's handbook: The bestselling guide to running 5Ks through marathons.* 2nd ed. East Rutherford, NJ: Penguin Group.

Glover, B., Shepherd, J., and Glover, S. 2007. *The runner's handbook.* 2nd ed. East Rutherford, NJ: Penguin Books.

Greene, L., and Pate, R. 2004. *Training for young distance runners.* 2nd ed. Champaign, IL: Human Kinetics.

Hawkins, J., and Hawkins, S. 2001. *Walking for fun and fitness.* 3rd ed. Belmont, CA: Wadsworth/Thomson.

Henderson, J. 2000. *Running 101.* Champaign, IL: Human Kinetics.

Henderson, J. 2004. *Run right now: What a half-century on the run has taught.* New York, NY: Barnes & Noble Books.

Henderson, J. 2004. *Marathon training.* 2nd ed. Champaign, IL: Human Kinetics.

Higdon, H. 2000. *Run fast.* Emmaus, PA: Rodale Press.

Higdon, H. 2002. *Marathoning A to Z: 500 ways to run better, faster, and smarter.* Guilford, CT: Globe Pequot Press.

Iknoian, T. 2005. *Fitness walking.* 2nd ed. Champaign, IL: Human Kinetics.

Laird, R. 2000. *Fast walking.* Mechanicsburg, PA: Stackpole Books.

McGregor, S., and Fitzgerald, M. 2010. *The runner's edge.* Champaign, IL: Human Kinetics.

Murphy, S., and Connors, S., 2008. *Running well.* Champaign, IL: Human Kinetics.

Miller, T. 2002. *Programmed to run.* Champaign, IL: Human Kinetics.

Noales, T., and Granger, S. 2003. *Running injuries: How to prevent and overcome them.* New York, NY: Oxford University Press.

Nottinghama, S., and Jurasin, A. 2010. *Nordic walking for total fitness.* Champaign, IL: Human Kinetics.

Pfitzinger, P., and Douglas, S. 2009. *Advanced marathoning.* 2nd ed. Champaign, IL: Human Kinetics.

Rosato, F. 2003. *Jogging and walking for health and fitness.* 5th ed. Stamford, CT: Wadsworth/Thomson.

Salazar, A., and Lovett, R. 2003. *Alberto Salazar's guide to road racing: Championship advice for faster times from 5K to marathons.* New York: McGraw-Hill Companies.

Sandrock, M. 2001. *Running tough.* Champaign, IL: Human Kinetics.

Seiger, L., and Hesson, J. 2009. *Walking for fitness.* 5th ed. Dubugue, IA: Kendull Hunt Publishing.

Svensson, M. 2009. *Nordic walking.* Champaign, IL: Human Kinetics.

Tanser, T. 2001. *Train hard, win easy: The Kenyan way.* Mountain View, CA: Track & Field News.

Ungerleider, S. 2005. *Mental training for peak performance.* Emmaus, PA: Rodale Press.

Yessis, M. 2000. *Explosive running: Using the science of kinesiology to improve your performance.* Chicago, IL: NTC Publishing Group.

RESOURCES

Videos

High-powered plyometrics. Insight Media, 2001. 40-minute videotape. www.insight-media.com/

Improving flexibility and strength with proprioceptive neuromuscular facilitation. Insight Media, 2002. 20-minute videotape. www.insight-media.com/

The myths and realities of stretching. Insight Media, 2002. 45-minute videotape. www.insight-media.com/

Preventing and managing common running injuries. Insight Media, 2002. 34-minute videotape. www.insight-media.com/

See how they run (analyzes the biomechanics of running in humans and other mammals). Insight Media, 2001. 24-minute videotape or DVD. www.insight-media.com/

See Appendix C for other video sources.

Organizations and Newsletters

American Running and Fitness Association 4405 East-West Highway, Suite 405, Bethesda, MD 20814. Web: http://www.americanrunning.org

Association of International Marathons and Distance Races. http://www.aims-association.org

McMillan Running, http://www.mcmillanrunning.com, email: support@mcmillanrunning.com. McMillan Running Company, Inc. 7710 W Sweetwater Trail, Flagstaff, AZ 86001

Peak Running Performance, 36 W. Randolph, Suite 303, Chicago, Il 60601. Call: 858-922-6613, Email: peakrunning@gmail.com web site: http://www.peakrunningperformance.com/webpages/home.html

Peak Performance Newsletter, http://www.pponline.co.uk, Email: pp@sports-performance.com US: 305-956-3992

Running Research News, P.O. Box 27041, Lansing, Michigan 48909. 517-574-4401. Email: info@runningresearchnews.com, web site: http://www.rrnews.com/

Running Times http://runningtimes.com/

Running USA Web: http://www.runningusa.org

Runner's World Online : http://www.runnersworld.com/ Email: customer_service@rodale.com Phone: 800-914-9363

Team Oregon: Links to online publications and workouts: http://www.teamoregon.com/

USA Track & Field, 132 EastWashington ST, Suite 800, Indianapolis, IN 46204. http://www.usatf.org/ This is the site of USA Track and Field, which is the national governing body for track and field, long-distance running and race walking in the US.

United States Institute for Distance Running. Web: http://usidr.com

WEB SITES

The World Wide Web provides a new area where information can easily be attained, but some Web sites do change their addresses (URL) or completely disappear. Hopefully most of the sites listed here will still be around, but if not, use your search engine to find a new site.

Shoe Company Sites: Some of the major running-shoe companies have some very nice video clips of the biomechanics of running.

Shoe Company Sites:

http://nikerunning.nike.com/nikeos/p/nikeplus/en_US/?sitesrc=uslp Nike Running site, which has information on shoe selection and training tips.

http://www.adidas.com/running/us/ Adidas running site, which has information on shoe selection and see the MYTV video clips.

http://www.saucony.com:80/store/SiteController/saucony/home Saucony website, which has information on shoe selection and shoe construction.

http://www.asicsamerica.com/sports/running/ Asics website, which has information on shoe selection and training information.

http://www.newbalance.com/performance/running/ New Balance website, which has information on shoe selection and shoe construction.

Some Running Sites:

1. http://www.iaaf.org/. International Association of Athletics Federations-Home of world Athletics.

2. http://www.runnersworld.com/. Races & Places: Extensive list of marathons, including dates and contact names and addresses, maintained by *Runner's World* magazine. Site also has many training articles and a shoe selection guide with video clips.

3. http://www.runningpage.com/. The Running Page has links to many running resources.

4. http://www.ultrarunning.com/. Ultra Running Magazine is a site for really long-distance runners maintained by Tia Bodington.

5. http://www.gbtc.org/home.html. Greater Boston Track Club. Homepage of prominent Boston track club, which has boasted such members as Bill Rodgers, Greg Meyer, Alberto Salazar, and Pete Pfitzinger.

6. http://www.americanrunning.org/. American Running Association is a site founded by doctors to help runners train smart and stay injury-free.

7. http://www.mcmillanrunning.com McMillan Running provides training tips on all aspects of running. Includes free video clips and training articles.

8. http://www.runnershangout.com/. This is a online discussion group for runners.

9. http://www.drpribut.com/sports/. This site is about running training and injuries by Stephen M. Pribut, D.P.M., F.A.A.P.S.M.

10. http://usidr.com/. This site provides both training information and individualized training programs.

11. http://www-rohan.sdsu.edu/dept/coachsci/index.htm. This site contains Coaching Science Abstracts of current research articles.

12. http://www.coolrunning.com/ A running magazine format with race information and training guides.

13. http://www.halhigdon.com/. Hal Higdon, a collection of columns by a senior writer for *Runner's World Magazine*. Site has different types of training programs, including virtual training.

14. http://www.runningnetwork.com. The Running Network is a site which feature various regional publications across the U.S. and training tips.

15. http://www.rice.edu/~jenky/mednav.html. A site with information on stretching, injuries, and training.

16. http://www.gssiweb.com. Gatorade Sports Science Institute provides endurance training and sports nutrition information.

17. http://www.runcoachjason.com/ Site with training tips and a free monthly running newsletter.

18. http://www.active.com/running Site with a variety of training and running tips.

19. http://www.runtheplanet.com. Site with locations and maps of different places to run all over the world.

20. http://www.jeffgalloway.com. Site with running advice and training schedules.

17 | Karate

After completing this chapter, the reader should be able to:

- Appreciate the rich tradition behind this martial art
- Be familiar with the types of karate training
- Understand the ranking system used in karate
- Practice the etiquette and safety precautions of karate
- Explain the physical and psychological principles of karate

HISTORY

The martial art of karate as it is known today began in the late nineteenth and early twentieth centuries in Okinawa and Japan. Its origin as a system of self-defense, however, dates back many centuries. Legend relates how a Buddhist priest named Bodhidharma (Daruma) traveled overland from India to China around CE 525 to instruct monks of the Liang dynasty at the Shaolin-si (Small Forest Temple) regarding the tenets of Buddhism. There he taught the monks a combination of Indian fistfighting and yoga that eventually became known as *Shaolin-tsu* (Shaolin "fist-way").

As the art spread throughout China, many styles and systems appeared. The masters of these various fighting systems developed human movement combative patterns based on how they viewed and interpreted the world around them. Some chose to develop their systems based on (1) movements of various animals such as the tiger, snake, or monkey; (2) specific aspects of Chinese religion, culture, myths, or traditions; (3) major geographical locations where the arts were developed and practiced (e.g., northern China vs. southern China); or (4) whether their systems focused on "internal" (that is, "soft," emphasizing "qi," or spiritual energy) or "external" (that is, "hard," emphasizing physical attributes such as muscular strength and flexibility) development. Although there exists a myriad of names for the many Chinese martial arts practiced today, the two most popular terms used to refer to them collectively are *kung-fu* (a general term meaning individual accomplishment or skill) and *wushu* (a more precise term to describe actual Chinese martial arts).

As cultural trade increased, the fighting techniques of China were carried to other Asian countries, the most significant of which was Okinawa. It was here that the empty-handed fighting systems of China were combined with the empty-handed fighting systems of Okinawa (known as *te*), and a rough form of karate was developed.

It was not until the twentieth century, when Gichin Funakoshi (an Okinawan karate instructor and school teacher) introduced Okinawa-te to Japan, that it acquired the name *karate*.

It is important to note that the original Chinese characters that made up the name *karate* translated as "Chinese hands." While Funakoshi is credited with substituting the first character, *kara* (meaning "Chinese"), with that of *kara* (meaning "empty"), it was Chomo Hanashiro who first used this new character when he wrote his notes on kumite (free fighting) in 1905. The kara of "empty" has the meaning of not only empty-handed or weaponless fighting but also keeping one's spirit of inner self hollow (meaning both selflessness and unselfishness).

Karate was introduced into the Okinawan middle-school system in 1905, where it became a required part of the physical education curriculum. It was not until the period between 1917 (in Kyoto at the Butokuden "Hall of Martial Virtues") and 1923 (at the National Athletic Exhibition in Tokyo) that karate began to spread into the universities in Japan, where the art received its greatest impetus. Following World War II, from 1945 to 1965, many U.S. servicemen studied karate, judo, and other martial arts in Japan. On their return to the United States, a number of these servicemen opened martial arts schools. Here, too, the martial arts spread rapidly, and today they are practiced by thousands of students.

Currently there are more than 100 styles of karate. The word *style* refers to a specific system or tradition in the way that karate and other forms of empty-handed combat are taught. Generally, styles of karate and other forms of empty-handed combat can be classified according to national systems, such as Japanese, Korean, Chinese, and Okinawan. Under each of these national systems there are many different styles. Table 17.1 provides an overview of some of the major styles of empty-handed combat taught throughout the world today.

PRONUNCIATION OF JAPANESE

To better understand the terms used in this chapter, it is necessary to provide a short explanation of some of the relevant Japanese terms.

In the Japanese language, each syllable consists of a vowel or of a vowel and a consonant, except for the syllabic *n* and the letters *k, p, t,* and *s* when they occur as the first letter of

Table 17.1. MAJOR STYLES OF EMPTY-HANDED COMBAT

Japanese	Okinawan	Korean	Chinese
Shotokan	Goju-ryu	Tae Kwon Do	T'ai Chi Ch'uan
Wado-ryu	Isshin-ryu	Hapkido	Siu-Lum
Shito-ryu	Shorei-ryu	Tang Soo Do	Hsing-I
Goju-ryu	Shorin-ryu	Taekyon	Wing Chun
Kyokushinkai	Uechi-ryu		Hop Gar

a double consonant. In pronouncing Japanese, each syllable receives approximately equal stress and time.

Vowels

There are only five vowel sounds in Japanese:

a sounds like "ah" as in father (not the *a* in back or gate)
i sounds like "ee" as in machine (not the *i* in hit or flight)
u sounds like "oo" as in glue (not the *u* in cut)
e sounds like "eh" as in met (not the *e* in free)
o sounds like "oh" as in rope (not the *o* in pot)

Length of vowel sounds

The length of vowel sounds is important in the pronunciation of Japanese, because the meaning of some words will change according to the length of the vowel. For example, *o-ba-san* (aunt) and *o-ba-a-san* (grandmother) are distinguished by the length of the vowel *a*.

Unvoiced vowels

The vowels *u* and *i* are sometimes not voiced (not pronounced) at all when they appear between unvoiced consonants (*f, h, k, p, s, ch, sh*) or when *u* appears at the end of a sentence after an unvoiced consonant. Examples:

u between two voiced consonants:
su:

desu ka?	(is it?)	sounds like deska
sukoshi	(a little)	sounds like skoshi
suki	(like)	sounds like ski

ku:

kushami	(sneeze)	sounds like kshami

tsu:

tsukue	(desk)	sounds like tsuke

fu:

futatsu	(two)	sounds like ftatsu

i between two unvoiced consonants:
shi:

shite	(doing)	sounds like shte

chi:

chikai	(near)	sounds like chkai

ki:

kitte	(stamp)	sounds like ktte
Kippu	(ticket)	sounds like kppu

hi:

hitori	(one person)	sounds like htori

u at the end of a sentence:

Hon desu.	(It is a book.)	sounds like Hon des

Consonants

Most Japanese consonants are pronounced almost the same as English consonants, except for the following:

f is made by blowing air between the lips, without letting the lower lip touch the teeth. The sound produced is approximately halfway between the *h* sound and the *f* sound of English.

g is hard, like the *g* in go or get (not the *g* in *generation* or *judgment*).

n is sometimes considered to be a full syllable itself (without any vowel). It sounds something like the *ng* in *singer* or *ping-pong*, but without the slightest hint of a *g* sound.

r is pronounced between the *l* and *d* sounds of English. It is a flap-*r*, in which the tip of the tongue briefly touches the roof of the mouth just behind the teeth.

ch is pronounced like the *ch* in *church*.

ts is pronounced like the final *ts* in *cuts*.

Double Consonants

kk is pronounced like the *kk* in *bookkeeper*. The first *k* (*p, t, tch,* or *s*) is a momentary pause (silence) equivalent in time to the pronunciation of one syllable of Japanese; the second *k* (*p, t, tch,* or *s*) is pronounced as usual.

pp is pronounced like the *p* sounds connecting two words in English such as "flip past" (not like the *pp* in a single word such as *supper*).

tt is pronounced like the *t* sounds connecting two words in English such as "flight time" (not like the *tt* in a single word such as *butter*).

tch is a variation of the *tt* sound, the pronunciation of *ch* in Japanese begins with the *t* sound.

ss is pronounced like the *s* sounds connecting two words in English, such as "less shame" or "let's sing."

THE MEANING OF KARATE-DO

The modern Japanese martial arts of karate and judo are practiced the world over as forms of sport competition, self-defense, physical education, and aesthetics. However, their primary focus is to serve as systems of self-cultivation and to transmit the ideals, norms, and behaviors associated with the traditional cultural setting of the martial arts. These include loyalty, bravery, and the acceptance of physical and mental hardships through disciplined training. Of paramount importance is the development of a strong fighting spirit.

The martial arts are considered to be both physical and mental disciplines that focus on self-cultivation through a combative mode. The *do* suffix in the words *karate-do* and *judo* suggests that they are philosophical paths or ways to travel throughout one's life in the pursuit of perfection of character. Japanese culture is replete with such activities. Those more familiar to the Westerner include the tea ceremony (*chado*), calligraphy (*shodo*), and Zen meditation. The martial arts, however, serve as a unique system of *seishin kyoiku* (spiritual education) through a combative mode of training and instruction. The highest aim of all of the martial arts such as karate-do, kendo, judo, kyudo, and aikido is to

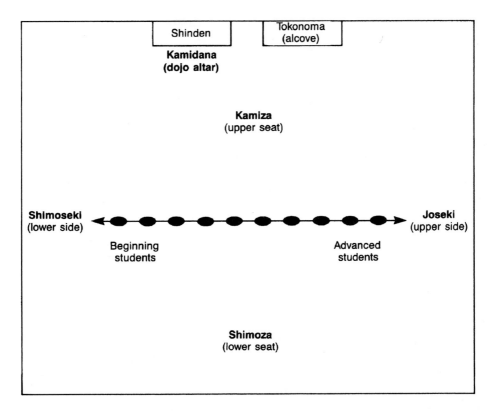

Figure 17.1. Dojo schematic.

develop one's character through physical, mental, and moral education.

DOJO

Every *dojo* (martial arts training hall) is arranged so that there is a front and back wall and an upper and lower side (see Figure 17.1). The point of reference for training activity and etiquette is the front wall (*shomen*). At the front wall in most traditional dojo, there is a Shinto or Buddhist deity shelf (*kamidana*). It is the kamidana specifically that serves as the focal point for all training activity and etiquette. In place of the kamidana, many dojo outside of Japan elect to place either a national flag or a picture of the founder of their particular karate style on the front wall. Some dojo also have a *tokonoma,* or a special place on the front wall in which may be placed a fine sword or a piece of calligraphy (*kakemono*) depicting a martial arts training concept.

The upper seat in the dojo is known as the *kamiza*, while the lower seat in the dojo is known as the *shimoza*. The kamiza is the approximate location that the teacher occupies at the beginning and end of class for formal salutation. The shimoza is the location where the students line up before and after class for the same purpose. Generally, the higher-ranking students line up toward the right, or *joseki*, side of the dojo, and the lower-ranking students line up toward the left, or the *shimoseki,* side.

Ideally, a dojo should be clean, simple, and without ostentatious display of trophies or other encumbrances. The floor should be of smooth wood and should be thoroughly cleaned by all students at the end of each training period.

UNIFORM

The uniform worn while training is called the *karate-gi*. It consists of a jacket, pants, and a belt that is about 8 feet (2.44 m) long. Most traditional dojo require the karate-gi to be white, although there are exceptions. While the belt primarily serves to keep the jacket closed, its color also denotes level of expertise.

Karate-gi are manufactured in light-, medium-, and heavy-weight material and are available in a variety of costs and sizes. It is important that it fit somewhat loosely and not restrict movement while training. Table 17.2 illustrates the most common sizes available.

RANKING SYSTEM USED IN KARATE

Karate uses the *kyu-dan* system to rank its exponents in terms of proficiency, knowledge, and experience. The *kyu* ranks, also known as the *mudansha* (ungraded) ranks, begin with either the tenth, ninth, or eighth kyu for beginners and proceed up to the first kyu (usually designated in most dojo by the brown belt). The *dan* ranks, also known as the *yudansha* (graded) ranks, begin with the first-degree black belt (*shodan*) and progress up to the tenth-degree black belt (*judan*). In most traditional dojo, it takes 4 to 5

Table 17.2. KARATE UNIFORM SIZE CHART

Uniform Size	Clothing Size	Height	Weight
000	Child 2–4	3′–3′5″	30–40 lbs.
00	4–6	3′5″–3′10″	40–55 lbs.
0	6–8	3′10″–4′3″	55–70 lbs.
1	8–10	4′3″–4′8″	70–90 lbs.
2	10–12	4′8″–5′1″	90–110 lbs.
3	Adult Small	5′1″–5′6″	110–140 lbs.
4	Medium	5′6″–5′11″	140–170 lbs.
5	Large	5′11″–6′2″	170–200 lbs.
6	X–Large	6′2″–6′5″	200–230 lbs.
7	XX–Large	6′5″–6′8″	230–260 lbs.
8	XXX–Large	6′8″–6′11″	260–290 lbs.

Table 17.3. KARATE RANKING SYSTEM*

Rank	Age	Title
Ju-Dan (10th) over 10 years after Ku-Dan	70 years or over	Hanski (master)† over 15 years after Kyoshi 55 years old or over
Ku-Dan (9th) 10 years after Hachi-Dan	60 years or over	
Hachi-Dan (8th) 8 years after Shichi-Dan	50 years or over	Kyoshi (teacher)† over 10 years after Renshi 40 years old or over
Shichi-Dan (7th) 7 years after Roku-Dan	42 years or over	
Roku-Dan (6th) over 5 years after Go-Dan	35 years or over	Renshi (instructor)† over 2 years after 5th Dan 35 years old or over
Go-Dan (5th) over 3 years after Yo-Dan	under 35 years	
Yo-Dan (4th) over 3 years after San-Dan	under 35 years	
San-Dan (3rd) over 2 years after Ni-Dan	under 35 years	No formal title
Ni-Dan (2nd) over 1 year after Sho-Dan	under 35 years	No formal title
Sho-Dan (1st) at least 3 years‡	under 35 years	No formal title
Ikkyu (1st Brown) Nikyu (2nd Brown) Sankyu (3rd Brown) Yonkyu (4th class) Gokyu (5th class) Rokkyu (6th class) Shichikyu (7th class) optional Hachikyu (8th class) optional	No age specified	Kyu (below brown identified by different colors) However, all kyus are considered white relative to the black belt.

*Ranking system adopted by the Federation of All Japan Karate-Do Organizations (FAJKO) on March 27, 1971.
†Title may not be given irrespective of how high the rank; awarded for exceptional achievement and outstanding character.
‡Daily practice.

years to achieve the rank of first-degree black belt if a *kara-teka* (karate practitioner) trains three to five times per week with no breaks in training. Belt colors most often used in the mudansha class include white, orange, blue, purple, green, red, and brown. The black belt is used to denote those in the yudansha class. The Japan Karate Federation (JKF) uses the ranking system shown in Table 17.3.

It is considered axiomatic in most karate circles that to progress from one martial arts rank to a higher one, the practioner must demonstrate significant improvement in both martial arts skill and technique as well as character. This necessitates that karateka pursue not only physical training, but academic training as well, if they are to acquire the requisite skill and knowledge required for their rank. In addition, examinees are tested on *kihon* (basics), *kata* (formal exercises), and *kumite* (sparring). More advanced karateka must demonstrate sufficient skill in *tameshiwari* (board breaking) and self-defense. Some schools require that advanced karateka demonstrate technical proficiency in the use of a traditional martial arts weapon. The highest yudansha levels require that the karateka produce a written thesis or completed research on some aspect of martial arts theory or practice.

In addition to the kyu and dan ranks given in karate, karateka may also be awarded one of three honorary titles after reaching the rank of *Yo-Dan* (fourth-degree black belt). The three special titles are those of *renshi* (instructor), *kyoshi* (teacher), and *hanshi* (master). Refer to Table 17.3 for the requirements for these titles.

A head instructor of a style of karate is usually referred to as *kancho* (literally, "building chief"). *Shihan* (master) is the term of address usually given to those of sixth-degree black belt or higher. *Sensei* (teacher) is the term of address given to those black belts who head an individual dojo or who have the primary responsibility of teaching within a dojo. *Sempai* (senior) is the term usually given to the more experienced

and higher-ranking students within a group, while the term *kohai* (junior) is used to designate those karateka of lower rank and lesser experience. It is important to note that while the terms *sensei, sempai,* and *shihan* are used as formal forms of address, *kohai* is never used in this manner.

KARATE TRAINING

Karate training is generally divided into three basic aspects: kihon, kata, and kumite. Kihon (basics) training consists of fundamental practice in the execution of blocks, punches, strikes, kicks, stances, stepping, and body-shifting techniques. Generally, these are performed by *karateka* on an individual basis or during group practice. Kata training consists of learning and executing prearranged traditional routines of attack and defense against imaginary opponents. Most schools require karateka to learn two to three kata per rank for advancement purposes. Kumite training consists of learning and executing basic, intermediate, and advanced levels of fighting. Basic sparring, sometimes referred to as "one-attack fight," or *yakusokugeiko* ("promise" practice), consists of two opponents executing basic attack and defense techniques against prearranged targets such as the opponent's face or mid-section.

Kihon (Fundamental Practice)

1. *Blocking techniques:* These are employed to defend vital areas of the body against punches, strikes, and kicks primarily by deflecting them from their intended target of attack. The more common techniques include the downward block, the middle forearm chest block, the high block, and the knife-hand block (Figure 17.2).
2. *Punching and striking techniques:* These are used to attack vital areas of the body. The two basic techniques are the lunge punch (or straight punch) and the reverse punch. Basic striking techniques

Figure 17.2. Blocking techniques. A, Route of downward block. B, Route of forearm block against body attack. C, Route of upper block against head attack.

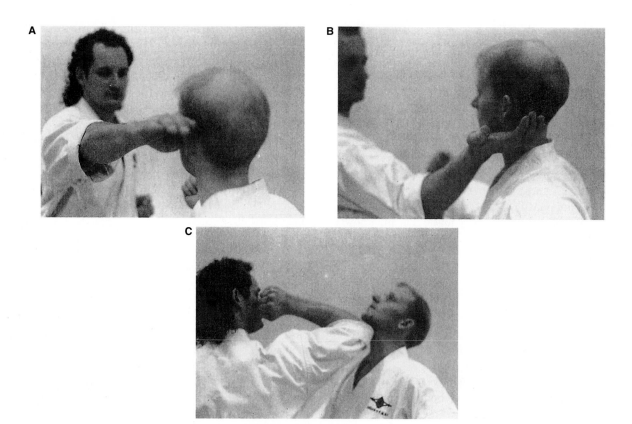

Figure 17.3. Punches and strikes. A, Ridge hand strike. B, Knife hand strike. C, Elbow strike.

Figure 17.4. Kicking techniques. A, Route of side thrust kick. B, Route of side snap kick. C, Route of roundhouse kick.

include the ridge hand strike, knife hand strike, and elbow strike (Figure 17.3).

3. *Kicking techniques:* The front, round, side, and back kicks comprise the basic kicking techniques used in karate. Like the punching and striking techniques, these may be delivered to vital target areas in attack or counterattack modes (Figure 17.4).

4. *Stances:* For the karateka, strong stances (*tachikata*) and combative postures (*kamaekata*) serve as the foundations from which to deliver strong offensive and defensive techniques. Some of the more common stances used in karate include the front stance, back stance, rooted stance, horse-riding stance, free-fighting stance, and cat-leg stance (Figure 17.5).

Figure 17.5. Karate stances. A, Front stance. B, Back stance. C, Rooted stance. D, Horse-riding stance. E, Free-fighting stance. F, Cat-leg stance.

5. *Stepping and body-shifting techniques:* Stepping techniques allow the karateka to move from one position to another for attack and defense purposes. During basic practice, the front stance is used to execute many of the attacking techniques while the back stance and rooted stance are used to execute many defensive techniques.

Kata (Practice of Forms)

Kata are exercises of offensive and defensive techniques arranged in formal sequences and executed against imaginary opponents. They are loosely analogous to compulsory floor routines in gymnastics. Formulated and transmitted down through the ages by past true masters of the art of karate, they consist of a number of movements that must be performed in a strict sequence with correct power, speed, focus, rhythm, and movement interpretation. Historically, they represent a condensation of the fighting knowledge of the master who developed the kata. Kata were originally designed to have no unnecessary movements. Each movement in the kata has a very specific combative application. As the karateka practices each kata, the vast amount of information within the kata, under the guidance of a knowledgeable teacher, gradually begins to reveal itself to the practitioner.

In performing kata, execution of techniques must not be rigid and robotic, but must effectively contrast the active (do) and passive (sei) elements of the kata to demonstrate proper rhythm and fluidity of human motion. Years of practice are required to master even the most basic kata. Figure 17.6 shows an example of a kata known as *Heian Yondan*.

Japanese karate kata are traditionally divided into the two styles of Okinawan karate from which they were derived, the Shorin-ryu and the Shorei-ryu. Kata from the Shorin-ryu tradition emphasize movements that are light and flexible, while those of the Shorei-ryu tradition emphasize movements that are strong and powerful. Generally, kata were commonly named by the originator according to a particular technique, movement, or philosophical meaning of the kata itself. At other times, the kata were assigned the name of the originator. Table 17.4 lists the Japanese names and meanings of some of the kata that are practiced by karateka who train in the Shotokan tradition of karate-do.

Kumite (Free-Fighting)

Kumite, or free-fighting, is the application of skills learned in kihon and kata practice to practical fighting and self-defense situations. This aspect of karate training allows karateka to practice their fighting skills against one another. Beginning karateka train to execute all attacking and counterattacking techniques with maximum power and speed and stop just short (*Sun-dome* = about 3 cm)

Table 17.4. NAMES OF KATA PRACTICED IN THE SHOTOKAN KARATE TRADITION

Name of kata	Meaning of kata	Outstanding feature(s)
Ten-no Kata	"Form of the universe"	Basic attack and defense techniques
Taikyoku	"Chaos" or "Void"	Fundamental stances, blocks, and punches
Heian	"Peaceful"	Comprehensive techniques that, when mastered, should be "comfortable" in most basic self-defense situations
Bassai Sho and Dai	"To penetrate a fortress"	Strong movements intended to change disadvantage into advantage by employing differing degrees of power and rapidly switching blocks
Kanku Sho and Dai	"To view the sky"	Variation of fast and slow technique, jumping
Jion	Name of originator	Turning, shifting, various stepping patterns
Jutte (sometimes "Jitte")	"Ten hands"	Fast and slow movements, high and low body positions, reversal of body positions
Empi	"Flying swallow"	Fast and slow movements, high and low reversal of body positions
Hangetsu	"Cresent" or "Half moon"	Coordinating stepping and breathing with circular arm and leg movements
Gankaku	"Crane on a rock"	Balancing on one leg, side kick and back fist
Chinte	"Small hands"	Small, but powerful, hand blocks and strikes
Unsu	"Cloud hand"	Strong forceful arm and hand blocks with stances and high-level ridge-hand strikes
Sochin	"Preservation of peace among men"; "immovable"	Low, powerful movements in stances
Nijushi	"24 hands"	Strong blocking and striking techniques
Tekki	"Iron horse"	Strong hand and leg techniques from horse stance
Jion	Named after Chinese monk who visited Okinawa	Multiple hand punches, strong hand and foot techniques

Figure 17.6. Heian Yondan.

Figure 17.6. (continued)

Figure 17.6. (continued)

Figure 17.6. (continued)

of actual contact to prevent intentional injury. More-advanced karateka, after undergoing disciplined training and conditioning, are allowed to make light contact to restricted target areas during kumite. Kumite teaches the concepts of proper distancing and timing, the proper moment to initiate an attack or defense, and recognition of different offensive and defensive maneuvers made by an opponent. Additionally, it is necessary to master effective body shifting (*taisabaki*) techniques and quick-witted changing techniques (*henka waza*).

Kumite is arbitrarily categorized into basic, intermediate, advanced, and specialized levels. Basic kumite, also called *yakusoku* or "promise" (agreement to attack only a predesignated target area) kumite, consists of *sanbon* (three-step) kumite, *gohon* (five-step) kumite, and *ippon* kumite (one-attack

fight). In sanbon or gohon kumite, the attacking karateka attacks either three to five times consecutively to the *jodan* (upper level), *chudan* (middle level), or *gedan* (lower level) with a lunge-punch-front stance technique while the defending karateka steps backward in a front stance at the same time executing the appropriate high, middle, or low blocking technique. On the last block, the defending karateka counters with a reverse punch technique.

In the initial attack in *ippon kumite* (one-attack fight), the offensive karateka launches a prearranged attack to the face with a lunge-punch-front stance technique while the defending karateka steps to the rear in a defensive stance (usually an immovable stance or a back stance) and executes a counter offensive technique. It is important here for the offensive karateka to hold position after the attack so that the defending karateka has time to deliver a counteroffensive technique with good form. In the second attack, the offensive karateka executes a lunge-punch-front stance technique to the middle level and the defending karateka counters with an appropriate counteroffensive technique. In the third attack, the offensive karateka launches a prearranged front-kick-front stance attack and the defending karateka again counters with an appropriate counteroffensive technique. At the completion of the first high, middle, and low attack-counter sequence, both karateka change roles to gain equal practice in attack and defense training.

Ippon jiyu kumite (one-attack fight from fighting stance position) is performed almost like ippon kumite. Two exceptions are that both karateka use a free-fighting stance position and the attacking karateka instantaneously returns to the original preattack position after attack delivery so that the defending karateka does not have time to counter the initial attack.

Jiyu kumite allows both karateka to move about at will and execute offensive and defensive maneuvers as opportunities arise. Again, as in the other forms of kumite, all punches, kicks, and strikes are stopped just short of contact to avoid injury. When training in a karate dojo (training hall), the kumite usually continues until one karateka scores what is considered to be a decisive blow on the opponent. A decisive blow is one in which good technique, posture, timing, balance, and power can be demonstrated. In competitive sport matches, kumite bouts usually last for a designated period (e.g., 3 or 5 minutes) or number of points scored (e.g., one to three).

Specialized free-fighting may include activities such as circle fighting (*enjin*) kumite or seated free-fighting (*suwari geiko*) kumite. In *enjin kumite*, one karateka is located in the center of a circle of six to eight other karateka. Each karateka on the circle takes turns in rapidly attacking the karateka in the center with a strong technique. The karateka in the center is responsible for avoiding, blocking, and countering each attack. In *suwari geiko kumite*, two karateka face each other about 1 m apart in a formal Japanese kneeling posture known as *seiza*. The offensive and defensive karateka follow the same sequence of attack and defense as in ippon kumite, described previously.

ETIQUETTE

Proper behavior in the dojo is considered to be the hallmark of a martial art that is taught within traditional contexts. Dojo protocol and etiquette create a teaching and learning environment that is conducive to disciplined training according to Japanese customs and traditions. Rituals followed within the dojo have a purpose, and it is not one of religious conversion. They serve to establish decorum, develop an attitude conducive to disciplined training, prepare for the learning process, and show respect for the karate tradition.

There is agreement among practitioners regarding the general behavior that is allowed when visiting or training in any dojo. It is customary not to wear shoes on the training surface even if you are in everyday clothes. Prior to beginning a training session, karateka should present themselves with a clean body and clean *karategi* (uniform). This shows respect for those you are going to train with and for your martial art. While training, it is inappropriate to wear jewelry, watches, or the like. Your training uniform must always be kept neat and clean. It is important to bow when entering and leaving a dojo, before and after training with an opponent, and before and after speaking with an instructor or senior student. Acts of profanity, loud talking, laughing, socializing, and misconduct are out of place. When in the dojo, one should use the time to either train or meditate. Karate and other martial arts begin and end with courtesy.

SAFETY

Because the martial art of karate is a combative activity, safety is extremely important. Following a few basic rules will reduce the potential for injuries. When attacking or counterattacking during kumite, one must remember to stop all techniques just short of contact. It is recommended that karateka, especially beginners, use protective equipment to cover the shins, forearms, and hands when engaged in free-fighting. It is strongly encouraged that one wear a protective mouthguard and refrain from wearing eyeglasses or hard contact lenses when sparring. If eyeglasses are worn, it is important to wear some type of associated protective device. Keeping toenails and fingernails trimmed and not wearing jewelry during training will also reduce injury.

CONDITIONING

Karate involves the balanced use of almost all major muscle groups. Speed, power, flexibility, balance, agility, and reaction time are important components of training sessions. Although practicing kihon, kata, and kumite provides an adequate conditioning stimulus to the body, supplemental conditioning such as jogging, cycling, swimming, and weight training will enhance cardiorespiratory fitness, muscular strength, endurance, flexibility, and body composition.

Serious karateka make extensive use of the *makiwara* (straw-wrapped punching board) and the heavy bag to develop precision and power in performing effective punches, strikes, and kicks. Use of these two pieces of training equipment helps karateka develop the focus necessary in tensing and relaxing muscles during various techniques.

PHYSICAL AND PSYCHOLOGICAL PRINCIPLES

Being successful at karate requires an understanding and application of fundamental physical and psychological principles to training. The proper use of speed, strength, technique, balance, timing, distance, and focus is necessary to effectively use karate skills.

Tachikata (Importance of Stances)

To maintain balance, the center of gravity must be within the base of support. There are times in karate when you need a stable stance and times when you need an unstable stance. Stable stances are needed to strike with force or when you are receiving a strong attack. Unstable stances are required when it is necessary to change your stance and move rapidly from one position to another.

Chikara (Power)

The ability to generate power is necessary in karate. Because power is a product of speed and strength, it is important to emphasize both of these in training. Energy generated from the slower but larger and more powerful muscles of the hips and trunk should be coupled with those of the smaller, weaker, but faster muscles of the extremities to generate maximum power in blocking, punching, striking, and kicking.

Kime (Focus)

The ability to focus (*kime* means "to penetrate the spirit") your technique results from contracting muscles at the moment you make contact with your target. At the same time, it is important to exhale forcefully to help augment the power generated.

Kiai (Spirit Cry)

Associated with karate is the traditional spirit cry known as the *kiai!* Kiai represents a willful activation and union of the karateka's vital energy and should not be misconstrued as merely "shouting."

Koshi Kaiten (Hip Rotation)

The importance of the lower central torso region in generating power and maintaining stability in karate and other martial arts cannot be overemphasized. This region, known as the *seika tanden*, is the focal point of thought and motion. Without effectively employing the hips in karate techniques, there can be no true power.

Jun Kaiten (Regular Hip Rotation)

Jun kaiten is a motion that occurs when the direction of rotation and direction of technique are the same. As an example, when the hips are rotated to the left, the right fist is used for punching. When the hips are rotated to the right, the left arm may be used for an outward-to-inward block.

Gyaku Kaiten (Reverse Hip Rotation)

Gyaku kaiten is a motion that occurs when the direction of rotation and direction of the technique are opposite to one another. In this motion, the hips rotate to the right and the technique is executed to the left. Reverse rotation is used in executing the down block, middle block, and knife hand block. As an example, during a left down block, the block is executed moving toward the left hip while the hips are rotated to the right.

Kokyu (Use of Proper Breathing)

As a general rule, when attempting to generate power to execute any technique, it is necessary to exhale forcefully only about two-thirds of the air from the lungs. In doing so, less time is needed to refill the lungs prior to the next technique. Additionally, exhaling all the air from the lungs may weaken the power of a technique.

Mizu No Kokoro (Mind Like Water)

Mizu no kokoro refers to the need to make the mind calm and serene, like an undisturbed body of water. Just as undisturbed water accurately reflects objects, so does the undisturbed mind accurately reflect that which it sees. A composed mind, devoid of distractions and apprehensions, will accurately reflect the physical and mental posture of the opponent and will be able to respond with appropriate offensive and counteroffensive techniques. Conversely, if the surface of the water is disturbed, the images it reflects will also be disturbed. In like manner, if the mind is preoccupied with thoughts of attack, defense, or apprehension, it will not be able to anticipate the opponent's intentions and thus will create an opportunity for the opponent to attack.

Tsuki No Kokoro (Mind Like the Moon)

Just as moonlight shines equally on everything within its range, the karateka can be constantly aware of the totality of the opponent's movements and intentions. Clouds that block out the light of the moon are similar to nervousness and distractions that interfere with the interpretation of your opponent's intentions. This makes it impossible to find openings in your opponent's defenses to deliver an effective attack or counterattack. When watching an opponent, a karateka should envision looking at a distant mountain (*enzan no metsuke*). This ensures that the opponent's entire body, as well as the background, is in the field of vision. Better detection of the relative motion of the opponent's technique is then possible.

Ma (Timing)

Ma deals with the principle of correct timing in attack and defense situations.

Maai (Combative Engagement Distance)

Maai is the principle of correct distancing in delivering offensive and defensive techniques. For training, distancing is generally divided into close, middle, and far distance. Opponents practice modifying techniques so that they can be used at these ranges.

Kuzushi (Off-Balancing)

Kuzushi refers to unbalancing your opponent, either psychologically or physically, to create an opening for an attack or counterattack.

Tsukuri (Fitting In)

Tsukuri refers to "fitting in," or closing the combative engagement distance between you and your opponent with an appropriate technique.

Kake (The Attack)

Kake is the attack or counterattack in a combative situation.

Ki, Ken, Tai Ichi (Spirit, Sword, and Body Are One)

This combative concept comes from Japanese swordsmanship and indicates that for a technique to be effectively employed, one's resolute will, proper technique, and body must all be used simultaneously.

Suki (Opening)

Suki refers to a physical or psychological "opening" in your opponent through which to deliver an attack or counterattack.

Waza o Hodokoso Koki (Proper Moment to Attack)

Closely related to the concept of suki is that of *waza o hodokoso koki*, which is the psychological moment to execute an effective technique. Generally, there are four instances in which a karateka may deliver a technique against an opponent. These are (1) at the start of the opponent's technique, (2) when the attack comes, (3) when the opponent's mind is motionless, and (4) when creating an opening in your opponent.

Kobo Ichi (Appropriateness of Attack and Defense)

Kobo ichi refers to the appropriate timing of offensive and defensive techniques. Three levels of timing are recognized:

1. *San no sen:* to take the initiative with one's attack.
2. *Tai no sen:* to take the initiative when the enemy attacks.
3. *Go no sen:* to take the initiative later. This is not the same as engaging in defensive karate. It refers to setting up or leading an opponent into a situation in which you have an advantage.

Zanshin (Remaining Heart)

Zanshin translates literally as "remaining heart" or "remaining mind." It refers to the psychological domination or awareness remaining or "lingering" over an opponent, even after an offensive or counteroffensive technique has been completed.

RULES FOR SPORT COMPETITION

The martial art of karate is an international sport and is practiced in almost every country of the world. In most karate tournaments, karateka may participate in either kata or kumite competition, or both. The specific rules under which karateka compete in sport competition vary according to the sponsoring organization. Some of the major organizations under whose auspices international and national karate sport competition is held are the Japan Karate Federation (JKF) in Japan, the FMK (Fédération Mondiale de Karate—also known as the World Karate Federation or WKF) in France, and the World Karate Confederation (WKC) in Switzerland. In the United States, karate sport competition is held under several different organizations, including the United States of America–National Karate-do Federation (USA-NKF), which is a member of the U.S. Olympic Committee and is the U.S. representative to the WKF; the United States Karate Federation (USKF), which is associated with the WKC; and the Amateur Athletic Union (AAU), which has a separate membership with the WKC. There are, however, a multitude of national and international karate organizations and styles that have no affiliation with the aforementioned bodies and who host their own competitions.

Kata competition takes the form of individual and team matches. Team matches usually consist of three contestants, either all male or all female. The individual kata competition consists of solo performance in separate female and male divisions. Kata are judged according to correct sequence of movements (*embusen*), good form, proper body rhythm (*unsoku*), proper speed (*waza no kamkyu*), development of power, proper tension and relaxation of techniques (*karada no shin-shuku*), correct breathing, continuity (*renzokusei*), and awareness of imaginary opponents (*waza no imi*). They must be executed with competence and must demonstrate a clear understanding of the kata *bunkai* (practical applications). Contestants are expected to perform compulsory (*shitei*) and self-selected (*tokui*) kata.

Kata competition is organized into three rounds. The first round selects sixteen contestants, the second round selects eight contestants, and the third round selects the winner and final placings. Each kata judge displays the score by means of points on a card held in the hand. To minimize ties generally, scoring is held to between 5 and 7 points in the first round, between 6 and 8 points on the second round, and between 7 and 9 points on the final round. Deductions for a momentary hesitation in a smooth performance, an inappropriate pause in the kata, and instabilities range from -0.1 to -0.4 points. If the contestant loses balance completely or falls, a disqualification will result. In some scoring systems, each judge (the number of which may vary according to the rules used) awards a score, and the highest and lowest scores are deleted; the remainder of the scores are added together to form a total score. Deductions ranging from 20.1 to 21.0 points may be made in each area. The karateka with the

Table 17.5. ONE BASIS FOR AWARDING POINTS IN KATA COMPETITION

Perfect	10
Excellent	9
Very good	8
Good	7
Average	6
Fair	5
Poor	4
Very poor	3

highest total score at the end of the competition is declared the winner. One of the point systems used to judge kata is shown in Table 17.5.

Kumite competition is divided into team and individual matches. The individual match may be divided into weight or rank divisions and open category. Weight divisions are divided into bouts, with a "bout" being competition between opposing pairs of team members. Duration of the kumite bout is defined as 3 minutes or 3 points for senior male kumite (both teams and individuals) and 2 minutes for women and junior bouts. The result of a bout is determined by either contestant scoring three *ippon* (1 full point for each ippon awarded), six *waza-ari* (6.5 points), or a combination of the two totaling *sanbon*, or obtaining a decision, or by *hansoku* (foul), *shikkaku* (disqualification), or *kiken* (renunciation) imposed against a contestant. An ippon is awarded when a valid strike is delivered to a valid target area (head, neck, face, abdomen, chest, back, and sides). A valid strike consists of a technique that is delivered with good form (*shisei*), correct technique (*kohon waza*), correct fighting attitude, vigorous and correct application of power (*chikara no kyojaku*), perfect finish (*zanshin*), speed (*waza no kamkyu*), and proper timing (*ma*) and distance (*maai*). The actual kumite consists of a free exchange of punches, blocks, strikes, and kicks employing rapidly changing offensive and counteroffensive movements until one karateka scores an effective "hit" (stopped just short of actual contact) against a valid target area. The competition area (*shiaijo*) is generally a flat surface, preferably a wood floor, with an area about 8 meters square. Located within the match area itself are usually two judges (*fukushin*), one referee (*shushin*), and one arbitrator (*kansa*).

Target Areas of the Human Body

Effective attacks and counterattacks are aimed at a vital target area. In self-defense, this means that the technique delivered will strike an area in such a way as to cause the assailant to quit the assault. In sport competition, it means that if the technique were to make contact, it would cause the opponent to quit the assault also. Figure 17.7 shows the most common target areas of the body against which techniques may be delivered to disable an assailant.

GLOSSARY

Tachikata (stances)

fudo-dachi Immovable stance.
hachiji-dachi Open-leg stance.
hangetsu-dachi Half-moon stance.
heiko-dachi Parallel stance.
heisoku-dachi Attention stance.
jiyu-dachi Free-fighting stance.
kiba-dachi Horse stance.
kokutsu-dachi Back stance.
kosa-dachi Cross-legged stance.
neko-ashi-dachi Cat-leg stance.
renoji-dachi L-stance.
sanchin-dachi Hourglass stance.
shiko-dachi Square stance.
shizentai-dachi Natural stance.
sochin-dachi Diagonal straddle-leg stance.
teiji-dachi T-stance.
uchi-hachiji-dachi Inverted open-leg stance.
yoi-dachi Preparatory stance.
zenkutsu-dachi Front stance.

Ukewaza (blocking techniques)

age-uke Rising block.
gedan-barai Downward block.
haishi-uke Backhand block.
juji-uke X-block.
kake-uke Hooking block.
kakiwake-uke Reverse wedge block.
kakuto-uke Bent-wrist block.
keito-uke Chicken-head wrist block.
morote-sukui-uke Two-hand scooping block.
morote-tsukami-uke Two-hand grasping block.
morote-uke Augmented forearm block.
nagashi-uke Sweeping block.
osae-uke Pressing block.
otoshi-uki Dropping block.
seiryuto-uke Ox-jaw block.
shuto-uke Knife-hand block.
sokumen-awase-uke Side two-hand block.
soto-uke Outside block.
sukui-uke Scooping block.
teisho-awase-uke Combined palm-heel block.
tekyubi-uke Wrist-hook block.
tsukami-uke Grasping block.
uchi-uke Inside block.

Tsukiwaza (punching techniques)

age-zuki Rising punch.
awase-zuki U-punch.
choku-zuki Straight punch.
dan-zuki Consecutive punching.
gyaku-zuki Reverse punch.
hiraken-zuki Fore-knuckle fist straight punch.
hasami-zuki Scissors punch.
heiko-zuki Parallel punch.
ippon-ken-zuki One-knuckle fist straight punch.
kagi-zuki Hook punch.
kizami-zuki Jab punch.

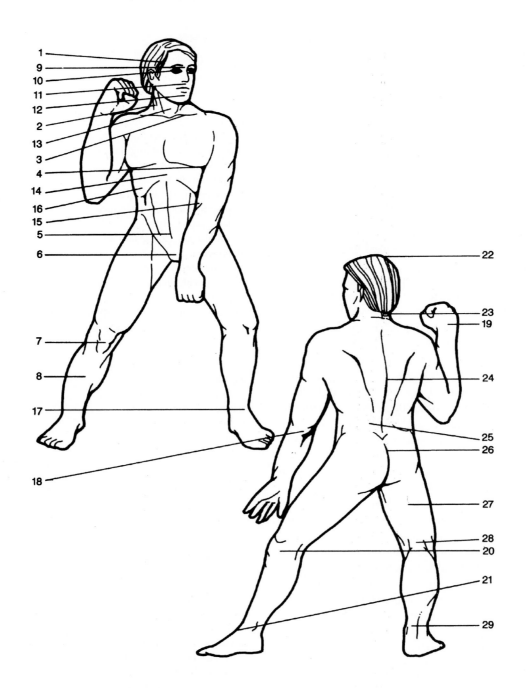

Figure 17.7. Target areas.

1. Temple
2. Side of neck
3. Collarbone
4. Armpit
5. Abdomen
6. Testicles
7. Knee
8. Shin
9. Bridge of nose
10. Eye
11. Just below nose
12. Chin
13. Throat
14. Solar plexus
15. Front of elbow

16. Ribs
17. Ankle
18. Back of elbow
19. Wrist
20. Side of knee
21. Instep
22. Skull
23. Back of neck
24. Center of back
25. Kidneys
26. Coccyx
27. Back of thigh
28. Back of knee
29. Achilles tendon

morote-zuki Double-fist punch.
nagashi-zuki Flowing punch.
nakadaka ippon ken Middle-finger one-knuckle fist.
oi-zuki Lunge, or chase, punch.
seiken choku-zuki Fore-fist straight punch.
tate-zuki Vertical fist punch.
teisho-zuki Palm-heel punch.
ura-zuki Close punch.
yama-zuki Mountain punch.

Keriwaza (kicking techniques)

age-uke-kake-uke Upper block (reverse foot).
ashibo-kake-uke Leg-hooking block.
ashikubi-kake-uke Ankle-hooking block.
fumikiri Cutting kick.
fumikomi Stomping kick.
gyaku-mawashi-geri Reverse round kick.
mae-geri Front kick.
mae-tobi-geri Jumping front kick.
mawashi-geri Round kick.
mikazuki-geri Crescent kick.
nidan-geri Double jump kick.
sokutei-mawashi-geri Circular sole kick.
sokutei-osae-geri Pressing sole block.
tobi-geri Jumping kick.
yoki-tobi-geri Jumping side kick.

Uchiwaza (striking techniques)

empi-uchi Elbow strike.
haishu-uchi Back-hand strike.
haito-uchi Ridge-hand strike.
hiji-uchi Elbow strike.
kentsui-uchi Bottom-fist strike.
nukite Spear hand.
riken-uchi Back-fist strike.
shuto-uchi Knife-hand strike.
tettsui-uchi Bottom-fist strike.
uraken-uchi Back-fist strike.

Commands and directions

hajime Begin.
hidari Left.
mae Front.
mawatte Turn.
migi Right.
modotte Return to original position.
narande Line up.
otagai ni rei Bow to each other.
rei Bow.
seiretsu Line up by rank.
sensei ni rei Bow to teacher.
shomen ni rei Bow to the front of the dojo.
ushiro Back.
yame Stop.
yasume Relax.
yoi Ready.

Other important terms

aite Opponent.
dan Black-belt rank.

dojo Martial arts school.
embusen Kata performance line.
enjin kumite Circle fight.
jiyu kumite Free-fighting.
kamae Posture.
kancho Building chief ("chief instructor of organization").
karate Empty hand.
kata Formal exercise.
kiai Spirit cry.
kihon Basic exercise.
kohai Junior.
kumite Sparring.
kyu Colored-belt rank.
makiwara Punching post.
mokuso Meditation.
nagewaza Throwing technique.
obi Belt.
okyu teate First aid.
osotu-gari Major outside leg sweep.
osu Greeting that shows respect.
ouchi-gari Major inside leg sweep.
renzuki Alternate punching.
ryu Tradition.
sanbon-kumite Three-step sparring.
seiza Formal sitting position.
sempai Senior.
senjin kumite Line fight.
sensei Teacher.
shihan Master.
shotokan Pine-sea style (*kan* translates here as "building").
suki Opening.
suwari-geiko Seated sparring.
teki Enemy.
tori Attacker.
uke Defender.
ukemi Falling practice.

SUGGESTED READINGS

Beasley, J. 2003. *Mastering karate*. Champaign, IL: Human Kinetics.

Cochran, S. 2001. *Complete conditioning for martial arts*. Champaign, IL: Human Kinetics.

Cook, H. 2009. *Shotokan karate: A precise history*. 2nd ed. Norwich, Norfolk County, England: Page Brothers, Ltd.

Gibson, A. 2004. *Competitive karate*. Champaign, IL: Human Kinetics.

Johnson, W. 2001. *The complete martial artist*. Champaign, IL: Human Kinetics.

Park, D., and Schein, A. 2006. *Tae Kwon Do: The indomitable martial art of Korea*. Montpelier, VT: Invisible Cities Press.

Kim, S., and Lee, K. 2007. *Complete Tae Kwon Do Poomsae*: Santa Fe, NM: Turtle Press.

RESOURCES

Videos

See Appendix C for video sources.

Organization

AAU Headquarters P.O. Box 971
Lake Zurich, IL 60047
847-540-9567
847-797-0510 (Fax)

WEB SITES

AAU

http://www.aaukarate.org/
http://www.aautaekwondo.org/
http://www.usankf.org

Shotokan Karate

http://www.iskf.com/
http://www.ska.org/
http://www.jkadojo.com/

Shindo Jinen-Ryu (Japan Karate-Do Ryobukai)

http://www.jkr.com/

Taekwondo

http://www.wtf.org/wtf_eng/main/main_eng_html
http://www.itftkd.org/

Goju Karate

http://www.imgka.com/
http://www.naha-te.com/

Wado-Ryu Karate

http://www.wadokarate-usa.org/

Shito-Ryu Karate

http://www.usakaratedokai.com/

Wing Chun Kung Fu

http://www.winchunkuen.com/

Kayaking and Canoeing

After completing this chapter, the reader should be able to:

- Describe the history and development of canoeing and kayaking
- Select and care for proper equipment
- Describe and execute fundamental canoeing and kayaking techniques
- Practice proper safety procedures
- Practice boating etiquette
- Instruct a group of students in basic canoeing and kayaking techniques

HISTORY

Canoeing and kayaking have evolved over hundreds of years. The first boating vessels were probably single logs or logs strapped together (rafts). With the use of fire and primitive tools, crafts such as the dugout canoe emerged. Natives from Central America, the Fiji Islands, Africa, and the Solomon Islands, and Indian tribes in North America used the dugout canoe for travel, trade, and war.

The canoe and kayak can be traced to the Indian tribes and Alaska natives of North America. In areas where trees were scarce, frame-and-skin craft were constructed. A wooden or bone frame was designed to form the gunwales, keel, and ribs, and the skins of buffalo, moose, or cattle were sewn together and stretched over the frame. Seams were sealed with pitch or tallow. In the north-central parts of the United States and Canada, where trees were plentiful, bark from birch trees was stretched over a wooden frame.

Decked (covered) boats were used by tribes mainly in Alaska and Greenland. These boats were called "kayaks" or "umiaks." Kayaks were smaller, for one person, and were paddled with double-blade paddles. Umiaks were larger, up to 30 feet (9.14 m), and were paddled by up to eight paddlers using single-blade paddles. Open boats were called "canoes." Canoes for one person were 12 to 17 feet (3.7 to 5.2 m) long, while those built up to 30 feet (9.14 m) long could carry more people. They were mainly paddled with single-blade paddles. Sometimes poles were used for steering and navigating upstream.

Canoes and kayaks were a primary source of transportation. They were used for hunting and for transporting furs to trading centers. When the settlers from Europe and Great Britain came to North America, they often had the help of Indians in facilitating travel. Canoes were fast, had good maneuverability on the water, and were lightweight for portaging between lakes or rivers. Many French immigrants—known as *voyageurs*—settled in the Canadian North and found the adventurous life of hunting and trapping more attractive than clearing land and farming. They adopted the Indian lifestyle and became expert canoeists.

Unlike voyageurs, other European settlers employed the Indians to help them. Samuel de Champlain, Jacques Marquette, Louis Joliet, Lewis and Clark, and others had Indian guides and used Indians to paddle canoes. Therefore, paddling expertise was never attained by these explorers.

Canoeing, both paddling and sailing, and kayaking enjoyed considerable recreational and competitive participation between the 1880s and 1940s. The American Canoe Association, which included Canada, was founded in 1885. One of the works that helped popularize North American canoeing was *Voyage of the Paper Canoe,* published by Nathaniel H. Bishop in 1878. The book recounts a canoe trip from Quebec through the lakes, rivers, and coastal waters of the eastern seaboard to the Gulf of Mexico. This was also a time of very widespread interest in outdoor recreational pursuits. A number of exceptionally talented boat builders, such as J. Henry Rushton, emerged at this time.

Interestingly, Europeans who traveled in the United States and Canada saw the canoe or kayak and popularized it as sport in their countries. In 1865, John MacGregor made his famous 1000-mile trip throughout England and Europe in the *Rob Roy.* Because the *Rob Roy* and others like it were closed or decked boats, kayaking became known as *canoeing* throughout Europe. Because of the influence of French fur trappers who preferred more open Indian-style vessels, the term *un canadien,* or "a Canadian," became a popular name for the canoe, and it is still used throughout Europe. Whitewater paddling in Europe was pursued as a leisure activity, and Europeans dominated international canoe and kayak racing throughout the twentieth century.

Canoeing and kayaking have enjoyed ongoing popularity in North America and Europe. Many times the canoe is used in conjunction with other outdoor recreational pursuits like fishing and hunting. Private camps, YMCA camps, military academies, and the like have done an excellent job in introducing many youth to the sport. The American Canoe Association and the American Red Cross worked in tandem for many years in presenting excellent canoe instruction and safety programs. The traditional wood covered with canvas, Old Town, and plywood veneer canoes were supplanted by the very durable aluminum models, Grumman, after World War II. However, these specialty craft have been undergoing a revival recently and can often be seen along with new hand-built wood strip canoes.

The development of such synthetics as fiberglass, acrylonitrile butadiene styrene (ABS), and Kevlar, along with a maturing of social, economic, and environmental values, has resulted in a growing popularity of canoeing and kayaking (Figure 18.1). The popularity of flat-water boating and whitewater canoeing has stabilized in the recent past. However, interest in sea kayaking has flourished since the 1990s. Sea kayaking now represents the area of greatest growth. The term *sea kayaking* is now used interchangeably with *touring kayaking* and includes paddling on inland lakes and flatwater rivers. In states with coastal waters or large inland bodies of water, sea kayaks provide opportunities for exploring saltwater marshes and intercoastal waterways, whale and dolphin watching, and cruising barrier islands in open expanses of water with some degree of stability.

Play-boating, hotdogging, and freestyle are also being explored by canoeists and kayakers. As people gain expertise in controlling their vessels, there is always an urge to test the limits of what can be done, just as in skiing, surfing, and rock climbing. As a result, the art of quick turning by laying a boat on its side, pirouettes, and the like is continually evolving.

One of the driving forces behind the introduction of canoeing into the Olympic Games was Wally Van B. Clausen, who helped organize a demonstration event at the 1924 Games. Canoeing was introduced as a permanent event in 1936 in Berlin with distances of 1,500 and 10,000 meters. It has continued as an official sport in the Summer Games since and is now contested in

Figure 18.1. Canoeing rivers offers many recreational opportunities.

men's and women's single, tandem, and 4-person sprint kayaks, and single and tandem canoes for men. The race distances are now 500 and 1,000 meters. Slalom canoe and kayak events were held in Munich, Barcelona, Atlanta, and Sydney and added to the regular program in the Athens and Beijing Olympics. With 16 Olympic events, kayaking and canoeing together make up the fourth largest sport in the Summer Olympic program. In addition to the Olympic Games kayak and canoe events are held in continental championships such as the Pan American Games. International kayak and canoe racing is governed by the International Canoe Federation (ICF). In addition to conducting Olympic events, the ICF is responsible for an annual racing calendar that includes the World Cup and World Championships. These events include single, double, and four-person races over 200 m, 500 m, and 1,000 m.

The Americans were highly respected international competitors in the late '40s and into the early '60s. After a long period of mediocre performance in the competitive arena, Greg Barton became the first Olympic medallist in 20 years in 1984 in Los Angeles, winning a bronze medal in the 1,000-meter single kayak. In 1988 in Seoul, he accomplished an unprecedented feat by winning the single and teaming with Norman Bellingham to win the double kayak. The first World Whitewater Competition in the United States took place on the Savage River in Maryland in 1989, after being held in Europe for decades. Kathy Hearn, Davey Hearn, Jon Lugbill, and others have led the resurgence of whitewater slalom racers. In the 1992 Olympics in Barcelona, Spain, Joe Jacobi and Scott Strausbaugh became the first Americans to win a gold medal in whitewater competition. Dana Chladek also won a bronze medal in women's solo canoe for the United States. The 1996 Olympics in Atlanta had venues in both flat-water canoeing and kayaking, as well as in downriver and slalom whitewater canoeing and kayaking. The whitewater events were held on the Ocoee River in southeastern Tennessee. Once again the Europeans dominated the events, although Dana Chladek from the United States won a silver medal in women's singles kayak. At the 2000 Olympic Games in Sydney, Australia, the German and Hungarian participants took home nearly one-third (15 of 48) of the possible medals. The rest of the medals were distributed among participants from 15 other countries. The highest finish by the United States was a 6th place by Peter Newton and Angel Perez in the 2-man 500-meter kayak sprint.

The 2004 Olympic Games in Athens, Greece, featured both whitewater slalom and flat-water sprint events. The whitewater slalom competitions were held at the Olympic Canoe/Kayak Slalom Center at the Helliniko Sports Complex, and the flatwater sprint events took place at the Olympic Rowing and Canoeing Center in Schinias. Much like the 2000 Olympics, the Germans and Hungarians proved to be the dominating forces, finishing at the top of the medal standings, earning again 15 out the 48 total medals. Nevertheless, highlighting the U.S.'s Olympic Team was Rebecca Giddens, who took home a silver medal in the women's single kayak whitewater slalom race. This was the first medal for the U.S. Olympic Canoe/Kayak Team since the 1996 Olympic Games.

The only two United States athletes to make the Olympic finals in 2008 in Beijing were Benn Fraker, who finished 6th in the canoe-single slalom event, and Heather Corrie, who was 8th in the kayak-single slalom event. The biggest winners at the Beijing Games were the Germans with 3 gold, 2 silver, and 3 bronze medals and the Australians with 1 gold, 1 silver, and 4 bronze medals.

VALUES

Whereas most outdoor recreation and sports develop the muscles of the lower limbs, canoeing and kayaking primarily develop muscles of the back, abdomen, shoulders, and arms. It is an excellent aerobic activity because most canoe and kayak outings last for at least half an hour and many take from half a day to several days. Canoeing and kayaking may begin as recreational activities or as a sports interest. As skill is developed, the number of options becomes almost limitless. One can canoe or kayak solo or with a partner. Canoeing and kayaking can offer solitude as well as the companionship of groups. Canoeing and kayaking are done by both sexes and by people of all ages.

The versatility of canoes and kayaks is amazing. One can paddle on the smallest creek, river, lake, or even the sea. After developing skill in a selected vessel, it is possible to combine paddling with picture-taking, sightseeing, fishing, hunting, bird-watching, and the like. If one wishes to become competitive, there are flat-water sprint racing or whitewater slalom and downriver racing competitions. More recent modifications include marathon kayaking on lakes and rivers and surf-ski racing on open water and the sea. Competition varies from citizens races (friendly, novice racing) to Olympic events.

EQUIPMENT

Paddles, boats, personal gear, and clothing have changed greatly in recent years. Natural materials in clothing and boats have given way to synthetics, which have brought about changes in the sport.

In the past, equipment such as an aluminum canoe served many purposes. Today specialized equipment exists for different boating and paddling styles. Because the diversity of equipment can be overwhelming, asking instructors or boat outfitters appropriate questions concerning equipment and gear will enhance the chance of making good choices.

CLOTHING

On a hot summer day, you may be comfortable in a swimsuit or a cotton shirt and shorts. However, during the spring or fall and on cold-water rivers or lakes, always consider the prospect of hypothermia. Long-sleeve shirts and pants made of a lightweight UV blocking fabric protect the skin from harmful sun while allowing the skin to radiate heat. Lotions and creams including UV block can reduce the radiating ability of the skin and can lead to overheating.

Layering clothes increases warmth and comfort. A wicking layer next to the body transfers moisture from the skin to the outer layers. Silk and polypropylene serve this purpose. Absorbing material should be the middle layer. Wool, pile, and bunting moves moisture to the outer layer. The outer layer protects against wind and water and is usually made of nylon or Gore-Tex. Although it may not be necessary to wear all these clothes at all times, harsh weather conditions and water temperature should always be considered. Clothes not needed immediately should be packed in a dry bag. Wet suits and dry suits are often worn by paddlers under some conditions.

Shoes should also be considered. Entry, exit, and portage conditions cannot always be predicted. Old sneakers, hiking boots, river shoes, and booties are all choices. Many accidents have been caused by poor traction or stepping on cut glass. It is important to protect the feet from injury.

Other personal choices are hats and sunglasses. Hats help keep the body warm and protect the eyes from the sun's glare. Sunglasses protect eyes from glare and from harmful ultraviolet rays.

ACCESSORY GEAR

Accessories for canoeing and kayaking include paddles, life vests, flotation devices, spray covers, first-aid kits, and rescue equipment. Next to choosing a proper canoe or kayak, the choice of a paddle is the most critical. Paddles are constructed of wood, fiberglass, carbon fiber, plastic, or aluminum. Grips are either pear-shaped or T-shaped. Shafts are straight or angled from 5 to 15 degrees. Blade width may vary from 6 to 9 inches (15.2 to 22.9 cm) or more. Length is determined by the paddler's height and whether the paddle will be used from a sitting or kneeling position. When standing, a canoe paddle should be long enough to come up approximately to the chin of a person. High-performance paddles are light, stiff, and expensive, but sometimes not very durable. Paddles used on rugged, remote trips should be durable. Aluminum shafts are light and durable, but they may feel cold to bare hands. Beginning paddlers usually use whatever the outfitter provides, but as one becomes serious about canoeing or kayaking, one must learn about the available choices before buying.

Paddlers should always wear a U.S. Coast Guard–approved life vest for adequate buoyance, physical protection, and warmth (Figure 18.2). Type III and Type V personal flotation devices (PFDs) are most commonly used. In challenging conditions, persons in decked boats (kayaks, C-1s, etc.) or open boats in difficult rivers with a probability of capsizing should use helmets. Helmets have a plastic or fiberglass shell with a liner to cushion blows.

Type I PFD — Off-Shore Life Jacket
Best for open, rough, or remote water, where rescue may be slow coming.
Advantages: Floats you the best.
  Turns most unconscious wearers face-up in water. Highly visible color.
Disadvantages: Bulky

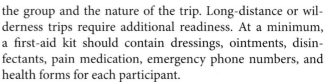

Type II PFD — Near-Shore Buoyant Vest
Good for calm, inland water, or where there is a good chance of fast rescue.
Advantages: Turns some unconscious wearers face-up in water. Less bulky, more comfortable than Type I PFD.
Disadvantages: Not for long hours in rough water.
  Will not turn some unconscious wearers face-up in water.

Type III PFD — Flotation Aid
For calm, inland water, or where there is good chance of fast rescue.
Advantages: Generally the most comfortable type for continuous wear. Designed for general boating or the activity that is marked on the device.
Disadvantages: Wearer may have to tilt head back to avoid going face-down. In rough, water, a wearer's face may often be covered by waves. Not for extended survival in rough water.

Type IV PFD — Throwable Device
For calm, inland water with heavy boat traffic, where help is always nearby.
Advantages: Can be thrown to someone.
  Good backup to wearable PFDs.
  Some can be used as seat cushion.
Disadvantages: Not for unconscious persons.
  Not for nonswimmers or children.
  Not for many hours in rough water.

Type V PFD — Special-Use Devices
For special uses or conditions such as rough whitewater canoeing and kayaking, boardsailing, etc.
Advantages: High level of flotation.
  Good for continuous wear.
  Turns most unconscious wearers face-up in the water.
Disadvantages: Approved for limited use.

Figure 18.2. Classes of personal flotation devices.

Flotation is necessary for canoes and kayaks so that they will not sink when swamped. Many aluminum and composite canoes have flotation in sealed compartments in the bow and stern. Decked boat flotation includes airbags and Ethafoam or Styrofoam walls that also prevent the deck from collapsing on the boater's legs in the case of a pin. Open-boat flotation may include inflatable air bags, Styrofoam blocks, and tire inner tubes. Extra flotation causes greater displacement of water when the boat is capsized, making rescue easier.

Spray covers and spray skirts are used in some canoeing conditions and most kayaking conditions to keep water from entering the vessel. Spray covers and skirts must release reliably, but not prematurely, under normal boating conditions so the paddler can get free of the boat.

First-aid equipment is a must for all boaters. The extent of readiness depends on the qualifications of the personnel in the group and the nature of the trip. Long-distance or wilderness trips require additional readiness. At a minimum, a first-aid kit should contain dressings, ointments, disinfectants, pain medication, emergency phone numbers, and health forms for each participant.

Rescue equipment is important for unexpected emergencies. Throw lines or rescue bags are often necessary for rescuing people or boats. "Painter lines" on canoes and grab loops on kayaks are helpful in rescue because they allow a person to get away from the boat while still maintaining contact. Other rescue equipment could include pulley-and-rope systems and repair kits for remote travel.

BOATS

The characteristics of canoes and kayaks vary widely. Paddlers can select boats geared to their strength, body size, and purpose (racing, touring, or pleasure). The most important features of canoes, kayaks, and paddles are shown in Figure 18.3.

Length
The overall length of a boat is the distance from one end to the other. If the width remains the same, an increase in length will increase the speed and tracking ability of the craft.

Width (Beam)
Width is measured at two points for canoes: the molded beam and the waterline. The molded-beam width is the distance between the tops of the two sides. The narrower this width, the easier it is to paddle because the canoeist does not have to reach out as far to the side. The waterline width is the widest point where a boat rests in the water. More weight added to a boat will generally increase its waterline width. Kayak width is measured at the widest point. Whitewater models generally are widest near the middle. This allows for increased maneuverability.

Symmetry describes the shape of the kayak from bow to stern. If the shape of the front half matches the shape of the rear half, the kayak is symmetrical. If the two halves differ in shape, the kayak is asymmetrical. Symmetrical kayaks are generally more maneuverable than their asymmetrical counterparts.

Asymmetrical kayaks are divided into two types: Fish-form and Swede-form. These terms are used to describe the location of the kayak's widest point in relation to its true middle. If the kayak is widest forward of true middle, it is a Fish-form kayak. If the kayak is widest to the rear of true middle, it is a Swede-form kayak. Fish-form kayaks have roomier cockpits and greater directional stability. They tend to hold a straight course better. Swede-form kayaks ride drier, cruise at slightly faster speeds, and feel as though they have slightly better stability, but they will require more effort to turn.

Parts of a Canoe

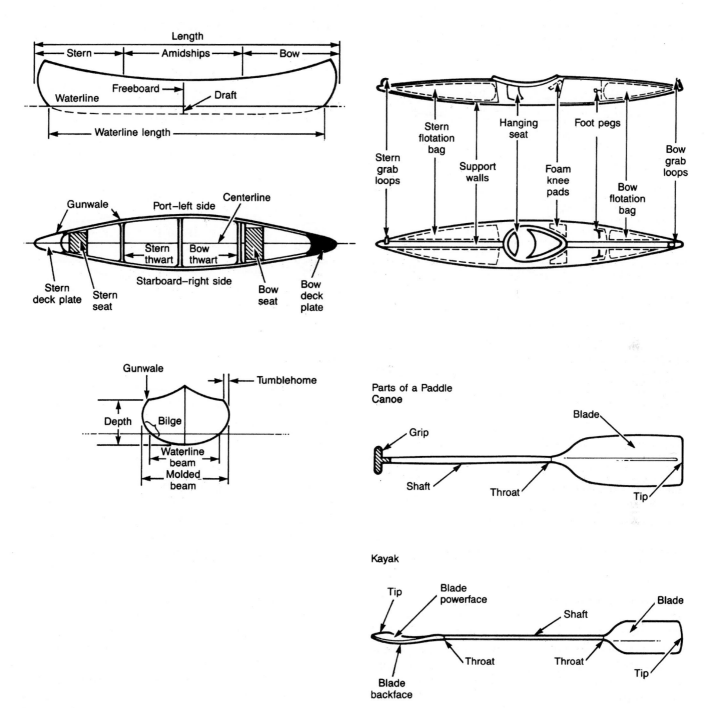

Figure 18.3. Features of canoes, kayaks, and paddles.

Depth

In a canoe, depth is measured at the centerline from the gunwale down. A taller boat deflects spray and waves, but may catch more wind than one with less depth. A shallow boat minimizes wind resistance, but increases the probability of shipping water. Depth in a kayak influences the amount of room for the legs and gear storage.

Rocker

The rocker is the shape of the hull along the underwater keel line (Figure 18.4). A straight keel line improves tracking ability. Turning is made easier (less drag) when a rocker is added. Rocker can be added by keeping the ends in the water or by reducing volume in the ends.

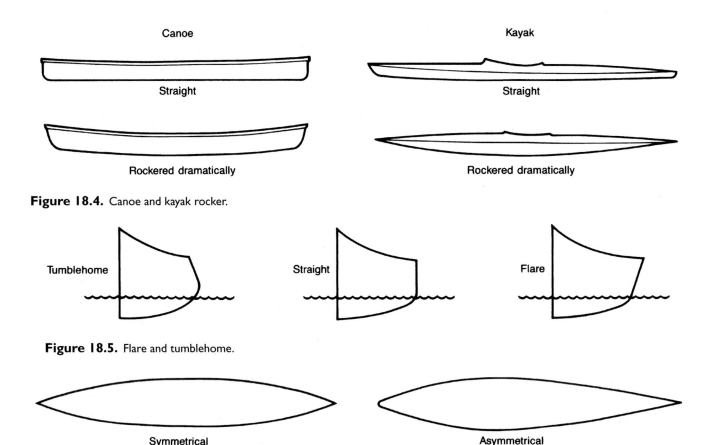

Figure 18.4. Canoe and kayak rocker.

Figure 18.5. Flare and tumblehome.

Figure 18.6. Symmetry.

Flare and Tumblehome

Flare and *tumblehome* are terms used to refer to the shape of the boat above the waterline (Figure 18.5). Flared sides provide increased stability. Boats with tumblehome have less molded beam width than waterline width and allow canoeists to paddle without banging knuckles on the gunwales. When boats with tumblehome are leaned extremely, stability is decreased dramatically.

Symmetry

As mentioned above, symmetry refers to the shape of the boat from front to back at the waterline (Figure 18.6). Symmetry affects a boat's movement through the water and its ability to turn. Symmetrical boats are used for quick maneuverability. Asymmetrical boats usually lengthen and streamline the shape of the bow to increase the efficiency of passage through the water. In asymmetrical boats, directional control is increased, but turning ability is decreased.

Arches and Flat Bottoms

Arches and *flat bottoms* are terms used to describe the bottom shape of the boat (Figure 18.7). Flat-bottom boats tend to be very stable. Rounded hulls are initially less stable than

flat bottoms if they have flare. They have good stability and are forgiving, however, when the boat is leaned. The greater the boat's V shape, the better the directional ability but the poorer its stability.

The cross-sectional shape of the bottom and sides of the canoe influence its performance, especially its stability. Stability is categorized as initial (primary) and final (secondary). If a boat has good initial stability it feels quite stable when first entered and it would take much effort to flip it on flat water. It resists leaning until it reaches a point of no return, but then it can upset quickly without much warning. In this type of boat secondary stability was sacrificed for the stableness of initial stability. Secondary stability refers to how the boat behaves as it tilts. A boat with good secondary stability, although somewhat unstable on first entering, is easy to lean onto its side. It feels stable and predictable in the lean. This is a useful characteristic for whitewater moves and rough-water paddling.

Flat-bottomed canoes have great initial stability at the expense of speed and rough-water performance. Because they are quite secure on calm water, they are great for sportsmen and recreational paddlers. Round-bottomed boats are the other end of the extreme. Rounded bottoms have less

Canoe

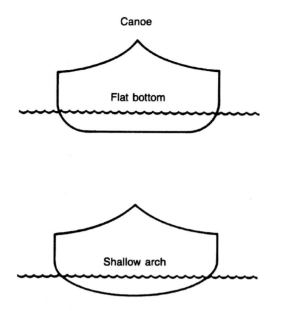

Kayak

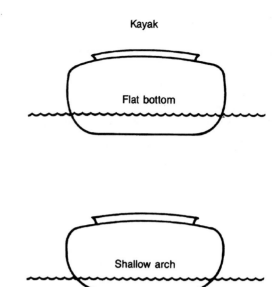

Figure 18.7. Arches and flat bottoms.

surface area with the water and they have great speed and efficiency but sacrifice initial stability. Most canoe designs are a compromise between flat and round with a shallow-arch bottom. They sacrifice varying degrees of initial stability for good secondary stability and all-around performance.

Volume

Volume indicates the fullness of a boat's shape and how much weight it can carry. High-performance vessels for racing have low volume. Medium-volume boats can carry some gear and are suited for general recreational paddling. High-volume boats can carry more than 200 pounds and are used for extended travel.

Boat Types

Canoes are classed into two divisions: tandem (for two people) and solo. (There are "multiple" canoes as well, varying in length from 18 feet to 30 feet, such as Canadian war canoes and Oriental Dragon boats that can carry crews of up to 22 people. These canoes will not be described in detail in this chapter.) Each division has several classes based on the purposes for which the canoe may be used. Within the tandem division, the casual-recreation, day-tripper, touring, and downriver boats are the most popular. Casual-recreation canoes are generally built with cost as a primary consideration, along with low maintenance, casual storage, and safety (Figure 18.8A). Performance is not a primary consideration. Tripper and touring canoes have a medium volume (Figure 18.8B). They are designed to carry two paddlers with gear yet have low profiles, are lightweight for portability, and are fairly quick in the water. Downriver canoes are valued primarily for their directional integrity or fast straight-ahead paddling (Figure 18.8C). They are good performers in waters

ranging from millponds and open bays to nontechnical class II and class II whitewater rivers. Competition cruising, whitewater play boat, whitewater slalom, and Olympic sprint are further types of tandem canoes used for racing in various conditions.

Solo canoes are the second division of canoes. Types of solo canoes are cruising, racing, sport, whitewater, and Olympic sprint (Figure 18.9). Cruising canoes are designed for the traveler. Sport canoes are ideal for day-tripping or "just messing around" on a lake or millpond. They combine maneuverability and directional integrity.

Kayaks also have many designs (Figure 18.10). They include casual recreation, touring, sea kayak, downriver, whitewater slalom, whitewater playboat, squirt, and Olympic sprint. Casual-touring kayaks are primarily touring boats, but they will handle nicely in moderate whitewater. Touring kayaks and sea kayaks are high-volume boats designed to carry generous loads without compromising handling qualities in moderately rough water and are designed to cover long stretches of unpredictably rough open water with comparative ease. Because of the interest in exploring the open water and coastline, this is the fastest-growing segment of the kayak industry. The remaining kayaks are generally for racing or recreation in whitewater.

GENERAL RULES AND WATER ETIQUETTE
Be Kind to Others

There is an old rule that good friends or spouses should never paddle together because of disagreements over route selection, fault for capsize, and so on. Communicate with your partner. Help or compensate for your partner. Offer assistance when asked. Don't be loud and obnoxious. Don't hog the best practice place, view, and the like.

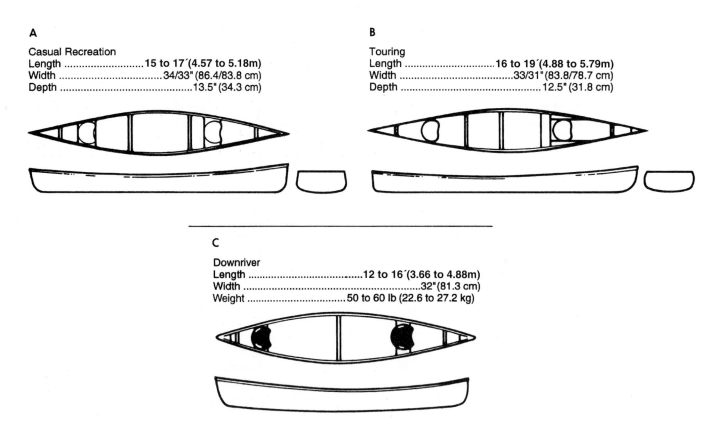

Figure 18.8. Types of tandem canoes.

A

Casual Recreation
Length ....15 to 17´(4.57 to 5.18m)
Width ....34/33" (86.4/83.8 cm)
Depth ....13.5" (34.3 cm)

B

Touring
Length ....16 to 19´(4.88 to 5.79m)
Width ....33/31" (83.8/78.7 cm)
Depth ....12.5" (31.8 cm)

C

Downriver
Length ....12 to 16´(3.66 to 4.88m)
Width ....32" (81.3 cm)
Weight ....50 to 60 lb (22.6 to 27.2 kg)

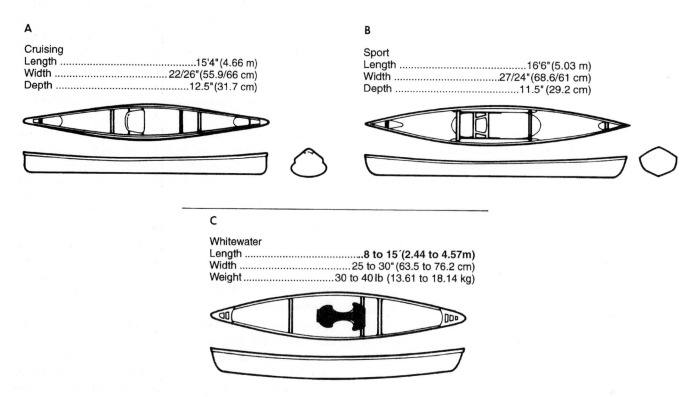

Figure 18.9. Types of solo recreational canoes.

A

Cruising
Length ....15'4" (4.66 m)
Width ....22/26" (55.9/66 cm)
Depth ....12.5" (31.7 cm)

B

Sport
Length ....16'6" (5.03 m)
Width ....27/24" (68.6/61 cm)
Depth ....11.5" (29.2 cm)

C

Whitewater
Length ....8 to 15´(2.44 to 4.57m)
Width ....25 to 30" (63.5 to 76.2 cm)
Weight ....30 to 40 lb (13.61 to 18.14 kg)

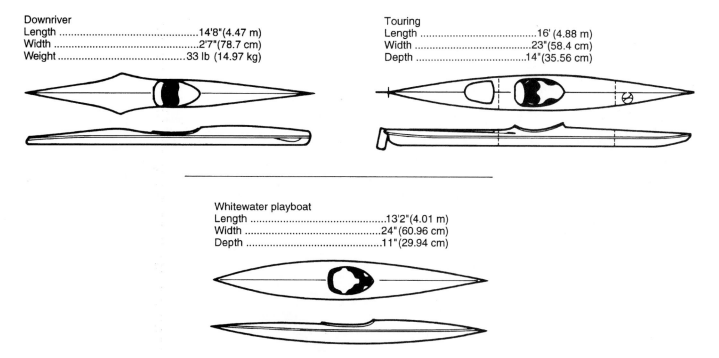

Downriver
Length ....14'8"(4.47 m)
Width ....2'7"(78.7 cm)
Weight ....33 lb (14.97 kg)

Touring
Length ....16' (4.88 m)
Width ....23"(58.4 cm)
Depth ....14"(35.56 cm)

Whitewater playboat
Length ....13'2"(4.01 m)
Width ....24" (60.96 cm)
Depth ....11"(29.94 cm)

Figure 18.10. Types of kayaks.

Stay with Your Group

If you are in a group, paddle as fast or as slow as the rest while maintaining a reasonable distance between boats. Getting too far ahead or behind puts you in a position to get lost, reduces the safety of the group as a whole, and generally causes ill feeling toward you. All group members, regardless of level of experience, are responsible for the integrity and safety of the group. If necessary, break your group into two units—one faster, one slower.

Respect Others' Property

Make sure you have permission to put your boats in the water and take them out. When stopping along a lake or river to eat, rest, or sleep, get permission and respect the trees, animals, fences, and land. Don't litter; and when you can, clean up the litter of others. See the section "Leave No Trace" in Chapter 5.

Follow Established Rules

The U.S. Coast Guard and other governing bodies, such as the American Whitewater Affiliate of the American Canoe Association, have rules for safety on the water. Know and follow them. Some general rules are:

1. Boats propelled by oars or paddles have the right-of-way over noncommercial motorboats.
2. In a crossing situation, the boat to the right has the right-of-way.
3. Use the universal river signals to communicate to others (Figure 18.11).
4. Right-of-way is never taken—only yielded.

FUNDAMENTAL SKILLS AND TECHNIQUES

Orienting the Paddler to the Boat

Canoes and kayaks are lightweight and shallow-draft crafts. They are sensitive to weight distribution (fore and aft as well as side to side). The key is to keep the center of gravity (CG) over the base of support (BS). In a canoe, the base of support may be thought of as that part of the canoe that is in direct contact with the water. As weight of packs or paddlers is added to a canoe or kayak, there is a potential for both the CG and BS to shift fore, aft, or to one side.

Maintaining balance in a canoe or kayak is regulated by keeping the CG over the BS and by keeping the CG as low as possible. A sudden change in trim caused by an outside force—such as a wave, collision, or by leaning to one side—results in a shift where the CG may begin to fall outside the BS. If this happens, it is necessary to use a righting action called a "hip flip" to recenter the CG over the BS. As one leans the canoe to the left, for example, the left gunwale lowers and comes close to the water. If one continues to lean left, the CG may fall outside the base of the canoe, causing it to capsize. To guard against this when kneeling, the canoeist can use the paddle to shift his or her weight thereby rebalancing or leveling the canoe again, bringing the CG over the BS. If additional righting force is needed, the paddler on the left side can brace and use the paddle to push the CG of the paddlers' bodies back to the center.

The recommended position for canoe paddling is kneeling. This offers a low center of gravity with three points of contact with the canoe. The knees are spread wide with the buttocks resting against the seat, or thwart. One can also

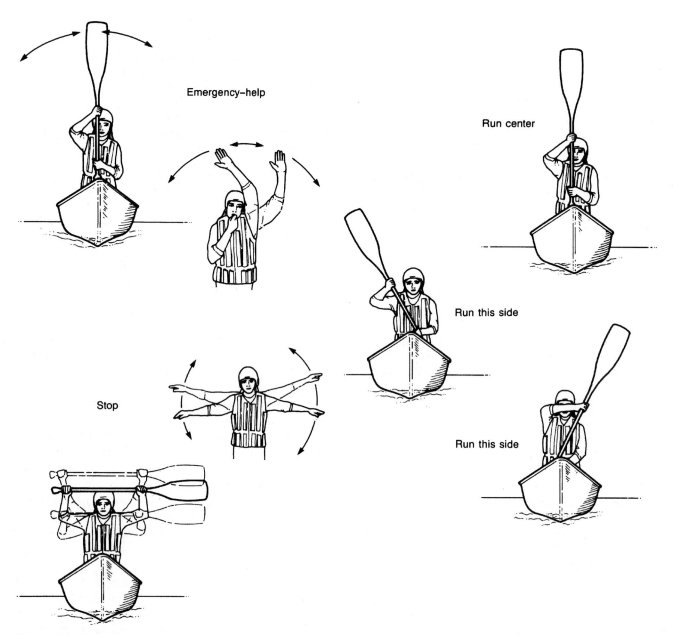

Emergency–help

Run center

Run this side

Stop

Run this side

Figure 18.11. Universal river signals.

perform the righting action (hip flip) from this position quite well. Other paddling positions—sitting, high-kneel, or standing—are possible. However, each causes the canoeist to have a higher CG relative to the BS and should not be tried until one has a feel for the canoe and has become competent in basic paddling strokes.

Kayakers always sit in their vessel with their legs out in front. To get a good fit, or to "wear the kayak," the knees should be bent up and out to fit snugly yet comfortably in the thigh braces under the deck of the kayak. Foot braces should be adjusted so the balls of the feet press against the braces. This snug fit gives a low CG and allows a good hip flip for maintaining stability.

A good stability drill is to get into position in the boat, lean slightly to one side, and then flip the hips back under to correct the BS and regain equilibrium. Another good stability drill is to rock from side to side while keeping the navel, shoulders, and head in a centered position. In both instances, paddlers can get a good feel for the boat and learn that by making adjustments, the craft can maintain stability under changing conditions.

Correct launching and docking (getting in and out) of canoes and kayaks are essential to a successful experience. Canoes may be boarded end-first, with the canoe perpendicular to shore, or from the side, with the side parallel to the shore or dock. When two people board a canoe, the

Figure 18.12. Launching.

Figure 18.13. Launching parallel to dock.

bowman usually boards first to maintain trim. The stern person assists by straddling the canoe and holding the gunwales. The bow person places the first foot on the center, or keel line, of the canoe while keeping the weight centered over the leg on the bank or dock. Next, while keeping low by bending at the hips and knees, the bow person graps each of the gunwales then brings the trailing leg into the canoe, at which time the canoeist assumes the kneeling position to assist the stern person in getting in (Figure 18.12). When getting out, the process is reversed. Launching and docking a canoe from a position parallel to the dock involves the same procedures. Step into the center. Grasp both gunwales. Keep your weight low (Figure 18.13).

Getting into and out of a kayak, with its tiny cockpit, is more of a challenge. The best way is to place the kayak parallel and next to shore or the loading dock. Place the paddle across the kayak, just behind the cockpit, with one of the blades lying flat on shore for support. With the hand nearest the kayak, grip the junction of the kayak paddle and the cockpit along the centerline of the boat to keep the boat steady. While keeping your weight leaning toward shore, place the leg nearest the kayak just to the front of the seat (Figure 18.14). Follow it with the other leg. Then lower yourself into the seat, being careful not to scrape your shins across the front of the cockpit. Exiting is a reversal of this process.

In both canoeing and kayaking, it may be necessary to perform what is called a *wet entry* and exit. The exit part is easy. In a canoe, rather than jumping out or capsizing, it is safer to place both hands on one gunwale, maintain contact, and slip over the side of the canoe into the water. When doing a wet entry, it is important for a partner or another canoe to provide support and assistance. With this assistance being provided from the opposite side, place both hands on the gunwale, perform a scissors kick to gain lift, and push up with the arms into a support position with the hips near the

gunwale and lean the torso across the canoe. Hook one leg inside the gunwale and roll into the canoe resulting in sitting upright on the bottom of the boat. Staying low through this process is important. A wet exit from a kayak is accomplished by capsizing, stretching forward to release the skirt, then pressing on the sides of the kayak next to the cockpit and rolling forward—the legs follow the hips out of the boat. After righting the kayak and approaching it diagonally from the rear, a wet entry can be performed by placing both hands on the cockpit and using the arms to pull up onto the back deck of the kayak in straddle position. Then, by placing both hands behind the hips, both legs are lifted simultaneously (bilaterally) and smoothly back into the kayak and slid back down into a sitting position. This is an advanced skill and requires a great deal of practice.

Mechanics of Paddling

There are three major types of canoe and kayak strokes: power strokes; turning, lateral, or corrective strokes; and bracing strokes. Power strokes primarily provide forward or reverse propulsion. Turning and lateral strokes pivot the boat or make it go sideways, while corrective strokes adjust the path of the boat to keep it on a straight course. Bracing strokes provide stability for the craft.

Strokes are also divided into onside and offside strokes. Onside strokes are executed on the selected paddling side. Offside strokes are executed on the other side. There are two phases to all strokes. The *propulsion phase* is the application of force on the paddle against the water. The *recovery phase* is the return of the paddle to a "catch" position, where the blade is braced against the water, ready to begin the propulsion phase. Recoveries can be feathered above the water or sliced through the water.

Strokes can be dynamic or static. A dynamic stroke moves the blade actively against the water. A static stroke is a fixed-position

Figure 18.14. Launching the kayak.

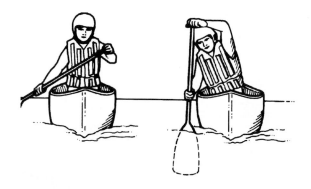

Figure 18.15. Paddle position for linear motion.

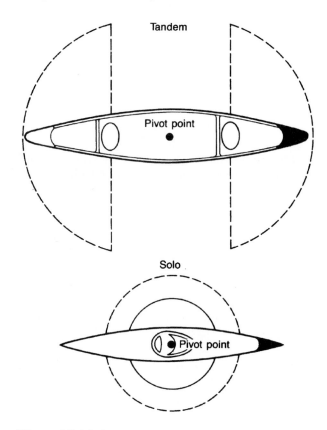

Figure 18.16. Rotary motion.

stroke used to turn or veer the boat. Static strokes require the boat to be moving faster than the water to be effective.

Paddling strokes utilize leverage to gain propulsion through the water. With a firm grip of the top hand, the paddler reaches in a chosen direction with the bottom hand to propel the load (canoe/kayak) through the water (forward, backward, sideways, or turning). As the paddle blade enters the water, one can think of it like placing it in molasses or cement. While there is some slippage of the paddle through the water, the resulting muscular action on the paddle propels the craft in the desired direction. Speed and range of motion are gained at the blade end of the paddle. Mechanical advantage is the result. In selected strokes such as the J and pry, or push-away, the paddler can attempt to use the middle of the shaft against the gunwale of the canoe and transfer the power of the stroke directly to the canoe, utilizing fulcrum mechanics, and make the stroke more effective.

The power face is that side of the blade that is pressed against the water during a forward stroke. The back face is the reverse side of the paddle and is pressed against the water during a backstroke. Turning, lateral, correcting, and bracing strokes will be identified according to whether they use the power face or back face of the paddle for execution.

To establish linear motion in a canoe or kayak, it is best to have the paddle in a vertical position and follow a straight path parallel to the keel line of the boat (Figure 18.15). To establish rotary motion (Figure 18.16) in a vessel, it is best to apply force to the paddle as far forward, or aft, of midships as possible to establish an arc around a pivot point.

Newton's Third Law of Motion states that for every action, there is an equal and opposite reaction. In paddling, the action is the application of force to the blade. The reaction is the movement of the craft in the opposite direction. To go forward, pull the water back. To go to the right, push or pull the water to the left.

The most powerful stroking action is accomplished with the arms in a relatively fixed, straight, extended position and by using the large, strong muscles of the back and torso. This concept is called *torso rotation* (Figure 18.17). During the recovery phase, the shoulder of the onside arm is rotated forward to "coil" the body. During the power phase, the torso is unwound.

Three types of wind and water resistance that can affect a craft are frontal, surface, and vortex resistance (Figure 18.18). Frontal resistance occurs where the force of wind or water strikes a craft first. It exerts the greatest pressure against a boat. Surface resistance occurs when the wind or water slides

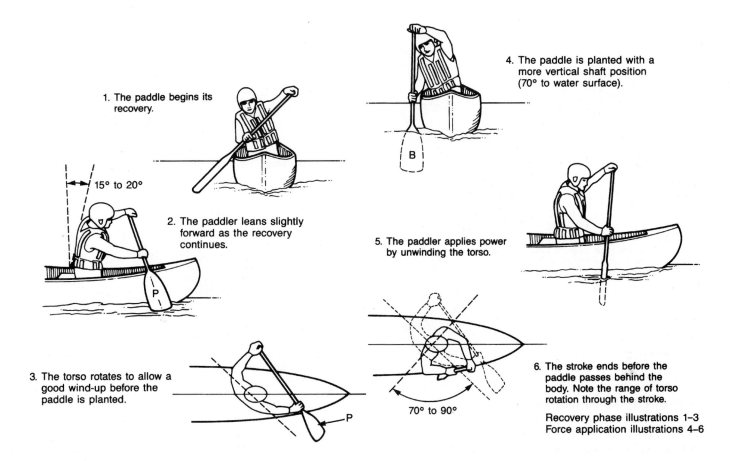

1. The paddle begins its recovery.

15° to 20°

2. The paddler leans slightly forward as the recovery continues.

3. The torso rotates to allow a good wind-up before the paddle is planted.

4. The paddle is planted with a more vertical shaft position (70° to water surface).

5. The paddler applies power by unwinding the torso.

6. The stroke ends before the paddle passes behind the body. Note the range of torso rotation through the stroke.

70° to 90°

Recovery phase illustrations 1–3
Force application illustrations 4–6

Figure 18.17. Torso rotation in forward stroke.

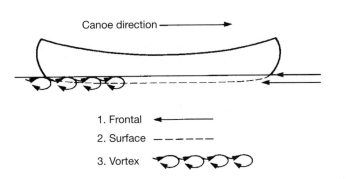

Canoe direction

1. Frontal
2. Surface
3. Vortex

Figure 18.18. Three types of resistance.

along the craft. Vortex resistance is created when a craft displaces wind or water at its widest point. The resulting vacuum is filled in by an unstable whirl of displaced water. An understanding of these resistances helps paddlers determine which stroke to use in a given situation. For example, corrective strokes are most effective in the vortex resistance end. When paddling forward, the stern person can best steer the craft. When paddling backward, the bow person can best steer the craft.

Paddling Strokes

Power strokes

Forward. The forward stroke is used in solo and tandem canoeing and kayaking. For clarity, the forward canoe stroke is discussed separately from the kayak stroke.

In the catch position, the body is rotated with the bottom, or shaft, arm reaching as far forward as possible. Both arms are relatively straight. The top, or control, arm is across the midline of the body to allow the paddle to be vertical in the water. The torso remains fairly upright, with no more than a 20-degree bend (Figure 18.19). Lunging and straightening the back causes the canoe to bob in the water. To catch, drive the onside hand down so the blade is fully immersed. Once the blade is in the water, the propulsion phase of the stroke involves unwinding the torso. The arms remain relatively straight, with the most movement occurring at the shoulder nearest the paddle as it unwinds like a spring.

At entry, the paddle is angled forward, blade ahead of the grip, between 30 and 45 degrees. As power is applied, it appears that the paddle is drawn backward through the water; however, the canoe is actually moving past the blade that only "slips" a little. The primary propulsion is accomplished from the time of entry until the shaft is angled backward about 15 to 30 degrees. Recovery should begin before the shaft reaches the hip. During

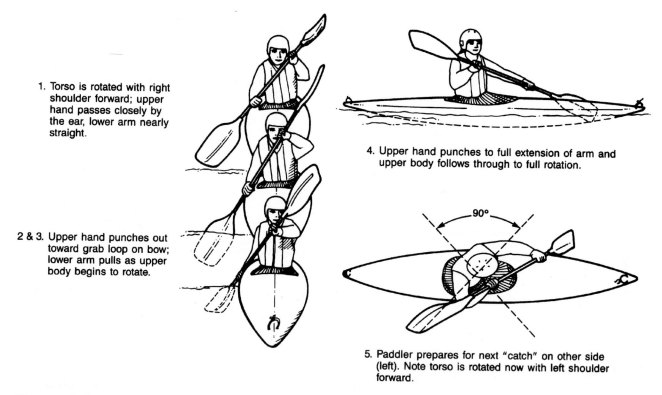

1. Torso is rotated with right shoulder forward; upper hand passes closely by the ear, lower arm nearly straight.

2 & 3. Upper hand punches out toward grab loop on bow; lower arm pulls as upper body begins to rotate.

4. Upper hand punches to full extension of arm and upper body follows through to full rotation.

5. Paddler prepares for next "catch" on other side (left). Note torso is rotated now with left shoulder forward.

Figure 18.19. Forward stroke—kayak.

recovery, the blade should be angled to cut through the air like a knife to reduce air resistance.

The forward kayak stroke involves significant torso rotation and a push-pull action with the upper body (Figure 18.19). The top of the paddle shaft is stabilized by a static push while the torso and lower arm pull on the shaft to move the kayak forward.

Although the apparent path of the canoe paddle in the water is straight and parallel to the direction of travel, the blade of the kayak paddle will move in a line just inside the bow wake away from the boat because of the enhanced torso rotation. This is especially true with wing-shaped racing paddles. Exit and recovery begins when the lower hand reaches the hip. The paddle blade is removed from the water by lifting the wrist and elbow to shoulder level. This action promotes a clean exit and a quick recovery for the next stroke.

Common inefficiencies include failing to submerge the blade fully, leaning forward (lunging), pulling the paddle too for through the water, and sweeping the blade in an arc rather than pulling vertically parallel to the keel line. Keeping a boat on a straight course requires timing and power, which may be elusive at first.

Back. The backstroke for canoes and kayaks retraces the forward stroke with the same body techniques. The catch position is just behind the hip nearest the blade, and the power phase ends when the upper hand is near the shoulder. The back face of the paddle blade is used. Beginners should look over one shoulder to see where they are going.

Turning, lateral, and corrective strokes

J stroke. When using the forward stroke, a canoe will begin to veer off course to the soloist's or stern person's off paddling side. For this reason, a corrective stroke is needed to keep the vessel on track. The J stroke (Figure 18.20) is used for this. It is not a kayaking stroke because kayakers paddle on both sides and can compensate with the next stroke.

The initial part of the J stroke, including the catch and beginning of the propulsion phase, resembles the forward stroke. A vertical paddle shaft and torso rotation are keys to success. However, as the paddle comes back to the hip, departure from the forward stroke begins. Rather than an immediate recovery, the paddle shaft is brought against the gunwale. The top, or control hand, with the paddle shaft in a vertical position (blade under the boat), rotates the thumb downward to present the power face of the paddle to a ver-

Figure 18.20. J stroke.

tical position, facing away from the canoe. In this position, the paddler uses the control hand to curve the blade sideways away from the canoe, tracing the pattern of a "J" on the water surface, pushing the stern of the canoe back on course behind the bow.

This movement is smooth and continuous yet powerful, allowing the paddler to keep an uninterrupted pace, or stroke rate. The use of the J stroke will vary according to factors such as solo or tandem paddling, wind and current, and strength/weight ratio of the tandem pair. Sometimes it is used every stroke in combination with the forward stroke; at other times it is used every two to four strokes. The trick is to gauge its use to anticipate and counteract the effects of veering.

Draw stroke. The draw stroke is used in canoeing and kayaking to move a boat laterally or to turn a boat, depending on the conditions under which it is applied. The basic draw stroke (Figure 18.21) is performed at a right angle to the paddler's side. With the arms making a C shape and the paddle in a vertical position extended out and away from the boat, the paddle is inserted fully into the water. The boat is then pulled to the blade. Most of the force is provided by the lower, or shaft, arm as it pulls into the hip. The hip simultaneously is thrust toward the paddle blade, thereby moving the boat back under the paddler's center of gravity. The stroke ends with the blade parallel to and near the boat. The recovery is initiated by turning the thumb of the top hand so it points away from the boat and then in an outward slicing action of the blade above the water or a knifing action of the blade through the water back to the catch position. Variations on the draw stroke include performing a stationary draw or a dynamic draw (several in a row). The stationary draw is used when the boat has built up some speed and the paddler wants to use one powerful stroke to sideslip the boat sideways to his or her onside or to initiate a turning action. The dynamic draw is used for lateral or turning maneuvers requiring continuous action or where the boat has no for-

Figure 18.22. Cross draw.

ward momentum. If the draw is used from midships, lateral movement will occur. If the paddler is positioned fore or aft or lowers the top hand fore or aft, the draw can be used to turn the boat. Other variations of the draw stroke are bracing strokes and the Duffek stroke, which will be discussed later.

Cross draw. The cross draw (Figure 18.22) requires the paddler to lift the paddle across the boat to the offside without changing hand position on the paddle. The body and arms are twisted to face the offside. The top hand is kept stationary at or near the armpit. The paddling action is done entirely by the lower arm. The hand on the shaft is palm down. The grip palm faces forward. The power face of the paddle blade is in a vertical position and is pulled toward the bow. Recovery is above the water. The stroke is used as an alternate to the pry stroke, especially in strong current. It is used to turn or move the canoe laterally. It may be used dynamically or from a static position.

Pry stroke. The pry, sometimes called the *push-away,* moves the canoe in the opposite direction of the draw. It moves the boat to the paddler's offside and can be used to

Figure 18.21. Basic draw stroke.

turn or move the boat laterally, depending on where the force is applied and whether the canoeist is paddling solo or in tandem. The pry is not a kayak stroke.

To execute the pry (Figure 18.23), place the paddle in a vertical position with the shaft in contact with the gunwale. The bottom hand holds the paddle and simultaneously cups the gunwale to stabilize the paddle, making it a first-class lever. The top hand, knuckles out, pulls sideways toward the midline of the body. A short, quick, powerful action is used with the back face of the paddle used for the stroke. The recovery can be out of or through the water. In each case, the paddle is knifed or sliced back to the catch position.

The pry can be used dynamically (several in a row) or singly. It can be used in combination with other strokes, such as a forward stroke into a pry.

Sweep strokes. Sweep strokes, as the name implies, are wide-sweeping arcs of the paddle. Solo sweeps in a canoe or kayak involve a 180-degree arc and are called *one-half sweeps* (Figure 18.24). Tandem sweeps are intended to account for one's position in a boat and thus cover 90 degrees and are referred to as *one-fourth sweeps* (Figure 18.25).

Unlike previous strokes in which the paddle was in a vertical position, the paddle position is low and angular. The forward sweeping action is with the power face of the blade. The reverse sweep is with the back face. Because the stroke's purpose is for turning, the torso of the body twists early for the catch and follows the blade through the exit.

When performed from a solo position at midships, a forward sweep enters at the 12 o'clock position and exits at the 6 o'clock position as the paddler follows with the torso, head, and arms until the shoulders are parallel to the keel line. The

forward sweep turns the boat to the paddler's offside. The reverse sweep for a solo boater begins at the 6 o'clock position, ends at the 12 o'clock position, and turns the boat to the paddler's onside.

When paddling tandem, the bow paddler's arcs are from the 12 o'clock position to the 3 o'clock position (or to the 9 o'clock position). The stern paddler's strokes are from the 3 o'clock position (or the 9 o'clock position) to the 6 o'clock position. If the bow does a forward one-fourth sweep and the stern does a reverse one-fourth sweep, the canoe will pivot in one direction, toward the stern paddler's paddling side. If the bow does a reverse one-fourth sweep and the stern does a forward one-fourth sweep, the boat will pivot in the opposite direction.

Duffek. The Duffek stroke is a turning stroke. It was first used in kayaking, but it can be used in canoeing by a solo paddler or by the bow paddler when tandem canoeing. The purpose of the Duffek is to make a 180-degree turn to enter or exit currents and eddies or to turn behind a solid object, such as a dock or pier. Because the boat has forward momentum, a sweep stroke (forward or backward) is used to initiate the turn.

A left turn in kayaking, for example, would be initiated by a forward sweep on the right. The Duffek would then be executed on the turning side, or left side (Figure 18.26). In many ways, the Duffek is like the stationary draw. The paddle is vertical in the water. However, in the catch position, the blade is opened until it broaches the current. The wrists are cocked to present the power face of the paddle perpendicular to the boat. As the boat turns around the paddle, which is acting as a fulcrum, or anchor, the wrists uncock. Other important aspects of the Duffek are a turning of the torso so that one can see the stern at the beginning of the stroke. The top hand is also kept about shoulder height with the elbow below the shoulder. The lower arm is bent, relaxed, and extended slightly forward and over the boat. All of these factors are important to prevent shoulder dislocation. A cross Duffek, like a cross draw, can be executed in canoeing on the canoeist's offside.

Bracing strokes

High brace. Bracing strokes are used to help stabilize a vessel and prevent capsizing (Figure 18.27). The high brace is a variation of the draw stroke. The power face of the blade is used on the water. Instead of drawing the boat to the paddle from a vertical position, there is more of an angle to the blade. This allows for part of the force to be applied in a downward direction, giving the paddler time to regain balance and reposition the CG above the center of buoyancy (COB) of the boat by pulling the hips toward the paddle and moving the boat back within one's base. Sweeping the blade slightly forward or backward with the blade angled slightly upward increases the righting force of this stroke and moves the boat toward the paddle.

Figure 18.23. Pry stroke.

Figure 18.24. One-half sweep.

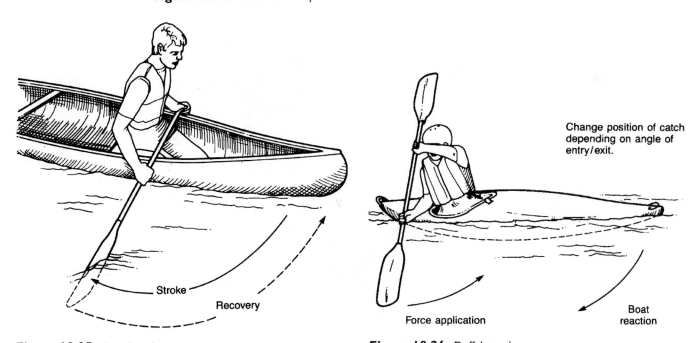

Figure 18.25. One-fourth sweep.

Figure 18.26. Duffek stroke.

Low brace. The low brace is used in canoeing and kayaking to lean the boat into turns and to correct an impending capsizing (Figure 18.28). In the low brace, lay the back face of the paddle flat in the water behind the hips. The position of the knuckles of both the grip and shaft hands is down. The elbows are bent and above the paddle. From the entry position, the blade is simultaneously pushed down and swept to the side, perpendicular to the boat. A quick push down on the paddle and a thrust of the hips toward the paddle will pull the CG back over the COB. In an extreme crisis, the head and torso can be put into the water and the boat brought around the knees and hips (hip flip). The body is brought back aboard (over the vessel) only at the end of the recover, just as in an Kayak roll.

Kayak roll. The kayak roll is an advanced maneuver used mostly in turbulent whitewater conditions. Because the potential for danger always exists, the kayak roll should be learned carefully in calm water first. The kayak roll, or modified C-to-C roll, is a two-part process using a sweep stroke combined with a hip snap (Figure 18.29). The forward sweep brings the paddler's body from under the boat and up to the water's surface in a C position. Then the lower body can snap the boat upright with a hip snap (a high brace maneuver) to the second C position.

The "low" high brace.

Figure 18.27. High brace.

Figure 18.28. Low brace.

Calm-Water Practice of Maneuvers

Boat maneuvers in ponds, lakes, and slow-moving rivers involve moving in a straight line, moving sideways, spins, and U-turns (Figure 18.30). Each involves one or more of the strokes previously discussed. The choice of a stroke is often dependent on whether one is in a canoe or a kayak and whether one is paddling solo or tandem.

Spins

Spins are discussed first because they can be taught to a group of people and executed under various practice conditions while allowing the group to remain in one place. Spins, full or partial, are used when moving around a bend in a river or positioning around another object, such as a boat or a dock.

The setup

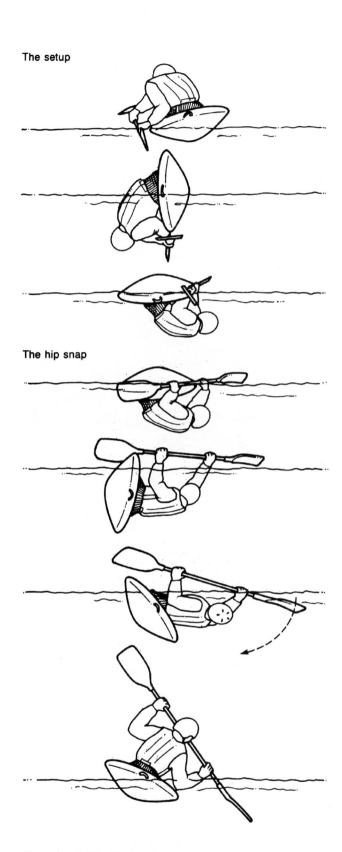

The hip snap

Figure 18.29. Kayak roll.

From a kayak or from a solo position in a canoe, a forward one-half sweep will turn the bow to the offside of the stroke. A reverse one-half sweep will move the bow to the onside of the stroke. From a tandem paddling position, several combinations of strokes will spin the canoe. If both people draw, the canoe will turn to the onside (Figure 18.31A). If both paddlers pry, the canoe will turn to the offside. If the bow paddler executes a forward one-fourth sweep while the stern does a reverse one-fourth sweep, the canoe will spin to the offside (Figure 18.31B). If the bow does a reverse one-fourth sweep and the stern does a forward one-fourth sweep, the canoe will spin to the onside.

The farther away from the side of the boat the paddle is placed, or swept, the more the boat turns away from that side.

Moving sideways

Moving laterally in a canoe or kayak is helpful to pull up beside another boat or the shore or to move sideways to avoid an object, such as a rock or branch in the water (Figures 18.32 and 18.33).

In kayak or solo canoe paddling, drawing to the right or left from midships will move the boat sideways in the direction of the onside, or paddling side (Figure 18.34). Use of a pry or cross draw will move the boat to the offside (Figure 18.35). In tandem paddling, the use of opposite strokes (draw/pry) will move the boat sideways (Figure 18.36).

Moving in a straight line

Moving in a straight line (or tracking) is most often the intent of paddling. Going forward is the obvious choice because it is the most powerful and efficient stroke. Also, you can see where you are going!

In a kayak, forward movement occurs with the power stroke on alternate sides (Figure 18.37). Remembering that the boat and paddle are bilaterally symmetrical, equal amounts of force should be applied on each side to enhance

Figure 18.30. Learning stroke technique on a flat-water pond.

A

Draw (P)

Draw (P)

B

Forward ¼ sweep (P)

Reverse ¼ sweep (B)

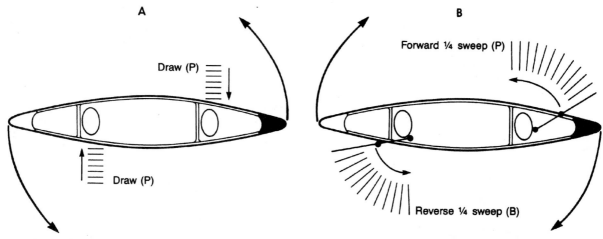

Figure 18.31. Spins.

Figure 18.32. Canoeists using proper ferry technique to run laterally across the river.

Figure 18.33. Sideslipping technique allows canoeists to negotiate rock formations.

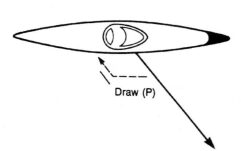

Draw (P)

Draw (P)

Figure 18.34. Moving sideways by drawing.

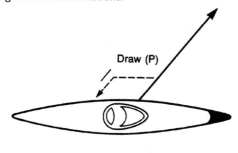

Draw (P)

going straight ahead. In a solo canoe, the J stroke is preferred to go forward. Sometimes a C stroke is used, which is in essence a draw moving directly into a J stroke. Both C and J strokes prevent a canoe from veering to the paddler's offside (Figure 18.38). When tandem canoeing, the bow person uses a forward power stroke. The stern paddler uses a forward stroke with a J or forward one-fourth sweep as needed to keep the boat moving in a straight line (Figure 18.39).

An alternative method of traveling on a straight course in a tandem canoe is to have the stern paddler call switches; both paddlers change and paddle on their opposite side every few strokes. The tandem canoe will generally go

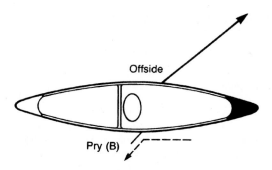

Figure 18.35. Moving sideways using a pry.

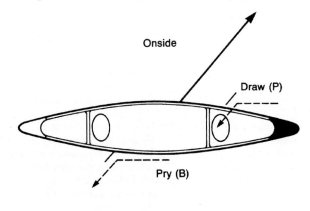

Figure 18.36. Moving sideways in tandem paddling.

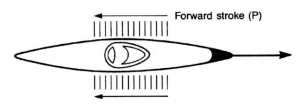

Figure 18.37. Moving forward in a kayak.

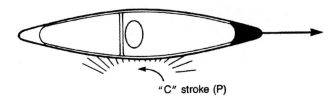

"C" stroke (P)

Figure 18.38. Moving forward when solo in a canoe.

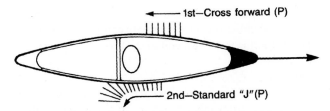

Figure 18.38. Moving forward when solo in a canoe.

reasonably straight with one paddler on each side; however, the boat will usually gradually turn away from the stern paddler's side. This technique of switching sides every few strokes takes some time to learn but allows directional stability without using steering strokes.

At times one may also want to go backward—for example, backing away from shore, from another boat, or from danger.

In a kayak, one uses a backstroke on alternating sides (Figure 18.40). In a solo canoe, one uses a backstroke in combination with a reverse J because the steering is now done at the bow (eddy) end of the canoe (Figure 18.41). In tandem

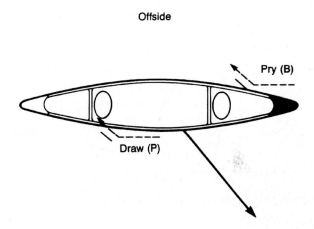

paddling, the stern person does the backstroke, while the bow person steers with a reverse J (Figure 18.42).

Turns

While moving forward through the water, all of the techniques discussed under "Spins" will cause the boat to turn. Additionally, the curvature of the hull can be used to assist in turning. Canoes and kayaks will turn away from the side to which they are leaned. Caution must be employed to learn the finesse required with this technique.

U-turns

A U-turn (an abrupt 180-degree turn) in flat-water paddling, though not an essential skill, can be taught to develop proficiency in using combinations of strokes. However, the value of a U-turn becomes apparent when you need to stop behind a rock (eddy turn) or reenter the current (peel out). U-turns can also be helpful on flat water in windy conditions.

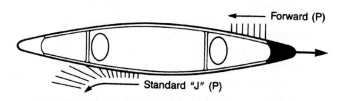

Figure 18.39. Moving forward when tandem in a canoe.

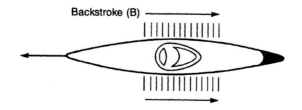

Figure 18.40. Moving backward in a kayak.

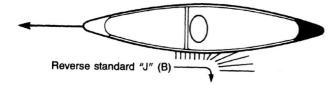

Reverse standard "J" (B)

Figure 18.41. Moving backward when solo in a canoe.

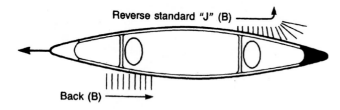

Reverse standard "J" (B)

Back (B)

Figure 18.42. Moving backward when tandem in a canoe.

In a kayak with forward momentum, a U-turn is done with a sweep on the outside to initiate the turn and carry the momentum forward. Then a Duffek is executed on the inside of the turn. In solo canoe paddling, the choice of strokes depends on the side of the turn. To turn to the onside, begin with a reverse sweeping low brace and follow with a Duffek and forward stroke (Figure 18.43). To turn to the offside, begin with a forward stroke followed by a cross Duffek (Figure 18.44). In tandem paddling, to turn to the onside, the stern uses forward one-fourth sweeps while the bow uses a Duffek followed by a forward stroke. To turn to the offside, the stern uses a reverse sweeping low brace while the bow uses a cross Duffek followed by a cross forward stroke (Figure 18.45).

Rescue

Principles of rescue

Swamping or capsizing a canoe or kayak on flat water may be caused by wind, waves, wake from powerboats, a paddler's poor balance, or improper trim from improper loading. If a boat does capsize, paddlers must evaluate the situation and determine a course of action. The following guidelines should be observed:

1. Alert other boaters that your boat has capsized.
2. Victims should initiate self-rescue procedures immediately and be ready to accept assistance from others.

POSSIBLE ERRORS AND CORRECTIONS

Possible Errors	Corrections
Canoe veers to the stern paddler's offside.	Stern paddler must make a more effective J stroke—paddle blade must be vertical at the end of the stroke, and the blade must push the water sideways away from the canoe.
Canoe gradually turns in a sweeping curve.	Make sure in the power paddling strokes that the paddle is held vertically and that the paddle follows a straight pathway back rather than the curved path of the gunwale line.
Path of the canoe makes an S pattern through the water.	Anticipate changes of direction; don't overcorrect in one direction or the other.
Canoe appears to bob up and down in the water.	Entry and exit of the paddle stroke must be corrected—avoid reaching too far forward and pushing down on the water and pulling up at the end of the stroke while lifting water.
Turning strokes are ineffective, resulting in slow turns.	Make sure that the draw and pry strokes are done with the paddle vertical in the water—the paddle must push/pull the water directly sideways.
Ferry maneuvers are ineffective.	Paddlers must establish a proper angle to the river current and flow of the water—maintain a slight angle in the direction of movement.
Eddy turns are ineffective.	Paddlers must enter the turn with proper speed, at a 45-degree angle, and lean into the turn.
Peel-outs are ineffective.	The bow of the canoe must reenter the downstream current, the appropriate Duffek maneuver must be made in the downstream current, and paddlers must lean into the turn.

3. Other paddlers can assist in the rescue when it is safe to do so.
4. Paddlers not involved in the rescue should keep their distance and continually evaluate the rescue in the event that more help is needed.

There are rescue priorities to help reduce confusion in a potentially hazardous situation. The first priority is saving the paddler in the water. Once in the water, the paddler should initiate self-rescue procedures and remember to stay with the boat. Paddlers of decked boats should attempt a roll. If a paddler has a partner, he or she should establish visual and voice contact. Capsized paddlers, after assessing the situation, should not swim to shore without the boat. The boat is the number one piece of safety equipment. In moving water, stay at the upstream end of the boat.

Self-rescue

Paddlers can rescue a swamped craft in deep water without assistance from other boats using a Capistrano flip or a shake-out technique. The Capistrano flip is accomplished

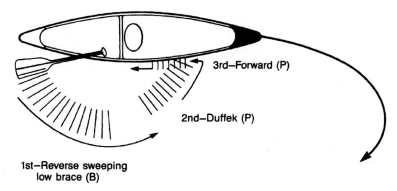

3rd—Forward (P)

2nd—Duffek (P)

1st—Reverse sweeping
low brace (B)

Figure 18.43. Onside U-turn.

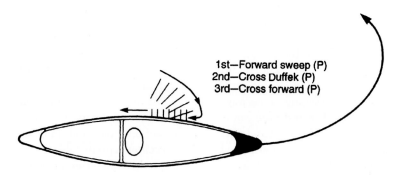

1st—Forward sweep (P)
2nd—Cross Duffek (P)
3rd—Cross forward (P)

Figure 18.44. Offside U-turn.

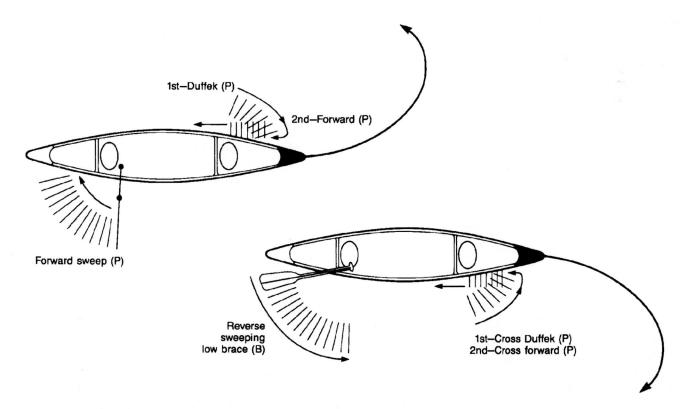

1st—Duffek (P)

2nd—Forward (P)

Forward sweep (P)

Reverse
sweeping
low brace (B)

1st—Cross Duffek (P)
2nd—Cross forward (P)

Figure 18.45. Tandem canoe U-turns.

by ducking under the capsized canoe and coming up in the air pocket. In unison, the paddlers use a scissors kick and a forceful lifting action to one side to push the craft above the water and roll it upright. A shake-out is done while the boat remains upright. One paddler pushes down on an end of the canoe while also pushing forward. The end must then be lifted before the water flows back in. Another way to accomplish the shake-out is to rock the canoe from side to side and then quickly pull up on the gunwale before water flows back in. These techniques rarely get all the water out of the canoe. The paddler then must decide what to do with the partially submerged boat. The choices are to reenter the boat and paddle to shore or to bail the boat to empty it further. Swamped boats can be paddled, though progress is slow and unbalanced.

Group rescue

Where other boats are available to assist in the rescue, the process changes. Get the swimmers to the ends of the rescuing canoe. If a dangerous situation exists or if the victim is cold or injured, get him or her into the rescuing canoe, have the victim lay down on the bottom and then do the canoe over canoe maneuver. With the boat upside down and perpendicular to the rescue boat, one end is lifted and pulled over the craft. The tipped craft is moved up and over the rescue craft until it is balanced, rolled upright, and slid back into the water (Figure 18.46). The boat is then moved into position beside the rescue craft and held so that the swimmers can reenter the craft.

SAFETY

Canoeing and kayaking are challenging, adventurous activities with inherent risks. Therefore, it is important to develop an awareness of safety and develop skills that promote safe

Figure 18.46. Group rescue.

paddling. Risks in boating cannot be eliminated, but they can be managed to an acceptable level. It is highly recommended that instructors be certified to teach canoeing and/or kayaking by an organization and that participants enroll in certified courses.

The recent increase in popularity of canoeing and kayaking has brought with it an increase in accidents and fatalities. Much can be learned from accident reports compiled by the U.S. Coast Guard. They reveal that most accidents are the result of ignorance. The majority of small-craft fatalities involve unknowledgeable, inexperienced boaters. Accident reports indicate five common problems.

1. Paddlers are often not wearing lifejackets, which are either forgotten or used for other purposes, such as padding, sitting on, or kneeling on.
2. Cold water or cold weather is present. Hypothermia inhibits reasoning abilities, including the ability to paddle effectively, and the ability to self-rescue.
3. Most victims are inexperienced, having had no formal instruction or practice.
4. Alcohol is a contributing factor. Drugs and alcohol affect coordination and judgment. Slow response time and poor decisions in hazardous conditions make accidents predictable.
5. Victims often cannot swim. The ability to be at ease in or around water increases the ability to perform well in stressful situations.

INTERNATIONAL SCALE OF RIVER DIFFICULTY

The American Whitewater Affiliation's International Scale of River Difficulty is a useful tool to determine the severity of sections in a river. These guidelines offer a general classification for rivers, but be aware that the system is not exact. Rivers do not always fit neatly into the various classifications. Also, rivers are constantly changing as water pushes rocks around and water levels rise and fall. Regional interpretations of the classification system can create misunderstandings. In addition, if rapids on a river generally fit into one of the following classifications but the water temperature is below 50°F or the trip is an extended trip in a wilderness area, the river should be considered one class more difficult than normal.

There is no substitute for a cautious approach to rivers with which a paddler is unfamiliar.

Moving water has three classifications:
1. Class A—Flowing under 2 mph
2. Class B—2 to 4 mph
3. Class C—Greater than 4 mph
Whitewater has six classifications:
Class I: Easy
- Few obstructions—all obvious and easily missed.
- Fast-moving water with riffles and small waves.
- Risk to swimmers is slight.
- Self-rescue is easy.

Class II: Novice

- Straightforward rapids with wide, clear channels that are obvious without scouting.
- Occasional maneuvering may be required, but rocks and medium-size waves are missed easily by trained paddlers.
- Swimmers are seldom injured, and group assistance, while helpful, is seldom needed.

Class III: Intermediate

- Rapids with moderate, irregular waves that can be difficult to avoid and capable of swamping an open canoe.
- Complex maneuvers in fast current, and frequent narrow passages requiring good boat control.
- Large waves, holes, and strainers might be present but are easily avoided.
- Strong eddies and powerful current effects can be found, particularly on large-volume rivers.
- Scouting is advisable for inexperienced parties.
- Chance of injury while swimming is low, but group assistance may be required to avoid long swims.

Class IV: Advanced

- Intense, powerful rapids requiring precise boat handling in turbulent water.
- Depending upon the character of the river, there may be long unavoidable waves and holes or constricted passages demanding fast maneuvers under pressure.
- A fast, reliable eddy turn may be needed to negotiate the drop, scout rapids, or rest.
- Rapids may require "must" moves above dangerous hazards.
- Scouting is necessary the first time.
- Risk of injury to swimmers is moderate to high, and water conditions can make rescue difficult.
- Group assistance is often essential but requires practiced skills.
- A strong kayak roll is highly recommended.

Class V: Expert

- Extremely long, obstructed, or violent rapids that expose the paddler to above-average risk of injury.
- Drops may contain very large, unavoidable waves and holes or steep, congested chutes with complex, demanding routes.
- Rapids often continue for long distances between pools or eddies, demanding a high level of fitness.
- What eddies exist may be small, turbulent, or difficult to reach.
- Several of these factors may be combined at the high end of this class.
- Scouting is mandatory.
- Rescue is extremely difficult even for experts.
- A very reliable kayak roll and above-average rescue skills are essential.

Class VI: Almost Impossible

- Difficulties of Class V are carried to the limits of navigability.
- Nearly impossible and very dangerous.
- Risks are high and rescue may be impossible.
- For teams of experts only at favorable water levels, after close study and with all precautions.
- The frequency with which a rapid is run should have no effect on this rating, as there are a number of Class VI rapids that are regularly attempted.

TEACHING CONSIDERATIONS

1. Always consider the teaching site. Pools, ponds, lakes, and calm places in a river are acceptable. Make sure the site will be free from such distractions as loud noises and groups of other people and free from the danger of trees, branches, debris, broken glass, or other objects.
2. Initial instruction can occur onshore or at the side of the water or pool. It is then possible to work on technique with the paddle and walk about freely to give feedback to people who need correction.
3. Use visuals—such as miniature boats and paddles, charts, or mock drawings of boats in the sand—to help illustrate points about stroke technique and maneuvers.
4. Move from simple to complex. Boats can actually be paddled by hand to see the action and reaction of strokes on water. With this simple understanding, paddles can be added early and you can then proceed with more complex drills.
5. Teach spins and turning strokes first so the group can stay close to you. Then teach power and bracing strokes when the group has beginning control and knowledge of the paddle.
6. Teach and refine for good technique and stroke mechanics. For example, if a stroke is intended to turn the boat, it must be applied away from the center at an angle that creates torque. If a stroke is intended to propel a boat in a straight line (forward, backward, or sideways), the paddle must be vertical in the water and pulled in a line opposite the intended motion.
7. Allow students to gain expertise paddling on one side or position before asking them to change. Then, to create versatile paddlers, encourage them to transfer their learning to paddle on the opposite side, to change positions (bow to stern), to paddle with a different person, and to switch from tandem to solo paddling.
8. After students have learned strokes and simple maneuvers, develop drills in which they have to respond automatically. For example, have them respond to verbal commands to turn right, turn left, sideslip right, sideslip left. Mix the commands so their responses become second nature.
9. Move from simple singular maneuvers to combining several maneuvers. Make up a course on a flat-water pond, lake, or river using obstacles such as bleach bottles or milk carton buoys to be negotiated. For example, enter the vessel, sideslip away from shore,

paddle forward, turn left around a bend (obstacle), back up, go between two rocks (obstacles), turn right, paddle forward, and so on.

10. Move from a more controlled obstacle course to a natural setting where students negotiate moving between two rocks, around a tree or bend, laterally beside a dock, and so on.

11. Learn all strokes and maneuvers on flat water before proceeding to moving water.

12. Help students to learn to read river signs in a classroom setting before encountering them on the water. For example, upstream and downstream Vs, strainers, hydraulics, and standing waves should all be discussed before practicing on a river.

13. Practice map and compass reading and discuss trip-planning procedures before going on any day trips.

14. Practice safety and rescue procedures along with a paddling sequence. For example, paddle out with another boat and have one capsize (stay near shore). Follow rescue procedures and then paddle back to shore.

15. Instructors should be certified to be aware of standards of practice.

16. If having enough boats is a problem (one boat for every two students), consult local outfitters, YMCAs, canoe clubs, and so on. They are often willing to help.

GLOSSARY

amidships The area midway between the bow and stern. Often shortened to *midships*.

astern Behind the canoe, kayak, or other craft.

back paddle Paddling backward to slow or check forward motion.

bail To remove water from a craft.

bar An accumulation of sand, gravel, or rock, usually located along the inside bend of a river.

beam The width of a craft measured at its widest point.

blade The broad, flat section of a paddle.

bow The area in the forward end of a watercraft.

bow person Person who tandem paddles from the bow, front thwart, or front seat.

bracing stroke Paddle stroke providing stability against the capsizing force of a lateral current. May also be used for turning.

broach To turn a craft broadside to oncoming waves or obstructions.

capsize To overturn.

closed boat Boats having the deck as an integral part of the craft.

combination stroke A blended stroke maneuver consisting of two or more simple strokes.

confluence The point where two or more rivers flow together.

control hand The upper hand on a canoe paddle, which controls turning of the paddle blade.

cross draw A stroke used to move the canoe, or part of the canoe, to the paddler's normal offside.

current General movement of water in a river caused by gradient differentials.

deck On a traditional open canoe, the triangular piece found at bow and stern to which the gunwales attach at their ends; often called *deck plates*. On a closed canoe or kayak, a covering for the entire hull.

double blade Paddle with a blade at each end; usually used in a kayak and sometimes in an open or decked canoe.

downstream V A clear deep-water path for canoes or kayaks to negotiate through between two rocks.

draw stroke A paddle stroke designed to move the craft to the onside of the paddler or toward the power face of the blade.

Duffek stroke A high bracing stroke first used in the kayak by Milovan Duffek of Czechoslovakia. Used mainly to enter or leave an eddy as an eddy turn (entering) or a peel-out (leaving).

eddy Place where the current either stops or moves upstream below obstructions and on the inside of bends.

eddy turn A dynamic technique used by boaters to enter an eddy.

feather Returning the paddle to the "catch" position (ready for a propulsive action) with one edge leading, thus reducing resistance by water or air.

flotation Material placed in a canoe to keep it floating high when upset or swamped.

forward stroke The standard propulsion stroke used in paddling a canoe directly ahead. Also called *basic forward* or *power forward*.

freeboard The shortest distance from the waterline to the top of the gunwale of a canoe or to the seamline of any decked boat.

gunwale Strips along the top of a canoe's sides, extending from bow to stern, where the deck and topsides meet.

hull The frame, or body, of a craft, exclusive of rigging and flotation systems.

hydraulic A water formation caused by a sudden drop of the river over a dam, rock, or ledge, causing an upstream current on the surface of the water, which tends to hold or spin boats.

hypothermia A serious, life-threatening physical condition caused by a lowering of the body's core temperature.

inside bank In a river bend, the edge of the river with the slower, shallower water.

inverted J A reverse J stroke, used by the tandem bow or solo paddler when canoeing in reverse.

J stroke Stroke used by tandem stern or solo paddler to correct the characteristic swing of the craft to the offside when only a forward stroke is used.

K-1 A kayak with one paddler who sits on his or her buttocks, keeps the legs extended forward, and uses a double-bladed paddle.

keel A thin projecting strip of material running down the exact center of the outer hull of a craft from bow to stern.

lee, leeward, leeway A protected area downwind or downstream of an obstruction that breaks the normal direction and force of the wind or water. Leeward means "downwind." Leeway means "the drift of a boat downwind."

life vest Personal buoyancy device that is worn like a vest; provides upper-body protection and warmth. Also called a *PFD* (personal flotation device).

low brace Brace stroke in which the entire paddle is nearly flat on the surface of the water.

mouth Area where a river joins another body of water.

nonpower face The face of a paddle blade opposite the power face.

offside Side of the canoe on which the paddler is not usually paddling.

paddle The tool used to propel the boat in the desired direction.

painter A length of rope attached to an end of a canoe.

pillow A smooth bulge on the river's surface created by water flowing over an underwater obstruction.

port The left side of a craft when facing toward the bow.

portage The act of carrying a canoe and gear around an obstacle. Also, the place where the canoe has to be taken from the water and carried on land around an obstruction or dangerous spot in the river.

power face The face of the paddle blade that bears against the water.

pry A type of stroke that uses the craft as a fulcrum to move the boat away from the blade.

recovery The component of a stroke preparing for the next propulsive action.

rocker The upward sweep of the keel line toward both ends of a canoe.

ruddering Holding the paddle blade stationary in the water at a fixed angle to steer.

scull, sculling To propel or align a craft by moving a paddle side to side in a continuous figure-eight pattern using the same power face throughout.

sideslipping Situation in which a canoe's center of gravity continues in the initial direction of movement even though the boat is turning.

skirt Garment worn around the waist of closed-boat paddlers. It attaches around the coaming (a raised frame to keep out water) to make the cockpit watertight.

standing wave A wave formed at a right angle to the flow of the current. Usually occurs in several sets and most often indicates a deep-water channel.

starboard The right side of a craft when facing the bow.

stem The curved section at the ends of a canoe that slices through the water when paddling forward or backward.

stern The rear section of a watercraft.

strainer A solid object in the water (such as a fallen tree) that allows the water to pass but prevents boats and people from continuing downstream.

swamp When a canoe fills with water but does not capsize.

sweep canoe The last canoe in a group, usually containing experienced paddlers, extra equipment, rescue lines, and a first-aid kit.

sweep stroke A wide, shallow stroke used for turning or pivoting the canoe.

tandem Two paddlers in a canoe.

throat The flare of the paddler's shaft where it starts to form the blade.

through The low point, or hollow, found between the crests of two standing waves.

thwart Cross braces, running from gunwale to gunwale, which provide reinforcement for the gunwales. Also known as a *spreader* or *crossbar*.

track Paddling in a straight line.

trim The manner in which a canoe rides on the water.

tumblehome The inward-curving upper portion of a canoe that produces a narrowing of the beam at the deck level.

upstream V A single rock in the river that deflects water to both sides of the downstream current, creating a current differential behind which is often created an eddy pool.

yoke A cushioned shoulder harness that clamps to the gunwales of a canoe permitting the canoe to be carried upside down on the paddler's shoulders.

SUGGESTED READINGS

American Canoe Association. 2009. *Canoeing*. Champaign, IL: Human Kinetics.

Curran, D. 1999. *Canoe trip*. Mechanicsburg, PA: Stackpole Books.

Dillon, P., and Oyen, J. 2009. *Kayaking*. Champaign, IL: Human Kinetics.

Glickman, J. 2003. *The Kayak companion*. North Adams, MA: Storey Books.

Hanson, J. 2006. *Complete sea kayak touring*. Camden, ME: Ragged Mountain Press.

Harrison, D. 1998. *Kayak touring*. Mechanicsburg, PA: Stackpole Books.

Harrison, D. 1998. *Whitewater kayaking*. Mechanicsburg, PA: Stackpole Books.

Jackson, E. 1999. *Whitewater paddling*. Mechanicsburg, PA: Stackpole Books.

Kearney, J., and McKenzie, D. 2000. *Physiology of canoe sport in exercise and sport science*. Philadelphia, PA: Lippincott, Williams and Wilkins.

Kuhne, C. 1998. *Canoeing*. Mechanicsburg, PA: Stackpole Books. Includes information on equipment, basic and advanced paddling techniques, and safety measures. Checklists and resources for preparing a canoe outing are also provided.

Kuhne, C. 1998. *Kayaking*. Mechanicsburg, PA: Stackpole Books. Contains illustrated techniques for basic and advanced paddling, conditioning, trip planning, and safety.

Kuhne, C. 1999. *Kayak touring and camping*. Mechanicsburg, PA: Stackpole Books.

Ray, S. 1999. *The canoe handbook*. Mechanicsburg, PA: Stackpole Books.

Rizzetta, S. 2009. *Canoe and kayak building the light and easy way*. Camden, ME: Ragged Mountain Press.

Robinson, J. 2003. *Sea kayaking illustrated: A visual guide to better paddling*. Camden, ME: Ragged Mountain Press.

Rounds, J. 2003. *Basic canoeing*. Mechanicsburg, PA: Stackpole Books.

Rounds, J. 2005. *Basic kayaking*. Mechanicsburg, PA: Stackpole Books.

Stuhaug, D. 2004. *The complete idiot's guide to canoeing and kayaking*. New York, NY: Primedia Enthusiasts Publications, Inc.

Historical References

Adney, E., and Chapelle, H. 1964. *The bark canoes and skin boats of North America*. Washington, DC: Smithsonian Institution.

Bishop, N. 1878. *Voyage of the paper canoe*. Cambridge, MA: John Wilson & Son.

Manley, A. 1968. *Rushton and his times in American canoeing*. Syracuse, NY: The Adirondack Museum/Syracuse University Press.

Toro, A. 1986. *Canoeing: An Olympic sport*. San Francisco, CA: Olympian Graphics.

RESOURCES

Magazines

American Whitewater, American Whitewater Affiliation, 1343 N Portage, Palatine, IL 60067.

Canoe & Kayak Magazine.

Paddler, Paddling Group, 4061 Oceanside Blvd., Suite M, Oceanside, CA 92056.

Organizations

American Canoe Association, 7432 Alban Station Blvd., Suite B226, Springfield, VA 22150; 703-451-0141. Membership plus a complete book and film library.

American Red Cross, 2025 E Street NW, Washington, DC 20006; 202-303-4498. A good source for courses, books, and films.

Canadian Recreational Canoeing Association, P.O. Box 398, 446 Main St. West, Merrickville ON KOG INO.; 1-888-252-6292.

Sierra Club, 85 Second St., 2nd Floor, San Francisco, CA 94105; 414-977-5500.

USA Canoe & Kayak, 301 S. Tryon Street, Suite 1750, Charlotte, NC 28282; 704-348-4330.

There are many local and state canoe clubs. Consult a phone book under River Outfitters to obtain locations and contact persons.

Videos

Cold, wet, and alive. Nichols Productions, 17000 Carwell Rd., Silver Springs, MD 20904. This video follows a group of early season paddlers down a cold-water stream and documents their encounter with the silent killer hypothermia.

Heads up! River rescue for river runners. Russ Nichols/Walkabout Productions, American Canoe Association, 7432 Alban Station Blvd., Springfield, VA 22150. Fundamentals of river rescue, from simple self-rescue techniques to technical group rescues.

The kayaker's edge. Whitewater Instruction, 160 Hideaway Rd., Durango, CO 81301. For kayakers looking for instruction on how to begin whitewater paddling or for seasoned veterans wanting a tune-up on their skills.

Path of the paddle: Quiet water. Blue Heron Enterprises, 6212 W Cermak Rd., Berwyn, IL 60402. Bill Mason demonstrates basic paddling strokes for solo and tandem paddlers; filmed in rugged Canadian Shield country.

Path of the paddle: Whitewater. Blue Heron Enterprises, 6212 W Cermak Rd., Berwyn, IL 60402. How to read the rapids, plan a course, and follow it while in complete control of the boat.

Performance sea kayaking. American Canoe Association, 7432 Alban Station Blvd., Springfield, VA 22150. This video demonstrates and explains paddling, rescue and surf technique, and basic seamanship.

Sea kayaking: Getting started. American Canoe Association, 7432 Alban Station Blvd., Springfield, VA 22150. A comprehensive, indexed reference for both beginning and experienced paddlers. With clear demonstrations of strokes, rescue, basic navigation, and general knowledge, this video provides an excellent overview of the diversity of sea kayaking.

Solo playboating. Whitewater Instruction, 160 Hideaway Rd., Durango, CO 81301. Intermediate whitewater open-canoe paddlers who are ready for advanced skills will find this fast-paced video an excellent learning tape.

Uncalculated risk. American Red Cross, General Supply Office, 17th and D Sts. NW, Washington, DC 20006. Concentrates on the risk and dangers of river running.

Whitewater self-defense: The Eskimo roll. Nichols Productions, 17000 Carwell Rd., Silver Springs, MD 20904. Slow motion and stop action, using underwater cameras, help demonstrate the skill and clearly show components of the Eskimo roll (kayak roll).

Wild Americans. Watershed Films, P.O. Box 551, Lotus, CA 95651. Big action, obligatory wipeouts, original music, and outrageous humor combine to make this an instant boating classic. Catch a glimpse of California's wet and wild side!

WEB SITES

This Web site includes where to buy a kayak, types of kayaks, paddling schools, basic equipment and clothing needs, links to other paddle Web sites, and allows you to subscribe to their *Canoe & Kayak* magazine.
http://canoekayak.com

USA Canoe/kayak (USACK) is the national governing body for canoe and kayak racing in the United States.
www.usacanoekayak.org

U.S. Canoe Association (USCA) is a non-profit, educational group that encourages the growth of recreational and competitive paddling.
www.uscanoe.com

The American Canoe Association (ACA) promotes the health, social and personal benefits of canoeing, kayaking, and rafting.
www.acanet.org

Information on canoeing, sea kayaking, whitewater boating, and paddling skills—all aimed at making you a better boater.
http://paddling.about.com/

This Web site includes a comprehensive list of related Web sites.
http://sportsvl.com/water/canoeing.htm

Online paddling magazine.
http://www.paddlemagazine.com

Sea kayak touring.
http://www.seakayakadventures.com

19 *Lacrosse*

After completing this chapter, the reader should be able to:

- Appreciate the history, development, and values of lacrosse
- Understand the rules of both the men's and women's versions of lacrosse
- Be aware of considerations of equipment selection and care
- Demonstrate the basic lacrosse skills of cradling, catching, throwing, scooping, shooting, and dodging
- Understand basic offensive and defensive strategies
- Instruct a group of students in the basic skills of lacrosse

HISTORY

With a history that is centuries old, lacrosse is the oldest sport in North America. The sport is rooted in Native American religious ceremony, in which it is referred to as *baggitaway*. Early explorers of North America found different forms of lacrosse widely played by the Indians. French missionaries gave the game its present name because the sticks the Indians used resembled the crosier *(la crosse)* carried at religious ceremonies by a bishop as a symbol of his pastoral office.

The first use of the word *crosse* in reference to the game was made in 1636 by the Jesuit missionary Jean de Brébeuf, who saw the Hurons play the game near Thunder Bay, Ontario, and mentioned it in a report to his ecclesiastical superiors. Indian lacrosse was a mass game, played not only for recreation but also as a means of training warriors. Most teams were made up of about a hundred players, sometimes nearly a thousand. The distance between goals was usually between 500 yards (457 m) and half a mile (805 m), but occasionally the goals were several miles apart! Games lasted as long as three days, starting at sunup and ending at sundown.

French pioneers began playing the game avidly in the early 1800s. On the same day in 1867 that the Dominion of Canada was created, lacrosse was declared its national sport. In 1861 Dr. W. George Beers, a Montreal dentist, formed the Canadian National Lacrosse Association and drew up the first set of written rules for the game. Later that year an Indian team traveled to England to play, and as a result of interest aroused in the game there, the English Lacrosse Association was formed in 1868. The sport was introduced into Australia in 1874 and has been played there ever since.

Development of the Men's Game

A group of Indians from Canada demonstrated lacrosse at the Saratoga Springs, New York, fairgrounds during the racing season in 1867. This event brought the first mention of lacrosse in American newspapers, and soon there were club teams in the Midwest, North, and East. In New York City, in the fall of 1877, intercollegiate lacrosse began when New York University played Manhattan College. The Intercollegiate Lacrosse Association was formed in 1882, and the development of the game in the United States was under way.

Lacrosse on the high school and college levels in the United States took great strides forward beginning in the late 1950s. At that time there were 80 high schools and 40 colleges playing the game. By 1997 there were 890 high schools and 179 colleges playing lacrosse on the varsity level. There are also approximately 250 high schools and 200 colleges that support lacrosse on the club level.

The International Lacrosse Federation (ILF) sponsors a World Championship Series every four years, with teams from Australia, Canada, Czech Republic, England, Germany, Ireland, the Iroquois Nations, Japan, Korea, New Zealand, Scotland, Sweden, the United States, and Wales. Affiliate members include Argentina, Denmark, Hong Kong, Finland, Italy, and Tonga. The 2006 Senior World Championships were held in London, Ontario, Canada, and the team from Canada defeated the U.S. team, 15 to 10. It was only the second time since 1967 the U.S. team hasn't won the championship. In 2008 the ILF merged with the former governing body for women's lacrosse and formed the Federation of International Lacrosse (FIL). This new organization now sanctions World Championships, such as the one held in July 2010 in Manchester, England, at which the U.S. team defeated their archrival Canada 12 to 10 to claim their ninth title.

Development of the Women's Game

By the 1870s, lacrosse had been transported to England, where the rules were modified to eliminate roughness and body contact, and in 1890, St. Leonard's and St. Andrew's Schools of Scotland played the first women's game. The success of this game was immediate, and soon women's lacrosse was being played throughout England.

In the early 1900s women's lacrosse recrossed the Atlantic with English teachers who introduced the game at Bryn

Mawr and Sargent Colleges. Women enjoyed the game so much that it spread into the other women's colleges, and the demand for qualified instructors kept England's Constance M. K. Applebee, Joyce CranBarry, and Joyce Riley in the United States for years as coaches.

The game continued to expand in popularity on both the college and high school levels so that in 1932 the United States Women's Lacrosse Association (USWLA) was formed to promote its growth and to prepare rules and standards. By 1933, the first USWLA National Tournament was held in Greenwich, Connecticut. This tournament continues to be held each year with schoolgirls, club, and, as of 1994, masters divisions.

Collegiate tournament play was introduced in the late 1970s by the Association for Intercollegiate Athletics for Women (AIAW) and continues today through the National Collegiate Athletic Association (NCAA), with tournaments for Divisions I, II, and III.

Worldwide, women's lacrosse is played in England, Scotland, Wales, Australia, Japan, Canada, the Czech Republic, Sweden, France, Germany, Ireland, and the United States, with programs being developed in New Zealand and Denmark. The international game is governed by the International Federation of Women's Lacrosse Association, and a World Cup competition is held every four years.

VALUES

Lacrosse is one of the great team games on the American sports scene. Nearly everyone who has played it or watched it loves the game. Lacrosse gets in your blood because it is such a fast-moving and exciting sport. It has been accurately characterized as "the fastest game on two feet."

Lacrosse is a beautiful game, too—above all, for the skill of the stick handlers in throwing and catching either long, looping passes or bulletlike short passes. But that is just the beginning. There are frequent changes in the action: the defensive team geting possession of the ball and dashing downfield; the dodging and the stick checking; the quick pass to an attacker on the crease and an equally quick shot at the goal; the amazing saves of a good goalie; and the sudden body checks that are so different from the constant pounding of bodies in football. Also in contrast to the often obscured contact in football, all action takes place in the open, so that the knowledgeable spectator can follow and appreciate the fine points of strategy and tactics.

This wide-open, action-packed game presents many scoring opportunities. In fact, one of the foremost reasons for the popularity of lacrosse is the high number of climactic plays that occur during a game. In a typical college game, a combined total of 70 or more shots will be taken at the goal by the two teams and as many as 25 goals will be scored. This makes for excitement, geared to the action-loving players and fans of today.

Lacrosse is played in the spring, and in most areas this means green grass, budding leaves, and blooming flowers. Except in areas that have a year-round warm climate, this provides a refreshing change from the winter season, when most sports are played indoors. How invigorating it is to leave the heated gymnasium and get outside to the beautiful spring weather to play or watch lacrosse! There is a certain magic to springtime, and those who have been exposed to lacrosse know there is a touch of magic in this great American game.

Authors' note: It is interesting to watch the evolution of sports and their rules over the years. In the past many sports have had different sets of rules for men and women, and in some cases these rules have begun to merge (e.g., basketball and, in this book, the rules for speedball). In lacrosse, however, the rules for the men's and women's games are still considerably different, so we will present each game separately in this book. We will begin by noting the major differences between men's and women's lacrosse:

1. There are no boundary lines in women's lacrosse. Men's lacrosse is played within a lined, rectangular field.
2. The men's center draw starts on the ground. The women's center draw starts from a standing position.
3. Men's lacrosse is a body contact sport. Body contact is strictly forbidden in women's lacrosse.
4. Field players in the men's game are heavily padded. Women do not wear heavy gloves or helmets, due to the noncontact nature of the game.
5. Women's field sticks must be woven with four or five vertical thongs, and they do not have a loose pocket. Men's sticks have a very loose pocket and are often made of a mesh material.

Men's Lacrosse

RULES

Field and Goals

The playing area of a lacrosse field is bigger than that of a football field. It is 110 yards (about 100 m) long and 60 yards (about 55 m) wide. The goals are 80 yards (about 73 m) apart, and there is a playing area of 15 yards (13.8 m) behind each goal, which permits considerable behind-the-goal action. The length of the field is divided in half by a centerline. A circle with a 9-foot (2.76 m) radius is drawn around each goal and is known as the *crease*. A rectangular box, 35 yards × 40 yards (32 m × 36.6 m), surrounds each goal and is called the *goal area* (see Figure 19.1 for field markings).

The goal consists of two vertical posts joined by a top crossbar. The goalposts are 6 feet (1.84 m) apart, and the top crossbar is 6 feet from the ground. A goal line is drawn between the goalposts to indicate the plane of the goal. Attached to the goal is a pyramidal cord netting, which is fastened to the ground at a point 7 feet (2.15 m) in back of the center of the goal.

Players

There are 10 players on a team, plus a number of substitutes for each of the four positions: goal, defense, midfield,

The Lacrosse Field of Play

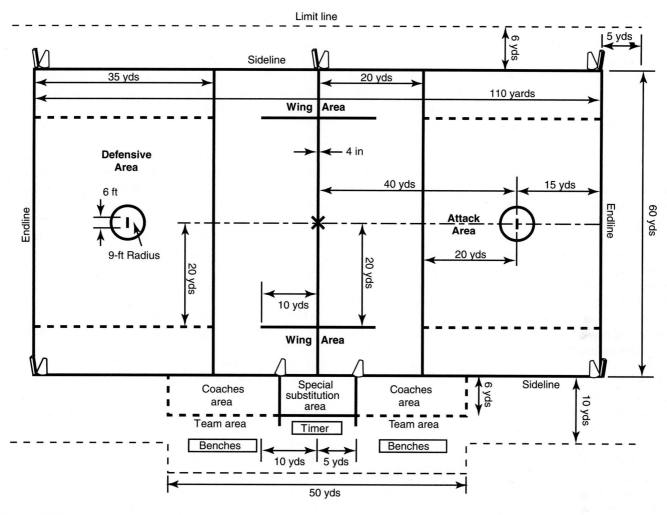

Figure 19.1. Lacrosse field. (To convert yards to meters, multiply by 0.91.)

and attack. The goalkeeper, or goalie, protects the goal and receives primary support from three defensive players. Because they are normally near the goal, they are known as the *close defense*. Three midfielders cover the entire field, operating as both offensive and defensive players. One of the midfielders handles the face-offs and is called either the *center* or the *face-off player*. Three attackers spend most of their playing time around the opponent's goal and are referred to as the *close attack*.

Ball and Sticks

The lacrosse ball is solid rubber and white, yellow, orange, or lime green in color. It is slightly smaller than a baseball and just as hard. When dropped from a height of 6 feet (1.84 m) on a concrete floor, it must bounce 43 to 51 inches (1.1 to 1.3 m). The ball may not be touched by the hands except by a goalie while in the crease. Although it is legal to kick the

ball with the foot or bat it with the stick, most of the action takes place with the ball being controlled in the pockets of the players' sticks.

The lacrosse stick—or *crosse,* as it was originally called—may have an overall length of 40 to 72 inches (1.02 to 1.84 m). The inside measurement of the head of every stick, except the goalie's, is between 6.5 and 10 inches (16.6 and 25 cm). Attackers normally use sticks with the smallest heads to aid them in ball control and dodging.

The stick is made of wood, plastic, or any other synthetic material. The net of the stick is constructed of gut, rawhide, clock cord, linen, nylon, or any other synthetic material and is roughly triangular in shape. A guard stop, which is made of a rubberized material, is located at the throat of the stick, a minimum of 10 inches (25 cm) from the outside edge of the head. The pocket of the stick may not sag to such a depth that it becomes unreasonably difficult for an opponent to dislodge the ball. This is determined by placing a ball in the pocket: If the top surface of the ball is below the bottom edge of the wall, the pocket is too deep and must be adjusted. This ruling does not apply to the goalie's stick.

Personal Equipment

The rules require all players to wear a pair of gloves and a helmet equipped with a face mask. A chin pad is secured to the mask and acts as a cushion to keep the mask from being pushed into the face. A cupped chin strap must be fastened on both sides of the helmet to keep it in the proper position. A lacrosse helmet is considerably lighter than a football helmet because the amount of physical contact in lacrosse is minimal compared with that in football. The lacrosse helmet mainly provides protection from the ball and from blows by the opponent's stick. Gloves are worn for the same reason. They are similar to ice hockey gloves but more flexible.

Arm or elbow pads and a shoulder pad are worn for protection from stick checks, and are also required by rule. The remaining pieces of equipment worn by the lacrosse player are shoes, a jersey, and shorts. The cleated shoes worn for football or soccer are used for lacrosse. The jerseys are similar to football jerseys, and the shorts are similar to those worn in soccer or basketball.

All players are required to wear protective mouthguards of a visible color.

PLAY OF THE GAME

Time

The regulation playing time of a college varsity game is 60 minutes, divided into four periods of 15 minutes each. High school teams play four 10-minute periods. In the event of a tie score at the end of a regulation game, sudden-victory play will begin, with the winner being the team scoring the first goal.

Officials

The game is controlled by two officials: a referee and an umpire. If both teams agree, a third official, designated the field judge, may be used. The referee has the final word in all decisions. The officials start the play at the beginning of each period and after each goal with a face-off.

Offside

The offside rule, which is peculiar to the game of lacrosse, requires each team to have three players located on its attack half of the field (between the centerline and the endline) and four players on its defensive half of the field (between the centerline and the endline). This rule prevents all 10 players from jamming in front of the goal in an effort to prevent a score, as is done at times in the game of soccer. It enables lacrosse to be a wide-open, freewheeling game with ample opportunity for scoring attempts.

Out-of-Bounds

When a player throws or carries the ball out-of-bounds, the opposing team gets possession. This is a basic rule for all team sports, but in lacrosse there is one exception to this rule: When a loose ball goes out-of-bounds as a result of a shot taken at the goal, it is awarded to the team whose player is closest to it at the exact time it crosses the boundary line. This gives the offense the opportunity to maintain control of the ball after a missed shot goes out-of-bounds.

Substitutes

There are two methods of substituting players in lacrosse. The regular method allows players to enter the game whenever play has been suspended after the ball has gone out-of-bounds at any point along either sideline. The other method is similar to ice hockey's substitution of players while the game is in progress. One player at a time may enter the game when a teammate leaves the playing field. This takes place at a special substitution area at the centerline.

Penalties

Although the uninitiated spectator often thinks lacrosse is a wild, stick-swinging game, it is not nearly as rough as it appears. There is physical contact in lacrosse, but not nearly as much as in football, with its continuous hitting on every play. Injuries in football are more numerous and more serious. Even though body and stick checks are part of lacrosse, there are definite limitations on them, which prevent injuries. In addition, the protective equipment worn by the lacrosse player minimizes injuries. Body checking of an opponent is legal as long as the opponent either has possession of the ball or is within 5 yards (4.6 m) of a loose ball and the contact is from the front or side and above the knees. A player can check the opponent's stick with his own stick when the opponent has possession of the ball or is within 5 yards (4.6 m) of a loose ball. The opponent's gloved hand on the stick is considered part of the stick and can be legally checked. However, no other part of his body may be checked.

Lacrosse is similar to ice hockey in that a player who violates the rules must spend time in a penalty box. This forces the violator's team to operate with one less player than its opponent—or even more, if other penalties occur at the same time or while a player is already in the penalty box. The team that has been fouled then plays with one player more than the other team and usually ends up taking a close-range shot at the goal. There are two types of fouls: personal and technical.

Personal fouls, the more serious type, consist of illegal body checking, slashing with the stick, tripping, unnecessary roughness, and unsportsman like conduct. The penalty for a personal foul is suspension of the offending player from the game for 1 to 3 minutes, depending on the official's judgment of the severity and intention of the foul. Most personal fouls call for only a 1-minute suspension.

Technical fouls are those of a less serious nature, and they consist of interference, holding, pushing, offside, and stalling. The penalty for a technical foul is suspension from the game for 30 seconds if the offending team does not have possession of the ball at the time the foul is committed.

A player who has committed a violation of the playing rules must serve time in the penalty box. The player must remain there until substituted for or informed by the timekeeper that it is time to reenter the game. The player is also released from the penalty box when the opposing team scores a goal. Expulsion fouls and unsportsman like conduct fouls, however, are such serious violations that they require that the full time always be served.

If a defending player commits a foul against an attacking player who has possession of the ball, a slow-whistle technique, similar to that used in ice hockey, is enacted. The official drops a signal flag and withholds his whistle until a scoring play is completed. The scoring play is considered to have been completed when the attacking team loses control of the ball, takes a shot, or the ball leaves the attack-goal area.

FUNDAMENTAL SKILLS AND TECHNIQUES

Holding the Stick

The player must hold the stick properly to control the ball effectively in the pocket. Figure 19.2 shows a right-handed player with the proper grip of the stick. The left (lower) hand, with the palm facing down, grasps the stick at the end of the handle for protection. Failure to do so, resulting in a portion of the stick (even just 1 or 2 inches) being exposed, gives the defender a good chance of making a successful poke check on the end of the handle and dislodging the ball. The right (upper) hand, with the palm facing up, is placed on the handle about 12 inches (30.7 cm) from the left hand. Both hands are in front of the hips or slightly outside them.

Beginners often feel more comfortable grasping the stick with the upper hand closer to the head of the stick, giving them more control in catching and cradling the ball. However, they lose a considerable amount of leverage and power when releasing the ball with their hands too far apart on the stick. More-advanced players like to shoot the ball with their hands about 6 inches (15.4 cm) apart, giving them greater leverage. As a general guide, the hands are placed in the basic position of about 12 inches (30.7 cm) apart when catching, throwing, cradling, shooting, and scooping the ball.

The fingers hold the stick with a firm but not tight grip. Beginners often make the mistake of "squeezing the stick to death" with a viselike grip and consequently lose the feel for controlling the ball. The stick rests more in the fingers than in the palm of the upper hand. The thumb is on top of the handle. The elbow of the upper arm is pointed toward the ground and not out to the side. These points allow for a free and easy motion to cradle the ball and keep it in the pocket.

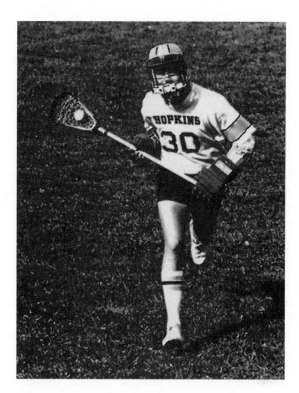

Figure 19.2. Grip and two-hand front cradle.

Cradling

Cradling is probably the most difficult technique for the beginner to learn, and it is obviously the most important. Each player must be able to run at top speed, often surrounded by opponents, and still control the ball in the pocket of the stick. The key to cradling is the looseness of the upper hand and wrist. The loose wrist motion of the lacrosse player's upper hand while cradling can be compared to the symphony conductor's handling of the baton. When conducting, the maestro moves the entire arm as well as the hand, and so does the lacrosse player when cradling.

Most youngsters have played around with either a table tennis paddle or tennis racquet, trying to keep the ball on the flat surface of the paddle or racquet by moving their arms and turning their wrists in a swinging motion. This technique is similar to cradling a lacrosse ball, and it may be helpful for the beginner to hold the stick in front of the body with only one hand and cradle the ball this way. The ball is not shaken or jiggled around in the pocket of the stick by the wrist action alone; it is rocked back and forth with a smooth, rhythmic motion of the entire upper arm as well as the hand. If the wrists are not locked but are allowed to move with the swinging motion of the arms, which results normally from running, the ball will come to a more positive rest in the pocket. Both hands are involved with the cradling, although the upper hand carries the bulk of the load. The lower hand has to have a loose enough grip to allow the stick to be turned in it. Beginners can look at the ball when cradling just to make sure it is under control in the pocket. As confidence is gained in handling the ball, the player does not need to look at it because he has a feel for its position in the stick.

There are different types of cradles, but each has the same basic motion. Figure 19.3 shows the two-hand upright cradle, which is used when a defender is playing the opponent with the ball. This cradle gives good protection of the ball and keeps the stick in a position to release the ball quickly and accurately. The one-hand cradle (Figure 19.4) gives excellent protection because the lower hand is placed in front of the body to prevent the defender's checks from getting to the stick.

Throwing

The techniques used in throwing a football or baseball are the same ones used in throwing a lacrosse ball with the stick. Figure 19.5 shows a right-handed player in the three phases of the throwing motion. The body is turned to the side and the feet are staggered. The upper hand is even with the shoulders or slightly above, and it controls the stick throughout the throwing motion. When one throws a football or baseball, the upper hand is well above the shoulder. However, the

Figure 19.4. One-hand cradle.

Figure 19.3. Two-hand upright cradle.

lacrosse player uses the stick to place the ball in this position, and therefore the upper hand remains at shoulder level or slightly above. The upper hand is primarily responsible for accuracy, but it also shares in providing the power with the lower hand, which is about 6 to 8 inches (about 15 to 20 cm) from the body. The stick is held at about a 45-degree angle from the horizon and with the head of the stick facing in the direction the ball is to be thrown. The ball rests in the pocket, and the thrower should have a feel for it.

In the actual throwing motion, the following takes place:

1. The body weight is drawn back first to the rear leg and then transferred to the front leg.
2. The upper body is turned from a side position to one facing directly to the front. The whipping of the shoulders gives added power.
3. The upper hand is drawn back several inches and then follows through with a snapping motion. This wrist snap is the key to throwing with the lacrosse stick, just the same as it is in throwing the football or baseball, because it gives both accuracy and power.
4. The lower arm is bent at the elbow, which places the lower hand in a position closer to the body than the upper hand.

Figure 19.5. Three phases of the throwing motion.

5. The lower hand pulls down on the end of the handle, making a small arc toward the middle of the body.
6. The ball leaves the stick from the center of the pocket.
7. The ball is aimed for the head of the receiver's stick.
8. The stick ends up pointing directly at this target in a nearly horizontal position.

To emphasize the similarity between throwing a baseball or a football and a lacrosse ball with the stick, the beginner can throw with just one hand, the upper hand, on the stick. The wrist snap is of primary importance, and the throw can be made with the identical motion used by a pitcher or quarterback. The accuracy and power with one hand on the stick are obviously more limited, but it is easy to feel the similarity in the throwing techniques.

The most common error the beginner makes is pushing the ball out of the pocket rather than throwing it. This is caused either by the failure to draw the stick back several inches just prior to the forward motion or by a failure to snap the wrist when making the throw. When the ball is pushed out of the stick, it has limited power and control. The beginning thrower also tends to use primarily the pull-down move by the lower hand to release the ball instead of using the joint action of both the upper and lower hands.

Catching

When a player catches the ball, the positions of both the body and the stick are important (Figure 19.6). The upper body squarely faces the ball in its flight. The feet are about shoulder width apart and in line rather than staggered. This position allows the receiver to move quickly to either the left or the right, depending on where the ball is thrown. The stick is placed slightly above the head as a target for the pass. The pocket of the stick is positioned so that it completely faces the ball. The catch is made in front of the body, with the head of the stick reaching out for the ball, much the same as a baseball player using a glove to catch the ball. The baseball player doesn't catch the ball when it is even with the body or with the arm completely straightened out in front of the body. Rather, the player reaches out with the gloved hand as the ball approaches and then cushions the ball into the glove, actually making the catch about 6 inches in front of the body.

The lacrosse player uses the same techniques in catching the ball with the stick. The idea of catching in lacrosse is also much the same as trying to catch a thrown tennis ball with a tightly strung racket. The stick must be withdrawn or the ball will rebound. The receiver cushions the ball in the pocket by bringing the head of the stick back toward the body and making use of a quick but soft wrist action. This cradle motion controls the ball in the pocket and keeps it from bouncing out.

Catching the ball on the backhand side—that is, the side opposite the receiver's stick—requires a different maneuver. The receiver swings the stick across the front of the body into the backhand position (Figure 19.7). The entire stick is moved to the backhand side, not just the head of the stick. Beginners will often move just the head of the stick and leave the butt end on the forehand side. This makes for a very awkward catch. The wrist or cradle action is the same, except that it is done in the backhand position. The receiver will either

Figure 19.6. Three phases of the catching technique.

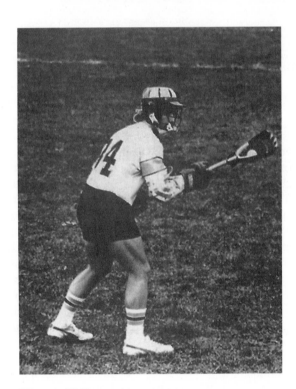

Figure 19.7. Backhand catch.

Once the catch is made, the receiver always turns into a position with the body between the stick and the nearest opponent. This gives the best possible protection of the stick. Beginners—and even some advanced players—often make the mistake of turning the wrong way and bringing the stick in front of the body, where the opponent can check it.

Scooping

Control of the ball is a significant factor in a team's success. Because the ball is on the ground for a portion of every game, it is vital for a team to try to gain possession of it more than 50 percent of the time. Scooping a ground ball that is being contested by as many as five players requires not only mastering the basic skills of actually scooping the ball, but also a determination and fierce competitiveness. A team's mental attitude is usually reflected in its play of the ground ball, and in most cases the team controlling the ground ball wins the game.

Maintaining the proper body and stick position is essential for the scooper. Starting within several yards of a ground ball, the scooper bends the knees and upper body in a semi-crouch position. If holding the stick right-handed, then the right foot is forward on the scoop to give a free-flowing scooping motion with the arms (Figure 19.8). The left (lower) arm determines the angle that the stick makes with the ground in the scoop. The angle will vary according to the size of the player, but a general guideline of approximately 30 degrees can be established. The lower arm will be slightly bent in the scoop. If the angle approaches 60 degrees, it is going to place the stick at too steep an angle, which minimizes the effectiveness of controlling the ball in a fast-moving

sidestep or cross over to get to a ball thrown to the backhand side. If the ball is close to the body, a right-hander will sidestep with the left foot. Figure 19.7 shows a right-hander who has pivoted on the left foot and made the crossover with the right foot because the ball was not near the body. The crossover step provides extra reach.

Figure 19.8. Scooping the ball.

pressure situation. Instead of getting their nose down near the ground to play the ball, players will often take the lazy approach: scooping the ball with the body in an upright position and with the stick at a sharp angle. This technique, referred to as *spiking* the ball, should be avoided.

The end of the handle is held to the side of the body rather than in front, where the stick could dig into the ground and force the butt end of the handle into the scooper's groin or midsection. The head of the stick hits the ground 1 to 2 inches (2.6 to 5.2 cm) from the ball. A common mistake is for the scooper to try to place the head of the stick right next to the ball, which may cause the stick to hit or go over the ball. The scooper must keep his or her eyes on the ball until it has been scooped into the stick with a shovel-like motion and should keep moving. Do not flip the ball into the air as it is scooped. If a player is completely ambidextrous, the ball may be scooped either left- or right-handed. However, if one hand is obviously stronger than the other, the stronger hand should be used to scoop the ball in a pressure situation, not the weaker hand.

Stress should be placed on the importance of scooping the ground with both hands on the stick. It may seem easier to scoop with just the lower hand gripping the stick at the butt end of the handle, but the percentages are not good with the one-handed scoop. The one-handed scoop using just the upper hand should also be avoided, because the end of the handle is exposed to the opponent's check. The chance for error is far less in the two-handed scoop because the scooper gets the body closer to the ground and can control the stick better.

Once the ball is in the stick, the scooper's primary concern is protecting it. There are several courses of action, depending on the circumstances. Determine the location of the opposition as soon as the ball is scooped. If surrounded, tuck the stick close to the body and try to dodge out of trouble. This maneuver is referred to as the *scoop and tuck*. If, after the scoop, an open area is available, regardless of whether it's toward the offensive or defensive half of the field, burst full speed for daylight. If pressure comes from the side once on the run, the player can hold the stick with one hand and protect it with the other.

INDIVIDUAL OFFENSE

Dodging

Every player on the team must strive to master the face, roll, and bull dodges. These three dodges give the player with the ball the capability of going by an opponent and advancing the ball toward the goal. Most dodges occur as a result of an opponent's mistake or overcommitment. Incorrect body or stick position by the defender can also encourage the dodge. The ball carrier can initiate the dodge by baiting the opponent into making a mistake and then taking advantage of it.

Protection of the stick by the dodger is probably the most important factor in completing a successful dodge. A simple rule to achieve this protection is: Keep your head between and in direct alignment with the head of your stick and the opponent. If you maintain this head-on-head position, the defender cannot check the ball carrier's stick without hitting him on the helmet and committing a foul.

Face Dodge

The face dodge is best used when an opponent delivers a check at the ball carrier's stick. The ball carrier pulls his own stick across the front of the body when he sees the stick coming. Actually the stick goes in front of the face—hence the name *face dodge*. The ball carrier can help set up the face dodge by faking a pass to a teammate. Use a head-and-eye fake, looking in the direction of the anticipated pass and even calling a player in that area by name. Have two hands on the stick when faking the pass to make it more realistic. If the opponent raises the stick in the air to block the faked pass, this will open up the opportunity for the face dodge just as well as the opponent's using an aggressive slap check.

Figure 19.9 shows a right-handed player executing the face dodge. In one simultaneous motion, the player pushes off with the right foot, sidesteps to the left with the left foot, and pulls the stick across the face. When the face dodge is done with quickness and agility, the dodger gains at least a step on the opponent in the new direction.

Roll Dodge

Of all the dodges, the roll dodge is probably used most frequently. It is effective when the opponent is very aggressive with stick checks, especially with a horizontal thrust that

Figure 19.9. Two phases of the face dodge with a side step.

almost turns or pushes the ball carrier in the opposite direction. The check actually helps to roll away from the pressure. The roll dodge can be done in either a slow-moving or a fast-moving situation. It is not necessary to keep two hands on the stick because the success of the dodge is dependent more on footwork than on the handling of the stick. Figure 19.10 shows a right-handed attacker who, while driving toward the goal, has reacted to the check of the defender with a roll dodge. The roll dodger pivots on the left (lead) foot, then pushes off the left leg and takes a step with the right foot in the direction opposite the original path. This step is sizable, 2 to 3 feet (0.6 to 0.9 m), and is the key to the roll dodge. It should be as close to the defender as possible to facilitate rolling by in the new direction. If the dodger rounds out on the first step, moving away from the defender, no advantage will be gained because the defender will have a chance to recover position.

When taking the first step on the roll dodge, the ball carrier faces away from the opponent and throws his hips into him. The head of the stick stays even with the player's own head while making the pivot. If the head of the stick is kept well above the head, the defender may be able to check it. If the head of the stick is trailed, the defender can reach around and also make the check. However, if it is even with his own head, the stick is well protected and the defender will either jeopardize his positioning by making a reckless swing with his stick or foul him.

Bull Dodge

Whereas both the face dodge and roll dodge have the dodger changing direction and going in a direction opposite to the original path, the bull dodge starts one way and climaxes in the same direction. The name of the dodge indicates brute strength overpowering the defender, but in many cases it is the burst of speed that gives the dodger the advantage. Because the dodger has the advantage of knowing when the burst of speed is going to start, the dodger will be able to beat even a defender who is as fast. If the defender is slower, the attacker should have no trouble gaining the advantage by running at full speed throughout the dodge.

If the defender has similar or greater speed and size than the attacker, the attacker can make use of change-of-pace maneuvers, head fakes, and stick fakes to throw the defender off balance. By driving hard and using one of these techniques, then by bursting full speed in the original direction, one can gain a jump on the opponent.

There are other dodges that are for the most part combinations of the basic three: face, roll, and bull. Mastery of these three, however, will give a player all the weapons needed to dodge the opponent. This applies to players on all levels, from "little league" to college varsity. The dodges can be used by players in all positions, goalies and defensive players as well as midfielders and attackers.

Shooting

Because games are won by the number of goals scored, shooting plays a vital role in any team's success. Although being able to shoot the ball with power is important, the crucial factor in effective shooting is accuracy. One of the shocking statistics in lacrosse is the high percentage of shots that miss the goal completely. Emphasis must be placed on taking only good shots and keeping them on target, or on the goal. Shots can be classified in two general categories: outside shots and close-range shots.

Figure 19.10. Three phases of the roll dodge.

Outside Shots

Outside shots are those normally taken approximately 12 to 18 yards (11 to 16.5 m) from the goal. A shot taken past the 18- to 20-yard (16.5 to 18.3 m) mark is considered to be too long and not very effective against a good goalie.

Outside shots should be bounced, because they are harder for the goalie to follow than are shots thrown into the air. The shooter should aim the outside bounce shot at the center of the goal, anticipating it to go about 8 to 12 inches (20.5 to 30.7 cm) to either side of center and thus inside the pipes of the goal. Aiming for a spot just inside the pipes is asking for trouble, because the margin of error will cause the ball to go outside the pipes too many times.

Close-Range Shots

Any shot taken between the 12-yard (11 m) mark and the crease can be considered a close-range shot. These shots are high-percentage scorers because of the proximity to the goal. The shooter keys on the body and stick position of the goalie and tries to place the ball where the goalie is most vulnerable. If the goalie's stick is high, the shooter can direct the ball low, and vice versa. The shooter also has the option of bouncing the ball or firing it in the air. But most important, the ball should be shot hard and accurately for an open area. Because the shooter is close to the goal, the ball should be aimed about 6 to 12 inches (15 to 30.7 cm) inside the pipes. Trying to place the ball just an inch or two inside the pipes usually results in hitting the pipe or missing the goal completely.

Shooting Technique

The same basic techniques that apply to throwing the ball also apply to shooting it. The upper hand of the shooter is in a position over the shoulder, in much the same way that most baseball pitchers and football quarterbacks hold their arms when throwing. This over-the-shoulder shot is the most effective of shots because it is the most accurate. The upper hand follows through in a vigorous throwing motion with a snap of the wrist as the lower hand pulls down hard on the butt end of the handle. The body weight transfers from the rear to the front leg in much the same fashion as an outfielder in baseball catches a fly ball and fires to home plate to put out a runner trying to score from third base. The head of the stick actually ends up pointing to the ground because the body follow-through is so complete.

TEAM OFFENSE

The structuring of a team's offense is vital to its success. Games are won by scoring goals, and a team must utilize the talents of its ballplayers to give them the opportunity to score. This requires detailed organization by the coach and a thorough understanding of the offensive strategy by each attacker and midfielder. A disorganized offense can completely demoralize a team. Confusion will reign if there is little coordination between the attack and midfield units and players are allowed to freelance and "do their own thing" without their teammates' awareness and cooperation.

A team usually scores nearly half its goals on unsettled play: intercepting a clearing pass, taking the ball away from the goalie or a defensive player, dodging an over-aggressive defender who forces the attacker to dodge, gaining possession of a ground ball after a big scramble and pressing for the goal, and fast breaks initiated at the defensive end of the field. The goals scored in these situations are easy because

the defense is not settled and ready to meet the attack. The more goals a team can score this way, the better its chances of winning.

The other half of a team's goals come from settled, all-even play. A team has to work persistently and patiently to score in this situation. Some offenses are attack-oriented; others are midfield-oriented. The capabilities of the players determine the emphasis. In any offensive play, all six players are involved if it is to be successful. Some players may have to be good "actors" while others are carrying out the primary effort to score. However, no player can just stand around and watch play and consequently allow a defender to help stop the play.

There are different styles of offense, and most teams make use of a combination of them. Dodges and flip-offs when double-teamed, the cutting game, set plays, inverts, and a fast-break, move-the-ball offense are the basic ways to score in the settled situation. Regardless of the style, discipline is a key factor. Each player must know his responsibilities within the system and carry them out to the letter.

INDIVIDUAL DEFENSE

A complete understanding of the basic skills of defending against an opponent with the ball is essential to every player on the field. Each defensive player and midfielder obviously becomes involved with the primary responsibility of neutralizing the opponent when in possession of the ball. Attackers make use of the same principles when they play an opponent who is attempting to clear the ball. The goalie must know the defensive techniques to assist defensive teammates with positive verbal instructions.

The techniques for playing one-on-one defense in lacrosse are identical with those used in basketball, although the lacrosse player has the advantage of using a stick. However, it is imperative the stick be handled more like a foil than a bludgeon. Too many defensive players feel they must be extremely aggressive with the stick and show their superiority over their opponents by pounding them with the stick and trying to gain possession of the ball. They believe that this style is more challenging to them personally and that it gives them more notoriety than the patient, position-conscious defensive game. A defender who has an easy time handling a weak attacker might run into trouble when playing against one who is an equal or better. The take-the-ball-away approach will often lead the defender to committing a foul or being dodged. Therefore, the conservative style of defense (play your position, apply pressure, and be patient) should be emphasized.

Stance

The stance of the defensive player is vital to effectiveness in defending the player with the ball. Control of the body and readiness to move in any direction are essential. The feet should be spread a little wider than shoulder width and staggered in a heel-to-toe alignment. The defender must maintain balance by keeping most of the weight on the balls of the feet. The heels should make contact with the ground to provide stability. Knees should be flexed and the upper body bent slightly forward. This semicrouch position resembles that of a boxer (Figure 19.11).

Eyes

The defender's eyes do not center on any one thing, but rather look through the attacker's hands, stick (pocket), and eyes, as each of these can give a tip-off. If the attacker has only one hand on the stick, he normally will not be able to shoot or feed effectively. Therefore, the defender can concentrate primarily on maintaining proper position and getting ready to execute a poke or slap check (discussed later) when the attacker puts the other hand on the stick. However, the defender can use the poke check to annoy an attacker who is carrying the stick in one hand. When the attacker has two hands on the stick, the defender should be ready to apply pressure. The attacker's eyes will often betray when and where the ball will be thrown. Only the best attacker will look one way and then throw the other way. Most players look exactly where they are going to throw the ball, and their faces will almost light up when they spot the open player and prepare to release the ball. The defender must be ready for the clever attacker who fakes with the eyes and then makes a countermove.

Positioning

Being in the proper position when the offensive player gets the ball is extremely important for the defender. The defender assumes a squared-up position with the body in a direct line with the ball carrier's stick side and the center of the goal. The alignment of the feet is also determined by the attacker's stick position. If the attacker has the stick in a right-hand position, the defender should have the left foot back and right foot forward in a staggered alignment (Figure 19.11). The feet are reversed when the attacker has the stick in the left hand. This allows the defender to move quickly in the direction the opponent is facing.

Footwork

The speed at which the offensive player moves will determine the footwork of the defender. A "shuffle" with short, choppy steps and no crossover steps is used when the opponent moves at a slow to half-speed pace. When shuffling, the feet should remain spread about shoulder width to provide a solid base. They should never come closer than about 8 to 10 inches (about 20 to 25 cm) apart. This footwork is similar to a boxer's maneuvering in the ring. The body is squared off and facing the opponent when using the shuffle. When the attacker increases speed to the point where the defender would not be able to keep up using the shuffle, the defender should change to a hip-to-hip running position (Figure 19.12). The defender's body is turned in the same

Figure 19.11. Defensive position (player on right).

Figure 19.12 Hip-to-hip running defensive position (player on right).

direction as the opponent's body, and the hips are even with those of the offensive player. This allows the defender to maintain the proper defensive position between the opponent and the goal. If the attacker slows up, the defender can resume shuffling.

Handling the Stick

Proper handling of the stick by the defender when playing the ball is almost as important as proper footwork. If using a stick of attack or midfield length, the hands should be about 12 inches (30.7 cm) apart. If using a long-handled stick, the hands should be farther apart to better control the bigger stick. With either stick, the lower hand should be at the butt end of the handle and the upper hand should be the proper distance up the handle, never at the throat of the stick. Placing the stick across the chest or on the number of the opponent's jersey can be most disconcerting. From this position, the defender can execute any check.

A player who is basically a right-hander should play right-handed when on defense—vice versa for the left-hander. It is not a good idea to change hands when on defense because the switching of the hands will result in less than complete control of the stick. Trying to change hands every time the attacker changes direction will place the defender at a decided disadvantage. Another reason for not changing hands is to ensure that the defender will be holding the stick with the stronger hand when the ball is on the ground. This will allow scooping the ball more easily if he does check it out of the opponent's stick. The extra second or two of delay

to change hands for the scoop in this situation could cause the ball to be lost.

It is debatable whether the forehand or backhand stick position is stronger on defense. The forehand position can be defined as that used by a right-handed defender who is guarding a left-handed driver. The backhand position (Figures 19.11 and 19.12) is used when a right-hander plays against a right-handed driver. There are two important advantages to the backhand position:

1. The stick rests across the chest of the opponent and acts as a natural deterrent to his taking a shot at the goal. If the attacker is forcing his way into a good shooting area, the defender can use a backhand hold to stop penetration and turn him back. The arms of the defender and the stick act as a natural "hook" on the attacker.

2. When the attacker runs toward the goal at full speed, the defender can keep pace and still keep the stick resting across the attacker's body and deliver checks that will interfere with shooting. It is extremely difficult, if not impossible, for the defender to do this when holding the stick in a forehand position and moving at full speed.

Basic Checks

Poke check

The poke check is one of the most effective checks because the opportunity to dislodge the ball from the opponent's stick without overcommitting is greater than in the other checks. The poke check consists of a thrust of the stick, propelled through the upper hand by the lower hand. This technique is similar to the billiard player's handling of a cue stick. The lower hand draws the stick back slightly just prior to the stroke to provide additional power. It is important for the upper hand to remain in contact with the handle as it slides through the fingers to provide control. If the upper hand loses its grasp, the lower hand will not be able to control the stick, thereby giving an advantage to the attacker. If the attacker is holding the stick with one hand, the thrust can be directed at any part of the handle that is showing. If he has two hands on the stick, it can be aimed at the cuff of the glove holding the butt end of the stick. The defender must guard against an overaggressive poke that will cause him to step into the opponent, resulting in an opening to roll by on the side opposite the check.

Slap check

The *slap check,* as the term implies, is merely a short, slapping blow directed at the attacker's lower, gloved hand or the handle of the stick just above it. It is used mainly when the attacker either has both hands on the stick or is about to put his lower hand on it. The slap check will not be effective if the attacker is holding the stick in one hand and protecting it well with the other. The wrist action of the upper hand on the stick delivers the check, and it should be as quick as possible. The head of the stick will be directed at the target anywhere from a horizontal position up to an angle of approximately 45 degrees above horizontal. The check should not cover a distance any greater than about 18 inches (46 cm). In fact, the shorter the check, the less it is "telegraphed." When the defender hauls back with the stick as if to bludgeon the opponent, not only is the maneuver tipped off, but also this usually results in a check that generates so much power it gets out of control and exposes the defender to a face or roll dodge. The head of the defender's stick should not go beyond a position horizontal to the ground when it is in the downward motion. If it does, it can cause a foul by tripping or hitting the attacker on the lower part of the body. When making the slap check with the stick moving in a horizontal path, the defender must guard against using too vigorous a check, which will give the attacker an easy roll dodge.

Over-the-head check

The over-the-head check is a risky one, and it requires extreme caution. If it does not knock the ball out of the opponent's stick, the defender is in a vulnerable position and will probably be dodged. There are various techniques for executing the over-the-head check:

1. The defender takes the upper hand off the stick and raises the lower hand over the opponent's head. The defender's arm will be straightened out, and with a quick flick of the wrist, the stick will swing like a pendulum, checking the head of the opponent's stick.

2. The defender takes the lower hand off the stick and raises the upper hand over the opponent's head. The arm is straightened out, and with a quick snap of the wrist, the butt end of the stick will make the pendulum swing and check the opponent's stick. This technique is best used when the attacker is facing the defender.

3. The defender can make the over-the-head check with both hands on the stick and directing them over the opponent's head. The arms almost straighten out completely, and the check is made by snapping both wrists. This check is not as popular as one-hand checks.

Wraparound check

The wraparound check is almost as dangerous as the over-the-head check because it is a one-handed maneuver, and the defender does not have complete control of the stick. However, it can be effective if the attacker has worked his way into a good shooting position close to the goal. The defender takes the lower hand off the stick, straightens the other arm, and directs the stick in a horizontal position toward the opponent's stick. This check is more effective when a right-handed defender is playing against a left-handed attacker who is going to the left, and vice versa when a left-handed defender is playing against a right-hander going to the right.

TEAM DEFENSE

Defense is the most important phase of team play in lacrosse. The goalie, three defensive players, and three midfielders must blend together into a well-coordinated group that presents a solid, unified front to the opposition. Defensive players must be concerned not only with guarding their opponents but also with assisting each other. If the game were strictly a series of one-on-one confrontations, the defense would lose out most of the time because the offensive player would find it easy to get a close-range shot at the goal given the liberty to maneuver the defender over the entire field without interference from any other defensive players. It is reassuring for each member of the defense to know that the strong support of teammates is available.

The mission of the defense is obviously to prevent the opponent from scoring. The philosophy for team defense follows the pattern established for individual defense. Position and patience are the watchwords, as opposed to an aggressive, take-the-ball-away approach.

The goalie is the backbone of the team defense and directs all the action. The defensive players and midfielders have definite responsibilities concerning both the opponents and their defensive teammates. Even attackers must know defensive strategy because they may find themselves at the defensive end of the field when they are forced to go over the centerline in a riding situation.

There are three types of team defense: one-on-one, zone, and a combination of one-on-one and zone. If a team plays more than one defense in a game, it is imperative that each player knows which defense is being used at a given time.

TIPS TO REMEMBER

1. Keep your hands approximately 12 inches (30.7 cm) apart on the stick when throwing, catching, scooping, and shooting the ball.
2. When throwing the ball, snap the upper hand/wrist and follow through with a motion similar to that used in throwing a baseball or football.
3. Throw the ball to a teammate on the stick side and at a height that is slightly above the head.
4. When cradling the ball; move the entire upper arm and keep a loose wrist.
5. When scooping the ball, keep two hands on the stick and bend at the knees.
6. A defender's mistake or overcommitment will normally dictate the type of dodge to be used by the ball carrier.
7. When dodging, the ball carrier should keep his head between and in direct alignment with the head of his stick and the opponent's stick.
8. Stress accuracy in shooting rather than power. Don't try to place the ball just inside the pipes of the goal because this will frequently result in missing the goal completely or hitting the pipe.
9. When defending against the ball carrier, handle the stick like a foil and don't bludgeon the ball carrier with stick checks that could result in a foul. Keep the stick across the numbers of the opponent's jersey and use short, quick, 6-inch (15 cm) checks.
10. Repetition is the key to learning. Be sure to execute all the fundamental skills on the run. Move your feet!
11. Remember that lacrosse is a team game and must be undertaken with enthusiasm, fair play, and a positive attitude.
12. While playing the game, respect everyone (opponents, teammates, coaches, and referees) and you will gain self-respect, which is most important.

TEACHING CONSIDERATIONS

1. Handling the stick should dominate practice sessions for beginners. Catching, throwing, and cradling drills will enable players to feel comfortable in controlling the ball in their sticks.
2. Learning the three basic dodges will enable players to gain more confidence with stick handling and their ability to maneuver with the ball.
3. Players enjoy shooting at a goal, and emphasis should be placed on teaching proper, accurate shooting techniques.
4. Team offense can be developed by first working with three-on-three maneuvers for both attack players and midfield players. Then all six offensive players can be coordinated in a basic pattern of offense.

5. When teaching the techniques for playing one-on-one defense, stress should be placed on proper positioning, footwork, and use of the various stick checks.
6. The natural progression is to follow one-on-one defensive play with three-on-three, and finally team defense, which is six-on-six.
7. Developing a team defense and a team offense should not be too difficult to teach because lacrosse, with its six-on-six play, is very similar to basketball's five-on-five play. Making sure that each player understands his offensive and defensive responsibilities is most important. There must be organized and controlled play at both ends of the field.

Women's Lacrosse

RULES

General

Women's lacrosse is played by two teams of 12 players on a grass field or artificial surface. The playing area is 110 to 140 yards (100.6 to 128 m) in length, 60 to 70 yards (54.9 to 64 m) in width, and goals are placed 90 to 100 yards (82.3 to 91.4 m) apart from one another. There are no restrictions as to player movement (other than related to specific strategy and safety considerations in front of the goal area), and play may continue behind the goal cage area. For safety reasons, when attacking, only 7 players may be on the opposing team's side of the restraining line (30 yards [27.45 m] from the goal line) and at least 5 players must be on the defensive side of the restraining line.

The game is played in an upright position, and the ball is thrown from a stick through the air from player to player. The aerial nature of the game combined with the freedom of movement makes lacrosse a dynamically creative and fast-moving game. Players generally match up player to player; and because no body contact is permitted, it often becomes a game of quickness and interceptions, with the focus on scoring goals. The only player with special equipment and privileges is the goalkeeper.

Young players may be introduced to the game through keep-away games with just a few players per side or the game of seven-on-a-side lacrosse. These games enable each player to maintain a maximum amount of activity time through the learning phases.

Ball and Sticks

Ball

The ball is solid rubber, with a circumference of not less than 7.75 inches (19.8 cm) nor more than 8 inches (20.5 cm). It must weigh not more than 5.25 ounces (149 g) and not less than 5 ounces (142 g). It must have a bounce of not less than 43 inches (1.1 m) and not more than 51 inches (1.3 m). Balls used in formal competition must be smooth or slightly textured rubber solid yellow or bright orange in color and, unless agreed to by both coaches, the same type and color ball must be used throughout the game.

Sticks

Field player. Field players propel the ball through the air with a *crosse,* or stick. The stick may be constructed of wood (Figure 19.13) or with a plastic head (Figure 19.14) and a wooden or aluminum handle. The stick must be a minimum of 35.5 inches (.9 m) and a maximum of 43.25 inches (1.1 m) in length. The head of the stick resembles a woven basket in which the ball is carried, or cradled, and thrown. This pocket must consist of four or five thongs laced through the top of the stick with stitches cross-lacing the thongs. Mesh is not allowed. The pocket must be kept tight at all times, and the ball must be visible above the sidewall of the stick. The head of a field player's stick may range from 7 to 9 inches (17.8 to 22.9 cm) wide.

Goalkeeper. Goalkeepers may use a stick with a 12-inch (30.7 cm) head. The overall length of the goalkeeper's stick is 35.5 inches (.9 m) minimum and 48 inches (1.22 m) maximum. Most goalkeepers use a plastic-headed stick that is allowed to have a deep mesh pocket.

Personal Equipment

Clothing

For play on grass or turf, cleated shoes may be worn. The cleats may be rubber or plastic but not metal. For play on turf, players may wish to wear turf shoes. Uniforms are usu-

Figure 19.14. Plastic lacrosse stick.

ally short skirts, kilts, or loose-fitting shorts. The shirt should fit loosely enough to allow the arms full movement. Some teams wear knee socks, but because the playing season tends to be in warm weather, many wear short socks. All players must wear a professionally manufactured intraoral mouthpiece, and all field players must wear proper eye protection.

Gloves

Field players may choose to wear thin, close-fitting gloves for warmth or knuckle protection. These gloves have padding on the back that still allows for maximum flexibility. Many players do not wear gloves, as they are not required.

Goalkeeper's Equipment

Helmet

Because the ball is shot directly at the goal face, where the goalkeeper stands, head protection is required. Lightweight, close-fitting helmets are manufactured specifically for women's lacrosse goalkeepers. The face is covered with a mask that comes down below the chin.

Throat and mouth protection

Throat protection is required. The protector may be attached to the bottom of the face mask and be made of plastic or foam, or a protective collar may be worn around the neck. A dental guard is also required.

Figure 19.13. Wooden lacrosse stick.

Chest protector

Although a body pad covering the upper body and continuing down along the thighs may be worn, more movement and greater flexibility are achieved by wearing a separate chest protector. Several styles of compressed foam are available that cover the chest, clavicle area, and stomach.

Thigh protection

Slip-on pants with built-in pelvic protector and foam padding covering the thighs and hip bone area are recommended.

Leg protection

With the use of the large-headed stick, many goalkeepers elect to keep their legs free to allow maximum speed and ease of movement. When protection is used, it generally consists of a slip-on foam shin guard. Occasionally knee pads are worn.

Gloves

Large padded gloves similar to men's lacrosse gloves are worn by goalkeepers. Rules require that the padding should not be excessive and not exceed 1 inch (2.5 cm).

Dimensions of the Field

The playing area for women's lacrosse shall be rectangular and marked with a solid-lined boundary. Optimal field dimensions are 120 yards (109.7 m) in length and 65 yards (59.4 m) in width. The field consists of two goals 6 feet by 6 feet (1.8 m by 1.8 m) placed 100 yards (91.4 m) apart. There must be minimum of 10 yards (9.1 m) and a maximum of 20 yards (18.2 m) of space behind each goal line, extending to the end line and running the width of the field. The goals sit in the middle of a circle with a radius of 8.5 feet (2.6 m) called the *crease*. Coming off of the crease are two fan-shaped areas of 8.75 yards (8 m) (arc) and 13.1 yards (12 m)

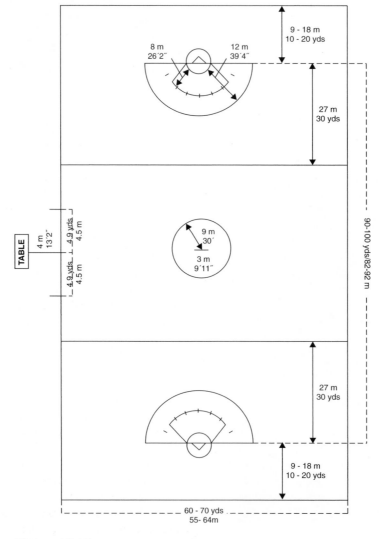

Figure 19.15. Women's lacrosse field dimensions and playing positions.

(fan) that demark the critical scoring area. A restraining line is located 30 yards (27.4 m) from and parallel to each goal line. The center of the field is marked by a large circle, with a radius of 10 yards (9.14 m) and a centerline of 3.3 yards (3 m) drawn horizontally to the goal lines (Figure 19.15).

Rules

Women's lacrosse is played by two teams of 12 players each with one being designated as goalkeeper. The game is started with three line-attack players (first home, second home, third home), five midfield players (two attack wings, one center, two defense wings), and three line-defense players (third person, cover point, point). The goalkeeper completes the defense line (Figure 19.15). Time of play for high school competition is generally 25-minute halves with a 10-minute halftime. At the collegiate level, teams play 30-minute halves.

Draw

The game is started by a center draw. The opposing centers toe the centerline facing their attacking goal and place their sticks back to back horizontally at a level above their waists. The ball is placed between their sticks, not resting on the sidewalls but cushioned between the pocket weave. At the umpire's command "Ready," the players remain motionless until the umpire blows the whistle, when they push their sticks up and away in an effort to raise the ball above their heads and out of the circle to one of their teammates. All other players must remain out of the center circle during the draw, and a maximum of five players from each team may be between the restraining lines at the start of the draw. Once the whistle is blown, players may cross the lines. Midfield players usually position themselves around the circle in anticipation of the drawn ball and move into the circle toward the ball when the umpire blows the whistle.

Scoring

The ball may be shot from any position on the field. The whole ball must cross the goal line for a goal to count. The attacking player's body may not enter the crease at any level during a shot. When a goal is scored, play is restarted at the center draw. If the ball does not cross the goal line or if an attacking player has entered the crease, the goalkeeper may place the ball in her stick and, within 10 seconds, pass the ball out of the crease to a teammate.

Stand

One of the unique rules in women's lacrosse is the stand: When the umpire blows the whistle, the ball is considered dead and all players are required to "stand" in the position they were in when the whistle blew. They may not move until the umpire restarts the game. Any player who moves after the whistle has blown, either intentionally or by the momentum of her original movement, is returned to her original position before play is restarted.

Throw

When the game needs to be restarted without giving an advantage to either team, a throw is taken. One player from each team, standing at least 1.1 yard (1 m) apart and on the side nearer to the goal she is defending, faces the umpire, who is about 6 yards (5.5 m) away. On the whistle, the umpire throws the ball in the air a little higher than head height and between the players so that they may move toward it and into the game. All other players must be 4 yards (3.7 m) away from these players and may move (stop standing) on the umpire's whistle.

A throw is taken when:

1. The ball goes in the goal off a nonplayer.
2. It cannot be determined which team caused the ball to go out of bounds.
3. Simultaneous fouls occur.
4. The ball lodges in the clothing of a field player or umpire.
5. Two players commit off setting fouls (major and/or minor), or after the attacking team fouls during a slow whistle situation.

Fouls

(See www.uslacrosse.org for a more complete list of fouls.)

Major fouls. A player may not:

1. Roughly or recklessly check/tackle another player's crosse.
2. Hit or cause her opponent's crosse to hit the opponent's head (mandatory card).
3. Slash (mandatory card).
4. Hold an opponent's crosse when the opponent is in possession of the ball.
5. Hold her crosse within the sphere around the face or throat of an opponent.
6. Initiate crosse-to-body or body-to-crosse contact.
7. Use the crosse in a dangerous and/or intimidating manner.
8. Use the webbed area of her crosse to hook the bottom end of an opponent's crosse.
9. Reach across an opponent to check the crosse when she is level with or behind her.
10. Hold, with or without cradling, the head of her crosse in front of her face or her teammate's face, within the sphere or close to her body, or her teammate's body, making a legal/safe check impossible.
11. Block her opponent by moving into her path without giving her a chance to stop or change direction.
12. Charge, shoulder, or back into an opponent.
13. With any part of her body, guard the goal outside the goal circle so as to obstruct the free space to goal—Shooting Space (Figure 19.16).
14. While defending within the 8-meter arc, remain in that area more than 3 seconds unless one is marking an opponent within a stick's length—3 Seconds.

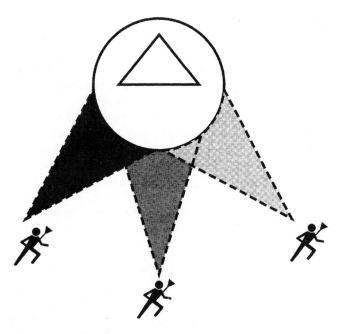

Figure 19.16 Free space to the goal.

15. Set a moving or stationary pick out of the visual field of an opposing player which does not allow enough time or space to stop or change direction and contact occurs.
16. While in possession of the ball, try to force her crosse through an opposing crosse(s) in such a way as to cause her own crosse to contact her body.
17. Move before the whistle to start play.
18. Propel the ball with her crosse in a dangerous or uncontrolled manner at any time.
19. Shoot dangerously or without control.
20. Shoot from an indirect free position.

Minor fouls. A player may not:
1. Cover a ground ball with the foot or crosse.
2. Check an opponent's empty crosse.
3. Guard one's crosse with the hand or elbow.
4. Touch the ball with the hand.
5. Allow the ball to play off the body, unless the player is the goalkeeper and is inside the crease.
6. Throw the crosse.
7. On the center draw, step into the circle before the whistle blows.
8. Play with a crosse that does not meet measurement and pocket requirements.
9. Fail to be ready to start play after a 2-minute team timeout or following halftime.
10. Substitute illegally.
11. Request more than two timeouts.

Goal circle (or crease) fouls. A field player must not enter or have any part of her body or crosse on or in the goal circle at any time except in the following circumstances:
1. She is deputizing for the goalkeeper.

2. The shooter may follow through with her crosse over the goal circle; however, her feet must not touch the goal circle, and her shooting motion must be initiated from outside the goal circle.
3. The player(s) directly defending the shooter may reach into the goal circle with her crosse(s) to block the shot or check the shooter's crosse; however, the defender's feet must not touch the goal circle.

Once a team gains possesion of the ball in the goal circle and the ball is cleared, the team must not intentionally return the ball to their goal circle until the ball has been played by another player.

Goalkeepers may not:
1. Allow the ball to remain in the crease longer than 10 seconds.
2. Play the ball outside of the circle with the hand.
3. Step back into the crease while in possession of the ball.
4. Place one foot outside of the goal circle and drag the ball inside.
5. Score a goal with a crosse that does not meet specifications for field players.

Penalty for major and minor fouls. The penalty for fouls is the *free position*. On the umpire's whistle, all players stand. The umpire then awards the ball to the fouled player while moving all other players 4.4 yards (4 m) away. For major fouls, the offending player is moved 4.4 yards (4 m) behind the player awarded the free position. Play is restarted by the umpire's arm signal and whistle.

Penalty for major fouls inside the 13.1-yard (12-m) fan. The penalty for a major foul by a defensive player awards a free position to the fouled attack player on the spot where the foul occurred. All other players and their crosses must be moved sideways out of the penalty lane (Figure 19.17). The goalkeeper may remain within the goal circle.

Penalty for major fouls inside the 8.75-yard (8-m) arc. Major fouls committed by the defense within the 8.75-yard (8-m)

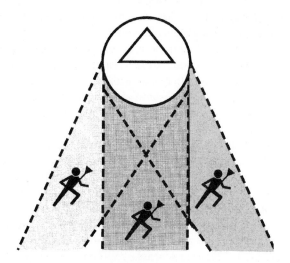

Figure 19.17. Penalty lanes.

arc result in a free position to the fouled attack player, which is placed on the closest hash mark on the 8.75-yard (8-m) arc. All other players are cleared from the 8.75-yard arc and penalty lane, and the offending defense player is placed on the 13.1-yard (12-m) fan, directly behind the fouled attack player. If a major foul occurs to the side of the 8.75-yard arc, the fouled player is positioned 8.75 yards from the goal, and all other players must be moved from the penalty line (Figure 19.17).

Penalty for minor fouls inside the 13.1-yard (12-m) fan. Minor fouls by the defense within the 13.1-yard (12-m) fan result in an *indirect free position* awarded to the fouled attack player, who is placed on the nearest spot on the 12-meter fan. The ball must be touched by another player before a shot on goal is attempted. The offending defense player is placed 4.37 yards (4 m) behind the fouled player. All other players may remain in their positions, as long as they are 4.37 yards (4 m) away from the player taking the free position.

Basic Skills

Cradle

The cradle allows a player to move with the ball remaining securely within the laced pocket of the stick. Because the rules require the stick to have a tight pocket, continuous movement is required to keep the ball in place. Cradling is a natural movement that mirrors the body's movement while running. To teach a natural cradle, the following progression should be used:

1. Have players run 20 yards with their arms in a natural pumping movement.
2. Focus players' attention on the natural movements of their arms.
3. Have players clasp their hands in front of the body, elbows bent, with the hands held slightly above the waist (Figure 19.18).
4. With clasped hands, players should run 20 yards again, overemphasizing the arm-pumping movement. This results in the arms moving together from one side of the body to the other, which is the movement of a natural full cradle.
5. Players should hold the stick in a vertical position, with the middle of the stick clasped in both hands. Remind players to keep their arms bent at waist level.
6. Have players run 20 yards with the stick remaining vertical and moving naturally from one side of the body to the other as the arms pump during the running motion (Figure 19.19).
7. Players should gradually spread their hands apart on the stick (Figure 19.20) and continue to reinforce the natural arm-pumping motion until they have one hand just below the head of the stick and one hand at the bottom (Figure 19.21). Both arms should still remain above waist level. Teach players to be comfortable with either the right hand or the left hand at the top of the stick.

8. Once players are comfortable with the full cradle, teach them the half-cradle, which has the stick movement coming from midbody to one side and back again.

Grip during cradle. (See Figures 19.13 and 19.14.) Lay the stick, with the open pocket facing up, on the ground. While looking at the back of the hand, spread the thumb away from the other fingers to form a V between the thumb and index fingers. Wrap this hand around the stick just below the pocket with the V and back of the hand on the same side of the stick as the open pocket. Place the other hand at the bottom of the stick and bring the stick to a vertical position, with the bottom hand slightly above waist level. With this grip and relaxed shoulder and arm movements, the cradle will keep the ball in the pocket.

Throw

Lacrosse is a passing game, which means that players must have several ways in which to throw the ball. The most common are the overarm throw (a lever-type action when not closely guarded or a punch-type throw when closely guarded) and the underarm throw. To teach the overarm throw, the following progression should be used:

Overarm: lever style

1. Without a stick, the player should throw the ball to another player.
2. Focus player's attention on taking back the hand, opposite foot forward, shoulder rotation, and follow-through, as in the softball throw.

Figure 19.18. Learning the cradle.

Figure 19.19. Learning the cradle: hands together.

Figure 19.20. Learning the cradle: hands spread.

Figure 19.21. Learning the cradle: final position.

3. Freeze the player in the position of "hand back and ready to throw the ball" (Figure 19.22).
4. Place a stick in the throwing hand with the pocket facing toward the sky and the end of the stick pointed toward the target. Remember to maintain the body's correct throwing position.
5. With only the throwing hand holding the stick, throw the ball toward the target, making sure that the stick face remains open toward the target, the bottom of the stick moves in a lever action under the arm, and a correct body rotation position is maintained.
6. Repeat this process, adding the second hand to the bottom of the stick (Figure 19.23).
7. Start cradling while walking. As the cradle comes to the side of the body, move into the throwing position and throw the ball while walking through the throwing action. The stick moves in a lever action and finishes with the throwing arm straight toward the target and the bottom hand in the armpit (Figure 19.24).
8. Gradually increase speed from a walk to running and throw on the run.

Overarm: punch style

1. The punch style is very similar to the lever style, but limit the upper-hand preparation of the throw to a position in front of the throwing shoulder instead of behind the shoulder.

2. Body position and motion remain the same. Because of the starting position, there is a much smaller lever action. The power loss is compensated for by a push from the upper arm and hand.

Grip during overarm throws. When throwing overarm, the grip is relaxed to allow the stick face to open up toward the target. This results in the hand moving around the stick, where the back of the pocket is. As the ball is thrown, the hand should be firm on the stick. Immediately after the throw, the hand should return to the cradling position.

Underarm throw. When another player is guarding the ball carrier, there are times when the carrier must be able to throw the ball when the stick is on the wrong side of the body for an overarm throw. To accomplish a throw, either switch hands—placing the other hand on the top of the stick—or use an underarm throw. If the thrower is trying to throw under the opponent's stick, the underarm throw is the better choice. A description of this movement follows.

Body position. The body is turned sideways, with the shoulder aimed at the target. Both feet can be turned sideways. The arms are pulled across the body away from the target, the hand of the aiming shoulder on top, in a cradle position (Figure 19.25). At the start of the throw, the stick is held in a vertical position.

Arm and stick movement. In one continuous movement, the stick is turned almost upside down and moved in a shovel/sweep across the body, ending with the top of the

Figure 19.22. Ready to throw.

Figure 19.23. Adding the stick.

Figure 19.24. The throw.

stick pointed at the target and the arms extended. The foot closest to the target may step toward the target during the movement (Figure 19.26). The stick movement simulates a canoe stroke or snow shoveling.

Grip during underarm throw. The grip during the underarm throw remains the same as during the cradle, with the V positioned just below the open pocket face of the stick.

The catch. (Figure 19.27) The catch is an extension of the cradle. The player must make sure that the pocket on the stick face is open toward the oncoming ball and must continuously watch the ball move into the pocket of the stick. As soon as the ball enters the pocket, the player should absorb its shock with a "soft give," as in baseball, and continue into a cradle. The feeling of the give is an important skill because most catches are made while moving toward an oncoming ball.

Grip during the catch. The V of the top hand may be slightly relaxed during the catch. However, this should result in a minimal amount of repositioning of that hand. Once the ball enters the stick, a natural wrap into a continuous cradle will keep the ball in place. If the V is moved too far out of the

Figure 19.27. The catch.

cradle position, it will be difficult to move smoothly into a cradle, with the result of the ball jumping out of the pocket.

Ground ball pick-ups

Because passing and catching are skills that require some practice to consistently be successful, it is inevitable that the ball will sometimes hit the ground. Because players may not touch the ball with their hands, ground balls must be picked up with the stick.

Body position. The body is turned sideways (as in throwing) when executing a ground ball pick-up. Which side turns, or opens up, is determined by where and how closely one is being defended. The player who is picking up the ground ball should position the body between the opponent and the ground ball. As the ball is approached, the player should slowly move into a crouch position by bending the knees and lowering the hips (Figure 19.28). As the front foot outdistances the ball, the player should already be low enough to scoop the stick through it as it moves toward the front foot (Figure 19.29). As the player scoops, she continues to run through the ball and gradually assumes an upright cradling position (Figure 19.30).

Stick position. The stick is lowered and scrapes the ground with the lip of the stick moving under the ball. As the ball enters the stick, a gradual cradle is immediately started and continues as the player slowly moves into an upright position. Players should also practice a one-handed ground ball pick-up with each hand.

Figure 19.25. Underarm throw (side view).

Figure 19.26. Underarm throw (front view).

Figure 19.28. Approach for picking up a ground ball.

Figure 19.29. The scoop.

Grip. The grip is the same as with the cradle, with the V of the hand positioned just below the open pocket. This position enables a smooth transition into the cradle.

Body checking

No matter what strategy is used, lacrosse always comes down to a level of one player competing against another. When playing against an opponent who possesses the ball, it is critical to maneuver into a safe playing position before making an attempt to dislodge the ball. This skill is called body checking. There is no body or stick contact. The player who is body checking positions her body about a stick's length away from the opponent and moves with her in an effort to slow her down, keep her from moving in the desired direction, or move her into a position where the defense player or a teammate can legally check her stick.

Double-teaming

Double-teaming refers to two defense players who, through their body-checking skills, maneuver their opponent into a position where one of the defense players has a clear opening to the attacker's stick and is able to legally check her stick.

Stick checking

The ball may be dislodged from a player's stick by the opponent's stick. There are strict rules on how this should be accomplished. The stick checker must be in a position where she can reach the opponent's stick without crossing the body or reaching from behind. When the checking stick makes contact with the ball carrier's stick, all stick movement must be away from the ball carrier's body and must never occur within the imaginary sphere around her head. The checking movement must also be combined with a short jab-and-release motion. In youth competition, stick checking is not permitted.

Cutting

As the ball is moved down the field, it is each player's responsibility to maneuver herself into a position that gives the ball

carrier a passing option. Each player accomplishes this by first eluding the defense and then timing a movement, or "cut," toward the ball carrier. If the cutter does not receive the ball, she should then pull away from the play, reposition, and cut again. Sometimes this is accomplished by making one cut and immediately following it with a second cut.

Cutting practice. Place the ball carrier at one corner of a square. Place the cutter at the corner diagonally across from the passer. As the passer turns toward the cutter, the cutter runs toward one of the other corners, showing with her stick where she wishes to receive the ball. A double cut can be practiced by using two sides of a square. Be sure to time the cut based on the passer's readiness to throw.

This pattern can then be transferred to any position on the field. When a defensive player is added, the cutter should execute a fake before making a cut.

Attack Movement

Attack movement is generated by moving the ball down the field in twos, then in threes, and then by adding interchanging movements. The next step would be a two-on-one situation, along with a continuous "give-and-go" passing formation. This is built upon to create situations of three-on-two and three-on-three. Small games with these formations can then be played in any area of the field.

A popular small game used to practice ball movement up and down the field is to create a three-on-three or four-on-four formation in a line. Each player stays with her opponent while the ball is passed up and down the line. Each time the ball is intercepted by an opponent, the direction of play is changed.

In lacrosse, when your team has the ball, you are an attack player. Although some positions are known as attack positions, this distinction arises due to their proximity to the goal.

The ball is moved down the field through a series of cutting and passing movements. Although players are constantly repositioning after a cut and interchanging their

Figure 19.30. Moving from the scoop to the cradle.

positions, there are general areas of the field for each position. The following are general guidelines only and are not meant to restrict movement.

As the goalkeeper clears the ball, the line defense—point (P), center point (CP), and third man (3M)—the defense wings (DW), and the center (C) cut in order to give the goalkeeper passing options. The line defense players' roles are to move the ball away from their defensive goal and to either the midfield players (wings or center) or into the attack. The role of the midfield players—defense wings (DW), attack wings (AW), center (C)—is to act as connectors between the defensive end of the field and the attacking end of the field.

The attack wings cover the outside of the field from the center area to the goal (Figure 19.31). Occasionally they will cross over to the other side of the field. When this occurs, the

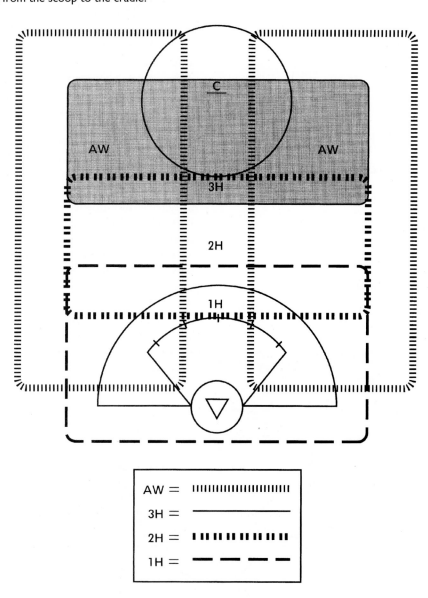

Figure 19.31. Playing areas of the homes and attack wings.

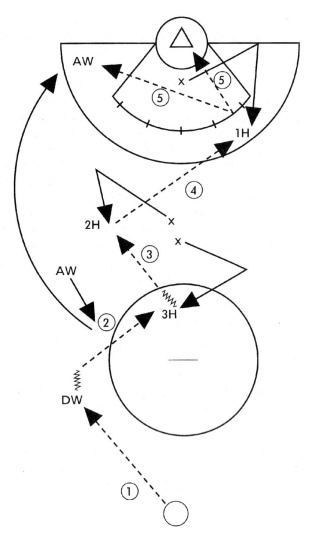

Figure 19.32. Passing during an attack.

other wing often crosses to keep the field balanced. Each of the homes covers the width of the playing area and approximately one third of the area between the center of the field and the goal area.

An example of this kind of movement is shown in Figure 19.32, where the DW receives a clear, turns and passes to the third home (3H), who has made a movement toward the outside of the field in order to make the space for a cut directly to the DW. The AW has also cut to receive the ball, but the DW chose to pass to the 3H. The 3H turns and passes to the second home (2H), who has moved out and down to make space and then cut toward the ball. The 2H then turns and passes to the first home (1H), who has repositioned herself away from the goal so that her cut enables the 2H to pass directly to her. The 1H then turns and has an opportunity to shoot at the goal or pass off to the opposite AW, who has repositioned herself below the ball. Another option would be a pass to the ball-side AW or the 2H, who would be repositioning in an attempt to be available should the 1H need an outlet pass.

Once the ball has reached the attacking end and a goal has not been scored, the attack players need to reposition themselves while keeping the ball in motion. They should continuously send cutters through the attacking area in an attempt to gain a position that would allow a shot on goal. Teams devise numerous plays to cover this situation.

Defense Movement

All defense movement starts with the ability to effectively and safely bodycheck. After the initial skill is learned, players should begin in one-on-one situations and build into two-on-one situations. At this point, double-teaming concepts can be introduced and continued into three-on-two situations.

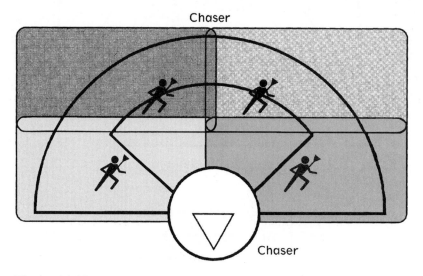

Figure 19.33. A zone formation with a chaser.

When a member of the opposing team has the ball, all players become defense players and play in a one-on-one formation until the ball crosses the center of the field. At this point, some teams elect to continue to play with one-on-one formations, while others choose to create a zone formation. A common zone using five players, four in boxed areas and one chaser, is shown in Figure 19.33. Another common zone defense uses seven players with the middies (faster players), who are circled in Figure 19.34, chasing and applying pressure.

Teams who play a one-on-one formation often have a plan to account for fast breaks. The one shown in Figure 19.35 shows the DW who is not on the ball side (weak side) dropping off to cover the center of the field and often picking up the 2H or 3H. The 3M or the CP may pull off and pick up the ball-carrying AW, who has lost her opposing DW. If the opposing DW has stayed with the attacking AW, the 3M may still pull off and, along with her DW, create a double-team situation that should lead to a turnover.

Seven-a-Side Lacrosse

A great small game and lead-up to full field lacrosse is seven-a-side lacrosse. Each team has one attack, two attack wings, a center, two defense wings, and one defense player (Figure 19.36). All play is person-to-person, with no restrictions on where players may move. However, keeping a balance to the playing area is an important concept and should be constantly stressed.

The game can be played outdoors in a small area or indoors on a court similar to a basketball court. Goals could be basketball backboards or official goals, which are basketball-type hoops placed 5 feet off the ground on a standard and angled 45 degrees toward the floor, with the open face toward the playing area. The hoop has a net with a closed bottom.

Play is started from the center circle when the official blows the whistle. Only one player, usually the center, may be in the center circle with the ball. She has 10 seconds in which to pass the ball out of the circle to a teammate after the whistle has blown. Play is continuous and follows all the field game rules until a foul occurs or a goal is scored. When a goal is scored, play is restarted from the center circle with a center throw by the nonscoring team.

Any player may attempt to score a goal from any space within the playing area. The ball carrier may also run to the goal and place the ball in the goal while making contact with the goal rim or standard. Because there are no goalkeepers, full field game rules pertaining to the crease, arc, and fan do not apply.

TEACHING CONSIDERATIONS

1. Cradling, throwing, and catching can be taught immediately and practiced in small game-type activities. From the start, encourage all skills to be practiced on the move and with either hand at the top of the stick.
2. Ground ball pick-ups should be taught next, combined with throwing in different directions on the run.
3. Introduce small keep-away games with no resistance, slowly building to passive resistance. Slowly build the numbers of players within these games.

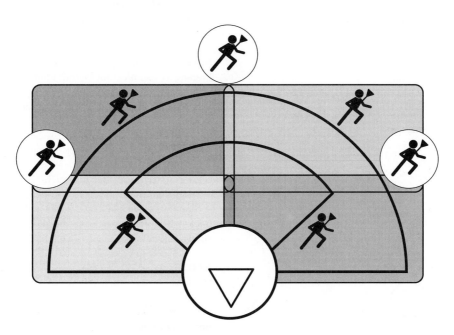

Figure 19.34. A zone defense.

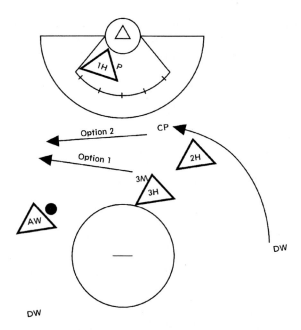

Figure 19.35. Fast-break defense.

Attack

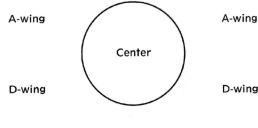

Defense

Figure 19.36. Positions for a seven-a-side lacrosse.

4. Be sure that players are aware of their body space and stick space as they work with and compete against other players.
5. Emphasize the importance of safe body checking before introducing stick checking.
6. Once stick checking has been introduced, apply the rules of the game tightly and consistently in practice and game situations. In some environments, stick checking may be eliminated.

GLOSSARY—MEN'S

attackmen The three offensive players who operate around the goal area.

ball stop A piece of foam rubber that adheres to the throat of the stick and facilitates holding the ball in the pocket.

body check A deliberate bumping of an opponent from the front—above the knees and below the neck—when the opponent is in possession or within 5 yards of the ball.

checking Attempting to dislodge the ball from your opponent's stick.

clear Running or passing the ball from the defensive half of the field to the attack goal area.

cradling The rhythmical coordinated motion of the arms and wrists that keeps the ball secure in the stick and ready to be passed or shot.

crease The circle with a 9-foot radius around each goal.

cross check An illegal check or hold using the area of the stick handle between the hands.

cutting A movement by an offensive player without the ball, toward the opposition goal and in anticipation of a feed and subsequent shot.

dodges Ball-carrying maneuvers used for eluding defenders.

ground ball A loose ball anywhere on the playing field. Opposing teams fight for possession using body and stick checks as well as scooping techniques.

handle A metal alloy pole connected to the head of a stick; the part of the stick that players grasp when executing any maneuver with their sticks.

head The plastic part of the stick connected to the handle.

holding A technical foul committed either by grabbing an opponent or by hindering a ball carrier's progress with one's stick.

interference A technical foul committed by preventing the free movement of an opponent who is neither in possession of the ball nor within 5 yards of a loose ball.

midfielders The three players who play in the center of the field and play both offense and defense.

offside A technical foul in which the offending team has either fewer than three players in its offensive half of the field or fewer than four players in its defensive half of the field.

pocket The strung part of the head of the stick that holds the ball.

riding The act of preventing a team from clearing the ball.

GLOSSARY—WOMEN'S

blocking Occurs when a player moves into the path of the ball carrier and creates contact without giving the ball carrier time to change direction.

body checking When a defender moves with an opponent and causes the opponent to slow down, change direction, or pass.

bridge In a wooden stick, the area on the bottom of the pocket made of heavy gut or nylon that connects the woven sidewall to the wooden wall.

charging When a player with the ball pushes through the opponents by using the body.

cradle The arm and stick movements used to keep the ball in the stick.

crease The circle around the goal cage. Sometimes called the "goal circle."

critical scoring area An area at the end of the field where the attacking team is shooting for a goal. It's boundaries are about 16.4 yards (15 m) in front of the goal circle, 9.8 yards (9 m) behind the goal line extended, and 16.4 yards (15 m) to each side of the goal circle.

crosse A lacrosse stick is often called a crosse.

crosse checking An extension of the body checking whereby the defender attempts to dislodge the ball from her opponent's crosse by using controlled crosse to crosse contact.

cutting A movement made into a space on the field toward the ball carrier in order to receive a pass.

deputy A player on the defensive goalkeeper's team who may only enter or remain in the goal circle when her team is in possession of the ball and the goalkeeper is out of the goal circle.

8-meter arc The area in front of each goal circle inscribed by 2 lines drawn at 45 degree angles extending from the intersection of the goal circle and the goal line and connected by an arc marked 8.7 yards (8 m) from the goal circle.

free space to goal A path to the goal within the critical scoring area as defined by two lines extending from the ball to the outside of the goal circle. No defense player will be penalized if positioned below the extension of the goal line.

gut Sticks made of wood are often woven with a fine gut thread. Bridges may also be woven of a thicker gut.

penalty lane The path to the goal that is cleared when a free position is awarded to the attacking team inside the critical scoring area in an area in front of the goal line. The path is defined by imaginary lines that extend from the width of the goal circle. Players must clear this lane when a free position is awarded in front of the goal.

sidewall The side edge of a stick. In wooden sticks, one sidewall is woven from a stiff nylon material.

slashing The swinging of a crosse at an opponent's crosse or body with recklessness, whether or not the opponent's crosse or body is struck.

slow whistle A held whistle, with flag raised, once the attack has entered the critical scoring area and is on a scoring play.

sphere An imaginary area of 7 inches (15 cm) surrounding the head.

stick checking A controlled tap on an opponent's stick designed to dislodge the ball.

12-meter fan A semicircle area in front of each goal circle bounded by an arc 13.1 yards (12 m) from the goal circle.

thongs, or leads Leather or synthetic strips that run vertically in the pocket of the crosse and around which the pocket is woven.

throat The part of the head of the stick where the plastic meets the handle.

SUGGESTED READINGSE

American Sport Education Program. 2003. *Coaching youth lacrosse*. 2nd ed. Champaign, IL: Human Kinetics.

Amonte Hiller, K., Gersuk, A., and Elliott, A. 2010. *Winning women's lacrosse*. Champaign, IL: Human Kinetics.

Maddox, J. 2009. *Lacrosse attack*. Mankato, MN: Capstone Press.

National Collegiate Athletic Association. Current ed. *NCAA lacrosse rule book*. Overland Park, KS: NCAA.

Pietramala, D, and Grauer, N. 2006. *Lacrosse: Technique and tradition*. 2nd ed. Baltimore, MD: The Johns Hopkins University Press.

Swissler, B. 2009. *Winning lacrosse for girls*. New York, NY: Facts on File Publishers

Tucker, J. and Yakutchik, M. 2003. *The baffled parent's guide to coaching girls' lacrosse*. New York, NY: McGraw-Hill.

United States Women's Lacrosse Association. Current ed. *Official lacrosse rules*. Hamilton, NY: USWLA.

Weston, J. 2000. *Lacrosse goaltending for coaches*. Rockville MD: Weston Lacrosse.

RESOURCES

Videos

On the attack; Defense, the long sticks; Goalie, the last defense; and *The middie* are available from the Lacrosse Foundation, 113 W University Parkway, Baltimore, MD 21210.

Skills and techniques and *The goalkeeper* are available from the United States Women's Lacrosse Association, Hamilton, NY.

See Appendix C for other video sources.

WEB SITES

Men's lacrosse statistics
www.ncaa.org/stats/m_lacrosse

NCAA Lacrosse
www.ncaa.lacrosse.com

Intercollegiate Women's Lacrosse Coaches Association
www.iwlca.org

International Federation of Women's Lacrosse Associations
www.womenslacrosse.org

U.S. Lacrosse www.uslacrosse.org
The national governing body for men's and women's lacrosse.

Mountaineering

After completing this chapter, the reader should be able to:

- Understand the evolution of modern mountaineering from practical endeavor to sport
- Recognize a number of mountain hazards and the crucial role of decision making and risk management in mountaineering
- Recognize the range of mountaineering equipment utilized on different climbs
- Understand the nature of climbing movement on rock, snow, and ice
- Recognize the range of protective systems and strategies employed by climbers

Mountaineering evolved from a desire to fulfill the need for adventure, to test abilities and limits, and to venture to some of the most challenging and beautiful terrain on earth (Figure 20.1). As sport and outdoor recreation, it is a difficult activity to define, or at least to limit one's definition—a boulderer working gymnastic moves on a 10-foot rock is doing something very different from a backpacker hiking down a trail, but both the backpacker's and the boulderer's skills are part of mountaineering. Climbing mountains requires moving well on rock, snow, and ice, and knowing the risks, methods, and protective systems for each. It also involves living, sometimes for a day, sometimes for months, in the mountains, and this requires backpacking and camping skills—knowing how to stay warm, fed, hydrated, and rested in foul weather and difficult conditions. Mountaineering involves a wide range of risks and hazards—from hypothermia to heat stroke, from falling to being struck by falling rock and ice. Climbing safely requires good judgment based on experience, instruction, and an intimate knowledge of personal skills and limits. This chapter (or any climbing text) can only serve as a general introduction to mountaineering—it is not an activity that can be learned out of the mountains.

HISTORY

For all of human history, man has lived and traveled in the mountains. Hannibal crossed the Alps with elephants to attack Rome. Spanish conquistadors climbed 17,000-foot Popocatepetl in Mexico in 1519 to obtain sulfur to make gunpowder. The first ascent of Mont Blanc in the 18th century was led by a geologist who wished to ascertain the true elevation; he was guided by shepherds who had learned mountain craft herding their flocks in the mountains. As these examples show, mountaineering developed for practical reasons—shepherds, soldiers, and scientists. Climbing for sport, for challenge, developed slowly—perhaps Whymper's climb of the

Matterhorn in 1865 marks the dividing line, perhaps that line is not clearly crossed until Mallory in the 1920s replies "Because it's there," when he is asked why he wishes to climb Mount Everest. Even so, most large mountaineering expeditions into the 1960s combined at least token scientific objectives with purely recreational goals. Today, while scientific studies are still conducted in the mountains, and most militaries have climbing specialists and schools, sport and recreation drives the vast majority of mountaineering. In the United States, climbing clubs such as the American Alpine Club, the Sierra Club, the Mountaineers, and the Colorado Mountain Club developed early in the 20th century and helped create interest in the sport; these and other clubs still thrive, as do Outdoor Adventure Programs at many high schools and universities. But the majority of modern climbers belong to no organizations other than perhaps the local rock gym; it is estimated that 9 million Americans engage in climbing at some level each year, and about 40 percent of enthusiasts are women.

TRAINING FOR MOUNTAINEERING

Mountaineering makes incredible demands on the body. The training goal is to make oneself as fit and indestructible as possible before going into the mountains. Mountaineering climbs are marathons, requiring great cardiovascular endurance. Technical climbing requires significant upper-body strength; both power and power-endurance are needed, plus good whole-body flexibility. Climbing builds climbing-specific strength more efficiently than anything else—mountaineers away from the mountains climb rock and ice on smaller cliffs and train indoors in commercial climbing gyms. Most lift weights, run, and stretch as well.

MOUNTAINEERING TERRAIN

This chapter focuses on skills and equipment needed for mountaineering in the classic alpine terrain of North

Figure 20.1. Sometimes the view from the summit (Nepal Himalaya) makes it all worthwhile.

America, for example, the U.S. and Canadian Rockies, the Sierra Nevada, and the Cascades. Some of the information in Chapter 5 (Backpacking) might be repeated here, since backpacking and camping skills are essential for mountaineering. To avoid redundancy, backpacking will be defined as what happens on the trail, mountaineering as what begins when one leaves the trail and travels over rough and increasingly steep terrain toward the summit of a peak. The focus is on the movement and technical skills needed for travel on rock, snow, and ice, the mixed terrain of the mountains. The many hazards of the alpine environment and the methods of mountain decision making and risk management are also discussed.

EQUIPMENT

The equipment needed for mountaineering can vary greatly with the nature of the mountain climbed, as the following examples show. All technical terms are defined in the glossary at the end of this chapter.

One-Day Climb

This section details gear needed for a one-day climb of a nontechnical peak, for example, Longs Peak in Colorado via the Keyhole Route in July. Such a route would involve a long approach over trails, then increasingly steep off-trail rock scrambling; the hands would only occasionally be needed to assist balance or upward movement. By July, the climb would be entirely on rock; there would be little to no travel over snow and ice. On the climb, temperatures in the pre-dawn might be in the 20°F range; the temperature in the heat of the day could approach 80°F. Almost certainly, there will be clear skies in the morning and rain (and lightning) in the afternoon. An average party will take 12 hours car to car; 20 hours is not uncommon. Total weight of gear required would be 15 to 20 pounds.

Backpack

Small and light, approximately 2000 cubic inches or 30 to 35 liters.

Clothing. In general, cotton clothing is hazardous in mountaineering; most mountaineering clothing is made of wool or synthetic fabrics that better preserve heat when the wearer is in cold, wet conditions.

 socks: perhaps a liner pair plus a heavier pair, though many modern mountaineering boots are designed to be worn with a single pair of heavy socks (wool or synthetic).
 boots: for this climb, lightweight approach shoes that climb rock well might work better than a heavy leather or synthetic hiking boot.
 lightweight long underwear: top and bottom.
 pants: a water-resistant soft-shell fabric is ideal.
 expedition-weight shirt, wool or synthetic fabric.
 windshirt.
 synthetic jacket or light parka.
 rain shell.
 warm hat, waterproof gloves.

Food. Plan more for continuous snacking than for sit-down meals. Several thousand calories total achieved from a mix of trail snacks, energy bars and gels, and maybe a sandwich or two.

Water. Two- to three-liter water bottles, with some means of water purification and replenishment because the body may lose as much as a liter/hour of water on a climb. Many climbers prefer sports drinks such as Gatorade or Endurox since these replace electrolytes as well as water and also provide an additional source of calories. Most climbers hope to consume 4 to 6 liters over the course of the entire day, including pre- and postclimb.

Miscellaneous.
first aid kit
headlamp
map/compass
sunglasses
sunscreen, insect repellent, and lip balm

Multi-Day Ascent

The following gear is needed for a multi-day ascent of a route involving technical movement on rock, snow, and ice, for example, the North Face of Forbidden Peak in the Washington Cascades in September. The temperature range is roughly the same as in the first example, and the chance of rain (possibly snow) remains high. Let's assume a two-person team.

Backpack

To accommodate camping and technical gear, the pack must be larger, 50 L or 3000 cubic inches, which will weigh approximately 3 pounds. A much larger pack could be stuffed with gear that might be used, but the weight and size of the pack would not allow efficient movement, and that is dangerous in the mountains.

Clothing. Same as in the previous example, except for the **boots.** The boots must now be crampon compatible to climb the ice sections of the route. Weaker rock climbers might also consider bringing **rock shoes** as well, for the technical rock sections of the climb.

Food and water. Caloric expenditure on a multi-day mountaineering route can easily be upward of 5000 calories per day. A realistic plan for each day might be 750 calories for breakfast (instant oatmeal, breakfast bar, and hot drink would achieve this), 2000 calories over the course of the day (same mix as before), and 1000 calories at night (simple and lightweight, from soups and dry pasta mixes to the add-water freeze-dry packages). With drink mixes adding another 1000 calories for the day, this would be a reasonable caloric intake. Water goals are the same, 4 to 6 liters per day. Of course, to do this on a multi-day trip, you now need:

Stove, fuel, lighter, pot, personal mug, and spoon. Because snow must be melted for water, plan on 16 ounces of white gas per day or an 8-ounce butane cartridge.

Sleep and shelter. Sleeping bag, pad, two-person **tent** or **bivouac sacs** in lieu of the tent if the weather forecast looks favorable.

Miscellaneous gear. Much the same as before, to be discussed under the **10 Essentials.**

Technical gear. A vast range of possibilities exist here. The Union Internationale des Associations d'Alpinisme (UIAA)

sets climbing equipment standards worldwide; look for the UIAA logo on all gear you purchase. All terms are defined in the glossary; their use is discussed in the movement and technical systems section.

Personal climbing gear. Crampons for moving on ice; **two 50-cm technical ice tools** as a single **ice axe** (normally 60 to 70 cm in length) would not be adequate for the technical demands of the route; **harness**—an alpine style with adjustable/droppable leg loops to accommodate various amounts of clothing and also calls of nature; **helmet,** a mountaineering essential, as falling rock and ice are constant hazards; this helmet should have features to allow a **headlamp** to be attached since you will be climbing pre-dawn. **Belay/ rappel device**—a modern plate, or tube-style device; the same device will work equally well for belays and rappels.

Team climbing gear

Rope. Two ropes are needed to efficiently manage the rappels.

Climbing rack. This will be matched to the demands of the route and to your skills as a climber, and these will vary enormously (Figure 20.2). A typical rack for an average climber on this route might include:

Figure 20.2. Climber with modern rock-climbing rack-stoppers, cams, slings, and carabiners.

slings: perhaps eight single-length sewn slings (24-inch loops of sewn material), two double-length sewn slings (48-inch loops), one or two cordelettes (20-foot strands of 6- to 7-mm Perlon cord).

carabiners: at least 20 nonlocking and 3 to 4 locking carabiners.

protection: for building climbing anchors in rock, snow, and ice. **Rock:** 6 to 10 **nuts**, 5 to 6 **cams**, perhaps 3 to 4 **pitons** (mostly to replace old rappel anchors). **Snow:** 2 **pickets. Ice:** 6 to 8 **ice screws**, from 10 to 20 cm in length. 1 **v-thread device** for building ice rappel anchors.

The total equipment needed for this climb is much greater than in example 1. Going as light as possible, the total gear weight remains upward of 40 pounds per person (Figure 20.3). Yet this is a more difficult climb, and the harder the climb, the more difficult it is to climb with additional weight. This brings us to what is known as the "alpine dilemma." If you bring everything you could possibly need or want, you are too heavy to climb at all.

The 10 Essentials

These were once a simple list of items, but have evolved more into functional systems. They include:

1. Navigation: map and compass, perhaps altimeter watch and GPS unit
2. Sun protection: sunglasses, sunscreen, lip balm
3. Insulation: adequate clothing for the climb, more to survive emergencies
4. Illumination: a headlamp works better than a flashlight as it leaves the hands free
5. First-aid supplies
6. Fire: matches or lighter
7. Repair kit and tools
8. Nutrition: adequate for the climb; extra for emergencies
9. Hydration: water or drink mixes
10. Emergency shelter: such as a light bivy sack

Mountaineering is a sport that emphasizes decision making and judgment over equipment lists and protocols. The "10 Essentials" are a useful concept, but the alpine dilemma remains in force. All mountaineers know that success and safety are both largely entwined with the ability to move light and fast. Moving slowly on a route means longer exposure to mountain weather and mountain hazards. Also, many mountain hazards worsen later in the day—thunderstorms and snow conditions are two examples. As the day grows warmer, snow softens; it becomes more difficult to climb on, bridges over crevasses weaken, and odds of wet avalanches increase. The goal is to climb quickly and be down before the hazards rise. With experience, rather than blindly following the 10 Essentials, mountaineers try to envision all the events that could happen on their intended climb. They assess the likelihood of each event and the consequence if it was to occur. The final decision of what to bring and what can be left is situational, suited to the specific conditions of each climb.

MOUNTAINEERING HAZARDS

Mountaineering is dangerous. While field sports such as football have a much greater risk of injury, few sports in this text have the risk of mortality that mountaineering has. While the risks of mountaineering can be diminished by choosing routes within ability levels and by exercising good judgment, they cannot be eliminated—they are part of the experience. Traditionally, mountain hazards have been divided between those that are subjective (created by human errors) and those that are objective (inherently part of the mountain). There is considerable interaction between the two. Rockfall is an objective mountain hazard, for example, that frequently increases at specific times of the day—after temperatures warm above freezing, for instance. If a climber chooses to enter a couloir during the warmth of the

Figure 20.3. Packing for an expedition. A large technical peak can require a lot of gear.

afternoon, the risk of being struck by rockfall is much greater than early in the morning when the rocks are still frozen in place. Here, a human error has increased an objective hazard. Following are some of the most prevalent hazards; it is not an exhaustive list.

Subjective Hazards
Falling

Not surprisingly, falling is the cause of the vast majority of mountain accidents. Often, the length of mountain routes, the broken nature of much mountain rock, and the insecure nature of ice and snow mean that the ropes, belays, and other protective systems of technical climbing do not safely protect a climb. Even a short fall, when all the protective systems work as they should, can easily cause a broken ankle or a sprain. Such an injury is inconvenient at a roadside cliff, but the climber can hobble to the car and drive to the hospital. In the mountains, days from treatment, exposed to other mountain hazards, the same injury can be fatal. "The leader must not fall" is an anachronistic statement in many climbing genres today, but it still largely applies in the mountains.

Fatigue and ignorance

Many mountain accidents are caused by a combination of these factors. Mountaineering is a demanding physical sport. Many modern climbs involve continuous movement for days, with little chance to sleep or eat. As fatigue sets in, coordination and judgment suffer, and the risk of an accident increases exponentially. No piece of equipment replaces mountain judgment in terms of reducing risk. Knowledge helps one see the easiest route up a mountain, helps choose a route through crevasses on a glacier, helps determine when an avalanche slope is stable and when it is not, or whether an anchor is solid or not. Lack of knowledge increases risk.

Objective Hazards
Rock and ice fall

Other than falling, these probably claim the most lives in the mountains. To some extent, these hazards are always part of the mountain environment. But the risk does tend to rise and fall, and mountain judgment can help to lessen this risk.

Avalanche

Avalanches kill many mountaineers and skiers, approximately 25 a year in North America and over a 100 a year in Europe. Here again, knowledge, experience, and good decision making can greatly reduce but never eliminate the risk. Every mountaineer should take a course in avalanche safety.

Glacier crevasse falls

Here, knowledge of protective systems can almost completely eliminate the hazard, but these falls continue to claim victims each year.

Environmental Hazards
Altitude

All mountaineering is not equally dangerous. The most dangerous peaks are the biggest and highest. There are 14 8000-m peaks on earth, and the mortality rate on climbs of these peaks far exceeds the mortality rate on lower peaks. The bigger the peak, the longer in general it takes to climb, and that increases the exposure to risk. The higher the peak, often the fouler the weather, and this increases the risk of hypothermia and frostbite. Altitude affects judgment and coordination, thus increasing almost all risks. In addition, a host of altitude illnesses exist, from **acute mountain sickness** to **high-altitude pulmonary and cerebral edema.** In North America, with elevations less than 5000 m, the risk of these illnesses can be almost entirely eliminated with careful acclimatization. That is not as true at higher elevations.

Hypothermia and frostbite

Hypothermia is when body-core temperatures drop below normal, leading first to discomfort and loss of coordination and eventually to death. Frostbite is frozen tissue. Both of these conditions are far easier to prevent than to treat. Hydration, food, a good strategy of layering with clothes (non-cotton fabrics)—these tactics normally will prevent these conditions.

Mountain weather

Mountains tend to be wet, cold, and stormy. The most obvious mountain weather hazard is lightning. In much of the Rocky Mountains, lightning can occur almost every day of the summer, usually in the afternoons, and an experienced mountaineer plans a route to be down before the lightning strikes. Storms can also make movement impossible in the mountains, and a stormbound team is eventually a team at risk—food, fuel, and water run out; avalanche danger worsens; hypothermia and frostbite risks increase. Team members grow impatient to get off the mountain and judgment lapses. Wet rock is slippery, and that increases the risk of falling.

MOVEMENT AND TECHNICAL SYSTEMS FOR ROCK, SNOW, AND ICE

Big mountains are not the best places to learn rock and ice climbing techniques. These are better learned in the somewhat more controlled environments of small crags. Learning to belay and rappel, to place protection and build anchors, to lead pitches on rock and ice—these need to be mastered on short climbs before going into the mountains. Getting good instruction is essential in this development—ideally from a certified climbing guide, or at least from a skilled and caring friend.

A key difference between technical climbing at a small crag and mountaineering is that mountains usually have a large amount of easy and moderate terrain in addition to sections of more difficult climbing. A typical mountain route might be approached on a trail (class 1 terrain), then by more uneven and steeper climbing off-trail (class 2 terrain). The route itself probably involves large sections of rock scrambling or moderate snow climbing where only the legs are needed for upward movement; the upper body might only be used to hold a ski pole or ice axe for balance (class 3 terrain). As the hands and upper body are used more and more to grab holds and pull upward and as the consequences of a fall increase, we enter more technical (class 4 and 5) terrain. The ropes and climbing racks emerge, and the climber has to choose among many different techniques to manage risks effectively. Since the level of difficulty and risk can vary continuously on a mountain climb, so, too, do the methods of protecting and reducing the risks.

MOUNTAIN WALKING—CLASS 2 AND 3 TERRAIN: ROCK, SNOW, AND ICE

In this terrain, which covers most angles up to approximately 45 degrees, only the legs are needed for movement. The arms might assist balance by using ski poles or an ice axe, but they are not needed to pull the body upward. The principles of mountain walking evolved from the need to conserve energy on long, steep climbs. Mountain walking techniques use predominantly the larger thigh muscles and allow a rest at each step—frequently the technique is called the "mountaineer's rest step." The leg is straightened completely with each step, the foot is flat on the ground, and weight is transferred completely from one foot to the other. This places the weight on the skeleton of the body and allows the muscles to relax. This flat-foot technique, as opposed to the rolling off the ball of the foot that is the more normal human stride, covers more ground with less energy expended.

The same flat-foot techniques are used on all surfaces—hard ground and rocky slopes, ice, and snow slopes. As the terrain steepens, initially one can maintain a flat foot by angling the feet outward, feet splayed like a duck. Steeper yet, the climber faces sideways to the hill and sidesteps, crossing one foot over the next with each step. The climber can climb quite steep terrain by choosing a line that zigzags up the hill while still maintaining flat-foot technique.

On snow, the climber adds an ice axe to the technique, but the purpose of the ice axe is primarily to aid with balance. If the terrain feels exposed or tricky, the ice axe is plunged into the snow deeply on each step, and serves as an effective self-belay (Figure 20.4). Lastly, on some snow slopes, if the climber does fall, an ice axe can be plunged into the snow during the fall to help the climber stop or self-arrest (Figure 20.5).

If the snow surface is hard or icy, crampons are used to gain purchase. Again, the techniques are the same, but it is highly unlikely the ice axe can be used effectively for self-belay or self-arrest. If the climber judges that the probability of a fall is high, then additional protective methods are needed. Descending, the principles are still the same, to

Figure 20.4. Ice axe self-belay. Climber using mountaineer's rest step.

keep your weight over your feet (Figure 20.6), to transfer weight completely from step to step, and to place the entire foot on the surface. The same steps can be used as well, zigzagging, sidestepping, and splaying the feet. An additional technique for descending on snow is the plunge step (Figure 20.7); it is quick and effective but can be very tiring on steep slopes. The plunge step is executed by keeping the leg fairly straight. When the heel is about to contact the ground, the leg is extended backward forcefully to plunge the heel into the ground or snow. This technique can aid in descending a slope as steep as 30 to 35 degrees.

CLASS 4 AND 5—TECHNICAL CLIMBING: ROCK AND ICE

In 4th- and 5th-class climbing, the consequences of an unprotected fall are severe, and both arms and legs are needed to make progress. Both 4th- and 5th-class climbing are considered technical climbing, and ropes, harnesses, and a wide range of protective strategies are employed to make climbs safer. The terms 4th class and 5th class refer to a continuum of difficulty; 5th class is harder than 4th class. Presently, 5th-class rock climbing is subdivided from 5.0 to 5.15, with the higher the number, the harder the climb.

Figure 20.5. Ice axe self-arrest.

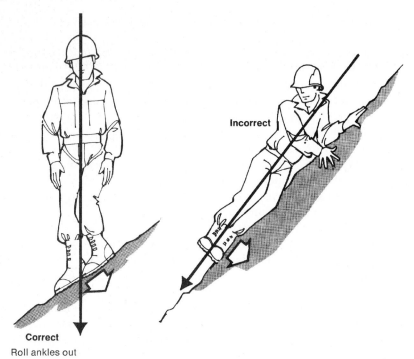

Correct
Roll ankles out

Incorrect

Figure 20.6. On steep ground, body weight should be directly over the feet, not leaning into the hill. If leaning into the hill, the climber will slide.

Rock climbing takes many forms and so do the techniques of climbing them. Slab climbing, face climbing, crack climbing, chimneys and off-widths—all of the primary sub divisions of rock climbing have their own nomenclature and specialized techniques, some of which are illustrated here in photos.

Ice-Climbing Movement

Flat-foot techniques become ineffective on angles greater than 45 degrees. Up to 45 degrees, it is normal to find both ice and consolidated snow, and normal to climb both using a single ice axe. Crampons are almost always used on ice slopes and well-frozen snow slopes. Soft snow is better climbed without crampons, by kicking steps in the snow with boots. Snow rarely sticks to slopes much steeper than 50 degrees, however. Mountaineering in steeper terrain involves ice climbing, or ice climbing mixed with rock and loose unconsolidated snow. Two ice tools (one for each hand) are standard for steep ice, as are crampons. Whenever possible, climbers still place the entire foot on a surface, because it is a much more relaxed and comfortable position. As the ice steepens, this is less and less possible, and climbers kick their

Figure 20.7. Plunge step for descent.

Technical ice climbing has its own scales, with WI for Water Ice, and M for Mixed, where the climber climbs both rock and ice simultaneously. Snow climbing is often represented simply by its angle. A guide book might describe a route, VI, 5.9, WI5, M5, 50 degrees. The Roman numeral describes the length of the route; VI means that more than one day is needed to complete the climb; 5.9, WI5, and M5 mean that steep, technical climbing will be found on both rock and ice. The steepest snow slopes will be 50 degrees.

Rock-Climbing Movement

A good rock climber moves efficiently and confidently, rarely wasting energy. Fundamental principles include:

- Keep most of your weight over your feet, and drive upward movement with the large muscles of the legs, not the smaller muscles of the arms (Figure 20.8).
- Climb relaxed, exerting just enough effort to make the move—many climbers overgrip and tense their bodies unnecessarily, wasting effort and energy.
- Move decisively, learning to read the rock and see the sequence of hand and footholds that best yield progress. The steeper the climb, the more quickly one tires and the more important it is to move quickly.

Figure 20.8. Climber using footholds to take weight off of the arms.

crampons directly into the ice, front-pointing (Figure 20.9) their way up vertical and even overhanging ice climbs.

Most ice climbers climb rock as well, and the principles of movement are the same in both mediums. A good climber is relaxed and confident, moves without wasted motion or effort, and drives upward progress with the legs more than the arms. Climbing steep ice is extremely strenuous—efficient technique maximizes a climber's strength and energy. This is particularly important on long mountaineering routes, which tax all of a climber's endurance.

Technical Systems

Belayed climbing with intermediate protection

This is the standard form of protection on technical climbs (both ice and rock), particularly on smaller cliffs (Figure 20.10). It provides the most security to a climbing team. Its disadvantage in mountaineering is that it is also the slowest method of climbing.

Imagine two climbers at the base of a technical climb. It is several rope-lengths to the top of the cliff. In belayed climbing, only one climber moves at a time. First one climber leads the rope up, while being belayed (protected) by the second. The leader places pieces of protection en route, which would shorten the length of any fall. Note that a fall for the leader could still be considerable—double the distance above the last placed piece (Figure 20.11). When the leader runs out of rope or reaches a convenient stopping point, the leader stops and places several pieces of protection and arranges them into an anchor. The follower is then belayed up to the anchor—since the rope runs upward from the follower to the anchor, the follower will not go any distance in the event of a climbing fall, and the rope can be kept tight. When both climbers are at the anchor, the process is repeated as many times as necessary until they reach the top of the climb. They could take turns leading, or the stronger climber could lead all the pitches.

Figure 20.9. Front-pointing on steep ice.

A

B

C

Figure 20.10. A, Placing protection. B, Spring-loaded cramming device protection. C, Stopper protection placed in a crack.

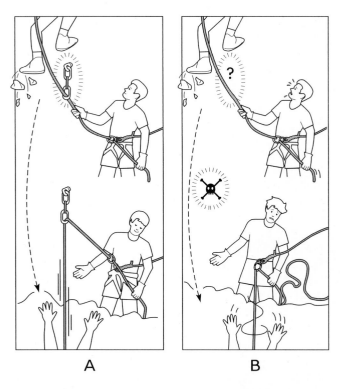

Figure 20.11. A, Proper belay. B, Improper belay due to dangerously high forces transmitted to belayer's body.

Figure 20.12. Climbing on lead.

Technical Systems for Mountaineering

Because of the need to move quickly on big mountains, combined with the ever-changing technical demands, mountaineers change tactics and systems frequently. The goal is to travel as efficiently as possible while still addressing the risk of a fall. These tactics fall along a continuum, with unroped soloing at one end (maximum speed, minimum security) and belayed climbing with intermediate protection (maximum security, minimum speed) at the other (Figure 20.12). Midway along the continuum, climbers travel together, moving simultaneously, placing protection as they go. Sometimes, no protection is placed, but the rope is weaved in and out of natural features as the climbers move together, thus providing some security. Along a ridge, if a climber falls to one side, sometimes the only protection necessary is an alert climber dropping down to the other side, thus stopping the fall when the rope comes tight.

A NOTE ON GLACIER TRAVEL

On glaciers, the primary risk is often crevasse fall. Usually, climbers travel roped together, spaced on the rope so that no more than one member of the party is exposed to a crevasse at a time (Figure 20.13). If a climber does fall into a crevasse, the others hold the fall. Then, if uninjured, the climber in the crevasse can usually ascend the rope to regain the surface. If the rope cannot be ascended, the team members build a mechanical system to haul the fallen climber back up.

TECHNICAL SYSTEMS—RAPPELS

Descending a mountain also calls for a number of tactics. In general, if a route can be down-climbed safely, then that will be the quickest, most efficient way down. When the route grows too steep to down-climb, climbers rappel. To rappel, the rope is doubled through a climbing anchor, and the climbers slide down the rope using a rappel device to create the friction needed to control the speed (Figure 20.14). Since the rope has not been tied to the anchor but doubled through, the climbers can pull the rope down to them and rappel again, as many times as necessary to get down the climb or to reach a section of the route where they can again down-climb. Note that if a rope is 200 feet long, the maximum length of a rappel using that rope is 100 feet. To make

Figure 20.13. Alpine simul-climbing. Roped and moving together in the mountains.

Figure 20.14. On rappel.

rappels more efficient, climbers frequently bring two ropes, which they tie together so that they can rappel longer distances at a time.

DECISION MAKING, ROUTE-FINDING, AND RISK MANAGEMENT

On a typical mountain route, a climber will be asked to make literally hundreds of decisions in a day. For some, this is much of the appeal and challenge. Many of the decisions will come back to the same goal—to travel as efficiently as possible while still addressing the risk of a fall. Frequently, the mountaineer who climbs most efficiently is not the strongest technical climber (though technical skills are essential). The most efficient climber is the one who sees the best route. Mountains are huge, and the terrain often infinitely complex. Developing an eye for the easiest or safest line on a peak is one of the most essential skills of a mountaineer. Seeing the best route makes all the other decisions easier.

Other mountaineering decisions center on weighing the various hazards and how significant or imminent they are. Will avalanche slopes worsen as the sun warms them in the afternoon? Does an ice chimney offer a quick way up, or will the risk from falling rock and ice in the chimney outweigh the apparently easy climbing? Does it look like the weather is holding, or is a thunderstorm approaching? Did we bring the gear necessary to survive an unplanned bivouac caused by a storm? Or do we need to climb more quickly to avoid being caught in the storm? All climbs have hazards. The hazards are not constant in nature but ever-changing. The climber is forever trying to be aware of all hazards and continually assessing them for probability of occurrence and consequence if they do occur.

TEACHING CONSIDERATIONS

As the preceding section illustrates, mountaineering judgment is not developed easily; it is a product of training and experience, skills, and intuition. No one should attempt to instruct mountaineering without a qualified program of training and great experience.

The American Mountain Guides Association (AMGA) offers the only guide training program in the United States that meets international standards. As yet, only a minority of instructors and guides in the United States have received training or certification from the AMGA, but that number is increasing yearly.

Mountaineering is a difficult sport to learn from a textbook; it requires a great deal of time in the mountains. That said, a new wave of instructional literature has recently been published in the United States, in particular the Mountaineers Outdoor Expert Series from Mountaineers Books. Those books (see suggested readings) would be an excellent next step for readers of this chapter; they would also be appropriate as instructional texts in a college or secondary school outdoor adventure program focused on mountaineering.

GLOSSARY

altitude illness A number of illnesses are caused by climbing at high elevations. **Acute mountain sickness (AMS)** is the mildest, consisting of headache and nausea among other symptoms. **High altitude pulmonary and cerebral edema (HAPE and HACE)** are life-threatening illnesses resulting from fluid on the lungs (HAPE) and swelling in the brain (HACE).

approach shoes Lightweight shoes that combine features of both a hiker and a technical climbing shoe.

avalanches A large snow or ice mass in motion down a mountainside. A leading cause of mountain fatalities.

belay Techniques used to manage the rope so as to catch a falling climber, hold a climber in place, or lower a climber. Often, the belayer uses a **belay-rappel device,** a mechanical device (many varieties) that creates a sharp bend in the rope and thus provides friction for belaying or rappelling.

bivouac A lightweight, rarely comfortable overnight camp, often unplanned.

bouldering Climbing without a rope on smaller rocks where falls usually do not have serious consequences. A growing subgenre of climbing.

cam A generic term for mechanical spring-loaded devices of varying size which can be inserted into cracks to secure a climbing rope.

carabiners A high-strength snap-link used to connect components of the climbing system. Usually made of aluminum, some carabiners have gates that can be locked in place; others do not.

climbing anchors Any means of attachment that can be used to protect a climber against a fall. Some anchors are natural—trees and large rocks. Others modify natural features—digging a large snow bollard and running the rope around it. Others involve placing artificial protection (nuts, cams, ice screws, pitons, bolts) and linking them into an anchor system.

cordelettes A piece of cord, often made of Perlon 6 to 7 mm thick and tied in a 20-foot loop, which is commonly used to link protection into a climbing anchor.

crampons Used for ice and alpine climbing, crampons attach to climbing boots and have a number of sharp points (usually 12, including two points in front) to penetrate and grab the ice.

couloir A steep mountain gorge.

glaciers Glaciers form in places where more snow falls each year than can melt away. Large glaciers flow downhill; the stress of the movement creates **crevasses,** or holes within the glacier that can be hazardous to mountaineers.

harness Web nylon belts (usually consisting of both a waist belt and leg loops) that the climber wears and to which the rope is attached.

ice axe An axe designed specifically for mountaineering, usually 60–75 cm in length. The axe head has an adze on one end and a sharp point or "pick" on the other. The shaft is metal (usually) and ends in a sharp spike used for plunging the shaft into hard snow.

ice and snow climbing protection Ice screws are metal tubes with sharp points and threads that can be easily screwed into the ice. A **v-thread** is a type of ice anchor made by drilling intersecting holes into the ice, then threading (using a wire v-thread device) and tying a section of cord or webbing. An ice or snow **bollard** is a teardrop-shaped groove chopped in the ice, around which a rope or sling is placed. **Pickets** are simple metal shafts that can be hammered into hard snow or slung and buried in softer snow. In good snow and ice, the protection can be very strong. Ice and snow vary greatly in strength (they melt); sometimes strength changes even over very short time intervals, and this means the strength of ice and snow protection is hard to predict.

ice tools Similar to an ice axe but shorter (most often 50 cm) and more useful for technical ice climbing. Normally, an ice climber uses two tools, with one in each hand. Ice tool heads are modular—both ice tools have sharp picks, and the other end of the head may hold an adze or a hammer.

leading Climbing first up a pitch. Only the lead climber usually risks a long fall in belayed climbing. If the leader places no protection, the fall equals twice the amount of rope used—for example, after climbing 10 feet above the belay, the climber falls until the rope stops him 10 feet below the belay, 20 feet total. If the leader places protection while climbing, the fall is twice the distance to the last piece of protection (or farther if the piece fails). The **second** or **follower** climbs on a tight belay from the leader above and should not fall any significant distance before stopping.

multipitch climbing A **pitch** is the section of a climb between belays; the maximum length of a pitch is determined by the length of the rope. A multipitch climb is a climb long enough to require multiple pitches with intermediate belays.

Perlon A type of nylon used in climbing cordage such as ropes and slings.

rack The collection of protection anchors, slings, and carabiners that climbers carry on a route to build the protection system.

rack stopper A trapezoidal metal wedge attached to a loop of flexible wire which is fitted into cracks and depressions in the rock to provide protection for an ascending climber.

rappel A method used for descending a rope.

rock climbing protection Cams are spring-loaded camming devices (SLCDs) for fitting in parallel cracks. **Nuts** are metal wedge-shaped anchors that lock into constrictions in a crack. **Pitons** are steel spikes that are hammered in cracks. **Bolts** are metal shafts placed within a drilled hole in the rock—they can be glued in place or the shafts expand when tightened. Nuts and cams are "clean pro" in that they can be placed and removed many times without harming the rock. Bolts and pitons are permanent protection, staying in the rock. Rock protection is considered more reliable than ice and snow protection, but rock types also vary considerably in strength, and no piece of rock protection can be stronger than the rock in which it is placed.

rock shoes Shoes designed specifically for rock climbing. Normally, they fit the feet very closely and have sticky rubber soles to better adhere to the rock.

rope A climbing rope consists of an outer protective nylon sheath and an inner core of woven nylon fibers. Depending on the rope system chosen, modern climbing ropes are between 8 and 11 mm thick, 50–70 m long, and can hold tremendous forces.

slings Nylon fibers woven flat and then tied or sewn into a loop. Typical climbing webbing has a breaking strength of 5500 pounds.

SUGGESTED READINGS

The Mountaineers Outdoor Expert series, including:

Gadd, W. 2003. *Ice and mixed climbing: Modern technique.*

Houston, M., and Cosley, K. 2004. *Alpine climbing: Techniques to take you higher.*

Luebben, C. 2004. *Rock climbing: Mastering basic techniques.*

Soles, C. 2008. *Climbing: Training for peak performance.* 2nd ed.

All the books in this series are published in Seattle by Mountaineers Books.

Also suggested:

Horst, E. 2008. *Training for climbing: The definitive guide to improving your performance.* Guilford, CT.: Falcon Guides.

Hunter, D. and Hague, D. 2006. *The self-coached climber.* Mechanicsburg, PA: Stackpole Books.

Lewis, S.P., and Cauthorn, D. 2000. *Climbing: From gym to crag.* Seattle, WA: Mountaineers Books.

Long, S. 2007. *The climbing handbook.* London, U.K: Marshall Editions.

Loomis, M., and Tyson, A. 2006. *Climbing self rescue: Improvising solutions for serious situations.* Seattle, WA: Mountaineers Books.

Renner, J. 2005. *Mountain weather: Backcountry forecasting for hikers, campers, climbers, skiers, snowboarders.* Seattle, WA: Mountaineers Books.

Shepherd, N. 2004. *The complete guide to rope techniques,* 2nd ed. Guilford, CT: Falcon Guides.

Soles, C., and Powers, P. 2003. *Climbing: Expedition planning.* Seattle, WA: Mountaineers Books.

Soles, C. 2004. *The outdoor knots book.* Seattle, WA: Mountaineers Books.

The Mountaineers. 2003. *Mountaineering: The freedom of the hills.* 7th ed. Seattle, WA: Mountaineers Books.

Tremper, B. 2008. *Staying alive in avalanche terrain,* 2nd ed. Seattle, WA: Mountaineers Books.

Tyson, A., and Clelland, M. 2009. *Glacier mountaineering: An illustrated guide to glacier travel and crevasse rescue.* Guilford, CT: Falcon Guides.

Volken, M., Schell, S., and Wheeler, M. 2007. *Backcountry skiing: Skills for ski touring and ski mountaineering.* Seattle, WA: Mountaineers Books.

Williamson, J. (ed), annual. *Accidents in north american mountaineering.* Golden, CO: American Alpine Club.

RESOURCES

Videos

Goddard, D., and Neumann, U. 1993. *Performance rock climbing.* Salt Lake, UT. Self-produced.

Hunter, D., and Hajue, D. 2006. *The self-coached climber.* Mechanicsburg, PA: Stackpole Books.

The largest climbing video collection in the United States is available through Chessler Books, www.chesslerbooks.com

Climbing organizations

American Alpine Club, 710 10th St., Suite 100, Golden, CO 80401. (303) 384-0110. www.americanalpineclub.org

American Mountain Guides Association, P.O. Box 1739, Boulder, CO 80302. (303) 271-0984. www.amga.com

WEB SITES

Expanded climbing dictionary.
climb.mountainzone.com/glossary_a_l.html

Excellent instructional articles and videos.
www.animatedknots.com
www.alpinist.com
www.climbing.com
www.mountainproject.com
www.petzl.com

Community climbing site with educational forum discussions.
www.realknots.com
www.rockandice.com
www.rockclimbing.com

This Web site gives participation data for a number of outdoor sports, including rock and ice climbing.
www.outdoorindustry.org/research.current.html

21 Orienteering

After completing this chapter, the reader should be able to:

- Appreciate the development, values, and objectives of orienteering
- Use maps and a compass for navigation
- Organize an orienteering event
- Teach others map- and compass-reading skills
- Conduct orienteering lead-up games
- Organize orienteering variations
- Understand how to arrange a course setting for a meet

The sport form of land navigation is called orienteering. It is a cross-country race in which participants use a map and compass to navigate between checkpoints along an unfamiliar course. The activity can be a means of enjoying other outdoor pursuits or a sport complete with competition, rules, and organizational structure. Both aspects of orienteering qualify its inclusion in the "environmental sports" family, along with running, cross-country skiing, hiking, kayaking, and similar activities.

VALUES

Orienteering has many appealing attributes for modern physical education and recreation. People from 5 to 90 years old can participate in this lifetime sport with no extraordinary physical or mental abilities. Orienteering is appropriate for both males and females. Groups, pairs, or individuals can navigate an orienteering course in a competitive or cooperative fashion, involving the participants in a wide range of commitment and challenge. Orienteering for the disabled has been developed in a special form called Trail Orienteering. Finally, orienteering can be organized on commonly found, accessible tracts of land. Schoolyards, parks, and town forest preserves are all adequate.

HISTORY

Orienteering began when humans first ventured from their familiar environs into an unmapped world, seeking new horizons. Organized orienteering, however, is a relatively new addition to the sports world, particularly in the United States. The first time an event was labeled an orienteering race was in 1900 at a meet organized by Club Tjalve in Oslo, Norway. By 1919, orienteering meets were attracting as many as 200 people, with Capt. Ernst Killander organizing these meets outside of Stockholm and generally being credited as the father of orienteering.

The sport's next boost came in the early 1930s with the invention, by Bjorn and Alvar Kjellstrom, of the one-piece protractor compass, or base plate compass, which provided a simple tool for land navigation. By 1942, orienteering was a compulsory activity in Swedish physical education programs. Orienteering continued to grow, rivaling soccer as the most popular sport in Sweden and spreading to other Scandinavian countries.

In 1946 Bjorn Kjellstrom, now living in the United States, sponsored the first orienteering meet in the United States at Indiana Dunes State Park. However, the sport remained relatively unpracticed in North America until 1965, when Geoffrey Dyson and John Disley introduced orienteering in Canada, where it steadily gained popularity. Since 1967 the sport has grown in the United States, beginning with permanent orienteering groups centered at the Marine Physical Fitness Academy in Quantico, Virginia, in the Delaware Valley, and in New England. The United States Orienteering Federation, founded in 1971, now represents 71 clubs spread from coast to coast and has a membership of 1,400.

Today some orienteering meets rank as the largest participative athletic events in the world; the Oringen, held in Sweden each July, attracts over 15,000 competitors for 5 days of competition. National and regional competitions are held annually in countries all over the world, as well as a World Orienteering Championship.

OBJECTIVES

Before organizing an orienteering event, a physical educator or recreation leader should have experience and a solid understanding of the following components of the sport: equipment, techniques using map and compass, safety precautions, teaching methodology, and sources of information.

Orienteering in whatever setting it might be offered can provide the unique contribution of fostering the attitude that the outdoors is a safe and interesting place. The following objectives are considered outcomes of an orienteering program. The participant will:

1. Gain the basic skills of land navigation using a map and compass

2. Improve his or her physical fitness
3. Know what to expect at a standard competition
4. Acquire an increased awareness of the environment

EQUIPMENT

Limitations

The only navigational aids that may be carried on the course are magnetic compasses, watches, and copies of the competition map. The possession of other navigational aids, including pedometers, altimeters, and GPS receivers, on the course is prohibited. The use of relevant maps other than those expressly sanctioned by the organizers is prohibited (USOF rule 5.2). Note: Some specialized and local orienteering events might allow the use of GPS devices, but typically participants who choose to do so are not allowed to be listed in the final standings. All A and B orienteering meets must be conducted under all rules laid out by the USOF.

Maps

The map serves as the primary tool of navigation for the participants. To the trained eye, it can yield an enormous amount of information. The most common maps used for orienteering are specially created five-color topographical maps that are made by experienced orienteering mapmakers. United States Geological Survey (USGS) maps do not have the detail, or a large-enough scale, that is necessary for the sport. Orienteering maps can be purchased from local orienteering clubs around the United States. The Web site for the United States Orienteering Federation has the contact information for all clubs. USGS maps can be useful as a starting point for making a suitable orienteering map. A base map can be created, using the topographical lines, but detail must be filled in by doing careful surveying in the field. Many sporting goods stores, bookstores, and camping stores stock government topographical maps of the local area.

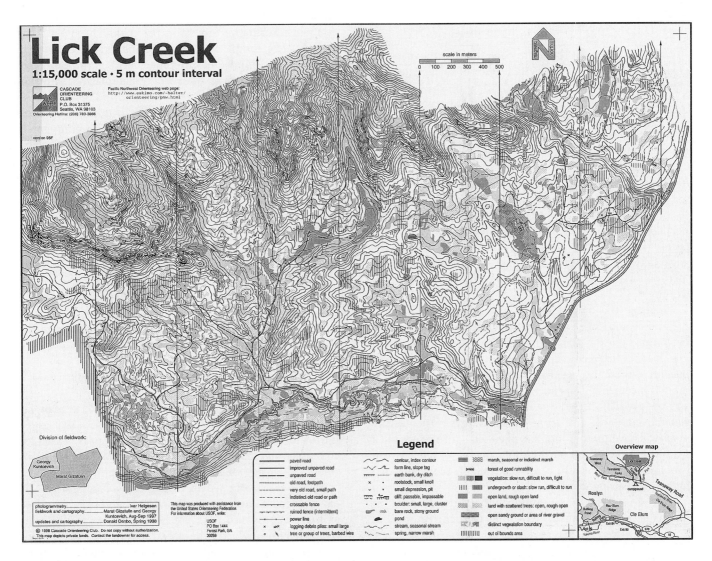

Figure 21.1. Orienteering topographical map. Reprinted by permission of the Cascade Orienteering Club, Seattle, WA.

An index of maps that can be ordered is available from the Map Information Office, U.S. Geologic and Geodetic Survey, Washington, DC 02042.

Specialized orienteering maps (Figure 21.1) have a large scale, usually 1:10,000 or 1:15,000; they have a contour interval of 3 or 5 meters, and are created on a computer using recent, precise aerial photographs and a drawing program called OCAD. The added detail and accuracy allow course setters to design orienteering courses that are suited to various skill levels of competitors.

Orienteering maps contain much the same kinds of information that other maps have, but in addition they will show details such as boulders, cliffs, distinct trees, vegetation density, open areas, and many other features. Below is a list of items that will be found on any orienteering map.

Location. Each map has a title describing the location, and often a small locator map will be included, which shows the proximity to known urban areas. Unlike a USGS map, they will not contain longitude and latitude coordinates that locate the area on the earth's surface.

Date. The map must be up-to-date; the year the map was created will be noted along with the years of any updates that have been made.

Distance. Orienteering maps contain a bar scale given in a ratio of centimeters to meters. For example, on a 1:10,000 scale map, 1 centimeter on the map equals 10,000 centimeters or 100 meters on the ground.

Direction. The top of the specialized orienteering maps indicates magnetic north, not true north, because such maps are used exclusively by orienteers using magnetic north-seeking compasses. On a USGS map, the top indicates true north and magnetic north is indicated by an arrow that points slightly off to one side of the true north line. The angle between true north and magnetic north is known as "declination." The angle of declination varies throughout the world.

Elevation. The unique feature of topographical maps is their description of elevation in the land mass. This is shown by contour lines in the form of irregular concentric rings. The distance between each contour line, termed the *contour interval,* represents a vertical change in elevation of the terrain. The center of the rings is the high point of elevation, and the broader circles show progressively lower areas. In general, land will rise from water features. Orienteering maps will have contour intervals of either 3 or 5 meters. On a map with 3-meter contour intervals, the rise or fall between two contour lines will be 3 meters, which is the height of a high diving springboard.

Natural-terrain features. Important natural features of mappable size are shown. Examples of such features are bodies of water, including lakes, streams, and swamps; cliffs; earth banks, erosion gullies, and boulders; and open areas.

Other features. Buildings, roads, bridges, power lines, and various manmade objects listed as "special features" are among the other features symbolically displayed on the map. The explanation for each symbol is contained in the map's legend (Figure 21.2).

Legend. Orienteering maps are five-color maps, and the various types of features will be indicated in the legend and will fall into categories that are depicted with the colors listed below.

Blue: water features
Green: vegetation features
Yellow: open areas
Brown: land forms
Black: manmade features
White: runnable forest, with minimal ground clutter

Compass

The compass, second in importance only to the map among the orienteer's tools, serves to supplement and confirm information given on the map. The most commonly used compass in orienteering is the base plate compass. The important difference between the base plate compass and others is the rectangular plastic plate that serves as a protractor and assists in taking a bearing. Base plate compasses are available in the United States from several commercial sources, including sporting goods stores and mail-order orienteering equipment vendors. Models featuring a liquid-filled compass housing that dampers and stabilizes movement of the magnetic needle are well worth the additional expense.

Types of compasses

A variety of compasses is available, each having features designed for different functions:

Plain watch compass. This compass looks like a pocket watch and is suitable for general travel that requires limited accuracy.

Lensatic compass. Also commonly called the army or the prismatic compass, the lensatic compass features excellent sighting devices but lacks a protractor base, so it cannot be used to take a compass bearing. Because of its high accuracy, it is popular in mapmaking.

Mirror compass. The mirror compass is similar to an orienteering compass, but it also has a sighting device that uses a mirror for added precision. The mirror compass is used for course setting, mapmaking, and backpacking, but it is considered too heavy for conventional orienteering.

Thumb compass. Used in orienteering competitions by experienced navigators. It allows one hand to remain free as the compass and map are held together in the same hand. It has an elastic thumb strap, an irregular-shaped base plate, and generally, the compass housing is fixed and cannot dial a bearing.

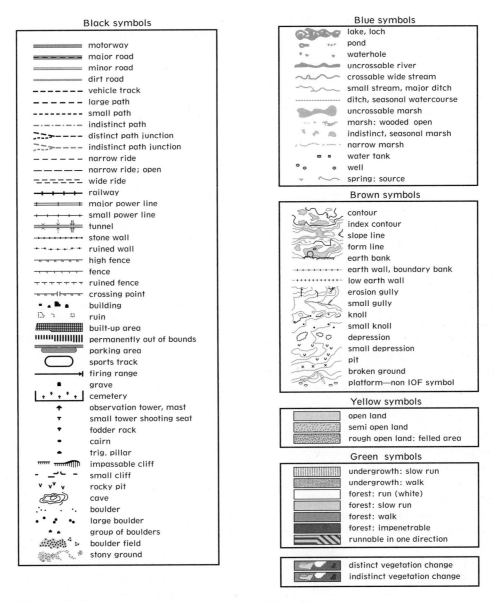

Figure 21.2. Orienteering map symbols, grouped by color.

Protractor, or base plate compass.

Used most commonly by orienteers, this compass has measuring scales on the base, a rotating housing for taking bearings, and often a magnifying lens. The following are the main components of the base plate compass (Figure 21.3).

Base plate. The Plexiglas rectangle under the compass itself is referred to as the base plate, or protractor, and serves two purposes: it measures distance using the scale (in centimeters) that is imprinted on the edges, and assists the orienteer in determining a course of travel.

Compass housing. The compass housing is mounted on the base plate and appears as a basic watch compass. It must rotate freely on the protractor and should have a transparent bottom and be dampered with liquid.

Direction-of-travel arrow. The only arrow on the base plate, located in the center of the long end of the protractor, is the direction-of-travel arrow.

Orienting, or north, arrow lines. The north arrow is drawn on the bottom of the compass housing. This arrow is flanked by a series of parallel, orienting lines.

Magnetic needle. Suspended in the compass housing is a freely rotating, floating needle. The red end of the needle points to magnetic north when not influenced by nearby iron objects.

Magnifying lens. A small lens is embedded in the base plate to aid in reading map detail.

Wrist strap. A strap attached to a compass with a slip knot at the distal end provides protection from loss in the event of a fall.

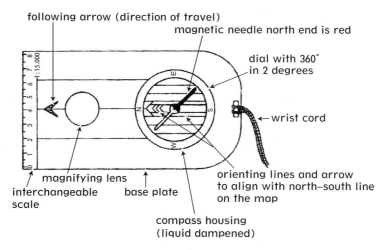

following arrow (direction of travel)

magnetic needle north end is red

dial with 360° in 2 degrees

wrist cord

orienting lines and arrow to align with north–south line on the map

compass housing (liquid dampened)

magnifying lens

interchangeable scale

base plate

Figure 21.3. Parts of a base plate compass.

Other Equipment

Personal equipment other than a compass that is required for orienteering includes:

Clothing. Athletic clothing that is breathable, and snag proof, and that covers the extremities of the body is best. Orienteering suits, made of thin fabric, and usually bright in color, are recommended for optimal comfort.

Footwear. There are orienteering shoes available that provide the best traction and have waterproof properties. These shoes have knobby soles, which sometimes have small spikes embedded in the knobs. Running shoes, trail shoes, or hiking boots can be used, and those with the knobbiest soles work best.

Whistle. A whistle is often required at events. Small, flat versions can be purchased and carried easily in a pocket of the orienteering suit.

Punch card holder. A plastic sleeve that has a finger, wrist, or arm strap for attaching it to the body, is used to protect the punch card.

Electronic punching device, with finger strap. Many events are now featuring electronic punching systems, and this requires competitors to carry a chip that automatically records their visits to the controls. The "E-Punch" (Figure 21.4) is attached to the body with a finger strap, but it can also be secured with a wrist strap for additional protection against loss. E-Punches can be purchased and used at multiple orienteering events, or rented from meet organizers.

Control description holder. Control descriptions can be carried in the punch card holder, but if electronic punching is being used, it will be necessary to have a case to hold and protect the descriptions. This case can be attached to the hand, sleeve, or chest by a strap or a safety pin.

All of the above items can be ordered from mail-order orienteering gear vendors. (See resources at the end of this chapter.)

In organizing a meet, several items (aside from maps) are necessary: punch cards, control markers, punches, plastic map cases, red pens for copying courses from master maps onto individual maps, digital watches or a clock for timing, clipboards, master maps for each course, and control description sheets for each individual and course.

Control descriptions are an important supplement to the map, and they have course information needed by competitors. The course setter prepares the descriptions, using special computer programs. At major events, as a backup, descriptions will also be printed on the map—usually the back side. Descriptions are denoted using international symbols, so it is possible to participate in events in foreign countries despite language differences (Figure 21.5). Beginner course descriptions will not use symbols, but instead, in the United States, descriptions will be written in English (Figure 21.6). Control descriptions give the orienteer extra information that cannot be derived from the map, including the control code numbers. Each column of the control description sheet, which is sometimes referred to as the "clue sheet," gives the following information:

Column A—control number
       B—control code
       C—which of a number of similar features
       D—the control feature
       E—details of appearance
       F—dimensions of the feature
       G—position of the marker on the feature
       H—other information

CHARACTERISTICS OF A CROSS-COUNTRY ORIENTEERING EVENT

The most commonly practiced form of orienteering is the cross-country or point-to-point event resembling a car rally or treasure hunt. The event occurs in an area of 75 to 2,000 acres (0.3 to 8 square km), ideally consisting of wooded

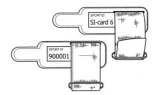

Figure 21.4. Electronic punching finger chip, with elastic finger strap.

acreage with varied terrain. The course setter, using an orienteering map (see Figure 21.1), places from 6 to 15 markers, or "controls," in the field at distinct terrain features, such as those mentioned above under "Legend." The positions of the controls are precisely circled on a master map, numbered sequentially, and connected with a straight line, forming a course for the event. Participants in the event are then assigned the task of copying the control locations shown on the master map to their personal copy of the map.

Courses may be printed on the maps already, thus no copying would be required. Courses for different skill levels will generally be offered at an orienteering meet. Courses are color coded, like "belts" in karate, to indicate difficulty. In the United States these colors are used:

Course Colors	Distance	
White—Beginner	3K or less	(1.86 miles or less)
Yellow—Advanced beginner	3.5–4.5K	(2.17–2.79 miles)
Orange—Intermediate	4.5K	(2.79 miles)
Brown—Advanced, but short	3.5–4.5K	(2.17–2.79 miles)
Green—Advanced, somewhat longer	4–5K	(2.48–3.1 miles)
Red—Advanced, even longer	5–7K	(3.1–4.34 miles)
Blue—Advanced, very long	7–12K	(4.34–7.44 miles)

When meet participants register, they will be given a punch card and a control description sheet for their course, and their start time will be written on the punch card.

Individuals are started at intervals and will not see their course until start time. A competitor from each course may start at the same time (Figure 21.7). Each will proceed to locate their markers in the correct sequence, using their skills of navigation in moving from one control to the next in the most efficient or fastest manner. Controls are not hidden but are visibly placed exactly on the features in the terrain that are circled on the map and described in the control description. It is expected that competitors will not communicate with each other if they are competing individually. They should not distract or purposely attract others to the control locations. Route choice, navigational techniques, and rate of travel (running versus walking) are at the discretion of each participant. At each control a punch pattern is made by the competitor, using the punches that hang on each

control marker. The patterns are imprinted in the sequentially numbered boxes on the punch card (Figure 21.8). In the case of electronic punching, the "e-card" will be inserted into a control box for a brief moment, until a beep sounds and a light flashes. These procedures ensure that the competitors were present at each control. Before the start, the competitor's punch card will have the starting time written on it. Upon finishing, the card will be collected, and the competitor's finish time will be written on the card as well. Meet officials calculate the "actual time on the course" and place the card in rank order on a results string, or a computer-generated results list, that is displayed for review of all competitors. The fastest, or shortest, time will win the competition. Most events have gender and age class divisions, which gives everyone the opportunity to be competitive among their peers. Because of the challenge of locating all the controls on a course, some participants consider completion of the race a satisfying goal and position in the meet of secondary importance.

BASIC ORIENTEERING TECHNIQUES
Map Reading

The map is the primary tool of navigation, with the compass used to ensure that the map is oriented to north. To get the most information from an orienteering map, use the following basic techniques of map reading:

1. Before going out with a map, be familiar with the map's scale, contour interval, and symbols (legend—Figure 21.2).
2. Competitors should always keep the map "oriented," that is, keep the top facing north regardless of your direction of travel. This will keep the map properly aligned with the terrain. It is possible to orient the map in two ways: visually or by using the compass. It is done visually simply by noting the features that can be seen in the terrain and holding the map so that the corresponding symbols are lined up in the same configuration (Figure 21.9). Orient the map using the compass in the following manner:
   a. While holding the map flat and parallel to the ground, place the compass in proximity to a north line on the map.
   b. Turn both the compass and the map together until the magnetic needle lines up parallel to the map's north lines, being certain that the north end of the magnetic needle points toward the north edge of the map. (The north lines have arrow heads that indicate which edge of the map is north.)
   c. The map now corresponds to the surrounding terrain (Figure 21.10).
3. Fold the map to a readable, holdable size (approximately 4 inches square). Concentrate on the

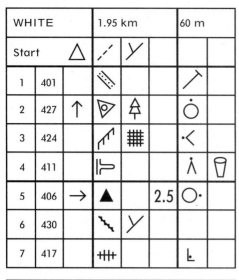

Course WHITE Length 1.95 km Climb 60 m

Start Path Junction

No.	Code	Description
1	401	Dry ditch northeast end
2	427	Northern single tree coniferous north side
3	424	Fence overgrown west outside corner
4	411	Spur north tip refreshments
5	406	Eastern boulder height 2.5 m east side
6	430	Stream junction
7	417	Earth bank at foot

110 m marked route to finish

Figure 21.5. Control descriptions.

Course: Yellow Length 3080K Climb 87 m

No.	Code	Description
Start		open land
1	303	E-most, dry ditch junction
2	205	Knoll, on top
3	212	Spur, NW foot
4	306	SW-most knoll, on top
5	235	Re-entrant, upper part, H_2O
6	311	Special item
7	224	Re-entrant
8	219	Gully, NW end
9	123	Thicket, NW edge, H_2O
10	217	Hill, SW part
11	315	Fence, SW outside corner, H_2O
12	200	NE-most thicket, E edge

70 mm funnell tapes to finish

Figure 21.6. Written control descriptions for beginner courses.

part of the map you are using; the remainder will only confuse you. Walking or running is best accomplished with a small, neatly folded map that will not get caught on tree branches. Pinch the map between the first two fingers, using the thumb to trace your progress. Fold the map so the folds are parallel to the north lines.

4. When reading the map, visualize the terrain through which you will soon be passing. Try to imagine how the ground will be sloping from your position—either upward or downward. For example, contours between you and a creek slope down. Visualize the type of vegetation and other terrain features you encounter as you move along your planned route. Picture these features in your mind before seeing them in the field.

Compass Technique

On some occasions the compass must be heavily relied on to determine a direction of travel, usually when adequate terrain features for navigating are lacking or if the orienteer simply wishes to be absolutely certain that he or she is heading in the desired direction. This procedure is called taking a compass bearing, and it is accomplished using these steps:

1. Establishing direction. Place the long side edge of the compass base on the map along the line of intended travel. Be sure that the direction-of-travel arrow, which is on the base plate, is pointing from your location to your destination (Figure 21.11).

2. Setting the north-south lines. While pressing the base plate firmly to the map with your thumb, turn the compass housing around so that the north lines of the compass housing are parallel to the north lines of the map. Be sure that the north arrow of the compass housing is pointing to the north of the map (Figure 21.12).

3. Reading the bearing. Now hold the compass level in your hand with the direction-of-travel arrow pointing away from you. Turn around so that the north end (red) of the magnetic needle coincides with the north arrow of the compass housing. The direction-of-travel arrow on the base plate is now pointing toward the destination (Figure 21.13). When reading a compass, always hold it parallel to the ground and at the midline of the body.

4. Running the bearing. Look down at the compass and focus on the direction-of-travel arrow. Slowly lift your head, sighting directly in line with the direction of travel arrow. Pick out a prominent landmark, which can be a

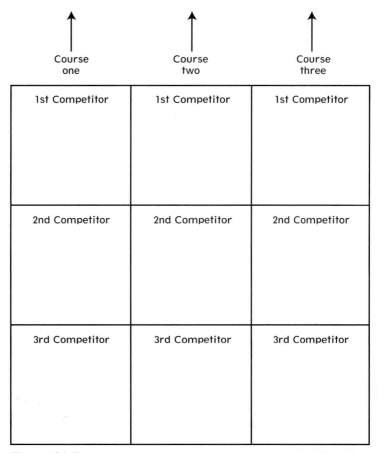

Figure 21.7. Interval start. The start system organizes competitors into lanes—a different lane for each course offered.

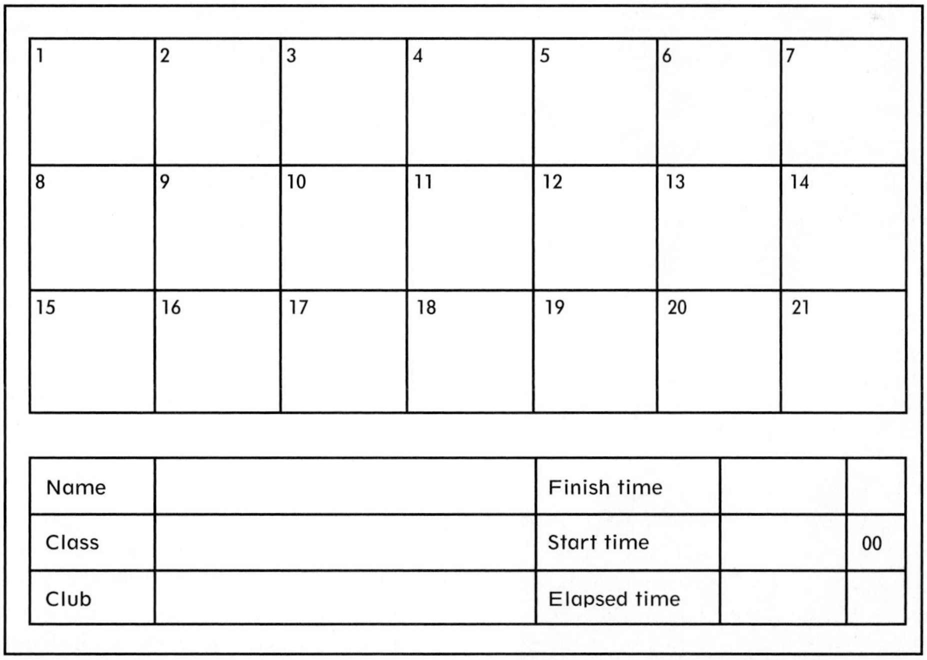

1	2	3	4	5	6	7
8	9	10	11	12	13	14
15	16	17	18	19	20	21

Name		Finish time		
Class		Start time		00
Club		Elapsed time		

Figure 21.8. The punch card, with competitor information and start time written on it, is carried on the course. It is imprinted with punch patterns at each control and turned in to officials at the finish.

Figure 21.9. Orienting the map can be done visually, by aligning the features on the map with the corresponding features that can be seen on the ground.

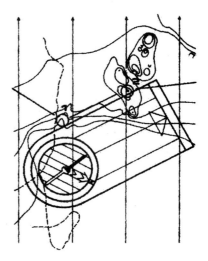

Figure 21.11. Step one, taking a bearing: Place the long edge of the base plate on the map along the desired route so that the direction-of-travel arrow on the base plate points from your present location to your destination point.

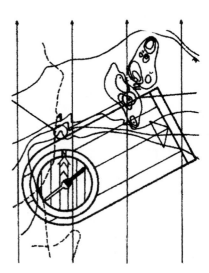

Figure 21.12. Step two, setting the north lines: Keeping the compass firmly in position on the map, rotate the compass housing until the arrow on the housing is parallel to the north lines on the map.

Figure 21.10. Getting a bearing with a map and compass.

rock or tree about 50 to 100 meters ahead of you. Take the easiest route to the landmark, avoiding obstacles, and then repeat this step again by sighting new landmarks until you reach your destination (Figure 21.14).

Remember that the compass is used to supplement the map; so while running on a bearing, consult the map often to help confirm your position.

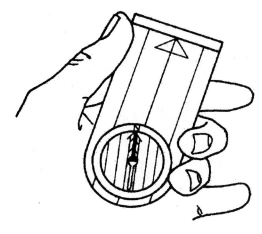

Figure 21.13. Step three, reading the bearing: Still keeping the compass firmly pressed to the map, turn your body until the floating, red end of the compass needle lines up with the housing arrow. The direction of travel arrow on the base plate will point in the direction that you need to travel, and the map will be oriented.

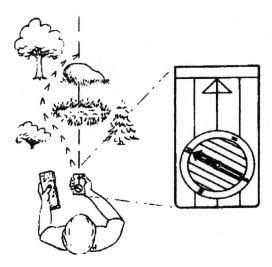

Figure 21.14. Step four, running the bearing: Looking straight along the line of direction-of-travel arrow on the base plate, pick a prominent object in the distance and travel exactly to that location. Repeat this again by sighting new landmarks until you reach your destination.

Route Choice

Good route choice is the essence of successful orienteering and must be learned by experience. The fastest route around an orienteering course is different for every individual and is based on fitness, orienteering skill level, and experience. Overriding these factors, however, is the terrain of the course, which ultimately dictates route decision. Commonly, one must make decisions concerning path versus woods travel, elevation gain versus distance, and easy, nontechnical navigational routes versus difficult and intricate navigational routes.

Aiming Off

When taking a compass bearing toward a control located near a linear feature, such as a path across your direction of travel, you have a 50/50 chance of arriving at the path either to the right or the left of the control. You will not know in which direction your bearing is off, so many orienteers purposely aim slightly to one side of the control, and when arriving at the path—knowing the direction of their "error"—they move down the path in the correct direction to the control. By aiming off, the orienteer knows for certain in what direction to turn to seek the marker (Figure 21.15).

Attack Point

The orienteer should identify an obvious or visible feature as near the control as possible to use as the last relocation or attack point on the way to the marker. The larger and more definite the feature and the nearer it is to the control, the more desirable it is as an attack point. Path, fence, or stream junctions, corners of fields, and the like provide excellent reference points on the orienteer's last portion of a control leg.

Precision Compass

Precision compass is the precise application of the method of taking a compass bearing cited earlier. Extreme accuracy is required in this technique, which is often employed while traveling from the attack point to the control. This method is time consuming but necessary in those parts of the course containing difficult navigation problems and should be used in conjunction with the technique of pace counting.

Precision Map Reading

Precision map reading could be referred to as aggressive map reading and is used in areas containing numerous detailed terrain features that can confuse the competitor. Continuous glances at the map should be made every few seconds. At all times the thumb should be kept on the map at the point where the orienteer is currently located, and the thumb should be moved as the orienteer progresses through the terrain. Features along the route should be mentally checked off as they are passed and thus these features are called "check off features."

Control Finding

Once in the immediate locale of the control marker, the orienteer must use cautious awareness to quickly find the control. Good skills in this area can save minutes:

1. Always read the control description carefully and know what you are looking for—for example, the marsh, eastern edge.
2. Choose a good attack point.
3. Slow down as you near the control. Use precision map reading, compass bearing, and pace counting.

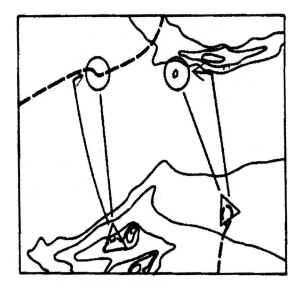

Figure 21.15. Aiming off: Select a route to either the left or right side of the direct route. This ensures that you know your position in the terrain and simplifies the route.

4. Concentrate on your task, ignoring other orienteers in the area.
5. Use extra caution on the first and last control of the course because both are critical in finishing the course.

Traffic Light Orienteering

Each competitor's pace throughout a course should be controlled by an imaginary traffic light in the mind. Through experience, the participant learns the appropriate light for existing terrain conditions, but the following can serve as a general guide:

1. Green light: Go. Travel at the fastest speed possible while still maintaining navigational control. This technique is used when traveling along obvious handrails, such as trails, roads, and stone walls.
2. Yellow light: Proceed quickly but cautiously under more difficult conditions. More precise navigating is employed. This technique is often used in arriving at an attack point.
3. Red light: Stop or go slowly. This technique is used when temporarily lost or disoriented, when a control has been missed, or during particularly critical navigational portions of the course. Good orienteers can sense when to use this light and to slow down, avoiding a major mistake. While traveling from the attack point to the control, use this light.

Collecting or Catching Features

These are two similar terms for any distinct feature across the direction of travel that will aid in navigation. It can be used effectively to funnel the orienteer toward an attack point or

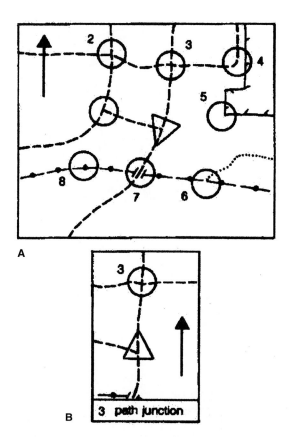

Figure 21.16. Star Exercise. A, Map showing the start, a north arrow, and all of the numbered controls. B, A "single" map with start triangle, one numbered control, a north arrow, and a written description of the control.

the control, and it can also serve as an alert that the orienteer has gone too far beyond the control.

Handrails

Terrain features that are parallel to the direction of travel serve as "handrails" to a control. Paths, roads, streams, or ridges that orienteers can travel along can serve as excellent handrails. A series of land-shape features such as knolls or marshes that form a line can serve as a handrail.

Rough Compass

Frequently an orienteer must travel quickly to get to a large collecting feature or handrail that will be easy to locate. A rough compass bearing coupled with a sense of direction will lead one to the feature. The standard method is used in taking the compass bearing, but it is done quickly. Sightings using the compass along the direction of travel are done less frequently and often on the run.

Distance Judging

This essential skill is done with varying degrees of accuracy but is accomplished so that the orienteer knows his or her location at all times. Distance judging requires a two-step approach, first measuring the distance and then pace counting while traveling. To measure the distance to be traveled, place the measuring edge of the compass base plate along the direction of travel and calculate the number of centimeters on the map between the current location and the destination. Then refer to the map's scale to translate centimeters on the map to meters on the terrain. This gives the distance to be traveled, but if additional precision is required, this can be translated into the orienteer's paces. By taking repeated trials over a 110-yard (100 m) stretch in varying terrain, the orienteer should know the number of paces (a double stride) required to cover 110 yards. This personal yardstick of pace counting takes time to develop but is indispensable in precise compass and map-reading situations. Some typical measures for pace count per 110 yards for adults are:

Hiking	60 paces
Running in dense woods	45 paces
Running in flat woods	40 paces
Running on open trails	36 to 38 paces

Orienteers should determine their own pace-count values so they can use this technique for keeping track of distance covered.

INSTRUCTIONAL GAMES

Orienteering teachers rely on their ingenuity to devise orienteering lead-up games, so imagination is the only limit. Following are some instructional activities that can be used for training exercises.

Follow the Leader

Both leader and followers have a map, and the leader chooses a destination point without telling the group where it is. Starting from a known location, the leader orienteers to the point and the rest follow, trying to determine the route on their map. Periodically the leader stops along the route to quiz the group on their location and how they got there. When the destination is reached, the process is repeated with a new leader.

Star Exercise

Obtain copies of a large-scale map of a playing field area or a park. Select a central starting point where it is easy to orient the map to the ground by looking at nearby features. Place several markers with code letters and marking devices, like different colored pencils, within 200 meters around the central point, and use very distinct features. Make "single" maps for each participant that only have the central point start triangle and one control drawn on them. Make a separate map for each control. The control circle must have the code letter indicated, and it must be possible to locate north on each map. Have students orient their single map to the ground, and then start them together. They will head out in different directions. The

students will locate the control on their map, punch or mark their punch card, and return to the start triangle. After checking that the punches are correct, they swap maps and repeat until they have located all of the markers. Later, "minicourses" can be designed by using the same controls with a connecting line between three or four of the controls (Figure 21.16).

Map Walks

This informal activity is instructive for beginners in groups of up to a dozen people with one leader and resembles a slow-paced version of Follow the Leader. At the start, the leader teaches map orienting and basic elements of map reading, such as scale, elevation, and symbols. After this brief lecture, the group, armed with the preceding skills, goes for a walk in an area containing many terrain features. During the walk, map orienting and thumbing are stressed and appropriate items discussed as terrain features appear along the route. The length of the walk should be adjusted to the group's attention span and physical abilities. This activity is most successful with novices.

Score Orienteering

This activity is a variation of orienteering that is often used for competitions, but it can be useful as a training exercise. Controls are placed at terrain features. Each control is assigned a point value from 5 to 30, depending on its difficulty and distance from the start. The purpose of the event is for each individual to accumulate points by locating as many high-valued controls as possible within an allotted time. There is a stiff point penalty for returning after the time deadline. Controls can be located in any order. Whoever accumulates the most points within the time limit wins.

This activity has a number of benefits:

1. Students are encouraged to work efficiently and quickly.
2. The time limit is helpful in working within a class schedule. All participants will be at the finish at a determined time.
3. It is suitable for parks and even school yards because many controls can be placed in a small area.

Trim Courses

A trim course is a group of permanent markers that are set out in a park or school ground. The markers are generally weatherproof and resistant to destruction. They have code numbers that correspond to a master control description list that matches the master map of the trim course. A park or school office can be responsible for making the maps and control descriptions available to the public. Contact local orienteering clubs in order to determine if there is a trim course in your area, as the clubs are normally the bodies that install the courses and print the maps and descriptions.

The advantages of trim orienteering include the following:

1. People can try orienteering at their convenience and at their own pace.

2. Families can enjoy orienteering in a noncompetitive fashion.
3. Schools can use parts of the course for instruction.
4. Competitive orienteers can use the course for training.

TRAINING

Orienteering requires mental and physical abilities, so it follows that training should develop one's capabilities in both areas. To excel in the sport, one must devote adequate preparation to the mental and technical aspects of orienteering as well as the physical. It is necessary to keep in mind the unique demands of orienteering while planning a training program.

Navigation Technique Training

Basic techniques can be sharpened through a variety of activities, including:

1. Reading books that discuss navigation
2. Looking at orienteering maps daily
3. Doing physical training while reading a map
4. Practicing pace counting during physical training; determining a personal pace count
5. Acquiring the "guidelines for course setting" and planning courses (See resources)
6. Drawing a simple map; making a map of your garden or a school yard
7. Practicing a personal, consistent system to use at each control
8. Taking part in instructional games (including those previously mentioned)
9. Participating in as many training meets as you can

Some of these training activities can produce physical benefits when done at a sufficiently high workload.

Physical Training

Orienteering places distinct physical requirements on the participant: cardiovascular endurance, agility, strength, and flexibility. Physical training should be molded to meet these demands. Training that simulates running through rough terrain is beneficial, but actually training in rough terrain is optimal for developing the physical skills needed for orienteering.

Cardiovascular endurance can be improved in a variety of methods—most commonly, walking, running, bicycle riding, and cross-country skiing. In training for cardiovascular fitness, it is necessary to keep in mind that the objective of doing aerobic training is to gain the ability to maintain a high work level for 60 to 90 minutes. This is the sort of endurance that is required to complete a typical orienteering race.

Agility is probably the most ignored physical requirement for successful orienteering. Running at high speeds in the woods places different demands on the body than running at a similar pace on a track. Increased agility can be obtained by training over the same terrain that orienteering meets use—woods, paths, boulder fields, meadows, and hills—adapting the running stride to the undulating, varied footing of the outdoors. Training runs should incorporate the specific demands of completing an orienteering course. Along with agility, strength and flexibility will be developed with this sort of training.

The ability to vary running speeds in a race is developed by changing the pace of training runs or using instructional games that force the participant to travel using the traffic lights system. Varied-pace training runs can include interval training, fartlek, and hill climbing. Instructional games, such as follow the leader and score orienteering, will develop the ability to know how to vary running speed.

SAFETY PRECAUTIONS

A few precautions when organizing an orienteering event can eliminate most safety problems:

1. Check the area to be used. With bright tape, mark any ruined barbed-wire fences, cliff edges, etc. Avoid planning courses that pass through hazardous areas.
2. Always employ a check system to track all registered participants. The start list will have names of all participants. This list should only have about 10 names per age so that the first portions of the list can be sent periodically to the finish officials. They can use this list to check off participants as they finish. Competitors are reminded to always report to the finish regardless of whether they complete the course.
3. Establish a time limit, at which time participants must return to the finish. A 3-hour limit is standard at competitions, but this can be shortened to any suitable length. The last starter must have as much time as the first starter. Anyone going over the time limit will be given an "overtime" score, which is a disqualification.
4. Designate a safety bearing or specific direction (north, south, etc.) at each event so that participants will know which direction to go if they are completely disoriented. For example, if a major road borders the south edge of the meet area, the safety bearing would be 180 degrees, or south, bringing anyone in need of help to a civilized area.
5. Respect private property and cultivated fields or gardens. Always request permission from landowners before mapping an area, training there, or setting courses on their property.
6. When using large forests for an event, have all competitors carry a whistle. If they are injured, they can summon other orienteers by blowing three sharp blasts with the whistle.

COURSE SETTING

For orienteering meets to take place, an organizer or leader must prepare a course and place orienteering markers in the woods. The skill of the course setter along with the quality of the map play a major role in the success of an orienteering meet. The course setter's task is to test the orienteer's running and navigational skills at the appropriate level. This is difficult for inexperienced persons to accomplish, so it would be advisable to contact a local orienteering club for assistance. The course setter follows these important rules:

1. Keep the competition fair. The quality of the map should be adequate for orienteering competition and verified by field checking on the part of the course setter. Controls should be correctly placed and not hidden, thus eliminating the element of luck.
2. Design a course to meet the different skill levels of the orienteers. If a diverse population of orienteers will attend the meet, several courses must be designed to meet the needs of all levels of ability. The difficulty of a course can be controlled by varying the number of controls, course distance, and control placement. Placing markers nearer or farther away from navigational "handrails" and good attack points will determine the degree of difficulty for locating the markers. Courses that travel along linear features, such as trails, streams, fences, power lines, ridges, etc., are appropriate for beginner courses. The advanced orienteer needs to be challenged to find handrails and attack points in less obvious features, which are often denoted only with contour lines.
3. Ensure that the course measures both physical and mental skills. Every part of a good orienteering course will present navigational problems that require the orienteer's concentration and continuous reading of the map. Distances on a course that require merely running skills with no map reading are a waste.

The course setter should always plan the course well in advance of the competition and preferably have the course checked in the field by another individual. Obtaining course setter's guidelines from the U.S. Federation (see resources) and following them closely is imperative. Orienteering has been standardized throughout the world, so that participants will always know what to expect, within limits, when they attend a meet. Therefore, organizers and course setters should adhere to the United States Orienteering Federation's guidelines as closely as possible. The satisfaction of watching a participant enjoy his or her studied creation is the course setter's reward.

ORIENTEERING VARIATIONS
Night Orienteering
Only orienteers with experience should participate in this event. A few modifications of the basic point-to-point orienteering format will provide safety:

1. Use a relatively civilized area, such as a park or athletic field.
2. Place controls at readily distinguishable features, such as path junctions or fence corners.
3. Shorten the course to a maximum of 3 kilometers (1.86 miles) (less for young participants).
4. Use track relay batons, for example, wrapped with reflective tape, as control markers.
5. Insist on everyone checking in at the finish regardless of whether they complete the course.
6. Require flashlights and whistles for all participants.
7. Avoid meet sites containing cliffs, rivers, or busy highways.

Ski Orienteering
This is an approved but yet-to-be-implemented Olympic sport that combines orienteering with cross-country skiing. Ski orienteering differs from orienteering primarily in the placement of control markers (nearer paths). The meet organizer ensures a number of routes between each control, making route choice the primary navigational problem.

Bicycle Orienteering
Road maps as well as orienteering maps could be used for this variation of the orienteering theme, and it can be an enjoyable activity. Relatively traffic-free roads are necessary, and participants should be able to find controls without leaving the pavement or trail. Distances of 15 to 30 kilometers (9.3 to 18.6 miles) are not uncommon. Like ski orienteering, several route choices should be possible per control.

Canoe Orienteering
A map that has waterways is ideal for this form of the sport. Lakeshores, rivers, streams, inlets, etc., can be used as features along which markers can be placed. Any type of maneuverable boat can be used for transport.

Horseback Orienteering
A map, with trails that are not restricted for horseback riding, is suitable for this type of orienteering. Markers should be hung high enough so that participants do not have to dismount to punch in at the controls.

Trail Orienteering
Specifically designed for the physically disabled, this is orienteering where the competitor remains on the trail. It is defined as "untimed courses where the challenge is mental and achievement is based upon the ability to interpret correctly the map and its relationship to the ground." This will allow access for the physically disabled, those temporarily disabled through injury, people with learning difficulties, and others unable to compete in rough terrain. Able-bodied competitors can do this form of orienteering as well.

String Orienteering

This type of orienteering is specifically for very young children and toddlers. A short course is laid out in a very safe area, where parents can see the children or accompany them. A string connects all of the controls. Children begin to learn about moving from control to control, where they will then punch or place a sticker on their punch card. They will begin to learn very basic procedures. A large-scale orienteering map, or a picture-style map that depicts the features in the area, can be used.

ROGAINE

The name comes from the phrase: "Rugged Outdoor Group Activity Involving Navigation and Endurance." Competitors always have a partner, and they locate markers in any order they wish, as in score orienteering. The area of competition usually is large in size, and often maps with less detail than orienteering maps are used. The common time limit is 24 hours, but there are short versions lasting 3, 6, and 12 hours, as well as a long 48 hour version.

Map Hiking

This is a term used to describe recreational, rather than competitive, orienteering. Map hikers can go out on courses in a group or alone, they are not timed, and at large competitions their courses may be different from the competition courses. It is recommended that each person in a Map Hike group always have their own personal copy of the map; otherwise, they will just be hiking and not orienteering.

TEACHING CONSIDERATIONS

1. Orienteering is best learned by doing. Encourage beginners to experience navigational problem solving as soon as possible by getting them out on a course after only brief classroom instruction.
2. Limit the amount of lecture time each period to allow sufficient time for practice of techniques.
3. Begin activities in a familiar setting with a simple orienteering course for a group or partners, but be sure that each individual has his or her own personal map. Later, have students attempt more difficult courses in less-familiar surroundings.
4. Allow time at the end of each lesson for discussion of route choices, techniques, and strategies.
5. Consider doing "Assignment Orienteering." This interdisciplinary approach can incorporate many school subjects into an orienteering format. A standard orienteering course is used, but once an individual or group arrives at a control, an assignment must be accomplished. The task can be related to school subjects or to orienteering and may require an instructor at the control.

GLOSSARY

aiming off Aiming to one side of the precise target in order to avoid making a wrong turn. This technique is most often used when the marker is on a linear feature that is being approached at a right angle.

angle of declination The angle representing the difference between north and magnetic north.

attack point An easily located feature from which an orienteer begins to navigate carefully to a control.

bearing A direction to travel, measured in degrees from north and determined by a map and compass.

beeline Straight line from one point to another.

check-off feature An easily identifiable feature on the map and in the terrain that can be mentally checked off as it is passed.

collecting or catching feature A long or large feature that will "collect" you when you are nearing a control or "catch" you when you have gone too far beyond a control.

contour interval The vertical distance between contour lines on a topographical map. On orienteering maps the interval is generally 3 or 5 meters.

control A prism-shaped, usually orange-and-white marker, made of fabric and wire, that is hung in the terrain to mark the site that is identified on the map as the control point. A patterned punch, or electronic punch box and a control code number, will be provided with each control marker.

control code Identification numbers that are attached to the control marker. Codes are indicated in the control description list for the course and will enable the competitor to insure that they have arrived at the correct control.

control descriptions A brief description of the precise locations of the control markers. They are printed on a sheet and carried by participants during the event to assist in locating and identifying the correct control features on their courses. The control description provides information that is not available from the map, such as the code numbers on the marker, the size of the feature, and where, on the feature, the marker is placed. Descriptions are given with international symbols, but beginner courses will have descriptions written out in English.

control extension Plotting a course to a larger adjacent feature rather than to the easy-to-miss, smaller actual target.

fartlek Swedish word meaning speed play; a form of running training incorporating increased efforts over various distances at different paces.

fight Impenetrable forest, shown as dark green on an orienteering map.

finish symbol A double circle, marked on the map, which marks the location of the finish area for a course.

form line An intermediate or extra contour line showing ground detail. It is drawn with a dashed brown line.

handrail A linear feature, or a series of features, running parallel to one's direction of travel and thereby serving as a handy navigational aid.

index contour Every fifth contour line is drawn with a heavy line. This serves as a guide for the eye and makes the shape of the ground more obvious.

interval training Repeated fast-paced runs of 100 yards to three-quarters of a mile interspersed with recovery walks or jogs.

knoll A small hill—shown by a brown dot, a small brown ring, or a form line.

leg A section of the course between two controls.

legend A written description and examples of the symbols that appear on the map.

magnetic north lines North lines that are shown on all orienteering maps, so that the compass can be used accurately. Magnetic North is slightly different than True North.

master map This map shows the course so that competitors can copy from it to their own blank map. Often courses are pre-printed and there is no need for hand copying.

oriented map A map where the symbols on the map are in the same position as the features they represent on the ground. The map can be oriented either by visibly comparing the map directly with the terrain or by using the compass and the map's north arrows.

pace counting Counting the number of double steps it takes to travel 100 meters.

precise or fine compass When extra care is taken in following the compass reading.

punch A pin punch found at each control for competitors to use to mark their punch card. It is a bent piece of strong plastic about 4 inches long with a distinctive set of needles at one end. The pattern of needles is different at each control.

punch card A card with numbered boxes in which to place the punch pattern from each control. Printed on the card will be competitor information, including start time. Punching the card is how the orienteer verifies his or her visit to each control on the course.

reentrant An elongated, sloping valley. It can be shallow or deep and water would flow downward through it.

rootstock A mound of soil that has been raised up around the roots of a fallen tree. Generally the mound should be at least 1 meter high to be considered for mapping.

rough compass Running on a compass bearing without being precise in keeping to the line of travel.

saddle A low point on a ridge connecting two summits.

spur A narrow, sloping ridge.

start triangle An even-sided triangle drawn on the map to indicate the starting point for a course. The precise starting spot indicated on the map may also be marked by a large triangle on the ground.

thumbing A technique used to mark one's location on the map. As the orienteer moves through the terrain, he moves his thumb position on the map to reflect his progress.

topographical map The graphic depiction of natural and man-made features that shows their relative position to each other and their elevation.

SUGGESTED READINGS

Boga, S. 1997. *Orienteering: The sport of navigating with map and compass.* Mechanicsburg, PA: Stackpole Books. Contains information on map and compass reading, conditioning and nutrition, and rules for competitors.

Bratt, I. 2002. *Orienteering.* Mechanicsburg, PA: Stackpole Books.

Garrett, M. 1996. *Orienteering and map games for teachers.* Forest Park, GA: U.S. Orienteering Federation. A stimulating set of orienteering lesson plans and game ideas especially for elementary school teachers.

Lowry, R., and Sidney, K. 1989. *Orienteering skills and strategies.* 3rd ed. North York, Ontario: Orienteering Ontario. A textbook intended for middle to high school ages, but good for all levels.

McNeill, C., et al. 1998. *Teaching orienteering.* 2nd ed. Champaign, IL: Human Kinetics. Encyclopedic collection of orienteering lesson plans and exercises.

Renfrew, T. 1997. *Orienteering.* Champaign, IL: Human Kinetics.

Seidman, D., and Cleveland, P. 2001. *The essential wilderness navigator.* 2nd ed. Camden, ME: Ragged Mountain Press.

RESOURCES

Books

Bratt, I. 2002. *Orienteering.* Mechanicsburg, PA: Stackpole Books.

Davenport, G. 2006. *Advanced outdoor navigation: Basics and beyond.* Guilford, CT: Falcon Press.

Kjellström, B. 1994. *Be expert with map and compass.* Hoboken, NJ: Wiley Publishing Co.

Mattern, J. 2004. *Orienteering.* Mankato, MN: Capstone Press.

McNeill, C., Renfrew, T., Cory-Wright, J. 1998. *Teaching orienteering.* 2nd ed. Champaign, IL: Human Kinetics.

Palmer, P. 1997. *The complete orienteering manual.* Ramsbury, UK: Crowood Press.

Films and Videotapes

Cassone, C. 1998. *Orienteering—all welcome.* USA, revised 1998, 111/2-minute VHS tape.

Daniels, J. 1995. *Orienteering—a map and a compass,* 30-minute VHS tape. Video production: J. Daniels Video RR#1 Box 265A Wapwallopen, PA 18660

Jones, K. 1990. *Finding your way in the world.* Minneapolis, The Richard Diercks Company, Inc. International Film Bureau, 332 S. Michigan Ave., Chicago, IL 60604. Orienteering Service/USA, PO. Box 547, North La Porte, IN 46350. Silva, 2466 State Road 39 N, North La Porte, IN 46350.

Organizations

United States Orienteering Federation, P.O. Box 1444, Forest Park, GA 30298. Tel: 404-363-2110.

Map and Information Office, U.S. Geological and Geodetic Survey, Washington, DC 02042. USGS topo maps can be ordered from this agency. For areas west of the Mississippi River, write to Western Distribution Branch, USGS, Building 41, Box 25286, Federal Center, Denver, CO 80225. For areas east of the Mississippi River, write to Eastern Distribution Branch, USGS, 1200 S. Ends St., Arlington, VA 22209.

WEB SITES

A great deal of information about orienteering is available on the Internet. The simplest way of finding this information is to go to the U.S. Orienteering Federation's home page (http://www .us.orienteering.org) where you will find useful categories:

Education—provides information on course setting, event organization, and other topics, including a special section for teachers.

Orienteering Gear—list of equipment vendors for online orders.

Club Resources—how to start a club, organize an event, and conduct an orienteering clinic.

Links—takes you to countless orienteering pages and sites for other branches of orienteering such as Trail-O, Bike-O, and Canoe-O.

A list of specific sites follows:

Aerial Photo Site— http://terraserver.homeadvisor.msn.com/default.asp

Bay Area Orienteering Club, San Francisco: http://www.baoc.org

International Orienteering Federation: http://www.orienteering.org/

International ROGAINE Web site
http://rogaine.asn.au/ara/irf/irf.htm

OCAD—mapmaking software
http://www.ocad.com/

Trail O
http://www.trailo.org

United States Orienteering Federation
http://www.us.orienteering.org

U.S. Geological Survey
http://www.usgs.gov/index.html

Finally, if you go to an Internet search engine such as Google and type in "orienteering," there will be a vast selection of topics available.

Pickle-Ball

22

After completing this chapter, the reader should be able to:

- Have a basic knowledge of the origin of Pickle-Ball
- Understand the equipment used in the game
- Perform and demonstrate the fundamental skills for effective playing
- Know the principles of strategy for competitive play

HISTORY

The original purpose of Pickle-Ball was to provide a game that the whole family might enjoy regardless of athletic ability or strength. In 1965, Joel Pritchard, the congressman from Washington's First Congressional District, and Bill Bell, a successful businessman, returned to Pritchard's home after playing 18 holes of golf and found their families sitting around complaining that there was nothing to do. Pritchard's home was located on the resort island of Bainbridge, a short ferry ride west of Seattle, Washington.

There was an old badminton court nearby, so Pritchard and Bell decided that would be the activity for the afternoon and began trying to find usable equipment for the children. They could not find a full set of playable equipment, so they began to improvise with what was available. They cut off the shafts of the damaged racquets, found a perforated plastic ball, and began to play. The players had trouble hitting the ball with the short-handled, small-headed racquet, so the determined fathers came up with four solid wooden paddles that are very similar to the official paddles of today.

At first the badminton net was placed at regulation height of 5 feet, and the players volleyed the balls back and forth over the net with pleasure and excitement. The players soon realized that the ball would bounce well and true on the solid asphalt surface of the court. By allowing the ball to bounce, a new dimension was added to the game. The next morning upon waking, Pritchard and Bell discovered that the women and children were already outside playing the new game. The net had been lowered to approximately the height of a tennis net. The next weekend, Barney McCallum came out for a visit and was introduced to the game. He was instantly hooked. They all enjoyed just hitting the ball over the net but soon became bored. They decided it was time to decide on some rules for the game. The original purpose was for the whole family to play together, so this was a prime consideration as rules were formulated. They relied heavily on the rules of badminton. In the first version, only the serving team could score points; and the service was alternated so that first one opposing player and then the other received it. The server was allowed to step over the baseline with one foot so that a tree in one corner of the court would not obstruct the delivery. (Only one foot had to remain behind the baseline before the ball was hit.) As in badminton, only one serve was allowed and the paddle had to meet the ball below the server's waist. The competitive players soon discovered that the best position was right on top of the net. From here it was very easy to put the ball away with a volley or smash. They decided that some control was needed at the net, so they created the "penalty zone" between the short service line of the badminton court and the net and ruled that no volleying could take place by a player standing within it. Only after a short shot had bounced in that area of the court could the player enter the penalty area to make a return. This new rule controlled the net player's advantage and actually contributed to the making of the game. Later the line was moved back to 7 feet (6.4 m) from the net and the area renamed the non-volley zone.

The Pritchards had a dog named Pickles who became interested in the new game. He would lie and watch the game from a distance, and when any loose ball would come his direction, he would take the ball and disappear with it. Hence, the name Pickle-Ball. During the following winter, Barney McCallum kept wanting to play the new game. He realized that the street in front of his house was about the width of a Pickle-Ball court, and a few minutes later, he determined that the street was 22 feet (20.1 m) wide. He and his son David lined off a court and set up net posts that could be tipped over if any vehicles came by. Not long after, another innovation was added to the game by McCallum, the double-bounce rule. This rule stated that the first opposing team could hit its first shot only after the ball had first bounced on the playing surface. The receiving team had to let the ball bounce and the serving team had to let the return of serve bounce. Only after these two bounces happened could the ball be volleyed in the rally. This diminished the advantage of the serving team and gave some edge to the receiving team, as they could take the net by executing a deep approach shot when receiving the serve.

During the winter of 1967, the first permanent Pickle-Ball court in the United States was constructed in Joel Pritchard's backyard in Seattle, Washington. Soon after, another followed at a neighbor's house across the street from Barney McCallum's. From 1965 to 1973, the game was played faithfully by the founding fathers and friends with fewer than 10 courts established during the eight-year span. The most effective advertising for this new game was word of mouth, as most people who played it enjoyed it and told their friends about it. Some of the local high schools and colleges added the game to their physical education programs. They already had badminton courts, so Pickle-Ball was easily added.

In 1972 a corporation was formed to protect the new creation, although the three original stockholders did not expect to give their full time to the business. The corporation published playing rules and copyrighted them, and the name Pickle-Ball was registered. By the mid-1970s, Pickle-Ball had spread into almost all high schools and junior colleges in the Seattle area. The Seattle Parks and Recreation Department also included the sport in its citywide athletic programs. Pickle-Ball is now played worldwide in schools, camps, YMCAs, Boys and Girls Clubs, health clubs, churches, senior centers, and many other venues.

Pickle-Ball is presently being introduced at state physical education conventions and advertised in recreation and physical education journals, and equipment is carried by the majority of school supply companies.

EQUIPMENT

Paddle

The paddles are presently made of plywood as well as composite material. The paddle's overall length should not exceed 15½ inches (39.4 cm), with a maximum head width of 8 inches (20.3 cm) and a maximum weight of 13 ounces (404 g). The head of the paddle is distinctly squared off rather than oval. The head may not be strung, nor any perforations or texturing materials allowed on the surface (Figure 22.1).

Ball

This sport's projectile is a plastic sphere with small holes. The maximum diameter of the ball is 3 inches (7.6 cm). The Dura 56 ball is a seamless plastic polyball that has been specially designed and manufactured for Pickle-Ball use. The rotationally molded ball can be used indoors or outdoors on any hard surface. This unique ball will provide truer flight and extended durability when compared to other plastic balls (Figure 22.1).

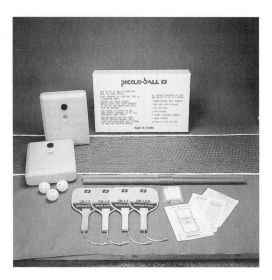

Figure 22.1. Pickle-Ball equipment.

Net

The official Pickle-Ball net is 21 feet by 30 inches (6.4 m by 76.2 cm). The net is constructed of quality knotless nylon with ⅜ inch (.95 cm) cord running through the top binding. A badminton net may also be used for Pickle-Ball play (Figure 22.1).

COURT

The official rules of Pickle-Ball set the dimensions of the court to be 20 feet by 44 feet (6.1 m by 13.4 m), which also happen to be the dimensions of the badminton doubles court. The same size court is used for both singles and doubles. The court is divided by a net that is 36 inches (.91 m) high on the sides of the court and that slopes to 34 inches (.86 m) in the middle. The non-volley zone is the area 7 feet (2.1 m) on each side of the net. The centerline divides the area behind the non-volley zone into two equal service courts. The short service line on the official badminton court is 6 feet, 6 inches (1.98 m) from the net, but this line may be used for the non-volley zone when Pickle-Ball is played on the badminton court in the gymnasium. There should be space of at least 3 to 5 feet (.91 to 1.5 m) beyond the end lines and 1 to 2 feet (.3 to .6 m) beyond the sides to provide for adequate player movement (Figure 22.2). All Pickle-Ball equipment and publications may be obtained from Pickle-Ball, Incorporated, 4700 9th Avenue NW, Seattle, WA 98107; phone: 206-784-4723.

RULES AND SCORING

Serve

Player must keep one foot behind the back line when serving. The serve is made underhanded. The paddle must pass below the waist. The server must hit the serve. The service is made diagonally crosscourt and must clear the non-volley

Official Pickle-Ball court

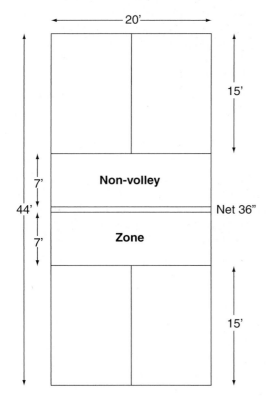

Figure 22.2. Pickle-Ball court.

zone. Only one serve attempt is allowed, except if the ball touches the net on the serve and lands in the proper service court. Then the serve may be taken over. If the server attempts to serve the ball and misses the ball with the paddle, it shall count as an attempted serve. In doubles, at the start of each new game, the first serving team is allowed only one fault before giving up the ball to the opponents. Thereafter both members of each team will serve and fault before the ball is turned over to the opposing team. When the receiving team wins the serve, the player in the right-hand court will always start play.

Volley

To volley a ball means to hit it in the air without first letting it bounce. All volleying must be done with player's feet behind the non-volley zone line. Note: It is a fault if the player steps over the line on his volley follow-through.

Double Bounce Rule

Each side must play the first shot off the bounce. That is, the receiving team must let the serve bounce, and the serving team must let the return of serve bounce before playing it. After the two bounces have occurred, the ball can be either volleyed or played off the bounce.

Faults

Hitting the ball out of bounds
Not clearing the net
Stepping into the non-volley zone and volleying the ball
Volleying the ball before it has bounced once on each side of the net

Scoring

A side shall score a point only when serving. In doubles, a player who is serving shall continue to do so until a fault is made by his or her team. The game is played to 11 points; however, a team must win by 2 points.

Determining Serving Team

Players may toss a coin or rally a ball until a fault is made. Winner of the toss or rally has the option of serving first or not serving first.

Other Rules

In doubles, if a player serves out of turn, or from the wrong service court, or receives in the wrong court, and that side wins the rally, it shall be called a let, providing that such let be claimed before the next succeeding service is delivered. If a player standing in the wrong service court takes the service, and that side wins the rally, it shall be called a let, provided that such let be claimed before the next succeeding service is delivered. If in any of the above cases the side at fault loses the rally, the mistake shall stand and the player's position shall not be corrected during the remainder of the game.

The server may not serve until the opponent is ready, but the opponent shall be deemed ready if a return of service is attempted.

If a player is playing a ball that has bounced in the non-volley zone and touches the net with the paddle or any part of the body, it shall constitute a fault for that player.

A service fault occurs when the server swings the paddle with the intent of striking the ball but misses. However, the server may toss the ball into the air and then catch it or allow it to fall to the court without penalty, so long as no attempt to deliver that ball is made.

The server must take up a position with at least one foot behind the baseline without touching that line, and between an imaginary extension of the centerline and the sideline. Both feet must be inside the imaginary extensions.

In doubles, only the player served to may receive the service, but should the ball touch, or be struck by the receiver's partner, the serving side scores the point.

A fault is called when a player is hit by the ball whether standing inside or outside the court boundaries.

A ball seemingly going out-of-bounds must be allowed to hit the floor out-of-bounds. It is a fault to catch the ball and claim that it is going out.

FUNDAMENTAL SKILLS AND TECHNIQUES

Grips

Eastern grip

To position your hand for this grip, hold the paddle in the nondominant hand with the hitting surface perpendicular to the floor. Slide the hand onto the paddle as you would to shake hands with someone. The right forefinger is spread slightly away wrapped around the handle to make contact with or lie close to the inside of your middle finger.

The paddle should be lying across the palm and fingers with the thumb and index finger forming a V on the top of the handle with the wrist slightly to the left. Spread your fingers comfortably around the handle.

Western grip

This grip is used primarily to impart topspin on the ball during the forehand drive. To obtain the western forehand grip, simply lay the paddle on the floor and then pick it up by the handle. The hand will be approximately an eighth turn to the right of the eastern forehand.

Continental grip

This grip is midway between the eastern forehand and backhand. No change is made from the forehand to the backhand, thus offering a distinct advantage in an exchange of rapid strokes at the net when volleying.

The Ready Position

The efficiency with which you return the ball is dependent on how you prepare to stroke the ball. The ready position allows you to move in any direction for the return of the opponent's shots. The feet should be spread to be shoulder width and the knees slightly flexed with the weight on the balls of the feet. The back should be fairly straight and inclined slightly forward, head up, and eyes on the opponent. The paddle should be held in front of the body about waist level and pointed toward your opponent.

Court Coverage

Good footwork means moving into position in a way that enables you to take an efficient hitting stance. An open stance is when the outside foot is closer to the net than the inside foot and the body is facing the net. A closed stance is when the forward foot is several inches nearer the sideline than the back foot.

The Forehand Drive

The forehand drive is actually a natural hitting movement, similar to batting a baseball. The ball is played from the paddle side of the body after it has bounced once. If the ball is allowed to bounce twice before it is returned, a fault is called. The term "not up" should be used when this happens. From the ready position, pivot toward the sideline and simultaneously draw the paddle back at waist level. This must be a complete pivot with the feet, hips, and shoulders all facing the sideline. Beginners often fail to do this movement fully.

The Backhand Drive

Basically the backhand drive involves the same mechanics as the forehand, but it is executed on the opposite side of the body, the nonpaddle side (Figure 22.3).

Ball Spin

The kind and amount of spin on the ball are determined by the position of the paddle and the direction in which the paddle is traveling upon contact with the ball. Understanding spin and the effect it has on the flight and bounce of the ball will assist you in your stroke production and in preparing for groundstroke and service returns. When you are able to control ball spin and can also play the spinning ball after it bounces, you will be well on your way to achieving a well-rounded game.

Serves

To put the ball in play, you must use an underhand motion and the paddle must pass below the waist. You must hit the ball in the air and keep one foot behind the back line when serving. You are not allowed to bounce the ball and then hit it. Use a forehand grip for the service.

Drive serve

A hard, deep drive serve will keep the opponent at the baseline and on the defense. A poor return of service will allow the server to take the attacking position. To execute this serve, take a forward stride position with the dominant foot forward and at least one foot behind the end line.

Lob serve

The lob serve can be used for a change of pace and will also keep the receiver at the baseline on the defense. The ball will have a high bounce and be difficult to return effectively.

The Lob

The drive down the line, a short crosscourt, or a lob, can be used when your opponent rushes the net. There are two types of lobs, the offensive and the defensive. The offensive lob is used to force the net player back to the baseline into a less advantageous position. The defensive lob usually provides time for the player drawn out of position by an opponent's placement to recover and get back into position on the court.

Volley

The volley is used to play the ball before the bounce and from a position just behind the non-volley zone of the court. The basic volleying position is about 1 foot behind

Figure 22.3. Executing a backhand drive.

the non-volley zone. With the volley, you are trying to stop the progress of the ball rather than slam the ball back over the net.

The Drop Shot and the Drop Volley

Drop shots and drop volleys add excitement and flavor to the game and are necessary for you to be a complete player. They require a very soft touch and knowledge of when and when not to use them to be successful. A baseline player may be drawn to the net, a slow player may be caught deep in the court, and an opponent may be tired out by tactical use of the drop shot. This shot is usually attempted when you are in a good position on the court, usually about midcourt. The drop shot is executed after the ball has bounced. It is gently hit with underspin so that it will just barely clear the net and land in the non-volley zone close to the net. The drop volley is used when you are at the net. This is also a surprise shot and should be used carefully. It is hit with underspin so that it barely clears the net and lands short in the opponent's non-volley zone.

The Half-Volley

The half-volley is a defensive shot when the ball is hit immediately after the bounce. The ball has usually been hit directly at your feet in the backcourt, and you do not have time to get into position to drive the ball.

Smash

The smash is used to hit the ball downward with authority and placement from midcourt prior to the bounce.

STRATEGY

The Singles Game

The serve

The most advantageous positions from which to serve are near the centerline when serving into the even court, and a couple of feet from the centerline for the odd court. Make a decision before your service about how and where you are going to serve the ball. Generally there are three placements for the serve: (1) deep to the far corner in both courts,

(2) down the middle close to the centerline, and (3) right at the receiver. Vary the pace and the placements of your service; do not let your opponent be able to guess how and where you are going to serve the ball. Do not try to serve the ball too close to the lines; give yourself some room, about 1 foot inside the lines of the service court.

The return of service

The return of service is an important element in the game of Pickle-Ball and should be practiced by all players. The receiver must allow the ball to bounce before returning it. The receiver should assume a position of readiness: the head up, hips and knees flexed slightly, weight on the balls of the feet. The feet should be spread a little more than shoulder width with the paddle held in front of the body at about shoulder height. Your position on the court must allow freedom to move wide for serves hit in the far corners or toward the centerline for serves hit in the middle. The distance you stand from the net is determined by the speed of your opponent's serve. For a very fast, hard serve, you must take a deep position behind the baseline so that you can prepare for the return. Also for the fast serve, you must stroke the ball with a firm wrist and utilize the power that the server has already applied to the ball. Most serve returns should be hit deep to the server's forehand or backhand corners. Hard serves that come wide to the forehand in the even court and wide to the backhand in the odd court are easily returned with crosscut shots, since they allow time to play the ball and give a better angle for shot placement.

Net play

Due to the small size of the Pickle-Ball court, net play becomes a very important facet of the singles game. A player can control the pace of the game from the net and gain a distinct advantage. However, you must remember the non-volley zone of the court and that a player cannot step into this area on the follow-through of a stroke. A player can move into the area if the ball has already bounced but should retreat back to a legal position to play the next ball. An advance to the net must be made carefully and be well planned. It should always follow a forcing shot that has put your opponent on the defensive. Most opportunities to rush the net follow short returns by your opponent. A deep placement to one of the corners, usually the backhand, will prepare you for your advance to the net. As you move to the net, drift toward the side of your placement to bisect the angle of the return. The wider your shot, the more you must crowd the sideline. Moving to the net following an approach shot must be done quickly, keeping your paddle in readiness on the way. Watch your opponent as you move to the net, and as the opponent is about to make the return, you should pause and be ready to move in any direction for the ball. If you are caught in a poor net position, you may be forced to hit a defensive volley or half-volley. If this happens, put the volley deep down the middle to cut down the angle of return.

Baseline play

Baseline play is very basic to Pickle-Ball. Without good baseline play, the net rusher will have difficulty in going to the net. Strategy from the baseline begins with simply keeping the ball in play. Let your opponent make the error. When playing from the baseline, you must also learn to keep the ball deep. Any ball that you return short will allow your opponent to be aggressive and take the net. This does not mean that you have to hit the ball as hard as possible, but just keep it as close to the baseline as possible. Baseline strategy involves, first of all, running your opponent from side to side. This will cause the opponent to anticipate moving from side to side, and then you can use the element of surprise by hitting to the same side twice in a row. You may also hit balls to one side of the court and then send one deep to the opposite corner. When your opponent seems to play both sides of the court well, you will want to play the ball deep down the middle of the court.

The Doubles Game

Some basic doubles tactics should be followed that will lead to exciting, well-played games. The team that has control of the net will in most instances win the game. The offense in doubles is built around the serve, volley, and smash, with the lob being the major defensive stroke. The receiving team begins with one player at the net, and the partner who receives the serve will want to follow the return to the net and locate even with the partner already at the net. Because of the double bounce rule, both members of the serving team must remain in the backcourt until the ball has bounced twice; they must let the ball bounce in their court one time before going to the net to volley the ball. The serving team must be prepared to lob its first return if the opponents are aggressive at gaining the net. The serving team must play the ball down the middle to create confusion for the opponents.

The serve

The game of doubles is based on positioning, and the receiving team has an advantage over the serving team since the partner of the receiver is already at the net at the beginning of each point. The net player has the responsibility of guarding the sideline but should move to the center to cut off any weak return. The appropriate position at the net is about 2 feet (1.8 m) behind the non-volley zone and about 3 feet (2.7 m) inside the sideline. The net player must not slowly drift toward the center of the court during a rally, giving the opponent an opening down the line for a winner. The server should take a position halfway between the centerline and the sideline on the server's side of the court, and on or slightly behind the baseline. The serving team must remain in the backcourt until it has played the ball after it has bounced one time (double bounce rule).

The return of service

The return of service in doubles is very important. It may help the receiving team to gain control of the net, since the return must be allowed to bounce on the serving side of the court. The depth and strength of the service will determine how deep the receiver will stand. The receiver should be ready to play a forehand or backhand serve. The partner of the receiver should take a position about 2 feet (1.8 m) behind the non-volley zone and 3 feet (2.7 m) inside the sideline. The receiver should come to the net, even with the partner, on the return of service to gain the offense position.

Net play

The total strategy for doubles is to gain possession of the net by both partners. The receiving team has the advantage to begin each point and must protect it with good return of service shots. The serving team's best opportunity to gain the net is to force the receiving team away from the net with a well-placed lob over their heads on their first return of the ball after it has bounced. The lob should be hit either to the backhand corner or up the middle to create confusion between the two partners as to who will return the shot. A team that has been pushed away from the net will many times lob the ball back, hoping to regain the net position. The serving team may also try to gain the net with a well-placed drop shot just over the net into the non-volley zone on its first hit after the serve. The opponents must let the ball bounce in the non-volley zone before hitting it and will probably have to hit the ball up on the return. This will allow a possible put-away by the opposing team, which has gone to the net following the drop shot. This well-placed drop shot may also cause the opponents to foot fault by trying to play the ball before it bounces and stepping into the non-volley zone on the hit or follow-through. The basic net position for both partners is about 2 feet (1.8 m) behind the non-volley zone and midway between the sideline and the centerline.

Baseline play

All play from the baseline should be in preparation for an advance to the net. This is usually accomplished by a lob, by a low crosscut return, or when both opponents are confused as to who will play the ball. Many times a drive right at a net player will result in a point because of lack of a quick reaction by that player.

ETIQUETTE

1. Dress according to the rules established by the center or school where you play.
2. Be on time for your game.
3. Do not distract other players by walking behind their court during play. Wait until the point is finished.
4. Always know your opponent. If you have never met, introduce yourself in a friendly manner.
5. Take a brief warm-up period before each game. All practice serves should be taken by all players before any points are played.
6. Make sure that your opponent is ready before serving.
7. It is the server's responsibility to keep score and to announce the score clearly to the opponent before serving each point. The server's score should be given first.
8. Do not return a serve that is obviously out. Let it go past you or block it into the net so that it will not be in the way. Returning faulty serves is a very discourteous action in Pickle-Ball.
9. Make calls on your side of the net fairly, giving your opponent the benefit of the doubt on close calls. A ball should be considered good unless it is clearly seen to be out.
10. Retrieve balls from adjacent courts by waiting until the point is over and then politely saying "thank you" or "ball please."
11. Return balls from adjacent courts by waiting until play has stopped and then tossing them softly and accurately to the nearest player.
12. Stop play immediately and play a "let" if a ball enters your playing area.
13. Recognize a good play by your partner or opponent.
14. Pickle-Ball is a game of concentration. Talk only when it pertains to the game or while changing sides.
15. Quickly collect all balls on your side of the court after each point. Hustling after stray balls makes the game go much faster.
16. Control your feelings on the court. Abide by the rules and always display sportsmanlike conduct.
17. Cracked balls should be replaced as quickly as possible.

TEACHING CONSIDERATIONS

1. For large beginning classes, have players practice hitting the ball against the wall 10 times. This exercise gives them practice hitting forehands, backhands, and the like by themselves. They progress to the net when they can hit 10 in a row.
2. Use a modified two-bounce-limit rule for beginning classes or less-fit players.
3. Have players feed the ball to each other using half the court. This method encourages practicing technique and provides numerous practice trials.
4. Volley the ball in the air with a partner. The goal is to see how many times you can hit the ball back and forth keeping the ball in the air. This drill is good for eye-hand coordination.
5. Score on every serve. The side-out rule can be modified so that a point is scored on every serve. One player serves for a total of five serves, then the opponent serves for five serves until one player scores 10 points.
6. Provide challenge drills, modified games, games or tournaments set up before class.

GLOSSARY

ace A serve that the receiver cannot get to and that scores a point for the server, a winner.

all When the score is tied, as in 6–all.

approach shot Usually a groundstroke hit deep into the opponent's court, allowing the hitter to go to the net.

backcourt The area around the baseline.

backhand A stroke used to play the ball on the nonpaddle side of the body.

backspin Spin applied to the ball by hitting down behind it, causing it to spin in the opposite direction of its flight.

change of pace The strategy of changing the speed of the ball from stroke to stroke.

chop A movement in which the paddle is drawn down and under the ball, imparting backspin to the ball.

crosscourt shot Placing the ball from one side of the court across the net to the side diagonally opposite.

deep A shot that lands within the court near the baseline.

doubles A game played between two teams of two players: two men, two women, or a man and a woman in mixed doubles.

down the line shot A ball that travels low over the net and parallel to the sideline.

drive A ball hit after the bounce with medium speed so that it will travel to the end of the opposite court.

drop shot A ball hit softly with backspin so that it just clears the net and lands very close to it in the non-volley zone.

earned point A point won by the skill of the player rather than by error of an opponent.

error A point lost because of poor play, not caused by your opponent. Many more points are lost on errors than are won on placements or on earned points.

even court The right court, because when serving from this court, an even number of points have been played in the game. Partners will be on the side of the court on which they started the game.

face The hitting surface of the paddle. A closed face is when the hitting surface is turned down toward the floor. An open face is when the hitting surface is turned toward the ceiling. A flat face is when the hitting surface is perpendicular to the floor.

fault A served ball that does not land within the proper service court; sometimes referred to as an illegal serve or return.

foot fault Stepping into the non-volley zone before the served ball bounces.

forcing shot Usually a fast, deep, and well-placed attacking shot designed to force a weak return or an error by your opponent.

forehand A stroke used to play the ball on the paddle side of the body.

game Completed when one side has won 11 points, with at least a 2-point lead.

ground stroke Hitting the ball after it has bounced.

half-volley Usually a defensive stroke in which the ball is contacted immediately after it begins to rise from a bounce.

head The part of the paddle used to hit the ball.

kitchen Another an name for the non-volley zone.

let A point that must be replayed.

let serve A ball that hits the top of the net on the serve and lands in the correct service court; must be replayed.

lob A high, arching shot over the reach of the net player that lands near the opponent's baseline.

mixed doubles Team composed of male and female partners.

net game Strategy where the player usually advances to the net to use the volley and smash to end the point.

non-volley zone The area 7 feet (6.4 m) on either side of the net; the player may not step into this area to play a ball before it has bounced. The player also may not step into this area on the follow-through of a stroke.

not up Allowing the ball to bounce twice before returning it. This is a fault.

odd court The left court, because when serving from this court, an odd number of points have been played. Partners will be on the opposite sides of the court from which they started the game.

passing shot To send the ball quickly over the net past an opponent's reach.

poach Usually in doubles when the net player moves across the court to cut off a ball that would normally be played by his partner.

put-away A ball hit so well that the opponent cannot return it; a winner.

rally The continuation of play after the serve; the players keep the ball in play for several strokes.

rush the net A style of play where the player hits an approach shot and takes the net to be in a better position to win the point.

serve The underhand stroke used to put the ball in play at the beginning of each point.

service foot fault A service that is illegal; usually the server fails to keep one foot behind the end line.

singles A game played between two players.

smash An overhead stroke used to put the ball away.

spin the paddle At the beginning of a game, a paddle is spun so that it will land flat on the floor. The nonspinner will call which side the paddle will fall on. The winner of the spin may choose to serve or receive first, or which court to play in. The other player or team then makes the remaining choice.

topspin Spin applied to the ball by bringing the paddle up behind it, causing the ball to spin in the direction of its flight.

volley Hitting a ball before it bounces.

SUGGESTED READINGS

Curtis, J. 1998. *Pickle-Ball for player and teacher.* 3rd ed. Stamford, CT: Wadsworth/Thomson Learning. Includes information on the origin and development of the game, basic skills, rules, and tactics and strategy.

Free Catalog and Brochure can be obtained from the following: Pickle-Ball, Inc. 810 NW 45th, Seattle, WA 98107. Phone: 206-632-0119 or 1-800-377-9915.

Friedenberg, M. 1999. *The official pickleball handbook.* Seattle, WA: PB Master.

Leach, G. 2008. *The art of pickleball: Techniques and strategies for everyone.* Ban Harber, ME: Acadia Publishing.

WEB SITES

www.pickleball.com
www.pickleballcentral.com
www.pickleballstuff.com
www.thepickleballstore.com

23

Racquetball, Paddleball, and Handball

After completing this chapter, the reader should be able to:

- Understand the similarities and differences among racquetball, handball, and paddleball
- Select equipment properly
- Recognize the court markings for these sports
- Understand the rules of scoring procedures for games involving two, three, or four players
- Execute the basic skills, including court positioning and various shots and serves
- Display a knowledge of offensive and defensive strategies
- Recognize and use racquetball, handball, and paddleball terms correctly and instruct a group of beginning players in the fundamentals of the sports

The popularity of racquetball as a recreational activity increased significantly in the mid-1960s and has been a popular pastime ever since. The game is a variation of handball and paddleball, activities that have long been popular. The popularity of racquetball can be partially explained by the fact that even beginners can achieve early success in contacting and placing the ball using a stringed racquet, whereas the skills are more difficult to master in handball and paddleball. Although the rules for all three activities are similar, each has its advocates, claiming their favorite to be the best of the three.

HISTORY

Handball

There is evidence that handball originated in Rome and that it is one of the oldest of sports. Ireland is credited with first developing the game and holding the first championship tournament. John Kavanagh of York, England, was the leading player and champion in 1840, the same year handball was introduced to the United States.

The first international match was played in 1887 for a purse of $1,000. The match was between Phil Casey of Brooklyn and John Lawler, the Irish champion. Casey won seven straight games and the championship. The matches were played on a four-wall court. Casey retained the championship for many years and was called the father of the game in the United States. In 1897 the Amateur Athletic Union (AAU) sponsored the first American tournament, won by Michael Egan.

In the early years of the game, four-wall courts were used. Later, around 1913, a one-wall court game on the beaches of New York became popular. This was a modification of the four-wall game. The use of one wall brought the game outdoors. A three-wall court is sometimes used for play in which abbreviated side walls abutting the front wall permit corner shots and some sidewall shots.

The first four-wall championship was held in Los Angeles in 1919, and the first one-wall AAU Championship was held in New York in 1924. The first YMCA National Championship was held in Cleveland in 1925.

The AAU, the YMCA, the United States Handball Association (formed in 1951), and the Jewish Community Recreation Association hold joint regional and national championships. Now, the USHA holds annual state, regional, and national tournaments for the open and age-group divisions for juniors, males, and females.

Paddleball and Racquetball

The game of paddleball is generally believed to have been formulated at the University of Michigan in the early 1920s. The rules are similar to those for handball except that a wooden paddle is used instead of the hand and a different type of ball is used. Racquetball, which developed from paddleball in 1949, has rules similar to paddleball except that a stringed racquet is used. Racquetball is a much faster game than paddleball. There is more emphasis on the serve, and the rallies are shorter in racquetball. However, paddleball is still popular because its longer rallies provide excellent physical conditioning, and there is an emphasis on control and placement of the ball. The USA Racquetball Association (USAR) conducts annual state, regional, and national tournaments for the open and age-group divisions for juniors, males, and females in racquetball.

NATURE OF THE GAMES

A rubber ball is batted alternately by the players against the front wall of a one-, three-, or four-wall court. The object is to cause the ball to rebound to such a position and in such a manner that the opponent cannot return it before the second bounce on the floor. The ball may be played either on the fly from the front wall or after one bounce from the floor or ground. It is put in play by a serve that must first hit the front wall. A point is scored only by the player or team serving.

VALUES

One of the best of the many features of these great recreational sports is that they combine a vigorous workout in a short time with a great deal of fun. The proper ball, a pair of gloves (or a paddle or racquet), protective eyewear, and suitable clothing and shoes are the only equipment needed. Most YMCAs, recreation centers, universities/colleges, and athletic clubs have courts. The popularity of these activities grew so fast that commercial racquetball and handball facilities have been built all around the United States. A one-wall court can be marked off in any gymnasium or erected outdoors on a tennis court or similar playing area. The rules are simple and can be learned in a short time. These games require only two, three, or four persons to play, so it is easy to play a game almost anytime without getting a lot of people together.

These games can be played at any age. However, because they require fast reactions, quick reflexes, and good eye-hand coordination, it is best to play with partners and opponents of comparable ability.

EQUIPMENT

Balls

The balls used for paddleball and racquetball are slightly smaller than a tennis ball. They are manufactured by several companies and come in different colors and degrees of "liveliness." The ball used in paddleball is much slower than the ball used in racquetball. The official racquetball is 2¼ inches (5.7 cm) in diameter and weighs about 1.4 ounces (40 g). Common colors for racquetballs are blue, black, green, or red. The official handball is 1⅞ inches (4.8 cm) in diameter with a 1/32-inch (.08 cm) variation and weighs 2.17 ounces (62 g), with a variation of .07 ounces (2 g). Color is optional but is usually black or blue. It is often suggested that beginners use a softer, larger ball, such as a tennis ball, until some of the basic footwork and shot fundamentals are mastered.

Gloves

In handball, gloves must be worn. The gloves may be made of leather or a soft material and must be light in color. The fingers of the gloves cannot be webbed, and no foreign substance (tape, rubber bands, or the like) can be worn on the gloves. Padded gloves are available and are recommended for beginners. After the hands become toughened and the player's skill increases so that batting the ball does not result in sore hands, tight-fitting, unpadded gloves are recommended to allow increased control of the ball. It is recommended that gloves be worn by paddleball and racquetball players to improve the grip on the paddle or racquet.

Racquet

With the increase in popularity of racquetball has come an increase in the number, types, and sizes of racquets available. The phenomenon is similar to the proliferation of types of tennis racquets. The USRA rules now state that the racquet length is limited to 22 inches (58.9 cm). Frames are made of fiberglass, graphite, titanium, tungstun, and various kinds of metals, plastics, and compositions of differing shapes. The racquet strings may be made of gut, nylon, monofilament, graphite, plastic, metal, or some combination of these.

Of course, prices vary considerably. For the beginner, a lightweight frame has advantages. Most importantly, the racquet should feel comfortable when gripped. When selecting a racquet, it is important to grip the handle with the wrist thong attached in the correct manner.

Paddle

The paddle, although much the same size as the racquet, is made entirely of wood. Some models have a leather-wrapped handle similar to that of the racquet, and all paddles should have a wrist thong attached to the handle. Most paddles have regularly spaced holes drilled through the face to reduce air resistance.

Eyeguards

Because of the possibility of eye injury, special eyeguards have been introduced and are highly recommended for all levels of play. In fact, in many tournaments and recreational facilities, lensed eyewear is required. Because the ball travels at such a high rate of speed, if it hits a player directly in the eye, it is possible to injure the eye seriously. The wearing of eyeguards is especially important for beginning players because of their tendency to turn the head to look for the ball. The eyewear should be unaltered, worn as designed at all times, and meet or exceed the American Society for Testing and Materials specifications.

COURTS

One-Wall Court

The one-wall court is 20 feet (6.10 m) wide, 34 feet (10.36 m) long, and 16 feet (4.88 m) high, with at least 6 feet (1.83 m) of clear space beyond the side and long lines. (The 34-foot line is called the "long line.") There are no official specifications for playing surfaces. The surface is usually wood, cement, or clay (Figure 23.1).

The short line is drawn across the court 16 feet (4.88 m) from the front wall and parallel to it. The service line is drawn across the court 9 feet (2.74 m) behind the short line and parallel to it. The space between the service line and short line is the service zone.

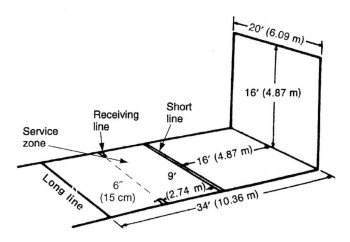

Figure 23.1. One-wall court.

Four-Wall Court

The four-wall court should have a hardwood floor, and sidewalls should be constructed of smooth plaster, tile, concrete, glass, or brick. The court should measure 20 × 20 × 40 feet (6.10 × 6.10 × 12.19 m) (Figure 23.2).

Three-Wall Court

Three-wall courts are occasionally used and are identical to four-wall courts in dimensions, except that there is no back wall.

RULES

One-Wall Court

The rules for the four-wall court also apply to the one-wall court, with the exception of those rules pertaining to sidewalls, back wall, and ceiling plays where there is no ceiling adjoining the front wall, and with the following other considerations.

Serving

The server drops the ball to the floor within the service zone and on the first bounce strikes it in such a manner that it hits the front wall and returns to the floor beyond the short line and in front of the long line. The opposing side must make a legal return by striking the ball after the first bounce or on the fly.

Following are terms that pertain to serving:

long ball A ball that passes over the long line on the serve.
short ball A ball that does not pass beyond the short line on the serve.
out An out results from serving any combination of two faults; serving the ball out-of-bounds; or the served ball hitting the floor before the wall.

Special rules for paddleball

1. In paddleball doubles, the server's partner must stand off the court in the extension of the service area while the teammate is serving. Violation will be a fault. In addition, the server's partner must not enter the court until the served ball has passed him or her. Violation will be a fault.
2. A striker must call "Block" whenever there is danger of hitting the opponent while taking a normal swing. Upon the block call, the striker must refrain from hitting the ball. The point is then replayed. An opponent may call "Block" if he or she foresees danger. If the game is being refereed, the referee will either confirm or deny the legitimacy of the call.

Four-Wall Court

1. The game may be played by two (singles), three (cutthroat), or four players (doubles).
2. In handball and paddleball, a game consists of 21 points. A match consists of two games of 21 points with a tiebreaker of 11 points if the first two games are split.

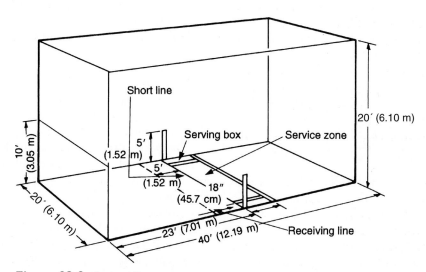

Figure 23.2. Four-wall court.

3. In racquetball, a game consists of 15 points; a match, two games of 15 points, with a tiebreaker of 11 points if the first two games are split.

4. Only the racquet, paddle, or one hand may be used to strike the ball. The use of the foot or any other portion of the body to return the ball is not permitted.

5. In attempting to return the ball, a player cannot strike it more than once.

6. Serving:

   a. To make a legal serve, the server drops the ball to the floor within the service zone and strikes it on the first bounce, so that it hits the front wall first and on the rebound lands on the floor back of the short line. It may strike one of the sidewalls or rebound directly from the front wall.

   b. Drive-serve zones in racquetball (Figure 23.3): The drive-serve lines are 3 feet (0.91 m) from each side-wall in the service box, dividing the service area into two 17-foot (5.18 m) service zones for drive-serves only. The player may drive-serve to the same side of the court on which he or she is standing, so long as the start and finish of the service motion take place outside of the 3-foot line. The referee watches the 3-foot line to see that none of the server's body or racquet passes over the line, preventing the receiver from plainly seeing the served ball. Violation is a fault.

   c. The four types of serve are legal serve, out serve, dead ball, and fault serve. If the serve is legal, play continues; if the serve is an out serve, the server is retired; if the serve is a fault serve, another serve is permitted, and if the serve is a dead ball serve, the serve is replayed. What constitutes each of these types of serve is explained under "Playing Regulations."

d. After the ball has been legally served, the opposing side makes a legal return by striking the ball on the fly or the first bounce, causing it to hit the front wall before hitting the floor. The ball may go directly to the front wall, or hit the front wall after hitting the ceiling, back wall, either one or both of the sidewalls, or any combination of these surfaces.

e. The serving and receiving sides alternate in attempting to make legal returns until one side fails. If the serving side fails, it scores an out; if the receiving side fails, a point is scored for the server.

Three-Wall Court

Three-wall handball is played similarly to four-wall, with the exception of the back wall. In place of the back wall, a line is drawn on the floor parallel to the front wall and is called the "long line." A ball in play striking behind the long line is a point or a handout depending on the side last to hit the ball. A served ball that lands behind the long line is a long ball. Hitting two long balls or one long and one short ball in succession puts the server out.

PLAYING REGULATIONS
Service

1. The choice for the right to serve is decided by a coin toss, and the player winning the toss has the option of serving or receiving the first game. The player who wins the most points in the first two games has the option of serving first for the third (tiebreaker) game. In the event that both players or teams score an equal number of points in the first two games, another coin toss will take place and the winner will have the option of serving or receiving. In informal matches a common procedure to determine who serves is to see which player can rebound the ball off the front wall and come closest to the short line.

2. With the exception of the racquetball drive-serve, the server may start serving from any place in the serving zone.

3. In serving, the server must begin the serve with both feet in the service zone. The server can step on, but not completely over, the service line. Stepping completely over is a foot fault. At no time can the server or the server's partner break the plane of the short line until the served ball has passed it. Violation is a loss of serve.

4. In serving, the ball must be bounced on the floor and struck on the rebound from the floor. The server is out if the attempt to hit the ball on this rebound fails. The server and receiver each have 10 seconds from the time the server or referee calls the score to resume play. Failure to do so can result in a technical foul for delay of game (deduct one point from guilty player or team score).

5. A served ball that first hits the front wall and on the rebound passes so closely to the server (or the server's partner, in doubles) that it prevents the receiver from

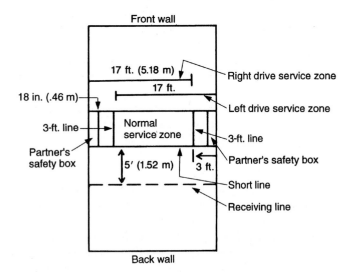

Figure 23.3. Drive-serve zones in racquetball.

having a clear view of the ball, called a screen serve, and results in a fault.

6. In singles, when the server loses the service, a sideout is called. The server becomes the receiver; the receiver then becomes the server, and so on alternately in all subsequent services of the game.

7. In doubles, only one player on the team who serves first is allowed to serve in the first inning. When this player is put out, a sideout is called. Each of the opponents is allowed to serve until put out. When the first server loses serve, handout is called, and when the second server loses serve, a sideout is called. On resuming service, the player who served first serves again until put out, and then the partner serves.

8. The server may not serve until the opponent has had a chance to get placed or the referee calls play.

9. In doubles, the server's partner must stand within the service box, with his or her back to the wall and both feet flat on the floor until the ball passes the short line on each serve. Failure to stand in the correct position is a foot fault.

10. A served ball that hits the doubles partner while he or she is standing correctly in the service box is ruled a fault.

11. In doubles, each partner must serve in the regular order of service. Failure to do so counts as a handout, and the points scored on the illegal serve do not count.

12. Every effort should be made to keep the ball dry, particularly on the service. Deliberate violation of the spirit of this rule results in forfeiture of serve. The ball may be inspected at any time during a game, and the referee puts a new ball in play if advisable.

Defective Serves

1. Defective serves are of three types resulting in penalties as follows:
   a. Dead ball serve—A dead ball serve results in no penalty, and the server is given another serve (it does not cancel a previous fault serve).
   b. Fault serve—Server is permitted another opportunity to serve a legal serve. Any combination of two faults and server loses serve.
   c. Out serve—No second serve, server out.

Dead Ball Serves

1. Court hinder—A serve that takes an irregular bounce because it hit a wet spot or an irregular surface on the court.

2. Broken ball—If the ball is determined to have broken on the serve, the serve shall be replayed.

Faults

1. Foot Faults: These occur if the server steps beyond the service line before the ball passes the short line on the

serve or if the server's partner is not standing correctly in the doubles partner box while the server is serving.

2. A serve is considered short when the served ball hits the front wall and fails to carry beyond the back edge of the short line.

3. A serve is considered long when the served ball rebounds from the front wall and touches the back wall before touching the floor.

4. A serve is also considered a fault if the ball rebounds from the front wall and touches the ceiling.

5. A serve is considered a fault (three-wall serve) if it first hits the front wall and on the rebound strikes both sidewalls before touching the floor.

6. Bouncing the ball outside the service zone as part of the service motion.

7. A drive serve in which the player fails to observe the 17-foot drive service zone.

8. A screen serve as previously described.

9. Serving before the receiver is ready.

Out Serves

1. Two consecutive fault serves.

2. A served ball touches the server in singles or doubles.

3. A served ball strikes the server's partner when the latter is outside the service box.

4. A served ball hits the ceiling, floor, or sidewalls before striking the front wall.

5. A served ball hits the front wall and sidewall, front wall and floor, or front wall and ceiling at the same time (crotch ball).

6. A partner serves out of turn. Any points scored are erased.

7. Missed serve attempt. Any attempt to strike the ball that results in a total miss.

8. Fake or balk serve. Any movement toward the ball during the serve that is noncontinuous and done for the purpose of deceiving the receiver.

9. Illegal hit. Includes contacting the ball twice, carrying the ball, or hitting the ball with the handle of the racquet or part of the body.

10. Out-of-court serve. A served ball that rebounds from the front wall and, before striking the floor, goes out of the court.

11. Safety-zone violation. If the server or server's partner enters the safety zone before the served ball passes the short line, it will result in a loss of serve.

Receiving Service

1. In handball, paddleball, and racquetball, the receivers must stand at least 5 feet (1.52 m) in back of the short line, as indicated by the receiving or restraining line.

2. In handball the receiver can hit the ball after it passes the short line; however, no part of the body may extend over the plane of the short line when and after contacting the ball.

3. In racquetball and paddleball the receiver may not enter the safety zone (the 5-foot [1.52 m] area between the short line and receiver's line) until the served ball bounces in the safety zone or crosses the receiving line.

4. A receiver may play the service either on the fly or after the first bounce. In making a fly return, the receiver must play the ball after it passes over the short line in handball and the receiver's line in racquetball and paddleball.

Hinders

A *hinder* is defined as interference with an opponent's fair chance to see and play the ball. There are two types: replay (rally replayed) and penalty (player or team is penalized).

1. Replay hinders (resulting in the rally being replayed):
   a. A returned ball striking an opponent on the fly, on its way to the front wall. It has to be obvious that the ball would have reached the front wall.
   b. Screen ball (not on serve): any ball rebounding from the front wall so close to the body of a player on the team that hit the ball that the opponent is interfered with or prevented from seeing the ball.
   c. Straddle ball: a ball going between the legs of a player on the side that just returned the ball, so that the opponent does not have a fair chance to see or return the ball.
   d. Body contact with an opponent that interferes with opponent's seeing or returning the ball.
   e. Any other unintentional interference that prevents an opponent from seeing or returning the ball.
   f. Court hinders.
   g. Backswing hinders.
   h. Safety holdups.

2. Penalty hinders (resulting in an "out" or a "point," depending upon whether the serving side or the receiving side was at fault):
   a. A player fails to move enough to allow his opponent a fair shot or moves in such a way that blocks a shot.
   b. Intentionally pushing an opponent during play.
   c. Blocking an opponent by moving into the path or by moving in front of an opponent as your partner plays the ball.
   d. Intentionally wetting the ball.
   e. Interfering with an opponent's stroke.
   f. Unnecessary equipment hinder.
   g. Verbal—deliberate shouting, stamping of the feet, waving of the racquet, or any manner of disrupting the player who is hitting the ball.
   h. Diving—diving in an attempt to return a ball that prevents further action.

3. Considerations: It is the responsibility of the side that has just hit the ball to move so the receiving side may go straight to the ball and have an unobstructed view and shot at the ball.

   a. There has to be a reasonable chance to return the ball in order for a hinder to be called.
   b. Be consistent.
   c. Must be called immediately.
   d. Cannot be appealed/judgment call.

4. It is NOT a hinder when a player interferes with his or her partner.

Outs during Rally

1. A player commits a penalty hinder.
2. A legally returned ball strikes the partner of the player returning the ball.
3. Player fails to return a properly returned ball.
4. Player hits ball out of court.
5. A ball that obviously does not have the velocity or direction to hit the front wall but strikes an opponent.
6. Switching hands with the racquet/paddle in racquetball/paddleball.
7. Failure to wear a wrist thong in racquetball/paddleball.
8. Touching the ball with the body or uniform during a return attempt.
9. Carrying or slinging the ball.

SPECIAL POPULATIONS

Rule modifications have been made in these sports to accommodate special populations, such as wheelchair athletes and athletes with visual or hearing disabilities. In general, the standard rules governing the sports are followed, except for some modifications. For example, there is typically a two-bounce or multibounce rule in effect. In wheelchair play, rules referring to feet are adapted to indicate where the wheels touch the floor. Players with visual disabilities may make multiple attempts to strike the ball until the ball has been touched or has stopped bouncing (USRA 2005, Rules 8, 9, and 10).

SAFETY

All players should be careful to avoid swinging wildly at the ball because the hand, paddle, and racquet can injure a partner or opponent. In fact, paddles and racquets have a thong attached to the handle that must be secured to the player's wrist, which helps prevent a paddle or racquet from slipping from the hand. The wrist thong was added to prevent a player from switching the paddle or racquet from hand to hand during play. This does assist in safety. Failure to properly apply the wrist thong is a loss of the rally.

FUNDAMENTAL SKILLS AND TECHNIQUES

The beginner watching an experienced player soon learns that there are fundamentals common to most sports. The beginner is often out of position, off-balance, and unable to get a good, accurate shot, while the more experienced opponent seems to always be in the correct position. The beginning student should work on these fundamentals.

Position on Floor

Study the possible angles that a ball can travel and rebound within the four rectangular walls of the court as you would in studying angles while playing billiards. Throw or hit the ball at the walls at different angles and heights and observe the rebounds. Try to move to that spot where the ball is expected to be best played (Figure 23.4).

Footwork

The fundamental skill of correct footwork is essential for proficiency and accuracy in these activities. For a right-handed player, the left foot and side should be toward the front wall when a forehand stroke is called for; if a backhand or a left-hand stroke is called for, the right foot and side should face the front wall. While waiting between shots, the front of the body should face the front wall, the feet should be approximately shoulder width apart, the weight should be evenly distributed on both feet, and the player should be ready to move in any direction. While waiting and when contacting the ball, the knees are usually bent and the body is crouched (Figure 23.5).

Accuracy of Playing Shots

Accuracy depends on proper footwork, good balance, and keeping the eyes on the ball with correct early arm preparation, stroke, and follow-through. The player, by experience, should gain the ability to choose the angle and spot that is desirable to hit without looking at the spot. (The player should be watching the ball.)

Practice low corner shots that have little or no rebound. These shots are called "kill shots." The sidearm stroke is most accurate for this shot.

The Hand

Snug-fitting gloves should be worn for handball. The tips of the fingers should be slightly squeezed together, and the entire hand should be slightly cupped like a swimmer's hand. The wrist and elbow should be flexible to accommodate a wrist-snap shot or an overhead stroke similar to that of throwing a fast ball.

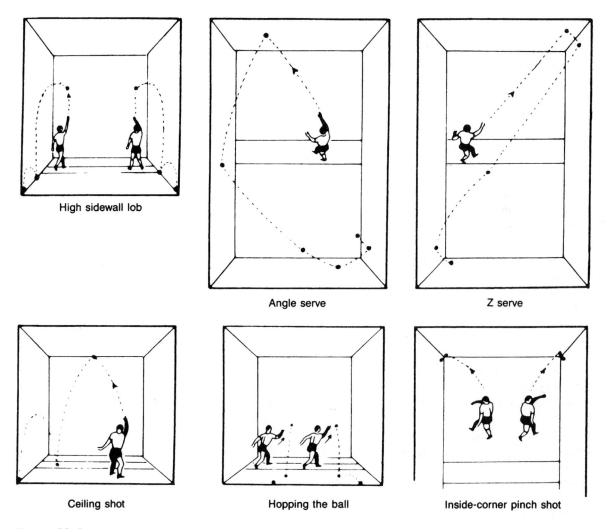

High sidewall lob

Angle serve

Z serve

Ceiling shot

Hopping the ball

Inside-corner pinch shot

Figure 23.4. Floor positions and ball placement.

Figure 23.5. Stance for an open-hand shot in handball.

Figure 23.6. Handball fist shot.

In stroking the ball, the hand should follow through toward the spot where the ball is directed before the arm swings across the body to complete the follow-through. The hand can also be held in a tight fist for certain kinds of shots (Figure 23.6).

Strokes

The arm strokes used in all three activities are similar except that in racquetball and paddleball a backhand stroke is often employed, whereas in handball the player must develop the ability to use the nondominant hand in striking the ball. In all three activities, the overhead, sidearm, and underhand strokes are used.

Overhead. The body position for the overhead stroke is similar to that in throwing a ball fast, for example, from a catcher to second base. The arm swings back so that the racquet or the hand begins the stroking action from behind the ear. If a ball is hit from a high reach, the arm is usually held almost straight while stroking. A quick, flexible wrist snap is desirable.

Sidearm. The sidearm stroke on the dominant side of the body is similar to a sidearm throw except that the elbow is tucked in for the forehand stroke. If the player is right-handed, the left foot should be in front of the right, and vice versa. Often the stroke is made without changing feet and with a quick, flexible wrist snap. However, the feet should always be ready to react if a more accurate stroke can be delivered by shifting the feet.

Underhand. This stroke is not as common in racquetball or paddleball as it is in handball. In all three activities, the underhand stroke is usually less effective than bending low at the knees and waist and using the sidearm stroke.

In handball, where power is desired, the ball may contact the heel of the hand, which is strong and muscular and can withstand repeated contact with the ball.

In all three activities, the use of the wrist to impart speed to the ball is critical. Because of the velocity with which the ball travels, often a player will not be able to get in the proper position to effectively use the proper body, leg, and arm movements, and the wrist snap in these situations is the only remaining movement to achieve a decent return. In racquetball and paddleball, this motion is aided by the use of light racquets and paddles. In handball, it is helpful to contact the ball toward the tips of the fingers when possible. This permits a longer leverage to the hand, and a wrist snap gives the ball added speed and accuracy. To master this stroke requires a great deal of practice. The ball can be hit with the palm of the hand, but this shot is not very accurate, nor can speed or power be obtained from it.

Kill Shots

A kill shot is one that hits the front so close to the floor that there is practically no bounce before an opponent can reach the ball and play it. There are many varieties of kill shots (Figure 23.7).

Straight kill shot. The straight kill is a shot to the front wall that does not touch either sidewall, but hits the wall low.

Outside-corner pinch shot. In the outside-corner pinch shot, the ball first hits the sidewall, bounces to the front wall, and then bounces to the floor. Either the right or left corner may be used.

Inside-corner pinch shot. In the inside-corner pinch shot, the ball first hits the front wall, bounces to the sidewall, and then bounces to the floor. Again, either the right or left corner may be used.

Figure 23.7. Racquetball forehand kill-shot position.

Fly kill shot. In the fly kill shot the ball is hit on the fly from a front wall rebound so fast that the opponent has no opportunity to play the ball.

A player should constantly strive to direct a ball into an area or at such an angle into the sidewalls that the opponent has little opportunity to play the ball. This is a skill that can be mastered only by practice and experience.

Back-Wall Shot

A hard shot that hits moderately high on the front wall will often rebound all the way to the back wall without hitting the floor. A player sensing such a situation should move into a position to return the ball as it comes off the back wall (or floor) and is moving toward the front wall. By waiting until the ball is near the floor, the player can execute a kill or pass shot.

Occasionally a player may not have time to get into the proper position to return a back-wall shot. It may be possible to hit the ball hard and moderately high against the back wall to cause it to rebound to the front wall before hitting the floor. This shot should be used only in desperation because it often results in an easy return for the opponent. The shot should be used only when the player is out of position and needs to buy time to regain proper court position.

Ceiling Shot

The ceiling shot is basically a defensive shot used when a player is out of position or when a change of pace is needed. It may also be used offensively to move an opponent out of the center-court position. It is executed by hitting the ball relatively hard and directing it toward the ceiling a few feet in back of the front wall. The intent should be to cause the ball to bounce on the floor in the front court area and then come down in a back corner near a sidewall. By hitting the ceiling and front wall, the ball develops an overspin and bounces higher than normal, possibly causing the opponent to misplay the ball.

Pass Shot

A shot directed in such a way that it travels along the sidewall that is farthest away from the opponent is a pass shot. It should not be hit with so much force that it rebounds off the back wall, but instead it should drop into one of the back corners.

Serve

There are many types and variations of serves, such as the drive serve (see Figure 23.8). A serve is begun by dropping the ball on the floor behind the service line. On the first bounce, the server hits it with the racquet, paddle, or hand. To be a legal serve, the ball must hit the front wall; it can then either rebound directly back behind the server or from the front wall onto the sidewalls, as long as it rebounds to the floor behind the short line. The server is permitted another serve if a fault is committed. Two faults retire the server.

Drive serve. In the drive serve the player, while standing in the drive service zone (see Figure 23.3), contacts the ball close to the floor so that it hits the front wall close to the floor and rebounds just behind the short line. It is usually directed at an angle and with a velocity so that, if not hit by the receiver, it will take a second bounce just prior to going into the corner.

Z serve. In the Z serve the player serves from an area so that the ball rebounds from the front wall to the near sidewall opposite the server at such an angle that the ball lands behind the short line. This serve can also be hit high so that the ball rebounds to the back wall and corner behind the receiver.

High or half lob. The server serves the ball high or midway up on the front wall and close to the sidewall so that the ball rebounds close to the receiving line and stays very close to the sidewall on its entire flight. These serves often drop dead in the back corner and are difficult to return. Some of these serves may just touch the sidewall on their rebound flight, causing the ball to drop dead.

Two-wall serve to back corner. The server serves the ball about head high and about 4 or 5 feet (1.5 m) from a sidewall. The ball rebounds to a sidewall just back of midcourt, rebounds to the floor and on back to the opposite corner, and hits the back wall before hitting the floor.

The flight of this serve causes the receiver to run around, following the ball and looking for an opportunity to play it, which is difficult.

HINTS ON PLAY AND STRATEGY

1. Throughout a game, keep in mind that situations like those described in the various serves may arise, and the ball can be directed and played like a serve. In these situations, there is a need to quickly size up an opponent's weaknesses and strong points and play to the weaknesses.
2. Keep your eyes on the ball. Follow it constantly.
3. Protect your eyes by wearing lensed eyeguards.

Figure 23.8. Racquetball drive serve.

4. Watch your opponent's feet and position. He or she will usually telegraph the return shots.
5. Avoid rushing the ball. It is important to wait before attempting the return shot.
6. Concentrate on your serve.
7. Develop several different types of serves. Analyze your opponent's return of various serves. Concentrate on the serve that is most difficult for your opponent to return.
8. Change from fast play to lob shots and runaround plays to keep an opponent off balance. Strive to place shots accurately.
9. Be constantly on the alert for balls that can be contacted close to the floor or for the opportunity to hit accurate pass or kill shots.
10. Constantly work for a desirable position on the court. A good spot is usually the "hole," or "well," near the center of the court and around the receiving line. This is also known as the *offensive spot*, and the backcourt is known as the *defensive spot*. Try to keep the opponent out of the well.
11. Strive to think ahead and set up a series of plays that will keep the opponent off balance and therefore at a disadvantage.
12. Continue to practice your weakest strokes. In handball it is usually necessary to practice hitting with the nondominant hand. In racquetball and paddleball, regularly practice hitting backhand strokes. On either a serve or rebound, concentrate on hitting a spot on the front wall, but keep the eyes on the ball until it is hit. After a serve, come quickly to the "well." Continue to maneuver for the offensive position throughout the game.

SKILLS TO PRACTICE ALONE

Serving Drills: Drive Serve

Purpose. To develop accuracy in the drive serve and be able to drive-serve to a variety of court positions.

Method. From the center of the service zone, hit three drive serves to each of the four designated court positions. Repeat the circuit three times. Score 1 point for each correct placement. Total points possible = 36. (Note: You can total points scored to each designated area to indicate your most accurate placement. Total points to each area = 9) (Norton and Bryant 1991, p. 96).

Defensive Shots: Lob, Ceiling, High Z, Around-the-Wall

Purpose. To practice hitting a defensive shot from two court positions and develop accuracy in ball placement.

Method. Using a dropped ball, hit each defensive shot 10 times, from center and backcourt positions (five to each corner). Use the same target area as designated for the lob and high Z serves. Total points possible for each serve from each

position = 50. To vary this drill, begin the defensive shot with a side wall toss (Norton and Bryant 2004a, p. 101).

30-Second Drill

Purpose. To learn to react quickly to the ball's court position and improve movement time, and to work on ball control.

Method. Begin in a center-court position. Drop the ball and return it to the front wall. Continue to return the ball off the rebound, counting the number of times the ball is returned in 30 seconds. Count only shots that would be legal returns in a game. Do this drill at least every other practice session. Try to improve by one to three shots each time (Norton and Bryant 2004a, p. 99).

Forehand and Backhand Shots from Side-Wall Toss

Purpose. To practice hitting forehand and backhand shots to the back corners of the court from a ball bouncing off the side wall.

Method. Stand with your hips pivoted and facing the side wall appropriate for either a forehand or backhand stroke. Toss the ball into the side wall. After the rebound, hit the ball to a back corner of the court. Hit eight balls from each of the three court positions, four to each corner, then repeat eight shots each from the same court positions with the other stroke (Norton and Bryant 2004a, p. 99).

Suicide Drill

Purpose. To develop muscular endurance and anaerobic capacity, and to practice moving to the ball and returning it to the front wall.

Method. Begin in the center court, drop the ball, and hit it to the front wall. Continue to return the ball as quickly as you can, moving to hit all balls after one bounce. Work at positioning yourself correctly for each hit. Continue this drill for 2-minute intervals, allowing yourself to rest 30 to 60 seconds after each hitting session. Repeat the drill 10 times. Record the number of balls hit during each 2-minute interval (Norton and Bryant 2004a, p. 99).

Ceiling Ball Rally

1. Stand in the rear court and direct the ball to the ceiling.
2. As the ball rebounds toward the back court, adjust your court position to strike the ball, attempting to repeat the ceiling ball return.
3. Continue executing ceiling ball returns until either the ball bounces twice or the return does not contact the ceiling.
4. During the return, the ball can hit either the ceiling or the front wall first (although ceiling first is preferred), as long as the ball contacts both the ceiling and the front wall.

5. The score is determined by the number of successful returns made before the ball either bounces twice or fails to contact the ceiling or the front wall on the return.

6. A good score for a beginner is ten successive returns in a row in any one of five repetitions of the test (Kozar and Catignani 1997, p. 58).

Off-the-Back-Wall Kill

1. Using masking tape or other temporary marking material 1 to 2 inches wide, make a line along the width of the front wall 1.5 feet up from the floor.

2. Stand 5 feet from the back wall in the center of the court and toss the ball about waist high against the back wall.

3. As the ball strikes the back wall, pivot into a forehand (or backhand) striking position and slide toward the front wall with the ball as it rebounds off the back wall and contacts the floor.

4. Slide your feet and adjust your body position while waiting for the ball to drop to knee height or lower near the lead leg, which is the prime striking position.

5. Strike the ball and direct it so that it contacts the front wall between the floor and the marked area.

6. A good score for a beginner would be five successful attempts out of ten trials.

Once you are able to consistently hit directly to the targeted area on the front wall, attempt to improve your accuracy by hitting either side wall before the ball contacts the marked area on the front wall (Kozar and Catignani 1997, p. 57).

Deep Lob Serve

1. Using masking tape or other temporary marking material 1 to 2 inches wide, outline a 5-foot-square area on the sidewall in each rear corner.

2. Assume the appropriate position in the service zone for the lob serve.

3. Execute the lob serve so that it contacts the front wall three-fourths of the way up, rebounding in a slow arc to the left or right rear corner.

4. Note the number of times the ball hits the targeted 5-foot-square area on the sidewall before contacting the floor.

5. A good score for a beginner would be three successful attempts out of ten trials (Kozar and Catignani 1997, p. 56).

Drive and Short Lob ("Garbage") Serve

1. Using masking tape or other temporary marking material 1 to 2 inches wide, outline a 3-foot-square area in each of the rear corners of the court.

2. Assume the appropriate position in the service zone for the drive or garbage serve.

3. Execute either a drive or a garbage serve and attempt to land the ball on the second bounce in one of the outlined target areas.

4. Note the number of successful attempts after 10 trials. Be sure to attempt both serves an equal number of times to each corner targeted area.

5. A good score for a beginner in attempting each of these serves would be a total of five successful attempts out of ten trials (Kozar and Catignani 1997, pp. 55–56).

COURT COURTESY

If there is any doubt about a play, it should be played over. It is not fair play to deliberately hit an opponent with the ball in order to get a hinder on the play. An opponent is entitled to a fair, unobstructed opportunity to play the ball.

TEACHING CONSIDERATIONS

1. Many school situations will be limited to games on one-wall courts. Taped lines on the walls and floor can be used to mark off playing areas.

2. Teach students basic sidearm and underhand patterns, beginning with tapping the ball easily against the wall rather than hitting strokes requiring maximum force. Start with forehand strokes before introducing backhand strokes. Emphasize action of the wrist and open stance as well as returning to a ready position in the play area. Emphasize getting the racquet in proper position.

3. Use partners to practice alternating hits in a cooperative way before introducing competitive strategies. Emphasize interference rules as soon as you introduce partner work. When two players can keep the ball going fairly consistently (at least six hits) without losing control of the ball, begin to increase the demand for greater force levels by increasing the distance of the players from the wall.

4. When players can consistently keep the ball going against the wall, encourage them to begin placing the ball to make their partners move to unused spaces in the playing area. Teach for changing the level of the ball against the wall, changing the angle of the shot, and changing the force level of the ball as offensive strategies. Name the shots and teach for form.

5. Introduce the serve and game rules as players begin to need more formal regulation of play (after some consistency is developed in ability to return the easier shots).

6. Modify and develop rules as necessary to meet the needs of the facilities available.

7. Require all players to wear lensed eyeguards. Emphasize eye safety in early instruction. Insist that players wear a wrist thong on racquets and paddles at all times and constantly remind them about racquet safety.

GLOSSARY

ace A serve that completely eludes the receiver.

court hinder A ball that takes an irregular bounce due to hitting a wet spot or irregular surface on the court, or a ball that breaks during play.

crotch ball A ball hitting at the juncture of the front wall and the floor or the ceiling, sidewall, or corner.

fault An infraction of the rules during serving that involves a penalty other than an out.

first service In doubles, only the first player serves to start the game.

handout A handout occurs when the first server of a doubles team loses the serve.

hinder An accidental interference or obstruction of the flight of the ball not involving a penalty.

kill A ball returned to the front wall in such a manner that it rebounds from the front wall or sidewall so close to the floor that it is impossible to return.

long ball A ball that, on the serve, either hits the back wall directly or passes over the long line (three wall).

match Winning two out of three games.

out Sometimes called a *handout*. It is scored against the serving side when the server fails to serve legally or loses a rally. In a doubles game, when each of the two partners has been put out, it is a *sideout*. In a singles game, retiring the server retires the side.

penalty hinder A hinder that results in the loss of a rally. It may be intentional or unintentional.

point Scored only by the serving side and made when an opponent fails to play a legal serve or a legally returned ball.

receiver The player or players to whom the ball is served; also called the "receiving side."

receiving line The line running parallel with and 5 feet (1.52 m) in back of the short line.

receiving zone The back court is the receiving zone for the serve.

replay hinder Play resumes without penalty to either player or side.

screen serve A served ball that passes so close to the server (or partner) that the receiver is unable to get a clear view of the ball.

server The person serving the ball.

service line The line running parallel with and 5 feet (1.52 m) in front of the short line.

service zone The space between the outer edges of the short and service lines in which the server must remain while serving the ball.

short line The line running parallel with the front wall and dividing the court into two equal parts.

sideout The loss of serve for the server in singles or for the serving team in doubles.

SUGGESTED READINGS

Fisher, D. 2008. *Racquetball: Steps to success.* Champaign, IL: Human Kinetics.

Kozar, A., and Catignani, E. 1997. *Beginning racquetball.* Winston-Salem, NC: Hunter Textbooks.

Metzler, M. 2001. *Racquetball: Mastering the basics with the personalized sports instruction system.* Needham Heights, MA: Allyn and Bacon. Contains well-written, easy-to-follow instructions.

Norton, C., and Bryant, J. 2004a. *Beginning racquetball.* 6th ed. Stamford, CT: Wadsworth/Thomson Learning. Contains more than 200 photographs illustrating basic skills. Includes chapters on safety, strokes, serves, strategy, drills, etiquette, interpreting rules, and an instructor's manual.

Norton, C., and Bryant, J. 2004b. *Instructor's manual for beginning racquetball.* 6th ed. Stamford, CT: Wadsworth/Thomson Learning.

Official racquetball rules. Current edition. Colorado Springs, CO: USA. Racquetball.

Official rules for one-wall, three-wall, and four-wall paddleball. Current edition. New York: National Paddleball Association.

The new and official U.S. Handball Association handball rules. Current edition. Tucson, AZ: U.S. Handball Association.

Turner, E., and Clouse, W. 1996. *Winning racquetball: Skills, drills and strategies,* Champaign, IL: Human Kinetics.

Tyson, P., and Martin, L. 2000. *Four-wall handball for the teacher and student.* 3rd ed. Tucson, AZ: United States Handball Association.

Walker, D. *Racquetball.* 1999. Scottsdale, AZ: Holcomb Hathaway Publishers.

Winterton, J. 2004. *Racquetball fundamentals.* Champaign, IL: Human Kinetics.

RESOURCES

Videos

Graffiti Entertainment. Racquetball: The video game for wii. Signature services, Inc. (SDUI) 2010.

See Appendix C for sources of videos.

WEB SITES

National Paddleball Association
www.paddleball.org

United States Handball Association
www.ushandball.org

United States Racquetball Association
www.usaracquetball.com

Rugby

After completing this chapter, the reader should be able to:

- Appreciate the development and values of the game of rugby
- Select rugby equipment and lay out a rugby field
- Describe the rules and scoring procedures of the game
- Practice the fundamental techniques of rugby
- Explain the skills and duties required of the various positions
- Use lead-up activities and other suggestions to teach the fundamentals of rugby

HISTORY

Ball games resembling football have been played for well over 2,000 years. Many descriptions, paintings, and drawings surviving from the Middle Ages show that the game has been played in the British Isles for centuries.

Rugby football was devised accidentally at Rugby School in England in 1823, when one of the players on Rugby's team, William Webb Ellis, tucked the ball under his arm and ran across the goal line, an act recognized as unsportsmanlike conduct. However, this form of the game gained tremendous popularity over the next 40 years, and when the word *football* was used, some people asked, "Which kind?" Over the last half of the 19th century, five distinct codes of football were developed, including codes for rugby football, American football, and Gaelic and Australian rules.

Rugby football changed even further at the beginning of the 20th century. A group of clubs in northern England formed what eventually became known as Rugby League. Rugby League developed as a result of players wanting to be paid; an early form of professionalism. Rugby Union supporters refused to support the idea of payment, thus resulting in two separate codes of rugby after the early 1900s. Rugby Union and Rugby League now support two totally distinct games.

Rugby has been played in the United States since the late nineteenth century but has been overshadowed by gridiron football and soccer, both of which developed from a rugby framework.

For much of its history in the United States through the first half of the 20th century, rugby was played primarily between colleges and universities. Harvard University is widely credited with having played the first game of rugby in the United States. McGill University (Montreal, Canada) challenged Harvard to a home and home series in 1874. From there, rugby spread to most of the Ivy League schools, such as Yale and Columbia on the East Coast. By 1900, Walter Camp of Yale introduced the concepts of downs and blocking, eliminated the scrum and line-out, and reduced the number of players from 15 to 11. These changes forever resulted in the separation of gridiron football from rugby.

After the separation, there is little evidence to describe how rugby further evolved in the early 1900s. West Coast universities, such as Stanford and Cal Berkeley, started playing rugby as a result of gridiron's reputation for violence. Additionally, the presidents of these schools had heard of the English Rugby Football Union's belief that rugby helped develop moral character in young men. At this time California became a hotbed for rugby in the West by forging relationships with Canadian universities. The pinnacle of American rugby occurred when teams of predominantly California-based players won Olympic gold medals in 1920 and 1924, defeating the French teams both times. Because the Olympics dropped rugby after the 1924 Games, interest in the United States waned.

During the 1950s interest was rekindled, and today there are more than 75,000 members and over 2,000 registered clubs in the United States. In 1975 the American governing body, now known as USA Rugby, was formed. It is composed of seven territorial unions—the Northeast, Mid-Atlantic, South, Midwest, Western, Pacific Coast, and Southern California Rugby Football Unions. USA Rugby sponsors 16 different national championships for men, women, colleges, and high schools. USA Rugby is a member of the United States Olympic Committee (USOC) and International Rugby Board (IRB). Internationally, the men's national team usually ranks around 15th in the world. New Zealand and South Africa usually rank at the top of the world rankings each year.

There are six American national teams (Men, Women, Collegiate Men, Collegiate Women, Men under 19, and Women under 23) altogether. The men's senior team is known as the Eagles, and they compete every spring and summer in the Churchill Cup Championship, played between the United States, Canada, Argentina, and England. The United States also hosts a number of international teams each year. Since

2004, the United States has hosted the USA Sevens international tournament as the fourth leg of the IRB Sevens World Series, an annual international series of the seven-a-side version of rugby. In 2010, the U.S. tournament was hosted in Las Vegas, Nevada. Sevens rugby is a condensed version of the game with a faster and more exciting style, which has gained popularity worldwide to the point that the sevens version of rugby was readmitted to the Olympic Games for London 2012.

Internationally, rugby is played in four professional leagues in Europe (Guinness Premiership League, Magners League, French League, Heineken Cup) and three in the southern hemisphere (Super 14, Air New Zealand Cup, Currie Cup). Players in these competitions compete for positions on their respective national teams in order to play in the IRB's World Cup, which ranks third in viewership after the Olympics and FIFA's World Cup. The following chart lists the year, host country and winner of the five World Cups for rugby:

1987	New Zealand	New Zealand
1991	England	Australia
1995	South Africa	South Africa
1999	Wales	Australia
2003	Australia	England
2007	France	South Africa
2011	New Zealand	

The United States has not fared well internationally, due to limited professional opportunities for American players. The top men's league is the Super League, consisting of the top 16 teams in cities around the country. Recently, there have been attempts to professionalize American rugby with the short-lived North America 4 competition (2 Canadian, 2 American) and the most recent Americas Rugby Championship started in 2009. This competition was funded by grant money from the IRB to fund professional development in Canada, Argentina, and the U.S.

The U.S. women's senior side has fared better than the men's. They won the inaugural Women's World Cup in 1991, and came in second in 1994. Since that time teams from England and, most recently, New Zealand, have become dominant on the international circuit. The women do not have professional opportunities, but a US Women's Premier League was started in 2009, which is composed of the top eight teams in the U.S., similar to the men's Rugby Premier League. Both men's and women's rugby have benefitted from the infusion of IRB money that started in 2004 in an attempt by the IRB to improve rugby union competition worldwide, thereby improving the quality of the World Cup.

VALUES

Rugby is a team game that requires players to use their skill in conjunction with others to achieve success. It is a running game that requires active involvement of each player for the duration of the game. It develops team spirit and cooperation and affords a high level of satisfaction for the participants.

Because players are in constant motion, rugby helps develop cardiovascular endurance. The basic skills of the game require speed, balance, coordination, strength, and power, important in any physical development program. By virtue of the structure of the game, rugby requires a unique combination of cardiovascular and strength endurance, as well as power. It is a contact sport, and players should physically equip themselves to meet this requirement. Fitness, strength training, and power development are strongly recommended. Much of the cardiovascular training should be done with a ball in hand, particularly since most American athletes are not acculturated to the sport as quickly as they are to basketball, football, or soccer. Strength and power can be developed on-field but should be coordinated with a proper off-field regimen. All top clubs have developed power endurance programs to improve their athletes.

Preseason conditioning involves building endurance and strength, with a strong emphasis on the development of the core and on individual skills. Just prior to the season, a power regimen should be included to supplement the strength training. During the season much of the time is spent building the team, developing and coordinating plays, and sharpening basic and individual skills. Stretching is important before and particularly after training: 10 to 15 minutes should be allowed for a gradual cool down of the major muscle groups in the neck, chest, lower back, arms, thighs, hamstrings, and calves.

EQUIPMENT
Clothing

Rugby can be played by persons of all ages and requires little equipment. Proper cleats, called boots, are required. They should be leather and have rubber, plastic, or aluminum cleats to give the player a secure grip on the ground. High-topped boots are popular with prop forwards and lock forwards, but most players wear low-cut boots. Some boots are available with additional forward toe protection for the rigorous action inherent in rucks and mauls. Backs are not likely to prefer this because the toe protection layer interferes with all forms of kicking necessary for the game. Rugby laws prohibit boots that have a single stud in the middle of the toe. Socks, shorts, and a rugby shirt make up the rest of the basic uniform. It is advisable to wear a mouthguard to protect against concussions. Some players wear scrum caps and soft shoulder padding. Rugby laws require the padding in scrum caps and shoulder pads to be no thicker than 1 centimeter and of a soft material. Women are allowed chest protection, but it must conform to the same regulations as scrum caps and shoulder padding. No jewelry, sharp objects, or rigid materials are allowed, covered or otherwise.

Ball

The rugby ball is oval and made of four panels of leather or other approved synthetic material. It weights 13½ to 15½ ounces (378 to 434 g).

FIELD

Rugby is played on a rectangular field not exceeding 100 meters by 70 meters (109.3 yd × 76.8 yd) (Figure 24.1). It is often played on a shorter and narrower field, depending on the space available and the age of the players. A line drawn across the center, the halfway line, divides the field. The goal-posts, placed in the center of the goal line, consist of two uprights exceeding 3.4 meters (3.7 yd) in height and a crossbar 5.6 meters (6.1 yd) wide. The crossbar is attached to the uprights 3 meters (3.3 yd) from the ground. The in-goal area between the goal line and the dead-ball line must not exceed 22 meters (24 yd).

In rugby, the field is referred to as the "pitch," and sidelines are called "touchlines." Kicking or running the ball out-of-bounds is called "putting the ball into touch."

The 22-meter (24-yd) line is marked 22 meters out from the goal line of each half. The significance of the 22-meter (24-yd) line is that a player may kick the ball directly into touch (out of bounds) from inside his or her own 22-meter (24-yd) line and the goal line, thus stopping play where the ball, still in the area, crosses the touchline. If a player kicks the ball directly into touch in front of the 22-meter (24-yd) line on the fly, the out-of-bounds play (or line-out) must begin on the sideline perpendicular from where the player kicked the ball, not where it went out-of-bounds. Recent rules do not permit the player to retrieve the ball and then bring it behind the 22-meter line and then attempt to kick the ball in touch on the fly. The ball must be caught or retrieved behind

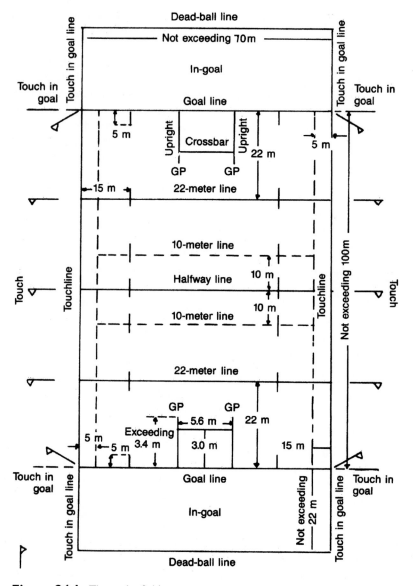

Figure 24.1. The rugby field.

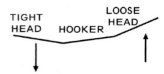

Figure 24.10. Opposing players' shoulders should look like this before engaging.

tackling is as much attitude as it is skill. After ball handling, tackling is the next most necessary skill. The best way to learn how to tackle is to practice one step at a time and build up confidence. With the correct technique it is possible to knock down the opponent without getting hurt. The three basic types of tackle are head-on, side-on, and from behind. A fourth type, smothering, is sometimes used. In this tackle, the arms are wrapped around an opponent to prevent him or her from advancing or passing the ball.

Head-on tackle

1. Judge the approach of the opponent so as to make contact with the shoulder and body weight.
2. As the opponent approaches, drive into the tackle from one leg.
3. Contact the opponent at about waist height, keeping the head to the side. Close the arms tightly around the opponent's legs.
4. Follow through using momentum to bring the opponent to the ground (Figure 24.12).
5. Get to your feet to play the ball.

Side-on tackle

The basic principles for the head-on tackle apply for the side-on tackle.

1. Line up the opponent.
2. Drive in off one leg and contact the opponent just above the knees.
3. Keep the head behind the opponent's back and wrap the arms around the opponent's legs.

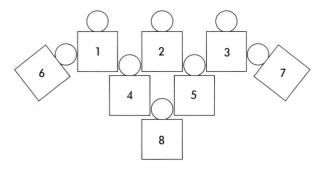

Figure 24.11. Flankers (6 and 7) pushing inward in the scrum.

Figure 24.12. Head-on tackle.

4. The momentum and the arm lock will cause the opponent to fall.
5. Get to your feet to play the ball.

Tackle from behind

1. Drive in off one leg, keeping low.
2. Keeping the head clear, contact the opponent above the knees and close the arms tightly around the legs.
3. The locked legs and momentum will cause the opponent to fall.

PLAYING POSITIONS

Forwards

The eight forwards—known as "the pack"—play as a unit. They are the platform from which the backs play. The forwards are in the front line of attack and are the main source through which their team gains possession of the ball. On gaining possession of the ball, the forwards have the option of trying to advance the ball forward among themselves or of transferring the ball to the backs. Physical makeup and natural ability often determine the position one plays.

Although different skills are required for each forward position, forwards as a group need to be strong, powerful, and mobile. They are generally larger and more physical than the backs. The back row of the scrum needs to be fast and aggressive, whereas the front five forwards provide much of the power. The hooker must be quick with the feet in the scrum, and the two locks, usually the tallest players on the team, provide useful targets in the line-out, as well as the power behind the push in the set scrums. Props are usually the most dependent on sheer strength. They also rely on power, but props need the most strength to fully support the hooker while providing the stability necessary for the clashes and engagements in the scrums.

Backs

Each back position has its particular skills, but in general backs must learn to handle, run, pass, tackle, and kick a ball with ease. Speed, coordination, and ability to read the play are important. The scrum half is the link between the forwards and backs and must be able to transfer the ball to the back line when it is made available by the forwards. The fly half marshals the back line, determines the play, and keeps the backs in position. The back-line players have an important role in halting an opposition attack, because they present the main line of defense.

Offense or Attack

The offense should advance forward as a unit, creating gaps in the opposition defense. This may be done by beating the opposition in a one-on-one situation, by creating an extra player situation, or by driving the opposition back by strength. The offense tries to maintain possession of the ball while advancing and to support the player with the ball. They should vary the attack and prevent the defense from organizing. Attack usually disorganizes the defense when the ball carriers are closely supported by their teammates, quick rucks occur that launch another immediate attack, and ball carriers exploit the weaknesses of opposing defenses. American players are not as adept at understanding the strategic play necessary for effective attack due to the cultural influence of American football.

Defense

Organization, discipline, and pressure are the keys to defense. The defense tries to maintain position and to halt the advancing team before they can mount a full attack. Strong decisive tackling, support for the tackler, quick thinking, and ability to adapt to the situation presented will make things difficult for the advancing team. Since rugby is a "continuous" sport that doesn't stop when a tackle is made, as in American football, regrouping and organizing defense at every tackle is very important.

Good defenses communicate as they attempt to prevent the offense from moving forward. They must prepare for the unexpected and communicate where new offensive players are coming from and what might happen next. Good defenses make for good tacklers because they are in the correct location.

LEAD-UP ACTIVITIES

Mini-rugby

Mini-rugby is used as an introduction to the 15-a-side game. Its advantages are that it requires a much smaller playing area and fewer players, and it is simple yet exciting and an ideal game for beginners. Participants are afforded an opportunity to play many of the positions of the full game.

The playing area is 69 × 38 meters (75.4 × 41.5 yds). Each team has nine players: four forwards—two front row, one lock, one flanker—and five backs—one each scrum half, fly half, center, wing, fullback.

The game may be played on a full-sized rugby pitch, using only one half from touchline to touchline. The game is started from the center and "drop outs" from the existing 15-meter line.

The adapted rules include the following:
1. There are no line-outs.
2. Kicking is not encouraged.
3. Direct kicking to touch is only allowed inside the 15-meter area.
4. There are no kicks at goal for penalties.
5. When a try is scored, a kick at goal is taken from in front of the posts.

When penalties are awarded, the opposition retires 7 meters (7.6 yds) and the attacking team "taps the ball" and plays on. Tackling is unrestricted. The rules for offside, onside, knock-on, throw forward, and so on apply as usual. Each period lasts 20 minutes. The objectives of this type of training are to work on and improve straight running, good tackling, creating quick overlap situations in attack, and pressuring defense.

Touch Rugby

Touch rugby may be played during training. The size of the field should correspond to the number playing. The idea of the game is to score a try by touching the ball down behind the opposition's goal line. Players advance the ball by passing and running with the ball.

Tackling and kicking are not allowed. The opposition attempts to touch the player with the ball. Each team has four plays in which to advance the ball. A play is considered finished when a member of the opposition touches the advancing player in possession of the ball. After four plays, the other team has four plays in which to score. Each play is started by touching the ball on the foot and passing it to a teammate.

There are no line-outs or scrums, but knock-ons and offsides result in the ball being automatically turned over to the other team. The goals for players in touch rugby are improving ball-handling skills, recognizing attack situations quicker, and practicing continuous support running.

Grids

Teams of 2 to 10 players oppose each other in a playing area approximately 5 meters (5.5 yd) square. The objective is to develop fundamental skills in a simulated situation. Games in the grids may be organized for drill in a particular skill, such as passing. For example, with five players, three players can attempt to score a try and the other two attempt to stop them. This develops skills for tackling, decision making, passing, using the extra player, and running with the ball. The number of players and rules of the games can be modified to suit the objective of practice.

TEACHING CONSIDERATIONS

1. Because of safety considerations involved, tackling should probably not be part of the game taught to younger students. Touch rugby, with teams of 3 to 10 players, and modified rules, is probably more appropriate.
2. The weight and shape of the ball make rugby a unique activity, requiring different ball handling and kicking than in soccer and football. Experience in other field sports such as speedball, soccer, and football will help. However, practice time with the rugby ball is a necessity.
3. Practice in ball-handling skills should be designed for maximum participation. In most instances this means passing, catching, and kicking skills should be practiced with partners. Distances, directions, and force level requirements should vary as they do in actual games.
4. Offensive and defensive play can be introduced in two-on-one situations. Additional offensive and defensive players may be added as strategies are improved. Actual game play can begin in two-on-two situations.
5. Add scoring options and out-of-bounds rules gradually as the need arises. Maintain offside rules to differentiate rugby from football.
6. Stay with the game long enough for skill and appreciation of it to develop.
7. Some suggested drills are:
   a. Passing drill "pass at pace." In rugby, passing is the most fundamental of all skills. The rugby pass must combine the elements of rhythm, speed of pass, speed and acceleration of the run, and length and accuracy.
      (1) A group of four players separate about 4 meters (4.4 yds) apart. They begin by quickly passing from 1 to 2, to 3, to 4.
      (2) Once the ball is in 4's hands, 4 sprints ahead to a cone 20 meters (22 yds) in front. The other three must sprint to keep up with 4.
      (3) At the cone 4 passes back to 3 who sprints 10 meters (11 yds) to the next cone.
      (4) At this cone 3 passes to 2 who likewise sprints 10 meters (11 yds) to the next cone.
      (5) At this cone, 2 passes to 1, who then ensures the line is realigned for the final quick hands passing 1 to 2 to 3 and finally to 4.

This drill encompasses all of the techniques necessary to pass properly in a game: accuracy, pace, length, alignment, and, if done with a great deal of repetition, fitness.

   b. Loop or outside support drill. One of the most important skills a rugby player needs to develop continually is support of the ball carrier.
      (1) As in the preceding drill, 4 players about 4 meters (4.5 yds) apart begin by passing the ball laterally 1 through 4. After each player passes, he or she sprints to the outside of the last player in support.
      (2) Each player "loops" once as this is accomplished, and it should be done within 30 meters (33 yds). At the 30-meter mark, 4 places the ball on the ground, waits for a realignment of the other three players, and then begins the drill again going in the same direction.
      (3) The width of the drill should be no more than 15 meters (16.7 yds). This forces all players to step into each pass, creating space on the outside.
      (4) As the drill is completed, the players have traveled 50 to 60 meters (55 to 66 yds), so again these handling drills can also be used for fitness.

   c. Standing tackle drill. Since rugby is a contact sport, a ball carrier must know what to do when hit. In many cases a defensive player will try to hold up a ball carrier. This is called a "standing tackle." This is done to help strip the ball carrier of the ball. To prevent this is obviously an important objective for the offense.
      (1) Four players line up across a similar grid as in preceding drills *a* and *b*. Either player 2 or player 3 runs the ball forward, with the other three players behind. This player runs about 10 to 15 meters (11 to 16.5 yds), places the ball on the ground, and retreats 5 meters (5.47 yds) and faces the others.
      (2) One of the trailing players shouts "ball," scoops up the ball (using the proper technique of stationary hand in front of the ball and scooping hand coming in from behind), and then drives into the stationary player.
      (3) After contact, and while keeping in balance, the charging player abruptly rotates the shoulders perpendicular to the tackler, keeping *both* hands on the ball.
      (4) The next player drives into the teammate ball carrier, utilizing the outside shoulder. This player drives the shoulder into the ball carrier with a ripping motion over the ball to help secure it from the tackler.
      (5) The last player stands off at depth and, when he or she sees the ball rewon, shouts for the pass and takes it a pace, runs up 10 to 15 meters (11 to 16.5 yds), places the ball on the ground, and retreats. The entire process is repeated three to four times in this 60-meter grid.

   d. Continuous tackling drill. This is a drill that emphasizes that the tackle situation is not the end of the play as it is in American football. Players line up in line about 5 meters (5.47 yds) apart, each with a rucking bag in hand (rucking bags can be found at rugby supply companies online). The object is for players to hit the bag, drive and move onto the next bag to demonstrate the drive necessary to help make good tackles.

i. Five players line up with the bags while another group of 5 stands in front. The first player runs at half speed toward the first bag holder.
    1. The bag holder must stand with a good supportive base and a shoulder behind the bag.
ii. As the player approaches the bag, he or she should break down into a good driving position: leaning forward, head up, and leading with a shoulder.
iii. The player should hit the bag with either shoulder and head to the side, then wrap his or her arms around the bag and holder while driving through the bag at the same time.
iv. The drive should only be for a step or two, whereupon the player releases and moves on to the successive bags in line, repeating the action.
v. While reinforcing proper tackling technique and continuous action, the drill also should replicate the driving forward technique necessary in rucking and mauling.

GLOSSARY

accidental offside A player is offside unintentionally.

attacking team Team that has possession of the ball.

conversion Attempt to gain 2 extra points by kicking the ball over the crossbar after a try has been scored.

dead-ball line Line at the end of the field of play.

defending team The team that is attempting to stop the attacking team from scoring while also trying to gain possession of the ball.

drop goal The ball is drop-kicked over the bar during the continuous flow of play.

dropkick Kicking the ball on the half volley.

foul An infringement of the rules.

goal Obtained by scoring a try and a conversion. Worth 7 points.

halfway line Line that marks the center of the field.

in-goal area Area between goal line and dead-ball line; end zone.

in touch A ball that goes out-of-bounds is said to be in "touch."

kickoff Used to start the game at the beginning of each period and after a team has scored a try.

knock-on The ball is knocked forward during an attempt to catch it.

line-out Used to restart the game when the ball goes out of bounds.

mark Given to a player who catches the ball cleanly while standing still; player must call, "Mark."

maul One or more players from each side surround and hold the player with the ball and start to struggle for it.

pack The eight forwards.

penalty goal Worth 3 points when a player placekicks or dropkicks the ball over the crossbar after a penalty given by the referee for an infringement of the rules of the game.

ruck One or more players from each side in the field of play are on their feet and shoving each other, with the ball on the ground between them.

scrum Used to restart the game after an unintentional infringement of the rules.

throw-in A means of putting the ball into the line-out to restart the game after the ball has gone out-of-bounds.

try Score when a player carries the ball over the opposition goal line and touches the ball on the ground. Worth 4 points.

22-meter (24-yd) drop-out Dropkick from the 22-meter line to restart the game after the ball has been touched down in the end zone by the defending team or when the ball has crossed the dead-ball line.

SUGGESTED READINGS

Biscombe, T., Drewett, P., and Rutherford, D. 2010. *Rugby: Steps to success.* 2nd ed. Champaign, IL: Human Kinetics.

Brown, M., Guthrie, P., and Growden, G. 2007. *Rugby for dummies* Ontario, Canada: John Wiley & Sons.

Chandler, T. J. L. 1999. "Recognition through resistance: Rugby in the USA." In *Making the world: Race, gender, commerce,* Timothy J. L. Chandler and John Nauright, eds. Portland, OR: Frank Cass Publishers. This book provides historical reading for rugby.

Greenwood, J. 2003. *Total rugby.* 5th ed. London: A + C Black.

Greenwood, J. 2004. *Think rugby: A guide to purposeful team play.* 4th ed. London: A + C Black.

Hale, B. 2002. *Rugby tough.* Champaign, IL: Human Kinetics.

Luger, Dan. 2004. *Complete conditioning for rugby.* Champaign, IL: Human Kinetics.

Rugby, Football League. 2007. *Rugby League.* 3rd ed. London: A & C Black.

Sheryn, C. 2006. *Youth rugby drills.* London: A & C Black.

Williams, T., and Bunce, F. 2008. *Rugby skills, tactics, and rules.* 2nd ed. Willowdale, Canada: Firefly Books.

RESOURCES

Videos

Focus on rugby, Trace Videos, Reedswain, Inc, 62 Byers Rd., Chester Springs, PA 19425.

Mini rugby barbarians style, Rugby Football Union, Twickenham, Middlesex, England.

This is mini rugby, Welsh Rugby Union, 28 St. Marys St., Cardiff, Wales.

Film of the United States—International Games may be obtained through *Rugby* (newspaper), published by Rugby Press, Ltd., 527 Madison Ave., New York, NY 10022.

Rugby skills training, Queensland Rugby, Union, Australia, On Set Production (Telephone: 07 875-1651).

Video films of international games may be obtained through Trace Video Sports Club, c/o Brandon Hall, Box 1167, Natchez, MS 39120.

See Appendix C for other video sources.

Wall charts

Wall charts may be obtained from the Welsh Rugby Union, 28 St. Marys St., Cardiff, Wales.

WEB SITES

International Rugby Board (Rules, regulations, etc.) www.irfb.com
Planet Rugby www.rugbyrugby.com
Rugby Information www.uidaho.edu
Rugby Magazine (Monthly News—U.S.) www.inch.com/rugby
Rugby Newsletter www.scrum.com
Rugby Today (daily news—international) www.rugbytoday.com
Touch Rugby http://touch-canada.hypermart.net
    www.austouch.com.au
Ultimate Rugby http://ultimaterugby.on.ca
United States of America Rugby Football Union www.usarugby.org
World of Rugby www.worldofrugby.com

Self-Defense

25

After completing this chapter, the reader should be able to:

- Appreciate the importance of self-defense strategies and techniques in relation to daily living
- Explain the basic self-defense principles by describing various strategies related to awareness, prevention, escape, and recovery
- Demonstrate and execute proper stance, kicks, strikes, and releases employed in self-defense
- Utilize the information contained within this chapter to teach an effective self-defense curriculum to a group of individuals

HISTORY

Self-defense is a human behavior that has existed for thousands of years. Records indicate that individuals in the Eastern world have used various strategies to protect their physical selves and property from external threats. Yet it was not until the 1600s that the concept of self-defense spread to the Western world. By the late 19th and early 20th centuries, public discussions and printed materials began to present tactics and strategies for personal protection. These early documents were primarily focused on specific martial arts fighting forms, such as karate, jiu-jitsu, taekwondo, and judo. It was not until the 1980s and 1990s that the modern concept of self-defense education began to be presented in printed form.

Modern self-defense is described as a mixture of basic protection skills and common sense. Simple physical skills are employed that can be learned in a short time frame and effectively executed by anyone. These skills often are rooted in traditional martial art formats. In addition to physical skill development, modern self-defense curricula educate about awareness and prevention tactics. The goal of self-defense education is to teach how to make good choices, recognize potentially dangerous situations, and take action to prevent a physical altercation.

Personal protection is a basic human need. When individuals feel specifically threatened or generally uncomfortable, the resulting anxiety decreases the opportunity for personal development. This concept is theoretically supported by Maslow's theory of human motivation, also known as the "Hierarchy of Needs." As Maslow's Hierarchy of Needs indicates, an individual cannot fully self-actualize until his/her basic needs are met, including personal safety and security. It is vital that human beings exist in an orderly world where injustice is addressed and a sense of security is present. In modern times, Americans tend to worry about their safety. It has been estimated that more than one-third of Americans chronically worry that they will be assaulted at any given time. Through participation in a self-defense unit of instruction, students can generate knowledge and develop skills related to personal preservation that allow them to live a confident and purpose-driven life.

FACILITIES, EQUIPMENT, AND SPACING

Self-defense can be taught in any facility, including a gymnasium, a classroom, or any playing field. A unit of study could be taught with virtually no equipment; however, it is ideally taught with the following equipment and conditions available:

1. Striking Pads—9″ × 12″ striking pads are the ideal. It is recommended that one pad be used for every two students.
2. Surface Area—Mats for rolling or practicing ground techniques are very beneficial. Often a wrestling room, a gymnastics studio, or an area where gymnastic mats may be rolled out to provide a safe learning center can be utilized.
3. Floor Lines—Lines on the floor are beneficial to organize the classroom and appropriately space students when sliding and performing distractions.
4. White Board—It is helpful to have access to a white or chalk board as the instructor may wish to utilize it for class discussion or to outline the day's activities.
5. DVD Player and Television—Technology to play videos illustrating major concepts further stimulates the learning environment.

BASIC PRINCIPLES AND STRATEGIES

The four basic principles of self-defense are awareness, prevention, escape, and recovery.

Awareness

The ability to remain alert, attentive, and responsive to the environment around you is the most effective form of self-defense that can be taught. By focusing your attention outward, you are more likely to notice concerns, or "red flags," within your surroundings. Additionally, the alert individual sends a clear message to predators that he or she is not an "easy" target, decreasing the likelihood of being victimized. In short, self-defense units should include information about who assailants are, how assaults happen, and why assailants target certain victims. Making students familiar with this type of information helps achieve the primary goal of self-defense training: to help students trust intuitive messages and not to hesitate or freeze in the event of an impending assault. Instilling the realization that crime can and does happen, even in the most remote areas, should be a basic tenet of all self-defense units. Becoming familiar with general knowledge about assaults will drastically reduce a person's chance of becoming a victim of crime. Bring students' attention to the following issues related to increasing their general sense of awareness.

1. Recognize that it could happen to you!
2. Understand the types of crimes that concern you. The average citizen is most vulnerable to crimes of violence and property loss. These types of crimes are of concern within self-defense education not necessarily because of the financial loss, but more importantly because of the physical and emotional consequences associated with being victimized.
3. Attempt to identify potential assailants.
4. Familiarize yourself with the tactics used by criminals.
5. Understand the various reasons why criminals commit crimes.
6. Take steps to avoid being targeted by a criminal.

Prevention

Prevention refers to perceiving an impending assault and taking the necessary steps to keep that assault from occurring. Several steps may be enacted during the prevention phase; however, the two most prominent steps are **avoidance** and **deterrence.** Avoiding an assault altogether is the preferable choice for any potential victim. Therefore, self-defense educators should teach avoidance strategies by helping students to critically observe their physical surroundings and the behavior of others, and to listen and trust in their own intuition.

Once an assailant has begun the process of asserting dominance, however, the immediate threat of the situation has been escalated. Self-defense educators should teach students to utilize deterrence options to thwart an assailant from escalating this behavior to the level of physical violence. Deterrence strategies often include confident and assertive behaviors involving body posture, eye contact, facial expressions, and a commanding voice when utilizing communication skills. Listed below are several strategies to help students develop appropriate avoidance and deterrence behaviors.

Avoidance

1. Eliminate the potential for danger. You may employ several preventive measures to avoid becoming a victim of crime in all areas of life. The following is a list of some simple strategies related to:
   a. Home Safety—Secure locks on all doors and windows, draw the shades in the evening hours, install a motion detector light, and place a hold on your delivered mail when on vacation.
   b. Parking Lot Safety—Park under a light so that when you return to your vehicle visibility is enhanced. Approach your vehicle with your keys in hand and visually scan the area for others. Do not loiter inside your vehicle, rather start the engine and drive away.
   c. Driving Safety—Common courtesy on the highways can prevent a negative reaction by other motorists. Use turning indicators and avoid talking on the phone or playing with the radio. Do not return crude hand gestures, as remaining patient and polite is always an appropriate defense. If you are driving in a part of town with which you are unfamiliar, either use a mapping system or GPS to provide accurate directions, or call the store, restaurant, or venue to which you are heading and ask for clear directions and suggestions on parking. Additional suggestions include packing a first aid and winter survival kit in the trunk and being able to change a flat tire.
   d. Exercise Safety—When walking or jogging in a natural environment, listening to music through headphones is not recommended, as this decreases one's awareness of his/her surroundings. It is a good idea to vary your exercise times and routes. Other suggestions include never exercising alone and avoiding trails or paths that are lined with thick foliage.
   e. Dating Safety—Approximately one in three teenagers or young women have experienced violence in a dating relationship. Violence is often used to maintain power and control over another individual. Early warning signs indicating potential abuse include jealousy, controlling behavior, unpredictable mood swings, the use of alcohol or drugs, intense anger, a belief in rigid sex roles, or verbal and emotional abuse. Early identification of these warning signs may also stop an impending sexual assault, another serious issue facing young women. It is estimated that 25 percent of women will be the victims of sexual assault and that 90 percent of the time the crime will be committed by someone known to the victim.
   f. Technology Safety—A cellular phone is a wonderful device to aid in a time of need. A common mistake is to talk on your phone as a way to avoid being victimized. You may do this to give the impression that there is "safety in numbers," but the reality is that

talking on your phone distracts you and thus you become a potential target for assault.

2. Recognize and avoid dangerous situations. It is important to take precautionary steps to avoid being victimized. However, the potential for danger still exists. The following are examples of some ways to recognize and avoid danger:
   a. Safety in numbers—It is always better to travel in a group than alone.
   b. Avoid dangerous situations—Avoid isolated and darkened areas where there are not a lot of other people.
   c. Give up your valuables—When confronted by an attacker, especially one with a weapon, it is best to quickly give up your valuables. Money and material items may be replaced; however, your physical health may not. Get to safety as soon as possible.
   d. Never go to a secondary location with the attacker—It is better to fight for your life at the first crime scene, as the odds of survival are much higher.
   e. Trust your intuition—Countless testimonials from victims of crime reveal that their intuition was attempting to communicate that they were in danger.

Deterrence

1. Display confident behaviors and determined actions. Most assailants capitalize on the weaknesses and vulnerabilities of others. You can lessen the chance of being victimized by portraying confident behaviors and a determined demeanor. The following actions can be practiced to help develop these qualities:
   a. Developing body posture—A classic athletic stance contains most characteristics evident within a confident body posture. Head up, shoulders back, arms relaxed and at sides, standing up straight, knees slightly bent, and feet shoulder width apart are all elements that can be practiced.
   b. Facial expressions and voice—Other elements that indicate confidence during tense situations are your facial expressions and command of voice. Be positive.
   c. Establishing adequate personal space—A general rule of thumb sets your personal space as the length of your outstretched arms.
2. Communicating with assertiveness. Simple strategies that can help develop assertive communication include:
   a. Recognizing assertive behaviors—When confronted with a situation where tensions are rising and the chance of physical aggression is escalating, assertive and aggressive behaviors are very appropriate.
   b. Develop and practice various assertive techniques—Practice simple strategies that demonstrate an assertive, confident persona.

3. Take action now! By avoiding potentially dangerous situations, trusting your intuition, and displaying confident and assertive behaviors, you are less likely to become the victim of crime. Take action to remove yourself from potentially dangerous situations prior to the situation escalating out of control.

Escape

Once an assault has escalated to the point of physical aggression, numerous strategies, including physical defense skills, may be employed to help you escape from an already progressive assault. Escape techniques include the psychomotor actions and knowledge of proper stance, balance, movements, blocks, strikes, kicks, throws, floor, and release techniques. Through practice and the refinement of skills, you can build confidence in your abilities.

In the following section, many physical skills are presented that effectively target vulnerable body parts to incapacitate an aggressor. Once the threat is lessened, the immediate goal is to escape from the present danger and find safety in a secure environment. Prior to discussing these physical techniques, however, it is important to understand some general principles presented below:

1. Basic Elements—Effective self-defense includes four basic elements of accurate strikes, forceful blows, speed associated with timing, and an active follow-through.
   a. Accurate strikes—It is important that your strike actually hit the intended target. Often you will only have one opportunity to strike a specific body target. If the target is missed, the situation could escalate to a higher degree of severity as the assailant becomes enraged. Therefore, accuracy is imperative.
   b. Forceful blows—Self-defense curricula includes physical skills that can be utilized by anyone, regardless of physical strength, size, or limitations. The more physically strong you are, the more force you can generate. Nevertheless, an all-out effort combined with accuracy can yield devastatingly positive results. When practicing skills and refining technique, it is important to engage with a full effort. Although progression from slow to medium to fast is appropriate and recommended, you must practice at full pace to develop appropriate motor patterns.
   c. Speed and timing—In any altercation there is typically a "window of opportunity" that presents itself. This would be defined as the opportune time to employ a physical technique to immobilize an assailant.
   d. Active follow-through—When attempting to incapacitate an assailant, it is crucial that you follow through with active strikes and blows. An active follow-through will increase the force of the blow and is more likely to yield the intended result: incapacitation of the perpetrator. To reiterate, your goal is to avoid and de-escalate a situation from becoming

physically violent. However, if you must engage in physical contact, do so with full effort.

2. Make Some Noise!—A very effective strategy to utilize prior to and during an assault situation is to make as much noise as possible. Yelling and screaming brings attention to the assault. Making noise has been shown to be effective in countless attack situations as even the most determined assailants become unnerved. Specific words that you should say are "no", "fire", and "hey." The word "no" is particularly effective. The use of the word "help" is discouraged by most self-defense educators, as onlookers either tend not to want to get involved or assume others will come to your aid. This phenomenon, known as the bystander effect, has been well researched and replicated within the field of social psychology.

3. Vulnerable Body Parts—There are seven vulnerable areas that exist on the human body that may be effectively exploited to incapacitate an individual. These areas include the eyes, nose, chin, throat, solar plexus, groin, and knees. The physical skills presented later target these seven areas of vulnerability.

4. Strike First—The goal of self-defense is to avoid physical altercations whenever possible. By recognizing and avoiding contact with potential danger, or by simply walking away from a tense situation, a physical assault may not occur. In the event that awareness and prevention tactics have not de-escalated the intensity of a situation and you fear for your personal safety or life, you may need to take action. When an aggressor has physically entered one's personal space with the intention of causing harm, you may strike first. *Striking first* is defined as quick and decisive actions with the intention of immediately immobilizing an assailant when no other options are available. Primary points of target are the eyes, chin, and throat. Once the assailant has been disabled, you should flee the environment and call for help.

5. Unleash the Beast—Once the physical altercation has begun, you are fighting for your life. Strike as often and as viciously as possible to disable the aggressor. It only takes a few seconds to disable an individual in an assault situation, whether it be you or the aggressor. Therefore, it is important that you not only focus on technical accuracy, force, and follow-through when you are practicing these skills, but also that you become proficient with the deliverance of successive blows.

Recovery

Issues relating to recovery arise both during and after an assault. Surviving an assault is a great accomplishment; however, once the victim or assailant has left the scene, the assault is not over. Often psychological and emotional trauma produced by the confrontation, sometimes referred to as *fall out,* must be dealt with properly. Important information and services are required to help an assaulted individual regain confidence in his or her personal safety. These services include:

1. Local police contact information.
2. Local hospital and clinic information.
3. Drug and alcohol abuse helplines.
4. National and local sexual assault contact information.
5. National and local domestic violence contact information.
6. Suicide prevention helplines.

BASIC TECHNIQUES
Balances and Stances

Understanding how to establish and maintain balance is an important concept when defending yourself. To remain mobile you must be able to stay balanced while standing, regardless of the external forces being imposed by an assailant. Balance is defined as stability when your weight is evenly dispersed. In simple terms, balance is comprised of two elements: center of gravity and base of support. When your center of gravity extends beyond your base of support (feet), you are likely to fall down, putting you at increased risk. To maintain balance, it is important that you develop an appropriate stance that is comfortable, mobile, and efficient. The following activities aid you in developing an understanding of and comfort level with balance and stance.

Balance drills

(see Figure 25.1)—You should gain a physical understanding of what it feels like to be properly and improperly balanced. To begin, stand face to face with a partner and clasp your hands at shoulder height. With feet together, push against your partner to knock him or her off balance. Try this drill again with feet at shoulder width and then again with feet as wide as they will go. A majority of people feel most comfortable with their feet at shoulder width; however, they are still at risk for being knocked off balance. For the final drill, stand with your feet at shoulder width but this time take a step back with your dominant foot. You are now in a position that allows for dynamic balance in forward, sideways, and backward planes.

Figure 25.1. Balance drills.

Balance position

(see Figure 25.2)—A balance position is an efficient stance that provides comfort, mobility, efficiency, and ultimately safety for the individual. It is important that you stand sideways to the aggressor, with your hips approximately 45 degrees from the threat. Beginners tend to stand square to their attacker, creating the largest target possible. The balance position is the first and most important physical skill to be taught in any self-defense educational unit. The balance position is the primary stance used within self-defense.

Instructional cues

- Feet are shoulder width apart with dominant leg one step back.
- Weight is evenly distributed on the balls of your feet.
- Hips are located at 45 degrees from the assailant.
- Shoulders are squared to the assailant.
- Arms are up, elbows in, and fists are clenched (thumbs outside of fingers).
- Head is protected "in the box."
- Eyes are on the horizon.

Sumo-style balance position

(see Figure 25.3)—In certain situations a secondary stance, known as a sumo-style balance position, is more efficient to maintain balance or deliver a blow than the previous stance. As the name suggests, you establish a position indicative of a sumo-style wrestler. Positive characteristics of this stance include a wide base and lowered center of gravity.

Instructional cues

- Feet wider than shoulder width and placed out to your sides.
- Bottom is lowered by bending at the knees.
- Body posture is erect with head up and shoulders back.
- Arms are up with palms facing forward.
- Eyes are on the horizon.

Kicking Techniques

Kicking techniques incorporate the use of your knees and feet as body weapons. Typical targets include an assailant's groin, thighs, hips, and knees. The groin area, particularly for males, is a sensitive body region that may be targeted to immobilize an assailant for a brief moment. It should be noted that groin strikes may prove effective in less threatening situations, but in tense situations where adrenaline is flowing in both victim and attacker, the blow could be rendered useless. Therefore, it is important to practice delivering successive blows to increase the likelihood of a favorable response. The knee is a hinge joint that locks when fully straightened. As is the case with any hinge joint, when pressure is applied to a straightened leg, damage to or dislocation of the knee joint may occur. It is not recommended to practice kicking techniques above knee height. Distractions are to be delivered quickly and efficiently so that balance may be immediately reestablished. By bringing your foot high into the air, accuracy is decreased and balance is compromised. The following kicking techniques can provide the novice with immediate success.

Figure 25.2. Balance position.

Figure 25.3. Sumo-style balance position.

Knee lift

(see Figure 25.4)—The objective of the knee lift is to strike the assailant's groin, thighs, or hips with a hard blow delivered by aggressively driving your knee into the targeted area. To be

successful the strike must be delivered when in close proximity to the assailant. It is important to place both of your feet firmly on the ground after striking to regain balance and/or strike again with force. Extreme force can be realized by holding on to the assailant's shoulders and driving the knee upward while pulling down. The back, or dominant, leg in the balance position is used to develop the most power; however, both legs will work.

Instructional cues
- Balance position.
- Square hips to assailant.
- Raise back leg so thigh is parallel to ground.
- Drive knee into assailant's groin.

Front snap kick

(see Figure 25.5)—The objective of the front snap kick is to strike the assailant's knee with the ball of your foot, making sure you have raised your toes up to reveal the proper striking surface of the foot. The back, or dominant, leg in the balance position is used. The striking target is the patellar tendon, located just below the kneecap.

Instructional cues
- Balance position.
- Square hips to assailant.
- Raise back leg so thigh is parallel to ground.
- Extend leg toward target.
- Kick with ball of foot (toes up).

Figure 25.4. Knee lift.

Figure 25.5. Front snap kick.

Back kick

(see Figure 25.6)—The objective of the back kick is to strike the assailant's knee. However, this distraction is used when the assailant is behind you. Similar to the front snap kick, the target point is the patellar tendon below the kneecap. You should look over your shoulder, point your back hip at the assailant and then strike. An effective strike is delivered by kicking with the heel of the foot.

Instructional cues
- Balance position.
- Point back hip at assailant.
- Raise back leg so thigh is brought toward chest.
- Extend leg toward target.
- Kick with heel of foot (foot perpendicular to ground).

Side kick

(see Figure 25.7)—The objective of the side kick is to strike the assailant's knee with the heel or outside blade of your foot. The front, or non-dominant, leg in the balance position is used. The striking target is the patellar tendon, located just below the kneecap. When attempting to deliver this strike, point the front hip at the assailant and bring the front leg to your chest prior to delivering the blow. The side kick is effectively used when the assailant is in close proximity or you do not have the ability to dynamically move throughout the area.

Instructional cues
- Balance position.
- Point front hip at assailant.
- Raise front leg so thigh is brought to chest.
- Extend leg toward target.
- Kick with heel of foot (foot perpendicular to ground).

Shuffle side kick

(see Figure 25.8)—The shuffling side kick incorporates the same technique as the side kick; however, this distraction is employed when there is distance between you and the assailant. If an opening to strike presents itself, previously discussed as the "window of opportunity," you may strike quickly by simply stepping with your front foot, bringing your back foot together with the front, and then performing the side kick technique.

Instructional cues
- Balance position.
- Step with front foot toward assailant.
- Bring back foot together with front foot.
- Perform side kick.
- Simple cue—"step-together-strike."
- This is a very powerful, quick movement.

Pivot side kick

(see Figure 25.9)—The pivoting side kick utilizes the same technique as the side kick to deliver the blow; however, you are able to use the back, or dominant leg, in the balance position. To deliver the blow, you drive your back knee around and toward the attacker, basically turning 180 degrees. In doing so your back hip is now pointing at the attacker with your knee tucked close to your chest. You may now deliver the side kick.

Instructional cues
- Balance position.
- Rotate back hip to point at assailant by pivoting 180 degrees on front foot.
- While rotating, back thigh is brought to chest.

Figure 25.6. Back kick.

- Extend leg toward target.
- Kick with heel of foot (foot perpendicular to ground).

Hand Blow Techniques

Hand blows are delivered with one's hands to distract an assailant long enough to either remove yourself from a dangerous situation or completely immobilize an assailant. Typical targets include the nose, eyes, chin, throat, head, or back of neck. Each of these target areas is highly sensitive when struck with adequate force, speed, and accuracy. It is not recommended to use a closed fist when striking in self-defense, as this is a collapsible object and prone to injury.

Furthermore, the development of closed fist striking techniques requires time and training to realize the maximum potential of the weapon. The following hand blows, which may be utilized immediately and with success, have been shown effective:

Cupped hand blow

(see Figure 25.10)—The objective of the cupped hand blow is to strike any of the head targets listed above, including the side of the neck, Adam's apple, nose, and back of the neck at the base of the skull, with the outside (pinky side) blade of your hand. The hand should be held in a "cupped" fashion

Figure 25.7. Side kick.

Figure 25.8. Shuffle side kick.

with all fingers being squeezed together to strengthen the weapon. Your back, or dominant, arm in the balance position is used. Similar to throwing a baseball, an effective blow is delivered by squaring your hips, pulling back the throwing arm, and following through with force.

Instructional cues
- Balance position.
- Square hips to assailant.
- Pull back arm (striking arm) into position while establishing cupped hand.
- Strike target (similar to throwing a ball).

Open hand blow

(see Figure 25.11)—The open hand blow is primarily intended to strike the nose of the assailant; however, it may be used effectively when striking other head targets such as the chin. This is a strike that could potentially prove fatal when the nose or chin is struck in an upwardly powerful motion. Care should be taken when practicing this move. To perform the blow, all of your fingers are bent over and the thumb is brought tightly in to meet the first (index) finger. The strike is delivered using the palm of your hand. Again, use your back, or dominant arm, in the balance position. The motion of the arm is similar to that of putting the shot rather than throwing a baseball.

Figure 25.9. Pivot side kick.

Instructional cues
- Balance position.
- Square hips to assailant.
- Pull back arm (striking arm) into position while establishing open hand.
- Strike target (similar to putting a shot).

Finger jab

(see Figure 25.12)—The finger jab is intended to be used as a strike into an assailant's eye, but may prove effective when directed to the neck region. Simply bring all your fingers and thumb together to make one point. Keeping the wrist straight, your arm and hand take on the appearance of a spear. The point of the "spear" is used to strike the intended target and is much more stable than a single or pair of fingers would be. The back, or dominant arm, would the most powerful. Nevertheless, any of the hand blows may be attempted using the front, or non-dominant, arm in the balance position.

Figure 25.10. Cupped hand blow.

Figure 25.11. Open hand blow.

Instructional cues
- Balance position.
- Square hips to assailant.
- Pull back arm (striking arm) into position while establishing point.
- Strike target (similar to throwing a ball).

Elbow Blow Techniques

Elbow blows are most commonly delivered with the area above or below your elbow. The intended targets are the solar plexus, head, throat, base of the skull, chin, chest, or rib cage, depending on which blow is being employed. Great force, equivalent to the striking power of a baseball bat, can be

Figure 25.12. Finger jab.

Figure 25.13. Backward elbow blow.

generated with the use of your elbows. Elbow blows are typically utilized when an assailant is in very close proximity or has physically grasped you.

Backward elbow blow

(see Figure 25.13)—The objective of this blow is to strike the assailant's abdominal region, or solar plexus, when you are being grabbed from behind. If you are grasped at or near shoulder level, you immediately know that the assailant's mid section is exposed because his or her arms are up and extended. You can capitalize on this vulnerability by taking two actions. First, aggressively step backward or into the assailant in an effort to "close the gap" and ensure an accurate strike. Next, drive your elbow directly into the assailant's solar plexus. Continue striking until the assailant has released his or her grip.

Instructional cues
- Balance position.
- Drive back foot between assailant's legs.
- Extend same-side arm straight out with palm up (leg and arm are in opposition).
- Make fist and cover with other hand.
- Drive elbow back into solar plexus of assailant.
- Continue to strike.

Over-the-shoulder elbow blow

(see Figure 25.14)—This is similar to the backward elbow blow in that the assault is occurring from behind you; however, one key difference exists. Rather than being grasped at shoulder level, now you are held at or near your waist level.

This indicates that the assailant's hands are at his or her waist, exposing the head and neck region for possible distraction. When grabbed from behind at the waist, you should immediately establish a sumo-style balance position. Once you see where the head of the assailant is by physically looking over your shoulders, you strike with the back of your elbow into the assailant's head.

Instructional cues
- Sumo-style balance position.
- Turn your head from side to side to see where assailant is.
- Make fist with one hand (palm down) and cover with other hand.
- Drive elbow over shoulder into head of assailant.
- Continue to strike.
- If you cannot see the assailant's head, it means he or she is directly behind your head. In this case a backward head butt (discussed later) may be appropriate.

Forward elbow blow

(see Figure 25.15)—The objective of the forward elbow blow is to strike the assailant's head, chin, neck, throat, base of the skull, chest, or rib cage when the "window of opportunity" presents itself. Unlike the backward or over-the-shoulder elbow blows, the forward elbow blow is utilized when you are face to face with the attacker. To successfully use this strike, simply step with the back, or dominant leg, from the balance position toward the attacker. Twist your torso backward while stepping forward with the lower body, creating torque. You now follow through by releasing the torqued position and striking the assailant with the forearm area.

Figure 25.14. Over-the-shoulder elbow blow.

Instructional cues
- Balance position.
- Step toward assailant with back leg.
- Twist upper body while stepping (as right leg steps forward the right shoulder should be twisting backward in opposition).
- Make fist with arm rotated backward.
- Cover fist with other hand.
- Strike assailant with forearm strike.

Releases from Wrist Grabs

The following wrist grab releases have proven to be effective when employed properly. To break the grab, you exploit the weakest point of the assailant's grasp. This area is typically the open space between the attacker's thumb and forefinger. Wrist grab situations tend not to be life threatening; nevertheless, the goal is to immediately reestablish your personal space by breaking the connection between you and the attacker.

Figure 25.15. Forward elbow blow.

Figure 25.16. Straight across wrist grab (single hand).

Straight across wrist grab (single hand)

(see Figure 25.16)—A common scenario likely to occur in a face-to-face assault situation is for an attacker to reach straight out and grasp your arm or wrist. More specifically, if the attacker reaches out with the right arm, he or she will grab your left arm or wrist. You can break the hold by first establishing a balance position and countering the attacker's strength by backing away, or distancing yourself, from the attacker. It is important for you to remain relaxed, as the first instinct is to contract muscles and limbs when physically assaulted, thus bringing the attacker closer to your body. It is also important to remain balanced and mobile throughout. Next, you turn the thumb side of your grasped hand toward the attacker's weakest link, mentioned above as the gap between the attacker's thumb and forefinger. In one fluid motion you "rip" your hand toward your chest by bending at the elbow, a motion similar to a biceps curl.

Instructional cues
- Balance position.
- Establish distance between you and the attacker by backing away/resisting attacker.
- Turn thumb side of hand toward weakest link of attacker.
- Pull your hand through attacker's weakest link—sideways motion, not a tugging motion.
- Balance position and back away.

Cross wrist grab (advanced wrist release)

(see Figure 25.17)—Another common scenario in a face-to-face assault situation is for the attacker to reach across your body, grabbing the opposite arm or wrist. For example, the attacker reaches with his or her right arm, grabbing your right arm or wrist. As is the case with the straight across wrist grab, you immediately establish a balance position and distance yourself from the attacker.

Figure 25.17. Cross wrist grab (advanced wrist release).

Next you break the hold by reversing the attacker's grip. This is done by leading with the pinky-side of your hand and rotating under and around your wrist. Depending on the intensity of the situation, you now have two options. First, you can completely break the grasp, freeing yourself from the hold, and back away from the situation. The second option is more advanced and intended for use in a tense situation. Rather than breaking the grip, you reverse the hold and now you have a firm grasp on the attacker's wrist. From this vantage point the attacker's elbow is vulnerable. You step with your back leg from the balance position toward the attacker's elbow. Meanwhile you rotate your upper body against your lower body, developing torque, and setting up a forward elbow blow. You now deliver a forward elbow blow to the elbow of the attacker.

Instructional cues

- Balance position.
- Establish distance between you and the attacker by backing away/resisting attacker.
- Reverse attacker's grip—use "pinky-side" of your hand to reverse.
- Step with back foot toward attacker's isolated elbow.
- Forward elbow blow to attacker's isolated elbow.
- Disengage.

Two hands on one wrist grab

(see Figure 25.18)—In the event that an attacker grabs your wrist with both hands, your first response is to establish a solid balance position. When balance is achieved and the "window of opportunity" arises, you turn the palm of your grasped hand toward the sky and make a fist. Next, you reach between the arms of the assailant, grabbing onto your clenched fist. Finally break the hold by pulling your grasped hand through the attacker's weakest link in the hold.

Instructional cues

- Balance position.
- Establish distance between you and the attacker by backing away/resisting attacker.
- Turn grabbed hand palm up and make a fist.
- Reach in-between attacker's hands and cover your clenched fist.
- Pull hand through attacker's weakest link.
- Balance position and back away.

Releases from Lapel Grabs and Choke Holds

The following techniques may be used to break a hold in which an assailant has grabbed your lapel or neck. As is the case with wrist grabs, lapel grabs are not necessarily life threatening. However, you should take action to break the connection and flee the situation. In the event that an assailant has attempted to secure a choke hold on your throat, immediate action is imperative. As pressure is applied to the neck region, you may lose consciousness in 4 to 14 seconds. Therefore, every second counts and quick, decisive distractions must be employed.

Figure 25.18. Two hands on one wrist grab.

Figure 25.19. Aikido release technique.

Aikido release technique

(see Figure 25.19)—The objective of an Aikido release is to disengage the assailant's hold on your lapel when grabbed in a straight across or cross body fashion. The key to success with this release in a face-to-face assault situation is to use the hand on the same side of your body as that of the attacker. In other words, if the attacker has grasped your lapel with the right hand, you should use your left hand to break the hold. You simply drive your thumb into the back of the assailant's hand and grasp the assailant's thumb with your fingers. You are now in position to "peel away" the attacker's grasp. You may now release the assailant by releasing the hold or continue to distract the attacker with toe stomps, kicks to the shin, or knee lifts. An Aikido release may be used on one-hand or two-hand lapel grabs.

Swim release technique

(see Figure 25.20)—The swim release is effectively used when a two-hand lapel grab or choke hold has been employed by an assailant. You should first establish a solid sumo-style balance position. Once balance has been attained, you "swim" through the assailant's grasp by reaching up and over the attacker's arms with one of your arms. Once your elbow has risen above the attacker's arms, you aggressively drive your elbow down and to your side. The power generated is typically enough to break a two-hand lapel grab or choke hold.

Figure 25.20. Swim release technique.

Figure 25.21. Wedge release technique.

Wedge release technique

(see Figure 25.21)—Another effective response to a two-hand lapel grab or choke hold is a wedge release. You first establish a solid sumo-style balance position. Next you clasp your hands together, bend at the elbows, and push them outward, creating a "wedge." The "wedge" is then driven straight up in-between the attacker's arms, releasing his or her grip. From this position you may drive your clasped hands down upon the assailant's nose or facial region.

Additional distractions

If the aggressor has established a very firm grip, or you are physically smaller or weaker than the attacker, the Aikido, swim, or wedge releases may not be effective. In this event, you should use other techniques to distract the assailant, loosening his or her grasp, prior to using any of the above mentioned release techniques. Strike as often as you can and as many times as necessary. Additional distractions, which are described below, indicate effective targets from the base to the head of the human body and are likely effective in any assault situation.

- Foot stomps (see Figure 25.22)—Using the heel of your foot, drive down with all of your force onto the arch of your aggressor's foot or toes.
- Shin scrapes (see Figure 25.23)—Using either the inside or outside of your foot, scrape down the front of an aggressor's shin with the edge of your shoe.
- Shin kicks (see Figure 25.24)—Repeatedly kick into the front of your aggressor's shin bones.

- Knee lift—Drive your knee powerfully into the groin, hip, or thigh region of your aggressor.
- Eye gouge (see Figure 25.25)—This technique is particularly successful in a chokehold situation. To execute this distraction, bring your hands either around or inside the arms of the assailant. Place your hands on the aggressor's head to stabilize it and drive your thumbs deeply and directly into his or her eyes. This technique may temporarily or permanently blind an assailant.
- Ears, lips, and hair pulls (see Figure 25.26)—Another useful distraction is to aggressively grab and pull on the ears, lips, or hair of an assailant.
- Head strikes (see Figure 25.27)—If both hands are free, hold the back of your attacker's head with one hand while striking with the other. Particularly effective strikes include cupped hand blows, open hand blow, or finger jabs directly focused upon the eyes, nose, and throat. Clawing, scratching, pinching, and biting are also recommended.
- Head butts—The use of your head as a weapon can be very effective, particularly when the blow is delivered at an assailant's jaw, face, or temple region. To safely execute this distraction, you should strike with the thickest part of your skull, located at the hairline of your forehead. Failure to strike with this region of the head could result in injury. Further, it is not recommended to use your neck muscles to "snap" the head forward. Rather, you should keep your head locked in a neutral position, tighten your core abdominal muscles, bend at the knees, and drive your body upward

Figure 25.22. Foot stomps.

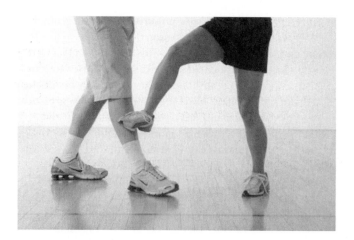

Figure 25.23. Shin scrapes.

Figure 25.24. Shin kicks.

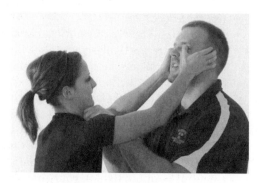
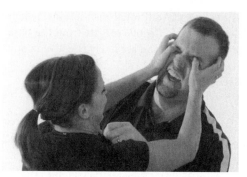

Figure 25.25. Eye gouge.

Figure 25.26. Ear pull.

Figure 25.27. Head strikes.

and forward by straightening your knees and bringing your chest toward the threat. The result is a "hammering" action with the upper body that increases force and ensures neck and head safety.

Releases from Rear Body Grabs

The following techniques may be used to break a body hold from behind. When you are grabbed from the rear it is typically around the waist or chest regions of the body. If your arms are "pinned" against your body, this escalates the intensity and difficulty of breaking the hold. The primary purpose for a rear body grab is to displace balance and force you to the ground. If an you are grabbed from the front side of your body, you may utilize any of the distractions listed in the Lapel Grabs and Choke Holds section to break the grip. When held from behind, it is important to first establish a balance position. In this case the appropriate balance position is the sumo-style stance. Once balance is maintained, you may break the hold.

Rear body grab with both arms free

(see Figure 25.28)—When grabbed from behind with both arms free, you are in the least restricted position. You should first establish a sumo-style balance position, ensuring that your legs are as wide as possible and your center of gravity is lowered appropriately. When the "window of opportunity" presents itself, utilize various distractions to loosen the assailant's hold. Effective distractions include over-the-

shoulder elbow blows, backward head butts, foot stomps, shin scrapes, and backward shin kicks. When the assailant's grip is loosened, you perform a finger-release technique (see Figure 25.29) to pivot out and away from the assailant's hold. This is accomplished by grabbing the attacker's forefinger with the hand on the same side of your body, compressing the attacker's knuckle joint by pushing in and pulling back the finger in an effort to dislocate or break the bone. You are now able to pivot out and away from the aggressor.

Instructional cues

- Sumo-style balance position.
- Foot stomps, shin scrapes, backward shin kicks, and backward head butt.
- Over-the-shoulder elbow blow with both arms.
- Once assailant's grip is loosened, perform finger release.
- With same side hand, grab attacker's forefinger, compress joint, pull back in attempt to dislocate or break.
- Allows you to disengage hold while pivoting away from attacker.

Rear body grab with one arm pinned

(see Figure 25.30)—With one arm pinned, you are in a somewhat restricted position. The appropriate response to breaking this grasp is the same as a rear body hold with both arms free. However, there is one additional distraction that is noteworthy, entitled the Side-Step Groin Strike. Because one arm is pinned within the attacker's arms, you are able

Figure 25.28. Rear body grab with both arms free (over-the-shoulder elbow blow).

Figure 25.29. Finger release technique.

Figure 25.30. Rear body grab with one arm pinned (side-step groin strike).

to strike the groin region of the aggressor. To accomplish this task, you bring your feet together, stepping in a sideways fashion. It is recommended that the victim step with the same side foot as the arm that is pinned, for example, stepping with the left foot when the left arm is pinned down. There is now a clear path to strike or "grab, twist, and pull" the groin region of the aggressor.

Instructional cues
- Sumo-style balance position.
- Foot stomps, shin scrapes, backward shin kicks, backward head butt.
- Over-the-shoulder elbow blow with free arm.
- Bring one foot together with other foot—clearing a path to strike (grab-twist-pull) assailant's groin.
- Once assailant's grip is lessened, perform finger release.
- With same side hand, grab attacker's forefinger, compress joint, pull back in attempt to dislocate or break.
- Allows victim to disengage hold while pivoting away from attacker.

Rear body grab with both arms pinned
(see Figure 25.31)—This is the most restricted position you can experience when held from behind. Because both arms are pinned, a finger-release is not possible. However, a strike to the groin of the aggressor is now possible with both hands. Continue to utilize distractions until the assailant's hold is loosened enough to break free.

Instructional cues
- Sumo-style balance position.
- Foot stomps, shin scrapes, backward shin kicks, backward head butt.
- Bring one foot together with other foot, clearing a path to strike (grab-twist-pull) assailant's groin.
- Attempt to break hold by pushing arms out, against the aggressor's hold.

ETIQUETTE
In the real world, there are no rules when it comes to self-defense. You should be willing to do whatever it takes to ensure your personal safety. A very different attitude must be taken to ensure the safety of participants when learning and practicing these techniques. The following suggestions pertain to the development of etiquette within the self-defense classroom:

1. Know Your Rights—It is important that you know and understand your legal rights and responsibilities regarding the use of force for personal protection. If you feel you are in a life-threatening situation, you have the right to use physical force to keep an aggressor at bay or to disable an attacker. Once the threat posed by the attacker has been minimized, you should cease the use of force, remove yourself from the situation, and call police for help. It is not within your rights to "teach" the assailant "a lesson" by continuing to physically strike the attacker once incapacitated.

2. Respect Individual Differences—The self-defense curriculum is available for and applicable to everyone, regardless of one's gender, race, ethnicity, social class, disability, religion, or sexual orientation.

3. Establish a Safe Zone—In a self-defense unit of instruction, the safety of the teaching and learning environment is a shared responsibility between instructor and students. Class rules and expectations should be discussed, posted, and practiced. Safety concerns include:

   a. Appropriate dress—Inappropriate dress may result in injury or exposure. Self-defense is a "hands on" endeavor that will be extremely physical in nature at times. Students should dress in clothing that allows for full physical participation without hindering movement or creating potential safety hazards. Appropriate dress would include comfortable shorts, shirts, or sweat suits. It is also recommended that fingernails be trimmed and all jewelry removed, including body piercings. Allowing students to wear street clothes for this unit may also be appropriate, as the likelihood of being attacked in active wear is minimal.

   b. Full participation/effort—Students should practice at a level conducive to developing an appropriate motor pattern. It is recommended that students begin simply and progress with increased speed and effort as their skills are refined. A lack of effort will

not only hinder skill development, it could result in injury.

   c. Follow Instructor's Directions—Off-task behavior could easily result in injury, hence the importance of closely following directions. The instructor has a duty to clearly outline each day's content for students, to break down each skill, and teach each skill in a progressive format.

4. Respect Equipment—Encourage students to remove their shoes and all jewelry prior to striking pads with their feet and/or hands.

TEACHING CONSIDERATIONS

Attempting to address the four basic principles (awareness, prevention, escape, and recovery) within a self-defense unit of instruction can be an overwhelming task. Therefore, it is suggested that individuals instructing a self-defense unit consider the following:

1. Anyone Can Teach Self-Defense—Self-defense is a difficult and intimidating topic when one has a limited background with the content. Nevertheless, any educator may teach basic awareness, prevention, and recovery strategies. This information is primarily common sense, and most students have already constructed knowledge related to these topics through exposure to mass media and life experiences. It is highly recommended that the instructor practice these skills to gain proficiency prior to teaching students.

2. Safety First!—It is important that safety is reiterated in every class session. Whenever reviewing a previously learned skill or introducing a new skill, the instructor should identify potential safety concerns. If the instructor perceives a skill being practiced as a safety issue, immediately stop all activity and correct the issue.

3. Class Organization—Simple classroom organizational strategies increase the effectiveness of a self-defense unit and promote the quality use of time.

   a. Teaching styles—Whenever possible the instructor should organize class for practice primarily using partners. It is recommended that students change partners often in order to experience differences between genders, height, weight, strength, and effort.

   b. Skill progression and refinement—It is recommended that students practice skills in a progressive format from slow to medium to fast pace. As the speed increases, skill refinement becomes a challenge. Educators and student-partners should pay special attention to the accuracy, force, and follow-through of each strike. Specific skill-related feedback will aid in the refinement of skill and the development of appropriate motor patterns. Providing resistance through the use of striking pads will further aid in the development of a refined motor pattern.

Figure 25.31. Rear body grab with both arms pinned.

c. Structuring the lesson—The effective design of the lesson should lead to skill acquisition, quality use of time, and a fun teaching and learning atmosphere. The following lesson sequence is suggested:

(1) Warm-up and review—Begin the class with fitness-based warm-up activities. This is also a good opportunity to review and practice skills taught the previous day, and to establish focus through student response to instructor cues during the *Balance Position Slides* (described next).

(2) Practice balance position slides—The development of an appropriate balance position is vital to safety because mobility is essential to surviving an assault. An attack situation is very dynamic, and depending upon the context in which it takes place, an individual must be able to move and react accordingly. To develop forward, sideways, and backward movements, begin by spreading students evenly throughout the gymnasium and utilize the following instructional drills:

(a) With students spread throughout the gymnasium, the instructor first calls "balance position." All students should immediately drop into the appropriate stance. The instructor is able to visually monitor the gymnasium and provide specific feedback to the group or individuals.

(b) Once the class has begun to respond to the instructor's "Balance position" cue, add the "No" response. From this point forward, any time the class hears the cue "Balance position," they will drop into the appropriate stance and loudly shout "No!" in unison. Research indicates that by simply taking one or two actions, such as establishing a balance position and loudly yelling, the majority of assailants will immediately flee as they were not expecting any resistance from their victim.

(c) Balance position slides + pivots—As students begin displaying proficiency with balance position slides on their dominant body side, the instructor can encourage the development of the non-dominant body side by calling "Pivot." When a "Pivot" is called, the students simply rotate 180 degrees on the balls of their feet. They need not lift their feet off the ground. The instructor may now move the class forward, sideways, and backward. It is important to note that all skills contained within the *Basic Techniques* section are taught using the dominant hand or foot. Nevertheless, students should be encouraged to develop proficiency with their non-dominant hand and foot through daily review and practice using both sides of the body.

(d) Balance position slides + escape skills—It is recommended to slide the students every day as a review and application technique. As new escape skills are taught, such as the snap kick, cupped hand blow, or forward elbow blow, these skills may be added to the slide practice. The instructor simply calls out "Balance position," "Slide forward," "Snap kick," etc. By incorporating escape skills into the balance position slides, students are able to apply self-defense technique while dynamically moving throughout the gymnasium. This is an important element to developing proficient movement on both sides of the body, practicing within a contextually fluid environment, and building confidence in one's skills.

(3) Introduce new course content—When introducing new material, do not simply focus on physical skills. Identify one topic that is of concern to students and present relevant information. For example, discuss pertinent awareness statistics and preventive strategies related to home safety. There are many topics recommended for discussion (see Table 25.1). When teaching physical skills, remember that "less is more." Introduce two or three simple skills. Provide quality physical models, break the skill into parts, and progress in a sensible fashion. Remember to exchange partners and provide ample time to develop comfort and confidence. Conclude skill practice with

Table 25.1. SELF-DEFENSE INSTRUCTIONAL CONTENT IDEAS

- Home Safety/Precautions
- Internet Safety/Precautions
- Bullying Concepts and Cyber Bullying Precautions
- Domestic Violence Prevalence/Precautions
- Dating Safety/Precautions
- Parking Lot Safety/Precautions
- Walking Home from School Safety/Precautions
- Outdoor Exercise Safety/Precautions
- Socializing Precautions
- Sexuality Concepts
- Bystander Effect
- Drugs/Alcohol/Date-Rape Drugs
- Trusting Your Intuition
- The "Interview": Tactics Used by Predators
- Awareness of Physical Surroundings
- Statistics on Violence/Crime
- Trusting Strangers
- Dog Attacks

application opportunities utilizing *Balance Position Slides* or *Student Attack Scenarios*.

(4) Application of escape skills—As students begin to demonstrate escape skill competency through individual and partner practicing, the instructor can further enhance skill development by creating situational attack scenarios. In essence, students will be "attacked" within the gymnasium by a fellow peer; however, they will not know how the attack will occur. Victims will simply respond to the situation based upon the attack "cues" provided by their aggressor. Student attack scenarios provide an authentic context in which students are able to practice their skills. The ultimate goal is that students are able to respond without thinking, or that their natural instincts engage when cued and that an appropriate motor pattern ensues. Should the student "freeze" or respond incorrectly or inefficiently, an effective teachable moment presents for everyone in the class.

(5) Student attack scenarios—To organize the gymnasium for student attack scenarios, students are paired. Each set of partners stands facing one another with about 5 feet of distance separating the duo. It is ideal if there is a line that the entire class can fit on, with half of the students on one side and the other half on the other side. The instructor walks between the lines, holding up a cue card with a specific skill indicated, so that one half of the group (the "attackers") know what to do. When the instructor gives permission with a verbal cue, such as "Go," the "attackers" perform the identified body hold or grasp. The "victims" attempt to respond to their "attacker's" advances. By having one line rotate, or slide to the right after each attack, students are able to experience physical differences in height, weight, strength, and effort as they practice with new partners. The following skills are appropriate for student attack scenarios:

- Straight across wrist grab
- Two hands on one wrist grab
- Cross wrist grab
- Backward elbow blow
- Over-the-shoulder elbow blow
- Single and double arm lapel grabs—Aikido release and swim release
- Single and double arm choke holds—swim release, wedge release, and additional distractions listed in *Lapel Grab and Choke Holds* section
- Bear hug from behind with both arms pinned
- Bear hug from behind with one arm pinned
- Bear hug from behind with both arms free

GLOSSARY

avoidance The use of preventive strategies to avoid becoming a victim of crime.

awareness The development of general knowledge regarding situational awareness to reduce the chance of becoming a victim of crime.

balance The ability to remain stable regardless of the external forces acting upon the individual.

balance position The ideal stance to remain upright and mobile in a dynamic assault situation.

deterrence Actions taken to de-escalate tensions in a stressful situation in order to avoid the use of physical force.

elbow blows The use of the area below and/or above the elbow to strike vulnerable body parts.

escape Physical skills used to help a victim immobilize an aggressor and halt an already progressive assault.

hand blows Various surfaces of the hands used to strike vulnerable body parts.

kicking techniques The use of the knees and feet to strike vulnerable body parts.

prevention Perceiving an impending assault then using avoidance and deterrence tactics, taking the necessary steps to keep the assault from occurring.

recovery Survival actions taken by the victim after a physical altercation has occurred.

releases A sequence of actions performed by the victim to loosen an aggressor's hold on any body part.

self-defense The use of awareness, prevention, escape, and recovery strategies to defend oneself against external threats by mixing basic protection skills with common sense.

strike first Quick and decisive physical distractions directed at the eyes and throat with the intention of immediately immobilizing an assailant when no other options are available.

vulnerable body parts The six areas of the human body that may incapacitate an individual, including the eyes, nose, throat, solar plexus, groin, and knees.

SUGGESTED READINGS

Banks, A. L. 2006. Developing student affect in a university self-defense course. *The Physical Educator, 63(1),* 8–17.

Banks, A. L., and Reed, J. A. 2003. Applying mass media to self-defense instruction in physical education. *The Journal of Physical Education, Recreation, and Dance, 74(2),* 41–45, 52.

Chen, G. 2008. *A comprehensive guide to self-defense.* Dubuque, IA: Kendall Hunt Publishing Company.

Conklin, J. E. 2010. *Criminology.* 10th ed. Needham Heights, MA: Allyn & Bacon.

DeBecker, G. 1997. *The gift of fear: And other survival signals that protect us from violence.* New York, NY: Little, Brown & Company.

DeBecker, G. 2000. *Protecting the gift: Keeping children and teenagers safe (and parents sane).* New York, NY: Dell Publishing.

Domitrz, M. 2003. *May I kiss you? A candid look at dating, communication, respect, & sexual assault awareness.* Greenfield, WI: Awareness Publications.

Katz, J. 2006. *The macho paradox: Why some men hurt women and how all men can help.* Naperville, IL: Sourcebooks, Incorporated.

Mattingly, K. L. 2007. *Self-defense: Steps to survival.* Champaign, IL: Human Kinetics.

Neide, J. 2009. *Teaching self-defense in secondary physical education.* Champaign, IL: Human Kinetics.

Perkins, J., Ridenhour, A., and Kovsky, M. 2009. *Attack proof: The ultimate guide to personal protection.* 2nd ed. Champaign, IL: Human Kinetics.

Walker, J. B. 2003. *Self-defense techniques & tactics.* Champaign, IL: Human Kinetics.

RESOURCES

Videos

A Comprehensive Guide to Self-Defense. Video that accompanies Gong Chen's book by the same title, available from Kendall-Hunt Publishing Company.

Boys to Men? available from Media Education Foundation: www.mediaed.org

Breaking Our Silence: Gloucester Men Speak Out Against Domestic Violence, available from Media Education Foundation: www.mediaed.org

Date Rape Backlash: Media and the Denial of Rape, available from Media Education Foundation: www.mediaed.org

Game Over: Gender, Race, & Violence in Video Games, available from Media Education Foundation: www.mediaed.org

Help! My Teen is Dating: Real Solutions to Tough Conversations, by Mike Domitrz: www.canikissyou.com

Killing Us Softly 3: Advertising's Image of Women, available from Media Education Foundation: www.mediaed.org

Spin the Bottle: Sex, Lies, and Alcohol, available from Media Education Foundation: www.mediaed.org

Tough Guise: Violence, Media, & the Crisis in Masculinity, available from Media Education Foundation: www.mediaed.org

War Zone, available from Media Education Foundation: www.mediaed.org

Wrestling with Manhood: Boys, Bullying, and Battering, available from Media Education Foundation: www.mediaed.org

See Appendix C for other video sources.

WEB SITES

Alcohol and Drug Information
www.ncadi.samhsa.gov

Association for Women's Self-Defense Advancement
www.awsda.org

Child Protection
www.missingkids.com

Cyber Bullying
www.cyberbullying.org and www.stopcyberbullying.org

Domestic Violence
www.domesticviolence.org

Equal Rights Advocates
www.equalrights.org

Family Violence Prevention
www.endabuse.org

Gavin De Becker
www.gavindebecker.com

Hate Crimes
www.civilrights.org/hatecrimes/

Internet Safety for Teens
www.safeteens.com

Men Against Sexual Violence
www.pcar.org/menagainst-sexual-violence-masv

Men Can Stop Rape
www.mencanstoprape.org

National Center for Victims of Crime
www.ncvc.org

National Sexual Violence Resource Center
www.nsvrc.org

Rape, Abuse, and Incest National Network
www.rainn.org

Self-Defense Forums
www.talks.self-defender.net

Self-Defense Statistics
www.ojp.gov/bjs/

Self-Defense Training
www.nononsenseselfdefense.com and www.impactpersonalsafety.com

Sexual Aggression Services
www.sapa.cmich.edu

Sexual Harassment Support
www.sexualharassmentsupport.org

Silent Witness National Initiative
www.silentwitness.net

Stalking Resource Center
www.ncvc.org/src/

Teen Victim Project
www.ncvc.org/tvp/main

U.S. Department of Justice Office of Justice Programs
www.ojp.gov

U.S. Department of Justice Violence against Women
www.ovw.usdoj.gov

Where's the Outrage?
www.wherestheoutrage.org

26 | *Soccer*

After completing this chapter, the reader should be able to:

- Appreciate the history and sociocultural values of the most popular sport in the world
- Understand the rules and spirit of the game
- Demonstrate proper technique associated with the fundamental skills of the game
- Understand the game's basic offensive and defensive principles
- Understand effective teaching progression involved with skill acquisition
- Demonstrate a thorough knowledge of soccer terminology

HISTORY

The roots of soccer are grounded in antiquity. Some believe that soccer's origins can be traced to the ancient (2500 BCE) Chinese game of tsu-chu, or kickball. The Egyptians (2000 BCE), Japanese (600 BCE), ancient Greeks (Epis-kyros), and Romans (Harpastum) have also been intimately linked with the evolution and spread of the game. The Roman legions under Emperor Claudius (CE 43) are credited with carrying the game to Britain, where it was integrated into the local games and evolved, grew, and developed from the Middle Ages through the industrial revolution.

The modern form of soccer gained its renowned shape and identity in October 1863, in London's Freemason's Tavern, where the first football association (English Football Association) was established and the laws of the game were formulated. The laws served to separate association—"assoc" football (soccer)—and rugby. The kick-in was replaced by the throw-in (1863); offsides (1866), corner kick (1872), and referees (1874) were added, as were the whistle (1878), the penalty kick (1891), and various numbers of substitutions. Thus, the modern game of soccer was off and running, and wherever England's ships gained port, soccer was soon to follow.

Contemporary soccer is truly an international game, with the Fédération Internationale de Football Association (FIFA), established in 1904, representing approximately 208 nations. Soccer was introduced to the Olympic Games in Paris in 1900, and the inaugural World Cup was played in 1930 in Montevideo, where the Uruguayan hosts defeated Argentina. Since then, such luminaries as Pele, Charlton, Cruyff, Beckenbauer, Maradona, Romanrio, Ronaldo, Ronaldinho, Zidane, Messi, and Mia Hamm have served to spread the passion for the game around the world.

The United States Soccer Federation (USSF), founded in 1913, serves as the governing body for most U.S. soccer interests. Since 1972, the USSF has offered coaching certification, as does the National Soccer Coaches Association. The United States Youth Soccer Association (USYSA), formed in 1974, is charged with the development and promotion of the game for those under age 19. Each of these affiliated organizations is attempting to build positive links to all communities by offering bilingual coaching courses, to promote not only the sport but also community solidarity. Today soccer is one of the most popular participatory sports for young boys and girls and has emerged as an intercollegiate favorite, with over 1,200 teams competing each year. The U.S. women's team captured the inaugural Women's World Cup in Beijing, China, in 1991 and again in 1999 in the Rose Bowl. In 1994 the United States opened its doors to the global soccer community to host the World Cup for the first time. It was won by Brazil over Italy, 3-2 in penalty kicks. France won at home in *1998,* Brazil won for a record fifth time in 2002, and Italy captured their third Jules Rimet Trophy in 2006. The World Cup was hosted for the first time in Africa (South Africa) in 2010, where Spain won its first World Cup competition.

The impact of the United States' hosting the 1994 World Cup led to the emergence of the Major League Soccer (MLS), which initiated play in the summer of 1996.

In the 1996 Olympic Games in Atlanta, the United States women's team won the gold medal, and the men's team held its own with the rest of the world. The United States women won again in Helsinki in 2004 and repeated in Beijing in 2008. London awaits in 2012.

THE NATURE AND SPIRIT OF THE GAME

Soccer is the most popular sport in the world, and it is also one of the most demanding. Soccer's intricacies have been described as playing chess at 30 miles per hour—referring to its cardiovascular, cognitive, competitive, and psychomotor challenges. Soccer can be played in industrial and less developed nations, by young and old, by boys and girls, by elite and physically or mentally challenged, and on beaches or in multimillion-dollar stadiums. All that is needed is a ball and willing participants, and the spirit of the game (unwritten laws of fair play and honor).

THE GAME, BALL, AND PLAYERS

A soccer match is contested by two teams of 11 players each (with an appropriate number of substitutes), one of which is designated the goalkeeper. The object of the game is to score by propelling the 14- to 16-ounce (400- to 457-g) no. 5 ball (27 to 28 inches [69 to 71 cm] in circumference) completely across the goal line and within the confines of the 8 × 24 foot (2.44 × 7.32 m) goalposts and crossbar. The game is begun—after one team has won the coin toss and has elected to defend a goal—by a kick-off from the center of the field (the ball must move or be touched before it can be played by another player). The game is restarted in a similar fashion after each goal and at each half, or period. The duration of the game consists of two 45-minute halves and typically a 10- to 15-minute halftime break, after which the teams exchange ends. High schools and colleges have adopted an overtime procedure for those games ending in a tie score. The high schools play two 10-minute periods (although in some states it is two 15-minute periods), while the colleges play two 15-minute periods. All phases and dimensions of the game may be modified to accommodate the individual needs of the participants. Examples of game durations, ball and field sizes, and age modifications are shown in Table 26.1.

Once play has been legally initiated, each team attempts to gain possession, and through planned and creative combinations of the fundamental skills (passing, shooting, heading, trapping, dribbling, tackling and marking, and goalkeeping) attempts to place the ball in the back of the opponent's net. It is hard to believe that these seemingly simple skills placed in a competitive environment have captured the hearts of hundreds of millions of players and spectators. Indeed, more people watched the 1994 World Cup than watched man take the first step on the moon!

FIELD OF PLAY

The field, sometimes referred to as a pitch, is rectangular, typically 120 × 70 yards (110 × 64 m) (Figure 26.1). International FIFA-sanctioned matches must be played on grass fields that are between a minimum of 110 × 70 yards (100 × 64 m) and a maximum of 120 × 80 yards (110 × 73 m). The field is bounded by lines no more than 5 inches (12.7 cm) in width running the length of the field (touchlines), as well as the field's two goal lines. The field is divided into two equal parts by a halfway line, upon which is centered a circle with a 10-yard (9.1-m) radius, where play is started at the beginning of each half or after a goal is scored. There is a penalty area at each end of the field that begins 18 yards (16.5 m) beyond each goalpost on the goal line and extends at right angles another 18 yards (16.5 m) into the field. The capstone line (44 yards [40.2 m]) enclosing the box designates where the goalkeeper can legally handle the ball, as well as the area where a penalty kick may be awarded. Within the penalty area is the penalty kick mark, located 12 yards (11 m) from the center of the goal line. The goal area is also found within the penalty box, extending 6 yards (5.5 m) from each goalpost and boxed in with a 20-yard (18.3-m) capstone line paralleling the goal mouth line. Goal kicks are taken within this rectangular area. At each corner of the field, an arc (quarter circle) with a radius of 1 yard (0.9 m) is drawn where corner flags at least 5 feet (1.5 m) high are placed and corner kicks are taken.

GOALS

The goals, centered on each goal line, consist of two upright posts 8 feet (2.44 m) high and 24 feet (7.32 m) apart, joined at the top by a horizontal crossbar measuring 24 feet (7.32 m). Goalposts are typically made of wood, tubular metal, or plastic, not exceeding 5 inches (12.7 cm) in width or depth.

Table 26.1. GAME'S MODIFICATIONS FOR AGE

Player age	Game length	Overtime periods
Adults	Two 45-minute halves	Two 15-minute halves
Under 16	Two 40-minute halves	Two 10-minute halves
Under 14	Two 35-minute halves	Two 10-minute halves
Under 12	Two 30-minute halves	Two 10-minute halves
Under 10	Two 25-minute halves	Two 10-minute halves
Under 8	Two 25-minute halves	Two 5-minute halves
Player age	**Ball number and weight**	**Ball circumference**
Under 14	No. 5, 14–16 ounces (400–457 g)	27–28 inches (69–71 cm)
Under 12	No. 4, 11–13 ounces (314–371 g)	25–26 inches (64–66 cm)
Under 8	No. 3, 8–10 ounces (229–286 g)	23–24 inches (58–61 cm)
Player age	**Goal size**	**Field size**
Under 12	7 × 21 feet (2.13 × 6.40 m)	90 × 50 yards (64 × 46 m)
Under 8	6 × 18 feet (1.83 × 5.49 m)	70 × 35 yards (73 × 50.3 m)

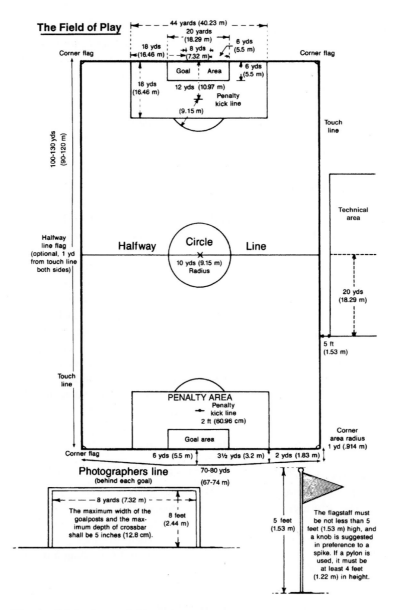

Figure 26.1. Soccer field.

Nets are made of hemp, jute, or nylon, and they should be attached to the back of the crossbar and goalposts, extending behind the goal so as not to interfere with the play of the goalkeeper.

TECHNICAL AREA

The technical area (coaching box) can be helpful in the management of the game. A box is marked at least 5 feet (1.53 m) from and parallel to the touchline and extending 20 yards (18.29 m) in both directions from the halfway line. Coaches and players should remain inside the technical area, except when players are warming up in preparation to substitute, which typically occurs with permission of the referee at the halfway line of the field.

EQUIPMENT

Soccer is one of the most economical team sports played. The only requirements are a ball, appropriate footwear (flats or spikes), shin guards, mouthguard, athletic supporter (for males), shorts, shirt (in a different color for the goalkeeper), and socks, along with the field equipment consisting of goals, nets, corner flags, and a lining machine. Cones are also very useful for practice sessions and are a solid investment. Rings, jewelry, and glasses should be left at home or with a friend!

OFFICIALS

Soccer matches are presided over by a referee and two assistant referees. The center referee makes all final decisions regarding fouls and technical infringements. The proper signals to indicate these are illustrated in Figure 26.2. The two assistant referees run the touchlines (opposite sides and halves) and signal when a ball completely crosses the touchline (throw-in), goal line (goal kick or corner kick), or goal. They also may indicate fouls and offside infractions, usually by snapping their flags in the direction of the team that is to maintain ball control. In all cases, however, it is the referee who calls (whistles) or does not call the infraction and awards possession of the ball or goal. The assistant referees serve as "advisors" in this regard. The referee usually keeps the official time on the field, at least for the last several minutes of the game to allow for injury or extra time. The officials' objective is to allow play to be free-flowing and within the spirit of the game while maintaining optimal safety for the participating players.

OUT-OF-BOUNDS (RESTARTS)

Once the ball completely crosses (either in the air or rolling) the touchline or goal line or a violation is whistled, the referee will designate by hand signal the team that is to be awarded pos-

session of the ball. Depending on the situation, any number of restarts may occur. Restarts can be direct (goal can be scored without touching another player) or indirect (ball must be touched by another player, even the opposition, before a goal is awarded). Direct restarts include the following:

Penalty Kick

A penalty kick is taken from the penalty kick, or 12-yard (10.97-m), mark. All players—with the exception of the penalty kicker and the goalkeeper—must be outside the penalty area and at least 10 yards (9.14 m) from the ball until the ball is struck forward. The goalkeeper may move on the goal line with his or her feet until the ball is kicked. The ball remains in play if it rebounds off the goalpost or the goalkeeper. The penalty kicker may legally play the ball again if it bounces off the goalkeeper; however, the penalty kicker may not play the rebound off the goalpost or crossbar until the ball has been touched by another player. A penalty kick is awarded when deliberate handling of the ball, holding, charging, tripping, pushing, or striking occurs inside the penalty area

Figure 26.2. Official soccer signals.

by the defending team. Any member of the offended team may take the penalty kick except a substitute brought in to take the penalty kick.

Corner Kick

When the ball crosses the defender's goal line and is last played by a defender, a corner kick is awarded from within the 1-yard (0.9-m) arc of the corner of the field (by the flag) closest to where the ball crossed the goal line. Players defending the corner kick must be 10 yards (9.14 m) from the corner kick arc when it is taken.

Direct Kick

Whenever any of the infractions cited in the "Penalty kick" or "Fouls and misconduct" sections occur, but are outside the penalty area or are committed by the offensive team in the defensive penalty area, then ball possession via a direct kick is awarded. The referee will signal the direct-kick violation by an upward tilting arm pointed in the attacking direction of the team that is to be awarded the ball. Defending players must always be 10 yards (9.14 m) from the ball before it is played, or a retake may be awarded.

Indirect restarts identified by the referee's straight, upraised arm signal include the following:

Goal Kick

When the ball crosses the defensive goal line and is last touched by the attacking side, the ball is awarded to the defending team. The goal kick is taken from the goal area and must clear the penalty area before being touched by either team. If such a violation occurs, the goal kick is retaken.

Throw-In

When the ball crosses completely over the touchline, a throw-in is awarded to the team that did not last touch the ball. A throw-in is a two-handed overhead movement that must be taken with both feet on the ground. An improper throw-in results in loss of possession and a throw-in for the opponent. If a throw-in fails to enter the field of play, the ball is awarded to the opposing team. There are no offsides on a throw-in.

Indirect Free Kick

An indirect free kick is offered to the opposing team following a technical infraction, such as offsides, obstruction, dangerous play, or delay of game (see "Fouls and Misconduct" section). The indirect-kick restart is similar to that for the direct kick in that opposing players must be 10 yards (9.14 m) from the ball; however, another player must touch the ball before a goal can be awarded directly off an indirect shot.

Offsides

A player is in an offsides position if he or she is nearer to the opponent's goal line than the ball at the moment the ball is played or passed by a member of his or her team unless:

1. The player is in his or her own half of the field.
2. There are two opponents (including the opposing goalkeeper) nearer to their own goal line than the attacking player.
3. The ball was last played by the attacker.
4. The attacking player receives the ball directly from a goal kick, corner kick, throw-in, or drop ball.
5. An offensive player even with the second-to-last defender is on-side (Figure 26.3).

Drop Ball

A drop ball is called for after the referee stops play due to an injury or emergency or when a call is unclear or in doubt. The ball is usually dropped in a nonthreatening or neutral territory and must hit the ground before being played. If the ball is played before hitting the ground (a violation), it is dropped again.

FOULS AND MISCONDUCT

When a player commits a foul or some other form of misconduct or illegal behavior, the opposing team is awarded a direct or indirect free kick. A direct free kick is awarded for intentionally fouling an opponent in any of the following ways (referred to as penal fouls):

- Kicking or attempting to kick an opponent
- Tripping
- Jumping at an opponent
- Charging in a violent or dangerous manner
- Striking or attempting to strike
- Holding
- Pushing
- Handling the ball (except by goalkeepers in their own penalty areas)
- Spitting at an opponent

Offside **Not offside**

Figure 26.3. Offsides. Measure relative position by players' torsos, not their arms or legs. The torso of the attacking player must be no nearer the opponents' goal line than that of the second-last defender. It is not necessary to "see daylight" between them for one to be considered nearer than the other.

If a defending player intentionally commits one of the penal offenses within his or her penalty area, a penalty kick is awarded from the 12-yard (10.97-m) mark to the opposing team.

Indirect free kicks are awarded to the opposing team when a player commits one of the following technical infractions:

- Playing in a dangerous manner, such as high kicking
- Charging with the shoulder when the ball is not within playing distance of the players involved (playing the opponent rather than the ball)
- Intentional impedance of an opponent when not playing the ball
- Charging the goalkeeper, except when the goalkeeper is holding the ball, is obstructing an opponent, or is outside the goal area
- When the goalkeeper has taken more than four steps without releasing the ball or has used tactics with the intention of delaying the game
- Offsides

CAUTIONS AND GAME EXPULSIONS

When, in the judgment of the referee, a player is not playing within the laws and spirit of the game by committing any number of serious violations, the referee may issue to the player a caution, or yellow card. Any repeat offense (flagrant violation) shall result in ejection from the game. If the referee finds a player guilty of any of the following:

- Violent conduct or serious foul play
- Abusive language
- Persistent misconduct after receiving a yellow card

A red card is awarded and immediate expulsion results. The player who is expelled may not be replaced, thus placing his or her team at a serious disadvantage.

- At the high school level, any player receiving a red card must sit out the next regularly scheduled game at the same level of competition. Also at the high school level, the National Federation Soccer Rules Committee has implemented a "soft" red card system. In this scenario, a player who receives a "soft" red card is still removed from the game, but he or she may be replaced so the player's team does not have to play short a player. Players sent off with a "hard" red card cannot be replaced and the team must play short a player for the remainder of the game.

FUNDAMENTAL SKILLS AND TECHNIQUES

Soccer is a game of movement, speed, physical and mental control, space, timing, flow, creativity, improvisation, and imagination. To safely play and enjoy the game, the acquisition, practice, and mastery of certain basic fundamental skills are required.

Passing

Passing (Figure 26.4) is the foundation of the game. Most short passes are made with the inside of the foot (Figures 26.5, 26.6, and 26.7), although the outside of the foot, the "touch" of a toe, and even the heel are often used during a match. Longer passes are either chipped, by placing the foot under the ball, or struck with force, while leaning the body backward to create the desired loft. During a match, the ball is passed to teammates at various angles, including a

Figure 26.4. Passing drill.

Figure 26.5. Instep kick instructions.

Figure 26.6. Instep kick, close up.

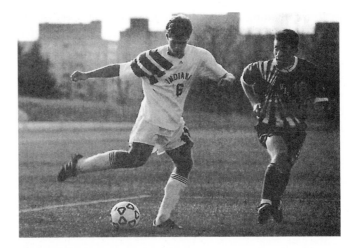

Figure 26.7. Instep kick in action.

Shooting

Shooting is obviously a key element of soccer. The basic technique can be described as a powerful instep blast, although, like the pass, any surface of the foot or body can be employed. If the shot is struck forcefully with the right instep, the shooter's right foot will also hit the ground first as full force, momentum, and low follow-through are enacted. The skill of shooting is very difficult, and it often seems that the potential scorer is "never in the right position." Sometimes the ball is rolling; sometimes it is up in the air, and a volley shot (Figure 26.8) must be used; and sometimes the ball must be taken after a "quick bounce," or half-volleyed. The technique of shooting includes accuracy, deception, discipline, and optimal concentration; and practice in all game situations is paramount.

Heading

Heading is used by the player to pass or to shoot the ball. The proper technique for safe heading is crucial, and injury

Figure 26.8. Volley kick.

square pass made at a right angle to the attacker in the hope that the passer will continue the momentum and receive a return pass (wall pass, or give and go). The through pass is the most direct forward pass in the game because the ball is thrust behind the opponents into their defensive space as your teammate runs onto the ball. Of course, when thwarted or attempting to delay the game, or to create a planned opportunity, the ball can be passed backward, laterally, or "around," including to your own goalkeeper, who in this case may not play the ball with his or her hands.

to the neck area should always be a consideration when warming up, teaching, and practicing the skill. The ball should be attacked by the header with the frontal bone of the forehead near the hairline and directed to a teammate or space that will permit a teammate to collect the ball or afford time to reorganize, especially in the defensive third of the field. Heading technique includes concentration, awareness of players around you, proper body posture and positioning, including the use of the arms as a protective shield, and keeping your eyes on the ball as it is directed.

Trapping and Collecting

Trapping and collecting the ball from a teammate's pass or opponent's miscue is the technique necessary for bringing the ball under complete control. Various parts of the body may be used, depending on the ball's position upon arrival. The chest (Figure 26.9), thigh (Figure 26.10), and instep (Figure 26.11) are often employed to control the ball if it arrives in flight, while the sole of the foot, or the inside or outside of the foot trap, is often used for ground balls. The key to control is knowing and using your immediate space to gain possession of the ball. Another key to successful trapping and collecting is to utilize muscular control and bodily momentum-absorption techniques (give and take) to ease the ball into your control space. Concentration and knowing

Figure 26.10. Thigh-high trap (with marker).

Figure 26.9. Chest trap.

Figure 26.11. Collecting the ball with inside of foot trap.

the opponents' whereabouts are mandatory so that the ball can be collected, protected, and distributed to a teammate.

Dribbling

Dribbling (Figure 26.12) is one of the most exciting and creative elements of the game and should be encouraged. Dribbling requires the player to use a series of soft touches, or pushes, as the ball is dribbled into appropriate space. Effective dribbling is done with both feet employing feints, or fakes; change of pace; and rapid, deceptive moves. Dribbling technique also requires proper body position because the ball often needs to be shielded, screened, and protected from a defender or marker (Figure 26.13). Dribbling can be used to advance the ball, move into position to get off a quick shot, delay the game, or take the ball into open space. Dribbling is also a great warm-up and aerobic and anaerobic conditioner. All practices should include dribbling.

Tackling and Marking

Tackling (Figure 26.14) is a defensive technique that is designed to dispossess an opponent from the ball so that you or your teammate can gain ball possession. It involves marking (Figure 26.15), or playing the opponent with the ball until the optimal time (usually just after the opponent has touched the ball) to make your tackling move. Tackling is usually accomplished by blocking, poking, or sliding in a

Figure 26.13. Shielding.

Figure 26.12. Dribbling.

calculated effort to win the ball. It requires sound judgment, assertive play, mental toughness, and teamwork.

Goalkeeping

The goalkeeper, or goalie, is unique in that he or she may legally use the hands (the W position, connecting the two thumbs for high balls, and palms open, fingers down for low shots) to stop, control, and catch a ball within the penalty area if it is not intentionally passed to him or her by a teammate (Figure 26.16). Upon collection of the ball (Figure 26.17), the goalie is also permitted to clear the ball or initiate "instant offense" by throwing (distributing), dropkicking, or punting the ball. Defensively, the goalkeeper must know when and how to challenge, come off the line, and cut down the attacker's angle and effectively smother and deflect shots. Often sound judgment, common sense, and coolness under pressure (mental ability) are as important as physical skill in a solid goalkeeper (Figure 26.18).

SYSTEMS OF PLAY

A system, or style, of play (Figure 26.19) describes the organization and configuration of the players on the field, as well as their responsibilities within the team structure. The beauty of soccer is that it is fluid, spontaneous, and constantly changing pace and configuration. Current systems of play have evolved from the original English 2–3–5 offensive

Figure 26.15. Marking.

Figure 26.14. Tackling drill with coach.

Figure 26.16. Goalkeeping with W grip.

Figure 26.17. Goalie smother.

Figure 26.18. Goalkeeping in a crowd.

set of the early 1990s to the Arsenal Football Club's 3–2–5 WU system of the 1930s, from the famous Brazilian World Cup 4–2–4 formation to Italy's more defense-minded Catenaccio, or 5–4–1, system to "total futbol," where total interchangeability is the optimal objective and weapon.

Regardless of the system of play, numbering begins from the defensive posture and works its way through the midfield to the most forward players. It is interesting to note that all the great systems of play had players like Pele, Cruyff, Beckenbauer, and Messi to carry them to prominence. Typically, the team's players and the skill and style of the opponent determine how a coach chooses to implement a particular style of play.

OFFENSIVE AND DEFENSIVE PRINCIPLES

The basic principles of soccer appear to be simple, but they take a great deal of practice, communication (verbal and nonverbal), discipline, and dedication. One primary principle often overlooked is that when your team is in possession of the ball, everyone attacks; and when the ball is lost, everyone becomes a defender.

Attacking Principles (Moving, Support, Penetration, Finishing)

Ball possession dictates who is the attacker and who is the defender. A good attacking player must be able to move without the ball, not only to create space, but also to receive a pass from a teammate. These moves, or runs, often take the form of near- and far-post runs, corner-flag runs, and runs away and off the ball, as well as overlapping runs, where a player, usually from the midfield position, runs forward past the ball being held by a teammate and into open space behind the defense. The pass is then fed to the penetrating overlapper, who collects the ball and goes to the goal.

Also critical to the team and the player who possesses the ball is support from teammates (at least two should always be 10 to 15 yards from the teammate with the ball). With proper support (depth and width) and communication, combination play, such as wall passing and "give and goes," can be initiated and space can be created and exploited for penetration (via passing and dribbling) behind the defense. After the defense has been penetrated and a scoring opportunity has been created (usually by improvising a combination of runs, passing, and dribbling), the principle of finishing, or scoring, must be effectively applied. Shooting is the only way to score, and functional practice makes perfect.

Defensive Principles (Chase, Delay, Support, Balance and Concentration, Challenge, Counterattack)

Defense is soccer's great equalizer. A team well schooled in defensive principles and sound judgment should have a chance to be competitive in every match. Defense begins as soon as the ball is lost to the opposition. Immediate chase and pressure should be applied to the player who has taken control of the ball.

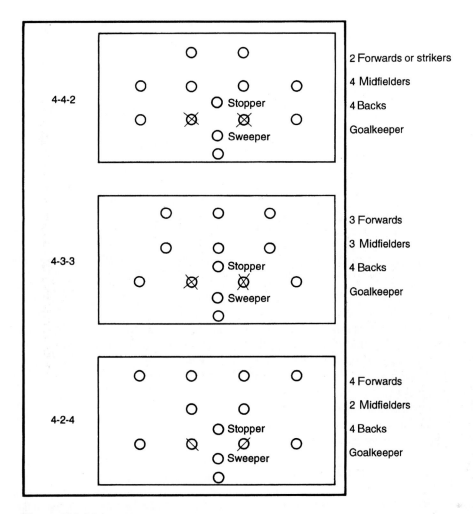

Figure 26.19. Sample systems of play.

The objective is to delay the player with the ball and force him or her to the nearest touchline, thereby preventing a quick penetration toward the goal. This delay permits the defense time to retreat, organize (find, mark, track), or regroup to support the defender playing the ball. This support involves balance, depth, and cover in order to restrict the amount of space that the opponent has to exploit. This is especially crucial in the defensive third of the field, where the defensive team must concentrate to force the attacking team to its least desirable offensive options (usually away from the center of the field, where the shooting angle is most favorable).

Once proper defensive support and cover are implemented, the defender playing the ball can challenge, or tackle, the ball. Often the ball is won by the cover person after the ball is challenged by the primary defender. When the ball is won, a counterattack (quick offensive penetration) or more deliberate offensive buildup is constructed, depending on where the ball is won. Thus, the game of soccer is a 90-minute, continuous series of attacks, recalculations, defensive destroys or offensive breakdowns, counterattacks, combination passing and buildups, and creativity.

TEACHING CONSIDERATIONS

Teaching the game of soccer should be an enjoyable and positive experience for all. It is important to note that teaching/coaching responsibilities first and foremost include the health and safety of the players, so a thorough medical examination should be required and placed on record and the instructor should possess current first-aid and CPR certification. All involved should be made aware "in print" of the emergency medical considerations involved in both practice sessions and matches.

Seasonal and practice plans should include the appropriate fitness level to be attained before strenuous practice and games are conducted. Practices should be conducted in a safe learning environment, and the instructor should always check the facilities (field, locker rooms, and security) before and after practice.

Practice should be fun, fast paced, and well organized and should begin with an informal "get to know each player" before a more structured 7- to 10-minute warm-up (dribbling, jogging, passing, static flexibility). The warm-up should include both individual (e.g., ball juggling) and cooperative group activities (e.g., cooperative stretching). Practices can be divided into a table of specifications, where each component can be manipulated by the instructor depending on the age, fitness and skill levels, season, and the particular goals to be accomplished daily or long range. A sample hour-long table of specifications may look like the following:

Warm-up	7 to 10 minutes
Functional fitness	7 to 10 minutes
Aerobic endurance (circuit-training course)	
Anaerobic (speed)	
Strength (power)	
Individual skill instruction and evaluation	5 to 10 minutes
Small sided games	5 to 10 minutes
Tactical considerations and economical training	5 to 10 minutes
Scrimmage (small grid, half or full field)	5 to 10 minutes
Cooldown (static stretching)	5 minutes

INSTRUCTIONAL STRATEGIES

It is important that each player master both the technique (skills) and the tactics (strategy) of the game. The skills should be introduced with varying degrees of time, space, pace, rest, and opposition being progressively adapted and manipulated in the following order:

- Individual instruction (foundational stage)
- Individual feedback and mastery
- Individual versus single opponent (1v1, 2v1, 3v1, passive resistance)
- Small groups (2v1, 2v5, 2v3, at progressively faster rates)
- Small sided related games (6v4, 5v4)
- Small grid, half- or full-field game conditions (7v7 or 8v8 continuous pressure and opposition)

At all phases of the progressive instructional plan, players should receive concise hands-on instruction, positive feedback, and accurate evaluation. Although soccer skills are individually taught, they must eventually be placed into the ever-changing game environment (opposition, pace, flow, timing), and these often neglected concepts must be effectively integrated into all practice sessions. Fun, mastery of skills, confidence, and individual and team self-worth must also be emphasized at every practice. The teaching of soccer is an ongoing process, and there is nothing more rewarding than watching a player develop in all phases of the game and become part of the most popular sport in the world.

GLOSSARY

attacking team The team that possesses the ball.

banana shot A shot or pass that curves (like Beckham).

blocking Tackle using the inside of the foot to block the ball from an opponent who is dribbling.

center A pass made by a wing player from the outside to the center of the field.

charge Body contact between two opponents that may be judged legal or illegal depending on the intent to play the ball.

chip To lift or lob the ball into the air and over another player.

clear To send the ball by foot or head away from the goal.

collecting A technique of receiving and gaining control of the ball.

CONCACF Confederation of North American and Caribbean Association Football, of which the United States is a member and must win the CONCACF title to gain a World Cup berth.

corner kick A restart after the ball crosses the opponent's goal line when last touched by the opponent.

cover To provide defensive support for teammates, especially when marking or tackling.

cross To kick the ball from the wings (outside) toward the goal area or to a teammate cross-field.

defending team The team that is trying to gain possession of the ball.

defensive concentration The defending team overloads the middle of the field, usually in the defensive third of the field.

depth Proper support of teammates on attack or defense.

diagonal run A run designed to penetrate the defense while drawing defenders from the middle of the field.

direct free kick A free kick from which a goal may be scored directly.

dribbling A succession of forward pushes or touches in which the player keeps the ball under control.

drop ball Ball held waist high and dropped by a referee.

dropkick A ball that is dropped on the ground by the goalie and kicked just after it bounces.

economical training Practice sessions involving at least two of the four components of the game: fitness, technique, tactics, psychology.

far post Goalpost farthest from the ball and the target of attacking runs.

functional training Repeated skill work under matchlike conditions.

goal area The rectangular area in front of the goal line (6 yards out—5.47 m) where the ball is placed for a goal kick.

grids The use of confined space for practice and small sided games.

half-volley Contacting the ball just as it contacts the ground after being airborne.

heading Playing the ball with the head.

holding Impeding the progress of a player by placing the hand or extended arm in contact with the player.

impedance The illegal use of the body to prevent an opponent from getting to the ball.

indirect free kick A free kick from which a goal cannot be scored unless touched by another player.

kickoff The free kick that starts play at the beginning of the game, each half and after each score. A goal may be scored directly from the kickoff.

man-on Popular term used to signal a teammate that defensive pressure is approaching, suggesting an immediate touch or pass to a teammate.

mark To stay close to an opponent for defensive purposes.

offsides Usually a player who does not have two defensive players between him or her and the goal when receiving the ball from a teammate.

own goal A goal scored by the defending team.

penalty area The large rectangular area in front of the goal that defines the area the goalkeeper can use his or her hands to play the ball, and the area in which a penal foul by the defense results in a penalty kick for the offense.

poke tackle Use of the defender's toe to push the ball away from an attacker.

restart The starting of play whenever the ball is out of play or the game is stopped. Also referred to as "dead ball."

shielding When the dribbler stays between the ball and the marking opponent.

square pass A pass played laterally to a teammate or space.

stopper The central defender located in front of the sweeper.

striker The most forward attacking player(s).

sweeper The last defender.

tackle The act of taking the ball away from an opposing player.

target player Usually a striker, who receives the ball a large share of the time.

through pass A pass that goes between and past defenders.

throw-in To put the ball in play from the touchline by a two-hand overhead throw.

touchline Side boundary of the field.

trapping A technique used to gain possession and control of the ball. Usually accomplished by the sole of the foot, thigh, or chest.

volley Meeting the ball in the air with some part of the body and directing it to a teammate or on goal.

wall Defensive tactic in which several players line up 10 yards (9.14 m) from a direct or indirect kick in the defensive third of the field.

width Attacking team's attempt to spread the defense in the attacking third of the field.

SUGGESTED READINGS

Bangsbo, J. 2004. *Offensive soccer tactics.* Champaign, IL: Human Kinetics.

Coaching youth soccer. 2006. 3rd ed. Champaign, IL: Human Kinetics. Part of the American Coaches Effectiveness Program. A basic book for the parent-coach or the first-time coach. Follows a step-by-step teaching progression for most skills.

Fédération Internationale de Football Association. Current ed. *FIFA laws of the game.* Zurich: FIFA.

Garland, J. 2003. *Youth soccer drills.* 2nd ed. Champaign, IL: Human Kinetics. Provides coaches and parents of youth players ages 5 to 12 with 84 progressive drills for optimal learning and having fun.

Getz, G. 2009. *Complete conditioning for soccer.* Champaign, IL: Human Kinetics.

La Prath, D. 2009. *Coaching girls' soccer successfully.* Champaign IL: Human Kinetics.

Luxbacker, J. 1999. *Attacking soccer.* Champaign, IL: Human Kinetics.

Luxbacker, J. 2002. *The soccer goalkeeper.* 3rd ed. Champaign, IL: Human Kinetics.

Luxbacker, J. 2005. *Soccer practice games.* 3rd ed. Champaign, IL: Human Kinetics. Details enjoyable games to develop fitness, skills, and tactical awareness in players of all ages.

Luxbacker, J. 2005. *Soccer: Steps to success.* 3rd ed. Champaign, IL: Human Kinetics. Features management and safety guidelines, rating charts, 155 drills, teaching cues, suggestions for identifying and correcting errors, and test questions.

Mielke, D. 2003. *Soccer fundamentals.* Champaign, IL: Human Kinetics.

National Collegiate Athletic Association. Current ed. *NCAA soccer rules manual.* P. O. Box 6222, Indianapolis, IN 46206. KS: NCAA.

NSCAA. 2004. *The soccer coaching bible.* Champaign, IL:]Human Kinetic.

Rees, R., and Van der Meer, C. 2003. *Coaching soccer successfully.* 2nd ed. Champaign, IL: Human Kinetics. Discusses the factors that must be considered to build and maintain a winning soccer program.

Reyna, C. 2004. *More than goals.* Champaign, IL: Human Kinetics.

Simon, J., and Reeves, J. 1999. *Soccer restart plays.* 2nd ed. Champaign, IL: Human Kinetics.

U.S. Soccer Federation. 1998. *FIFA laws of the game: A guide for referees.* Hitzigweg, Switzerland: FIFA.

RESOURCES

Videos

Soccer on video, Soccer Learning Systems, San Ramon, California 94583.

Soccer series: *Laws of the game, Fair and unfair challenges, Unsporting behavior.* United States Soccer Federation, U.S. Soccer House, 1801 S. Prairie Ave., Chicago, IL 60616.

Soccer series: *The world's greatest goals; Great goals; The world's greatest saves; The world's greatest players.* HIJ Coerver Goal Series. ACME, One Acme Plaza, P.O. Box 811, Carrboro, NC 27510.

In excess of 125 videos on soccer can be found on the Internet. See Appendix C for other video sources.

Computer software

Let's play soccer: ESPN soccer. Multimedia PC CD-Rom. Champaign, IL: Human Kinetics.

WEB SITES

www.FIFA.com
www.NCAA.com
www.nscaa.com
www.socceramerica.com
www.soccercoaching.net
www.ussoccer.com
www.usysa.org

More than 10,000 Web sites for soccer can be located using various search engines.

27 | Softball (Slow-Pitch)

After completing this chapter, the reader should be able to:

- Appreciate the development of softball and the popularity of the slow-pitch variation
- Know the basic rules of the game
- Perform the basic softball skills of throwing, catching, fielding, batting, pitching, and baserunning
- Know basic offensive and defensive softball strategy
- Teach softball skills and strategies to a group of beginning students

HISTORY

The YMCA perhaps did more than any other organization to inaugurate softball by transferring the game of baseball from outdoors to indoors about 1900. Softball is an adaptation of baseball. Because of limited indoor space and the hardness of the baseball, the YMCA directors originally made the softball softer, the bat smaller, and the baselines and pitching distances shorter. They also changed the delivery of the pitch to an underhand motion.

Several years later, the Playground Association of America, now known as the National Recreation and Park Association, needed a game that could be adapted to small outdoor spaces and could be played by all ages, especially by young boys and girls. The game acquired different names at different times, such as "playground ball," "kitten ball," "recreation ball," and "ladies' ball," but in 1933 "softball" was adopted as the official name by the Amateur Softball Association (ASA). That year a national tournament was held at the World's Fair in Chicago. At the same time, this organization set up and standardized rules that are the basis for rules today. During the Depression, when thousands of people were unemployed, the game was a great source of recreation at community centers.

Before World War II, public interest in softball grew so much that teams were organized into leagues all over the country, and it was estimated that well over 5 million people engaged in this popular American game. Because of its great appeal to all ages and because little equipment is needed and any ordinary playground is adequate, softball has become one of the most popular of all activities. It is now played by over 35 million Americans. The game has even been modified for the blind by use of a ball that emits a beeping sound.

Modifications of the basic rules have produced many types of games and leagues, such as fast pitch and slow pitch; leagues for men's teams, women's teams, and coed teams; games using the regulation-size softball (12 inches, or 30.5 cm, in circumference), games using a much larger ball, and games for women using a softball 11 inches (27.9 cm) in circumference; rules forbidding the use of gloves; and many other interesting variations. Presented here are the abridged rules and techniques of slow-pitch softball. As mentioned, many variations are enjoyed in different parts of the country.

The most popular style played in physical education activity classes and also very popular in most recreation programs is slow-pitch softball. Because of the arced delivery of the pitch, it is suitable for all ages and skill levels. Therefore, the focus of this chapter will be on slow-pitch softball rules, skills, and strategies.

EQUIPMENT AND FIELD

The bat should be round and made of hardwood, metal, plastic, graphite, carbon, magnesium, ceramic, or any other composite material approved by the ASA. It shall be no more than 34 inches (86.36 cm) long, 2¼ inches (5.72 cm) in diameter at its largest part, and weighing no more than 38 ounces (1.08 kg).

The ball should be regular, smooth seamed, flat surfaced, and pebble textured or dimple textured with concealed stitches. The 11-inch (27-cm) ball shall weigh at least 6.0 ounces (170.1 g), whereas the 12-inch (30-cm) ball shall weigh at least 6.75 ounces (193 g).

The bases shall be 65 feet (19.81 m) apart. For boys and girls under 12, the bases shall be 60 feet (18.3 m) apart. The distance from the pitcher's rubber to home plate is 50 feet (15.24 m) with the following exceptions—for boys and girls under 10, it shall be 40 feet (12.2 m), and for boys and girls under 12, it shall be 46 feet (14.0 m).

Gloves may be worn by any player, but mitts are limited to first basemen and catchers.

A mask, throat guard, and chest guard are recommended for catchers in slow-pitch. Spikes or any other type of sharp projections on the shoes are prohibited. Molded rubber cleats are acceptable.

Playing field dimensions are given in Figure 27.1.

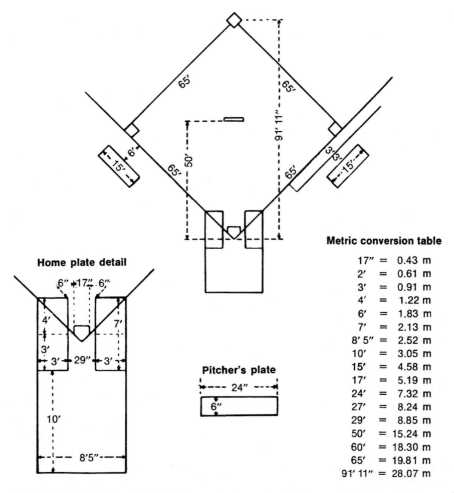

Figure 27.1. Slow-pitch softball playing field. Pitching distance is 50 feet (15.24 m). Bases are 65 feet (19.81 m) apart. Distances from home plate to the fence are 275 feet (83.87 m) for men and 250 (76.2) for women.

Metric conversion table

17"	=	0.43 m
2'	=	0.61 m
3'	=	0.91 m
4'	=	1.22 m
6'	=	1.83 m
7'	=	2.13 m
8' 5"	=	2.52 m
10'	=	3.05 m
15'	=	4.58 m
17'	=	5.19 m
24'	=	7.32 m
27'	=	8.24 m
29'	=	8.85 m
50'	=	15.24 m
60'	=	18.30 m
65'	=	19.81 m
91' 11"	=	28.07 m

ABRIDGED RULES

Teams, Players, and Substitutes

A team shall consist of 10 players, whose positions shall be designated as pitcher, catcher, first baseman, second baseman, third baseman, shortstop, and four outfielders (left fielder, left center fielder, right center fielder, and right fielder). An extra player may be added to the batting order. (Note: for classes or recreational games, any number of players can bat.) For coed games, two females must play in the infield and in the outfield. Either the pitcher or the catcher must be female. The batting order must alternate between male and female players. Defensive substitutions are unrestricted.

The Game

1. A regulation game consists of seven innings, unless the team second at bat (home team) scores more runs in six innings than the team first at bat (visiting team) has scored in seven innings.

2. It is a regulation game if the home team in the seventh inning scores the winning run before the third player is out.

3. It is a regulation game if it is called by the umpire because of darkness, rain, or other cause, provided five or more innings have been played by each side or the home team has scored more runs at the end of its fourth inning or in any part of its fifth than the visiting team has scored in five complete innings.

4. When a game is called in any inning after the fifth, the score is what it was at the time the game was called if the home team has more runs than the visiting team. If the home team has fewer runs than the visiting team when the game is called, the score is that of the last inning completed by both sides.

Pitching Regulations

Preliminaries

1. The pitcher must take a position with both feet firmly on the ground and with one or both feet in contact with the pitcher's plate. The pitcher's pivot foot must be in contact with the pitcher's plate throughout the delivery.
2. The pitcher must come to a full and complete stop with the ball in front of the body. The front of the body must face the batter. This position must be maintained at least 1 second before starting the delivery.
3. The pitcher shall not be considered in the pitching position unless the catcher is in position to receive the pitch.
4. The pitcher must not make any motion to pitch while not in contact with the pitcher's plate. Violations of 1–4: A dead ball should be called, an illegal pitch ruled, a warning issued, and repeated action would result in the pitcher being ruled illegal, and removed from the pitching position.

Starting the Pitch

The pitch starts when the pitcher makes any motion with the ball that is part of the delivery after the required stop. While on the pitching plate prior to the required stop, any motion may be used.

Legal delivery

1. The pitcher must not make any motion to pitch without immediately delivering the ball to the batter.
2. The delivery is a continuous motion.
3. The pitcher must not use a delivery in which there is a stop or reversal of the pitching motion.
4. The pitcher must deliver the ball toward home plate on the first forward swing of the pitching arm past the hip with an underhand motion. The palm of the hand may be over or under the ball.
5. The pivot foot must remain in contact with the pitcher's plate until the pitched ball leaves the hand. If a step is taken, it can be forward, backward, or to the side, provided the pivot foot is in contact with the pitcher's plate and the step is simultaneous with the release of the ball.
6. The pitcher must not pitch the ball behind the back or through the legs.
7. The pitch shall be released at a moderate speed. The speed is left entirely up to the judgment of the umpire. The umpire shall warn the pitcher who delivers a pitch with excessive speed. If the pitcher repeats such an act after being warned, the pitcher shall be removed from the pitcher's position for the remainder of the game.
8. The ball must be delivered with perceptible arc and reach a height of at least 6 feet (1.83 m) from the ground, while not exceeding a maximum height of 12 feet (3.66 m) from the ground.
9. The pitcher must not continue the pitching motion after the ball is released.
10. The pitcher has 10 seconds to release the next pitch after receiving the ball, or after the umpire indicates "play ball."
11. The pitcher shall not deliver a pitch from the glove.

Foul Tip

A foul tip is a ball that is batted by the batter while standing in the lines of the batter's position and that goes sharply and directly to the hands of the catcher and is legally caught. In slow-pitch softball, a foul tip is considered to be like any other strike.

Out

Besides grounding out, flying out, or being tagged out, a batter is declared out if any of the following occur:

1. The batter makes a foul hit other than a foul tip as just defined and the ball is caught by a fielder before touching the ground, provided it is not caught in the fielder's hat, cap, protector, pocket, or other part of the uniform or does not strike some other object before being caught.
2. The ball is batted illegally.
3. The ball is bunted or chopped.
4. The batter attempts to hinder the catcher from fielding or throwing the ball by stepping outside the lines of the batter's position or in any way obstructs or interferes with that player.
5. Immediately after three strikes. If the batter fouls the third strike, it is still considered to be an out.
6. Before two players are out, while first and second bases or first, second, and third bases are occupied, the batter hits a fair fly ball that is handled or, in the opinion of the umpire, could have been caught by an infielder with reasonable effort (infield fly rule).
7. The batter steps from one batter's box to the other while the pitcher is in position ready to pitch.

FUNDAMENTAL DEFENSIVE SKILLS AND TECHNIQUES

The basic skills of softball, like those of any other sport, must be learned and practiced often. The techniques necessary for good performance are given here.

The Grip

Initially, beginning players should be taught the correct *grip* of the ball. If the players do not grip the ball correctly, it will be difficult for them to throw the ball accurately. The correct grip should be a two- or three-finger grip across the wide seams (Figures 27.2 and 27.3). The thumb placement is critical in that the thumb needs to be placed directly underneath the fingers so when the throwing arm comes to release, the thumb is pointed directly at the target. If this does not occur,

Figure 27.2. Two-finger grip.

Figure 27.3. Three-finger grip.

then some lateral deviation of the ball will result, making it more difficult to throw the ball in the desired direction. To check this grip, there are several things that can be done. A half-and-half ball can be used, with half the ball colored dark and the other portion remaining light. This half-and-half configuration should run across the wide seams so that the players become used to gripping the ball in this fashion. Using the half-and-half ball it is relatively simple to check finger placement and thumb placement before the ball is thrown. An excellent preliminary drill is to have the players hold the ball in their glove with their bare hand in such a way that they cannot see the ball and have them twist the ball around in their hand until they feel the wide seam and immediately pull it out and show it to you with the thumb pointed directly at you. This should create a situation where the fingers are behind the ball. This is the position that the hand should be in at release to ensure a straight throw.

There are modifications that can be done on this drill, such as having the players hold the ball behind their back

and have them flip it to themselves and then show you the correct grip as quickly as possible. You can also toss them the ball and have them catch the ball bare-handed and assume the correct grip as soon as possible. These are all fun drills that can be done on breaks or before or at the end of practice.

Ready to Catch

The next skill to be taught after the grip is the *Ready to Catch Stance* (Figure 27.4). Players should be in the Ready to Catch position any time they are thrown a ball. Anticipation and reaction are important in softball. In the Ready to Catch position, the feet should be at least shoulder-width apart and the toes pointed directly toward the thrower. The knees should be bent and directly over the toes. The player should be bent at the waist so that the shoulders are directly over the knees. This brings the center of gravity forward and provides the most stable position to allow movement in any direction. The elbows are bent, and the thumbs are brought together in front of the chest.

Mechanics of Catching

Once this basic position has been taught, the fundamentals of throwing and catching should be introduced. With novice players, the use of a glove simply hinders development. Initially they should be taught to catch bare-handed with the majority of the catch being accomplished by the non-throwing hand, but with the throwing hand directly next to the catching hand and in a position to cover the ball and get it ready to throw as soon as possible. Before discussing this action further, some definitions are needed. The side of

Figure 27.4. Ready to catch—thumbs together.

the body on which the throwing hand is located is called the throwing side. The side of the body away from the throwing hand is called the glove side. When describing positions to beginning players, this terminology is useful. When a player is preparing to receive a thrown ball, the glove should be held directly in front of the chest with the throwing hand positioned right next to the glove in a thumbs-together position. It is important that the glove be held chest high with the fingers pointing upward so that the glove can be moved in any direction in case an off-target throw is made.

The correct mechanics for receiving the ball involve moving in such a way that the ball is caught in the middle of the body. If this is not possible, then both hands should be moved to the ball to help insure a safe, efficient catch. If this is not possible, then the glove should be moved as quickly as possible in the direction of the thrown ball with concomitant movement of the body if necessary. The coach should flip several balls to the player to check mechanics and make sure that if the throw is above the waist, the ball is caught with the fingers of the glove pointed up in a "thumbs together" position. If the ball is thrown waist high or below, then the player should change the position of the hands so that the little fingers are together, again palms facing the ball, fingers pointing slightly down in this case (Figure 27.5). This is the correct position for catching the ball. Players should be encouraged to receive the ball with a soft, giving motion. They should not stab at the ball, slap at the ball, or move to try to keep it from hitting them. They should let the ball come to them.

One simple drill beginning players can use is to toss the ball to themselves. The toss should be at least 3 feet above the head. Initially they should try to catch the ball with little fingers together in an underhand fashion and the emphasis should be on watching the ball all the way into the hands. They should be encouraged to let the ball come down and catch it between chest and waist high, rather than reaching up for the ball. This is called tracking. Also emphasis should be placed on receiving the ball with soft hands. After they have attempted 10 or so repetitions of this catch, they should step under the ball and attempt to catch it above the head in a thumbs-together position. This approximates the correct receiving pattern for a fly ball or a thrown ball and may be somewhat more difficult for most of the beginning players. Once the players feel reasonably comfortable performing these skills, the ball can be tossed to them by a coach or a partner.

Throwing Drills
Flick drill

The first throwing drill that should be taught is the *flick drill* (Figure 27.6). The purpose of the flick is to teach the thrower the proper relationship of the throwing elbow to the shoulder, to check the grip and release, and to emphasize the correct throwing actions of the elbow and wrist. Players should initially start out about 15 feet (4.6 m) apart. They should assume the ready to catch position, but once they catch the ball, they should transfer it as quickly as possible to the throwing hand, assuming the correct grip, and place the glove with the finger side against the glove side of their chest in what is termed the tuck position. This tuck position becomes important when the full throwing motion is used because this is where the glove should reside when the glove

Figure 27.5. Ready to catch—little fingers together.

Figure 27.6. The flick position.

side is pulled in to help give increased throwing velocity to the throwing side. The elbow of the throwing arm is held at shoulder height and in the same plane as the shoulder. The elbow is bent at 90 degrees so that the forearm is basically vertical. The forearm is turned so that the thumb is facing the target, and the fingers are directly behind the ball. The ball is thrown with extension of the elbow and flexion of the wrist. There will be some anatomical action at the shoulder joint; however, it is minimized because the emphasis of this drill is the release and the wrist and elbow action, not distance or velocity of the ball. The ball should be flicked toward the chest of the partner in a relaxed, easy motion. The rotation of the ball can be checked and the follow-through on the flick should be held so that the coach can check the extension of the elbow and the flexion of the wrist.

There are several actions that *should not* take place in the flick drill. For one, there is no step involved since the purpose of the drill is to isolate the elbow and wrist action. That is why the feet are placed parallel to one another facing the target. This is not how they would be placed when throwing with the full throwing motion. The arm should not be drawn back. The elbow should stay in the plane of the shoulders, and the force should be provided simply by elbow extension and wrist flexion. Many players will try to accomplish this throw by flexing the wrist in a kind of pushing action. This should be discouraged. It should be a smooth coordinated extension of the elbow and flexion of the wrist to accomplish the flick correctly. The ball should rotate tightly. If a half-and-half ball is used, then the colored half should stay on one side and the white half on the other with the line basically vertical between the two colors.

Next, the Ready to Throw position should be taught. In the *Ready to Throw* position (Figure 27.7) the players are turned so the body faces a line perpendicular to the flight of the ball. This is imperative for teaching the correct throwing mechanics. Many beginning players exaggerate trunk action and shoulder action rather than throwing with the correct trunk rotation and the correct arm action. To complete the ready to throw position, the ball is placed in the throwing hand and the throwing hand with the ball in it is placed in the glove. The glove should be held about chest high or slightly lower, and the eyes should be turned and focused on the target.

Break and throw drill

The next throwing drill in teaching the throwing progression should be the *break and throw drill*. The purpose of the break and throw drill is to teach the correct ready to throw position and the correct arm mechanics for the full throw. The only element not included in the break and throw drill is the movement to the ready to throw position and the foot movement to maximize throwing accuracy and velocity. These will be taught later. To assume the ready to throw position, the players turn so the glove shoulder is pointed at the target.

Figure 27.7. The ready to throw position.

For this drill, partners should be 30 to 40 feet (9.1 to 12.2 m) apart depending on their skill level. Again, the basic ready position with the feet shoulder width apart, knees over toes, and shoulders over knees should be assumed. However, the feet should be at right angles to the target.

The commands on the break and throw drill are as follows:

The player assumes the ready to throw position previously explained. On the *break* command, the thrower should extend both elbows with the ball coming out of the glove and the glove coming down. In this position the ball should be behind the thrower (Figure 27.8). The thumbs on both hands should be pointed down. There should be slight flexion in the elbows. A point of emphasis in this position is that the back of the throwing shoulder should be actually rotated toward the target to provide a little additional torque. This position should be tension free. The shoulders should be relaxed. The elbows should be relaxed, and the eyes should still be focusing on the target. On the *throw* command, three motions should occur. The player should step with the glove foot directly toward the target. The glove foot should stay closed until just prior to landing. The player should pull the glove side in to reduce the rotational axis and increase the angular velocity of the trunk. And the throwing arm needs to traverse an arc with the elbow popping the arm up to a position similar to the flick position, which is followed by a rigorous extension of the elbow and flick of the wrist toward the target.

The words *step, pull,* and *pop* can be used at this point to reinforce the movement pattern. On the step command, the thrower will pick up the glove foot and step directly toward

Figure 27.8. The break position.

the target. They should land on the ball of the foot as the foot turns naturally toward the target, although the toes should not be pointed at the target as they step. With the step, the glove should be pulled vigorously in toward the tuck position to reduce the radius of rotation and help speed up the trunk rotation. As the trunk starts to rotate and the torso turns toward the target, the elbow pops up as the shoulder rotates through the throwing motion, and as the foot lands, the elbow should be extending and the wrist should be flexing to deliver the throw. The follow-through should consist of the throwing elbow ending up by the glove side knee. The throwing side hip should roll, and the eyes should remain on the target throughout the entire throwing action.

The next two throwing drills that should be taught are the *step and throw* and the *skip and throw*. These throws help the player learn to coordinate the total body actions that are involved in throwing.

Step and throw drill

This drill is similar to the break and throw drill except the thrower does not pause in the break position. Also, footwork is added to increase throwing velocity and to make the throw more game-like.

From the ready to throw position, the thrower steps with the glove foot in the direction of the target. The foot should be facing 90 degrees to the target. The player then takes a short step with the throwing side foot and executes a break and throw. The key is that the step be taken from ball of foot to ball of foot. Balance is maintained; the throwing shoulder is rotating as the pull-pop action takes place and as the glove foot is planted to make the throw. This becomes a left, right,

left step pattern for right-handers or a right, left, right action for left-handers. This is the most commonly executed throw and should be practiced often. The starting distance for partners in this drill should be 50–60 feet (15.2 to 18.3 m) apart based on the level of ability of the players.

Skip and throw drill

The foot mechanics on the skip and throw are used less often in the game of softball but are still used occasionally by outfielders and sometimes by infielders when throwing in the opposite direction from which they face (e.g., the shortstop wheeling to throw to third might execute a skip and throw to get the body turned). This allows the thrower to get the body turned more quickly. Skip and throw is executed by picking up the glove foot, skipping on the throwing foot as the body turns, and then completing the throwing motion.

Ready to Field

The next position that should be taught is the *ready to field* position (Figure 27.9). Players should assume the ready to field position any time they are preparing to receive a batted ball. In this position the player is bent at the knees and at the hips, leaning slightly forward, and the glove and the throwing hand are placed close to the ground out in front of the player with the palms facing the batter. The weight should be on the balls of the feet, and the player should be ready to move in any direction. To teach the fielding mechanics of ground balls, the first element to stress is the importance of moving to the ball. Whether the ball is hit to either side or in front, the player should move directly to it. In the case of the ball being hit directly in front of the player, this movement is called *charging* the ball. To practice this skill, the ball can either be placed several feet in front of the player or it can be rolled slowly to the player. In either case, the player assumes a ready to field position, charges the ball, and upon catching the ball, hops to a ready to throw position. This hopping

Figure 27.9. The ready to field position.

movement is very critical and is very difficult to do if the glove foot is not forward. Good preliminary steps to teach this action are to have the player (1) assume a ready to field position, (2) charge the stationary ball making sure to take short choppy steps and to keep the center of gravity low to the ground, and (3) field the ball with two hands with the throwing hand beside the glove in a little-fingers-together position (Figure 27.10). This is a safer position for teaching beginners than the hinge position where the heel of the throwing hand is placed above the heel of the glove hand.

Fielding Grounders

After the basic fielding form for grounders is taught, the following progression should be followed: (1) field easy rollers, (2) field easy bouncers, (3) field glove side grounders, and (4) field backhand grounders. Basic points to emphasize in these drills are: charge the ball, field with glove foot forward, hop to the ready to throw position, and step and throw. If the player does not field the ball cleanly, it should be picked up with the throwing hand; then the player should assume the ready to throw position and step and throw. The mechanics for fielding backhand grounders involve executing a crossover step with the glove foot to get the body turned in the correct way. After the player fields the ground ball in the backhand position, the throwing foot should be planted, the ball brought to the throwing position, and a step or throw executed. The movement of the glove is critical in fielding backhand grounders. Many beginning players tend to stab at the ball and let the ball roll under the glove as they are bringing it down. The glove should be moved in a swinging motion from a ready to field position to a backhand position, never getting much higher than the ground itself. It is important that it be opened up in the direction of the ball and that it is placed in front of the foot. Many beginning players as they step will put their foot in front of their glove, making it extremely difficult to field the ball. A good way to

Figure 27.10. Fielding the ground ball.

practice this is to have the players line up at the shortstop position close to second base and have them execute a backhand and then pivot and flick the ball to the second baseman. This allows them to execute a number of backhands fairly quickly without having to worry about planting and making a long throw to first. As they progress with their fielding mechanics, they can practice longer throws.

Fielding Fly Balls

The next element of fielding is *catching fly balls*. Catching fly balls is a difficult skill for beginning players to execute. It should be practiced early in a very controlled situation. Coaches can get fairly close to the players and toss the ball either overhand or underhand to the players. The players should start in a ready to field position even if they are outfielders. They should start with their gloves higher than infielders, but not in a ready to catch position. They should not get in the habit of starting with their gloves in a ready to catch position. They should not start with their hands on their knees. This is what is considered a rest position. They can be in this resting position until the pitcher gets ready to pitch the ball, but then they should assume the ready to field position. When a player goes after a fly ball, and is unsure of where it is coming down, the first step should always be backward because it is common to underestimate the distance of the hit, and it is much easier to come in on a ball than to go back on one. Once it is determined where the ball is coming down, the player should run to that position as quickly as possible, and set up under the ball to catch it with the glove in front of the body, about chest high. The player should be able to see the ball come down into the glove this way. A fault that many outfielders make is to place the glove directly in front of the face, therefore making it very difficult to track the ball into the glove. Catching the ball off to the side should be discouraged because this makes it more difficult to throw the ball. The ball should be caught either in midline or it should be caught over the throwing shoulder to make for an easy release.

The progression for teaching fielding fly balls is to start by having the players move to fly balls hit to their left or right. These should be easiest to track since they have an angular perspective as to where the ball is coming down. Again, this can be done with the coach tossing the ball to them to make them run back and forth. After they achieve success at this task, the ball can be hit to them by a batter who has good bat control. It is a very good idea to use safety balls at first. Even tennis balls can be used because they force the players to catch the ball with soft hands.

The next step in the progression is fielding balls that are short and deep. This often results in rolling catches close to the ground (the shoestring catch) or over-the-shoulder catches like a wide receiver in football. Throwing balls will allow for more repetitions and more quality work early in the season with beginning players, and as the season progresses, the balls can be hit to the players.

Fielding ground balls for the outfielders is slightly different than for infielders. Three situations can arise when outfielders are fielding ground balls. If there are no runners on base and the ball is hit directly to the outfielder, it is imperative that the ball be stopped. The outfielder should get in front of the ball, get to one knee with the leg turned to the side, and place the glove down between the legs to provide the biggest target for the ball to hit. As soon as the ball is caught, the outfield should come up quickly and execute a step and throw toward second base. If the runner does not attempt to go to second base, the cut-off player (a player positioned between the fielder and the base) should catch the ball. If the runner makes a big turn and thinks about possibly trying for second, the ball should go through to the second baseman or shortstop, and they can make the play.

If there are runners on base and a ball is hit directly to an outfielder, the outfielder should execute the catch of the ground ball as an infielder would, with the glove foot forward, being ready to bring the ball to the ready to throw position and step and throw toward the lead base. One important axiom in baseball is to always throw ahead of the runner. If the runner is moving from first to second on a hit, the throw should go toward third base. Occasionally an outfielder might be able to get a force-out at the preceding base, but these situations need to be talked about specifically and used judiciously. It is best to teach beginning outfielders to throw in front of the runners.

The last ground ball fielding situation occurs when a runner is attempting to score, and it is imperative that this runner be stopped. In this situation, the outfielder charges the ball as quickly as possible and fields the ball off to the glove side. This allows the fielder to run through the catch, execute a modification of a step and throw called a "crow hop," which is hopping from the glove foot to the throwing foot and throwing the ball as quickly as possible. The outfielder will never actually be in the complete ready to throw position. It is important in this action that the ball be caught and released as quickly as possible; therefore, actually getting players into the ready to throw position is not beneficial in this drill. It needs to be practiced at full speed.

Plays at Bases

Other important elements of fielding involve plays around the bases. Two situations need to be taught: (1) fielding for a force play, such as a force-out at first or any other base, and (2) the tag play at a base, especially home plate.

Force-outs

The key element in both situations is safety. It is important that the fielder be positioned in such a way as not to get run over by the runner. On any force play, the fielder should position the throwing foot on the bag closest to the direction from which the throw is coming. The glove foot should be placed right next to the throwing foot and slightly to the side to give balance, and both knees should be bent so that as the ball is thrown they can step out (stretch) and reach

in the direction of the throw. Care needs to be taken to not stretch until the ball is thrown because the player must be sure to know where the ball is going. The glove should basically be in a modified ready to catch position with the fingers pointed so that the palms of the glove and throwing hands are facing each other and the fingers are pointed in the direction of the throw (Figure 27.11).

If a good throw is made, the glove can be rotated one-fourth of a turn upward to make the catch. If the throw is low, the glove can be rotated one-fourth of a turn downward with the fingers down to make a catch. The stretch should be made by simultaneously reaching with the glove hand as far as possible in the direction of the throw while stepping with the glove foot in the same direction. The throwing hand is left back for balance, and when the ball is caught, the ball of the foot should be in contact with the base (Figure 27.12).

To teach this skill, the ball is tossed first to the glove side, then directly in front, and finally to the throwing hand side. In game

Figure 27.11. Ready to stretch position.

Figure 27.12. The stretch position.

situations, when an errant throw takes the fielder down the first base line, it is important to stay out of the baseline to avoid being run over by the oncoming runner. Once the ball is caught, the fielder should step off the base to see if there is a succeeding play. Catching the ball is the primary objective. If it is necessary to come off of the base to catch the ball, so be it!

Tag plays

Tag plays are difficult to teach because the footwork depends on the direction from which the throw is coming. Whenever possible, the fielder should be on the side of the base from which the throw is coming for safety purposes. For example, if the third-base player is taking a throw from a left fielder, he or she should be positioned next to the base and just slightly toward second base. The body should be turned to receive the throw (Figure 27.13). As the throw comes in, the ball should be caught, covered with the throwing hand, and the glove placed in front of the bag, allowing the person sliding in to slide into the tag. If the throw is coming from the outfield to second base, then the fielder's position depends on where the throw is coming from and whether the runner is coming into second or returning to second after having made a turn. If the throw is coming from right field, the technique just described works best. If the throw is coming from center or left, the fielder needs to straddle the bag to be in the best position for the tag.

The tag play at home is a critical one because runners are allowed to overrun this base. If the catcher is making a tag play at home, it is important to position the left foot in front of the front edge of the plate to take it away from the runner. The toe should be pointed down the third-base line. This

Figure 27.14. Applying the tag.

allows the runner to run past the catcher if the throw is late or to slide past the catcher without making contact. In either situation, since runners are not allowed to run over fielders, this does give the runner some place to go, minimizing the possibility of a collision. Once the ball is caught, it is covered with the throwing hand and the glove is placed in front of the exposed part of the plate so the runner would slide into it (Figure 27.14). For throws that are going to bounce, it is important that fielders in all tag plays let the ball come to them. If they leave the base to make the catch and then come back, it is very difficult to execute the tag correctly. However, if the throw is off-line, it is important that the fielders go get the throw and then come back to make the tag.

Other Fielding Concerns

When the team is on defense, it is important that all players know how many outs there are, where the runners are, and where their next play should be if the ball is hit to them. They also should be aware of what batted balls they may have to back up and what thrown balls they should back up. This should all be thought out before each pitch or before each batter. Some key concepts to remember are to get the lead runner, always be sure of one out, and on a slowly hit ball, get the easiest out. The easiest out is usually at first base. Another way to determine where the easy out is, is by determining the direction the fielder is moving. For example, with a runner on first, if the second base player moves toward first to field a ground ball, the easy out is at first.

BATTING

Good batting ability and clever base running are the keys to successful offensive softball. It is therefore essential that beginners remember the following: the golden rule of hitting dictates that the hitter who waits the longest and swings the quickest will hit the hardest. This is especially true in slow-pitch softball. With the high arc of the pitch, the batter has the ability to evaluate each pitch over

Figure 27.13. Getting ready to catch the ball for a tag.

a much longer period of time than hitters in other games (e.g., fast-pitch or baseball). The mechanics involved in slow-pitch batting are similar to those of fast-pitch and baseball. The distinction comes in the increased decision time available to the softball batter.

Grip

The initial consideration is how to grip the bat. Often the alignment of the knuckles of each hand is emphasized. Because of different hand sizes and finger lengths, this can be difficult to evaluate. The key element is to have the batters hold the bat as much in their fingers as they can. If they have small hands, there will be a lot of palm contact, but as they grow, the key to a quick bat is finger control. Have the batter lean the bat in front of the body with the barrel on home plate and lay it in the fingers like a golf club (Figure 27.15). Then curl the fingers around the handle so there will be a *V* between the thumb and forefinger of each hand (Figure 27.16). This grip helps in bat control and bat speed. Also it is important to remember that relaxed muscles are quick muscles. The emphasis should be on a quick swing, not a hard swing.

Figure 27.16. Batting grip with V between thumb and forefinger of each hand.

Stance

The stance is often an overtaught or overcoached area. However, with beginning hitters it is critical that they have a basically sound stance. The goal should be to develop a comfortable stance with the feet at least shoulder-width apart. For most hitters, it is difficult when you have a narrower stance to keep the weight back—to keep from lunging.

The toes should be pointed directly toward home plate or toward the inside edge of the batter's box. Batters should be balanced in the box. The easiest way to teach this balance is to have the batter assume a ready to catch position—bend at the knees so that the knees are out over the toes, and bend at the waist so that the shoulders are over the knees. This is a good balanced position. The knees should be slightly bowed in. You want a good strong triangular base. Now the weight is going to be slightly toward the front part of the body (balls of the feet), which is facing the plate (Figure 27.17).

To discuss the mechanics of hitting, the term "lead" side will refer to the side closest to the pitcher and the term "rear" or "trail" side will refer to the side closest to the catcher. To

Figure 27.15. Initial position for batting grip.

Figure 27.17. Batting stance.

Figure 27.18. Batting stance. Checking the distance from the plate.

check the location in the box, the batter should be able to reach the far edge of the plate when reaching out with the bat with the lead hand—the hand closest to the pitcher (Figure 27.18). Make sure that the feet are positioned first before checking distance. The knees should be bent. From there if the bat is brought back toward the trailing shoulder and the trailing hand is placed on the bat, the result should be a relatively good bat position. The bat should be relatively close to the rear shoulder, and the hands should be about even with the rear shoulder. The hands should not be too low because they will tend to hitch and swing under the ball. If the hands are too high, the bat will have to be lowered to get to the launch position.

At this point, the arms resemble two letters. The lead arm is shaped like the letter *L*. The elbow should be relaxed and pointing down. If it is too high, it causes a tendency to drop the barrel of the bat. The elbow should not be tucked in but rather held out away from the body. It should be in a comfortable position. The rear arm has a *V* shape and is also relaxed. If the rear elbow is too high, it will cause the batter to swing under the ball. If it is pressed up against the side, there will be a tendency to push the ball. (Note: when you are trying to hit to the opposite field, this could be beneficial.) Again, a good relaxed position is best. Many beginning hitters will have trouble with the angle of the bat. If the bat is too heavy, they will tend to hold it straight up because it is easier to balance. Some will try to wrap it way around the head, which makes it difficult to get into the hitting position. One good way to describe the position of the bat in a general stance is to imagine a clock positioned in front of the

hitter. If a right-handed batter holds the bat straight up, it corresponds to noon. If the hitter holds the bat parallel to the ground, almost resting on the shoulder, it would correspond to three o'clock. The ideal position is somewhere between one and two o'clock. For a left-handed hitter, it would be between ten and eleven o'clock.

There can be a lot of variations in batting stances, but there is no point in teaching some strange stance because it will be harder to get the bat to the hitting position.

Mechanics of Hitting: The 4 Ts

There are four primary Ts in hitting: Track, Tuck, Turn, and Throw. The first T is track. Track means watch the ball until contact. To accomplish this, the head and eyes need to be level. This is the best position to efficiently track the ball. Also, in the stance, the chin should be close to the lead shoulder. As the swing is taken, the chin moves to the trailing shoulder. The head actually moves minimally, but the body rotates around it to generate force.

The second T is the tuck. This is often described as the stride. Hitting is a rotational skill, and this is best taught by employing a tuck. The tuck is executed by bringing the lead knee back toward the trail knee (Figure 27.19). This helps keep the weight back. The idea is to get the weight going backward before it goes forward. This transfer of weight allows you to hit efficiently. As the lead knee tucks, the bat is taken back slightly to provide additional force before the swing is started. The lead leg returns to basically the same place it started as the lead foot is placed down lightly. This provides a stable base from which to begin the swing (Figure 27.20).

Figure 27.19. The tuck position.

Figure 27.20. The hitting position.

The third T is the turn. The turn initiates the swing. It involves the hips starting to turn toward the pitcher. The trailing foot begins to pivot, but the hands stay back to create a coil effect (Figure 27.21).

The fourth T is throwing (the hands). This produces a quick swing. The best swing is relaxed and quick, not long, sweeping, and slow. Ideally, at contact the hips have turned and the feet have twisted to allow a full rotation. The hip movement is very important. If the hips are not turned, full rotation with the upper body will not occur. Throwing the trail hand will bring the bat down through the ball. The arc of the swing is also very important. The barrel of the bat should be kept above the hands until the bat reaches the plate, and the barrel of the bat should be forcefully swung toward the ball. At contact the bat should be an extension of the arms (Figure 27.22).

Figure 27.21. The turn.

Figure 27.22. Batting position just after contact.

After contact, the follow-through should be checked to ensure that an efficient swing has taken place. After contact, the wrists roll over and the bat continues around the body, ending up curled around the lead shoulder. The chin should be very close to the trailing shoulder at contact and should stay there briefly at follow-through. The lead leg should be straight, but not straight up and down (Figure 27.23). The trailing leg should be pivoted in a reverse L. The trailing foot should have twisted on the ball of the foot. This is often described as "squishing the bug." If this occurs the proper weight shift has probably been maintained.

A summary of the mechanics of hitting is presented in the Hitter's Guide (Table 27.1). It should be noted that individual differences will occur in hitting styles. Examination of Figures 27.23 and 27.24 shows that the position of the trailing foot is different for each hitter. As long as the hitter does not lunge forward at the ball, either of these finishing positions is acceptable.

Power and Choke Hitters

A power hitter stands farther back from the plate, with the feet well apart and parallel to the sides of the batter's box. The power hitter grips the bat at the end of the handle just above the knob.

Figure 27.23. Batting follow-through.

Table 27.1. SOFTBALL HITTER'S GUIDE

Golden Rule:	The hitter who waits the longest and swings the quickest will hit the hardest!
The 4 Primary Ts:	TRACK, TUCK, TURN, THROW
Gripping:	In the fingers (lead hand firm; trailing hand loose) **CRC:** Concentration, Relaxation, Confidence
Stancing:	Feet at least shoulder-width, toes pointed at home plate, knees flexed, bend at waist (shoulders over knees), weight on balls of feet, hands at top of strike zone by trailing shoulder, L and V, bat at 2 o'clock, head and eyes level **BALANCE**
Tracking:	Head and eyes relatively still throughout swing, chin starts out close to lead shoulder, eyes track ball until contact, chin ends up on trailing shoulder at contact (nose on the ball)
Tucking:	Front knee to rear knee (to load weight back), wrists cock (bat in slot), head still, front foot lands about where it started with weight on inside ball of foot, weight stays back (step on thin ice) **RHYTHM**
Turning:	Swing is initiated with hip turn, front foot stays closed, trailing foot begins to "squish the bug," trailing knee turns toward pitcher, hands stay back **ROTATION**
Throwing:	Contact is achieved by taking your hands directly to the ball, bat barrel stays above hands until just prior to contact, front leg is straight, belly button facing pitcher, weight over trailing hip **EXPLOSION**

Figure 27.24. Another batting follow-through.

A choke hitter stands closer to the plate than the power hitter when first learning. The trunk should be slightly inclined toward home plate. The choke hitter grips the bat several inches above the knob of the bat.

BASE RUNNING

The first running skill that should be taught to the beginning softball player is how to run to first base. There are two situations that are taught. In either case the first thing the batter does after making contact with the ball should be to drop the bat. Beginning players have a tendency to throw the bat.

The first situation involves the ball being hit to the infield, and there is a high probability that a play will be made at first base. In this case, the runner should leave the batter's box as quickly as possible and run directly to first base. Beginning in 2004, the safety base (double base) was approved for use at first base. Half of the base (white) is in fair territory and is to be used by the fielder. The other half of the double base (colored) is in foul territory and is what the runner must touch. The rules state that if there is a play at first and the runner, running in fair territory, interferes with the play, the runner is out. Runners should be taught that for the last half of the way to first they should run in foul territory. This is also important from a safety standpoint to keep them from getting hit with a ball and to prevent a collision with the first-base player who might be on the middle of the base. The runner should learn to run through the base and not to slow down until well past the base. The runner should hit the front part of the base (nearest home plate) with either foot and stay on stride. Runners should not take a last long lunging step at the base because this tends to slow them down. After passing first base, the runner should take a quick look over the right shoulder to see if an overthrow occurred. If not, the runner should be taught to turn to the right and immediately return to first base. Technically it does not matter which way the turn is made as long as no attempt to go to second is made; however, it is simpler and safer to teach that the turn should always be made toward foul territory.

The second base running situation involves a ball that is clearly hit to the outfield or a ball that is hit between infielders and goes through to the outfield. In this situation, the runner should run directly toward the base until told by the first-base coach to turn and look or turn and go. In this situation, when the runner has passed halfway to the base, a small banana turn into foul territory should be made and first base should be contacted in such a manner that the runner is going directly toward second base. The runner should hit the inside portion of the base closest to home plate with either foot. It doesn't matter which foot is actually used to push off of as long as the turn is directly toward second and not into right field.

The "turn and look" command is given by the coach when the ball is hit directly to the outfielder. On any ball hit directly to the outfield or any grounder that gets past an infielder,

the batter should be thinking about getting to second base right out of the batter's box. The runner should make a turn as if going to second by taking several steps toward second base while watching the play in the outfield. If the outfielder bobbles the ball, the runner can continue on to second. If the outfielder makes a bad throw to the relay person or overthrows the base, the runner can continue on to second. The runner should not return to first base until the ball is clearly in possession of an infielder. At that point, the runner should return to first without losing sight of the ball.

The next step in teaching base running is to practice the turn and go making sure that the runner makes a good turn at first base, running hard into second and stopping on the base. It is imperative that coaches give clear, concise verbal *and* visual commands. To get the runner to run through the base at first, the coach should yell something like "go-go-go." The commands to turn are "turn and look" or "turn and go." The command to stop on second should be "stop on the base, stop on the base." The third-base coach should be pointing at second base. If there are no other runners on base, the third-base coach should be telling the runner to stop on second base. If the third-base coach is involved with getting a different runner around third, then it is the responsibility of the first-base coach to get the runner to stop at second.

It is important for runners to be aware of where the ball is at all times. They should not just watch a ground ball that is batted to the infield, but they should have a feel for where it is hit. Once it comes off the bat, they should have a basic idea of where it is going and they should simply look to the coach and run through the base. On an overthrown ball at first, the runner does not have to retouch first base but instead can go directly to second base. However, once they have made an attempt to go to second, they do not have a free return to the base.

Running from second to home can also be practiced, since home is the only other base that can be overrun. The technique is similar to running from home to second. The runner should take off directly toward third base. The third-base coach should be slightly down the third-base line toward home plate and using the commands "turn and look," "turn and go," or "stop on the base." The hand signals associated with these commands are waving an arm in a circular fashion for a turn. On a turn and go, the coach would continue waving the arm. On a turn and look, both arms should be put up after the runner has hit the base, and for stopping on the base one hand should be placed up in the air and the other hand should be pointing at the base. It is important that these visual and verbal commands are clear to the runners, and they should be practiced.

BASE-RUNNING STANCE

Slow-pitch rules do not allow the runner to leave the base until after the ball is hit, it hits the ground, or crosses the plate. This is called a fixed base (as opposed to a lead-off situation).

The best way to be positioned on a fixed base allows the use of a rolling start. This involves placing the left foot on the side of the base facing the next base. The ball of this foot should be on the dirt and pressed up against the side of the base. The heel of this foot is actually in the air. The right foot should be placed directly beside the base (Figure 27.25). For example, when on first base, the right foot should be on the

Figure 27.25. Base-running stance.

Figure 27.26. Rolling start.

outfield side of the base slightly in fair territory. When the pitcher delivers the pitch, the runner should pick up the right foot and start leaning toward second base (Figure 27.26). It should be timed in such a way that the right foot hits the ground as the ball crosses the plate. This allows the runner to overcome inertia and be heading toward second base if the ball is hit. If the ball is not hit, the runner repositions the right foot and waits for the next pitch.

Sliding is difficult to teach and can be dangerous. For the beginning player, sliding should not be allowed. For those interested in teaching sliding see the section in Johnson, Leggett, and McMahon (2001).

POSITIONAL SKILLS

Catcher

The catcher should be in a half-squat or kneeling position comfortably behind the batter. The glove should be placed on the ground, pocket up, and several feet behind home plate. There is little need to catch the pitch before it bounces. The catcher should be ready to field a dribbler or a pop-up as well as making force plays and tag plays at home. For safety purposes, the catcher should be taught to let the pitch come to him or her rather than reaching forward to catch the ball.

Pitcher

Because of the arc rule, the direction the pitcher steps is a matter of preference. The two most common styles are (1) stepping directly toward home with the glove foot, and (2) pitching with no step and then retreating several steps to become a fifth infielder. The first style is the easiest to teach, but it brings the pitcher closer to the batter. Many pitchers have trouble mastering the second style, but it does provide more safety and better team defense. In either style, the pitcher should assume a ready to catch position prior to the batter swinging. This is again for safety purposes.

There are three main grips and releases of the ball used in slow pitching: (1) forehand position, (2) mid position, and (3) backhand position. To deliver the ball with a forehand release, grip the ball like you would be making an overhand throw. As the arm is taken back past the hip, the palm of the pitching hand is facing home plate (Figure 27.27). As the arm is swung forward, the ball is released with a gentle wrist flick to give the ball the appropriate arc. To pitch from the mid position, the ball is gripped with the thumb and first two fingers of the throwing hand. The forearm is rotated inward so the thumb is next to the pivot leg (Figure 27.28). As the arm is brought forward, the release is executed with a gentle wrist flick. Many slow-pitch pitchers prefer the backhand release (Figure 27.29). In the backhand release, as the arm is taken back past the hip, the back part of the pitching hand is facing home plate. As the arm is brought forward, this allows for more backspin and a better feel at release.

Figure 27.27. Forehand pitching grip.

Figure 27.29. Backhand pitching grip.

Figure 27.28. Mid-position pitching grip.

First Base

The person playing first base should cover the base in a way that does not cause interference with the runner, but allows balls from all directions to be played. The first-base player should be stationed on the infield side of the base when receiving throws from the infield. The player normally stands about 6 feet (1.83 m) off the base and a few feet behind the baseline. The first-base player is normally tall to allow a longer stretch for errant throws. Mobility is not as necessary for the first-base player as for other infielders.

Second Base

The person playing second base must have the ability and agility to run to the left or right for ground balls. The best position is a little nearer second base than first base and in back of the baseline. It is important for this player to back up other infielders whenever possible. The second baseman does not need as strong an arm as the other infielders.

Shortstop

The shortstop should play about 10 to 12 feet (3.05 to 3.66 m) behind the baseline and approximately one-third of the way toward third base. A shortstop must be agile, quick, and able to move equally comfortably to the left or right. Generally the shortstop covers second base when the ball is hit to the right side of the infield or to the pitcher. The shortstop backs up or covers third base when the person playing third base is fielding the ball. Other important functions of the shortstop are to be the pivot person on a normal double play and to serve as the cut-off or relay person on many hits to the outfield.

Third Base

The person playing third base should play about 6 feet (1.83 m) from the base and behind the baseline. They should have a strong arm and quick reactions. This player may have to dive for more balls than the other infielders and should be taught to play any balls they can reach to the left since this is an easier play for the third-base player than the shortstop.

Outfielders

Outfielders must have running speed, be able to accurately judge the flight of a fly ball, and be able to throw accurately and hard. In slow-pitch outfielders are normally positioned in a four-across alignment (Figure 27.30). Outfielders should study hitters to know where they normally hit the ball. An outfielder should watch every pitch and be ready to move in any direction with each pitch. When playing a ground ball with no runners on base, the outfielder should drop to one knee and place the body in front of the ball to block it. With runners on base, the outfielder should field the ground ball like an infielder and be sure to throw in front of the lead runner. When trying to throw a runner out at home or other bases, the ball should be fielded on the move with a scooping action of the glove. This is a high-risk play, but it allows the fielder to get rid of the ball quickly.

On fly balls, the outfielder should move to a position that allows the ball to be caught in a thumbs-together fashion. If unsure of the distance of the fly ball or line

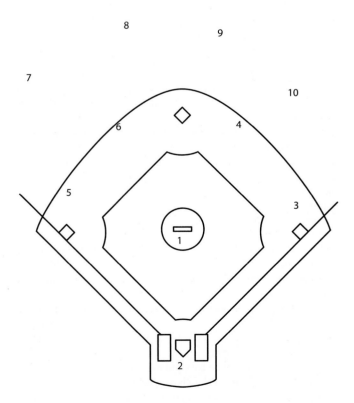

Figure 27.30. Fielding positions. 1, Pitcher. 2, Catcher. 3, First base. 4, Second base. 5, Third base. 6, Shortstop. 7, Left field. 8, Left center field. 9, Right center field. 10, Right field.

drive, a step backward should be taken to make sure to keep the ball in front of the outfielder. Verbal communication about balls hit between outfielders or between an outfielder and an infielder is a must. Outfielders have priority over infielders. Fly balls will normally tail toward the foul line, so corner outfielders would have priority over interior outfielders. On balls hit to center, the fielder having the shortest route to the ball should call it. Besides fielding batted balls, outfielders should be involved backing up plays of infielders or adjacent outfielders as well as backing up bases on potential thrown balls.

SELECTED RULES OF PLAY

A *ball* is called for a pitched ball that does not enter the strike zone. The strike zone is over any part of home plate between the back shoulder and the front knee of the batter when in a natural batting stance.

A *fair* ball is one that (1) lands in fair territory (between first and third bases), (2) lands on any one of the bases, including home base, (3) falls on fair ground beyond first or third base, or (4) bounds over first or third base but then lands in foul territory. It should be noted that home base is in fair territory.

The *infield-fly rule* states that, with base runners on first and second or first, second, and third, with less than two outs, and in the judgment of the umpire the batted ball could be caught by an infielder making a normal effort, the batter is out and the runners may advance at their own risk. The ball must be a fair ball.

A *foul* ball is a legally batted ball that (1) settles on foul ground outside the first or third baseline or behind home plate, or (2) bounds past first or third base on foul ground, or outside of bases. If a foul fly is caught, *the batter is out.* Runners may advance at their own risk as if it were a fair fly. The batter is out if there are two strikes and the next batted ball is a foul.

A *foul tip* is a batted ball that goes from the bat, not higher than the batter's head, to the catcher's hands and is legally caught.

The batter is *out* under the following circumstances:
1. On three strikes.
2. When the ball is bunted or chopped downward.
3. When a fly ball is legally caught.
4. On an infield-fly rule.
5. When the batter interferes with the catcher.
6. When the batter is tagged or thrown out at first base.
7. Intentional interference puts a runner out plus the batter who hit the ball.

Base-Running Rules

1. *All* bases must be touched in order.
2. If two base runners are on the same base, the last runner to reach the base can be tagged out.

3. The batter becomes a base runner when four balls are called.
4. When a fair *batted ball* bounds or rolls into a bleacher or over, under, or through a fence or other obstruction marking the boundaries of the playing field, the ball is dead and all base runners are awarded two bases from the time of the pitch.
5. When a *thrown ball* bounds or rolls into a bleacher or over, under, or through a fence or other obstruction marking the boundaries of the playing field, the ball is dead and all base runners are awarded two bases from the time of the throw.
6. There is no base stealing. Only after the pitched ball has passed home plate and has been batted can the base runner leave a base. Note: In some adult men's slow-pitch leagues, steals are allowed.
7. The base runner is out if running outside the baseline to avoid a tag. The runner is allowed 1 step on either side of the baseline, approximately 3 feet (0.91 m). The runner is out if he or she interferes with a fielder fielding a batted ball. The base runner is not out if it is necessary to run around a fielder taking the batted ball.
8. The base runner is out if he or she passes another base runner.
9. The base runner is out if off base and struck by a fair batted ball before it passes a fielder other than the pitcher.

TEACHING CONSIDERATIONS

1. Establish a reasonable level of consistency in fielding and throwing skills before using these skills in game or gamelike conditions.
   a. Consider beginning with a softer ball.
   b. Start with fielding slow balls thrown directly to the fielder. Increase the speed gradually and cause the fielder to move to either side, forward, and back to receive the ball.
   c. Include throws of different distances and directions from the fielder. Acknowledge appropriate throwing patterns for different situations.
   d. Include fielding of batted balls as soon as learners are ready for balls coming with more force.
2. The basics of the game can be taught without batting a pitched ball (by replacing with batting with a throw or batting off a tee) and with a smaller number of players. There are many lead-up and modified games that permit more practice and have much higher levels of participation than the official game. Teachers should consider using these. Base-running and defensive strategies are best taught without batting to permit more offensive play opportunities.
3. Practice pitching as a separate skill. Give all students opportunities to play all positions. Do not permit weak players to be "left out in the field." However, do not put a weaker player in harm's way.
4. Emphasize safety at all times:
   a. Pair weaker players together when playing catch.
   b. During warm-up, be certain that all pairs are throwing in parallel lines.
   c. Also make sure that there is enough space between pairs so they are not likely to get hit with errant throws.
   d. If using stations, make sure that batted balls and overthrows will not go into another station.
   e. Any time a player is holding a bat, bat safety must be emphasized. Hitters should make certain no one is close to them if they are swinging at a ball or taking a practice swing. When carrying a bat from one place to another, it should be held by the handle with the barrel down by the ankle.
5. To teach batting, consider the following methods:
   a. Use whiffle balls and bats.
   b. Bat off a tee.
   c. Have the pitcher (or coach) pitch with a lower arc.
6. Start with only basic rules. Add more technical rules as learners are ready for them.
7. Give students the responsibility for leadership (being captain or in charge of equipment), but teach them what is expected of these individuals and maintain those expectations.
8. Keep safety in mind (e.g., playing especially weak players where they will receive many thrown balls could result in injuries).

GLOSSARY

appeal play A play on which an umpire cannot make a decision until requested by a player. The request must be made before the next play.

assist Throwing or deflecting, by a player, of a thrown or batted ball by which an out is made.

base on balls Reaching first base after four balls are called by the umpire.

base path An imaginary line 3 feet (0.91 m) to either side of a direct line between bases.

battery The pitcher and catcher.

batting average The number of hits made by a batter divided by the times at bat. Walks and sacrifice flies are not counted as a time at bat.

batting order The official listing of the sequence of the players to bat.

double play A play in which two players are legally put out on the same hit ball.

error A play that fails to cause the out of a runner or that allows advancement of a runner.

extra player A player who bats and may play in the field.

fair territory The part of the playing field within or including the first- and third-base foul lines from home plate to the bottom of the extreme playing-field fence and perpendicularly upward.

foul tip A ball that goes directly from the bat to the catcher's glove.

infield That portion of the field within the baselines.

infield-fly rule The batter shall be declared out when hitting an infield fly with runners on first and second or first, second, and third, with fewer than two outs. The ball must be fair and, in the umpire's judgment, must be catchable by an infielder making a normal effort. The ball remains alive, and runners may advance at their own risk.

inning That portion of a game in which a team plays both offense and defense, starting with the first team at bat.

pivot foot The foot that the pitcher must keep in constant contact with the pitcher's plate until the delivery of the ball.

play ball "Play ball" means to begin the game or resume play.

sacrifice fly A fly ball hit to the outfield, allowing a runner to score after tagging up when the ball is caught.

strike zone The area between the batter's back shoulder, front knee, and over the plate.

switch hitter A batter capable of batting both right-handed and left-handed.

Texas leaguer A looping ball that lands safely between the infield and outfield.

SUGGESTED READINGS

American Sport Education Program. 2001. *Coaching youth softball.* 3rd ed. Champaign, IL: Human Kinetics.

DeMichele, D., and Majeski, D. 2004 *Softball everyone.* 3rd ed. Winston-Salem, NC: Hunter Textbooks.

Garman, J. 2001. *Softball skills and drills.* Champaign, IL: Human Kinetics.

Joseph, J. 2001. *Coaching youth softball: A baffled parents' guide.* Dubuque, IA: McGraw-Hill.

Kempf, C. 2002. *The softball pitching edge.* Champaign, IL: Human Kinetics.

Noren, R. 2005. *Softball fundamentals.* Champaign, IL: Human Kinetics. Contains over 48 gamelike drills.

Potter, D. L., and Johnson, L. 2007. *Softball: Steps to success.* 2nd ed. Champaign, IL: Human Kinetics. The authors identify the keys to correct technique, describe common errors, provide practice drills, and suggest performance goals for softball skills.

Rikli, R. 1991. *Softball skills test manual.* Reston, VA: American Alliance for Health, Physical Education, Recreation and Dance. Contains skills tests with national norms, instructions for administration, and suggestions for their use.

Southworth, H., and Pullins, G. 2000. *Teaching the complete baserunner.* Dubuque, IA: Kendall/Hunt.

The Amateur Softball Association of America. Current edition. *Official rules of softball.* Oklahoma City, OK. The official rules of slow-pitch as well as fast-pitch and modified pitch.

U.S. Olympic Committee Sport Series. 2004. *A basic guide to softball.* Torrance, CA: Griffin Publishing Group. Includes how-to information for beginning players.

RESOURCES

Videos

thepitchmaster.com/

www.kellysultimatesports.com/categories
.asp?Slowpitch-Softball-Videos

www.mefeedia.com/tags/slowpitch

www.youtube.com Malach's Slow Pitch Softball Pitching Primer, August 18, 2007

www.youtube.com Slowpitch Softball Tips with Combat Softball, July 26, 2007

www.wellsphere.com/wellpage/slow-pitch-softball

See Appendix C for sources of other videos.

WEB SITES

www.angelfire.com/sd/slopitch/

www.asasoftball.com/

www.eteamz.com/slowpitch/

www.usasoftball.org

28 | Speedball

After completing this chapter, the reader should be able to:

- Appreciate the wide variety of skills that can be developed in this game, which is a combination of basketball, football, and soccer
- Understand scoring procedures and rules of the game
- Demonstrate the many physical skills involved in speedball
- Modify the game to fit specific circumstances
- Instruct a group of students in the fundamentals of speedball
- Be familiar with speedball terminology

HISTORY

Before 1920 the main team sports used for fall outdoor participation in physical education classes and intramural programs were touch football, soccer, and field hockey. Many recreation directors, physical education teachers, and coaches felt the need for a vigorous outdoor game through which participants could develop a variety of basic skills. After much experimentation, Elmer D. Mitchell of the University of Michigan developed the rules for speedball, combining many of the fundamental elements and skills found in basketball, football, and soccer. Because speedball is designed to permit all players on a team to participate in all phases of the game, including catching, throwing, and kicking, it developed rapidly and became widely used in recreation and physical education classes and in intramural programs throughout the United States.

Speedball was originally designed as an activity for men. As the game gained popularity a second set of rules was developed to accommodate female participants. Following the passage of legislation mandating coeducational physical education classes, multiple sets of speedball rules became unnecessary. Speedball continues to be utilized as a non-traditional game within recreation and physical education classes and intramural programs. Although traditional rules may be used to guide play, most recreation leaders, physical educators, or coaches elect to modify the rules, field dimensions, game tactics, and player positions to fit the needs of a specific context. To date, no official governing body oversees the game of speedball.

GENERAL DESCRIPTION OF TRADITIONAL SPEEDBALL

Speedball is a game that is similar in nature to soccer, basketball, and football. A variety of techniques are used in speedball, including kicking and dribbling the ball with the feet as in soccer, catching and throwing the ball as in basketball, and punting and passing the ball as in football. Adolescents

and youth tend to enjoy this game due to its dynamic and inclusive nature. In the modern physical activity literature base, speedball is considered an excellent activity because it can exist within popular curricular areas, such as sports education, skills and tactics mastery, and fitness education.

Speedball provides an opportunity to practice and implement the skills and tactics traditionally taught within individually isolated units of instruction in a challenging and fun setting. Played by two teams, with 11 players constituting a side, the object of the game is to invade the opponents' territory and score points in a variety of ways. The opponents of the team in possession of the ball try to intercept it. Once the opponents have obtained possession of the ball, they move it toward the opposite goal line in an attempt to score. Because speedball combines elements of soccer, basketball, and football, generally soccer rules apply when the ball is on the ground, basketball rules apply to fly balls, and football rules apply in the forward passing of the ball and in scoring. Playing positions are shown in Figure 28.1.

FIELD DIMENSIONS

Speedball may be played on a variety of fields, such as football, soccer, or field hockey. Regardless of the dimensions, the field should have a halfway line, and each side of the field should have a restraining line, end zone/penalty area, and penalty kick mark. Figure 28.1 illustrates the dimensions of a speedball field.

- Halfway Line—The halfway line divides the playing area in half and is utilized during kickoffs to ensure that the kicking team remains on its own half of the field.
- Restraining Line—Two restraining lines are 5 yards (4.57 m) from and parallel to the halfway line. The purpose of the restraining line is to ensure that the opponents of the kickoff team remain behind their restraining line until the ball is contacted.
- End Zone/Penalty Area—There is an end zone/penalty area at each end of the field that extends the width of the

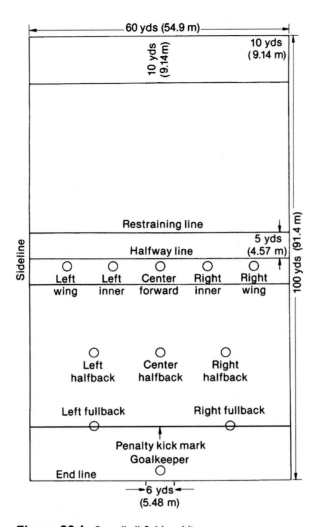

Figure 28.1. Speedball field and lineup.

field and encompasses the area between the end line and a parallel line 10 yards (9.14 m) ahead of the end line. This area serves two primary purposes: to score points and to enforce any personal fouls and/or contact fouls.

- Penalty Kick Mark—The penalty kick mark designates the placement spot from which a penalty kick is awarded. It is 10 yards (9.14 m) in front of the end line.

EQUIPMENT

Speedball is a basic game in which the only required equipment is a ball and two goals. As such, modifications often occur regarding the type of ball and goal that are used during game play. The official ball used for speedball is slightly larger than a soccer ball. Although the regulation ball is recommended, many organizations simply use a soccer ball because it is readily available. Any type of goal may be used when the rules have been modified; however, soccer and/or football goals are most commonly available. In traditional speedball, an "H"-styled football goalpost was the original goal.

Goalies should be provided with gloves, shin guards, and, if desired, knee pads. Mouth guards are also recommended. All other players may wish to use shin guards and soccer, or cleated, shoes for better traction. Multi-colored jerseys are helpful for identifying teams.

SCORING

The scoring procedures and rules presented within this chapter derive from Elmer Mitchell's original speedball design. The following methods of scoring and differing points awarded are described in Table 28.1. Points may be scored as follows:

- Field Goal—A field goal is scored when a ball that has been kicked or legally played with any part of the body passes between the goalposts and under the "H"-styled crossbar. A field goal counts 3 points.
- Drop Kick—A drop kick is made when the ball passes over the "H"-styled crossbar after having been drop-kicked from the field of play outside of the penalty area. A drop kick counts 2 points.

Table 28.1. VALUES OF DIFFERENT TYPES OF SCORING

Types of Scoring	Points
Field Goal	3
Dropkick	2
Touchdown	1
Penalty Kick	1
End Goal	1

- Touchdown—A touchdown is scored when an offensive player passes the ball to a teammate who catches it behind the opponent's goal line. A touchdown counts 1 point.
- Penalty Kick—A penalty kick is scored when the player awarded the try kicks the ball between the goalposts and under the "H"-styled crossbar. A penalty kick counts 1 point.
- End Goal—An end goal is scored when an offensive player who is in the end zone legally causes the ball to pass over the end line but not between the goalposts. An end goal counts 1 point.

RULES

Speedball is officiated according to a specific set of rules. When an infraction of a rule occurs, a penalty is enforced depending on the severity of the rule infraction. The following list differentiates between less and more severe infractions. Less severe infractions are classified as *Violations* while more severe infractions are termed *Technical Fouls.*

Violations

The following infractions of rules are considered violations:
1. Traveling with the ball
2. Touching a ground ball with one's hands or arms
3. Dribbling overhead more than once
4. Kicking or kneeing a fly ball before it is caught
5. Causing the ball to go out-of-bounds
6. Interfering with a kickoff or jump ball
7. Illegally interfering with a penalty kick
8. Illegally interfering with a player returning the ball from out-of-bounds

Violation Penalties

The penalty for a violation committed on the field of play outside of the end zone is the awarding of the ball to the opponents out of bounds at a spot nearest the violation for a throw-in. If a violation is committed within the penalty area, one penalty kick is awarded to the opponents. If the penalty kick is missed, the ball continues in play.

Technical Fouls

The following infractions are considered technical fouls:
1. Unsporting conduct, including pushing, holding, kicking, tripping, charging, or blocking an opponent
2. Illegal substitutions, or failing to report to the officials before going into the game
3. Unnecessary delay of the game
4. Taking more than three time-outs
5. Having more than 11 players on the playing field at one time

Technical Foul Penalties

A penalty kick is awarded for a technical foul committed outside the penalty area. Any member of the team may take the penalty kick. If the penalty kick is not successful, the ball is dead and a touchback is awarded to the opponents. When an unsporting conduct is committed by a player within the penalty area, the offended team is given two penalty kicks. If the second kick is missed, the ball remains in play.

FUNDAMENTAL REGULATIONS

The following section describes the various regulations for proper speedball play.

Officials

The officials for a game of speedball consist of two umpires, two time keepers, and two scorers. The umpires have final authority in all decisions pertaining to the conduct of the game. Two linespersons may assist. In physical education settings, the physical educator and/or students serve as the officials to monitor game play.

Duration of the Game

A regulation speedball game consists of four 12-minute quarters with a 10-minute rest period between halves and a 2-minute interval between quarters. Each team is allowed three time-outs during a game. Each additional time-out taken by a team constitutes a technical foul.

Beginning the Game

The game and each quarter are started by having one team commence play by placekicking the ball into its opponent's territory from the center of the field. The members of the kicking team line up on the halfway line. They remain behind the ball until it is kicked. The opposing team members must remain behind their restraining line until the ball is put into play. The kickoff must travel the length of the circumference of the ball and may be lifted by the foot to a teammate. The ball may not be touched by the kicker until another player has touched it. Goals are changed at halftime. As in soccer, after a score, the team that did not score begins play by kicking off.

Playing the Game
Fly ball

A ball that has been kicked into the air is referred to as a fly ball. A fly ball that has been caught may be passed from one player to another, as in basketball, or moved by a forward pass, as in football. It can continue to be played in this manner until it again touches the ground, becoming a ground ball. A player catching a fly ball is allowed to take one step in making a pass if the ball is caught while the player is standing still; two steps, if the player catches the ball while running.

Ground ball

A ball that is in contact with the ground is called a ground ball, whether it is stationary, rolling, or bouncing. The ball remains a ground ball, even though it may bounce into the air, until it is lifted into the air by a direct kick or a kick-up. A ground ball can be kicked, headed, or played with any part of the body except the hands and arms.

Dribbling the ball

A player may dribble a ground ball with the feet using a succession of short kicks. A player may use one overhead dribble; that is, after catching the ball, the player may toss it into the air and catch it again. The player may toss it in any direction and run to catch it before it strikes the ground. Any number of steps may be taken before catching the ball after tossing it. Only one overhead dribble is permitted before passing to another player. A touchdown cannot be scored by an overhead dribble.

Goalkeeper

The main work of the goalkeeper is to keep the ball from going through the goal. The goalkeeper has no privileges or restrictions, but is governed by the same rules as other players.

Illegal play

Although defensive play is allowed in speedball, blocking and tackling (as in football) are illegal. A player must attempt to secure the ball legally and without undue body contact or roughness.

Tie ball

A tie ball is called when two opposing players catch the ball simultaneously, hold the ball without gaining possession, commit a double foul, or when the officials are in doubt as to which side last touched the ball before it went out-of-bounds. In case of a tie ball, the official puts the ball into play by a jump ball (as in basketball). All players must remain at least 5 yards (4.57 m) from the spot where the ball is being put into play as a jump ball until it is touched by one of the jumpers. Following a jump ball, the ball may be played as a fly ball. A score may not result from a jump ball that is caught in the end zone, even though the ball is still in play. The jump ball is used at the spot of the foul in the case of a double foul. If the ball drops to the ground after the jump, either jumper can kick it.

Out-of-bounds

When a player causes the ball to go out-of-bounds over the sidelines, it is put into play with a pass by a player of the opposing team. In returning the ball to the field of play, the player can use either an underhand or overhand pass and can use one or both hands. In the case of a double foul over the sideline, a jump ball is used 5 yards (4.57 m) in from where the foul was committed. When a player causes the ball to go over the end line without scoring, the opponents put the ball into play by a pass or a kick.

Penalty kick

A placekick is used in making a penalty kick. A penalty kick is awarded as a result of a technical foul. The kick is made from the 10-yard line. The defensive players may be behind the goal or in the field, as long as no one is within 5 yards (4.57 m) of the kicker.

FUNDAMENTAL SKILLS AND TECHNIQUES

The game of speedball blends various techniques from the sports of soccer, basketball, and football, with only a few skills that are specific to speedball. The following section identifies necessary skills and techniques for proper speedball play. Skills and techniques have been categorized according to their sport of origin.

Soccer Skills

Dribbling with the feet

Dribbling with the feet is used in moving the ball toward an opponent's goal line, most often in situations where it is not advisable to kick up or kick to a teammate. In dribbling the ball, it is extremely important to control the ball at all times, which means that it must not be kicked with too much force. In most cases the inside surface of the foot should be used for best control, although experienced players may use the outside of the foot along the area of the little toe. Ordinarily, for best control, the ball should be kicked from an even run about every third step.

Instep kick/pass (Figure 28.2)

This type of kick is the most accurate because the individual generally has control of the ball. The player should place the non-kicking foot next to the ball and then the kicking foot strikes the ball along the arch area of the inside of the foot.

Outside-of-the-foot kick/pass (Figure 28.3)

This kick, performed with the outside of the foot, is used to push/pass the ball to a teammate.

Trapping (Figure 28.4)

Trapping the speedball may be done in various ways, such as with one's foot, leg, or body. The primary method of trapping, however, is done with the foot. In trapping the ball with the foot, the player extends the leg forward toward the ball with the heel 4 to 5 inches (10 to 13 cm) above the ground and the toe pointing upward. The sole of the foot is presented to the ball as it approaches. When the ball comes within reach of

Figure 28.2. Instep kick/pass.

Figure 28.3. Outside-of-the-foot kick/pass.

the foot, the player presses down and traps the ball between the sole of the foot and the ground.

Placekicking (Figure 28.5)

The placekick is used in an attempt to score after a foul. The ball is placed on the penalty kick mark. The object is to kick the ball past the goalkeeper, between the goalposts, and under the "H"-styled crossbar. The goalkeeper is the only player on the opposing team who is permitted to defend against the placekick.

Basketball Skills

Passing (Figures 28.6, 28.7, and 28.8)

Many types of basketball passes may be used. Any kind of one-hand or two-hand throw, including chest and overhead, is acceptable depending on the particular situation. The basketball-type pass is used extensively in speedball because of the wide playing field available.

Catching

The ball should be caught with the entire hand, because many passes are vigorously thrown. After the catch, the ball should be held with the fingers. Since catching a speedball is similar to catching a basketball, the same technique should be practiced in perfecting this skill.

Pivot

A player with the ball may pivot as in basketball if one foot is stabilized. This sometimes helps in finding a teammate open to receive a basketball-type pass.

Football Skills

Punting (Figure 28.9)

Punting in speedball is used to advance the ball toward the opponent's goal line as quickly as possible. Techniques of punting in speedball are similar to those in football. The ball should be kicked with the upper surface of the instep. Take one step forward with the left foot, drop the ball from extended arms, and kick the ball with the right foot. The ball should be dropped as the foot starts its upward swing. If the player kicks with the left foot, the reverse technique should be used.

Figure 28.4. Trapping with the foot and leg.

Figure 28.5. Placekicking.

Dropkicking (Figure 28.10)

For the best control of the ball in dropkicking, hold the ball just above the knees, flex at the waist, drop the ball to the ground, and kick it just as it bounces; take one step with the left foot and kick the ball with the right foot, or vice versa.

Speedball Skills

Overhead dribble

The overhead dribble is made by tossing the ball into the air and running to catch it before it strikes the ground. There is no restriction on the number of steps that may be taken after

Figure 28.6. One-hand pass.

tossing the ball and before catching it again. Only one overhead dribble is allowed. The overhead dribble is particularly useful when a closely guarded player tosses the ball over the head of the opponent to attain free space.

Kick-up

In many situations a ground ball may be played advantageously by converting it into a fly ball, thus allowing the various basketball and football skills described above. A player may convert a ground ball into a fly ball by kicking it into the air in one of two ways.

1. Kick-up with two feet (Figure 28.11)—With the ball held firmly between the insides of the feet and ankles, the player jumps into the air, lifting the ball upward. After releasing the ball from the ankles and feet, the player catches it before it drops to the ground. Because the kick-up with two feet is one of the easiest ways to pick up a ground ball, players should practice and develop considerable skill in its use.
2. Kick-up with one foot—A one-footed kick-up may occur when the ball is either stationary or moving.

   a. Stationary One Foot Kick-Up—This play can be made on a stationary ball by placing the foot on top of the ball and drawing it backward to start the ball rolling toward the player. The toe is quickly placed under the ball so that it will roll onto the instep. When it rolls onto the instep, the player quickly flips the ball into the air and catches it before it drops to the ground.
   b. Moving Ball One Foot Kick-Up—This play can be made on a rolling ball by flipping the ball into the air with the foot and catching it after it leaves the foot but before it drops to the ground. As the rolling ball approaches, the player should extend the leg forward with the pointed toe touching the ground. As the ball rolls onto the instep of the foot, the player flips the ball into the air and catches it. The kick-up technique for stationary or moving balls may also be used effectively to lift the ball to a teammate.

OFFENSIVE AND DEFENSIVE PLAY

Speedball is an invasive game in which teams score by moving the ball into another team's territory. Scoring occurs by either kicking the ball into the appropriate goal or moving the ball across the end line. The defending team attempts to prevent scoring by not allowing the offense to invade its territory. There are several skills and strategies that are employed to aid in offensive and defensive success. Incorporating a tactical games approach to the teaching of speedball fosters student understanding and increases success.

The development of tactical awareness is critical to student success in speedball. It is important that students develop an understanding of various offensive and defensive tactical problems that present themselves within the game context. Once a student has developed the ability to identify a tactical problem, the appropriate response, or solution to the problem, may be employed. Primary tactical problems in speedball include on-the-ball skills and off-the-ball movements regarding *scoring* (offense) and *preventing scoring* (defense). By reviewing general offensive and defensive strategies from previous experience, such as soccer, basketball, or football, instructors help participants draw parallels between the similarities of invasive games, thus increasing success.

Players must have the opportunity to practice skills, refine and develop technique, and comprehend when and how to apply speedball skills and tactics in a game-like setting. When playing an invasive game, such as speedball, players must be able to not only score when possessing the ball, but more importantly, move and position themselves without the ball. Offensive success depends on the ability to create space to receive a ground or aerial pass and threaten the goal. In contrast, defensive success relates to players individually guarding opponents and pressuring the ball. Table 28.2 identifies specific tactical problems related to speedball that may be taught to encourage offensive and defensive knowledge.

Figure 28.7. Two-hand chest pass.

Table 28.2. TACTICAL PROBLEMS, MOVEMENTS, AND SKILLS IN SPEEDBALL*

Tactical Problems	Off-the-Ball Movements	On-the-Ball Skills
SCORING		
Maintaining possession of the ball	• Supporting the ball carrier • Cutting to open space	• Passing • Dribbling for control • Trapping for control • Kick-ups
Creating and using space in the attack	• Using a target player • Crossover play • Overlapping runs • Shielding • Using the entire width and depth of the field	• Lead throws and kicks • Overlapping runs • Using the entire width and depth of the field
PREVENTING SCORING		
Defending space	• Marking and pressuring opponents • Making recovery runs • Player to player vs. zone coverage	• Clearing the ball • Receiving and blocking the ball • Distributing the ball
Defending the goal	• Creating an outlet • Player to player vs. zone coverage • Positioning of the goalkeeper	• Position player placement • Goalkeeping skills
Winning the ball	• Providing support • Denying the pass	• Tackling—block, poke, slide • Player to player vs. zone coverage
RESTARTING PLAY		
Free kick	• Offense provides support • Cutting and utilizing space	• Offensive ball placement • Defensive coverage

*Contents of Table 28.2 adapted from Pleban & Wiersma (2003) and Griffin, Mitchell, & Oslin (1997).

Figure 28.8. Two-hand overhead pass.

Figure 28.9. Punting.

Figure 28.10. Dropkicking.

Generally speaking, the offensive and defensive playing positions of speedball are very similar to traditional soccer. In essence, the wings and forwards move the ball down the field in an attempt to score. Halfbacks remain in position to back up the forwards or try to score if an opportunity presents itself. If the ball is intercepted and lost to the opposing team, the halfbacks are in position to support the ongoing opposition of the fullbacks and goalkeeper.

TEACHING CONSIDERATIONS

Instructional Considerations

1. Provide a historical overview of the game.
2. Emphasize game characteristics, such as player and official roles, the invasive nature of the game, field dimensions, and necessary equipment.
3. Develop knowledge of the rules, including scoring, violations, fouls, and penalties.
4. Incorporate fundamental regulations, such as beginning the game, maintaining game play, and restarting play.
5. Develop speedball skills, including soccer, basketball, and football skills for use during game play.
6. Incorporate speedball game tactics, specifically on-the-ball skills and off-the-ball movement, into modified game play.
7. Develop positional play, such as the roles of forwards, wings, halfbacks, fullbacks, and goalkeepers.
8. Participate in ongoing regulation game play.

Designing the Speedball Unit

When designing the speedball instructional unit, it is important that instructors implement a learning experience to allow each individual participant to have success. Through various instructional modifications, the opportunity for players to acquire, develop, and refine skills increases. Additionally, the instructional design has the potential to increase comprehension of relevant skills and tactical strategies. The following teaching considerations are presented to help aid in teaching and instructional effectiveness:

1. Evaluate the Participants' Backgrounds—For example, if the participants are familiar with soccer, less time need be spent on dribbling and passing skills with the feet. However, if not familiar with soccer, this part of the game will need more work than passing and throwing skills using the hands.
2. Modify the Rules—Decide on the rules applicable for the specific situation. Most participants will have had previous experience with basketball, soccer, or football; therefore, speedball should be taught as a combination of these sports. Confusion often exists regarding methods of scoring and playing aerial or ground balls; hence it is important to clarify the rules regarding these points.
3. Modify Game Conditions—When students are first learning to play speedball, instructors might consider some of the following game modifications:
   a. Use a modified soccer ball for young learners or beginners. It is also effective to add multiple balls to game play.
   b. Allow the use of one's hands when first beginning play.
   c. Decrease the number of players per team when play begins to four, six, or eight with the purpose of applying appropriate skills to game-like situations.

Figure 28.11. Kick-Up with Two Feet.

d. Decrease field size when first beginning play. For example, divide the length of the field to make three widthwise fields.

e. Change playing time by shortening quarters.

f. Incorporate smaller, bigger, or more goals when practicing and/or playing.

g. Increase the number of goalies used at once or remove the goalkeeper altogether.

h. Introduce penalty kicks after continuous play has been achieved.

i. Change the number of points awarded for different types of scoring. For example, by increasing the value of a touchdown to 3 points, players will be increasingly likely to utilize this method of scoring.

4. Develop Skills through Proper Progressions—Teach how to move the ball down the field, emphasizing both aerial and ground balls. It is important to develop the ability to convert ground balls to aerial balls. Practice until these skills are developed with some consistency. Work with executing the punt and catching punts as a way to move the ball down the field. Help players to understand that dribbling with the feet is the slowest way for groups to move the ball. Use small groups of partners or groups of three to practice moving the ball.

5. Refine Skills with Application Activities—Various lead-up games may be used to introduce, develop, and refine speedball-related skills. A review of the lead-up activities described in the soccer, basketball, and football chapters of this text may provide several options for unit development. Some examples of lead-up game activities that might be taught are:

a. Keep away

b. Dribble, kick-up, and pass to a teammate

c. Toe pick-ups to a teammate while running down the field

d. Punting and punt receiving

e. Aerial-only game, in which students are only allowed to advance the ball down the field with aerial passes.

f. Mini-games (smaller fields, fewer players)

g. Task stations possibilities include
   (i) Dribble through and around obstacles
   (ii) Conditioning activities
   (iii) One-foot lift to a target area
   (iv) Volleying with partners
   (v) Goal shooting and goalkeeping

6. Develop Game Play—Add defensive players only after students have some control of both aerial and ground balls. Start with 2 on 1, 3 on 1, and 3 on 2 situations to introduce defensive and offensive play of both aerial and ground balls. Gradually add additional offensive and defensive players. Practice the types of scoring possibilities first without defense and then with defense, again initially giving the offense the advantage.

7. Alternative Indoor/Outdoor Settings—If a traditional football field and/or "H"-style football crossbar is not available, speedball may be played by modifying the location or goal. Pleban & Wiersma (2003) provide the following suggestions for playing in various settings and on differing goals:

a. Soccer—Whether utilizing an indoor or outdoor soccer facility, speedball may be played with soccer nets. To play in this setting one would simply identify the end-zone scoring areas on both sides of the soccer net.

b. Basketball—When playing indoors, speedball rules and game conditions may be modified to incorporate the backboard or net into the scoring regime.

c. Baseball—Speedball may be played on a diamond field, either indoors or outdoors, by allowing the "batter" to commence play by placekicking the ball from home base. The "batter" attempts to score by rounding the bases as the defense works to eliminate the threat. The defenders may only eliminate the runner through aerial methods. Defenders may play an aerial ball with their hands and throw to a base to eliminate the runner. If the ball has touched the ground, the defenders must convert it to an aerial ball through any of the kick-up skills discussed earlier.

GLOSSARY

aerial dribble A ball that is tossed or tapped into the air and caught by the same player.

attackers The team in possession of the ball.

blocking the ball Intercepting the ball with any part of the body. A player cannot block a ground ball with the arms or hands unless a ground ball is in contract with the body.

closely guarded Being guarded within 3 feet (0.9 m).

dead ball A ball no longer in play: out-of-bounds, after a score, after a foul, during time-out, or a tie ball.

defenders The team not in possession of the ball.

double foul Fouls committed at the same time by both teams; a jump ball is used to put the ball back into play.

dribble Advancing the ball by a series of kicks.

dropkick Dropping the ball to the ground and kicking it just as it bounces from the ground.

end goal Passing the ball over the endline but not between the goalposts; counts 1 point.

field goal Passing the ball between the goalposts and under the "H"-styled crossbar; counts 3 points.

fly ball A ball that has been raised into the air by either a one- or two-foot kick; a punt, dropkick, kick-up, or thrown ball that has not touched the ground.

foul An infringement of the rules for which a free kick, free throw, or penalty kick is awarded the opponents.

free kick A placekick from which a goal can be scored directly.

free throw A throw taken by any player on the team that has been fouled during the play of an aerial ball.

goalkeeper A player whose duty is to defend the goal.

ground ball A stationary, rolling, or bouncing ball that is in contact with the ground.

handling the ball Putting the hands or arms on a ground ball.

indirect free kick A free kick from which a goal cannot be scored directly.

kick-up The play converting a ground ball into an aerial ball.

own goal The goal one's team is defending.

own half The half of the field in which one's own goal is located.

passing Means of moving the ball by passes or batting with the hands to another player.

penalty kick A free kick awarded as the result of a foul; a placekick from the 10-yard (9.14 m) line, and the ball must go under the crossbar.

placekick A stationary ball kicked by a player.

punt A play in which a player drops a caught ball and kicks it before it touches the ground to quickly advance the ball down the field.

trapping Stopping the motion of the ball by placing the sole of the foot on the top of the ball.

volley A play in which a player fields a fly, or aerial, ball with some part of the body, such as the head, hip, or shoulder.

SUGGESTED READINGS

Darst, P. W., & Stillwell, B. 1997. Speed-a-way for middle school students. *Teaching Secondary Physical Education, 3,* 14–15.

Diagram Group. 1995. *Rules of the game: The complete illustrated encyclopedia of all the sports of the world.* New York, NY: St. Martin's Press.

Fronske, H. 2005. *Teaching cues for sport skills for secondary school students.* 3rd ed. San Francisco, CA: Benjamin Cummings.

Griffin, L., Mitchell, S., & Oslin, J. 1997. *Teaching sport concepts and skills: A tactical games approach.* Champaign, IL: Human Kinetics.

Lamb, M. (1986). Indoor speedball. *Oklahoma Health, Physical Education, and Recreation, 18*(27).

Mitchell, E. D. 1926. *Official speedball rules.* Ann Arbor, MI: G.L. Moe.

National Association for Girls and Women in Sport. 1982. *NAGWS guide: Flag football, speedball, speed-a-way.* Reston, VA: American Alliance for Health, Physical Education, Recreation, and Dance.

Pleban, L. A., and Wiersma, L. 2003. "Speedball: The 'oldest new game around.'" *The Journal of Physical Education, Recreation, and Dance, 74*(3).

Schmottlach, N., McManama, J., and Hicks, L. 2010. *Physical education activity handbook.* 12th ed. San Francisco, CA: Benjamin Cummings.

White, J. R. 1990. *Sports rules encyclopedia.* 2nd ed. Englewood Cliffs, NJ: Prentice-Hall.

29 | Swimming

After completing this chapter, the reader should be able to:

- Be familiar with the evolution of swimming and the various strokes
- Assist students in being comfortable and able to maneuver their bodies in water
- Instruct novice swimmers in basic swimming skills, such as floating, gliding, and beginning propulsion
- Teach beginning and advanced swimming strokes
- Recognize the proper progressions for teaching beginning, intermediate, and advanced swimmers

HISTORY

Early humans probably learned swimming by observing animals that used a running motion to move about, on, or in the water. Water is an unnatural medium for humans because it interferes with the breathing mechanism; animals are usually better equipped anatomically for swimming. Humans cannot easily keep the nose above water while horizontal.

Ancient carvings showing people swimming have been found dating as early as 9000 BC. In the Middle Ages, accounts in the Greek, Roman, Anglo-Saxon, and Scandinavian classics dealt often with great feats of swimming of the heroes of the day.

In 1538 Nicolaus Wynman, a German professor of languages, wrote the first book on swimming, titled *Colymbetes*. In 1696 a Frenchman named Thevenot wrote a more scientific book titled *The Art of Swimming*.

The strokes listed here are still fundamental and seaworthy for utility purposes, but have been considerably refined for competitive swimming.

These strokes evolved in the following order:

1. The "doggy" or human paddling strokes.
2. The breaststroke (sailor stroke), the first scientific stroke taught.
3. The underarm sidestroke. This stroke was still too slow for speed because both arms recovered under the water as they did in the breaststroke. The kick was scissorslike.
4. The side, or English, overarm stroke. This stroke was faster than either the breaststroke or the side underarm stroke because the uppermost arm recovered above the surface and thereby reduced undesirable resistance.
5. The trudgen stroke. This stroke was discovered in South America in 1860 by an Englishman, John Trudgen. It employed the method of recovering both arms above the water hand-over-hand. It further reduced resistance to water and created greater speed. It was similar to the side overarm stroke except that the body turned

over to permit the under arm to lift out of the water for recovery. In this stroke the scissors kick was used.

6. The Australian crawl. Introduced to England by Richard Cavell of Australia in the 1902 championships, this was the first true hand-over-hand stroke with alternating vertical movement of the legs. Cavell explained the stroke as "crawling through the water." The scissors kick was eliminated for speed swimming because the leg recovery caused great resistance.
7. The American six-beat leg-kick crawl. The Australian stroke was scientifically refined by American coaches. This style broke all existing freestyle records in speed swimming and became known as the fastest human stroke in water.
8. The inverted breaststroke (elementary backstroke). This is the breaststroke executed while swimming on the back.
9. The back crawl. About 1900 the crawl was turned onto the back and was much faster in competition than the inverted breaststroke. Since there was no recovery of arms or legs underwater as in the inverted breaststroke, it minimized resistance and created faster speed on the back.
10. The butterfly breaststroke. This stroke began to make its appearance in competition about 1934. The kick remained the same as in the breaststroke, but both arms recovered above the water simultaneously. They lifted out of the water at the hips and were swung laterally forward to the entry, resembling a butterfly in flight, thus the name.
11. The butterfly (dolphin) stroke. The newest of all the swimming strokes was created by D. A. Armbruster through the ability and skill of Jack Sieg. The purpose of this stroke was to obtain greater speed with the breaststroke by eliminating the recovery underwater of the legs in the kick. This was accomplished by moving the legs up and down in unison from the hips. This kick

actually created greater speed when used without arms than did the alternating flutter kick. It synchronized beautifully with the butterfly arm stroke and created greater speed.

All of these strokes have been developed and refined, and have been put to practical use by the average swimmer. They are used in many different water activities, commonly referred to as *aquatics*. Some aquatic activities are:

1. Recreational swimming
2. Lifesaving
3. Competitive swimming
4. Synchronized swimming or ballet
5. Springboard and platform diving
6. Water games: polo, basketball, baseball, and similar activities
7. Water safety
8. Water survival
9. Skin diving and scuba diving

Most of these aquatic activities use the fundamental skill strokes.

It is strongly recommended that the beginner be taught all of the basic strokes to gain self-assurance in the water and experience the joy and relaxation of recreational swimming. To accomplish this, the beginner must know the fundamental skill strokes. This method of learning is the "all-stroke method for beginners."

UNITED STATES OLYMPIC SWIMMING HISTORY

Men

In the 1896 Olympic competition at Athens, there were only four swimming events. They were held in a lake, and competitors could use any stroke. Over the years competitions have become increasingly organized in terms of distances, strokes, and facilities. By 1912, there were seven men's swimming events and two women's swimming events. In addition there were three men's and one women's diving events.

Early outstanding U.S. swimmers were Charles Daniels, who won four golds in 1904 and 1908, and Duke Kahanamoku, who won the 100 m freestyle in 1912 and again in 1920. His new style of kicking (the flutter kick) was later adopted by most freestyle swimmers. In 1924 Johnny Weissmuller, the next dominant U.S. swimmer, emerged. He was the first person to swim the 100 m freestyle in under a minute, and he won a total of five gold medals at two Olympiads.

In 1932 the Japanese men won five of six events, and three of six events in 1936. In the years that followed, the U.S. and Australian men became the swimming powers.

Then in 1964, Don Schollander of the United States matched Johnny Weissmuller's feat of five gold medals by winning four in 1964 and one in 1968. Schollander's gold medal in 1968 was in the 4 × 200 m relay. Mark Spitz, a team member on that relay team, was destined to win seven gold medals in 1972. Each medal involved a world record (four were individual events and three were relays).

One of the most dominating team performances occurred at the 1976 Olympics when the U.S. men's team won 12 of 13 possible golds and 10 silvers in the 11 individual events. In 1980, when the United States boycotted the Olympics, the Soviet men's team dominated by winning 7 of the 13 gold medals. In 1984, when the Soviets boycotted, the U.S. men returned to dominance by winning gold medals in 9 of 15 swimming events, plus both gold medals in diving.

In 1988 a record 22 different nations earned medals in swimming (both men's and women's), but the men's events were once again dominated by a U.S. swimmer. Matt Biondi gathered five golds, one silver, and a bronze, for a performance eclipsed only by Mark Spitz.

The Unified team (formerly the Soviet Union) and the Hungarian team were surprisingly strong at the 1992 Olympics in Barcelona, but the U.S. men's team brought home six gold medals and seven silver or bronze medals.

In the 1996 Olympics at Atlanta, the Centennial Olympic games, the United States men's swim team ruled the pool. They won gold in six events, including all three relays and silver in six individual events. The Russians won 4 of the 16 events.

In the 2000 Olympics in Sydney, Australia, the U.S. men's team again dominated by winning gold medals in seven of sixteen events and a total of seventeen medals. Anthony Ervin and Gary Hall Jr. tied for gold in the 50-m free and Lenny Krayzelburg finished his career winning gold in the 100 and 200 m back.

The 2004 Oylmpics returned to Athens, Greece, where modern Olympics began in 1896. The U.S. men's team won 18 medals, including nine gold, which is the most they've won in two decades. The team was led by 19-year-old Michael Phelps. He won eight medals in all, including six gold and two bronze, becoming the first swimmer to go to the podium eight times in a non-boycotted Olympics.

The men had a very successful 2008 Olympic Games in Beijing, China, by winning 17 total medals with 10 of them being gold. The story of the Games was Michael Phelps, who won 8 gold medals, surpassing Mark Spitz's 36-year-old record of 7 golds. Two of Phelps's races were won in dramatic fashion; the 100 m butterfly against Milorad Cavic, which he won by .01 seconds, and the 4 × 100 m freestyle relay (Phelps, Garrett Weber-Gale, Cullen Jones, and Jason Lezak), who touched out France on the anchor leg.

Women

The first Olympic women's swimming events were held in 1912, and the next several Olympics were dominated by swimmers from Australia, Great Britain, and the United States.

In 1920, Ethelda Bleibtrey of the United States won the 100 m freestyle, the 300 m freestyle, and anchored the

4×100 m freestyle relay to sweep all three events at the Antwerp Olympics. In 1932 the U.S. women's swim team, led by Helene Madison, won four of the five swimming and diving events, but it won only three bronze medals in 1936.

After World War II (from 1948 to 1960), the U.S. women's teams won eight gold medals in four Olympic Games. The women's team from the United States emerged as a power at this same time, winning five golds in 1960. The United States continued to emerge as a swimming power in 1968 when Debra Meyer won three gold medals. In 1972, when Mark Spitz was winning seven golds, the dominant woman swimmer was Shane Gould of Australia with three golds, one silver, and one bronze. However, Melissa Belote of the United States also won three golds in two individual events and a relay.

In 1972, when the U.S. men had the great team performance, the U.S. and Australian dominance in the women's events continued, but it came to an end in 1976 as the East German women won 11 of the 13 golds. Shirley Babashoff of the United States did manage a gold and three silvers, giving her eight Olympic medals in her career and establishing her as one of the United States' great female swimmers.

When the United States boycotted the Olympics in 1980, the East German women repeated their feat of garnering 11 golds. In 1984, when the East Germans boycotted, the U.S. women swimmers returned to power with 9 of the 12 individual events and two relays.

In the 1988 Olympics, the stars of the women's swimming competition were Kristin Otto of East Germany and Janet Evans of the United States. Otto's six gold medals broke the record for most golds won by a woman in any sport at one Olympics. Seventeen-year-old Janet Evans won the 400 m individual medley, the 800 m freestyle, and the 400 m freestyle in a world record time of 4:03:85.

The U.S. women's team remained a world swimming powerhouse with 14 medals, although the Chinese women's team was surprisingly strong at the 1992 Barcelona Olympics. Janet Evans again won the 800 m freestyle and took the silver in the 400 m freestyle.

At the 1996 Olympics in Atlanta, seven countries won gold medals in the women's swimming events. The United States won 7 of the 16 gold medals. The star woman swimmer was Michelle Smith from Ireland, who won three individual gold medals. Amy Van Dyken was the bright star for the United States with two golds in individual events and two more golds in the relays.

In the 2000 Olympics in Sydney, Australia, the women's team prevailed by winning gold medals in 7 of 16 events and a total of 16 medals. The women not only swept the relay events; they dominated them by breaking two world records and one Olympic record. Megan Quann (now Jendrick) won gold in the 100 m breast stroke at the age of 16. Brooke Bennett dominated distance events, winning gold in both the 400 m and 800 m freestyle events.

At the 2004 Athens Olympics, the U.S. team brought home 28 medals: 12 gold, 9 silver, and 7 bronze. The women's team was led by Olympic veteran Jenny Thompson, who competed in her fourth Olympics. The 4×200 m freestyle relay team of Natalie Coughlin, Carly Piper, Dana Vollmer, and Kaitlin Sandeno, broke the oldest world record on the books.

The 2008 Olympic Games the U.S. women's team dominated the scene once again by winning a total of 14 medals. Led by Natalie Coughlin (1 gold, 2 silver, 3 bronze), the women's team made their mark on the competition. Coughlin's 6 medals in one Olympics made her the most decorated woman in Olympic history. Dara Torres, at the age of 41, competed in her fourth Olympics and took home 3 silver medals.

SWIMMING SAFETY RULES
Indoor Swimming Pools

1. Do not enter the pool or swim unless a lifeguard or qualified instructor is present.
2. Do not run on the pool deck.
3. Do not engage in horseplay in the pool or pool area.
4. Do not use glass bottles or containers in the pool area.
5. People with communicable diseases or infectious conditions such as open sores, eye infections, etc., will not be allowed in the pool.
6. Never swim near the diving area when diving boards are being used.
7. Only one person at a time is allowed on diving boards.
8. Before using diving boards, be familiar with the depth of the pool and configuration of the bottom of the pool.
9. Diving boards are to be used only for diving.
10. Diving into the pool from the deck is prohibited, unless water depth is sufficient.
11. All swimmers must wear bathing suits. T-shirts, cutoffs, or other clothing will not be allowed.

Open Swimming Areas

1. Do not remain in the water during an electrical storm.
2. Before participating in any aquatic activities—such as canoeing, boating, sailing, skin diving, scuba diving, and water skiing—understand all safety rules and procedures.
3. Air-filled flotation devices will not compensate for lack of swimming skills.
4. Never dive into water of unknown depth or into water that has not been checked for floating or partially submerged foreign objects.
5. Always be aware of the temperature of the water. Do not remain in cold water for excessive periods of time. Do not enter the water if you are chilled.

THE ALL-STROKE METHOD FOR TEACHING BEGINNERS

The all-stroke method begins by adjusting students to water. When the student is comfortably adjusted to water, the basic skill strokes can be learned quite rapidly.

Beginners make reasonable progress learning all strokes; however, not everyone can swim all strokes equally well. (People differ anatomically and in their individual ability to acquire new skills.) Therefore, by teaching all of the students all of the strokes, each one will naturally find the stroke most comfortable and suitable through a distance orientation program after the stroke skills are learned. The stroke that takes the least effort will naturally be selected most often, even though the students are basically "grounded" in every stroke. This also prepares students for advanced swimming, lifesaving, or any other form of aquatic interest.

The secret of the all-stroke method is to work the legs by challenging them in different kick skills. Legs are composed of big muscles that in everyday living are used to move our bodies. To get the legs to move in new and unfamiliar patterns, the swimmer must train them.

Correct breathing habits are the next essential skill to teach. Water interferes with a human's breathing mechanism. Humans have to learn to exhale completely under the surface and inhale above the surface. They must develop breathing patterns for different strokes.

Instructors should emphasize skill learning by progressive drills and action. Action creates interest and results in interested students who will work hard if they know they are learning. Swimming taught progressively and intensively accomplishes that. If students become fatigued (not exhausted) from constant exercise, they will naturally take it easy, and when they take it easy, the response is relaxation. Relaxation is learned through repetition and learning to feel comfortable in a relatively new environment (water).

OBJECTIVES

1. To orient students to water, a medium that presents new physical, physiological, and psychological stimuli and produces:
   a. Instability
   b. Apparent loss of body weight
   c. Decreased sense of balance
   d. Change in body position for locomotion
   e. Change in heat-regulatory mechanism
   f. Change in respiration
   g. Change in normal muscle tonus
2. To develop confidence, using drills that have the following goals:
   a. To eliminate mental barriers to being in the water
   b. To learn the proper techniques of inhalation and exhalation
   c. To relax in the water
   d. To enjoy swimming
3. To teach self-reliance for self-preservation
4. To teach an appreciation of swimming distance no matter how short or long
5. To teach respect for water while swimming
6. To impart confidence in skill and techniques
7. To teach strokes in such a way as to motivate persistent practice
8. To teach distribution of effort and conservation of strength
9. To teach how to delay fatigue
10. To teach how to dive into water
11. To encourage swimming as a source of lifelong pleasure and fitness

BASIC SKILLS AND TECHNIQUES

Adjustment to Water

1. Examine the pool markings to know its depth at all locations before entering the water
2. Sit on the side of the pool with the feet in the water. Reach into the water with the hands and splash water onto the legs, arms, and body. This will help to adjust to the water temperature.
3. Wade waist deep into the pool and submerge the hands in the water. Practice sculling motions in the water to gain a feel for the water and movements of the body in the water.
4. Stand in waist-deep water and submerge the body repeatedly to chin level, rising up and down and splashing the face.
5. Hold on to the overflow gutter and allow water to lift the legs and body to the surface. Stay relaxed.

Breath Control

Depending on the level and maturity of swimmers, the following activities can be performed while holding on to the pool gutter, holding on to a partner, or without support: If the student is wearing contact lenses, the lenses should be removed prior to completing these skills or goggles should be worn.

1. Standing in waist-deep water with the body inclined forward, practice breath holding: Inhale through the mouth, close the mouth, shut the eyes, and submerge the face flat beneath the water; hold for 3 seconds and recover. Repeat several times, lengthening the time underwater. If the student is wearing contact lenses, the lenses should be removed prior to completing this skill or goggles should be worn.
2. Inhale through the mouth, submerge the face with the eyes closed, exhale slowly through the nose and mouth, and recover. Repeat several times.
3. Inhale through the mouth, submerge the face with the eyes closed, and exhale through the nose, mouth, or both, steadily but as slowly as possible. Recover and repeat several times.

Use of Eyes Underwater

Inhale, close the eyes, submerge, open the eyes, count the number of fingers visible on a partner's hand, and recover. Repeat.

Balance and Control of the Body

The following activities are designed to aid the student in developing confidence in the water. To ensure that fear is not reinforced, it is important to discuss and practice (with partners) the procedures of returning to a stable position before assuming the various floating and gliding positions.

Jellyfish float

This float may be performed in either the pike or tuck position. Take a deep breath, submerge the face, raise the knees to the chest or extend the legs, and hold with the arms for 3 seconds. Release the hold, elevate the back and head, allow the legs to extend to the bottom of the pool, let the arms float up a little, and then push them down and toward the hips while at the same time raising the head. The instructor should pay close attention to the swimmer in these initial floats as individual differences, especially in amount of leanness and fat, will result in large differences in ability to float (Figure 29.1). Repeat.

Streamline (prone) float position

(Water must be at least waist deep.) The streamline float is done on the stomach. The position is taken by lifting and extending the arms forward beyond the head beneath the surface, with the head held low in the water, and extending the legs (Figure 29.2). To recover to the standing position, pull the knees to the chest, round the back, then simultaneously press firmly downward with the extended arms, extend the legs to the bottom of the pool, and lift the face from the water. With the legs extended downward, the feet will settle on the pool floor. Keep the eyes open. After recovery, exhale through the nose, open the mouth, inhale, and flutter the eyes open.

Streamline (prone) glide and stand

For the streamline glide, bend forward at the waist, with the arms extended forward. Lay the upper body and arms in the water, just under the surface. Take a deep breath, bend the knees, and roll the face under the surface. Straighten the knees, push the feet off the bottom, glide into the prone position, and glide. At the end of the glide, draw the knees into the chest and recover, as in the prone float.

Back floating position

With a partner standing directly behind, assume a back floating position by submerging to the chin and, with the partner supporting the back of the neck with one hand and the small of the back with the other, lift the hips and extend the arms sideward. The ears will be underwater. The partner gradually removes support, first from the small of the back and then from the neck. The body will not necessarily stay horizontal in the water. Some swimmer's legs have a tendency to sink. The important elements are to relax, keep the arms extended, and hold the neck back to keep the face above water. The partner should help in the recovery the first few times. To gain recovery from the back float, move the arms downward and forward in the water, round the back, bring the knees to the chin, and lift the head slowly forward. When the body moves to a vertical position, extend the legs to the bottom and stand (Figure 29.3).

Back glide and stand

For the back glide, crouch until the shoulders are submerged, lie back until the ears are submerged, push off with the feet, and glide until forward motion stops. During the glide, keep the arms at the side and the legs straight and together.

Recover by bringing both knees up toward the chest and the head forward. At the same time bring both arms forward.

Simple Leg Movements to Keep Body Horizontal and to Aid Propulsion

Kick glide, streamline position

For the kick glide, streamline position, start with the streamline glide, but as the body straightens out on the surface, move the legs alternately up and down with the knees and ankles fairly loose; continue to the limit of breath-holding ability. (For additional practice, hold on to the gutter or a kickboard and kick the legs as above.)

Kick glide, back position

In the kick glide, back position, assume a back floating position but with the back flat, the chin tucked well into the throat, and the arms kept by the sides. Move the legs in a slightly bent-kneed flutter kick. Snap each knee into extension when finishing the kick. (For additional practice, hold on to the gutter and execute the flutter kick.)

Simple Arm Movements for Support, Propulsion, and Balancing of Body

Arm stroke on the front

For the arm stroke on the front (dog paddle or human stroke), assume the prone position in the water and extend the arms alternately forward and downward, following with a press backward under the body. Keep the fingers together and hands straight on the pull backward. In the recovery forward of each arm, straighten the hand, draw it up under the chin, and extend it to a forward position; cup the hand and repeat the stroke.

Arm stroke on the back

The arm stroke on the back (finning) is a paired movement of the hands and arms in a back position. The arms are first extended by the sides and then drawn up about 1 foot (30 cm), extended outward so the hands are perpendicular to the body; then push water backward toward the feet using a fishtail flip of the hands and wrists.

Coordination of Breathing with Leg and Arm Movements

Combined stroke on the front

The combined stroke on the front is composed of up-and-down alternating beats of the legs and the dog paddle with the arms, with breathing done entirely above the surface or alternately inhaling above and exhaling below the water. Two or more beats of the legs should accompany each cycle of arm strokes.

Rotary breathing should be done with the head rotated to the side. If the head is rotated to the left to get air, inhale when the right arm is extended forward. Rotate the head into the water on this cycle, and when the left arm is extended, exhale underwater through the mouth. To inhale to the right side, the left arm should be extended, and on this cycle, as the right arm is extended, rotate the face into the water and exhale.

Figure 29.1. A, Jellyfish float, pike. B, Jellyfish float, tuck position. C, Recovery from jellyfish float.

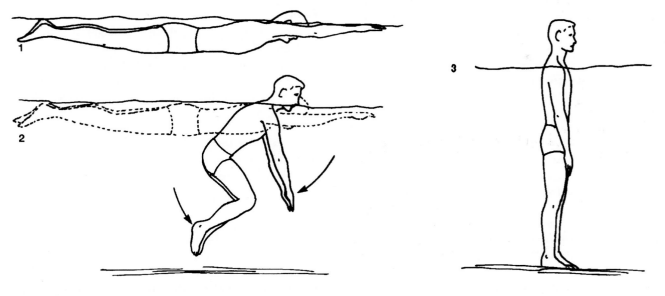

Figure 29.2. Streamline float and recovery.

Combined stroke on the back

The combined stroke on the back consists of finning with the hands and flutter kicking with the legs. Assume the back floating position with the back flat and the chin tucked well into the throat. First, the leg beat is started using greater speed and more flexibility than is used in the front kick. The thrust of the hands (finning) is put into the stroke at regular intervals. Breathe naturally.

Turning, right and left

Begin the front stroke (human stroke), maintaining the body nearly horizontal, and execute a right turn and then a left

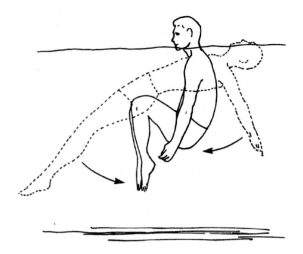

Figure 29.3. Back float and recovery.

turn in the middle of the pool. Try executing a complete turn. Extend the hands and pull in the opposite direction of the turn.

Change positions

In changing position or turning over from the front to the back, start swimming, keep the body nearly horizontal, and at the point of changing positions, roll the body either right or left to a back floating position. Keep the shoulders and head low in the water. The head, arms, hips, and legs will aid in rolling the body. In changing from a back float to the front, roll in a similar manner to a front position and resume the stroke.

SAFETY AND SURVIVAL STROKES

The first three strokes are presented for their use as water safety and survival strokes. They require the least amount of energy and skill. They are not competitive strokes.

Resting Backstroke

The resting backstroke (Figure 29.4) should be the first stroke taught to beginners. It requires little coordination and gives the student a sense of security. This is principally a resting stroke for an emergency or for easy swimming while resting, and it lays a sound foundation for the breaststroke and elementary backstroke as well as for treading water. The face is never underwater, and thus breathing is not a disturbing factor.

Inverted breaststroke kick

The recovery is executed by spreading the knees to approximately hip-width while holding the heels together. Keep the heels down as they are drawn toward the buttocks so that the knees do not lift out of the water, and at the same time lift the hips to prevent the drop. Separate the heels and cock the feet outward toward the knees. Start the drive by sweeping the legs out and pushing against the water with the inside

of the feet, extending the feet as they kick. During this kick, when the knees are not quite straightened, squeeze the thighs together forcefully with the knees relaxed to give a whiplike motion to the legs from the knees down and to the forelegs and feet, resulting in increased propulsion. This stroke can also be introduced using a flutter kick first, because the inverted breaststroke kick can be difficult for some students to master.

Arm stroke

The arm recovery starts from the sides of the thighs by turning the palms downward toward the bottom of the pool, the little-finger side of the hand leading and knifing through the water. The arms are held straight. The arms move outward away from the thighs to a point just above the shoulders.

The arm pull is executed by turning the palms to the rear and slightly downward and moving the straight arms forcefully to the sides of the thighs.

At no time during either the recovery or the pull of the hands or arms should they be above the surface.

Whole stroke

This stroke is easy to execute because the arms and legs work in unison. The arms and legs recover at the same moment and kick and pull at the same moment. When the stroke is closed, stretch out straight and pause until the momentum is spent. Repeat.

Elementary Backstroke

This stroke (Figure 29.5) should be taught after the resting backstroke has been mastered. This style affords a little more speed than does the resting backstroke, but is still restful and easy to learn. However, more coordination is required to execute it because the arms are partly recovered before the legs recover.

Inverted breaststroke kick

The inverted breaststroke kick is executed exactly the same as in the resting backstroke.

Arm stroke

The arm recovery in the elementary backstroke differs from that in the resting backstroke. The arm recovery is executed by bending the elbows downward and sliding the hands from the sides of the thighs up along the sides of the body toward the shoulders. Then the hands, palms facing up, reach out diagonally from the armpit under the water until the arms are straight. Turn the palm facing backward and pull, straight-armed, to the sides of the thighs. Pause until the momentum from the pull subsides.

Whole stroke

In the propulsive phase the arms and legs start at the same time, although the legs will usually finish before the arms

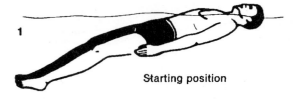

1

Starting position

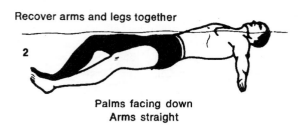

2

Recover arms and legs together

Palms facing down
Arms straight

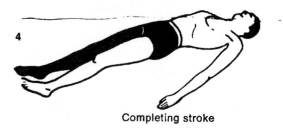

3

Kick and pull together

4

Completing stroke

5

Glide until momentum subsides

Figure 29.4. Progressive steps in the resting backstroke—the first skill stroke to learn.

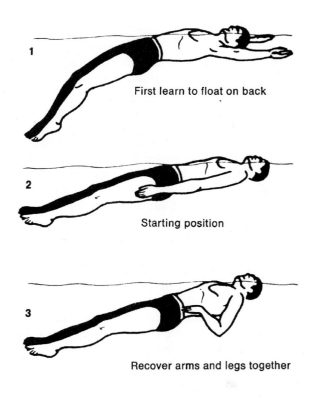

1

First learn to float on back

2

Starting position

3

Recover arms and legs together

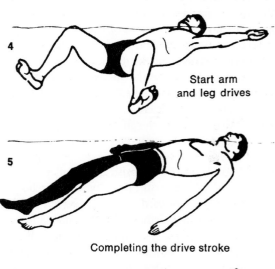

4

Start arm
and leg drives

5

Completing the drive stroke

6

Glide, stroke closed

Figure 29.5. Progressive steps in swimming the elementary backstroke.

because of a shorter range of motion. Stretch the body and legs straight, though relaxed, and pause until the momentum is spent. In the recovery phase, hold the legs straight while the arms recover to about armpit level; then start the leg

recovery at the same slow speed as the arms recover. When the arms have reached the pulling position, the legs have recovered to the kick position; that is, the knees and heels are apart, feet pointed outward. Breathe regularly.

Underarm Sidestroke

The underarm sidestroke (Figure 29.6) is easy to learn. It is the basic stroke for lifesaving. Breathing is not difficult because the nose and mouth are turned to the rear and water passes by the side of the face.

Scissors kick

The scissors kick is perhaps the most powerful of all kicks in the water, which is why it is used so much in lifesaving.

First the kick is learned on both sides by holding on to the side of the pool. The body is held straight on its side, legs straight, feet extended, and one leg on top of the other. The legs remain parallel with the surface of the water throughout. To start the recovery movement, flex at the knees and slowly draw the heels backward with both legs together and moving simultaneously. This drawing of the heels backward gives just the proper amount of flexion at the hip joint. In this position, if an imaginary line were passed through the midpoint of the shoulder and hip joints, it would project out over the legs at a midpoint between the knees and ankles when the legs are in a full recovery position. The scissors is now opened by moving the bottom leg back and the top leg forward, still maintaining the fully flexed knees. The foot of the top leg flexes toward the knee. The under foot remains extended. From this position, the legs start the drive, sweeping outward and together by extension of the knees and the foot of the top leg. The under leg hooks the water like it is kicking a ball. The top leg uses a whip motion similar to a horse's pawing. With a powerful yet smooth movement, the legs come together stretched straight and relaxed and pause long enough for momentum to be spent in the glide.

Arm stroke

While the body is on its side, with the shoulders in a true vertical plane, the lower arm (arm closer to the bottom of the pool) is extended forward directly under the head, with the palm facing down and the hand just under the surface. The upper arm pulls back, hugging closely along the upper front part of the body with the palm of the hand resting on the front side of the upper leg—never on the top of the leg.

The learner should first get a clear mental picture of the arm stroke from the starting position—that is, both arms moving simultaneously along the longitudinal plane of the body. They meet just under the head, change direction, and simultaneously extend again to their starting position. The lower arm moves forward; the upper arm moves backward. As the upper arm slides forward to meet the lower arm, the lower arm should pull diagonally downward and backward to a line under the head. Here it changes direction and starts the recovery movement, with the hand and fingers pointing forward to their starting position. Even though the hands move in and out together, the lower arm is always pulling on the "in" movement, while the upper arm is pulling on the "out" movement.

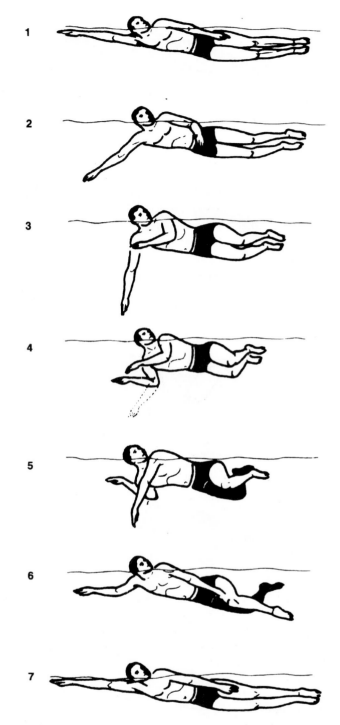

Figure 29.6. Progressive steps in swimming the underarm sidestroke.

Whole stroke coordinated in four steps

It is recommended that each of the following four steps be learned thoroughly before advancing to the next step (Figure 29.7).

Step 1: Scissors kick only. Take a deep breath and lie on the side floating position with the body straight and the lower

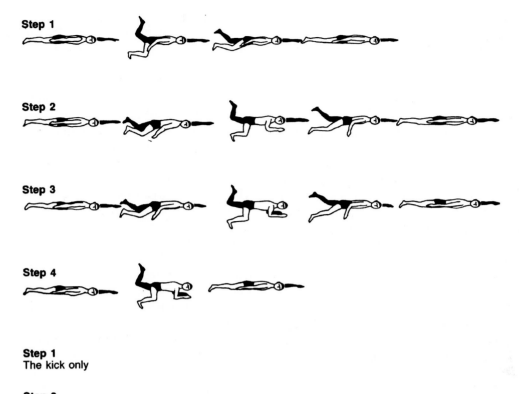

Step 1
The kick only

Step 2
The kick and upper arm; must be timed to work together

Step 3
The kick, upper arm, and lower arm; timed to start the stroke simultaneously with the kick

Step 4
Whole stroke

Figure 29.7. Progressive steps in learning the sidestroke (as seen from the side).

arm extended in a line with the body. Turn your face into the water on top of the lower arm and hold your breath. The upper arm is in front of the upper thigh. Take at least four kicks in succession and pause between each stroke for the glide. After at least four kicks, switch sides. The upper hand is in front of the upper thigh and remains on it during these kick exercises. This trains the upper arm to work in unison with the kick, as it must do in the whole stroke.

Step 2: The kick and upper arm. The body is positioned as in step 1. To execute step 2, the upper hand and arm recover at the same time as the legs. The hand moves forward beyond the face, with the elbow and hand submerged to a point beyond the face. The arm pull starts at the same time as the kick. The upper arm and legs recover at the same time, and the kick and pull occur at the same time.

Step 3: The kick, upper arm, and lower arm. The body and face are still in the same position as in step 1. To execute step 3, press—do not pull—the lower arm diagonally down and backward to a point under the face. At the same time that the lower arm starts its press, the legs and upper arm are recovered. The hands meet, cross over, and repass as the lower-arm hand recovers and thrusts forward to guide the glide. At the same time the lower arm recovers, the upper arm and legs start the pull and kick. Pause and glide. This makes it easy for the arms and legs to coordinate into the whole stroke. Repeat at least four strokes before stopping for air.

Step 4: Breathing. Take one or two strokes in the step 3 position and then turn your face out of the water and face to the rear, with the chin in line with the upper shoulder. Breathe in as the arms and legs come in; breathe out as the arms and legs go out. Now repeat the same four-step procedure on the right side. The water level should remain constant at your face, leveling at the corner of the lower eye and lower corner of the mouth.

Note: These four-step procedures can also be performed with flotation devices, such as kickboards.

COMPETITIVE STROKES

Breaststroke

The breaststroke was the first competitive stroke and is still used in competitive events. It is also an excellent utility stroke and is used in lifesaving.

Kick

There have been many modifications of the breaststroke kick in order to increase the speed of the entire stroke. In general, the main characteristic of these modifications has been to reduce unwanted resistance by narrowing the knee spread and increasing the desired resistance by adding a slightly downward thrust in the propulsive phase of the kick. However, for the beginner, the traditional kick is probably easiest to learn initially.

The breaststroke kick is almost the same as used in the inverted or the resting backstroke. The body is prone, arms extended, face below the surface of the water with the water line at the top of the forehead, and the heels close together. The recovery begins by drawing the heels forward toward the buttocks and then separating them to hip width with the angle of the thighs to the upper body slightly greater than 90 degrees. The thighs should not go as far as to be directly under the pelvis (Figure 29.8). The heels are then flexed in preparation for the drive. The drive is made forcefully but smoothly by pressing the feet first outward and then backward and inward until they are together, with the toes pointed. During the drive, the knees should remain hip-width apart while the lower leg whips outward and backward. Glide with the legs fully extended until momentum from the kick is spent. During the propulsive phase of the kick, water is pushed backward by the inside of the feet and the lower part of both legs. Then the legs whip together by driving the thighs in toward each other before the knees have fully extended. This final movement gives the kick extra power at the finish.

Arm stroke

In the streamline position, the arms are extended forward with the hands close together. The arms press slightly outward and downward simultaneously until the hands are slightly wider than the shoulders. The elbows then bend and the hands press downward so the palms face the feet. The hands then press inward together until they are under the chin. This part of the arm pull is the power phase of the pull. At the chin the hands

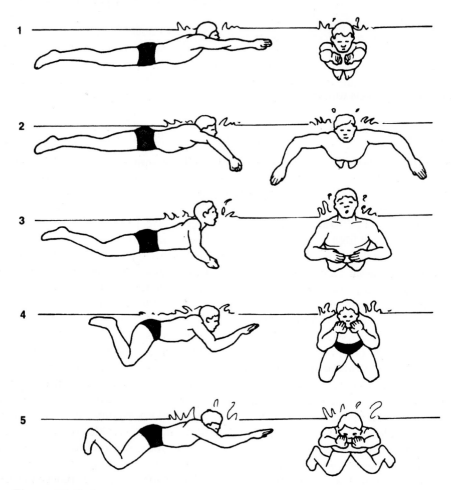

Figure 29.8. Progressive steps in swimming the breaststroke.

release the water and immediately begin to recover by pushing them from the chin until the arms are extended forward. Pulling too wide removes the support from under the shoulders and head, causing them to drop and sink, which disturbs the body balance. Furthermore, a wide arm pull provides little power while increasing resistance to a point that is not beneficial. As the arms sweep in toward the chin and the shoulders rise, the face will also rise to breathe. At this point, the knees begin their flexion for the kick recovery. The recovery of the arms begins under the chin as the hands join each other and are thrust forward to the starting position. At this point pause to allow for a glide. Practice walking across the pool without the breathing action first. Then coordinate the breathing with arm action technique.

Whole stroke

Push off from the side of the pool with the body prone on the surface, fully extended, the face underwater. The arms pull as just described, the breath is taken as the arms begin their recovery, and the legs are recovered with the feet spread and cocked for the drive. The legs begin their recovery and then perform the propulsive kick when the arms are fully extended.

The legs then pause for the glide when they have closed at the end of the drive. The body is now fully extended. Exhale slowly during the glide. Repeat several strokes to time the movements smoothly and continuously from the start of the stroke to the end of the leg drive (Figure 29.8). The breaststroke can be executed with the face of the water, as may be required in some lifesaving situations. The glide is shortened, and the stroke requires more effort.

Crawl Stroke (Freestyle)

The crawl stroke, usually called freestyle in competition, (Figure 29.9) is the fastest of all swimming strokes. Engineering and mechanical principles have been applied to this activity and have made it one of the most refined of all sports skills.

Flutter kick

The body is prone, with arms and legs fully extended, face under, and ankles stretched and feet and toes close together. From this position the flutter kick is executed by alternately moving the legs vertically from the hips, forcefully and regularly. On each downward beat, the foot turns slightly inward (pigeon-toed). This occurs naturally if the ankles and feet are held loosely. This increases the surface area of the foot. In the upward beat, the foot is extended with the sole pushing up against the water. Beginners should first attempt this kick with the legs straight yet not rigid in order to move from the hips. As the leg drives up, the sole of the foot is pulled upward with the knees slightly flexed and remains there until the knee is almost straight on the downward beat. (See action of right leg in Figure 29.9, 1 through 3.) This movement results in a quick down-up whip of the fore leg and foot at the end of the downbeat. This skill can be learned by daily drills with the aid of a kickboard. Three important points regarding the flutter kick are that the heels should just "brush" the surface of the water, the upward and downward motions of the legs are equally important in developing propulsive forces, and the feet should remain flexible and flipperlike.

Arm stroke (alternating)

This stroke is executed by alternately reaching hand-over-hand forward into the water and pulling the body forward. The arm stroke has six components: (1) entry, (2) catch, (3) pull, (4) push, (5) finish, and (6) recovery.

For the entry, place the hand in the water at a natural arm's length, directly in front of or slightly outside of the shoulder. The fingers should enter the water before the elbow or shoulder. A comfortable reach should be made; never overreach (Figure 29.9, 1 through 3.).

An opposition-rhythm type of stroke is maintained. This means that the arms are nearly opposite each other at all times.

The catch (the position the hand assumes when it is in the optimal position to begin propulsion) and pull should start first in the wrist and then in the elbow, bending slightly for good leverage (Figure 29.9, 2). The pull shifts into a push as the arm passes by the side of the chest toward the hip. Then the push continues the drive to the finish with the forearm and hand. (The finish of one hand coincides with the catch of the other hand.) At this point, the shoulder begins to lift in preparation to recover the arm until the hand clears the surface at the hip.

The arm is then recovered to the entry by lifting the shoulder, bending at the elbow, and turning the hand so that the palm faces to the rear and gradually faces the water at entry. The arm recovery movement is up and forward with the elbow high. The hand enters the water first, followed by the forearm. The hand reaches forward as the shoulders and hips rotate. The desired high elbow position on the recovery, entry, and catch is made easier if the shoulders and hips are allowed to roll to both sides during a complete stroke. The rolling action should be symmetric, with the head held in a relatively stable position and eyes looking at the bottom of the pool (Figure 29.9).

Whole stroke

While the arms execute a complete revolution, the legs complete some number of evenly measured beats. In walking, the arms and legs move in a 1:1 ratio, an opposite-arm-and-leg counterbalancing movement. In swimming the crawl, a preferred leg-to-arm ratio is 3:1; that is, the legs perform three beats to each armstroke, or six beats to each complete cycle of both arms. If speed is desired, the fundamental mechanics of the stroke become quite complex and highly technical in obtaining the ease and balance necessary for good performance as well as speed.

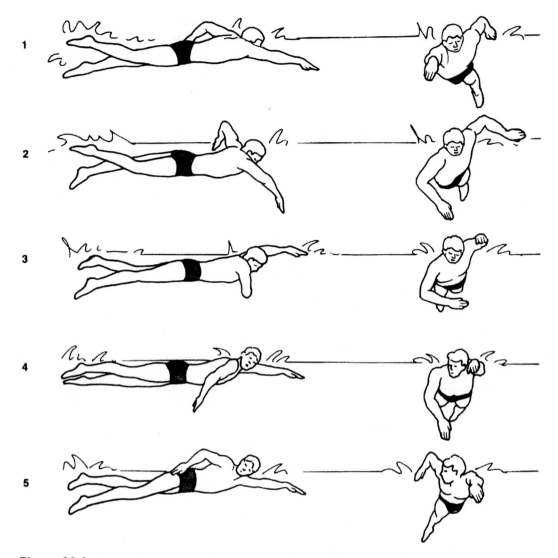

Figure 29.9. Progressive steps in timing the arms and legs with breathing in the crawl stroke.

Breathing

Breathing in the crawl stroke is executed as follows: Just as the arm opposite the breathing side has entered the water and is stretching for the catch, the hips are rotating and the arm on the breathing side has completed two thirds of the pull; the head rotates with the body to inhale and then immediately follows the roll of the body back into the water. When rotating the head for air, keep the chin close to the throat and the mouth inside the trough of the bow wave formed by the head. To keep from rotating the head too far, one eye should be kept below the surface while the other eye is above the surface. Take a quick breath as the mouth is opening; do not pause after opening the mouth. Curl the lips out away from the teeth when opening the mouth (Figure 29.9, 4 and 5).

Back Crawl Stroke (Backstroke)

The back crawl stroke (called the backstroke in competition) (Figure 29.10) is the fastest stroke done on the back.

Inverted flutter kick

Essentially the kick is the same as the flutter kick in the crawl stroke. The body is extended on its back, legs held closely together and ankles and toes pointed but flexible. The legs move alternately up and down with action originating from the hips. On the upward beat, the toes turn in. At the end of the upward beat, the kneecap should not break the surface and the toes should barely "brush" the surface. The kick should create a "boiling" action on the surface of the water. To accomplish this skill, the thigh, as in other styles of kicks, forcefully drives down

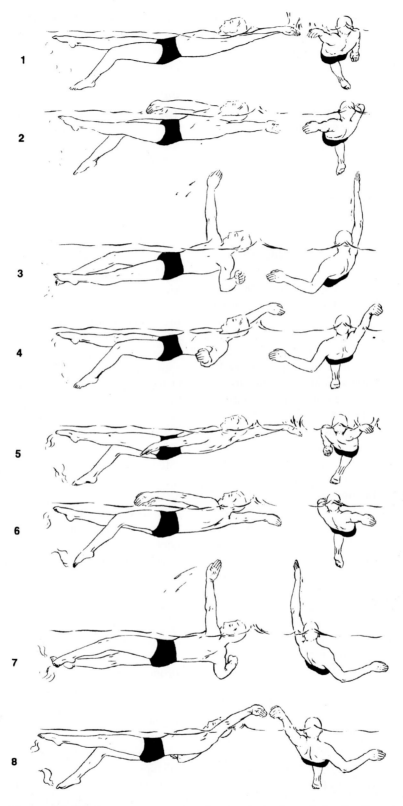

Figure 29.10. Progressive steps in swimming the back crawl, showing the six leg beats and one revolution of the arm cycle.

just before the knee has straightened. This action gives the fore leg and foot an effective propulsive up-down whip. The ratio of leg kicks to one complete cycle of arm (left and right) stroke revolution is 6:1, the same as in the front crawl stroke.

Arm stroke

The arms move in opposition to one another as in the front crawl stroke. The hands exit the water thumb-first and enter the water with the little finger first.

The arm is bent slightly at the elbow at the beginning of the recovery phase, but it is straightened for the entry. The arm recovers to the entry with an upward swing and continues to the entry at a point not more than 6 inches (15 cm) outside the shoulder line. The hand and forearm should not be slowed as they near the point of entry, but should accelerate so that they are in the water before the shoulder can sink under.

The power, or pull, phase of the stroke can be done with either a bent or straight arm. The bent-arm stroke is used by high-level competitive swimmers and is more difficult to learn than the straight-arm pull. In the initial part of the straight-arm pull, the arm is shallow, about 2 to 6 inches (5 to 15 cm) underwater. As the arm reaches a point directly out from the shoulder, the depth should be about 6 to 10 inches (15 to 25 cm). From here, the arm continues until it reaches the leg and begins the recovery phase (Figure 29.10).

The bent-arm pull is initiated with the hand entering the water, little finger first, palm out, facing away and slightly backward, with the arm straight. Body roll is crucial to perform the bent-arm stroke. Simultaneous with the hand entry, the body rolls onto the side of the arm entering the water. The hand enters the water and presses outward and downward until it catches the water. The catch with one hand and finish with the other hand should coincide. The catch is made 12 to 18 inches (30 to 45 cm) below the surface. As the pulling hand presses downward, outward, and backward, the elbow bends. Next the hand presses upward, backward, and inward toward the hip and surface. The arm will have a maximum bend of about 90 degrees at this point and will be about 6 inches (15 cm) below the surface. The hand now increases its pulling speed and presses downward and outward. The moment the arm has finished its pull along the side of the thigh, the hand gives a final downward press as the shoulder is lifted out of the water and the hand is turned to face outward. In both types of pulls, the arm stroke should be smooth and relaxed throughout. A pronounced hip roll and shoulder roll permit an easier recovery and catch, as well as more efficient action of the opposite arm.

Breathing and head position

Breathing should be continuous and rhythmic. The chin is always lined up on dead center, and the head should never move from side to side. The ears should be below the water surface. The head should be propped up slightly as if it were on a pillow. The swimmer should use his or her abdominal muscles to sit up slightly in the water. The body stretch will prevent sagging at the hips (Figure 29.10).

Butterfly (Dolphin) Stroke

The butterfly stroke was created in 1935 by David A. Armbruster, the swimming coach at the University of Iowa, with the aid of one of his swimmers, Jack Sieg. The legs in this stroke move in unison in an up-and-down wavelike action that resembles the movement of a dolphin. The arms also move in unison. The arms recover bilaterally, low above the surface; are held nearly straight; and resemble the wings of a butterfly in flight.

The stroke is definitely dominated by the kick. This wavelike kick by the legs has become the fastest means of kicking through water. It is even faster than the alternating flutter kick.

The butterfly stroke is very exhausting to the untrained individual, but it provides a learning challenge. The dolphin kick can also be used with the crawl and backstroke turns for increased speed and power. Except for use as a competitive swimming stroke, it has little, if any, value to humans. It is certainly not a survival stroke due to the high energy demands it requires of the swimmer. However, the stroke is included here because many students desire to learn it, if for no other reason than for its rugged, challenging action and for the satisfaction of being able to perform it.

Kick

As practice progresses, the student should first practice the kick on the surface of the water, with the hands finning at the sides of the hips. As a final step of conditioning and training, and before the whole stroke is attempted, the student should submerge and practice the kick underwater during breath-holding intervals. The hands should be finning at the sides of the hips rather than extended in front of the head. By practicing the kick underwater, the student is able to assure forward progress. It is also essential while performing underwater to relax the entire spine from the shoulders through all the joints to the end of the toes. Swim fins help beginners become familiar with this movement. When the true shortened up-and-down beat of the kick and the up-and-down action of the hips have been mastered, the student can progress to the arm action.

Downbeat. Both legs sweep downward simultaneously. The hips flex, the knees flex, and the thighs move downward at the beginning of the downbeat. At the end of the downbeat, the legs are fully extended, with the toes pointed and the hips flexed. At the completion of the downbeat, the feet are pressing downward with the most velocity and force in the entire kick. Loose ankles provide the whipping action necessary to be propulsive.

Upbeat. Hip extension pulls the legs toward the surface while the legs are still straight. Gradually the knees start to flex as the legs move toward the surface, and the hips drop lower in the water. As in the flutter kick, the upward and downward drive of the legs are equally important in the dolphin kick.

Arm stroke

The student should first practice the arm stroke by walking across the swimming pool, bent at the hips, chin at water level, stroking with the arms. The stroke can also be practiced while stationary, in the same position.

The arms start the stroke from the point of entry, in front of the head, pressing downward into a short lateral spread. The hands and forearms continue the pull backward with a quick inward action, with the hands coming close together, elbows bent until they reach a point just under and ahead of the shoulders. From this point, the power drive is completed backward and outward past the hips until the arms and hands have cleared the surface of the water. This final emphasis is delivered by straightening the elbows until shoulders, arms, and hands have cleared the surface of the water. This action forces the arms to swing laterally forward with the hands just above the water and the elbows slightly bent through the recovery phase to the correct point of entry. During the recovery, the arms are held nearly straight, palms facing backward. The recovery should be executed without hesitation at the end of the power phase. The hands and forearms should enter the water slightly ahead of the upper arms and shoulders, with the wrists slightly flexed. The catch of the next stroke is started without breaking momentum.

When walking or swimming across the pool practicing the arm stroke, the student should imagine the body moving toward the face of a large clock; the left arm should enter the water pointing to 11 o'clock, and the right arm should point to 1 o'clock.

There is no pause in the entire stroke turnover. This is what is known in swimming terms as a *fast turnover stroke;* that is, the moment the arms complete the power drive, they go into the recovery to start the next stroke. Not only must the arms recover quickly, but the power drive of the arms must also be rapidly executed. It is this fast turnover cadence that makes the stroke so strenuous, especially if the beginner is poorly conditioned. However, most students skilled in other strokes can learn the challenging, complex skills involved in performing this stroke.

Whole stroke

The stroke is started with one or two kicks with the head submerged and the arms in streamline position. The hands enter the water just outside the shoulders simultaneously, pointing to the 11 and 1 o'clock positions, respectively. As the hands execute the catch, with a slight spread and downward press, the first downward beat of the kick takes place (Figure 29.11,

1 and 2). This downbeat of the kick is a natural counteraction caused by the powerful downward catch and pull of the forearms, similar to the counterswing of the arms and legs in walking or running. While the hands and arms execute the inward drive or pull to a point just ahead of under the shoulders, the first upbeat of the kick takes place (Figure 29.11, 3 and 4). From this point, the arms continue to complete the final power drive as the second downbeat of the kick takes place (Figure 29.11, 4 and 5). This action is again a natural counterbalancing movement of legs and arms. As the arms drive out of the water at the hips and move into the recovery phase, the legs execute the second upbeat (Figure 29.11, 6 through 8). Note that during the entire arm recovery phase there is only one beat of the legs, which is up, and none supporting the body. For this reason it is essential that the swimmer move the arms quickly from the end of the drive to the entry. This quickened movement will prevent the body from sinking below swimming level. The most troublesome part in learning the stroke is this latter phase. If the arms move too slowly or hesitate at any point between the final drive and the entry, rhythm and timing are lost.

In executing the entry, the arms plunge lightly into the water and immediately go into the catch to start the next stroke. The stroke should first be practiced without breathing until reasonably satisfactory timing is attained. Beginners often make the mistake of starting the recovery of the arms prematurely, before the arms and hands have cleared the surface of the water well back of the hips and straightened elbows (Figure 29.11, 5 and 6).

Breathing

Correct breathing in the butterfly (dolphin) stroke is not too difficult, providing the beginner does not develop a tendency to lift the head too high or back. In learning this skill, the student should again walk the arm stroke across the swimming pool with the face submerged while executing the breathing and correct timing action of the head in the arm stroke cadence. Taking a breath every stroke should be practiced. Correct breathing habits in this stroke are essential to obtain ease of performance of the entire stroke.

To inhale, the swimmer should lift the head up and out just far enough for the mouth to clear the surface of the water. This action takes place just as the arms have passed backward under the shoulders and are completing their drive. Air is actually taken just as the arms clear the water and move into the recovery phase (Figure 29.11, 4 through 6). Note how the finishing "kick" of the arm stroke gives the head the necessary lift to inhale. The head drops quickly but not deeply into the water after inhalation, before the arm recovery has reached the point of entry (Figure 29.11, 7 and 8). A quick recovery of both the head and the arms gives support to the body during this phase of the stroke. Both the head and the arms are above the surface of the water during the second upward beat of the kick. If this phase of the

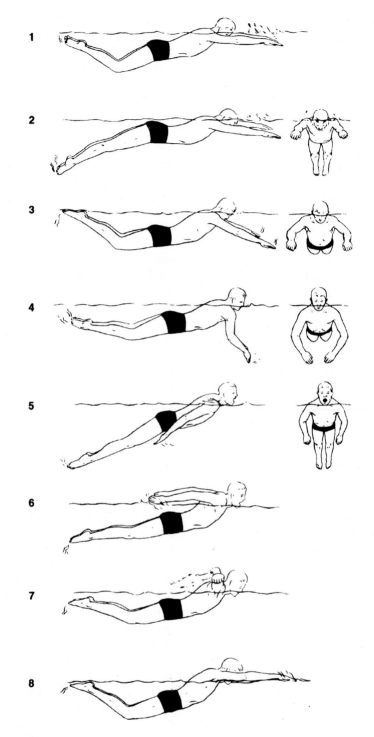

Figure 29.11. Progressive steps in swimming the butterfly (dolphin) stroke.

stroke is not well timed and executed, the torso and hips will tend to sink too deep in the water to continue forward. With practice, proficiency is acquired and the tiring, unnecessary movements are minimized.

LEARNING PROGRESSION FOR BEGINNERS

1. Study pool sanitation and personal health and hygiene.
2. Provide the opportunity to orient and adjust to water in order to overcome the loss of body weight,

loss of balance, and loss of body heat, all of which make the beginner psychologically, physiologically, and physically uncomfortable. Use the following exercises:

    a. Submerge the face, opening the eyes underwater, and hold the breath.

    b. Bobbing exercises, where the swimmer pushes him or herself down toward the bottom. Once the head is submerged, push off the bottom to go back to the surface.

    c. Floating, with the body tucked and straight, on both the face and back.

3. Adjustment of the hands and feet to paddling in shallow water.

    a. Sculling with and without the feet

    b. Finning with and without the feet

    c. Treading water with and without the feet

4. Unskilled strokes on the face, sides, and back.

5. Skilled strokes

    a. Kicks

       (1) Flutter

       (2) Scissors (both sides)

       (3) Breaststroke

       (4) Dolphin

    b. Arm strokes

       (1) Alternating stroke with breathing

       (2) Sidestroke with breathing

       (3) Breaststroke

       (4) Resting inverted breaststroke

       (5) Butterfly

6. Synchronize action of arms and legs in all strokes by using the part-whole method—that is, breaking down each stroke from the whole into its component parts and by progressive stages building it again into the whole stroke.

7. Orientation in distance swimming.

LEARNING PROGRESSION FOR INTERMEDIATE SWIMMERS

Instruction in intermediate swimming is given to those who have taken and passed the beginner's course; those who have never had instruction but can pass the beginner's test, although they have no knowledge of stroke technique; or those who can swim in deep water.

1. Review swimming pool landmarks regarding pool depths, any unique features of the pool, and personal safety rules.

2. Review strokes, and review techniques of proper breathing.

3. Drill on stroke techniques.

4. Start orientation to distance swimming, emphasizing relaxation and natural breathing.

5. Practice fundamental dives from the springboard.

6. Learn and practice safety factors for self and others, such as recognizing tired-swimmer's stroke; use a simple rescue, simple carries in towing, and resuscitation.

7. Swim distances, stressing ease in breathing, relaxation, and the distribution of effort over distance comfortably.

LEARNING PROGRESSION FOR ADVANCED SWIMMERS

Instruction in advanced swimming is open to those who have passed the intermediate course or have achieved the ability to swim ¼ mile (0.4 km) and demonstrated all of the standard strokes.

1. Practice timing the strokes to develop ease of performance with added power and speed, thereby gaining confidence.

2. Swim each stroke 100 yards (91 m) with correct technique and timing of breathing with strokes.

3. Kick 25 yards (22.9 m) on each side, holding the upper arm out of the water fully extended.

4. Kick 25 yards (22.9 m) on the back, holding both hands out of the water.

5. Swim ¼ mile (0.4 km) in 8 minutes or less.

6. Learn a good racing start and good technique in turning at the end of the pool.

7. Be able to do at least three dives from the springboard in good form.

8. Learn safety procedures and operations of small craft.

9. Swim safely for 20 minutes.

10. Learn how to wade properly in water of unknown depth.

11. Learn how to swim out of a swift current.

12. Learn how to assist another person temporarily in distress in deep water.

13. Learn how to swim for two people.

14. Swim underwater for a distance of 25 yards (22.9 m).

15. Learn how to conserve strength.

16. Learn how to rest when tired in deep water.

17. Learn boatmanship:

    a. Paddling and rowing

    b. What to do when capsized

    c. How to land safely when capsized

18. Be able to teach others how to swim.

19. Learn how and when to make a safe rescue.

20. Be able to demonstrate proper resuscitation.

TEACHING CONSIDERATIONS

1. Skilled lifeguards should be on duty in the pool for all instructional sessions.

2. Beginning classes should contain fewer students than intermediate or advanced classes. All classes should be ability grouped as specified in the chapter.

3. All sessions should include introduction, practice, and summary.

4. Basic stroke technique is easier to understand if demonstrations and initial practice take place out of the water.

5. Consider using a "buddy" system for safety and skill feedback.

6. Work first for technique and then use strokes for distance and conditioning.

7. With intermediate and advanced swimmers, identify why students are taking the course. Competition, endurance, and recreational goals require different teaching techniques.

GLOSSARY

catch Position of the hand when it is at the optimal point in the stroke to begin the propulsive phase of pulling.

finning The backward thrust of the hands.

pike position Position where legs are straight, back is bent, and arms extend out to reach for the ankles.

sculling Back-and-forth action of the hands in the water used to feel movement of the water and for propulsion.

tuck position Position where the kness are bent and pulled to the chest by the arms.

SUGGESTED READINGS

Colwin, C. 2002. *Breakthrough swimming.* Champaign, IL: Human Kinetics.

Counsilman, R. 1994. *New science of swimming.* 2nd ed. Needham Heights, MA: Allyn and Bacon. This is a classic reference on the science of swimming by the "father" of modern competitive swimming.

Evans, J. 2007. *Jonet Evans' total swimming.* Champaign IL: Human Kinetics.

Goldstein, M., and Tanner, D. 1999. *Swimming past 50.* Champaign, IL: Human Kinetics.

Gutzman, R. 2007. *The swimming drill book.* Champaign, IL: Human Kinetics.

Hannula, D. 2003. *Coaching swimming successfully.* 2nd ed. Champaign, IL: Human Kinetics.

Intercollegiate and interscholastic swimming guide: Official rules of swimming and diving. Published annually. New York: National Intercollegiate Athletic Bureau.

Jager, T. 1999. *Swimming.* Dubuque, IA: McGraw-Hill. Introduces beginning and intermediate swimming as well as facilities, equipment, and conditioning schedules.

Maglischo, E. 2003. *Swimming fastest.* Champaign, IL: Human Kinetics.

Montgomery, J., and Chambers, M. 2009. *Mastering swimming.* Champaign, IL: Human Kinetics.

Official NCAA swimming and diving guide. Current ed. Shawnee Mission, KS: National Collegiate Athletic Association.

Salo, D., and Riewald, S. 2008. *Complete conditioning for swimming.* Champaign, IL: Human Kinetics.

Thomas, D. G. 2005. *Swimming: Steps to success.* 3rd ed. Champaign, IL: Human Kinetics.

USA Swimming (current year) rule book. Colorado Springs CO: USA Swimming.

Periodicals

Aquatics International (quarterly), Communications Channels, P.O. Box 5111, Pittsfield, MA 01203.

Fitness Swimmer (monthly), Rodale's Fitness Swimmer, P.O. Box 5307, Pittsfield, MA 01203-5307.

Journal of Swimming Research (quarterly), 304 SE 20th St., Fort Lauderdale, FL 33316.

Splash Magazine, USA Swimming, Inc., 1 Olympic Plaza, Colorado Springs, CO 80909

Swim Magazine (monthly), Sports Publications, Inc., 228 Nevada St., El Segundo, CA 90245.

Swimming Technique (quarterly), Swimming World Publications, P.O. Box 45497, Los Angeles, CA 90045.

Swimming World (monthly), Sports Publications, 155 S. El Molino, Suite 101, Pasadena, CA 91101.

RESOURCES

Videos

American Red Cross. *Swimming and diving skills,* American Red Cross, 17th & D Street, Washington, DC 20006.

Gambril, D. *Don Gambril's gold medal series: Breaststroke; Backstroke; Butterfly; Freestyle and coach's drills* and *The fundamentals of swimming* (5 videos), Swimming World, P.O. Box 91870, Pasadena, CA 91109.

Naber, J., and Fletcher, J. *Teaching kids swimming with John Naber and Joy Fletcher.* West One Video, 1995 Bailey Hill Rd., Eugene, OR 97405. Takes the viewer through a thorough program that acquaints youthful swimmers with the water.

USA Swimming. *Swim Fast: Breaststroke.*

USA Swimming. *Swim Fast: Freestyle.*

USA Swimming. *Swim Fast: Butterfly* (available online at www.usaswimming.org).

See Appendix C for other video sources.

WEB SITES

www.fina.org
www.swiminfo.com
www.swimmingcoach.org
www.swimnews.com
www.usaswimming.org
www.usms.org

Table Tennis

After completing this chapter, the reader should be able to:

- Appreciate the historical development and social values of table tennis
- Select the proper equipment for the game
- Properly apply the rules for singles and doubles play
- Demonstrate and execute proper grips, footwork, and shots
- Understand singles and doubles strategy

HISTORY

The exact origin of the sport now called table tennis is in question. Most experts can narrow it down only to the late nineteenth century, although there are lithographs suggesting an origin as early as 1810. It is believed to have originated in England. At one point in history, table tennis was known as "ping-pong." It is believed that this name was derived from the sound of the ball hitting the table ("ping") and the ball hitting the hollow vellum battledore, which was the paddle at the time ("pong"). Now the title *Ping-Pong* is usually reserved for the recreational version of the activity, and *table tennis* is the name used for the sport. The sport has also been known as Gossima, Flim-Flam, and Whif-Whaf. After a brief period of popularity in the United States, table tennis fell into obscurity. It was revived around 1920 and gradually gained in popularity around the world. The International Table Tennis Federation (ITTF) was established in Berlin in 1926, and the United States Table Tennis Association (USTTA) was established in 1933. The latter changed to USA Table Tennis (USATT) in 1994.

Table tennis is now considered to be the world's second largest participation sport and is a major sport in Asia and Europe. It is the number one racquet sport in the world, with over 13 million playing competitively each year.

Although world championships have been held in table tennis since 1926, it did not become a full-medal Olympic event until 1988 in Seoul. Early years of international competitions were dominated by Central European countries, especially Hungary and Czechoslovakia. In the 1950s, the dominance in table tennis shifted to Japan. In the 1960s, 1970s, and 1980s, China dominated the sport. China captured six of the possible seven titles at the world championships in New Delhi in 1987. South Korea spoiled the sweep by winning the women's doubles. In the 1988 Olympics, the Chinese and the South Koreans split the four gold medals, with China winning the women's singles and the men's doubles and South Korea winning the men's singles and the women's doubles. Sweden had a short period of dominance,

winning three titles in a row at the World Championships in 1989, 1991, and 1993. However, China has since won six of the seven men's team titles and eight women's titles in a row.

At the 1992 Barcelona Olympics, the four table tennis events (men's and women's singles and doubles) were dominated by the Chinese teams. They won 6 of the possible 12 medals, including three of the four gold medals.

At the 1996 Summer Olympics in Atlanta, Georgia, the four table tennis events (men's and women's singles and doubles) were all won by China. At the 2000 summer Olympics in Sydney, Australia, China won a total of eight medals (4 gold, 3 silver, and 1 bronze) out of a possible 12.

In the 2004 Olympics in Athens, Greece, the Chinese won the gold medal in three of the four events (a Korean, Ryu Seung Min, won the men's singles) and won a total of 6 of the 12 medals in all. The other 6 medals went to Korea (3), Hong Kong (2), and Denmark (1).

In the 2008 Olympics in Beijing, China, the Chinese won eight of twelve possible medals including all four gold medals. The remaining four medals went to South Korea (2), Germany, and Singapore.

VALUES

Table tennis is an excellent club or home game for everyone because it requires a minimum of equipment, is relatively inexpensive, and can be played almost anywhere by all age groups. It is very popular at recreation and community centers. Many table tennis tournaments are held each year. Table tennis causes little or no damage or injury because a small racquet and light-as-a-feather ball are used.

Finding opponents to play singles or doubles is usually easy. If unequal in ability, the better player can spot an opponent a few points to increase the competitive enjoyment of the game.

EQUIPMENT

Any type of clothing allowing freedom of movement and comfort is acceptable. Rubber-soled shoes that facilitate safe side-to-side movements should be worn. However, in tournament play, USATT rules specify that clothing may be of any color, except that the main color shall be clearly different from that of the ball in use. Whenever an orange ball is used, white but not orange clothing is allowed.

Racquet (Blade)

A variety of satisfactory racquets are available from commercial sources. At least 85 percent of the blade by thickness shall be natural. An adhesive layer within the blade may be reinforced with fibrous material such as carbon fiber, glass fiber, or compressed paper, but shall not be thicker than 7.5 percent of the total thickness or 0.35 millimeter, whichever is smaller. The striking surface (racquet covering) of the racquet blade must be covered with a pimpled rubber with the pimples facing inward or outward. A single layer of cellular (sponge) rubber is located underneath the rubber surface. The two surfaces of the blade may have different striking surfaces, but must be different colors, namely black and red.

In 2004, the International Table Tennis Federation and the USATT passed rules to regulate the adhesives used to adhere the racquet coverings to the blade. Beginning in September 2008, it became illegal to use adhesives containing volatile organic compounds (VOCs). Prolonged or continued exposure to these compounds is thought to be a health risk. Water-based adhesives are now produced and marketed by table tennis manufacturers.

Ball

The ball is small, celluloid, spherical, matte in color, 40 millimeters in diameter, and 2.7 grams in weight. It is fragile but quite hard to break unless stepped on. The USATT-approved standard ball has a uniform bounce. If it is dropped from a height of 12 inches (30.5 cm) on an approved table, it should bounce 8¾ to 9¾ inches (22 to 25 cm).

Table

The table is usually constructed of ¾-inch (1.9-cm) material, commonly plywood or particle board, and must be 9 feet (2.74 m) in length and 5 feet (1.52 m) in width. The playing surface should be dark (usually green or blue) and nonreflecting and should lie on a horizontal plane 2 feet 6 inches (76 cm) above the floor. The sidelines and endlines are white and should be ¾ inch (1.9 cm) wide. The centerline is also white, but only ⅛ inch (3 mm) wide (Figure 30.1). It is best to use tables approved by either USATT or ITTF. There should be sufficient room around the table to permit players to "go after" the ball without running into obstructions. Official rules state that the minimum playing space for each table is 40 feet (12 m) long, 20 feet (6 m) wide, and 11.5 feet (3.5 m) high.

Net

The net is lightweight. It is stretched taut across the center of the table and attached to the outside by supporting posts. The top of the net should be 6 inches (15 cm) above the table and extend to attached posts 6 inches (15 cm) outside of the sidelines. The bottom of the net should be as close to the table as possible and the ends of the net as close to the supporting posts as possible.

RULES (ABRIDGED)

Singles

A game is won by the player who first scores 11 points, unless both players have scored 10 points, in which case the one who first scores 2 points more than the opponent is the winner.

The choice of playing position at the table and order of service are determined by the toss of a coin. If the winner of the toss prefers to have first choice of playing positions,

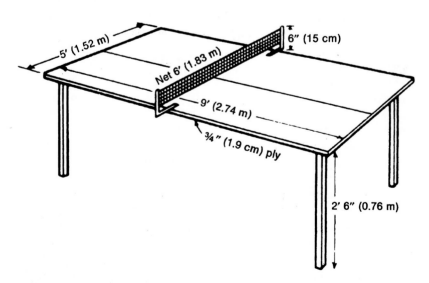

Figure 30.1. Table and net.

the opponent then has the choice of whether to serve first or receive first, and vice versa.

The change of service takes place after 2 points have been scored. A point is normally awarded when the play of a service is concluded. The receiver then becomes the server and the server becomes receiver, and so on, after each 2 points until the end of the game or the score is 10–all. Whenever the score becomes 10–all, the receiver becomes the server and the server the receiver, and so on, after each point until the end of the game.

In the start of a new game, the player who served first in the previous game becomes receiver and the receiver becomes server, and so on, alternating after each game.

The players also exchange ends after each game, and if play consists of more than one game, in the deciding game of the match, the players change ends when one player reaches a score of 5. A match is the majority of five (or seven) games.

Service

A good service is delivered by projecting the ball from the free (nonserving) hand, which must start from above the playing surface. The ball must be resting in the palm of the free hand, which is flat and the thumb free of the fingers. Without imparting spin to the ball, it is projected nearly vertically upward at least 6 inches. As it starts to descend, the ball is struck so that it touches the server's court first and then, passing directly over or around the net, touches the receiver's court. At the instant of contact of the racquet on the ball in service, both handle and ball must be behind the endline of the server's court, but not farther back than the part of the server's body, other than his or her arm, leg, or head, whichever is farthest from the net.

A good return of a served ball must be struck by the receiver on the first bounce so that it passes directly over or around the net and touches the opponent's court.

Points

Unless the rally is a let, a point is awarded to the opponent in the following circumstances:

1. Failure to make a good service
2. Failure to make a good return
3. If the player, the racquet, or anything that the player wears or carries touches the net or its supports while the ball is in play
4. If the player, the racquet, or anything that a player wears or carries moves the playing surface while the ball is in play
5. If the player's free hand touches the playing surface while the ball is in play
6. If, after being struck by the opponent, the ball comes in contact with the player or anything the player wears or carries before it has passed over the endlines or sidelines, not yet having touched the playing surface on the player's side of the table

7. If at any time the player volleys the ball—that is, before the ball hits the table top—except as provided in number 1 under "Let" (below)
8. If a player strikes the ball twice in succession

Let

A let ball, which is then replayed, is called in the following cases:

1. If the served ball, in passing over or around the net, touches it or its supports, provided that the service would otherwise have been good or is volleyed by the receiver
2. If a service is delivered when the receiver is not ready, provided always that the receiver may not be deemed unready if an attempt to strike the ball is made
3. If either player is prevented by a disturbance not under his or her control from serving a good service or making a good return
4. If either player gives up a point, as provided in number 3 to 7 under "Points," owing to an accident not within his or her control
5. If a game is interrupted for correction of an error in order or ends

Scoring

A point is scored by the side that makes the last successful return prior to the end of a rally. An unsuccessful return occurs whenever the ball is missed, struck with the side of a racquet blade having an illegal surface, hit off the table, sent into the net, or hit onto the player's own half of the court on the return. Failure to make a good serve also scores a point for the opponent unless it is a let.

In play

The ball is in play from the moment it is projected from the hand in service until the rally is decided as a let or a point.

Doubles

Good service

The service is delivered as previously described, except that it must touch first the right half of the server's court and then, passing directly over or around the net, touch the right half of the receiver's court. The centerline is considered part of each right-hand court.

Choice of order of play

The official rules specify that the team winning a coin toss has the choice of ends or the right to receive or serve. After the choice is made, the other team makes the remaining choice.

The pair who have the right to serve the first two services in any game decide which partner shall serve, and the opposing pair decide similarly who will first be the receiver.

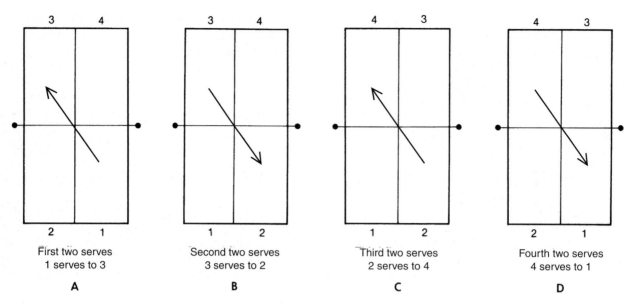

Figure 30.2. Order of service for doubles.

Order of service

The first two services must be delivered by the selected partner (1) of the pair who have the right to do so and must be received by the selected partner (3) of the opposing pair (Figure 30.2A). The second two services must be delivered by the receiver of the first two services (3) and received by the partner of the server (2) of the first two services (Figure 30.2B). The third two services must be delivered by the partner of the first two services (2) and received by the partner of the receiver (4) of the first two services (Figure 30.2C). The fourth two services must be delivered by the partner of the receiver (4) of the first two services and received by the server (1) of the first two services (Figure 30.2D). The fifth two services must be delivered in the same manner as the first two services, and so on in sequence until the end of the game or a score of 10–all, at which point each player serves only one service in turn until the end of the game.

The team (or player in singles) who served first shall receive first in the next game. In each game the initial order of serving is the opposite of the preceding game.

In a one-game match or in the deciding game of a match of more than one game, the pair that served the first two services has the right to alter its order of receiving or that of its opponents at the first score of 5.

FUNDAMENTAL SKILLS AND TECHNIQUES

Shakehands Grip

Shakehands grip is both highly versatile and popular. With the blade perpendicular to the floor, the racquet is grasped as if shaking hands with it. The index finger is pointed along the bottom of the blade surface with the thumb on the surface of the other side.

Forehand grip

In the forehand grip, the short handle of the racquet is gripped very closely to the blade, with the blade itself partially held in the hand and the forefinger and thumb bracing opposite sides of the blade (Figure 30.3A).

Backhand grip

The backhand grip is the same as for the forehand (Figure 30.3B).

Penhold Grip

The same side of the blade is almost always used for both backhand and forehand shots. Thus, the grip position remains unchanged unless the racquet is deliberately rotated between rallies in order to use the striking surface on the other side of the blade. With the racquet pointing down, hold the racquet where the handle meets the blade with the thumb and index finger. This is similar to holding a pen. Either curl up or straighten the remaining fingers. Figure 30.3C, D depicts the penhold grip.

Points to Remember

1. Do not grip the racquet too tightly; relax.
2. Hold the wrist firmly and rotate the forearm as needed to obtain the correct blade angle.
3. Whenever possible, angle your body toward the ball when making forehand and backhand shots in order to move forward when striking the ball.
4. Constantly check the racquet head, making sure that it is not dropped because the wrist is bent.
5. Regularly check the thumb and index finger to keep them in the proper place.

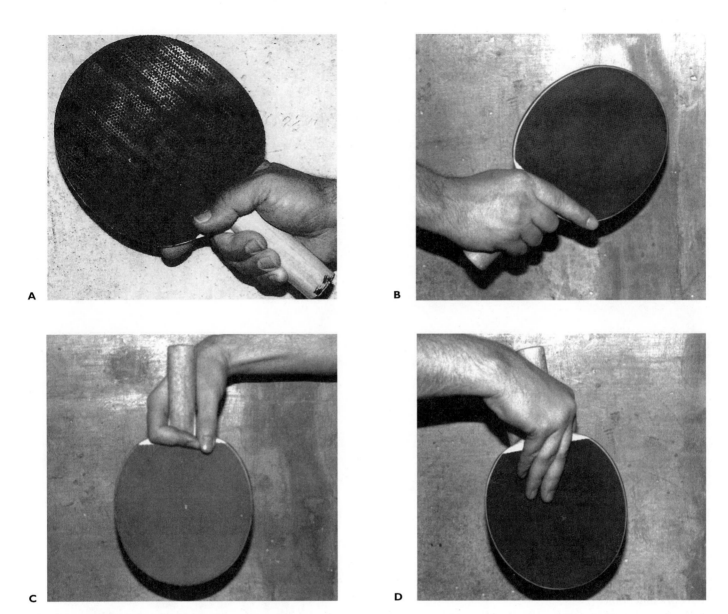

Figure 30.3. Grips: A, Shakehands, forehand. B, Shakehands backhand. C, Penhold, striking-surface side. D, Penhold, backside.

Serving

For a topspin serve with either a forehand or backhand stroke, the ball is put into play by projecting it upward from the flat free hand (Figure 30.4). As the ball is descending, it is met by the racquet, which is swung forward and upward and the racquet face is closed (facing toward the tabletop and net).

For a backspin (chop) serve, the ball is struck with a downward, forward motion of the racquet (Figure 30.5). The racquet face is open (facing upward from the tabletop and net). The player will need to practice adjusting the angle of the racquet to find the most effective one. More advanced players might want to work on the forehand and backhand side-spin serves.

For a forehand side-spin serve, the racquet is brought across the ball from right to left (if right-handed) just as the racquet strikes the ball, with the racquet head moving to a nearly vertical position and the ball being struck in front of the server.

For a backhand side-spin serve, the racquet is swung across the ball from left to right and (if the player is right-handed) the ball is released from the left hand just as the racquet passes in front of the server. Effective spin serves require giving the ball considerable spin.

In putting the ball into play, the server must keep the fingers straight and together and the thumb free. No cupping or pinching of the ball is permitted. The ball must be tossed vertically. The ball must remain visible by the receiver throughout the toss (neither the non-racquet hand nor the server's body may be used, to block the receiver's view of the ball). If this rule is violated, a let is called and the server

Figure 30.4. Start of the forehand topspin serve.

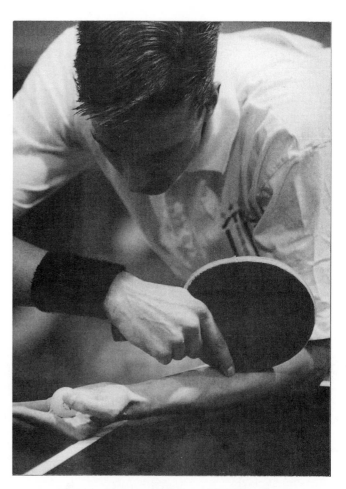

Figure 30.5. Backhand serve.

warned. If the violation is repeated, a point is awarded to the opponent.

Footwork and Stance

Proper stance and footwork in serving or receiving are just as important in learning table tennis as they are in tennis, badminton, or any sport that requires a constantly alert player. See Figure 30.6 for an excellent example of the stance that is often called the "ready position."

A good beginner's stance in serving the ball is a position where your playing elbow is about 1½ to 2 feet (45 to 60 cm) directly behind the centerline of the table. Face slightly to the right side with the feet well apart and the left foot forward (for a right-handed player). Remember the service rule stating that at the moment of impact, both the racquet and ball must be behind the endline on the table. In addition, the service toss must start at table height or above.

A good stance for receiving is a position where your playing elbow is about 2 to 2½ feet (60 to 75 cm) directly in back of the centerline of the table. The feet are spaced well apart, the knees are slightly bent, and the body is inclined forward in an alert position. From this position one can quickly step

Figure 30.6. Stance, or ready position.

forward, backward, or to the side to make either a backhand or forehand shot. After the shot is made, recover to this position in preparation for the next return.

For a forehand or backhand return, the feet should be placed, at the moment of contact of the racquet with the ball, so that they are perpendicular to the line of flight of the ball. The feet should be well spread in order to shift weight forward and backward in delivering a shot.

Whenever possible, attempt to be moving forward when striking the ball. In going after a ball for an effective shot, remember to face the ball as you play it. Also remember to return quickly to midcourt after the shot is made. Watch the ball at all times as demonstrated in the backhand return shown in Figure 30.7.

Stroke Techniques

Push shot

The push shot is the easiest way to return a backspin serve or shot. A backhand push is accomplished by meeting the ball as it touches the table and gently hitting it back over the net with a racquet that is rotated toward the body and is slightly down. This lifts and carries the ball forward at the same time. The backhand push occurs in front of the body while the forehand push occurs to the forehand side of the body.

In addition, by holding the racquet almost motionless when contacting the ball, it will rebound back over the net. This is called a "block shot," and it resembles a miniature drive shot, which is described next.

Forehand topspin shot

The forehand topspin shot (Figure 30.8) is the basic offensive drive shot. It is accomplished by striking the ball with a vigorous upward forward motion. The ball should be struck in front of and to the right side of the body (if right-handed) when it is at or just past its maximum bounce. The racquet is tilted forward at the point of contact with the ball. The upward motion imparts the overspin. This shot, at first, is best played on deep or high-bouncing returns because it requires both skill and accuracy. Shifting the body weight forward adds power to the shot, as does rotating the arm backward at the elbow.

Forehand and backhand loop shots

Loop shots begin with the knees bent and the racquet pointing downward and below tabletop height (Figure 30.9). A long, high, looping, striking, or grazing of the ball when it is dropping allows considerable topspin to be placed on the ball. In turn, it will bounce high and deep off the table. Finish with the racquet head held high. Snapping the wrist at contact increases the spin and speed placed on the ball. The emphasis during the stroke may be either upward or forward, depending on the kind and amount of spin on the incoming ball.

Backhand drive

The backhand drive is similar to the forehand drive, except that it is often shorter because the arm may cross in front of

Figure 30.7. Watching the ball.

Figure 30.8. Completion of forehand drive.

the body if not turned sideways. The ball is hit in front of and slightly to the left side of the body (if right-handed) and preferably as it is rising. The wrist may be snapped at contact, but the racquet continues forward in the direction of the new ball path (Figure 30.10). The racquet is held nearly perpendicular; and as the ball is struck, the racquet rotates downward (clockwise) toward the tabletop.

Forehand chop

The forehand chop is primarily a defensive stroke. It is executed with a hatchet-chopping motion. The stroke starts from nearly shoulder height, whenever possible, hitting forward and downward with the top of the racquet blade open (tilted back away from the ball). The stroke is finished with the arm almost fully extended in front of the body. Cutting with the blade down behind and under the ball gives the ball a backspin as it leaves the face of the racquet. This stroke should be executed with considerable speed. Chop shots are primarily defensive returns.

Backhand chop

The backhand chop also requires that the racquet be tilted backward (open). It is like the forehand chop, except that it is a shorter stroke and employs stronger use of the forearm and wrist. The stroke is started at about chest height and ends at about waist height. This shot, like most shots, requires a great deal of practice to acquire a worthwhile degree of control and accuracy.

Drop shot

The drop shot is executed by moving the racquet as if beginning a drive, but stopping the forward motion of the racquet and opening its face just before hitting the ball and letting the ball hit the racquet, returning the ball just over the net. This shot should be used only occasionally as a change of pace, to catch an opponent off guard, or when an opponent has moved back from the table on a preceding shot.

Smash shot

The smash shot is what its name suggests. It is used on a higher-than-net bounce—the higher the better. It is hit straight forward and downward, with little or no spin, onto the opponent's court. Attempt it only when an advantageous situation presents itself. Play it accurately and put weight behind the smash. It is a kill, or point-making shot. Remember to avoid contact with the table.

Points to Remember

1. Vary your shot and strategy; make your opponent guess what stroke you will make.
2. Exploit your opponent's weakness and work toward eliminating yours.
3. Practice spins for control and accuracy.
4. Do not smash when a drive is more desirable and safer.
5. Concentrate on the ball.
6. Do not smash too soon or be overanxious.
7. Do not telegraph your intentions or your shot.
8. If shots are hitting the net too often, try an upward, lifting motion instead of a straightforward swing.
9. In a drive, be sure to follow through.
10. Vary your serves and returns.
11. Do not hit harder than your form justifies.
12. Always strive to perfect form.

Figure 30.9. Start of the backhand loop shot.

Figure 30.10. Finish of backhand drive shot.

13. Always assume that the opponent will return the ball.
14. Adhere to form and do not sacrifice it for speed or power; speed and power will naturally follow well-executed form and good technique.

Strategy

It is very important to recognize as early as possible the kind and amount of spin imparted to the ball by the opponent. Different shots produce different spins; consequently, the appropriate countershot must take this into account. Becoming skilled in this facet of the game requires considerable study and practice.

For singles play

Probably the safest strategy for both the defensive and the offensive games is similar to that of tennis: rely on the opponent to commit an error. Concentrate on returning the ball safely to the opponent's court. Vary the speed of returns. Try different shots and study the opponent's weaknesses and strong points. Size them up quickly and play to an opponent's weaknesses. Keep the opponent guessing, and avoid setting up easy shots. Keep the ball in play.

For doubles play

Essentially, strategy in doubles play is the same as in singles play. Alternating successive shots between team partners makes doubles play actually a singles game. Offensive strategy therefore consists of keeping the opponents running and off balance, as in tennis. Do not drift into a slow, deliberate game, but mix the type of shots and tempo of the game.

If one wins the toss at the start of the game, it is sound strategy to choose to receive first. This causes the opponents to determine who is to serve first, and the receiving team can then choose wisely who is to receive (the same player must receive from the same opponent throughout the game). Receiving first puts one in a strategic position in the possibly crucial closing moments of a close game.

Keep your eyes on the ball. Learn to react quickly in choosing which type of shot to make in each game situation. Use cross-court angling shots and keep opponents off balance. Constantly strive for a versatile, deceptive attack and defense to keep opponents from anticipating your shots in advance.

It is especially important to assume the correct playing position between shots. Ordinarily, a player, after hitting a shot, moves back away from the table to avoid blocking the partner's pathway to the ball while also remaining as close to the playing area as possible (Figure 30.11). Moving to one side or the other often results in being out of position when it is your turn to hit the ball.

TEACHING CONSIDERATIONS

1. Have students first practice bouncing the ball up and down on the forehand, backhand, and alternate sides of the racquet. In addition, hitting a ball off a wall from various distances, as well as having two students volley back and forth in the air without a table, is helpful practice.
2. Begin practice with two students at a table when possible.
3. Teach the grip and a simple courtesy serve (hitting the dropped ball as it bounces up from the table) to beginners. The objective is to be able to put the ball into play. Later teach the legal serve and spin.
4. Teach the ready position and forehand and backhand racquet positions. Let beginning students practice hitting the ball back and forth in a cooperative way before introducing specific offensive strokes. When the ball crosses the net at least eight times consecutively, students should be ready to begin keeping the ball low to the net and placing the ball at various spots on the table in game situations.
5. After basic ball control has been mastered, teach specific offensive and defensive shots and introduce spin shots.

Figure 30.11. Positioning for doubles play.

6. Teach singles rules before doubles rules.

7. Include an opportunity for game or gamelike play in each lesson. Give game play a focus in the beginning of the unit by changing the scoring or rules to encourage skill development (e.g., "Keep ball less than 6 inches [15 cm] above the net" or "The ball must bounce in the alternate side of the opponent's court").

8. Match students of equal ability for game play. In large groups, play for time rather than points so that games finish at the same time for rotation.

GLOSSARY

ace A point scored on a shot that is impossible for the receiver to return.

ad Advantage.

angle shot Moving a shot diagonally across the table, also called a crosscourt shot.

backhand Hitting the ball with the back of the hand facing the direction of movement.

backspin Revolving the ball the opposite way of its flight (counterclockwise spin); mainly used on defensive shots.

blade The racquet face minus any covering.

block A quick return performed by holding the racquet directly in the ball's path and blocking it soon after it bounces.

chop Hitting the ball downward on the back of the ball, giving the ball a backspin. Used primarily on defense when not close to the table.

closed racquet A position of the racquet where the top edge is pointing away from you.

dead A ball with no spin.

deep A ball that bounces very close to the endline.

deuce A tie game at 10–all; 2 points scored consecutively are needed to win.

drive Giving a stroke topspin by turning the racquet slightly forward as the ball is hit; hitting the ball with a closed racquet face.

drop shot A shot that barely crosses the net. It is most effective when an opponent is away from the table.

flat A ball without any spin, usually traveling very fast.

flip, or flick A return striking the tabletop near the net that is produced with considerable wrist action and has topspin.

follow-through Continuing the swing after hitting the ball.

forehand Hitting the ball with the palm of the hand facing the direction of movement.

kill shot See "smash."

let Playing the ball over; occurs when the ball hits the top of the net and passes over it on the serve, when the receiver is not ready, or when an accident prevents a good service or return.

loaded A ball imparted with a lot of spin.

loop A long sweeping upward motion that just grazes the ball and puts tremendous spin on it.

match A 2-of-3 or 3-of-5 games contest.

mixed doubles A game in which each team consists of one male and one female.

open racquet A position of the racquet where the top edge is pointing toward you.

penhold One of two major racquet grips. It is similar to holding a pen.

pips Small conical bits of rubber located on one side of a sheet of table tennis rubber.

playing surface The tabletop, including the edges.

points Games are to 11 points and must be won by 2 points.

push A backspin return of a backspin shot.

rally The serve and all intervening legal returns; it ends when a point is won.

rating A number assigned to competitive players that changes based on personal match results. The higher the number, the better the player.

rubber The generic term for the material used as a racquet covering.

score The server's score is always called first.

serve Used to put the ball in play.

shakehands One of two major racquet grips. It is similar to shaking hands.

smash Executing a high-speed shot, usually after receiving a high bounce.

spin The rotation of the ball.

topspin A forward-rotating ball (clockwise spin).

two-step footwork This starts with a short step taken with the foot facing the direction one is moving followed by a step with the other foot so that both feet move together.

USATT USA Table Tennis; the national governing body for the sport of table tennis in the United States.

volley Illegal stroking of the ball while it is in the air before it hits the table.

SUGGESTED READINGS

Boggan, T. 2010. *History of U.S. table tennis, Vol I-X.* Geneva, Switzerland, Below the Line Productions S.A.

Charyn, J. 2001. *Sizzling chops and devilish spins: Ping pong and the art of staying alive.* New York, NY: Four Walls Eight Windows.

English Table Tennis Association. 2006. *Know the game: Table tennis.* London, England: A & C Black Publishers.

McAfee, R. 2009. *Table tennis: Steps to success.* Champaign, IL: Human Kinetics. Contains over 120 drills and 140 illustrations.

The laws of table tennis. Current ed. Colorado Springs, CO: USA Table Tennis.

Messins, D. 2000. *Table tennis from A to Z.* Athens, Greece. Published by author.

Pollisco, R. 2009. *Superior table tennis: The art and science.* Published by author. www.sportdominance.com

Periodical

USA Table Tennis Magazine. Published by USA Table Tennis, One Olympic Plaza, Colorado Springs, CO 80909.

RESOURCES

Videos

Available at http://www.Alphatt.com

Two videos—*Modern table tennis 101* and *Modern table tennis 102.* See Appendix C for other video sources.

WEB SITES

ITTF Web site
   www.ittf.com

NCTTA
   www.nctta.org (national collegiate table tennis association)

Table-Tennis.Com
   www.table-tennis.com

USATT-Net
   www.usatt.org

31

Team Handball

After completing this chapter, the reader should be able to:

- Appreciate the evolution, development, and values of an Olympic sport that is gaining popularity in the United States
- Construct a team handball court
- Demonstrate knowledge and understanding of team handball rules
- Execute the fundamental skills of passing, running, dribbling, and shooting
- Demonstrate offensive and defensive principles of the game
- Teach a group of students how to play team handball

HISTORY

Team handball, as it is called in the United States to distinguish the fast-paced and popular Olympic sport from the four-wall court sport that is played in the United States, developed in Europe (Bohemia, Germany, Denmark, and Sweden) during the early 1900s. Handball, as it is known in the rest of the world, evolved from combining several middle-European games, including German raffball and torball and Danish handbold, which resulted in a new sport (field handball) that could be contested across international boundaries.

In 1928, the Amateur Handball Federation was formed by the representatives of 11 countries with the inaugural rules calling for 11 players on a side and for the sport to be played outdoors on soccer fields. In 1933, this version of handball, "field handball," was included in the events in the 1936 Berlin Olympics. This was the only time that this version of handball was included as part of the Olympic program. When the Olympics were resumed in London in 1948, field handball was not included, and the sport, for the most part, lay dormant until it was reinstated at the Munich Olympic Games in 1972.

Handball, as it is played today, developed in the Scandinavian countries, where the sport moved indoors to escape the severe winters of northern and eastern Europe. Due to a lack of indoor facilities that would accommodate the 11-person teams, the number of players on each team was reduced to seven—a goalkeeper and six court players. This is the version of handball that the International Handball Federation (IHF) embraced at its seminal meeting in 1946. At that time the IHF was comprised of 54 nations representing almost 3 million players. Handball was recognized as an international sport by the International Olympic Committee in 1965 and was included as a new Olympic event for men in 1972 at Munich and for women in 1976 at the Montreal Olympic Games.

Since its reinstatement in Munich, team handball has experienced growth all over the world and gained increasing popularity. In general, the most powerful handball teams have

been from Eastern European countries and the former Soviet Union. From 1972 to 1992, the gold medal in men's handball has been won by Yugoslavia (1972), the Soviet Union (1976), East Germany (1980), Yugoslavia (1984), the Soviet Union (1988), and the Unified team (1992). The women's handball gold medal has gone to the Soviet Union (1976 and 1980), Yugoslavia (1984), and South Korea (1988 and 1992). Asian countries, notably South Korea and China, are beginning to serve notice on the sport, as indicated by South Korea's gold medals in the 1988 and 1992 women's competition and silver in the men's competition at the 1988 Seoul Olympics.

At the 1996 Summer Olympic Games, Denmark won the women's gold medal while the United States women's team finished last out of eight teams. Croatia won the men's team gold and the host American men's team finished ninth. Significantly, the Atlanta Games served as a showcase for team handball to all of North America.

At the 2000 Summer Olympics in Sydney, Australia, Russia won the men's gold medal, Sweden won the silver, and Spain took home the bronze. In the women's competition, Denmark defeated Hungary and Norway earned the bronze.

The 2008 men's competition in the Beijing Games marked a shift from Eastern European dominance as the gold medal was won by France. Additionally, Iceland took the silver, and Spain won the bronze. The final results for the women showed Norway winning the gold over second-place Russia, and South Korea earning the bronze.

USA Team Handball (USATH) was originally formed as the United States Team Handball Federation (USTHF) in 1959, and is a member of the IHF and the Pan-American Handball Federation. In 2008, the USOC certified USA Team Handball as the new national governing body and the headquarters was moved from Colorado Springs, Colorado, to Salt Lake City, Utah. Regional offices are located in Illinois, California, Texas, and Florida.

The men's gold medal at the 2004 Summer Olympics in Athens, Greece, was won by Croatia. Germany won the silver, and Russia took home the bronze. In the women's competition, Denmark needed two overtime periods to defeat South Korea for the gold, and the bronze went to the Ukraine.

While rapidly expanding worldwide, team handball has grown at a modest but steady rate in the United States. During the past two decades, it has gained a large number of participants and enjoys its most avid following on the East Coast. Team handball's growing popularity is due to its fast, exciting action and low cost of participation in comparison with other team sports. As of July 2009, the IHF listed 166 member federations and approximately 20 million participants.

VALUES

Team handball is an excellent sport for physical education and recreation programs. The equipment required is minimal and relatively inexpensive. Existing facilities, such as basketball courts, can be modified to accommodate the sport.

Team handball is a fast-moving sport that can provide an intense cardiovascular workout. It requires motor skills common to other popular sports, including running, jumping, throwing, and catching. The rules are simple, and when played competitively, it ranks as one of the fastest and most demanding of team sports.

The sport may be played with as few as five and as many as seven players on each team. It is similar in concept to basketball, lacrosse, soccer, and water polo. The objective is to score a goal by moving the ball past the defensive team and throwing the ball past the goalkeeper into the goal. Dribbling, passing, and defensive techniques are similar to those used in basketball. A goal counts as 1 point.

Team handball can be modified to be played by 5 to 15 players on a team, depending on available space. It can be played by elementary school students (where it lends itself well to coed activity) as well as those at the junior high, secondary, and collegiate levels. Additionally, it is a tremendous intramural, collegiate, and recreational sport.

In summary, team handball is a sport for all seasons, ages, and those who are enthusiastic to participate in a vigorous and exciting game. It is easily learned, may be played indoors or outdoors, is adaptable to almost any location or environment, and can be modified to meet the needs of special populations.

EQUIPMENT

The equipment required is minimal. A basketball-type shoe may be used for indoor and outdoor play, and a cleated shoe may be used on grass. Team uniforms with special identification for the goalkeepers are necessary. Players may wish to wear knee and elbow pads and mouthguards, and goalkeepers may want to wear additional protective equipment.

The only other piece of equipment needed is a ball. The USA Team Handball ball requirements for men and youths over 16 are a weight of 15 to 16¾ ounces (425 to 475 gm) [IHF size 3] and a circumference of 23 to 24 inches (58 to 60 cm), while for women and male youths over 12 and female youths over 14, the ball must weigh 11½ to 13 ounces (325 to 375 gm) [IHF size 2] and have a circumference of 21 to 22 inches (54 to 56 cm). Balls for youths aged over 8 must weigh 10 to 11½ ounces (290 to 330 gm) [IHF size 1] and have a circumference between 19 and 21 inches (50 to 52 cm). Balls may be constructed with 12, 18, or 32 panels. At least two balls should be available at the beginning of a game. (When handballs are not available for physical education and recreational use, appropriately sized playground balls can be substituted.)

THE FIELD OR INDOOR COURT

The following discussion of the playing area reflects dimensions established by USA Team Handball, which allows for variation from the standard IHF rules. Precise international measurements can be found in the IHF rules, which may be obtained from the IHF or USATH.

The official indoor or outdoor field may be not more than 147 by 75 feet (44 by 22 m) and no less than 126 by 60 feet (38 by 18 m) (Figure 31.1). The field for international competition is 131 feet 4 inches by 65 feet 8 inches (40 by 20 m). An indoor basketball court can be modified without difficulty (Figure 31.2).

Located centrally on each goal line is a goal 6 feet 8 inches (2 m) high and 10 feet (3 m) wide. The goal is usually made of 3 by 3-inch wood and pipe, fitted with a nylon net tensioned so that the ball cannot immediately rebound (Figure 31.3). In front of each goal are two semicircles. The inside arc (the goal area line or the 6-meter line) identifies the goal area and is a solid line drawn at a radius of 20 feet (6 m) from the goal. The next arc is the free-throw or 9-meter line. It is drawn as an interrupted line parallel to and outside the goal area line, 3 meters farther from the goal. Two marks are drawn directly in front of each goal—the 7-meter mark (or penalty mark) is at a distance of 23 feet (7 m) from the goal while the other mark lies between the penalty mark and the goal at a distance of 13 feet (4 m) from the goal. When a player is awarded a penalty throw, the mark at 13 feet (4 m) identifies the closest the goalkeeper may approach toward the penalty shooter. Midway between the goal lines a centerline is drawn, and on the sideline closest to the players' benches each team's substitution area is delineated by a 6-inch (15-cm) hash mark that is 14 feet 7 inches (4.45 m) from the centerline. The width of all the lines in marking the court is 2 inches (5 cm). A complete diagram of court dimensions with all markings is illustrated in Figure 31.1.

RULES

The detailed IHF "Rules of the Game" along with clarifications and depictions of the officials' signals are available at http://www.ihf.info/upload/PDF-Download/rules_english.pdf.

Officials

There are two referees who are in charge of the game. Both have the right to warn and disqualify players, and their decisions are final. The most frequently used referee signals are illustrated in Figure 31.4.

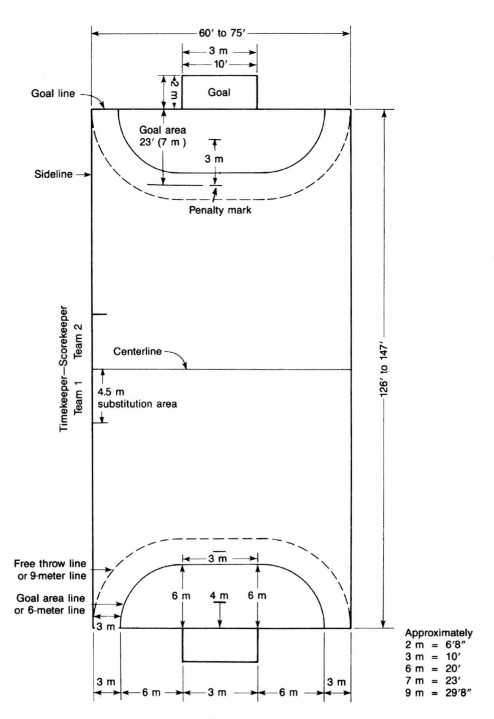

Figure 31.1. Team handball field dimensions and markings.

The field referee is stationed behind the play. The field referee's duties are to announce penalties, give warnings, and order suspensions and disqualifications. The field referee concentrates on the player with the ball and that player's opponent or marker. Responsibilities also include checking the proper distance of the defense on free throws. The decision of the field referee prevails over the goal referee on contradictory decisions.

The goal referee's positioning should be ahead of the play and on the goal line. His or her duties include enforcing goal area rules; whistling penalty throws, goals scored, and corner throws; and supervising throw-offs and throw-outs.

In addition to the two referees, a scorekeeper and a timekeeper are required. These officials are responsible for controlling time, monitoring substitutes entering and leaving the field of play, keeping the time for suspensions, and

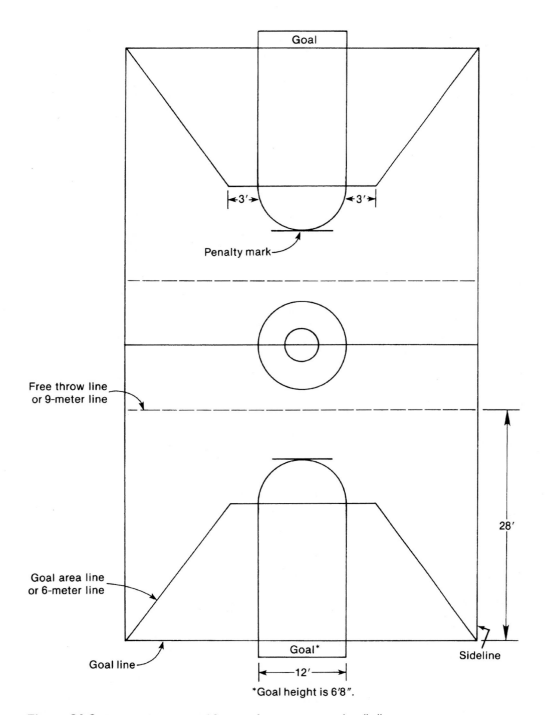

Goal

←3'→   ←3'→

Penalty mark

Free throw line
or 9-meter line

28'

Goal area line
or 6-meter line

Goal line

Goal*

Sideline

←——12'——→

*Goal height is 6'8".

Figure 31.2. Basketball court modifications for use as a team handball court

generally helping the referees by keeping them abreast of these concerns.

Duration of Game

Game duration can be adjusted to accommodate age, gender, and competitive variables. Competitive conditions include official USA Team Handball games and tournament competitions play. Time periods for official team handball games are as follows:

Players 16 years of age and above play two 30-minute periods with a 10-minute halftime; youths aged 12 to 16 play two 25-minute periods with a 10-minute halftime, while youths from 8 to 12 play two 20-minute periods with a 10-minute intermission. In competitions where teams may play several games during a 1- or 2-day tournament, rules allow for games without intermission—adults play two 15-minute periods, while juniors and all other teams play two 10-minute periods.

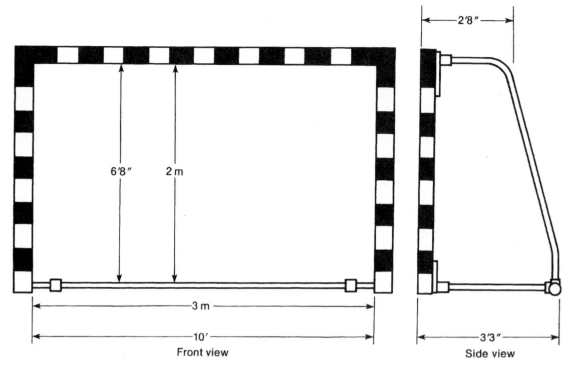

Figure 31.3. Team handball goal specifications.

Each team is entitled to one 1-minute timeout per half. There are, however, no timeout allocations during overtime periods of play.

In case of a tie at the end of regulation play, there is a provision for two 5-minute periods for overtime with a 1-minute break. If a winner is not decided by the end of two overtime sessions, the outcome may be decided by a 7-meter-throwing tiebreaker. In the tiebreaker, each team chooses 5 players to take alternating throws. Court players and goalkeepers are both eligible to be nominated. If the score remains tied following one tiebreaker, a second tiebreaker follows; however, the winner is decided when one team holds an advantage when both teams have had the same number of throws.

No players may be added to the roster for the overtime periods, and only players eligible during the game may be nominated for the tiebreaker. Players may be disqualified during the tiebreaker for significant or repeated unsportsmanlike conduct.

Number of Players, Substitutions, and Suspension

The game may be played with 5 to 15 players of either or both sexes. An official USA Team Handball team has 14 players—12 court players with only 6 playing at a time, and 2 goalkeepers with only 1 playing at a time. The positions of the players are goalkeeper, center halfback, right and left halfbacks, center forward, and right and left wings.

Substitution is from the bench area near midcourt. Once a court player is off the playing field, a substitute may enter. Substitutes need not notify the timekeeper. The procedure is the same for the goalkeeper, but the goalkeeper substitute must have a distinctive uniform. Illegal substitution may result in a free throw or penalty throw for the opponent.

Players may receive a warning, a suspension from play, or disqualification, depending on the severity of the infraction. A warning carries no penalty, but a second similar infraction results in a suspension. Suspensions are for two minutes, but flagrant violations may result in 4-minute penalties. Disqualifications result in the player being removed from the court for the remainder of the game, but after 2 minutes a substitute player (who is eligible) may enter the game.

Rules Governing Court Players

1. A player may hold the ball for up to 3 seconds, pass, shoot, dribble, or run three steps with the ball.
2. Players may not double dribble, hold the ball for more than 3 seconds, kick the ball, or travel (take more than three steps with the ball) (penalty: free throw).
3. Passive play or stalling is not permitted (referee's judgment).
4. A defensive player may obstruct an opposing player by using the body or arms. A player is not permitted to strike, grab, or tackle an opponent, and the ball must be the object of attack by the defensive players.

Figure 31.4. Team handball referee signals.

5. No player except the goalkeeper may dive for a ball lying or rolling on the ground.

Rules Governing Goalkeeper

1. The goalkeeper may defend the goal in any way using the hands, feet, and body.
2. Usual time and step restrictions are placed on the goalkeeper with possession of the ball.
3. The goalkeeper is free to move outside the goal area anytime without the ball, but must then abide by the rules for other players.
4. The goalkeeper may not touch the ball when it is stationary or rolling on the floor outside the goal area while he or she is inside the goal area.
5. The goalkeeper is prohibited from leaving the goal area when in control of the ball (penalty: free throw).
6. The goalkeeper may not re-enter the goal area from the playing area with the ball (penalty: 7-meter throw).
7. When the goalkeeper recovers a blocked or missed shot for a throw-out, opponents can block it from outside the 6-meter line, a goal can be scored directly from it, and the goalkeeper cannot touch the ball again until it has been touched by another player.
8. A court player substituting for a goalkeeper must notify the official before entering the goal area (penalty: 7-meter throw). This court player cannot enter the goal area until the goalkeeper is off the court (penalty: 7-meter throw).
9. The ball may not be thrown to a player's own goalkeeper while the goalkeeper is in his or her goal area (penalty: 7-meter throw).

Start of Play

The game officially must be started with seven players per team: six court players and one goalkeeper. A coin toss determines the option of side or throw-off, which places the ball into play. The game starts within 3 seconds after the referee blows the whistle. All players must begin on their own half of the court. A goal cannot be scored from a throw-off.

A throw-off is taken from the center of the court in any direction, typically to one's own team. All players must be in their respective halves of the court when the throw-off is taken, the opposing players being at a distance of at least 10 feet (3 m) from the ball. Whenever a goal is scored, play begins again at center court with the team that conceded the goal taking a throw-off. When taking a throw-off, throw-in, free throw, or 7-meter throw, the thrower must keep part of one foot in constant contact with the floor. The player may, however, repeatedly lift and put down the other foot.

Ball Out-of-Bounds

A ball is not out-of-bounds until the entire ball crosses the goal line or sideline. A ball crossing the sideline is put back into play with a throw-in by the team that did not last touch the ball before it went out-of-bounds. A throw-in must be executed from outside the sidelines, with one foot remaining stationary during the throw. The ball may be thrown with one or two hands. A goal cannot be scored from a throw-in.

A ball crossing the goal line outside the goal and last touched by the offensive team, or touched by the goalkeeper on a shot on goal when the goalkeeper was the only defender touching the ball, results in goalkeeper's throw. The goalkeeper executes the throw-out from within the goal area in whatever manner is desired. A goal cannot be scored directly from a throw-out. Opposing players must stay behind the 9.9-yard (9-m) line on a throw-out.

When a ball crosses the goal line outside the goal, and was last touched by a member of the defensive team other than the goalkeeper, a throw-in is awarded to the offensive team (Figure 31.5).

Fouls—Common (Penalty: Free Throw)

Common fouls are called for such violations as faulty substitution, faulty throw-in, intentionally playing across goal line or sideline, and body contact or striking an opponent that results in loss of possession or failure to complete the play. Furthermore, the defender must be between the player and the goal. These violations result in the fouled team being awarded a free throw. If contact is not too blatant or the defender had good defensive position, a foul is not always called. Free throws are also awarded for double dribbling; taking more than three steps with the ball; holding the ball more than three seconds; offensive player charges; illegal picking, holding, or pushing; or unnecessarily rough play.

Fouls—Flagrant (Penalty: 7-Meter Throw)

Flagrant fouls are called for violations such as taking the ball away from a player; obstruction with arms, hands, or legs; grabbing an opponent; pushing or forcing an opponent into the goal area; and intentionally shooting or throwing the ball at an opponent. These fouls result in the awarding of a penalty shot to the opponent. If the foul is severe, by the referee's judgment, the player may be suspended from the game.

Free Throw

In a free throw the ball is put into play at the point of the infraction. If the foul occurs between the 6.6- and 9.9-yard (6- and 9-m) lines, however, the ball is put into play from the 9.9-yard (9-m) line closest to the point of infraction. All offensive players must be outside the 9.9-yard (9-m) line, and all defensive players must be at least 10 feet (3 m) from the ball. A direct shot at the goal and a pass are the options for a free throw.

7-Meter Throw

The 7-meter throw is a free shot at the opponent's goal from the penalty mark (7-meter line) with only the goalkeeper defending and being at least 10 feet (3 m) from the thrower until the shot is taken. Any player may take the shot, and one

Figure 31.5. Player executing a throw-in.

foot must be stationary at all times during the throw. The shot must be taken within 3 seconds after the referee blows the whistle. All other players must be outside the 9.9-yard (9-m) line (Figure 31.6).

Goal Area

Legal entry

1. Goalkeeper is legal in the goal area.
2. A court player may not enter the goal area except after playing the ball when no advantage is gained.

Penalties for illegal entry

1. A court player in possession of the ball in the goal area (penalty: free throw).
2. A court player not in possession but gaining an advantage (penalty: free throw).
3. A court player gaining defensive advantage (penalty: 7-meter throw).

FUNDAMENTAL SKILLS AND TECHNIQUES

Inasmuch as team handball is similar to basketball in terms of running, dribbling, passing, and taking shots on goal, many of the basic skills that should be practiced parallel those of basketball.

Passing

Passing is basic to the game and is a good skill with which to begin a program. Passes may be made with one hand or two. Beginners should master the chest or push pass, bounce pass, overhead pass, shovel or underhand pass, baseball pass, reverse pass, and hook pass (Figure 31.7). Advanced players may be able to use the close hand-off pass, the jump pass, the behind-the-shoulder pass, and the wrist pass (Figure 31.8). A handball is about the size of a softball, and beginning players tend to want to grip the ball, which is an incorrect technique for control. The ball should rest in the hand on the fingertips, and considerable wrist snap should be used in passing. Players should be reminded to make short, crisp passes, and to pass frequently. Just as in basketball, a good passing team will have a distinct advantage over a group of individuals that underestimates the value of good passing.

Shooting

Although team handball shots are for the most part different than those in basketball, there are many similarities and several of the shot names are the same. Shots that are similar to those in basketball and may be practiced with some technical changes are jump shots, dive shots, lob shots, underhand shots, and any of the twisting moves that might be used with

Figure 31.6. Player taking a 7-meter throw.

Figure 31.7. Passes. A, Bounce pass. B, Baseball pass. C, Hook pass.

dunk shots. Changes in technique include not gripping the ball and using a great deal of wrist snap and strong forearm moves similar to those used in throwing a softball. It is preferable for players to learn to shoot with one hand rather than two in order to shoot with optimal power. Furthermore, jump shots following a run are desirable. Finally, players should learn to shoot at the high and low corners of the goal (Figure 31.9), to shoot while diving, and to utilize bounced shots. See Figure 31.10 for illustrations of various shots.

Dribbling

The ball may be bounced once or repeatedly with one hand. As soon as the ball is held by one or both hands, it must be played within three seconds or no more than three steps. As

Figure 31.8. Advanced passes. A, Close hand-off pass. B, Jump pass. C, Behind-the-shoulder pass. D, Wrist pass.

Figure 31.9. Player taking a shot at the goal.

in basketball, it is important that, when dribbling, the body is low and protecting the ball from the defensive players and the head is up to watch for an opening in which to pass or shoot. Remember that a pass can move the ball down the court much faster than a dribble, so one should look for the pass before taking the dribble (Figure 31.11).

Running

Running is a key component in team handball, so it is important that players are in sound condition. The player able to help the team with or without the ball is the best kind of team player. Agility drills for quickness in changing directions and lateral movement are important, but time should also be devoted to promoting aerobic and anaerobic endurance, as well as overall strength, power, and flexibility.

Offensive Play

The three basic offensive player positions in team handball are the wing player, circle runner, and back-court player. Each position has responsibilities.

The wing player (usually two) should be quick and agile and able to lead the fast-break attack. This player attacks the goal when shooting and should be able to protect the ball. The circle runner is usually the biggest and strongest player on the court and is generally a blocker, setting picks for the wing players and back-court players. The circle runner (usually only one) needs strength to handle the ball in heavy traffic and coordinate moves with the other players. The back-court players (usually three) should be strong, hard throwers who can pass, run, dribble, and shoot well. These players should be the best all-around athletes on the court and usually provide most of the team scoring.

The most basic offensive setup is called the 3–3 attack (Figure 31.12). The back-court players are the ball handlers and the playmakers. The wings and circle runner continuously move around the arc trying to set screens and picks to create an open scoring opportunity for any member of the attacking team. There are many options that can be created from this basic attack system.

Just as in basketball, there are set plays in team handball, and they rely heavily on players setting screens and picks for teammates to take shots at the goal. Offensively, players should focus on total team movement, remain spread out, think pass before dribble, move the ball quickly, and always pose a scoring threat.

Because defensive teams employ either a one-on-one or zone defense and follow many of the principles of basketball defense, the offensive team should practice against both of these defensive alignments.

Defensive Play

Most defensive schemes in team handball involve the positioning of defenders between the free-throw line and the goal area line. The 6–0 arrangement is the most common defensive system utilized (Figure 31.13). This is a combination of a zone and a one-on-one defense. Each player has an individual responsibility in addition to helping his or her teammates. Like any team sport using a basic defense, there are a large number of options that can be developed to counter the offense being run by the opposing team. The basic defense patterns are the one-on-one defense and the zone defense. In one-on-one defense, each player is responsible for one opponent. In zone defense, each player is responsible for a zone or designated area on the court. A zone defense is designed to prevent close shots at the goal and to force the opponents to shoot from much farther away. Team members must continually communicate to make each system successful.

In summary, each defender should strive to stay between the goal and his or her designated opponent; the defense should shift as a unit; no defense will fit all offensive systems; the defender should not jump too soon when attempting to block a shot or pass (Figure 31.14); and constant communication between defenders is necessary.

Goalkeeping

Goalkeeping is probably the most important and difficult position in team handball. A goalkeeper should be quick, unafraid of the ball, possess good hand-eye and foot-eye coordination, and be able to throw the ball to start the fast break. The goalkeeper should not catch the ball unless it

Figure 31.10. Shots. A, Jump shot. B, Dive shot. C, Lob shot. D, Side shot. E, Reverse shot. F, Underhand shot.

Figure 31.11. Player dribbling toward the goal in a team handball game adapted as a class activity.

is thrown directly at him or her, but should block shots by knocking them down, to the side, or over the goal line. The team that has a talented and well-trained goalkeeper has a great advantage during match play (Figure 31.15).

BEGINNING ACTIVITIES AND DRILLS

1. Practice dribbling with each hand; dribble while moving; dribble in and out of cones or around classmates; play tag while dribbling.
2. Practice throwing and catching: overhand throws, underhand passes, reverse passes, bounce passes.

3. Position students in pairs approximately 30 feet (9 m) apart to combine the above throws and catches. Thrower jogs forward to throw, then retreats before catching partner's return throw. Increase the distance between partners as students' proficiency and strength increase.
4. Position two lines of three to four students approximately 40 to 50 feet (12 to 15 m) apart facing the other group. First player in line 1 performs a 3-step jog toward the other line, jumps and throws to first player in line 2, then continues to the end of

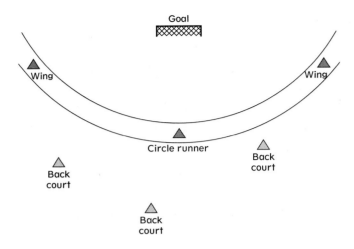

Figure 31.12. Basic offensive attack.

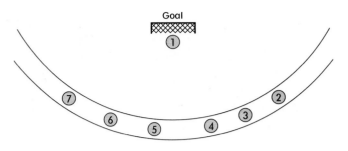

Figure 31.13. Common defensive arrangement.

line 2. First player in line 2 catches the thrown ball, then performs 3-step footwork, jump, and throw to student in line 1 and continues to the end of line 1. The drill continues with students moving from line to line—catch the ball, execute the 3-step footwork, jump and throw, and continue to the end of the other line.

TEACHING CONSIDERATIONS

1. Ensure that the size and weight of handballs used in class are appropriate for the students by following the recommendations stipulated in the rules of team handball.
2. The basic skills of team handball are very similar to those of basketball with the exception of shooting. Some court placement strategies are similar to those of soccer. See the chapters on basketball and soccer for additional teaching suggestions.
3. Students should practice footwork in combination with passing and shooting. They must also learn to jump before shooting.
4. Maximize opportunities for practice and play by organizing students in small groups or teams. Use several small courts (or outside areas) with fewer players rather than a large area with many players.

Figure 31.14. A defensive block.

Figure 31.15. Goalie blocking a practice shot on goal.

5. Since the ball is lighter and smaller than a basketball, more students will be able to throw longer and harder passes than in basketball. Practice passing ahead of moving players and moving into open spaces to receive a pass in consort with two or three players. Stress the pass (rather than the dribble) as the quickest way to move the ball down the court.

6. Gradually add defensive players to practice moving the ball down the court (three-on-one and three-on-two situations). Initially, scoring can include passing the ball across the endline or into an undefended goal. Later a goalkeeper should be included, and three-on-three and four-on-four games can be played.

7. Supplement goalkeeping practice with play around the goal area line. Students must become familiar with the unique skills and strategies that are required by the sport.

8. When teams are ready for more than four-on-four players, introduce specific player roles (other than goalkeeper) if they have not begun to emerge from four-on-four play (wing, circle runner, and back-court player).

9. Introduce zone defense (particularly on larger courts) after students have mastered the basics of one-on-one play. Place as much emphasis on defense as on offense.

10. Provide opportunity for gamelike play each lesson (simplified in the beginning and gradually increasing in complexity). Encourage skill and strategy development by modifying the rules to reinforce the lesson content (e.g., no dribbling, shooting only after a specified number of passes, or scoring from the sides only).

11. Game-condition scrimmages should be frequent with positive feedback on each player's technique and tactical understanding of the game.

GLOSSARY

common foul Violations such as illegal substitutions, illegal throw-in, illegal body contact, double dribble, and more than three steps with the ball (penalty: free throw).

court player A team player other than the goalkeeper.

defensive player A player whose team does not possess the ball.

dive shot A means of scoring by launching the body into the air toward the goal while making the throw.

flagrant foul Violations such as rough body contact and unsportsman-like play (penalty: 7-meter throw and possible suspension or disqualifications).

free throw Results from a common foul and is used to put the ball back into play from the point of the infraction, unless the infraction occurs between the 6.6- and 9.9-yard (6 and 9 m) lines, in which case the ball is put in play on the 9.9-yard (9 m) line nearest the point of infraction.

goalkeeper The only person who can legally play the ball in the goal area and use the feet.

goalkeeper throw When the goalkeeper puts the ball back into play after he or she blocks or catches a shot that does not cross the goal line.

held ball A ball held more than 3 seconds.

offensive player A player whose team possesses the ball.

7-meter throw Results from a flagrant foul and is a free shot at the goal from the penalty mark with only the goalkeeper defending.

throw-in Used by the team that did not cause the ball to go across the sideline to put the ball back into play. Also used by the offensive team to put the ball back into play after it crossed the outer goal line and was last touched by a defensive player other than the goalkeeper, except when a shot was taken.

throw-off Putting the ball into play at the beginning of the game and after any score. It is taken from the center of the court.

SUGGESTED READINGS

Clanton, R., and Dwight, M. 1997. *Team handball: Steps to success.* Champaign, IL: Human Kinetics.

Frick, T. 2001. *Team handball.* Kingston, ON, Canada: Rainbow Horizons Publishers.

Hamil, B., and LaPoint, J. 1994. *Team handball, skills, strategies and training.* Dubuque, IA: Eddie Bowers Publishing.

International Handball Federation. (2010). *Rules of the game.* International Handball Federation. Retrieved April 16, 2009 from www.ihf.info/TheGame/BylawsandRegulations/abid/88/Default.aspx

USATH. (2008). *USA Team Handball competition rule book.* Retrieved October 9, 2010 from http://assets.teamusa.org/assets/documents/attached_file/filename/30594/USA_Team_Handball_Competition_Rule_Book_Revised_September_2010.pdf

WEB SITES

Chicago Inter Handball Club
  http://www.chicagointerhandball.org/
European Handball Federation Web sites
  http://www.eurohandball.com/
  http://www.eurohandball.com/publications
  http://www.eurohandball.com/article/011823/Annual+Mpeg+publications+on+the+internet
IHF Web site
  http://www.ihf.info/Home/tabid/40/Default.aspx
USA Team Handball Web site
  http://usateamhandball.org/

32 | Tennis

After completing this chapter, the reader should be able to:

- Have a basic knowledge of the historical development of tennis
- Understand the proper selection of equipment
- Know the rules and scoring of tennis and understand the etiquette of play
- Perform and demonstrate the fundamental skills for effective playing technique
- Know the principles of strategy for competitive play
- Teach others by using sound instructional and practice techniques

HISTORY

There is evidence that a form of tennis was played in the ancient Greek and Roman Empires and that a game in which a ball was batted back and forth with a type of racquet may have been played in the Orient more than 2,000 years ago. Still other indications are that tennis may have begun in Egypt or Persia 500 years before the Christian era.

Despite these obscure ancient origins, there is no doubt that a tennislike game was played in thirteenth-century France. Called *jeu de paume* (literally, "game of the hand"), it was first a bare-handed game of hitting a stuffed cloth bag over a rope. When paddles, and later racquets, were added, the game grew steadily in popularity. By the close of the fourteenth century, it was also well established in England.

It is believed the game received its present name when English visitors heard French officials call *tenez*, which means to resume play, an expression similar to "play ball" used by baseball umpires. The English thought *tenez* was the correct name for *le paume*. In time, the English word *tennis* was substituted.

At the beginning of the fifteenth century, there were 1,400 professional players in France, and yet the first standardized written rules of tennis did not appear until 1599. The game reached a peak of popularity in England and France during the sixteenth and seventeenth centuries; but soon after, the game almost disappeared due to the civil war in England and the French Revolution.

What remnant of the game was left in England seems next to appear at a garden party given in 1873 by British Army Major Walter C. Wingfield. His guests were introduced to a game called "sphairistike," later to become more descriptively referred to as "lawn tennis." In attendance at the party was an army officer who took the game with him to Bermuda as a diversion for the British garrison stationed there. Miss Mary Outerbridge, who was vacationing on the island during the winter of 1873–74, became intrigued with the game and took equipment with her upon returning to her New York home.

As a member of the Staten Island Cricket and Baseball Club, Outerbridge received permission to lay out a court in an unused corner of the grounds. Within a few years, tennis was included as an activity at nearly every major cricket club in the East, and soon it became a sport of the masses. But the rules were diverse, so in 1880 Outerbridge's brother called a meeting in New York to establish a standard code. An outcome of that meeting was the establishment of the United States Tennis Association (USTA), still the ruling body of American tennis today.

Later that same year, the first tournament for the National Championship of the United States was held at Newport, Rhode Island. The site was moved in 1915 to Long Island, and in 1978 it was relocated to its present site at the National Tennis Center in Queens, New York City. This tournament is now called the U.S. Open. The U.S. Open, the Australian Open, the French Open, and Wimbledon are the four "grand slam" events on the professional tour.

Tennis was played at the Olympics for the first time at the 1924 games in Paris, France. The singles and doubles gold medals were won by players from the United States: Vincent Richards won the men's gold, and Helen Wills won the woman's gold. In the doubles, Richards paired with Frank Hunter and Wills teamed with Hazel Wightman to win the gold medals. The 1996 Atlanta Olympics attracted the very best American tennis players, because it was the first Games held in the United States that also allowed professional players to compete. Andre Agassi and Lindsay Davenport, both from the United States, won the gold medals in singles play. In doubles, Australians Todd Woodbridge and Mark Woodforde won the men's gold medal while Americans Gigi Fernandez and Mary Joe Fernandez won the women's gold. International players did well at the 2000 Sydney Olympics with Yevgeny Kafelnikov from Russia winning the men's gold medal in singles, and Venus Williams of the United States winning the women's gold. In men's doubles, Canadian pair Daniel Nestor and Sebastien Lareau won the gold medal and

Venus Williams teamed with her sister Serena to win the women's gold medal.

At the 2004 Athens Games, athletes from the nations of Chile and China surprisingly took home several medals from the tennis competition. Chile had never won a gold medal in any Olympic sport, yet players from that nation went away from the tennis event with two golds and a bronze. Nicolas Massu won the men's gold medal by defeating Mardy Fish of the United States in a five-set final match. In the longest three-set singles match ever played at the Olympics, Fernando Gonzalez, also from Chile, defeated Taylor Dent from the United States 6–2, 4–6, 16–14 for the bronze medal. Massu added to his singles medal by winning the doubles gold medal along with compatriot Fernando Gonzalez by defeating Nicolas Kiefer and Rainer Schuettler (Germany) 6–2, 4–6, 3–6, 7–6 (7–5), 6–4. China also won its first Olympic tennis gold medal when its team won the women's doubles. The surprise gold medalists were Ting Li and Tian Tian Sun, who defeated Conchita Martinez and Virginia Ruano Pascual (Spain) in the final. In the bronze medal match, Paola Suarez and Patricia Tarabini (Argentina) defeated Shinobu Asagoe and Ai Sugiyama (Japan) 6–3, 6–3. In women's singles, the favorites going into the Games met expectations when top-ranked Justine Henin-Hardenne (Belgium) defeated second-ranked Amelie Mauresmo (France) 6–3, 6–3 for the gold medal, while Alicia Molik (Australia) defeated Anastasia Myskina (Russia) 6–3, 6–4 the bronze medal.

At the 2008 Olympic games in Beijing, China, Rafael Nadal won the first-ever tennis gold medal by a Spaniard with his 6–3, 7–6 (2), 6–3 win over Fernando Gonzalez (Chile) in men's singles. Novak Djokovic (Serbia) won the bronze medal with a tight 6–3, 7–6 (4) win over James Blake (United States). In women's singles, Elena Dementieva (Russia) defeated Dinara Safina (Russia) 3–6, 7–5, 6–3 in the gold medal match while Vera Zvonareva (Russia) took the bronze by defeating Li Na (China) 6–0, 7–5. The last time a team from one country won all three medals in tennis was at the 1908 Games in London, where British players swept men's indoor singles, men's doubles, and women's singles play.

Roger Federer and Stanislas Wawrinka (Switzerland) won the gold in men's doubles with a 6–3, 6–4, 6–7 (4), 6–3 victory over Simon Aspelin and Thomas Johansson (Sweden). Bob Bryan and Mike Bryan (United States), who were favored to win the gold, took the bronze medal instead with a 3–6, 6–3, 6–4 win over Arnaud Clement and Michael Llodra (France). Serena and Venus Williams won their second career Olympic gold medal in the women's doubles when they defeated Spanish teammates Anabel Medina Garrigues and Virginia Ruano Pascual 6–2, 6–0. The bronze medal was won by Yan Zi and Zheng Jie from China with a 6–2, 6–2 win over Ukrainian sisters Alona Bondarenko and Kateryna Bondarenko.

With his grueling 5–7, 7–6 (6), 7–6 (5), 3–6, 16–14 win over Andy Roddick (United States) at the 2009 Wimbledon tournament, Roger Federer won his 15th Grand Slam singles title and broke the previous record held by Pete Sampras (United States). The four Grand Slam tennis tournaments consist of the Australian Open (which dates back to 1905), the French Open (which dates back to 1891), Wimbledon (which dates back to 1877), and the U.S. Open (which dates back to 1881). Along the way toward his 15th title, Federer appeared in 21 Grand Slam finals and reached the semi-finals or better in the last 22 Grand Slam tournaments. He also holds the record of reaching 10 consecutive Grand Slam finals and 17 of the last 18 Grand Slam tournaments finals (through the 2009 U.S. Open). Given Federer's record of accomplishments, many tennis analysts and players consider him to be the greatest male tennis player of all time.

VALUES AND REASONS FOR POPULARITY

Tennis is a popular lifetime sport throughout the world for the following reasons:

1. It can be played by able-bodied individuals as well as many individuals with disabilities. The United States Tennis Association has a division devoted to the promotion of wheelchair tennis that offers instruction, league play, and tournaments.
2. It can be played by both men and women and is well-suited for mixed-gender competition.
3. It requires only two or four players.
4. It can be played indoors and outdoors.
5. It can provide a strenuous physical workout, requiring cardiovascular endurance, quick movement, and good flexibility.
6. Public and private courts are widely available.
7. Tennis lessons are widely available for players of all skill levels.
8. Organized leagues and tournaments for recreational players are available in most communities.
9. Equipment costs are relatively low.
10. It can be played both as an individual and a team sport.

EQUIPMENT

Clothing

Historically, tennis attire has been both fashionable and functional. For many years tennis attire was distinguished by its "all white" quality and its ability to signal the wearer's social status. Today, there is a much greater emphasis on the functional aspect of tennis apparel; clothes are made from microfibers designed to wick away perspiration, keeping the player more comfortable, and shoes are designed to fit well, absorb shock, and resist wear.

Ball

Tennis balls are made of two rubber cups molded together, covered with a colored felt, and inflated to a specific pressure. Most manufacturers produce a normal and a high-altitude ball. The high-altitude ball is inflated to a lower pressure than the standard ball for better playing characteristics at elevations above 4,000 feet (1,219 m). Manufacturers have experimented with a variety of tennis ball colors; of these, optic yellow is most widely available and is the color used on the professional tour.

Racquet

For many years, tennis racquets were made of wood and there was little variation in the size or shape of the frames. By the late 1970s, metal racquets began to replace wood racquets, and soon after that frames made of composite materials began replacing metal. Today, most tennis racquets are made from fibers such as graphite, Kevlar, or fiberglass.

With the introduction of the radical Profile widebody racquet in the mid-1980s, Wilson Sporting Goods started a revolution in frame design and development. The main advantage of the widebody racquet is that it is more rigid longitudinally, and therefore more powerful than a standard racquet design. The main disadvantages of widebody racquets are that they transfer more shock to the arm when striking the ball and strings tend to wear out quickly.

Since then, manufacturers have tried to produce frames with better playing characteristics by continuously modifying features such as frame width, length, and composition. In recent years, manufacturers have designed racquet frames with larger "sweet spots" so that shots hit off-center can still generate power. This is accomplished primarily with a triangular-shaped frame that both makes the sweet spot wider and moves it toward the head of the racquet.

Strings

Tennis racquet strings range from 14 (thick) to 18 (thin) gauge diameter, with 16 gauge the most popular size for recreational players. Strings are made from two basic materials: natural gut (cattle intestines) or synthetics. Professional players still primarily use natural gut strings; however, most recreational players use synthetic strings, which are normally more durable and less costly. Most tennis racquets are

strung with 55 to 70 pounds (25 to 32 kg) of tension. Higher tensions work well for players who hit the ball hard, while mid-range tensions are best for most recreational players. Because tennis racquet strings lose resiliency and wear out over time, they need to be replaced occasionally. The need to replace strings depends on frequency and level of play. In general, strings should be replaced annually for moderately active players. Active players typically have the strings replaced several times a year.

Grip

The area on the racquet where the player places his or her hand is called the *grip*. Adult tennis racquet grips range from 4 to 5 inches (10.2 to 12.7 cm) in circumference, measured in steps of ⅛ inch (0.32 cm). For adult males, common grip sizes are from 4½ to 4¾ inches (11.5 to 12.1 cm). For adult women, 4 to 4½ inches (10.2 to 11.5 cm) are most common. The grips on children's racquets are smaller, typically from 3 to 4 inches (7.65 to 10.2 cm). A good way to determine correct grip size is to hold a racquet using an eastern forehand grip (Figure 32.1); the thumb should just touch the top knuckle of the second finger. A proper grip is important because a grip that is too small can cause the racquet to twist in the hand when the ball is struck off-center, whereas a grip that is too large can make it difficult to hold on to the racquet while hitting the ball.

Courts

Most tennis court surfaces are constructed from one of four types of material: clay, grass, cement or asphalt, and synthetic rubber. In the United States, public courts are generally cement or asphalt owing to the durability and low maintenance costs of these surfaces. Clay courts are still common in Europe, South America, and the southeastern United States. In recent years, clay courts have regained some popularity in other regions of the United States as well because they are less stressful on the body and easier on tennis balls and shoes than hard courts. In addition, clay is particularly

A
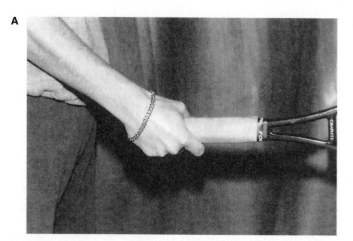

B
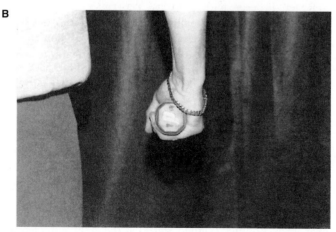

Figure 32.1. Eastern forehand grip. A, Side view. B, Back view.

suited for match play because the ball tends to bounce rather high, allowing a player more time to get in position to play a return. As a result, rallies are longer and more involved than on faster courts. Grass courts have the advantage of providing a cool and soft surface that is easier on the body and equipment; however, high maintenance costs and low durability limit the availability of these courts. Grass courts are most often found at private clubs and resorts. Synthetic rubber court surfaces are primarily used for professional tournaments conducted indoors in multipurpose arenas or for gymnasiums such as those at universities.

Most tennis courts are constructed and lined for both singles and doubles play. A few tennis courts are lined for singles play only. Some professional tournaments, primarily indoor events, also use singles-only courts.

Dimensions

1. Singles court: 78 × 27 feet (23.8 × 8.23 m)
2. Doubles court: 78 × 36 feet (23.8 × 10.97 m) (4½ foot [1.37 m] alley added to each side)
3. Height of net at center: 3 feet (0.914 m), commonly measured by taking the length of the racquet plus the width of the racquet head (using a normal-size racquet)
4. Height of the net at the singles sideline: 3½ feet (1.07 m)
5. Height of the posts: 3½ feet (1.07 m)
6. Distance of the posts away from the sidelines: 3 feet (0.914 m)
7. Distance between the baseline and the service line: 18 feet (5.49 m)
8. Distance between the service line and the net: 21 feet (6.40 m)

The endlines are called "baselines," and the sidelines are called "sidelines." The forecourt is near the net, and the backcourt is near the baselines (Figure 32.2).

RULES AND SCORING

Singles Game

The United States Tennis Association (USTA) sets the rules for tennis, along with the International Tennis Association (ITA). The USTA booklet "Friend at Court" is a complete guide to the rules of tennis, the tennis code of conduct, USTA regulations, solutions to common rules problems, and officiating techniques and procedures. Many serious recreational players keep a copy of "Friend at Court" in their gear bags. The booklet is available from USTA Publications, 70 West Red Oak Lane, White Plains, NY, 10604. The USTA address on the World Wide Web is http://www.usta.com/.

1. One player remains the server for all points of the first game of a match, after which the receiver becomes the server for all points of the second game, and so on, alternately for subsequent games of the match.
2. To start a match, the player who wins a "toss" may choose (a) to serve or to receive for the first game, whereupon the other player shall choose the end of the court on which to start, or (b) the end, whereupon the other player shall choose to serve or to receive. The "toss" is typically a spin of a racquet where one player guesses if an identifying mark will land up or down.
3. The server must take up a position behind the baseline, without touching that line, and between an imaginary extension of the center mark and the singles sideline. From that position, the server must project the ball into the air by hand and strike it in any fashion (an underhand serve is legal) before the ball hits the ground.
4. For each point the server is given two opportunities to make one good service into the proper court. To start a game, the server stands to the right of the center mark and attempts to deliver the ball diagonally across the net into the receiver's right service court. When the first point has been completed, the server then stands to the left of the center mark and serves diagonally. Thus, when the total number of completed points is an even number, service attempts are made from the right of the center mark; service attempts are made from the left when the completed points are an odd number. If a player inadvertently serves from the wrong side of the center mark, play resulting from that service is to be counted, but the improper position of the server must be corrected as soon as it is discovered.

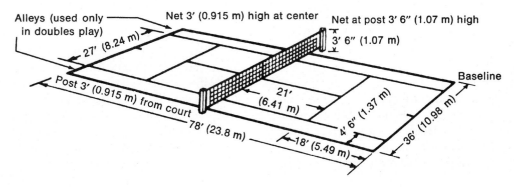

Figure 32.2. Tennis court.

5. A *fault* is an invalid serve and is counted as a service attempt. The *foot fault* occurs when the server steps on the baseline or into the court before the racquet contacts the ball or when the server is in contact with the imaginary extension of the center mark or singles sideline. However, the serve may legally be made while the server is completely in the air. Another service fault occurs when the server swings with the intent of hitting the ball but misses (although the ball may be tossed and then caught without penalty, so long as no serve is attempted). Finally, the service is a fault if the delivered ball does not land in the proper service court or on a line bounding that court. If the ball touches the net and then lands within the proper service court (including its lines), it is not a fault but a *let*.

6. Any service that is a let does not count as an attempt and is retaken. In addition, a let may be called by a receiver who was not ready to receive the serve, unless the receiver makes an attempt to return the ball. Any other interruption in normal play from an outside source is also a let, and the point is replayed. For example, if a ball from a neighboring court interrupts a rally or either of the services, the entire point is replayed, including the two service opportunities for the server.

7. There are no rules that govern the position of the receiver; a station may be taken anywhere, including within the service court. However, the receiver may not strike the served ball until after it has bounced.

8. With the occurrence of a legally served ball, play is continuous as long as the players succeed in making legal returns, even though a returned ball may strike another ball lying within the boundaries of the court. As is true with the service, a ball that lands on a line is considered to have landed in the court bounded by that line. After the service, it is not necessary for either player to allow the ball to bounce before making an attempted return.

9. After the service, a player has made a good return and play continues:
   a. When the ball lands from flight within the proper court.
   b. If the ball strikes and passes over the net and then lands within the proper court.
   c. When a player strikes a ball on his or her side of the net, even though the follow-through carries the racquet over the net without touching it. Note, however, that if a ball has bounced on a player's side of the net and the spin of the ball causes it to rebound or it is blown back over the net again, that player may then reach over the net to strike the ball, provided the player does not touch the net or the opposing court.

10. The server wins a point when a legal service is not returned or when a service hits the receiver or the receiver's racquet before it touches the ground. The receiver wins a point when the server commits two consecutive faults (double fault) or otherwise delivers the ball in an illegal manner. After the service, a player loses a point:
    a. When the ball bounces twice before the player strikes it.
    b. When a returned ball lands outside the opposing court.
    c. When a ball lands within a player's court and then strikes a permanent fixture before its second bounce.
    d. Any time a player strikes a ball before it has bounced and fails to make a good return, no matter where the player was standing when the ball was struck.
    e. If the player or the player's clothing or racquet touches the net or net post while the ball is in play.
    f. If the player hits a ball from flight before it has passed to that player's side of the net.
    g. If the ball in play touches a player or anything the player wears or carries except the racquet. A return may legally be made off any part of the racquet.
    h. If the player throws the racquet at and hits the ball.
    i. If the player intentionally interferes with an opponent.

11. Players change sides of the court at the end of the first, third, and every subsequent odd game of each set and at the end of each set, unless the total number of games in a completed set is an even number, in which case the change is not made until the end of the first game of the next set.

Scoring

A player must win at least four *points* to win a game, then at least six games to win a set, and usually at least two sets to win a match. When a player has no points in a game, the score is called *love*; the first point is called 15; the second point, 30; the third point, 40; and on winning the fourth point, that player has won the game, provided that the player is ahead by at least two points at that time. When both players have won one point, the score is called 15–all, and when both players have won two points, the score is called 30–all, but when both players have won three points, the score is called *deuce*. A score of deuce means that one player must win two consecutive points to win the game. The first point won by a player after a deuce score is called *advantage* for that player (often shortened to *ad*). If that point is won by the server, it is called *ad in*; and if that point is won by the receiver, it is called *ad out*. If the same player who won the advantage point also wins the next point, the game is won by that player. However, if the other player wins the next point, the score returns to deuce, and so on, until one player wins two consecutive points after a deuce score.

When a player wins six games and has at that time a lead of at least two games, that player wins the set. If a player wins six games and the opponent has won at least five games, traditional scoring requires that the set be extended until one player has a two-game lead. However, this custom has been replaced by playing a tiebreaker game if the set becomes tied at six games each. In this game the first player to win seven points with a two-point advantage wins the set. To start the tiebreaker game, if it is player A's turn to serve the thirteenth game (with the set tied at six games each), that player serves for the first point. Then, player B serves for points 2 and 3. Note that player B serves from the left of the center mark for point 2, then from the right of the center mark for point 3. Next, player A serves points 4 and 5, left then right of the center mark. Player B then serves point 6, the players change sides, and player B serves for point 7. The game continues with players alternately serving for two points each until one player has won at least seven points with the necessary two-point advantage. Players continue to change sides whenever the total number of points played is any multiple of six.

Points won in a tiebreaker game are called by their numerical value rather than the traditional scoring. After the tiebreaker game, player B becomes the server for the first game of the next set, and the players stay on their sides of the court for that game (Table 32.1).

Doubles Game

1. The server may stand anywhere between an extension of the center mark and the doubles sideline, behind the baseline. One player serves for the first game of the set, then a player on the opposing team serves for the second game. The partner of the player who served for the first game then serves for the third game, and the partner of the player who served the second game then serves for the fourth game, and so on, for all subsequent games of the set, each player serving every fourth game. A team may elect to change its order of service for the next set.

2. Should a partner serve out of turn, a correction must be made as soon as the mistake is discovered, but play that has been completed before the discovery must be reckoned. If a game has been completed before the

erroneous serving order is discovered, the order as altered must then remain for the continuation of the set.

3. One player of each team must receive all serves in the right service court, and that player's partner must receive all serves in the left service court for the entire set. At the end of any set, a team may change its order of receiving for the next set. The order of receiving is not determined by the order of serving.

4. Should a team receive out of turn, the altered receiving order must remain as is until the end of the game in which the discovery is made, whereafter the partners must resume their original order for the next game they receive.

5. If a served ball strikes the server's partner (including that partner's racquet), it is a service fault; but if a served ball strikes the receiver's partner or racquet before it touches the ground, it is a point for the serving team.

6. If both partners strike the ball for any return, it is a point for their opponents.

7. To play a tiebreaker game, the player whose turn it was to serve for the thirteenth game of the set (with the score tied six games each) serves for the first point of the game. Thereafter each player serves for two points, holding to the same rotation as was used in the set and following the same change of ends after every six points, as is true for singles.

ETIQUETTE

There is a code of etiquette in tennis that obliges every player to maintain a certain spirit within the rules, including giving an opponent the benefit of the doubt on line calls, avoiding foot faults during serving, never intentionally distracting an opponent, never stalling in an effort to upset an opponent, and always conducting oneself in a fashion that makes the game enjoyable for everyone. Specific situations are:

1. Any call of "out" on an opponent's ball must be made as soon as possible, before you have sent the ball back across the net.

Table 32.1. TENNIS SCORING

Points	Games	Sets	Tiebreaker	Match
Love, 15, 30, 40, deuce, ad in, ad out.	First player or team to win 4 points with a 2-point margin.	First player or team to win 6 games with a 2-game margin.	First player or team to win 7 points with a 2-point margin.	The first player or team to win 2 out of 3 or 3 out of 5 sets.
Either the server or receiver can win points. The server's score is announced first, followed by the receiver's score, prior to each point.	When the score is tied 40–40, it is called deuce. The first player to win 2 consecutive points wins the game.	When a set is tied at 6–6, a tiebreaker is played to determine the winner of the set. The server's score is announced first, followed by the receiver's score, prior to each game.	The player or team that wins the tiebreaker wins the set 7–6. The server's score is announced first, followed by the receiver's score, prior to each point in the tiebreak.	Most matches are played using the 2-out-of-3-set format. Some men's professional tournaments use a 3-out-of-5-set format.

2. You cannot ask for replay of a point where you are unable to make a sure call. The rules do not allow it, so the doubt must be resolved in favor of your opponent.

3. You may, however, ask your opponent to make the call on a ball that lands on your side, but that you did not clearly see.

4. If you hit a point-ending shot that you see as clearly out but your opponent thinks is good, you should make the correct call. This applies also to your own serve.

5. However, if you hit a first serve that you saw as out and the receiver, nevertheless, returns the ball for a point-winning placement without making an out call, you must assume the receiver made the return in good faith; therefore, the point counts and you cannot make an out call (which would then allow for your second serve).

6. Whenever a player realizes he or she has committed a violation, that player should make the call immediately. This includes such things as hitting the ball after two bounces, touching the net, or hitting the ball before it has crossed over the net.

7. The server should announce the score of the game prior to serving each point, always calling the server's score first and the receiver's second.

8. If there is a disagreement as to the score and it cannot be resolved, the score should revert back to the last score on which there was agreement.

9. The server should never hit a serve until the receiver has had time to assume a ready position.

10. A serve that is clearly out should not be returned by the receiver.

11. After a point has been played, you should return balls directly to the server; do not hit them back carelessly.

12. If your ball goes into the adjoining court, wait until the players on that court finish their point before calling for the ball.

13. If a ball from an adjoining court comes into your court, return it to the owners as soon as possible. If it interferes with your point, play a let.

14. In doubles, call service faults for your partner when he or she is the receiver.

15. Try for every point. Tossing points and playing to the audience are insulting to your opponent.

16. In nontournament play, insist on furnishing the balls half of the time—perhaps more often if you are much the inferior player.

17. Do not damage the court unnecessarily.

FUNDAMENTAL SKILLS AND TECHNIQUES

All strokes in tennis depend on a solid foundation of hitting techniques that give substance to every shot. These are the basic skill performances that should become automatic for any court situation, as follows:

Stay relaxed. Tense muscles produce rigid shots that are scattered and faulty. The first requisite for smooth, coordinated hitting is to remain relaxed—not lethargic, but calm. Stay loose, yet alive and energetic.

Think rhythm and timing. Give each swing a fluid motion with an unhurried start, a solid middle, and an unrestrained finish.

Be ready to respond. Between shots, maintain a ready-to-react position with a low center of gravity, feet shoulder-width apart, knees bent, weight mostly on the toes, and buttocks down. Relax your shoulders, and ease your grip on the racquet.

Pivot the whole body. From the ready-to-respond position, as soon as you sight the oncoming ball, begin to rotate your entire body by turning shoulders, arms, and hips, all together in a neat, packaged backswing that coils the body ready for uncoiling into the foreswing. This is especially critical for hitting a backhand, in which the shoulders play an important power role.

Go forward at impact. At contact with the ball, your weight should be going forward, toward the direction of the intended shot. Bring everything (racquet, arm, shoulders, hips, and knees) forward with the stroke. Feel the energy of your body driving the ball where you want it to go.

Hit the ball early. Contact the ball in your groundstrokes diagonally in front rather than alongside or behind your body. Intercept the ball early in its flight during a volley. Reach up and forward for serves.

Hit through the ball. Make sure the racquet is not quitting its forward speed as it meets the ball. Keep your racquet alive, actively moving through the hitting zone for all shots, including a volley or a lob.

Bend your knees. Never lock your knees when hitting, waiting to hit, serving, or receiving the serve, or playing the net. Flexed knees will allow a smooth shift of weight and provide a uniform, rhythmical swing.

Keep your eyes on the ball. Focus on the ball as it leaves your opponent's racquet, then refocus again after the bounce. Notice how much the ball slows down from its bounce, giving you time to clearly set your sights and organize the coordination of your swing. And on the serve, keep your chin up to see the actual contact.

Coil and uncoil. Every swing is a continuous motion of winding and unwinding—coiling into the backswing, then uncoiling for the foreswing. No matter how strong the swing, every shot should be a flowing coil-uncoil of effortless energy in motion.

GRIPS

How a tennis player grips the racquet might not seem like an important aspect of the game, yet in fact the grip plays a vital role in a player's ability to hit the ball effectively. The function of the grip is to help the player maintain control of the racquet while orienting the racquet face with the ball. Because of the mechanical differences between forehand and backhand shots, many players find that using different grips for different shots improves their game.

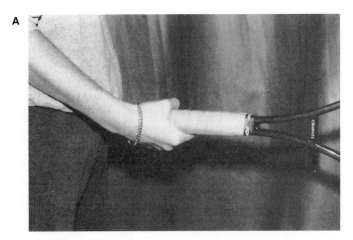

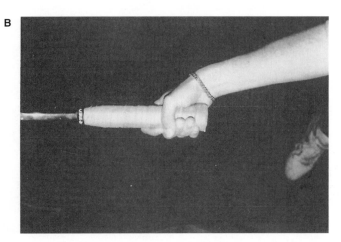

Figure 32.3. Western forehand grip. A, Side view. B, Top view.

Forehand Grips

Eastern forehand grip

The eastern forehand grip is sometimes called the "shake-hands" grip because the hand is positioned on the grip of the racquet in the same way as the hand is positioned when shaking hands. Notice in Figure 32.1A that the palm of the hand is in contact with the right surface of the grip and in Figure 32.1B that the heel of the hand is in contact with the top-right bevel. The eastern forehand is a good grip for the beginner and intermediate-level players because the angle of the racquet face can be effectively controlled when hitting groundstrokes. In addition, the eastern forehand can also be used when serving and playing forehand volleys.

Western forehand grip

The western grip is often preferred by advanced players who hit forehand groundstrokes with topspin. Notice in Figure 32.3A that the hand is rotated to the right so that the palm is in contact with the bottom-right bevel of the grip. Figure 32.3B shows that the hand is, in effect, positioned *under* the racquet. The main disadvantage of the western forehand grip

is that it requires a relatively large shift in the position of the hand when playing either backhand groundstrokes or volleys, and it cannot be used for serving.

Continental grip

The continental grip is very similar to the eastern forehand, with the main difference being that the hand is rotated slightly to the left on the grip. Notice in Figure 32.4A that the palm is in contact with the top-right bevel of the grip. In Figure 32.4B the heel of the hand is essentially in the same position as the eastern forehand grip. The continental grip is an *all-purpose* grip and can be used for forehand and backhand groundstrokes, serves, and volleys. The main disadvantage of the continental grip is that it might not be the most effective grip for any of these shots individually. As a result, few players today use the continental grip except perhaps for a volley or serve.

Backhand Grips

Eastern backhand grip

The eastern backhand is the most commonly used grip for the one-handed backhand groundstroke. Many advanced

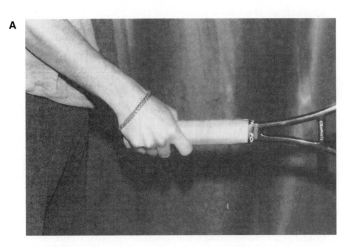

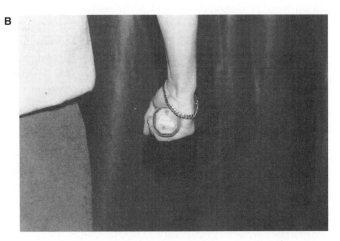

Figure 32.4. Continental grip. A, Side view. B, Back view.

A

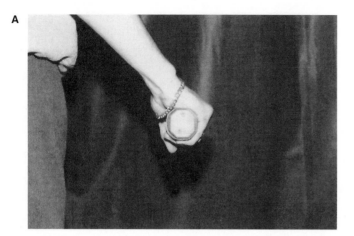

B

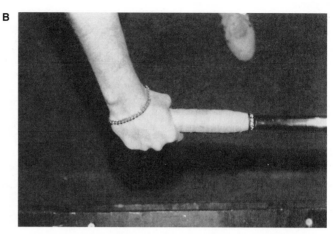

Figure 32.5. Eastern backhand grip. A, Back view. B, Top view.

A

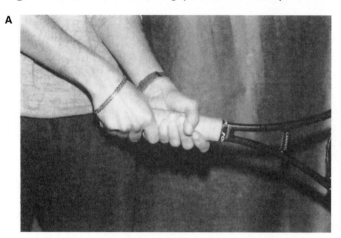

B

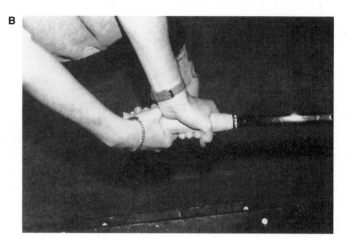

Figure 32.6. Two-handed backhand grip. A, Side view. B, Top view.

players also used the eastern backhand for the serve. Figure 32.5A shows that the palm of the hand is in contact with the top bevel of the grip. Notice in Figure 32.5B that the palm of the hand faces the surface of the court. The eastern backhand is the best one-handed grip for hitting topspin groundstrokes, although most recreational players find this shot difficult to master. The main disadvantage of the eastern backhand grip is that it requires a very strong forearm and hand to control the racquet at impact with the ball. Another potential disadvantage is that the eastern backhand can lead to tennis elbow in players who lack the strength necessary to play groundstrokes with this grip.

Two-handed backhand grip

The two-handed grip is the most common and effective alternative to the eastern backhand grip. Notice in Figure 32.6A that the right hand is positioned on the grip with an eastern forehand or continental grip and the left hand is positioned up the grip toward the head of the racquet with essentially a western grip. Figure 32.6B shows that the thumb of the right hand is in contact with the heel of the left hand.

The two-handed backhand grip is a much stronger grip than the eastern backhand, and for some players it is easier to use and more effective than a one-handed grip. There are two disadvantages to using a two-handed backhand. First, it can be difficult to play very low shots with it. Second, the ability to reach wide shots is somewhat reduced.

Continental grip

As discussed in the section on forehand grips, the continental grip is an *all-purpose* grip that can be used for hitting forehands and backhands. The main advantage of the continental grip (see Figure 32.4) is that changes in hand position are not needed when playing different shots. Also, the continental backhand is a good grip for hitting backhands with underspin. One disadvantage to using this grip is that it is difficult to hit topspin. Another disadvantage is that, like the eastern backhand, this grip requires good forearm and hand strength.

Grip Recommendations

One of the first things the beginning player has to learn before starting to hit the ball is how to grip the racquet. One of the difficulties inherent in learning tennis is that different shots are easier to hit if the player can adjust the grip of the racquet to suit a particular shot. What follows are grip recommendations for beginners, based on a combination of shot effectiveness and ease of finding when hitting the ball.

The eastern forehand (Figures 32.1A and 32.1B) is the most effective general-purpose grip for most short hits on the forehand side of the body, including the groundstroke, the volley, the lob, the overhead, the serve, and the return of serve. The biggest advantage of using a single grip for a variety of shots is that the player does not have to adjust the grip from shot to shot. The disadvantage is that relying on a single grip for a wide range of shots may not be the most effective choice for each of the shots. Nonetheless, the eastern forehand grip can work well for each of these shots, and the beginning player can use this grip effectively through at least an intermediate skill level. The two-handed backhand grip is the best choice for most players for the backhand, the groundstroke, the volley, and the return of serve (Figure 32.6). The main advantage of the two-handed grip is that it is much stronger and more intuitive for most players just learning to play. Another advantage is that most players can use the same eastern forehand grip that is used for forehand shots, so that the only thing the player needs to do when hitting a backhand is to grasp the racquet with the other hand with the western grip.

When returning the serve, it is best to initially use a two-handed backhand grip and then switch to the eastern forehand grip to play serves hit to the forehand side of the body. This is usually relatively easy to do since an eastern forehand grip is used as part of the two-handed grip. If the serve is hit to the backhand side, the player is ready since the two-handed grip is already in place.

TYPES OF SHOTS

To play tennis well, players need to be able to effectively hit each of the seven types of shots that form the basis of the game. These shots include *groundstrokes,* the *serve* and *return of serve,* the *volley,* the *overhead,* the *lob,* and the *approach shot.* While players who are still learning the game cannot be expected to be able to play all of these shots, anyone who is serious about playing a well-rounded game will need to be able to play each of these with some level of proficiency.

Of all the shots tennis players hit, *groundstrokes* are the single most fundamental shot in the game and are played with the greatest frequency of all the shots. Groundstrokes are played during a rally between players and are hit with either a forehand or a backhand swing of the racquet following the bounce of the ball. The *serve* is the stroke that is used to put the ball into play at the beginning of a rally. The serve is virtually always hit from the forehand side of the body and must be hit following an underhand toss of the ball into the air and before it bounces. The rules of the game specify that the serve must be hit from behind the baseline

and either from the ad court or the deuce court, depending on the game score. The *return of serve* is played in reply to a serve. The return is always hit following the bounce of the ball and is usually played from the vicinity of the baseline. The return, similar to groundstrokes, can be hit with either a forehand or a backhand swing. The *volley* is a shot that is hit before the ball bounces and is usually hit during a rally when one or both of the players are close to the net. The volley can also be played with either a forehand or a backhand stroke. The *overhead* is hit using a stroke that resembles the serve and is played most often in reply to a lob. An overhead can be hit either before or after the ball bounces and can be played from any position on the court. Like the serve, most overheads are hit on the forehand side of the body; on occasion, skilled players may attempt the difficult-to-execute backhand overhead. The *lob* is a high-arching shot that is usually hit from the backcourt with the goal of guiding the ball over a player who is close to the net. The lob is hit in a fashion similar to a groundstroke, and can be hit with either a forehand or a backhand stroke. The *approach shot* is hit as a player moves forward into the court from the vicinity of the baseline to a position near the net. The approach shot is hit with either a forehand or backhand swing that resembles a volley, but with the exception that it is hit following the bounce of the ball.

A few variations on the basic shots exist, such as the half-volley, the lob-volley, and the underhanded serve, to mention a few. While not often played, these shots are necessary in certain situations and skilled players will play them as the need arises.

Groundstrokes

Backhands (Figure 32.7) and forehands (Figure 32.8) are collectively called *groundstrokes.* They are the framework upon which all other aspects of the game are built. To produce effective groundstrokes, you should do the following:

1. Keep the grip loose to start, firm to hit. Between shots, ease your grip. You will automatically squeeze the racquet harder as you come into the ball.
2. Get a good shoulder turn for the coil into the backswing, especially for backhand shots, and emphatically if hitting a two-handed backhand.
3. When coiling for a backhand, look over the forward shoulder to sight the approaching ball. Pretend that an arrow extending through both shoulders would point at the ball. Bring the front shoulder down low for a low ball, high for a high ball.
4. Watch the ball all the way into the hitting zone. You do not need to see the ball actually hitting the strings, but keep a keen focus on the ball as it approaches the area of contact.
5. Take your weight off your front foot as you coil into the backswing so that you can step forward into the shot.
6. Point the handle of the racquet at the target (the area you want to hit the ball into) in your backswing.

Figure 32.7. Backhand drive.

7. Get all your weight into the shot. Accelerate the racquet into the contact point and have your weight going toward the target.
8. On two-handed backhands, keep the trailing arm directly behind the handle at contact, not lifted up with a hunched shoulder (Figure 32.9).
9. Extend your swing fully through the ball without hesitation, easing up only after contact.
10. Try to carry the ball on the strings as long as you can. Imagine that each ball has three other balls behind it. Try to thread the racquet through all four as you swing.

The Serve

When playing a game, all points begin with the serve, and as such, the serve is one of the most important skills needed to play tennis effectively. Figure 32.10 shows the basic service motion and illustrates the two key elements of the serve: the ball toss and the swing of the racquet. The following pointers provide several key reminders that contribute to an effective serve.

1. Serving is a dynamic, whole-body act. Start with an attitude of mental and physical freedom. If you hold back, you tighten your muscles and the swing has a cement-arm feeling. Instead, relax your whole body. Let your arm go limber.

Figure 32.8. Forehand drive.

2. To prepare for the serving motion, take up a throwing stance behind the baseline. Stand as if you are going to toss a ball over the net.

3. Imagine the spot, in the air, where your racquet will meet the ball. Hold the ball in your tossing hand directly beneath that spot. Cradle the ball in your fingers, not in your palm, and point your thumb toward the imagined spot of contact.

4. Hold the ball and racquet in front of you, together, more or less pointed toward the target service court.

5. Start the serving motion with both arms, then continue into the windup without pause. There is no hurry at the start, but there is no static halt at any point in the windup.

6. Lift the ball up unhurriedly, using your thumb as a guide to point toward the final destination of the toss.

7. Coil your body, similar to preparing for a forehand, and bring the racquet around behind you with the handle pointing toward the tossed ball.

8. Most or all of your weight should come to the back foot as you toss and wind up. Add some bend to your knees.

Figure 32.9. Two-handed backhand drive.

9. Start your foreswing into the ball from the ground up; that is, the knees rebound from their bend, the backbone uncoils, the hitting shoulder catapults toward the ball, and the arm thrashes up and over with the elbow unbending and the wrist adding a final vigorous snap that makes the racquet feel like a whip.

10. Build speed as you go. At the moment you hit the ball, your swing should still be gaining momentum. The whole swing is upward and forward in a clean arc that starts slow and finishes fast.

Return of Serve

Since every game point begins with the serve, the next shot is always the return of serve. As with the serve, this is a key skill and one that should be practiced along with all of the other basic shots in the game. While the return is most similar to the groundstroke, there are a few important differences that help distinguish the return from a groundstroke.

1. Stand in the middle of the widest possible area into which the server can hit, and as close to the net as you can be and still feel confident of being able to hit under control.

2. Hold the racquet loosely, directly in front of you, with your body flexed and your weight on the front of your feet.

3. Go to meet a wide serve by moving diagonally forward, on a path 90 degrees to the flight of the ball. Move toward the ball, not away from it.

4. The harder the serve, the more the swing for the return must be compact, with less backswing, but with no restriction on the follow-through.

5. Keep a solid, firm wrist as you come into the ball, especially on hard serves.

6. Have a "scrambling" attitude. Do anything to get the ball back.

PLAYING THE FORECOURT

The liveliest tennis occurs at the net. Go up to the net often, not only for the tactical advantage it presents, but also because it adds dimension to the game. However, approach the net only after your opponent hits a ball that lands

Figure 32.10. Service.

shallow in your court or when you hit a ball that you believe will force your opponent to reply with a weak return. Once at the net, your two offensive weapons are the volley and the overhead.

Doubles are played almost exclusively at the net. A good serve, volley, and overhead are essential to play competitive doubles.

Volley

1. A volley is a short stroke (Figure 32.11). It is a compact and firm block of the ball—a punch rather than a swing.
2. However, the weaker the opponent's return is, the more your volley stroke can resemble a regular groundstroke.
3. The ball should be contacted early, before it gets to the side of your body.

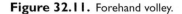

Figure 32.11. Forehand volley.

4. Generally, use the continental grip so that both forehand and backhand volleys can be played.
5. Reach for a wide ball by quickly turning your shoulders and pushing into a short step with your lead foot and, if necessary, following with a crossover step with your trailing foot.
6. Stay ready with your racquet head chin-high, in front of you.
7. Defend the net like an ice hockey goalie. Attack the ball! Hit every ball you can reach, aggressively when you can.

Overheads

1. You must get under and *in back* of the lofted ball. Skip-step into position. Keep your legs limber, with knees unlocked, for last-minute adjustments.
2. The overhead is like a serve, but the windup is more compact. Forget any fancy windup. Just get the racquet up and over your shoulder, as if you were an archer reaching back to pull an arrow out of the quiver.
3. Turn sideways as you arrive at your hitting place and rivet your eyes on the ball.

4. Make contact with the ball more in front of you than for a serve.
5. Hit the ball with as much power as you can control. The overhead is not a push or a punch, so crack off a point winner.

Lob

Use a lob to loft the ball over an opposing net player or when you need time to recover court position.

1. Let the racquet do the work. There is no need to lift your whole body into the shot.
2. Shorten the backswing. Get the racquet *under* the point of contact, then hit upward and forward in the same plane as the height you want to give to the ball.
3. Try to hold the ball on the strings as long as possible, and follow through into the path of the ball.
4. Maintain a firm wrist for the stroke.
5. Whenever you can, hit the ball just over the reach of your opponent's racquet. Always provide enough clearance—hit too high rather than too low.
6. When under pressure, do anything to get the ball up and give it extra height.

Half Volley

This is a difficult shot and should be avoided by playing either at the net or in the backcourt. When this shot is necessary, use the following techniques:

1. Bend the knees to get down to the ball.
2. Watch the ball all the way to the racquet.
3. Use no preliminary swing, but execute a full follow-through, hitting with a great deal of lift to make the ball drop into the court.
4. Stop and balance the weight forward at contact.
5. Use a firm, rigid twist and get the proper angle to the racquet. This angle is somewhat over the ball.
6. After hitting the shot, move to the net rather than remain in the middle of the court.

SPIN

While it may not be obvious to novice tennis players or casual fans, the ability to control the spin of the tennis ball is an important feature of the game. Skillful players very consciously try to impart a certain type and magnitude of spin to the ball on each shot. These players understand that the ability to manage spin helps to control the flight of the ball and improves the ability to place shots accurately in the court. A tennis ball typically rotates in one of two possible directions each time it is struck: either with topspin or with backspin. Both the directional rotation and rate of rotation strongly affect the flight of the ball through the air as well as how it bounces when it lands. A tennis ball hit with topspin tends to drop down toward the court surface more quickly than it would without spin, while a ball with backspin tends to sail a little farther than it would otherwise. When the ball

lands, topspin tends to result in a high bounce while backspin results in a low bounce off the surface of the court.

To hit the ball with topspin, the racquet is swung following a low-to-high path (Figure 32.8), while a high-to-low swing is used to apply backspin to the ball. Largely for mechanical reasons, certain shots favor one type of swing path or another, with the resulting spin being dictated by the path of the racquet. For example, the forehand and the two-handed backhand groundstroke are usually hit with topspin while the one-handed backhand groundstroke is often hit with backspin. Most approach shots and volleys are hit with backspin, while lobs can be hit with either topspin or backspin. Some players also use another type of spin, called a slice, when serving or when hitting overheads.

EFFECTIVE PRACTICE

Practice is the basis of improvement. It is the time to discipline your muscles so that in the next match, your mind can focus on the enjoyment of the game instead of the mechanics of your swing.

Develop automatically. If there is no structure to practice, it becomes too easy to slip into lazy habits such as not bending the knees or failing to transfer the weight properly. Keep your thoughts on the fundamentals of the game, looking first at your grip, then checking your pivot and backswing. Give special attention to accelerating the racquet into the ball. Try to train your muscles with free-flowing strokes.

Rehearse offense and defense. Offensive tennis is built around hitting the ball consistently deep into your opponent's court and hitting powerful serves. Practice these by trying to land every groundstroke behind the opponent's service line and hitting serves with extra effort. But also rehearse the defensive shots you'll need in competition, such as a well-lofted lob and returns of strong serves.

Make practice like a game. Part of every practice should simulate the game or segments of the game so that practice is not merely hitting the ball back and forth without purpose. Creating gamelike circumstances makes practice more interesting and gives incentive to do well.

Practice specific shots. Have a partner feed you the type of shot you want to practice. For instance, if you want to rehearse overheads, ask to have lobs hit to you. Often it is better if your partner hits a bucket of balls to you, without attempting to return your shots. After the bucket is exhausted, switch roles so that you can aid your partner's practice.

Play specific points. Try to stage playing situations. Be inventive with these drills, but make them as close to reality as possible. For example, you can play a three-ball rally whereby your partner feeds a ball to you that you hit for a deep shot and then follow with a charge to the net. Your partner, not bothering to flag down your shot, hits another ball to you that you can volley and then lifts another ball for you to hit as an overhead. Or, while your partner is practicing serves, you could practice returns by attempting to return every serve, in or out, while your partner does not chase your returns but attends only to serving.

Include aerobic conditioning. Practice can be arranged to incorporate rehearsal of skills and aerobic conditioning for tennis play. A good drill is an all-court scramble where your partner has a bucket of balls and hits a variety of placements to any part of your court. You chase down and return every ball you can, and your partner continues to act as a feeder without retrieving shots.

Practice in logical sequence. Warm up properly, then hit easily for the first few minutes. Next, give your shots plenty of depth, then try for placements into a particular area of the court. Play some "rapid fire," when you and your practice partner stand across the net from each other, just inside the service line, and hit volley after volley to each other. Then hit serves and returns of serve. Play match situations. Then do drills that include aerobic conditioning, and finish off the session with free hitting, in which you focus solely on rhythm and form.

Make practice fun. Add variety to the sessions. Experiment with different techniques or add spin to the ball. Or, play some points when the only rule is that the ball must cross over the net. Let practice be therapeutic and spark renewed interest in the game. Remember that tennis is a game. Its purpose should be to add enjoyment to your life.

USING A BACKBOARD OR BALL MACHINE

Practicing against a backboard or with a ball machine is an effective way to refine groundstrokes, serves, and volleys. Because the ball returns consistently from a wall or machine, a player can concentrate on proper stroke mechanics, movement, and positioning rather than on returning the ball to another player. In addition, an hour or two of backboard or ball machine practice can provide a vigorous physical workout. Backboards can often be found at public parks, schools, and private tennis facilities, some of which may also provide the use of ball machines.

Most backboards are 10 to 12 feet (3–3.6 m) high and have a 2-inch (5 cm) wide horizontal line painted 3 feet (0.9 m) above the ground to simulate a net. Some good practice drills include hitting forehand and backhand groundstrokes cross-court and down the line, hitting groundstrokes with underspin and topspin, and hitting first and second serves. As you alternate cross-court and down-the-line strokes, you will learn to distinguish between the subtle differences in the timing of your swing and body positioning, allowing you to better play these shots. By practicing hitting the ball with spin, you will learn the difference between a low-to-high stroke used for topspin and the high-to-low stroke used for underspin. Backboard practice is also an effective way of learning forehand and backhand grip changes. As you practice, you will learn to automatically, without conscious effort, shift hand position on the grip when changing from forehand to backhand. The main disadvantage of backboard practice is that there is no way to tell whether a given shot would actually land in play on a real court. When practicing with a backboard, it is best to think about actually hitting the ball into a tennis court, and not just hitting the ball hard.

Ball machines are even more effective than backboards because they allow for practice on an actual court. These machines are designed to "throw" tennis balls to a player in a consistent manner, using either pneumatic pressure or spinning wheel mechanisms. Sophisticated machines can throw tennis balls with different spins, at different speeds, and at different angles.

Like backboards, ball machines can provide effective practice for forehand and backhand groundstrokes, such as hitting cross-court and down-the-line groundstrokes, and for hitting with spin. Machines are more effective than backboards for volley practice, and some machines can also be used for overhead practice, which is not possible with a backboard. Although the serve cannot be practiced with a ball machine, some machines can be used to practice the return of serve. The main disadvantage of ball machines is that they do not simulate actual play because human opponents are less predictable and hit with more variability than a machine. The ability to successfully play the wide variety of shots hit by human players is difficult to learn with machines.

PRACTICE VERSUS PLAY

People participate in sports for many reasons: for example, for the pleasure of the activity, for exercise, for the competition, for social interaction, and to test and improve motor skills. One reason why tennis is so popular is because it is both physically and mentally challenging to master the many varied skills needed to play well. Many enthusiastic players become proficient enough to play tennis in a relatively short time with some instruction and practice, but they are generally quick to realize that continued practice and play are necessary to improve their overall game.

Many players assume that playing a match serves as practice, and indeed a player can learn things during a match that are not well learned during practice, such as how to apply strategy. However, during match play, the goal is to win points and games, so players tend to rely on their strengths and avoid their weaknesses. Although practice might not be inherently enjoyable, because it requires physical and mental effort, the best way to correct weaknesses and improve overall performance is through deliberate practice. In contrast to playing games, deliberate practice involves specific activities designed to improve skills and performance during matches.

Practice Drills

The following drills can be used to practice tennis fundamentals. A playing partner or ball machine is needed to practice groundstrokes, approach shots, and volley drills, whereas the serve drill can be practiced alone.

Deep rally practice

Two players (P1 and P2) hit groundstrokes with the objective of hitting consecutive shots into the shaded areas. Players can hit forehands, backhands, or a combination of the two (Figure 32.12).

Cross-court practice

Two players (P1 and P2) hit groundstrokes with the objective of hitting consecutive cross-court shots into the shaded areas. For example, players exchange forehands from areas A2 to B1 or backhands from A1 to B2 (Figure 32.13).

Down-the-line practice

Two players (P1 and P2) hit groundstrokes with the objective of hitting consecutive down-the-line shots into the shaded areas. Players hit forehands to the right side of the court only and backhands to the left side only (Figure 32.14).

Approach shot practice

Two players (P1 and P2) rally two or three groundstrokes deep (GD), then P1 hits a short ball (GS); P2 moves forward and plays an approach back to P1. P1 plays a return shot that P2 volleys from the net position (Figure 32.15).

Volley practice—1

The net player (V) practices forehand and backhand volleys by returning balls hit by the player at the baseline (B). Forehand volleys are hit to area A1 and backhand volleys to area A2 (Figure 32.16).

Volley practice—2

Both players take a position near the net and practice forehand and backhand volleys (Figure 32.17).

Serve practice

The player (P) practices four types of serves: wide serves (A1) and down-the-center serves (A2) to the deuce court, and down-the-center serves (B1) and wide serves (B2) to the

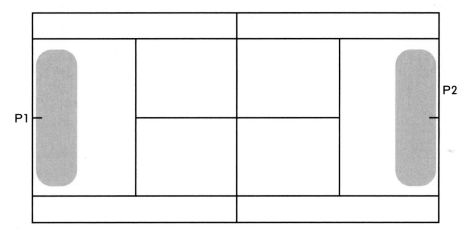

Figure 32.12. Deep rally practice.

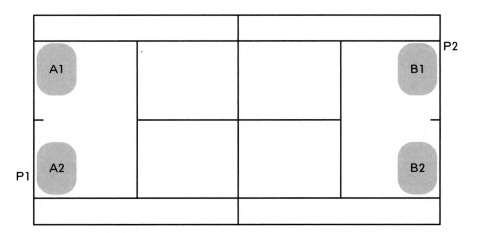

Figure 32.13. Cross-court practice.

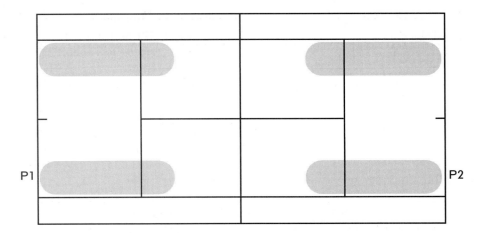

Figure 32.14. Down-the-line practice.

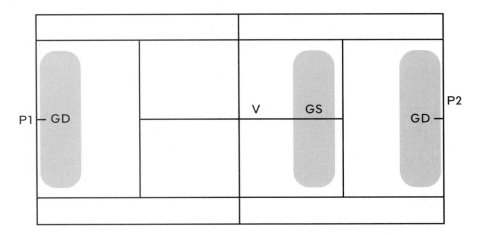

Figure 32.15. Approach shot practice.

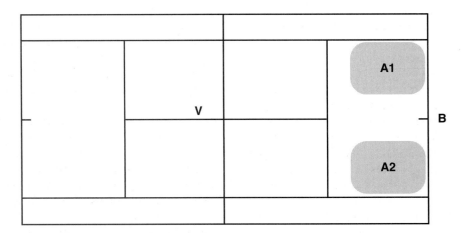

Figure 32.16. Volley practice—1.

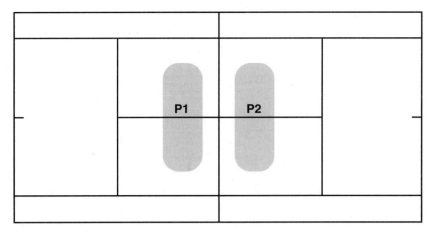

Figure 32.17. Volley practice—2.

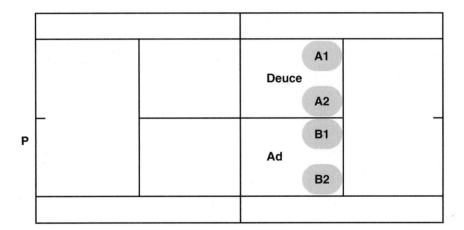

Figure 32.18. Service practice.

ad court. More-advanced players should practice hitting first and second serves to the targets (Figure 32.18).

STRATEGY

The strategy for effective play in tennis is remarkably uncomplicated. Most situations in a game have automatic answers or, at least, sensible responses.

Singles

Keep the ball in play. The first rule of tennis strategy is to hit the ball over the net, land it inbounds, and do this one more time than an opponent on each point. The worst mistake is to hit the ball into the net. It is a dead loss, never giving an opponent a chance to commit an error. Rather than trying constantly for point winners, loft the ball with enough room to clear the net by several feet. Give your opponent opportunities to misplay the ball.

Keep the ball deep. An associated tactic is to consistently place the ball deep. This will compel an opponent to stay back, hitting incessantly from behind the baseline, with little chance to come up to the net to hit point winners. You will also give yourself more time between points as the longer returns from your opponent allow you to move into a better hitting position on each ball and to collect yourself for a rhythmical, free-flowing swing.

Know when to use angles. When your opponent offers a shallow ball, take advantage of the expanded angles for placing your return. The farther inside the court you can move to hit, the greater the potential is for hitting an angled shot toward either sideline. If you are also pulled off to one side of your court for this shallow ball, the situation then becomes more favorable for hitting a cross-court return.

Use the forecourt often. Go up to the net as often as you can, even if you are still uncertain about your ability. Your presence alone may be enough to force a jittery opponent into committing errors. And once at the net, finish the point off as quickly as possible. Try to hit every ball out of your opponent's reach.

Get the first serve in. Too often players assume they should bash away at the first serve and, upon failure, push the second. Instead, slow down the pace of the first serve and increase the pace of the second. This makes first serves successful more often and keeps your opponent from stepping up to hit winners off your second serve.

Play percentage tennis. An overall guide is to ask (1) What do you do best? And (2) Where is your opponent weakest? Use your strengths. Note what an opponent cannot do well and play to that flaw often. That way you will win instead of trying to avoid losing.

Doubles

Take the net. Doubles is a net game. The basic and overriding objective is to gain control of the net, from where most points are won. Both players should get into the forecourt at every opportunity to take command of the point.

Hit high-percentage serves. Control the pace of your serve. If you can, hit it mostly to the receiver's backhand side, where it will generate a softer return, giving your net-playing partner more time to reach the ball and volley a winner.

Hit away from a net player. When one opponent is at the net and the other back, hit the ball past the net player. It is especially important to return a serve back toward the server as deep as you can. Alternatively, lift a lob over the net player.

Exploit open space. Doubles teams are often overprotective of the alleys and thus play too far apart. Send the ball up the middle often, where the two of them may hesitate an instant due to uncertainty over who will take the ball. However, when given a chance to hit cross-court, take advantage of the wide doubles court. Use the angle opportunity, but provide a margin of error by aiming to land the ball on the singles sideline.

Cover the empty space. Tie an imaginary rope between you and your partner. If your partner is forced off the side of the court, let the rope pull you over to cover the now-wider area of return space that is presented to your opponents. Always stay in the middle of the court space that is left over when your teammate is pushed out of position.

TEACHING CONSIDERATIONS

1. The techniques of skilled hitting have a common denominator of physics. Regardless of how contradictory different players' styles appear to be, at the critical microsecond when racquet and ball are in contact, everyone must impart the same force to achieve the same end. Learn the physics that apply to hitting a tennis ball, then help students to understand those laws and evaluate how well they are doing in relation to them.

2. Keep instructions simple. It is easy to become overloaded with instructional facts about each stroke. At some point, a learner will no longer handle all the information while simultaneously trying to organize commands about what the muscles should do. The best method is often the simplest. Focus on only the most important aspects of hitting.

3. Attend mostly to the rhythmical patterns of the swing. Encourage learners to first develop smooth, flowing motions for each swing, without necessarily judging their swings on the basis of where the ball goes. Emphasize the coiling and uncoiling and the position of the body relative to the ball. Have them think of the *art* of tennis. Make them "look good" as they hit. Focus their attention on the sensation of rhythm and timing for every swing.

4. Play lots of "minitennis" games to emphasize rhythm and proper position. Have one partner stand at the net and toss the ball on one bounce to the hitter; then switch roles. Or have partners stand on opposite sides of the net at the service lines and rally the ball, trying to keep it within the boundaries of the service court. Provide students with games in which they can have instant success by making it possible to develop a feel for the game.

5. Become target oriented. Introduce rallying for specific targets. For example, to improve the depth of everyone's shots, stretch a piece of cord across the court several feet inside the baseline to act as an aiming point for deep groundstrokes. For the serve, stand a ball can (as a target) inside each corner of the service court. Or exchange groundstrokes using the alley as in the inbounds area.

6. A common mistake is to turn one's head prematurely, looking up to see where the ball is going before it is hit. Have players attend to all the dimensions of the ball as they follow it into the hitting zone. Focus on the spin, trying to actually see the seams of the ball. Or note the color of the ball and try to heighten its hue as it approaches. Create the habit of refocusing on the ball after its bounce. Then play "bounce-and-hit," whereby both partners say "bounce" every time the ball bounces (including on the opposite side of the net), and "hit" every time a player strikes the ball. This will help players to refocus after the bounce and to concentrate on the ball rather than on mechanical parts of the swing.

7. The service toss is a major headache for many players. Too often they throw it into the air with an exaggerated lift of the knees. Isolate the toss by practicing it alone, perhaps starting with the tossing hand resting against the inside of the forward thigh, then lifting and releasing the ball as if settling it on a shelf at hitting height. Place a racquet on the ground, the head in front and inside the forward foot. Toss the ball to the proper height and allow it to drop to see if it will land on the racquet face.

8. Teach beginners to serve with a four-part but continuous sequence, as follows: (1) start with both hands held together, elbows bent, racquet pointed in the direction of the target court; (2) drop both hands

down at the same time, toward the forward thigh; (3) bring both arms up together to release the ball, and arc the racquet behind the hitting shoulder; then (4) deliver the racquet into the back of the ball with an accelerating forward swing. Have students say "down-together, up-together, swing" as they practice the motion of the serve.

9. Arrange variants of the game to encourage certain skills. For example, play a groundstroke game without the serve, in which each point begins with one player hitting a groundstroke and the ball crossing the net three times before a point can be scored (this will encourage controlled rallies). Or practice second serves by playing games in which only one serve is allowed. Or play games in which the server hits half-speed and only backhands are allowed thereafter.

10. Make practice fun. Add variety to the sessions, sometimes doing such things as hitting the ball with the racquet held in the nondominant hand. Play some points where the only rule is that the ball must cross over the net and land in front of the fence. Or have a rule that after every shot, players must run up and touch the net with their racquets. Try a game in which, on each side, a player hits a shot and then hands the racquet off to another player for the next shot.

CLASSIC WORKS ON TENNIS

Books about tennis have been published since at least the early 1900s, and many well-known professional players of the day, such as Don Budge, Jack Kramer, and Bill Tilden, wrote books designed to help amateurs better understand the game and improve their play. Although the basic rules of the game and the dimensions of the tennis court have not changed over the years, other elements, such as the apparel worn by players, playing style, and game strategy, have evolved. Books that have been written over the years provide an insight into the history and the evolution of the game of tennis.

The Suggested Classic Tennis Readings section in this chapter includes a listing for many of these books about tennis. Most of the books have long since gone out of print; however, many of them can still be found in public libraries and used copies can sometimes be found at Web sites such as Amazon.com or Powellsbooks.com.

Two highly recommended classic works include *The Game of Singles in Tennis* (1962) and *The Game of Doubles in Tennis* (1968), by William F. Talbert and Bruce S. Olds. Both books include some historical information on the games of singles and doubles, nice drawings showing various strokes, statistical analysis of some classic matches, and an extensive set of diagrams depicting rallies that typically take place during games. These books are of particular interest to tennis enthusiasts not only for historical reasons, but also because they contain considerable information that contemporary players find quite valuable.

GLOSSARY

ace A point-winning serve that is hit beyond the reach of a receiver.

ad court The left service court; also that court into which the serve is hit when the total number of points played in a game is an odd number.

ad in When the server has a score of advantage.

ad out When the receiver has a score of advantage.

advantage The next point after a deuce score. The player who wins the point is said to have the "advantage"; and if that player also wins the following point, the player will have won the game; if not, the score returns to deuce.

alley The area on either side of the singles court that is included as inbounds for doubles play.

approach shot A groundstroke hit by a player to prepare the way for an approach to the net.

backcourt An undefined area in the vicinity of the baseline.

backhand A stroke used to play a ball on the opposite side of a player's dominant hand.

baseline The line marking the end of the court.

break (service break) To win a game that the opponent serves.

center mark A short line extended inward from the baseline as a continuation of the center service line that marks the two halves of the court and indicates the sides of the court in which the server must stand.

cross-court shot Hitting the ball from one side of the court across the net to the side diagonally opposite.

deuce An even score in a game after six or more points have been played or an even score in games after 10 or more games have been played.

deuce court The right service court; also that court into which the serve is hit when the total number of points played in a game is an even number.

double fault Failure of a player to get either of the two service attempts into the proper service court.

down-the-line shot A ball hit across the net parallel to a sideline.

fault A served ball that does not land within the proper service court, or any other violation of the rules of service.

foot fault A service delivery that is illegal because the server stepped on the baseline or into the court before the racquet contacted the ball.

forecourt That area of the court between the net and the service line.

forehand A stroke used to play a ball on a player's dominant side.

game A unit of a set completed when one side wins four points before the other side wins three or, if both sides have won three points, when one side thereafter gains a two-point margin.

groundstroke A forehand or backhand stroke used to hit the ball after it has bounced.

let Any point that must be replayed. Most often it refers to a serve that hits the top of the net, then lands in the proper service court.

lob A high, arcing shot that lands near the opponent's baseline.

love A score of zero. In a love game, one side wins no points; in a love set, one side wins no games.

match A contest between two or four players in which one side must win a predetermined number of games or sets to be declared the winner.

match point Term used when a side needs only one more point to win the match.

overhead (smash) A free-swinging stroke used for a ball that is over the player's head.

rally The exchange of shots between opponents after the serve, usually referring to prolonged play.

serve The stroke used to put the ball into play at the start of each point. The more inclusive term *service* applies to the right to be the server and the served ball itself.

service break A game won by the receiver.

set A unit of a match completed when one side wins six games or when one side wins the tie-breaker game.

set point When a side needs only one more point to win the set.

sideline The line that marks the outside edge of either the singles or the doubles court.

slice Shots that are hit with a high-to-low swing that results in a backward rotation of the ball, causing it to sail farther and bounce lower than it would without spin.

tie-breaker A scoring system designed to eliminate prolonged sets in which one player must win seven points with a two-point advantage to win a set. Played when a set becomes tied at six games each.

topspin Shots that are hit with a low-to-high spin that results in a forward rotation of the ball, causing it to drop to the court more rapidly and to bounce higher than it would without spin.

volley A short punch stroke used to hit the ball before it bounces.

SUGGESTED READINGS

The American Sport Education Program. 2008. *Coaching youth tennis.* 4th ed. Champaign, IL: Human Kinetics.

Bollettieri, N. 2001. *Bollettieri's tennis handbook.* Champaign, IL: Human Kinetics.

Brown, J. 2004. *Tennis Steps to success.* 3rd ed. Champaign, IL: Human Kinetics.

Bryant, J. E., and Bryanz, J. S. 2007. *Game-set-match.* 7th ed. Belment, CA: Thompsons Wadsworth.

Cayer, L. 2004. *Doubles tennis tactics.* Champaign, IL: Human Kinetics.

Chafin, M., Thornquist, R., and Daglis, T. 2007. *Tennis everyone.* 6th ed. Winston-Salem, NC: Hunter Textbooks.

Claxton, D. 1999. *Tennis.* New York City, NY: McGraw-Hill.

Collins, B. 2008. *The Bud Collins history of tennis: An authoritative encyclopedia and record book.* Washington, D.C: New Chapter Press.

Dinoffer, J. 2003. *Tennis practice games.* Champaign, IL: Human Kinetics.

Gould, R. H. 2000. *Tennis anyone?* 6th ed. New York: McGraw-Hill.

Greenwald, J. 2007. *The best tennis of your life: 50 mental strategies for fearless performance.* Cincinnati, OH: Betterway Books.

Hoskins, T. 2003. *The tennis drill book.* Champaign, IL: Human Kinetics.

Johnson, J., and Xanthers, J. 2003. *Tennis.* 8th ed. New York City, NY: McGraw-Hill.

Johnson, M. L., Hill, D. L., and Hill, K. 1999. *Tennis: The game for any age.* 6th ed. Winston-Salem, NC: Hunter Textbooks.

Kattan, K. 2006. *Raising big smiling tennis kids: A complete road map for every parent and coach.* Austin, TX: Mansion Grove House.

Little, A. 2009. *Tennis and the Olympic Games.* London: Wimbledon Lawn Tennis Museum.

Matsuzaki, C. 2004. *Tennis fundamentals.* Champaign, IL: Human Kinetics.

Roetert, E., and Ellenbecker, T. 2007. *Complete conditioning for tennis.* Champaign, IL: Human Kinetics.

Rutherford, J. 1999. *Skills, drills & strategies for tennis.* Scottsdale, AZ: Holcomb Hathaway Publishing.

Salvino, N. 2003. *Maximum tennis.* Champaign, IL: Human Kinetics.

Schwartz, B., and Dazet, C. 1998. *Competitive tennis.* Champaign, IL: Human Kinetics.

Smith, S. 2002. *Winning doubles.* Champaign, IL: Human Kinetics.

Smith, S. 2004. *Coaching tennis successfully.* 2nd ed. Champaign, IL: Human Kinetics.

U.S. Tennis Association. 1996. *Tennis tactics: Winning patterns of play.* Champaign, IL: Human Kinetics.

U.S. Tennis Association. 1998. *Complete conditioning for tennis.* Champaign, IL: Human Kinetics.

U.S. Tennis Association. 2004. *Coaching tennis successfully.* 2nd ed. Champaign, IL: Human Kinetics.

U.S. Tennis Association. with Kink Anderson. 2009. *Coaching tennis technical and tactical skills.* Champaign, IL: Human Kinetics.

Wardlaw, P. 2000. *Pressure tennis.* Champaign, IL: Human Kinetics.

Werthelm, L. J. 2009. *Strokes of genius: Federer, Nadal, and the greatest match ever played.* Orlando, FL: Houghton Mifflin Harcourt.

Williams, S., and Peterson, R. 2000. *Serious tennis.* Champaign, IL: Human Kinetics.

Woods, K. and Woods, R. 2008. *Playing tennis after 50.* Champaign, IL: Human Kinetics.

Suggested Classic Tennis Readings

Budge, J. D. 1939. *Budge on tennis.* New York: Prentice-Hall.

Cochet, H. 1966. *Le tennis de A à Z; une nouvelle méthode d'enseignement acceleré, par Henri Cochet et Jacques Feuillet.* Dessins de Marc Feuillet. Paris: La Table Ronde.

Connolly, M. 1954. *Power tennis.* New York: Barnes.

Gallwey, W. T. 1974. *The inner game of tennis.* New York: Random House.

Gonzales, P. 1962. *Tennis, by Pancho Gonzales and Dick Hawk.* New York: Fleet Pub. Corp.

Hardwick, M. 1937. *Lawn tennis for women, by Mary Hardwick.* New York: M. S. Mill Co., Inc.

Kramer, J. 1949. *Winning tennis.* London: Marston.

———. 1977. *How to play your best tennis all the time.* New York: Atheneum/SMI.

Lacoste, J. R. c1928. *Lacoste on tennis, with an introduction by William T. Tilden.* New York: W. Morrow & Company.

Lenglen, S. 1937. *Initiation au tennis, principes essentiels et préparation physique.* Paris: A. Michel.

Little, R. D. 1913. *Tennis tactics, by Raymond D. Little.* New York: Outing Publishing Company.

Sedgman, F. 1954. *Winning tennis; the Australian way to a better game.* New York: Prentice-Hall.

Talbert, W. F., and Old, B. E. 1962. *The game of singles in tennis.* Philadelphia: J. B. Lippincott Co.

———. 1968. *The game of doubles in tennis.* 3rd ed. New York: J. B. Lippincott Co.

Tilden, W. T. c1921. *The art of lawn tennis.* New York: George H. Doran Company.

———. 1922. *Lawn tennis for club players.* London: Methuen & Co. Ltd.

———. 1923. *The expert.* New York: American Sports Publishing Co.

———. c1925. *Better tennis for the club player.* New York: American Sports Publishing Company.

———. c1925. *The junior player, formerly "the kid"; a tennis lesson.* New York: American Sports Publishing Company.

———. 1925. *Match play and the spin of the ball.* 2nd ed. New York: American Lawn Tennis.

———. c1931. *Tennis for the junior player, the club player, the expert.* New York: American Sports Publishing Company.

———. 1950. *Tennis A to Z.* London: Gollancz.

Vaile, P. A. c1906. *The strokes and science of lawn tennis.* New York: The American Sports Publishing Company.

———. *Modern tennis.* 2nd ed. New York: London, Funk & Wagnalls.

Vines, E. c1938. *How to play better tennis, by Ellsworth Vines.* Philadelphia: David McKay Company.

———. c1939. *Ellsworth Vines quick way to better tennis; a practical book on tennis for men and women.* New York: Sun Dial Press.

Wills, H. 1928. *Tennis, by Helen Wills.* New York: London, C. Scribner's Sons.

RESOURCES

Videos and DVDs

A wide selection of videotapes and DVDs on tennis is available from Human Kinetics Publishers. Search using the keyword tennis at www.humankinetics.com for a complete listing of available titles.

See Appendix C for other sources of videos.

WEB SITES

Adjusting the Net
  http://adjustingthenet.wordpress.com/
Association of Tennis Professionals:
  www.atpworldtour.com/

GOTOTENNIS
  www.gototennisblog.com/
History of Tennis
  www.historyoftennis.net/
International Tennis Federation
  www.itftennis.com/
International Tennis Hall of Fame
  www.tennisfame.com/
Junior Tennis
  www.juniortennis.com/
Official Website of the Davis Cup
  www.daviscup.com/
Sony Ericsson WTA Tour
  www.sonyericssonwtatour.com/
Tennis.com
  www.tennis.com/
Tennis Channel
  www.tennischannel.com/index.aspx
Tennis Country
  http://www.tenniscountry.com/
Tennis Insight
  www.tennisinsight.com/
TennisOne
  www.tennisone.com
Tennis Online
  www.tennisonline.com/
Tennis Served Fresh
  http://cornedbeefhash.wordpress.com/
The Tennis Server
  www.tennisserver.com/
Tennis W—The Online Tennis Community
  www.tennisw.com/
Tennis Week
  www.tennisweek.org/
USA Tennis
  http://tennis.teamusa.org/
United States Professional Tennis Association
  www.uspta.org/
United States Tennis Association
  www.usta.com/
Women's Tennis Blog
  www.womenstennisblog.com/

33 | Touch Football and Flag Football

After completing this chapter, the reader should be able to:

- Appreciate the historical development of touch and flag football
- Know the rules for each of these activities
- Demonstrate the basic skills of blocking and touching (removing flags), kicking, passing, and receiving a football
- Understand the fundamentals of offense and defense for touch and flag football
- Correctly execute several offensive and defensive formations used in the two activities
- Teach the fundamentals of touch and flag football to a group of novice players

Touch and flag football are similar to regulation American football except that the ball carrier is downed differently. In touch football the ball carrier is stopped by being touched with both hands rather than being tackled. Flags being removed will down a ball carrier in flag football versus tackling or touching. In addition, noncontact blocking (screen blocking) is utilized in both flag and touch football. These changes lessen the danger of injury and encourage a more open game. Forward passing is usually the principal offensive weapon, with all players eligible to receive a pass.

With the exception of a few rules, flag and touch football in all aspects are virtually the same (e.g., equipment, field of play, scoring). Therefore, they will be discussed together, and any differences will be noted.

HISTORY

Football as it is played today is derived from soccer and rugby. Harvard, Yale, Princeton, and Rutgers universities were early players of the game, which at the time was not much more than a gang fight over a round ball.

However, since 1869, rules have been formulated, equipment has been adopted and qualified, and coaches and members of the medical profession have worked toward making football a relatively safe game.

Touch football is a modification of football that can be safely played without pads. Playing the game without costly equipment has increased the age span and number of possible participants. Touch football is an interesting and beneficial game for all who desire competition and fun.

In 1932, the Intramural Sports Section of the College Physical Education Association adopted rules for school and college play.

The National Touch and Flag Football Rules were first developed after considerable study of the variations of the game played in colleges and universities throughout the United States and Canada by a National College Touch Football Rules Committee of the College Physical Education Association. In 1950, this committee, in addition to an advisory committee and subcommittees, submitted questionnaires to more than 100 schools concerning the rules and recommended their standardization. The recommendations were then approved by the Intramural Section of the College Physical Education Association. Through cooperation with the Athletic Institute, the first rule book was published in 1952. The latest version (2004–2005) of the Official U.S. Flag and Touch Football Rules can be ordered online from the United States Flag and Football League (www.usftl.com). Even though official rules exist for these sports, local custom, available facilities, and tradition often dictate the rules used.

EQUIPMENT

Playing field

The field is 40 yards (36.6 m) wide by 100 yards (91.4 m) long (Figure 33.1). It is suggested to modify the size of the field to fit the needs of the participants. For example, if the group is very large and there is a desire to provide maximum time on task and increase participation, a field may be divided into two smaller fields with four teams.

Ball

A regulation American football is used for men, and a junior-sized football is used for women.

Uniforms

No special uniform is necessary, and a typical gym uniform is adequate. Teams should be equipped with distinctively colored jerseys. However, two groups of different-color flag belts will suffice. Cleated shoes are recommended; however, basketball, tennis, and gym shoes are suitable. Cleated shoes have some restrictions covered in the rules and regulations section. In team play mouthguards are mandatory.

THE GAME

Length of Game

The length of the game is up to the discretion of the participants, based on group size and time limit. However, the

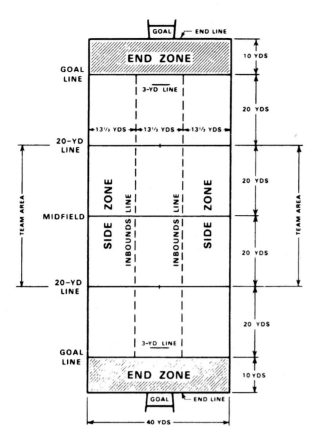

Figure 33.1. Football field.

following time frame is suggested: a game with two 24-minute halves on a running clock with a 10-minute intermission. The clock will start when the ball is legally snapped or the kickoff is legally touched. It will run continuously for 24 minutes unless stopped for a:

1. Score; starts when the kickoff is legally touched
2. Team time-out; starts on the snap
3. Referee's time-out; starts on the ready-for-play signal

At the end of the second 24-minute period, 2 minutes of plays will be executed without the game clock. When the official announces that regulation time has expired and that only 2 minutes remain, the play continues normally.

Overtime

An overtime period is played in case of a tie. There are two common methods of playing an overtime period:

1. Each team is given four downs from the first 20-yard (18-m) zone line heading away from the nearest end zone; the team advancing the ball the farthest in the four downs is the winner. If both teams score, repeat the procedure.
2. Each team is given four downs from the same 10-yard (9.1-m) line heading into the nearest end zone. The team that scores is the winner. If the score is tied or there is no score after the four downs, the procedure is repeated.

One additional option is to award the win to the team with the most 20-yard (18-m) zone line penetrations during

the game. If penetrations are also tied, one of the overtime procedures mentioned previously may be employed.

Time-Outs

Many leagues and flag/touch football organizations limit the number of time-outs per game to speed up play. It is recommended to limit each team to two or three 30-second time-outs per game.

Scoring

1. Touchdown: 6 points men; 9 points women
2. Safety: 2 points and possession of the ball by punt
3. Forfeited game: 1 point
4. Point after touchdown: 1 point from the 3-yard (2.7-m) line and 2 points from the 10-yard (9.1-m) line.

If there are goalposts available, there may be kicks for extra points from the 3-yard (2.7-m) line for 1 point. Two points are awarded for running or passing. In addition, a team may be allowed to attempt a field goal for 3 points. Many leagues and organizations do not use kicks because of the lack of goalposts. If kicks are used, the defense should not be allowed to rush the kicker, for obvious safety reasons. To have kicks without a defensive rush would give the offense an unfair advantage; therefore, kicks are rarely used.

Players and Substitutions

1. A team consists of 7 to 11 players. The offensive team must have at least 3 players on the line of scrimmage.
2. It is advised, for safety and maximum participation, to keep the number of players to 11 or below. Having four teams of 5 players each is better than two teams of 10.
3. Any number of substitutions may be made during the game. Substitutes must report to the referee before entering the game.

Playing Regulations

1. Start of the game: The game is started by the following procedures:
   a. A coin is tossed, and the winner gets the choice of which goal to defend and whether to receive the ball or defer the choice until the second half.
   b. Putting the ball into play: The ball is put into play at the beginning of the game, at the beginning of the second half, and after a score by one of two ways depending on league or organization requirements. The ball may be put into play by a kick, a dropkick, or a punt from the 20-yard (18-m) line. If kicks are not allowed, the team that would normally receive the ball puts the ball into play by starting its offensive series from its own 20-yard (18-m) line.
   c. Recovery of a kickoff or punt: A punt or kickoff is only a live ball for the receiving team. If the receiving team touches the ball in the air but does not catch it, the ball becomes dead when it touches the ground.

If the ball hits the ground before a receiving player touches it, it is still a live ball and can be picked up and advanced by the receiving team only. If a kicking-team player touches a ball that is live on the ground or in the air, the ball becomes dead and the receiving team remains in possession. No member of the kicking team may interfere with a receiving-team player's attempt to catch the ball.

2. Ball kicked or punted over opponent's endline (back of the end zone): If the ball goes through the opponent's endline, it goes to the opponents for scrimmage on their own 20-yard (18-m) line.

3. Ball kicked or punted out-of-bounds: If the ball goes out-of-bounds, the receiving team gets possession of the ball where it went out-of-bounds.

4. Fumbled ball: If a ball is fumbled and touches the ground, it is a dead ball and the offense retains possession of the ball.

5. A down: A down is a unit of the game that starts with a legal snap or legal free kick and ends when the ball next becomes dead. "Between downs" is any period when the ball is dead.

6. Series of downs: A team in possession of the ball shall have four consecutive downs to advance to the next zone by scrimmage. Any down may be repeated or lost if provided by the rules.

7. Zone line-to-gain: The zone line-to-gain in any series shall be the zone in advance of the ball, unless distance has been lost due to penalty or failure to gain. In such cases, the original zone in advance of the ball at the beginning of the series of downs is the zone line-to-gain. The most forward point of the ball, when declared dead between the goal lines, shall be the determining factor.

8. Awarding a new series: A new series of downs shall be awarded when a team moves the ball into the next zone on a play free from penalty; or a penalty against the opponents moves the ball into the next zone; or an accepted penalty against the opponents involves an automatic first down; or either team has obtained legal possession of a ball as a result of a penalty, free kick, protected scrimmage kick, touchback, pass interception, or failure to gain the zone in advance of the ball.

9. Failure to advance: If, in four consecutive downs, a team fails to advance the ball to the next zone, the defense receives the ball. If, on the fourth down, the offense elects to punt, it must declare that intention to the officials. Quick kicks are not allowed. On the punt the offense must have every player except the punter on the line of scrimmage. No offensive player may move until the ball is kicked. The defense must have at least three players on the line of scrimmage, and they may not move until the ball is kicked. All punts must

be announced. The defense is not allowed to attempt a punt block.

10. Downed ball: The player is downed in touch football when touched by an opposing player with both hands anywhere between the offensive player's knees and shoulders. In flag football a player is downed when one or both of the flags are removed by an opposing player. If any of the offensive players' flags fall off inadvertently, a defensive player may down the offensive player by the rules of touch football.

11. Passing:
    a. All players on the offensive team are eligible to receive a pass. Any member of the defensive team may intercept a pass.
    b. Only one forward pass may be thrown per down. Any forward pass must be executed behind the line of scrimmage. There is no limit to the number of laterals a team may use on any given down. A lateral is any ball thrown or tossed parallel or backward from the line of scrimmage.

12. Snapping: The snapper shall pass the ball back from its position on the ground with a quick and continuous motion of the hand(s). It may be snapped between the legs or from a side snap position. Any player may receive the snap as long as he or she is a minimum of 2 yards (1.83 m) back from the line of scrimmage.

13. Motion: One offensive player may be in motion during the snap as long as three other offensive players are on the line of scrimmage. The player in motion must not be moving toward the line of scrimmage before the ball is snapped.

14. Mercy rule: If a team is 17 or more points ahead when the referee announces the 2-minute warning or that there are six plays left in the game, the game shall end.

15. Scoring:
    a. Touchdown: A touchdown shall be scored when a legal forward pass is completed or a fumble or backward pass is caught on or behind the opponent's goal line or when a player who is legally in possession of the ball penetrates the vertical plane of the opponent's goal line.
    b. Extra points: An opportunity to score 1 point from the 3-yard line or 2 points from the 10-yard line shall be granted the team scoring a touchdown. If the league has goalposts, a successful kick will be 1 point and running or passing into the end zone from the 3-yard line will be 2 points.
    c. Safety: A safety results when a runner carries the ball from the field of play to or across his or her own goal line, and it becomes dead there in his or her team's possession. Exception: When a defensive player intercepts a forward pass in his or her end zone and downs the ball, it is not a safety. If the interceptor runs the ball out of the end zone and re-enters the end zone and the ball becomes dead, it is a safety.

Fouls and Penalties

1. Ball in play; dead ball; out-of-bounds:
   a. A dead ball becomes alive when it is snapped or kicked. A ball is declared dead when:
      (1) It goes out-of-bounds.
      (2) A player catches a free kick and then drops it on the ground.
      (3) A backward pass or fumble touches the ground.
      (4) A runner is legally tagged (touched or flag pulled).
      (5) An official sounds a whistle.
   b. Out-of-bounds: A player is out-of-bounds when any part of the body touches anything other than another player or a game official that is on or outside the sideline or endline.
2. Fair-catch interference: While any free kick is in flight beyond the kicking team's scrimmage line, no kicking-team player shall touch the ball or receiver or obstruct the receiver's path to the ball. Penalty: Fair-catch interference; 10 yards (9.1 m) from the previous spot, and replay the down.
3. Encroachment: Following the ready-to-play signal and until the snap, no player on the defense may encroach (enter the neutral zone) nor may any player contact opponents or in any other way interfere with them. After the center has placed his or her hands on the ball, it is encroachment for any player to break the scrimmage line plane. Penalty: Encroachment; 5 yards (4.6 m) from the previous spot.
4. Snap: A player may pick up the ball and advance it to a player at least 3 yards deep in the offensive backfield. The ball does not have to be snapped between the legs.
5. Minimum line players: The offensive team must have three players on the line of scrimmage prior to the snap. Penalty: Dead ball foul, illegal procedure; 5 yards (4.6 m).
6. Motion: More than one player in motion during the snap or a motion player moving toward the line of scrimmage during a snap is illegal. Penalty: Illegal motion; 5 yards (4.6 m).
7. Illegal forward pass: A forward pass is illegal if:
   a. A passer's foot is in contact with the ground beyond the line of scrimmage when the ball leaves the hand.
   b. There is more than one forward pass. Penalty: 5 yards (4.6 m) from the spot of the foul and a loss of down.
8. Pass interference: Contact, while the ball is in flight, that interferes with an eligible receiver who is beyond the line of scrimmage is pass interference unless it occurs when two or more eligible receivers make a simultaneous and bona fide attempt to reach, catch, or bat a pass. It is also pass interference if an eligible receiver is deflagged or tagged prior to touching the ball. Penalty:
   a. Offensive pass interference: 10 yards (9.1 m) from the previous spot and loss of down.
   b. Defensive pass interference: 10 yards (9.1 m) from the previous spot and automatic first down. If it is ruled intentional or unsportsmanlike, an additional 10 yards (9.1 m).
9. Unsportsman-like conduct and personal fouls. These are left to the instructor's discretion. Any player displaying conduct that is deemed harmful to players or is unsportsman-like should be penalized. Penalty: Unsportsman-like conduct; 10 yards (9.1 m). If the action is flagrant, the offender shall be disqualified.
10. Roughing the passer: Defensive players must make a definite effort to avoid charging into a passer after it is clear the ball has been thrown. Penalty: 10 yards (9.1 m); automatic first down.
11. Blocking: The offensive screen block shall take place without contact. The screen blocker shall keep the hands and arms at the side or behind the back. Any use of the hands, arms, elbows, legs, or body to initiate contact during a block is illegal. Penalty: Personal foul; 10 yards (9.1 m).
12. Use of hands or arms by the defense: Defensive players must go around the offensive player's screen block. The arms and hands may not be used as a wedge to contact the opponent. Penalty: Personal foul; 10 yards (9.1 m).
13. Runner:
    a. Guarding the flag or deflecting a touch: Runners shall not flag-guard or guard their body by using their hands, arms, or the ball to deny the opportunity for an opponent to tag or remove a flag belt. Penalty: Guarding or flag guarding; 10 yards (9.1 m).
    b. Stiff-arm: The runner shall be prohibited from contacting an opponent with extended hand or arm. Penalty: Personal foul; 10 yards (9.1 m).

Officials

1. The referee has absolute charge of the game, and decisions made by the referee are final.
2. The umpire pays particular attention to holding and interference on forward-pass plays.
3. The line judge measures distance and reports offside and personal fouls, such as holding and roughness. The line judge may also be the timekeeper if no special individual is assigned this duty. (See Figure 33.2 for official football signals.)

FUNDAMENTAL SKILLS AND TECHNIQUES

Stance

The player must be positioned within 1 foot (30.5 cm) of the scrimmage line in a 2-point stance.

Offensive-line stance

The stance used by players on the offensive line must enable them to move forward, backward, and laterally; therefore, it

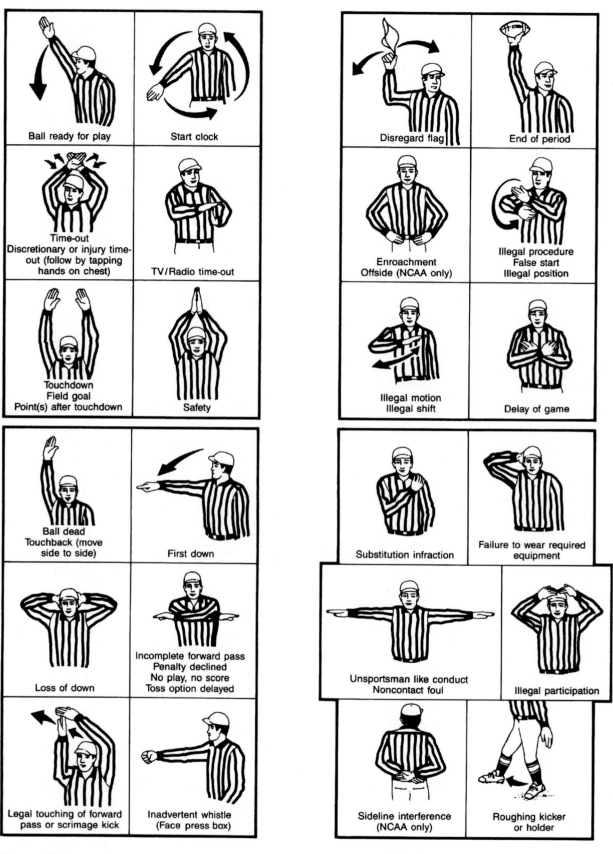

Figure 33.2. Men's and women's touch and flag football signals.

Figure 33.2. *cont'd.* Men's and women's touch and flag football signals.

must be a position with the feet comfortably apart and staggered, knees bent, with the body in balance to facilitate a quick movement in the desired direction.

Defensive-line stance
This stance is similar to the offensive stance, but the body is closer to the ground. Weight must be forward so a lineperson can charge forward.

Offensive-backfield stance (2-point stance)
1. The feet are about shoulder-width apart, with the toes pointed straight ahead.
2. Weight is equally distributed on the balls of both feet, and the knees are slightly flexed.
3. The hands or elbows are on the knees, arms are slightly flexed, thumbs are on the inside of the knees, the head is up, and the eyes are straight ahead.

Defensive-backfield stance
Players should stand in a natural but alert posture, feet apart and staggered. A semierect body position facilitates quick movements yet affords an effective position to observe movements of the offense.

Blocking
The object of blocking is to stop or deter a defensive rusher's attempt to reach the quarterback on a pass play. It may also be used to obstruct the path of the defender on a running play. Screen blocking is utilized in that the player on the line attempts to stay in front of the defensive player without making contact (Figure 33.3A, B).

Blocking techniques
1. Assume a 2-point stance.

2. Feet are parallel with the knees, which are bent to achieve a low center of gravity and afford maneuverability in any direction.

3. Keep your head up and concentrate on the defender's midsection.

4. Arms and hands are held behind the back or at the sides.

5. If pass blocking, take an inside-position step with the foot nearest the center to take away the inside rushing lane. Attempt to make the rusher take an outside path that will allow a pocket for the passer to throw from. If the rusher gets past, the blocker should immediately turn and face the passer while retreating backward and alert the passer of the oncoming rusher. This allows two things: (a) it reduces the traffic the passer must scramble through, and (b) it gives the passer a safety valve to throw to if pressured. At worst, the blocker will get to the original line of scrimmage.

6. If blocking for a run, attempt to maneuver between the rusher and the running lane.

Blocking strategies

1. If the passer wishes to stay in the pocket, the blocker should line up as near the offensive center as possible without interfering with the snap. This virtually takes away the inside path toward the passer. The blocker needs to be patient, protect the inside, and let the rusher commit to the outside rush. Once the rusher starts outside, pivot on the inside foot, staying low, and shuffle with the rusher on an inside-out path past the passer. Blockers should also be careful not to become overly anxious and step outside to an outside fake, thus leaving an opening to the inside.

2. If the passer wishes to sprint (roll) out to one side, the blockers should block as follows:

   a. Play-side blockers should line up wider than normal to entice the rusher to the inside. The passer can help entice the rusher by taking an initial step in the opposite direction of the rollout. The blockers then attempt to hook (reach) the rusher and make him or her take an inside path to the passer. This block can be assisted by lining up a receiver near the outside of the rusher. On the snap, the blocker and the receiver double-team the rusher.

   b. Off-side blockers should line up very tight to the center to make sure the rusher cannot take an inside path toward the rollout. Getting the rusher to take an outside path complements this type of play.

3. If the passer wishes to run to the outside or run an option, the blockers would block the same way as on a

Figure 33.3. Screen block. A, Arms behind back. B, Arms at sides.

sprint-out pass. Exception: If the team runs an option attack, the quarterback may option off the rusher instead of the defensive back. In this case, the blocker would not attempt to block the rusher and would release and block downfield.

Touching (Touch Football)

Touching is used as a substitute for tackling. The location of the ball carrier when touched by a defensive player will determine the location for start of the next play. Touch the opponent between the knees and the shoulders.

Flag Removal (Flag Football)

Pulling flags is used as a substitute for tackling. The flags are located on a belt around the runner's waist. If close enough, it is good strategy to use both hands to grab at the flags to reduce the chances of an unsuccessful grasp.

Passing

The forward (overhead) pass is an offensive technique used to advance the ball and to hold secondary defensive players deep enough to make the running game function.

Grip

1. Grip the ball slightly behind the middle with two to three fingers on and across the lace. How far behind the middle a player grips the ball depends upon the passer's hand size. Typically, throwers with smaller hands grip the ball near the back of the ball (Figure 33.4).
2. The fingers and thumb should be relaxed and well spread.
3. There must be space between the ball and the palm of the passing hand. Control the ball with the fingers, not the palm. Otherwise, proper wrist rotation cannot be achieved.
4. In the event that the front part of the ball fails to drop in flight, the index finger should be extended toward the rear point of the ball.

Ready position (stance and position before the throw)

1. The stance should be such that the line of the shoulders is perpendicular to the intended target.
2. Feet should be slightly less than shoulder-width apart.
3. The throwing hand is positioned on the ball as mentioned above, and the nonthrowing hand is placed lightly and on the opposite side for control.
4. The ball is held near the head and shoulder area. This allows the passer to deliver the ball as quickly as possible.

Throwing motion

1. The ball is raised toward the throwing shoulder with both hands. The nonthrowing hand releases the ball as the throwing hand is pulled back with the ball to a position behind the ear with the upper arm parallel to the ground (Figure 33.5).

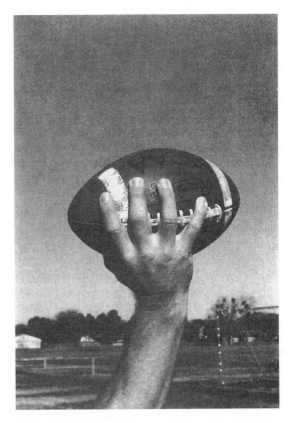

Figure 33.4. Passing grip.

Figure 33.5. Upper-arm and ball position for throwing.

2. As the forward throwing motion begins, the passer steps with the contralateral foot directly at the target, landing on the ball of the foot.

3. As the passer steps, the nonthrowing arm is pulled back sharply in the direction opposite to the pass. This aids shoulder rotation and promotes a stronger throwing motion.

4. As the nonthrowing arm is pulled back, the throwing hand is led by the elbow and moved directly over the shoulder in a sharp downward motion. The elbow must be at least shoulder height to facilitate proper wrist rotation. The thumb of the throwing hand should rotate downward and slightly outward. This type of rotation allows the ball to spiral.

Follow-through

1. The majority of the thrower's weight should be shifted to the front foot as the ball is delivered.
2. The throwing hand should finish across the body over the opposite knee.

Additional coaching points

1. A common error passers make is stepping toward the receiver instead of toward where the receiver will be when the ball arrives. This typically causes the ball to end up behind the receiver. Therefore, the passer should always step toward the point where the ball is intended to meet the receiver. The step also transfers momentum, allowing more force in the throwing motion.

2. The passer should concentrate on that point where the ball is intended to go until the ball reaches the receiver. Concentrating on the receiver during the throwing motion or ball during its flight will inhibit accuracy.

Lateral Pass

The lateral pass is one of the most successful methods of producing touchdowns, provided a few general rules are followed.

1. Use for passes under 5 yards (4.6 m).
2. Use when you are prevented from breaking away.
3. Do not wait for a lateral pass when you are in a position to block for the ball carrier.
4. Use a lateral pass as late as possible.
5. Do not throw lateral passes indiscriminately.
6. Practice either the basketball-type lateral or the one-handed underhand lateral pass.
   a. Basketball pass:
      (1) The ball is delivered by both hands with arm and wrist action, so that it turns relatively slowly end over end.
      (2) There is very little arc on the ball.
   b. One-hand underhand pass:
      (1) The ball rests in the dominant hand and is held there by the nondominant hand until the toss

is made, the ball rolling off the fingertips with a slight spiral action.

Pass Receiving

1. Concentration is the most important teaching point. The receiver should watch the ball from the time it leaves the thrower's hand until the catch is tucked away.

2. Whenever possible, the receiver should reach forward to meet the ball as it approaches and give with the ball by flexing the elbows and wrists on impact. This will cushion the impact and reduce the chances of the ball bouncing off the hands.

3. The arms and hands should be relaxed.

4. The fingers should be spread, with the palms facing the ball.

5. The hands should be very close together and if the pass is:
   a. chest high or higher, the rule is "thumb to thumb and index to index" (forming a triangle)
   b. below waist high, the rule is "little finger to little finger" (fingers pointing down). Keeping the hands close together and fingers spread creates a natural pocket for the ball.
   c. between the chest and waist, the receiver positions the hands as for a. or b., whichever is most comfortable.

6. As the ball is caught, the receiver should tuck the ball away into a protected position, with the arm close to the body.

7. In the protected carrying position there are four points of contact. The front nose of the ball is covered by a hand with the fingers spread. The back point of the ball is locked into the armpit. The outside edge of the ball rests against the forearm. The inside edge of the ball rests against the torso.

Pass-receiving drills

The following drills may also improve throwing.

1. Target drill
   a. With a partner, starting at 10 yards (9.1 m), the receiver makes a target with the hands above, below, or to the side. The arms are extended and the hands form a pocket. The passer attempts to hit the target, and the receiver catches the ball, concentrating on technique.
   b. The partners throw the ball back and forth, alternating targets and gradually increasing the yardage.

2. One-handed drill
   a. Partners face each other from 10 yards (9.1 m) and lightly throw the ball with a slight loft.
   b. The receiver attempts to catch the ball using one hand.
   c. The receiver may use the body to assist, but not the other hand or arm.

d. As the receivers become adept at this speed, the passer may increase the speed of the throw.

e. This drill teaches receivers to reach and give with the ball as well as to improve concentration.

3. Ball drill

a. Partners set up 15 yards (13.7 m) apart.

b. The receiver turns his or her back on the passer.

c. The passer throws a soft, lofted pass about the shoulder height of the receiver and to the outside (right or left).

d. As the ball is released, the passer yells "Ball!"

e. The receiver turns as quickly as possible and attempts to catch the ball.

f. The passer should never throw the ball at the receiver, but can increase the difficulty by increasing the ball speed or yelling "Ball" later.

g. This drill teaches the receiver to turn the head around quickly on a route to locate the ball and then make an adjustment to the ball's flight.

4. Toe dance drill

a. The passer lines up on a sideline.

b. The receiver lines up 10 yards (9.1 m) away on a yard line approximately 10 yards away from the sideline. For example, the passer stands on the intersection of the 10-yard line and the sideline facing the 20-yard (18-m) line. The receiver stands on the 20-yard line, 10 yards away from the sideline and facing it.

c. The receiver jogs toward the sideline, and the passer attempts to throw the ball so the receiver and the ball meet at the intersection of the yard line and the sideline.

d. Once there, the receiver tries to get possession of the ball before going out-of-bounds.

e. As the receivers become proficient at this task, the passer can widen the throw out-of-bounds, forcing the receiver to stretch to catch the ball and attempt to keep at least 1 foot (30 cm) inbounds.

f. This drill can also be used in the end zone. The passer sets up on the endline, while the receivers run toward the endline.

g. This drill promotes concentration and body awareness in relation to the sideline and endline.

Punting

The punt is one of the most important plays in football. It can determine the outcome of the game. The punt is used to gain yardage or to better a team's position on the field. Punting is highly specialized, and constant practice is necessary to develop into a good kicker.

1. Stand with the feet slightly apart and even with each other other, legs flexed at the knees, and weight equally distributed on the balls of both feet.

2. Incline the body forward from the waist, arms and hands extended in front of the body, fingers spread, and palms up.

3. Have either foot either ahead at the start of the kick.

4. Follow the ball with the eyes from the center and after the ball is caught; keep the eyes on it until it has been kicked.

5. Hold the ball with both hands, laces up and with the long axis of the ball perpendicular to the body.

6. Hold the ball on the kicking-foot side just below the chest.

7. Take a maximum of three steps before contacting the ball.

8. Keep the kicking foot plantar-flexed (pointed) at and through the impact with the ball.

9. Release the ball so that it remains in its long axis until after being kicked and before the nonkicking foot touches the ground.

10. Contact the ball between the toe and upper part of the kicking foot.

11. Swing the leg from the hip through the perpendicular arc, the center of the long axis of the ball meeting the instep approximately 2 feet (60 cm) above the ground.

12. As the foot meets the ball, extend the lower leg and lock the knee joint. The kicking motion should follow a path directly to the desired landing spot of the ball.

13. The follow-through extends along this line and should end up as high as the kicker's flexibility allows. A higher follow-through will probably result in a longer punt. A high punt allows for better punt coverage.

14. When advantageous, kick out-of-bounds.

Punting drills

1. Drop drill. One of the most common errors of punting is a poor drop. If dropped correctly, the ball will not tumble or turn and should land on the kicking foot in the same position as when dropped.

a. Assume the normal starting position.

b. Extend arms to the position used in a normal punt.

c. Release the ball with both hands simultaneously.

d. Do not attempt to kick the ball, but let it hit the ground.

e. Watch the path of the ball to see if it turns or tumbles.

f. If the ball is dropped properly, it will bounce straight up or back toward the kicker.

2. One-step drop drill. This incorporates a stepping motion with a drop.

a. Assume a normal starting position or one with the kicking leg slightly forward.

b. Take an elongated stride with the nonkicking leg and drop the ball before the foot touches the ground. Do not take another step.

c. Concentrate on the ball, and observe whether the ball tumbles or turns and how it bounces. Both of these drills work to improve the drop and can be done alone or with partners who can help watch for mistakes.

3. One-step drop, punch (pass). This works on the drop and proper foot contact. Have kickers choose partners and face each other approximately 5 to 7 yards (4.5 to 6.5 m) apart.
   a. Same as *a* in one-step drop drill above.
   b. Same as *b* in one-step drop drill above.
   c. Swing kicking leg through the correct motion but at one-quarter speed, and stop the motion after contact is made with the ball. Make sure the kicking foot is plantar-flexed at impact.
   d. If contact is made correctly, the ball should spiral. The objective is to kick the ball to the partner with a spiral.
   e. The distance between partners as well as the speed of the kicking motion can be gradually increased. Distance and speed of the kicking motion should not be increased unless the kicker is making correct contact with the ball and consistently spiraling the ball. This drill can be expanded by adding one step and then another until the desired number of steps is achieved. In addition, kickers should be reminded to attempt a full motion and not a full-speed motion until their level of skill allows it.

4. Coffin corner drill. This is a buildup drill that concentrates on technique and accuracy.
   a. Line up on a hash mark on the 20-yard (18-m) line and face the nearest corner of the end zone.
   b. Kick five punts and attempt to land in or near the corner out-of-bounds.
   c. After five punts, increase the distance by 10 yards (9.1 m) and repeat.
   d. Continue to increase the distance as the kicker's strength allows.
   e. This drill makes kickers use less force and concentrate on accuracy because the starting distance is short. In addition, it is an excellent warm-up for kickers.

Receiving Punts

1. Concentrate on the ball from the time it leaves the kicker's foot until it is safely caught.
2. Sprint to the point just below the ball and assume a good football position. This allows movement in any direction if the ball drifts.
3. Form a basket with the hands (fingers spread), arms, and forearms nearly parallel, and give with the arms and legs as the ball impacts.
4. The eyes should follow the ball into the arms, while making a nodding motion with the head.
5. The elbows should be "squeezed" inward. Otherwise the ball is liable to go through the receiver's arms.
6. Do not attempt to run upfield until the catch is ensured.

Punt-receiving drills

1. Throwing the ball

   a. Partner up by twos, start at 20 yards (18 m) apart, and throw the ball high in the air.
   b. Receivers position themselves under the ball and attempt to catch it.
   c. Gradually increase the distance between partners, but always attempt to throw the ball high.
   d. When possible, throw the ball sometimes so the nose turns over and sometimes with the nose staying up. This will change how the ball descends and will help the receiver work on judgment.

2. Punt drill. Have partners actually punt the ball to each other. As with the previous drill, start rather close and gradually increase the distance between partners.

3. Concentration drill
   a. Put players in groups of three: one punter, one receiver, and one distracter.
   b. The punter lines up approximately 35 to 40 yards (32 to 36.5 m) away from the receiver and punts the ball to the receiver.
   c. The receiver attempts to catch the ball.
   d. The distracter waits until the ball almost makes contact with the receiver and then screams or lightly touches the receiver as a distraction.
   e. After the kicker kicks five balls, have the partners rotate positions.
   f. This drill is an excellent concentration builder.

Placekick

The traditional and soccer styles of placekicks may be used. The soccer-style kick is a popular form that has evolved in recent years.

Traditional style

1. The kicker should stand so that the path of the kicking leg will be in line through the point of the kick and over the center of the crossbar.
2. A spot slightly below the center of the ball should be picked in advance and the eyes kept focused on this spot throughout the kicking action.
3. The feet should be comfortably spread, knees slightly bent, and body slightly inclined forward from the hips.
4. For the kickoff, any number of steps may be taken in the approach to the kick, but for a field goal or point after touchdown, only two-step approaches are valid.
5. The nonkicking foot should be planted slightly to the side and far enough back of the ball to allow contact to be made below the middle of the ball. Both side and back positions should be within 6 to 12 inches (15 to 30 cm).
6. As the nonkicking foot is planted, the kicking lower leg should reach a position at least parallel to the ground. The higher the backswing, the more force that can be imparted to the ball (Figure 33.6A).

Figure 33.6. Conventional-style kick. A, Backswing (ankle locked). B, Downswing/foot position. C, Dorsal-flexed position.

7. The eyes should remain focused on the ball from the start of the approach until contact is made with the ball. The kicker should actually see the foot contact the ball (Figure 33.6B).
8. On impact, the foot should be locked in a dorsal-flexed position of about 90 degrees. This allows a consistent point of impact and solid impact (Figure 33.6C).
9. The follow-through of the kicking leg is toward the intended line of flight.
10. If greater height is needed, the kicker should start the approach slightly closer to the ball. This makes the impact point lower, which achieves a higher trajectory. If more distance is needed, the kicker should move farther away. This causes the impact position to be higher so that the ball will travel farther but with less trajectory.

Soccer-style kick

1. The approach should have the same number of steps as the conventional kick, except from a different angle. The kicker should approach from approximately a 45-degree angle.

2. On the last step, the nonkicking foot should land in approximately the same spot as in the conventional style. The plant foot might land slightly wider in this style due to the approach. To prevent a "hook" or a "shank," the toe of the plant foot must point at the desired target.

3. On the last step, the backswing of the kicking lower leg should reach a position at least parallel to the ground. The higher the backswing, the more force that can be imparted to the ball.

4. The downswing should be made down and slightly across the kicker's body so that the foot makes contact behind the ball in line with the intended line of flight.

5. At impact, the kicking foot should be plantar-flexed and make contact slightly below the middle of the ball (Figure 33.7A, B).

6. The eyes remain focused on the ball from the start of the approach through the kicking motion.

7. The follow-through finishes close to the intended line of flight.

Note: In both styles of kicks, the follow-through does not have to be very high.

Drills for kicking (both styles)

1. No-step wall drill. Position partners 10 feet (3 m) away from a wall with a target taped to the wall 3 feet (90 cm) high. Partners take turns holding for each other and kicking.

   a. Conventional: Stand directly behind the ball with the feet parallel and the plant foot in the desired position. Soccer: Stand in the same manner but at a 45-degree angle to the intended line of flight.

   b. Lift kicking lower leg up past parallel to the ground and down into the ball slightly below the center.

   c. On impact, soccer-style foot is plantar-flexed and conventional style is dorsi-flexed.

   d. Follow-through is short, about 12 to 18 inches (30 to 45 cm) and toward the target.

   e. The object is to use good form, keep the head down, and hit the target.

2. One-step partner drill

   a. Drill is exactly like the preceding drill, except that the kicker stands in the same starting position and takes one elongated stride backward.

   b. From this position, the kicker takes a stride toward the ball and pulls the lower leg up past parallel in the backswing and then down through the ball.

   c. The follow-through is short to emphasize technique, not direction.

   d. The kicker attempts to kick the ball to the partner 10 yards (9.1 m) away.

Figure 33.7. Soccer-style kick. A, Body and foot position. B, Plantar-flexed position.

Figure 33.8. Centering. A, Two-handed snap. B, One-handed snap.

e. The distance can gradually be increased between partners. The kickers will find that they can kick the ball a great distance with only one step if done correctly.

f. This drill can also be expanded by increasing the number of back steps taken by the kicker until the desired number of steps is reached.

Note: Kickers may have a problem when taking back steps and then approaching the ball. Typically, they take normal steps backward but elongated steps toward the ball. Therefore, they will be too close to the ball at contact. Most kickers use a 3:1 ratio when determining how far back to go—for example, if using a one-step kick, the kicker would position himself or herself behind the ball in the desired plant position and take three normal steps backward from the ball. A conventional kicker would start here, and a soccer-style kicker would then take one or two lateral steps. It is important for soccer-style kickers to remember as they take lateral steps not to go directly lateral (parallel) to the line of scrimmage. This would put them farther away from the ball than they marked off. Therefore, the lateral steps should be slightly less than parallel to the line of scrimmage.

3. Accuracy and progression drill

  a. Position the ball at the extra-point mark and have the kickers attempt to make five in a row.

b. If they are successful, have them move back 5 yards (4.6 m) and attempt to make five more.

c. As long as they are successful, they can continue to move in 5-yard (4.6-m) increments.

d. Once a kicker misses, the partners switch.

e. This builds concentration and leg strength, and is an excellent warm-up.

Centering

Centering is much like a forward pass, but upside down.

1. Hold the ball on the ground with the dominant hand.
2. Place your fingers on the laces.
3. Use the nondominant hand to guide the ball, if necessary. A center may use a one- or two-handed snap (Figure 33.8A, B).
4. Spread the feet wider than shoulder-width.
5. With the quarterback right behind the center, pass the ball with the dominant hand only.

LEARNING SEQUENCE

1. Practice all the physical skills related to the game:
   a. Throwing
   b. Receiving
   c. Kicking/punting
   d. Blocking

e. Pass coverage
f. Deflagging
g. Lateral passing
h. Running with the ball and fakes
i. Pass rushing
2. Learn the positions, including duties and common formations
3. Learn kicking formations and assignments involved:
   a. Getting down field quickly and keeping the runner inside
   b. Kicker as safety
4. Practice offensive plays:
   a. Routes
   b. Blocking schemes
   c. Defensive-formations recognition
   d. Audibles
5. Practice defensive formations:
   a. Player to player
   b. Zones:
      (1) Two-deep straight
      (2) Two-deep rotation
      (3) Three-deep
   c. All defensive formations change depending on how many players rush the passer
6. Practice the kicking game:
   a. Punt return
   b. Punt coverage
   c. Extra point
   d. Kickoff
   e. Kickoff return
7. Playing suggestions
   a. Assignments should not be tipped off by players' leaning or pointing the eyes, head, or body or by changing facial expression.
   b. Remember that the passer is a ball carrier as long as the ball is in his or her hands.
   c. Vary your style of defensive play when flanked by an offensive player. Move out and set, move out and come back in motion, and move and dart through the split if it is wide enough.
   d. Early in the game, discover which defensive players are weak in covering passes.
   e. Set up plays by sacrificing one or two downs to make future plays function properly.
   f. Plays should be set up in a sequence, including both passing and running plays.

DEFENSE

With the rule changes that eliminated contact blocking, offensive football is almost exclusively passing. Therefore, the type of defense employed must be set up to stop the pass first. With any of the following defenses, a few adjustments will control any running attack.

There are three key factors for a successful defensive team:

1. A strong pass rush: The pass rush is not typically the primary focus of a defense. Mistakenly, teams put slower, weaker players in this position. However, just like all levels of football, pass rushing is the most important aspect of defending the pass. Nothing helps the defensive backfield more than a quarterback who is under tremendous pressure. The more time a quarterback has, the more difficult it is to cover the receivers.
2. Team speed: Rarely will an offensive team be completely stopped. Therefore, overall team speed allows maximum pursuit of the ball in all situations. Three vital positions where team speed and ability are needed most are pass rusher, linebacker, and safety. The three best athletes on the team should play in these positions. Team speed is also more vital if the defense runs a player-to-player defense.
3. Communication and cohesion: No matter what the skill level, if players are not communicating, there will be missed assignments and lack of unity in the defense. Therefore, players may line up incorrectly, and, by mere position alone, set themselves up to be beaten by an offensive player. For example, the defense is in a two-deep rotational zone that ends up in three-deep coverage if the quarterback rolls out. If the corner who is supposed to drop back as a safety does not, then one-third of the deep zone is uncovered. Therefore, the defense must never line up in a position where it cannot cover.

Player-to-Player Pass Coverage

Eligible receivers are covered by a single defensive player who follows the receiver wherever he or she goes.

Coverage rules

1. Concentrate on the receiver, not the quarterback.
2. Concentrate on the receiver's midsection, not the head.
3. Never let a receiver get behind you. Therefore, the initial distance between a receiver and a defensive back should be determined by the receiver's speed.
4. Never leave your player unless you see the ball has been thrown.

General strengths

1. Allows tighter coverage, especially in short-yardage situations.
2. Makes the receiver work harder to get open and catch a pass.

General weaknesses

1. Requires more-skilled, faster athletes to perform properly than do other defenses.
2. Requires more physical effort than the zone, so fatigue may become a factor. This is especially true if players are playing both offense and defense.

3. Overloads by receivers (three to one side) make it difficult to cover.
4. Crossing patterns by multiple receivers may cause a defender to be screened and not be able to pursue the receiver.
5. There is an offensive innovation that uses no players as blockers and two or more receivers lined up on both the right and left sides. A player-to-player defense would have a difficult time defending this offense, especially if the receivers run crossing patterns.

Player-to-Player Formations and Strategies

The following illustrations are for seven-player teams. For eight- or nine-player teams, use the additional player(s) to cover players where needed. For example, if the offense uses another wide receiver, cover this player with another defensive back. If the player lines up as a blocker or in the backfield, the extra defensive player may rush, take the back one-on-one, or play a rover and help where needed.

Two rushers, one free safety, one linebacker

See Figure 33.9.

Player responsibilities.

1. Rushers only have rushing responsibilities. They attempt to sack or pressure the quarterback.
2. The linebacker takes center or first blocker to release for a pass. If no release, linebacker reads the quarterback and plays a shallow (8 to 10 yards; 7 to 9 m) middle-zone coverage.
3. The free safety typically lines up in the middle of the field, favoring the strong receiver side (side with two or more receivers). The free safety plays like a center fielder, reading the quarterback's eyes, and breaks on the ball when it is released. The free safety has no one-on-one responsibilities, so he or she must alert the other defensive backs if there is a run.

4. The remainder of the backs each pick a receiver and run with him or her wherever he or she goes. These players cannot concern themselves with the run or other receivers. They must focus on the receiver and not the quarterback. Defenders should attempt to stay between their player and the end zone and never get beat deep. They should line up with enough distance between the receiver and defender to enable deep coverage.

Strengths and weaknesses.

1. Excellent for short-yardage plays. Allows tight coverage on receivers.
2. Allows free safety to help out on deep patterns or speedy receivers.
3. Allows maximum pressure on the quarterback.
4. If the quarterback gets outside of the rushers, the free safety must come up and make the play. Because of the distance the safety must travel, this usually results in a substantial gain.
5. If the center releases and is picked up by the linebacker and a second blocker releases, the free safety is again responsible for the play.
6. If both blockers and center release, one of the players will be uncovered.

Strategies.

1. Have rushers line up wide and rush from the outside and keep the quarterback in the pocket to stop the quarterback from running.
2. Not much can be done about multiple blockers releasing in this defense. Switching to a single-rusher defense would be the best tactic.

Two linebackers, two rushers, no free safety

See Figure 33.10.

Responsibilities.

1. Rushers and pass-coverage backs are the same.
2. With two linebackers, one is designated to take the first blocker to release. If another blocker releases, the

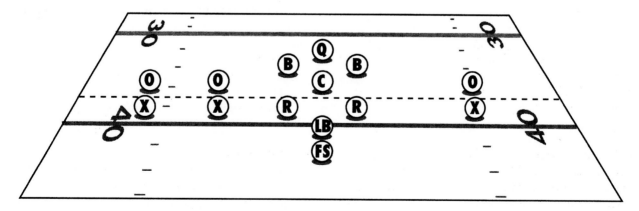

Figure 33.9. Two rushers, one free safety, one linebacker (player to player no. 1). (B: blocker; C: center; FS: free safety; LB: linebacker; O: receiver; Q: quarterback; R: rusher; X: secondary defender.)

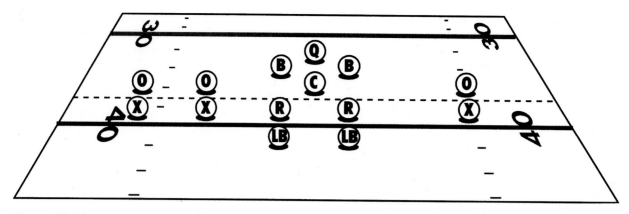

Figure 33.10. Two linebackers, two rushers, no free safety (player to player no. 2). (B: blocker; C: center; LB: linebacker; O: receiver; Q: quarterback; R: rusher; X: secondary defender.)

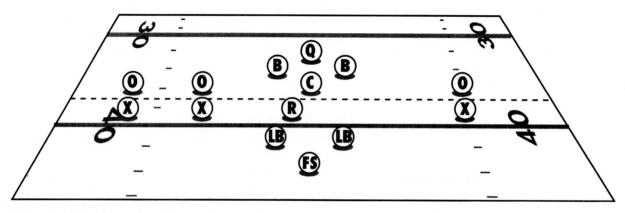

Figure 33.11. One rusher, two linebackers, one free safety (player to player no. 3). (B: blocker; C: center; FS: free safety; LB: linebacker; O: receiver; Q: quarterback; R: rusher; X: secondary defender.)

second linebacker covers this player. If another blocker does not release, the linebacker plays a shallow middle zone and takes the quarterback if he or she runs.

Strengths and weaknesses.

1. Allows maximum pressure on the quarterback.
2. Excellent for short-yardage plays. Allows tight coverage on receivers.
3. Reduces the success of the quarterback running.
4. Reduces the success of short passes to the second blocker releasing.
5. There is no free safety to help cover deep. Therefore, if a defensive back is beaten deep, it usually results in a long gain or a touchdown.

Strategies.

1. Defensive backs must play a little softer and not be fooled by a short fake, allowing the receiver to get behind the defender.
2. Rushers can take an inside or outside path to the quarterback, allowing more pressure.

One rusher, two linebackers, one free safety
See Figure 33.11.

Responsibilities.

1. Defensive backs and two linebackers play the same as the defense above.
2. Free safety plays the same as in the first player-to-player defense.

Strengths and weaknesses. This defense has all the strengths of the aforementioned defenses save one: Because there's only one rusher, the quarterback will have additional time to throw and the receivers will have additional time to get open.

Strategies.

1. Defensive backs can play tighter.
2. Have one of the linebackers line up like a rusher and drop back into position on the snap of the ball. This will keep the lone rusher from being double-teamed by the blockers.
3. In this defense, the lone pass rusher *must* be an aggressive, fast player to pressure the quarterback.

Zone Coverage

With the exception of pass rushers, each defensive player is assigned an area (zone) to be responsible for covering.

Receivers entering their zone should be guarded by release as the receiver enters another zone.

Coverage rules

1. Stay at home. Never follow a receiver into another zone.
2. Keep the receiver in front of you.
3. Safeties must stay as deep as the deepest player in the zone and wide as the widest player.
4. When the ball is released, all defensive backs attempt to break on the ball and/or pursue.

General strengths

1. Does not require exceptionally gifted athletes.
2. Is not as fatiguing as player-to-player defense.
3. Good at preventing the deep pass.
4. Has more players breaking on the ball than player-to-player defenses.

General weaknesses

1. Does not allow tight coverage in short-yardage plays.
2. Is weak in the seams between zones.
3. Is susceptible to the zone being flooded by multiple receivers.
4. Is typically weak in the flat area.

Zone Formations and Strategies

Two safeties, corners, rushers; one linebacker

See Figure 33.12.

Player responsibilities.

1. Rushers pursue quarterback.
2. Corners have the flat area on their side. The flat area is approximately 10 to 12 yards (9 to 11 m) deep, from the near sideline to the linebackers' hook/curl zone.
3. Linebacker has the hook/curl zone. This zone is about 10 to 12 yards deep and approximately 10 yards on either side of the linebacker.
4. Each safety has one half of the field, behind all of the other zones.

Strengths and weaknesses.

1. Allows maximum pressure on the quarterback.
2. Excellent against the run.
3. Can be hurt in the seams between zones.
4. Flooding the zones makes it difficult to cover.

Strategy. Have defenders line up with a player-to-player look and on the snap of the ball go into their zones. This may confuse the quarterback and not tip off the weak areas of this defense.

Two safeties, linebackers, corners; one rusher

See Figure 33.13.

Player responsibilities.

1. Strong-side rusher pursues the quarterback.
2. Weak-side rusher drops into linebacker position and plays the hook/curl zone on his or her side.
3. The linebackers widen to the strong side and play the hook/curl zone. Having two linebackers cover this zone helps the corners by decreasing their flat coverage.
4. Corners have flats. The flats will not be as wide due to the two-linebacker set.
5. Safeties play halves.

Strengths and weaknesses.

1. Excellent short-pass coverage, which allows more players to break on short passes.
2. Deep passes are more difficult to throw because the ball typically has to pass over one of the shallow defenders to a receiver. This helps the safeties because the ball is in the air longer and allows them additional time to pursue a pass.
3. Excellent against the run.
4. With only one rusher, the quarterback will have additional time to find a receiver, especially one on a deep route.

Strategy. Have the weak-side rusher move to the linebacker position on that side on the snap of the ball. This will help the single rusher from being double-teamed.

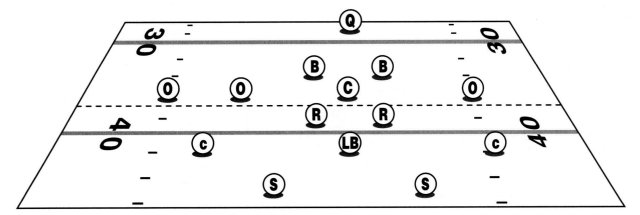

Figure 33.12. Two safeties, corners, and rushers; one linebacker (zone no. 1). (B: blocker; C: center; c: corner; LB: linebacker; O: receiver; Q: quarterback; R: rusher; S: safety.)

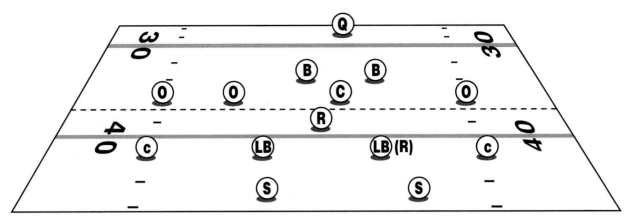

Figure 33.13. Two safeties, linebackers, and corners; one rusher (zone no. 2). (B: blocker; C: center; c: corner; LB: linebacker; O: receiver; Q: quarterback; R: rusher; S: safety.)

Three safeties, one corner, one linebacker, two rushers

See Figure 33.14.

Player responsibilities.

1. Rushers pursue quarterback.
2. Linebacker covers hook/curl zone.
3. Strong-side corner (corner on the two-receiver side) plays the flat.
4. Weak-side corner (corner on the one-receiver side) lines up in the flat zone and sprints to the deep, outside one-third of the field on that side.
5. Both safeties line up in halves and rotate toward the offense's strong side and play thirds. Therefore, in the illustration, the right corner plays the right outside one-third; the right safety plays the middle one-third; and the left safety plays the left outside one-third.

Strengths and weaknesses.

1. Excellent against the deep throw.
2. Puts maximum pressure on the quarterback.
3. Weak-side flat is uncovered.

Strategy. Have safeties and corners line up in Cover I prior to the snap and move to the new coverage on the snap of the ball. This will prevent the opponents from identifying an uncovered area. It may also lure the quarterback into throwing deep.

Three safeties, two corners, one linebacker, one rusher

See Figure 33.15.

Player responsibilities.

1. Strong-side rusher pursues quarterback.
2. Weak-side rusher lines up to rush and drops into the corner position on the snap of the ball and plays the flat.
3. Linebacker covers hook/curl zone.
4. Corners and safeties rotate toward the offensive strong side and play thirds, as in zone 3A (Figure 33.14).

Strengths and weaknesses.

1. Only one rusher allows the quarterback additional throwing time.
2. Excellent against the deep pass.

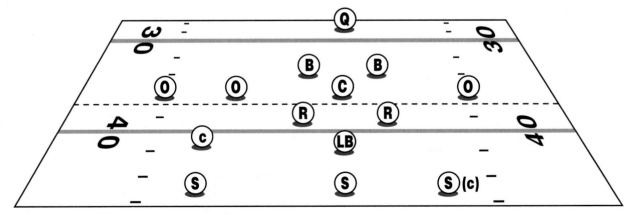

Figure 33.14. Three safeties, one corner, one linebacker, two rushers (zone no. 3A). (B: blocker; C: center; c: corner; LB: linebacker; O: receiver; Q: quarterback; R: rusher; S: safety.)

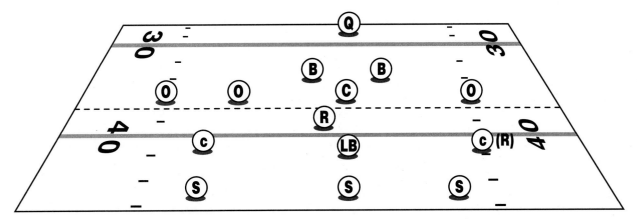

Figure 33.15. Three safeties, two corners, one linebacker, one rusher (zone no. 3B). (B: blocker; C: center; c: corner; LB: linebacker; O: receiver; Q: quarterback; R: rusher; S: safety.)

3. Does not give up the weak-side flat, as does zone 3A.

Strategy. As in zone 3A, line up in zone 1 and switch on the snap of the ball.

OFFENSE

Even though speed is an asset for an offensive team, it is not as important as for the defense. A team can have a very productive offense with receivers who run good routes and are excellent possession receivers.

There are two major factors for an effective offense:

1. A good quarterback is the most important individual in the offense.
2. Everyone on the offensive unit should have decent quickness and must be able to catch the ball.

Offensive Considerations

1. Types of offense:
   a. Drop back: Quarterback stays in the pocket to throw.
      (1) Quarterback needs a strong arm.
      (2) Must be excellent blockers for maximum protection.
      (3) Receivers must be fast to allow the deep pass.
   b. Sprint out: Quarterback rolls to one side of the field to throw.
      (1) Quarterback must be mobile and have decent throwing ability.
      (2) Do not need strong blockers.
   c. Option: Quarterback sprints out to one side of the field and throws or pitches to the option back. Option back may run or throw.
      (1) Must have a quarterback with excellent mobility, and would be very effective if he or she can throw on the run.
      (2) Option back needs good speed, lateral movement, and throwing ability.

      (3) Need quick blockers to slow the rush.
   d. One- or no-blocker set.
      (1) Quarterback must be quick and have a strong arm.
      (2) Receivers need to run hard, quick routes and move with the quarterback if he or she scrambles.
2. Personnel: Dictates what style of offense will be utilized. This is especially true with the quarterback.
   a. Quarterback:
      (1) If the quarterback is not very mobile but has a good arm, he or she should stay in the pocket formed by the blockers to throw.
      (2) If the quarterback is very mobile but does not have a strong arm, an option or sprint-out attack may be preferred.
      (3) If the quarterback has both mobility and throwing ability, the offense may utilize any attack.
   b. Receivers:
      (1) If they are not very fast, the offense must rely on short, quick passes and attempt to have a ball-control type offense.
      (2) If they have excellent speed, they can be used in all offenses.
   c. Blockers:
      (1) If they are slow, they would be better suited for the straight drop-back pass.
      (2) If they are quick, they can work in any offense, but would be excellent for the option and sprint-out style.

Offensive Formations

The following formations are composed of seven-person teams. If additional players are used, they may be lined up as receivers or blockers depending on the style of offense and the defense played against.

Option sets

See Figure 33.16.

Strengths and weaknesses.

1. This is a good ball-control offense.
2. There are fewer chances for interceptions.
3. Forces the defense to commit to cover the run, which opens up passing lanes.
4. It is excellent for running out the clock.
5. It is difficult to catch up when down by several points.
6. Limits the amount of field the offense can attack. Because the quarterback is running in one direction, it makes it very difficult to throw back to the other side of the field. This enables the defense to give up an area and use that player to help stop the run.

Strategies.

1. Do not always line up the running back in the backfield, but have him or her line up as a receiver and go in motion to start the option.
2. Do not always run the option. Mix the running plays with some passing plays to keep the defense from stacking up to stop the run.

Note: Sprint-out and drop-back formations may use motion with receivers and/or an option for formation.

Sprint-out and drop-back pass formations

See Figure 33.17.

Strengths and weaknesses.

1. Provides more opportunities for interceptions.

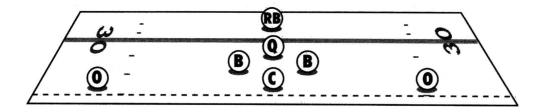

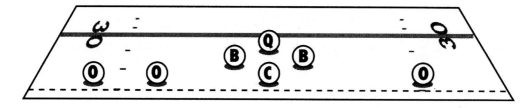

Figure 33.16. Option sets. (B: blocker; C: center; O: receiver; Q: quarterback; RB: running back.)

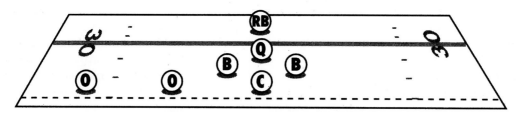

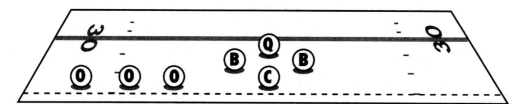

Figure 33.17. Sprint-out and drop-back pass formations. (B: blocker; C: center; O: receiver; Q: quarterback.)

2. May not provide as much ball control unless many short passes are thrown.

3. It is easier to catch up from a large deficit.

Strategies.

1. Alternate formations to confuse the defense.

2. Alternate the side receivers line up on, to confuse the defense by showing it something different almost every play.

3. Use motion to identify player-to-player coverage and to flood a zone.

One- or no-blocker formations

See Figure 33.18.

Strengths and weaknesses.

1. Allows maximum number of receivers into the pass pattern, which puts a tremendous strain on the coverage.

2. Excellent against player-to-player defense because so many receivers are releasing and many receivers are lined up on the same side.

3. Excellent for short-yardage passes.

4. Hard to make a long pass unless the quarterback can avoid the rush.

5. If the defense is in player-to-player coverage and the quarterback avoids the rush, there is no player left to guard the quarterback and the run becomes a viable option.

General Offensive Strategies

1. Take what the defense gives you.
   a. Player-to-player defense.
      (1) Have many crossing patterns.
      (2) Put many receivers on the same side. This makes it very hard to cover if the receivers cross.

   (3) Find the weakest defender and let the receiver he or she is covering line up alone to allow more room to get open.
   (4) Use the one- or no-blocker offense.
   (5) Clear out an area with the receivers, release a blocker there, and throw to him or her.
   (6) Quarterback should run if the rush can be avoided.
   b. Two-deep zone with two corners, one linebacker, and one rusher.
      (1) Flood zones with several receivers.
      (2) Throw passes between the seams of the zones.
      (3) Quick-outs and quick-ins with the wide receivers are difficult to stop if done correctly.
      (4) If the quarterback has time, flood the deep areas with receivers because each safety has to cover half the field.
   c. Two-deep zone with one rusher, two corners, and two linebackers.
      (1) Short patterns are going to be very difficult to defend.
      (2) Any medium-distance pattern that is between the linebackers is good.
      (3) Flood the deep safeties.
   d. Three-deep zone with two corners, one linebacker, and one rusher.
      (1) Throwing deep will be difficult, so concentrate on short patterns.
      (2) Flood the short patterns with several receivers.
      (3) Because there is only one rusher in this formation, the quarterback should have more time to throw and may run if the rush can be avoided.

2. Give the defense a different look as often as possible.

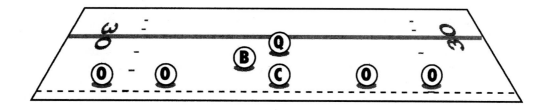

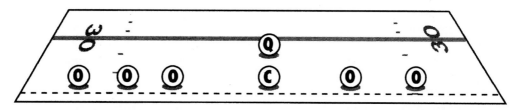

Figure 33.18. One- or no-blocker formations. (B: blocker; C: center; O: receiver; Q: quarterback.)

3. Build plays on one another—in other words, set the defense up. Throw to one area with a pattern of two or more receivers. On the next play, run the same pattern but throw to a different receiver.

4. All receivers must run their routes as if they were the primary receiver.

5. The quarterback should attempt to throw to as many receivers, including the lineman, as possible. This keeps the defense from keying on any one player.

SAFETY PRECAUTIONS

1. Inspect all equipment to ensure safety and minimize injuries.

2. Provide competent officials.

3. Inspect the field and clear it of all obstacles that might cause injuries.

4. Give immediate medical attention to injured players.

TEACHING CONSIDERATIONS

1. Use a modified ball (smaller, lighter) for young learners and women. Consider using a foam or plastic ball to establish skills.

2. In most school programs, contact blocking or tackling of any sort should not be permitted for safety reasons. Flag football is an acceptable substitute.

3. Passing and receiving skills should be taught first. Partner work can be used, first with stationary receivers at short distances and then with moving receivers at longer distances.

4. Two-on-one play can begin a player's introduction to defense. Encourage players to break up passing plays by staying with the receiver between the goal and receiver.

5. All players should practice kicking skills. This can be done in partners, with one partner kicking and the other receiving the ball.

6. When passing, kicking, and receiving skills have become somewhat consistent, modified games can be played, beginning with two-on-two and moving toward more players on each side. Having six players is adequate for the game and encourages more participation. Teach a few basic offensive and defensive plays and then encourage students to design their own plays.

7. Increase the size of the playing field as the number of players increases. Add centering and specific positioning as students begin to understand, through their play, the need for differentiated positioning. Keep rules at a minimum. Enforce no-contact rules consistently.

RULE MODIFICATIONS

The following sample rule and/or game modifications are used to increase time on task and participation and improve the chances for learning and success.

1. Favor more teams with smaller numbers of students per team. The field sizes might have to be modified, but a smaller number of students increases the number of opportunities for each player to touch the ball and be a more active participant.

2. Use smaller balls. The smaller balls will be more developmentally appropriate for students with smaller hands and weaker students.

3. Use nontraditional balls (e.g., Nerf, softcover balls, balls of various shapes that are easier to catch) to improve motivation and increase success.

4. If field goals are used, construct goals that are larger than normal to increase success.

5. If more adept players tend to "hog" the ball, change the rules to promote cooperation of typically weaker or excluded students. For example, though it is erroneous thinking, girls are typically avoided because they are thought to be not very good. The following coed rules could be applied to increase participation by the girls:

   a. Any boy-to-boy touchdown equals 6 points. Any boy-to-girl or girl-to-boy touchdown equals 9 points.

   b. After a successful boy-to-boy play (completed pass), the next play is deemed "closed" and must include a girl. This could entail a girl throwing to a boy, a girl throwing to a girl, or a boy throwing to a girl. This play must be successful, in that at least 1 yard is gained. If the play is unsuccessful, the next play is also deemed "closed."

   c. Award extra points at the end of the game (6 or instructor's choice) if all players on a team attempted to throw a pass or made an attempt to catch a pass. If all team members were part of a completed pass (either the thrower or receiver) the team is awarded double the extra points for attempts (12 or teacher's choice).

6. The actual game could be structured like a scrimmage. For example, for two teams of 8 players:

   a. Each team has eight consecutive offensive plays.

      (1) Normal zone-line-to-gain rules apply. If the team makes a first down, they continue to score.

      (2) If a first down is not made after the first four plays, the team returns to the original zone line and continues until all eight plays have been attempted.

      (3) If a score is made on the first play, the team returns to the original zone line and continues until all eight plays have been attempted.

   b. Each player has a chance to be the quarterback. The participants can determine the order, but after the first quarterback calls and executes a play, another player gets a chance to do the same. This way of playing the game effectively moves the ball around. For example, students who typically do not get the ball thrown to them tend to choose another avoided player to throw a pass to.

    c. During the offense's eight plays, the defense also rotates positions; therefore, everyone is afforded the chance to play each position, and its players are not relegated to positions they do not want to play.

    d. Once the offense has completed eight plays, the ball is turned over to the defense.

7. Invoke a "secret play" rule into your game. For example, each team is allowed one secret play per half. Rules:

    a. At any given time, the quarterback may elect to punt the ball instead of throwing a pass.

    b. Wherever the ball lands is where the opposing team must start their next offensive series.

    c. If the ball goes into the end zone or beyond, the opposing team starts on the first zone line.

    d. However, to award the defense for being alert and thinking, if they catch the punt, the offense is charged with an incomplete pass, must proceed with the next down, and lose their secret play for this half.

GLOSSARY

backfield The players behind the line, who usually handle the ball.

backward pass A pass that travels toward the goal line a team is defending; may be made by any player.

balanced line Same number of players on each side of the center.

block Using the shoulder, but not the arms, to intercept a defensive player or to stop a defensive player from touching the ball carrier.

bootleg play Faking a handoff or a pass to another player, then running with the ball shielded with the body from the defensive team's view.

button hook A pass route in which the receiver turns and runs back to catch the ball.

centering The act by the center of putting the ball in play from the ground by handing or passing the ball between the legs to a backfield player.

clipping Landing on the back of the leg(s) of a player not carrying the ball.

cross-back An offensive play in which two backs cross, one of them taking a handoff from the quarterback.

cut back To change direction; usually done by the receiver or ball carrier.

disqualifying foul Unnecessary roughness, for which a player is removed from the game.

double wingback An offensive formation: two backs are placed about 1 yard (0.9 m) outside of their ends, one back is placed either to the right or left behind a guard, and the tailback is about 5 yards (4.5 m) behind the center.

down A unit of the game that starts with the centering of the ball and ends when the ball is declared dead.

end zone The 10-yard (9-m) area between the goal line and endline.

fair catch A catch designated by the player receiving a kicked ball by raising the hand.

flag guarding Using the hands, arms, or clothing or spinning more than once to prevent another player from pulling the flag. Penalty: 15 yards (13.7 m) and loss of down.

flanker An offensive receiver lining up closer to the sideline than the team.

handoff A play in which one back hands the ball to another back.

lateral pass Passing the ball backward or sideways.

line of scrimmage An imaginary line through the front tip of the ball and perpendicular to the sidelines.

offsides Advancement of a player beyond the line of scrimmage before the ball is snapped.

safety A score made when a free ball, or one possessed by a player defending his or her own goal, becomes dead behind the goal, provided the impetus that caused the ball to cross the goal was supplied by the defending team.

shotgun offense A formation, used primarily for passing, in which the quarterback lines up 5 to 6 yards (4.5 to 5.5 m) behind the center.

SUGGESTED READING

Chamness, D. 2002. *Coaching kids flag football.* Lincoln, NE: Writers Club Press.

Coaching YMCA champions flag football. 2001. Champaign IL: Human Kinetics.

Guy, R., and Sang, R. 2009. *Football kicking and punting.* Champaign, IL: Human Kinetics.

Johnson, J. 1992. *Flag football: The worldwide game.* Boston, MA: American Press.

Reed, J. 1999. *Coaching youth flag football.* Alamo, CA: J. T. Reed Publishers.

The United States Flag and Touch Football League. Current ed. *The United States flag and touch football rules.* Mentor, OH: USFT Football League.

RESOURCES

Videos

Football skills analysis: A practical guide for observing performance. 1997. Dubuque, IA: McGraw-Hill.

NIRSA: Flag and touch football rules and *First and twenty* are both available from NIRSA, 850 SW 15th St., Corvallis, OR 97333.

See Appendix C for other video sources.

WEB SITES

American Flag and Touch Football League
  www.aftfl.com

Coaching Flag Football
  http://www.coachflagfootball.com

Flag Football Magazine
  www.flagmag.com

National Women's Flag Football Association
  www.keywest.com/nwffa3.html

NFL Youth Football Network
  www.nflyouthfootball.com

Pro-Flag Football
  www.pro-flagfootball.com

United States Flag Football League
  www.usftl.com

34 Track and Field

After completing this chapter, the reader should be able to:

- Understand and appreciate the history and development of the sport of track and field
- Become familiar with the events included in a track-and-field competition and the equipment and facilities required
- Understand the various skills involved in the running, jumping, vaulting, and throwing events
- Be aware of the rules governing competition in these events
- Teach basic skills in these events to a group of students

HISTORY

Track-and-field events originated almost with the beginning of humanity. To survive, humans had to be gymnasts, sprinters, hunters, and warriors. Survival depended on the ability to outperform the challenger, human or animal. When not being pursued or in search of sustenance, early humans kept physically fit by engaging in running, jumping, or throwing activities with families or other groups.

Games involving the fundamentals of track and field were formulated by the Greeks during their Golden (Homeric) Age. The most famous of these games were the Olympics, which began in 776 BC and were held every 5 and then 4 years until CE 392, when they were abolished by the Romans. In 1894 they were reorganized by Pierre de Frédy, Baron de Coubertin, and since then they have been conducted in different countries as an international festival.

The U.S. men's Olympic track-and-field teams have done well since the first modern-era Olympic Games, held in Athens in 1896. They have been one of the dominant teams, with strong competition coming from the Soviet Union, Great Britain, East Germany, and West Germany. The breakup of the Soviet Union and other Eastern European countries has weakened these teams. The U.S. women's Olympic track-and-field teams have also fared well since their first competition in the 1928 Games, where they won 1 gold, 2 silver, and 1 bronze. The Soviet and German women's teams dominated the competition through 1976. In 1980, the U.S. women's team began to improve, and in 1984 it became a world contender with 16 medals. In the 1992 Olympics at Barcelona, the U.S. track-and-field team won 30 medals, 20 by the men and 10 by the women. This total included 12 of the possible 43 gold, 8 silver, and 10 bronze medals. The U.S. team won both of the men's relay events, and the women took a gold and silver in their two relays. Nineteen of the 30 medals were in track events (11 men and 8 women). Carl Lewis, Mike Powell, and Joe Greene swept the men's long jump while Jackie Joyner-Kersee was the only double-medal winner in

individual events (bronze in the women's long jump and gold in the heptathlon).

The U.S. track teams continued their dominance in the 1996 Olympic Games in Atlanta, winning 13 gold, 5 silver, and 5 bronze for a total of 23 medals. The men won 16 and the women won 7 medals. Russia was second with 10 total medals, and Germany finished third with 7 total medals. The U.S. total of 23 medals was down from the 30 medals won in the 1992 Games, but the 1996 Games had the largest participation in history. Over 100 countries competed, with 45 countries winning medals. The memorable moments of the 1996 Games were Carl Lewis's and Jackie Joyner-Kersee's long-jump performances, Canada's Donovan Bailey's 100-meter victory, France's Marie-José Pérec's 200–400 double victory, and Michael Johnson's remarkable double in the 200 and 400 with a 200 world record of 19.32 seconds, 0.50 second under the old world record.

Research continues to have an impact on improving performances with the application of scientific principles. Improvements in training techniques, nutrition, and psychological preparation are helping athletes achieve their goals of faster sprint and endurance times, longer distances in the horizontal jumps and throws, and higher heights in the vertical jumps. Humans have not yet reached their limits. Records will continue to fall in the future.

In the 2000 Olympic Games in Sydney, Australia, no world records were set. It was the first time since the 1948 Games that this has happened. The lower performances of the Sydney Olympics were offset by the outstanding competition. Some of the key highlights were Haile Gabrselassie's (Ethiopia) victory as he strained to catch Paul Tergat (Kenya) at the line in the 10,000 meters; Jan Zelenzny's (Czech Republic) come-from-behind victory in the javelin, defeating Steve Backley (Great Britain) for his third Olympic title and Olympic record; Stacy Dragila's (USA) dramatic pole-vault; 35-year-old Heike Drechsler's (Germany) recapture of the long-jump crown she lost eight years earlier; Cathy

Freeman's (Australia) win in the women's 400-meter amid thunderous emotional cheering that shook the stadium; Maurice Greene's (USA) returning the 100-meter title to the United States after sitting tearfully in the stands in 1996; Michael Johnson, at age 33 becoming the oldest person to win the 400-meter and the first in history to successfully defend it; Marion Jones's failure to win 5 gold medals, but walking away with 5 total medals and 3 golds, becoming the first individual to win 5 track-and-field medals with the current Olympic events. Ville Ritola won 6 in 1924. Irving Baxter and Walter Tewksbury won 5 medals in 1900, and Paavo Nurmi won 5 in 1924 but all did so in events no longer run.

The U.S. team's medal count continued to drop in Sydney. They won only 20 total medals, down from the 23 won in 1996. The men won 13 and the women won 7. Total gold medals were 10, down from 13 in 1996. The men won 6 and the women won 4. Marion Jones won 3 of the 4. Russia finished second again with 12 total medals (3 gold). Newcomer Ethiopia finished third with 8 (4 gold) and Kenya and Jamaica both had 7 medals. The Sydney Games also had over 100 countries competing, with 44 winning medals. The U.S. women's team lost potential medal winners Regina Jacobs, Gail Divers, and Inger Miller just before the Games with injuries and illness. The men lost Michael Johnson and Maurice Greene in the 200 meters with injuries in the U.S. Olympic Trials. Notable past U.S. Olympians who did not make the team were Carl Lewis, Jackie Joyner-Kersee, and Johnny Gray.

The 2004 Olympic Games returned to its birthplace, Athens, Greece. This historic site for the world's premier track meet was full of Greek theater and drama. Faced with the challenges of completing the facilities on time, meeting the enormous security needs, and piling up debt on their small economy, the Greeks drew on their national pride and staged a spectacular, peaceful show on time.

Team USA 2004 lost many of its premier stars to drug scandals, injuries, and poor performances in some events, but new young athletes emerged to carry the torch. The 25 total medals in Athens represent a significant improvement over Sydney (20) and Atlanta (23) (Table 34.1). The men had 19; 6 were gold. They had 6 gold in Sydney. The women were down to 6 medals with only 2 gold. They were hurt by lower performances from Marion Jones and key injuries to other athletes.

The Russian team continued to hold up for second place, but most of their medals came from their women's team, who won 15 of their 20 medals. Ethiopia and Kenya tied for third place. They dominated the long-distance races from the 3000 meters, 5000 meters, 10,000 meters, and the marathon.

The United States made a return to the medal count in the marathon. Meb Keflezighi ran in the footsteps of the legendary Greek hero Phedippides and won the silver medal. This was the first U.S. marathon medal in 28 years. Deena Kastor won the bronze. This was the first marathon medal for the women in many years.

The United States' new shining highlights were the 1-3 finish of Justin Gatlin (1) and Shawn Crawford (2) in the 100 meters; the 1-2-3 finish of Shawn Crawford (1), Bernard Williams (2), and Justin Gatlin (3) in the 200 meters; the 1-2-3 finish of Jeremy Wariner (1), Otis Harris (2), and Derrick Brew (3) in the 400 meters; the 1-2 finish of Dwight Philips (1) and John Moffitt (2) in the long jump; and the 1-2 finish of Tim Mack (1) and Matt Hemingway (2) in the pole vault. The women's loss of medal production from Marion Jones was replaced by young sprinters Lauryn Williams's silver medal in the 100 meters and Allyson Felix's silver medal in the 200 meters. Joanna Hayes and Melissa Morrison won the gold and bronze, respectively, in the 100-meter hurdles. They helped to mend a disappointing loss of Gail Devers in the hurdles. The women's 4 × 400 relay won its third Olympic gold in a row. The men continued to dominate the 4 × 400 relay. They have rarely lost this race.

The 2008 Olympic Games were held in Beijing, China. The United States team nearly equaled its Athens total medal count of 25 by bringing home 23 medals (7 gold, 9 silver, and 7 bronze). Russia, Kenya, and Jamaica were next with 18, 14, and 11 total medals, respectively. In Beijing both the men's 4 × 400 relay (Jeremy Wariner, LaShawn Merritt, David Neville, and Angelo Taylor) and the women's 4 × 400 relay (Sanya Richards, Mary Wineberg, Monique Henderson, and Allyson Felix) teams continued the United States' dominance in this event by capturing the gold medals. The other United States gold medal winners in 2008 were Bryan Clay in the men's decathlon, LaShawn Merritt in the men's 400 (Jeremy

Table 34.1. TOP 5 TEAM MEDAL COUNT

| | Men | | | | Women | | | | |
	Gold	Silver	Bronze	Total	Gold	Silver	Bronze	Total	Overall
United States	6	10	3	19	2	2	2	6	25
Russia	1	1	3	5	5	6	4	15	20
Ethiopia	1	2	0	3	1	1	2	4	7
Kenya	1	2	2	5	0	2	0	2	7
Cuba	0	0	1	1	2	1	1	4	5

Wariner and David Neville completed a United States medal sweep by finishing second and third), Dawn Harper in the women's 100 hurdles, Angelo Taylor in the men's 400 hurdles (once again swept by the United States with Kerron Clement and Bershawn Jackson winning the silver and bronze), and Stephanie Brown Trafton in the women's discus.

NATIONAL LEADERSHIP

United States America Track and Field (USATF) is the national governing body for track and field in the United States. USATF came into existence in 1980 pursuant to the Amateur Sports Act. The vision and leadership of USATF over the past two decades has made it possible for the sport of track and field to grow into the most viable and successful national sport in the world.

Restructuring

In 1998 USATF began to restructure to become more effective and efficient. The governance of USATF changed drastically. The Executive Committee was eliminated and a smaller Board of Directors took over the operation. Four divisions were developed from the many standing committees: High Performance, Long Distance Running, General Competition, and Administration. An Audit Committee was established to work with budgeting. The bylaws and operating regulations were overhauled. In 1999 standards for associations and accreditation were established. The associations represent the basic constituency and grassroot programs throughout the nation.

Sponsors

USATF has significantly increased cooperate sponsorships to support athletes and the sport. Nike, XEROX, Visa, Fuji, USC, Mondo, GMC, Adidas, Pontiac, Envoy, Polo Sport, Ralph Lauren, Fragrance, Air Force, and Power Bar are examples of key sponsors.

Strategic Planning

A better business blueprint has been created for successful events, national championships, bidding procedures, member services, athletes, agent and team services, international teams, development, coaches' education, club and school services, and meet and race management. The five objectives critical to the future success of USATF are:

1. *Increase the business value* with new sponsorships.
2. *Build the brand* with marketing and media coverage.
3. *Grow the grassroots* with better services to the associations and building and supporting the youth programs
4. *Enhance the dynasty* by better identifying our most talented athletes at a young age, and nurturing them through their scholastic, collegiate, and post-collegiate careers. Expanding the Golden Spike Tour will give more athletes the chance to compete in high-level meets

at home, earn prize money, and build their reputation. This should help Team USA to remain the world's best.
5. *Bolster partnership* by building a better relationship with the IAAF, the USOC, and the U.S. Track Coaches Association. USATF continues to work hard to give more people a chance to compete in the world's greatest sport and helping Team USA get to the victory stand.

USATF added the "Visa Championship Series" in 2005. American athletes will have the opportunity to compete for more than $1 million in prize money. They will also race toward a combined $50,000 jackpot and other prizes for the Visa Championship. Some of the other prizes are invitations to the Super Bowl, Daytona 500, Kentucky Derby, Tony Awards, or a Pebble Beach weekend.

EVENTS

Track-and-field events involve running, jumping, and throwing activities (Table 34.2). The running activities make up the *track* events; the jumping and throwing events make up the *field* events. The track events are sprints, hurdles, relays, middle distances, and long distances. The field events are the

Table 34.2. ONE-SESSION MEETS ORDER OF EVENTS

When no preliminary flights or heats are required.

Boys

4 × 800 (3200 m) relay	400 m dash
110 m high hurdles	300 m intermediate hurdles
100 m dash	800 m run
4 × 200 (800 m) relay	200 m dash
1600 m run	3200 m run
4 × 100 (400 m) relay	4 × 400 (1600 m) relay

Girls

4 × 800 (3200 m) relay	400 m dash
100 m high (33") hurdles	300 m low hurdles
100 m dash	800 m run
4 × 200 (800 m) relay	200 m dash
1600 m run	3200 m run
4 × 100 (400 m) relay	4 × 400 (1600 m) relay

Field Events

Should begin at least 30 minutes before first track event.

Boys	Girls
Long jump	Long jump
High jump	High jump
Shot put	Shot put
Javelin	Javelin
Pole vault	Pole vault

Immediately following the long jump and shot put

Triple jump	Triple jump
Discus	Discus

long jump, triple jump, high jump, pole vault, shot put, discus, javelin, and hammer throw. Below is an example of an outdoor high school competition and order of events.

Track Meet

A track meet consists of contests in a presented number of races of different length and of contests in jumping and/or throwing. Competition is by individuals except in the relays, which involve competition of teams consisting of four individuals.

Running Events

Sprints

Outdoor sprints include 100-, 200-, and 400-meter dashes. Indoor sprints vary with the facility and range from 50 to 400 meters. These events are 80 to 100 percent anaerobic in nature (maximum intensity).

Middle distances

Outdoors or indoors, any race between 600 and 1,000 meters is considered middle distance. These distances require approximately 50 percent aerobic and 50 percent anaerobic power (speed and endurance). The most common races are 800 meters (half mile) and 1500 meters (1 mile equivalent).

Long distances

The long-distance running events in both indoor and outdoor competition are the 3000 meters (just short of 2 miles) and the 5000 meters (3.1 miles). Additional events run outdoors are the 10,000 meters (6.2 miles), the 3000-meter steeplechase, and the marathon (26 miles, 385 yards). Race walking is included in some competitions, with common distances of 10K to 20K.

Hurdles

A confusing array of races are run over varying hurdle heights and race distances. The heights of hurdles, the distance between them, and the total distance run vary among men, women, youth, master, and senior athletes. The outdoor hurdle sprint race for the men is the 110-meter high hurdles. The hurdles are 42 inches high (1.07 m). For high school boys they are 39 inches high (1.01 m). The hurdle sprint endurance race is the 400-meter hurdles, also called the intermediate hurdles. The hurdles are 36 inches high (0.91 m). High school boys run 300-meter hurdles that are 36 inches high (0.91 m). Women run the 100-meter short sprint distance with hurdle heights of 33 inches (0.84 m) for open and collegiate women and for high school girls. The women's sprint endurance hurdle race is 400 meters for open and collegiate women with hurdles 30 inches high (0.76 m) and 300 meters for high school girls (30 inches high also). The indoor races vary between 50 to 55 and 60 meters or yards for both men and women. The indoor hurdle heights are 42 inches for open and collegiate men, 39 inches for the high school boys, and 33 inches for open, collegiate, and high school girls (Figure 34.1).

Figure 34.1. Hurdles.

Relays

Relay teams consist of four members (except in the shuttle hurdle relays). Each runner carries a baton a specific distance, passing it to the next runner within a marked zone until the last runner carries it across the finish line. The relays include 4 × 100 meters, 4 × 200 meters, 4 × 400 meters (mile relay), 4 × 800 meters (2-mile relay), and 4 × 1500 or 1600 meters (4-mile relay). The sprint medley relays consist of two types: (1) 100, 100, 200, and 400 meters; and (2) 200, 200, 400, and 800 meters. The women run both sprint medleys and the men run only the 200, 200, 400, 800. The distance medley consists of 400, 800, 1200, and 1600 meters. Both men and women run this race.

Steeplechase

The standard distance is 3000 meters. Races at 2000 meters may also be contested. The 3000-meter steeplechase has 28 hurdle jumps and 7 water jumps. The 2000-meter steeplechase has 18 hurdle jumps and 5 water jumps. There are 5 jumps per lap. The water jump should be fourth if feasible. The jumps should be evenly distributed. Because of different track designs and water jump placements, each steeplechase course must be individually measured. Typical measurements and diagrams are shown in Figure 34.2. This is a relatively new event for women (1966). The men's hurdles are 91.4 centimeters (± 3 mm) high (3 ft). The women's hurdles should be 76.2 centimeters (± 3 mm) high (2 ft 6 in).

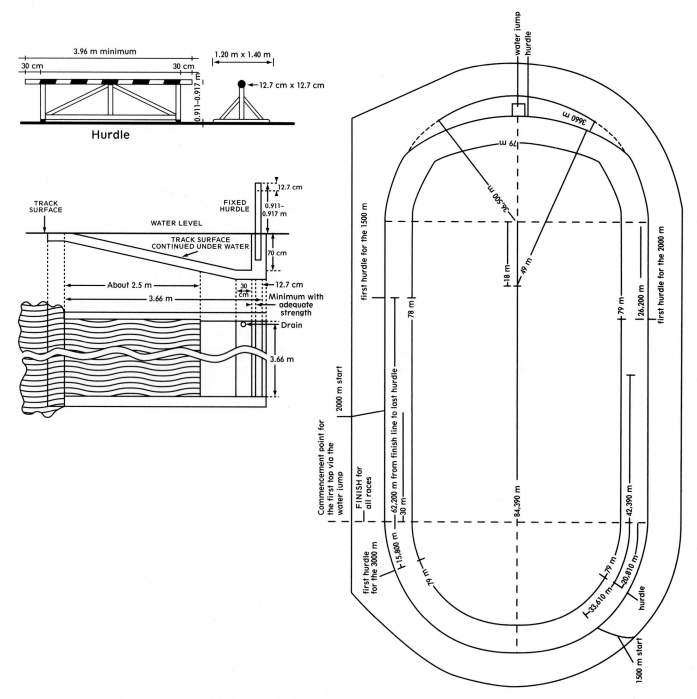

Figure 34.2. Water jump and hurdle measurements.

The hurdles should be at least 3.96 meters (13 in) wide and placed on the track so that 30 centimeters of the top bar will be on the inside of the field. The top bar of the hurdles and the water jump should be 12.7 centimeters (5 in).

The water jump, including the hurdle, should be 3.66 meters (± 2 cm) in length for events using 91.4-centimeter or 76.2-centimeter hurdles. The width of the hurdle should be 3.66 meters for all events. The water should be 70 centimeters (2 ft 3½ in) in depth immediately in front of the

hurdle and slope to the level of the field at the farther end. The hurdle should be firmly fixed in front of the water.

Jumping Events

Long jump and triple jump

The runway generally varies from 120 to 160 feet (36.6 to 48.8 m) for men and 90 to 140 feet (27.4 to 42.7 m) for women. The takeoff should be from a board made of wood or other suitable rigid material 7.8 to 8 inches wide (19.8 to

20.32 cm) and at least 4 feet long (1.22 m) and not more than 3.94 inches thick (10 cm). The landing area must not be less than 9 feet in width (2.74 m) and identical in elevation with the takeoff board. The area shall be filled with sand. The styles of long jump used are the sail, hitch kick, and hang (Figure 34.3). The triple jump has three phases, previously known as the "hop, step, and jump." The jumper must make the first jump (sometimes called the hop) by landing on the takeoff foot, the second jump (sometimes called the step) by landing on the nontakeoff foot, and the third jump into the landing pit.

High jump

The two primary styles of jumping are the straddle and the "Fosbury Flop" (Figure 34.4), named after Dick Fosbury, who used a back layout technique with a curved approach. This back layout style dramatically increased high-jump performances by allowing the athlete to use more speed in the approach and provided for a very efficient bar clearance.

Pole vault

The modern pole vaulter must have exceptional speed and strength and the agility of a gymnast. The combination of speed, strength, and coordination makes this a spectacular event. The introduction of the fiberglass pole has revolutionized this event. Tremendous increases in performances have resulted since its introduction. Records have moved from 16 feet to over 20 feet (4.9 to over 6.1 m). The runways vary from 125 to 140 feet (38.1 to 42.7 m) in length. The poles have increased in length from 14 feet to over 16 feet.

Figure 34.3. Long jump.

Figure 34.4. Back layout.

Throwing Events

Shot put

The 16-pound (7.26-kg) shot is used for college, USA Track and Field (USATF), and Olympic men's competition. High school boys use a 12-pound (5.45-kg) shot. College, USATF, Olympic women, and high school girls use an 8-pound-13-ounce (4-kg) shot. The shots are made of a cast iron, bronze, or brass shell with a lead center. The indoor shot has a plastic or rubber shell. The shot is thrown from a circle 7 feet (2.13 m) in diameter with a stop board in front.

Discus

The discus is usually made of wood with a metal rim. Some are made of rubber, but these are not legal outside of high school competition. Collegiate and open men's discus must have a minimum weight of 4 pounds 6.55 ounces (2 kg) with a diameter of 8.67 inches (219–221 mm). The high school boys' discus weight is 3 pounds 9 ounces (1.62 kg) with a diameter of 8.2 inches (209–211 mm). For high school, college, and open events for women, the discus must weigh no less than 2 pounds 3.25 ounces (1 kg) with a diameter of 7.1 inches (180–182 mm). All divisions throw the discus from a circle 8 feet 2.5 inches (2.5 m) in diameter.

Hammer

The hammer consists of a round weight attached to a triangular handle by a wire. The men's collegiate and open hammer weighs 16 pounds (7.27 kg). The high school boys' hammer weighs 12 pounds (5.45 kg). High school girls, open, and collegiate women all throw the 8-pound-13-ounce (4-kg) hammer. The hammer may not exceed 48 inches (1.22 m) in length for men and high school boys and 47 inches (1.195 m) for women and high school girls. The hammer is thrown from a circle 7 feet (2.13 m) in diameter. The indoor equivalents of the hammer are the 56-pound (25.4-kg) weight, the 35-pound (15.88-kg) weight, the 25-pound (11.34-kg) weight, the 20-pound (9.08-kg) weight, the 16-pound (7.26-kg) weight, or the 12-pound (5.45-kg) weight. These weights are thrown with a shorter handle than the hammer, and the weight used depends upon the level of the competition. Women and high school athletes throw the lighter weights.

Javelin

The javelin consists of three parts: head, shaft, and cord grip. The shaft must be constructed of metal and should have fixed to it a metal head terminating in a sharp point. The grip should be about the center of mass and shall not exceed the diameter of the shaft by more than 0.3 inches (8 mm) with uniform thickness. The length of the men's and boys' javelin is 8.7 feet (2.7 m). The weight must be not more than 1 pound 12 ounces (800 g) with a cord grip of 6 inches (16 cm). The women's and girls' javelin is 7 feet 4 inches (2.3 m) long with a minimum weight of 1 pound 9 ounces (600 g) and a cord grip of 5.7 inches (15 cm).

Other Track-and-Field Events

Some Olympic events are not always standard in U.S. competitions (e.g., 20-kilometer walk).

Race walking

Race walking is advancing through a progression of steps so taken that unbroken contact with the ground is maintained. The advancing leg must be straightened (i.e., not bent at the knee) from the moment of first contact with the ground until the leg is in the vertical upright position. Failure to adhere to this rule can lead to a warning and then to disqualification. The race walk is generally conducted over a distance of 3 to 10 kilometers (1.86 to 6.2 miles) on the track and 10 to 50 kilometers (6.2 to 31 miles) on the road.

Decathlon and heptathlon

The tests of all-around skill and ability are the decathlon for men and the heptathlon for women. The participants in these events are often considered the "world's best athletes."

The decathlon consists of 10 events that are run over 2 days in the following order: first day: 100-meter dash, long jump, shot put, high jump, and 400-meter dash; second day: 100-meter hurdles, discus, pole vault, javelin, and 1,500-meter run. The heptathlon consists of seven events that are scheduled over 2 days in the following order: first day: 100-meter hurdles, high jump, shot put, and 200-meter dash; second day: long jump, javelin, and 800-meter run.

FACILITIES

Building a track-and-field facility can be a very difficult task. Many complicated factors must be considered in the planning and construction phases. Some of the considerations include the unique needs of each track program, site selection and analysis, choice of surface, amenities and accessories, markings and specifications, and hiring a qualified contractor and consultant.

Specifications

A track site will require an area of approximately 5 acres (600 feet long and 300 feet wide). Additional area will be needed for grading, curbs, draining, grandstands, bleachers, lighting, fences, walkways, and so on. A 400-meter oval track is the standard size for all levels of competition. Some tracks are built around a football or soccer field; this provides for multipurpose usage. Some high school tracks don't have curbs. Curbs are required for NCAA, national, and international competition. Most tracks have 6 to 8 lanes (36–42 inches wide), and some affluent programs have the more expensive 9- to 10-lane tracks. The two most common shapes for tracks are (1) an oval equal-quadrant track with two 100-meter straightaways and two 100-meter curves and (2) a nonequal oval quadrant track where the straightaways are larger or smaller than the curves. The oval is slightly stretched or slightly compressed in these tracks (Figure 34.5).

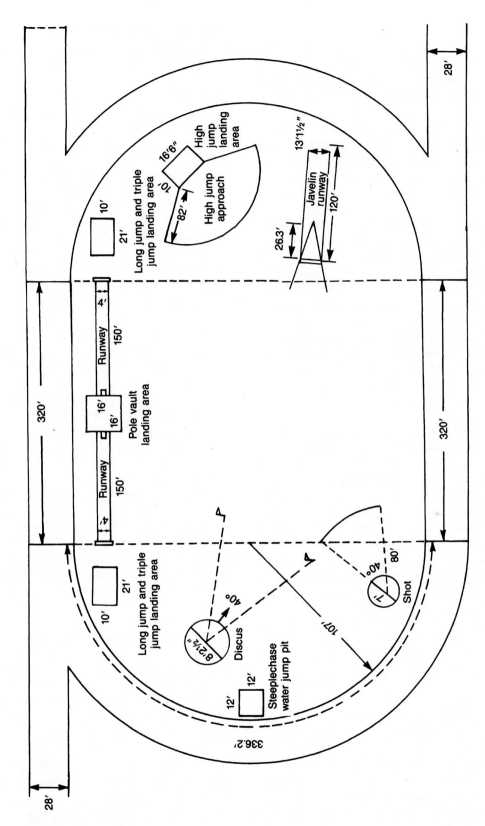

Figure 34.5. Track-and-field facility.

Choice of Surfaces

There are many types of surfaces to choose from. Financial resources, type of usage, geographical location, maintenance capability, durability, and performance characteristics all influence the special needs and circumstances.

Types of Surfaces

1. Natural material track systems (cinder and clay): These tracks are relatively inexpensive to construct, but they have two major disadvantages: They have constant and costly maintenance, and rain usually causes soggy conditions, cancellations, or postponements.

2. All-weather (rubber-asphalt emulsion): A combination of rubber with asphalt emulsion and sand. These were popular in the 1960s. These tracks were durable and unaffected by ordinary weather. However, summer heat softens the surface, and winter cold hardens the surface. It also becomes harder as it ages. These disadvantages make this surface no longer cost-effective.

3. Rubber-latex/polyurethane: Most tracks today are constructed with rubber particles bound with latex or polyurethane. These surfaces are installed on top of asphalt, concrete, or some other existing surfaces. The depth of these surfaces is ⅜ to ½ inch. The rubber used may be black or colored. Natural rubber, styrene-butadiene rubber (SBR), and ethlene-propylene-diene rubber (EPDM) are the standard choices. The rubber may be virgin or recycled. Virgin rubber is more expensive than recycled rubber, and colored rubber is more expensive than black rubber.

Consultants and Contractors

It is highly recommended to hire experienced consultants (i.e., architect, landscape engineer, contractors) who are trained and who specialize in building tracks. Colleagues who have recently completed a project should be contacted to check a contractor's references, business, and work performance.

SHOES

With the advent of new training and racing surfaces in the past few years, many types of shoes have been introduced. There now seems to be a specific shoe for every event in the sport of track and field. Most shoes have interchangeable spikes and are built for protection and comfort as well as style and fit. The type of shoe worn can make a great difference in terms of traction on a racing surface and therefore can represent the winning edge.

BASIC TECHNIQUES

Sprinting

The basic components of sprinting are:

1. Start: incorporates reaction time, block clearance time, and velocity out of the blocks

2. Accelerations: the ability to reach maximum velocity in the shortest time

3. Velocity maintenance: the length of time or distance the maximum velocity can be maintained

4. Mental and psychological aspects: relaxation, coordination, rhythm, concentration, and self-confidence

Sprint start

Starting blocks are essential to the sprinter. They provide a solid base from which to push off and prevent slipping or injury to the runner. Adjustable blocks that can be used either indoors or outdoors are the most effective.

1. Reaction times can have a positive effect on sprint times by providing a winning margin measured in hundredths of a second. However, this is only 1 percent or less of the racing distance. The most important factor is that the runner leaves the blocks with the greatest possible velocity in a balanced position that sets up a maximum acceleration pattern. There is a pronounced forward lean in this position, with force being applied against the blocks in a straight line drawn from the head through the shoulders, hips (center of mass), drive leg, and lead foot. The angle of this line should be between 30 to 40 degrees (Figure 34.6). Size, strength, flexibility, and agility dictate this angle.

2. Selection of block spacings significantly affects block clearance time and velocity out of the blocks. Studies have shown that the bunch start (10 to 12 inches [25 to 30 cm] between the blocks) provides the fastest block clearance time, including reaction time, but produces the slowest velocity and momentum out of the blocks. Research by Franklin Henry on acceleration patterns indicates that velocity out of the blocks appears to be more important than block clearance time. The medium start (14 to 21 inches [35 to 53 cm] between blocks) provides the most efficient spacing for maximum velocity and block clearance time.

These findings can be used as guidelines in selecting block spacing. However, they do not allow for individual differences of body type, size, and comfort. Research on angles of

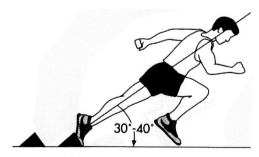

Figure 34.6. A well-balanced starting position for maximum acceleration.

flexion in related body joints of the knee, hips, ankles, and the like suggest optimal starting positions based on these angles. To find the optimal starting position for each athlete, the following procedure should be used:

a. Place the athlete in the set position and establish an angle of 90 degrees in the knee joint of the front leg. The greatest amount of force can be exerted in the shortest amount of time in this position. The front leg should be the athlete's stronger leg, but he or she should use whichever is more comfortable.

b. Establish an angle of approximately 120 to 135 degrees in the rear knee. This facilitates a fast, forceful drive of the rear leg. Pulling the rear leg off the rear block results in a loss of power. The rear leg should push forcefully against the rear block for maximum force.

c. Elevate the hips and establish a forward lean to provide a forward horizontal component. The hips should be slightly above the shoulders, and the forward lean should not place too much pressure on the hands.

d. The starting blocks are placed under the runner while maintaining these angles. The block spacings are established at this point. Application of the medium-start principles supplements these spacings, and adjustments are made to fine-tune the start (Figure 34.7).

3. Starting fundamentals:

a. "On your mark": The runner moves in front of the blocks and backs into position, carefully placing the feet in the blocks one at a time. The feet should be straight, with the toes in contact with the surface of the track. The hands are placed directly under the shoulders, with the fingers and thumbs bridged just behind the starting line about shoulder-width apart. The arms are fully extended, with the weight evenly distributed between the hands, rear knee, and foot. The front knee is relaxed, extending just inside the forearm. The head is in natural alignment with the trunk, and the eyes are focused just about a yard in front of the starting line (Figure 34.8).

b. "Set": The runner raises the hips to the desired level and extends the knee joints to the appropriate angles. The shoulders move slightly forward in front of the hands to provide a horizontal component. In competition, the runner should focus on a sensory response to the gun (see Figure 34.7).

c. "Go": The starting action is initiated by reacting immediately to the sound of the gun. Movement is initiated by picking up the hands and driving the lead arm forward and up, the other arm backward. Simultaneously, force is applied against both blocks as the legs extend against the blocks. The rear foot clears the blocks first as it is driven into the first stride. The shoulders gradually rise as the front leg fully extends. The body is now placed in the appropriate driving angles (30 to 45 degrees) to prepare the runner for maximum acceleration (see Figure 34.6).

4. Acceleration: Studies have shown that elite sprinters reach their maximum velocity between 60 and 70 meters (66 and 77 yards). Less-talented sprinters may reach maximum velocity in 50 to 60 meters (55 to 66 yards). The main objective of sprinting is to accelerate over the longest possible distance in the shortest possible time. Clearing the blocks with maximum force in a balanced position sets up the acceleration pattern.

a. Speed is the product of stride length and stride frequency. The actual stride length is the distance between the touchdown of the toes for each stride. Top sprinters have an average stride length of 7 feet 2½ inches to 7 feet 9¾ inches (2.20 to 2.38 m). Stride length will vary because of individual muscle strength, leg length, flexibility, speed of running, and/or any injuries.

The foot strike should be less than 12 inches (30 cm) in front of the athlete's center of mass to prevent overstriding. The sprinter should develop a stride length that combines with stride frequency to produce the fastest time because increasing actual stride length results in decreased stride frequency.

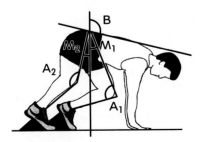

Figure 34.7. Recommended leg and body angles while in the set position. Angle B—104° (98°–112°); Angle M2—13° (8°–17°), Angle M1—21° (19°–23°), Angle A1—100° (92°–105°), and Angle A2—129° (115°–138°).

Figure 34.8. "On your mark" position.

The effective stride length is the distance the center of mass is projected with each stride. Increasing strength and flexibility in the relative muscle groups can increase the effective stride length by applying additional force to the ground. This increases stride length without decreasing stride frequency.

b. Stride frequency is the number of strides per second. For the best sprinters it is 2¼ to 2½ strides per second for both sexes. Research seems to indicate that very little improvement can be made in stride length, although improving strength, conditioning, technique, and relaxation can result in some gains. Improving stride frequency has a positive effect on maximum velocity, but this must be achieved without reducing stride lengths. This can be produced by a combination of stride length and stride frequency that meets the individual skills of each runner.

Research indicates that significant gains in improving speed can be made by increasing stride frequency (rate). The elite sprinters have shown 15 percent faster stride rates than good-to-average sprinters. The elite sprinters were able to do this by reducing ground time and utilizing efficient sprint mechanics. (They get on and off the ground quickly.) These sprinters developed a high level of explosive power in their legs. This is the weak link to speed development. Bounding, specific strength work, and activities that simulate getting on and off the ground develop explosive power, help sprinters get on and off the ground quicker, and significantly improve stride rate and speed. Here are a few explosive activities:

1. Speed squats
2. One leg squats
3. Step-ups on box or bench
4. Depth jumps from boxes
5. Multiple hops
6. Leg extensions and leg curls
7. Toe lifts
8. Lunges
9. Speed bounding
10. Jump squats

5. Maintenance of maximum velocity: After reaching maximum velocity (about 50 to 70 meters [55 to 75 yd]), the runner can only maintain maximum velocity for a few strides (about 15 to 25 meters [16 to 27 yd]) before fatigue causes a gradual deceleration. Deceleration can be minimized by relaxation, conditioning, and concentration on proper technique.

Basic running mechanics for sprinters

Running mechanics are influenced by the distance run and the speed required for each race. Long- and middle-distance runners require running mechanics that place an emphasis on economy of motion, pace judgment, and relaxation to conserve energy. Sprinting requires more vigorous and explosive action to produce a greater stride length and stride frequency. The sprinter must focus on the following mechanics to improve stride length and stride frequency:

1. **Posture:** The initial body position (lean) is a product of acceleration. During the start, the forward lean is greatly exaggerated to provide maximum horizontal forces through the center of mass. As the sprinter continues to accelerate, the body becomes more erect until maximum velocity is reached. Only a slight forward lean is required at this point to counter wind resistance and to maintain effective driving angles to the ground. The forward lean comes from the ankles, not the hips. The hips must stay tucked to prevent flexion at the waist and loss of driving angles and force. Running too erect or leaning backward will contribute to a loss of driving force and deceleration. This is usually a result of a lack of strength, conditioning, or concentration by the sprinter. The runner should focus on maintaining correct posture throughout the race. This prevents the foot from striking too far in front of the body, causing additional deceleration.

2. **Leg action:** The runner's ability to coordinate and place each body segment in the most efficient positions will help improve stride length and stride frequency, and reduce air and ground time. Analysis of the sprint striding phases can help coaches evaluate the runner's efficiency. The coach should study the following technical phases.

   a. **Takeoff (driving) phase.** This phase is characterized by the supporting leg driving through the athlete's center of mass (hips) and pushing the body into the flying trajectory. The athlete should keep this flight angle small. The lower this flight angle, the less time spent in the air and the sooner the return to the ground. During this phase, the support leg should be maximally extended at the hip joint, but not at the knee joint. This incomplete knee extension reduces ground time and increases stride frequency. The amount of force produced by the driving leg into the ground affects stride length (Figure 34.9A).

   b. **Recovery phase.** This phase begins as the drive leg leaves the ground, flexes at the knee joint, and rotates up and under the buttocks into the next stride. The tighter this knee and hip flexion, the faster the folded leg segment swings through. This shorter leg lever enhances stride frequency by allowing the thigh to rotate through faster. The ankle should be dorsal flexed to also shorten the lever, relax the hamstrings and to prepare for an explosive touchdown. The foot should pass over the knee of the support leg as it moves forward. This high thigh position applies force to the ground (Figure 34.9B, C).

   c. **Amortization phase.** This phase is responsible for absorbing the impact forces and resisting the forces of gravity. The center of mass (hips) moves over the supporting leg, and the body prepares for another takeoff phase with the opposite leg. The breaking

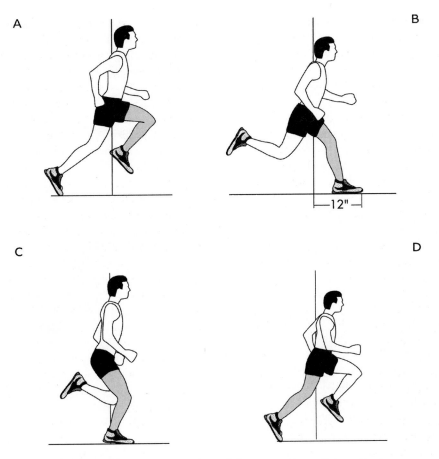

Figure 34.9. A, Takeoff or driving phase. B, Recovery phase. C, Amortization or support phase. D, Landing phase.

forces at the hip, knee, and ankle should be minimized. This increases ground time, loss of ground force, and velocity. These joint angles should be kept as straight as possible (Figure 34.9C, D).

   d. **Landing (ground contact).** The foot should be placed no more than 6 to 12 inches (15 to 30 cm) in front of the body at impact. The closer under the body the better. The foot and lower leg should have a negative acceleration (moving backward) with a pawing action. This reduces the breaking force at impact. High-speed photography reveals that sprinters land on the outside toes of the foot, roll to the ball of the foot, settle back to the heel during amortization, and push off with the big toe during the drive phase. "Toe-heel-toe" (Figure 34.9B).

3. **Arm action:** Current research indicates that the hands and arms are not significant contributors to the differences in sprint performance between good sprinters and elite sprinters. The arms are primarily used for absorbing forces created by the thrust of the legs. They balance the body and assist in maintaining stride rhythm. The hands are driven to the shoulder or chin level on the front swing to the midline of the body, and they are driven past the hips with the elbow driven to shoulder height on the backswing. The backswing is a neglected technical aspect in poor-to-average sprinters. Incomplete backswings can limit the full range of motion and may limit stride length. Too much backswing could decrease stride frequency. The runner should focus on keeping the shoulders down and square for relaxation and efficiency of movement. Cupped hands or extended fingers are an individual choice. Relaxation should be the main focus.

Sprint training (100-200-400)
Periodation plan
A speed-training program should start with a basic plan for the competition years with considerations for future goals. Overall development is important in the early training phase rather than specific speed training, especially for young athletes. Dividing the season into four phases allows the body to gradually and systematically develop its physiological systems to higher levels, minimizing injuries. The four phases are listed below.

preparation phase. (General conditioning and technique.) This phase starts with low volumes of work and intensities. Flexibility, strength, muscle balance, and specific physical weaknesses are assessed at this time. Performance tests can be given to assess ability and fitness levels.

strengthening phase. (Increasing muscle strength, endurance, and explosive power.) The specific muscle groups to develop for sprinters are gluteals, hamstrings, quadriceps, gastrocnemius, soleus, hip flexors, and achilles. Training volumes and intensities gradually increase during this phase.

pre-competition phase. (Work volumes begin to decrease and intensities continue to decrease.) The athlete begins to sharpen and prepare for competition.

competition phase. (Final preparation for major competition begins.) High-quality work, racing experience, and rest and recovery are key concerns during this period. Each phase takes 4 to 6 weeks depending on the needs of the athlete.

200 Meters

The 200-meter runner must be able to run the curve efficiently and then carry the speed for an additional 100 meters. The runner must run as close to the lane line as possible on the curve to cut down the distance run, without running on the lane line. Technically you can run less than 200 meters by doing this. Also, to maintain balance and fight the centrifugal force that tends to push the athlete outward, the athlete should look inside, lean inside, and drive the outside arm across the body to help maintain balance. Runners in the 400 meters should practice this curve-running technique also (Figure 34.10).

400 Meters

The basic mechanics of sprinting also apply to the 400-meter race, but the runner must develop the ability to distribute his or her speed and energy over the total racing distance in the most efficient manner. It is not physiologically possible to run the 400-meter all-out. Pace judgment and effort distribution are critical skills. Outstanding runners can maintain 90 to 95 percent of their best 200-meter speed while running the 400-meter. They are capable of running with a 1-second differential between the first and second 200 meters (e.g., 21.5 + 22.5 = 44 seconds). A good formula for predicting potential 400-meter times is to double the runner's best time for 200 meters and add 3.5 seconds.

The first 150 meters should be run in a relaxed and smooth manner while trying to maintain rhythm and velocity with the least effort. At the 200-meter mark, the runner must gradually start to increase the arm drive and stride frequency. This controlled pickup will allow the runner to come off the final turn with good momentum and in good position. In the final 100 meters, the runner must stay as relaxed as possible and try to maintain form and concentration. Success in this event requires maximum development of the anaerobic endurance energy system. Training in a high state of lactic acid buildup will

Figure 34.10. Curve-running technique for 200-meter dash.

develop this ability (40 to 45 seconds of near maximum effort). There are two types of 400-meter runners, the 200 to 400 type and the 400 to 800 type. The best tend to be 200 to 400 types. The mental aspects of 400-meter runners are just as important as the physical abilities. They must be aggressive, focused, and have the ability to withstand pain and fatigue.

Relays

Relays are popular and exciting events. They require teamwork and timing. Relays employ two types of baton passes: the nonvisual and the visual pass. The *nonvisual (blind) pass* is one not seen by the receiver, and it is used in sprint relays. The baton must be passed in a 20-meter (22-yard) zone, and the outgoing runner has an additional 10-meter (11-yard) zone in which to accelerate. Sprint relay runners usually alternate hands, with the first and third runners carrying the baton in the right hand and the second and fourth runners carrying the baton in the left hand.

The *visual pass* is a pass that is seen by the receiver. It is primarily used in long (1600 m and above) relays, when fatigue may lessen coordination, decreasing the runner's ability to pass accurately. The pass must be made in a 20-meter (22-yd) zone.

Nonvisual pass technique

The outgoing runner should accelerate maximally into and through the passing zone as the incoming runner hits the go mark. Start with 18 to 20 feet (5.5 to 6 m) for the go mark and gradually increase to 20 to 30 feet (6 to 9 m) as the timing and conditioning improve. Visual or vocal cues can be used to initiate the pass. Some teams still use the upsweep-V technique (Figure 34.11A). However, the extended arm position of the outgoing runner—with the open-palm, thumb-down hand position—is a much more efficient technique (Figure 34.11B)

because it provides a bigger target, a natural hand-baton fit, better control, and a longer free distance between runners. (The arms are completely extended by both runners.) The incoming runner uses an upsweep push into the target hand of the outgoing runner. The main objective is to keep the baton moving through the passing zone at top speed.

Visual passing technique

The outgoing runner should turn and go as the incoming runner hits the go mark (about 10 to 15 feet [3 to 4.5

Figure 34.11. A, Nonvisual baton pass—underhand upward pass. B, Nonvisual pass—upsweep push pass.

m]). The outgoing runner accelerates into three to five fast strides and turns about 10 meters (11 yards) into the zone. The outgoing runner reaches back with the left hand, chest facing the curb. The hand should reach high into the face of the incoming runner. This provides a good target, with the fingers extended and the thumb open in a natural reaching position (Figure 34.11C). The incoming runner places the baton in the target hand of the outgoing runner. As the outgoing runner turns, she or he must judge the strength and speed of the incoming runner. The outgoing runner has about 10 meters (11 yd) to slow down or speed up to complete the pass. As soon as the pass has been completed and the runner is clear of traffic, the baton should be switched to the right hand, and the runner should sprint hard through the first turn and establish position (Figure 34.12).

Hurdles

Hurdling is an event that requires outstanding sprinting ability to be successful. The best hurdlers are excellent sprinters. Other necessary physical characteristics are rhythm, flexibility, coordination, balance, and efficient technique.

Technique

The start is basically the same as for sprinting, but adjustments must be made to achieve the correct stride number to the first hurdle. Eight strides is the most common pattern to the first hurdle, but some taller athletes may use seven strides. The lead leg should be placed in the rear block in preparation for eight strides to the first hurdle, in the front block for seven strides. The takeoff distance from the hurdle is important to establish

Figure 34.12. Visual pass in 1600-meter relay.

Figure 34.11. *Cont'd* C, Visual passing technique.

an efficient flight path over the hurdle. The hurdler's size, speed of approach, and lead-leg action determine the proper takeoff distance for each hurdler. The average distance is 6½ to 7½ feet (2 to 2.3 m) for men and 6 to 6½ feet (1.8 to 2 m) for women.

Hurdle clearance

Efficient hurdle clearance depends on a proper takeoff and lead-leg action. The takeoff should be high on the balls of the feet, with a highly flexed lead knee and a large split between the legs. This lifts the center of gravity high into an efficient flight path over the hurdle while minimizing vertical forces. The lead leg should not swing up with a straight or locked leg, which slows down the action significantly. The lead leg should not swing to the inside or the outside, which can create balance problems during landing. The lead leg should be directly in front of the hip, with the toe straight up (Figure 34.13A). The takeoff (trailing) leg is driven up and around to the side of the body in a tightly folded position. The toe of the trailing leg is turned out. This should be a fast, continuous action.

Arm action

The single-arm action is the most efficient technique because it simulates the running action. The lead arm is driven forward about shoulder level, with a bent elbow. This balances the lead leg. The trailing arm swings backward for balance and rhythm. The hurdler leans forward with the shoulders square. This gets the hurdler down to the ground quicker.

Landing

The hurdler should land on the ball of the foot with the center of mass (hips) over or slightly in front of the landing foot. The trailing leg comes through with a high knee action and flows into a full sprint stride (Figure 34.13B). The hurdler takes three sprint strides between hurdles, with the last stride being shorter. Hurdling is sprinting, so the hurdler should sprint through the first hurdle out of the blocks, between the hurdles, and off the last hurdle through the finish line.

Technique for women

Women require some different techniques because their hurdles are lower. The center of mass does not have to be lifted as high. The technique is closer to sprinting, and the hurdling action is less pronounced. The lead-leg action is quicker and more explosive. The female hurdler leads with a bent knee, then explosively kicks out the lower leg. This is

Figure 34.13. A, Takeoff, lead-leg action, and hurdle clearance technique. B, The landing and sprint off of the hurdle. C, The women's 100-meter hurdle technique.

immediately followed by a quick snap of the leg down and under the body for landing (Figure 34.13C).

The trailing-leg action is also less pronounced for women. It is not brought around, as it is for male high hurdlers. It is kept tight under the body, with the toe turned out to clear the hurdles. Women do not have to lean as much as men do; they are very close to their sprint posture throughout the race. Some smaller women may need to lean somewhat. The other technical aspects are similar to those in men's hurdling.

Endurance Events

Whether you are training for health, fitness, or competition, the training systems are basically the same. The goals, training intensities, and workloads will dictate the specific differences. Modern training systems utilize many of the old systems, but mix and modify them to meet individual needs, abilities, events, and local environmental conditions. With the exception of a few philosophical differences regarding how much, how fast, and how far to run, the main emphasis is on development of the aerobic metabolic oxygen transport system (the lungs, heart, and vascular systems). There is a strong correlation between a high aerobic capacity (VO_2 max) and success in endurance events.

Training methods

Middle-distance runners are more balanced in their use of the aerobic and anaerobic systems in their training; they use about a 50 percent to 50 percent ratio. Runners and marathoners in both the 5K and 10K use from 70 to 80 percent of their training from the aerobic energy systems. Long continuous runs, fartlek, interval training, and various types of speed work (anaerobic) make up most programs.

Long continuous runs. This is the major part of endurance runners' training programs where they build a strong aerobic base first. The runs will range from 3 to 10 miles for the middle-distance runner, and 10 to 20 miles for longer-distance runners. These runs may average a pace of 5 to 7 minutes per mile for men and 6 to 9 minutes per mile for women, depending on the level of competition and fitness.

Interval training. Interval training was developed by Drs. Hans Reindell and Woldemar Gerschler with their world-record-setting athlete Rudolph Harbig in the 1930s. They used alternating measured runs of 200 to 400 meters on a flat track, at a measured pace with easy recovery jogs for a measured length of time. Precise measurement of each phase of work is essential to get the specific training effect to produce the developmental heart stimulus. These are the basic elements: (1) *The distance run:* Groups of 100, 200, or 400 m, etc. (2) *The recovery interval:* 30, 60, or 90 seconds. Heart-rate recovery of 120 beats/minute has also been used. (3) *The pace* of the run. How fast each interval is run depends on the fitness of the athlete and the race pace desired. (4) *The number of repetitions:* The number of times the run is repeated

depends on the planned workload. Example: a 20×200 m run at a pace of 30 seconds, with a 90-second jog recovery.

Fartlek. This was developed by the great Swedish coach Goster Homer in the 1940s. Homer trained the great distance runner Gunder Haegg. Fartlek alternates hard and easy running over varied and interesting terrains. It takes the athlete away from the confines of a track to a more natural setting. However, fartlek can be done on the track. Fartlek means "speed play." The runners usually run fartlek in pine-needled forest, parks, on golf courses, and in the hills. The runner can develop speed and endurance at the same time in a fun and stimulating environment. It is a flexible and wide-ranging system.

Training plans

With a basic understanding of the various training systems, coaches and athletes must develop a training plan to meet their special needs and situation. The following are basic principles of training:

1. A medical evaluation should precede each year's training.
2. Workloads should be increased gradually over days, weeks, and years.
3. A strong aerobic base should be developed first, with long continuous runs.
4. Gradually reduce the resting heart rate and raise the steady state (an increase in pace without an increase in lactic acid).
5. Develop anaerobic power (speed). All distance races need some training done at race pace or faster. Even the marathon.
6. Use variety in the terrains, training runs, environment, and competitions.
7. Training systems must adapt to the individual.
8. Develop a periodation training plan with specific phases, goals, and objectives.
9. Training must be consistent with regularity of workouts, diet, rest, recovery, and mental development.
10. Training should include some work on running mechanics and pace judgment.
11. Fun and enjoyment should be a major part of the training program. Variety and clear expectations play a part in these goals.

Running the Steeplechase

The key to the steeplechase lies in mastering the barriers. Running workouts combining long distance, intense distance intervals, and speed work are necessary, but the method for jumping the barriers deserves special attention. The key to jumping the barriers is momentum. It is important not to slow down in front of the hurdles or the water jump. Lack of momentum causes landing with the center of gravity far behind the lead leg and coming to a near halt on the far side of the barrier. The usual method for attacking the water jump is to place the lead leg on the barrier, allow momentum to move the body across the barrier, push off the barrier, and land in the water on the other foot far enough out so that the leg that pushed off the barrier can land next on the track beyond the water. It is important to get back to proper running form as quickly as possible.

Jumping Events

Long jump

Approach. The distance of the run-up is determined by strength, skill, conditioning, and the acceleration pattern of the jumper. Young jumpers may need only 14 to 16 strides, although more-experienced jumpers may require 18 to 23 strides. The main objective of the approach is to develop maximum controllable speed at takeoff. Many techniques have been used to achieve this goal: a gradual buildup, an explosive buildup, or a two- to four-step walk-in to the first check mark. All have been effective, but the key factors are a fast, relaxed, consistent stride pattern. One or two check marks are the most commonly used number. One check mark is placed at the start, and one is placed four to six strides from the takeoff board. The jumper should establish the takeoff foot and starting mark by "running through" the jump a few times to check for accuracy.

Takeoff. Speed down the runway is more important than jumping ability by a 2:1 ratio. Jumping ability is important, obviously, but not at the expense of losing horizontal velocity at takeoff. The most efficient takeoff action is one that allows the jumper to get lift at the appropriate angle with a minimum loss of horizontal velocity.

The position of the takeoff foot and the center of mass at takeoff are the most important technical considerations for successful jumps. If the foot is too far in front of the body at takeoff, the jumper will get good lift but lose horizontal velocity; and if the hips are too high, the jumper will not get enough lifting force. The jumper should use a long/short stride pattern in the last two strides because this lowers the center of mass on the next-to-last stride and catches the hips on the rise in the final stride. This provides an efficient transfer of horizontal velocity at takeoff. A short/long final two strides may place the foot too far in front of the body, resulting in a loss of velocity and shorter jumps. The takeoff action should be fast, with a short duration on the board. A foot plant that is too far in front of the body with a long duration on the board should be avoided (Figure 34.14A).

Flight in the air. Long jumpers have traditionally used three types of in-the-air styles: the sail, the hang, and the hitch kick (running in the air). All three styles have been used effectively, and each has its strengths and weaknesses. All styles are basically used to counter forward rotation created at takeoff. They allow the athlete to maintain balance and prepare the legs for an efficient landing.

The hitch kick is the most difficult to learn, but it is the most efficient. It is a natural extension of the run; it puts the athlete in a better landing position; and it can effectively reverse or delay forward rotation. The hitch kick is divided into one-and-a-half and two-and-a-half strides. The two-and-a-half hitch delays forward rotation longer and has the most potential for longer jumps, but it requires great strength, skill, and coordination.

Regardless of the style used, once the athlete leaves the ground, there is nothing he or she can do to change the parabolic flight curve of the center of mass (Figure 34.14B).

Landing. The most effective landing position is with the feet as far as possible in front of the center of mass (hips) without falling backward into the pit. Arriving in the landing position too early will result in a premature entry into the pit because of forward rotation. Stomach muscles or leg strength cannot hold the legs up once in this position because forward rotation causes the legs to rotate down into the pit.

The landing action is initiated by extending the legs parallel to the pit or slightly above parallel, with the toes up. The head, chest, and arms are thrust forward. The arms sweep down and back, then forward, as the heels contact the sand. At this point, the knees flex and allow the hips to move forward. The athlete can fall forward into a tight tuck position or execute a sit-out technique that employs a pivot to the side with a hip thrust that strikes the sand with the buttocks near or past the feet (Figure 34.14C).

Triple jump

As in the long jump, horizontal velocity is a very important factor for success in the triple jump. This is a speed event. The major differences between these events are the lower takeoff angle and three jumps that require an even distribution of effort and conservation of horizontal velocity on each jump. The triple jumper must take off and land on the same foot in the first jump; on the second jump the jumper must land on the opposite foot; and on the third jump the jumper may land in any manner. The triple jumper must also possess good balance and a high level of leg strength and power.

Approach. The approach is essentially the same as for the long jump, but it requires additional control. The jumper may have to slow down the approach if he or she does not have the skill or leg strength to handle a faster speed. The takeoff in the first phase is characterized by a single- or double-arm action. The latter provides lifting force and balance, but it disrupts or decreases takeoff velocity. The single-arm action is recommended because it is a more natural extension of the run. The stronger leg should be used for this phase.

First jump. The jumper runs off the board with a single-arm action and pulls the takeoff leg tightly through under the buttocks to a high-thigh position in front of

Figure 34.14. A, The hitch kick takeoff. B, The hitch kick flight pattern. C, The landing.

the hips. The fore leg is extended slightly forward, and the ankle is cocked (dorsal-flexed). The arms are simultaneously extended backward into a double-arm position (Figure 34.15A). The jumper is now prepared to execute the second phase.

Second jump. This is initiated by a forward swinging of the arms, an explosive firing and pawing action by the extended takeoff leg and flexed ankle into the ground under the body, and a forward drive of the opposite knee into a high-thigh position. The jumper must hold this position as long as possible to achieve the greatest distance possible in this phase (Figure 34.15B). The jumper must again extend both arms backward, and the foreleg of the lead leg extends forward, with the ankle cocked. The jumper is now prepared to execute the final phase.

Third jump. This jump also begins with the forward swing of the arms, the driving, pawing action of the lead leg under the body, and the forward and upward drive of the opposite knee. The flight path and landing of the third phase is similar to the long jump. Triple jumpers usually use a sit-out landing technique because of a lack of momentum to carry them over the legs in the traditional tuck position (Figure 34.15C).

Triple jumpers use a variety of percentages in each jump phase. This helps them to distribute their efforts more efficiently. These are called ratios.

Table 34.3 is a chart of ratios that coaches and athletes can use to gradually achieve a specific distance. The ratios of 35.5%/28.8%/35.7% were developed by averaging the ratios of world-class triple jumpers.

A

B

C

Figure 34.15. A, Phase I of the triple jump. B, Phase II of the triple jump. C, Phase III of the triple jump.

Example: For a 40-foot jump (12.20 m), the athlete must jump 14 feet 2¼ inches (4.32 m) on the first jump, 11 feet 6½ inches (3.52 m) on the second jump, and 14 feet 3¾ inches (4.36 m) on the third jump. The 25 feet 8 inches (7.82 m) on the first two jumps is the most important to achieve.

High jump

The two basic styles of high jumping that have produced the highest jumps are the flop and the dive straddle. Currently, the flop is the more popular and has produced the best jumps. The dive straddle is an old technique, but is still a very efficient technique used by many eastern European jumpers successfully. The flop is easier to learn and does not require as much strength.

Straddle. The approach is from a 20- or 30-degree angle to the plane of the uprights. A proper approach should provide enough speed to allow the jumper to transfer this energy into maximum vertical velocity. The jumper should take off at the appropriate takeoff angle to allow for an efficient rotation around the bar. The approach is from 10 to 14 strides out. The jumper uses a gradual buildup, and the last three strides are the fastest and the longest. The arms and the free leg swing upward explosively together toward the bar. This creates takeoff momentum that adds to the forces created by the speed of the approach and the drive of the takeoff foot. The straddle jumper takes off on the inside foot. After takeoff, the outside arm reaches around the bar, and the head and shoulders dive down below the bar as the hips rise. The takeoff leg flexes and the body rotates around the axis of the bar. During the bar clearance, the flexed takeoff leg abducts (opens up) at the hip, and the jumper continues to rotate and lands on the back (Figure 34.16).

Flop (back layout). Because the movements are simple and natural, the flop seems to be easier to learn than the straddle. The approach is J-shaped. It begins with a straight line and gradually curves into the takeoff. The flopper uses 8 to 12 strides with two check marks. The marks are placed at the start and at the beginning of the curve (the turn mark). The turn mark can only be used in practice; it is not allowed in competitions. At the curve, the jumper gradually leans into the inside of the curve and accelerates into the plant and takeoff. The inside lean is critical in placing the jumper in an

Table 34.3. TRIPLE JUMP RATIOS

Conversion	35.5%/28.8%/35.7%			
	Hop	Step	Jump	1st and 2nd Phase
9.14 m = 30'	10'7¾"	8'7½"	10'8¾"	19'3¼"
9.75 m = 32'	11'4¼"	9'2½"	11'5¼"	20'6¾"
10.35 m = 34'	12'¾"	9'9½"	12'1¾"	21'9¾"
10.97 m = 36'	12'9¼"	10'4¼"	12'10¼"	23'1¾"
11.58 m = 38'	13'5¾"	10'11½"	13'6¾"	24'5¼"
12.20 m = 40'	14'2¼"	11'6½"	14'3¼"	25'8¾"
12.50 m = 41'	14'7"	11'9½"	14'7½"	26'4½"
12.80 m = 42'	14'11"	12'1"	15'	27'
13.11 m = 43'	15'3½"	12'4"	15'4½"	27'7½"
13.41 m = 44'	15'7½"	12'8"	15'8½"	28'3½"
13.72 m = 45'	15'11¾	12'11½"	16'¾"	28'11¼"
14.02 m = 46'	16'4"	13'3"	16'5"	29'7"
14.33 m = 47'	16'8"	13'6½"	16'9½"	30'2½"
14.63 m = 48'	17'½"	13'10"	17'1½"	30'10½"
14.94 m = 49'	17'4¾"	14'1½"	17'5¾"	31'6¼"
15.24 m = 50'	17'9"	14'4½"	17'10½"	32'1½"
15.55 m = 51'	18'1¼"	14'8¼"	18'2½"	32'9½"
15.85 m = 52'	18'5½"	14'11¾"	18'6¾"	33'5¼"
16.16 m = 53'	18'9¾"	15'3¼"	18'11"	34'1"
16.46 m = 54'	19'2¼"	15'6½"	19'3¼"	34'8¾"
16.77 m = 55'	19'6¼"	15'10¼"	19'7½"	35'4½"
17.07 m = 56'	19'10¾"	16'1¾"	19'11½"	36'½"
17.38 m = 57'	20'2¾"	16'4¾"	20'4½"	36'7½"
17.68 m = 58'	20'7"	16'8½"	20'8½"	37'3½"
17.99 m = 59'	20'11½"	17'	21'½"	37'11½"
18.29 m = 60'	21'3½"	17'3½"	21'5"	38'7"

Figure 34.16. The dive straddle takeoff, bar clearance, and landing.

Figure 34.17. A, The flop takeoff, accent, layout, leg clearance, and landing. B, The flop.

efficient takeoff position to take advantage of proper takeoff angles and centrifugal force (Figure 34.17A, B).

Plant and takeoff. The jumper should plant the outside foot almost parallel to the bar, 3 to 4 feet (0.9 to 1.2 m) directly in front of the near standard (Figure 34.18). The jumper plants with the heel and rotates to the toe. The ankle and the knee extend fully to the toe for maximum drive. The inside knee is driven up and across the body at takeoff. This rotates the body into a back-to-the-bar position. The lead knee must be driven away from the bar, and the body must be perpendicular to the ground at takeoff. This ensures maximal takeoff force with the most efficient takeoff angle to clear the bar. Both the single- and double-arm action have been used effectively. The single-arm action facilitates a faster takeoff with a short, quick takeoff impulse. The double-arm action uses a greater backward lean, a deeper drop (lower center of mass), and a longer takeoff impulse.

Bar clearance. The jumper prepares to clear the bar as soon as he or she leaves the ground. From the back-to-the-bar position, the jumper drops the head back and lifts the hips to clear the bar. This places the jumper in a back-layout position around the bar. Spreading the knees with the heels kept close together facilitates flowing into this position. The arms and hands generally rest on the thighs (see Figure 34.17A). Once the hips clear the bar, the jumper drops the hips and lifts the arms and legs to clear the feet (action-reaction). The jumper lands on the shoulder and back in the pit.

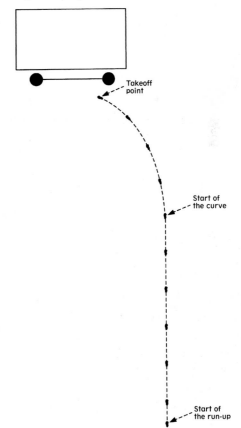

Figure 34.18. A 10-stride approach for a left-leg takeoff for the flop.

Pole vaulting

With the advent of the fiberglass pole, pole vaulting performances improved markedly, requiring new coaching techniques. The fiberglass pole does for the vaulter what the parallel bars and the horizontal bar do for the gymnast. In both cases, the resiliency of the apparatus actually aids the performer. There are five phases in vaulting.

Approach. The vaulter should use an approach allowing the greatest buildup of controlled speed. The handhold should be slightly wider than shoulder width (Figure 34.19).

Pole plant. The pole should be planted early and out in front of the body. The upper arm is extended as straight as possible overhead or slightly in front of the head. The vaulter should continue to drive into the pole. The plant foot should be directly under or slightly behind the upper hand at takeoff.

Swing. After the takeoff, the lower arm should be locked. This aids in the transfer of linear velocity to angular velocity. The knee opposite the plant foot should be driven up, whereas the plant foot is left hanging until the next phase: the rollback.

Rollback. During the rollback phase, the hips should be brought higher than the head and the knees flexed into the chest. The vaulter should remain in the rollback position until the pole is well into its recoil.

Pull-up/push-up/push-off. The final phase starts with a pull-up, which should be done when the pole is almost straight for maximum efficiency and greatest height potential. The push-up is done much like the handstand push-up. After maximum height is realized, the vaulter pushes off, dropping the legs and rotating around the bar (Figure 34.20).

Throwing Events

All throwing events are described for a right-handed individual.

Shot put

The technique for throwing the shot is a putting action (elbow and forearm extension). A legal put must be made from the shoulder with one hand only so that, during the attempt, the shot does not drop behind or below the

Figure 34.19. The pole vault approach.

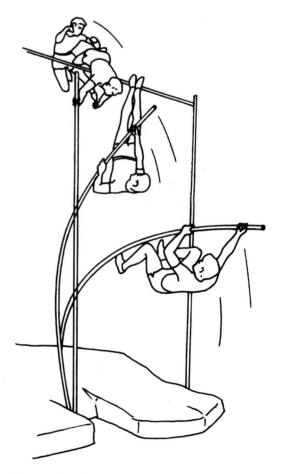

Figure 34.20. Flexibility of fiberglass pole.

shoulder. There are currently two basic techniques being used effectively: the glide and the spin.

The glide. The glide technique is a modified version of the Perry O'Brien shift, named after the man who used it. It is slowly being replaced by the spin, but it is still a very effective technique. The thrower starts at the back of the circle facing the opposite direction of the sector (Figure 34.21). The shot is held at the base of the first three fingers and is placed in the neck below the level of the chin (Figure 34.22). The knees should be flexed and the trunk leaning forward over the right leg. The hips and shoulders are square to the back of the circle at this point, and the weight is over the right foot. The throw is started by driving the left leg in the direction of the throw. This action causes a falling backward in the direction of the throw. At the same time, the right leg should begin a driving action. The line of movement is nearly horizontal during this phase. *The landing and throw:* The right foot lands near the center of the circle, and the left foot makes contact with the inside edge of the toeboard. The hips and the body begin to rotate in the direction of the throw. The forearm and elbow of the right arm should remain directly behind the shot. The throwing arm extends explosively and chases after the shot, and the wrist is snapped. The release angle should be about 40 to 42 degrees. During the follow-through and reverse, the thrower should lower the center of mass and extend the arms and legs to maintain balance and stay in the circle (Figures 34.21A, B, and 34.23).

Figure 34.22. Starting position at the back of the circle.

The spin. The current men's world record holder and leading throwers are using this technique. This technique seems to be easier to master, and greater speed or velocity of release can be achieved with the spin. Balance and control of direction may be difficult for some throwers to master. Multievent athletes have been very successful with this technique. The spin or rotational style of throwing is similar to the discus turns. The thrower starts at the back of the circle

Figure 34.21. O'Brien shot put technique. A, Glide and landing. B, Throwing positions.

Figure 34.23. The release angle and position.

and rotates into the power position like the discus thrower instead of gliding (Figure 34.24). The remaining movements are the same as the glide. Foot movements are the same as for the glide (as shown in Figure 34.25). Foot movements for the spin are the same as the discus (Figure 34.26).

Discus

Most beginners are under the mistaken impression that the discus is thrown with the arm. Actually, the force is generated primarily by the hips, legs, and trunk.

The hand is placed on the discus with the fingers slightly separated and the first joint of each finger curled slightly over the rim. The thumb rests on top of the discus, and the wrist is slightly cocked toward the little finger. At the release, the discus should spin clockwise (for a right-handed thrower); the index finger is the last finger to lose contact with the discus.

To achieve the greatest force, the thrower starts in the extreme back position of the circle and will eventually complete one-and-three-quarters turns before the release. The beginning of the spin is usually preceded by a few preliminary swings of the discus back and forth to establish a

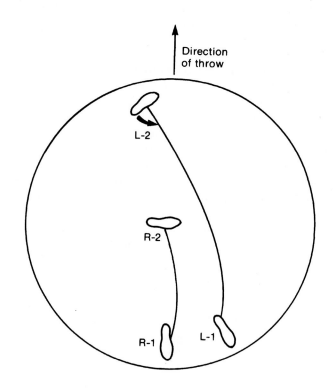

Figure 34.25. Foot movement for shot put.

Figure 34.24. The spin.

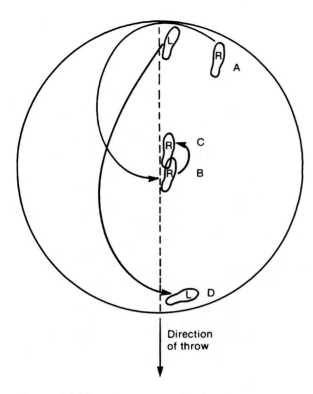

Figure 34.26. Foot movement for discus.

rhythm. The beginning position of the spin should be with the feet slightly wider than shoulder width and the top part of the body rotated more than 180 degrees to the right. (See Figure 34.27A for position of feet.)

The spin is then initiated by the legs and the hips as the weight is shifted to the left. The upper body remains relaxed, and the throwing arm trails behind with the discus at shoulder height. A key here is to keep the feet in contact with the ground as long as possible.

As the weight continues to shift to the left, the right foot will be lifted off the ground and driven forward toward the center of the ring to establish a new support. Before the right foot contacts the ground, the thrower will face the front of the ring, pass through this position, and again face the back of the ring. Once the right foot contacts the ground, the performer pivots on this foot. The left foot comes off the ground to eventually be placed at the front of the circle a little past the centerline. Once the left foot makes contact, the thrower enters the explosive part of the throw.

With the right foot now planted at the center of the circle and the left foot planted at the front of the circle, the thrower explodes and accelerates the turning of the upper body against the firmly anchored lower body. The discus at the beginning of this explosion should be at about shoulder height, then it is dropped to hip height, and released at shoulder height (Figure 34.27A, B).

Figure 34.27. A, The discus turn. B, The discus throwing action.

Javelin

The most important aspect of the javelin throw is the velocity of the release. Velocity is developed in the run-up, the torque created by the thrower's body, and the transfer of these forces over the thrower's plant leg.

Approach. The approach covers 110 to 130 feet (33.5 to 40 m), with crossover steps in the final five or six strides. The crossover steps allow the thrower to place the body in a strong throwing position.

Plant. The thrower plants the leg opposite the throwing arm in front of the body with a long last stride. The javelin is pulled back, and the shoulders are rotated back to create torque in the body (Figure 34.28A).

Throw. The throw is initiated by an explosive push by the rear leg that drives the body over the plant leg. The shoulders and the arms follow the leg drive as they rotate into the throw. The final wrist flick and body follow-through further accelerate the javelin at release (Figures 34.28B, 34.29).

The javelin's flight path is affected by aerodynamic factors. Because of the design of the javelin, air resistance causes it to follow a nonparabolic curve. Recent design changes that move the center of mass forward have been made to reduce the danger of the javelin traveling too far. Javelin distances initially declined, but they have recently increased again as throwers have learned to throw the new javelin. The angle of release is dependent on the ability of the thrower. The beginner thrower releases at approximately 33 degrees, and the advanced thrower releases at 28 degrees.

Figure 34.29. The power position in the javelin.

Figure 34.28. A, The javelin crossover and plant. B, The javelin throw and follow-through.

A

B

Figure 34.30. A, Acceptable method of holding the javelin. B, Preferred method of holding the javelin. The first finger aids javelin rotation, which stabilizes the line of flight.

Grip. Many varieties of grips are used, but for all of them the hand must be in contact with the cord grip (Figure 34.30). The palm should face upward, and the thrower should pull straight through the shaft to the tip into the proper release angle and direction. The final wrist and finger drive should be against the cord grip and through the tip, to impart spin on the javelin and stabilize its flight.

Hammer throw

The hammer throw is a very complex event, requiring a high degree of skill, as well as balance, strength, power, speed, and very specific motor patterns. To be successful, the thrower's training must provide specific input that develops the correct motor patterns. Incorrect training patterns can lead to injury and slow development. The hammer is a rhythm event, and many hours of drills are needed to coordinate the balanced movements of the body. The basic parts of the throw are preliminary swings, entry, turns, low and high points of the swings, and the release. The throw must be viewed as a whole, linked by its various parts.

Technique. The thrower begins from a position facing the opposite direction of the throw and toward the edge of the circle. The thrower begins with the feet approximately shoulder-width apart, arms extended, and body weight over the leg on the side of the hammer. The throw is initiated with one or two preliminary swings around the head while facing the starting position in the back of the circle. The thrower then accelerates into three-and-a-half complete turns with the hammer. The hammer thrower attempts to build maximum velocity in the hammer head during the turns. While rotating through the three-and-a-half turns, the hammer moves progressively from a low point to a high point and reaches a final angle of approximately 45 degrees at the release. The most successful hammer throwers can move the feet, hips, and shoulders progressively faster and farther ahead of the hammer to maximize the muscular forces acting to increase the hammer's velocity (Figure 34.31).

BASIC RULES
Running Events

1. Starting blocks must be used for all races up to and including 400 meters and the leadoff leg of relays where that leg does not exceed 400 meters. They may not be used in any other event. Masters and youth have exceptions to the use of blocks.
2. Up to 400 meters the start command is "on your mark, set" and the gun is fired about two seconds after everyone is up and motionless.
3. For races over 400 meters, the starting command is "set," and the gun is fired.
4. Two methods of timing are considered official, hand timing (manual-mt.) and fully automatic timing (FAT). Hand times are recorded to the next higher tenth of a second. Add .24 seconds to hand times to convert to fully automatic times.
5. A false start is declared if the runner jumps the gun. In NCAA or high school competition, one false start disqualifies the runner. In IAAF and international competition, a runner is disqualified after the second false start.
6. A competitor who cuts in front of another runner without proper clearance of one full stride shall be disqualified.
7. In all races run in lanes, runners shall start and finish in their assigned lanes.

Hurdles

1. All competitors must clear, within their lane, the required number of hurdles.
2. The hurdler may not run around the side of the hurdles, trail the leg below the level of the hurdle bar, run out of her or his lane, impede another hurdler, or deliberately knock down a hurdle with the hand or foot.
3. The entire body must pass over the hurdle.

Figure 34.31. The hammer's three-and-a-half turn sequence.

Relays

1. The baton must be passed in a 20-meter passing zone.
2. The runner must remain in his or her lane and not interfere with other team exchanges.
3. The baton's position, not the body of either athlete, is the decisive point in determining if the exchange occurred within the zone.
4. The baton must be carried in the hand, and if dropped, must be recovered by the athlete who dropped it.
5. The last runner of the race must have the baton.

High Jump

1. A legal high jump is one in which a competitor jumps from one foot.
2. The crossbar must be cleared without displacement.
3. It is a failed attempt when, after clearing the bar and landing in the pit, the jumper stumbles against the uprights and displaces the crossbar.

Pole Vault

1. The crossbar must be cleared without displacement caused by either the body or the pole.
2. It is a failed attempt if the vaulter leaves the ground in an attempt to vault and fails to clear the bar.

3. It shall not be counted as a trial or failure if a vaulter's pole breaks during an attempt to clear the bar.
4. The pole may be of any material or combination of materials, and it may be of any size and weight.
5. The landing pad measured beyond the vertical plane of the stopboard shall be a minimum of 16 feet wide and 12 feet deep (4.88 m and 3.66 m).

Long Jump and Triple Jump

1. The jumper's shoe must not extend over the foul line.
2. The jumper must leave the pit under control beyond his or her mark made in the sand.
3. The triple jumper must take off and land on the same foot in the first jump, the opposite foot in the second jump, and any landing is permissible following the final jump.
4. In attempting a jump in the long jump and triple jump, it is a foul jump if the jumper runs beyond the foul line extended.

Shot Put—Discus

1. Must start from a stationary position.
2. Must not leave the circle until the implement has touched the ground.

3. Must not exit from the back half of the circle once the implement has landed.
4. The implement must land in the sector.
5. The proper implement must be used.
6. The shot must be held in close proximity to the chin, and the throwing arm must not drop behind or below the shoulder level.
7. No tape is allowed on hands unless there is an open cut or wound. Gloves are not permitted.
8. There are no form requirements while throwing the discus.
9. You may not touch the tip of the stopboard or ring, or outside of the circle.

Javelin

1. The throw must land within the sector.
2. The javelin must be held by the cord grip.
3. A regulation javelin must be used.
4. It shall be a foul and not measured if during an attempt to throw, the thrower touches with any part of the body, any surface of the foul line, the run-up lines, or the area outside of the foul line or run-up lines.

Hammer Throw

1. The throw must land within the sector.
2. During the throw, the competitor must not leave the circle.
3. The hammer must be legal.
4. Gloves may be used.

SAFETY PRECAUTIONS

1. Warm up with a few flexibility and conditioning exercises before practice or competition to prepare the body and prevent injury.
2. Wear shoes that are suitable for the individual events, and make sure they fit properly.
3. Take proper care of equipment.
4. Use caution in all throwing events. Carry the implements back to the thrower and make sure the throwing area is clear.
5. Check all jumping surfaces for stability and firmness. Take special precautions for wet, slippery conditions.

TEACHING CONSIDERATIONS

In teaching or coaching track and field, the first consideration is to have a basic understanding of the physical and mental responses to training. A general knowledge of exercise physiology and biomechanical principles should be used as guidelines in planning training programs. These guidelines should include the following principles:

1. Specificity of training: Training should be specific to the requirements of the event in terms of the development of strength, power, speed, flexibility, and the aerobic and anaerobic energy systems.

2. Training loads: The appropriate intensity, frequency, and duration of training should be well planned. The principle of gradual progressive overloads should be followed to allow for training adaptation.
3. Individuality: Each individual has unique abilities and skills. A sensitivity to genetic and acquired differences should be considered when planning training programs. Body size and composition and muscle type should be evaluated. Individual temperament and tolerances should also be considered.
4. Adaptation to stress: Adequate rest and recovery cycles should be included in the training to allow for positive adaptation. The "hard day, easy day" principle is a good policy to follow. Overtraining can lead to injury, staleness, and burnout. The athlete needs regular recovery periods, both physically and psychologically.

Class or Team Management

Management requires careful planning to achieve the various training goals. The following tasks should be considered:

1. Setting individual and group goals
2. Designing daily, weekly, and monthly practice times
3. Providing for equipment needs
4. Staffing and teaching strategies
5. Proper selection and grouping of athletes into appropriate events
6. Testing and evaluation of performances
7. Motivational techniques and strategies

Teaching Specific Events

In teaching specific event skills, athletes should be divided into the appropriate event groups with similar carry-over value. This provides efficient use of time for skill development.

Group 1: Sprints, hurdles, relays

The movement skills for these events are very similar. Drills that emphasize arm action, rhythm and relaxation, posture, increased stride length and frequency, starting skills, and maximum acceleration patterns are excellent for these events. Hurdlers require additional work to develop the technical aspects of stride patterns and the hurdling technique and rhythm. Relays can also be worked in with this group. Relay practice should focus on the skills of taking and passing the baton through the passing zone. A variety of standing, jogging, and running drills can be used to improve passing skills.

The conditioning for this group is primarily anaerobic, but some aerobic work is done for general fitness and cardiovascular efficiency. The development of strength, explosive power, and flexibility are important training components of these events. Sprint, hurdling, and relay drills can also be incorporated in warm-up sessions.

Sprint drills. The objectives of these drills are to teach anticipation of the correct sequence of muscular firing and coordination (recruitment of fast-twitch fibers) to teach correct posture for optimal force application in the support phase, and to specifically strengthen muscles throughout the support, landing, and driving phase.

1. A-skip drill: High knee drills done by driving the right or left knee waist-high every other step for 20 to 30 yards. Do 1 to 2 sets with the right and 1 to 2 with the left.
2. B-skip drill: Drive the knees up as in the A-skip, followed by extending the fore leg out and then snapping it explosively under the body. Do 1 to 2 sets with the right leg and with the left.
3. Butt kicks: Drive 20 to 30 yards down the track with quick armswings, and rapidly pull the heels to the butt and extend back down to the track on alternate steps. Do 1 to 2 sets.
4. Straight-leg bounding: With the knees locked out, extend the legs and feet out forward and pull the body down the track with a backward clawing action. Do 1 to 2 sets of 20 to 30 yards.
5. Ins-outs: Speed control drills from 30, 60, or 100 meters. *Example:* For 60 meters, accelerate for 20 meters, relax without slowing down for 20 meters, and accelerate for 20 meters. Do 8 to 10 repetitions.
6. Standing long jumps, to work on timing and landing: 4 to 6 repetitions.
7. Standing triple jump, to work on timing, phases, and landing: 4 to 6 repetitions.
8. Bounding up hills or stairs (20 to 60 yards): 4 to 6 repetitions.
9. Starts: 6 to 8 repetitions 30-, 40-, or 60-meter starts with a gun. Work on reaction time and starting mechanics.

Hurdle drills.

1. Practice 7- to 8-stride rhythm to the first hurdle, with and without starting blocks and the gun.
2. Run 5-step rhythm between the hurdles to work on form, balance, and quickness. Move the hurdles an extra 2 to 3 yards apart. Do 6 to 10 repetitions over 5 to 10 hurdles.
3. Place the hurdles 1 to 3 yards closer and work on the three-stride rhythm and quickness.
4. Focus on the lead leg, trailing leg, and arm action.
5. Hurdling is sprinting, so follow the same drills and workouts as the sprinters.

Relay drills.

1. *4 × 100 relay drill:* Stand in the alternate pass position and pass the baton between the runners focusing on getting the hand back in a high position, and placing the baton firmly in the target hand. Do this at slow, medium, and fast speed. This can also be done while jogging.
2. *4 × 100 relay drill:* Run through each 20-meter passing zone checking the timing of the go marks of the outgoing runners, the technique of receiving and making the pass, and the time through the zone. Run easy, medium, and fast.
3. *4 × 400 relay drill:* Work with the outgoing runner getting out fast through the first 10 meters, turning to adjust to the incoming runner, taking the pass in the middle of the zone, and running aggressively into the curve.
4. Incorporate both the blind and visual passes in the workouts focusing on smooth, efficient passes.

Group 2: Horizontal jumps (long jump, triple jump)

The horizontal jumps require excellent sprinting ability. They are speed events, and thus the speed component of the training should be with the sprinters. An equal portion of their training for individuals interested in the long and triple jumps should also be used for specific skill development. Training patterns and drills for these events should include the following:

1. Visual aids are used to illustrate the technical phases of the jumps.
2. Run-up drills are used to develop consistency and accuracy in the approach. Check the touchdown pattern on the takeoff board and make any necessary adjustments.
3. Pop-up drills: Use 6- to 10-stride short-approach jumps to practice the technical aspects of takeoff, flight, and landing phases of the jumps.
4. Strength and power development: In addition to weight training, use plyometrics (bounding and box drills), hills, and harness pulls to supplement power development.

Group 3: Vertical jumps (high jump, pole vault)

These two events are quite different and require individual approaches. The physical requirements of these events are similar to the sprints and horizontal jumps. The pole vault requires upper-body strength and flexibility, agility, and gymnastic skills.

High jump. The high jump requires a slower, more controlled run-up than vertical jumps. Ninety percent of the jumping height is determined by what the jumper does in the run-up and takeoff. Therefore, most technical training should be focused on developing these skills. Emphasis should be placed on a fast, smooth approach that the jumper can control, and placing the body in a sound takeoff position that efficiently transfers horizontal velocity into maximum vertical lift. Bar clearance is only 10 percent of the jumping height, but time should be spent on drills that develop timing and efficient rotation around the bar.

Training tips

1. Use soft (plastic or rope) crossbars and the required landing pits to reduce injury and the fear of injury.
2. Teach both the straddle and the flop, and allow athletes to choose the style they would like to develop.

3. Determine the takeoff foot and work out an 8- to 10-stride approach. Use the athlete's strongest leg and a straight or curved approach, depending on the style used.

4. Take 10 to 15 approaches and jumps, one or two times a week, at a comfortable height to establish consistency, rhythm, and confidence.

5. Use 1- to 3-step jumps for bar-clearance drills. Ramps or boxes can be used for easy takeoff action, but make sure they do not move or slide.

6. Use 3- to 5-step jumps, working on takeoff and bar clearance.

7. Use backward double-leg takeoffs, working on bar clearance.

Pole vault. Executing a pole vault requires speed, strength, flexibility, and agility. The basic technical skills are the approach, plant, takeoff, swing-up, timing of the pull-turn, bar clearance, and landing.

Training tips

1. Teaching progressions
   a. First, teach the grip and pole-carry.
   b. Second, teach the 3- to 5-step pole-planting action.
   c. After the planting action is established, allow the athlete to take off, swing up, and ride the pole into the pit, landing in a sitting position (assisted and unassisted).
   d. When comfortable with these skills, the vaulter is now ready to develop the pull, turn, bar clearance, and landing.
   e. At this point, the approach distance and speed are gradually increased and the full movements are executed.

2. Two check marks are used in the approach, one at the start and one at the takeoff point. Practice run-throughs to establish consistency in hitting the takeoff mark.

3. Full jumps are practiced one or two times a week. Start at a comfortable height and gradually move the bar higher. Take 10 to 15 jumps in a session, placing the bar 2 feet (60 cm) over the vaulter's best height and attempting to get the ankles over the bar help the vaulter get into a vertical, inverted position.

4. Gymnastic work on the rings and other apparatus has great carryover value for vaulting skills.

5. Use 3- to 5-step pole-plant drills, working on the rhythm of the pole-plant preparation, plant, and takeoff.

6. Pole carry drills: 8 to 10 20- to 40-yard runs on the track with the pole.

Group 4: Throwing events
(shot put, discus, javelin, hammer throw)

These events all require maximum development of speed of release of the implement. An increase in the speed of release generally produces an increase in distance. All throwers must exert maximum force against the ground with the entire body (action-reaction) to produce optimal release velocity. The legs and hips initiate these movements (importance of the lower body), and the back, shoulders, arms, wrist, and fingers further accelerate the implements. The greater the forces transferred to the ground, the greater the force potential available to accelerate the implements.

Training tips

1. Use drills that simulate the sequential, coordinated movements of the legs, hips, back, shoulders, arms, wrists, and fingers. They have great carryover value for all throwing events.

2. The use of implements that are slightly lighter or heavier than the standard weight can be used to develop speed or power in specific throwing events.

3. The specific technical skills vary with each throwing event, but they all require the development of very high levels of strength and power in the specific muscle groups. The bench press, incline press, leg squats, power cleans, and other dynamic, explosive exercises are essential for these events.

4. Start beginners from the power position or half circle. Gradually add the glide, turns, or steps in the approach. Hammer throwers should learn the foot movements and weight shifts with and without the hammer. Practice the turns, glides, and foot movements down a line, keeping the weight over the landing leg. Add the complete movement.

Shot put drills.
1. Half-circle throws from the power position, with and without the reverse (10–20 throws).
2. Execute 8 to 10 repetitions—glides or spins into the power position and the toeboard.
3. Execute throws from the kneeling position with emphasis on shoulder rotation and wrist flick.
4. Execute 10 to 20 full throws, some for easy rhythm and control, and some for speed and explosive power.

Discus drills.
1. *Release drills:* Toss the discus in the air with proper spin and catch it, and roll the discus on the ground to a partner.
2. *Half-circle throws:* In the power position, from the front of the circle with and without the reverse.
3. *Spin drills:* Into the power position down the track 10 to 20 yards.
4. *Full throws:* some for control, some for maximum effort, 10 to 20 throws.

Javelin drills.
1. One step: Release drills with throws into the ground emphasizing pulling through the tip.
2. 1- to 3-step throws: Emphasis on driving up and over the plant leg.
3. 5-step throws: Emphasis on speed and explosive power.
4. Throwing balls and stubby javelins into nets.
5. Approach: Runs with crossover steps and full throws.

Hammer drills.

1. The most important skill to teach beginning hammer throwers is the correct legwork and footwork.
2. During the turns, the left foot (for a right rotation) rotates from the heel to the ball of the foot, but it never loses contact with the ground. The right foot, however, is always on the ball of the foot when on the ground, during the turns.
3. Proper grip and starting position.

First part

Drill 1: Start without the hammer, in a standing position with the legs shoulder-width apart, slightly flexed at the knees. The left foot is placed on the heel, and the right foot is placed on the ball. Perform 90-degree turns to the left (right-hand throwers). At 90 degrees, place the ball of the foot on the ground. Repeat for rhythm and control.

Second part

Drill 2: Start with the finish position of Drill 1. Lift the right foot off the ground and step around 270 degrees using an active rotation on the ball of the left foot. Continue the rotation on the balls of both feet from 270 to 360 degrees.

Full turns

Drill 3: With and without the hammer, start with the left foot forward. Make continuous turns without stopping. It is not important at this point for the left foot to move from heel to ball of the foot absolutely correctly. The correct movement will occur when using the hammer due to its pull.

Drill 4: Progress when ready by completing the turns holding a stick, broomhandle, weighted bags, and finally the hammer.

Throwing

The athlete is now ready to throw.

Drill 5: Start with preliminary swings. Make two swings, the first slightly to the right and the second to the front, and turn and throw.

Drill 6: Use two preliminary swings, execute 1, 2, or 3 turns and throw.

Drill 7: Carry out as many turns as possible with the hammer, without throwing. Four to 5 sets of at least 4 turns. Work up to 5 to 10 sets of 15 to 20 turns.

Group 5: Endurance running
(800 m, 1500 m, 3 km, 5 km, 10 km)

The basic running mechanics of endurance running are similar to those for sprinting, but, depending on the distance, they are less vigorous and more economical. The main training objective is to develop aerobic endurance and the speed required for the race distance.

1. General training: Include a proper warm-up and warm-down, flexibility exercises, light strength training, and hill work.
2. Specific training: Include hard endurance runs of 3 to 10 miles, speed work, fartlek, slow-recovery runs, and interval training. These should all be worked into the training schedule with the proper rest and recovery.

3. Tactical considerations: Include pace work, surge training, drafting, running in groups, and preparing for environmental factors.

Group 6: Special events

Multievents (pentathlon, heptathlon, decathlon).

1. The multievents require a well-balanced training program with an emphasis on maximizing the athlete's strong events and improving the weak events. The scoring tables will also influence event training priority.
2. The pentathlon and heptathlon are speed-oriented events, while the decathlon requires more balance in the development of speed, strength, and endurance. However, all multievents require the development of speed, endurance, strength, power, flexibility, aerobic endurance, and specific technical event skills.
3. The athlete must be patient and develop sound fundamental skills for each event. The athlete must view multievents as one event, with 5, 7, or 10 individual parts.
4. Maintaining emotional control and mental concentration is critical for consistency and maximum performance.

Race walking (10K, 20K, 50K).

1. Training for race walking is similar to the endurance events: The main objective is to increase cardiovascular (aerobic) capacity. The development of legal walking speed is also a consideration.
2. The development of strength and flexibility in the arms, shoulders, hips, trunk, and legs is important for race walking.
3. Start the athlete out with walking normally; then gradually increase the speed without breaking into a run. The elbow angle is nearly 90 degrees, and the heel touches the ground first. The walker pushes off on the toe, and the leg tends to land straight at the knee.
4. Posture should be between vertical and a slight forward lean. A posture too far forward causes the knees to bend and leads to disqualification. Leaning too far backward results in a loss of power.
5. The athlete should walk on a straight line, with one foot over the other. Any other foot placements result in a loss of power and distance.
6. Proper hip rotation allows the walker to gain extra distance without overstriding. The walker must simultaneously rotate the hips in a horizontal and vertical direction. Walking on a line and crossing the left foot over the right side of the line, the right foot over the left side, helps to develop proper hip rotation.

GLOSSARY

AAF/CIF The Amateur Athletic Foundation of Los Angeles, and the California Interscholastic Federation.

acceleration zone An area the width of one lane, 11 yards (10 m) long, which may be used by a relay runner to begin running before receiving the baton in the exchange zone.

aerobic activity Activity of moderate intensity that uses large muscle groups and requires oxygen to produce energy while a person is working.

alley May consist of two or three lanes used as a single lane for running the 800-meter run or 3200-meter relay from a one-turn stagger when more runners are competing than the number of lanes available.

amortation The absorption or loss of force due to flexion at the ankle, knee, and hip during the ground-contact phase of running.

anaerobic activity High-intensity activity in which the energy produced to perform work is done without the presence of oxygen.

anchor The last runner on a relay team.

approach Run used by the competitor before the actual takeoff in the jumps and the javelin throw.

apron Area in front of the high-jump pit.

artificial aid Any object, equipment, or device used illegally to enhance performance. Not legal by the rules of competition.

backswing Driving the arms back past the hips to improve stride length and frequency.

baton The stick carried and passed on by the runners of a relay team.

blind pass A sprint relay passing technique where the outgoing runner does not look back to take the baton.

breaking for the pole Cutting over to the inside lane of the track.

butt kicks Sprint drills designed to improve heel recovery and stride frequency.

cardiovascular system Related to the ability of the heart, lungs, and blood vessels to deliver oxygen and other nutrients to the cells for energy production.

center of gravity Also known as the center of mass. The center of a body's mass. In the human body and all objects, the point at which all parts are in balance with each other, and the axis of rotation.

continuous runs Long aerobic runs for 10 minutes to an hour or longer.

cord grip The middle part of the javelin where it is grasped.

course Path of the runner.

crossbar Bar over which high jumpers and pole vaulters jump.

curb Inside border of the track.

curved starting line An involuted (waterfall) starting line used in 1500-, 3000-, 5000-, and 10,000-meter races.

dead heat A race in which two or more runners cross the finish line at exactly the same moment.

dorsal flex A vertical cocking or flexion of the ankle or wrist.

exchange zone An area the width of one lane, 22 yards (20 m) long, used in relay races. The baton must be passed from one runner to a teammate while they are in this zone. Also called the "passing zone."

false start Leaving the starting blocks or starting line before the gun sounds, or making a movement from the set position.

fartlek A system of endurance training that alternates strenuous runs and easy runs over varied terrain. Also known as "speed play."

finish line A line drawn on the track, the edge nearest the runner marking the legal completion of the distance raced.

flight The breaking down of a large field of competitors into smaller competitive groups. Used in the horizontal jumps and the throwing events so that competitors may warm up and compete within a reasonable time. Also refers to a lane or row of hurdles.

foul jump or throw A jumper throw counted as a trial but not measured because of some violation of the field event rules.

glide The backward explosive push-off, or shift from the back of the circle to the toeboard, in the shot put.

grip The handhold on a baton, discus, shot, or javelin; or, specifically, the cord wrapping on the middle of the javelin.

heat A preliminary round of a race from which the designated places advance to the next round.

high-jump standards Uprights used to hold the crossbar for the high jump.

horizontal velocity The rate of speed in a forward or linear direction.

IAAF International Amateur Athletic Federation.

ins-outs Sprint training drills that alternate fast runs with easy runs for 20, 30, 40, 60, or 100 meters (tempo changes).

interval training A fitness workout that alternates hard work with light recovery work.

jostle To run against or to elbow; a form of crowding or bumping together that may hamper or impede a runner.

kilometer A metric unit of measuring distance, equal to 1000 meters (1,093 yds.).

lactic acid A by-product of anaerobic metabolism known to cause localized muscle fatigue (lactate workouts).

lane The path marked on the track for a race or that part of a race during which a runner must stay in a prescribed path.

lap One complete circuit of the track.

leg of a relay The distance over which one member of a relay team must run.

mechanics Biomechanics; the physics of the human body in motion; the forces produced by the body and the forces acting on the body in temporal (time) and spatial (space) dimensions.

medley relay A relay race in which the members of the relay team run different distances.

metabolism The process of physical and chemical changes by which energy is produced for the maintenance of life.

meter A metric unit of measuring distance, equal to 3 feet 3½ inches.

multievents The decathlon, heptathlon, and pentathlon.

NCAA National Collegiate Athletic Association. The governing body for collegiate athletics.

nonvisual exchange A blind relay pass, used in the short sprint relays.

pass Voluntary giving up of one of a competitor's preliminary or final jumps or throws. Also refers to the actual exchange of a baton or the overtaking of one runner by another in a race.

passing zone See *exchange zone*.

periodation plan A training plan that divides the training stimulus into days, weeks, months, and years. The training phases gradually manipulate the training intensities, loads, and other factors.

pole Inside, or curb, lane of the track.

power position The dynamic throwing position in the shot put, discus, and javelin where the shoulders are parallel to the back of the circle (closed), the hips are perpendicular to the front of the circle (opened), and the weight is back over the rear foot. Produces torque and rotational momentum.

qualifying round Competition in which performances qualify athletes for positions in the trials, but times or distances are not considered for final placing. Marks can be considered for record purposes.

recall Calling back of runners after a false start.

recovery period The rest interval between runs to allow the athlete to recover and return to a resting or normal state.

reverse The switching of the feet in the air as part of the follow-through in the shot put, discus, and javelin. The thrower lands on the nonthrowing leg for balance and control to stay behind the foul line.

scratch Decision not to compete in an event after confirmation or declaration.

scratch line Curved or straight line behind which throws must be made.

sector lines Boundary lines within which a throw must land to be a fair throw.

shuttle hurdles A relay race where hurdler 1 runs 100 or 110 meters in one direction, hurdler 2 runs back in the opposite direction, hurdler 3 runs back as hurdler 1 did, and hurdler 4 runs in the same direction as 2 to finish the race.

staggered start Start of a race in which runners do not start on a straight line. Used in races run around a curve up to and including 800 meters.

starting block A device against which runners may place their feet in order to get a faster start at the beginning of a race.

straightaway Straight area of the track between one curve and the next.

stride Distance covered by one step.

takeoff board A board from which a long jumper begins the jump.

takeoff mark A spot at which a competitor leaves the ground, as in the high jump and long jump.

toeboard A curved piece of wood or metal used as a foul line for the shot put and the javelin throw.

trailing leg Takeoff (rear) leg in hurdling.

trial An attempt in a field event.

turn Curved portion of the track. A standard 400-meter track has two turns, or curves, in one lap.

USATF USA Track and Field. The national governing body for competition in track and field, road racing, and race walking in the United States.

vertical velocity The rate of speed in an upward direction.

visual exchange A baton exchange in which the receiver watches the incoming runner until the pass is completed.

VO₂ max The maximum oxygen used by the body during a hard workout. A measure of stamina and endurance.

warm-up Preparation of the body through light exercise for more vigorous exercise.

SUGGESTED READINGS

Carr, G. 1999. *Fundamentals of track and field.* 2nd ed. Champaign, IL: Human Kinetics. Includes 13 chapters on specific track-and-field events, focusing on safety, techniques, teaching steps, common errors, and standards and assessment.

Daniels, J. 2005. *Daniels' running formula.* 2nd ed. Champaign, IL: Human Kinetics.

Green, L., and Pate, R. 2004. *Training for young distance runners.* 2nd ed. Champaign; IL: Human Kinetics.

Guthrie, M. 2003. *Coaching track and field successfully.* Champaign, IL: Human Kinetics. Contains information on season planning, event coaching, meet preparation, postmeet analysis, and athlete-coach communication.

Jacoby, E. 2009. *Winning jumps and pole vault.* Champaign IL: Human Kinetics. This book contains advice on techniques, training, strategy, and mental preparation for the long jump, triple jump, high jump, and the pole vault events.

Jacoby, E., and Fraley, B. 1995. *Complete book of jumps.* Champaign, IL: Human Kinetics.

National Collegiate Athletic Association. Current ed. *Official collegiate track and field guide.* New York: NCAA.

Pfitzinger, P., and Douglas, S. 2009. *Advanced marathoning.* 2nd ed. Champaign, IL: Human Kinetics.

Silvester, J. 2003. *Complete book of throws.* Champaign, IL: Human Kinetics. Contains in-depth information on the discus, javelin, hammer, and shot put events.

RESOURCES

Track and Field News, 2570 El Camino Real, Suite 606, Mountain View, CA 94040 (415-948-8188).

Videos

Championship Video Production, Tafnews, 2570 El Camino Real, Suite 606, Mountain View, CA 94040.

See Appendix C for other video sources.

WEB SITE

Track & Field News
  www.trackandfieldnews.com
USA Track & Field
  www.usatf.org

35 Volleyball

After completing this chapter, the reader should be able to:

■ Appreciate the development of volleyball and describe the general rules and equipment used
■ Practice the fundamental skills of passing, setting, spiking, serving, and blocking
■ Explain aspects of team play and offensive and defensive strategies
■ Teach the fundamentals of volleyball

HISTORY

Volleyball was invented in 1895 by William J. Morgan, who was the physical education director of the YMCA in Holyoke, Massachusetts. He developed the game to provide an indoor game for the winter months in which relatively large groups of men could participate in a small gymnasium. The principal features of tennis were employed, but the net was raised, and the players struck the bladder of a basketball with their hands instead of racquets.

The YMCA is chiefly credited with promoting this very fine game throughout the United States and in many foreign countries. In the United States, volleyball is played regularly on playgrounds and in recreation centers, camps, and school and college classes and intramural programs. It recently has become one of the most popular sports in high school and college women's athletic programs. Also, it has become an excellent recreational game in the armed services and was played in both World War I and World War II.

The YMCA held its first National Volleyball Championships in 1922. The annual YMCA tournament and the addition of the United States Volleyball Association (USVA) Open Championship in 1928 further popularized the game, not only as a pleasurable sport but also as a competitive game.

Volleyball was adopted as an Olympic sport in 1964 at Tokyo. Although at the time it was a sport played around the world, it was the Soviets and Japanese who took it most seriously. The Japanese women's teams introduced tenacious defense and increased the level of play by scraping and diving for every ball hit by an opponent. The Soviets' contribution to the game was the power offense. With the exception of 1976, when the Polish men's team defeated the Soviets for the gold medal, the Soviets or the Japanese won every men's and women's volleyball gold medal through 1980 (Soviet men three gold, women three gold; Japanese men one gold, women two gold). In fact, in the women's competitions from 1964 through 1980, the only time the gold or silver medal failed to go to the Soviets or Japanese was in 1980, when the Japanese boycotted the Olympics (silver to East Germany).

Until 1984, the highest finish by a U.S. men's team was seventh in 1968, and the highest placement by a U.S. women's team was eighth in 1968. But in 1984 (when the Soviets boycotted), the U.S. men won the gold and the U.S. women won the silver (China won the gold). In 1988 the Soviet women's team regained the gold by beating Peru (with China capturing the bronze), but the U.S. men's team repeated its gold medal performance, this time by beating the Soviets 13–15, 15–10, 15–4, and 15–8. Both the men's and women's U.S. volleyball teams took the bronze medal at the 1992 Barcelona Olympics. The men's gold was won by Brazil and the women's gold by Cuba. In the 1996 Olympic Games, neither U.S. team medaled. The men's gold was won by the Netherlands, and the women's gold was captured by Cuba. In the 2000 Olympics in Sydney, Australia, the U.S. women's team lost to Brazil in the bronze medal match and the U.S. men's team finished 11th with a 0–5 record. The women's gold medal went to Cuba and the men's gold medal was won by Yugoslavia.

In 2004, neither the United States men's nor women's team medaled at the Olympics. Brazil won the men's gold medal and China won the women's gold medal. In 2008, the United States men's team defeated Brazil for the gold medal and the United States women's team won the silver medal, losing to Brazil in the championship match. Both the United States men's and women's beach pairs won gold medals in the 2008 Olympics.

Today the game of volleyball requires team strategies involving offensive and defensive plays and highly refined individual skills. Another popular modification, especially on sand courts and beaches, is played with just two players on each side. Most recently, four-person volleyball has become popular across the nation.

DESCRIPTION AND EQUIPMENT

Volleyball for men and women is played on a rectangular court divided by a tightly stretched net. The top of the net is 7 feet 11⅝ inches (2.43 m) from the floor for men and for coed matches and 7 feet 4⅛ inches (2.24 m) from the floor for women (Figure 35.1). A backcourt spiking line is drawn across the court 9 feet 10 inches (3 m) from and parallel to the centerline. At a point 8 inches (20 cm) behind and perpendicular to each end line, two lines, 6 inches (15.2 cm) wide, are drawn to mark the service area for each team. These lines are extensions of the sidelines. The server may serve from anywhere behind the end line between the sidelines. Six players constitute a team: three frontline players and three backline players.

An inflated leather ball 25⅝ inches (65 cm) in circumference and weighing between 9 and 10 ounces (260 to 280 g) is used. It is somewhat smaller than a basketball and resembles a soccer ball or water polo ball in size. Knee pads are not required equipment although they are highly recommended for safety purposes.

The play begins with a serve by the right back player. The server stands with both feet in the service area, which must be at least 6 feet 6 inches (1.98 m) deep and is designated as the entire end line. The right boundary line of this area is an extension of the right sideline, and the left boundary line is an extension of the left sideline, of the court. The serve consists of hitting the ball with the open hand or any part of the arm so that it goes over the net and within the boundaries designated by vertical extensions of the sidelines called the "net antennae." If the ball hits the top of the net and goes over, it is in play. The receiving team must return the ball over the net before it touches the floor. Each team may hit the ball a maximum of three times in returning it across the net (a block is not considered one of the three hits). The ball is returned back and forth until one team makes an error. All levels of volleyball, the international, collegiate, junior club, and high school, now use rally scoring where a point is scored on every legally served ball by either the receiving team or the serving team.

The ball must be cleanly hit in volleyball; it may not come to rest momentarily in the hands or on the arms. A player may not hit the ball twice in succession. (*Exceptions:* Blocking rule and successive contacts are allowed on the first attempt to play the ball when coming from the opponents' court. This now includes any overhead or use of finger action, as in setting, during the attempt.) The server continues to serve until loss of serve or completion of the game. Following a side-out, the opposite team must rotate clockwise one position before serving. This rotational system is used so that every player rotates not only in serving but to every position on the floor. Both teams must be in correct rotation order at the time the ball is served. However, after the serve, players may exchange court positions.

ABRIDGED RULES AND REGULATIONS

USVA rules and regulations are described here and apply to international, collegiate, and junior club levels. High school rules are somewhat different.

Playing Area and Court Specifications

The height of the net is the only difference between court specifications for men and women. For the official measurements of the court and playing area for men, see Figure 35.1.

Officials and Their Duties

1. The first referee is the superior official and decides whether the ball is in play or dead and when a point or side-out is made, and imposes penalties for rule

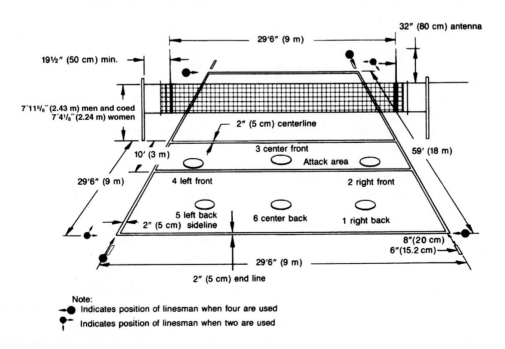

Figure 35.1. Volleyball court.

infractions. The first referee is in full control of the match and any judgment decisions rendered by the first referee are final.

2. The second referee assists the first referee wherever possible but is primarily responsible for net and centerline violations, supervision of substitutions, and overlap violations of the receiving team. This referee stands outside the court behind the standard, constantly changing positions as the ball changes sides of the court, and should be positioned on the side of the net opposite the ball.

3. The scorer, seated on the side of the court opposite the referee, keeps the record on points scored, substitutions made, and time-outs called, and supervises rotations of servers.

4. When two line judges are used, they are stationed diagonally opposite each other (Figure 35.1). They are responsible for decisions concerning boundary plays and serving errors.

Players and Substitutes

1. In official matches each team must consist of only six players. Player positions along the net are designated right front, center front, and left front; those in the backcourt are called right back, center back, and left back.

2. When the ball is served, players must be in their rotational order. Side-to-side and front-to-back relationships of players must be maintained until the serve is contacted. In the frontline, the center front must be between the right and left front. In the backline, the center back must be between the right and left back. Also, back-row players may not overlap with their corresponding frontline player. In other words, the left back player must be deeper in the court than the left front player. However, the left back player does not need to be deeper in the court than the center forward because they do not have a side-to-side or front-to-back relationship. As soon as the serve is contacted, players may move anywhere on their side of the court. However, even though a backline player could move into the front row area after the serve, the rules prohibit backline players from hitting the ball over when contacting the ball above the level of the top of the net.

3. A substitute may replace any player when the ball is dead, provided the player has reported to the scorer and received permission of the referee. Each level of play has limits on the number of team substitutions allowed, but if a player reenters a game, it must be to the original position in the serving order.

4. In international, college, or club rules, the "libero" rule allows a backcourt player to substitute in multiple times for different players. The libero can serve for one rotation unless international rules are being used—then the libero may not serve. This player must also wear a different color uniform, shirt, or jacket in contrast to the other team members. This substitution rule will probably be adopted at the other levels of competition in the near future. In collegiate and high school rules, a maximum of 12 team substitutions are allowed with no entry limitations per player.

Service and Rotation of Positions

1. Choice of playing area or service at the start of a match is determined by the toss of a coin. After each game, the teams alternate who serves first. When teams are tied in the number of games won and the next game is the deciding game, the first serve in this game is determined by a second coin toss.

2. The player in the right back position makes the serve and continues as the server until a side-out is called. After a side-out is called, an opponent becomes the server.

3. Each member of a team, on receiving the ball for service, rotates clockwise one position and remains in this new position until side-out has been called on an opponent's serve.

4. When a game is completed, teams change courts, and alterations in rotation of players must be made at that time. In collegiate and junior club level volleyball, during the deciding game of a match, the teams change courts when one team reaches 8 points. At the high school level, teams do not change sides in the middle of the final game.

5. The server must stand entirely outside the court and anywhere behind the end line until the ball is struck. The server must contact the ball with one hand clearly over the net so that, if untouched, it will land within the opponent's court. A serve is good if it clears or touches the net and is touched by an opponent, regardless of where it might have fallen. Most levels of volleyball competition now play "let" serves as good. This is another recent rule change.

Returning the Ball

1. A return may be hit in any direction. A player may use any part of the body to hit the ball.

2. A return that passes over that part of the net between the net posts or their imaginary extensions is in play even if it touches the top of the net while in flight.

3. A return may be recovered from the net, provided the player avoids contact with the net.

4. After once contacting the ball, a player may not touch it again until it has been touched by some other player. (*Note:* After the ball has been blocked at the net, any of the blockers may make the next contact.)

Restrictions in the Play of Backline Players

1. Backline players may not participate in the action of blocking.

2. Backline players may not spike from the attack area, but may from behind the attack line.

3. Inasmuch as the attack line extends indefinitely, a backline player may not hit a ball into the opponents' court from above the height of the net while outside the court and within such limits of the attack area.

Infractions

If any member of a team commits any of the infractions listed, 1 point is credited to the other team.

1. Serving illegally or serving out of turn.
2. Catching or holding the ball or failing to make a legal return.
3. Touching the ball twice in succession with any part of the body, unless the attempt is on the first hit over the net from the opponent, including a blocked ball.
4. Contacting the net. A player is not considered to have contacted the net if a hard-driven ball causes it to touch him or her. (*Note:* Should two opponents contact the net simultaneously, both are called for a violation; however, neither team is penalized and the serve is repeated.) Insignificant net contact by a player not involved in an action of playing the ball is not an infraction. This includes any contact made by a player's hair. Players attempting to play the ball, or attempting to fake attack on the ball, or attempting to block the ball are considered to be involved in the action of playing the ball, and net contact during these examples would be an infraction.
5. Touching the ball when it has already been played three times without passing over the net.
6. Completely crossing the centerline when not directly involved in a play on the ball is permitted. For example, a setter in attempting to push off from the net position could step across the centerline and not be called for this action. Another example is if the setter is running in from the back row to the net and in planting the feet, he or she crosses the centerline, this is legal. However, if a player is across the line before beginning a jump, or lands from a set and crosses the line, this would be illegal because it was part of the play on the ball. Note that any time the player crosses the centerline, whether involved in the play of the ball or not, and makes contact with an opponent, an infraction will have occurred.
7. Reaching under the net and intentionally or unintentionally interfering with the opponent's play of the ball.
8. Changing player positions before the serve has been made. Until the serve is made, players on each team must be in their relative court positions.
9. Violating substitutions or time-out regulations.
10. Unnecessarily delaying the game. (One verbal warning will be given before a point is credited to the other team for delaying the game.)

Time-Out

1. Time-out can be called only by the referee on request of a team captain or coach when the ball is dead.
2. Time-out for substitutions is not charged against a team, provided play is resumed immediately.
3. The length and number of time-outs vary by level of play.
4. Time-out between games is customarily 3 minutes, depending on the level of play.

Scoring

1. Failure of a team to return the ball legally over the net into the opponent's court scores 1 point.
2. At the high school and the junior club level, a match consists of three out of five games to 25 points with the fifth game to 15 points. At the collegiate levels, a match consists of three out of five games to 25 points with the fifth game to 15 points. In all cases, a game continues until a team wins by 2 points if tied at the end of the regulation score.
3. Some local rules may put a 17-point cap on the first four games of a five-game series with no cap on the deciding game. Also sometimes the need to win by 2 points is eliminated so a 17–16 score is possible.

FUNDAMENTAL SKILLS AND TECHNIQUES

Volleyball is a game that challenges the participant's skill in the use of the hands and agility in jumping, twisting, reaching, and hitting. Hitting motions that require the use of proper body control and muscular coordination are constantly demanded.

Passing

The most fundamental skill to be learned is the ability to pass the ball to a teammate, which is required on almost all plays. This skill will go a long way in determining the level of success a team at any level may achieve.

Forearm pass

A forearm pass should be used to receive serves, low balls, and spikes (Figure 35.2). The forearm pass used to recover the opponents' attack is called a "dig." In the "dig" the body is much lower and wider than the posture for a normal forearm pass. The official rules do not permit carrying the ball. To avoid carrying the ball when it is hit underhanded, the player should clasp the hands together in one of two methods: (1) Fist inside a fist or (2) palm inside a palm. In both cases, the thumbs should be together and wrists extended toward the floor to form a flat platform for passing and digging (Figure 35.3).

When possible, the passer should move quickly to a position behind the ball, with knees bent, feet shoulder-width apart, and trunk slightly forward. The hands and

Figure 35.2. The forearm pass. (Source: Photo by Brian Lewis, Media Relations, Intercollegiate Athletics, University of Colorado)

Figure 35.3. Hand positions for the forearm pass. A, Fist inside fist. B, Palm inside palm.

arms should be extended and together and parallel, with the elbows locked during contact. The hands should point toward the floor, and the ball should be contacted on the forearm above the wrist. The arm movement should be an arc from the shoulders, with the legs actively involved.

Setting

The setter moves to a position so that the forehead is in line with the descending ball and faces the direction of the intended set. The setter's hands "form a window" approximately 6 inches in front of the forehead, with the upper arms nearly horizontal, wrists cocked, and fingers spread. The ball should be contacted with the inner surface of the thumb and fingers. A synchronized springing action of the fingers, wrists, and arms, as well as extension of the legs, pushes the ball forward. There should also be a noticeable weight transfer from the left foot to the right foot when setting (Figure 35.4).

Spiking

Spiking is the act of striking the ball with great force in a downward direction into the opponent's court. To accomplish this powerful offensive skill, the player must learn to coordinate the approach, takeoff, and arm movements.

The outside spiker's preliminary position is near the sideline and attack line. Three or four steps are taken during the approach, with the last step taken with the dominant foot.

The step-close takeoff is one method of transferring the momentum of the body into a vertical direction.

During the last steps, the heels of both feet contact the floor, and then the weight is shifted forward to the toes. Both arms swing backward to approximately shoulder height when the heels contact the floor. The arms are swung forward and upward during the takeoff. For a right-handed spiker, the left arm extends directly upward above the shoulder, and the right arm bends into a throwing position. The left elbow leads the swing, followed by an extension of the spiking arm, contacting the ball with the heel of the open hand. The wrist should snap quickly over the ball to impart a topspin (Figure 35.5). Attackers should develop the ability to spike the ball to a variety of angles or kill zones (areas of the court, depending on the defense that are uncovered and thus vulnerable to the spike). Attackers should also develop the skill of "using the block" when no hitting angles are available. This means to hit the ball in such a way that it bounces off the blockers and goes out-of-bounds.

Figure 35.4. The set.

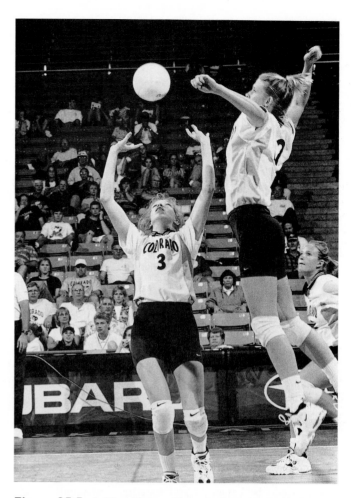

Figure 35.5. Spiking. (Source: Photo by Brian Lewis, Media Relations, Intercollegiate Athletics, University of Colorado)

Tipping

A tip is a soft shot contacted with the fingertips. The arm action is similar to the spike, but the attacker reduces the speed of the swing. The ball is contacted high above the net so that the tip is just over the opponent's attempted block or to any open area of the court. Tips and other off-speed shots advance the abilities of the successful attacker.

Serving

Serves should never be missed at the beginning of a game, after a time-out or substitution, or near the end of a close game. Players should study the opposing team and serve to deep corners, weak players, areas between players (seams), and substitutes. Players should always concentrate on keeping the serve inbounds.

A player should learn to serve accurately and carefully because the serving team has an offensive advantage, and a poor serve can give that advantage back to the receiving team. The success of a serve depends primarily on accuracy, control, and consistency. Regardless of the type of serve used, the server should attempt to place the ball in the opponent's backcourt, preferably in the corners or to the opponent's weakest receivers, or to serve short, just over the net, to cause the front-row spikers to pass the ball.

Types of service

The underhand serve is the easiest to learn and control. The use of the overhand serve can give greater speed to the served ball as well as a floating line of flight deceptive to the opposing receivers. Sidearm serves can also be made. The jump serve is becoming increasingly common at all levels of play.

Underhand serve

The underhand serve is the easiest and simplest for beginners to use to start play.

In executing this serve, the player faces the net with the left foot in front (if right-handed) of the right, rests the ball in the left hand at about waist height, and hits the ball just after releasing it off the holding hand. The hitting arm swings as in bowling a ball. The hand follows the ball straight through in the direction of the flight of the ball (Figure 35.6A).

Overhand serve

There are two types of overhand serves: the floater and the topspin. The chief asset of the floater is its speed and its weaving line of flight, making it difficult for opponents to

Figure 35.6. Contact for the underhand (A) and overhand floater serve (B).

return. The topspin serve, while resulting in a more predictable path than the floater, tends to dive toward the floor after it crosses the net.

For a right-handed server, the overhand serve is executed by tossing the ball 2 or 3 feet (about 0.8 m) in the air above and in front of the right shoulder. It is important to take a minimum of steps prior to contacting the ball in the serve. As with any technical skill, the more motion, the more opportunity for error. The left side of the body faces the net, with the feet in a stride position. As the ball falls to the desired hitting spot, the arm extends from a cocked position to contact the ball. The ball should be contacted first by the heel of the hand and then nearly simultaneously with the palm and the pads of the fingers. Contacting the ball momentarily at its midpoint and with little follow-through results in a floater, while contacting the ball on its lower midsection, snapping the wrist, and rolling the hand over the top of the ball imparts the topspin. The overhand serve is the one most used by players participating in power volleyball (Figures 35.6B and 35.7).

Sidearm serve

The sidearm serve is infrequently used at any level of play. Its chief assets are its deceptive curves and the twist that the line of flight often has. Accurate use requires practice, but the serve can be used as a change of pace.

The ball is held at about hip level and is tossed about a foot into the air while the arm swings parallel to the floor. For a right-handed server, the left side of the body faces the net, left foot forward as in a forehand stance in tennis, and the swing of the arm is similar to the forearm swing.

Jump serve

Hitting the serve while jumping allows the server to contact the ball at a higher point, thus permitting a steeper angle. The similarity of the body actions of this serve to the spike (except the angle of contact with the ball) makes this serve a natural, and its use is increasing in most levels of competition.

Receiving the Serve

The ball should be advanced from the backcourt to the frontline in preparation for setting the ball to designated attackers. The success of the receiving team depends on anticipating the flight of the serve and then on accurate passing.

Because the overhand serve is such a potent offensive weapon, formations for receiving the serve are necessary. An effective approach for beginning level players to receive the serve is called "the W formation." The two frontline outside players move back and toward their respective sidelines, and the frontline center player stays near the net with the right shoulder turned slightly toward the net. The backline center player becomes the primary serve returner by being positioned in the center of the court approximately 12 feet (3.7 m) ahead of the backline. The backline outside players move back to about 6 or 7 feet (about 2 m) from the backline. This results in the receivers forming into a W arrangement as shown in Figure 35.8. In this formation, the receiving team is best prepared to react to the rebound from the center back player, whose job is to nullify the effects of the opponent's serve. Advanced level teams may use four, three, or even two players as designated serve receivers.

Blocking

Blocking is a defensive play by a player or players against the spike or any other placement play near the net. Essentially, the block consists of a defensive player or players jumping into the air directly in front of the spiker, with arms extended in an effort to block the ball and at the same time to rebound it off the arms back into the spiker's court (Figure 35.9).

Figure 35.7. Overhand serve.

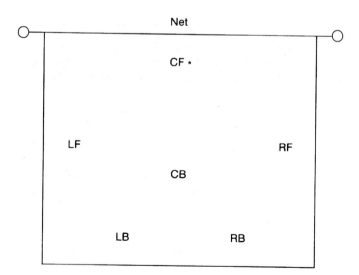

Figure 35.8. Formation for W-serve receive (back toward net).

To block effectively, one should time the jump with that of the spiker. Multiple contacts by a player(s) participating in a block are legal, provided they are during one attempt to intercept the ball.

Figure 35.9. Blocking.

Retrieving the Ball from the Net

To play the ball from the net, crouch low, legs spread and bent, with the body facing the sideline. As the ball rebounds from the net, use a forearm pass and an upward-backward striking motion so that a teammate may be able to play the ball. If the ball hits the net near the top, it will drop almost straight down. If it hits low in the net, it may rebound several feet, and the retriever must be stationed accordingly.

Of course, the best advice is to save the ball before allowing it to get to the net.

Team Play

The idea of the game of volleyball is not merely to hit the ball back and forth over the net. Essentially, the game offers many opportunities for team play, both offensive and defensive. When these skills are smoothly developed and executed, a real sense of enjoyment is derived by all players.

Offense

The basic offense consists of passing the ball from the backline to a setter at the net. The setter delivers the ball above and within 2 or 3 feet (about 0.8 m) of the net to the spiker for the attack plays selected to take advantage of the opponent's weaknesses.

The attack is used to develop and establish a playing situation that will deliver to the opponent an unplayable ball. This requires team play. The spiker should aim the ball into an unguarded area of the opponent's court. Sometimes as a surprise play, the spiker tips the ball just over the blockers' heads or directs it to either side of the blockers' hands.

Offensive systems are labeled by using numerals, such as the 4–2, 6–2, or 5–1. The first numeral identifies the number of attackers available to spike in all six possible rotations. The second numeral reflects the number of setters in the system. In the 6-2 offense, the setters set while they are in the backline and spike when they are in the front line, so they are counted twice.

The four-two is a simple, basic offense. Four players are designated as attackers and the two best ball handlers as setters. In this system, a setter always switches to the center of the frontline. Success depends on the ability of the five remaining players to pass the ball to the designated setter. The service order should be arranged so that the two setters and two best spikers are diagonally opposite each other. In the four-two offense, the setters are always setting from the front row, which allows for a two-hitter offense throughout the system (Figure 35.10). Both hitters may be placed in front of the setter or one in front and one behind. In a more advanced offense (six-two), the setter is in the back row and this provides for three hitters (Figure 35.10). Another advanced option is the five-one offense in which one of the setters runs the offense. See Figure 35.10.

Defense

Primarily, good defensive methods are formation plays to most effectively block or recover a hard-hit or well-placed ball. A block is usually set up by grouping two (or occasionally three) frontline players. The backline players are the secondary line of defense. The diggers must crouch low with hands held waist high, ready for a low, fast spiked ball.

A base defense is used before the ball is set by the other team (Figure 35.11). This defense protects the middle of the

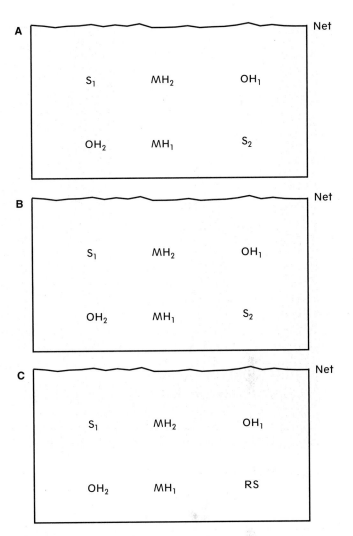

Figure 35.10. Offensive formations. A, 4-2 in which S₁ sets to the two frontline hitters. B, 6-2 in which S₂ sets to the hitters—S₁ becomes or is replaced by a hitter. C, 5-1 where one setter is used.

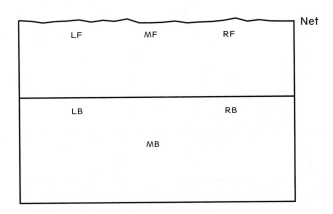

Figure 35.11. Base defensive positions.

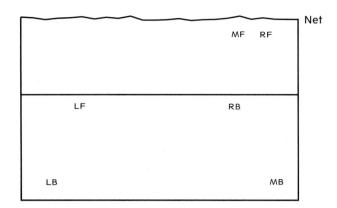

Figure 35.12. Rotation defense.

court, then adjusts when the set is made. A rotation defense is shown in Figure 35.12 to combat a high outside set (left side) by the opponent. The middle front and right front become the blockers, the right back and left front protect against tips, and the left back and middle back cover the rest of the court.

TEACHING CONSIDERATIONS

1. Along with fundamental movements involving shuffles and hop steps, the first skill to be taught should be passing. This is the most fundamental skill in volleyball, and until it is mastered, other skills will be difficult to learn. Progression for teaching the forearm pass is as follows:

   a. Establish a proper body position and rebounding surface with which to play the ball. The feet should be slightly wider than shoulder width, with one foot slightly advanced. The shoulders are tipped forward at the hip and should be out in front of the knees. The arms are extended out, and the elbows are in full extension to create a firm rebounding platform for ball contact. Think of the pass as a rebounding skill first. As the students become more familiar with the correct body position, add a slight armswing from the shoulders to direct the ball to the target. With novice students, having them practice against a wall is often a good step in developing effective passing skills.

   b. Utilizing a partner and a ball, assume the correct position and simply rebound the ball off the passing platform. Add slight movement to position behind the ball and rebound.

   c. Add the slight armswing to give impetus up to the setting target (this can still be done in partners). Then begin adding greater movement for positioning prior to contact.

   d. Utilizing groups of three in volleyball as quickly as possible is a valuable teaching concept. The game is really a game of triangles in many instances. Using three people and two balls, create a triangle for practicing the pass.

   ^^^^^^^^^^^^^^^^Net
     Th.   T.
        P

Th—Thrower	Using two balls increases the pace of the drill and the number of repetitions for the player. Increase difficulty and create a more gamelike drill by placing the thrower on the other side of the net.
P—Pass	
T—Target	
.—Ball	

   Whenever possible, always have passers in drills passing toward the net to develop correct spatial awareness.

2. The overhead set is the next basic skill upon which continuous play can be built. Teach the set using the following guidelines:

   a. Begin teaching the fundamentals of the set in partners off of simple tosses. Once a basic degree of skill is accomplished, move into a triangle formation.

   ^^^^^^^^^^^^^^^^Net
    T.   S
       Th.

T—Target	Drill sequence is throw, set to target (positioned at net where the spike should occur), and T catches the ball.
Th—Thrower	
S—Setter	
P—Pass	
.—Ball	

   A variation of this drill would be to position the target behind the setter, and the setter can then practice the back set.

   b. To create a more gamelike drill, change the formation as follows:

   ^^^^^^^^^^^^^^^^Net
    Th.   S

        P

   Th throws (tosses) the ball to P, who passes the ball to S (setter), who sets a high outside set to Th (who is also the target for the set). The drill can be repeated with a backset and by positioning the Th on the back side of the setter.

   c. To create a more gamelike drill, use a group of 4 and change the formation so that the Th is across the net on the other side. The formation would look as follows (use 2 balls):

    Th.

   ^^^^^^^^^^^^^^^^Net
    T.   S
     P

   Th throws over the net to P (passer), who passes to S (setter), who sets the high outside set to the target. The drill can be varied to put T on the back side of the setter to practice back sets.

   Use a group of 5 and position a second target on the backset side at the right sideline. The setter can then front set or backset the ball off the pass.

3. Once the set is established one-on-one, two-on-two, and four-on-four, cooperative and competitive play can be introduced to teach positioning and basic offensive and defensive strategy. Offensive strategy includes:

   a. Playing the ball to an empty space on the opponents' court (back and to the sides).

b. Changing the direction of the ball.

c. Changing the dynamics of the hit (tip or spike).

d. Defensive strategy for beginning players includes primarily returning to home base to cover space.

4. The serve can be introduced as court size increases. Introduction of the serve requires introduction of the forearm pass.

5. Combine practice of the forearm pass with the set and serve until students can receive a serve with the forearm pass from different directions and can set it in different directions.

6. Introduce the spike and dig only after consistency with the set and forearm pass is established.

7. When introducing attacking skills, it is good to start from a toss so that accuracy is controlled.

8. Build new skills into the basic game gradually. Provide opportunities to play the game in modified form through the unit, gradually increasing the number of players, size of the court, and skills used as students develop consistency. Do not permit students to swing at the ball with one hand (make it illegal in game play if necessary). Modify rules to encourage good play (e.g., must be three hits on a side, or use as many hits as needed).

GLOSSARY

ace A serve that results in a ball not able to be hit a second time.

blocking A defensive play; attempting to block or stop the returning ball over or near the net. To be recorded as a block, it must end the rally.

carrying the ball It is illegal to hold or catch the ball. It must be deflected or rebounded cleanly.

catch Allowing the ball to come to rest on any part of the body.

cover Being positioned behind a spike or a block to field a ball glancing off a team member or tipped over the block.

dead ball Ball that is out of play.

defaulted game Game in which one team does not have six players to start.

delaying the game Deliberately slowing down the game.

dive A defensive maneuver to recover a ball by extending to a prone position to contact it.

double foul Simultaneous fouls.

foot fault To step on or over the endline before or during the serve, or to step completely over the centerline.

game point The last point in the game.

held ball The ball coming to rest momentarily in the hands or arms.

kill A spike that is not able to be contacted a second time by the defending team and cannot be blocked.

let serve A served ball that touches the net on its way over the net. In some competitions, a let serve is in play; in others it results in loss of serve or a point for receivers.

libero A player who is allowed to replace any player in a back-row position. There are special limitations and substitution rules associated with this player.

match To win two of three or three of five games depending on the competitive level of play.

point Awarded to a team for any infringement of the rules by the opponent or for an unreturned shot.

roll A defensive maneuver to recover a ball. Rolls may be executed in all directions for recovery.

rotation Clockwise movement of the players following a side-out and prior to a team's term of service. Also a type of defensive system.

run-through A passing skill used to play a dropping ball while remaining on your feet and running through contact in a passing posture.

service Putting the ball into play by the right back.

service area Anywhere behind the end line.

set A contact with your fingers that is generally the second play by a team to position the ball for a spiker.

side-out A successful play by the receiving team causing the rally to end.

spike A ball hit forcibly from a height above the net.

switch A change of playing positions on the court for strategic reasons.

term of service Serving the ball until side-out is called.

time-out Stopping the game for rest, substitutions, or injuries.

tip A change-of-pace attack.

violation A foul, such as a lift, double hit, or four hits on one side.

SUGGESTED READINGS

Dearing, J. 2003. *Volleyball fundamentals.* Champaign, IL: Human Kinetics.

Dunphy, M., and Wilde, R. 2000. *Volleyball today.* 2nd ed. Stamford, CT: Wadsworth/Thomson.

Kenny, B., and Gregory, C. 2006. *Volleyball: Steps to success.* Champaign, IL: Human Kinetics.

Kluka, D. A., and Dunn, P. J. 2000. *Volleyball.* 4th ed. Dubuque, IA: McGraw-Hill. Presents the unique characteristics of volleyball with clear photos of sequential movements, visual skill enhancements, a chapter on officiating, and a discussion of volleyball's history.

Kus, S., 2004. *Coaching volleyball successfully.* Champaign, IL: Human Kinetics.

Miller, R. 2005. *The volleyball handbook.* Champaign, IL: Human Kinetics.

Pellett, T., and Lox, C. 2000. *Skills, drills and strategies for volleyball.* Scottsdale, AZ: Holcomb Hathaway Publishers.

Scates, A., and Linn, M. 2003. *Complete conditioning for volleyball.* Champaign, IL: Human Kinetics.

Schakel, D. 1997. *Volleyball inside out.* 3rd ed. Boston: American Press Press

Shondell, D., and Reynaud, C. 2002. *The volleyball coaching bible.* Champaign, IL: Human Kinetics.

Stokes, R., and Haley, M. 2001. *Volleyball everyone.* 4th ed. Winston-Salem, NC: Hunter Textbooks. Contains numerous illustrations, teaching/learning aids, checklists, quizzes, resources, defensive and offensive strategies, and drills.

U.S. Volleyball Association. Current edition. *Official volleyball reference guide.* Colorado Springs: U.S. Volleyball Association.

Waite, P. 2009. *Agressive volleyball.* Champaign, IL: Human
Kinetics.
Wise, M. 1999. *Volleyball drills for champions.* Champaign, IL:
Human Kinetics.

RESOURCES

Videos

See Appendix C for sources of videos.

WEB SITES

American Volleyball Coaches Association
www.avca.org
Links to volleyball organizations
http://dmoz.org/Sports/Volleyball/organizations/
USA Volleyball
www.usavolleyball.org

36

Water Polo

After completing this chapter, the reader should be able to:

- Describe the history of and equipment and facilities for water polo
- Explain rules and officiating practices
- Execute the swimming skills required of a water polo player
- Demonstrate defensive and offensive skills and tactics
- Teach a group of students how to play water polo using proper drills and teaching techniques

HISTORY

Bored with conventional swimming races and stunts, a group of British aquatic athletes created a new type of game during the 1860s. Played originally in lakes, with 11 players per side and rafts as goals, water polo has undergone numerous refinements. Today it ranks as perhaps the most demanding of all aquatic sports.

Introduced to the Olympic Games in 1900, water polo has always appealed to swimmers throughout the world, especially in Europe. Until recent years, however, it remained a rather obscure sport. Great Britain and Belgium dominated early Olympic competition (Great Britain won four gold medals in the five Olympics between 1900 and 1920, and Belgium won four silver medals and a bronze medal in the six Olympics between 1900 and 1924). Incredibly, beginning in 1928, Hungary won a medal in every Olympics through 1980, amassing six golds (1932, 1936, 1952, 1956, 1964, and 1976), three silvers (1928, 1948, and 1972), and three bronzes (1960, 1968, and 1980).

With the increase in the number of swimming pools and the availability of well-trained professional swimming coaches, resulting in the tremendous increase in the number of competent swimmers around the world, water polo is one of the fastest growing sports. In fact, of the 30 sports on the Olympic agenda, the U.S. Olympic Development Committee rated water polo as the third-fastest growing sport in the United States.

In the past, for various reasons, the United States did not conform to the rules used by most other nations—that is, the FINA (International) rules. Now, however, water polo in the United States follows almost exactly the FINA rules so that its teams can gain experience to enable them to do well in international competition.

Earlier in this century the United States promoted what was called "softball" water polo, in which a soft, semi-inflated ball was used; the ball could be taken underwater, and much of the action occurred beneath the surface. This game attracted few spectators because no one could see what was happening underwater. Furthermore, the referee, who was situated at poolside, could not see what was taking place, and, therefore, an increasing number of underwater injuries occurred.

In the late 1940s and throughout the 1950s, a small group of California swimming coaches brought U.S. water polo back to the surface of the water and created a style of play that appealed to California high school and college swimmers and that, during the 1960s, spread rapidly across the country.

Until 1984 the United States had managed only three bronze Olympic medals (1924, 1932, and 1972) in water polo. The United States did win the gold, silver, and bronze medals in 1904, but the only foreign team (Germany) withdrew because of the "strange" rules adopted in St. Louis. In both 1984 and 1988, however, the U.S. teams finished with the silver medal, losing in both cases to Yugoslavia in close games. The 1984 final score was 5–5, but the gold medal went to Yugoslavia because they had scored more total goals in the tournament. In 1988 the Yugoslavian team defeated the U.S. team 9–7 in the first overtime game in Olympic history.

In July 1991 the U.S. men's water polo team defeated Yugoslavia 7–6 in overtime to win the first gold medal for the United States in major international competition since 1904. This was in the FINA World Cup tournament in Barcelona, Spain. In the 1992 Olympics Italy won the gold, with Spain taking the silver and the United States taking fourth place. In 1996 Spain captured the gold medal with Croatia winning the silver and Italy the bronze.

In June 1991 the U.S. women's water polo team won a bronze metal at the FINA World Cup. Women's water polo became an Olympic event for the first time in 2000, where the U.S. women won a silver medal and the gold medal went to Australia.

At the 2004 Olympics in Athens, the men's team from Hungary won the gold medal, with Serbia and Russia winning the silver and bronze, respectively. In the women's competition, the gold medal went to Italy, the silver to Greece, and the U.S. women won the bronze medal.

The United States continued to demonstrate its strong development in water polo at the 2008 Beijing Olympic Games. Both the women's and men's teams brought home silver medals. The women's team narrowly lost to the Netherlands (9 to 8) in the gold medal match, and the men's team lost to Hungary, 14 to 10, in the battle for the gold medal. Australia and Serbia won the women's and men's bronze medals, respectively.

EQUIPMENT

Each team must have two sets of caps—one white set and the other set a dark, contrasting color, except they cannot be yellow/orange or the color of the ball. The visiting team shall wear white caps and the home team dark caps. Plastic ear guards shall be worn on all caps and must match the caps (e.g., dark guards on dark caps and white guards on white caps) (Figure 36.1).

Figure 36.1. Swim caps with guards.

Goalkeepers must wear solid-red caps. The goalkeeper's ear guard shall be red or the same color as the field players on his or her team. Goalkeepers' caps shall be numbered 1 or 1A.

The ball is of rubber fabric composition, yellow/gold in color, waterproof, four-ply, with a self-closing valve. The ball shall weigh 14 to 15.75 ounces (400 to 450 g). For men the circumference of the ball shall be between 26.75 and 28 inches (0.68 to 0.71 m), and its pressure shall be 13 to 14 pounds per square inch (90 to 97 kilopascals). For women the circumference of the ball shall be between 25.6 and 26.4 inches (0.65 to 0.67 cm) and its pressure shall be 12 to 13 pounds per square inch (83 to 90 kilopascals).

FINA RULES

Play is based on two popular sports: swimming and lacrosse.

The game is played on the surface of the water by teams of seven players each. The distance between goal lines shall be not less than 65.6 feet or more than 98.4 feet (20 to 30 m) for men and not less than 65.6 feet or more than 82 feet (20 to 25 m) for women. The width of the field of play shall not be less than 32.8 feet or more than 65.6 feet (10 to 20 m). The deeper the water, the better. If the entire playing area is deep—6½ feet (2 m) or more—it is ideal, but most indoor pools have a shallow end. The goalposts must be 10 feet (3.05 m) apart, and the crossbar must be 3 feet (0.91 m) above the water surface when the water depth is 5 feet (1.52 m) or more; when the water depth is less than 5 feet, the crossbar must be 8 feet (2.44 m) from the floor of the playing area. Canvas or net backing and sides must enclose the goal area. The goals may be wall-mounted or "floating"—secured in play by lane lines or buoyed ropes. The depth of the goal space must be a minimum of 18 inches (46 cm). Both sides of the field of play shall be marked as follows: from the goal line to the 2-meter line in red, from the 2-meter line to the 5-meter line in yellow, and from the 5-meter line to the half distance line in green. Also, a red mark shall be placed at each end of the field of play, 2 meters from the corner of the field of play, to denote the re-entry area.

At the start of the game, each team consists of six field players and a goalkeeper, each wearing a swimsuit and a cap with ear protectors. The captain of each team can be any player on the team.

Substitution rules resemble those of hockey as substitution is allowed during play. At any time during the game, a player may be substituted by leaving the field of play at the re-entry area (see Figure 36.2) nearest to his or her own goal line. The substitute may enter the field of play from the re-entry area as soon as the player has visibly risen to the surface of the water within the re-entry area. A substitute may enter the field of play from any place during the intervals between periods of play, after a goal has been scored, during a timeout, or to replace a player who is injured or bleeding.

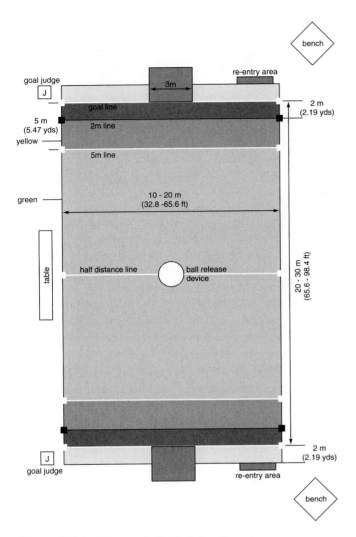

Figure 36.2. Water polo field of play dimensions.

The goalkeeper is the only player on a team who can stand or jump from the bottom (if the water is shallow enough to permit this), catch and pass the ball with both hands at the same time, or hit the ball with a clenched fist, provided he or she is inside the 5-meter (5.47-yd) line.

The field players on each team may swim freely up and down the pool as they see fit, interchanging positions as often as they wish. They may not stand on or jump from the bottom, nor may they touch the ball with more than one hand at a time when catching, passing, or shooting it, nor may they enter inside the opposing team's 2-meter (2.18-yd) line unless preceded by the ball.

Over the years water polo rules have changed frequently because of influences of the NCAA, USA Water Polo, and FINA. The rules are beginning to stabilize, as demonstrated by the fact that USA Water Polo and NCAA rules are now identical, except for a few minor differences for the goalkeeper. A current rule book from both organizations and the

appropriate state high school rule book should be consulted to ensure that players are familiar with the differences.

PLAYING TIME

In intercollegiate competition the game consists of four 8-minute quarters, the teams normally changing ends at halftime. However, if conditions (sun, wind, vision, etc.) are favoring one side of the pool, at the coin toss to start the game the winner can choose to switch sides every quarter. In high school competition the game consists of four quarters of varying length, depending on the level of the competition. Varsity play 7-minute quarters; junior varsity, 6 minutes; and fresh-soph, 5-minute quarters. The teams change ends after every period. There is a 2-minute interval between quarters and a 5-minute interval between halves. Time is stopped for 3 seconds when there is a foul. In the event of a tie at the end of a game, after a five-minute interval, two periods of three minutes each shall be played with a two-minute interval between the two periods. If at the end of the two extra periods the score is still tied, a shoot-out similar to that in ice hockey (except five poloists from each team participate) will be used to determine the winner.

Each team is allowed three one-minute timeouts per game. The third timeout may only be requested during extra time.

STARTING THE GAME

At the start or restart of a game, one player (usually the goalkeeper) must be in position between the goalposts, and the field players must take up their positions about 1 meter (3.3 ft) apart on their respective goal lines and at least 1 meter from the goal posts. They may grasp the wall of the pool, ready to push off (Figure 36.3).

The game is started with a blast of the whistle by the referee, who then drops or throws the ball at the halfway line into the lane closest to the referee. If the ball is not dropped or thrown properly, it may be done again. If a player on one team jumps the whistle, the ball is given to the opposing team on the 2-meter (2.18-yd) line where the infraction occurred.

OFFICIALS

The head referee walks along one side of the pool, watching for infractions, and is aided by the assistant referee, who patrols the opposite side of the pool. The referees shall have absolute control of the game and are both equipped with shrill whistles.

Whenever one of the referees sees an infraction committed by a player, the referee blows the whistle and uses hand signals to indicate what has occurred.

In addition to the two referees, other necessary officials include timekeepers, goal judges, and secretaries. The timekeepers' duties include recording the exact periods of play, timeouts, and intervals between periods, to keep track of exclusion times of players sent out of the game and the

Figure 36.3. Lineup and start of a game just after referee's whistle.

re-entry times for such players, and to announce the start of the last minute of the game. The secretaries' functions include maintaining a record of the game (players, score, timeouts, exclusion fouls, penalty fouls, and personal fouls) and to signal any improper re-entry. The goal judges monitor the correct positions of the players at the start of a period, signal when a goal has been scored, and indicate directions for various throws awarded. Depending on the importance of the game, the actual number of officials can vary from four to eight.

As in all sports, it is important that the officials be skilled and competent. This is especially true in water polo, in which the players are somewhat submerged and out of sight, thus inviting underwater holding and kicking unless the referees are adept at interpreting what is happening beneath the surface.

ORDINARY FOULS

The following are ordinary fouls:

1. Starting before the referee blows the whistle to begin the quarter
2. Holding on to or pushing off from the sides of the pool during play
3. Taking or holding the entire ball underwater when tackled by an opposing player ("tackled" meaning to have made body contact)—called "ball under"
4. Swimming inside the opposing team's 2-meter (2.18-yd) line unless preceded by the ball
5. Touching the ball with both hands at the same time (goalkeeper excepted)

6. Standing on, walking on, or jumping from the bottom when taking an active part in the game (goalkeeper excepted)
7. Causing the ball to go out-of-bounds.
8. Striking at the ball with a closed fist (goalkeeper excepted)
9. Impeding an opponent who is not holding the ball
10. Pushing or pushing off from an opponent who is not holding the ball
11. Taking a penalty throw in other than the correct manner
12. Delaying unduly when taking a free, goal, or corner throw
13. Goalkeeper going or touching the ball beyond the half-distance line
14. Team retaining possession of the ball for more than 30 seconds without taking a shot at the opponent's goal

When an ordinary foul occurs, the referee blows the whistle and by hand signals awards possession of the ball to the team against which the infraction was committed. The player on the team awarded possession who was nearest the point of infraction then has 3 seconds to put the ball back into play with a free throw; this may be done by passing to a teammate or by dropping the ball into the water and swimming with it. The ball must visibly leave the hand.

EXCLUSION FOULS

The following are exclusion fouls:

1. Pulling back a player who does not have the ball
2. Any penalty-shot foul

3. Interfering with a free throw, goal throw, or corner throw
4. Entering the water incorrectly
5. Leaving the water or sitting or standing on the steps or side of the pool during play, except in the case of accident, injury, or illness.
6. Splashing in the face of an opponent intentionally
7. Kicking or striking an opponent intentionally
8. Being guilty of misconduct (e.g., use of unacceptable language, persistent foul play, disrespect for an official)
9. Committing an act of brutality (kicking or striking with malicious intent)
10. Interfering with a penalty throw
11. Goalkeeper failing to take the proper position when a penalty throw has been awarded

Exclusion fouls are punished by excluding the offending player for a brief period of time or for the remainder of the game (replaced by a substitute). The excluded player or a substitute may re-enter the game after the earliest occurrence of one of the following:

a) when 20 seconds of actual play have elapsed
b) when a goal has been scored
c) when the excluded player's team has retaken possession of the ball
d) when the excluded player's team is awarded a free or goal throw

The player who is ejected may be substituted for at the coach's discretion or must be substituted for if it is the third foul. Accumulating three exclusion fouls results in fouling out of the game. When this occurs, a red flag is waved by the scorer's table.

PENALTY FOULS

The following penalty fouls are punished by the awarding of a penalty shot.

1. Any foul committed by a defending player within the 5-meter area that probably prevented a goal from being scored.
2. A defending player within the 5-meter area kicking or striking an opponent or committing an act of brutality. The offending player shall also be excluded for the remainder of the game and a substitute may not enter until four minutes of actual playing time have elapsed
3. An excluded player intentionally interfering with play.
4. A goalkeeper or other defending player pulling over the goal to prevent a probable goal.
5. A player or substitute who is not entitled to participate entering the field of play.
6. A coach of the team not in possession of the ball requesting a timeout.

PENALTY THROW

A penalty shot can be awarded by either of the referees when a player commits a penalty foul. When one of these infractions occurs, the head or assistant referee should immediately blow the whistle and extend the hand with five fingers spread, signaling that a penalty shot has been awarded.

A penalty shot is taken from the 5-meter (5.47-yd) line in front of the goal. All players except the defending goalkeeper must leave the 5-meter line until the shot is taken, and no player can be within 2 meters (2.19 yds) of the shooter.

After ascertaining that the shooting player is on the 5-meter line and ready to shoot and that the goalkeeper is on the goal line, the referee gives a sharp, quick blast of the whistle and lowers the arm from vertical to horizontal. At the whistle, the shooter must shoot without delay and without faking at the goal. The goalkeeper may try to block the shot; if the shot is blocked or is otherwise missed, the ball is immediately in play and action continues.

WHEN A GOAL IS SCORED

A shot must be attempted within 30 seconds from the time a team obtains the ball. The goal counts if it is made after the 30-second whistle blows but the ball left the player's hand before the whistle blew. The offensive team loses possession of the ball if a shot is not taken within the 30-second time period. The shot clock is reset when the ball changes possession or when a shot is taken.

When a goal is scored, either from a shot taken by a player out in the field or by virtue of a penalty shot, all players must move back to their respective sides of the pool. No part of a player's body shall be beyond the half-distance line at water level. The referee restarts the game by blowing the whistle. Play resumes when the ball leaves the hand of a player of the team not having scored the goal.

OTHER THROWS

Goal Throws

A goal throw is a free throw awarded to the goalkeeper after the offensive team has caused the ball to go over the goal line but outside of the goal.

Corner Throws

A corner throw is awarded when the ball passes over the goal line but not into the goal and was last touched by the goalkeeper of the defending team or when a defending player deliberately sends the ball over the goal line. The corner throw is taken by a player of the offensive team from the 2-meter mark on the side nearest where the ball crossed the goal line. No player of the attacking team shall be within the 2-meter area when a corner throw is taken.

Neutral Throws

A neutral throw is awarded when, at the start of a period, the referee determines that the ball has fallen in a position advantaging one team, when one or more players of each team commit a foul at the same time and it cannot be determined which player offended first, when both referees blow their whistles simultaneously to award ordinary fouls to opposing teams, and when the ball strikes or lodges in an overhead obstruction.

Free Throws

Free throws shall be taken at the place an ordinary foul occurs unless the foul is committed by a defending player within the defender's 2-meter area. In this case the throw shall be taken on the 2-meter line opposite to where the foul was committed.

SWIMMING SKILLS

The better one can swim, the better chance one has at becoming a competent water poloist. It is practically impossible for a swimmer of limited ability to play a respectable game of water polo because the rules place a premium on speed and continual action.

The ordinary *freestyle,* or *crawl, stroke* is used most commonly in water polo. However, because each player must remain alert to the positioning of other players and the location of the ball, it is necessary to swim with the head raised. This results in a type of crawl stroke in which the arms are a bit higher and the legs a little lower than normal. Also, the stroke in water polo is much shorter and wider than the regular crawl stroke. This short stroke is used when you have the ball to "dribble" as well as to protect the ball. When swimming without the ball, the stroke is longer and resembles the regular crawl stroke.

The second most important stroke for the water poloist is a specific version of the *breaststroke* in which a whip, or frog, kick is used. This type of kick, especially when refined into the eggbeater kick, does the best job of enabling the player to raise the body high out of the water. The higher a player rides in the water, the more advantageous it is.

To perform the *eggbeater kick,* the poloist simply uses the familiar breaststroke frog kick but moves the legs alternately rather than simultaneously; in short, when one leg is bent in the frog position, the other is extended, and vice versa. This kick, when mastered, enables the player to raise the body several inches—sometimes as much as a foot—out of the water.

The *sidestroke kick* is also important because a single sidestroke or scissors kick, done from a prone, stationary position, will quickly provide momentum with which the player may get started, after which the crawl stroke is usually used.

The *backstroke* is useful because there will be times in every game when the player is sprinting downpool ahead of the ball. By turning over on his or her back, the player can look and see where the ball is while continuing to swim down the pool.

The *butterfly stroke* is not used much in actual water polo competition, but many coaches use it during practices to help players build up their shoulder and arm muscles.

Normally the first 30 or 40 minutes of every water polo practice is devoted to the swimming skills just discussed because a poloist must be able to perform several different strokes with finesse and speed. Inasmuch as a game lasts from 20 to 28 minutes in high school competition and 32 minutes or somewhat longer in college competition (not including the time used for changing ends after each quarter or for time-outs, during which time the player remains in the water either swimming or treading water), a high degree of stamina is necessary. A poloist participating in a water polo game from start to finish will usually be in the water twice as long as a swimmer competing in a mile-long race! Furthermore, the necessity for making continued stops, pivots, and directional changes in midpool adds to the requirement for stamina.

Many champion swimmers have used water polo for conditioning purposes, and an increasing number of swimmers are finding that they enjoy the tactics provided by water polo more than mere swimming up and down the pool.

DEFENSIVE SKILLS AND TACTICS

Recent rule changes have resulted in alternative defensive tactics. For example, the full-pool press is used less than it used to be because of the new method of starting the game after each goal is scored (all players moving to the center of the pool). Because the goalkeeper can now throw the ball anywhere in the pool, the offensive team has increased forward mobility. The standard defense is the half-pool one-on-one, but because of the exclusion rules (personal fouls), the zone defense must be employed at times as well.

Half-Pool One-on-One

The defensive team members fall back toward their half of the pool area whenever the opponents capture possession of the ball. As soon as possible, the defenders pick up the opponents and guard them one-on-one. The half-pool one-on-one is effective at shutting off the opposing team's fast break, but it allows the opponents to take their time setting up their attack, and it also removes all defensive players from the opposing team's goal area and, therefore, eliminates a quick counterattack in case the ball is intercepted or stolen.

Zone Defense

The defensive team members fall back into a cluster around their goal and defend a particular segment of the goal area rather than a player on the opposing team. Thus the defensive team shuts off almost all close-in shots that the attacking team might want to take but challenges the attackers to shoot freely from far out. This necessitates good goaltending by the defensive goalkeeper. This defense is rarely used when teams are at full strength.

Exclusion fouls committed by the defensive team shall result in the removal (ejection) of that player immediately from the playing area by the quickest way for 20 seconds, until a goal is scored by either team or that player's team regains possession of the ball or restarts play after a stoppage of play, whichever occurs first.

When an ejection occurs, the zone defense becomes a necessity because of the six-on-five situation. The typical defense for an ejected-player situation is a 3-2. Three players shift back and forth on the 2- or 5-meter line while the ball is passed back and forth. The two outside players guard the two outside offensive players and sluff (leave their assignments and move toward the ball) when the ball goes inside.

Slow-swimming teams have used the zone defense successfully to stop faster-swimming opponents, but it places an emphasis on defense rather than offense and does not lend itself well to much scoring by the team relying on it.

No matter what tactics are used by a team defensively, each player must possess individual skills. Guarding an opponent is not easy. Each player when guarding must determine whether the opponent likes to swim around a lot or remain in one position, handles the ball with the right or left hand, is intimidated by close breathing-down-the-neck guarding, or uses illegal underwater tricks to gain an advantage.

Guarding

Guarding is defined as when a defensive player from one team makes bodily contact with any offensive player from the other team. This maneuver is only permitted when the offensive player has possession of the ball. Holding, striking at the ball with the open hand, pulling, and sinking an opponent are permitted while the opponent has the ball. When the ball is released, no bodily contact is allowed. If there is bodily contact after the ball has been released, it results in a foul being called.

A good player stays close to the opponent, prepared to guard whenever possible. It may be permissible to guard an opponent by impeding the arm or leg movement, by swimming over, or by sinking the opponent, *provided the opponent is touching the ball*. This makes water polo a rough sport at times. Swimming over or sinking often results in a foul, but it is a must in aggressive defense.

Many beginning water poloists are competent swimmers and have enough ball-handling ability to do a good job offensively at the start, but good guarding is a separate skill that must be practiced often. The poloist who can keep a particular opponent from scoring while causing some bad passes to be thrown and some good passes to be fumbled is an asset to any team.

GOALTENDING

As in soccer, field hockey, and other sports, the goalkeeper in water polo has special privileges and restrictions. The goalkeeper's position in the field of play and duties are unique.

In water polo the goalkeeper should play about 2 or 3 feet (0.6 or 0.9 m) in front of the goal being defended. A good goalkeeper can block at least half the good shots taken at the goal. In short, a skilled goalkeeper's value cannot be underestimated; the goalkeeper is the backbone of the team, always being in position to compensate for errors being made by teammates and often positioning teammates when on offense.

The goalkeeper may stand on or jump from the pool bottom (shallow pool), may go up to the half distance but not beyond it, and may use two hands or strike the ball with clenched fists.

It is true that a goalkeeper needs swimming speed less than the other players, but there will come times when a loose ball falls in front of the goal, and the goalkeeper's speed in swimming to it might save a score by the opposition. Furthermore, the goalkeeper must tread water (in a deep pool) throughout the entire game. Inasmuch as a game can last as long as 45 minutes, including between-quarter breaks and timeouts, stamina and strong leg conditioning are necessary.

From the position in front of the goal, the goalkeeper can see all that is taking place in the pool and should not hesitate to shout directions to teammates.

The goalkeeper should be able to move quickly from side to side across the goal when opposing players swim in from various angles to shoot and should also be able to stand up to strong shots without flinching. More than any other player, the goalkeeper's ability to execute the eggbeater kick and raise the body high out of the water is important; a goalkeeper who is high in the water, with outstretched arms and a confident expression, can be an intimidating sight to a player swimming in and preparing to shoot.

The goalkeeper should be an adept ball handler. The goalkeeper is the only member of the team allowed to catch and pass the ball with both hands at the same time, and poor ball handling is inexcusable.

To summarize, the goalkeeper should have some swimming speed and stamina, a good eggbeater kick, the ability to "talk it up" to teammates, fast reactions, better-than-average ball-handling skill, courage, and enough strength to withstand a degree of physical contact, because the goalkeeper, like any other player, can be tackled when touching the ball.

Goalkeeper is a demanding position to play, and only the best athletes can succeed at it.

OFFENSIVE SKILLS AND TACTICS

The team in possession of the ball has one objective: to advance the ball down the pool by dribbling and passing and then to score by shooting the ball into the opposing team's goal.

Dribbling is done by controlling the ball between the arms while swimming the crawl stroke with the head raised. The arms are carried a bit higher than normal in the recovery to protect the ball from opponents. Proficient poloists can dribble with amazing speed, but a better way to advance the ball is by passing. This seemingly simple skill is actually difficult to perform. The passer can pick up the ball with only one hand, but when doing so can immediately be tackled by an opponent. Therefore, the passer must first assume a position to make the pass without being grabbed, ducked, or otherwise impeded; this requires adroit body maneuvering.

Because players are usually low in the water, the passer frequently has a tough time seeing a teammate to whom to pass with all the splashing that is taking place, so sharp eyesight is helpful (Figure 36.4).

Finally, the passer must lift the body up out of the water with a powerful eggbeater kick so that the passing arm clears the surface of the water and the thrown ball clears the outstretched arms of the opposing team.

It is essential that the pass arrive on target; if it is even a foot or two off target, the receiver may have trouble catching it, because just one hand can be used and the catch must be made in a manner so as to avoid being tackled.

If the pass receiver is stationary in the water and has secured an advantageous position over an opponent, the pass thrown to the receiver should be a dry pass, one that travels from the passer to the receiver entirely in the air without touching the water.

If the pass receiver is swimming down the pool or is closely guarded by an opponent, the pass thrown to the receiver should be a wet pass, one that lands in the water in front of the receiver if the receiver is swimming or at the side away from the opponent if the receiver is closely guarded.

Whether wet or dry, the pass must be thrown with accuracy and must then be caught and handled adeptly. The mark of a good water polo team is its ability to advance the ball down the pool with accurate passes and without losing control or possession (Figure 36.5).

As with defensive tactics, offensive play in water polo has recently changed dramatically because of the new rules. Two commonly used attacks involve the fast break and a motion type of offense.

Fast Break

If all players on a team are in top physical condition, the team is likely to use a fast-break offense. When the team gains possession of the ball, all the players break as swiftly as possible toward the opposing team's goal. This takes some practice and coordinated effort so the players do not swim into each other. But when these techniques are executed properly, one or two players are almost assured of breaking into the open and will have a good shot at the goal if given an accurate pass.

A fast-breaking team can often run up many goals against an inferior opponent, but this type of attack requires a whole team of swift, well-conditioned athletes, much practice, and accurate passing. Furthermore, if the attack does not result in a score, the team members will have to use their speed to get back on defense hurriedly (Figure 36.6).

Figure 36.4. Water polo game in progress.

Figure 36.5. Player about to make a pass.

Figure 36.6. Fast break (white caps) after an intercepted pass.

Motion Offense

In the motion offense, one or two players (usually one and usually one of the most talented players) drive to the 2- or 5-meter line. They set the "hole." When the ball comes to them, a foul usually occurs. Then the other players make a break to get free for a shot. If a good shot does not result, the ball is returned to the hole and worked again for a foul, pass, and shot. The hole guard's fouls often result in an ejection and a six-on-five situation. To a great extent, the offense works off of the fouls.

Whether a team uses a fast-breaking offense, depends on a single shooter stationed near the opposing team's goal to do most of the scoring, or uses two or three players breaking in and around the player on the 2- or 5-meter line, no scores can be recorded without some strong, accurate shooting.

SHOOTING SKILLS

The goal at which the players are shooting is large: 10 feet (3.05 m) across, with the crossbar 3 feet (0.91 m) above the water surface when the water is 5 feet (1.52 m) or more in depth and 8 feet (2.44 m) from the floor of the playing area when the water is less than 5 feet deep. Yet when a goalkeeper is positioned in front of the goal, with the body held high and the arms outstretched, the goal looks surprisingly small to the attacking player. Furthermore, whenever the attacker touches the ball or lifts it up in preparation for taking the shot (Figure 36.7), opponents can tackle the attacker.

It takes much practice to become a good shooter, one who can handle the ball easily with one hand, outmaneuver opponents to avoid being tackled, and shoot past a waiting goalkeeper. A player who under these conditions can score on 50 percent or more of shots over a season of competition is doing well.

Water polo players should take at least 50 practice shots daily and should learn to master as many different shots as possible. Every player should be able to score through hard, accurate shooting when the opportunity presents itself.

Frequently Used Shots

Power shot

When unguarded and unhurried, the shooter can simply assume a vertical position in the water, rear back, and shoot (Figure 36.8) as hard as possible toward the goal.

Bounce, or skip, shot

From the same unguarded and unhurried vertical position, the shooter can throw the ball so that it hits the water in front of the goal and bounces up into the goal.

Lob shot

Taken from almost any position facing the goal, the lob shot is designed to be thrown high into the air so that it sails gently over the goalkeeper's outstretched arms into the corner of the goal in the rear.

Pop shot

When swimming in toward the goal and closely pursued, a player often cannot stop and shoot without being caught from behind and tackled; therefore, from the swimming

Figure 36.7. Attacker preparing to shoot at goal.

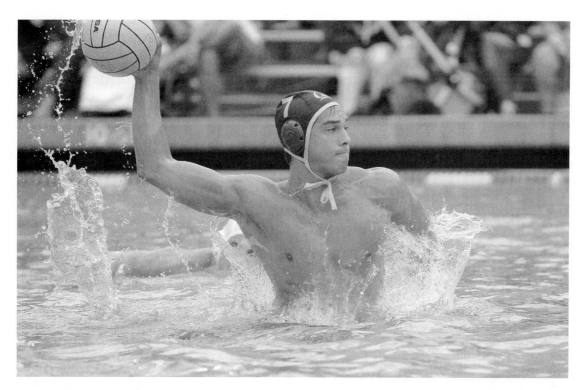

Figure 36.8. Power shot.

position the player can lift the ball a few inches into the air with the underwater arm and then hit (no closed fist) the ball goalward with the other arm as it swings forward on the recovery. This is called a "t" or "wet" shot.

Shooting Drills

Two shooting drills are shown in Figure 36.9. These drills should be practiced without defensive players in position and with the players in the drill changing position. As skills develop, the same drills may be practiced with defensive players in position.

PASSING DRILLS

Circle Drill

The circle drill is excellent for practicing the dry pass. Catching the ball softly with the fingers spread wide should be emphasized. All players should practice with both the left and right hands. If the group is large enough for two or more circles, competition can be easily established by having each circle count the number of good passes and receptions without the ball touching the water.

A keep-away drill could also be used by having three or four defenders in the center of the circle try to intercept the ball. Such a drill emphasizes sharp, quick passes to the open player on the part of the offense and quick reaction and hustle on the part of the defense.

Three-Player Passing Drill

The three-player passing drill is good for practicing the wet pass (Figure 36.10). Leading the receiver should be emphasized, but not so much that the defense has a chance at the ball. Have all players vary positions and use both hands.

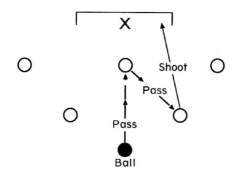
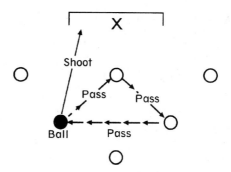

Figure 36.9. Two shooting drills.

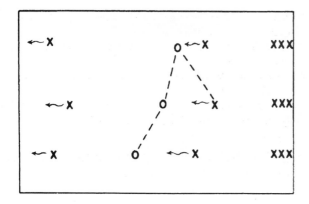

Figure 36.10. Three-player passing drill.

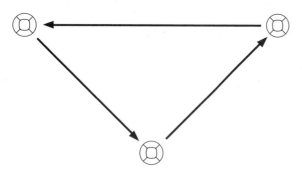

Figure 36.11. Triangle passing drill.

Triangle Passing Drill

Three players form a triangle and continuously pass in one direction. Switching direction every so often allows work on the cross-face pass (Figure 36.11).

TEACHING CONSIDERATIONS

1. Water polo requires highly conditioned players with skilled swimming techniques. If students do not have the stamina to participate with official rules, consider modifications that permit resting on the side of the pool, two-handed ball handling, or no guarding. Excessive fatigue in an unconditioned or unskilled swimmer can be dangerous.

2. Include conditioning and practice of the basic swimming strokes used in water polo as a large part of all classes (crawl, breaststroke, sidestroke kick, and backstroke).

3. Teach passing as a basic individual skill in shallow and then deep water, first to stationary receivers and then to moving receivers. Add a passive defender (no guarding) and a moving receiver as soon as basics are established. As the technique becomes consistent, give guarding privileges to the defender.

4. Teach guarding as a separate skill, first with a passive offensive player and then with an active offensive player.

5. Combine practice of dribble and pass, dribble and shoot, and receiving a pass and shooting, first without defense, next with passive defense, and then with active defense. Move from practice situations using one individual moving the ball to a partner and then three players moving the ball. When adding defensive players, give the offense the advantage initially.

6. Teach shooting skills first without a goalkeeper, then with a goalkeeper, and then with a defender.

7. Teach player-to-player defense initially as the basic defense. Later teach zone defense around the goal and zone defense as a basic defense.

8. Begin game play in two-on-one, three-on-two, and three-on-three situations using a smaller play area.

9. All practice situations should be organized to permit maximum ball-handling opportunities. Waiting for a turn should be avoided.

10. Skills involving positioning in game play should be gradually integrated into practices as defense is added and the number of players increases. Because swimmers can tire easily and cannot quickly recover from poor positioning, strategies on player movement in the play area are critical and should be taught specifically.

GLOSSARY

backing Canvas or net backing to enclose goal space.

caps Each team must have two sets of caps, one white and the other a contrasting color. The visiting team wears white. All caps must have plastic ear guards.

exclusion Penalty accompanying a personal foul. Offending player must swim to ejection area, exit the water, and remain out for 20 seconds (or less, if a goal is scored).

free throw A throw used to put the ball in play after a foul, goal, ball out-of-bounds, or any other situation in which one team is directly given the ball. The free throw is later taken at the point of infraction. The player has 3 seconds to get rid of the ball. It may not be thrown directly at the goal.

game Thirty-two minutes of actual play, in four periods of 8 minutes each. There should be 2-minute intervals between quarters and a 5-minute period at the half.

goal throw A free throw taken by the goalkeeper after the offensive team causes the ball to go over the goal line outside the goal.

guarding When a defensive player from one team makes bodily contact with an offensive player from the other team. This maneuver occurs when the offensive player has possession of the ball. Holding, striking at the ball with the open hand, and pulling the opponent are permitted. When the ball is dropped or released, no contact is permitted.

hole The area in front of the goal at the 2-meter (2.18-yd) line.

illegal player A player who has committed a third personal foul or has been excluded for the entire game.

impeding When a player intentionally hinders or slows the progress of an opponent by swimming on the back, legs, or shoulders of the opponent or swims under any swimming opponent with or without the ball.

penalty throw A throw taken by any member of the offended team from the penalty line. A one-handed, over-the-shoulder shot is taken.

pop shot, or tee shot Executed by a player swimming in with the ball (dribbling) toward the goal; she or he, without stopping, lifts the ball slightly out of the water with one hand and hits it with the other hand.

signals The hand positions used by the referee to denote the game situations.

30-second clock (shot clock) The visible digital timer used to indicate how long any team may have possession/control of the ball before attempting a shot at the goal. A shot must be attempted within the 30-second time limit or the offensive team loses possession.

time-outs There may be two time-outs of not more than 2 minutes each per team in the first four quarters. In overtime each team may have one time-out.

SUGGESTED READINGS

Books

Cicciarella, C. 2000. *Water polo.* 3rd ed. Boston: American Press.

Cutino, P., Cutino, P., and Topper, R. 2001. *101 offensive water polo drills.* Monterey, CA: Coaches Choice Books.

Cutino, P., Cutino, P., and Topper, R. 2002. *101 defensive and conditioning water polo drills.* Monterey, CA: Coaches Choice Books.

Dettamanti, D. 2009. *A practical guide to coaching water polo.* Raleigh, NC: Lulu Enterprises, Inc.

Dettamanti, D. 2009. *Understanding water polo.* Raleigh, NC: Lulu Enterprises, Inc.

NCAA official water polo rules. Current ed. Kansas City, MO: NCAA.

Swimming, diving, and water polo rules. Annual. Kansas City, MO: National Federation of State High School Associations.

Periodical

Water Polo Scoreboard (monthly), U.S. Water Polo, 201 S Capitol Ave., Suite 520, Indianapolis, IN 46225.

RESOURCES

Videos

www.swimoutlet.com/water-polo

Several DVDs available covering all aspects of water polo.

See Appendix C for video sources.

WEB SITES

www.collegiatewaterpolo.org

www.usawaterpolo.com

37 | Weight Training

After completing this chapter, the reader should be able to:

- Describe the history of weight lifting and distinguish the differences among the activities in this chapter
- Set up a personal weight-training and circuit weight-training program
- Recognize the importance of safety in these activities
- Identify appropriate exercises for various parts of the body
- Explain the competitive lifting events
- Teach basic weight-lifting techniques to a group of beginning students

OVERVIEW

Weight training or resistance training is a form of exercise that utilizes progressive resistance movements, typically with free weights or weight machines, to build muscular strength, endurance, and/or size. The activity of weight training has become very popular, with several different purposes. Some perform weight training for sport; that is, they participate in weight lifting, powerlifting, or bodybuilding competitions. Athletes of other sports, such as football or track and field, use weight training to enhance sports performance. Many people also use weight training for general fitness; they just want to look and feel better. The value of weight training in the promotion of health has been recognized and recommended by the surgeon general of the United States. Weight training has been used by physical therapists, athletic trainers, and occupational therapists to restore the musculoskeletal system to health from disease or injury. It is now clear that weight training, by improving strength and increasing lean body mass, has an important role in lowering the risks of osteoporosis, loss of function with increasing age, and obesity. Although these reasons for lifting stem from different goals, all those who participate in a weight-training program expect the program to produce certain benefits such as increased strength and muscle size and an improvement in body composition, or the ratio of fat-free mass to body fat.

HISTORY

The exact period in history when weight training became a practice or part of a training regimen is not known. Strongmen such as Samson, Hercules, and the Greek wrestler Milo are part of ancient myth and folklore.

In its earliest form, weight lifting was a part of everyday life. Weight training also played an important role in preparing soldiers for battle in the days of the Greeks, Egyptians, and Romans. During the Middle Ages, Romans trained their soldiers by marching them over long distances with heavier-than-normal loads. Throughout the seventeenth to nineteenth centuries, most of the empires and armies of Europe followed the Greek and Roman examples and trained with overloaded packs.

Weight "lifting" was introduced to the United States between 1859 and 1872, when Dr. G. B. Winship toured the United States and Canada, giving lectures and presenting exhibitions.

Weight "lifting" soon found its way into carnivals and circuses and onto vaudeville stages, where men and women performed unbelievable feats of strength that in fact were tricks—which probably was responsible for most of the myth and mystery that has surrounded weight lifting until recent times. Weight training survived this era and went on to find its way into YMCAs and athletic health clubs. With these organizations promoting the activity, evidence of the value of weight training began to grow.

Through most of the early 1900s, weight training was practiced, almost exclusively, by those who competed in one of the weight-lifting sports.

The sport of weight lifting has been included in the Olympic Games since 1896. At first there were two events, a one-handed lift and a two-handed lift, and the lifter's body weight was not considered. In 1920 the press, snatch, and clean and jerk were introduced, and this system remained until 1972, when the press was eliminated. In the United States, organized competition began in 1929 when the Amateur Athletic Union (AAU) held its first national championship. In 1932 the United States entered its first team in Olympic competition.

The sport of bodybuilding first began in the United States in 1938 when the AAU held the Mr. America contest. This was the only group to organize national contests until the International Federation of Bodybuilders (IFBB), formed in 1946, created the IFBB Mr. America Competition in 1948. In 1950 the National Amateur Bodybuilders Association (NABBA) began the Mr. Universe contest. Then, in 1965 the IFBB began the Mr. Olympia contest. Today this is the biggest and most prestigious bodybuilding competition. In 1965 the NABBA held its first Miss Universe competition. In 1980 women began competing in the Miss Olympia contest.

The sport of powerlifting involves three lifts: the squat, deadlift, and bench press. In recent years it has been the most popular form of competitive lifting in the United States. In less than 10 years the sport grew to the extent that more than 40 nations compete in the International Powerlifting Federation World Championships.

Using weight training for other sports was not done until the late 1960s when the San Diego Chargers and the University of Hawaii both had strength coaches and had successful seasons. The University of Nebraska followed suit and won national championships in 1970 and 1971. They credited their success to their strength program. Strength and conditioning quickly became popular for the sport of football. Today strength and conditioning for sport is done for most all sports and is being used even at the high school level.

Medical doctors, physical therapists, athletic trainers, and occupational therapists began experimenting with strength exercise for injury rehabilitation and muscle rebuilding soon after World War II. Their efforts were successful, so they encouraged physical educators to include weight training in gym classes. Magazines devoted to weight lifting and bodybuilding also helped to make the public more aware of the benefits of this activity. More gyms opened up throughout the country, but they were still used by mostly hardcore lifters. In the 1970s, weight machines were introduced into many gyms and weight training became more popular among the general population.

In the 1990s *Physical Activity and Health: A Report of the Surgeon General* established that increased risks for a variety of chronic diseases are associated with physical inactivity and a sedentary lifestyle. This report contained specific recommendations indicating that a physically active lifestyle should produce sufficient levels of all components of health-related fitness—cardiorespiratory endurance, body composition, muscular strength, muscular endurance, and flexibility. Weight or resistance training was specifically recommended for improving muscular strength and endurance and increasing or maintaining lean body mass. Reduced risks for osteoporosis (bone mineral loss), loss of functional capacity, and loss of lean body mass are related to a lifetime of weight or resistance training. The United States is facing an epidemic of obesity and the many chronic diseases associated with obesity. As Figure 37.1 illustrates, in the last decade there has been a dramatic and accelerating increase in the percentage of adult Americans classified as obese. This increase in obesity is occurring in a similar fashion for American children. As individuals age, lean body mass and resting metabolic rate (energy expenditure) decrease (Figure 37.2). Lean body (muscle) mass has a high resting energy expenditure. Resting metabolic rate represents

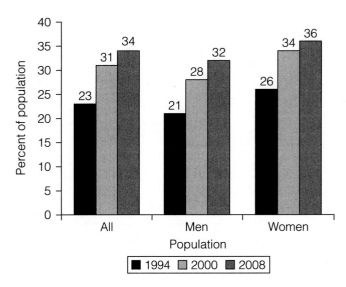

Figure 37.1. Increasing obesity in the United States, 1994 to 2008.

between 60 percent and 75 percent of daily energy expenditure. Thus, a lifetime of weight training can make a contribution to maintaining energy balance by increasing caloric expenditure through the physical action required to maintain lean body mass, which will decrease the age-related reduction in resting metabolic rate. Numerous studies indicate that weight bearing is important in reducing bone mineral loss, as well as maintaining functional capacity and the ability to perform the activities of daily living as people age.

Weight training and bodybuilding are continuing to increase in popularity in colleges and health clubs throughout the country. It is not uncommon to find a set of barbells or other weight-training equipment in the recreation room of many American homes. In an age that has provided us with countless labor-saving devices, weight training has provided the much needed vigorous exercise that our inactive lifestyle has taken away.

TRAINING CONSIDERATIONS

When it comes to weight training, the goals of lifters are different. Weight lifters and powerlifters are concerned with improving power and strength, bodybuilders are concerned with size and definition, and athletes are concerned with improving performance. Goals for noncompetitive lifters are numerous. With lifters having different goals as well as different levels of experience, how lifters train will vary also. There is no one correct method of weight training but rather a variety of methods that can produce strength gains. The following suggestions are to help beginners with starting a weight-training program.

A weight-training program designed to improve strength, like other physical training programs designed to improve

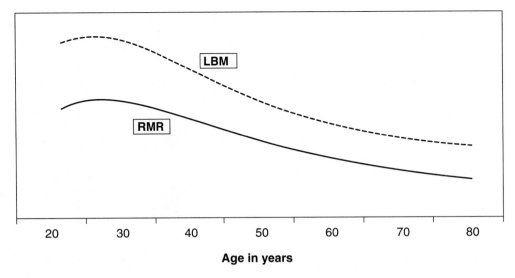

RMR = Resting Metabolic Rate
LBM = Lean Body Mass

Figure 37.2. The reduction in RMR and LBM with age.

cardiorespiratory endurance, speed, or flexibility, is governed by the following six basic principles:

- **Overload**—to create an adaptation, such as muscular size, strength, or endurance, a greater load must be applied to the body than it is normally accustomed to.
- **Progression**—As adaptations occur, overload must continually be increased to produce improvement.
- **Specificity**—For general fitness the overload principle must be uniquely applied to the training objectives and the muscles that are to become stronger. For example, if one wishes to increase the strength of the biceps, one should select an exercise that emphasizes this musculature. For improved performance, specific exercises that replicate the gross movement patterns related to the primary actions of the sport should be utilized. For example, the squat is an exercise more similar to athletic performance when compared to a leg extension or leg curl.
- **Individuality**—This refers to the concept that people respond differently to the same training stimulus.
- **Reversability**—If training is discontinued, training gains will cease and individuals return to pretraining or near pretraining levels.
- **Diminishing Returns**—Performance gains are related to the level of training experience of the individual. The closer an individual is to his or her genetic potential, the more marginal the improvements they will experience when compared to the beginner.

In essence these principles indicate that to become and stay stronger, individuals should plan their own programs with their own goals and monitor individual progress. The weight loads or resistances must be greater than normal, and the strength-building exercises must stress the muscles to be strengthened. The program must be continued if the strength gains are to continue or be maintained.

All human movement, including simple movements like those used in weight training, requires complex motor control from the central nervous system. Almost every complete physical movement uses three types of muscular actions: concentric, eccentric, and isometric. In concentric action, the muscle shortens, generates force, pulls the tendon attached to the bone, and movement results. In eccentric action, the muscle generates force while it is lengthening. Isometric muscle actions are characterized by force generation without noticeable changes in muscle length. The bicep barbell curl from a standing position can be used to demonstrate concentric, eccentric, and isometric actions. When the participant lifts the barbell, the bicep muscles shorten (concentric) and generate force. When the participant lowers (not drops) the barbell, the biceps lengthen (eccentric) and generate enough force to control the weight as it is lowered. During the lowering and raising of the barbell, the muscles of the shoulders and trunk must contract isometrically to stabilize the upper body and resist any unwanted movements. Almost all physical movements are a series of concentric and eccentric contractions controlled by the central nervous system.

Five variables, frequency, intensity, volume, type, and rest, must be manipulated to develop an appropriate weight-training program. A summary of each follows:

- Frequency—How many weight-training sessions should be performed each week?
- Intensity—How much weight or resistance should be used in each session?

Table 37.1. STRENGTH-TRAINING GUIDELINES

Variable	Recommended Prescription
Frequency	2 to 3 days per week
Intensity	8 rm to 12 rm per set
Volume	Minimum of 1 set per exercise Three sets if time allows
Type	Free weights, rack-mounted weights, dynamometers, or body weight
Rest	Variable, depending on goals

In the table, the abbreviation *rm* represents repetition maximum. An rm is the maximum amount of weight an individual can lift through a complete range of motion, once. The 8 rm is a training load or intensity of that set.

- Volume—In relation to weight training, how many lifts or repetitions and how many sets of lifts or repetitions should be performed in a session?
- Type—What type of equipment or resistance, free weights, rack-mounted weight machine, body weight, or mechanical dynamometers will be used?
- Rest—How much time should elapse between sets in a workout?

As mentioned previously, there is no one absolutely correct method for developing a weight-training program. In Table 37.1, strength-training guidelines are provided.

A weight-training program usually has one of three general goals: improve or maintain muscular strength, muscular endurance, or improve body composition. In Figure 37.3, the relationship between resistance or weight-lifted repetitions and the goals of muscular strength or endurance are illustrated. Heavier weights and fewer repetitions are associated with improving strength while lighter weights and higher numbers of repetitions improve muscular endurance.

Specific Training Tips
Order of exercises

During a workout the order of the exercises performed is important. The following are points to consider:
- First perform larger muscle mass exercises or multijoint exercises. For example, do the bench press (pectoralis major, anterior deltoids, triceps—shoulder and elbow) before triceps or arm extension (triceps—elbow).
- Alternate among upper body, trunk, and leg exercises. This will allow progression through a workout in less time without excess fatigue, which might negatively affect the quality and intensity of the exercises. Rest and recovery time is essential to optimize your training results. If seeking to improve strength or power, a minimum of 3 to 5 minutes between sets should be used. If the main goal is to increase muscular size or fitness, approximately 1 to 1½ minutes of rest should be allowed between sets. Finally, if striving to improve muscular endurance, rest periods of 1 minute or less should be used.

Progressive resistance exercise (PRE)

To continue to improve strength, overload conditions must be maintained. As the weight trainer gets stronger, he or she gradually needs to increase the weight load or resistance. Various strategies have been used to establish the initial weight loads in weight lifting. The best approach is to use experience as well as trial and error to establish the initial weight loads and resistances. The following uses the ACSM guidelines with the bench press as an example:
1. A male participant has established his initial 8 rm as 130 pounds.
2. Over a period of weeks, he gradually improves his strength and muscular endurance and his 130 pounds becomes a 12 rm instead of an 8 rm.

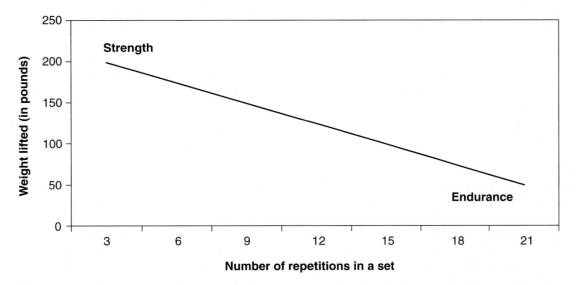

Figure 37.3. Strength or endurance repetitions and resistance.

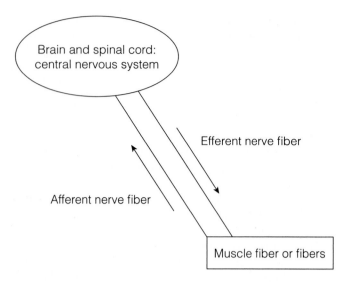

Figure 37.4. Neural activation and motor control of muscular contractions.

3. Since strength is his primary goal, he increases his weight load to 145 pounds and this becomes his new 8 rm.

Using PRE, a weight trainer will gradually increase weight load or resistance or repetitions depending upon his or her goals.

Workout variability and improvement

Performance in weight training will not be perfectly consistent across workouts. Some days a participant will perform better than others. A participant may also experience training plateaus where improvements may stop. A beginner may experience large gains that are related to improved motor control and neural activation, recruitment of motor units (nerve fiber and muscle fibers that are stimulated). Figure 37.4 depicts neural activation and motor control of muscular contractions. The central nervous system sends signals via the efferent nerve fibers for the motor units to function and produce movement. The central nervous system receives feedback for the muscles via the afferent nerves. This feedback allows the central nervous system to modulate neural activation and produce the motor unit recruitment required for the needed muscular force. Essentially, greater force demands require more motor units. Figure 37.5 illustrates the improvement profile of weight training. Note that initial gains are fast and related to neural activation; secondary and lasting gains are related to hypertrophy (increase in muscle fiber size). Athletes, competitive weight lifters, and bodybuilders have used anabolic steroids as an ergogenic aid to further enhance performance as genetic potential is reached. While anabolic steroids do improve strength and power, a variety of serious diseases and health problems have been associated with their use, including sexual dysfunction, sexual anatomy abnormalities, heart disease, and cancer. The use of anabolic steroids is a dangerous health behavior and should be avoided.

Periodization

The planned progression of workouts over time is called periodization. A participant can adapt his or her program from high resistance or weight loads with lower repetitions (strength goal) to lower resistance or weight loads with higher repetitions (muscular endurance goal) over a period of weeks. Periodization allows diversity in training and may prevent mental and physical staleness.

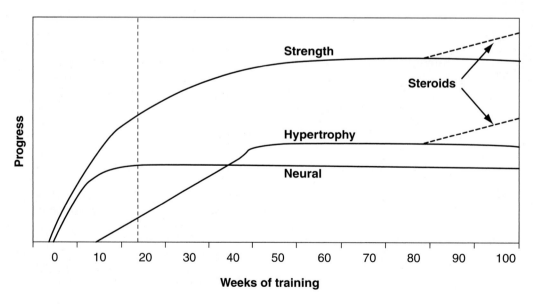

Figure 37.5. Improvement profile of weight training.

Weight Training

GENERAL TECHNIQUES FOR ALL LIFTS

Warm-up. All resistance training sessions should begin with a light 3 to 5 minute general warm-up, such as jogging, skipping rope, or cycling. This helps prepare the body for more vigorous activity and warms the muscles up for the specific warm-up. After the general warm-up a specific warm-up should be performed. This part of the warm-up should be specific to the exercise; for example, a light bench press should be done in preparation for the bench press exercise. Usually a warm-up consists of 10 repetitions with a light, comfortable weight.

Breathing. In general, one should inhale during the negative, or lowering, phase of all lifts and exhale during the working, or positive, phase. Beginners should avoid holding the breath during any part of a lift. Advanced level lifters, such as power lifters, who use maximal or near maximal loads may find temporarily holding the breath, also referred to as the Valsalva maneuver, is beneficial for improving the rigidity, or stability, of the torso, making it easier to lift heavy weights. However, the Valsalva maneuver also can cause a transient elevation of blood pressure, making an individual more likely to black out. For this reason, this technique should be used with caution and only by experienced lifters who are able to avoid increasing pressure to the point of blacking out.

Full range. It is recommended that individuals always complete the full range of motion during any lift, while learning basic exercises.

Spotting. For any exercise in which a weight is lifted over the head or over the face, a spotter should be used. The spotter should stay in communication during the set of exercises so that aid is provided when necessary to prevent a training accident and subsequent injury. See Figure 37.6 for an example of the correct spotting technique.

FUNDAMENTAL SKILLS AND TECHNIQUES

Exercises for the Upper Body

Free-weight bench press
(for chest, shoulders, and upper arms)

Starting position. Using a flat bench, the lifter will position himself or herself on the bench using five main points of contact, with the head, shoulder blades, and glutes in contact with the bench and both feet flat on the floor. The lifter will grab the bar with an overhand grip, slightly wider than shoulder width. The eyes should line up directly with the bar. The spotter should assume an athletic stance and grab the bar using an alternated grip (Figure 37.6).

Movement. With assistance from the spotter, the lifter will move the bar off the rack until it is positioned directly over the chest. The lifter will then lower the bar in a controlled manner to the chest (Figure 37.7), touch the bar to the chest lightly, and push the weight back to the starting position.

Technique and safety tip. The spotter should hold the bar throughout the set to aid the lifter should they fatigue before completing a repetition, or should they need assistance to re-rack the barbell.

Rack-mounted bench press

The technique for this exercise is similar to the free-weight bench press, but rather than aligning the bar with the eyes, the lifter should be positioned so that the barbell is aligned with the middle of the chest (Figure 37.8).

Figure 37.6. Free-weight bench press—starting position.

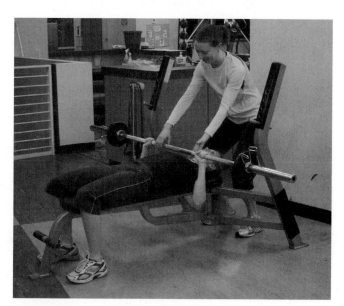

Figure 37.7. Free-weight bench press.

Figure 37.8. Rack mounted bench press.

Figure 37.10. Lat pull.

Lat pull
(for upper back, biceps, and posture muscles)

Starting position. Grasp the bar with a slightly wider than shoulder-width overhand grip. Sit on the seat with the leg pad snug against the thighs. Keep your head up and back neutral (Figure 37.9).

Movement. Pull the bar down in front of the head until the bar reaches the collar bone (Figure 37.10). Return the bar to the starting position.

Technique and safety tip. Return the bar slowly to avoid any loss of control or stabilization. No spotter is necessary.

Free-weight bent-over row
(for posture muscles, biceps, and upper back)

Starting position. Stand with the feet shoulder-width apart and the toes pointed out slightly. Bend over until the torso is nearly parallel to the floor, and bend the knees slightly. Grasp the barbell with an overhand grip, with the hands at about shoulder width.

Movement. Pull the barbell up until it reaches the lower rib cage (Figure 37.11). Then return it to the starting position.

Figure 37.11. Free-weight bent-over row.

Technique and safety tip. Concentrate on raising the elbows as high as possible. No spotter is necessary. Keep the knees bent and use relatively light weights to avoid lower-back injury.

Standing free-weight overhead press
(for shoulders and upper arms)

Starting position. Stand with the feet shoulder-width apart and the toes pointed slightly out. Using a shoulder-width overhand grip, lift the barbell off the rack. Place the barbell at shoulder height (Figure 37.12).

Movement. Push the barbell straight up until the arms are fully extended (Figure 37.13). Return to the shoulder-high position.

Technique and safety tip. Never bend or arch the back. Always look straight ahead or down during the lift to prevent lower-back arching.

Free-weight arm curl (for biceps)

Starting position. Stand with the feet shoulder-width apart and the toes pointed straight ahead. Bend at the knees, grasp

Figure 37.9. Lat pull—starting position.

Figure 37.12. Standing free-weight overhead press—starting position.

Figure 37.14. free-weight arm curl—starting position.

the bar with an underhand grip, then return to the standing position (Figure 37.14).

Movement. With the elbows tucked tightly against the rib cage, flex the arms at the elbows and pull the bar up to the chest, then return to the starting position (Figure 37.15).

Technique and safety tip. The lifter should not use momentum to lift the weight, and arching of the back should be avoided.

Parallel-bar dip
(for lower chest, shoulders, and upper arms)

Starting position. Use an overhand grip on the parallel bar, and jump up to an arms-extended position (Figure 37.16). Cross the legs and arch the back slightly.

Figure 37.13. Standing free-weight overhead press.

Figure 37.15. Free-weight arm curl.

Movement. Bend or "dip" until the chest touches the crossbar or the elbow is bent to approximately 90 degrees (Figure 37.17). Push back up to the starting position.

Technique and safety tip. Avoid arm swinging and rocking during the movement.

Side lateral raise
(for shoulder and upper back)

Starting position. Stand with the feet approximately shoulder-width apart, with a slight bend in the knees and an upright torso. Hold a dumbbell in each hand and rest them at the sides of the body against the outer part of the thigh (Figure 37.18).

Movement. With a slight bend in the elbows, maintain good posture and raise the arms out to the sides to shoulder height (Figure 37.19), then slowly lower the dumbbells back

Figure 37.16. Parallel-bar dip—starting position.

Figure 37.17. Parallel-bar dip.

Figure 37.18. Side lateral raise—starting position.

Figure 37.19. Side lateral raise.

to the starting position. The only movement for this exercise should occur at the shoulders. Do not use momentum to assist in performing the movement

Technique and safety tip. Keep head erect and back straight. This exercise can also be done with the trunk bent at the waist (Figures 37.20 and 37.21).

Exercises for the Lower Body
Free-weight parallel squat
(for thighs, hips, lower back, and buttocks)

Starting position. Stand with feet shoulder-width apart and the toes pointed slightly out. Grasp the bar with a comfortable, wide overhand grip. (The distance between the hands will vary with the individual.) Squeeze the shoulder blades together to create a shelf and position the bar on the top of the shoulder blades across the back. (Figure 37.22).

Movement. With the head up and the back slightly arched, squat until the tops of the thighs are approximately parallel to the floor (Figure 37.23). Then extend the legs and return to the starting position.

Technique and safety tip. Prior to adding weight to this exercise, the lifter should demonstrate proficiency squatting with proper technique. To avoid rounding the back, keep the head up and the eyes focused ahead. The lifter should emphasize sitting back at the hips prior to bending the knees. The knees should be aligned directly over the toes while in the squat position. The rate of descent should be slow and controlled. Never try to bounce out of the squat position. The lifter should always perform this exercise in a safety rack with appropriate safety settings in place to prevent getting trapped beneath the weight should he or she fail to achieve the lift. Also, use at least one spotter when doing this exercise.

Figure 37.20. Bent lateral raise—starting position.

Figure 37.21. Bent lateral raise.

Figure 37.22. Parallel squat—starting position.

45-degree leg sled
(for thighs and buttocks)

Starting position. Sit on padded seat and place the feet high up on the metal platform. Push up on platform and move safety catch. Grasp the handles on the sides of the chair (Figure 37.24).

Movement. Flex at the hips and knees to lower the weight. Push weight back up smoothly until legs are almost straight, leaving only a slight bend in the knees (Figure 37.25).

Technique and safety tip. Position the seat so that the knees are flexed approximately 90 degrees at the start of the exercise. Control the weight in the extended position. Return slowly to the starting position. Push smoothly, keeping most of the weight on the heel of your foot.

Leg curl (for hamstrings)

Starting position. Lie facedown on the bench with the back of the ankles touching the ankle pads. The knees should be positioned just over the edge of the bench and aligned with the pivot axis of the machine lever arm.

Movement. Bend the knees and pull the ankle pad as close to the buttocks as possible (Figure 37.26). Then return to the starting position.

Figure 37.23. Parallel squat.

Figure 37.25. Leg press on 45° leg sled—movement.

Figure 37.24. Leg press on 45° leg sled—starting position.

Figure 37.26. Leg curl.

Technique and safety tip. The hips and buttocks have a normal tendency to rise during the movement, but this can be corrected by using a flexed bench.

Heel raise (for calves)

Starting position. Position the balls of the feet over a board or stair step.

Movement. Stretch the calves by lowering the body until the heels are lower than the toes, then extend to a "tiptoe" position (Figure 37.27).

Technique tip. Additional weight can be added to this exercise by grasping dumbells while performing this movement.

Abdominal crunch or trunk curl (for abdominals)

Starting position. Lie flat on an exercise mat or stability ball with knees bent and feet flat on the floor. Place the hands behind the head or on the opposite shoulders with the arms crossed on the chest.

Movement. Roll forward, lifting the head, shoulders, and upper back off the surface. Let the lower back remain in contact with the surface at all times to stress the entire rectus abdominus muscle.

Technique and safety tip. Roll forward enough to stress the abdominals and keep the lower back in contact with the surface to protect the low-back area. There are an infinite number of variations in training using this exercise, including

Figure 37.27. Heel raise.

Figure 37.29. Abdominal crunch.

Figure 37.30. Stability ball—abdominal crunch.

Side bridge
(for external obliques, internal obliques—stabilizers of the lumbar spine)

Starting position. The side bridge is a static or isometric exercise requiring no movement. Establish the position demonstrated in Figure 37.31 and maintain it.

Technique and safety tip. Maintain the static position for 10 seconds as the exercise is introduced into the training program. Increase the length of contraction time to 30 seconds as performance improves. Perform the exercise on both sides of the body. Be sure to have the elbow positioned directly under the shoulder to prevent shoulder strain (see Figure 37.31).

Back hyperextension
(for back extensors and hamstrings)

Starting position. Lie facedown on hyperextension bench with the end of the bench positioned at the waist.

Movement. With hands across the chest touching the opposite shoulders, extend the back slowly, hold, relax, and repeat (Figures 37.32 and 37.33).

Figure 37.28. Abdominal crunch—starting position.

changes in foot position, use of external weight loads, and repetitions and sets (Figures 37.28 and 37.29). When using a stability ball, be certain to position the lower back in full contact with the ball (Figure 37.30).

Figure 37.31. Side bridge—starting position.

Figure 37.32. Back hyperextension—starting position.

Technique and safety tip. Resistance can be increased by holding a weight across the chest.

Leg extension (for quadriceps)

Starting position. Sit on the bench of a leg extension machine with ankles behind the pads. Lean back slightly and hold the bench.

Movement. Raise the legs to a position parallel with the floor, lower slowly, and repeat (Figures 37.34 and 37.35).

Technique and safety tip. Resistance can be increased or decreased by adjustment of the machine. If legs cannot reach a parallel position, reduce the weight resistance.

Figure 37.33. Back hyperextension.

Pull-up (for upper body)

Starting position. Hang from a horizontal bar using a wide overhand grip (palms away from the face) (Figure 37.36).

Movement. Starting from a straight hanging position, pull up until the chin is above the bar (Figure 37.37), then return to the down position, straightening the arms completely.

Technique and safety tip. To increase the resistance, a hanging weight can be strapped to the waist.

Shoulder shrug (for upper body)

Starting position. Start from a normal standing position while holding the barbell in front of the thighs (Figure 37.38).

Movement. Raise the shoulders as high as possible, shrugging them toward the ears, while keeping the arms straight (Figure 37.39).

Technique and safety tip. Keep the back straight and avoid the temptation to lean backward.

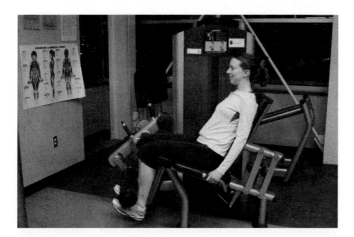

Figure 37.34. Leg extension—starting position.

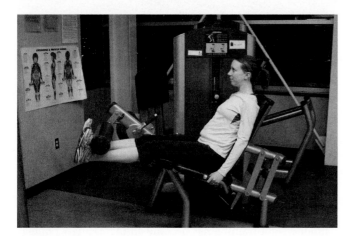

Figure 37.35. Leg extension.

Figure 37.36. Pull-up (wide overhand grip)—starting position.

Figure 37.37. Pull-up.

Squat Jump (for lower body)

Starting position. Begin by standing with the feet about hip-width apart. The chest should be up, the shoulders should be back, and the hands should be placed on the hips.

Movement. Rapidly, but under control, sit back at the hips and squat until the upper portion of the leg is parallel to the ground. Before coming to a complete stop, immediately extend the knees and hips, jumping as high as possible off of both feet. Land in the same position as the take-off and immediately repeat the jump (Figures 37.40 and 37.41).

Technique and safety tips. Do not initiate this movement with the knees first, rather sit back at the hips to start the movement. The knees should remain in alignment with the toes at all times. Do not allow the knees to move either inward or outward, putting excess stress on the knees and hips. In the bottom position of this exercise the shoulders should be directly over the toes. Leaning too far forward compromises the safety of the lower back.

Resistance push-up (for the chest, shoulders, and upper arms)

Starting position. Assume a push-up position with the arms fully extended, back neutral, and brace the trunk by isometrically contracting the abdominals (Figure 37.42).

Movement. This exercise is performed like a traditional push-up, but a partner will place his or her hands on the exerciser's shoulder blades and apply the appropriate resistance as the push-up is performed (Figure 37.43).

Figure 37.38. Shoulder shrug—starting position.

Figure 37.39. Shoulder shrug—movement.

Figure 37.40. Squat jump—starting position.

Technique and safety tips. The partner applying the resistance should make this exercise challenging, but not impossible. Apply only the appropriate amount of resistance to allow the exerciser to perform the desired number of repetitions. The exerciser should make certain that the hips do not sag or the lower back does not arch excessively during this exercise.

Circuit Weight Training

Circuit weight training has become an increasingly popular form of exercise because it is believed to be one of the best forms of total-body conditioning. Circuit weight training involves the aerobic (using oxygen) as well as the anaerobic (not using oxygen) energy systems. Normally, circuit weight training consists of 8 to 12 stations, with different weight-training exercises at each. The participant moves from one station to another with little or no rest between exercises. This provides the aerobic system with only enough time to get ready for the next exercise. Usually 8 to 12 repetitions are completed at each station. This helps improve the strength and local muscle endurance. Rest time between stations is normally 10 to 15 seconds. The exercises should progress from the large, major muscle groups to the smaller groups and alternate between the upper and the lower body.

TYPICAL CIRCUIT PROGRAM

1. Frequency: Program should be done 2–3 days per week on nonconsecutive days.
2. Intensity: Approximately 30 to 45 seconds at each station, performing 8 to 12 repetitions at each station.
3. Rest time: No greater than 1 minute.
4. Order of exercises:
   a. Abdominal crunch (Figures 37.28, 37.29, and 37.30)
   b. Back hyperextension (Figures 37.32 and 37.33)

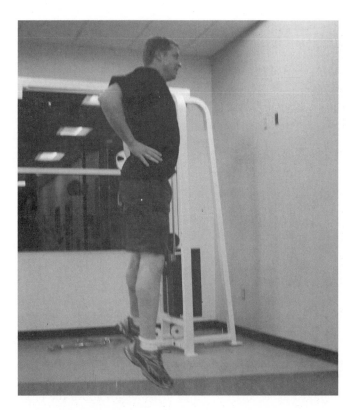

Figure 37.41. Squat jump.

Figure 37.43. Resistance push-up.

Figure 37.42. Resistance push-up—starting position.

    c. Parallel squat (Figures 37.22 and 37.23)
    d. Bench press (Figures 37.6 and 37.7)
    e. Leg press (Figures 37.24 and 37.25)
    f. Lat pull (Figures 37.9 and 37.10)
    g. Overhead press (Figures 37.12 and 37.13)
    h. Leg curl (Figure 37.26)
    i. Arm curl (Figures 37.14 and 37.15)
    j. Leg extension (Figures 37.34 and 37.35)
    k. Side lateral raise (Figures 37.18 and 37.19)

After the circuit has been completed, the individual should rest 3 to 5 minutes before starting another cycle.

SETTING UP A PERSONAL CIRCUIT

Below are a few stations, listed by upper and lower body core, or primary exercises, and secondary, or assistance exercises. When setting up a circuit, choose one or two exercises from each section. (Be sure to choose exercises that can be done with available equipment.) Next, decide time intervals to be used; and finally, determine how many repetitions will be used at each station.

Another technique is to complete as many repetitions as possible in a chosen time limit (e.g., 30 to 45 seconds). If this style is adopted, the resistance should be set so that approximately 12 to 15 repetitions can be performed in the allotted time. Approximately 15 to 30 seconds should be allowed between stations and 3 to 5 minutes between circuits.

Section 1: Lower Body Large-Muscle Group Exercises
1. Parallel (Figures 37.22 and 37.23)
2. Leg press (Figures 37.24 and 37.25)
3. Squat jump (Figures 37.40 and 37.41)

Section 2: Upper Body Large-Muscle Group Exercises
1. Bench press (Figure 37.6 and 37.7)
2. Lat pull (Figures 37.9 and 37.10)
3. Resistance push-up (Figures 37.42 and 37.43); done like a normal push-up, but with partner supplying resistance by pushing on the back
4. Overhead press (Figures 37.12 and 37.13)

Section 3: Trunk Assistance Exercises
1. Back hyperextension (Figures 37.32 and 37.33)
2. Abdominal crunch (Figures 37.28, 37.29, and 37.30)

Section 4: Upper Body Assistance Exercises
1. Side lateral raise (Figures 37.18 and 37.19)
2. Parallel-bar dip (Figures 37.16 and 37.17)
3. Arm curl (Figures 37.14 and 37.15)

Section 5: Lower Body Assistance Exercises
1. Leg extension (Figures 37.34 and 37.35)
2. Heel raise (Figure 37.27)
3. Leg curl (Figure 37.26)

KEEPING A RECORD

When beginning a weight-training or circuit-training program, write down your goals and chart your progress toward them. Fancy charts and printed graphs are not necessary. However, to keep track of current status and future plans, a journal or log is often helpful.

Most journals start with the date and personal observations, such as body weight and current condition (for example, tired, energetic, strong, weak). This is followed by a short-term training goals (e.g., "Add two more repetitions to every exercise this week"). Next entered are the exercises to be performed, and finally, the number of sets, number of repetitions, and amount of weight used for each exercise.

Competition Lifts

The following descriptions are for the lifts used in competitions. This section is meant to familiarize you with how the lifts are performed in their respective competitions and not as instructions for doing these lifts. **Because these lifts are much more advanced, they should be done with instruction and supervision from a weight-lifting coach (Olympic lifts) or powerlifting coach.**

OLYMPIC LIFTS

Snatch

Place the bar horizontally in front of the legs. Grip the bar with both hands and pull it in one motion from the floor to the end of the arms vertically above the head, either splitting or bending the legs. The bar should pass with a continuous nonstop movement along the body, of which no part other than the feet may touch or graze the floor during execution of the movement. The lifted weight must be held in the final motionless position, arms and legs stretched and feet on the same line, until the referee gives the signal to lower the weight (Figure 37.44).

Clean and Jerk

Place the bar horizontally in front of the legs. Grip the bar with both hands and pull it up in a single, distinct motion from the ground to the shoulders while splitting or bending the legs. While resting the bar on the chest or arms, bring the feet back to the original position—that is, on the same line. Bend the legs, then extend the legs and the arms suddenly, thus jerking the bar to arm's length above the head. The weight must be held in the final motionless position until the referee's signal to replace the bar on the platform (Figure 37.45).

POWER LIFTS

Squat

Place the bar horizontally across the back of the shoulders. Assume an upright position with the hands gripping the bar and the feet flat on the platform. After the referee's signal, bend the knees and lower the body until the surface of the legs at the hip joint is lower than the tops of the knees. Then recover to the standing position (Figures 37.22 and 37.23).

Bench Press

Assume a supine position on the bench, with the feet flat on the floor. The proper lift does not officially start until the bar is brought down and is absolutely motionless on the chest. When the referee's signal is given, the bar must be pressed vertically to arm's length (see Figures 37.6 and 37.7).

Dead Lift

Place the bar horizontally in front of the feet. Bend at the knees, grip the bar with both hands, and lift it upward with one continuous motion, with the arms remaining extended until standing erect with the knees locked and shoulders thrust back.

LIFTING EQUIPMENT

There are several pieces of weight-training gear that can be used to make lifting weights safer or more comfortable.

Figure 37.44. Snatch.

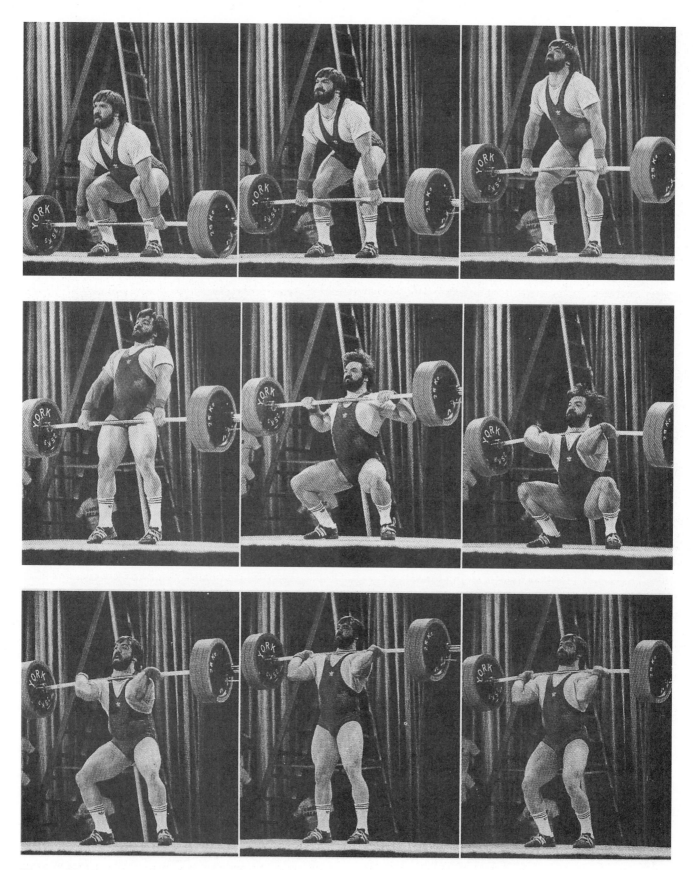

Figure 37.45. Clean and jerk.

Figure 37.45. *cont'd.* Clean and jerk.

Weight belts. Weight belts provide some support for the lower back. A belt should be used for lifts that involve the lower back (squats, dead lift) or when lifting weights over the head (shoulder press, clean and jerk). However, it is important to remember that weight belts should only be utilized when attempting to lift maximal or near maximal loads (less than 6 repetitions) Otherwise the development of the muscles surrounding the lower back may not be adequately achieved.

Lifting gloves. Lifting gloves are used to make gripping weight bars more comfortable. They help to prevent or minimize calluses on the hands.

Wrist straps. Wrist straps are used to improve the lifter's grip. They are helpful with most lifts for the back (pull-ups, pull-downs, rows) where you pull the weight toward your body. However, while utilizing wrist straps may aid in the lifting of heavier weight, one must remember that grip strength will not be developed to the same extent when using this equipment. As a result, lifters often become reliant on straps to lift increasingly heavier loads. Therefore, the use of straps on a regular basis is not recommended.

Wraps. Wraps (knee, elbow) provide support and stabilization for joints.

TEACHING CONSIDERATIONS

1. The decision to include weight training in a program should be based in part on the availability of equipment in relation to the number of students involved. A vigorous workout two or three times a week for a minimum of 6 weeks can provide gains for each student in both strength and muscular endurance.

2. For a school program, consider circuit weight training because of the total-body effect. For units with specialized training goals, teach students the principles and possible effects of both weight training and circuit weight training.

3. Individual pretesting to assist with goal setting programs should be conducted before a full program is begun. Students can design their own programs if they are taught the principles of program design and if the teacher checks the programs before the students begin. Goal setting should be part of each program, with periodic checks of progress in relation to goals.

4. Partner work is a necessity for many exercises and is necessary for spotting.

5. Proper form and safety need to be taught and emphasized. Partners can be used to check form, and weight room mirrors are also beneficial for this purpose.

6. If students are kept off the equipment when they are not using it for exercising, accidents are less likely to occur.

GLOSSARY

anabolic steroids Muscle, strength, and power-enhancing drugs with dangerous health side effects.

assistance exercise An exercise that requires only a single joint action (e.g., biceps curl or leg extension), used to develop a single muscle or muscle group.

barbell A specialized steel bar 4 to 7 feet (1.2 to 2.1 m) long with one or more disks of various weights.

cheat Do an exercise improperly.

circuit weight training A type of weight training done in a continuous manner until an entire cycle of exercises is completed.

clean Raise the barbell in one explosive motion to the standing bent-arm press position.

core exercise An exercise that requires multijoint action and works at least one or several major muscle groups.

dumbbell A short-handled barbell used in one hand.

hypertrophy The increase in muscle fiber size.

isokinetic exercise A type of resistance exercise in which the amount of resistance offered is regulated by a mechanical device to be proportional to the effort applied.

isometric exercise A type of exercise involving the static contraction of a muscle or muscle group. Resistance is greater than force applied.

isotonic exercise Exercise involving muscle contraction that produces movement through a partial or complete range of motion. Resistance remains constant.

motor units Nerve fiber and muscle fiber or fibers the nerve fiber stimulates.

neural activation Central nervous system recruitment of motor units.

Olympic lifts Snatch, and clean and jerk.

periodization The planned progression of training changes in a weight-training program.

power lifts Squat, bench press, and dead lift.

press Push a barbell or dumbbell to arm's length.

progressive resistance exercise The process of gradually increasing training intensity or time to maintain overload conditions.

repetitions (reps) Number of times an exercise is repeated without stopping.

resistance Amount of weight or pressure the muscles work against.

set A specific number of repetitions.

spotter Person responsible for assisting the lifter if needed for safety.

weight lifting A competitive sport; Olympic weight lifting or power lifting.

weight training A form of exercise in which muscle groups are worked against resistance. Apparatus is usually a barbell, dumbbell, or weight machine.

SUGGESTED READINGS

Allsen, P. 2009. *Strength training: Beginners, body builders, and athletes.* 5th ed. Dubuque, IA: Kendall/Hunt.

Baechle, T., and Earle, R. 2005. *Fitness weight training.* 2nd ed. Champaign, IL: Human Kinetics.

Baechle, T., and, Earle, R. 2006. *Weight training: Steps to success.* 3rd ed. Champaign, IL: Human Kinetics. Presents a self-paced program and the knowledge to design a customized weight-training program.

Beckwith, K. 2008. *Weight training.* Dubuque, IA: Kendall/Hunt.

Bompa, T., Di Pasquale, M., and Cornacchia, L. 2003. *Serious strength training.* 2nd ed. Champaign, IL: Human Kinetics.

Fahey, T. 2010. *Basic weight training for men and women.* 7th ed. New York, NY: McGraw-Hill. Along with instructions for designing a training program, includes topics such as ACSM guidelines, aging, and current trends.

Faigenbaum, A., and Westcott, W. 2009. *Youth strength training.* Champaign, IL: Human Kinetics.

Hesson, J. L. 2009. *Weight training for life.* 9th ed. Belmont, CA: Wadsworth. Presents a lifetime approach to weight training. Topics include goal setting, stretching, guidelines for all ages, exercises for women, setting up a personal program, and advanced techniques.

Newberry, D., Kaufman, K., and Baker, J. 2000. *Strength training.* Scottsdale, AZ: Holcomb Hathaway Publishers. Key elements are skills, drills, and strategies.

Sandler, D. 2003. *Weight training fundamentals.* Champaign, IL: Human Kinetics.

Shepard, G. 2009. *Bigger, stronger, faster.* 2nd ed. Champaign, IL: Human Kinetics.

Stone, M., Stone, M., and Sands, W. 2007. *Principles and practices of resistance training.* Champaign, IL: Human Kinetics.

Stoppani, J. 2006. *Encyclopedia of muscle and strength.* Champaign, IL: Human Kinetics.

U.S. Weightlifting Federation. Current ed. *Official rules.* Colorado Springs: U.S. Weightlifting Federation.

Wescott, W. 2003. *Building strength and stamina.* 2nd ed. Champaign, IL: Human Kinetics.

Westcott, W., and Baechle, T. 2007. *Strength training past 50.* Champaign, IL: Human Kinetics.

Wuebben, J., and Stoppani, J. 2009. *Stronger arms and upper body.* Champaign, IL: Human Kinetics.

Periodical

National Strength and Conditioning Association Journal (bimonthly), National Strength and Conditioning Association, 300 Old City Hall Landmark, 920 O St., Lincoln, NE 68508.

RESOURCES

Videos

See Appendix C for video sources.

WEB SITES

National Strength and Conditioning Association
www.nsca-lift.org/

The American College of Sports Medicine
www.acsm.org/

38 | Wrestling

After completing this chapter, the reader should be able to:

- Display a knowledge of the various forms of wrestling and the equipment and facilities used
- Explain the rules of the sport and the differences that exist between high school and college wrestling
- Demonstrate fundamental skills, including starting positions, takedowns, escapes, reversals, and pointing holds
- Teach a beginning group of students the fundamental skills of wrestling
- Explain safety and scientific principles of wrestling

HISTORY

Wrestling is the most natural and, therefore, one of the oldest forms of combat in which two individuals can engage. Even today children left to their own devices and without instruction do not hesitate to take hold of each other and wrestle about, so it is not surprising that wrestling is one of the oldest known sports.

At the dawn of civilization wrestling was an art of war. Even before written history, we are reasonably sure, people of the Stone Age developed a form of wrestling that bordered on the scientific. They had to provide for themselves by means of strength and cunning, so physical combat was essential, not only between individuals but also with animals.

Carvings and drawings found on cave walls in France, estimated to be between 15,000 and 20,000 years old, illustrate combatants in holds and leverage positions similar to many present-day wrestling positions.

An ancient vase from about 2800 BC featuring two wrestlers in action was discovered by archeologists in Mesopotamia, near present-day Baghdad, Iraq. And from other ancient paintings, reliefs, vases, mosaics, and writings we know that wrestling was important in Egyptian culture. For example, more than 200 pictographs of wrestlers from approximately 2500 to 3000 BC were discovered on the walls of the temple-tombs of Beni Hasan, a village on the Nile in central Egypt, indicating that wrestling had already reached a high stage of development in Egypt 5,000 years ago. It was competitive, with definite objectives, and it was controlled by strict rules that determined the winner, with successful performance requiring know-how, strength, and endurance.

Wrestling as combat was an ancient method for settling disputes. Many references are made to wrestling in the Bible—for example, "And Jacob was left alone; and a man wrestled with him until daybreak" (Genesis 32:24). Wrestling progressed through the ages until it developed into a sport in the modern sense of the word.

Heroes of antiquity—such as Gilgamesh, Jacob, Ulysses, and Milo—all earned a certain degree of fame as wrestlers, but it was the Greeks who raised wrestling to its zenith as a sport. It flourished not only as exercise in athletic training, but as an integral part of national life, rooted in the need to prepare citizens for war and in Greek ideals of beauty and harmony. Wrestling was the heart of Greek sport and formed the chief event of the pentathlon. The Greeks believed that wrestling displayed strength, agility, and grace better than any other activity, and their language is full of expressions borrowed from the terminology of the wrestling match.

Although Greek tradition ascribed wrestling's invention and original rules to Homer's legendary hero Theseus, it is generally accepted now that wrestling in its systematic and scientific form was probably introduced into Greece from Egypt or Asia. Historians are quick to point out that Homer's description of holds corresponds closely with the Beni Hasan figures in Egypt.

Historians attest that the Greeks competed in two styles of wrestling: Orthopali, "proper wrestling," and Pankration, "anything goes wrestling." In the former, the objective was to throw the opponent to the ground from a standing position. The victory went to the competitor who successfully executed two out of three falls. In Pankration, victory was gained by forcing the opponent to give up. Anything except biting was allowed. Therefore, punches and kicks were common in this form of wrestling.

It was not until the last quarter of the second century BC that wrestling was introduced into Rome, but it never attained the same degree of popularity as in Greece. Wrestling was also popular in the Orient, particularly Japan. The first recorded wrestling match in Japan took place in 23 BC. In China, many famous wrestlers were produced during the period of the Five Dynasties (CE 907–960).

During the later Middle Ages, wrestling bouts were frequently held between English towns, and almost every village festival included this sport as part of its entertainment.

One of the more notable contests reported in the sporting annals was held in 1520 between Henry VIII of England and Francis I of France, the so-called Cloth of Gold meeting. At the time of this match, the English and French kings were the foremost monarchs in Europe. Unfortunately, although records document the contest, they do not clearly describe the outcome.

Long before Christopher Columbus set foot in the New World, the Indians of North and South America were holding wrestling matches as sport. Later, wrestling matches were popular entertainment at social gatherings of the early European settlers. George Washington was well known as the colonial champion in the collar-and-elbow style of wrestling, long before he led colonists against the British in the Revolutionary War. Abraham Lincoln, best known of all presidents for his wrestling skills, was famous for his success in free-for-all and catch-as-catch-can competitions. Even though America's wrestling heritage dates back to the days of the Revolutionary War and wrestling was popular among Union soldiers during the Civil War, the first organized American national tournament was not held until 1887.

Although wrestling is one of the oldest sports, it did not come into prominence as an amateur sport in the United States until the last 50 or so years. The first organized intercollegiate wrestling meet was held between the University of Pennsylvania and Yale in 1900. Perhaps the greatest single influence on the development of amateur wrestling in this country was the formation of the Wrestling Rules Committee by the National Collegiate Athletic Association (NCAA) in 1927. Before 1900 it was necessary for coaches to agree on the rules, weights, length of matches, etc., before engaging in any meet or tournament. Dr. R. G. Clapp, head of the Physical Education Department, University of Nebraska, served as the chairman of this committee for many years. Dr. Clapp's background, insight, and dedication provided the guidance for this committee in establishing the rules that greatly aided the development of amateur wrestling in American universities and colleges. With an official set of rules in place, college wrestling held its first national (NCAA) tournament in 1928. The new rules, a variation of international freestyle wrestling, led to the American style of wrestling, referred to as catch-as-catch-can, or folkstyle, wrestling.

Today, the value of wrestling is universally recognized. Wrestlers are among the best-conditioned and best-disciplined athletes. By its very nature, amateur wrestling invites a wider range of individuals to participate, from 100-pound dynamos to behemoths up to 285 pounds. Both boys and girls participate in wrestling at the secondary school level and receive instruction together in physical education settings. Vision- and hearing-impaired people and those with other physical disabilities find wrestling an excellent sport in which to participate.

Wrestling is basic stuff: speed, strength, intelligence, and courage. There are several distinct styles of wrestling, including catch-as-catch-can, freestyle, Greco-Roman, judo, and sumo. Both freestyle and Greco-Roman are international styles of wrestling and are contested in the Olympic Games. The American interscholastic and intercollegiate styles are really modifications of international freestyle wrestling and are commonly referred to as folkstyle or catch-as-catch-can wrestling. In international freestyle and Greco-Roman, the emphasis is on executing throws or takedowns that lead to immediate pins. In freestyle no points are awarded for time advantage or escapes. The action is much faster than in folkstyle and requires three officials. The Greco-Roman style has the same basic rules and scoring as freestyle, but unlike freestyle and folkstyle wrestling it does not allow for the use of the legs in holds or application of any holds below the waist. The overall goal of these two forms of wrestling is to use holds and techniques to put the opponent on the ground, pinning both shoulders to the mat long enough for the referee to signal a fall. A fall is an automatic victory. However, if a fall (pin) is not obtained, a wrestler can win by scoring more points than the opponent. On the other hand, the American style places a greater emphasis on the ability to gain control over the opponent after he or she has been brought to the mat. From this position on the mat, the contestant in control attempts to work the opponent into position for a fall.

From the first modern Olympic Games until 1924, wrestling rules varied greatly, usually favoring the country hosting the event. In Paris in 1924 some order was achieved, and both freestyle and Greco-Roman events were contested. Over the years many countries have produced great Olympic individual wrestlers and wrestling teams. Turkey, Sweden, the United States, West Germany, and the Soviet Union all were successful until around 1960. Since 1972, Russia and the 15 former Soviet states of Eastern Europe and Central Asia have dominated the sport. With a total of 48 medals (16 medals within each of the three categories of men's freestyle, women's freestyle, and Greco-Roman), wrestling is a sport worth concentrating on to gain international attention.

In the 1972 Olympics held in Munich, 15 of the gold medals were won by Eastern Bloc wrestlers (nine by the USSR). The United States won three golds, including one by Dan Gable, who did not give up a point in six matches. Between 1972 and 1980 the Soviet wrestlers continued to dominate the sport. In 1984 in Los Angeles the U.S. wrestlers put together a competitive team and did well (seven golds and two silvers in freestyle and the first-ever golds [two] in Greco-Roman events), but the performance was somewhat tainted by the Soviet boycott. In 1988 the United States captured only two gold medals and five medals overall. The USSR captured nine medals, four of them gold.

In 1992 in the freestyle events, the U.S. Olympic team picked up six medals, including three gold, two silver, and one bronze. John Smith (136 lb), Kevin Jackson (180 lb), and Bruce Baumgartner (286 lb) were all Olympic champions.

In the Greco-Roman events the United States captured only one silver (Dennis Koslowski at 220 lb) and one bronze (Rodney Smith at 150 lb).

In the freestyle events in the 1996 Olympics, the U.S. team captured five medals—three gold, a silver, and a bronze. Kendall Cross (125.5 lb), Tom Brands (136.5 lb), and Kurt Angle (220 lb) were Olympic champions. Townsend Sanders (149.5 lb) brought home a silver, and Bruce Baumgartner (286 lb), a bronze. In the Greco-Roman events Brandon Paulson (114.5 lb), Dennis Hall (125.5 lb), and Matt Ghaffari (286 lb) all won silver medals.

In the 2000 Olympic Games Rulon Gardner stunned the world by winning the gold medal in the 97–130 kilogram Greco-Roman event. He beat Alexandre Kareline, 1 to 0 in overtime. Kareline had virtually ruled this event for many years. Terry Brands and Lincoln McIlravy also brought two bronze medals home to the U.S. by winning third place in the 54–58 kilogram and 63–69 kilogram classes of the free-style wrestling competition.

At the 2004 Olympics in Athens, Greece, Rulon Gardner again medaled in the 120-kilogram Greco-Roman weight class, capturing the bronze in his final amateur wrestling event. Overall, the United States tied Japan for second place in total wrestling medals with six. Russia was first with ten. For the United States men's team, Cael Sanderson won a gold at 84 kilograms, Stephen Abas won a silver at 55 kilograms, and Jamill Kelly took a silver at 66 kilograms. For the women's team, Sara McMann won a silver at 63 kilograms and Patricia Miranda won a bronze at 48 kilograms.

The United States sent a 16-member wrestling team to the 2008 Beijing Summer Olympics. Henry Cejudo won a gold medal in the men's freestyle under 55 kilograms (121 lb) weight class. Adam Wheeler took home a bronze medal in the men's Greco-Roman 84–96 kilogram (185–211.5 lb) class, while Randi Miller won bronze in the women's free-style 55–63 kilogram (121–138.5 lb) weight class.

Title IX of the 1972 Education Amendments Act is a federal law that requires high schools and colleges that receive federal funds to not discriminate on the basis of gender in the provision of any educational activity—including athletics. Since the passage of Title IX, young women have competed on male teams against males but until recently women have not competed against other women in the sport of wrestling. Women's freestyle wrestling features the exact same rules as men's freestyle, except that matches are 4 minutes instead of 5.

Women's wrestling is growing very rapidly at all levels. Today both genders participate in wrestling at the junior high, senior high, and college levels and receive instruction together in the physical education setting. In 1997, the state of Michigan sponsored the first-ever women's state high school championships. A total of 120 female wrestlers competed in 10 weight classes. In 1993, the University of Minnesota–Morris was the first college in the nation to sponsor women's wrestling as an official varsity sport. Since that time, women's programs have been developed at a number of other colleges as an official varsity sport and countless women have also joined their collegiate men's programs.

USA Wrestling, the national governing body, has sponsored the women's freestyle national team and has been participating in the Women's Freestyle World Championships since 1989. As the national governing body, USA Wrestling is responsible for the development of amateur wrestling in the United States and has been a major contributor in the growth of women's wrestling. USA Wrestling is providing new opportunities for young women to participate and grow as athletes in the sport.

THE MAT

For high school competition the wrestling mat shall be a circular area a minimum of 28 feet (8.53 m) in diameter. Surrounding and secured to the wrestling area of the mat shall be a safety mat approximately 5 feet (1.52 m) wide. The wrestling mat shall be of uniform thickness not more than 4 inches (10.2 cm) nor less than the thickness of a mat that has the shock-absorbing qualities of at least 1-inch (2.54-cm) PVC-covered foam (Figure 38.1A). At the college level the wrestling area of the mat is no less than 32 feet (9.75 m) square or, if circular, 32 feet in diameter, and not more than 42 feet (12.8 m) square or a circular area 42 feet in diameter. There should be at least a 5-foot (1.52-m) width of mat around this area. The mat should have the shock quality of a 2-inch (5-cm) thick hair felt mat. In the center of the mat there should be painted a circle 10 feet (3.05 m) in diameter (Figure 38.1B).

Two 1-inch (2.54-cm) starting lines are placed in the center of the mat. One of the lines lies on the diameter of the 10-foot circle, and the other starting line is parallel to the first line and 10 inches (25.4 cm) from it. One-inch (2.54-cm) lines close the ends of the starting lines, forming a box in the center of the mat. One starting line should be green (toward the home team) and one red (toward the visiting team) (Figure 38.1C).

EQUIPMENT

The uniform (Figure 38.2) consists of a one-piece singlet that may be worn with or without full-length tights. A properly cut one- or two-piece uniform is optional. A minimum 4-inch (10-cm) inseam is required. Lightweight over-the-ankle wrestling shoes, without heels and laced through eyelets, must be worn, and a protective earguard is required. In addition, contestants must be clearly identified by some means (such as red or green anklets).

ABRIDGED RULES

The rules for wrestling are subject to change each year by various rules committees and are the most variable of any sport. It is not uncommon for both the point values and the

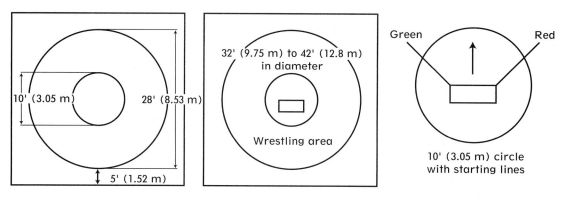

Figure 38.1. Recommended mat sizes. A, High school. B, College. C, Starting lines.

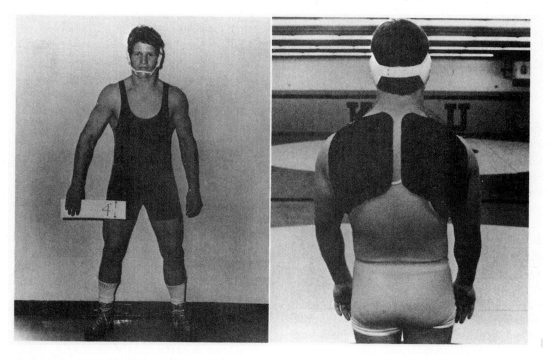

Figure 38.2. Front and rear views of official uniform. Front view shows 4-inch inseam. Rear view shows pinning areas.

required weight classes to change frequently. The abridged rules presented here should be compared to a current rule book for the most recent changes. It is recommended that reference be made to the *NCAA Intercollegiate and Interscholastic Wrestling Guide* and *The National Federation of State High School Associations Wrestling Rules Book.*

Weight Classification

Intercollegiate

The classes for intercollegiate wrestling are as follows:

125 pounds (56.7 kg) and under
133 pounds (60.3 kg) and under
141 pounds (63.9 kg) and under
149 pounds (67.6 kg) and under
157 pounds (71.1 kg) and under
165 pounds (74.8 kg) and under
174 pounds (78.9 kg) and under
184 pounds (83.4 kg) and under
197 pounds (89.3 kg) and under
Heavyweight (183–285 pounds) (82.9–129.2 kg)

In all dual college meets there is no weight allowance at weigh-in.

High school modification

103 pounds (46.7 kg) and under
112 pounds (50.8 kg) and under
119 pounds (54.0 kg) and under
125 pounds (56.7 kg) and under
130 pounds (59.0 kg) and under

135 pounds (61.2 kg) and under
140 pounds (63.5 kg) and under
145 pounds (65.8 kg) and under
152 pounds (68.9 kg) and under
160 pounds (72.6 kg) and under
171 pounds (77.5 kg) and under
189 pounds (85.7 kg) and under
215 pounds (97.5 kg) and under
285 pounds (129.5 kg)

High school competition is governed by the National Federation of State High School Athletic Associations.

One of the many problems facing wrestlers, their coaches, and their parents is the practice of dieting and dehydrating in order to wrestle at a lower weight class. In no other sport are we so consistently determined to have our athletes weigh in at a weight considerably below their usual weight. The extent to which wrestlers diet and dehydrate in order to compete at a lower weight class becomes a serious medical problem for many. The overwhelming medical evidence indicates that this practice is both physically dangerous to the contestant and completely illogical from the standpoint of improved performance.

In 2005, the National Federation of State High Schools Association Wrestling Rules Committee passed a number of rule changes and revisions regarding weight control and weight reduction in high school wrestlers. The NFHS board of directors subsequently approved these rules. The most significant revision outlines a weight-management program that utilizes fat assessment and discourages dehydration. The revised rule mandates that specific gravity may not exceed 1.025, a body fat assessment no lower than 7 percent (males)/12 percent (females), and a monitored weekly weight-loss plan not to exceed 1.5 percent a week.

From a health standpoint, crash diets designed to produce rapid or extreme weight loss are to be condemned. Disturbing the fluid balance of the body by dehydrating also has serious health hazards. These dangers are intensified in the immature organism of the growing, adolescent athlete.

Because rapid weight reduction ("cutting weight") through caloric restriction, dehydration, and excessive exercise in heated environments exposes wrestlers to decreased performance, heat-related trauma, and hazard to health and life, USA Wrestling has adopted the following rules:

1. With regard to the practice of dehydration, the use of hot rooms, hot showers, hot boxes, saunas, steam rooms, heating devices, diuretics, laxatives, excessive food and fluid restriction, and self-induced vomiting is prohibited.
2. Regardless of purpose, the use of vapor-impermeable suits (e.g., rubber or rubberized nylon) is prohibited.
3. Violation of these rules shall cause the individual(s) in question to be suspended from the competition for which use of the prohibited methods were intended.

Major Differences between Scholastic and Collegiate Rules
Injury time
HIGH SCHOOL: One-and-one-half cumulative minutes to recover.
COLLEGE: Two minutes to recover.

Riding time
HIGH SCHOOL: No riding time.
COLLEGE: One point for 1 minute or more net time advantage more than opponent.

Fall
HIGH SCHOOL: Two seconds.
COLLEGE: One second.

Number of matches
HIGH SCHOOL: No wrestler shall compete in more than five full-length matches in any day.
COLLEGE: No similar rule.

Weight allowance
HIGH SCHOOL: Two-pound growth allowance may be added to each weight class any time after the date of certification. Additional weight allowance for consecutive days of competition is limited to a maximum of 2 pounds, regardless of the number of consecutive days teams may be competing.
COLLEGE: No allowance for growth.

Weigh-in
HIGH SCHOOL: Maximum of 1 hour and minimum of 30 minutes before dual meet is scheduled to begin.
COLLEGE: Maximum of 1 hour or less before the first match begins.

Duration of bout
HIGH SCHOOL: Three 2-minute periods. (See current rule book for sudden victory and tournaments.)
COLLEGE: Three periods: first period, 3 minutes; second and third periods, 2 minutes (tournaments—overtime, three 1-minute periods, consolation—three 2-minute periods).

Weight class restriction
HIGH SCHOOL: May wrestle one weight class above actual weight at time of weigh-in.
COLLEGE: May wrestle any weight class above actual weight; unlimited contestant must weigh a minimum of 183 pounds (83 kg). Wrestlers weighing in two weight classes above the original certified weight class are not allowed to return to the original wrestled weight class.

Conduct of Match

The first period starts with the wrestlers opposite each other on their feet, one standing on the green area and the other on the red. The wrestlers will first come forward and shake hands and then go back to their 3-foot starting lines. When the referee blows the whistle, they begin wrestling. A fall during this or one of the other periods terminates the match. If no fall occurs in the first period, a disk is tossed. The winner of the disk toss may choose top, bottom, or neutral position, or defer choice until the third period. If the wrestler with the choice defers, the opponent may select top, bottom, or neutral. If the wrestler with the choice does not defer, the opponent will have the choice of top, bottom, or neutral to begin the third period. The referee starts all wrestling with the whistle. If during the match no falls occur, the winner is decided by the point system. Wrestlers must return to and remain in their respective areas until the winner is declared or a penalty (Table 38.1) will be imposed. If the contestants are tied at the end of the three regular periods, they will wrestle a 1-minute sudden-victory period with no rest between the regular match and the sudden-victory period. The sudden-victory period will begin with wrestlers in the neutral position. The wrestler who scores the first point(s) will be declared the winner. If no winner has been declared at the end of the sudden-victory period, two 30-second tiebreaker periods will be wrestled. The two tiebreaker periods will be wrestled in their entirety. The choice for position in the first tiebreaker period will be determined at the conclusion of the regulation match and granted to the wrestler who scores the first points other than penalty points and escapes in the regulation match. In intercollegiate wrestling, time advantage of 1 minute or more for either wrestler shall be included in this determination.

When the only points scored are either escapes and/or penalty points, the choice of position will be granted to the winner of a toss of a colored disk. The referee will toss the disk at the conclusion of the sudden-victory period and allow it to fall to the mat unimpeded. The wrestler winning the toss may select only the top or bottom position. A wrestler choosing the defensive (bottom) position in the first 30-second tiebreaker period is required to assume the offensive (top) position in the second 30-second tiebreaker period.

If no scoring occurs in the 30-second ultimate tie-breaker, the offensive wrestler will be declared the winner.

In college a maximum of one point can be earned for 1 minute or more of *net* riding time advantage over an opponent.

In college and high school wrestling, if the wrestlers go off the mat, they are brought back to the center of the mat with the wrestler that had advantage on top. If neither had control, they start again on their feet.

For the most recent wrestling rule changes, refer to the current rule book.

Scoring for High School and College
Definitions

fall   A fall terminates the match and occurs when any part of both shoulders or part of both scapulas of either wrestler are held in contact with the mat for 1 second (college) or 2 seconds (high school). The opponent securing the fall is declared the winner of the match.

technical fall   A technical fall terminates the match and occurs when a wrestler has earned a 15-point advantage over the opponent.

major decision   A major decision occurs when the margin of victory after three periods is 8 through 14 points.

decision   A decision occurs when the margin of victory is fewer than 8 points.

default   A default is awarded in a match when one of the wrestlers is unable to continue for any reason.

disqualification   A disqualification is a situation in which a contestant is banned from participation in accordance with the Penalty Table.

forfeit   A wrestler receives a forfeit when the opponent, for any reason, fails to appear for the match.

medical forfeit   A medical forfeit may be declared when a contestant is injured or becomes ill during the course of the match or tournament.

Point-scoring system for matches in which no fall occurs
1. For takedown, or bringing the opponent to the mat from standing: 2 points.
2. For escaping from a defensive position on the mat: 1 point.
3. For reversal of position from a defensive position on the mat: 2 points.
4. For a near fall or a situation in which the offensive wrestler has control of the opponent and a fall is imminent: 2 points when near-fall criterion is held for 2 seconds, 3 points when held for 5 seconds. If the defensive wrestler is injured or bleeding occurs after a 3-point near fall has been earned, a 4-point near fall should be awarded.
5. For 1 minute or more of accumulated time advantage over an opponent, a wrestler will be awarded 1 point. One point is the maximum awarded for the match for time advantage.

Dual-meet scoring (team points)
In dual meet competition, team scoring is based upon the results of each individual match as follows:
1. Fall (any part of both shoulders held in contact with the mat for 2 seconds in high school and 1 second in college competition): 6 points
2. Decision
   a. Five points if winning wrestler has 15 match points more than losing wrestler (technical fall)
   b. Four points if winning wrestler has between 8 and 14 match points more than the losing wrestler (major decision)
   c. Three points if winning wrestler has 8 or fewer match points than losing wrestler (major decision)
3. Forfeit: 6 points
4. Default: 6 points
5. Disqualification: 6 points

Table 38.1. INFRACTION PENALTY TABLE*

PENALTY CHART (Available in PDF format on Web site - nfhs.org)

	Rule	Warning	First Penalty	Second Penalty	Third Penalty	Fourth Penalty
Illegal Holds/Maneuvers	7-1	No				
Technical Violations	7-3	No				
Stalling	7-6	Yes				
Unnecessary Roughness	7-4-1	No	1 Pt.	1 Pt.	2 Pts.	Disqualify
Unsportsmanlike Conduct by Contestants During a Match	7-4-2	No				
Not Reporting to Scorer's Table Properly Equipped	8-1-1	No				
False Start or Incorrect Starting Position	8-1-3		Following two cautions there is a 1-point penalty for each subsequent infraction.			
Coach Misconduct (during the match)	5-5 6-6-6 7-5-4 8-1-5	Yes	Deduct 1 Team Point	Removal of head coach from premises immediately on second penalty and deduct 2 team points. Removal is for the remainder of the day.		
Unsportsmanlike Conduct - Contestants (not during the match), Coaches and Other Team Personnel	7-4-2 7-5-3 8-1-4	No	Deduct 1 Team Point	Remove from premises immediately on second penalty and deduct 2 team points. Removal is for the remainder of the event, day/dual meet or tournament.		
Flagrant Misconduct - Contestants	7-4-3 8-1-6	No	Disqualify on first offense, deduct 3 team points and remove from premises immediately for the duration of the event. Contestant is eliminated from further competition for the remainder of a dual meet, multiple school event or tournament and no team points can be earned in an individual tournament.			

	Rule	Warning	First Penalty
Flagrant Misconduct - Coaches and Other Team Personnel	7-5-5 8-1-3 8-1-6	No	Remove from premises immediately on first offense and deduct 3 team points. Removal is for the dual meet, remainder of a multiple school event or tournament.
Greasy Substance on Body or Uniform, Improper Grooming, Objectionable Pads and Braces; Illegal Equipment or Uniform	7-3-7 8-1-1		Any contestant reporting to the scorer's table in violation of this article shall be disqualified if not removed or corrected within the 1½-minute injury time.

Summary of Technical Violations

Going out of Wrestling Area (Fleeing) (7-3-1)
Grasping Clothing, Etc. (7-3-2)
Interlocking Hands (7-3-3)
Leaving Wrestling Area Without Permission (7-3-4)
Figure 4 Head From Neutral (7-3-5)
Reporting to the Scorer's Table Not Properly Equipped or Not Ready to Wrestle (7-3-6)

Note 1 — Disqualification due to technical violation, illegal hold, stalling, unsportsmanlike conduct during a match or unnecessary roughness does not eliminate a contestant from further competition in tournaments. Disqualification for unsportsmanlike conduct not during the match eliminates a contestant or coach for the remainder of the event. Disqualification for flagrant misconduct will disqualify any individual for the remainder of a multiple school event or tournament. They are removed for the duration of the event.

Note 2 — Points for unnecessary roughness, grasping clothing, locking hands or fleeing the mat are awarded in addition to points earned.

Penalty Chart | 2009-10 NFHS Wrestling Rules | Page 42

Page 43 | 2009-10 NFHS Wrestling Rules | Penalty Chart

Because of the many levels of American folkstyle wrestling and the numerous organizations involved with the sport, there has been a tendency for repeated annual changes in rules, match scoring, tournament scoring, and weight classifications. Therefore, it is important for anyone using this text to secure the current National Collegiate Athletic Association (NCAA), National Federation of State High School Athletic Associations (NFSH), and the USA Wrestling rule and interpretation guides.

Illegal Holds

The following holds are illegal: hammerlock above the right angle, the twisting hammerlock, front headlock, headlock without the arm, the straight head scissors, over scissors, full nelson, strangle holds, all body slams, toe holds, twisting knee lock, key lock, overhead double-arm bar; bending; twisting, or forcing of the head or any limb beyond its nor-

mal limit of movement; locking the hands behind the back in a double-arm bar from a neutral position; full back suplay from a rear standing position; and any hold used for punishment alone. Illegal holds are signaled by the referee. See Figure 38.3 for this and other signals.

FUNDAMENTAL SKILLS AND TECHNIQUES

Descriptions are given from one side only. However, the techniques may be applied from the other side by changing the approach from right to left and left to right.

Wrestling Positions

The neutral position

The first period starts with the wrestlers in the neutral position (Figure 38.4). One foot of one of the wrestlers must be on the green starting line and the opponent's foot on the red starting line (Figure 38.1). The other foot of each wrestler

Revised 2009

Figure 38.3. High school and college referees' wrestling signals.

Figure 38.4. The neutral position.

must be extended on the starting lines, or behind the foot on the starting line. The wrestlers will shake hands and when the referee sounds the whistle, they will begin to wrestle. In matches involving sight-disabled wrestlers, a finger-touch method shall be used in the neutral position and contact shall be maintained throughout the match.

Starting position on the mat (referee's position)

Defensive wrestler. The defensive wrestler's starting position requires the wrestler to be at the center of the circle stationary on hands and knees so both knees are on the mat behind the rear starting line. The heels of both hands shall be on the mat in front of the forward starting line. (See Fig. 38.5.) The elbows shall not touch the mat. This position must also allow the offensive wrestler to be able to assume a legal starting position on either side.

Offensive wrestler. The offensive starting position requires the wrestler to be positioned on either side of an opponent with at least one knee on the mat on the near side of the opponent. The near side is the one on which the offensive

Figure 38.5. Basic starting position on the knees.

wrestler places the palm of the hand on or over the back of the opponent's elbow. The offensive wrestler's head shall be on or above the spinal column of the opponent's back. The other arm (right or left) is placed loosely around the defensive wrestler's body perpendicular to the long axis of the body. The palm of the hand is placed loosely over the defensive wrestler's navel. A knee or foot may be placed behind the defensive wrestler's feet, but may not be in contact with the defensive wrestler. (See Fig. 38.5.)

Optional offensive starting position. The offensive wrestler may be positioned on either side or to the rear of the opponent, with all weight supported on both feet, one knee, or both knees. The offensive wrestler must place the hands on the opponent's back with thumbs touching. Only the hands can touch the defensive wrestler's back. If the offensive wrestler selects the optional starting position, the wrestler must indicate this to the referee. The defensive wrestler must be positioned as described above (Figure 38.6).

Wrestling Objectives
Offensive
1. Takedown: to take the opponent to the mat.
2. Controlling: to keep the opponent under control on the mat.
3. Breaking: to force an opponent off-balance when down on the mat.
4. Pinning: to bring the opponent's shoulder blades in contact with the mat for 2 seconds.

Defensive
1. Reverse position: to change from a defensive position on the mat to an offensive position.

2. Escaping: to free oneself from the grasp of an opponent while in a defensive position on the mat.

Takedown skills
In preparation for a takedown, the wrestlers move around, tie up, and use various setups to gain an advantage. The eyes should be focused ahead but past the opponent so that one can be aware of anything that moves in the range of vision. An example of a tie-up is to hook the back of the opponent's head with your right hand and at the same time put your left hand on the opponent's bicep. Pull with the right hand and push with the left hand. A setup is any movement or act that distracts the opponent to make him or her vulnerable to a takedown move.

The penetration step, with slight variations, is the basic initial step used to penetrate while executing takedowns. Bend the knees to lower the hips, drive off the inner edge of the back foot, and step as far forward as possible while keeping good balance. Keep the head up and the arms in, close to the body. Concentrate on getting your hips close to the opponent (Figure 38.7).

Duck under. From the standing position, grasp the opponent's right elbow with the left hand, drop to the right knee, and force the arm up. Grasp one or both of the opponent's legs and force the opponent off-balance (Figure 38.8).

Counter. Defensive wrestler resists by moving the feet back, dropping to the knees, and forcing the opponent's head to the mat.

Arm drag and go-behind. Start from the standing position. The objective is to get behind the opponent while standing. Grasp the opponent's right wrist with the left hand, and then with the right hand grasp opponent's right arm above

Figure 38.6. Optional offensive starting position.

Figure 38.7. Penetration step.

the elbow and pull with both hands to the right until the opponent is partly turned. Then slip the left arm around the opponent's waist and with the left foot step behind the opponent. Lock the hands around the opponent's waist (Figure 38.9).

Counter. Resist and keep facing the offensive wrestler when the opponent attempts to pull your arm.

Drop with leg trip. The objective is to take the opponent down from a position behind. Lock your hands with your arms around the opponent's waist and your head resting on the opponent's left hip. Drop to the left knee and grasp the opponent's left ankle with the left hand. Place your right leg in front of the opponent's right leg. Then force your right shoulder to the opponent's buttock and force the opponent forward while pulling the opponent's ankle.

Counter. Open the body lock by tearing the opponent's hands apart.

High-crotch to single-leg takedown. From a tie-up position, lift the opponent's elbows and simultaneously step in quickly. Once in close, duck the head and shoulder under the opponent's right arm, and bring your right arm between the opponent's legs. Grasp your right hand with your left hand and pull up. This is the high-crotch position (Figure 38.10). This can be followed by a single-leg takedown by moving down on the opponent's left leg while dropping to the mat on your right knee. By pulling the opponent's left leg and foot toward you and pushing forward with your shoulders, the opponent can be dumped backward for the takedown (Figure 38.11).

Counter. Keep the leg the attacker is trying to control between the opponent's legs to prevent him or her from lifting it.

Fireman's takedown. From the collar-biceps tie-up, move the left hand from the biceps to the opponent's triceps. Step the right foot between the opponent's legs and drop to the left knee. Move your head under the opponent's right arm and pull down (Figure 38.12). Move your right hand from the opponent's neck and go between the legs and reach up the back. Drop your left hip to the mat, pull down with your left hand or arm, and lift the opponent's body with the right arm. Pull your head out and reach across the opponent's body with your right arm to hold under the left shoulder with your right hand (Figure 38.13).

Counter. Free up the right arm (being held at the triceps by the attacker) and cross face and get the left arm under the attacker's midsection or between the legs to avoid being lifted off the mat.

Breakdowns and rides

To break a wrestler down means to put the wrestler on hands and knees on the mat from the starting position. A wrestler's first objective after bringing an opponent to the mat is to flatten the opponent into a prone position on the mat. Because of the low center of gravity and the four points of support, this is difficult. The technique is to disengage one or more of the points of support.

Bar arm and waist lock. From the starting position, pull the near arm out from under and force the opponent to the mat by pulling the opponent down with the arm that is around the waist (Figure 38.14).

Counter. After the tie-up, the bottom wrestler rolls toward the top wrestler. Then the bottom wrestler takes the left arm, which is free, wraps it over and around the top wrestler's arm, and grasps the top wrestler's wrist and pries it loose.

Far ankle and far arm. The object is to quickly reach under the wrestler and grasp the far arm above the elbow. Now pull this arm to you, and at the same time grasp the far ankle with the other hand. Turn the opponent over by applying body leverage (Figure 38.15).

Counter. The best way to counter this move is for the bottom wrestler to pull the right arm away (or the left arm if the approach is from the other side).

Grapevine and arm bar. This can be accomplished only if the top wrestler is extremely fast. The top wrestler must quickly move on the bottom wrestler's back and wrap the right leg between the bottom wrestler's arm and leg. The top wrestler then places the body across the bottom wrestler. While in this position the top wrestler grasps, from above, the bottom wrestler's arm.

Counter. The bottom wrestler should expect this and not allow the top wrestler to place a foot between arm and leg. However, if the top wrestler's leg does go through, the bottom wrestler should push it through farther than the opponent wanted it to go (Figure 38.16).

Figure 38.8. Duck under and takedown.

Figure 38.9. Arm drag and go-behind.

Figure 38.10. High-crotch position.

Grapevine and bar nelson. Execute a grapevine as previously described, placing the right forearm behind the opponent's neck, pushing the left arm under the opponent's left arm, and locking the hands (bar nelson).

Grapevine and half nelson. Execute a grapevine as described previously, placing the left arm under the opponent's left arm and the forearm behind the opponent's neck (half nelson).

Spiral breakdown. The top wrestler moves the right hand to inside the bottom wrestler's right thigh and pries outward.

The top wrestler also moves the left forearm behind the bottom wrestler's left forearm and pushes forward. At the same time, the top wrestler is circling in a clockwise direction.

Head pry and near arm. To execute this breakdown, the top wrestler moves the right knee to a position between the bottom wrestler's legs. The top wrestler then slides the left hand down to the wrist of the bottom wrestler. While lifting the bottom wrestler's arm up and slightly to the side, the top wrestler places the head in back of the bottom wrestler's arm and applies pressure. This pressure and the pressure forward of the right thigh force the bottom wrestler to the mat (Figure 38.17).

Counter. The bottom wrestler should try to pull the arm forward as the top wrestler moves the hand from the elbow to wrist.

Escapes and reversals

Stand-up. The wrestler in the defensive position pushes off the mat with both hands, brings the elbows back and toward the ribs, raises the head and trunk, and steps out with either foot. By sitting on the rear foot and leg, which are still on the mat, the wrestler prevents the opponent from grasping this ankle or stepping over the near leg. Next, the defensive wrestler grabs the opponent's hands, pulls them apart, and pushes back with the back. The opponent is forced to resist this action (which helps the bottom wrestler to stand) or else be pushed over backward. Finally, when both wrestlers are standing, the defensive wrestler continues to pull the opponent's hands apart and then turns to face the opponent (Figure 38.18).

Counter—far-ankle pick-up. The offensive wrestler releases the arm that is around the defensive wrestler's wrist and

Figure 38.11. Single-leg takedown.

Figure 38.12. Fireman's takedown—initial move.

Figure 38.13. Fireman's takedown—completion.

Figure 38.14. Bar arm and waist lock.

Figure 38.15. Far ankle and far arm.

moves this arm to grasp and lift the far ankle of the bottom wrestler (Figure 38.19).

Counter—forward jam. Remaining in the referee's position, the top wrestler jams the defensive wrestler forward and down to prevent a stand-up (Figure 38.20).

Counter—near-ankle pick-up. The offensive wrestler releases the near arm in the referee's position, moves behind, and grasps and lifts the near ankle of the bottom wrestler (Figure 38.21).

Counter—body lock and forward trip. If the defensive wrestler gets to a standing position, the offensive wrestler should keep the hands tightly clasped around the defensive wrestler's body, step outside and in front of the bottom wrestler's leg, and push forward, thus tripping the defensive wrestler back to the mat (Figure 38.22).

Sit-out. Step the right foot forward first. Then shoot the left foot out and forward. At this point (Figure 38.23, 2) the defensive wrestler can turn out (to the right) by pushing down with the right elbow to break the offensive wrestler's grasp around the waist and swinging the left arm forcefully forward, or turn-in (as illustrated).

Counter. The top wrestler should break the left arm down as the bottom wrestler attempts to execute the kickout with the left leg.

The switch. Begin the switch by crossing the right hand over the left (if the referee's position is on the right side). Now place the weight on the left foot. Kick the right foot forward and to the left. Keep the hips off the mat. With the left arm, reach over the top wrestler's left arm and grasp the left thigh from the inside. Lean back and apply force to the opponent's shoulder. Now pivot on the right foot and grasp the top wrestler around the waist (Figure 38.24).

Figure 38.16. Grapevine and arm bar.

Counter. Break down the bottom wrestler's right arm as the opponent attempts to pivot just after kicking out.

Side roll. The wrestler in the defensive position locks the opponent's right wrist by pressing the arm close to the body, then rolling to the right, bringing the opponent over and under (side roll) or holding the right arm between the opponent's legs (crotch hold). See Figure 38.25.

Pinning holds

Farside-roll to reverse nelson and cradle. This move is executed from the referee's position. The bottom wrestler straightens the left leg and at the same time grasps the top wrestler by the wrist (right). The bottom wrestler then brings the right leg to the left, drops on the right shoulder, and rolls the top wrestler over. As the top wrestler hits the right side, the bottom wrestler turns to face the opponent (Figure 38.25, 4). The bottom wrestler now places the left arm over the top wrestler's right shoulder and around the head to a half nelson. Finally, the bottom wrestler inserts the right arm between the opponent's legs, raises the left leg, and then locks the hands. Locking the hands or arms around the opponent's leg and head is called the cradle.

Arm bar and half nelson. The top wrestler uses the near-arm breakdown described earlier, then brings the left hand up and puts it on the bottom wrestler's back. The top wrestler then applies a half nelson with the right hand, moves to the right side, and "sinks" the half nelson in as far as possible.

Figure 38.17. Head pry and near arm.

He or she circles counterclockwise on the knees to turn the bottom wrestler on the back. This combination of moves is called the "chicken wing" (Figure 38.26).

Three-quarter nelson. This also is executed from the referee's position. The top wrestler places the right knee behind the bottom wrestler. The top wrestler then moves the right arm from the bottom wrestler's waist, reaches under the wrestler with the right hand, and locks hands over the back of the wrestler's head. Next, the top wrestler pulls the bottom wrestler's head under and moves to the left. To keep the bottom wrestler from rolling out, the top wrestler retains control of the bottom wrestler's leg with the right leg (Figure 38.27).

Half nelson and crotch hold. Starting in the referee's position and using a breakdown, the offensive wrestler puts the defensive wrestler flat on the mat. The offensive wrestler then secures a half nelson on the bottom wrestler by moving the arm closest to the bottom wrestler's head under the near arm and behind the neck. With the other arm, the offensive wrestler grasps the defensive wrestler's top leg, lifts it up, and pushes the bottom wrestler over to the back. The top

Figure 38.18. Stand-up.

Figure 38.19. Far-ankle pick-up.

Figure 38.20. Forward jam.

Figure 38.21. Near-ankle pick-up.

Figure 38.22. Body lock and forward trip.

Figure 38.23. The sit-out and turn-in.

Figure 38.24. The switch.

Figure 38.25. Side roll.

wrestler continues to maintain a half nelson with one arm and an inside crotch hold with the other (Figure 38.28).

Near cradle. Assume the wrestlers are in the referee's position, with the top wrestler on the left side of the bottom wrestler. If the bottom wrestler tries to stand up by raising the left knee off the mat, the top wrestler should release the right arm from around the bottom wrestler's waist and move that arm behind the opponent's left knee. At the same time, the top wrestler should shift to a position in front of the bottom wrestler and move the left arm from the bottom wrestler's left elbow to a position around the head and try to lock hands under the wrestler's chest. By pulling the hands together and pushing the wrestler to the right and forward, the top wrestler should be able to move the opponent into a pinning position (Figure 38.29).

Figure 38.26. Chicken wing.

Guillotine. This is done from either the kneeling or the referee's position. Starting from the cross-body ride, the top wrestler reaches over the body of the bottom wrestler and places the right hand on the mat for support. Then the top wrestler grasps the bottom wrestler's left wrist with the left hand. The top wrestler then lifts the bottom wrestler's left arm up over the head and falls back, pinning the bottom wrestler's shoulders (Figure 38.30). The guillotine is a potentially dangerous hold when the arm is forced to such an extent as to endanger a contestant.

Counter. The bottom wrestler should not allow the top wrestler to lift the left arm.

SAFETY

All possible precautions should be used to ensure the safety of the participants. The rules in wrestling are continuously being altered to help prevent injuries and to make the sport safer and more rewarding for the participants. Wrestlers should be monitored continually and reminded regularly regarding the use of illegal holds, including slam, headlock, head scissors, twisting knee lock, neck wrench, and figure-four overscissors (refer to current rule book). In one of the very early class periods the instructor should explain and demonstrate all illegal holds, as well as potentially dangerous situations, including guillotine, chicken wing, standing front headlock, and takedown with arms tied up.

It has become traditional to begin wrestling instruction by first teaching those skills that can be employed as takedowns. It seems only natural that instruction should begin with standing techniques (takedowns) because regulation matches begin from the starting positions. However, one of the most overlooked safety concerns in the teaching of

Figure 38.27. Three-quarter nelson.

wrestling is the well-known fact that a vast majority of injuries occur during the early stages of instruction and are often the result of falling to the mat from a standing position. Too often it is assumed the primary cause of injury is the failure to warm up properly. The fact that the first stage of a wrestling match is conducted in a standing position is commonly ignored. The novice wrestler is more susceptible to injury as a result of a tenseness that accompanies a fall to the mat because of a lack of experience and/or confidence.

A safer method of teaching wrestling skills is to depart from the conventional approach and begin teaching skills from a down position on the mat. This method will accomplish three major objectives: (1) allow the participants time to gain confidence in performing basic skills, (2) provide the participants time to develop a certain amount of mat sense, and (3) cut down on the number of injuries from the standing position due to eliminating landing (a) on another wrestler, (b) off the edge of the mat, or (c) into an awkward landing position.

In addition to proper instruction and knowledge of the rules prohibiting dangerous holds, the following are some general safety suggestions:

1. Have a telephone available in an area near the wrestling room. Emergency number(s) should be posted in a conspicuous place near the telephone.
2. A well-equipped first-aid room should be maintained near the wrestling room.
3. A supply of accident record forms should be kept in the wrestling room. The teacher/coach should complete the accident form in detail within 24 hours following any accident.

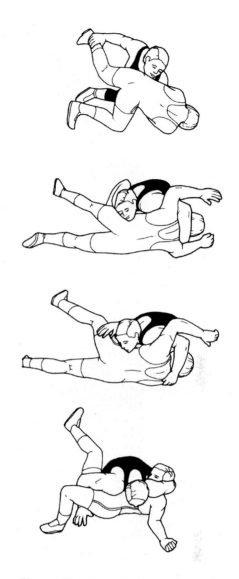

Figure 38.28. Half nelson and crotch hold.

4. A daily record of each wrestler's weight before and after each workout should be kept adjacent to the weighing scale. A careful monitoring of each wrestler's weight is one step toward maintaining the well-being of the wrestler.
5. Participants should not be permitted to wrestle without a proper warm-up. Only semiresistance should be allowed when practicing new holds.
6. Pair the contestants, as nearly as possible, according to weight, height, and athletic temperament.
7. Place spotters around the edges of the mats to prevent the participants from going off the mats and onto the floor.
8. Condition wrestlers gradually.
9. Have wrestlers trim fingernails and toenails short.
10. Participants should not be permitted to wear rings or other jewelry when wrestling.

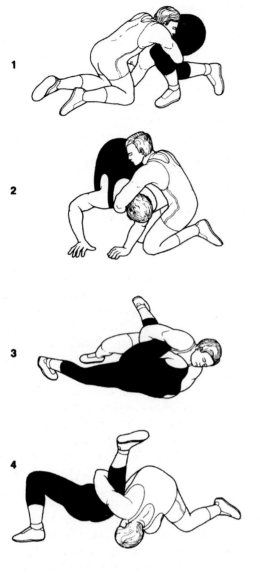

Figure 38.29. Near cradle.

11. Participants should keep all personal equipment clean.
12. Begin teaching holds from the referee's position first.
13. All lacerations or abrasions should be treated immediately.
14. All mats should be checked at least once a year to be sure they have adequate resiliency.

Communicable-disease control procedures should be followed, including those to protect against the spread of blood borne pathogens.

1. Be certain that mats are cleaned and disinfected.
2. Wrestlers should take hot, soapy showers after each workout and clean their equipment and clothing. This practice will help prevent skin infections.
3. Wrestling mats in a high-use facility should be disinfected after each class. In a facility that does not have high use, the mats can be cleaned at the end of

Figure 38.30. Guillotine.

each day. The frequency of use, the temperature and humidity of the room, and the type of activity are significant factors in determining how often mats should be cleaned.

4. There are two commercial disinfectants recommended for mats that are OSHA approved: O-Syl Disinfectant and Amphyl Disinfectant. Both disinfectants are super concentrates that must be mixed with water; they are available from Baxter Scientific Products. The Nevada Department of Environmental Health and Safety suggests that laundry bleach—i.e., a solution of sodium hypochloride—should be used to clean and disinfect mats.

5. If regular laundry bleach is used, be certain to dilute it by mixing one part bleach with nine parts water. The bleach should be mixed daily and put into spray bottles for application. Following the application of disinfectant, the mats should be dried with towels. Contaminated towels should be properly disposed of or disinfected.

6. Mats should be periodically removed from the floor so that the floor can be cleaned. Mats should be cleaned and dried on both sides before being replaced. Under no circumstances should mats be cleaned with mops and pails of water; this practice is a source of mold, mildew, and other microorganisms.

7. To clean up blood, use paper towels to cover the soiled area, spray cleaning solution onto paper towels, wait 1 minute, and then clean up the wet towels and dispose of them in a medical waste bag. Spray the mat area again with the cleaning solution and wipe dry with a towel. Latex gloves should always be worn when coming in contact with blood.

8. All human blood and certain body fluids should be treated as if they are known to contain HIV, HBV, or other bloodborne pathogens. (Check your institution's bloodborne pathogen policy and procedure.)

9. All individuals who are responsible for cleaning mats should be directed to wear rubber gloves and approved eye and respiratory protection.

10. Although saliva has not been implicated in HIV transmission, mouthpieces, resuscitation bags, and other ventilation devices should be available for use to minimize the need for emergency mouth-to-mouth resuscitation.

WRESTLER'S CODE OF CONDUCT

1. *Live right.* Watch how you eat, drink, and party. Consistently maintain your class weight. Retain your maximum strength by not undertraining or overtraining. Get sufficient rest. Keep clean even when just working out.

2. *Train right.* Challenge your coach. Set up a training schedule and follow it. Always attempt to practice with a superior wrestler. You should hurt sometimes during your training program.

3. *Watch and ask.* Do not fool around when not wrestling. Try to pick up new skills. Get into the middle of the action. Ask questions about new moves that you see and then learn them.

4. *Be prepared.* Know the scientific principles involved in wrestling. Know all the skills of wrestling so you can successfully counter them. Know the method of scoring points. Be aware of the penalty system.

5. *Wrestle.* Plan ahead what move you are going to make and what you will do if your opponent successfully counters it. Try to outguess your opponent. Watch your opponent's center of weight and move quickly.

6. *Shake hands.* Be courteous when the match is over, whether you win or lose.

SCIENTIFIC BASIS OF WRESTLING

On what basis does a teacher or coach make sound judgments on training, practice, and skill analysis? The answer is via the study of the sciences of exercise physiology, biomechanics, and motor learning. The reader may wonder why these sciences are important. In brief, a working knowledge of the scientific bases of motor learning equips a teacher or coach to make sound judgments concerning methods of instruction and length, frequency, and nature of practice. A knowledge of exercise physiology equips one to make sound judgments concerning the amount and type of training to prescribe in a given case. A knowledge of biomechanics equips one to choose appropriate techniques and to detect the root cause of faults that may arise in performance. These sciences are not always able to provide immediate solutions, but they do offer the means whereby an answer can ultimately be obtained.

Biomechanical Principles

Wrestling coaches are concerned with the forces that act on the human body and the effects that these forces produce during the performance of the various skills comprising the sport. Their ability to understand and/or teach the various wrestling techniques (takedowns, breakdowns, reversals, escapes, counters, and pinning combinations) depends largely on their appreciation of both the effects they are trying to produce and the forces that cause them.

The wrestler, in applying various holds, takes advantage of the fundamental principles of biomechanics. An example of this knowledge is an understanding of the principle of mechanical advantage. Mechanical advantage for a wrestler is the application of a comparatively small force (f) acting through a comparatively long distance (D) that produces a large force (F) acting through a comparatively short distance (d). The common automobile bumper jack offers us an everyday example of the application of this principle. You must push the jack handle up and down many times (a small force); consequently, through a distance of several feet, you are able to lift the car a few inches.

Wrestlers want to maximize their mechanical advantage so that they can get a large resulting force from a much smaller applied force. The main principle used by the wrestler to gain this mechanical advantage is the lever. For the wrestler the lever is generally a portion of the leg or arm free to turn on some fixed point (axis), which is called the *fulcrum*. The point of the fulcrum is usually established by the wrestler applying the hold.

Conditioning Principles

Many people have suggested that amateur wrestling is one of the most rugged sports because of its great requirements of physical conditioning. It is generally agreed that attaining a high level of physical conditioning is one of the necessary components leading to successful performance in wrestling.

The general overriding principles that are considered necessary for any individual who hopes to attain improvement in physical performance and upon which all athletic training and conditioning should be based are:

1. *Overload.* This principle states that all organs or systems in the human body must be taxed beyond their accustomed loads to increase their physical capacity. The body tends to adapt to the various demands imposed upon it as a result of prolonged muscular activity. Workouts need to be of such frequency, intensity, and duration that the level of stress is near its maximum for the present level of conditioning.

2. *Progression.* Training should begin at a comfortable level and over time systematically progress to much higher levels. This can be accomplished by manipulating the variables of frequency, intensity, duration, or a combination of these variables.

3. *Retrogression.* Training on an almost daily basis is necessary to improve the state of conditioning. Several consecutive days of complete inactivity may intrude on the overall performance, and longer periods of inactivity lead to retrogression.

4. *Recovery.* Sufficient periods of recuperation must be included in both the daily and the overall training programs. Schedule hard workouts only every other day.

5. *Principle of diminishing returns.* The closer one gets to maximum performance, the greater the time and effort that must be exerted in terms of training and conditioning in order to gain even slight improvement in performance.

6. *Individual differences.* Even when athletes receive the same conditioning program, each individual's rate of improvement and level of development may be different.

7. *Specificity.* Training must be specific to the particular requirements and strategies of that sport.

Aerobic and Anaerobic Training

During the course of a wrestling match, all of the physiological systems of the body are taxed. As such, planning a training program for the wrestler that will ensure a high level of sport-specific conditioning requires an understanding of physiological training principles, an awareness of which parameters are called upon during the course of a match, and an appreciation of the relationship between general physical condition and sport-specific conditioning.

During a match, a wrestler will use two basic energy pathways to furnish the required energy for the required performance. The contribution made by each pathway is dependent upon the intensity and duration of the activity. If the activity is intense and prolonged up to 60 seconds, the anaerobic pathway will prevail in energy delivery. If the activity persists beyond 60 seconds, the energy will start to be produced by the aerobic pathway. Although this system is more efficient, it does not produce the same quantity of energy as the anaerobic pathway, and subsequently a reduction in intensity will result.

Wrestling is an activity characterized by short-duration, high-intensity bursts of action that use great amounts of explosive strength and are repeated intermittently during the course of a 6- or 7-minute match. It is a sport requiring high levels of training for each of the energy pathways mentioned above.

The aerobic system is considered the basis of all athletic conditioning. Before engaging in any sport-specific training, a well-established aerobic base should be developed. Attaining this base will provide for higher levels of sport-specific conditioning to be achieved and subsequently, higher-level performances. Additionally, a highly developed aerobic system will allow for more rapid recovery from anaerobic work and for quicker resynthesis of the high-energy phosphate during the easier, submaximal phases of the bout.

During training, the aerobic energy pathway the teacher/coach must be concerned with has two components: the ability of the cardiovascular system to deliver oxygen to the working muscles, and the ability of the muscle tissue to extract and use the oxygen delivered. Exercise physiologists suggest that continuous training is the best method to increase this oxygen transport component, whereas interval training appears to be the best means to increase oxygen utilization at the muscle cell level. In the first training component, training specificity is important but sport specificity is not—that is, continuous activity at a heart rate level of 75 percent of the maximum for periods of 20 minutes or more is necessary, but the activity producing the increased heart rate can be jogging, cycling, swimming, cross-country skiing, etc. However, for the second component (oxygen utilization), adaptation occurs only in the working muscles, so training must be sport-specific and must utilize muscle groups, movements, and resistance patterns encountered during the performance of specific skills. To improve the extraction and utilization rate of oxygen in the muscle tissues, the wrestler must follow an interval training system using specific wrestling movements.

Anaerobic capacity refers to the maximum amount of energy that can be produced and made available for use in the first 30 to 90 seconds of all-out effort. Training for the anaerobic energy pathway is similar to the second component of aerobic training in that it requires both training and sport specificity. The major limitation of anaerobic capacity is the accumulation of lactic acid in the working muscles. The effect of training is to increase the muscles' tolerance to lactic acid accumulation. The result is that the wrestler will be able to sustain an all-out effort for a longer period of time. It is this repeated exposure to high levels of lactic acid accumulation that produces training adaptation.

Coaches do not agree on the best method of training for this pathway. However, some exercise physiologists have indicated that any of the following approaches will produce a significant training effect:

1. Maximal effort for 1 minute followed by a rest period of 4 to 5 minutes, or an exercise-to-rest ratio of 1:4 or 1:5.
2. Maximal effort ranging between 30 to 80 seconds, with an exercise-to-rest ratio of 1:2 or 1:3.
3. Ninety to 100 percent effort at maximum aerobic capacity for 2 to 3 minutes, with an exercise-to-rest ratio of 1:1.

Motor Learning Principles

Teachers and coaches need to understand the general nature of the processes involved in learning and performing various motor skills. With a foundation in motor learning, coaches/teachers will be able to develop appropriate methods for conducting practice and for teaching specific wrestling skills. The following is a list of some general principles related to practice:

1. The amount of practice affects the quality of learning, although the effect is not always proportional.
2. The spacing or distribution of practice appears to affect performance and/or learning (massed practice, distributed practice).
3. Practicing while being physically fatigued appears to affect performance to a greater degree than learning does.
4. The decision to practice a motor skill as a whole or by parts should be made on the basis of the complexity and organization of the skill (task organization, task complexity).
5. Variability of practice is important for motor skills where novel responses must be made.
6. Practice that occurs mentally can be beneficial to the acquisition of a new motor skill and to the performance of a well-learned skill.

TEACHING CONSIDERATIONS

1. Match students for weight.
2. Begin with holds from the referee's position before the standing position.
3. Walk through beginning holds with a passive defense until proper technique is established. Increase resistance gradually.
4. Combine offensive and defensive moves in practice. Give both offense and defense a choice of several moves in drill-like practices, focusing the wrestlers on the decision-making process involved in selecting a move.
5. Introduce illegal holds as they may occur in drills, and be firm about calling them.
6. As soon as several offensive and defensive skills have been developed, provide opportunities for mini-matches in each lesson. Use these times as opportunities to teach rules and scoring. Structure the matches to require or encourage the use of particular moves as part of the lesson (e.g., give more points for a particular move).
7. Go back to basics when students revert to poor technique. Provide for repetition. Continually return to earlier moves as you introduce advanced moves.
8. Modify the rules as needed to make illegal any move beginners cannot perform safely, either because of skill level or conditioning.
9. Change matched partners as often as possible within a weight class.

DRILLS

Wrestling drills should emphasize the proper wrestling mechanics. Use of these drills can be a real time-saver because they are an effective way to integrate the teaching and perfecting of wrestling skills with physical and mental conditioning. Take care that the drills do not become too complicated or tedious. Here are some suggestions for the teacher/coach to keep in mind when developing and using wrestling drills:

1. Proper administration of the drill is of paramount importance.
2. An explanation of the drill should be accompanied by a demonstration of how it is to be performed.
3. Drills are beneficial if characterized by discipline, order, and good management.
4. Drills should be programmed from the simple to the complex.
5. All drills should reinforce proper wrestling mechanics.
6. Drills should not be allowed to drag along after interest is lost.

Warm-Up Drills

Run, sprawl, cuddle, and recover drill

Many outside of wrestling see this drill as four separate drills, but in teaching wrestling it is considered a single drill. This drill is designed to (1) teach basic wrestling skills (sprawl, cuddle), (2) introduce chain wrestling, and (3) provide warm-up.

Wrestlers begin by running in place; on the whistle they are asked to *sprawl* (drop hands straight to the mat, throw legs back with feet spread and back arched); immediately they should *cuddle* left or right (roll to left or right and take a fetal position, raise and throw leg toward the head to the defensive starting position and then *recover* to the neutral standing position). Recovering includes bringing both knees to the mat, shifting the weight back over the feet, pushing off the mat with the hands to return to the standing position, and continuing to run. The circuit is repeated as often as the teacher or coach feels appropriate for the state of training and experience of the class or team.

Preliminary Mat Drills

Passive-resistance drill

The wrestlers are paired off. One member of each pair is designated as being the offensive wrestler. The designated wrestler executes setups, takedowns, rides, breakdowns, pins, escapes, reversals, and counters as directed by the coach. The other wrestler offers only token resistance. This wrestler is not to be completely submissive, but rather sufficiently resistant to require the move to be correctly applied for it to work. After a reasonable period of time the position of the two wrestlers is reversed.

Point-of-contact drill or "floating drill"

From the referee's position, the top wrestler places the chest on the opponent's back but does not use the arms or legs to secure a wrestling hold. The underneath wrestler attempts to displace the top wrestler by moving, turning, sitting out, twisting, or rolling about the mat, but is not permitted to use any lock, grip, or wrestling hold. It should be the purpose of the wrestler to expend a minimum amount of effort while maintaining the position of advantage.

Spinning drill

Spinning is an excellent conditioning activity and also contributes to effective wrestling skills. One wrestler assumes the down defensive position. The other wrestler assumes the floating position by placing the chest on the back of the underneath wrestler. The top wrestler spins to the right or left on command, keeping the chest on the bottom wrestler's back. The top wrestler pivots on the chest and moves in a circular motion around the bottom man, who remains stationary. The spinning wrestler should attempt to travel 180 degrees on each move, completing the entire circle (360 degrees) in two moves. The wrestlers reverse positions every 20 to 30 seconds.

Change-of-Pace Drills

Challenge drill

This game-type drill gets its name from the fact that both sides or teams are challenged. The game or drill begins by dividing the class or team into two groups. The teacher/coach assigns one group a challenge. The other group is told to prevent it. Examples are as follows:

1. The members of one group are told to remain standing on their feet. The other group is given the task (challenge) of taking them down and keeping them from regaining a standing position.
2. One group is told to remain prone while the other is told to turn them over onto their backs and hold them there.
3. One group is told to maintain at least some part of their bodies in contact with a line on the mat while the other group is to prevent this action.

At the conclusion of the assigned challenge, wrestlers are instructed to remain in their last position in order to be counted. Scores are totaled at the end of each challenge. The roles of each group are then reversed. In this way each group has to accomplish and prevent the same tasks. The number of tasks that can be assigned is only limited by the coach's imagination and creativity.

WRESTLING LEAD-UP STUNTS/GAMES

Here is a description of a few stunts and games that can be used in classes and wrestling programs as lead-up games. It is suggested that several stunts might be used during each physical education class in leading up to the unit on wrestling.

Chicken or Rooster Fighting

Contestants grasp their own ankle from behind and while balancing on the opposite foot attempt to knock the opponent off balance.

Dog Wrestling

Two contestants face each other on hands and knees, with a strap or towel tied in a circle placed behind each of their heads. The heads are kept up and back. Each contestant attempts to pull the other over a line on the mat.

Foot Push

Contestants sit on the floor or mat facing each other. The feet are placed in contact and the knees bent. Contestants support themselves with their hands behind their backs with fingers pointing away from the back. The object is to straighten the legs against the pressure exerted by the opponent.

Hand Wrestle

Contestants grasp left or right hands and stand with right or left foot against the outside of the opponent's right or left foot. The object is to make the opponent move either foot from the starting position.

Hop and Pull

Divide the class or team into two sides. Each side forms a line facing each other. Contestants from both sides advance and grasp the right hand of the opponent and lift their own left foot. At a signal, contestants attempt to pull the opponents to their goal line. If the left foot touches the floor or mat, that contestant loses.

GLOSSARY

arm drag A preliminary move to execute a takedown from behind.

breakdown From the referee's position, the wrestler on top forces the bottom wrestler off the hands and knees to a position flat on the mat.

bridge A position on the mat in which the wrestler is supported on the head and feet with the back arched.

control This condition exists when a wrestler has gained restraining power over the opponent.

counter Stop a move made by the opponent.

cradle A move made to force the opponent's head and knees together.

decision If no fall occurs in a match, the wrestler with the greater number of points is declared the winner.

default Winning a match through the inability of an opponent to continue the match.

disqualification A situation in which a contestant is banned from participation in accordance with the Infraction Penalty Table (Table 38.1).

escape Gaining a neutral position by the defensive wrestler while the supporting points of either wrestler are within the wrestling area.

fall Holding both of an opponent's shoulders to the mat simultaneously for 1 or 2 seconds; also termed a *pin.*

folkstyle The popular form of wrestling found in American schools and universities. Similar to but not the same as freestyle.

forfeit Winning a match through failure of an opponent to appear.

freestyle An international form of wrestling that emphasizes domination by taking the opponent to the mat and turning the opponent with the intent to pin.

Greco-Roman An international form of wrestling that has its roots in ancient Greece. This form of wrestling allows no holds below the waist, and the legs cannot be used for any purpose other than standing.

half nelson A hold executed from the rear by reaching either the left or right arm under the opponent's corresponding arm and using the hand behind the head to apply pressure.

hammerlock Holding the opponent's arm behind the back. This is illegal if the hand is pulled away from the body or if the angle at the elbow is less than 90 degrees.

judo A recent (1850) alteration of the ancient Japanese martial art of jujitsu. Judo emphasizes defensive tactics, physical training, and character development.

near fall Position in which the offensive wrestler holds the opponent's shoulders or the scapula area in contact with the mat for a designated time, less than that required for a fall.

neutral position Position in which neither wrestler has control.

out-of-bounds The supporting parts of either wrestler outside the boundary lines.

overtime When the contestants are tied at the end of the three regular periods, they will wrestle overtime. The overtime will consist of a 1-minute sudden victory period, and if needed two 30-second tie-breakers. If the score remains tied at the end of the two 30-second tie-breakers, a 30-second ultimate tie-breaker shall take place.

pin Synonymous with *fall.*

position of advantage Having control of an opponent.

potentially dangerous hold Hold causing a body part to be forced to the limit of normal range of motion.

reversal Act of moving from a defensive position to an offensive position.

riding time or time advantage The offensive wrestler who has control in the advantage position is gaining time advantage. If a contestant has 1 minute or more of net time advantage, that wrestler is awarded one point.

sit out A maneuver executed from the referee's position in which the bottom wrestler throws the legs forward to a sitting position.

stalemate Neither wrestler is able to improve the situation; the referee stops and restarts the match.

stand-up A breakaway (escape) move resulting in getting up to the feet quickly.

starting position on the mat Position in which the defensive wrestler is kneeling with hands in the center of the mat. The offensive contestant is kneeling at the side of the opponent, with the nearest arm around the opponent's body perpendicular to the long axis with the palm of the hand placed on the navel and the other hand placed on the back of the opponent's nearest elbow.

sudden victory The first overtime tie-breaker.

sumo The national sport of Japan. The object of the event is to force your opponent out of the ring or make any part of his body, except for the soles of his feet, touch the floor. The emphasis is on strength and gargantuan size. Many of the sumo wrestlers weigh 350 to 400 pounds.

sweatbox or hot box An illegal device consisting of a confined heated space or box that wrestlers use to facilitate weight loss through sweating.

takedown Bring an opponent from a standing position to the mat and keep under control.

technical fall Occurs when a wrestler has earned a 15-point advantage over an opponent.

tie-breaker The second overtime.

time advantage Accumulated time during which a wrestler is in a position of advantage over the opponent; no more than 1 point may be awarded in any one match. (Not used in high school.)

ultimate tie-breaker The third overtime. If no scoring occurs during the ultimate tie-breaker, the offensive (most aggressive) wrestler is declared the winner.

SUGGESTED READINGS

Amateur Athletic Union of the United States. Current ed. *Official wrestling guide.* New York: AAU.

Carr, G. 2004. *Sport mechanics for coaches.* 2nd ed. Champaign, IL: Human Kinetics.

Chapman, M. 2005. *Wrestling tough.* Champaign, IL: Human Kinetics.

Coaching youth wrestling. 2008. American Sport Education Program. 3rd ed. Champaign, IL: Human Kinetics.

Gable, D. 2005. *Coaching wrestling successfully.* Champaign, IL: Human Kinetics. This book presents the keys to successful coaching in wrestling.

National Collegiate Athletic Association. Current ed. *Official wrestling guide.* New York: NCAA.

National Federation of State High School Associations. Current ed. *Wrestling Rules Book.* P.O. Box 690, Indianapolis, IN 46206.

U.S. Olympic *Committee's Sport Series.* 2004. A basic guide to wrestling. Torrance, CA: Griffin Publishing Group.

Walker, B. 2005. *The wrestling drill book.* Champaign, IL: Human Kinetics. This book features 200 match-tested drills.

RESOURCES

Videos

Dan Gable's wrestling essentials complete collection DVD 2005. Champaign, IL: Human Kinetics.

Fundamentals of wresting with Greg Shoemaker (2 videos). Includes stances, various setups, bridging the gap, takedowns, defensive takedowns, escapes, reversals, and pins.

Granby System videos. Grandby System Wrestling, 4817 Admiration Dr., Virginia Beach, VA 23464.

Wrestling classic and *Wrestling's greatest heroes* (2 videos). Corbin House, 227 Corbin Place, Brooklyn, NY 11235.

See Appendix C for other video sources.

Sources of Additional Information

USA Wrestling
6155 Lehman Dr.
Colorado Springs, CO 80918
719-598-8181
Fax: 719-598-9440

USA Wrestling, Women's Wrestling Committee
6155 Lehman Dr.
Colorado Springs, CO 80918
719-598-9440
Fax: 719-598-9440

WEB SITES

Intermat
http://www.intermatwrestle.com/

International Wrestling Institute and Museum
http://www.wrestlingmuseum.org/

National Wrestling Coaches Association—Amateur Wrestling
http://www.nwcaonline.com/

Nevada Wrestling Forum
http://nevadawrestling.proboards43.com/

TheMat.com
http://www.themat.com/

The Wrestling Megasite
http://www.wrestlingsbest.com/

United States Girls Wrestling Association
http://www.usgwa.com/

Welcome to Dan Gable.com!
http://www.dangable.com/

Wrestling International News Magazine
http://www.winmagazine.com/

The Wrestling Mall/Takedown Radio
http://www.thewrestlingmall.com/takedownradio/

WrestlingReport.com
http://www.wrestlingreport.com

Wrestling USA Magazine
http://www.wrestlingusa.com

39 | Yoga

After completing this chapter, the reader should be able to:

- Understand and appreciate the history of yoga practice and yoga philosophy
- Explain basic yoga postures and perform a general vinyasa in the Sun Salutation
- Demonstrate all sun saluation postures
- Utilize knowledge to continue exploring yoga in one's daily life

HISTORY AND OVERVIEW

The term "yoga" literally means "yoking" or "union" in the sense of bringing together a harmonious relationship with the physical and spiritual aspects of self. The practice of yoga dates back more than 5000 years and has gone through several resurgences around the globe in the last century. What was once seen as a practice by the fringe elements of society has now been fully embraced by mainstream America. In fact, yoga studios are now commonplace in most American cities. Yoga is not a religion, but rather a philosophy that encompasses many lineages and schools of thought. Most Americans practice hatha yoga, a branch of yoga that focuses on physical postures and breathing practices.

Teaching yoga to children and youth has many advantages. Traditionally people think of yoga as only improving flexibility; however, it also develops strength and stamina and enhances concentration and awareness. For example, the focused breathing used in yoga can actually help participants facilitate the performance of spatial cognitive tasks. Kinesthetic awareness can also be greatly improved, as yoga helps to fine-tune motor coordination and can help individuals gain control over their developing bodies. Yoga is an activity that can be pursued throughout life as it can be easily modified to accommodate differing abilities.

Although instructors may be intimidated by incorporating yoga into their curriculum (many poses seem impossibly difficult!), it should come as a relief to know that there are literally thousands of poses from which to choose. It may also seem that yoga is simply "stretching," but the variety and sequencing of postures coupled with the practice of deep breathing creates an extremely diverse and effective method of enhancing a range of health-related fitness skills.

FACILITIES

Yoga can be taught in any facility, including a gymnasium, a classroom, or any playing field. Classes should be arranged so that participants can easily view the instructor (mirrors can greatly assist with this) and the distance between participants should accommodate the full range of movement. Remember that participants will often be inverted or turned away from the instructor; therefore, it is also important that all can easily hear the verbal instructions given.

EQUIPMENT

A unit of study could be taught with virtually no equipment, however, it is ideally taught with the following enhancements:

Yoga mats. Mats provide individual space for each participant and allow the instructor to arrange the class for maximal visibility and safety. They also provide a nonslip, padded surface on which to practice postures.

Yoga blocks, bands, bolsters. These can be used to help participants who lack the flexibility or strength to safely achieve and/or hold a posture.

DVD player and television. Technology to play videos illustrating major concepts further stimulates the learning environment.

BASIC PRINCIPLES AND STRATEGIES

A typical yoga class will follow a traditional teaching format. A general warm-up will precede the body of the lesson, which is composed of skill practice, refinement, and application. A general cooldown will conclude each yoga session. The following section describes principles and strategies regarding the warm up, the body of the lesson, and the cool-down.

The Warm-up of the Yoga Lesson

Most classes begin with a few minutes of deep breathing. Instructors can use this time to allow participants to center and calm themselves before beginning the physical practice of yoga. The yoga warm-up allows participants to cleanse their minds and release their daily worries and has been shown to alleviate stress.

The Body of the Yoga Lesson

There are literally thousands of yoga asanas, or poses. Selecting the most appropriate poses and designing the proper sequencing of postures can be a daunting task to the novice. A sequence that many beginners start with is a variation called the *sun salutation.* Depending on the yoga tradition that is followed, this sequence has many different variations, but all essentially follow a similar pattern of movement.

The sun salutation series (Figure 39.1), or *vinyasa,* is thought to have a complete and total effect on the entire body, which is why it is such a popular sequence. Once the individual poses that comprise the sun salutation series have been mastered, the series may be executed continuously in a flowing movement.

The sun salutation is a series of poses that are practiced in a specific order. Two times through the order is considered one round. A complete cycle of the sun salutation is comprised of two rounds. The order of the sun salutation is as follows:

1. Standing mountain pose
2. Standing back bend pose
3. Standing forward bend pose
4. High lunge pose
5. Plank pose
6. Grasshopper pose
7. Cobra pose
8. Downward facing dog pose
9. High lunge pose
10. Standing forward bend pose
11. Standing back bend pose
12. Standing mountain pose

The Cooldown of the Yoga Lesson

Most classes will end with a few minutes of deep breathing and relaxation. Classes may practice the focused breathing activity, such as deep belly breathing, that is used to begin class. Another typical cooldown to elicit a relaxation response is to allow participants to assume the shavsana, or corpse pose. Encourage participants to relax completely prior to ending the lesson.

BASIC TECHNIQUES

Warm-up Activities

General breathing techniques are typically practiced to begin a yoga lesson. To begin practicing breathing techniques, it is often easiest to lie in a supine position on the floor and rest the hands on the belly (Figure 39.2). As one inhales through the nose, the belly will begin to slowly rise up, somewhat like

Figure 39.1. Circular illustration of the sun salutation.

filling a balloon. As the individual exhales through the nose, the belly will slowly deflate. Have participants practice this several times. Be mindful that they do not hyperventilate, as the purpose is to develop slow, even, and moderately deep breaths. As the participants advance, the instructor cues them to begin to slow their breathing down even more by utilizing a count. Count Breathing and the three-part breath are appropriate warm-up activities to prepare for the sun salutation.

Count breathing

"Inhale on 1-2-3—hold for 1—and exhale for 1-2-3." Beginners can usually manage counts of 3 to 6 seconds. This deep belly breathing stimulates the sympathetic branch of the autonomic nervous system and has a calming effect on the mind and body. Participants can and should strive to maintain this breathing pattern throughout the body of the yoga lesson. To assist in this, instructors will usually cue both the pose and the breathing for each posture.

Three-part breath

This is another breathing technique commonly used to help beginners become familiar with how the body responds during respiration. The three-part breath should only be used as a warm-up activity, while Count Breathing may be used throughout the body of the lesson, or yoga asana practice. Instructional cues:
- Place your hands on your belly.
- Breathe in and expand your belly for 3 counts.
- Exhale and let your belly relax for 3 counts (Part 1).
- Move your hands to your ribs.
- Continue to inflate and deflate the belly, but now add the ribs to the movement (Part 2).
- Finally, try to get the air to the very top of your lungs, right underneath your collarbones (Part 3).
- Keep breathing slowly through your nose throughout each breath. Do not force your breath; try to breathe as fully and naturally as you can.

- If you feel dizzy, stop and return to your normal breathing pattern.
- Pour the breath out as if you were pouring out a glass of water from the clavicles to the belly button. The last air in is the first air out, just like the water would flow.

The Middle of the Lesson—Poses of the Sun Salutation

It is important for instructors to be reminded that every body is built and put together a little differently. This becomes apparent when the practice of yoga postures begins. Remind participants that there is no one "perfect" posture for a pose, as each body will reveal the movement a little differently. Asking everyone to look identical in each pose is not required, and in fact, should be discouraged. A noncompetitive, internally focused atmosphere in the class should be cultivated. In the following section, each pose of the sun salutation has been described with instructional cues. Note that the poses are numbered and follow the appropriate order for completing a cycle within the sun salutation series.

1. Stand in mountain pose

Mountain pose is the position from which most standing poses start. If done correctly, this pose may feel like work; however, it should not feel like a rigid "soldier" posture. You should feel solid and "grounded like a mountain" in the pose (Figure 39.3). Instructional cues:
- Stand at the front of your mat.
- Feet are shoulder-width apart, balancing on the four corners of the feet, spreading the toes.
- All ten toes should be pointing forward with the outside edges of the feet parallel to the outside edges of the mat.
- The tailbone reaches downward, while the spine and head reach upward.
- Arms are at the sides with fingers reaching down.
- Thigh muscles are pulling upward and in toward the femur bones.
- Practice count breathing in this posture for several breaths. Eyes can be closed or open.

Figure 39.2. General breathing.

Figure 39.3. Stand in mountain pose.

2. Standing back bend pose

This posture is designed to open the upper torso. The legs are grounded while the upper torso is free to move like tall bamboo bending in the wind. In this pose, it is helpful to think about expanding the chest, rather than arching the back (Figure 39.4). Instructional cues:

- Inhale and extend the arms out to the sides and slowly reach them overhead. (You may choose to place your fully extended arms with the hands together overhead or leave them shoulder width apart.) Look up at your thumbs and reach your arms toward the sky.
- Exhale, lift, and open the chest. Slowly begin to let the head and eyes look up and begin to travel backward across the ceiling. Try to avoid just dropping the head back; rather, strive to keep the back long throughout the arch.
- Lift up and out of the pelvis and elongate the spine. Engaging the gluteus muscles can help to protect the spine.
- Inhale and come back to the extended standing position.
- Variation: Some might find it comfortable and stable to place the palms of their hands on their lower back during this posture.

3. Standing forward bend pose

The purpose of this pose is to allow your legs to be fully engaged and connected to the earth, feeling a stretch in the hamstrings. The energy of the earth is allowed to travel up the legs as the upper torso and head relax (Figure 39.5). Instructional cues:

- Exhale and allow yourself to fold forward at the hips.
- Feet stay grounded and pushing into the earth. Hips lift. Knees can be slightly bent to allow chest to drape on the upper thighs, which is the safest position for the low back.
- The head hangs like a ripe piece of fruit from a tree branch. Arms are also hanging next to the legs or the

Figure 39.5. Standing forward bend pose.

fingertips may be gently resting on the thighs, shins, or the floor for the very flexible participantss.
- Variations: Arms can be out to the side (like a swan dive) or straight down the center of the body.

4. High lunge pose

This is an excellent hip opener and is often referred to as the runner's stretch. To achieve full extension of the hip in this posture, the instructor should encourage a large backward step, approximately 3 feet in distance (Figure 39.6). Instructional cues:

- Inhale and step with the right foot, reaching with the heels, toward the back of the mat. Left leg stays at 90 degrees to the floor.
- Fingertips or palms rest on the floor.
- Right hip gently presses toward the ground, while right leg fully extends.
- Back should be flat and long, while the head can be either up or down.

Figure 39.4. Standing back bend pose.

Figure 39.6. High lunge pose.

Figure 39.7. Plank pose.

- Front knee presses forward, while back heel presses backward.
- The tailbone reaches toward the feet, while the top of the head stretches forward.

5. Plank pose

This posture will look like the top of a standard push-up. The Plank Pose encourages a union between the upper and lower body. The pose takes a lot of arm strength, so it is appropriate for beginners to go to their knees (Figure 39.7). Instructional cues:

- Step the left foot back in line with the right foot. Your body is now in a "push-up" position.
- Try to keep yourself straight like a board. Use your abdominal muscles to assist you.
- Pull the bellybutton upward as you extend through the heels of the feet.

6. Grasshopper pose

This pose visually resembles a grasshopper and is often called the *8-point pose,* as the participant has two feet, two knees, two hands, one chest, and one chin in contact with the floor (Figure 39.8). Instructional cues:

- Slowly lower yourself to the ground, touching only your knees, chest, chin, hands, and toes. When you get to the ground, your body will look like a grasshopper.
- The hips stay 2 to 6 inches (5–15 cm) off the floor.
- The pose is typically not held more than 1 to 2 seconds before you release to a prone position.

7. Cobra pose

This posture builds lower back strength and upper back flexibility (Figure 39.9). Instructional cues:

- Lie flat on the ground and lift your chest and torso slightly off the floor as if a group of ants was walking right under your nose and shoulders.
- Look at the ants under your nose, and when the last one has passed, lower yourself back down to the ground.

Figure 39.8. Grasshopper pose.

- Do not use your hands or arms to lift. Keep your elbows in tight to the sides.
- Think about expanding the chest and lengthening the spine instead of arching the back.

8. Downward facing dog pose

This is one of the best stretches in all of yoga for the back side of the body. Common errors of beginners are to tend to place too much weight on their hands and to take a stance that is too narrow (Figure 39.10). Instructional cues:

- Tuck your toes under and lift your buttocks as high as you can in the air. Your body will form an upside down letter "V."
- Imagine pushing your hands forward as if you had them on a rolling pin that was in wet cement.
- Keep your legs straight and try to push your heels to the ground. It is all right if they do not touch the floor.

9. High lunge pose

See above (#4) for specifics.

Figure 39.9. Cobra pose.

Figure 39.10. Downward facing dog.

10. Standing forward bend pose
See above (#3) for specifics.

11. Standing back bend pose
See above (#2) for specifics.

12. Stand in mountain pose
See above (#1) for specifics. You are now back at the beginning posture of the sun salutation.

As previously mentioned, two times through this series of poses is considered to be one round in this version of the sun salutation. At this point, one half of the cycle has been completed. When the second half of the cycle begins, the only variation is that the left leg goes into the high lunge pose first. If that is difficult to remember or cue, continue to allow the right leg to be the first high lunge. Beginning yoga instructors often find it helpful to visualize the postures of the Sun Salutation in a circular, rather than linear, format. Figure 39.1 provides a visual illustration of the circular nature of the sun salutation.

Cooldown Activities
Corpse pose (Shavasana)
It is believed that finishing a practice in this posture allows the nervous system and the rest of the body to integrate the movements practiced. Many argue that the time spent in resting corpse pose at the end of the practice is the most important of all (Figure 39.11). Instructional cues:
- Begin by resting on the floor on your back with palms facing upward about 6 inches (15 cm) from your sides. Eyes should be gently closed.
- Allow the body to relax and melt into the floor.
- Perform body scan—Talk participants through their body and encourage them to relax each part. For example, "Relax your left hand" (pause for 5 to 10 seconds). "Relax your left arm and shoulder" (pause for 5 to 10 seconds). "Relax your right hand" (pause for 5 to 10 seconds). "Relax your right hand and shoulder," and so on.

Figure 39.11. Corpse pose.

- Classes typically end with 5 to 10 minutes of this deep relaxation.
- To exit this pose, first roll gently with an exhalation onto one side, preferably the right. Take 2 or 3 breaths. With another exhalation, press your hands against the floor and lift your torso, dragging your head slowly after.
- The head should always come up last.
- Participants return to a comfortable sitting position and rest for a few moments to normalize circulation.

REFINING THE CURRICULUM WITH ADDITIONAL TECHNIQUES
The sun salutation provides both instructors and participants a common ground to begin the practice of yoga. Once the sun salutation poses and sequence of movements are refined and comfortably practiced, instructors may further challenge participants by incorporating additional postures and sequences. There are literally thousands of yoga asanas, so you will probably never know all of them.

The following section is designed to provide instructors with additional asanas that could be included in the yoga curriculum. These are common poses that may be easily incorporated within a session. It is important to be consistent in one's teaching style and to practice the postures in a safe and appropriate manner. Unless otherwise noted, the following postures are typically not held for longer than 15-30 seconds for beginners. Count breathing should continue to be practiced.

Additional Beginning Asana
Child's pose
This is a resting pose in which the participant remains from 30 seconds to a few minutes. This pose should be very comfortable for all. Do not worry if they cannot get their buttocks on their heels. This is a great pose to get participants to practice breathing and relaxing since they are usually not distracted by others in the class (Figure 39.12). Instructional cues:

Figure 39.12. Child's pose.

- Rest your forehead on the ground and focus on your breath.
- Allow the hips to relax and the belly to expand as it rests between the legs.
- Arms may rest by the sides or in front of the head on the mat.

Easy seated pose

In this pose, the participant sits cross-legged, with the shins aligned parallel to each other (Figure 39.13). Instructional cues:

- You can sit in this position for any length of time, but if you practice this pose regularly, be sure to alternate the cross of the legs.
- Sit tall and lengthen your spine while rooting your pelvis to the ground.
- Breath deeply and focus on the point between the eyebrows.

Warrior I pose

This is a standing lunge pose with arms held overhead. A slightly narrow stance and resting one hand on the sacrum

Figure 39.14. Warrior I pose.

can reduce the difficulty of this pose. Although it looks simple, this can be a very challenging asana. This pose builds leg strength and stamina (Figure 39.14). Instructional cues:

- Ensure that the rear foot is planted on the floor.
- Lift and expand the chest while sinking down into the hips.
- Allow the back to form a natural arch as the eyes look straight ahead or to the sky.

Warrior II pose

This is a standing lunge pose with the arms extended horizontally over the legs. Torso and front of the pelvis align. Head turns and eyes look out over the front fingers (Figure 39.15). Instructional cues:

- Most beginners do not step wide enough and often allow their torso to be "pulled forward" in this pose instead of keeping the armpits directly above the hips.
- Encourage participants to take up some space by elongating their spine and neck and stretching out their arms.
- This pose is sometimes called the *star pose* because of the energy flow it creates. Try to feel the energy flowing up through your legs and out through your fingers and head.

Figure 39.13. Easy seated pose.

Figure 39.15. Warrior II pose.

Figure 39.16. Triangle pose.

Triangle pose

This pose incorporates flexion, extension, and rotation all at once. Stay in the posture for more than 15 seconds and you will feel how it works the entire body, building strength and flexibility at the same time (Figure 39.16). Instructional cues:

- The most common error that beginners make is to reach for their feet and twist their torso instead of "tipping" their torso in the same plane.
- The upper torso reaches forward and the hips shift backwards slightly as you enter this pose almost as if your fingers were being pulled in one direction and your hips in another.
- Once you have reached as far forward as you can, simply tip yourself toward the floor or shin.
- The essence of this pose is lengthening the spine and staying in one plane, not touching the floor.
- If it bothers your neck to look upward, you can look straight ahead or at the floor.
- Pull energy up from the floor and firm up your legs.
- Try to turn from your torso and not from your shoulders.

Stick pose (Chaturanga)

You are usually getting into this posture from the plank pose. This pose is a more difficult version of the grasshopper pose in the sun salutation. It is used frequently in other versions of sun salutation. Although it does require strength, perhaps the most important thing in this pose is having the intention and courage to do it (Figure 39.17). Instructional cues:

- Start in the plank pose and then lower 1 to 2 inches (2.5 to 5 cm).
- Your eyes can look down or straight ahead.
- Elbows should touch your ribs as you lower down.
- Try to keep your entire body straight as you lower.
- Even if you just lower down by 1 inch (2.5 cm), that's a good start. The more you practice, the stronger you will get.
- If you need to, you can go to your knees and perform the grasshopper pose.

Figure 39.17. Stick pose.

Chair pose

This pose is a great example of yin and yang, or opposite energies. While the arms, upper torso, and face reach up, the hips and lower body settle and sink down (Figure 39.18). Instructional cues:

- As the feet and knees are a comfortable shoulder-width apart, reach the arms forward and fully extend the spine.
- Look up to the hands or straight ahead.
- Reach the tailbone back.
- Allow the upper body to be buoyant while it is anchored by the strength of the lower body grounding you to the earth.
- Breathe.

Upward facing dog pose

This is one of the best chest openers in yoga and also a good pose with which to begin to build upper body strength (Figure 39.19). Instructional cues:

- At the end of this pose, only the hands and tops of the feet remain on the floor. In many vinyasa sequences, this pose is done between the chaturanga and downward facing dog pose.

Figure 39.18. Chair pose.

Figure 39.19. Upward facing dog pose.

- In this pose there is often a tendency to "hang" on the shoulders, which lifts them up toward the ears and turtles the neck. To avoid this, slide your shoulders away from your ears and pull your shoulder blades toward your tailbone.
- Refrain from arching the back; rather, concentrate on lengthening through the front of the body.

Pyramid pose

This pose creates an intense hamstring stretch and can be felt along the anterior portion of the shins. The straighter the back is kept as you bend forward, the more the hamstring is engaged (Figure 39.20). Instructional cues:
- The feet are slightly closer together than they are in the warrior II pose.
- If it isn't possible for you to touch the floor in this pose, you can support your hands on a pair of blocks or the seat of a folding chair.
- Cast your spine forward as you bend. Keep the length throughout the spine and avoid rounding. If your hands do not touch the floor, simply rest them on your shins.
- Square your shoulders to the mat.

Figure 39.20. Pyramid pose.

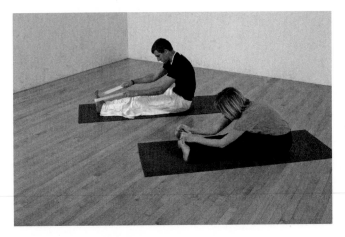

Figure 39.21. Seated forward bend pose.

Seated Forward Bend Pose

This is a nice hamstring stretch that can be intensified by striving to keep the torso and back long as you reach forward (Figure 39.21). Instructional cues:
- This pose is not about getting your nose to your knees; rather, imagine that your nose will touch your toes.
- Let your hips be grounded to the floor. Now extend and lengthen your spine from your hips. Each time you inhale, visualize yourself extending further toward your toes. Each time you exhale, relax and settle into the ground a little more deeply.
- Grab your big toes with your first two fingers if you can. If not, use a band. Keep your spine flat and your eyes on your big toes. Imagine that with each breath you are able to get your nose a little closer to your toes.
- In this posture, the hips actually are tilting backward to allow the back to remain flat while extending forward. You should not allow the pelvis to tilt forward, nor should the spine appear to round as you bend forward.

Tree pose

This is one of the simplest balance poses. Start in a position that you can easily hold. Work your way up to balancing for 1 minute. Notice how active the ankles are in the posture (Figure 39.22)! Instructional cues:
- In all balancing postures participants can use a *drysti,* or eye focusing point. Have them focus on one point either on the wall or floor.
- The purpose of the posture is to increase concentration; therefore it does not matter if the foot is all the way on the upper thigh or not as long as the participant is balancing on one foot.
- Press the standing foot firmly into the floor. Find your focus point. Extend your spine and neck from the hips.
- Breathe.
- Don't worry if you fall out of the pose. Just gather yourself back and try again.

Figure 39.22. Tree pose.

Additional Vinyasa Sequences: Putting Asana Together

Table 39.1 provides examples of additional vinyasa sequences that can be taught. Sequences usually begin on the right side and are repeated on the left side. One or two breaths in between sequences is helpful to allow for recovery. You may choose to hold postures for 3 to 5 breaths to work on alignment and develop strength or to move rapidly through the sequences to focus on cardiorespiratory endurance.

As you become increasingly familiar with yoga curricular design, you may wish to develop your own vinyasa sequences. A simple way to create sequences is to utilize yoga cards. On each index card, put the name of a single pose. Begin with five poses. Lay the cards out and complete the poses in order. As you progress you can add more cards. Participants can also participate in this process by putting their favorite pose on a card, designing their own cards and sequences, or researching a pose and teaching it to the group when their card is selected. There are also many texts, Web sites, and multimedia options to help you in the creation of new sequences.

ETIQUETTE

As is the case in teaching any physical activity, etiquette issues encourage proper and safe participation. Safety of the participant is always of paramount concern to the instructor. In a yoga unit of instruction, the safety of the teaching and learning environment is a shared responsibility between instructor and participant. Class rules and expectations should be discussed, posted, and practiced. When safety rules are violated, there is a potential for injury to both instructor and participant. Etiquette issues include:

1. Silent participation—participants are encouraged to be silent throughout their practice time. They should feel free to ask questions, but refrain from unnecessary chatter. They should focus on the sound of their own breathing and need a quiet environment to do that successfully.

2. Beginning/Ending class—because sessions typically begin and end with quiet time, it is important for participants to arrive to class on time and to not leave early, causing a disruption.

3. Appropriate dress—inappropriate dress may result in injury or exposure. Safely practicing yoga requires that individuals be able to move freely and without restriction. Participants should dress in clothing that allows for full physical participation without hindering movement or creating potential safety hazards. Appropriate dress would include comfortable shorts, shirts, or sweat suits. Participants should also practice without shoes in bare feet, as stocking feet can slide on the floor, creating possible unsafe situations.

4. Personal space—the yoga mat is considered one's personal space. Participants should refrain from walking on others' mats when they move around the classroom. Walking on someone else's mat with bare feet is also a hygiene issue.

5. Shared responsibility—participants should be encouraged to practice their skills to the level that is appropriate for their current fitness ability and any existing health conditions that they may have. It is important for the instructor to develop an environment in which participants are not competing with others in the class to achieve a posture that is outside of their abilities.

6. Cleaning supplies—it is important that yoga mats, blocks, or any other equipment be sanitized on occasion to ensure a hygienic environment.

TEACHING CONSIDERATIONS

The following teaching considerations will allow for the successful implementation of a yoga unit of instruction:

1. Young elementary school children may appreciate a less structured, more imaginative approach to yoga. Several postures are named after animals, and this can be a fun and appealing way to introduce yoga. cat, grasshopper, lion, crane, cobra, and turtle are common examples. Many of these poses look like the animals after which they are named. Children can also explore other movements that the animals might make after they have been introduced to the posture.

2. Yoga could also be incorporated at the beginning or end of other physical activities. Performing intentional breathing or working on one or many of the poses will be beneficial to participants in a variety of ways. Use yoga as a way to increase flexibility or muscular strength or simply to help individuals relax and unwind; create vinyasas that focus on balance or abdominal strength; use it as a way to explore other cultures or to introduce ethics.

3. Yoga's appropriateness for mainstreamed children makes it particularly appealing for today's educational

Table 39.1. ADDITIONAL VINYASA SEQUENCES

Sequence #1 8 Posture Vinyasa	Sequence #2 Great Salutation	Sequence #3 Warrior Vinyasa	Sequence #4 Balanced Vinyasa	Sequence #5 The Wheel Vinyasa
Mountain	Mountain	Warrior I—R leg forward	Child's pose—then move to Standing	Mountain
Chair pose	Standing back bend	Warrior II—R	Mountain	Chair
Forward fold with chest to thighs, gently straighten legs	Forward fold	Triangle—R	High lunge—R leg forward	Forward fold
Rise halfway to flat back with hands on floor or shins	High lunge—R leg back	High lunge—R	Warrior I—R	Plank
Jump or step to Plank pose	Warrior I—R leg back	Plank	Triangle—R	Upward facing dog
Lower to stick pose	Lunge—R leg back	Downward facing dog	Tree—R	High lunge—L leg forward
Upward facing dog	Plank—then lower all the way to the ground	High lunge—L	Tree—L	Warrior II—L
Downward facing dog	Cobra	Repeat—begin with L leg	Triangle—L	High lunge—L
Warrior I—R leg forward	Downward facing dog		Warrior I—L	Downward facing dog
Step back to plank pose	High lunge—L leg back		High lunge—L	High lunge—R
Lower to stick pose	Triangle—L leg back		Mountain	Warrior II—R
Upward facing dog	Warrior II—L leg back		Child's pose	High lunge—R
Downward facing dog	Pyramid pose—L leg back			Plank
Warrior I—L leg forward	High lunge—L leg back			Upward facing dog
Step back to plank pose	Forward fold			Downward facing dog
Lower to stick pose	Mountain			Forward fold
Upward facing dog	Repeat and use other leg in sequence			Chair
Downward facing dog				Mountain
Jump or step and rise halfway to a flat back				
Forward fold				
Chair pose				
Mountain				

environment. Yoga is an excellent way to include exercises that focus on coordination, physical fitness, and self-awareness, while also providing a structured environment for activity. By emphasizing physiological self-perception, yoga strengthens self-awareness. It has been shown to be especially suitable for children with ADD and ADHD.

4. Many communities now offer yoga in local studios or in health and fitness centers. Taking a few classes yourself or inviting an instructor to help you develop your curriculum are easy ways to get started. Yoga videos are also abundant. Appropriate instructional videos should target a beginning level and offer instruction rather than just a series of vinyasas.

GLOSSARY

asana Yoga position or yoga pose, also called yogasana.

hatha Sun and moon, or active and receptive life forces.

hatha yoga The branch of yoga devoted to the practice of asana for health and physical discipline.

namaste A common greeting simply meaning, "I bow to you." Often used at the beginning and end of classes with hands in a palms-together position over chest.

Sun Salutation A flowing series of 12 asana.

vinyasa A series of postures or poses.

yoga A "yoking" or "union" in the sense of bringing together a harmonious relationship with the physical and spiritual aspects of self.

SUGGESTED READINGS

Anderson, S. 2008. *Yoga: Mastering the basics.* Honesdale, PA: Himalayan Institute Press.

Bermsa, D. 2003. *Yoga games for children: Fun and fitness with postures, movements and breath.* Alameda, CA: Hunter House.

Brown, C. 2002. *Yoga: A system for harmonizing the mind, body, and spirit.* New York, NY: Parragon.

Calhoun, Y. 2006. *Create a yoga practice for kids.* Santa Fe, NM: Sunstone Press.

Christensen, A. 2002. *The American yoga association beginner's manual.* Whitby, ON: Fireside.

Dykema, R. 2006. *Yoga for fitness and wellness.* Belmont, CA: Thomson.

Fronske, H. 2005. *Teaching cues for sport skills for secondary school students.* 3rd ed. San Francisco, CA: Benjamin Cummings.

Gerstein, N. 2008. *Guiding yoga's light: Lessons for yoga teachers.* Champaign, IL: Human Kinetics.

Iyengar, B.K.S. 2001. *Yoga: The path to holistic health.* London, UK: Dorling-Kindersley.

Kaminoff, L. 2007. *Yoga anatomy.* Champaign, IL: Human Kinetics.

Kirk, M., and Boon, B. 2006. *Hatha yoga illustrated.* Champaign, IL: Human Kinetics.

Kraines, M., and Sherman, B. 2010. *Yoga: For the joy of it!* Sudbury, MA: Jones & Bartlett.

Shaw, B.J. 2001. *YogaFit.* Champaign, IL: Human Kinetics.

Solis, S. 2006. *Storytime yoga: Teaching yoga to children through story.* Boulder, CO: The Mythic Yoga Studio.

RESOURCES

Videos

All Day Yoga for Beginners, available from Gaiam, Inc.: www.gaiam.com

Power Yoga Stamina for Beginners, available from Health Arts Publishing, LLC.: www.livingarts.com

Yoga Fitness for Kids, available from Gaiam, Inc.: www.gaiam.com

Yoga Journal: Yoga for Stress, available from Yoga Journal: www.yogajournal.com

Yoga & Sculpting, available from Entertaining Fitness, Inc.: www.karenvoight.com

Task Cards

The Yoga Deck, developed by Olivia Miller: www.chroniclebooks.com

Yoga Fit Deck, developed by Phil Black: www.fitdeck.com

WEB SITES

Yoga Alliance
  www.yogaalliance.org
Yoga Asana
  www.santosha.com/asanas
Yoga Basics
  www.yogabasics.com
Yoga Directory
  www.yogadirectory.com
Yoga Journal
  www.yogajournal.com
Yoga Postures
  www.yogasite.com/postures.html
Yoga Research
  www.yrec.org
Yoga Routines
  www.yogamazing.com

A

Miscellaneous Field and Court Dimensions

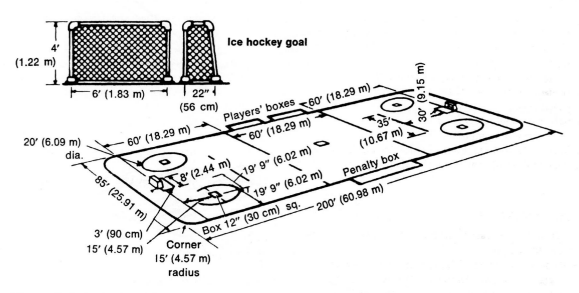

Figure A.1. Ice hockey rink.

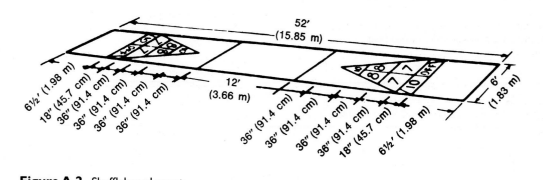

Figure A.2. Shuffleboard court.

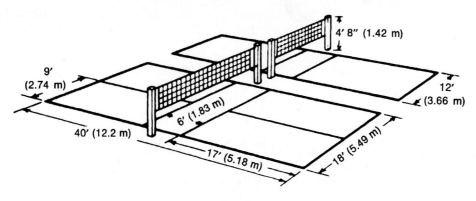

Figure A.3. Deck tennis (double and single) courts.

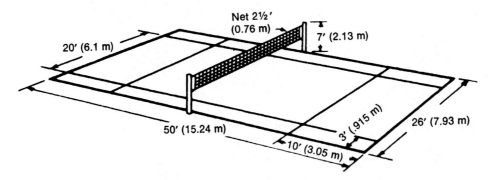

Figure A.4. Aerial tennis court.

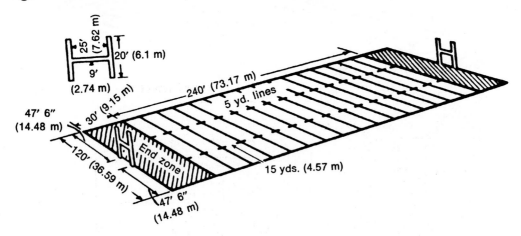

Figure A.5. Six-person football field.

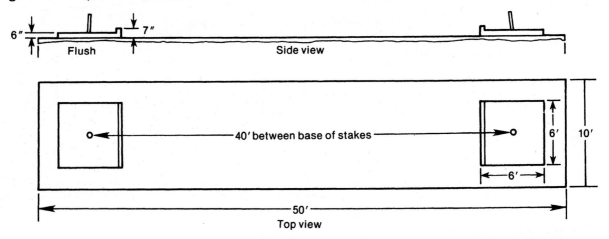

Figure A.6. Horseshoe pit. The 1-inch by 3-foot stakes extend 14 inches above ground and incline 3 inches toward each other. Stakes are 30 feet apart for women and boys under 16 years.

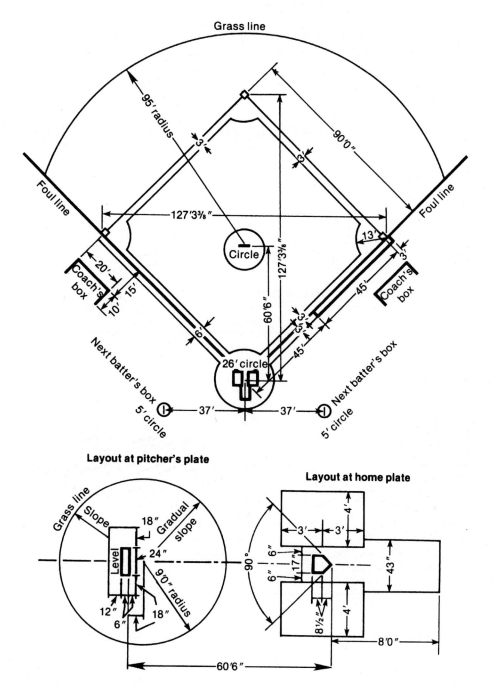

Figure A.7. Baseball diamond.

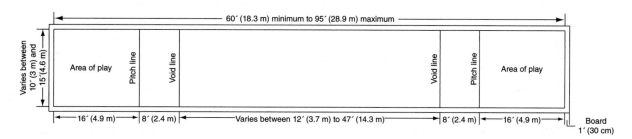

Figure A.8. Bocce court.

APPENDIX **B** | *Metric and English Equivalents*

Table B.1. CONVERSION

Length

1 millimeter (mm)	= 0.04 inch
1 centimeter (cm)	= 10 millimeters = 0.4 inch
1 meter (m)	= 39.37 inches = 3.3 feet = 1.1 yards
1 yard (yd)	= 0.91 meter
1 foot (ft)	= 30.5 centimeters
1 inch (in)	= 2.54 centimeters

Distance

1 meter (m)	= 39.4 inches = 3.3 feet = 1.1 yards
1 kilometer (km)	= 1000 meters = 0.62 mile
1 mile (mi)	= 1.61 kilometers

Weight

1 gram (g)	= 0.035 ounces
1 kilogram (kg)	= 2.2 pounds
1 ounce (oz)	= 28 grams
1 pound (lb)	= 0.45 kilogram

Table B.2. UNITS OF LENGTH IN TRACK-AND-FIELD EVENTS

Track Events

Meters	Miles	Yards	Feet	Inches	Yards	Meters
1	0	1	0	3.37	40	36.58
2	0	2	0	6.74	50	45.72
3	0	3	0	10.11	60	54.86
4	0	4	1	1.48	70	64.01
5	0	5	1	4.85	75	68.58
10	0	10	2	9.70	100	91.44
20	0	21	2	7.40	110	100.58
30	0	32	2	5.10	120	109.73
40	0	43	2	2.80	220	201.17
50	0	54	2	.50	300	274.32
60	0	65	1	10.20	440	402.34
70	0	76	1	7.90	600	548.64
80	0	87	1	5.60	880	804.67
90	0	98	1	3.30	1000	914.40
100	0	109	1	1.00	1320	1207.01
110	0	120	0	10.70		
200	0	218	2	2.00	**Miles**	**Meters**
300	0	328	0	3.00	1	1609.3
400	0	437	1	4.00	2	3218.7
500	0	546	2	5.00	3	4828.0
1000	0	1093	1	10.00	4	6437.4
1500	0	1640	1	3.00	5	8046.7
2000	1	427	0	8.00	6	9656.1
2500	1	974	0	1.00	7	11,265.4
3000	1	1520	2	6.00	8	12,874.8
5000	3	188	0	2.00	9	14,484.1
10,000	6	376	0	4.00	10	16,093.5

26 Miles − 385 yards = 42 kilometers − 195.1 meters

Field Events

Feet	Meters	Feet	Meters	Feet	Meters	Feet	Meters
1	0.305	6	1.829	20	6.096	70	21.336
2	.610	7	2.134	30	9.144	80	24.384
3	.914	8	2.438	40	12.192	90	27.432
4	1.219	9	2.743	50	15.240	100	30.480
5	1.524	10	3.048	60	18.288	200	60.960

Relation of metric to English scale. For measuring or checking courses where no metric tape is available, the following table is acceptable: 1 meter = 39.37 inches = 3.2808 feet = 1.0936 yards. 1 kilometer = 1000 meters = 0.621370 miles.

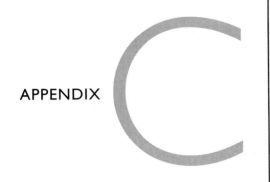

Video and DVD Sources

The following distributors of videos are presented in alphabetical order and numbered. This is followed by a listing of the sports and recreational activities in this book for which these distributors, identified by their number, provide videos.

1. Active Videos, www.activevideos.com
2. American Alliance for Health, Physical Education, Recreation and Dance, www.aahperd.org
3. Human Kinetics, www.humankinetics.com
4. Insight Media, www.insight-media.com
5. Instructional Videos for All Sports, www.school-tech.com
6. Just Push Play, www.justpushplay.com
7. Online Sports, www.onlinesports.com
8. Sports ID, www.sportsid.com
9. Sports Nation, www.sportsnationvideo.com
10. Sysko's Sports Books and Videos, www.syskos.com
11. Velo Press, www.velopress.com

CHAPTERS	DISTRIBUTORS
2. Health-Related Physical Fitness	1, 2, 3, 4, 5, 6, 7, 9
3. Aerobic Dance (Group Exercise)	1, 3, 4, 5
4. Archery	8
5. Backpacking	4, 5
6. Badminton	8
7. Basketball	1, 3, 5, 6, 7, 8, 9, 10
8. Bicycling	1, 3, 5, 6, 8, 11
9. Bowling	1, 8
10. Dance: Concert and Recreational Forms	1, 2, 3, 4, 5, 6, 7
12. Field Hockey	8
13. Golf	1, 3, 5, 6, 7, 8
14. Gymnastics and Tumbling	1, 3, 5, 7, 8
15. In-line Skating	1, 5, 6, 8
16. Jogging and Walking	1, 3, 4, 5
17. Karate	1, 3, 6
18. Kayaking and Canoeing	1, 5, 6
19. Lacrosse	5, 9
20. Mountaineering	6, 8
21. Orienteering	4
23. Racquetball, Paddleball, and Handball	1
24. Rugby	3, 8
25. Self-Defense	1
26. Soccer	1, 3, 5, 6, 7, 8
27. Softball (Slow Pitch)	1, 3, 5, 7, 9,
29. Swimming	1, 3, 5, 7, 8, 9
30. Table Tennis	1, 3, 8
32. Tennis	1, 3, 5, 6, 7, 8
33. Touch Football and Flag Football	1, 3, 5, 6, 7, 9, 10
34. Track and Field	3, 4, 5, 7, 8, 9
35. Volleyball	1, 3, 5, 8, 9
37. Weight Training	1, 3, 4, 5, 7, 8
38. Wrestling	1, 3, 5, 6, 7, 8, 9
39. Yoga	1, 3, 6

Credits

Chapter 1

p. 1 Photodisc.

p. 2 (left) Photo by Raili Filion. **(right)** From A. Lumpkin, *Physical Exercise and Sport,* 3rd ed. (St. Louis: Mosby).

p. 3 (top) Oliver Furrer/Brand X/Corbis. **(bottom)** From A. Lumpkin, *Physical Exercise and Sport,* 3rd ed. (St. Louis: Mosby).

p. 4 (left) Image Source/Alamy, **(right)** Photo by Raili Filion.

Chapter 2

Fig. 2.1. Reprinted with permission from *Research Quarterly for Exercise and Sport,* vol. 67, no. 2, 193–205. Copyright 1996 by the American Alliance for Health, Physical Education, Recreation, and Dance, 1900 Association Dr., Reston VA 20191.

Figs. 2.4 and 2.5. From S. Blair, et al. "Physical Fitness and All-Cause Mortality: A Prospective Study of Healthy Men and Women." *Journal of the American Medical Association,* 262 (1989): 2395–2401.

Table 2.7. Adapted by permission from E. T. Howley and B.D. Franks, *Health Fitness Instructor's Handbook,* 4th ed. (Champaign, IL: Human Kinetics, 2003), p. 308.

Table 2.10. Reprinted with permission from *Research Quarterly for Exercise and Sport,* 63(1): A52. Copyright 1992 by the American Alliance for Health, Physical Education, Recreation, and Dance, 1900 Association Dr., Reston, VA 20191.

Table 2.11. From J. Morrow, et al., *Measurement and Evaluation in Human Performance* (Champaign, IL: Human Kinetics, 2000).

Table 2.13. Reprinted with permission from American Society of Contemporary Medicine and Surgery. Michael L. Pollack, Donald H. Schmidt, and Andrew S. Jackson. "Measurement of Cardio-Respiratory Fitness and Body Composition in the Clinical Setting." *Comprehensive Therapy* 6(9) (1980): 12–27.

Table 2.14. Reprinted from *Y's Way to Physical Fitness,* with permission of the YMCA of the USA. 101 N. Wacker Drive, Chicago, IL 60606.

Table 2.15. Based on norms from *The Physical Fitness Specialist Manual,* The Cooper Institute for Aerobic Research Dallas, TX, revised 1988, used with permission.

Table 2.16. Reprinted from *Y's Way to Physical Fitness,* with permission of the YMCA of the USA. 101 N. Wacker Drive, Chicago, IL 60606.

Table 2.19. Reprinted by permission from J. F. Sallis and K. Patrick, "Physical Activity Guidelines for Adolescents: Consensus Statements," *Pediatric Exercise Science,* 6(4) (1994): 306–308.

Table 2.20. Reprinted from Tudor-Locke, C. and Bassett, D. Jr. "How Many Steps Per Day Are Enough? Preliminary Pedometer Indices for Public Health." *Sports Medicine,* 34 (2004): 1–8.

Chapter 3

Figs. 3.1, 3.3, 3.4, 3.5, 3.6, and 3.7. Photos by Lorna Francis.

Fig. 3.2. Photo by Raili Filion.

Chapter 4

Fig. 4.6. From Archer and Fencing Rules by NAGWS of the American Alliance of Health, Physical Education, Recreation and Dance. Copyright 1960.

Fig. 4.7. Photo by David C. Tyndall.

Figs. 4.9 and 4.10. From F. Bear, *Fred Bear's World of Archery* (New York: Doubleday & Co., Inc., 1979). Photos by George Bing.

Figs. 4.11 through 4.14. Photos by Frank Thomas.

Chapter 5

Fig. 5.1. Photo by Jeff McNamee.

Figs. 5.2 through 5.6, 5.8, and 5.9. Photos by Jeff Steffen.

Chapter 7

Figs. 7.1 and 7.2. Reprinted with permission of the National Collegiate Athletic Association.

Figs. 7.3 through 7.8, 7.15 through 7.18. Photos by Raili Filion.

Figs. 7.9 through 7.14. Reprinted with permission of James LaPoint.

Chapter 8

Figs. 8.2 and 8.16. Photo by Raili Filion.

Figs. 8.3, 8.5 through 8.7, 8.9 through 8.12. Photos by Chris Harnish.

Fig. 8.17. Photo by Paul Weiss.

Chapter 9

Figs. 9.4 through 9.10. Photos by Raili Falion.

Chapter 10

Fig. 10.6. Photo by Ashley Hartka.

Fig. 10.7. Photo by Alina Prax.

Fig. 10.8. Photo by David Andrews.

Figs. 10.9, 10.11, and 10.12. Photos by Raili Filion.

Chapter 11

Fig. 11.1. Harold Duvall, Innova Champion Discs, East Coast Sales Office, Rock Hill, SC 29732.

Figs. 11.2 through 11.4. Adapted from Frisbee Sports and Games, Charles Tipes and Dan Ruddick.

Figs. 11.5 through 11.10, 11.12, and 11.14. The Disc Course, Dan Ruddick.

Figs. 11.11 and 11.13. Frisbee Sports and Games, Charles Tips and Dan Ruddick.

Chapter 12

Figs. 12.1 and 12.2 Photos by Raili Filion.

Figs. 12.6 through 12.11 Photos by Nick Conway.

Chapter 13

Fig. 13.1 From *Rules of Golf*, by United States Golf Association, P.O. Box 708, Far Hills, NJ 07931.

Figs. 13.8b, 13.14, and 13.15: Photos by Raili Filion.

Figs. 13.11 through 13.13, 13.16, and 13.17. Photos by Kimber Westbrook.

Chapter 14

Figs. 14.39, 14.41 through 14.44. Photos by Raili Filion.

Fig. 14.45. Photo by Frank Musker.

Chapter 15

Figs. 15.1, 15.5, 15.7 through 15.10. Photos by Daniel R. Kibler.

Figs. 15.2 through 15.4, and 15.6: From Liz Miller, *Get Rolling* (Ragged Mountain Press, 1998). Reprinted by permission of McGraw-Hill Companies.

Chapter 16

Figs. 16.4 through 16.6. Courtesy of Washington University assistant track coaches.

Chapter 17

Figs. 17.2 through 17.5. Photos by Rick Schmidt.

Chapter 19

Figs. 19.2 through 19.12. Photos by Robert Scott.

Figs. 19.13, 19.14, 19.18 through 19.30. Photos by Polly Keener.

Chapter 20

Figs. 20.1 through 20.5, 20.7 through 20.9, and 20.12 through 20.14. Photos by John Bicknell.

Fig. 20.10. Photo by Tresa Gilchrest.

Chapter 21

Fig. 21.1. Reprinted by permission of the Cascade Orienteering Club. Seattle, WA.

Figs. 21.2 and 21.3 and 21.16. From C. McNeill, *Orienteering: The Skills of the Game*. (Wiltshire, England: The Crowood Press, 1996). Reprinted by permission.

Fig. 21.10. Courtesy of Silva Company, Orienteering Services, U.S.A. Box 547, LaPorte, IN 46350.

Chapter 22

Figs. 22.1 and 22.3. Photos by Janet Valentine.

Chapter 23

Figs. 23.7 and 23.8. Photos by Robert Maughan.

Chapter 25

Fig. 25.1 through 25.31. Photos by Aaron Banks.

Chapter 26

Figs. 26.4 through 26.18. Photos by March Krotee.

Chapter 27

Figs. 27.2 through 27.23 and 27.25 through 27.29. Photos by James Disch.

Chapter 28

Figs. 28.2 through 28.11. Photos by Aaron Banks.

Chapter 30

Fig. 30.3. Photo by Raili Filion.

Figs. 30.4, 30.5, 30.7 and 30.8. Courtesy USATT. Photos by Allsport.

Figs. 30.6, 30.9 and 30.10. Photos by Steve Hopkins.

Chapter 31

Fig. 31.4. From United States Team Handball Federation, *Rules of the Game,* 1981–1985 edition, (Colorado Springs, CO: USTHF).

Chapter 32

Figs. 32.1, 32.3 through 32.11. Photos by Randy Hyllegard.

Chapter 33

Fig. 33.2. From R. J. Grambeau, *The Official National and Touch Football Rules* (North Palm Beach, FL: The Athletic Institute, 1986). Used with permission from the Athletic Institute.

Figs. 33.3 through 33.8. Photos by Randy Bonnette.

Chapter 34

Figs. 34.1, 34.3, 34.4, 34.19, 34.22, and 34.30. Photos by Al McDaniels.

Figs. 34.10, 34.12, 34.19, 34.23, and 34.29. Photos by Kirby Lee.

Chapter 35

Figs. 35.2, 35.4, and 35.5. Photos by Brian Lewis, Media Relations, Intercollegiate Athletics, University of Colorado.

Chapter 36

Figs. 36.1, 36.7, and 36.8. Photos by Goldenbearsports.com.

Figs. 36.3 through 36.6. Photos by George Weiny.

Chapter 37

Figs. 37.7, 37.8, 37.10, 37.12 through 37.15, 37.18, 37.19, 37.22 through 37.25, and 37.27 through 37.43. Photos by Jay Dawes.

Figs. 37.16, 37.17, 37.20, 37.21, and 37.26. Photos by Raili Filion.

Figs. 37.44 and 37.45. From *The Clean and Jerk Lift* (Colorado Springs, CO: United States Weightlifting Federation).

Chapter 38

Fig. 38.2. Permission to reprint granted by the National Collegiate Athletic Association. From *NCAA Wrestling Rules and Interpretations* (Mission, KA: NCAA, 1989). NCAA specifications subject to review annually.

Figs. 38.4 through 38.13 and 38.26. Photos by Raili Filion.

Chapter 39

Figs. 39.2 through 39.22. Photos by Aaron Banks.